DISTANCE CHART

NEW YORK CITY								
233 375	WASHINGTON, DC							
779 1253	**688** 1107	CHICAGO						
1286 2069	**1050** 1689	**1371** 2206	MIAMI					
1300 2092	**1073** 1726	**922** 1483	**856** 1377	NEW ORLEANS				
1541 2479	**1315** 2116	**921** 1482	**1349** 2171	**515** 829	DALLAS			
1793 2885	**1669** 2685	**994** 1599	**2079** 3345	**1390** 2237	**878** 1413	DENVER		
2816 4531	**2725** 4385	**2030** 3266	**3329** 5356	**2690** 4328	**2178** 3504	**1306** 2101	SEATTLE	
2873 4623	**2782** 4476	**2106** 3389	**3106** 4998	**2272** 3656	**1729** 2782	**1248** 2008	**801** 1289	SAN FRANCISCO
2763 4444	**2640** 4248	**1989** 3200	**2736** 4402	**1902** 3060	**1445** 2325	**998** 1606	**1131** 1820	**38** 61	LOS ANGELES

EYEWITNESS TRAVEL GUIDES

USA

EYEWITNESS TRAVEL GUIDES

USA

DK

LONDON, NEW YORK,
MELBOURNE, MUNICH AND DELHI
www.dk.com

Statuary, Grand Central Terminal,
New York City

MANAGING EDITOR Aruna Ghose
ART EDITOR Benu Joshi
PROJECT EDITOR Vandana Mohindra
EDITORS Kajori Aikat, Rimli Borooah,
Nandini Mehta, Manjari Rathi
DESIGNERS Pallavi Narain, Supriya Sahai, Priyanka Thakur
SENIOR CARTOGRAPHER Uma Bhattacharya
CARTOGRAPHER Alok Pathak
PICTURE RESEARCHER Taiyaba Khatoon
ADDITIONAL PICTURE RESEARCH Kiran K. Mohan
DTP COORDINATOR Shailesh Sharma
DTP DESIGNER Vinod Harish

US EDITOR Mary Sutherland

MAIN CONTRIBUTORS
Andrew Hempstead, Jamie Jensen, Joanne Miller, Eric Peterson,
Kevin Roe, Kap Stann

MAIN PHOTOGRAPHERS
Andy Holligan, Jon Spaull, Peter Wilson

MAIN ILLUSTRATORS
Arun P, Gautam Trivedi

Reproduced by Colourscan (Singapore)
Printed and bound by South China Printing Co. Ltd. (China)

First published in Great Britain in 2004
by Dorling Kindersley Limited
80 Strand, London WC2R 0RL

Copyright © 2004 Dorling Kindersley Limited, London
A Penguin Company

A CIP CATALOGUE RECORD IS AVAILABLE FROM THE BRITISH LIBRARY.

ISBN 1 4053 0291 7

FLOORS ARE REFERRED TO THROUGHOUT IN
ACCORDANCE WITH AMERICAN USAGE; IE THE "FIRST FLOOR"
IS THE FLOOR AT GROUND LEVEL.

**The information in every
Eyewitness Travel Guide is checked regularly**.
Every effort has been made to ensure that this book is as up-to-date
as possible at the time of going to press. Some details, however,
such as telephone numbers, opening hours, prices, gallery hanging
arrangements and travel information are liable to change. The
publishers cannot accept responsibility for any consequences arising
from the use of this book, nor for any material on third party
websites, and cannot guarantee that any website address in this
book will be a suitable source of travel information. We value the
views and suggestions of our readers very highly. Please write to:
Publisher, DK Eyewitness Travel Guides,
Dorling Kindersley, 80 Strand, London WC2R 0RL, Great Britain.

CONTENTS

◁ Utah's Bryce Canyon, with its series of deep amphitheaters filled with flame-colored rock formations

Nighttime view of the US Capitol in Washington, DC

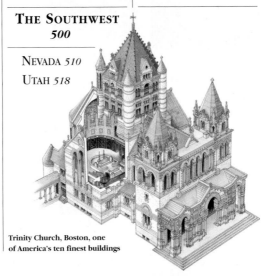

Trinity Church, Boston, one of America's ten finest buildings

How to Use this Guide

THIS DORLING KINDERSLEY travel guide helps you to get the most from your visit to the United States. *Visiting the USA* maps the country and gives tips on practical considerations and travel. *USA at a Glance* gives an overview of some of the main attractions and a brief history. The book is divided into 14 regional sections,

each covering from one to seven states. The chapter on each region starts with a historical portrait and a map of the area. The main sightseeing section then follows, with maps of the major cities. For each region there is a section of practical and travel information, followed by listings of recommended hotels and restaurants.

USA MAP

The colored areas shown on the map on the inside front cover indicate the 14 regional chapters in this guide.

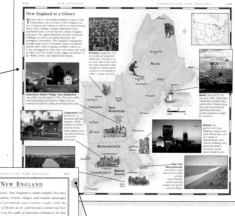

1 At a Glance
The map here highlights the different states in each section as well as the most interesting cities, towns, and regions.

Each region chapter has color-coded thumb tabs.

2 Introduction to a Region
This section gives the reader an insight into the region's geography, historical background, politics, and the character of the people. A chart lists the key dates and events in the region's history.

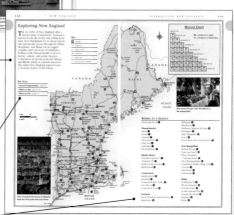

3 Regional Map
For easy reference, sights in each region are numbered and plotted on a map. The black bullet numbers (eg. ❸) also indicate the order in which the sights are covered in the chapter.

For each region there is an index of the practical and listings pages at the end of the chapter.

Sights at a Glance lists the numbered sights in sequential order.

4 City Map
This plots individual sights within the most important cities. The sights within a city such as Boston are indicated with clear bullet numbers (eg. ③), in contrast to the black bullets used on the regional maps.

Visitors' Checklist gives all the practical information needed to plan your visit.

Sights at a Glance lists the numbered sights within the city.

5 Major Sights
Historic buildings are dissected to reveal their interiors, while museums and galleries have color-coded floor plans to help you find the most important exhibits.

Stars indicate the features that no visitor should miss.

6 Detailed Information
Cities, towns, and other sights are described individually. Their entries appear in the same order as the numbering on the regional map at the beginning of the section.

Each entry begins with essential practical information, including the address and telephone number of the local tourist information office. Opening times are given for major sights and museums.

7 Practical Information
This section covers subjects such as travel, security, shopping, and entertainment. Some cities, such as New York, are covered separately.

Directory boxes give contact information for the services and venues mentioned in the text.

Climate charts are also provided for each region.

GUSTAFSON'S

MOTEL

RESTAURANT

SELF
SERVE

IT'S LIKE
MONEY IN
THE TANK

VISITING THE USA

Putting the USA on the Map

SPREADING OVER 3,000 miles (4,800 km) east to west between the Atlantic and Pacific Oceans, the United States covers the heart of the North American continent and has a population of 285 million people. Bordered by Mexico to the south and Canada to the north, it extends for over 1,500 miles (2,414 km), covering an area of more than 3.5 million sq miles (9 million sq km), and includes climates from the tropics to the Arctic Circle. The US is divided into 48 states. These, together with the two states, Alaska in the extreme northwest, and the islands of Hawai'i in the Pacific Ocean, comprise the 50 United States of America. The national capital is Washington, DC, a small federal district located between the states of Maryland and Virginia.

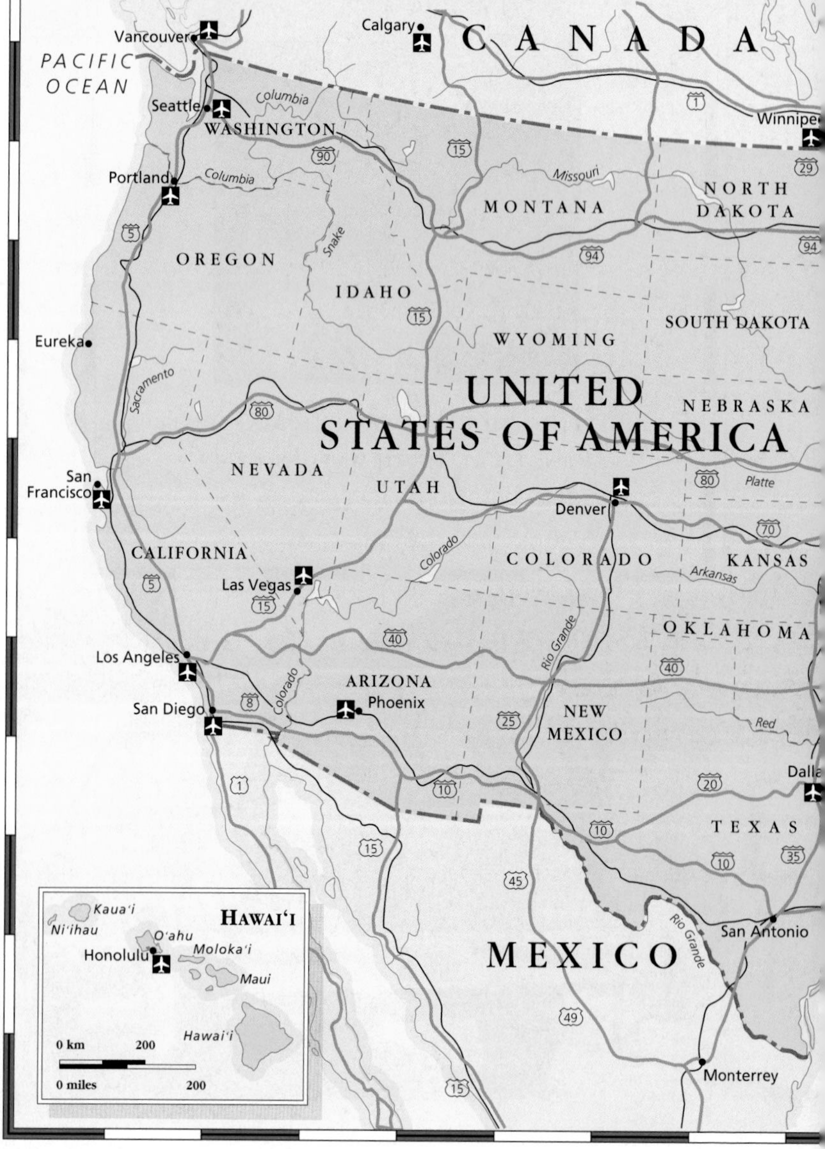

PACIFIC OCEAN

Lake Winnipeg

Vancouver

CANADA

Calgary

Seattle

WASHINGTON

Columbia

Winnipe

Portland

Columbia

OREGON

Snake

MONTANA

Missouri

NORTH DAKOTA

IDAHO

SOUTH DAKOTA

Eureka

WYOMING

UNITED STATES OF AMERICA

Sacramento

NEBRASKA

NEVADA

UTAH

San Francisco

CALIFORNIA

Las Vegas

Denver

COLORADO

KANSAS

Colorado

Platte

Arkansas

OKLAHOMA

Los Angeles

San Diego

ARIZONA

Phoenix

Colorado

NEW MEXICO

Rio Grande

Red

Dalla

TEXAS

Kaua'i
Ni'ihau
O'ahu
Honolulu
Moloka'i
Maui
HAWAI'I

Hawai'i

0 km   200
0 miles 200

MEXICO

Rio Grande

San Antonio

Monterrey

◁ **Gustafson's Motel in Brevort in Michigan's Upper Peninsula**

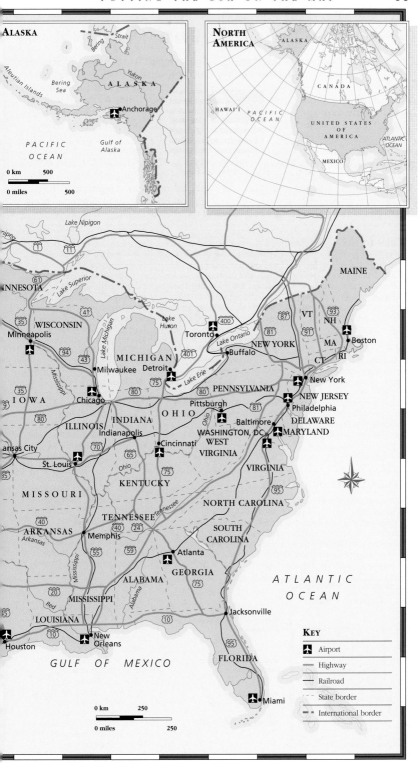

ALASKA

Aleutian Islands

Bering Strait

Yukon

Bering Sea

ALASKA

Anchorage

PACIFIC OCEAN

Gulf of Alaska

0 km 500
0 miles 500

NORTH AMERICA

ALASKA

CANADA

HAWAI'I *PACIFIC OCEAN*

UNITED STATES OF AMERICA

ATLANTIC OCEAN

MEXICO

Lake Nipigon

MINNESOTA

Lake Superior

WISCONSIN

Minneapolis

Lake Michigan

Lake Huron

Toronto

Lake Ontario

MICHIGAN

Milwaukee

Detroit

Lake Erie

Buffalo

NEW YORK

VT

NH

MA

Boston

RI

CT

IOWA

Chicago

ILLINOIS

INDIANA

OHIO

Ohio

Pittsburgh

PENNSYLVANIA

New York

NEW JERSEY

Philadelphia

DELAWARE

Indianapolis

Cincinnati

Baltimore

WASHINGTON, DC

MARYLAND

Kansas City

St. Louis

Ohio

WEST VIRGINIA

VIRGINIA

MISSOURI

KENTUCKY

TENNESSEE

Tennessee

NORTH CAROLINA

ARKANSAS

Memphis

Arkansas

SOUTH CAROLINA

Atlanta

Mississippi

ALABAMA

GEORGIA

Alabama

MISSISSIPPI

Red

LOUISIANA

Houston

New Orleans

GULF OF MEXICO

Jacksonville

FLORIDA

ATLANTIC OCEAN

Miami

KEY

Airport

Highway

Railroad

State border

International border

0 km 250
0 miles 250

Practical Information

Flag of the United States of America

MILLIONS OF VISITORS travel to the US from around the world every year, and millions of Americans also spend their leisure time exploring and enjoying their country. The nation's richly diverse history, culture, art, and landscape, as well as its tradition of hospitality and service, makes traveling in the US both enjoyable and stress-free. In all parts of the country, tourist facilities are generally of a very high standard. This section gives some basic information on the various transportation and accommodation options available. It deals with issues such as passport and visa formalities, travel insurance, banking, communications, and health care. This section covers the country as a whole, but more specific information is provided in subsequent *Practical Information* sections at the end of each regional chapter.

When to Go

THE BEST TIME to visit the US depends on a visitor's interests and itinerary. It is important to time your visit carefully, because the country's geography and weather patterns vary greatly from region to region, even at the same time of the year. Summer is generally the warmest and most popular time to travel, especially to the northern areas. Summer in the southern parts, especially in the deserts of the Southwest, can be unbearably hot, while in New England they are generally cool and pleasant. All over the country, the summer months are when children are out of school and on vacation, so most resort areas and national parks are full to capacity during these times. Summer is also the time when numerous outdoor cultural events, fairs, and festivals take place.

Spring can be the best time to visit the Rockies and the Deep South; the crowds are fewer, and discounts are often available. April and May in particular are ideal times to experience the wildflowers and gardens of the southern US. Fall is another good time to travel, since the leaves on the trees in the mountain forests, particularly in the northeast, are at their peak of color, and the high humidity of summer has decreased to more pleasant levels. Winter brings on the greatest diversity of weather, ranging from heavy snows in the winter sports capitals of New England and the Rocky Mountains, to tropical sunshine on the beaches of Florida and Hawai'i.

Passport & Visas

ALL TRAVELERS to the US are required to hold a valid passport, regardless of their age. Passports should be valid for at least six months longer than the last date you expect to remain in the country. Visas are not required for citizens of Canada, Australia, or the UK if the visit is for less than 90 days. Some form of government-issued photo ID, though, is required.

Citizens of many countries may take part in the "visa waiver" plan, using a Form I-94, which is available on all US-bound flights. However, due to increased security measures and constantly changing international conditions, it is wise to confirm visa requirements with the US embassy before traveling. Check with a travel agent for the latest requirements.

Travelers interested in studying, working, or staying for a longer period than the stated 90 days should request special visas from the nearest US embassy. If you are in the United States and need to extend your stay, you should

The Climate of the USA

Given the sheer vastness of its size, the United States is characterized by a diversity of climates. In addition to the many regional variations, the country also experiences dramatically shifting weather patterns, produced mostly by the Pacific westerlies that sweep across the entire continent. The *Practical Information* section for each region contains a panel like the one below.

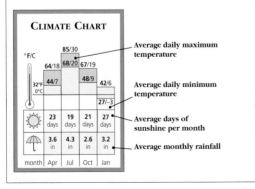

Climate Chart

°F/C		85/30	
	64/18	68/20 67/19	
32°F	44/7	48/9	42/6
0°C			27/–3
☀	23 days	19 days	21 days	27 days
☂	3.6 in	4.3 in	2.6 in	3.2 in
month	Apr	Jul	Oct	Jan

Average daily maximum temperature

Average daily minimum temperature

Average days of sunshine per month

Average monthly rainfall

contact the nearest office of the **Bureau of Citizenship and Immigration Services** *(see p17)* in the US, and apply for an extension. Failure to request an extension may result in a fine or deportation.

CUSTOMS ALLOWANCES & DUTY-FREE

ALL VISITORS to the US are required to complete a Customs Declaration before entering the country. On this form, which is available from airlines and customs officials upon arrival, you must state the value of any goods being brought into the US, and you may be charged duty on especially valuable items. Travelers are allowed to bring small quantities of tobacco and alcohol along with them, but certain goods are forbidden. These include meat products, plants or seeds, Cuban cigars, and ancient cultural artifacts. When you leave the US, make sure that you are aware of the duty-free allowances for tobacco products (200 cigarettes for each person over 18 years old), and for alcoholic beverages (0.2 gallons or one liter of spirits for each person over 21). No meat products, plants, seeds, fruits, or firearms may be taken out of the US.

PLANNING THE TRIP

SINCE THE COUNTRY IS so large and diverse, it is essential to plan ahead in order to make the most of your time

PUBLIC HOLIDAYS

New Year's Day (Jan 1)
Martin Luther King Jr. Day (3rd Mon in Jan)
Presidents' Day (3rd Mon in Feb)
Memorial Day (last weekend in May)
Independence Day (Jul 4)
Labor Day (1st Mon in Sep)
Columbus Day (Oct 2 weekend)
Veterans' Day (Nov 11)
Thanksgiving (4th Thu in Nov)
Christmas Day (Dec 25)

in the United States. Following a logical, efficient itinerary, and allowing enough time to get between places to enjoy them are two of the most important concerns. Also, bear in mind that the US is divided into six time zones *(see p20)*. All of the states and major cities offer a variety of information which can be ordered in advance over the telephone or accessed via web sites. A particularly useful web site is **www.SeeAmerica.org**. Local bookstores are also a valuable source of travel information, as are municipal libraries, travel agencies, and local and regional tourism bureaus across the country.

CHILDREN

CHILDREN ARE welcomed everywhere, and an amazing number of attractions exist primarily for the enjoyment of young people. From amusement parks and aquariums to national parks and children's museums, their enjoyment is catered to all over the United States.

Most restaurants have special children's menus, with simple foods, smaller portions, and lower prices. For a small charge, most lodgings will provide an extra bed or crib *(see p19)*, and many hotels or motels have adjoining or connecting rooms available especially for families. The main exceptions to kid-friendly status are most bed-and-breakfast accommodations, certain gourmet restaurants in the larger cities, as well as those deluxe resorts that focus on providing relaxing escapes or luxurious spa-like pampering to their guests. Restaurants and lodgings that welcome children are marked in the chapter-by-chapter listings.

SENIOR CITIZENS

OLDER TRAVELERS, or "seniors," make up a fairly large proportion of the traveling public, and most hotels and other establishments offer discounts and special services to attract

CONVERSION CHART

US Standard to Metric
1 inch = 2.54 centimeters
1 foot = 30 centimeters
1 mile = 1.6 kilometers
1 ounce = 28 grams
1 pound = 454 grams
1 US pint = 0.5 liter
1 US quart = 0.947 liter
1 US gallon = 3.8 liters

Metric to US Standard
1 centimeter = 0.4 inch
1 meter = 3 feet 3 inches
1 kilometer = 0.6 miles
1 gram = 0.04 ounce
1 kilogram = 2.2 pounds
1 liter = 1.1 US quarts

them. Visitors over the age of 50 can contact the **American Association of Retired Persons** or AARP *(see p17)* to request a membership, which costs about $13 per year. ElderHostel and a few other organizations cater to seniors who enjoy traveling both in and outside the US.

DISABLED TRAVELERS

DISABLED TRAVELERS will find traveling easy in the US, because the country has initiatives aimed at providing "barrier-free" access throughout. The Americans with Disabilities Act (ADA) requires most public buildings, including museums, hotels, and restaurants, to make their services and facilities accessible to all people, including those in wheelchairs. However, it is mostly only the newer hotels that have handicap-accessible bathrooms *(see p19)*. Two of the many organizations in the country that will help disabled visitors plan and enjoy their trips are **Access Adventures** (716-889-9096) and **Care Vacations** (780-986-6404/ www.carevacations.com). Hotels that offer facilities for disabled tourists are marked in the "Where to Stay" listings at the end of each regional section. For restaurants that offer similar facilities, look at the restaurant listings for the wheelchair access symbol.

Communications & Banking

A NY BANK IN THE US can accept transfer of funds from foreign banks. Many travelers already use credit cards or "automated teller" (ATM) cash/debit cards, so getting money from a bank or ATM should be relatively simple. It's best to buy traveler's checks in US dollar amounts before entering the country in order to avoid delays and extra charges. The country offers excellent telephone and mail services; cell phones and public Internet cafés have made keeping in touch easier and less expensive than ever, and most hotels also offer Internet hookups.

TELEPHONES

M ANY COMPANIES offer telephone services in the US at varying rates. Most public pay phones accept coins, but calls can also be charged to a credit card. Local calls cost between 25 and 50 cents, with additional charges for longer calls. Some hotels offer guests free local calls, but some levy hefty charges per call, so check ahead. Making international calls is very expensive. Consider using a calling card with discounted rates, as they allow you to charge calls to your home

REACHING THE RIGHT NUMBER

• The international code for the US is 1.
• For long distance calls within the US or to Canada: dial 1, the 3-digit area code, and the 7-digit local number.
• For local calls: dial the 7-digit local number.
• International direct-dial call: dial **011** followed by country code (UK: **44**; Australia: **61**; New Zealand: **64**; South Africa: **27**) then the city or area code (omit the first 0) and then the local number.
• International call via the operator: dial **01**, followed by country code, then city code (without the first 0), and then the local number.
• For operator assistance: dial **0**.
• An **800, 888, 877,** or **866** prefix indicates a free call.
• Directory inquiries: dial **411**.
• **For emergencies: dial 911.**

number, while others deduct charges from a prepaid account. Some foreign cell phones work in the US, but the charges can be high. Many car rental companies also rent cell phones for customers.

POSTAL SERVICES

P OST OFFICES ARE open from 9am to 5pm (weekdays) with some open on Saturday mornings. Postcards and letters can be dropped into big blue mailboxes on street corners. Domestic mail should include the five-digit zip code. Rates for international mail vary, so buy stamps from a local post office. To receive mail, General Delivery service is available, whereby letters are held for you at a specific post office for 30 days. Mail forwarding services also exist for a fee.

INTERNET ACCESS

L OCAL LIBRARIES, shopping malls, hotels, and university hangouts are perhaps the least expensive and easiest places to access the Internet. Most library computers will let you send e-mail and surf the web. Many large cities have designated stores that offer Internet access for a small fee.

BANKING

B ANKS CAN BE FOUND in all US cities and towns, and many have service centers in supermarkets and malls. Other financial institutions such as savings-and-loans and credit unions also offer banking services. Traveler's checks can be cashed as long as you have your passport. Banks also give cash advances against credit cards, but card companies

DIRECTORY

FINANCIAL SERVICES

Thomas Cook Currency Services
(415) 362-3452.

Thomas Cook Refund Assistance
(800) 223-7373.

American Express Travel Service
(415) 536-2600.

American Express Helpline
(800) 221-7282.

Cirrus
(800) 424-7787.

Plus
(800) 843-7587.

charge a high fee for this service. Most banks will not exchange foreign currency. Banking hours are 9am to 4pm, weekdays, but some banks remain open till 6pm on Fridays, and some open on Saturday mornings as well.

AUTOMATED TELLER MACHINES

A LMOST ALL BANKS have 24-hour ATMs, as do most train stations, airports, and malls. ATMs are connected to a number of bank-card networks and can dispense cash from accounts held in other states or countries. The primary US bank-card networks are **Plus**, **Cirrus**, **Star**, and **Interlink**. Be sure that your bank permits international cash withdrawals, and that your card and personal identification number (PIN) are compatible with US machines. Many ATMs charge a fee of $1 to $2.50 per trans-action. Exchange rates for ATM transactions, however, are better than those for traveler's checks or foreign currency.

CREDIT CARDS

T HE MOST commonly accept-ed credit cards are VISA, MasterCard, American Express, Japanese Credit Bureau (JCB),

Discover, and Diners Club (DC). Credit cards can be used in hotels, restaurants, stores, and to pay for such services as medical care or car rental. Having a credit card will make your stay much easier, and the exchange rates on cards are often better than those for traveler's checks or currency.

TRAVELER'S CHECKS

THE MOST WIDELY accepted traveler's checks are those issued by American Express and Thomas Cook in US dollars. It is easier to pay for purchases with traveler's checks and get cash as change, than go to the trouble of cashing the checks at a bank. Buy checks in a variety of denominations, with $10, $20, and $50 bills. It can be difficult to cash $100 bills except at a bank. Foreign currency checks are not accepted, and out-of-state checks are difficult to cash. Contact **Thomas Cook Refund Assistance** or **American Express Helpline** for lost, stolen, or destroyed traveler's checks.

FOREIGN EXCHANGE

TRY TO CHANGE your money into US denominations before traveling to the US. You may find it difficult to exchange foreign currency except in international airport terminals in major cities. The main foreign exchange companies in the US are American Express and Thomas Cook. If you are in the need of ready cash, you can always visit a duty-free shop and buy something so that you can cash a traveler's check.

10-cent coin (a dime)

5-cent coin (a nickel)

1-dollar coin

25-cent coin (a quarter)

Coins
American coins come in 2-dollar, 1-dollar, and 50-, 25-, 10-, 5-, and 1-cent pieces. 1-cent pieces are popularly called pennies, 5-cent are nickels, 10-cent are dimes, and 25-cent pieces are quarters.

Bank Notes
Units of currency are dollars and cents; 100 cents make a dollar. Notes (bills) come in $1, $5, $10, $20, $50, and $100s. All bills are green, so it is important to check the amount carefully. The only exception is the new $20 bill (not shown), which has other colors.

Accommodations

THE US OFFERS A WIDE VARIETY of accommodations to suit all tastes and budgets. At the high end of the comfort scale, visitors can choose from luxury hotels and resorts, found in most major cities. Country inns and bed-and-breakfasts (B&Bs), usually located in large, refurbished historic houses, offer a more personal and hospitable atmosphere. If you're traveling on a budget, there are thousands of convenient inexpensive motels all along the highways. Generally, hotels, motels, and inns offer impeccably clean surroundings. For those who wish to experience the country's wide open spaces, there are more than enough campgrounds in parks and forests.

HOTELS & RESORTS

THERE IS NO better place to experience the comfort of the US than to stay in one of the country's many chain hotels, such as the **Hilton**, **Marriott**, and **Renaissance**. Historic and ultramodern hotels and resorts are usually located in downtown areas, at the heart of the city. The best hotels, in major cities, often have the finest restaurants and pleasant cocktail bars. These hotels offer a full range of guest services, including swimming pools and health clubs, and their concierge can provide shopping and tourist information, as well as preferential seating at restaurants and theaters.

There are also a number of classic older hotels located in traditional vacation spots, notably the early 20th-century rustic lodges found in state and national parks. Some of the national parks' famous hotels, such as Yellowstone's Old Faithful Inn (*see p602*), are also located in unforgettably scenic locations. Most large resort hotels focus on relaxation and offer spa facilities or access to golf courses, tennis, and other outdoor activities.

An alternative to the large chain or resort hotels are the growing boutique hotels. These small, unique places all have their own personalities and stress service over amenities. These hotels are often quite expensive, so always ask for rates. For a complete listing of accommodations, see Where to Stay in each regional section.

BUSINESS TRAVELERS

MANY DOWNTOWN hotels cater mainly to business people, and some offer special "club-level" accommodations with extra-large rooms for long stays or occasional meetings. These club-level suites often provide breakfast, snacks, and evening cocktails, and on weekends they are great for the whole family.

MOTELS

MOST OVERNIGHT accommodations are provided by motels. Generally located along the main highways, they offer parking for your car right next to your room. Motels usually have fewer amenities than hotels, but they are less expensive and often include swimming pools and children's play areas as well as a restaurant. Motel rooms usually have one large or two smaller beds, a bathroom, a TV, and a phone.

Many motels are run as part of national franchises, but many of the more pleasant ones are locally owned. Some of the most popular chain motels include **Motel 6**, **Howard Johnson**, **Fairfield Inn**, **Holiday Inn**, and the well-known **Best Western**.

BED-AND-BREAKFAST & HISTORIC INNS

MOST HISTORIC INNS offer a much more luxurious experience. Generally located in beautifully restored historic homes or mansions, they are often decorated with heirlooms and antiques. B&Bs, on the other hand, offer a wider choice, from rooms in private homes, where you may have to share a bathroom, to luxurious private accomodations that differ from historic inns in name only.

Most inns and B&Bs rent rooms on a nightly basis, though some offer discounts for week-long stays. Most are run as full-time businesses by professional staff. B&Bs also offer a fully cooked breakfast, often served communally so guests can get to know each other. Breakfasts are usually fairly lavish, multi-course affairs, with eggs, pancakes, and pastries. Some B&Bs, especially in rural areas near popular tourist areas, may also serve gourmet dinners with regional specialties with advance notice.

HOSTELS

FOR SOLO TRAVELERS, one of the best ways to meet others and save money is to take advantage of the clean hostels run by **Hostelling International (HI)**, the American affiliate of the International Youth Hostels Association (IYHA). Hostels can be found in the centers of most major cities and near popular destinations. They offer inexpensive beds in dormitory-style shared rooms, segregated by sex, and many also have a few private rooms for couples or families. Some hostels are housed in unique buildings, such as lighthouses or renovated army barracks.

All hostels have kitchen facilities, bathrooms, and common rooms. HI Hostels have several rules, including no alcohol and sometimes a curfew, and guests are expected to bring their own bed linen. HI Hostels are open to travelers of all ages, although nonmembers are asked to pay a nominal surcharge in addition to nightly rates, which can run between $15 and $20. In many urban areas, there are also a number of privately run hostels that offer basic rooms or dormitory beds. Check the listings in the Yellow Pages.

CAMPGROUNDS

MOST LOCAL, state, and national parks, national forests, and other public lands provide parking and a single or double campsite for tents, along with a picnic table, a campfire pit, toilet facilities, and sometimes hot showers. Some are fancier, with electrical and water "hook-ups" for self-contained recreational vehicles (RVs). Overnight fees vary with location, facilities, and season but generally run from $8 to $20 a night. Many campgrounds accept advance reservations, but some operate on a "first-come, first-served" basis. **Campgrounds Woodalls** and **Trailer Life** carry listings of campsites.

Privately operated campgrounds, such as those run by **Kampgrounds of America** (KOA) offer several features, including game rooms, swimming pools, and small grocery stores. Some also feature log cabins, suitable for families with children. The most popular campgrounds fill up early during vacation weekends and in the summer. It is also a good idea to set up camp well before sunset. Overnight camping in highway rest areas or along public roads is not only illegal but dangerous as well.

RUSTIC OR BASIC ACCOMMODATIONS

THERE ARE several very basic "walk-in" primitive campgrounds in forest areas, used primarily by backpackers. These are generally free, but check with park rangers about wilderness permits and other regulations you might need. Vast portions of the West have such areas, managed by US government departments such as the **National Park Service**, the **US Forest Service**, and the **Bureau of Land Management** (see p37).

PRICES

ROOM RATES for overnight accommodations vary tremendously, from under $20 a night for a campground or hostel, to well over $500 a night in a deluxe downtown hotel. Most places quote the rate per room, but in some places, such as Las Vegas and New England, rates are often quoted per person, should two people share one room.

Room rates at all levels of comfort vary with demand. It is, therefore, worthwhile to ask for discounts, especially on the weekends in urban areas, weekdays in rural areas, or almost anywhere in the off-season, depending on the region.

RESERVATIONS

MAKING ADVANCE reservations can also secure lower rates. Short-notice discounts are also offered, often through advertisements in local newspapers. Many hotels offer package deals in conjunction with a special event, such as theater or concert tickets with overnight accommodations.

Most lodgings will request a credit card number when you make a reservation. If you choose to cancel, you may be charged for a night's stay, depending on the time. For example, if you don't cancel by 6pm or earlier, you may be charged for one night. At the most popular places in peak season, many hotels and resorts may insist on a two-night minimum stay.

Most of the large lodging companies operate toll-free telephone lines for reservations, which can be useful if you are heading to a new city. These lines give up-to-date information about room rates, availability, and are also a good way to compare prices. Most companies publish free directories of all their properties, with maps and full details of rates and facilities.

CHILDREN

MOST HOTELS welcome children and provide extra supplies, such as cots, for families. Babysitting services may also be available. In some family-oriented spots, hotels offer activities for kids and other fun programs. Children from the ages of 12 to 16, sometimes up to 18, can stay free of charge in their parents' room. Rooms often have sofas that unfold into beds; or extra beds may be set up for an additional fee. For more information see p13.

DISABLED TRAVELERS

THE US LAW requires that all businesses provide facilities for the disabled (see p13). However, lodgings do their best to accommodate all customers. If you have specific needs, give advance notice. Most places have wheelchair accessibility, wide doorways, handicap-accessible bathrooms, and support bars near toilets and showers.

DIRECTORY

HOTELS

Hilton
[(800) 445-8667.

Marriott
[(800) 228-9290.

Renaissance
[(800) 468-3571.

MOTELS

Holiday Inn
[(800) 465-4329.

Howard Johnson
[(800) 654-2000.

Motel 6
[(800) 466-8356.

HOSTELS

Hostelling International
733 15th St NW
Washington, DC 20002.
[(202) 783-6161.
w www.hiayh.org

CAMPGROUNDS

Campgrounds Woodalls
w www.woodalls.com

Kampgrounds of America
w www.koa.com

Trailer Life
w www.tldirectory.com

Travel by Air

THE UNITED STATES IS A NATION on the move, with a huge number of airlines that fly both within the country and all around the world. While international travel is offered by US airlines as well as by hundreds of airlines in other countries, domestic travel is limited to airlines based in the United States. Because the country is so enormous, and recent competition has reduced prices considerably, air travel has become an integral part of life. Today, most long-distance and medium-distance domestic travel is by plane.

FLYING TO THE US

MOST LARGE foreign cities have several daily flights to a number of US cities, especially pimary gateways to the East Coast, the West Coast, and throughout the Midwest. The main East Coast cities include New York, Boston, Washington, DC, Atlanta, and Miami; Chicago, St. Louis, Houston, Dallas, and Denver serve as main cities in the central region; and the West Coast is served by Los Angeles, San Francisco, and Seattle.

Most international flights from Europe travel across the Atlantic to New York, Washington, DC, Miami, Boston, and Chicago, taking roughly seven hours. Flights from Asia arrive at the West Coast airports, often stopping in Hawai'i on the way. These flights, as well as flights from Australia, take between 11 and 12 hours.

KEEPING COSTS DOWN

AIR FARES FLUCTUATE in the US depending on the season, sometimes doubling during the peak holiday periods, especially in summer, and around Thanksgiving and Christmas. Fares are usually less expensive between February and March, when round-trip transatlantic flights can cost significantly less. You often get a better deal, too, by flying mid-week.

The least expensive fares are the APEX (Advance Purchase Excursion) tickets for scheduled airlines. These must be bought 21 days in advance and are valid for a seven- to 30-day period. However, any changes that need to be made can cost an additional fee. Some airlines also offer cheaper fares if you limit your stay to a certain period of time. Senior citizens and children may also receive discounts on certain flights.

These tickets are not always available, though. Another option is the short-term Internet fares advertised by airlines if there are any available seats. These are valid within a few days of the announcement (fares may be announced on a Wednesday for traveling that weekend and returning the next weekend).

ARRIVAL AT THE AIRPORT

ALL INTERNATIONAL visitors must go through customs and immigration when they arrive in the US *(see p13)*. All major airports have multilingual information booths to answer your questions and give details on transportation into the city.

Most international airports are well connected to the nearest city either by public transportation or the vast array of rental car facilities. Many rentals supply shuttle buses to car pick-up points, usually located just outside the airport. Major airlines are connected to countless domestic airline services, and all have facilities for disabled passengers. Still, it is a good idea to prearrange any necessary services through your airline or agent.

SECURITY

AFTER THE September 11, 2001 terrorist attacks, airport authorities tightened their pre-flight security checks (especially for domestic flights). International visitors should expect to be frisked thoroughly and have their hand luggage examined. Items such as battery cells, scissors, nail files, knitting needles, and sharp objects are prohibited. Signs throughout the Customs areas explain which items are prohibited in checked luggage. New plans are in place for

---

TIME ZONES ACROSS THE UNITED STATES

The United States covers six different times zones – the "Lower 48" states are divided into Eastern, Central, Mountain, and Pacific time, while Alaska and Hawai'i have their own zones. The zones are divided into one-hour increments. For instance, when it is 8pm in New York, it is 7pm in Chicago, 6pm in Denver, 5pm in Los Angeles, 4pm in Anchorage, and 3pm in Honolulu.

Eastern Time is five hours behind Greenwich Mean Time, and Hawai'i is 11 hours behind Greenwich Mean Time. With a few variations, the United States observes Daylight Savings Time between spring and fall.

Pacific Time -8
Los Angeles

Denver
Mountain Time -7

Chicago
Central Time -6
Dallas

New York
Eastern Time -5

Miami

visitors with visas to be photo-graphed and fingerprinted on arrival, for details to be checked against a national security database. In light of increased security, expect a long wait to check in.

FLYING WITHIN THE UNITED STATES

VISITORS INTERESTED in seeing the entire country may want to take advantage of domestic flights. These are operated by more than a dozen different major airlines, many of which fly inter-nationally as well. An exten-sive domestic flight network serves most cities, making it easy to fly within the US.

The major US airlines operate what is known as a "hub-and-spoke" network, meaning that long-distance flights travel between regional airports, from where shorter flights continue on to your desired destination. Most **Delta Airlines** flights con-verge on their hub in Atlanta; **United Airlines** flights con-verge in Chicago and Denver; while **American Airlines** usually flies first to Dallas.

BOOKING A DOMESTIC FLIGHT

FOR FOREIGN visitors the easiest way to book a domestic flight is to have it agree with your itinerary. This way you have to buy only

one set of tickets and often get a better deal. Another money-saving option is to take advantage of "Visit USA" (VUSA) coupons, which are good for numerous domestic flights (between three and ten flights), for a pre-paid fee. However, these coupons must be bought before you arrive and can be redeemed only with the same airline on which you flew internationally.

The Internet and the deregulation of the airline industry have made planning trips and purchasing tickets much easier. The best prices now are on airlines' websites.

DOMESTIC AIRLINES

MOST INTERNATIONAL airlines have formed alliances with domestic flights, for instance, **British Airways** is partnered with American Airlines, and **Lufthansa** with United Airlines, making flight networks effectively inter-linked. Beside the major inter-national US airlines, there are a large number of domestic airlines that offer inexpensive flights. The most popular of these is **Southwest Airlines**, a "no-frills" carrier that connects to and from smaller airports rather than from major ones. These airlines are a less expensive and reliable means of travel. They offer basic snacks, and do not transfer to or from other carriers, which can make

connecting flights a hassle, but the fares are low, and there are fewer restrictions.

FLY-DRIVE

MANY AIRLINES, in addition to travel companies and agents, offer fly-drive pack-ages for tourists, which com-bine air fares and car rentals. These deals are well worth considering, since they give you flexibility and usually save you more money than if you were to book plane and car travel separately.

AIRPORT	C INFORMATION	DISTANCE FROM CITY	TAXI FARE TO CITY	AVERAGE TRAVEL TIME
Chicago (O'Hare)	*(800) 832-6352*	17 miles (27 km) from downtown	$35–40 to downtown	Road: 30 mins to downtown
Dallas–Fort Worth (International)	*(972) 574-8888*	18 miles (29 km) from Dallas	$38 to downtown Dallas	Road: 25 mins to downtown Dallas
Los Angeles (LAX)	*(310) 646-5252*	15 miles (24 km) from downtown	$27 to downtown	Road: 30 mins to downtown
Miami (International)	*(305) 876-7000*	10 miles (16 km) from Miami Beach	$24 to Miami Beach	Road: 20 mins to Miami Beach
New York City (JFK)	*(718) 244-4444*	15 miles (24 km) from Manhattan	$40 to downtown Manhattan	Road: 1 hr to down-town Manhattan
San Francisco (SFO)	*(650) 821-8211*	14 miles (22 km) from downtown	$35 to downtown	Road: 25 mins to downtown
Seattle (Sea-Tac)	*(206) 431-4444*	14 miles (22 km) from downtown	$30 to downtown	Road: 25 mins to downtown
Washington, DC (Dulles International)	*(703) 572-2700*	26 miles (42 km) from downtown	$44–50 to downtown	Road: 40 mins to downtown

Travel by Road

AWAY FROM MAJOR CITIES, where traffic can be frustrating, driving in the United States is a delightful experience. Driving is a favorite American pastime, and to see the country in all its glory, you have to drive a car. Major roads and most highways are rarely crowded, and drivers are generally courteous and safe. Gasoline in the US is inexpensive, and car rental rates are also reasonable. You can get by without a car in a few larger towns, and in cities like New York, Boston, or San Francisco you will probably be better off without one. However, in most of the country, if you want to explore the wide open spaces of the western US, you will need a car since public transportation there is limited.

Transcontinental Interstates run east-to-west and range from I-10 between Florida and California to I-90 between Boston and Seattle.

In and around cities, a complicated system of ring roads, link roads, and spur roads are also part of the Interstate system. These roads are often better known by name than number, for instance I-405 in Southern California is referred to as the "San Diego Freeway."

Most Interstates are free, but some states charge tolls. These sections, known as "turnpikes," have the same numbers as sections without toll booths.

Before the Interstate Highway System came into use, the primary long-distance highways were federal ones. Today, these are the main routes in rural areas and are officially signed as "US" and a number, ranging from US-1 along the East Coast to US-101 along the West Coast.

TYPES OF ROAD

THE US HAS AN excellent network of roads, with over 4 million miles (6 million km) of paved roads open to the public. For long distance travelers, the fastest and most convenient part of the US highway system is the Interstate Highway, a high-speed, limited-access highway. Some have between six and 12 lanes running both directions, while rural areas generally have two or three lanes.

Stretching all across the country in an east-to-west and north-to-south grid, Interstate Highways are abbreviated on signs with a capital "I," followed by a number. The main Interstates start with I-5 on the West Coast and end with I-95, the busy main route along the East Coast.

RULES OF THE ROAD

- All traffic drives on the right.
- All distances are measured in miles.
- Seat belts are compulsory, and children under the age of 4 are required to have special car seats.
- At traffic signals, green lights mean you can proceed safely; amber lights mean prepare to stop; and red lights mean stop. A flashing red light means stop before proceeding; and a flashing yellow light means proceed with caution.
- At a red octagonal stop sign, traffic must come to a complete halt before proceeding. When two or more cars reach a stop sign simultaneously from different sides of the intersection, drivers must yield to traffic on the right.
- A yellow triangular yield sign directs you to give way to other traffic.
- In towns and cities, roads are usually divided by a painted center line (usually white). Smaller streets may have no dividing line.
- On all roads, a double yellow line means do not pass or cross the lines.
- Some roads have a central lane, protected by painted single lines; this is a designated turning area for making left-hand turns.
- "U" turns are legal only where posted.
- On multi-lane highways, the fastest traffic travels in the left-hand lanes; slower traffic occupies the right-hand lane.
- Cargo-carrying heavy trucks generally stay in the slow lane. Keep your distance from these vehicles, because they have poor visibility and enormous weight and size.
- On multi-lane highways traffic can pass only on the left-hand side. On smaller roads safe passing places are indicated with a broken yellow line on your side of the double yellow line.
- Speed limits vary from state to state, but range from 25mph (40 km/h) in residential areas to 65–75mph (105–120 km/h) on highways.
- There is a minimum speed of 45mph (72 km/h) on highways and Interstate Highways. Farm traffic and pedestrians are not permitted on Interstates.
- Parking is allowed on most streets, subject to posted rules, but any restrictions are posted at the site. Park only in the direction of travel. If you receive a ticket, pay it immediately or it will be charged (with a penalty) to the rental car company, who will collect it from your credit card.
- Visitors should be aware of regional exceptions to the standard US driving laws. Some of these are pointed out in the "Practical Information" section of each chapter.
- Most foreign licenses are valid, but if your license is not in English, or does not have a photo ID, you must get an International Driver's License.
- Drunk driving is a serious offense and can result in a heavy fine or jail term.

Lined by neon-lit motels, and other classic landmarks of roadside America, these roads are slower but more enjoyable, and along with many other state and country roads, provide the country's most scenic routes (*see pp40–41*).

Road names vary from state to state. In the northeast, for example, highways are called "routes" while in Texas, roads are labeled "FM," farm to market or "RM," ranch to market.

TIPS FOR RENTING A CAR

MOST RENTAL CARS are relatively new and low on mileage, and rates are as low as $150 a week. The best rates are generally offered for cars rented for full week time periods, and for returning cars to the same location they were rented from. A more economical option is the fly-drive *(see p21)*.

Small economy or subcompact cars have the lowest rates. Many companies also offer upgrades to larger or more luxurious vehicles for very modest rates. Most rental cars have automatic transmissions, power steering, and air conditioning, but you should confirm this in advance. Also, check for any pre-existing damage to the car and note this on your contract.

To rent a car, you must be at least 25 years old, have a valid driving license, a clean driving record, and a major credit card. The car company will "authorize" an amount ranging between $250–1,000, to assure payment and return of the vehicle. Depending on your existing car insurance policy, you may want to accept the "damage waiver" and liability insurance that the rental company will offer you, and this will add $10–20 per day to the rental cost.

DRIVEAWAYS

AN INEXPENSIVE OPTION for a long-distance road trip is a driveaway car. Driveaways let you take a private car to a predetermined place in a specified amount of time. Most driveaways are offered to private members, but some ads may appear in magazines or newspapers.

Flexiblity is essential for a driveaway deal since the destination is beyond your control. You have to choose an efficient route and average about 400 miles (644 km) a day. However, since you have to pay only for the gas, the price is quite good. To use a driveaway car, you must have a clean driving record, and most companies require a minimum deposit to cover the insurance deductible.

One of the biggest driveaway companies, **Auto Driveaway**, has offices all over the US. Other firms are listed in phone books under "Automobile Transporters."

RV RENTALS

RECREATIONAL vehicles (RVs) or mobile homes, are great for families or groups, as they are equipped with beds, kitchens, and bathroom facilities. Costs run between $900–1,400 for seven nights plus a per-mile charge, but lodging is free and you have some flexibility, despite the vehicles' slow, stocky designs. Although rental RVs are usually older, conditions are similar to those for cars.

It is illegal in most places to pull over to the side of the road and camp. Many chain retail outlets, notably Wal-Mart, allow one night's free stay in their parking lots, with approval of the manager or front desk. Even with an RV, it costs about $20 a night to park in a campground (*see p19*). For more details contact **Recreational Vehicle Association of America** or **Cruise America**.

INSURANCE

IT IS EXTREMELY IMPORTANT that you have adequate insurance if you plan on driving around in the US. Rental agencies generally include insurance in the cost, but if you bring a car into the country, you must make absolutely sure that you are adequately covered by car and life insurance.

GAS STATIONS

EXCEPT IN THE most remote areas, gas stations are easy to find and conveniently located. Many stations require advance payment, either by cash or credit/debit card. Most gas stations also have attached convenience stores, where you can buy food, beverages, and newspapers.

REST AREAS

CONVENIENTLY located immediately adjacent to Interstates and major highways, rest areas are easily accessible and provide restrooms, telephones, picnic tables, dog-walking areas, and sometimes free coffee. Some even allow overnight stays, but be wary of strangers. It is a good idea to take a rest when driving long distances.

Travel by Motorcycle or Bike

For visitors with time on their hands as well as a sense of adventure, touring the United States by motorcycle or bicycle can be a rewarding experience. Ride the open road with a Harley-Davidson, or mountain bike throughout the beautiful and peaceful American wilderness for the adventure of a lifetime. Good planning, familiarizing yourself with the rules and regulations, and using the right equipment can make this an enjoyable way of seeing the country.

MOTORCYCLES

Fans of Marlon Brando's famous movie *The Wild One* (1954) or the Jack Nicholson's classic *Easy Rider* (1969) may dream of exploring the United States on a motorcycle. Today, there are several motorcycle rental companies, especially in bike-friendly areas, where licensed riders drive classic motorcycles such as Harley-Davidsons or BMWs.

An American motorcycle license or an International Driving Permit for motorcycles is necessary. Also, the law in most states requires that you wear a helmet.

MOTORCYCLE RENTALS & TOURS

Renting is expensive, since the rates and liability insurance can add up to well over $100 a day. Moreover, you have to pay extra for collision insurance. Most companies allow short-term rentals in a single location, but larger firms such as **Eagle Rider** have branches or affiliates all over the country. If you plan to stay for a longer period, it might be less expensive to buy a bike for a few months, then resell it.

For long-distance motorcycle trips, Eagle Rider offers guided tours along selected routes. **Blue Sky Motorcycle Tours** also offers a wide range of tours.

Riders may be interested in taking part in one of the many motorcycle rallies, when thousands of riders get together for annual gatherings held in places like Daytona Beach, Florida (early March); Laconia, New Hampshire (mid June); or Sturgis, South Dakota (August).

BICYCLES

Bicycles are another great way to see the country. Unlike motorcycles, bicycles can be brought on most airplanes as luggage. Check the requirements first with your airline – many carriers require that you disassemble and pack the bike into a special box, which is available in most good bike shops.

In a great many cities, there are extensive networks of bike paths, which are often separated from car traffic. In some larger cities, bikes can be strapped onto the outside of local buses or carried on the subway.

For serious long-distance biking, it's important to equip yourself with a good bike, tools and spares, maps, and preferably a helmet. Cyclists must obey all traffic laws and should be careful to lock up their bikes and gear.

· In the US, bikes are not as common as they are in many other countries. Car and truck drivers are not used to sharing the road with bikes, which can make cycling hazardous. Be aware of RV drivers in particular, because it is easy for them to misjudge the sizes of their vehicles. Bikes are prohibited on restricted-access highways and freeways.

BICYCLE RENTALS & TOURS

Bikes are available for rent in all major US cities for around $25 a day, or you can buy used bikes from flea markets or garage sales. Notices of second-hand sales appear in newspaper ads or hostel notices. Look in the Yellow Pages for local bike rental companies.

Backroads organizes a variety of guided bike tours, following some of the most spectacular scenic routes, with overnight stays in country inns or national park campsites. If interested in long-distance cycling, be sure to contact the **Adventure Cycling Association**, which has developed a network of bike-friendly routes following quieter and more scenic federal and state highways.

RECREATIONAL BIKING

In country areas, many bike paths have been reclaimed from unused railroad lines. Known as "rail trails," these are some of the best long-distance bicycling and walking routes in the country, often running alongside rivers and having moderate grades. In addition, there are miles and miles of country roads everywhere you go. Areas such as California's Wine Country and New England's river valleys are among the most popular.

The more athletic or daredevil travelers may also want to try off-road mountain biking, which is encouraged in many recreational areas such as downhill ski resorts in summer.

Travel by Bus or Train

ALTHOUGH MORE TIME-CONSUMING than flying, you can enjoy long-distance bus and train trips that let you see the beauty of the US. Greyhound – the major long-distance buses – offers clean, modern travel conditions with on-board movies and restroom facilities. Amtrak trains are spacious and comfortable. Amtrak provides restaurant cars, observation cars, and great social atmospheres. If you want to meet fellow travelers, buses and trains are the transportation options for you.

TRAVELING BY BUS

THE NATION-WIDE carrier **Greyhound Lines** serves all the major cities that airlines do, plus many smaller towns along the way, but the travel times are much longer. On long journeys, be sure to take something to eat and drink as meals are determined by where the bus stops.

Buses are also a good option for urban or suburban transportation, but because service can be limited in rural areas, you should plan your route carefully when visiting the countryside. Greyhound buses also provide links with major airports as well as Amtrak services.

TICKETS & RESERVATIONS

MANY BUS stations are located in low-rent parts of town, so it is usually a good idea to take a taxi home from the station at night.

Ask about discounts and special fares on Greyhound and other carriers. Most major bus lines offer discounts for children under 12, students, and senior citizens (with proper ID), as well as unlimited travel within a set period. Tickets can be bought on the same day of travel, although fares are much less expensive if they are bought in advance. For advance tickets, contact Greyhound directly or ask a travel agent.

International visitors should know that Greyhound tickets are cheaper if bought from an agent outside the US. If you plan to interrupt your trip to explore on your own, or tour the US on an extended trip, there may be a travel package just for you.

BUS TOURS

IN MOST STATES, bus companies offer short package trips in deluxe air-conditioned buses that tour major attractions. These guided tours provide a comfortable way of seeing the sights, without having to worry about time schedules, admission tickets, and opening hours.

For passengers with more time to spare, you may want to try certain bus companies, such as **Green Tortoise**, that offer leisurely trips between major cities. Passengers on these buses can take breaks to camp out, prepare meals, and explore the countryside. Unlike other buses, there are foam mattresses for sleeping. These tours are not for everyone, nevertheless they can provide an enjoyable, relaxed, and memorable tour of the country.

TRAVELING BY TRAIN

THE USE OF RAILROADS in the US is dwindling. Still, there is a small and enjoyable network of long-distance passenger train routes, operated by **Amtrak**, the national rail system. In spite of its limited network and sometimes inconvenient schedules, a scenic train ride can be a unforgettable experience.

TRAIN TICKETS & RESERVATIONS

TO MAKE THE most of an Amtrak trip, consider paying the extra money to get a sleeping compartment, which costs around $150 a night on a twin-sharing basis. Meal service is included in the price.

Amtrak travel is an especially good value for international visitors, who can take advantage of a number of rail tickets that give 15 or 30 days of train travel for a fee of $350–500, depending on the dates and regions of travel.

HISTORIC RAILROADS

MANY PIONEER railroads that braved the Wild West frontier are now back in business as tourist attractions, running short trips (often under coal-fired steam) through some spectacular scenery. Many trains, running along narrow-gauge tracks, were constructed by mining or logging companies over a century ago.

Among the most popular railroads are the **Durango and Silverton Narrow Gauge** in southwestern Colorado (*see p591*), the **Cumbres and Toltec** line in New Mexico, and the **Grand Canyon Railroad** in Williams, Arizona, which goes to the rim of the Grand Canyon.

(see p591)

DIRECTORY

LONG-DISTANCE BUSES

Greyhound Lines
C (800) 231-2222 (24 hrs).
W www.greyhound.com

BUS TOURS

Green Tortoise
C (415) 956-7500.
W www.greentortoise.com

RAILROADS

Amtrak
C (800) 872-7245.
W www.amtrak.com

Durango & Silverton Narrow Gauge
C (970) 247-2733.
W www.durangotrain.com

Cumbres & Toltec Railroad
C (505) 756-2151.
W www.cumbrestoltec.com

Grand Canyon Railroad
C (800) 843-8724.
W www.thetrain.com/gcinfo.cfm

USA at a Glance

USA Through the Year

THE SIZE AND SCOPE of the United States means that at almost any time of year you can find the right weather to suit any activity. In the middle of winter, for example, while skiers are enjoying the deep snows of the Rockies and New England, sun-seekers flock to Florida or the Arizona deserts. Both the weather and the calendar of events heat up in the summer with a proliferation of county fairs, arts and music festivals, and other

Jazz Festival musician, New Orleans

events, many celebrating the nation's diverse history and culture. October and November are prime time for harvest festivals, especially near Thanksgiving. The year ends with a variety of religious holidays, including Christmas, Hannukah, Ramadan, and the African-American celebration Kwanzaa, while the college and professional football seasons climax with a series of New Year's Day championship games and the Super Bowl finale.

Spring

SPRING INSPIRES a definite sense of renewal all over the country. Wildflowers carpet the deserts, the magnolias and cherry trees burst into bloom, and melting snows fill streams and waterfalls to their annual peak. Among the events that celebrate the season, the most symbolic are the first games of the baseball season, which begins in April.

March

Lahaina Whalefest *(early Mar)*, Lahaina, HI. Lectures, dives, and whale-watching activities celebrate the humpback whale that winters off the Hawaiian coast.
Bike Week *(early Mar)*, Daytona, FL. Motorcycle racers and enthusiasts congregate in one of the US's largest gatherings of bikers.
St. Patrick's Day Parade *(Sun nearest Mar 17)*, Boston, MA; New York City, NY; Chicago, IL; San Francisco, CA. Parades celebrating Irish heritage are held in these major cities. Towns such as Butte, MT, and Savannah, GA, also hold parties.
South by Southwest Festival *(mid-Mar)*, Austin, TX. An independent pop-music festival.
Academy Awards *(mid-Mar)*, Hollywood, CA. The movie industry honors its stars with golden Oscars.

Natchez Pilgrimage *(early Mar–early Apr)* Natchez, MS. A month-long celebration of Old South culture and antebellum architecture *(see p30)*.

April

Easter *(date varies)*. This spring holiday is a study in contrasts. Early morning outdoor "Easter Sunrise" services are held all over the country, while in New York City, outrageously dressed characters join in the Easter Parade down Fifth Avenue. At this time, college kids flock to warm climes in Florida, Texas, and California for their annual "Spring Break."
National Cherry Blossom Festival *(early Apr)*, Washington, DC. A number of events celebrate the blossoming of hundreds of the city's famous cherry trees.
Patriot's Day *(Mon nearest Apr 18)*, Lexington and Concord, MA. Early morning re-enactments of the first

battles of the American Revolution are followed by the country's most famous race, the Boston Marathon.

May

Cinco de Mayo *(May 5)*. Celebrations of Mexican culture featuring folk dancing and mariachi music, take place all over the US to mark the anniversary of the Battle of Puebla.
Kentucky Derby *(first Sat in May)*, Louisville, KY. The country's biggest horse race and the start of the "Triple Crown" championship takes place at the end of a two-week-long public party.
Wright Plus *(mid- or late May)*, Chicago, IL. You can tour architect Frank Lloyd Wright's buildings and residences during this annual housewalk at Oak Park.
Spoleto Festival USA *(late May-early Jun)*, Charleston, SC. The largest arts festival in the United States.

Jockeys at Churchill Downs for the Kentucky Derby, Louisville

◁ Silhouettes of tall saguaro cacti, unique to the Sonoran Desert, Arizona

Indianapolis 500 *(Sun before Memorial Day)*, Indianapolis, IN. The most famous auto race in the US draws over 100,000 fans.
Kinetic Sculpture Race *(Memorial Day weekend)*, Arcata, CA. Northern California's good-natured culture is evident at this three-day event, in which human-powered sculptures are raced over land and sea.

Independence Day fireworks light up the sky in Houston, Texas

SUMMER

THE MEMORIAL Day holiday, at the end of May, marks the unofficial beginning of summertime. This is prime vacation and travel time for students and families. It is also a good time to enjoy music festivals, usually held in idyllic rural locations. The weather is hot and frequently humid, with afternoon storms in much of the country.

The flamboyant Lesbian and Gay Pride Parade, New York City

JUNE

Harvard-Yale Regatta *(early Jun)*, New London, CT. This series of collegiate rowing races offers visitors a chance to observe the Ivy League elite at play.
Indian Bayou Blues Festival *(first Fri in Jun)*, Indianola, MS. One of the oldest and most popular of the many Deep South summer blues festivals.
Red Earth Native American Festival *(second weekend)*, Oklahoma City, OK. One the largest gatherings of Native American dancers and musicians is held at what was the last vestige of "Indian Territory."
Lesbian and Gay Pride Day *(Sun in late Jun)*, New York City, NY; San Francisco, California. Major parades and festivities fill the streets of both these cities.

JULY

Independence Day *(Jul 4)*, Bristol, RI; Boston, MA; Independence, MO; Stone Mountain near Atlanta, GA. Although the entire country celebrates the Fourth of July with parades and fireworks displays, these cities put on particularly good shows.
Taste of Chicago, *(first week in Jul)*, Chicago, IL. The city's best food and music can be experienced at an open-air party, held on the Lake Michigan waterfront.
Ernest Hemingway Days *(mid-Jul)*, Key West, FL. The city where the famous writer lived offers a week of theatrical productions, short story contests, and a Hemingway look-alike competition.
Tanglewood Music Festival *(Jul–Aug)*, Lenox, MA. The Boston Symphony and Boston Pops give outdoor concerts in a beautiful Berkshire Mountains estate.

AUGUST

Hawaiian International Billfish Tournament *(first week in Aug)*, Kailua-Kona, HI. This international fishing tournament draws people in search of record-sized marlin.
Sunflower River Blues Festival *(early-Aug)*, Clarksdale, MS. One of the country's most enjoyable blues festivals takes place in the home of the blues, the Mississippi Delta.
Elvis International Tribute Week *(mid-Aug)*, Memphis, TN. Also called "Deathweek," a series of events are held to celebrate the life and times of Elvis Presley, leading up to the anniversary of his death on August 16.
Alaska State Fair *(mid-Aug)*, Palmer, AK. This fair is especially famous for its super-sized vegetables, with pumpkins and cabbages grown to world-record sizes due to the state's 24-hour summer sunshine.
Newport Jazz Festival *(mid-Aug)*, Newport, RI. Sponsored by electronics firm JVC, this popular festival draws the very best jazz musicians from all over the country and the world.
US Open Tennis Championships *(Aug–Sep)*, New York City, NY. Professional tennis players from the world over compete in this Grand Slam tournament.

Opening ceremony of the 2002 US Open Tennis Championships

The famous fiery colors of New England's fall foliage

FALL

DURING FALL in New England, the leaves of the hardwood trees turn stunning shades of red and gold, drawing appreciative tourists from all over the country. In the West, wine-growing regions celebrate the annual harvest, and in the Great Lakes and Mid-west, beer lovers join the Oktoberfest celebrations in the nation's many German enclaves. The approach of winter and the start of the Christmas shopping season is kicked off by the nationally televised Macy's Thanksgiving Day parade down Broadway in New York City.

SEPTEMBER

Mississippi Delta Blues and Heritage Festival *(mid-Sep)*, Greenville, MS. A blues and African-American culture festival in the heart of the Mississippi Delta.
Miss America Pageant *(mid-Sep)*, Atlantic City, NJ. The nation's oldest beauty contest, held in the seaside resort of Atlantic City.
Festivals Acadiens *(late Sep)*, Lafayette, LA. Over 100,000 people flock to this Cajun Country capital to enjoy the unique sights, sounds, and tastes of Louisiana life.
Northeast Kingdom Fall Foliage Festival *(mid-Sep–early Oct)*, VT. Celebrating the change of seasons, as well as the

brilliantly colored fall foliage, several tours and events are held in small towns all over northern Vermont.
Major League Baseball Championships *(Sep–Oct)*. The nation's top professional teams face off, with the winners competing in October's World Series.

OCTOBER

Texas State Fair *(late-Sep–early Oct)*, Dallas, TX. One of the country's largest state fairs, with a focus on Texas.
King Biscuit Blues Festival *(early Oct)*, Helena, AR. Once sponsored by the King Biscuit flour company, the small Mississippi River town of Helena has been celebrating the blues since the 1920s.
Ironman Triathlon *(Sat nearest to full moon)*, Kailua-Kona, HI. More than 1,000 of the world's fittest athletes take part in a highly challenging series of trials, combining a 2.4-mile (3.8-km) swim, a 112-mile (180-

Giant cowboy balloon at the Texas State Fair in Dallas

km) bike ride, and a 26-mile (42-km) marathon run.
American Royal Rodeo *(date varies, mid-Oct to early Nov)*, Kansas City, MO. One of the country's largest and most prominent professional rodeo competitions.
Columbus Day Parade *(second Mon in Oct)*, San Francisco, CA. Columbus Avenue, winding through the city's Italian-American North Beach district, comes alive with a parade celebrating the achievements of the Italian-born explorer Christopher Columbus. Several other such parades are held throughout the country.
Fall Pilgrimage *(mid-Oct)*, Natchez, MS. *(see p28)*. A three-week-long series of events celebrate antebellum architecture and culture.
Oktoberfest *(late Oct)*. Modeled on the famous one in Munich, beer-flavored festivals are held in German neighborhoods of most large cities in the US, as well as small German towns like New Braunfels TX, Hermann MO, and Leavenworth, WA.
Haunted Happenings *(late Oct)*, Salem, MA. Leading up to Halloween, the historic home of the Salem Witch Trials stages a series of supernatural-themed events and activities.
Halloween *(Oct 31)*. While children dress up in scary costumes and beg for candy, many adults flock to raucous public parties in places like Key West, FL, and New York's Greenwich Village.

NOVEMBER

Dia de los Muertos (Day of the Dead) *(Nov 1)*, San Francisco, CA. Festivities in San Francisco's Mission District highlight this Catholic festival, when the souls of the dead are said to visit the living. Similar festivities take place in Mexican neigh-borhoods across the country.
Thanksgiving *(last Thu in Nov)*. Celebrating the sur-vival of the pilgrims who landed at Plymouth, MA, in 1620, this holiday sees

Turkey Float in Macy's Thanksgiving Day Parade, New York City

families coming together from all over the country to share in a massive meal of roast turkey, stuffing, cranberry sauce, and pumpkin pie. Many restaurants serve special Thanksgiving meals, and an old-fashioned celebration of the festival is held at Plimoth Plantation.
Macy's Thanksgiving Day Parade *(Thanksgiving Day)*, New York City, NY. Giant inflatable figures march down New York's Broadway to celebrate Thanksgiving and the start of the Christmas holiday season.

WINTER

P ERHAPS BEST KNOWN for the shopping mania that leads up to Christmas, winter in American cities is a time of twinkling lights, ringing cash registers, and occasional snowstorms. Department stores along New York's Fifth Avenue, Chicago's State Street, and other shopping districts attract shoppers with exuberant displays in their store windows. Many ski resorts stage special winter activities, such as sleigh rides and visits from Santa Claus. Winter is also the best time to watch the gray whale migration along the Pacific Ocean, or to observe the humpback whales on the way to their winter breeding grounds in Hawai'i. February also sees a number of public parades and parties, which range from the Chinese New

Year celebrations to the wild fun and festivity of Mardi Gras in New Orleans.

DECEMBER

Triple Crown of Surfing *(late Nov to mid-Dec)*, North Shore O'ahu, HI. The world's most prestigious surfing competition usually spans three weeks, waves and weather permitting.
Boston Tea Party Re-enactment *(mid-Dec)*, Boston, MA. Costumed performers and interpreters bring to life the famous Boston Tea Party, a protest that played an important role in precipitating the famous American Revolution.
 New Year's Eve *(Dec 31)*, New York City, NY. The country's foremost New Year celebration starts with the countdown in New York's Times Square, which is televised live across Eastern US and repeated (on tape) for viewers elsewhere in the country. Major New Year's Eve parties occur in most major cities, with great public celebrations in Las Vegas and San Francisco.

JANUARY

New Year's Day *(Jan 1)*. A variety of parades and lively festivities are held all around the country; these are very often connected with a championship college football game such as the well-known Orange Bowl in Miami, the Cotton Bowl in Dallas, the Sugar Bowl in

New Orleans, and the Rose Bowl in Pasadena, CA.
Martin Luther King Jr. Day *(Mon nearest Jan 15)*. Events are held around the country to honor the birth and life of the Civil Rights leader.
Mud Week *(mid-Jan)*, San Antonio, TX. While workers drain the water to clear out downtown's River Walk, musicians and artists have fun in the mud.
Cowboy Poetry Festival *(late Jan)*, Elko, NV. Cowboys come to this town to tell tales, quote their very own poems, and sing songs about the heroic American West.

FEBRUARY

Groundhog Day *(Feb 2)*, Punxsatawny, PA. The star of this festival is a small rodent who forecasts the beginning of spring.
Mardi Gras *(date varies, mid-Feb)*, New Orleans, LA. Colorful parades, lavish parties, and masked balls are held. Many smaller cities hold similar celebrations.

Lion dance during Chinese New Year, Chinatown, San Francisco

Chinese New Year *(date varies, late Jan to mid-Feb)*, San Francisco, CA. To celebrate Chinese New Year, colorful parades are held here, in New York City, and several other cities.
Iditarod Trail Sled Dog Race *(late Feb–early Mar)*, Anchorage, AK. This test of endurance takes packs of dogs and their drivers two grueling weeks.

Climate of the USA

MUCH OF THE US ENJOYS temperate weather, but the country is so vast that many regions experience climatic extremes. Alaska has the harshest winter, while the warmest temperatures are in Hawai'i and Florida. Even within the "Lower 48" states, the weather varies tremendously, from the heavy snows of the Rocky Mountains to the intense heat of Death Valley in the California desert. Beside the four main seasons, the US also sees some unusual weather, including destructive tornadoes that may form in spring and summer across the Great Plains; thunderstorms that burst over the South during summer; and powerful hurricanes that strike coastal areas in the Southeast in autumn.

Subarctic (Alaska)
Though temperatures drop well below freezing for most of the year, the warm summers are extended by the non-stop daylight of the "midnight sun."

Temperate (California)
The West Coast's mild climate is much like that of the Mediterranean regions, with mild winters and long, sunny summers.

Tropical (Hawai'i)
This island paradise is warm and pleasant year-round. Significant rain falls in winter, usually on the northeastern or windward coasts.

Arid (Southwest)
The hot, dry climate of the Southwestern desert draws millions of visitors. Winter snows can fall at higher elevations, but sunshine is guaranteed throughout the year.

Cool Temperate (New England)
Bright, sunny days followed by frosty nights cause the most intense color in New England's famous autumn foliage. The region experiences warm summers and cold winters with high snowfalls in certain areas.

Cool Continental (Great Lakes)
The Great Lakes states are famous for their frigid winters, when the region receives the country's heaviest snowfall.

0 km   500

0 miles   500

NEW ENGLAND

apolis

lwaukee ● ● Detroit
Buffalo
NYC & MID-ATLANTIC REGION ● Boston
● Chicago
New York
THE GREAT LAKES
Philadelphia ●
Indianapolis ● Cincinnati Baltimore ●
City
● St. Louis DC & THE CAPITAL REGION ● WASHINGTON, DC
Richmond

● Nashville ● Charlotte
THE SOUTHEAST
emphis ●
THE DEEP SOUTH ● Atlanta ● Charleston
Savannah
Mobile ● Jacksonville
on ● New Orleans
FLORIDA
● Miami

Cool Temperate (Great Plains)
Chilled by arctic winds in winter, and hit by fierce tornadoes in spring, the Midwest states usually enjoy long, hot summers.

Warm Tropical (Florida)
The sultry climate of Florida and the Gulf of Mexico is usually warm and frequently very humid. Hurricanes can hit the coast between June and late November, making December to April the most popular time to visit the region.

National Parks

FOR MANY VISITORS, the highlight of a visit to the US is to experience the country's sublime scenery and abundant wildlife. Some 80 million acres (32 milion hectares) of pristine splendor have been preserved as national parks, found in 49 of the 50 states. From Acadia National Park on the rugged coast of Maine to the deserts of Death Valley in California, the parks encompass a variety of terrain, as well as the habitats of several endangered species. Most have a full range of facilities, including delightful rustic lodges, and offer a variety of outdoor activities.

Yellowstone National Park (see pp584–5) *in Wyoming is the country's first and oldest national park. Highlights include geysers and the country's largest bison herd.*

Grand Teton National Park's *(see p583)* peaks make it one of Wyoming's top sights.

Badlands National Park *(see p444),* South Dakota's most important park, combines craggy sandstone formations with mixed grass prairie.

Olympic National Park (see p620), *a UNESCO biosphere reserve, preserves Washington's lush forests.*

Olympic NP
North Cascades NP
Mt. Rainier NP
THE PACIFIC NORTHWEST
Crater Lake NP
Redwood NP
CALIFORNIA
Lassen Volcanic NP
Yosemite NP
Kings Canyon NP
Sequoia NP
Death Valley NP
Joshua Tree NP
Glacier NP
THE ROCKIES
Yellowstone NP
Grand Teton NP
Badlands N
Rocky Mountain NP
Great Basin NP
Bryce Canyon NP
Arches NP
Mesa Verde NP
Grand Canyon NP
Petrified Forest NP
Saguaro NP
Carlsbad Caverns NP
Guadalupe Mountains NP
Big Bend NP
THE SOUTHWEST
TH GR PLA
TEX

Death Valley National Park *(see pp684–5)* in California's Mojave Desert, is one of the world's hottest places.

Mesa Verde National Park's *(see p596)* great cliff dwellings offer glimpses of Colorado's early inhabitants.

Yosemite National Park (see p718), *a wilderness of forests, meadows, and granite rocks, is California's prime destination.*

Grand Canyon National Park (see pp536–9), *perhaps the most-visited park in both Arizona and the US, is an awe-inspiring spectacle of magnificent rock formations.*

Voyageurs National Park (see p421), *an area of staggering natural beauty, was named after French-Canadian fur trappers. Although most visitors traverse the park's network of lakes and streams by boat, there are numerous hiking trails as well.*

Caribou in Denali National Park, Alaska

ALASKA

Kobuk Valley NP
Gates of the Arctic NP
Denali NP *(see pp742–3)*
Wrangell St. Elias NP
Lake Clark NP
Glacier Bay NP
Katmai NP
Kenai Fjords NP
  (see p739)

HAWAI'I

Haleakalā NP
Hawai'i Volcanoes NP
  (see pp752)

0 km   500

0 miles   500

ʋageurs

Acadia NP

NEW
ENGLAND

NYC &
MID-ATLANTIC
REGION

Cuyahoga
Valley NP

THE
GREAT LAKES

Shenandoah NP

DC &
THE CAPITAL REGION

Mammoth
Cave NP

Great Smoky
Mountains NP

Great Smoky Mountains National Park *(see p262)*, in Tennessee and North Carolina, supports an incredible diversity of plant life.

Hot Springs NP

THE
SOUTHEAST

THE
DEEP SOUTH

FLORIDA

Biscayne NP

Everglades NP

Acadia National Park (see p172), *a wild, unspoiled island paradise in Maine, is crisscrossed by hiking trails that offer breathtaking coastal views. Its main attraction, however, is the scenic 27-mile (43-km) Loop Road.*

Everglades National Park (see p321) *covers a vast expanse of low-lying wetlands at the southern tip of Florida. This unique ecosystem is characterized by tree islands or hammocks that support a fantastic variety of flora and fauna. Alligators are the park's best-known and most-feared residents.*

Exploring the National Parks

A National Park ranger

IT'S NO EXAGGERATION to claim that one could spend a lifetime exploring the sprawling expanses of national parks such as the Grand Canyon or Yosemite. Most people visit parks simply because they happen to be near one, or to see specific sights such as the geysers of Yellowstone. To make their trip more worthwhile and enjoyable, visitors should restrict the number of parks they intend to visit, and instead explore a couple of the most appealing ones at leisure. Plan for a minimum of one full day per park. to enable you to get away from the crowds and the traffic, and to really enjoy the parks at close range.

PASSPORTS, FEES & PERMITS

TO HELP MAINTAIN their facilities, most parks charge admission fees, valid for seven days, which range from nominal amounts ($1–5) at the smaller sites to upwards of $20 at prime attractions. Some parks don't charge a fee but do collect charges for specific activities.

If planning to visit more than two or three parks, visitors should consider purchasing a **National Parks Pass**. Valid for one year, these cost approximately $50, and give admission to the bearer and all

BACKGROUND

THE WORLD's first national park was established in 1872 to protect the geothermal wonders and wild creatures of Yellowstone, on the crest of the Rocky Mountains. In the years since, a staggering 375 places of scenic or historical interest in the US have been given federal protection, including 56 parks in the National Park system.

America's national parks offer visitors some of the most unforgettable wilderness experiences anywhere in the world, from stunning glacial lakes and lush forests to arid expanses of desert.

In addition to the most prominent parks, the **National Park Service**, a unit of the US Department of the Interior, also manages national historic sites (such as Independence Hall in Philadelphia, Pennsylvania) and national memorials (such as Mount Rushmore in South Dakota).

PLANNING YOUR VISIT

THE NATIONAL parks draw millions of visitors each year. In fact, the immensely popular Great Smoky Mountains National Park sees over 10 million visitors, while more than 3 million people visit comparatively remote parks such as Yellowstone and Yosemite. To avoid the crowds, aim to visit the parks outside the peak summer season (June–August), when they are full to capacity.

While the most popular parks are the jewels in the crown of US public lands, there are many quieter parks where you can enjoy nature without the crowds. Also try to take advantage of the many well-maintained trails

TOP NATIONAL PARKS

Listed below, are some of the most popular national parks in the United States (in alphabetical order), including the top parks featured on the previous pages. This chart depicts the various types of landscape and geological formations that are found within each park.

	Volcanic/Geothermal	Mountainous	Glaciers	Climatic Extremes	Dramatic Erosion	Coral Reefs & Islands	Coastal Marshlands
Acadia NP, ME *(see p172)*				●			
Arches NP, UT *(see p520–21)*						●	
Badlands NP, SD *(see p444)*						●	
Biscayne NP, FL *(see p322)*							■
Bryce Canyon NP, UT *(see pp526–7)*						●	
Canyonlands NP, UT *(see p522)*						●	
Death Valley NP, CA *(see pp684–5)*					■		
Denali NP, AK *(see pp742–3)*		■					
Everglades NP, FL *(see p321)*							■
Glacier NP, MT *(see p579)*			●				
Glen Canyon & Lake Powell, AZ *(see p523)*						●	
Grand Canyon NP, AZ *(see p536–9)*						●	
Grand Teton NP, WY *(see p583)*		■					
Great Smoky Mts. NP, TN, NC *(see p262)*		■					
Hawai'i Volcanoes NP, HI *(see p752)*	●						
Mesa Verde NP, CO *(see p596)*					■		
Mount Rainer NP, WA *(see pp626–7)*	●						
Olympic NP, WA *(see p620)*					■		
Rocky Mountain NP, CO *(see p591)*		■					
Sequoia & Kings Canyon NP, CA *(see p719)*					■		
Shenandoah NP, VA *(see p219)*		■					
Voyageurs NP, MN *(see p421)*			●				
Yellowstone NP, WY *(see pp584–5)*	●						
Yosemite NP, CA *(see p718)*			●				
Zion NP, UT *(see p525)*						●	

Visitors overlooking Thunder Hole, Acadia National Park, Maine

visitors traveling in the same private vehicle. In parks where a per person fee is charged, the pass admits the pass holder, his or her spouse, and their children. This pass can be bought at any park entrance, or even in advance via credit card payment.

US citizens or permanent residents over the age of 62 are eligible for the **Golden Age Passport**, a lifetime entrance pass to national parks, monuments, historic sites, recreation areas, and wildlife refuges. It admits the pass holder and accompanying passengers in a private vehicle (if there is a per vehicle fee). It also provides a 50 percent discount on federal fees charged for various facilities and must be obtained in person from a federal area, such as a national park or monument.

ELK CROSSING NEXT 2 MILES

Wildlife warning sign

If visitors expect to see many national forests, recreation areas, or Bureau of Land Management lands, they may opt to pay an additional $15 and purchase a **Golden Eagle Pass**, which covers the fees for all US federal lands. For citizens or permanent residents who are disabled or blind, the **Golden Access Passport** is a lifetime pass for national parks, monuments, historic sites, recreation areas, and wildlife refuges.

TYPES OF ACCOMODATION

VISITOR FACILITIES vary from park to park. Some provide very basic amenities, while others, especially the popular ones, have deluxe hotels close by. It is advisable to make reservations for overnight accommodation well in advance. Some parks make reservations on a first-come-first-served basis only, so the sooner you arrive at your destination, the better.

Most parks have campsites for both tents and RVs but these are often "unserviced," with no RV hookups for electricity, water, or sewage. Campsites usually cost about $20 a night. The US Forest Service and **Bureau of Land Management** (BLM) campsites are less expensive and more readily available.

PRACTICAL TIPS FOR VISITING THE PARKS

- Wear appropriate clothing – sturdy boots, a protective hat, plus waterproof or warm clothing, depending on the conditions.
- Carry drinking water, a pair of binoculars, a first-aid kit, sun screen, and insect repellant.
- Do not litter. Use the litter bins provided, or carry your waste out of the park.
- Do not play loud music or blow car horns within park limits, as this disturbs everyone.
- Do not interfere, provoke, or try to feed any wildlife.
- Hunting is prohibited and visitors found in violation will face heavy penalties.
- Do not approach bears or other wild animals; they can be extremely dangerous.

- Talk softly when on park trails to improve your chances of spotting wildlife.
- Do not wander off on your own, and do not venture off on marked park trails; it is not only hazardous if you encounter dangerous animals but is also easy to get lost in the wilderness.
- Be sure to tell a friend or fellow traveler your itinerary; in case you don't return on time they can inform the park ranger.
- Observe and obey all signs throughout the individual park regarding speed limits, food, animals, water, and all other safety precautions. Following these rules and regulations will enhance your enjoyment of the park and keep both you and the wildlife safe.

Great American Cities

ONE OF THE MAIN ATTRACTIONS of visiting the US is the chance of enjoying its many great cities. They vary from Colonial-era, pedestrian-friendly places such as Boston, with its distinctly European ambience, to the frenzied modern metropolis of Los Angeles, where no one walks, except to and from the car. In between, there is a wide range of cities, each with its own history and culture. Washington, DC, the capital, is known for its political focus and national galleries; Miami offers a spicy taste of Latin America; New Orleans is packed with multicultural music, food, and fun; and New York and Chicago are famous for their architecture and exciting nightlife. On the West Coast, San Francisco and Seattle have picturesque settings and vibrant arts scenes. All in all, cities here have something for everyone.

Seattle (see pp616–19) has risen from the ashes of the Great Fire of 1889 to become a prosperous city of gleaming skyscrapers, upscale shops, and sophisticated hotels.

San Francisco's (see pp694–711) many hills, ocean views, and rich ethnic mix give it a distinctive character, in keeping with its status as the West Coast's cultural capital.

Seattle

Portland

THE PACIFIC NORTHWEST

Boise

THE ROCKIES

Sioux

Eureka

CALIFORNIA

Salt Lake City

Cheyenne

Denver

TH GRE PLAI

San Francisco

THE SOUTHWEST

Las Vegas

Santa Fe

Los Angeles

Albuquerque

Oklahoma C

San Diego   Phoenix

Tucson   El Paso

TEXA

| 0 km | 250 |
| 0 miles | 250 |

Dallas (see pp478–9) in many ways is synomous with the wealth of Texan oil fields and cattle. Today, it is both the state's financial and entertainment center.

Los Angeles (see pp658–77) is often associated with movies, the glamor of Hollywood, the luxury of residential Beverly Hills, and the excitement of Sunset Boulevard. Yet, this vibrant city is also home to some of the country's finest museums and galleries as well as the most popular beaches along the Pacific Ocean.

Chicago (see pp386–97), located on the southwestern edge of Lake Michigan, is famous throughout the world for its magnificent, innovative architecture. New building techniques were perfected here, and it was here too that architects, such as Frank Llyod Wright and others, created masterpieces of modern design.

Philadelphia *(see pp98–105)*, where the Declaration of Independence was signed on July 4, 1776, is the birthplace of America. Today, this "City of Brotherly Love" is one of the country's most popular destinations.

Boston (see pp132–49) is *justly proud of its past. While its Colonial heritage is reflected in its buildings, the city also includes numerous important sites directly related to America's fight for freedom.*

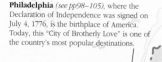

apolis
Iwaukee
Buffalo
NYC &
MID-
ATLANTIC
REGION
Boston
Detroit
New York
Chicago
Philadelphia
THE GREAT LAKES
Baltimore
Indianapolis
Cincinnati
DC & THE
WASHINGTON, DC
City
St. Louis
CAPITAL
REGION
Richmond
Nashville
Charlotte
mphis
THE
SOUTHEAST
Charleston
Atlanta
THE
EEP SOUTH
Savannah
Mobile
Jacksonville
on
New Orleans
FLORIDA
NEW
ENGLAND
Miami

New York *(see pp64–89), the "Big Apple," is one of the world's great cities. One aspect of its character lies in its striking modern architecture. Others revolve around its many outstanding museums, its ethnic neighborhoods, and the choice of entertainment.*

New Orleans *(see pp344–53)* is a fun city of bars, restaurants, and always lively Mardi Gras celebrations.

Miami's *(see pp290–99)* focus of action concentrates on South Beach, with its Art Deco hotels and trendy shops.

Washington, DC *(see pp196–211), the nation's capital, is an impressive city of classical architecture and grand, tree-lined avenues. Beside its political focus, the city also has a cultural heart, with museums located along the Mall.*

Best Scenic Routes

ONE OF THE GREAT PLEASURES of traveling in the US is the chance to explore its many scenic highways and byways. From quiet rural lanes to breathtaking coastal drives, they offer glimpses of the land's abundant natural beauty, and provide an opportunity to get to know its many inviting small towns. Many of the best-known routes are also historic and follow in the footsteps of the pioneer wagon trains, the Pony Express, or along trails taken by Civil War soldiers. For additional information on scenic routes, visit www.byways.org.

Going-to-the-Sun Road (see p579) *cuts across Glacier National Park, following the steep Rocky Mountain cliffs. The route offers breathtaking mountain views.*

Historic Columbia River Highway *(see p632)* offers incomparable views of Oregon's diverse landscape, including Mount Hood's snowcapped summit. It also passes several waterfalls and lush orchards.

Pacific Coast Highway *(Highway 1) was named California's first scenic highway in 1966. One of the world's most stunning drives, its most beautiful stretch is through Big Sur.*

0 km   250

0 miles   250

Route 66 (see p461), *from Chicago to Los Angeles, is perhaps America's best-loved highway. Much of the original route remains intact, offering a nostalgic cruise across the country's heartland.*

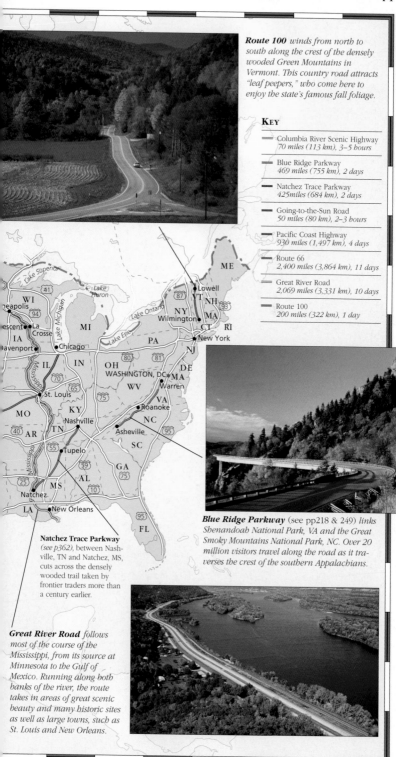

Route 100 *winds from north to south along the crest of the densely wooded Green Mountains in Vermont. This country road attracts "leaf peepers," who come here to enjoy the state's famous fall foliage.*

KEY

Columbia River Scenic Highway
70 miles (113 km), 3–5 hours

Blue Ridge Parkway
469 miles (755 km), 2 days

Natchez Trace Parkway
425miles (684 km), 2 days

Going-to-the-Sun Road
50 miles (80 km), 2–3 hours

Pacific Coast Highway
930 miles (1,497 km), 4 days

Route 66
2,400 miles (3,864 km), 11 days

Great River Road
2,069 miles (3,331 km), 10 days

Route 100
200 miles (322 km), 1 day

Blue Ridge Parkway (see pp218 & 249) *links Shenandoah National Park, VA and the Great Smoky Mountains National Park, NC. Over 20 million visitors travel along the road as it traverses the crest of the southern Appalachians.*

Natchez Trace Parkway (see p362), between Nashville, TN and Natchez, MS, cuts across the densely wooded trail taken by frontier traders more than a century earlier.

Great River Road *follows most of the course of the Mississippi, from its source at Minnesota to the Gulf of Mexico. Running along both banks of the river, the route takes in areas of great scenic beauty and many historic sites as well as large towns, such as St. Louis and New Orleans.*

HISTORY OF THE USA

M
AN FIRST ENTERED NORTH AMERICA *from Siberia some 13,000 and 30,000 years ago, migrating over the Bering Strait land bridge to Alaska. As the ice receded, they moved south into the rich gamelands of the Great Plains. Isolated from Eurasia by melting ice and rising sea levels, those early settlers were mainly hunter-gatherers, as agricultural life evolved sporadically.*

During this period of isolation, unique ecological, genetic, and social patterns emerged that proved disastrously fragile when confronted by the first Europeans in the late 15th century.

EARLY EUROPEAN EXPLORERS

European exploration began in earnest when improvements in shipping made the longer voyages of Columbus (1492) and Cabot (1497) viable. Early explorers were astonished by the quantity of natural resources they encountered here. Fur-bearing animals such as beavers were quickly exploited for their pelts. Once Europeans began to investigate further, they were able to draw heavily on the indigenous peoples' detailed knowledge, and use their pre-existing trails to explore the continent. An early map of 1507 displays the name "America," taken from one of the New World's early explorers, Amerigo Vespucci.

COMPETING COLONIES

The long rivalry between Spain, France, and Great Britain continued with the discovery of the New World in 1492. Spain founded the first successful North American colonies, in Florida in 1565 and New Mexico in 1598, combining commercial and religious interests. France's first permanent settlement was at Quebec (1608), while the Dutch set up a trading post (1624) at the mouth of the Hudson River. However, it was the English who gained control, with colonies in Virginia (1607), New England (1620), and Pennsylvania (1681). Many early colonists died of disease and malnutrition. Virginia eventually became the most lucrative New World colony, thanks to the production of tobacco. By 1700, these English colonies' population was 250,000, excluding Native Americans, while only some 1,000 non-Natives lived in Spanish or French regions.

Christopher Columbus sets foot in the New World on October 12, 1492

◁ **George Washington before Yorktown, painted by Rembrandt Peale between 1824 and 1825**

John Trumbull's 1786 painting of the Battle of Bunker Hill

THE AMERICAN REVOLUTION

The 18th century was a period of significant change throughout the world, and this was especially true in the New World. Colonists expanded their domain, displacing or killing the native tribes through a combination of land purchases, warfare, and disease. In the southern colonies of Virginia and Carolina, where the lack of available land discouraged new immigrants, African slaves were imported in great numbers, reaching a total of 150,000, 40 percent of the population, by 1750.

The American Revolution began swiftly, and transformed the face of the world in a few short years. The removal of a potential French threat, following Britain's conquest of Canada in the Seven Years' War, led to American complaints about British abuse, epitomized by the phrase "No Taxation without Representation." In 1770, British troops opened fire on a group of unruly workers, killing five in what became known as the Boston Massacre. In 1773, some colonial merchants disguised as Indians dumped a boatload of tea into Boston Harbor, to protest Britain's monopoly of the tea trade.

War broke out in April 1775, when British "Redcoats" marched on the town of Concord in an attempt to seize a stockpile of weapons from the American "Minutemen." As the British fought their way back to Boston, more than 75 Redcoats and over 90 Americans were killed. The British occupied New York City and Philadelphia, while the ill-equipped Americans struggled through a harsh winter. The war moved south, and frontier fighters under Daniel Boone and George Rogers Clark captured British outposts in Kentucky and Illinois. The Americans eventually succeeded, largely due to French support, and the war officially ended in 1783.

KEY DATES IN HISTORY

1763 The Seven Years' War ends, France surrenders its Great Lakes lands to Great Britain

1773 Boston Tea Party

April 19, 1775 The Revolutionary War begins

1776 The Declaration of Independence is adopted in Philadelphia

1783 Treaty of Paris puts an end to the Revolutionary War

1790 A 100-mile square on the Maryland/ Virginia border, Washington, the District of Columbia, is set aside as the new capital

1793 Samuel Slater's water-powered mill at Pawtucket, Rhode Island, brings the Industrial Revolution to the US

1803 Ohio is the first of the Northwest Territories to become a state

1803 The Louisiana Purchase

1814 Francis Scott Key composes "The Star-Spangled Banner"

1824 The Bureau of Indian Affairs, a division of the US War Department, is formed to handle relations with Indian tribes

1832 Resisting attempts to remove his people from their traditional homelands, Chief Black Hawk leads a militant band of 1,000 Fox-Sauk Indians but is destroyed by the US Army

Patriots disguised as Indians dumping tea into Boston Harbor, Boston Tea Party

George Washingtion holding a copy of the US Constitution, surrounded by Founding Fathers, 1787

BIRTH OF A NATION

By 1783, the newly formed United States of America had a draft constitution and a border that extended as far west as the Mississippi River. The new Constitution was officially adopted in 1788, and in 1791 the ten amendments of the "Bill of Rights" were added, enumerating each citizen's freedom of speech, press, religion, and public assembly. In 1800, the capital moved from Philadelphia to the newly created city of Washington, DC, which by now had a population of 3,200 people.

MANIFEST DESTINY

America expanded greatly in its early years, first opening the "Northwest Territory" lands along the Great Lakes in 1787. The Louisiana Purchase of 1803 added a huge area of western lands formerly controlled by France. This rapid expansion created the need to survey the new territories. Lewis and Clark's famed cross-continental expedition between 1803 and 1806, was funded by Congress at the express request of President Thomas Jefferson.

The first test of strength for this new independent country came in 1812, when the US found itself caught in the middle of an ongoing war between France and Great Britain. Though both countries agreed to stop interfering with American ships, US forces attacked British interests in Canada, and in retaliation the British burned the Capitol and White House in Washington, DC. Ironically, the war was ended by a peace treaty that was signed two weeks before its biggest skirmish – the Battle of New Orleans – took place in January 1815.

After the War of 1812, the US abandoned hopes of annexing Canada, and so began its great push westward. Settlers poured into the Great Plains, Oregon, and eventually the northern periphery of the Republic of Mexico, including Texas and California. The Santa Fe Trail, open for trade by 1823, brought New Mexico under US influence. By 1850, there was an extensive communications network. Steamboat traffic dominated the rivers, augmented by canals and cross-country railroads.

The consolidation of western lands encouraged millions of pioneers to migrate west and forge new lives for themselves. By the mid-19th century, people had grown accustomed to the idea that the country would stretch undivided across the continent, from ocean to ocean. This idea, in the words of populist journalist John L. O'Sullivan, was the country's "Manifest Destiny." Orderly settlement was made possible by the official survey and division of these lands into rectangular sections, each one square mile in area. Overland trails were opened leading west to the gold fields of California, which itself became a state in 1850. By 1860, more than half the population lived west of the Appalachian Mountains, compared to less than 10 percent in 1800.

An 1891 illustration depicting Indians fighting US soldiers

TERRITORIAL CONFLICT

Although involved in conflicts with Britain over Canada, the US managed to resolve these issues peacefully. However, this was not so with Mexico, who feared US territorial ambitions, especially after President Andrew Jackson offered to purchase Texas. The crisis accelerated after Texas declared independence from Mexico in 1835. Turning a blind eye to Native American tribes (and the legal ownership of much of the land by Spain), the United States took over Texas in 1845, a move that set off war with Mexico. This war in turn led to the US confiscation of California and much of the Southwest. In 1848, Mexico yielded nearly half of its territory; the cession of the northern Oregon territory by Britain in 1846, and James Gadsden's 1853 purchase of 30,000 square miles in the Southwest completed the westward expansion. Thus, in less than 50 years, the country had more than tripled in size.

THE DESTRUCTION OF THE INDIANS

Since the 1500s, diseases such as small pox and syphilis had wiped out almost 90 percent of some tribes. As European settlement increased, forced relocation of tribes became frequent. It reached its peak with the forced march of most of the Cherokee Nation from the southeast to Oklahoma along the "Trail of Tears." As Europeans spread westward, tribes were forced onto reservations, often the poorest and most desolate lands, where many remain even today.

The building of the transcontinental railroads in the late 19th century opened the West to hunters who eventually killed millions of buffalo. Within a few hundred years, North America's indigenous cultures had been destroyed or marginalized by Europeans, who transformed the continent into a world economic, industrial, and political power.

CIVIL WAR

Between independence in 1783 and 1860, two very different societies developed within the US. In the North, there emerged an industrialized society, committed to liberal banking and credit systems, and protective tariffs, whereas the South was a less populous, agrarian society opposed to the sale of public land in the Midwest, high duties, and restrictions on slavery.

The causes of the Civil War are still up for debate. Though slavery was clearly the divisive issue, the war was

KEY DATES IN HISTORY

1838 US Government forcibly expels native Cherokee Indians westward along the "Trail of Tears"

1846–1848 Mexican War. US acquires Arizona, California, Utah, Nevada, and New Mexico

1859 Abolitionist John Brown raids the Federal Armory at Harpers Ferry

1861 Confederates attack Fort Sumter in South Carolina

1861 The Battle of Bull Run (Manassas), the first major land battle of the Civil War

Jan 1, 1863 President Abraham Lincoln issues the Emancipation Proclamation, freeing slaves in areas controlled by the Confederate army

July, 1863 Union forces defeat General Robert E. Lee and the Confederacy at Gettysburg

April 9, 1865 Robert E. Lee surrenders to Union General Ulysses Grant at Appomattox Court House, Virginia

April 14, 1865 President Lincoln assassinated by a Confederate sympathizer, John Wilkes Booth, in Washington, DC

Dec 18, 1865 The 13th amendment to the US Constitution is adopted, effectively putting an end to slavery in the US

1870 African-Americans granted full citizenship

not fought to free the slaves. Instead, the battle lines were drawn over the question of extending slavery into the newly forming western states. The South, resisting the federal government's growing power, wanted each new state to decide this question independently. The northern states wanted to keep slavery within its current limits, in part to protect their own manual labor. The federal government left the decision to the new states, and riots between pro- and anti-slave campaigners raged across the west. In 1856, pro-slave guerillas burned the city of Lawrence, and 200 people were killed in retaliation. Three years later, 22 abolitionists led by John Brown attacked the Federal Armory at Harpers Ferry, Virginia, hoping to incite a slave rebellion. Instead, he and his forces were killed, but his efforts further polarized the already divided nation. By 1860, the country was composed of 18 "free states" – mainly in the North, and 15 "slave states" – mainly in the South. When Abraham Lincoln was elected president in 1860, South Carolina seceded from the Union, followed by six other southern states, which joined together to form the Confederate States of America.

The first shots of the Civil War were fired in April, 1861, when the Confederates attacked Fort Sumter in South Carolina. President Lincoln mobilized US soldiers to quell the rebellion, and soon four other slaveholding states, including Virginia, seceded from the Union. Richmond became the new Confederate capital, and Virginia provided most of the Confederate military leadership. Four slave states remained in the Union, and the western counties of Virginia separated to form West Virginia, which joined the Union in 1863.

The Confederates won the first major land battle at Manassas, Virginia, in July 1861, and for the next two years battles raged across Virginia and Maryland. With their defeat at Gettysburg in 1863, the Confederates were finally turned back. In the same year, Union forces gained control of the Mississippi River. Union forces destroyed Atlanta in 1864 and marched across Georgia, cutting off supply lines and virtually encircling the remaining Confederate army. By April 1865, the Civil War was over.

The destruction caused by the war was immense. Nearly three million soldiers (some 10 percent of the total population at the time) fought in the war, and 620,000 of them died. Entire cities lay in ruins, and it would be years before the nation recovered from the ravages of war.

Confederate forces occupy Fort Sumter, South Carolina, on April 15, 1861

THE WILD WEST

The end of the 19th century was a time of radical change across the country. The conquered South and the newly freed slaves suffered the ravages of the Reconstruction, while in the West, Native Americans saw their lands taken away and their lifestyles destroyed. Their culture's death knell was sounded in 1862, when the Homestead Act granted 160 acres of land to any white settler, freed slave, or single woman. The Army battled Indian tribes across the Great Plains in the 1870s and 1880s, and Indian resistance in the Southwest desert came to an end with the surrender of Apache chief Geronimo in 1886.

Buffalo Bill's Wild West poster, 1900

In the East and Midwest, massive mills and factories replaced local producers, as the population shifted from self-sufficient farms to the chaotic city life. In a relatively brief period, the pace of life was altered by the growth of railroads, the telegraph, the telephone, the airplane, and the automobile. Railroads brought the once-distant West within reach of eastern markets, and the frontier towns that appeared along the railroads were often lawless places. During this post-Civil War period, the US became an international power, buying Alaska from Russia in 1867, then taking over Hawai'i in 1893, the Philippines in 1899, and Panama in 1903.

IMMIGRATION, URBANIZATION, & INDUSTRIALIZATION

While stories of the Wild West captivated people's imagination, the most significant development was the increasing importance of industrialization. The rapid demographic shift from small towns and farms to big cities and factories was inevitable. This change was made possible in part by waves of immigration that doubled the population in a few decades.

In the 1880s, over six million immigrants arrived, and by the first decade of the 20th century a million people were arriving every year. By World War I, the population reached 100 million, 15 percent of whom were foreign born. The majority settled in East Coast cities, and for the first time in US history the population was predominantly urban.

The consolidation of the population was mirrored by a consolidation in industry and business. By 1882, John D. Rockefeller's Standard Oil Company had a monopoly in the petroleum industry, followed by other effective monopolies, legally organized as "trusts," in tobacco products, banking, and steel. These corporations' abuse of monopoly power was exposed by such writers as Upton Sinclair and Frank Norris. Political movements too resisted the rise of corporations, finding an ally in "trust-busting" President Theodore Roosevelt, who also made significant steps toward protecting the natural environment from the ravages of unrestrained industrial development.

KEY DATES IN HISTORY

1867 Russia sells Alaska for $7.2 million

1869 First transcontinental railroad is completed when the Union Pacific and Central Pacific meet at Promontory, Utah

1876 The Battle of Little Big Horn, Montana

1876 The US Supreme Court legalizes "separate but equal" facilities for whites and non-whites, sanctioning racial segregation

1884 New York and Boston telephone link

1886 The Statue of Liberty erected in New York

1898 USS *Maine* explodes in Havana, sparking Spanish-American War

1915 The Lincoln Highway from New York City to San Francisco is the first transcontinental highway

1915 The "Great Migration" of African-Americans to northern cities begins

April 6, 1917 US declares war on Germany

1925 Fundamentalist Christians ban the teaching of the theory of evolution in many states

1929 The US stock market crash

1934 Benny Goodman's orchestra popularizes "Swing" jazz

1939 The first regular commercial TV broadcasts begins

Cartoon of Uncle Sam welcoming immigrants into the "US Ark of Refuge"

The early 20th century also saw the growth of labor unions, which staged successful and sometimes violent strikes to improve pay and conditions, and helped protect children from working in factories.

BOOM & BUST

Involvement in World War I confirmed America's position as a world power, drawing the nation away from its long-cherished isolationism. But, after the war, soldiers returned home from Europe to severe unrest, with labor strikes and race riots. This economic depression caused enormous suffering and changed the domestic role of the government forever.

The 1920s, known as the "Jazz Age," saw an explosion of artistic creativity, especially in popular music. Architectural and engineering landmarks were constructed, and the rising popularity of the automobile encouraged the building of the first transcontinental highways, which linked the nation and gave rise to the first suburbs.

This creativity coincided with Prohibition, when the sale of alcohol was made illegal. Ironically, it was Prohibition itself that led to the freewheeling, drug-and-alcohol-fuelled lifestyles of the Roaring Twenties.

Duke Ellington, celebrated icon of the Jazz Age

THE GREAT DEPRESSION & THE "NEW DEAL"

The Wall Street Crash of 1929 shattered millions of dreams and left many Americans destitute. Farmers and black people in cities and rural areas were particularly hard hit, as banks withdrew funding. Unemployment and the gross domestic product dropped to half of what it was in the 1920s. Extended drought and sustained winds caused such destruction that the Great Plains was dubbed the "Dust Bowl," forcing some 200,000 Great Plains farmers to migrate west to California.

The Republican government, which had promoted the boom and was blamed for the crash, was rejected by the electorate, leading to the 1932 election of Democrat Franklin Delano Roosevelt. In his first 100 days in office, Roosevelt established federal government relief programs (the "New Deal") to revitalize the economy, provide jobs, and aid those who were hurt by the economic downturn. Roosevelt also set up regulatory bodies to help prevent economic turmoil in the future. Although millions of dollars of federal funding were spent on relief, 20 percent of Americans still continued to be unemployed in 1939.

**The battleships USS *West Virginia* and *Tennessee*
burning after the Japanese attack on Pearl Harbor**

The Cold War

The Japanese attack on Pearl Harbor in 1941 and the subsequent US entry into World War II marked the beginning of America's new role in international politics. With the onset of the Cold War, the numerous US military bases, established during World War II, gained renewed importance. The Cold War also encouraged alliances with other nations. America's powerful influence, and investment overseas was seen as a way to bind other nations to the capitalist sphere. The Marshall Plan of 1948 provided $13 billion to aid reconstruction of postwar western Europe and reduce Communist influence.

Economic and social developments were often overshadowed by the specter of nuclear war. The Korean War was the first of many fought to stop the spread of Communism. Fear on the domestic front inspired years of anti-Communist "Witch Trials," such as those conducted by Senator Joseph McCarthy. Cold War fears also led to numerous military operations around the world, including the takeover of Guatemala in 1954, an ill-fated invasion of Cuba in 1961, and the Vietnam War of the 1960s and 1970s, the longest and most costly of attempts to contain the perceived Communist threat.

After Vietnam, the US retreated from an active international role. The Soviet invasion of Afghanistan in 1979 revived the Cold War for another decade. With the collapse of the Soviet Union in 1991, the United States became the world's only superpower.

Key Dates in History

Dec 7, 1941 Japanese attack on Pearl Harbor

1945 The UN established in San Francisco

Aug 14, 1945 After US bombing of Hiroshima and Nagasaki, Japan surrenders, ending WW II

1950 The Korean War begins

1961 Alan Shepard is the first American in outer space; the Soviets erect the Berlin Wall

1962 Naval blockade against Soviet missile bases in Cuba

1963 Assassination of John F. Kennedy, Dallas

1968 Martin Luther King Jr. assassinated

1969 Neil Armstrong walks on the moon

1970 The Environmental Protection Agency (EPA) is established

1973 Energy crisis

1974 Richard Nixon resigns after Watergate

1988 The Indian Gaming Regulatory Act opens up tribal lands to legalized gambling

1989 Fall of Berlin Wall; end of Cold War

1990–1 The Gulf War

Sept 11, 2001 Terrorist attacks on NYC & DC

2003 Space shutte *Columbia* explodes, killing all on board

2003 George W. Bush declares war on Iraq

Postwar Prosperity

Unlike much of the rest of the world, this was one of the most prosperous periods in US history. The economy, stimulated by mobilization of industry during World War II, and the arms race with the Soviet Union were key factors in creating unprecedented affluence. As manufacturing switched to a peacetime mode, consumer durables flowed into the marketplace, generating a flourishing service sector. America's position at the hub of the international trading system gave her access to crucial

**Vietnam veterans marching toward the Democratic
National Convention, Miami Beach**

foreign markets. Home ownership was brought within reach of middle-class Americans, thanks to government supports and mass-production construction techniques. Most adults owned a car, and consumer products, such as refrigerators, washers, dryers, and dishwashers, multiplied within the home.

CIVIL RIGHTS MOVEMENT

As black Americans migrated from the rural south to urban centers in the 1940s and 1950s, whites abandoned city life for the suburbs, taking their tax dollars with them. The financial crisis was made worse by the decline of traditional industries, and many cities during the 1960s and 1970s suffered as well. Housing deteriorated, roads went unrepaired, and poverty, crime, and racial tension were common features of many urban areas. Poverty was not confined to the inner cities; people in rural areas in the Deep South and the Appalachians were some of the most deprived in the country.

The new postwar opportunities were denied to many African-Americans, particularly in the still-segregated South. Aided by a 1954 Supreme Court judgment that ruled segregation unconstitutional, African Americans fought for an end to discrimination. In 1955, a bus boycott in Montgomery, Alabama, forced the company to end segregation. The success inspired similar protests throughout the South. In 1964 and 1965, Congress passed legislation banning racial discrimination.

The 1960s also saw a rise in political consciousness among other groups; protests against the Vietnam War grew in number, as did the movement for women's rights. In the 1970s, the women's movement narrowly failed to achieve an end to sexual discrimination. During the AIDS crisis of the late 1980s, homosexuality became an increasingly accepted aspect of life, with gay and lesbian couples earning greater legal protections.

THE MODERN ERA

The postwar boom ended in the early 1970s, with the Vietnam War and the energy crisis producing prolonged

Reverend Martin Luther King Jr. delivering a sermon at the Ebenezer Baptist Church, Atlanta

inflation and recession. Europe and Japan challenged American economic domination. American firms tried to secure access to valuable raw materials, most importantly oil in the Middle East, and companies found ways to exploit cheap foreign labor by establishing factories overseas, which in turn threatened jobs at home.

In the 1980s, computers and other digital devices began to change the way Americans communicated. The Internet opened new ways of working and generated large amounts of wealth. By the turn of the millennium, the Internet-fuelled boom went bust, causing a stock market collapse, and the economy fell into recession for the first time in a decade. The controversial appointment of George W. Bush dominated the news and showed that the American public was deeply divided over crucial issues.

The terrorist attacks on New York and Washington, DC in September 2001, instigated President Bush to launch a war against terrorism. This resulted in a war against the Taliban in Afghanistan in 2002 and another one to oust Saddam Hussein in Iraq in 2003. Despite these setbacks, the US still embodies the ideas of freedom and indomitable optimism.

The American Presidents

THE PRESIDENTS OF THE United States have come from all walks of life; at least two were born in a log cabin – Abraham Lincoln and Andrew Jackson. Others, such as Franklin D. Roosevelt and John F. Kennedy, came from privileged backgrounds. Millard Fillmore attended a one-room schoolroom, and Jimmy Carter raised peanuts. Many, including Ulysses S. Grant and Dwight D. Eisenhower, were military men, who won public popularity for their great achievements in battle.

Benjamin Ha
(18

Chester A. Arthur
(1881–85)

Millard Fillmore
(1850–53)

Zachary Taylor
(1849–50)

Franklin Pierce
(1853–57)

James K. Polk
(1845–49)

W.H. Harrison
(1841)

Rutherford B. Hayes
(1877–81)

Andrew Johnson
(1865–69)

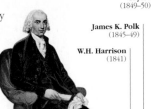

George Washington (1789–97) was a Revolutionary War general. He was unanimously chosen to be the first president of the United States.

James Madison (1809–17), known as the Father of the Constitution, was co-author of the Federalist Papers.

1775	1800	1825	1850	1875

1775	1800	1825	1850	1875

John Adams (1797–1801), a lawyer and historian, was the first president to live in the White House.

James Monroe (1817–25)

John Quincy Adams (1825–29)

John Tyler (1841–45)

Martin Van Buren (1837–41)

James A. Garfield (1881)

Ulysses S. Grant (1869–77)

G
Cleve
(188

James Buchanan (1857–61)

Thomas Jefferson (1801–1809), architect, inventor, landscape designer, diplomat, and historian, was the quintessential Renaissance man.

Andrew Jackson (1829–37) defeated the British at the Battle of New Orleans in the War of 1812.

Abraham Lincoln (1861–65) won the epithet, the Great Emancipator, for his role in the abolition of slavery. He led the Union through the Civil War.

Harry S. Truman
(1945–53) made the
decision to drop the
atomic bombs on
Hiroshima and
Nagasaki in 1945.

KEY TO TIMELINE

- Federalist
- Democratic Republican
- Whig
- Republican
- Democrat

iam
inley
7–1901)

Woodrow Wilson
(1913–21) led the country
through World War I and
paved the way for the
League of Nations.

John F. Kennedy (1961–63)
was one of the most
popular presidents. He
sent the first astronaut into
space, started the Peace
Corps, and created the Arms
Control and Disarmament
Agency. His assassination
rocked the nation.

Richard Nixon
(1969–74) opened up
China and sent the first
men to the moon. He
resigned after the Water-
gate scandal.

**Franklin D.
Roosevelt**
(1933–45) started
the "New Deal", a
reform and relief
program, during
the Great
Depression. He
was elected to
four terms.

Jimmy Carter (1977–81), who
brokered the peace accord
between Israel and Egypt, won
the 2002 Nobel Peace prize.

George W. Bush
(2001–)

George Bush
(1989–93)

| 00 | 1925 | 1950 | 1975 | 2000 |

| 00 | 1925 | 1950 | 1975 | 2000 |

**Dwight D.
Eisenhower**
(1953–61)

**William H.
Taft**
(1909–13)

Herbert Hoover
(1929–33)

Calvin Coolidge
(1923–29)

Warren Harding
(1921–23)

**Gerald
Ford**
(1974–77)

Lyndon B. Johnson
(1963–69) escalated the
Vietnam conflict, resulting
in widespread protests.

William J. Clinton's
(1993–2001) two-term
presidency saw unprece-
dented prosperity.

Ronald Reagan (1981–89), a one-time
movie actor and popular president,
cut taxes, increased military spending,
and reduced government programs.

heodore Roosevelt
901–9) created many
tional parks and over-
w the construction of
e Panama Canal.

nd
7)

THE ROLE OF THE FIRST LADY

In the 19th century, the First Lady acted
primarily as hostess and "behind-the-
scenes" adviser. Dolley Madison was
known as the "Toast of Washington."
Later, when Eleanor Roosevelt held
her own press conferences, the role
of First Lady changed greatly. Jackie
Kennedy gave unprecedented support

**First Lady & Senator Hillary
Clinton in New York, 1999**

to the arts, Rosalynn Carter attended Cabinet meetings, Nancy Reagan
told the world to "Just Say No" to drugs, Barbara Bush promoted
literacy, and Hillary Clinton ran her own political campaign.

NYC & THE MID-ATLANTIC REGION

NYC & the Mid-Atlantic Region at a Glance

THE THREE-STATE REGION surrounding New York City is one of the most fascinating areas in the US. New Jersey, the region's smallest but most densely populated state, extends between New York and Philadelphia. To its west, the idyllic pastoral landscape of Pennsylvania stretches almost all the way to the Great Lakes, with towns, green farm valleys, and the rolling folds of the Allegheney Mountains. Farther north, New York State has cities, towns, and rural hamlets spreading between the Hudson River Valley and Niagara Falls. Of the two main cities, New York City is a vibrant, cosmopolitan city and the financial capital of the world, while Philadelphia is more historic, in keeping with its status as the capital of Colonial America.

Niagara Falls (see p95), *located on the border between Canada and the US, is one of New York State's prime attractions, drawing more than 10 million visitors a year.*

0 km   100

0 miles   100

Pittsburgh (see p108), *in Pennsylvania, has rebuilt itself from the ashes of an industrial past to become one of the country's most attractive cities. The Andy Warhol Museum and the Carnegie Institute are popular tourist attractions here.*

Rochester

Buffalo

Jamestown

PENNSYLVANIA
(See pp98–109)

Willia

New Castle

Altoona

Pittsburgh

Harrisburg

Gettysburg

Gettysburg (see p106) *is one of Pennsylvania's most significant historic sites. In July 1863, this peaceful town was the scene of a devastating Civil War battle. It was here, four months later, that President Abraham Lincoln delivered his moving Gettysburg Address.*

◁ **A view of New York City's glittering skyscrapers as seen from Brooklyn Bridge**

New York State (see p90–95) *offers a diversity of landscapes, from the beauty of the Hudson Valley, to the craggy Adirondack Mountains and the lush wine country of the Finger Lakes. Other highlights include Albany, the state capital, and the awesome Niagara Falls.*

LOCATOR MAP

Plattsburgh

Glens Falls

NEW YORK
(See pp64–95)

Albany

cranton

New York

Philadelphia

NEW JERSEY
(See pp96–97)

Atlantic City

Cape May

New York City (see pp64–89), *with its world-class museums and wide variety of shopping, dining, and entertainment options, is one of the most frequently visited cities in the United States. Its most distinctive sight, however, is the Statue of Liberty, the symbol of freedom for millions who have now made this city their home.*

Philadelphia (see pp98–105), *the "City of Brotherly Love," was the focus of the revolutionary movement for American independence. Its historic Independence National Historic Park preserves structures and artifacts relating to those stirring times.*

Cape May (see p97), *at the southern tip of New Jersey, is a Victorian-period resort that draws many visitors. The state's other attractions include the opulent casinos of Atlantic City and the picturesque wilds of the Delaware Gap.*

NEW YORK CITY
& THE MID-ATLANTIC REGION

T HE TRI-STATE REGION AROUND NEW YORK CITY *truly embodies American diversity and dynamism. The vitality of New York City and Philadelphia is balanced by a surprisingly calm, almost pastoral hinterland. The Mid-Atlantic landscape is spectacular and ranges from dramatic mountain scenery, superb river valleys, and forests, interspersed with rolling farmlands.*

New York City, or the "Big Apple," dominates northeastern US, and to a large extent controls the country's economy and culture. It is, without exaggeration, one of the world's great cities, and it is hard to imagine visiting the region without spending some time here. Philadelphia, the other major city, was the nation's leading city during Colonial times, and its wealth of history offers unforgettable insights into early American ideals.

Fascinating as these cities are, the broader region around them paints a much fuller picture of the nation. New Jersey, despite its reputation for heavy industry and sprawling suburbia, has much to offer, from the Victorian-era coastal resort of Cape May to Ivy League Princeton University. Pennsylvania, to the west, juxtaposes peaceful scenes of rural farmland in the "Pennsylvania Dutch" country where Amish and Mennonite communities still speak German (Deutsch), with the industrial cities of Pittsburg and Reading. Farther north, the state of New York has majestic mountains, picturesque lakes, and the scenic Hudson River Valley.

HISTORY

The Mid-Atlantic Region's natural wealth supported some of early America's most powerful and accomplished Native peoples. The first main groups were the Algonquian tribes, including the Lenni Lenape who lived in what is now New Jersey and Pennsylvania. In the early 16th century, the Algonquian Indians were ousted by incoming tribes of Iroquois Indians. Settling in the Finger Lakes area in central New York State, the

Amish farmers harvesting corn in Lancaster County, Pennsylvania

◁ **Swirling mists surround the Niagara Falls, New York State's most famous natural wonder**

Iroquois, one of North America's most socially sophisticated tribes, formed a powerful alliance among their five constituent tribes – the Senecas, Cayugas, Oneidas, Mohawks, and Onondagas.

Around this time, the first Europeans were making efforts to forge trade relations. Although Giovanni da Verrazano visited New York as early as 1524, it was not until 1609, when the Dutch West India Company sent Henry Hudson to explore the river that now bears his name, that the first settlements were established. In the same year, a French explorer, Samuel de Champlain, laid claim to northeastern New York State, having ventured there by way of Quebec.

Detail from Benjamin West's monumental *Penn's Treaty with the Indians*, circa 1770

In 1624 the Dutch founded the region's first colony, Fort Orange, at present-day Albany, began another at New Amsterdam (later New York) the following year, and later expanded to make footholds in New Jersey and

Giovanni da Verrazano

Pennsylvania. Relations between the Dutch and the Indians were mutually beneficial, in that the Dutch supplied guns and other metal products to the Indians, who paid for them with valuable beaver and other pelts. However, contact with foreigners led to the spread of diseases, including smallpox and measles, which soon decimated Native populations.

From the 1660s onward, as England wrestled for power in the New World, upstate New York evolved into a battleground for distant European wars. To consolidate their control over trans-Atlantic trade, the English first acquired the Dutch colonies and established a new one of their own – Pennsylvania. This colony, which developed on land granted by King Charles II to wealthy Quaker William Penn in 1680, thrived, thanks to fertile soil, a healthy climate, and a group of comparatively wealthy and industrious colonists. Its capital, Philadelphia, flourished and became the key center of the nascent movement for American independence.

KEY DATES IN HISTORY

1524 Italian sailor Giovanni da Verrazano sails into New York harbor

1609 Henry Hudson explores and maps the Hudson River and New Jersey shore

1624 The Dutch establish Fort Orange

1664 England takes over New Netherland. The city of New Amsterdam is renamed New York

1731 Benjamin Franklin establishes the nation's first public library in Philadelphia

1776 The Declaration of Independence is adopted in Philadelphia

1825 The 363-mile (588-km) Erie Canal opens

1863 Union forces defeat Robert E. Lee and the Confederacy at Gettysburg

1929 Stock Market crash triggers the Great Depression

1933 New York Governor Franklin Delano Roosevelt is elected president

1978 Gambling legalized in Atlantic City

1987 Stock Market crash

1994 Rudolph Giuliani becomes mayor of New York City

2001 World Trade Center (WTC) destroyed in terrorist attack

Feb 2003 Architects for new WTC site selected

INDEPENDENCE & INDUSTRY

Throughout the first half of the 18th century, the English and their American colonists fought a series of frontier battles against the French and their Indian allies. The cost of these wars in loss of life and property was high, and to pay for them the English crown raised a series of taxes, many of which were especially onerous for the merchants of New York and Philadelphia. In 1774, and again in 1776, delegates to Philadelphia's Continental Congress debated the issues and eventually declared independence from

England. Soon after, the English military occupied New York and Philadelphia and held them until the end of the Revolutionary War in 1783.

Perhaps the most significant early battle took place in the summer of 1777 at Saratoga Springs, where patriots defeated the English under General John Burgoyne. Although this success earned the Americans the vital support of France, the revolutionary forces, organized into the Continental Army under George Washington, still suffered tremendous hardships. More than 3,000 soldiers died of disease at Valley Forge, outside Philadelphia, in the winter of 1777–78. After the British abandoned their American colonies in 1783, New York City served as the capital of the new nation until 1790, followed by Philadelphia from 1790 to 1800.

War memorial in Congress Park, Saratoga Springs

Although the battle for independence was fought and won by farmers and tradesmen, the following century saw the region emerge as a major industrial powerhouse. The Erie Canal was cut across upstate New York between 1817 and 1825, and Pennsylvania became the nation's biggest producer of coal and steel. Railroads crisscrossed the region by the mid-19th century, and it was this industrial might that enabled the North to withstand the divisive Civil War. The region sent more than 600,000 men to fight for the Union, but the main battle fought here was in July 1863, at the small town of Gettysburg in southeastern Pennsylvania. Known as the "high tide" of the war, this battle was the northern limit of Confederate success, the only time southern forces crossed the Mason-Dixon Line, the Pennsylvania–Maryland border that marked the divide between free and slave states.

PEOPLE & CULTURE

For nearly a century after the Civil War, the mines, mills, and factories of New York, New Jersey, and Pennsylvania attracted a huge influx of European immigrants. Between 1880 and 1910, some 12 million immigrants passed through New York City's port. During the World War years more people, including African Americans from the Deep South, came here to work in the several arms-related factories. Today, as much as one-third of the present population counts itself as ethnic minorities, and in many cities these "minorities" often comprise a large majority of the residents. Thus some neighborhoods are identified by their ethnic makeup – Chinatown or Little Italy in New York City, the Italian Market in South Philadelphia, or the Polish areas of Pittsburgh's South Side.

Years of labor strife, and many economic upheavals led to many industries closing down in the 1960s and 70s. New York City, the financial center of world capitalism, flirted with bankruptcy in the 1970s.

Today, however, things are different. "Heritage tourism" of battlefields, former industrial sites, historic canals, and railroads is a significant business, drawing almost as many millions of visitors as the natural wonders of Niagara Falls.

San Gennaro Festival in Manhattan's Little Italy

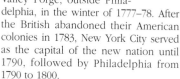

Exploring New York City & the Mid-Atlantic Region

THE TWO MAJOR CITIES OF New York and Philadelphia naturally dominate travel in the Mid-Atlantic Region. However, the region's other attractions include the exclusive summer retreats of the Hamptons, the collegian environs of Princeton, and industrial Pittsburg, today a vibrant cultural center. Equally attractive are its scenic wonders, ranging from the broad beaches of New Jersey and the tranquil beauty of Pennsylvannia's Amish Country to the wilderness of New York State's Adirondacks. A car is essential to explore the region's vast interior. All roads tend to lead through both New York City and Philadelphia, especially the New Jersey Turnpike (I-95), the main north–south artery. Heading west from the coast, the two main roads are I-80 across Pennsylvania and I-90, the New York Thruway. Many state and country roads connect the rural areas, while the major cities have good Amtrak and commuter train services.

Taughannock Falls surrounded by trees in fall foliage, Taughannock Falls State Park

SIGHTS AT A GLANCE

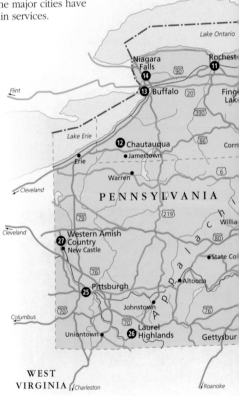

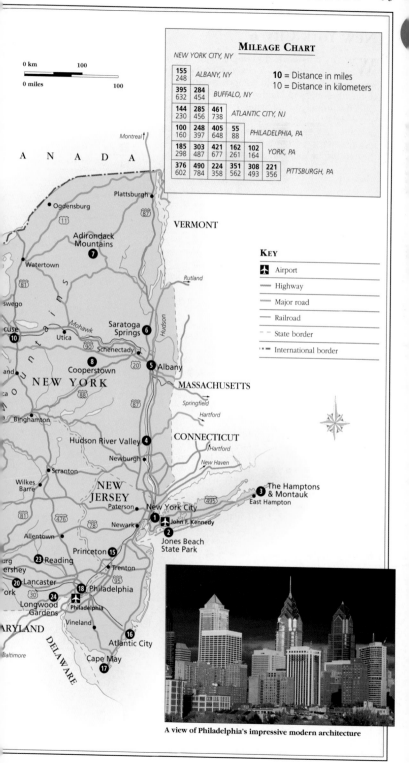

MILEAGE CHART

NEW YORK CITY, NY

155 / 248	ALBANY, NY			**10** = Distance in miles		
395 / 632	**284** / 454	BUFFALO, NY		10 = Distance in kilometers		
144 / 230	**285** / 456	**461** / 738	ATLANTIC CITY, NJ			
100 / 160	**248** / 397	**405** / 648	**55** / 88	PHILADELPHIA, PA		
185 / 298	**303** / 487	**421** / 677	**162** / 261	**102** / 164	YORK, PA	
376 / 602	**490** / 784	**224** / 358	**351** / 562	**308** / 493	**221** / 356	PITTSBURGH, PA

0 km   100

0 miles   100

Montreal↑

C A N A D A

Plattsburgh

Ogdensburg

⑪

⑧⑦

VERMONT

Adirondack
Mountains
7

Watertown

⑧①

Rutland

swego

cuse

10

Utica

Mohawk

Saratoga
Springs **6**

Hudson

⑨⓪

Schenectady

and

Cooperstown **8**

⑳

5 Albany

NEW YORK

⑧⑧

⑧⑦

MASSACHUSETTS

ca O

Springfield

Binghamton

Hudson River Valley **4**

CONNECTICUT
↑Hartford

Hartford

Newburgh

New Haven

Scranton

Wilkes
Barre

NEW
JERSEY

Paterson

New York City

3 The Hamptons
& Montauk

④⑨⑤

East Hampton

⑧①

④⑦⑥

⑦⑧

Newark

1 ✈ John F. Kennedy

2
Jones Beach
State Park

Allentown

Princeton **15**

urg

23 Reading

Trenton

ershey

⑨⑤

20 Lancaster

18 Philadelphia

ork

③⓪

24

Longwood
Gardens

Philadelphia

ARYLAND

Vineland

16
Atlantic City

Baltimore

DELAWARE

Cape May
17

KEY

✈	Airport
—	Highway
—	Major road
—	Railroad
- - -	State border
▪-▪-▪	International border

A view of Philadelphia's impressive modern architecture

New York City ●

WITH ITS SKYSCRAPERS and bright lights, this is a city of superlatives. It covers an area of 301 sq miles (780 sq km), and comprises the five distinct boroughs of Manhattan, the Bronx, Queens, Brooklyn, and Staten Island. Most of the major sights lie within Manhattan, the southern tip of which was the target of the September 11, 2001 terrorist attack. Glittering shops, museums, and theaters are in Midtown and along Central Park.

KEY TO STREET FINDER

- Place of interest
- ✈ Airport
- Ferry terminal
- Ⓜ Subway station
- Main railroad station
- Bus terminal
- ℹ Tourist information
- ✝ Church
- ✡ Synagogue
- Highway

SIGHTS AT A GLANCE

GETTING AROUND

With over 6,000 miles (9,600 km) of streets, walking around New York can be very strenuous. The city's taxis are convenient, except during rush hour. Other options are buses or the subway; the public transportation system is safe and an excellent way to get around the city.

SEE ALSO

- **Practical** pp88–9
- **Where to Stay** pp112–15
- **Where to Eat** pp118–19

GREATER NEW YORK

The Bronx

NEW JERSEY

La Guardia Airport

Manhattan

Jersey City

Queens

NEW YORK

Hudson River

Brooklyn

JFK Airport

Staten Island

0 km   5

0 miles   3

KEY

☐ Area of main map

0 km   1

0 miles   1

Trinity Church at the foot of Wall Street

Wall Street ①

Map B5. Ⓜ *2, 3, 4, 5 to Wall St, N, R to Rector St.* 🚌 *M1, M6, M15.*

NAMED FOR THE wall that kept enemies and warring Indians out of Manhattan, Wall Street is now the heart of the city's financial district. One of the prominent sites here is the **Federal Reserve Bank** on Liberty Street. Inspired by the Italian Renaissance, this is a government bank for banks, where US currency is issued. Five-stories below ground is a large storehouse for international gold. Each nation's hoard is stored in its own compartment within the subterranean vault, guarded by 90-ton doors.

Farther away is the **Federal Hall National Monument**, where a bronze statue of George Washington on the steps marks the site where the nation's first president took his oath of office in 1789 *(see p61)*. The present imposing structure, built between 1834 and 1842 as the US Custom House, is one of the finest Classical designs in the city.

At the head of Wall Street is **Trinity Church**. Built in 1846, this square-towered Episcopal church is the third one on this site in one of America's oldest Anglican parishes, founded in 1697. Designed by Richard Upjohn, it was one of the grandest churches of its day, marking the beginning of the best period of Gothic Revival architecture in America. The sculpted brass doors were inspired by Ghiberti's *Doors of Paradise* in Florence. Its 280-ft (85-m) steeple was New York's tallest structure until the 1860s. Many famous New Yorkers are buried here.

The hub of the world's financial markets, the **New York Stock Exchange** (NYSE) is housed in a 17-story building built in 1903. Initially, trading in stocks and shares took place haphazardly in the area, but 24 brokers signed an agreement in 1792 to deal only with one another. This formed the basis of the NYSE. Membership is strictly limited. In 1817, a "seat" cost $25; today it costs more than two million dollars, and a rigorous test of suitability is required. Visitors can watch the trading posts from a gallery overlooking the trading floor. The NYSE has weathered slumps ("bear markets") and booms ("bull markets") and has seen advances in technology, from tickertape to microchip, turn a local market into a global one.

🔒 Trinity Church
Broadway at Wall St. 📞 *(212) 602-0872.* ◯ *7am–6pm Mon–Fri; 8am–4pm Sat, 7am–4pm Sun.* ✝ *9am, 11:15am Sun.* 🎵 **Concerts** *Thu.* 🌐 *www.trinitywallstreet.org*

🚇 New York Stock Exchange
20 Broad St. 📞 *(212) 656-5168.* ◯ *9:30am–4pm Mon–Fri (last adm: 3:30pm).* ● *public hols.* ∅ ♿ 📷 🔲
Video displays. 🌐 *www.nyse.com*

World Trade Center Site ②

Map B5. Ⓜ *Chambers St, Rector St.* 📞 *212 SEAPORT.*

IMMORTALIZED BY countless filmmakers and photographers, the twin towers of the World Trade Center dominated the Manhattan skyline for 27 years, until the September 2001 terrorist attack. The enormous weight of each building was supported by an inner wire cage, which melted from the heat of the fire caused by the two aircraft that were flown into the towers. These towers were part of a buildings complex consisting of six office blocks and a hotel, connected by a vast underground concourse lined with shops and restaurants. A bridge linked the complex to the World Financial Center, which survived the attack.

The "Ground Zero" perimeter continues to shrink as buildings around the site are reoccupied. Things are moving quickly – the new design for the site has been approved, and construction began in late 2003.

In addition to rebuilding part of the 16 acre (6.5 ha) site as business and office space, a memorial to the thousands of people who died here is also being planned.

Bronze bull, symbol of Wall Street, near Custom House

Battery Park City's World Financial Center from the Hudson River

Battery Park City ③

Map B5. [M] *1, 9 to Cortland St.* ♿ 🍴 🛍 [W] www.batteryparkcity.org **World Financial Center** West St. ☎ *(212) 945-0505.* [M] *1, 2, A, C, & J, M, Z to Chambers St; 4, 5, 6 to Brooklyn Bridge/City Hall Station; E to WTC Station; N, R to City Hall.* ♿ 🍴 ☕ 🛍 [W] www.worldfinancialcenter.com

NEW YORK'S newest neighborhood is an ambitious development on 92 reclaimed acres (37 ha) along the Hudson River. This huge commercial and residential complex can house more than 25,000 people, at an estimated cost of $4 billion. A 2-mile (3-km) esplanade offers grand Statue of Liberty views.

The most visible part is the **World Financial Center**. A model of urban design by Cesar Pelli & Associates, this development is a vital part of the revival of Lower Manhattan, and its damage in the World Trade Center attack was attended to as a matter of urgency. Some of the world's most important financial companies are housed here. At the heart of the complex lies the dazzling Winter Garden (re-opened September 2002), a vast glass-and-steel public space often used for concerts and arts events. It is flanked by restaurants and shops, and opens onto a lively piazza and marina on the Hudson River.

Among the new attractions is the Skyscraper Museum, located at the Ritz-Carlton hotel.

Statue of Liberty ④

Map A5. Liberty Island. ℹ *(212) 363-3200.* [M] *1, 9, N, R to S Ferry, 4, 5 to Bowling Green.* 🚌 *M6, M15 to S Ferry, then Circle Line–Statue of Liberty Ferry from the Battery every 30–45 mins, 9:15am–3:30pm summer (winter hours vary).* ☎ *(212) 269-5755.* ○ *Jul–Aug: 9am–6pm daily; Sep–Jun: 9:30am–5pm daily.* ● *Dec 25. Ferry fare includes entry to Ellis & Liberty Is.* ♿ *elevator to observation deck only.* ☕ 🛍 [W] www.statueoflibertyferry.com

THE FIGURE presiding over New York harbor, titled "Liberty Enlightening the World," has been the symbol of freedom for millions since

Statue of Liberty, an enduring symbol of New York

her inauguration by President Grover Cleveland in 1886. A gift from the French to the American people to mark the US centennial in 1876, the statue was the brainchild of sculptor Frédéric-Auguste Bartholdi. In Emma Lazarus's poem, which is engraved on the base, Lady Liberty says: "Give me your tired, your poor, / Your huddled masses yearning to breathe free."

The 305-ft (93-m) high statue stands on a pedestal set within the walls of an old army fort. In one hand Liberty holds the new torch, with a 24-carat gold-leaf flame, while in the other is a book inscribed July 4, 1776, in Latin. The rays of her crown represent the seven seas and seven continents. The flight of 354 steps (22 stories) that took visitors right up to the crown, has been closed indefinitely since the September 11 terrorist attack.

After a $100 million restoration in time for its bicentennial, the statue was unveiled on July 3, 1986. The spectacular $2 million fireworks display to celebrate the occasion was the largest public party in the city.

Ellis Island ⑤

Map A5. ℹ *(212) 363-3200.* [M] *4, 5 to Bowling Green; 1, 9, N, R to Whitehall/South Ferry, then Circle Line/Statue of Liberty Ferry from the Battery.* **Departures** *every 30 mins 9am–3:30pm summer (winter hours vary).* ☎ *(212) 269-5755.* ○ *Jul–Aug: 9am–6pm daily; Sep–Jun: 9:30am–5pm daily.* ● *Dec 25.* 💲 *entry inc Ellis and Liberty Is.* ♿ ✋ 🎧 🍴 ☕ [W] www.ellisisland.org; www.statueoflibertyferry.com

MORE THAN HALF of America's population can trace its roots to Ellis Island, which served as the country's immigration depot from 1892 until 1954. Nearly 17 million people passed through its gates and dispersed across the country in the greatest wave of immigration the world has ever known. First- and second-class passengers were processed on board, but steerage passengers were ferried from arrival vessels and taken to the crowded island for medical and legal examinations. Immigrants with contagious diseases could be sent back. Ellis Island lay in ruins until 1990, when a $189 million project by the Statue of Liberty–Ellis Island Foundation, Inc., renewed the buildings.

Centered on the Great Hall or Registry Room, the site today houses the three-story **Ellis Island Immigration Museum** with permanent exhibits. Much of its story is told with photos and the voices of immigrants, and an electronic database traces ancestors. Outside, the American Immigrant Wall of Honor is the largest wall of names in the world. No other place explains so well the "melting pot" that formed the character of the nation.

A view of the main building, Ellis Island

South Street Seaport ⑥

Map C5. Fulton St. 🄲 *(212) 732-7678.* Ⓜ *Fulton St.* ⏰ *10am–9pm Mon–Sat, 11am–8pm Sun.* ♿ 🎫 *Concerts.* 🍴 🏛 🆆 *www.southstseaport.com* **South Street Seaport Museum** 207 Front St. 🄵 *(212) 748-8600.* ⏰ *Apr–Sep: 10am–6pm daily; 8pm Thu; Oct–Mar: 10am–5pm.* ⏸ *Tue; Jan 1, Thanksg., Dec 25.* 🏷 ♿ 🎫 *Exhibits, films.* 🍴 🏛 🆆 *www.southstseaport.org*

C ALLED THE "street of sails" in the 19th-century, the heart of New York's port has now been imaginatively restored as a tourist center. Glitzy stores and restaurants sit harmoniously beside seafaring craft, historic buildings, and museum exhibits, with spectacular views of Brooklyn Bridge and the East River from the cobblestone streets. The historic ships

The Ambrose lightship at a South Street Seaport pier on the East River

docked here range from the little tugboat *W. O. Decker* to the grand four-masted bark *Peking*, the second-largest sailing ship in existence. Mini-trips on the schooner *Pioneer* are a great way to see the river.

The **Fulton Fish Market** has been here since 1821. Once sold fresh from the boat, the fish now arrive in refrigerated trucks. The market is open only in the early morning. **South Street Seaport Museum** covers the 11 blocks of what was America's leading port. In addition to the six historic ships, it has more than 10,000 artifacts, artworks, and documents from the 19th- and early 20th-century maritime world. **Schermerhorn Row**, on Fulton and South Streets, was built as warehouses in 1813. The Row has been restored and now houses a visitor center, shops, restaurants, and an ice-skating rink.

A Frank Gehry-designed Guggenheim Museum being built here will add to South Street Seaport's attractions.

Brooklyn Bridge ⑦

Map C5. Ⓜ *4, 5, 6 to Brooklyn Bridge-City Hall (Manhattan side); A, C to High St, Brooklyn Bridge (Brooklyn side).* 🚌 *M9, M22, M101, M102.* ♿

A N ENGINEERING wonder when it was built in 1883, the Brooklyn Bridge linked Manhattan and Brooklyn, then two separate cities. At that time it was the world's largest suspension bridge and the first to be constructed of steel. The German-born engineer John A. Roebling conceived of a bridge

spanning the East River while ice-bound on a ferry to Brooklyn. The bridge took 16 years to build, required 600 workers, and claimed over 20 lives, including Roebling's. Most died of caisson disease

(known as "the bends") after coming up from the underwater excavation chambers. From the pedestrian walkway there are fabulous views of the city towers, seen through the artistic cablework.

Brooklyn Bridge, the first ever steel suspension bridge

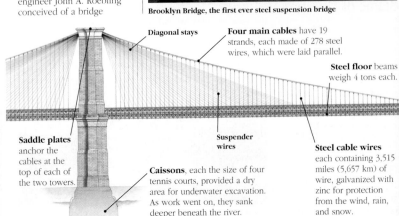

Diagonal stays

Four main cables have 19 strands, each made of 278 steel wires, which were laid parallel.

Steel floor beams weigh 4 tons each.

Saddle plates anchor the cables at the top of each of the two towers.

Suspender wires

Caissons, each the size of four tennis courts, provided a dry area for underwater excavation. As work went on, they sank deeper beneath the river.

Steel cable wires each containing 3,515 miles (5,657 km) of wire, galvanized with zinc for protection from the wind, rain, and snow.

City Hall's imposing early 19th-century façade

Civic Center ⑧

Map C5. Ⓜ *7th Ave/Broadway 2 & 3 to Park Pl; 8th Ave A, C, & E to Chambers St; N, R to City Hall.* **Woolworth Building** 233 Broadway. Ⓜ *City Hall.* Ⓞ *office hours.* **City Hall** City Hall Park. Ⓒ *(212) 788-6865.* Ⓜ *Brooklyn Br–City Hall.* Ⓞ *for prearranged tours only.* Ⓖ Ⓜ **Municipal Building** 1 Center St. Ⓜ *Brooklyn Br–City Hall.* Ⓖ

Mⁿᴬᴺᴴᴬᵀᵀᴬᴺ'ᔆ busy Civic Center is the hub of the city, state, and federal government court systems and the city's police department. The 1926 New York County Courthouse is adjacent to the 31-story pyramid-topped 1933 US Courthouse. The Tweed Courthouse, constructed by the infamous Boss Tweed, a corrupt politician, is being restored to house the Museum of the City of New York.

The monumental buildings here include the 1913 Gothic **Woolworth Building**, headquarters of Five-and-Dime mogul Frank W. Woolworth. Designed by architect Cass Gilbert, it was the city's tallest building until 1930 and set the standard for future skyscrapers. In contrast is the historic **City Hall**, the seat of government since 1812. This Georgian building with French Renaissance influences is considered one of the finest examples of early 19th-century American architecture. The City Hall Park was New York's village green 250 years ago. To its northeast, the **Municipal Building** is a wedding-cake fantasy of towers and spires, topped by the statue *Civic Fame*.

Eldridge Street Synagogue ⑨

Map C5. 12 Eldridge St. Ⓒ *(212) 219-0888.* Ⓜ *E Broadway.* Ⓞ *11am–4pm Sun.* ✱ *Fri at sundown, Sat 10am onward.* ▨ Ⓞ *11:30am & 2:30pm Tue, Thu, & by appt.* Ⓞ Ⓦ *www.eldridgestreet.org*

Tᴴᴵᔆ ᴹᴼᴼᴿᴵᔆᴴ-ᔆᵀʸᴸᴱ house of worship was the first large temple built in the US by Jewish immigrants from Eastern Europe, from where 80 percent of American Jews came. At the turn of the century, it was the most flamboyant temple in the neighborhood, and as many as 1,000 people attended services here. As congregants left the area, attendance waned and the temple closed in the 1950s.

Three decades later a group of citizens raised funds to restore the magnificent sanctuary. The synagogue is now a National Historic Landmark.

Chinatown ⑩

Map C5. Streets around Mott St. Ⓜ *Canal St.* **Eastern States Buddhist Temple** 64b Mott St. Ⓒ *(212) 966-6229.* Ⓞ *9am–6pm daily.*

Nᴱᵂ ʸᴼᴿᴷ'ᔆ ᴸᴬᴿᴳᴱᔆᵀ and most colorful ethnic neighborhood is Chinatown. In the early 20th century this was primarily a male community, made up of immigrant workers. Wages were sent to families back in China who were prevented from joining them by strict immigration laws. Today, more than 200,000 Chinese Americans live here.

The shops and sidewalks overflow with exotic foods and herbs, and gifts ranging from backscratchers to fine antiques. Most people, however, visit Chinatown to eat in one of the more than 200 restaurants or shop for Asian delicacies.

Other sights here include the **Eastern States Buddhist Temple**, with its incense-scented interior and more than 100 golden Buddhas; and tiny, crooked Doyers Street, called "Bloody Angle," reminiscent of the Tong wars between the 1920s and 40s. The Tongs were social clubs or rival criminal fraternities who gave the old locale its dangerous reputation.

Little Italy ⑪

Map C4. Streets around Mulberry St. Ⓜ *Canal St.* Ⓦ *www.littleitalynyc.com*

Tᴴᴱ ᴸᴼᵂᴱᴿ ᴱᴬᔆᵀ ᔆᴵᴰᴱ'ᔆ other ethnic neighborhood is Little Italy, home to southern Italian immigrants in the late 19th century. The immigrants preserved their language, customs, and food, making Mulberry Street lively with the colors, flavors, and atmosphere of Italy. Today, although Little Italy has shrunk to a few blocks, the 10-day Feast of San Gennaro in September draws crowds of joyful celebrants. Also on Mulberry Street is **Old St. Patrick's Cathedral**. It became a local parish church when the cathedral moved uptown (*see p77*).

NoLita, north of Little Italy, is filled with boutiques, and the city's fashionable flock here for the coolest small labels.

Little Italy, once home to thousands of immigrants

TriBeCa ⑫

Map C4. S of Houston St, N of Chambers St, & W of Lafayette St to Hudson River. Ⓜ *Prince St, Spring St, Canal St, Franklin St, Chambers St.*

UNTIL RECENTLY, the area named for its geographic shape – TRIangle BElow CAnal – consisted mostly of abandoned warehouses. Then Robert de Niro set up his TriBeCa Film Center in a converted coffee warehouse, and TriBeCa became the center of the city's movie industry. Known as Hollywood East, many screenings and events take place here. This is now one of New York's hottest neighborhoods, with stylish restaurants, art galleries, and big loft spaces occupied by celebrity residents.

SoHo Historic District ⑬

Map C4. S of Houston St. **Greene Street** Ⓜ *Canal St.*

THE LARGEST concentration of cast-iron architecture in the world survives in SoHo (south of Houston), a former industrial district. Its heart is Greene Street; 50 cast-iron buildings are stretched out over a five-block area. The finest are those at 72–76, the "King" and 28 –30, the "Queen." A 19th-century

The "Queen," SoHo Historic District

American innovation, cast iron was cheaper than either stone or brick and allowed decorative elements to be prefabricated in foundries from molds and used as building façades.

The **Singer Building** on Broadway was built by Ernest Flagg in 1904, at a time when steel-framed brick and terra-cotta were replacing cast iron. This ornate 12-story building, adorned with wrought-iron balconies and graceful arches painted in striking dark green, was an office and warehouse for the Singer sewing machine company. The original Singer name is cast in iron above the entrance to the store on Prince Street.

Nearby was the **Museum for African Art**. One of only two American museums devoted to African art, these galleries were ingeniously designed by architect Maya Lin, creator of Washington's Vietnam Veterans Memorial *(see p205)*. But the museum is now on the move and has taken temporary residence at 36–01 43rd Avenue, Long Island City (two blocks from the 33rd Street stop on the #7 subway line). Its final resting place will be at the top of Museum Mile on Fifth Avenue in early 2005. Meanwhile, the high-caliber changing shows continue, and the museum remains a pre-eminent organizer of exhibitions and publisher of books devoted exclusively to historical and contemporary African art. Besides museums, galleries, and cast-iron architecture, SoHo's streets are lined with trendy cafés, shops, and chic designer boutiques. It is also the city's favorite Sunday brunch-and-browse neighborhood.

🏛 **Museum for African Art**
Temporary location: 36–01 43rd Ave, Long Island City. 【 *(718) 784-7700.* 〇 *10am–5pm Mon, Thu, Fri, 11am–6pm Sat–Sun.* ● *Tue–Wed.* 🎟 *(free on Sun).* 🚪 🔲 *www.africanart.org*

Window on the corner of West 4th Street and Washington Square

Washington Square ⑭

Greenwich Vil. **Map** C4. Ⓜ *W 4th St.*

NOW ONE of the city's most vibrant open spaces, Washington Square was once a marshland that was filled to form a park. Stanford White's magnificent marble arch, completed in 1895, replaced a wooden version that marked the centenary of George Washington's inauguration. In 1916, a group of artists led by John Sloan and Marcel Duchamp broke in, climbed atop the arch, and declared the "free and independent republic of Washington Square, the state of New Bohemia." Decades later, Bob Dylan sang his first folk songs near the fountain in the small park's center.

Greenwich Village ⑮

Map C4. N of Houston St & S of 14th St. Ⓜ *W 4th St-Washington Square, Christopher St-Sheridan Square, 8th St.*

SIMPLY KNOWN as "the Village," this crazy-quilt pattern of streets is a natural enclave that has been a bohemian haven and home to many celebrated writers, artists, and jazz musicians. Later, it became a popular gay district, and the spirited gay Halloween Parade held here is a fantastic event. The Village comes alive at night, when cafés, theaters, and clubs beckon at every turn. A stroll through its narrow old-fashioned lanes reveal charming row houses, hidden alleys, and leafy courtyards. The 15 Italianate row houses, lining the north side of **St. Luke's Place**, date from the 1850s. Poet Marianne Moore lived here, and Theodore Dreiser wrote his *An American Tragedy* at No. 16.

The heart of the Village is **Sheridan Square**, where seven streets meet in such a maze that early guidebooks called it "the mousetrap." The Stonewall Inn, a gay bar on Christopher Street, was where a riot took place against police harassment on June 27, 1969. It was a landmark moral victory for the budding Gay Rights Movement. Stonewall Inn still stands, but is no longer a bar.

Jefferson Market Courthouse, "Old Jeff," is perhaps the Village's most treasured landmark. It was built as a courthouse in 1877 and voted the fifth most beautiful building in America. After remaining empty for over 20 years, it was restored and turned into a public library in 1967. Opposite is Patchin Place, a small pocket of 19th-century houses where playwright Eugene O'Neill, and poets e e cummings and John Masefield once lived.

Original furnishings in East Village's Merchant's House Museum

🏛 Jefferson Market Courthouse
425 6th Ave. 📞 *(212) 243-4334.*
⭘ *noon–8pm Mon, Wed, 10am–6pm Tue, Thu, noon–6pm Fri, 10am– 5pm Sat.* ⬤ *Sun, public hols.* ♿ Ⓦ *www.nypl.org*

Pointed tower of "Old Jeff," Greenwich Village

East Village ⑯

Map D4. 14th St to Houston St. Ⓜ *Astor Place.*

Prominent New Yorkers, such as Peter Stuyvesant, the Astors, and the Vanderbilts, lived in this fomer Dutch enclave until 1900, when they moved uptown. Thereafter, it was home to German, Jewish, Irish, and Ukrainian immigrants. In the 1960s the East Village became a haven for hippies, and this is the place where punk rock was born.

The six-story **Cooper Union** was set up in 1859 by Peter Cooper, a wealthy industrialist who built the first US steam locomotive and founded New York's first free, nonsectarian and coeducational college. Its Great Hall was inaugurated in 1859 by Mark Twain, and Abraham Lincoln delivered his "Right Makes Might" speech there in 1860. Cooper Union still provides free education.

The 1832 **Merchant's House Museum**, a remarkable Greek Revival brick town house, is a time capsule of a vanished way of life. It was bought by Seabury Tredwell, a wealthy merchant, and remained in the family until 1933. It still has its original fixtures and displays authentic Federal, American Empire, and Victorian furniture.

One of New York's oldest churches, the 1799 **St. Mark's-in-the-Bowery** is located on East 10th Street. Governor Peter Stuyvesant and his descendants are buried here.

The English-style **Tompkin Square** was the site of America's first organized labor demonstration in 1874, the main gathering place during the neighborhood's hippie era and, in 1991, an arena for violent riots when the police tried to evict the homeless who had occupied the grounds. A small statue of a boy and a girl looking at a steamboat commemorates the more than 1,000 local residents who died in the *General Slocum* steamer disaster on June 15, 1904.

🏛 Merchant's House Museum
29 E 4th St. 📞 *(212) 777-1089.*
⭘ *1–5pm Thu–Mon & by appt.*
📷 🚫 *(no flashes).* 🎧 *Lectures.*
Ⓦ *www.merchantshouse.com*

Union Square ⑰

Map D4. **M** *14th St-Union Square.*
Greenmarket *Mon, Wed, Fri, Sat.*

O PENED IN 1839, this park was once the hangout for drug dealers and soapbox orators. Today, renovations have transformed it into a flourishing section of Manhattan. A greenmarket fills the square where more than 200 farmers from all over New York State sell fresh produce four times a week, drawing patrons from all over the city. Herbs and berries, miniature vegetables, fresh flowers and home-baked pastries, honey, and newly woven yarns are all available at this bountiful market.

Flatiron Building ⑱

Map D3. *175 5th Ave.* **M** *23rd St.*
⬚ *office hours.*

T HIS UNUSUAL BUILDING, its shape conforming to a triangular plot of land, has intrigued New Yorkers since it was built by Chicago architect David Burnham in 1902. One of the first buildings to use a steel frame, it heralded the era of the skyscrapers.

It soon became known as the Flatiron for its triangular

Flatiron Building, New York's most famous early skyscraper

Appellate Court, said to be the world's busiest courthouse, Madison Square

shape, but some called it "Burnham's folly," predicting that the winds created by the building's shape would knock it down. It has, however, withstood the test of time.

The stretch of Fifth Avenue to the south of the building was once rather run down, but has come to life with chic shops such as Emporio Armani and Paul Smith, giving the area new cachet and a new name, "the Flatiron District."

Madison Square ⑲

Map D3. **M** *23rd St.*

Q UIET Madison Square opened in 1847 at the center of a fashionable residential district where politican Theodore Roosevelt and writer Edith Wharton were born. It was bordered by the elegant Fifth Avenue Hotel, the Madison Square Theater, and Stanford White's Madison Square Garden. The torch-bearing arm of the Statue of Liberty was exhibited here in 1884. Newly landscaped, this statue-filled park borders some of the city's hottest restaurants. Area residents stroll and walk their dogs at all hours.

Just off Madison Square is the spectacular **New York Life Insurance Company** building, designed in 1928 by Cass Gilbert of Woolworth Building fame *(see p69)*. The building has Gilbert's trademark pyramid-shaped tower, modeled on the Giralda in Seville. Its interior is adorned with hanging lamps, bronze doors and paneling, and a grand staircase leading to a subway station.

Opposite is the **Appellate Division of the Supreme Court of the State of New York**, a small marble palace designed by James Brown Lord in 1900. Considered to be the busiest courthouse in the world, appeals relating to civil and criminal cases for New York and the Bronx are heard here. During the week, the public can admire the fine interior, designed by the Herter brothers, including the courtroom when it is not in session. Displays in the lobby often feature some of the court's more famous and infamous cases. Among the celebrities whose appeals were settled here are Babe Ruth, Charlie Chaplin, Fred Astaire, Harry Houdini, Theodore Dreiser, and Edgar Allan Poe.

On the east side of Madison Square is the 54-story **Metropolitan Life Tower**. Built in 1909, this was the world's tallest building at that time, an appropriate corporate symbol for the largest insurance company in the world. The huge four-sided clock has minute hands said to weigh 1,000 lb (454 kg) each. A series of historical murals by N.C. Wyeth, the famed illustrator of such classics as *Robin Hood, Treasure Island,* and *Robinson Crusoe* (and the father of painter Andrew Wyeth), are now on display in the lobby.

🚇 **Appellate Division of the Supreme Court of the State of New York**
E 25th St at Madison Ave. ⬚ *9am–5pm Mon–Fri.* ● *public hols.* 🚫

Empire State Building ⑳

Map D3. 350 5th Ave. ☎ *(212) 736-3100.* Ⓜ *A, B, C, D, E, F, N, Q, R, 1, 2, 3, 9 to 34th St; 6 to 33rd St.* 🚌 *Q32, M1–M5, M16, M34.* **86th-floor Observatory** ○ *9:30am–last adm: 11:15pm; 11am–7pm Jan 1; 9am–5pm Dec 24; 11am–7pm Dec 25.* 🎥 ♿ 🍴 ⓦ *www.esbnyc.com*

THE EMPIRE State Building is New York's tallest and most impressive skyscraper. Construction began in March 1930 not long after the stock market crash, and by the time it opened in 1931, space was so difficult to rent that it was nicknamed "the Empty State Building." Only the immediate popularity of the observatories saved the building from bankruptcy – to date, they have attracted more than 120 million visitors – but the building soon became a symbol of the city

the world over. It only took 410 days to build this 102-story limestone and brick skyscraper, with an average of four and a half stories added every week. The 102nd floor has been closed to the public for several years. Each February, the annual Empire State Run-Up is held, when 150 runners race up the 1,576 steps from the lobby to the 86th floor (known for its outdoor observation decks), in 10 minutes.

102nd-floor observatory

The building was planned to be 86 stories high, but a 150 ft (46 m) mooring mast for zeppelins was added. The mast, now 204 ft (62 m), transmits TV and radio to the city and four states.

High-speed elevators travel at up to 1,200 ft (366 m) a minute.

Ten million bricks were used to line the entire building.

Colored floodlighting of the top 30 floors marks special and seasonal events.

The framework is made from 60,000 tons of steel and was built in 23 weeks.

Aluminum panels were used instead of stone around the 6,500 windows. The steel trim masks rough edges on the facing.

Sandwich space between the floors houses the wiring, pipes and cables.

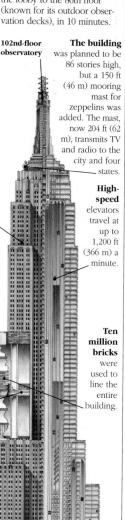

Fifth Avenue Entrance Lobby, Empire State Building

Macy's 34th Street entrance

Herald Square ㉑

Map D3. 6th Ave. Ⓜ *34th St-Penn Station.*

NAMED AFTER the New York *Herald*, which had its offices here from 1893 to 1921, the square was the hub of the rowdy, mid-19th century theater district known as the Tenderloin District. Theaters, dance halls, hotels, and restaurants kept the area humming with life until reformers clamped down on sleaze in the 1890s. The ornamental clock, on an island where Broadway meets 6th Avenue, is all that survives of the Herald Building.

Herald Square became a mecca for shoppers after the Manhattan Opera House was razed in 1901 to make way for **Macy's**. The "world's largest store" began modestly. It was founded by former whaler Rowland Hussey Macy in 1857; the red star logo was from his tattoo, a souvenir of his sailing days. The store was sold in 1888 and moved to its present premises in 1902. The 34th Street façade still has its original clock, canopy, and lettering.

Macy's sponsors New York's famous Thanksgiving Day parade *(see p31)* and the Fourth of July fireworks. Its annual Spring Flower Show draws thousands of visitors.

🏛 **Macy's**
151 W 34th St. ☎ *(212) 695-4400.* ○ *10am–8:30pm Mon–Sat; 11am–7pm Sun.* ● *public hols.* ⓦ *www.macys.com*

Times Square ㉒

Map D3. **M** *42nd St-Times Square.*
ℹ *1560 Broadway (46th St),*
8am–8pm daily. **✉** *noon Fri.*
W *www.timessquarebid.org*

N AMED FOR THE New York
Times Tower, Times
Square is the city's most
famous intersection. Although
the *New York Times* has
moved from its original headquarters at the square's
southern end, the crystal ball
still drops at midnight on
New Year's Eve, as it has
since the building opened
with fanfare in 1906.

Since 1899, when Oscar
Hammerstein built the
Victoria and Republic
theaters, this has also been
the heart of the city's theater
district. The district's transformation in the 1990s led
to the renovation of many
theaters, such as the New
Victory and the New Ams-
terdam. Their new produc-
tions, as well as the area's
bars and restaurants, attract
theatergoers each evening.

Old-world Broadway glamor
rubs shoulders with modern
entertainment in Times
Square *(see p88)*. MTV has its
studios here, and E Walk is a
vast entertainment and retail
complex. Exciting new buildings, such as the Bertlesmann
building and the fashionably
minimalist Condé Nast offices,
sit alongside the classic establishments, such as Sardi's, the
Paramount Hotel, and the
Baroque Lyceum Theater.

**The New York Public Library's Main
Reading Room**

The New York
Public Library ㉓

Map E3. 5th Ave & 42nd St. **C** *(212)
869-8089.* **M** *42nd St-Grand Central.*
◯ *Mon–Sat; hours vary.* **●** *public
hols.* **♿** **✦** *Lectures, workshops,
readings.* **▢** **W** *www.nypl.org*

A RCHITECTS Carrère and
Hastings won the coveted
job of designing New York's
main public library in 1897.
The white marble Beaux Arts
edifice they designed fulfilled
the library's first director's
vision of a light, quiet, airy
place, where millions of
books could be stored and yet
be available to readers as
promptly as possible. Built on
the site of the former Croton

Reservoir, it opened in
1911 to immediate
acclaim, despite having
cost the city $9 million.
The architects' genius is
best seen in the newly
renovated Main
Reading Room, a vast
paneled space as
majestic as a cathedral,
extending almost two
city blocks. Below it are
88 miles (140 km) of
shelves, holding over
seven million volumes.
It takes only minutes
for the staff or a com-
puterized dumbwaiter
to supply any book.
The Periodicals Room
holds 10,000 current
periodicals from 128
countries. On its walls
are murals by Richard
Haas, honoring New York's
great publishing houses. The
original library combined the
collections of John Jacob
Astor and James Lenox. Its
collections today range from
Thomas Jefferson's handwritten copy of the Declaration of
Independence to T.S. Eliot's
typed copy of "The Waste
Land." More than 1,000
queries are answered daily,
using the vast database of the
CATNYP computer catalog.

This library is the hub of a
network of 82 branches, with
nearly seven million users.
Other well-known branches
include the New York Public
Library for the Performing
Arts at the Lincoln Center
(see p83) and the Schomburg
Center in Harlem.

MIDTOWN MANHATTAN

**Elevator door at the
Chrysler Building**

Midtown Manhattan's skyline is
graced with some of the city's
most spectacular towers and
spires – from the familiar beauty
of the Empire State Building's
Art Deco pinnacle to the
dramatic wedge shape of
Citigroup's modern headquarters. As the shoreline progresses
uptown, so the architecture
becomes more varied; the
United Nations complex
dominates a long stretch, and
then Beekman Place begins a
strand of exclusive residential
enclaves that offer the rich and
famous some seclusion.

United Nations, founded in 1945, has
its impressive headquaters on an 18-acre
(7-ha) site on the East River *(see p76)*.

**Empire State
Building** *(see p73)*

**The
Highpoint**   **Tudor
City**

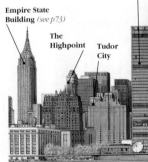

The skylit Garden Court, Morgan Library

Morgan Library ㉔

Map E3. 29 E 36th St. 📞 *(212) 685-0610.* 🆆 *www.morganlibrary.org* ⬤ *Closed for refurbishment until early 2006.*

THIS MAGNIFICENT palazzo-style building was designed in 1902 to house the private collection of banker Pierpont Morgan (1837–1913), one of the great collectors of his time. Established in 1924 as a public institution by Morgan's son, J.P. Morgan Jr, it has a splendid collection of rare manuscripts, prints, books, and bindings. However, because of an expansion program, the Morgan Library is currently closed and is due to re-open in early 2006.

The complex includes the original library and J.P. Morgan Jr.'s home. Pierpont Morgan's opulent study and his original library contain some of his favorite paintings, objets d'art, and priceless acquisitions. Prominent among the exhibits are one of the 11 surviving copies of the Gutenburg Bible (1455), printed on vellum, and six surviving leaves of the score for Mozart's Horn Concerto in E-flat Major, written in different colored inks.

The Garden Court, a three-story skylit garden area, links the library with the house. Exhibits are changed regularly to provide access to some of the world's most significant cultural artifacts.

Grand Central Terminal ㉕

Map E3. E 42nd St at Park Ave. 📞 *(212) 532-4900.* Ⓜ *4, 5, 6, 7, S to Grand Central.* 🚌 *M104, M42.* ⬤ *5:30–1:30am daily.* ♿ 📷 *Wed 12:30pm (free), call (212) 935-3960 & Fri 12:30pm (free), call (212) 697-1245.* **Baggage check; lost & found.** 🆆 *www.grandcentralterminal.com*

ONE OF THE world's great train terminals, this outstanding Beaux Arts building is New York's most visited, with 500,000 people passing through it daily. The present building, dating from 1913, is resplendent after its recent restoration. Its glory is the main concourse, dominated by three great arched windows that fill the space with natural light. The high vaulted ceiling of this vast pedestrian area is decorated with twinkling constellations. The information booth here is surmounted by a wonderful four-faced clock. The Grand Staircase, styled after the staircase in Paris' Opera House, is a reminder of the glamorous days of early rail travel. Adjacent to the main concourse is the Vanderbilt Hall, named after Cornelius Vanderbilt, the railroad magnate who opened the station in 1871.

Today, Grand Central is no longer limited to the city's commuters. It has become an attraction in its own right, with a museum, over 40 shops, and an extensive food court, including the famed Oyster Bar *(see p118).* This New York classic with a vaulted ceiling of yellow Guastavino tiles, has a huge dining concourse and specializes in seafood.

A fine clock on the Grand Central Terminal building

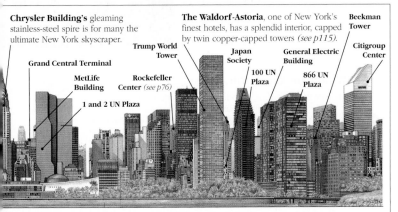

Chrysler Building's gleaming stainless-steel spire is for many the ultimate New York skyscraper.

The Waldorf-Astoria, one of New York's finest hotels, has a splendid interior, capped by twin copper-capped towers *(see p115).*

Beekman Tower

Trump World Tower

Japan Society

General Electric Building

Citigroup Center

Grand Central Terminal

MetLife Building

Rockefeller Center *(see p76)*

100 UN Plaza

866 UN Plaza

1 and 2 UN Plaza

The UN Buildings seen from the garden

United Nations ㉖

Map E3. 1st Ave at 46th St. (212) 963-8687. 4, 5, 6, 7 to 42nd St-Grand Central Station. M15, M27, M42, M50, M104. Mar–Dec: 9:30am–4:45pm daily; Jan–Feb: Mon–Fri only. Jan 1, Thanksgiving, Dec 25 (limited schedule during year-end hols). for tours. in 20 languages. **Lectures, films.** www.un.org

WHEN New York was chosen as the UN head-quarters, philanthropist and multimillionaire John D. Rockefeller Jr. donated $8.5 million for the purchase of the East River site. This complex was the creation of American architect Wallace Harrison and a team of international consultants.

The United Nations was formed near the end of World War II to preserve world peace, promote self-deter-mination, and to aid economic and social well-being around the globe. Currently 189 members meet regularly each year from mid-September to mid-December in the General Assembly, the closest thing to a world parliament.

The most powerful body is the Security Council, housed in the Conference Building. Here, delegates and their assis-tants meet around the horse-shoe-shaped table to confer on issues related to inter-national peace and security. In 1988, the UN was awarded the Nobel Peace Prize. The Trusteeship Council and the Economic and Social Council are in the same building.

The UN is an international zone and has its own stamps and post office. Daily guided tours show visitors the various council chambers and General Assembly hall.

Rockefeller Center ㉗

Map E3. 630 5th Ave between 49th & 52nd Sts. M 47th-50th Sts. www.rockefellercenter.com

A CITY WITHIN a city, and a National Historic Land-mark, this urban wonder is the world's largest privately owned complex. Begun in the 1930s, it was built on a site leased by John D. Rockefeller Jr. for a new opera house he had planned. When the 1929 Depression scuttled the plans, Rocke-feller, stuck with a long-term lease, went ahead with his own development. This was the first commercial project to integrate gardens, dining, and shop-ping with office space. The number of buildings has now grown to 19, though the newer structures do not match the Art Deco elegance of the original 14. The center's Channel Gardens, named after the English Channel because they separate the French and British buildings, change with the calendar.

The centerpiece of the center is the 70-story G.E. Building, headquarters of NBC studios. Backstage tours of the network's studios are a pop-ular attraction. The TV show *Today* can also be viewed live every weekday morning from the sidewalk in front of the studio. Another attraction is the 1932 Radio City Music Hall. Once a movie palace, it now hosts dazzling events, including the annual Christmas and Easter shows. Its reno-vation in 1999 brought back the glitter and sparkle of the original interior.

The center also houses a skating rink, and over 100 works of art, including a major mural in each building.

A view of Rockefeller Center

WORKS OF ART AT THE UN

The UN Building has acquired numerous works of art and reproductions by major artists; many have been gifts from member nations. Most of them have either a peace or international friendship theme. The legend on Norman Rockwell's *The Golden Rule* reads "Do unto others as you would have them do unto you." Marc Chagall designed a large stained-glass window as a memorial to former Secretary General Dag Hammarskjöld, who was accidentally killed on a peace mission in 1961. A Henry Moore sculpture, *Reclining Figure: Hand* (1979), graces the grounds. There are many other sculptures and paintings by the artists of many nations.

Reclining Figure: Hand (1979), a gift from the Henry Moore Foundation

The Great Bronze Doors in Saint Patrick's Church

Saint Patrick's Cathedral ㉘

Map E3. 5th Ave & 50th St.
📞 (212) 753-2261. Ⓜ 6 to 51st St; E, F to Fifth Ave. 🚌 M1, M2, M3, M4. 🕐 7:30am–8:30pm daily. ✝ frequent Mon–Sat; 7, 8, 9, 10:15am & noon, 1, 4, 5:30pm Sun. ♿ 🎥 🚻 **Concerts & lectures.**

NEW YORK's finest Gothic Revival building was designed by James Renwick Jr. and completed in 1878. This is also the largest Catholic cathedral in the United States and seats more than 2,500 people every Sunday. When Archbishop John Hughes decided to build a cathedral here in 1850, many criticized his choice of a site so far from the city's center at the time. Today his foresight has given the church one of the best locations in midtown Manhattan.

Museum of Modern Art ㉙

Map E2. 11 W 53rd St. 📞 (212) 708-9400. Ⓜ 5th Ave-53rd St. 🚌 M1, M2, M3, M4, M27, M50. ● Closed until 2005. See temporary location – MoMA, Queens.

ONE OF THE world's most comprehensive collections of modern art is on view at the Museum of modern art (MoMA). Founded in 1929, it set the standard for other museums of its kind. MoMA is currently undergoing a three-year, $650 million expansion project, and the museum is closed until 2005 (although the shop will remain open).

The museum has temporarily moved to a former factory in Queens, which provides 25,000 sq ft (2,322 sq m) of exhibition space in a dramatic building by architect Michael Maltzan. Several masterpieces from the main gallery, such as Picasso's *Les Demoiselles d'Avignon* (1907) and Vincent Van Gogh's *Starry Night* (1889), are on display. A major exhibit on Matisse and Picasso as well as other shows will be presented here until 2005, when MoMA will move back to its renovated premises.

🏛 **MoMA, Queens**
45-20 33rd St at Queens Blvd.
📞 (212) 708-9400. Ⓜ 7 IRT to 33rd St. 🕐 10am–5pm Thu, Sat–Mon, 10am–7:45pm Fri. ● Tue, Wed.
🎥 ♿ 🚻 Ⓦ www.moma.org

Fifth Avenue ㉚

Map E2. Ⓜ 5th Ave-53rd St.

FROM ITS inception in the early 1800s, Fifth Avenue has been the territory of New York's rich and famous. Then, it was lined with palatial mansions built by the Astors, Vanderbilts, Belmonts, and Goulds, giving it the sobriquet Millionaires' Row. But as retail and commercial ventures set up outlets here in the 1900s, society moved farther north.

Today, the heart of New York's best-known avenue extends from the Empire State Building (see p73) to the Grand Army Plaza, presided over by the 1907 Plaza Hotel. Along this stretch are a range of famous stores symbolizing wealth and social standing, which have made Fifth Avenue synonymous with luxury goods.

The Cartier store, at 52nd Street, is housed in a 1905 Beaux Arts mansion, originally the home of banker Morton F. Plant, who supposedly traded it for a perfectly matched string of pearls. Other well-known jewelry and accessory stores include Tiffany's, made famous by Truman Capote's 1958 *Breakfast at Tiffany's*, Harry Winston, and Henri Bendel. Among the high-quality department stores are Saks Fifth Avenue, Bergdorf Goodman, and the wonderful F.A.O. Schwarz toy store.

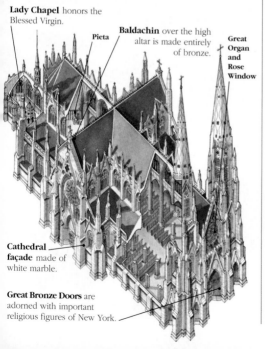

Lady Chapel honors the Blessed Virgin.

Pieta

Baldachin over the high altar is made entirely of bronze.

Great Organ and Rose Window

Cathedral façade made of white marble.

Great Bronze Doors are adorned with important religious figures of New York.

A Tour of Central Park ㉛

New York's "backyard," an 843-acre (340-ha) swath of green, provides recreation and beauty for residents and visitors. Designed by Frederick Law Olmsted and Calvert Vaux in 1858, the park took 16 years to create and involved the planting of over 500,000 trees and shrubs. A short walking tour from 59th to 79th Streets takes in some of Central Park's most picturesque features, from the dense wooded Ramble to the open formal spaces of Bethesda Terrace.

★ Strawberry Fields
This peaceful area was created by Yoko Ono in memory of John Lennon, who lived in the nearby Dakota apartments.

★ Bethesda Fountain
The richly ornamented formal terrace overlooks the Lake and the wooded shores of the Ramble.

Wollman Rink
was restored by tycoon Donald Trump in the 1980s for future generations of skaters.

Wildlife Conservation Center has three climate zones that are home to over 130 species of animals.

The Pond

Plaza Hotel

Frick Collection
(see p80)

★ The Dairy
This Victorian Gothic building houses the visitor center. Make it your first stop and pick up a calendar of park events.

Hans Christian Andersen's Statue
A favorite Central Park landmark for children, this is a popular site for storytelling in summer.

Bow Bridge
This cast-iron bridge links the Ramble with Cherry Hill by a graceful arch, 60 ft (18 m) above the Lake.

LOCATOR MAP
See Map pp64–5

San Remo Apartments
This is one of the five twin-towered apartments on Central Park West, famed for their grace and architectural detail.

Alice in Wonderland is immortalized in bronze at the northern end of Conservatory Water, along with the Cheshire Cat, the Mad Hatter, and the Dormouse.

STAR SIGHTS

★ **Belvedere Castle**

★ **Bethesda Fountain**

★ **Conservatory Water**

★ **Strawberry Fields**

★ **The Dairy**

The Dakota Apartment Building

American Museum of Natural History *(see p83)*

Metropolitan Museum *(see p80)*

Obelisk

Reservoir

Guggenheim Museum *(see p82)*

The Ramble is a wooded area of 37 acres (15 ha), crisscrossed by paths and streams. It is a paradise for bird-watchers – over 250 species have been spotted in the park, which is on the Atlantic migration flyway.

★ **Belvedere Castle**
From the terraces there are unequaled views of the city and surrounding park. Within the stone walls is the Central Park Learning Center.

★ **Conservatory Water**
From March to November, this is the scene of model boat races each Saturday. Many of the tiny craft are stored in the boathouse that adjoins the Lake.

Whitney Museum of American Art ㉜

Map F2. 945 Madison Ave. *(212) 570-3600.* M 6 to 77th St. ▪ M1, M2, M3, M4, 30, 72. ○ 11am–6pm Tue–Thu, Sat–Sun, 1–9pm Fri. ● public hols. ▨ ♿ ✓ *Lectures, film/video presentations.* ▮ ▯ W www.whitney.org

A N ENTIRE RANGE of 20th- and 21st-century American art is showcased in the Whitney Museum. Sculptor Gertrude Vanderbilt Whitney founded the museum in 1930 after the Metropolitan Museum of Art rejected her personal collection of works by living artists, such as George Bellows and Edward Hopper. Initially, the museum was set up behind Whitney's studio in Greenwich Village *(see pp70–71)* and moved to its present inverted pyramid building designed by Marcel Breuer in 1966. A midtown branch is now housed in the Philip Morris Building.

The Leonard and Evelyn Lauder galleries on the fifth floor have permanent collections, showing works by Calder, O'Keefe, and Hopper. Changing exhibitions occupy the second, third, and fourth floors. Highlights include Alexander Calder's fanciful sculpture *Circus* (1926–31),

James Whistler's second portrait of *Lady Meux* (1881), Frick Collection

The grand entrance of the Metropolitan Museum of Art

and works by realists such as Hopper, whose *Early Sunday Morning* (1930) depicts the emptiness of American city life. Other painters represented here are Jasper Jones and Roy Lichtenstein.

The Whitney Biennial show is today the most significant survey of new trends in American art.

Frick Collection ㉝

Map F2. 1 E 70th St. *(212) 288-0700.* M 6 to 68th St. ▪ M1, M2, M3, M4, 30, M72, M79. ○ 10am–6pm Tue–Thu, Sat, 10am–9pm Fri, 1–6pm Sun. ● most public hols. ▨ *(children under 10 not admitted).* ✗ ♿ ▮ *Concerts, lectures, film & video.* W www.frick.org

T HE PRICELESS art collection of steel magnate Henry Clay Frick (1849–1919) is exhibited in a residential setting amid the furnishings of his opulent mansion, providing a rare glimpse of how the extremely wealthy lived in New York's gilded age. Frick intended the collection to be a memorial to himself and bequeathed the entire house to the nation on his death.

The collection includes a suberb display of Old Master paintings, French furniture, and Limoges enamels. Of special interest is the skylit West Gallery offering oils by Hals, Rembrandt, and Vermeer, whose *Officer and the Laughing Girl* (1655–60) is a fine example of the Dutch painter's use of light and shadow. The Oval Room features Whistler, while the Library and Dining Room are devoted to English works. In the Living Hall are works by Titian, Bellini, and Holbein.

Metropolitan Museum of Art ㉞

Map F2. 1000 Fifth Ave. ❸ *(212) 535-7710.* M 4, 5, 6 to 86th St. ▪ M1, M2, M3, M4. ○ 9:30am–5:15pm Sun & Tue–Thu, 9:30am–8:45pm Fri, Sat. ● Jan 1, Thanksgiving, Dec 25. ▨ ♿ ▯ ▮ ▮ ▯ *Concerts, lectures, film & video presentations.* W www.metmuseum.org

O NE OF THE world's great museums, the Metropolitan houses treasures that span 5,000 years of culture from all over the world. Founded in 1870 by a group of artists and philanthropists who visualized an American arts institution to rival those of Europe, it began with three private European collections and 174 paintings. Today, its holdings number over two million, and the original 1880 Gothic Revival building by Calvert Vaux and Jacob Wrey has been expanded many times. Recent additions are inviting courts with huge windows overlooking Central Park, and the breathtaking **Byzantine Galleries**, located under the Grand Staircase.

Most of the collections are housed on the two main floors. On the first floor are the **Costume Institute**, and part of the **Robert Lehman Collection**. This extraordinary private collection, acquired in 1969, includes Old Masters, Dutch, Spanish, and French artists, Post-Impressionists, and Fauvists, as well as ceramics and furniture. The state-of-the-art Costume Institute covers fashion trends from the 17th century to the present day. On view are Napoleonic and Victorian ballgowns, Elsa

Cypresses (1889), painting by Vincent Van Gogh

Schiaparelli's shocking pink evening dresses, creations by Worth and Quant, and the costumes of the Ballets Russes.

The second floor includes the **American Wing**, European Sculpture and Decorative Arts, **Egyptian Art**, and the **Michael C. Rockefeller Wing**. Built by Nelson Rockefeller in memory of his son, who lost his life on an art-finding expedition in New Guinea, the wing showcases a superb collection of over 1,600 primitive artworks from Africa, the islands of the Pacific, and the Americas.

Among the African works are outstanding ivory and bronze sculptures from the royal kingdom of Benin (Nigeria). Also on view are pre-Columbian gold, ceramics, and stonework from Mexico and Central and South America. The American Wing has one of the world's finest collections of American paintings, including several by Edward Hopper. Prize exhibits include Gilbert Stuart's first portrait of George Washington, John Singer Sargent's notorious portrait of *Madame X*, and the monumental *Washington Crossing the Delaware* by Emanuel Leutze. There are also period rooms, including one designed by Frank Lloyd Wright, and Tiffany glass.

The Metropolitan has one of the largest collections of Egyptian art outside Cairo. Objects range from the fragmented jasper lips of a 15th-century BC queen to the massive Temple of Dendur. Many of the objects were discovered during museum-

sponsored expeditions during the early 20th century.

The **Lila Wallace Wing** holds the museum's growing contemporary art collection. Some great works include Picasso's portrait of *Gertrude Stein* (1905) and Jackson Pollock's *Autumn Rhythm*.

The heart of the museum, however, is its awe-inspiring collection of 3,000 **European Paintings**. Its highlights are masterpieces by Dutch and Flemish painters, specifically Brueghel's *The Harvesters* (1551) and Rembrandt's *Self Portrait* (1660), painted when he was 54. Among the finest Impressionist and Post-Impressionist paintings is *Cypresses* (1889), painted by Vincent Van Gogh the year before he died.

The third floor has a comprehensive collection of **Asian Art**, featuring textiles, sculpture, and ceramics from China, Japan, Korea, Southeast Asia, and India. The full-size Ming-style Chinese scholar's garden in the Astor Court was built by craftspeople from Souzhou. The **Cantor Roof Garden** has superb annual shows of 20th-century sculpture, displayed against the dramatic backdrop of the city's skyline. Guests can also visit the museum shops, located on the main floor and mezzanine.

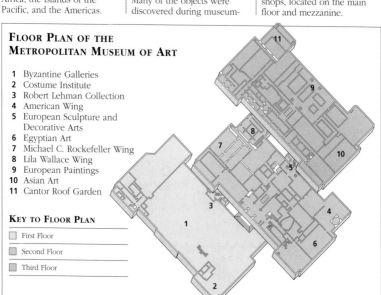

FLOOR PLAN OF THE METROPOLITAN MUSEUM OF ART

1 Byzantine Galleries
2 Costume Institute
3 Robert Lehman Collection
4 American Wing
5 European Sculpture and Decorative Arts
6 Egyptian Art
7 Michael C. Rockefeller Wing
8 Lila Wallace Wing
9 European Paintings
10 Asian Art
11 Cantor Roof Garden

KEY TO FLOOR PLAN

☐ First Floor

☐ Second Floor

☐ Third Floor

The Solomon R. Guggenheim Museum ㉟

1071 5th Ave at 89th St. *(212) 423-3500.* M 4, 5, 6 to 86th St. M1, M2, M3, M4. 10am–5:45pm Sat–Wed, 10am–8pm Fri. Jan 1, Dec 25. *Concerts, lectures, performing art series.* W www.guggenheim.org

O NE OF THE world's finest collections of modern and contemporary art is housed in a building that is considered one of the great architectural achievements of the 20th century. The only New York building to be designed by the celebrated American architect Frank Lloyd Wright *(see p396)*, it was completed after his death in 1959. Its shell-like façade is a New York landmark, while the interior is dominated by a spiral ramp that curves down and inward from the dome, passing works by major 19th- and 20th-century artists.

Over the years, Solomon Guggenheim's core collection of Abstract art has been added to by donations of several important collections. The museum now owns a large body of work by famous artists such as Kandinsky, and major holdings of Brancusi, Calder, Klee, Chagall, Miró, Léger, Mondrian, Picasso, Oldenberg, and Rauschenberg.

Not all of the permanent collection is on display at any one time. Only a small portion is on view as the main gallery, the Great Rotunda, usually features special exhibitions. The Small Rotunda shows some of the museum's famous Impressionist and Post-Impressionist holdings. The new Tower galleries feature exhibitions of work from the permanent collection and contemporary pieces. A fifth-floor sculpture terrace overlooks the scenic Central Park.

Cézanne's *Man With Arms Crossed* (1895-1900), Guggenheim Museum

Two important acquisitions of the museum are the Justin Thannhauser collection and more than a 100 photographs from the Robert Mapplethorpe Foundation.

Guggenheim SoHo, a downtown site, closed down recently in 2002 but a new Guggenheim, designed by Frank Gehry, is to be built near the South Street Seaport *(see p68)*. This museum will house the postwar collection and have two theaters.

THE SOLOMON R. GUGGENHEIM MUSEUM

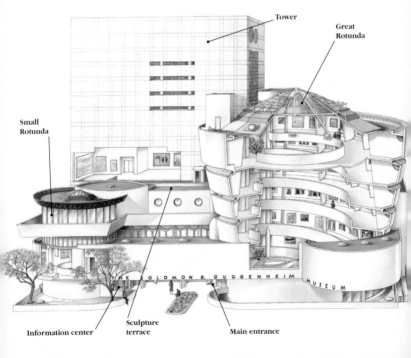

Tower

Great Rotunda

Small Rotunda

THE SOLOMON R. GUGGENHEIM MUSEUM

Information center

Sculpture terrace

Main entrance

American Museum of Natural History ㊱

Central Park West at 79th St.
C *(212) 769-5100.* **M** *B, C to 81st St.* **▬** *M7, M10, M11, M79.*
○ *10am–5.45pm daily. Donation.*
Rose Center **○** *until 8:45pm Fri.* **&**
✿ ▮▮ ▭ w *www.amnh.org*

THIS IS ONE of the largest natural history museums in the world, attracting more than 4.5 million visitors each year. Since the original building opened in 1877, the complex has grown to cover four city blocks, and today holds more than 30 million specimens and artifacts. The most popular areas are the dinosaurs, and the newly renovated Milstein Family Hall of Ocean Life.

Enter at Central Park West onto the second floor to view the Barosaurus exhibit, African, Asian, Central and South American peoples, and animals. First floor exhibits include ocean life, meteors, minerals and gems, and the Hall of Biodiversity. North American Indians, birds, and reptiles occupy the third floor. Dinosaurs, fossil fishes, and early mammals are on the fourth floor.

The new **Rose Center** for Earth and Space has as its centerpiece the Hayden Planetarium. The planetarium contains a technologically advanced Space Theater, the famous Cosmic Pathway, and a Big Bang Theater.

Barosaurus, American Museum of Natural History

The Lincoln Center for the Performing Arts complex

Lincoln Center ㊲

Broadway between W 62nd & W 65th Sts. **M** *1,9 to 66th St.* **▬** *M5, 7, 10, 11, 66, 104.*

A GIANT CULTURAL complex, built in the 1950s, Lincoln Center was conceived when both the Metropolitan Opera House and the New York Philharmonic needed homes. At that time, the notion of a single complex where different performing arts could exist side by side, was considered both daring and risky. Today, the Lincoln Center draws audiences of over five million each year.

The **Lincoln Center for the Performing Arts** was born in May 1959, when President Eisenhower traveled to New York to turn a shovelful of earth, composer Leonard Bernstein lifted his baton, and the New York Philharmonic and the Juilliard Choir broke into the *Hallelujah Chorus*. The center soon covered 15 acres (6 ha) on the site of the slums that had once been the setting for Bernstein's classic musical *West Side Story*.

Lincoln Center includes the **New York State Theater**, home to the highly acclaimed New York City Ballet and the New York City Opera, a troupe devoted to presenting opera at popular prices; and the **Metropolitan Opera House**, the focal point of the plaza. This fine building has five great arched windows, which offer views of the opulent foyer and two radiant murals by Marc Chagall. All the greats have sung here, including Maria Callas, Jessye Norman, and Luciano Pava-rotti. The other two significant institutions here are the

Lincoln Center Theater and Avery Fisher Hall, home to the New York Philharmonic, America's oldest orchestra (scheduled to return to Carnegie Hall in 2006). The best way to see the complex is by guided tour.

Although the **American Folk Art Museum** is now housed in a dramatic state-of-the-art building on West 53rd Street, the museum continues to operate the **Eva and Morris Feld Gallery** at the Lincoln Center. The gallery provides additional exhibition space for the museum, for displaying artwork from the museum's permanent collection, such as quilts, carvings, and paintings. The museum itself is well worth a visit to see its extensive collection of folk art.

The **Hotel des Artistes**, nearby, was built in 1918 as working artists' studios. Interesting residents have included Alexander Woollcott, Isadora Duncan, Noël Coward, Rudolf Valentino, and Norman Rock-well. The Café des Artistes is well known for its misty, romantic Howard Chandler Christy murals and fine cuisine.

▦ Lincoln Center for the Performing Arts
C *(212) 546-2656.* **&**
✿ *(212) 875-5350.* **▮▮**
w *www.lincolncenter.org*
🏛 American Folk Art Museum
45 West 53rd Street. **C** *(212) 265-1040.* **○** *10:30am–5:30pm Wed– Thu & Sat–Sun; 10:30am–7:30pm Fri.* **Ø &** **✿ ✿**
w *www.folkartmuseum.org*
🏛 Eva and Morris Feld Gallery
2 Lincoln Square. **C** *(212) 977-7170.*
○ *11am–7:30pm Tue–Sun; 11am–6pm Mon.* **Ø & ✿ ✿**
w *www.folkartmuseum.org*

Greater New York

THOUGH OFFICIALLY PART of New York City, upper Manhattan and the boroughs outside Manhattan are very different in feel and spirit. Away from the bustle of the inner city, they are residential and do not have the famous skyscrapers of New York. The difference is evident even in the way residents describe a trip to Manhattan as "going into the city." Yet these areas feature such attractions as Columbia University, the city's largest zoo, botanical gardens, museums, churches, beaches, and huge sports arenas.

View across Columbia University's quadrangle toward Butler Library

Columbia University ㊳

Map F4. Main entrance at W 116th St. 🅒 (212) 854-4900. Ⓜ 116th St-Columbia University (lines 1, 2). 🅟 Ⓦ www.columbia.edu

ONE OF America's oldest and finest universities, Columbia was founded as King's College under a charter granted by King George II of Great Britain, in 1754. Originally situated in lower Manhattan, the present campus was built in Morningside Heights. Architects McKim, Mead & White, who designed its first buildings around a central quadrangle, placed the university on a terrace, serenely above street level. A Classical, columned building, the **Low Library**, dominates the quadrangle. Daniel Chester French's statue *Alma Mater*, in front of it, became familiar as the backdrop to the 1968 anti-Vietnam War student demonstrations. The building now houses offices, and the rotunda is used for a variety of academic and ceremonial purposes. Its books were moved to Butler Library, across the quadrangle, in 1932. To the right, the 1904 **St. Paul's Chapel** is known

for its fine woodwork and vaulted interior. The whole chapel is bathed in light from above, and has fine acoustics.

Columbia, part of the Ivy League, is noted for its law, medicine, and journalism schools. Founded in 1912 by publisher Joseph Pulitzer, the School of Journalism is the home of the Pulitzer Prize awarded for the best in letters and music. Columbia's distinguished faculty and alumni, past and present, include over 50 Nobel laureates. Famous alumni include Isaac Asimov, J.D. Salinger, and James Cagney.

Visitors to the campus can stroll along the central quadrangle, where jeans-clad future leaders of America meet and mingle between classes. Across from the campus are the cafés where students engage in lengthy philosophical arguments, debate in the topics of the day, or simply unwind.

Also across the campus to the east on Amsterdam Avenue lies the **Cathedral of St. John the Divine**. Begun in 1892 and only two-thirds finished, with its

600 ft (180 m) long and 146 ft (45 m) wide interior, this Neo-Gothic cathedral, with its hand-carved gargoyles, is slated to be the largest in the world. Medieval construction methods, such as stone supporting buttresses, continue to be used to complete the structure, which is also a venue for theater, music, and avant-garde art.

🅗 **St. Paul's Chapel**
Columbia University. 🅒 (212) 854-1487 concert info. Ⓜ 116th St-Columbia Univ. 🕐 10am–11pm Mon–Sat (term time), 10am–4pm (breaks). ✝ Sun. 🅖

🅗 **Cathedral of St. John the Divine**
Amsterdam Ave at W 112th St. 🅒 (212) 316-7540. Ⓜ 1, 2 to Cathedral Pkwy (110th St). 🚌 M4, M5, M7, M11, M104. 🕐 7am–6pm daily. ✝ Vespers 7pm Sun. Donations. 🅖 🅟 🅗 *Concerts, plays, lectures, exhibitions, gardens.* Ⓦ www.stjohndivine.org

Riverside Church ㊴

Map F4. 490 Riverside Dr at 122nd St. 🅒 (212) 870-6700. Ⓜ 116th St-Columbia Univ. 🕐 10:30am–5pm Tue–Sun. ✝ 10:45am Sun. 🅾 with prior permission. 🅖 🅒 *Carillon Bell Concerts* 🅒 (212) 870-6784. noon, 3pm Sun. *Theater* 🅒 (212) 864-2929. Ⓦ www.theriversidechurchny.org

THE DESIGN OF Riverside Church was inspired by the cathedral at Chartres in France. This Gothic church with a 21-story steel frame was lavishly funded by John D. Rockefeller Jr, in 1930.

The Laura Spelman Rockefeller Memorial Carillon (in honor of Rockefeller's mother) is the largest in the world, with 74 bells. The 20-ton Bourdon, or hour bell, is the largest and heaviest tuned carillon bell ever cast. The organ, with its 22,000 pipes, is among the world's largest. The second gallery features a figure by Jacob Epstein, *Christ in Majesty*, cast in plaster and covered in gold leaf. Another Epstein

Carved stonework at the Cathedral of St. John the Divine

The 21-story Riverside Church, from the north

statue, *Madonna and Child*, stands in the court next to the cloister. The screen panels honor eight men and women including Socrates, Michelangelo, Florence Nightingale, and Booker T. Washington, whose lives exemplified the teachings of Christ.

For quiet reflection, enter the small, secluded Christ Chapel, patterned after an 11th-century Romanesque church in France. Visitors can take the elevator to the 20th floor and then walk the 140 steps to the top of the 392-ft (120-m) bell tower for a fine panorama of Upper Manhattan from the windy observation deck. There is no access to the bell tower during carillon concerts.

St. Nicholas Historic District ㊵

Map F4. 202–250 W 138th & W 139th St. **M** *135th St (B, C).*

A STARTLING CONTRAST to the run-down surroundings, the two blocks here, known as the King Model Houses, were built in 1891 when Harlem was considered a neighborhood for New York's gentry. They still comprise one of the city's most distinctive examples of row townhouses. A distinct feature of these houses is the provision of a central service alley that can be accessed from the avenue ends and at different points along the block. The alley serves a very useful feature in concealing garbage cans and service deliveries.

The developer, David King, chose three leading architects, who succeeded in blending their different styles to create a harmonious whole. The most famous of these was the firm of McKim, Mead & White, who were responsible for the northernmost row of solid brick Renaissance palaces. Their homes featured ground floor entrances rather than the typical New York brownstone stoops. The parlor floors have ornate wrought-iron balconies below, as well as carved decorative medallions above their windows.

The Georgian buildings designed by Price and Luce are built of buff brick with white stone trim. James Brown Lord's Georgian-style buildings feel much closer to Victorian, with outstanding red-brick façades and brownstone foundations.

Over the years, many distinguished professional and civic leaders made their homes here. Among them were celebrated musicians W.C. Handy and Eubie Blake, and one of the founders of the American Negro Theater, Abram Hill. He collaborated in the production of a play set in the historic district and called it "On Striver's Row," a name by which the district is now commonly known.

Studio Museum in Harlem ㊶

Map F4. 144 W 125th St. **C** *(212) 864-4500.* **M** *125th St (2, 3).* ◯ *noon–6pm Wed, Thu, noon–8pm Fri, 10am–6pm Sat, Sun.* ⬤ *Jan 1, Thanksgiving, Dec 25.* 🎟 *except Sat.* 🚫 ♿ 🎥 *Lectures, children's programs, films.* 🎁 📷 **W** *www.studiomuseuminharlem.org*

T HE MUSEUM WAS founded in 1967 in a loft on upper Fifth Avenue with the mission of becoming the premier center for the collection and exhibition of the art and artifacts of African Americans.

The present premises, a five-story building on Harlem's main commercial street, was donated to the museum by the New York Bank for Savings in 1979. There are galleries on two levels for changing exhibitions featuring artists and cultural themes, and three galleries are devoted to the permanent collection of works by major black artists, such as Romare Bearden and Elizabeth Catlett.

The photographic archives comprise one of the most complete records in existence of Harlem in its heyday. From the main floor a side door opens onto a small sculpture garden. In addition to its excellent exhibitions, the museum also maintains a national artist-in-residence program and offers regular lectures, children's programs, and film festivals. A range of books and African crafts are available in the small shop.

Exhibition space at the Studio Museum in Harlem

The Cloisters ㊷

Map F4. Fort Tryon Park.
☎ (212) 923-3700. Ⓜ A to 190th
St (exit via elevator). 🚌 M4.
🕐 Mar–Oct: 9:30am–5:15pm
Tue–Sun; Nov–Feb: 9:30am–4:45pm
Tue–Sun. ⬤ Jan 1, Thanksg., Dec 25.
💵 donations. No videos. ♿ ✉
book in advance. 🎫 **Concerts.**
ⓦ www.metmuseum.org

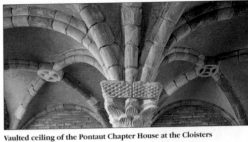

Vaulted ceiling of the Pontaut Chapter House at the Cloisters

THIS WORLD-FAMOUS branch of the Metropolitan Museum (see pp80–81), devoted to medieval art, resides in a building that incorporates medieval cloisters, chapels, and halls. The museum, organized in chronological order, starts with the Romanesque period (AD 1000) and moves to the Gothic (1150 to 1520). It is noted for its exquisite illuminated manuscripts, stained glass, metalwork, enamels, ivories, and beautifully preserved tapestries. Perhaps the most interesting exhibits in the Cloisters are the gardens, planted according to horticultural information found in medieval treatises and poetry. Early music concerts are performed regularly here and are extremely popular. Call in advance for tickets.

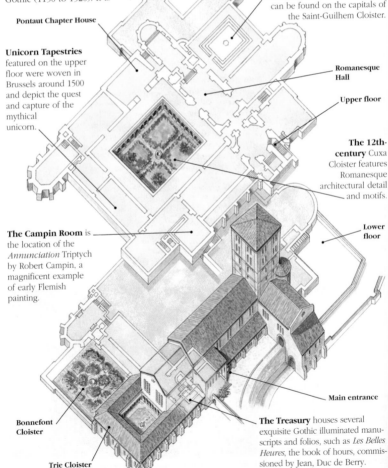

Pontaut Chapter House

Unicorn Tapestries
featured on the upper floor were woven in Brussels around 1500 and depict the quest and capture of the mythical unicorn.

The Campin Room is the location of the *Annunciation* Triptych by Robert Campin, a magnificent example of early Flemish painting.

Intricate floral ornamentation
can be found on the capitals of the Saint-Guilhem Cloister.

Romanesque Hall

Upper floor

The 12th-century Cuxa Cloister features Romanesque architectural detail and motifs.

Lower floor

Main entrance

Bonnefont Cloister

Trie Cloister

The Treasury houses several exquisite Gothic illuminated manuscripts and folios, such as *Les Belles Heures*, the book of hours, commissioned by Jean, Duc de Berry.

Jungle World, a climate-controlled tropical rainforest at the Bronx Zoo

The Bronx ㊸

Map F4. **M** *161st St (Yankee Std); 2, 5 to Pelham Pkwy (Bronx Zoo); 4, D to Bedford Park Blvd (NY Bot. Garden).*

ONCE A PROSPEROUS suburb with a famous Grand Concourse lined with apartment buildings for the wealthy, parts of the Bronx have now become a symbol of urban decay. However, visitors still frequent the area to escape the overwhelming city concrete for some beauty and quiet, while New Yorkers flock to the 1923 **Yankee Stadium**, home of the New York Yankees baseball team. Don't miss a sidetrip to one of the city's wealthiest and most beautiful parts – Riverdale – located between W 242 and Broadway.

But the most outstanding attraction of the Bronx is the **Bronx Zoo**. Opened in 1899, this is the largest urban zoo in the US, home to some 7,166 animals of 531 species, living in realistic representations of their natural habitats. The Park is a leader in the perpetuation of endangered species, such as the Indian rhinoceros and the snow leopard. Its 265 acres (107 ha) of woods, streams, and parklands include a children's zoo, camel safaris, a seasonal Skyfari cable car, and a shuttle train that takes visitors around the sprawling park.

Across the road from the Zoo's main entrance, visitors can experience 250 acres (101 ha) of beauty and hands-on enjoyment at the New York **Botanical Garden**. One of the oldest and largest botanical gardens in the world, it has 48 specialty gardens and plant collections, 50 acres (20 ha) of virgin forest, and a vast children's Adventure Garden. The Enid A. Haupt conservatory with 11 interconnected glass galleries has been wonderfully restored as "A World of Plants," with misty tropical rainforests and dramatic deserts.

🏊 Bronx Zoo

Fordham Rd /Bronx River Pkwy. **(** *(718) 367-1010.* ○ *Nov–Mar: 10am–4:30pm daily; Apr–Oct: 10am–5pm daily (5:30pm Sat & Sun).* (free Wed). 🚻 ♿ 🍴 Children's zoo. Ⓦ www.wcs.org

Brooklyn ㊹

Map F5. **M** *Prospect Pk (Brooklyn Bot. Gardens); 2, 3 to Eastern Pkwy (Brooklyn Mus); Kingston (Brooklyn Children's Mus); Stillwell Ave (Coney Is).*

ONE OF THE most ethnically diverse boroughs in New York, Brooklyn, if it were a separate city, would be the country's fourth largest. Many entertainment greats, such as Mel Brooks, Phil Silvers, Woody Allen, and Neil Simon, celebrate their birthplace with great affection and humor. Among the diverse neighborhoods are the historic residential districts of Park Slope and Brooklyn Heights,

Ibis Coffin (332–330 BC) in gold leaf and silver, Brooklyn Museum of Art

beautiful tree-lined enclaves that offer a wonderful stroll past Victorian houses and cafés. An oval gateway in the Grand Army Plaza, designed by Frederick Law Olmsted and Calvert Vaux, leads to the lush, green Prospect Park.

The adjacent **Brooklyn Botanic Gardens** feature a traditional Elizabethan-style "knot" herb garden, one of the largest bonsai and rose collections in the country, and some rare rainforest trees.

To its southeast, lies the 1897 **Brooklyn Museum of Art**, designed by McKim, Mead & White. Though only one-fifth completed, the museum is one of the most impressive cultural institutions in the US, with a permanent collection of some 1.5 million objects, housed in a grand five-story structure spanning 560,000 sq ft (41,805 sq m). Highlights include African, Oceanic, and New World art; a collection of classic Egyptian and ancient Middle Eastern artifacts, and some works of American and European contemporary art.

To the north on Brooklyn Avenue lies the imaginative **Brooklyn Children's Museum**, the world's first designed especially for young people. Programs and displays are based on a remarkable collection of 20,000 cultural artifacts and natural history specimens, live plants and animals, and interactive exhibits, all designed to satisfy the curiosity of young minds.

Brooklyn poet Walt Whitman composed many of his works on the borough's farthest point, **Coney Island**. It was billed as the "World's Largest Playground" in the 1920s, with its combination of hair-raising rides and lovely beaches. Today, Coney Island is a bit run down but holds historical memorabilia. A short trip to the New York Aquarium is a must.

🏛 Brooklyn Museum of Art

200 Eastern Pkwy, Brooklyn. **(** *(718) 638-5000.* ○ *10am– 5pm Wed–Fri, 11am–6pm Sat, 11am–11pm first Sat in month, 11am–6pm Sun.* ● *Jan 1, Thanksgiving, Dec 25. Donation expected.* ♿ 🎟 Concerts, lectures. Ⓦ www.brooklynmuseum.org

New York City Practical Information

Visitors to new york are treated very much the same as anyone else. While you may not be given special treatment, as long as you follow a few guidelines on personal security you'll be able to explore the city as freely as any native New Yorker. Buses and subway trains are reliable and inexpensive. Beside, the wide range of prices offered by the many hotels, restaurants, and entertainment venues means your New York trip can be both fun and affordable.

TOURIST INFORMATION

Advice on any aspect of life in New York City is available from the **New York Convention and Visitors' Bureau (NYC & Co.)**. Their 24-hour touch-tone phone service offers help outside office hours. Brochures and information kiosks are also found at the walk-in office of the **Times Square Visitors Information Bureau**.

PERSONAL SECURITY

Though New York is rated among the safest large US cities with around-the-clock foot, horse, bike, and car patrols by the police in tourist areas, it is always good to be cautious. Avoid certain areas, such as Chinatown and Lower East Side after dark. At night, if you can't afford a taxi, try to travel with a group. Walk as if you know where you're going. Avoid making eye contact and getting into confrontations with down-and-outs. If someone asks you for money, do not get drawn into conversation. Always keep change handy for phone calls or bus fares; carry your Metrocard in your pocket. Never carry too much cash, and lock your valuables in the hotel safe. Do not allow anyone except hotel or airport personnel to carry your luggage.

Public toilets in bus stations should be avoided. It is best to find a hotel or store if you want to use a restroom. Since parks are also often used for drug dealing, they are safest when there is a crowd for a rally or concert. If you want to go for a jog, avoid lonely areas and pathways, and follow a map of safe routes.

GETTING AROUND

New york's rush hours extend from 8 to 10am, 11:30am to 1:30pm and 4:30 to 6:30pm, Mon–Fri. During these times, every form of public transportation is crowded, and the streets are much harder to navigate on foot.

Buses are a comfortable way to get around, but they often tend to be slow. Subways are quick, reliable, and inexpensive, and make stops throughout central Manhattan. The vast system extends over 233 miles (375 km) and most routes operate throughout the year. You can buy a Metrocard for subway and bus fares. Cards come in $5 to $80 amounts depending on the number of trips you intend to take. Taxis are best for door-to-door service, but can be held up in traffic jams. You should hail only yellow taxis, as they are the only ones with licences. Accepting a ride from anyone else can be dangerous. If their roof numbers are lit up, they are available.

Heavy traffic and expensive rentals make driving in New York a frustrating experience. The speed limit is 30 mph (48 km/h) – which is hard to exceed due to traffic. Parking in Manhattan is difficult and costly. Many hotels include parking charges in their room rates. New York's tow-away crews are active, and one-third of cars towed suffer damage. If you cannot find your car at its parking place, first call the traffic department's tow-away office. For specific details call the **Department of Transportation**. If you receive a parking ticket, you have seven days to pay the hefty fine. If the car is not at the pound, report it to the police.

ETIQUETTE

It is illegal to smoke in *any* public place or building in New York. Bars all over the city also ban smoking.

Tipping for service is part of New York life. In general, 10 to 15 percent of your bill is sufficient, though 20 percent for outstanding service is always appreciated.

ENTERTAINMENT

New york city is a non-stop entertainment extravaganza, every day, all year round. Whatever your taste, you can be sure the city will satisfy it on both a grand and an intimate scale.

New York is famous for its extravagant musicals and its ferocious critics. The Times Square area hosts the "power productions" of Broadway – the big, highly publicized dramas, musicals, and revivals starring many Hollywood luminaries in sure-fire money earners, in theaters such as the **Ambassador** and the **Lyceum** (1903), the oldest theater still in operation. Off-Broadway and Off-Off-Broadway stages such as **Actors' Playhouse**, and **American Place** host experimental shows, ranging from the well-appointed to the improvised, in lofts, churches, and even garages.

The city is also a great center of traditional ballet and modern dance. The New York City Ballet, founded by the legendary choreographer George Balanchine, performs in the **New York State Theater**. The **Dance Theater of Harlem** is world famous for its modern, and ethnic productions.

There's every imaginable form of music in New York, from international stadium rock to the sounds of the 1960s, from Dixieland jazz or country blues, soul, and world music to street musicians. The city's music scene changes at a dizzying pace, with many new arrivals, so there's no way to predict what you may find when you arrive. The top performers such as Elton John, Bruce Springsteen, and the Stones perform in the huge arenas at **Shea Stadium** and **Madison Square Garden**. The **Knitting Factory** has live jazz and new music. The **Limelight** is a good bet for the latest sounds and newest groups.

New York's nightlife and club scene is legendary. Whatever your preference – noisy disco, stand-up comedy, or the soothing melodies of a Harry Connick Jr. – you'll be amazed at the choice. New Yorkers thrive on dancing. Dance floors available all over the city range from the ever-popular **SOB's** – for jungle, reggae, soul, jazz, and salsa – to huge basketball-court-sized places, such as **Roseland**. The historic **Copacabana** alternates live bands with a popular disco.

The city is also a film buff's paradise. Apart from new US releases, which show months in advance of other countries, many classic and foreign films are screened in this hotbed for new and innovative talent.

New Yorkers are sports crazy, and there are activities to suit every taste. Visitors can choose from health clubs and horseback riding to playing tennis or jogging. Spectator sports are provided by professional baseball (**Yankee Stadium**), ice hockey and basketball (**Madison Square Garden**), and football (Giants Stadium), while for tennis fans there is the US Open and Virginia Slims tournaments.

SHOPPING

NEW YORK IS the consumer capital of the world: a shopper's paradise, with dazzling displays and a staggering variety of goods for sale. Everything is available here, from high fashion to rare books, state-of-the-art electronics, and an array of exotic food. Keep in mind that the city's sales tax is a hefty 8.625%.

Known as the fashion capital of America, New York boasts such names as **Polo/Ralph Lauren** and **Calvin Klein**. There are fashion stores such as **Brooks Brothers** (menswear) and **Ann Taylor**

(women's wear), and shops of international names such as **Yves St. Laurent** and **Giorgio Armani**. Manhattan is also known for its world-class jewelry shops including **Cartier** and **Tiffany's**. The city is a bargain hunter's dream, with huge discounts on anything from household goods to designer clothes.

As the publishing capital of the US, New York has the country's best bookstores. Don't miss the **Barnes & Noble** stores, the **Strand** for rare and used books, and **Shakespeare & Co**.

Dozens of tiny shops around the city specialize in unusual merchandise, from butterflies and bones to toy firefighting equipment and occult potions. Don't miss a trip to the legendary **FAO Schwarz** for toys of all kinds. Some of New York's best souvenirs can be found in the city's many museum shops, including the **American Craft Museum** and the **American Museum of Natural History**.

DIRECTORY			
TOURIST OFFICES	**ENTERTAINMENT**	**Madison Sq. Garden** 7th Ave at 33rd St. (212) 465-6741. www.thegarden.com	**Brooks Brothers** 346 Madison Ave. (212) 682-8800.
NYC & Co. www.nycvisit.com www.ci.nyc.ny.us	**Actors' Playhouse** 100 Seventh Ave S. (212) 463-0060.	**New York State Theater** Lincoln Center. (212) 870-5570.	**Cartier** 653 5th Ave. (212) 753-0111.
Times Square Visitors' Bureau www.timessquarebid.org	**Ambassador** 219 W 49th St. (212) 239-6200.	**Yankee Stadium** River Ave at 161st St, Bronx. (718) 293-4300.	**FAO Schwarz** 767 5th Ave. (212) 644-9400.
TRANSPORTATION	**American Place** 111 W 46th St. (212) 840-3074.	**SHOPPING**	**Giorgio Armani** 760 Madison Ave. (212) 988-9191.
Department of Transportation Staten Island Ferry, S Ferry. (212) 487-5761 or 66.	**Dance Theater of Harlem** 466 W 152nd St. (212) 690-2800.	**American Craft Museum** 40 W 53rd St. (212) 956-3535.	**Polo/Ralph Lauren** Madison Ave at 72nd St. (212) 606-2100.
BARS & CLUBS	**Knitting Factory** 74 Leonard St, New York City. (212) 219-3055.	**American Museum of Natural History** W 79th St, Central Park W. (212) 769-5150.	**Strand Book Store** 828 Broadway. (212) 473-1452.
Copacabana 560 W 34th St. (212) 239-2672.	**Limelight** 660 6th Ave, New York City. (212) 807-7780.	**Ann Taylor** 645 Madison Ave. (212) 832-2010.	**Tiffany & Co** 5th Ave at 57th St. (212) 755-8000.
Roseland 239 W 52nd St. (212) 247-0200.	**Lyceum** 149 W 45th St, New York City. (212) 239-6200.	**Barnes & Noble** 105 5th Ave. (212) 807-0099.	**Yves St. Laurent Rive Gauche** 859 Madison Ave. (212) 517-7400.
SOB's 204 Varick St. (212) 243-4940.			

New York State

Stretching north for over 200 miles (322 km) to the Canadian border, and 400 miles (644 km) west to the Great Lakes, the "Empire State" is a world away from New York City. Due east of Manhattan, Long Island is the largest island adjoining the continental US, with miles and miles of suburbs, farmland, and beaches jutting out into the Atlantic Ocean. To the north, the Hudson River is an area of opulent mansions and small towns. The state capital, Albany, marks the start of the vast Upstate area, comprising the Adirondacks, rural farmland, and vibrant cities.

The octagonal Montauk Point Lighthouse, completed in 1796

Jones Beach State Park ❷

Wantagh. 🚆 *Long Island Railroad from Penn Station to Jones Beach. Operates Jun–Labor Day, (718) 217-5477.* 🚌 ℹ️ *(516) 785-1600.* ⏰ *Jun–Labor Day: sunrise–midnight.* ♿ 🎫 🅿️ Ⓦ www.visitjonesbeach.com

Located on Long Island, Jones Beach State Park is only 33 miles (53 km) from Midtown Manhattan. A popular destination since it was created in 1929, this barrier island resort features more than 2,400 acres (972 ha) of parkland, beaches, and a wide variety of outdoor and cultural activities.

The park's oceanside beaches are complemented by a stillwater bayside beach and several swimming, diving, and wading pools, and surf facilities. The park's other recreational options include golf courses, restaurants, fishing docks, and a 2-mile (3-km) boardwalk.

The 11,200-seat **Jones Beach Theater** is a popular venue for rock and pop concerts in summer. Another landmark, the 200-ft (61-m), brick-and-stone structure, the **Jones Beach Tower**, is modeled on the campanile of St. Mark's Cathedral in Venice.

The Hamptons & Montauk ❸

🏨 *15,000.* ✈️ 🅿️ 🚌 ℹ️ *(877) 386-6654.* Ⓦ www.hamptonstravelguide.com

At Riverhead, Long Island splits into two peninsulas – the mostly pastoral North Fork and the more urban South Fork. Most of South Fork's beaches and cultural attractions are concentrated in the expensive and trendy summer retreats of The Hamptons and Montauk.

Most New Yorkers tend to associate The Hamptons (from west to east, Westhampton Beach, Hampton Bays, Southampton, Bridgehampton, East Hampton, and Amagansett) exclusively with its many celebrity residents. However, the area also has a rich historical heritage. In the 19th-century whaling community of Sag Harbor, to the north of Bridgehampton, the **Old Custom House**, built in 1789, commemorates the town's post-Revolutionary War heyday as one of the first official ports of entry into the young US. On the Village Green in East Hampton, the **Home Sweet Home Museum** houses a variety of early Colonial, rough-shingled structures, including a classic saltbox house built in 1750, and the still-operational Old Hook Mill, constructed in 1806.

The easternmost Long Island community, Montauk is a busy summer resort, serving as a jumping-off point for the area's nature trails and beaches. Other activities are golf, horseback riding, and fishing. Montauk State Park contains the **Montauk Point Lighthouse**, commissioned by George Washington in 1792. Still in operation, the octagonal stone structure is an important landmark for oceangoing vessels.

🏛 **Old Custom House**
Main St. & Garden Sq, Sag Harbor. 📞 *(631) 692-4664.* ⏰ *Jul–Aug: 10am–5pm daily; Memorial Day–Jun & Labor Day–Oct: 10am–5pm Sat–Sun.* ● *public hols.* 🎫
Ⓦ www.splia.org/museum_custom.html

🏛 **Home Sweet Home Museum**
14 James Lane, East Hampton. 📞 *(631) 324-0713.* ⏰ *May–Sep: 10am–4pm Mon–Sat, 2–4pm Sun; Oct–Nov: 2–4pm Fri–Sun.* ● *public hols.* ♿
Ⓦ www.easthampton.com/homesweethome

One of the many swimming pools at Jones Beach State Park

Hudson River Valley ❹

☒ 🏛 🚃 ℹ️ *3 Neptune Rd,
Poughkeepsie.* ☎ *(845) 463-4000.*
🌐 *www.dutchesstourism.com*

Fᴿᴼᴹ ɪᴛs sᴏᴜʀᴄᴇ high in the Adirondack Mountains, the Hudson courses past bustling riverport towns and the dramatic Catskill and Taconic mountain ranges for nearly 315 miles (507 km) to its mouth at New York harbor. Strikingly beautiful and strategically located, the valley has played a pivotal role in North American military, economic, and cultural history.

Settled by the Dutch in the 1620s *(see p43)*, it was soon dotted with trading posts that grew up around the thriving fur trade with local Iroquois tribes. The area's Dutch heritage survives in names of places such as Catskill, Kinderhook, and Claverack, as well as in the early 19th-century fictional writings of Washington Irving (1783–1859), whose tales of *Rip Van Winkle* and *The Legend of Sleepy Hollow* made him America's first internationally recognized author. Irving's modest but whimsically eclectic Hudson River home, **Sunnyside**, is now a tourist attraction.

The Hudson's economic and transportation advantages also made it a key strategic objective of both British and American forces during the Revolutionary War, resulting in many pitched battles. Fort Putnam, one of the forts built along the river in 1778 to defend the colonies from British attacks, has been restored and is now part of the **United States Military Academy** at West Point. Established in 1802, the academy has trained the nation's leading military officers, including opposing Civil War generals Ulysses S. Grant and Robert E. Lee, and World War II commanders Douglas MacArthur and Dwight D. Eisenhower. The Military Academy Museum provides a comprehensive introduction to a tour of the fortress-like grounds.

The imposing exterior of the lavishly furnished Vanderbilt Mansion

Statue of George Washington at the US Military Academy

In the 19th century, many of New York's emerging elite constructed seasonal retreats along the Hudson. The largest of these is the **Vanderbilt Mansion** in Hyde Park. Completed in 1899, this Italian-Renaissance style palace was built by the architecture firm of McKim, Mead & White, for railroad baron Frederick W. Vanderbilt. The magnificent home offers a spectacular view of the river, and is laden with French furniture, art, tapestries, and architectural details taken from a Parisian château once occupied by Napoleon. An older and less ostentatious mansion is Springwood, the home of Franklin D. Roosevelt (FDR), America's 32nd president *(see p49)*.

Roosevelt was born here in 1882, and it was used as a summer White House during his 1933–45 term. The house is now part of the **Home of Franklin D. Roosevelt National Historic Site**, which also includes an extensive museum and library detailing Roosevelt's leadership during the Great Depression and World War II. Both FDR and Eleanor are buried here. The nearby Eleanor Roosevelt National Historic Site preserves Val-Kill, the First Lady's weekend and holiday cottage retreat.

🏛 **Sunnyside**
W Sunnyside Lane, off Rte 9, Tarrytown. ☎ *(914) 591-8763.* ◯ *Apr–Oct: 10am–5pm Wed–Mon; Nov–Dec: 10am–4pm Wed–Mon; Mar: 10am–4pm Sat–Sun.* ● *Thanksg., Dec 25.* 🅿️ 🎫 🌐 *www.hudsonvalley.org*

🏛 **US Military Academy**
W Sunnyside Lane, Rte 9 W, West Point. ☎ *(845) 938-2638.* ◯ *One hr ground tours by bus only. Mon–Sat: 9:45am–3:30pm every half hr. Photo IDs required for tours.* 🅿️ *(for tours only).* ● *Jan 1, Thanksg., Dec 25.* ♿ 🌐 *www.usma.edu*

🏛 **Home of Franklin D. Roosevelt National Historic Site**
4097 Albany Post Rd, Rte 9, Hyde Park. ☎ *(845) 229-9115.* ◯ *9am–5pm daily.* 🅿️ ♿ 🌐 *www.nps.gov/ hofr*
Library & Museum ☎ *(800) 337-8474.* 🅿️ ♿ **Museum** ◯ *Apr–Oct: 9am–6pm; Nov–Mar: 9am–5pm.* ● *Jan 1, Thanksg., Dec 25.*
Library ◯ *8:45am–5pm Mon–Fri.* 🌐 *www.fdrlibrary.marist.edu*

Sunnyside, Washington Irving's home

New York State Capitol in Albany, a blend of architectural styles

Albany ❺

🏙 101,000. ✈ 🚆 🚌
ℹ 25 Quackenbush Square, (518)
434-1217. ⓦ www.albany.org

ALBANY HAS BEEN a central
force in New York State
since 1614, when the explorer
Henry Hudson (see p60)
established a fur-trading post,
Fort Orange, at the northernmost navigable point on the
Hudson River. When the
British took over the settlement in 1664, they changed
its name to Albany. In 1797
Albany was selected as the
New York State capital, and
the town's political future was
secured. The city expanded
dramatically in the 1830s with
the completion of the Erie
Canal, which linked the
Hudson River to the Great
Lakes. When canal traffic
declined in the 1850s, Albany
retained its commercial
dominance, rapidly evolving
into a New York Central
railroad terminus and manufacturing center.
    While transportation and
industry are still important
components of the local
economy, government is the
main concern in today's
Albany. The majestic **New
York State Capitol**, built
over 30 years and completed
in 1898, occupies a central
location near the city's downtown. The massive stone
building is a curious amalgam
of Italian and French Renaissance and Romanesque,
replete with ornamented
stairways, soaring arches, and
an ornate Senate chamber
embellished with red granite,

yellow and pink marble,
stained glass, onyx, and
mahogany.
    The **New York State
Museum** chronicles the
state's rich heritage, beginning with its first Native
American occu-
pants and incor-
porating the stories
of New York's
many immigrants,
early settlers, and
business elite.
A reconstructed
Iroquois longhouse
and a restored
1940s subway car from
New York City's legendary
A-train are among the many
highlights here.

🏛 **New York State Capitol**
Empire State Plaza. 🅲 (518) 474-
2418. ◯ tours at 10am, noon, 2pm,
3pm Mon–Fri, 11am, 1pm, 3pm Sat–
Sun. ⬤ Jan 1, Easter, Thanksgiving,
Dec 25. ♿
🏛 **New York State Museum**
Empire State Plaza. 🅲 (518) 474-
5877. ◯ 9:30am–5pm daily.
⬤ Jan 1, Thanksgiving, Dec 25. ♿

Saratoga Race Track

Saratoga Springs ❻

🏙 25,000. 🚆 🚌 ℹ 297
Broadway, (518) 587-3241.
ⓦ www.saratoga.org/visitorcenter

THIS TOWN has been known
for its horseracing,
gambling, and high society
since it emerged as a resort in
the 19th century. The thera-
peutic waters from the town
springs at **Saratoga Spa State
Park** sparked an annual
influx of wealthy tourists
seeking relief from various
ailments. Other more
enjoyable distractions were
offered by the lavish casinos
and horseracing facilities.
One of Saratoga's original
gambling establishments, the
elegant Canfield Casino, is
now part of **Congress Park**.
The gabled grandstand of the
                Saratoga Race
                Track, built during
                the Civil War, is still
                in use, attracting
                large crowds
                during the racing
                season in August.
                For a glimpse of
                the area's more
                tempestuous
Revolutionary War past,
**Saratoga National Histor-
ical Park**, 15 miles (24 km)
southeast, was the site of the
1777 Battle of Saratoga. Here,
American commander Horatio
Gates led Colonial forces to a
decisive victory over 9,000
British regulars, Hessians, and
Native Americans commanded
by General John Burgoyne.
The victory ensured American
control of the Hudson River
shipping corridor, and
prompted the French King
            Louis XVI to send
            troops to the colonists'
            aid later that year.

🏛 **Saratoga Spa State
Park**
I-87, exit 13N. 🅲 (518)
584-2535. ◯ 8am–sunset
daily. 🚫 ♿ ⓦ www.
saratogaspastatepark.org
🏛 **Saratoga National
Historical Park**
Rte 4, 8 miles (13 km) S of
Schuylerville. 🅲 (518) 664-
9821. ◯ 9am–5pm daily.
⬤ Jan 1, Thanksgiving,
Dec 25. 🚫 ♿
ⓦ www.nps.gov/sara

Sprawling Saratoga National Historical Park

The tranquil waters of Otsego Lake, Cooperstown

Adirondack Mountains ❼

🏢 ❓ 216 Main St, Lake Placid
📞 (518) 523-2445.

SPANNING ALMOST one-fourth of the state, the Adirondack Mountains encompass various ecosystems and hundreds of lakes and rivers, with only 1,100 miles (1,770 km) of road. Rugged peaks such as the 5,344-ft (1,629-m) Mount Marcy are some of the scenic highlights. Two visitor centers serve as gateways to **Adirondack Park** and provide information about the conservation movement that led to the park's creation in 1894 as part of the nation's first forest preserve.

The picturesque village of **Lake Placid** straddles Mirror Lake and Lake Placid in the north-central section of the park. Home to the 1932 and 1980 Winter Olympic Games, it is both a summer resort and winter sports training and competitive center.

🏕 Adirondack Park
1 mile N of Rte 86/Rte 30,& 14 miles (22km) E of Long Lake, Rte 28N.
📞 (518) 327-3000. ⬤ 9am–5pm daily. ⬤ Thanksgiving, Dec 25. ♿

Cooperstown ❽

🏛 2,200. 🚌 ❓ 31 Chestnut St.
📞 (607) 547-9983.

OVERLOOKING Otsego Lake, this neat little village is the legendary birthplace of baseball and home of the **National Baseball Hall of Fame**. This engaging shrine and museum pays homage to baseball greats from the last 150 years, with a colorful array of gear, uniforms, audio-video features, and special exhibits. Founded in 1786, Cooperstown also has a superb collection of Native American artifacts, folk art, and Hudson River School paintings in the **Fenimore Art Museum**. The adjacent Farmer's Museum features exhibits on 19th-century rural life. Glimmerglass Opera, on the shores of Lake Ostego, is nationally renowned.

🏛 National Baseball Hall of Fame
25 Main St. 📞 (888) 425-5633.
⬤ Memorial Day–Labor Day: 9am–9pm daily; Labor Day–Memorial Day: 9am–5pm daily. ⬤ Jan 1, Thanksgiving, Dec 25. 📷 ♿
🌐 www.baseballhalloffame.org

BASEBALL

"America's Pastime," the country's first nationwide spectator sport, evolved from the British games of cricket and rounders, as well as town ball, a New England variant. The first recorded amateur game took place in 1845 in New York City. Since the 1870s, when professional play matured, baseball has seen many superstars such as Babe Ruth, Ty Cobb, and Ted Williams.

Babe Ruth

Finger Lakes ❾

☒ 🏢 🚌 ❓ 904 E Shore Dr,
Ithaca. 📞 (607) 272-1313.
🌐 www.visitithaca.com

ACCORDING TO the Iroquois tribes of west-central New York, the Finger Lakes were created when the Great Spirit placed his hand on the region, leaving behind a series of slender lakes. Seneca Lake is the deepest of these water bodies, at 630 ft (192 m), while Cayuga Lake is the longest, stretching 40 miles (64 km) between the lively town of **Ithaca** – containing the picturesque Cornell University campus – and historic **Seneca Falls**.

Downtown Ithaca, which has a diverse array of art galleries, bookstores, and excellent restaurants, is a pleasant place to start a tour of the Finger Lakes region. **Taughannock Falls State Park**, north of Ithaca, is a wooded oasis, with the 215-ft (65-m) falls tumbling gracefully into a cool, green pool, where swimming is permitted in season. At the top of Cayuga Lake, the quiet Seneca Falls is the spot where 19th-century feminists Elizabeth Cady Stanton and Susan B. Anthony held the first American women's rights convention in 1848, laying the foundation for the Suffrage Movement some 70 years later.

🏕 Taughannock Falls State Park
10 miles (16 km) N of Ithaca,
Rte 89. 📞 (607) 387-6739.
⬤ 8am–sunset daily. 📷
🌐 www.nysparks.state.ny.us/parks

Taughannock Falls State Park in the Finger Lakes region

Syracuse ⑩

🏛 *163,900.* ✈ 🚆 🚌 ℹ️ *572 S Salina St, (315) 470-1910.*
🌐 www.visitsyracuse.org

L IKE MANY UPSTATE New York cities, Syracuse prospered after the arrival of the Erie Canal in the 1820s. The informative **Erie Canal Museum**, housed in a restored canal-side building just east of downtown, has a full-size canal boat replica and a multimedia overview of the canal's important role in the city's history. The down-town Armory Square historic and entertainment district preserves many brick and cast-iron commercial and warehouse buildings from Syracuse's late 19th-century boom period, as well as the 3,000-seat **Landmark Theatre**, built in 1928.

A downtown surprise is the **Everson Museum of Arts**, which houses a remarkable collection that ranges from Ming dynasty porcelains to works by American painters from Gilbert Stuart to Jackson Pollock. The museum building is the first designed by architect I.M. Pei.

🏛 **Erie Canal Museum**
318 Erie Blvd E. 📞 (315) 471-0593.
🕐 *10am–5pm daily.* ⬤ *public hols.*
♿ 🌐 www.eriecanalmuseum.org
🏛 **Everson Museum of Arts**
401 Harrison St. 📞 (315) 474-6064. 🕐 *noon–5pm Tue–Fri, 10am–5pm Sat, noon–5pm Sun.*
🌐 www.everson.org

Old lithograph showing the inauguration of Erie Canal

The Kodak Company's office building in Rochester

Rochester ⑪

🏛 *231,600.* ✈ 🚆 🚌
ℹ️ *45 East Ave, (800) 677-7282.*
🌐 www.visitrochester.com

T HIS LOVELY CITY, with its abundant parkland and fine museums, evolved out of an industrial past, rooted in the milling industries that developed around the Genesee River's High Falls. The Center for High Falls includes a pedestrian bridge with scenic views of the still-roaring falls, an art gallery, a local history display, and a tour of an 1816 factory that lies three stories below street level. The city's top cultural attractions are the **Strong Museum's** vast collection of Americana, which features a restored 1956 working diner, and the **George Eastman House**, where the eccentric founder of the city's Eastman Kodak Company lived until his death in 1932. The George Eastman House is now the superb International Museum of Photography. It contains massive still, film, and video holdings, and cameras and books on photography.

🏛 **Strong Museum**
1 Manhattan Square. 📞 (585) 263-2702. 🕐 *10am–5pm Mon–Thu & Sat, 10pm–8pm Fri, noon–5pm Sun.* ⬤ *Jan 1, Thanksgiving, Dec 25.* 🎟 ♿
🌐 www.strongmuseum.org
🎞 **George Eastman House**
900 East Ave. 📞 (585) 271-3361.
🕐 *10am–5pm Tue–Sat, 1–5pm Sun.* ⬤ *Mon, Jan 1, Thanksgiving, Dec 25.* 🎟
🌐 www.eastman.org

Chautauqua ⑫

🏛 *4,600.* 🚌 ℹ️ *Chautauqua Institution, Chautauqua, (800) 836-2787.*

A SECLUDED community located on Chautauqua Lake in western New York State, this town doubles in population in summer, when its Victorian cottages and tree-lined streets are crowded with people attending the town's famous **Chautauqua Insti-tution**. Founded in 1874 as an instructional center for Methodist Sunday-school teachers, it spawned the Chautauqua Movement, spon-soring correspondence courses and lecture tours in an effort to make the liberal arts more accessible. The town is now one of the nation's premier venues for theater, classical music, and opera. The shady, open-air amphitheater on the timeless Chautauqua campus holds lectures, performances, and religious services from June until August.

Renoir's *Little Blue Nude*, Albright-Knox Art Gallery, Buffalo

Buffalo ⑬

🏛 *328,100.* ✈ 🚆 🚌
ℹ️ *617 Main St, (800) 283-3256.*
🌐 www.buffalocvb.org

B URNED BY THE British during the War of 1812, the fortunes of the frontier outpost of Buffalo revived some 13 years later, when it became the western terminus of the Erie Canal. This secured its economic future as the gateway to the prosperous Great Lakes trade.

Buffalo's skyline on a sunny morning from the city harbor

The **Buffalo and Erie County Historical Society** is housed in what was originally the New York State Pavilion, the only building to survive from the 1901 Pan-American Exposition. Its numerous exhibits focus on the town's rich ethnic and industrial heritage.

The nearby **Albright-Knox Art Gallery** overlooks bucolic Delaware Park, designed by Frederick Law Olmsted *(see p78)*. On display are works by Picasso and de Kooning, and a large collection of North American paintings by Jackson Pollock, Frida Kahlo, and others. Also worth a stop is the Jell-O Museum, on Main Street, containing displays and trivia relating to "America's favorite dessert."

🏛 **Albright-Knox Art Gallery**
Elmwood Ave, Off Rte 198. ☎ (716) 882-8700. ◯ 11am–5pm Tue–Sat, noon–5pm Sun. ⬤ Jan 1, Thanksgiving, Dec 25. ♿ ♿
ⓦ www.albrightknox.org

Niagara Falls 🄬

🏨 61,800. ✈ 🚉 🚌
ℹ Prospect St, (716) 282-8992.
ⓦ www.niagara-usa.com

Louis Hennepin, the French priest who was one of the first Europeans to gaze upon Niagara Falls in 1678, wrote that "the Universe does not afford its parallel." Even today the three Niagara water-falls, which plunge nearly 200 ft (61 m) into a rocky gorge, are as awe-inspiring as they were over 300 years ago. Despite the rampant development on both the US and Canadian sides of the Niagara River (which separates the Canadian province of Ontario from New York State), the spectacle still provides enough drama, mist, and romance to lure more than 10 million tourists a year to view this natural wonder.

Visitors on the American side often start their exploration with a visit to **Niagara Falls State Park**, where the 240-ft (73-m) Prospect Point Observation Tower provides a scenic overview of the falls. For a closer exploration, there are a number of paid excursions, such as the **Cave of the Winds** elevator ride to the base of the falls, and the **Maid of the Mist** boat ride, which departs from Prospect Park and passes directly in front of the falls and into the river's Horseshoe Basin, for a view of the more dramatic Canadian Falls.

The pedestrian-friendly Rainbow Bridge provides quick passage from downtown Niagara Falls to the Canadian side, where most of the area's commercial attractions are located. At night, the falls are dramatically illuminated by electricity generated by the **Niagara Power Project**. Its visitor center traces the development of hydroelectricity in the area and features an operating model of a hydropower turbine.

🚇 **Niagara Falls State Park**
Prospect St. ☎ (716) 278-1796. ◯ sunrise–sunset daily. ♿
ⓦ www.niagarafallsstatepark.com
Cave of the Winds Goat Island.
☎ (716) 278-1730. ◯ mid-May–Labor Day: 9am–10pm Sun–Thu, 9am–11pm Fri–Sat; post Labor Day–Oct: 9am–8:30pm Sun–Thu, 9am–10pm Fri–Sat. ♿ ♿ **Maid of the Mist Ride** Prospect Park.
☎ (716) 284-8897. ◯ timings vary depending on season. Check at office for details. ♿ ♿

The majestic Niagara Falls, one of the most dramatic spectacles the country offers

New Jersey

DESPITE THE INDUSTRIAL IMAGE earned by New Jersey's manufacturing and railroad towns such as Newark and Hoboken, the "Garden State" really does live up to its moniker. Outside the urban, industrial corridor that lies across the Hudson River from New York City and extends all the way into Philadelphia, New Jersey is a gentle country of green and orderly small towns, dairy farms, rolling hills, pine forests, and miles and miles of white sandy beaches along the Atlantic Ocean.

Strolling on the peaceful campus of Princeton University

Princeton ⓯

🏛 12,000. 🚗 🚌 🄷 *Princeton Chamber of Commerce, 216 Rockingham Row, Princeton Forrestal Village, (609) 520-1776.*

THE CENTRAL New Jersey village of Princeton witnessed considerable activity during the Revolutionary War period, changing hands between British forces under General Charles Cornwallis and the Continental Army, led by General George Washington. The once-sleepy agricultural village is now a pleasant tree-lined town, combining sophisticated shops, lodgings, and a variety of restaurants, with one of America's most prestigious universities.

The center of Princeton's shopping and dining area is Nassau Street. Located here is Bainbridge House, built in 1766, which now accommodates **The Historical Society of Princeton**. The Society offers local history exhibits and free walking tours, highlighting the town's fine 18th-century architecture. The popular Palmer Square, on Nassau Street, is home to Nassau Inn, Princetown's premier hotel since 1756.

The College of New Jersey, one of the 14 original Colonial colleges, moved to Princeton in 1756 and was renamed **Princeton University** in 1896. Nassau Hall, a landmark building on campus, was the site of the initial meeting of the New Jersey State Legislature in 1776. Renowned physicist Albert Einstein spent his final years here at the Institute for Advanced Study. Today, the campus covers 1,600 acres (647 ha), and the university enrolls 6,000 students annually. The grounds include sculptures by Picasso, Henry Moore, Louise Nevelson, and Alexander Calder. The Art Museum in McCormick Hall displays paintings and sculptures that range from ancient pre-Columbian, Asian, and African art to modern works. The University

Princeton's tiger mascot

Chapel is one of the world's largest – of special interest are the Gothic architecture, stained-glass windows, and the superb 16th-century French pulpit and lectern. About 30 gargoyles in different styles decorate buildings on the campus, including the Firestone Library, Princeton's central research facility. Inside the Library, the Cotsen Children's Library features a small museum focused on the works of C.S. Lewis, Lewis Carroll, and E.B. White.

🚇 Princeton University Visitors' Center

Welcome Desk, First Campus Center. 📞 *(609) 258-1766.* ◐ *Guided tours: 10am–3:30pm Sat, 1:30–3:30pm Sun.* ⬤ *mid-Dec–early Jan, public hols.* ♿ ✉

Atlantic City ⓰

🏛 38,000. ✈ 🚗 🚌 🄷 *Greater Atlantic City Convention & Visitors Bureau, 2314 Pacific Ave, (609) 449-7130.* 🌐 *www.atlanticcitynj.com*

CALLED THE "Queen of the Coast" by generations of beachgoers, Atlantic City has been a favored vacation spot since the mid-1800s. The first casino opened on the boardwalk in 1978, and since then the town has become one of the most popular destinations on the eastern seaboard.

All gambling – euphemistically referred to as "gaming"– takes place in the large, ostentatious, casino-hotels that lie within a block of the

Tourists in a rolling chair on the boardwalk at Atlantic City

Lucy, the Margate Elephant, near Atlantic City

boardwalk and beach. Although the casinos are justly famous for their nightlife, families will find plenty of other entertainment during the day. Atlantic City's boardwalk, lined with shops and amusement arcades, is always busy with people enjoying a stroll at any time of day or night. Another way to see the boardwalk is in a "**Rolling Chair**," a rickshaw-like wicker chair on wheels that seats up to three people. Beyond the boardwalk, white-sand beaches beckon sunbathers and swimmers.

Atlantic City also hosts the prestigious Miss America Pageant, which has been held here since 1928. In nearby Margate City, **Lucy, the Margate Elephant** stands tall in celebration of American marketing ingenuity. Built by real estate developer in 1881 to draw prospects to his holdings, "Lucy" has served as a residence and a tavern over the years. Today, guided tours take visitors into the 90-ton (90,000-kg) structure that has become instantly recognizable as part of the Jersey Shore and Atlantic City.

Rolling Chair
Atlantic City Famous Rolling Chair Co, 605 Boardwalk. 📞 (609) 347-7148.

Lucy, the Margate Elephant
9200 Atlantic Ave, Margate City. 📞 (609) 823-6473. 🕐 mid-Jun–Labor Day: 10am–8pm Mon–Sat, 10am–5pm Sun; Apr–mid-Jun & after Labor Day–last weekend in Oct: 10am–5pm weekends; Nov–Dec: hours vary. 🏛

Cape May ⑰

🚶 4,400. 🚗 🚌 ℹ Cape May Welcome Center, Lafayette & Elmira Sts, Cape May, (609) 884-9562.

FIRST EXPLORED by Cornelius Mey for the Dutch West India Company in 1621, Cape May is one of the oldest seashore resorts on the Atlantic Coast. Visited by a number of US presidents including James Buchanan, Ulysses S. Grant, Benjamin Harrison, and Franklin Pierce, it was popular with socialites from New York and Philadelphia during the late 1800s. Since then, this resort at the southernmost point of New Jersey, has continued to enjoy a fine reputation among beach lovers. A small boardwalk and sandy beach afford a lovely view of sunrise over the Atlantic Ocean.

Today, the area is characterized by the great Victorian building boom that took place in the 19th century. The central district is made up of so-called "cottages," two- and three-story buildings intended as summer homes for large families. They have been built in styles popular at the turn of the 20th century, ranging from lacy Queen Anne to Italianate. Most of the historic homes have been lovingly restored to period condition, and some are open to the public. Many others have been converted into B&B (bed-and-breakfast) lodgings. The town offers several tours of the Victorian homes, including a special trolley tour.

The **Historic Cold Spring Village** is a living history museum consisting of 25 authentically restored buildings set on a 20-acre (8-ha) wooded site. Costumed interpreters portray 19th-century lifestyles that would have been common in a southern New Jersey rural community. Trades and crafts such as pottery making, book binding, and blacksmithing are also demonstrated.

Nearby, the **Cape May County Park and Zoo** is home to 170 species of animals; some, such as Brazilian golden lion tamarins, are rare or endangered species. The park also features a 35-acre (14-ha) African savanna habitat accessed by an 800-ft (244-m) long boardwalk.

🏛 Historic Cold Spring Village
720 US 9, Cape May. 📞 (609) 898-2300. 🕐 mid-Jun–Labor Day: 10am–4:30pm Tue–Sun; after Labor Day–Sep 30 & Memorial Day–mid-Jun: 10am–4:30pm Sat–Sun. 🏛 ♿

One of Cape May's charming bed & breakfast lodgings

Philadelphia ⓲

PENNSYLVANIA'S LARGEST CITY, Philadelphia or the
"City of Brotherly Love," is also the birthplace of
the nation. In 1776, representatives from the 13
British colonies signed the Declaration of Independence here, and the city served as an early
capital of the fledgling United States. Since its
founding by English Quaker William Penn in the late
17th century, Philadelphia's port on the Delaware
River has welcomed thousands of immigrants from
all over the world. Their labor strengthened the
expanding city through two centuries of industrial
growth, wars, and economic reversals. Even today,
the city's neighborhoods and restaurants reflect this
ethnic mix. Philadelphia's rich history, world-class
art collections, special-interest museums, fine
restaurants and hotels, and the nation's largest
landscaped public park combine to make the city
one of America's most popular destinations.

**William Penn's statue on
Philadelphia City Hall**

KEY

▮	Sight/Place of interest
Ⓜ	Metro station
▯	Train station
🚌	Bus station
ℹ	Tourist information
P	Parking
✝	Church
═══	Expressway

GETTING AROUND

Philadelphia's excellent local transit system, SEPTA, operates
buses throughout Greater Philadelphia in addition to two
subway lines: the Market-Frankford line (east–west, under
Market St) and the Broadway Street line (north–south).
Purple-painted, tourist-oriented "Philly Phlash" shuttles
travel in a loop through downtown to all major attractions.
Taxis are plentiful and moderately priced.

SIGHTS AT A GLANCE

Independence Hall ①
Second Bank of the
  United States ②
US Mint ③
Independence Seaport
  Museum ④
Reading Terminal Market ⑤
Masonic Temple ⑥
Pennsylvania Academy of
  Fine Arts ⑦
College of Physicians
of Philadelphia/
  Mutter Museum ⑧

Greater Philadelphia
(see inset map)

Eastern State Penitentiary ⑨
Philadelphia Zoo ⑩
Fairmount Park ⑪
Philadelphia Museum of Art ⑫
The Barnes Foundation ⑬

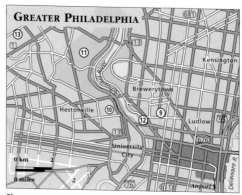

GREATER PHILADELPHIA

KEY

Area of main map

SEE ALSO

• **Where to Stay** p117

• **Where to Eat** p121

0 meters   250
0 yards   250

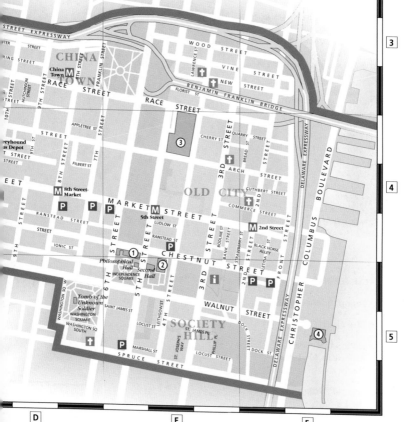

Independence National Historic Park

K NOWN LOCALLY AS Independence Mall, this 45-acre (18-ha) urban park encompasses several well-preserved 18th-century structures associated with the American Revolution. The Declaration of Independence that heralded the birth of a new nation was signed in this historic area. Dominated by the tall brick tower of Independence Hall, the park includes the oldest street in Philadelphia, the US Mint, and several special-interest museums exploring Philadelphia's Colonial and seafaring past as well as its ethnic heritage. Around 20 of the buildings are now open to the public.

Plaque commemorating Independence Hall

Arch St. Friends Meeting House

Christ Church Cemetery, where Ben Franklin, George Washington, and other notables are buried.

Constitution Center

African American Museum
Inspirational stories of Philadelphia's famous African-American citizens are displayed alongside exhibits of contemporary works.

★ National Museum of American Jewish History
This unique museum celebrates the history of Jews in America through artifacts such as this Torah scroll and ark (mid-1700s) from the collection of Congregation Mikveh Israel.

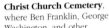

Independence Visitor Center

The Atwater-Kent Museum traces Philadelphia's history, from its infancy as a small country town to current times.

★ The Liberty Bell
Inscribed with the words, "Proclaim Liberty throughout all the Land," the Liberty Bell was rung when the Declaration of Independence was adopted. It is now located in the new Liberty Bell Center (see p102).

STAR SIGHTS
★ Independence Hall
★ The Liberty Bell
★ National Museum of American Jewish History
★ Second Bank of the US

KEY

– – – Suggested route

0 meter 200

0 yards 200

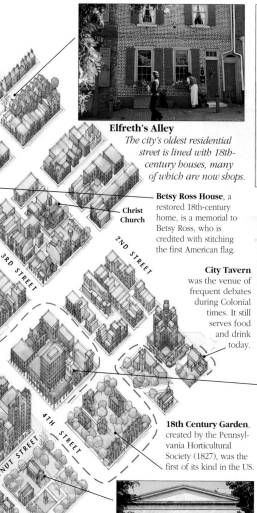

Elfreth's Alley
The city's oldest residential street is lined with 18th-century houses, many of which are now shops.

Christ Church

Betsy Ross House, a restored 18th-century home, is a memorial to Betsy Ross, who is credited with stitching the first American flag.

2ND STREET

3RD STREET

City Tavern was the venue of frequent debates during Colonial times. It still serves food and drink today.

4TH STREET

18th Century Garden, created by the Pennsylvania Horticultural Society (1827), was the first of its kind in the US.

STNUT STREET

WALNUT STREET

VISITORS' CHECKLIST

i *6th & Market Sts, (800) 537-7676.* ○ *8:30am–5:30pm daily.* **Independence Hall, The Liberty Bell** ○ *9am–5pm daily. Call (800) 967-2283 for Independence Hall tickets.* **National Museum of American Jewish History** ○ *(215) 923-3811.* ○ *10am–5pm Mon–Thu, 10am–3pm Fri, noon–5pm Sun.* ● *Sat & major Jewish hols.* **Second Bank of the US** ○ *9am–5pm daily.* **African American Museum** ○ *(215) 574-0380.* ○ *Tue–Sun.*

Franklin Court
Benjamin Franklin lived and worked in these buildings, which include the B. Free Franklin post office and museum.

★ Second Bank of the US
An extensive collection of portraits of luminaries involved in the military, diplomatic, and political events of 1776 is on display at this Grecian style building (see p102). ②

Washington Square Park

★ Independence Hall
The centerpiece of the park, this World Heritage Site was the place where the Declaration of Independence was signed on July 4, 1776 (see p102). ①

Independence Hall ①

Chestnut St between 5th & 6th Sts. *Philly Phlash.* ⬜ *9am–5pm daily, longer hours in summer.* 🚻 📷
🌐 *www.nps.gov/inde*

JUST WEST of the Delaware River, this unadorned brick building is the most important structure in the Independence Hall National Park. Previously designated the State House of Pennsylvania, it is the site of the drafting of the Declaration of Independence, the document that declared America's freedom from the British Empire.

Independence Hall, completed in 1748, was designed by master carpenter Edmund Woolley and lawyer Andrew Hamilton. The chambers of the meeting rooms are furnished simply, as they were during the late 1700s. Today, park personnel re-create history by pointing out the Windsor-style chairs from which Colonial leaders debated the contents of the Declaration. Although the Continental Congress rejected two passages in the first draft – an ill-tempered reference to the English people, and a bitter denunciation of the slave trade – the document was adopted without significant change and approved by Congress on July 4, 1776. The US Constitution was drafted in the same room in 1787.

The large, brass **Liberty Bell** that once hung in the tower has now been placed in the new Liberty Bell Center near Independence Hall. In 1846, a small crack developed and the bell could no longer be sounded. However, it remains the best-known symbol of the Colonial struggle for self-governance. The center incorporates interpretive displays that highlight Liberty Bell's importance to the story of America's independence.

The Liberty Bell on display near Independence Hall

Second Bank of the United States ②

420 Chestnut St. *Currently closed for renovation. Due to re-open in late 2004.*

BUILT BETWEEN the years 1819 and 1824, this is one of America's finest examples of Greek Revival architecture. Once a repository that provided credit for federal government and private businesses, it now houses a collection of late 18th- and early 19th-century portraits. On view are 185 paintings of Colonial and federal leaders, military officers, explorers, and scientists.

Many of the portraits are by Charles Willson Peale (1741–1827), his brother James, and their respective sons and daughters, who together form America's most distinguished family of artists. After the Revolutionary War, Peale began collecting portraits, and today, 94 of his original paintings, including likenesses of the American founding fathers George Washington and Alexander Hamilton, and the Continental Army's French ally, the Marquis de Lafayette, are on display along with the portraiture of other artists.

US Mint ③

5th & Arch Sts. *Closed to the public (group tours available on a limited basis by prior arrangement only).*

THE PHILADELPHIA mint, the oldest in the US, makes most of the coins that Americans use every day, and also produces gold bullion coins and national medals. The first US coins, minted in 1793, were copper pennies and half pennies intended solely for local commerce in the colonies. Today, 24 hours a day, five days a week, hundreds of machines and operators in a room the size of a football field blank, anneal, count, and bag millions of dollars worth of quarters, dimes, and pennies. Commemorative coins and numismatic collectables are available in the gift shop, opened on a limited basis.

Independence Seaport Museum ④

211 S Columbus Blvd. 📞 *(215) 925-5439.* *Philly Phlash.* *Market-Frankford line.* ⬜ *10am–5pm daily.* ⬛ *Jan 1, Dec 25.* 📷 🚻

QUARTERED IN a stunning modern building on the waterfront, this 100,000-sq-ft (9,290-sq-m) museum's mandate is to preserve US maritime history and traditions, with special focus on the Chesapeake Bay, and the Delaware River and its tributaries. Displays combine art and artifacts with hands-on computer games, large-scale models, and audio-

Aerial view of Independence Hall

ʼisuals. The Ben Franklin 3ridge, which connects Penn- ylvania with New Jersey, is e-created in the museum as a hree-and-a-half story replica hat straddles a working nodel of the Delaware River.

Other highlights include Divers of the Deep," eaturing underwater technol- ›gy through the ages, and Workshop on the Water," an ctive boat shop and gallery vhere visitors can watch ›oat building in progress s artisans craft traditional vooden 19th-century boats. The World War II submarine JSS *Becuna*, commissioned n 1943, and the USS *Olympia*, Admiral George Dewey's lagship in the Battle of Manila (1898), are berthed ıext to the museum.

Coffee shop in Philadelphia's Reading Terminal Market

Reading Terminal Market ⑤

2th & Filbert Sts. ☎ *(215) 922- 317.* 🚌 *Philly Phlash, SPREE bus.* ○ *8am–6pm daily.* ● *Jan 1, Dec 25.* ♿

THIS MARKET was created underneath a train shed fter two farmers' markets vere leveled to make space or a new terminal in 1892. So modern was the market hat people came from as far s the New Jersey shore to ›uy fresh Lancaster County ›roduce. Reading Terminal Market declined over the years nd was nearly destroyed in he 1970s. Today, however, t has been revitalized, and ishmongers, butchers, bakers, lorists, and greengrocers vie or space with quick-breakfast tands run by modestly lressed Amish women, and ›urveyors of Greek specialties.

Equestrian statue in the Masonic Temple courtyard

Masonic Temple ⑥

1 N Broad St. ☎ *(215) 988-1917.* 🚌 *Philly Phlash.* ○ *tours at 11am, 2pm, 3pm Mon–Fri; 10am, 11am Sat.* ● *Jul–Aug: Sat, Jan 1, Easter, Thanksgiving, Dec 25.* ♿ ✋

AN ARCHITECTURAL jewel dedicated in 1873 as the Grand Lodge of Free and Accepted Masons of Pennsylvania, this remarkable building contains a number of meeting halls in various decorative styles. Among them, the Oriental Hall's (1896) coloring and ornamentation has been copied from the Alhambra in Granada, Spain, the Renaissance Hall (1908) follows an Italian Renaissance motif, while the Egyptian Hall (1889) takes its inspiration from the Temples of Luxor, Karnak, and Philae. High arches, pinnacles, and spires form the Gothic Hall, and the cross-and-crown emblem of Sir Knights – "Under this sign you will conquer" – hangs over a replica of the Archbishop's throne in Canterbury Cathedral. The halls, still in use, were created to honor the building trades, and much of the stone and tilework are imperceptibly faux finished – an attestation to the skill of the men who made them. President George Washington wore his Masonic apron when he laid the cornerstone of the Capitol building in Washington, DC. The apron is on display, along with other Masonic rarities, in the museum on the first floor.

Pennsylvania Academy of Fine Arts ⑦

118 N Broad S at Cherry St. ☎ *(215) 972-7600.* 🚌 *Philly Phlash.* ○ *10am–5pm Mon–Sat, 11am–5pm Sun.* ● *public hols.* 🎟 *(free on Sun).* ♿

THE COLLECTION of this museum and school, founded in 1805, spans the history of American painting. Galleries display works by some of the art world's best-known denizens. One of them, the classical stylist Benjamin West (1738–1820), a Quaker from Philadelphia, helped organize the British Royal Academy in 1768, and four years later was named Historical Painter to the King. Impressionist and former Academy of Fine Arts student, Mary Cassatt (1824–1926), and modern abstractionist Richard Diebenkorn (1922–93) among others, share wall space. This distinctive building, with its ornate arched foyer, is considered one of the finest examples of Victorian-Gothic architecture in America.

The Foxhunt **by Winslow Homer, Pennsylvania Academy of Fine Arts**

The well-lit display of medical curiosities at Mutter Museum

College of Physicians of Philadelphia/ Mutter Museum ⑧

19 S 22nd St. 【 (215) 563-3737. 🚋 17, 21. ◯ 10am–5pm daily. ● Jan 1, Easter, Thanksgiving, Dec 25. 🅿 ♿ W www.collphyphil.org

Founded in 1787 for the "advancement of the science of medicine," the still-active college is a major source of health information. This is provided by the institute's C. Everett Koop Community Health Information Center, through the library, videotapes, and searchable computer system.

Mutter Museum, on the first floor of one of the buildings, is a fascinating collection of preserved specimens, skeletal constructions, and wax figures. These were originally used for educational purposes in the mid-19th century, when diseases and genetic defects were identifiable only by their physical manifestations. Some afflictions are quite grotesque, and may not be suitable for small children or those who have a tendency toward queasiness. The museum also contains medical instruments, exhibits on the history of medicine over the last 100 years, a re-creation of an early 20th-century doctor's office, and a medicinal plant garden. Special exhibits on medical phenomena, such as Siamese (conjoined) Twins, are an additional feature.

Eastern State Penitentiary ⑨

Fairmount Ave at 22nd St. 【 (215) 236-3300. 🚋 33. ◯ April–Nov: 10am–5pm Wed–Sun. ● Dec–Mar. ♿ 🅿 🎟

Named the "house" by inmates and guards, the Eastern State Penitentiary, established in 1829, was a revolutionary concept in criminal justice. Prior to this, criminals were thrown together in despicable conditions and punished by physical brutality. The Philadelphia Quakers proposed an alternative – a place where a criminal could be alone to ponder and become penitent for his actions. During incarceration, with sentences seldom less than five years in length, prisoners literally never heard or saw another human being for the entire duration of their stay. The prison had

Long corridor inside the Eastern State Penitentiary

a single entrance and 30-ft (9-m) high boundary walls. Each solitary cell had a private outdoor exercise yard contained by a 10-ft (3-m) wall. Eastern State's many "guests" included bootlegger and crime lord Al Capone. The prison was officially closed in 1971, but prison tours continue to draw many visitors today.

Philadelphia Zoo ⑩

3400 W Girard Ave. 【 (215) 243-1100. 🚋 Philly Phlash. ◯ 9:30am–5pm daily. ● Dec 25. 🅿 W www.philadelphiazoo.org

This zoo, the oldest in America, was founded in 1859. Set within verdant grounds, interspersed with statuary, the zoo is home to over 2,000 animals, including several rare species such as naked mole rats and bamboo-eating lemurs. A walk-through giant otter habitat shows the animals at their playful best.

The magnificent big cats – lions, clouded leopards, tigers (including rare white tigers), and jaguars – are kept in near natural habitats or inside the Carnivora House, in weather-protected cages that provide close-up views. Other features are an open birdhouse with uncaged finches and hummingbirds, a reptile house, where alligators bask in a tropical paradise, and a 3-acre (1-ha) reserve for 11 primate species, including the nation's only blue-eyed lemurs. The new zoo balloon takes passengers aloft for a panoramic view of the city.

Fairmount Park ⑪

🏛 John F. Kennedy Blvd & N 16th St (215) 685-0000. 🚋 Philly Phlash Market-Frankford line. ◯ daily.

Designed by Frederick Law Olmsted (1822–1903), America's pre-eminent landscape architect, Fairmount Park is an 8,900-acre (3,601-ha) greenway. It encompasses seven historic manor houses decorated in period style, dozens of sculptures, a horti-

Downtown Philadelphia rising above Fairmount Park

cultural center, and Japanese house and gardens among other features. A waterworks, innovative in 1840, was designed and built to pump water from the Schuylkill River, which divides the park into east and west. The grounds are interspered with roads, hiking, biking, and bridle trails. Visitors can also rent rowboats and canoes.

A handful of rowing clubs occupy Victorian boathouses along the river. The boathouses are turreted, gabled, and decorated with coats-of-arms. At night, when viewed from the West Fairmount Park shore, the houses are outlined with tiny lights and reflect magically on the river.

In 1894, wealthy manufacturer Richard Smith donated Smith Playground to the children of Philadelphia in memory of his son. Among the attractions are muscle-powered merry-go-rounds, a giant slide, and a renovated mansion and playhouse. Also in Fairmount Park is the 99-acre (40-ha) **Laurel Hill Cemetery**. This vast "park within a park" is dotted with obelisks, statuary, and classic Greek mausoleums. It was such a popular picnic and walking area during the late Victorian period that admission was by ticket only.

Philadelphia Museum of Art ⑫

26th St & Benjamin Franklin Pkwy. **€** (215) 763-8100. **▤** Philly Phlash, 38. **◯** 10am–5pm Tue, Thu, Sat–Sun; 10am–8:45pm Wed, Fri. **◯** Jan 1, Thanksgiving, Dec 25. **▨** **&** **✔** **W** www.philamuseum.org

THIS MUSEUM ATTRACTS major exhibitions to supplement its superlative permanent collection ranging from 15th-century illuminated manuscripts to modern sculpture by Constantin Brancusi. The full-scale medieval cloister courtyard and fountain on the second floor is a favorite, as are the French Gothic chapel and a pillared temple from Madurai, India. Scattered throughout the museum are computerized stations with information on the exhibits. A collection of Pennsylvania Dutch and American decorative arts adjoins galleries that feature paintings by American artists.

Medieval diptych, Philadelphia Museum of Art

The Barnes Foundation ⑬

300 N Latch's Lane, Merion. **€** (610) 667-0290. **▤** 17, 33. **◯** reservation only: Sep–June: 9:30am–5pm Fri–Sun; July–Aug: 9:30am–5pm Wed–Fri. **◯** public hols. **▨** **&** **✔** **W** www.barnesfoundation.org

ESTABLISHED IN the year 1922 to share the private collection of pharmaceutical magnate Albert C. Barnes with "people of all socioeconomic levels," this museum has one of the world's premier displays of French modern and Post-Impressionist paintings. Among the more than 800 works on view, there are 180 by August Renoir, 69 by Paul Cézanne, 60 by Henri Matisse, and more by Picasso, Seurat, Modigliani, Van Gogh, Rousseau, and almost every other noteworthy artist of that era. Other exhibits include ancient Greek and Egyptian art, medieval manuscripts, African sculpture, American furniture, ceramics, and handwrought ironwork. The art is displayed to highlight artistic affinities between diverse works. For instance, the Barnes Collection is displayed in accordance with Dr. Barnes' unique specifications – paintings, sculpture, and craft pieces – grouped into 96 distinct ensembles, without labels and with very little regard to chronology.

The glittering silhouettes of Victorian boathouses along Schuylkill River, Fairmount Park

Pennsylvania

PENNSYLVANIA HAS IT ALL – American history, beautiful scenery, varied recreation, lodging, and dining, ranging from the refined to the simple. Of its two main cities, Philadelphia *(see pp98–105)*, the birthplace of America, is a complex, stunning city, while Pittsburgh re-created itself from a grimy, industrial center to a sparkling gem on the forks of the Ohio River. Most of the state, however, is rural and bucolic, a green patchwork of dairy and produce farms, embroidered with forests and waterways, trim fields and small towns.

Memorial at Gettysburg National Military Park

Gettysburg ❶

🏚 *7,000.* 🚉 🚌 ℹ️ *PO Box 4117, (800) 337-5015.*

A PIVOTAL CONFRONTATION of the Civil War *(see p47)* took place near the small farming community of Gettysburg in early July 1863. Nearly 100,000 Union soldiers gathered here to confront some 75,000 invading Confederates led by Robert E. Lee. After three days of fighting, a staggering 50,000 soldiers lay dead or wounded, and the Confederates were turned back.

Though the war raged for another two years, Gettysburg was recognized as a turning point. To commemorate the site, a burial ground was purchased, and President Lincoln dedicated the **Gettysburg National Cemetery** with his now-famous three-minute-long speech, the Gettysburg Address. Several impressive monuments, honoring heroism on both sides, have been placed throughout the fields and forests of the battlefield, now the **Gettysburg National Military Park**. The Cyclorama, a giant circular mural painted in 1884, dramatizes a crucial battle scene – Picket's Charge,

in which more than 6,000 Confederate soldiers were killed or wounded.

🏛 Gettysburg National Military Park
📞 *(717) 334-1124.* ⏰ *Aug 17–Jun 13: 8am–5pm; Jun 18–Aug 16: 8am–6pm.* ♿ ✔️ 🌐 *www.nps.gov/gett*

Lancaster ❷⓪

🏚 *55,600.* 🚉 🚌 ℹ️ *501 Greenfield Rd, Lancaster, (800) 723-8824.* 🌐 *www.padutch.com*

THIS MARKET TOWN at the heart of the Pennsylvania Dutch Country *(see p59)* is surrounded by almost 5,000 small farms. The region is famous for the German-immigrant "Old Order Amish" Christians, who live and work without modern conveniences like electricity. The **Landis Valley Museum's** large outdoor collection focuses on the state's German rural heritage. Among the exhibits are a crossroads village and an adjoining farmstead with traditional breeds of animals and heirloom plants. Visitors can see demonstrations of skills such as sheep-shearing.

Ephrata Cloister, northeast of town in the village of Ephrata, is a collection of medieval-style buildings, founded in 1732. It was home to one of America's earliest communal societies, semi-monastics who practiced an austere lifestyle emphasizing spirituality, and the artistic use of music and the written word. In 1745, the colony set up one of the country's earliest printing presses. This tradition continues today; Ephrata is the home of the world-famous Rodale Press.

🏛 Landis Valley Museum
2451 Kissel Hill Rd. 📞 *(717) 569-0401.* ⏰ *9am–5pm Mon–Sat, noon–5pm Sun.* 🎟️ ♿ 🌐 *www.landisvalleymuseum.org*

Hershey ❷❶

🏚 *7,400.* 🚉 🚌 ℹ️ *1255A Harrisburg Pike, Harrisburg, (800) 995-0969.*

THIS FACTORY town, now a popular tourist destination, revolves around chocolate, so much so that even its streetlights are shaped like silver-foil-wrapped Hershey Kisses. The town's main attraction is **Chocolate World**, which features a 15-minute ride through a series of animated tableaux revealing Hershey's chocolate-making process. A free sample awaits at the end of the tour, while a series of shops sell souvenirs and every Hershey product made. Nearby is **Hershey Park**, a 90-acre (36-ha) amusement park. Hershey Park offers 80

"Sisters House" and "Meeting House" in Ephrata Cloister

rides including five water slides, four roller coasters, and one of the finest Philadelphia Toboggan Company four-row carousels in existence today.

Chocolate World
SR 743 & US 422, Hershey.
(717) 534-9400. hours vary throughout the year; generally 9am–5pm daily, later hours in summer.

York ②

42,200. 1425 Eden Rd, York, (717) 699-4430.

THE FIRST Pennsylvania settlement west of the Susquehanna River, York was laid out in 1741. At that time, its inhabitants were mainly tavernkeepers and crafts-people, catering to pioneers heading west. Since then, manufacturing has become the prime economic force. York's many covered public markets include the 1888 **Central Market**, the best place in town for local fresh produce, flowers, meats, baked goods, and inex-pensive restaurants.

Bikes being checked at the Harley-Davidson Assembly Plant in York

East of historic York, at the **Harley-Davidson Final Assembly Plant**, giant presses form steel sheets into fenders while gleaming motorcycles fly overhead. The plant is noisy, colorful, and easily the size of two football fields. A small museum covers Harley-Davidson's history from its establishment as a motorized bike company in 1903 to the present.

Harley-Davidson Final Assembly Plant
1425 Eden Rd. *(717) 848-1177.* reservation only: 8am–4pm Mon–Fri. hourly 9am–2pm Mon–Fri.

A lush greenhouse in Longwood Gardens

Reading ②

78,400. 352 Penn St, Reading, (800) 443-6610.
W www.readingberkspa.com

ONCE A CENTER of industry, Reading has reinvented itself as a discount-outlet capital, with clusters of buildings housing more than 80 name-brand stores from Brooks Brothers to Mikasa and Wedgewood. The **Read-ing Pagoda**, on the town's outskirts, is modeled after a Shogun dynasty castle that was built as part of an early 1900s resort. Today, cherry trees encircle the building, and there are walking trails throughout the adjacent park.

North of town, the **Mary Merritt Doll Museum** has over 1,500 dolls ranging in age and origin from 7th-century Egypt to 20th-century America. Also featured are dozens of mechanical dolls that blow kisses or dance.

Mary Merritt Doll Museum
843 Ben Franklin Hwy, (US 422), Douglassville. *(610) 385-3809.* 10am–4:30pm Mon, Wed–Sat; 1–5pm Sun. Tue.

Longwood Gardens ②

US 1, Kennett Square. *(610) 388-6741.* 9am–5pm daily; longer hrs in summer & at Christmas.
W www.longwoodgardens.org

PIERRE DU PONT, millionaire financier and industrialist, acquired the 1,000-acre (405-ha) Longwood Gardens in the beautiful, wooded Brandy-wine Valley in 1906. His aim was to preserve the property's unusual trees, and to provide a place of entertainment for his family and friends.

Over 11,000 varieties of plants including spectacular year-round seasonal displays, whimsical topiaries, and a children's garden are open to the public. The massive main greenhouse and conservatory are engineering marvels that shelter an array of exotics. But the real star of Longwood are the fabulous fountains whose choreographed erup-tions rise above the treetops and are highlighted at night by colored lights, creating dazzling displays that are often the backdrop for musical events.

HARLEY-DAVIDSON

What began as a tinkering project for 21-year-old William Harley and 20-year-old Arthur Davidson, grew into a company that has dominated racing since 1914. After World War I, the first American entered Germany astride a Harley-Davidson. In 1956, Elvis Presley posed on a model KH. Today, Harley Owners Group (HOG) has more than 500,000 members.

Harley-Davidson logo

Pittsburgh's Golden Triangle, with its downtown skyscrapers

Pittsburgh ㉕

369,900. 425 6th Ave, 30th Floor, (800) 359-0758. www.visitpittsburgh.com

LOCATED AT THE point where the Allegheny and Monongahela rivers come together to form the Ohio River, Pittsburgh is an American success story. It grew from a frontier outpost to become an industrial giant, home to the huge mills of the US Steel conglomerate as well as the food-processing company Heinz and the Westinghouse electric company. From the Civil War through World War II, Pittsburgh was a thriving metropolis, but in the 1950s and 60s its fortunes faded. Today, the city has rebuilt itself to become one of the most livable urban areas in the country.

Endowed by steel magnate Andrew Carnegie, the **Carnegie Institute's Museum of Art** offers a brilliantly lit suite of galleries with collections ranging from ancient Egyptian sculpture to Impressionist, Post-Impressionist, and modern American art by Roy Lichtenstein and Alexander Calder. The Hall of Sculpture is a two-storied columned hall that replicates the interior of the Temple of Athena in Athens. It is adorned with casts from the Greek classical era. Next door, the Hall of Architecture is filled with reproductions of some of the best examples of classical, medieval, and Renaissance architectural details. The

Carnegie Museum of Natural History, in the same complex, opens out on a central gallery and relies on filtered natural light as a part of its architectural charm. Exhibits change from time to time, but most of the displays in this museum consist of dioramas that feature taxidermy specimens.

At the **Carnegie Science Center** on Allegheny Avenue, the idea is to make science accessible through play. More than 40,000 sq ft (3,716 sq m) of the 186,000-sq-ft (17,280-sq-m) center is devoted to numerous interactive exhibits. The Miniature Railroad and Village displays the rich historical, architectural, and cultural heritage of

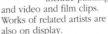

Students relaxing at Pittsburgh University

western Pennsylvania. In the four-story Rangos Omnimax® Theater – one of 13 in the country – audience members recline while images are projected onto a 79-ft (24-m) domed ceiling.

The 42-story **Cathedral of Learning** houses the University of Pittsburgh's Nationality Classrooms, which seek to reflect the different ethnic groups that contribute to the city's heritage. Started in the 1930s, each of the 26 rooms, the last of which were completed in 2000, has authentic decor and furnishings depicting a unique time and place from 5th-century BC Greece to 16th-century Poland.

In the city's north side, the tile-clad exterior of the **Andy Warhol Museum** reflects the workaday character of the neighborhood. Appearances are deceptive here, and this former warehouse conceals a brightly illuminated, ultra-modern interior. The museum celebrates the Pittsburgh-born founder of American Pop Art, Andy Warhol (1928–87) through selections of works from its archives. These include paintings, and video and film clips. Works of related artists are also on display.

Located 5 miles (8 km) southeast of Pittsburgh is **Kennywood Amusement Park**. It was built in 1905 as a Luna Park, a popular name for amusement parks that showcased the new electric light bulb. The park offers thrill rides, a stunt show, and a 1926 carousel made by the Dentzel Company – premier hand-carvers of carousel animals.

Hall of Sculpture at Carnegie Institute's Museum of Art, Pittsburgh

🏛 **The Carnegie Institute**
4,400 Forbes Ave. (412) 622-3131. ☐ Jul–Aug: 10am–5pm Mon–Sat; noon–5pm Sun; Sep–Jun: 10am–5pm Tue–Sat; noon–5pm Sun. www.cmoa.org

🏛 **Andy Warhol Museum**
117 Sandusky St. (412) 237-8300. ☐ 10am–5pm Wed–Thu, Sat–Sun 10am–10pm Fri. ● Mon.

Laurel Highlands 26

🅸 120 E Main St Ligonier, (800) 333-5661.

To THE SOUTH of Pittsburgh, ridges gather together, valleys become canyons, and mountain laurel covers the slopes, giving the region its name. The splendid 1,700-ft (518-m) deep Youghiogheny Gorge cuts through the scenic Laurel Ridge Mountains, where an area of nearly 19,000 acres (7,689 ha) forms the **Ohiopyle State Park**. The park includes more than 28 miles (45 km) of the Youghiogheny River. White-water rafting is popular here, as are hiking, jogging, biking, and cross-country skiing on the 43-mile (69-km) Youghiogheny River Trail.

Fallingwater, an architectural tour de force by renowned architect Frank Lloyd Wright, lies north of the park. Built in 1936, the house reflects Wright's interest in structures that were an integral part of the landscape. **Laurel Ridge State Park** stretches from the village of Ohiopyle in the west to the Conemaugh River in the east. The 70-mile (113-km) long Laurel Highlands Hiking Trail is open all year round. The Johnstown Flood Museum chronicles the Conemaugh River disaster that killed more than 2,000 people and destroyed Johnstown in 1889.

🏕 Ohiopyle State Park

7 Sheridan St, Ohiopyle. 📞 (724) 329-8591. 🔾 daily.

THE AMISH

All Amish trace their roots to the Swiss Anabaptist ("New Birth") movement of 1525, an offshoot of the Protestant Reformation, whose creed rejected the formality of established churches. Today's Old Order Amish are the most conservative of the sect, disdaining any device that would connect them to the larger world, including electricity, phones, and cars. Conspicuous because of their plain, dark attire – with white prayer caps for the women and straw hats for the men – and their horse-and-buggy mode of transportation, the Amish in America are little changed from their 17th-century ancestors who came seeking religious freedom.

Amish buggy on a rural highway

🏛 Fallingwater

SR 381, Mill Run. 📞 (724) 329-8501. 🔾 mid-Mar–mid-Nov: 10am–4pm Tue–Sun; Dec–mid-Jan: 10am–4pm Sat–Sun. ⬤ mid-Jan–mid-Mar, Jan 1, Easter, Thanksgiving, Dec 25. 🖼 📷

Western Amish Country 27

🅸 229 S Jefferson St, New Castle, (888) 284-7599.

THE SCENIC territory around the town of New Castle, 56 miles (145 km) from Pittsburgh, is a hand-stitched quilt of agricultural acreage, parks. and villages. Like the residents of the Pennsylvania Dutch Country near Lancaster *(see p106)*, a large population of Old Order Amish and Mennonites have plowed and planted farms in the Enon Valley, near New Castle.

Montgomery Locks and Dam, completed in 1936, is one of a series of 20 huge locks and dams on the Ohio River from Pittsburgh to Cairo, Illinois. The dam creates a pool more than 18 miles (29 km) long for recreational and commercial use.

McConnell's Mill State Park follows the path of Slippery Rock Creek and contains a former water-driven gristmill, now a museum. The untamed beauty of Slippery Rock Gorge is very popular with rock climbers and rappellers. **Moraine State Park**, which is about 5 miles (8 km) east of McConnell's Park, is a small paradise reborn from an industrial wasteland where underground and strip mining flourished until the 1950s. The mines were then sealed, gas and oil wells were plugged, and the 3,225-acre (1,305-ha) Lake Arthur was constructed.

🏕 McConnell's Mill State Park

Portersville. 📞 (724) 368-8091. 🔾 sunrise–sunset daily.

The Youghiogheny River looping through Ohiopyle State Park, Laurel Highlands

Practical Information

SUCCESSFUL TRAVELING AROUND New York, New Jersey, and Pennsylvania benefits from advance planning, simply because there is so much to see and do in such a concentrated area. The major cities are packed with attractions, hotels, and restaurants, while the expansive and diverse areas in between often double as resort areas, catering to city-dwellers in need of a change of pace. Depending upon the time, you can explore significant historical sights, appreciate stunning scenery, take in a local celebration, or simply relax along the coast.

TOURIST INFORMATION

NEW YORK, New Jersey, and Pennsylvania each publishes a wide variety of informative, richly illustrated travel guides. All of this information can be ordered by telephone or accessed via web sites, and further information is available from the multitude of local and regional tourism bureaus across the three states. The wealth of available information covers climate, transportation, attractions, accommodations, restaurants, recreation, festivals, regional history, and much more.

NATURAL HAZARDS

THUNDERSTORMS occur frequently across the Mid-Atlantic Region. A basic precaution that visitors should take if they find themselves in the middle of a sudden storm, is to never stand under a tree, as they are perfect targets for lightning strikes. Also, there is danger of the tree toppling due to strong winds. Western New York State and Pennsylvania experience extreme winter conditions; the Adirondacks face severe winter storms and sub-zero temperatures, while sudden heavy snowfalls often cause chaos in New York City. Visitors should listen for weather warnings and broadcasts on the radio and TV.

GETTING AROUND

UNLIKE MUCH OF the US, the Mid-Atlantic is a region where you can get around without a car. Some of the most modern, and fast **Amtrak** train services in the US link New York and Washington, DC with Philadelphia, bringing the two cities within an hour of each other. Other lines run across Pennsylvania, up the Hudson Valley between New York City and Albany then across to Buffalo and Niagara Falls, and between Philadelphia and Atlantic City. Seat belts are required for drivers and front seat passengers in the entire Mid-Atlantic Region. Most states also require seat belts for back seat passengers, and child seats are required for all automobile occupants age four and under. Speed limits vary but are usually 70 to 75 mph (113 to 121 km/h) on Interstate Highways outside of densely populated urban areas, weather permitting. Talking on a cell phone while driving is dangerous and against the law.

EVENTS & FESTIVALS

NEW YORK CITY and the Mid-Atlantic states stage a diverse range of annual community, regional, and national festivals. One of the nation's most unusual annual events takes place in central Pennsylvania on February 2, when a chubby rodent named "Punxsutawney Phil" wakes up from his winter hibernation on **Groundhog Day**. "Phil" forecasts the advent of spring, which in US folklore is related to whether he can see his shadow. In March, as an expression of New York City's strong Irish heritage, the city politicians and other characters march through the city as part of a boisterous **St. Patrick's Day** celebration. Summer brings a deluge of outdoor events, and fireworks, bands, and street festivals are the norm for community celebrations of the July 4 Independence Day holiday. County and state fairs crop up in the Mid-Atlantic countryside in July and August, as do music festivals like the **Glimmerglass Opera Festival** in Cooperstown. The "Miss America" pageant takes place toward the end of summer every year in Atlantic City, and the Christmas shopping season kicks off with the annual extravaganza of massive inflatable figures in the **Macy's Thanksgiving Day** parade in New York City.

SPORTS

WITH HIGH-QUALITY professional teams in every major sport, the New York and Mid-Atlantic Region is a

---

THE CLIMATE OF THE MID-ATLANTIC REGION

Weather across the vast Mid-Atlantic Region can be as varied as the scenery. New York's Adirondack Mountains are famed for the extremities of climate, while in Long Island and the coastal areas of New Jersey, the climate is milder. Western New York and Pennsylvania see some of the nation's heaviest snowfalls in winter. By late spring, the snows melt and the foliage returns to the gardens. Summer brings warm weather and high humidity, and thunderstorms that can put a sudden end to a pleasant day. Late summer and fall have comparatively stable weather.

NEW YORK CITY

°F/C	Apr	Jul	Oct	Jan
high	59/15	79/26	69/20	
low	43/6	63/17	49/9	37/3
	32°F 0°C			26/−3
☀ days	17 days	20 days	19 days	16 days
☂ in	3.8 in	4 in	3 in	3 in
month	Apr	Jul	Oct	Jan

great place to watch some of the world's greatest athletes perform. The cities here host a wide array of professional and amateur sports teams, with major pro baseball, football, and basketball franchises operating in New Jersey, New York City, Philadelphia, and Pittsburgh. Another extremely popular spectator sport is ice hockey.

There are also many "minor league" teams in smaller cities, and hundreds of high-quality sports teams fielded by the various public and private universities across the region.

The baseball season is from April to September, football from September through January, and basketball from winter through mid-spring.

However, an extremely popular sports event is the **US Open Tennis Championships**, held annually outside New York City in August. Horseracing's **Belmont Stakes** in early June is the last leg of the "Triple Crown" championship, while throughout the months of July and August racing continues at historic Saratoga Springs. Participant sports are also

prominent, with the New York Marathon in November being one of the more popular events.

OUTDOOR ACTIVITIES

NEW YORK STATE is also home to one of the country's prime winter sports resorts – Lake Placid in the Adirondack Mountains, where the 1932 and 1980 Winter Olympics were held. There are also ski areas in the Pocono Mountains of Pennsylvania and New Jersey, as well as Camelback Mountain and Hidden Valley in Western Pennsylvania, and Hunter Mountain and Catamount in Catskills, in New York State. For the best skiing, however, the most avid skiers head to the resorts of Vermont and New Hampshire.

ENTERTAINMENT

THE WORLD CAPITAL of the entertainment industry, New York City is a showcase for just about any form of performance. A quick read of the many local newspapers, like the *New York Times* or the *Village Voice*, and magazines such as *Time Out*

New York and the *New Yorker* will point you toward hundreds of events and activities. **Lincoln Center** is home to many ballet, opera, and orchestral performances, as is legendary **Carnegie Hall**. The region's other large cities, Philadelphia, Pittsburgh, and Newark, also host numerous cultural and entertainment events. The newest venue is the **New Jersey Performing Arts Center** in Newark.

SHOPPING

NEW YORK CITY can be called one of the world's greatest marketplaces, and it is safe to say that if you cannot buy a certain thing here, it probably does not exist at all. Everything ranging from fashionable boutiques to cut-price computers can be found in Manhattan, and some neighborhoods of New York City cater especially to the interest of shoppers and bargain hunters. Don't miss a trip to at least one of the city's exceptional department stores, such as **Macy's**, **Bloomingdale's**, **Saks Fifth Avenue**, or **Barney's**.

DIRECTORY

TOURIST INFORMATION

New Jersey
((800) 847-4865.
W www.visitnj.org

New York City
((212) 484-1200.
W www.nycvisit.com

New York State
((518) 474-4116.
W www.iloveny.com

Pennsylvania
((800) 847-4872.
W www.experiencepa. com

FESTIVALS

Bach Festival
Bethlehem, Pennsylvania.
((610) 866-4382.

Glimmerglass Opera Festival
Cooperstown, New York.
((607) 547-2255.
W www.glimmerglass.org

NJ Performing Arts Center
Newark, NJ.
((888) 466-5722.
W www.njpac.org

BASEBALL

New York Mets
((718) 507-8499.
W www.newyorkmets. mlb.com

New York Yankees
((718) 293-6000.
W www.yankees.com

Philadelphia Phillies
(215) 463-1000.
W www.philadelphia phillies.mlb.com

BASKETBALL

New York Knicks
((212) 465-6000.

Philadelphia 76ers
((215) 339-7600.

FOOTBALL

Buffalo Bills
((716) 649-0015.
W www.buffalobills.com

New York Giants
((201) 935-8222.
W www.giants.com

Pittsburgh Steelers
((412) 323-1200.
W www.steelers.com

OTHER SPORTS

Belmont Stakes
((718) 641-4700.
W www1.nyra.com/ belmont

Skiing
W www.goski.com
W www.merlink.org

ENTERTAINMENT

Carnegie Hall
((212) 247-7800.
W www.carnegiehall.org

Lincoln Center
((212) 875-5030.
W www.lincolncenter. org

SHOPPING

Barney's
660 Madison Ave NYC.
((212) 826-8900.

Bloomingdale's
Lexington & 59th St NYC.
((212) 750-2000.

Macy's
Broadway & 34th NYC.
((212) 695-4400.

Where to Stay

NEW YORK CITY AND THE MID-ATLANTIC REGION offers something for everyone in terms of accommodation. In New York City, the top hotels are not quite as expensive as those in Paris or London, but the best news for travelers is the increase in budget hotels. Other budget options are furnished apartments and studios and bed and breakfast in private homes.

NEW YORK CITY

EAST VILLAGE: *St. Mark's Hotel*
2 St. Mark's Place. ((212) 674-0100. FAX (212) 420-0854.
W www.stmarkshotel.qpg.com
In a city where ancient carpets and dingy walls are the norm in budget hotels, this bright and clean hotel offers welcome relief. Oak-and-marble hallways lead to sparse but neat rooms with small bathrooms. Shop-lined St. Mark's Place features a constant parade of tattooed youth, so don't expect quiet.
$ — Credit Cards; 70 rooms

EAST VILLAGE: *Union Square Inn*
209 E 14th St. ((212) 614-0500. FAX (212) 614-0512.
W www.unionsquareinn.com
Here's a wonderful find for discerning travelers who want standard comforts at a reasonable price. Rooms are small but have high-quality mattresses and brand-new bathrooms. A basic breakfast is included.
$$ — Credit Cards; 40 rooms

GARMENT DISTRICT: *Americana Inn*
69 W 38th St. ((212) 840-6700. FAX (212) 840-1830.
W www.newyorkhotel.com
Linoleum floors lend an institutional feel, but otherwise this is a winner in the budget-basic price category. Rooms have private sinks and bright, spotless baths. The location is central, and the friendly, professional service is of a higher caliber than most in this price range.
$ — Credit Cards; 50 rooms

GARMENT DISTRICT: *Hotel Chelsea*
222 W 23rd St. ((212) 243-3700. FAX (212) 675-5531.
W www.hotelchelsea.com
This legendary artists' haven has housed famous names from Sandra Bernhardt to Dylan Thomas and Sid Vicious. Good for short-term visitors with a bohemian spirit. Rooms are large and eccentrically outfitted.
$$ — Credit Cards; 400 rooms; Recommended Restaurant

GARMENT DISTRICT: *Holiday Inn/Martinique on Broadway*
49 W 32nd St. ((212) 736-3800. FAX (212) 277-2702.
W www.holiday-inn.com
This fine branch of the reliable Holiday Inn chain is housed in a landmark French-Renaissance building. Rooms are chain standard once you move past the marble lobby. The Little Korea location offers affordable Asian dining at all hours. Rates are high, so ask for discounts.
$$$ — Credit Cards; 532 rooms; Recommended Restaurant

GREENWICH VILLAGE: *Abingdon Guest House*
13 Eighth Ave. ((212) 243-5384. FAX (212) 807-7473.
W www.abingdonguesthouse.com
This lovely guest house is located in the brownstone-lined, boutique-dotted West Village, one of the city's most charming neighborhoods. Each artfully decorated room is outfitted with first-rate comforts.
$$ — Credit Cards; 9 rooms

GREENWICH VILLAGE: *Washington Square Hotel*
103 Waverly Place. ((212) 777-9515. FAX (212) 979-8373.
W www.wshotel.com
Facing Washington Square Park in the heart of New York University territory, this hotel offers small but recently refurbished rooms. Rates are a bit high, but the location is great for bar-hoppers and live-music fans.
$$ — Credit Cards; 170 rooms; Recommended Restaurant

GRAMERCY & THE FLATIRON DISTRICT: *Gramercy Park Hotel*
2 Lexington Ave. ((212) 475-4320. FAX (212) 505-0535.
W www.gramercyparkhotel.com
Huge rooms and an appealing old-world ambiance are the keynotes here. Rooms are large enough for families; suites and park-view rooms have kitchenettes. An extra-special amenity: guests have access to Gramercy Park, off-limits to everyone except area residents.
$$ — Credit Cards; 509 rooms; Recommended Restaurant

Price categories for a standard double room per night, inclusive of breakfast, service charges, and any additional taxes:

- $ under $100
- $$ $100–$150
- $$$ $150–$200
- $$$$ $200–$250
- $$$$$ over $250

CREDIT CARDS
Major credit cards accepted.

NUMBER OF ROOMS
Number of rooms in the hotel.

RECOMMENDED RESTAURANT
Good restaurant within the hotel.

CHILDREN'S FACILITIES
Hotel has various facilities for young children.

GARDEN OR TERRACE
Hotel has a garden, courtyard, or terrace.

	CREDIT CARDS	NUMBER OF ROOMS	RECOMMENDED RESTAURANT	CHILDREN'S FACILITIES	GARDEN OR TERRACE
GRAMERCY & THE FLATIRON DISTRICT: *Hotel Giraffe* $$$$	■	73	■		
LOWER EAST SIDE: *Off SoHo Suites Hotel* $	■	38			
LOWER MANHATTAN: *Holiday Inn Wall Street* $$$	■	138	■		
LOWER MANHATTAN: *Regent Wall Street* $$$$$	■	144			
LOWER MIDTOWN: *Clarion Hotel Fifth Avenue* $$$	■	189			
LOWER MIDTOWN: *Kitano* $$$$$	■	149	■		
MORNINGSIDE HEIGHTS & HARLEM: *Sugar Hill International House* $	■	25			
MORNINGSIDE HEIGHTS & HARLEM: *Ellington* $$	■	85			

GRAMERCY & THE FLATIRON DISTRICT: *Hotel Giraffe*
365 Park Ave S. **℃** *(212) 685-7700.* **FAX** *(212) 685-7771.*
W www.hotelgiraffe.com
The Flatiron District's finest hotel brims with inspired elegance – rich textiles and custom furnishings. Amenities include CD players and granite bathrooms; deluxe rooms have French doors on to a Juliet balcony. Complimentary breakfast, plus a stylish Euro-Asian fusion restaurant.

LOWER EAST SIDE: *Off SoHo Suites Hotel*
11 Rivington St. **℃** *(212) 979-9808.* **FAX** *(212) 979-9801.*
W www.offsoho.com
It used to be that this budget hotel was in no-man's-land – but hip downtown has expanded so much as to practically embrace it. Decor is nonexistent and beds are a bit too firm, but rooms are well tended. Deluxe suites have fully outfitted kitchens and baths, while economy suites share facilities.

LOWER MANHATTAN: *Holiday Inn Wall Street*
15 Gold St. **℃** *(212) 232-7800.* **FAX** *(212) 269-9569.*
W www.holidayinnwsd.com
Wall Street's most technologically mature hotel was designed with business travelers in mind. Standard features include a desk and personal computer with CD/DVD drive, fax/copier/printer, ergonomic chair, and portable phones. Good buffet breakfast.

LOWER MANHATTAN: *Regent Wall Street*
55 Wall St. **℃** *(212) 845-8600.* **FAX** *(212) 845-8601.*
W www.regenthotels.com
Financial District's finest hotel occupies an 1842 Greek Revival building. The grand Neo-Classical interiors have been preserved and updated into amenity-laden rooms. Weekend rates are a bargain.

LOWER MIDTOWN: *Clarion Hotel Fifth Avenue*
3 E 40th St. **℃** *(212) 447-1500.* **FAX** *(212) 213-0972.*
W www.hotelchoice.com
This freshly renovated chain hotel offers excellent value in a pricey neighborhood. Rooms are outfitted in comfort with a hint of smart Art Deco style. The location, near New York Public Library and Grand Central Terminal, is convenient for the Theater District.

LOWER MIDTOWN: *Kitano*
66 Park Ave. **℃** *(212) 885-7000.* **FAX** *(212) 885-7100.*
W www.kitano.com, www.summithotels.com
This elegant Japanese-owned hotel is a sea of tranquility in the bustle, chaos, and excitement of the city. Hotel rooms are elegantly appointed havens of restful Japanese luxury. The Kaiseki cuisine in the restaurant is exceptional, and the service is flawless.

MORNINGSIDE HEIGHTS & HARLEM: *Sugar Hill International House*
722 St Nicholas Ave. **℃** *(212) 926-7030.*
W www.sugarhillhostel.com
This quiet, well-run, all-nonsmoking hostel offers two-dozen dorm beds to shoestring travelers. Bunks fill spacious rooms; a few double rooms are available to early arrivals. Security is good, the neighborhood is quiet, there is a common kitchen, and the kind owners are happy to offer advice.

MORNINGSIDE HEIGHTS & HARLEM: *Ellington*
610 W 111th St. **℃** *(212) 864-7500.* **FAX** *(212) 749-5852.*
W www.nycityhotels.net
Smart Art Deco accents disguise the basic austerity of this budget hotel. Still, it makes a good choice for wallet-watching travelers who want a private bathroom and a few extras (like hairdryers), especially when rates drop below $150. A continental breakfast is included. Check for discounts.

For key to symbols see back flap

Price categories for a standard double room per night, inclusive of breakfast, service charges, and any additional taxes:

$ under $100
$$ $100–$150
$$$ $150–$200
$$$$ $200–$250
$$$$$ over $250

CREDIT CARDS
Major credit cards accepted.

NUMBER OF ROOMS
Number of rooms in the hotel.

RECOMMENDED RESTAURANT
Good restaurant within the hotel.

CHILDREN'S FACILITIES
Hotel has various facilities for young children.

GARDEN OR TERRACE
Hotel has a garden, courtyard, or terrace.

	CREDIT CARDS	NUMBER OF ROOMS	RECOMMENDED RESTAURANT	CHILDREN'S FACILITIES	GARDEN OR TERRACE
SoHo & TriBeCa: *Cosmopolitan Hotel – Tribeca* $ 95 W Broadway. (212) 566-1900. FAX (212) 566-6909. www.cosmohotel.com In the heart of hip TriBeCa is one of Manhattan's best budget hotels. Rooms are petite but well maintained and pleasantly furnished; the bathrooms are tiny but pristine. The location is super-convenient, and a wealth of first-rate restaurants are within walking distance. Highly recommended.	■	105			
SoHo & TriBeCa: *60 Thompson* $$$$ 60 Thompson St. (212) 431-0400. FAX (212) 431-0200. www.60thompson.com Despite its chic modernist lines, this smallish newcomer boasts a warm and surprisingly domestic ambience. Done in a soothing celadon-and-mahogany palette, rooms are plush and well equipped with DVD and CD players, Internet access, and marble baths. Location is first rate.	■	100	■		
Theater District: *Big Apple Hostel* $ 119 W 45th St. (212) 302-2603. FAX (212) 302-2605. www.bigapplehostel.com New York's best hostel caters to a world of young travelers with super-clean accommodations and a prime location. Most beds are in dormitories, but a few private doubles are available. Everything is newer and nicer than at most hostels. Book well in advance.	■	39			
Theater District: *Algonquin* $$$ 59 W 44th St. (212) 840-6800. FAX (212) 944-1419. www.algonquinhotel.com This restored legend, home to Dorothy Parker's literary "Round Table" of the 1920s, is one of Midtown's most evocative hotels. Rooms are small but comfortable; the literary-themed suites make a worthy splurge. The Oak Room offers star-quality cabaret.	■	174	■		
Theater District: *Ritz-Carlton* $$$$$ 50 Central Park S. (212) 308-9100. FAX (212) 207-8831. www.ritzcarlton.com This reliable luxury chain's first Midtown hotel opened in 2002. Expect all of the classic Ritz-Carlton hallmarks, which blend traditional stylings and premier comforts: state-of-the-art technology, a full-service spa, and staff who never say "no."	■	287	■		
Upper East Side: *Hotel Wales* $$$ 1295 Madison Ave. (212) 876-6000. FAX (212) 860-7000. www.waleshotel.com This quirky Victorian-style hotel offers pleasant relief in an expensive neighborhood. Comforts include beds dressed in Belgian linens, VCRs, and CD players. Rates include breakfast and self-serve cappucino all day. Sarabeth's is a favorite for homestyle cooking and afternoon tea.	■	87	■		
Upper East Side: *Surrey Hotel* $$$$ 20 E 76th St. (212) 288-3700. FAX (212) 628-1549. www.mesuite.com Experience the high life for less at this lovely all-suite hotel. The Old World suites are spacious and pleasing from tip to toe; each one has a fully equipped kitchen. In-suite dining, from Cafe Boulud, one of New York's finest restaurants, is reason enough to stay.	■	130	■		
Upper Midtown: *Kimberly Hotel* $$$ 145 E 50th St. (212) 755-0400. FAX (212) 486-6915. www.kimberlyhotel.com This low-profile hotel boasts mostly apartment-style one- and two-bedroom suites featuring home comforts, such as a full-size kitchen, dining area, and large, well-appointed rooms. Excellent for families and long-term business travelers. Check for discounts and packages.	■	185			

UPPER MIDTOWN: *Waldorf-Astoria/Waldorf Towers*
301 Park Ave. **(** *(212) 355-3000.* **FAX** *(212) 872-7272.*
W www.hilton.com
This New York legend is as great as ever. Rates are very reasonable in the main hotel, considering the glamorous air, extra-large rooms, and first-class dining and amenities. The exclusive Waldorf Towers has 24-hour butler service and a solid reputation for discretion.

$$$$ | 1242

UPPER WEST SIDE: *Jazz on the Park*
36 W 106th St, New York. **(** *(212) 932-1600.* **FAX** *(212) 932-1700.*
W www.jazzhostel.com
This funky, artsy hostel brings a downtown vibe to the Upper West Side. A coffeehouse with live music most evenings lends a party atmosphere. Dorm rooms are hostel-basic, and bathrooms are decent. Expect a young, energetic, and international crowd. Continental breakfast is a value-added touch.

$ | 220

UPPER WEST SIDE: *Trump International Hotel & Tower*
1 Central Park West, New York. **(** *(212) 299-1000.* **FAX** *(212) 299-1150.*
W www.trumpintl.com
Housed in a freestanding tower overlooking Central Park, this hotel is one of the city's finest. Smartly designed rooms are softened with soothing Tuscan hues; floor-to-ceiling windows offer great views. Each guest is assigned a personal concierge, making service unparalleled.

$$$$$ | 167

NEW YORK STATE

ALBANY: *Mansion Hill Inn*
115 Philip St. **(** *(518) 465-2038, (888) 299-0455.* **FAX** *(518) 434-2313.*
W www.mansionhill.com
This downtown inn, located near the Governor's Mansion and housed in an 1860s private home, has been fully modernized but still holds considerable charm.

$$$ | 8

BUFFALO: *Best Western Inn*
510 Delaware Ave. **(** *(716) 886-8333.* **FAX** *(716) 884-3070.*
W www.highlanderinn.com
This medium-sized mid-range hotel is conveniently located in the lively "Allentown" neighborhood downtown, with easy access to parks, museums, and other attractions.

$$ | 61

COLD SPRING (HUDSON RIVER VALLEY): *Hudson House Inn*
2 Main St. **(** *(845) 265-9355.*
W www.hudsonhouseinn.com
Set on the banks of the Hudson River, looking across to Storm King Mountain and the US Military Academy at West Point, this inn has been in business since the 1830s and is rich in period charm.

$$$ | 13

COOPERSTOWN: *Otesaga Hotel*
60 Lake St. **(** *(607) 547-9931.* **FAX** *(607) 547-9675.*
W www.otesaga.com
Recently restored to its 1909 splendor, this well-located downtown hotel is intimate and luxuriously appointed. Facilities include a swimming pool and a full-service gym. It is closed in winter.

$$$$$ | 136

ITHACA: *Buttermilk Falls Inn*
110 E Buttermilk Falls Rd. **(** *(607) 272-6767.* **FAX** *(607) 273-3947.*
W www.esbba.com/Inns/buttermilkfalls
Located near the foot of a waterfall, adjacent to a 750-acre (304-ha) state park, this B&B inn dates back to the 1820s.

$$$ | 5

LAKE PLACID: *Mirror Lake Inn*
5 Mirror Lake Dr. **(** *(518) 523-2544.* **FAX** *(518) 523-2871.*
W www.mirrorlakeinn.com
A lakefront landmark, rebuilt after a 1988 fire, this large old-fashioned hotel has a wide variety of luxurious rooms, as well as a full range of restaurants and activities, including a private beach and an ice-skating rink.

$$$$$ | 128

MONTAUK: *Shepherds Neck Inn*
90 Second House Rd. **(** *(631) 668-2105.* **FAX** *(631) 668-0171.*
W www.shepherdsneckinn.com
Set on 8 acres (3.2 ha), complete with tennis courts, a swimming pool, and an award-winning restaurant, this inn has a welcoming, easy-going feel.

$$$ | 70

Price categories for a standard double room per night, inclusive of breakfast, service charges, and any additional taxes:

$ under $100
$$ $100–$150
$$$ $150–$200
$$$$ $200–$250
$$$$$ over $250

CREDIT CARDS
Major credit cards accepted.
NUMBER OF ROOMS
Number of rooms in the hotel.
RECOMMENDED RESTAURANT
Good restaurant within the hotel.
CHILDREN'S FACILITIES
Hotel has various facilities for young children.
GARDEN OR TERRACE
Hotel has a garden, courtyard, or terrace.

	CREDIT CARDS	NUMBER OF ROOMS	RECOMMENDED RESTAURANT	CHILDREN'S FACILITIES	GARDEN OR TERRACE

NIAGARA FALLS: *Comfort Inn* $$
1 Prospect Pointe. [(716) 284-6835. FAX (716) 284-5177.
W www.comfortinn.com
This inn is located in a historic building just 1,200 ft (366 m) from Niagara Falls, so close you can feel the mist and hear the rumbling (though you cannot actually see the falls). True to its name, the inn offers comfortable accommodations at a good price.

Credit Cards / 118 / Children's Facilities

RHINEBECK: *Beekman Arms* $$
4 Mill Street. [(845) 876-7077. FAX (845) 876-7077.
W www.beekmanarms.com
In business since 1766, this is one of the oldest inns in America, having hosted everyone from George Washington to Franklin Roosevelt. Rooms in the original inn are somewhat small but comfortable. Larger rooms are available in adjacent buildings.

Credit Cards / 63 / Recommended Restaurant / Children's Facilities / Garden or Terrace

ROCHESTER: *Four Points Sheraton* $$
120 E Main St. [(585) 546-6400, (800) 223-9330. FAX (585) 546-1341.
W www.rrcc.com/fourpoints.asp
This is a very large, business-oriented downtown hotel, located right on the river across from the convention center. Four Points Sheraton offers all modern amenities at reasonable rates. Among the facilities provided are a full-service gym and swimming pool.

Credit Cards / 466 / Recommended Restaurant

SARATOGA SPRINGS: *Adelphi Hotel* $$$
365 Broadway. [(518) 587-4688. FAX (518) 587-0851.
W www.adelphihotel.com
Located right in the center of town, this historic hotel has been renovated with extravagant furnishings. Each room is decorated in a unique version of late Victorian excess, and the hand-painted murals in the opulent lobby have to be seen to be believed.

Credit Cards / 35 / Garden or Terrace

SKANEATELES (FINGER LAKES): *Hobbit Hollow Farm* $$$
3061 W Lake Rd. [(315) 685-2791. FAX (315) 685-3426.
W www.hobbithollow.com
Set on more than 300 acres (121 ha) of rolling fields overlooking Skaneateles Lake, this pleasant bread-and-breakfast inn offers a relaxing respite in the heart of the Finger Lakes. Each of the rooms is furnished with antiques and has a luxurious private bath.

Credit Cards / 5 / Garden or Terrace

NEW JERSEY

ATLANTIC CITY: *Quality Inn* $$
119 South Carolina & Pacific Ave. [(609) 345-7070. FAX (609) 345-0633.
W www.qualityinnatlanticcity.com
This modern, 18-story tower offers some of the best accommodation values in Atlantic City. The rooms are well-appointed with private baths, and the hotel is just a block away from the beach, the famous boardwalk, and major gaming casinos.

Credit Cards / 203 / Children's Facilities

ATLANTIC CITY: *Bally's Park Place Hotel* $$$
Boardwalk and Park Place. [(609) 340-2000, (800) 225--5977.
FAX (609) 340-4713. W www.ballys.com
One of the few remnants of historic Atlantic City, the 1860s-era Dennis Hotel has been restored as part of this mega-resort complex, which also includes a modern 37-story tower. Fans of the board game Monopoly will know that the hotel stands on the city's most valuable corner.

Credit Cards / 1270 / Recommended Restaurant / Children's Facilities / Garden or Terrace

CAPE MAY: *Chalfonte Hotel* $$$
301 Howard St. ((609) 884-8409. FAX (609) 884-4588.
W www.chalfonte.com
Like a living-history museum, this white-washed Victorian-era hotel offers
old-fashioned charms like rocking chairs on the wrap-around front porch.
Rooms have no TVs or phones, but the hotel is just two blocks from the
beach, and guests are invited to enjoy family-style communal meals. ⚡ P

| | | 66 | | ● | |

CAPE MAY: *Queen's Hotel* $$$
601 Columbia Ave. ((609) 884-1613.
W www.queenshotel.com
Built in the 1870s and fully restored in 1995, this mansard-roofed Victorian inn
is located in the heart of historic Cape May, just a block from the beach. Rooms
have antique furnishings, and free bicycles are available. ⚡ ⛳ TV 🔒 P

| | | 11 | | | |

PENNSYLVANIA

BIRD IN HAND: *Village Inn* $$
2695 Old Philadelphia Pike. ((717) 768-1535, (800) 914-2473.
FAX (508) 228-2446. W www.bird-in-hand.com/villageinn
Located in the heart of this picturesque, if oddly-named Pennsylvania Dutch
country village, this 1734 inn now welcomes travelers with all modern
comforts and conveniences. Great service and facilities. ⚡ ⛳ TV 🔒 P

| | | 11 | | | |

LITITZ: *General Sutter Inn* $$$
14 E Main St. ((717) 626-2115. FAX (717) 626-0992.
W www.generalsutterinn.com
Dating from 1764, this is the oldest inn in Pennsylvania and has retained
its stately period architecture and its position at the center of a very
quaint Pennsylvania Dutch country hamlet. Facilities include a good
restaurant and a lively bar. ⚡ ⛳ TV Y 🔒 P

| | | 17 | | | |

PHILADELPHIA: *Comfort Inn* $$
100 N Columbus Blvd. ((215) 627-7900. FAX (215) 238-0809.
W www.comfortinnphila.com
This budget-priced high-rise hotel has no frills but a great location, near
Penn's Landing and the historic Independence Hall. Rooms are sparse but
clean and comfortable, and all have large private baths. ⚡ ⛳ TV Y 🔒 P

| | | 185 | | | |

PHILADELPHIA: *Penn's View Inn* $$$
14 N Front St. ((215) 922-7600. FAX (215) 922-7642.
Overlooking the Delaware River from the heart of historic Philadelphia,
this small full-service hotel has well-appointed rooms and a welcoming,
European-style ambience. ⚡ ⛳ TV Y 🔒

| | | 52 | | | |

PHILADELPHIA: *Radisson Plaza Warwick* $$$
1701 Locust St. ((215) 735-6000. FAX (215) 789-6105.
W www.radisson.com/philadelphiapa
Located downtown in lovely Rittenhouse Square, this historic hotel is the
grand dame of Philadelphia. Excellent service, and all the usual amenities
make it great for the business traveler. ⚡ ⛳ TV Y 🍴 🔒 P &

| | | 545 | | | |

PHILADELPHIA: *Loews Philadelphia* $$$$
1200 Market Street. ((215) 627-1200.
W www.loewshotels.com/philadelphia
Housed in the PSFS building, a 1932 landmark of modernist architecture
at the heart of Philadelphia's Center City, this ultra-stylish luxury hotel
opened in 2002 and has set a new standard for comfort and service.
⚡ ⛳ TV Y 🏊 🍴 🔒 P &

| | | 581 | | ● | |

PITTSBURGH: *The Priory* $$
614 Pressley St. ((412) 231-3338. FAX (412) 231-4838.
W www.thepriory.com
One of the city's nicest places to stay, this charming B&B inn has been
brought back to life after its original incarnation as a rooming house for
traveling Benedictine monks. Guests today can enjoy complimentary
afternoon glasses of wine in the central courtyard. ⚡ ⛳ TV 🔒 P

| | | 24 | | | |

PITTSBURGH: *Omni William Penn* $$$
530 William Penn Place. ((412) 281-7100. FAX (412) 553-5252.
W www.omnihotels.com
Located in the heart of the downtown business district, this landmark
hotel offers a sumptuous lobby, spacious, comfortable rooms, and a full-
service gym. Very popular, so book early. ⚡ ⛳ TV Y 🍴 🔒 P &

| | | 595 | | ● | |

Where to Eat

A VARIED DINING EXPERIENCE IS OFFERED across much of the Mid-Atlantic Region. New York City, especially, has more than 25,000 restaurants catering to every taste. Here, "in" places and cuisine change with great regularity, while some favorite places remain popular. In the listings below, opening times are indicated by a "B" for breakfast, "L" for lunch, and "D" for dinner.

	CREDIT CARDS	OUTDOOR TABLES	VEGETARIAN	GOOD WINE LIST	CHILDREN'S FACILITIES

NEW YORK CITY

EAST VILLAGE: *Great Jones Café* $
54 Great Jones St. (212) 674-9304.
Cajun food lovers hie to this hole-in-the-wall NoHo neighborhood café for spicy gumbo made with andouille sausage, jambalaya, corn-meal fried catfish, and other delicious New Orleans fare. D.
(Vegetarian)

GREENWICH VILLAGE: *Babbo* $$$$$
110 Waverly Pl. (212) 777-0303.
The setting in a century-old duplex Greenwich Village townhouse, with its grand stairway and skylight, and the inventive, rustic Italian country fare of notable chef Mario Batali, make this one of the most popular Italian restaurants in the city; reserve well in advance. D. &
(Credit Cards, Good Wine List)

GRAMERCY & THE FLATIRON DISTRICT: *Union Square Café* $$$$
21 East 16th St. (212) 243-4020.
Restaurant entrepreneur Danny Meyer's first venue has been one of New York's most popular since 1985, loved for delicious fare served in friendly surroundings. Chef Michael Romano's new takes on American standards include the freshest ingredients from the neighboring Union Square Greenmarket. Mon–Sat L, D. &
(Credit Cards, Vegetarian, Good Wine List, Children's Facilities)

LOWER EAST SIDE: *Grand Sichuan* $
125 Canal St. (212) 625-9212.
For those who favor the spicy seasonings of China's Szechwan province, this is a Chinatown find, a no-frills storefront with authentic specialties of the region at reasonable prices. Its reputation has spawned two uptown siblings at 229 Ninth Avenue and 745 Ninth Avenue. L, D. &
(Credit Cards)

LOWER EAST SIDE: *Il Palazzo* $$
151 Mulberry St. (212) 343-7000.
One of the better choices on Mulberry Street: cozy, candlelit, and non-touristy. The menu includes all the Italian favorites, including tempting pastries. The serene garden with a fountain out back is a summer delight. L, D.
(Credit Cards, Outdoor Tables, Vegetarian, Children's Facilities)

LOWER MANHATTAN: *American Park at the Battery* $$$$
Battery Park, opposite 17 State St. (212) 809-5508.
A great location at the tip of the Battery with wall-to-wall harbor views makes this a popular choice. If you can sit on the expansive terrace on a sunny day, you won't mind if the generous seafood selection doesn't quite equal the view. Mon–Fri L, Mon–Sat D. &
(Credit Cards, Outdoor Tables, Children's Facilities)

LOWER MANHATTAN: *14 Wall Street Restaurant* $$$$
14 Wall St. (212) 233-2780.
Once J.P. Morgan's private dining room, this penthouse with wonderful views is a Wall Street expense-account favorite. The room with high ceilings, dark wood trim, and vintage French posters is a handsome setting for fine French cuisine. The service is impeccable. L, Mon–Fri D. & ♈
(Credit Cards)

LOWER MIDTOWN: *The Oyster Bar & Restaurant* $$$
Grand Central Station, lower level, 42nd St & Lexington Ave. (212) 490-6650.
A New York classic beneath a vaulted ceiling of Guastavino tiles, this big, noisy, 90-year-old restaurant serves only the finest seafood, from the formal menu with as many as 30 choices, to the long raw bar with two dozen kinds of oysters. Mon–Fri L, Mon–Sat D. &
(Credit Cards, Good Wine List, Children's Facilities)

MORNINGSIDE HEIGHTS & HARLEM: *Terrace in the Sky* $$$$
400 West 119th St. (212) 666-9490.
Off the beaten path, this elegant rooftop restaurant near Columbia University is so romantic that many weddings are held here. The view from the terrace is divine, the harpist adds to the ambience, and the Continental fare lives up to the setting. Tue–Sat D. & ♫
(Credit Cards)

Price categories include a three-course meal for one, a glass of house wine, and all unavoidable extra charges such as sales tax and service.
$ under $20
$$ $20–30
$$$ $30–45
$$$$ $45–60
$$$$$ over $60

CREDIT CARDS
Major credit cards accepted.

OUTDOOR TABLES
Garden, courtyard, or terrace with outside tables.

VEGETARIAN
A good selection of vegetarian dishes available.

GOOD WINE LIST
Extensive list of good wines, both domestic and imported.

CHILDREN'S FACILITIES
Small portions and/or high chairs available on request.

Restaurant	Price	Credit Cards	Outdoor Tables	Vegetarian	Good Wine List	Children's Facilities
SoHo & Tribeca: *Kin Khao*	$$	■		■		
SoHo & Tribeca: *Lupa*	$$$	■		■		■
Theater District: *Virgil's Real BBQ*	$	■				■
Theater District: *Le Bernardin*	$$$$$	■			●	■
Upper East Side: *Mocca Hungarian Restaurant*	$					■
Upper East Side: *Le Cirque 2000*	$$$$$	■			●	
Upper Midtown: *Dawat*	$$$	■		■		
Upper West Side: *Santa Fe*	$$	■				
Upper West Side: *Picholine*	$$$$$	■				

SoHo & Tribeca: *Kin Khao* $$
171 Spring St. (212) 966-3939.
The name means "eat rice" in Thai, but that's only the beginning of a vast menu offering regional Thai and Bangkok cuisine. Be sure to make reservations; the Soho location is very popular especially on weekends. Save room for the sticky-rice and papaya dessert. *D.*

SoHo & Tribeca: *Lupa* $$$
170 Thomson St. (212) 982-5089.
Much less expensive than his Babbo, Chef Mario Batali's rustic, candle-lit Roman trattoria serves elegant fare at affordable prices: appetizers like heavenly prosciutto with figs, and pastas such as squid ink tagliarini with spicy calamari. You may have to wait for a seat, but you won't be sorry you came. *L, D.*

Theater District: *Virgil's Real BBQ* $
152 West 44th St. (212) 921-9494.
This big, boisterous restaurant offers a tour of barbecue styles throughout the South, from Memphis to Carolina to Texas, 10 different platters of beef, pork, or chicken with a variety of sauces. Sides are flaky buttermilk biscuits with honey-butter and collard greens. *L, D.*

Theater District: *Le Bernardin* $$$$$
155 West 51st St. (212) 489-1515.
Seafood doesn't come any better than at this luxurious French restaurant lauded for revolutionizing the way fish is served in New York. It is considered one of America's best restaurants, and Chef Eric Lipert seems to have no critics. Perfection has its price, but the meal will be memorable. *Mon–Fri L, Mon–Sun D.*

Upper East Side: *Mocca Hungarian Restaurant* $
1588 Second Ave. (212) 734-6470.
Mocca brings to mind a simple European café with flowery china on the wall, lace curtains, and old-fashioned lighting. Chicken paprikash, beef goulash, stuffed cabbage, dumplings, and schnitzels are among the traditional choices. All are reasonable, and the prix-fixe dinners are a real bargain. *L, D.*

Upper East Side: *Le Cirque 2000* $$$$$
455 Madison Ave. (212) 303-7788.
Some love the bright neon and the playful curving furniture by Adam Tihany, although some find it jarring amid the gilded Old World splendor of the landmark Villard Houses. But no one doubts that Le Cirque is one of the city's better French restaurants. *Mon–Sat L, D.*

Upper Midtown : *Dawat* $$$
210 East 58th St. (212) 355-7555.
One of the more attractive Indian dining places in the city, Dawat features recipes inspired by Madhur Jaffrey, a noted Indian cookbook author. It is known for signature dishes such as salmon rubbed in coriander chutney and steamed in a banana leaf. *Mon–Sat L, D.*

Upper West Side: *Santa Fe* $$
72 West 69th St. (212) 724-0822.
A relaxing setting amid peach-colored walls and colorful rugs, and its location near Lincoln Center are among the reasons this Southwestern place has been a favorite for years. Popular dishes are the Masa shrimp appetizer, chipotle chicken with rice, steamed vegetables, and grated cheese over refried beans. *L, D.*

Upper West Side: *Picholine* $$$$$
West 64th St. (212) 724-8585.
For fine dining in the Lincoln Center area, the top choice is Terrance Brennan's elegant Mediterranean restaurant, where the chef's blending of subtle flavors transforms every dish. The cheese course is famous – be sure to save room. *Sat L, D.*

For key to symbols see back flap

	CREDIT CARDS	OUTDOOR TABLES	VEGETARIAN	GOOD WINE LIST	CHILDREN'S FACILITIES

Price categories include a three-course meal for one, a glass of house wine, and all unavoidable extra charges such as sales tax and service.
Ⓢ under $20
ⓈⓈ $20–30
ⓈⓈⓈ $30–45
ⓈⓈⓈⓈ $45–60
ⓈⓈⓈⓈⓈ over $60

CREDIT CARDS
Major credit cards accepted.
OUTDOOR TABLES
Garden, courtyard, or terrace with outside tables.
VEGETARIAN
A good selection of vegetarian dishes available.
GOOD WINE LIST
Extensive list of good wines, both domestic and imported.
CHILDREN'S FACILITIES
Small portions and/or high chairs available on request.

NEW YORK STATE

Entry	Credit Cards	Outdoor Tables	Vegetarian	Good Wine List	Children's Facilities
ALBANY: *Jack's Oyster House* ⓈⓈⓈ 4244 State St. 📞 (518) 465-8854. A popular haunt with state legislators and lobbyists, this lively restaurant specializes in seafood. *L, D.* 🍸 ♿ ⌁ 🪑	■		■	●	■
AMANGANSETT: *Lobster Roll* ⓈⓈ 1980 Montauk Highway. 📞 (631) 267-3740. Known locally as "Lunch," thanks to the huge sign that looms over the shack-like building, this informal beachfront café serves all kinds of fresh seafood and great fruit pies. *L, D.* ● *mid-Oct–May.* 🍸 ♿ ⌁	■	●	■		■
BUFFALO: *Roycroft Inn* ⓈⓈⓈⓈ 40 S Grove St. 📞 (716) 652-5552. If you want to appreciate the life and times of Buffalo at its turn-of-the-20th-century peak, enjoy a meal at this cozy restaurant, housed in a landmark Arts and Crafts-style hotel. *L, D.* ♿ ⌁	■	●	■	●	■
COOPERSTOWN: *Doubleday Café* ⓈⓈ 93 Main St. 📞 (607) 547-5468. Catering to the many baseball fans making a pilgrimage to the nearby Hall of Fame, with walls covered in baseball memorabilia, this family-friendly restaurant serves hearty American fare like soups and burgers. *B, L, D.* ● *Thanksgiving, Dec 25.* 🍸 ⌁	■		■		
HYDE PARK: *American Bounty* ⓈⓈⓈ 433 Albany Post Rd. 📞 (845) 471-6608. Located in the massive Culinary Institute of America (CIA), and operated by student chefs, this nationally famous restaurant is one of the best places to eat in the Hudson River Valley area. *L, D.* ● *Sun, Mon, late Jul.* ♿ ⌁ 🪑	■		■	●	
ITHACA: *Moosewood* ⓈⓈ 215 N Cayuga St. 📞 (607) 273-9610. One of the earliest and most influential natural-food restaurants in the country, this cooperatively owned and warmly decorated vegetarian café has excellent food and an easy-going ambience. The wine list is excellent. *Mon–Sat L, D.* ♿ ⌁	■	●	■		
MILLBROOK (HUSDSON RIVER VALLEY): *Millbrook Diner* Ⓢ Franklin Ave. 📞 (845) 677-5319. Set at the center of a quaint Hudson River Valley village, this classic 1950s O'Mahony stainless-steel diner serves up excellent breakfasts and other meals to a wide range of locals and visitors. *B, L, D.* ⌁	■		■	●	■
MONTAUK: *Gosman's Dock* ⓈⓈⓈ West Lake Dr. 📞 (631) 668-5330. Overlooking the harbor, this large and very popular restaurant has been serving fresh fish for over 50 years. The restaurant also features a well-stocked bar. 🍸 ♿ ⌁	■	●	■	●	■
SHARON SPRINGS: *American Hotel* ⓈⓈⓈ 192 Main St. 📞 (518) 284-2105. Located in the middle of a sleepy former spa town and inside a recently restored hotel that dates back to the mid-1840s, this stylish little restaurant offers urban sophistication in a relaxing setting. *L, D.* ● *Nov–Mar: Mon–Tue.* 🍸 ⌁	■	●	■	●	
SKANEATELES (FINGER LAKES): *Doug's Fish Fry* Ⓢ 8 Jordan St. 📞 (315) 685-3288. This Finger Lakes eatery offers truly delicious fresh fried fish, served up in an unpretentious setting that has hardly changed for 40-odd years. *L, D.* ● *Jan 1–15, major hols.* 🍸 ♿ ⌁	■	●	■		■

NEW JERSEY

ATLANTIC CITY: *Dock's Oyster House* $$$
2405 Atlantic Ave. ((609) 345-0092.
One of the oldest in the state, this wood-paneled restaurant has been run
by the same family since 1897. *D.* 🍸 ♿ ⚡

CAPE MAY: *Mad Batter* $$
19 Jackson St. ((609) 884-5970.
For an unforgettable breakfast, lunch, or dinner, head to this energetic
café, housed in a Victorian-era B&B inn. Generous portions are served in
a casual setting by a friendly staff. *B, L, D.* ● *Jan.*

PENNSYLVANIA

EPHRATA: *Doneckers Restaurant* $$$
333 N State St. ((717) 738-9501.
This stylish country French restaurant located in the heart of the
Pennsylvania Dutch Country, has an excellent wine list which
includes 500 different wines, and also has a less formal bistro. *L, D.*
● *Wed, Sun.* ♿ ⚡

GETTYSBURG: *Dobbins House* $$$
89 Steinwehr Ave. ((717) 334-2100.
Located in an old house that dates from 1776, this history-rich restaurant
serves old-fashioned hearty dishes like roast duck and a cherry-stuffed
pork tenderloin. *L, D.* ⚡

MOUNT JOY: *Groff's Farm* $$$
650 Pinkerton Rd. ((717) 653-2048.
For a taste of Pennsylvania Dutch Country cooking, plan to visit this
popular, family-style restaurant, where you can serve yourself as much as
you like of the well-prepared roasted meats, plentiful vegetables, and
heart-stopping desserts. *Fri–Sat D.* ♿ ⚡

PHILADELPHIA: *Reading Terminal Market* $
1200 Arch St. ((215) 922-2317.
Inside this historic downtown market, over 80 different stands sell all
kinds of lunch food from around the world, including Chinese, Japanese,
Greek, Middle Eastern, and Pennsylvania Dutch. Open since 1892, the
Reading Terminal Market now sits at the entrance to the city's convention
center. *L.* ● *Sun.* ♿ ⚡ 🎵

PHILADELPHIA: *Jim's Steaks* $
400 South St. ((215) 928-1911.
To sample the sandwich that's named for the city, the "Philly
Cheesesteak," come to this unique Art Deco stand, which has been
serving up these sliced steak and melted cheese concoctions for over 60
years. The original branch is still open at 431 N 62nd Street. *L, D.* ♿ ⚡

PHILADELPHIA: *City Tavern* $$
138 S 2nd St. ((215) 413-1443.
Part of the Independence National Historical Park, this is a faithful
re-creation of the city's most popular meeting place in the days leading
up to the American Revolution. *L, D.* ♿ ⚡

PHILADELPHIA: *Striped Bass* $$$$
1500 Walnut St. ((215) 732-4444.
The high ceilings and marble pillars of the main dining room set the tone
for one of the city's best restaurants, which features modern variations on
traditional fish dishes. Start the evening with fresh oysters at the adjacent
bar. *Mon–Fri & Sun L, D.* 🍸 ♿ ⚡

PHILADELPHIA: *Susanna Foo* $$$$
1512 Walnut Street. ((215) 545-2666.
French culinary techniques meet fresh American produce in these
wonderfully inventive versions of traditional Chinese dishes. *Mon–Fri L, D.*
♿ ⚡ 🍸

PITTSBURGH: *Primanti Brothers* $
6 18th St. ((412) 263-2142.
A blue-collar institution in this hard-working city, this is the first of many
locations around Pittsburgh serving excellent "cheesesteaks" and other
sandwiches, 24 hours a day. *L, D.* ♿ ⚡

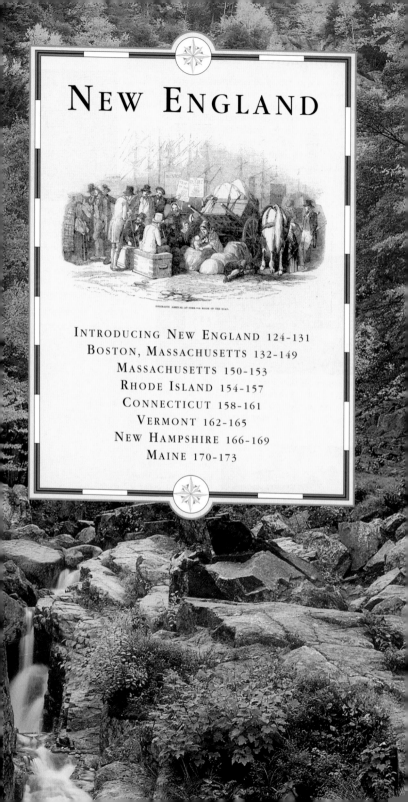

NEW ENGLAND

EMIGRANT ARRIVAL AT CORK—A SCENE ON THE QUAY.

New England at a Glance

Tucked away in the northeasternmost corner of the United States, the six states of New England are rich in history and culture as well as in natural beauty. Many of the country's earliest settlements were established here, as were the first centers of higher education. The region therefore abounds in historic buildings, as well as in superb museums and prestigious universities. New England's topography includes large tracts of farmland, dense woodlands, pristine lakes, and sweeping coastlines, which are rocky and jagged in some areas and serene and sandy in others. It is also home to the rugged peaks of the White, Green, and Appalachian Mountains.

Vermont (see pp162–5) *is an enclave of unspoiled wilderness. Vermont is at its scenic best in fall, when the Green Mountain State changes its verdant green cloak for a rich palette of yellow, orange, and red.*

Canterbury Shaker Village (see p168) *located in New Hampshire, was founded in 1792. This is one of the many picturesque historic villages that are scattered around the rolling farmlands of the state.*

Connecticut (see pp158–61) *is quintessential New England. Steepled churches around immaculate village greens are typical features of its serene landscape.*

Block Island (see p157) *in Rhode Island is one of the many tranquil havens situated along the pristine shoreline of this tiny state. Great Salt Pond has three marinas and is an excellent spot for kayaking and fishing.*

◁ **Silver Cascades, Crawford Notch State Park, New Hampshire, in the autumn**

<!-- map labels -->
Stowe
Burlington
Br
W

VERMONT
(See pp162–65)

NE
HAMP
(See pp1

Can
Sh
V

Killington

Manchester

MASSACHUSET
(See pp132–53)

Northhampton

The Berkshires

CONNECTICUT
(See pp158–61)

RI
IS
(See p

Hartford

Stamford

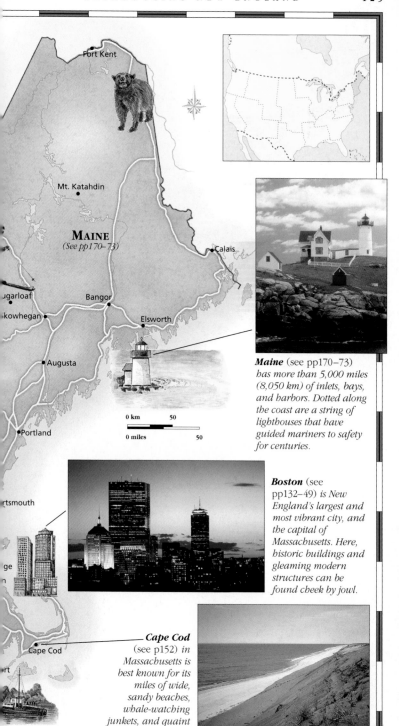

Fort Kent

Mt. Katahdin

MAINE
(See pp170–73)

Calais

ugarloaf

kowhegan

Bangor

Elsworth

Augusta

0 km 50

0 miles 50

Portland

rtsmouth

ge

Cape Cod

rt

Maine *(see pp170–73)
has more than 5,000 miles
(8,050 km) of inlets, bays,
and harbors. Dotted along
the coast are a string of
lighthouses that have
guided mariners to safety
for centuries.*

Boston *(see
pp132–49) is New
England's largest and
most vibrant city, and
the capital of
Massachusetts. Here,
historic buildings and
gleaming modern
structures can be
found cheek by jowl.*

Cape Cod
*(see p152) in
Massachusetts is
best known for its
miles of wide,
sandy beaches,
whale-watching
junkets, and quaint
Colonial villages.*

NEW ENGLAND

FOR MANY PEOPLE, *New England is white-steepled churches, craggy coastlines, historic villages, and timeless landscapes of tranquil farmlands and country roads, with the sophisticated city of Boston as its cultural and commercial hub. Many also regard it as the cradle of American civilization, for New England's early history is the history of the United States itself.*

From the beginning, the region has been shaped by both geography and climate. Early explorers charted its coastline, and communities soon sprang up by the coast, where goods and people could be ferried more easily from the Old World to the New. Early commerce depended heavily on the ocean, from shipping and whaling to fishing and boat-building.

The harsh, unpredictable climate, poor soil, hilly terrain, and dense virgin forests also helped shape the character of its people. To survive in this area required toughness, ingenuity, and a spirit of independence – all traits that became ingrained in the New England psyche. The slogan "Live free or die" on New Hampshire license plates is a reminder that the same spirit lives on. Indeed, New England today is as much a state of mind as it is a physical space. Despite this, New England is also home to the opulence of Newport, Rhode Island, the beautiful surburban communities of Connecticut, and the self-assured sophistication of Boston.

HISTORY

New England's historical connections are far richer than any other area in America, for it was here that much of the drama of forming a new country was played out. In 1614, the English explorer John Smith sailed along the coast of Massachusetts, named it New England, and declared that it was the best place to set up a new colony. On December 26, 1620, a group of 102 Puritans, who had left England to escape religious persecution, landed at Plymouth Rock after a grueling 66-day voyage on the *Mayflower* and established one of America's first permanent English settlements. Soon,

Stonington, a scenic town on Deer Isle, Penobscot Bay, Maine

◁ **Craggy Bass Harbor Head, a picturesque spot in Acadia National Park, Maine** large settlements had also grown up in Boston, Rhode Island, Connecticut, New Hampshire, and Maine.

As the colonists became more prosperous and self-sufficient, their resentment of British control and British taxes increased. The turning point came with the "Boston Tea Party" in 1773, when three British ships arrived at Boston Harbor laden with tea. About 60 local leaders, disguised as Indians, boarded the ships and dumped 342 tea chests, valued at £18,000, into the harbor as an act of defiance against an oppressive regime.

Meanwhile, locals had begun stockpiling arms in the countryside. In 1775, when British soldiers were sent to Concord to destroy these caches, American patriots (known as "Minutemen" for their ability to muster at a moment's notice) repelled them at Concord and nearby Lexington. They had been tipped off by a dramatic "midnight" horseback ride from Boston

Minute Man **statue in Concord**

by Paul Revere. The American Revolution had begun, with the first major battle at Bunker Hill in Boston on June 17, 1775. The Declaration of Independence, signed by Colonial leaders in Philadelphia on July 4, 1776, announced the birth of a new nation.

In the 19th century, New England's maritime trade grew more lucrative, as ships plied between the region's harbors and the West Indies, Europe, and the Far East. The whaling industry reached its zenith at this time, and cotton and wool manufacturing also flourished.

New England's role in 19th-century America was not merely one of economic powerhouse. It was the cultural heart of the nation as well. Boston was the center of a strong protest against slavery. Instigated by a newspaper called *The Liberator*, the so-called abolitionist movement set up what came to be known as the Underground Railroad which provided escape routes for fleeing slaves.

PEOPLE & CULTURE

New England has continued to play an important role in the life of the nation. It was this region that produced the first flowering of American culture, with influential 19th-century literary giants such as Henry David Thoreau, Herman Melville, Nathaniel Hawthorne, and Mark Twain. All these writers won international recognition and acclaim. The literary tradition still lives on in New England, led by such outstanding

---

KEY DATES IN HISTORY

1614 John Smith explores the Northeast coast

1620 The Pilgrims land at Plymouth

1630 Group of Puritans settle in Boston

1636 Harvard, America's first college, founded

1692 Salem witch trials begin

1770 British soldiers kill 5 in Boston Massacre

1773 New taxes spur Boston Tea Party

1774 British close Boston Harbor

1775 Battles at Concord and Lexington mark beginning of Revolutionary War

1776 Continental Congress ratifies Declaration of Independence

1783 Treaty of Paris ends Revolutionary War

1820 Maine breaks away from Massachusetts and becomes 20th state

1831 Abolitionist William Lloyd Garrison publishes first edition of anti-slavery newspaper

1851 Herman Melville publishes *Moby Dick*

1884 Mark Twain publishes *The Adventures of Huckleberry Finn*

1897 Country's first subway opens in Boston

1961 John F. Kennedy becomes president

1999 John F. Kennedy Jr. dies in plane crash off Martha's Vineyard

2004 Boston hosts Democratic National Convention

Harvard University's Widener Library, the third largest library in the United States

The New England shoreline, a haven for water sports

contemporary talents as John Updike, Saul Bellow, and Stephen King, who are all residents of this region. The beauty and majesty of the landscape, which inspired some of America's best-known creative spirits, such as the poet Robert Frost and the painters Norman Rockwell and Grandma Moses, still continues to exert its charm on contemporary artists, such as Sabra Field and photographer Nanocole.

In 1636, Harvard College was founded in Boston, making it the birthplace of higher education in America. Today, the region's concentration of educational institutions, including famous Ivy League universities such as Yale, and Brown, is a magnet for some of America's best and brightest.

By the mid-19th century, New England's population, which had earlier been quite homogenous, changed dramatically as waves of Irish immigrants arrived, driven from their homeland by the potato famines in the 1840s. Immigrants from Italy, Portugal, and Eastern Europe also arrived, flocking to the textile mills which had boomed in New England just after the Industrial Revolution. They have left a lasting impact on the region's social life and

politics, many of them ascending to the top of New England's social hierarchy – a fact that became evident to the country with the election of the Boston-born Democrat John F. Kennedy (1917–63) in 1960 as the very first Roman Catholic president of America. Nevertheless, even today there is a special cachet in New England's society for people known as "Boston Brahmins" popularly called WASPS (White Anglo-Saxon Protestants) – descendants of the earliest British settlers.

While industrialization and urbanization have left their stamp on the region, New England's stunning physical beauty still remains. The craggy coastline of Maine, the beautiful beaches located in Cape Cod, the picturesque Vermont villages, the magnificent mountains and forests of New Hampshire, and the places of historic interest found across the region attract thousands of visitors. In recent years, the growth of hi-tech industries in the area has brought a new dynamism and prosperity to New England. This seems fitting, since it was the area's natural beauty that convinced the early settlers of New England's viable future.

National Monument of Forefathers, Plymouth

Exploring New England

THE SIX STATES of New England offer a diverse array of attractions. Vermont is famous for its ski resorts and rolling farmland, New Hampshire for its dense forests and spectacular passes through the White Mountains, and Maine for its rugged coastline and vast tracts of wilderness. Farther south, Massachusetts is rich in history, culture, and scenic beaches, Connecticut in picture-postcard villages, and Rhode Island in opulent mansions. The entire New England region boasts a dazzling display of fall foliage.

KEY

- ✈ Airport
- — Highway
- — Major road
- — Railroad
- – – State line
- ▪▪▪ International border

SEE ALSO

- *Practical Information* pp174–5
- *Where to Stay* pp176–81
- *Where to Eat* pp182–5

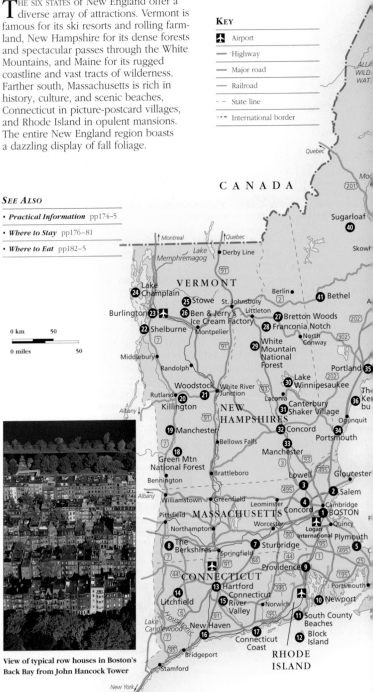

CANADA

Quebec

Montreal | Quebec

Lake Memphremagog | Derby Line

VERMONT

Lake Champlain 24

Burlington 23 ✈

22 Shelburne

25 Stowe | St. Johnsbury | Berlin

26 Ben & Jerry's Ice Cream Factory | Littleton

Montpelier | 27 Bretton Woods

28 Franconia Notch

29 White Mountain National Forest | North Conway

Middlebury

Randolph

Sugarloaf 40

Skowh

Bethel 41

Portland 35

Woodstock | White River Junction

Rutland | 21 | 20 | Lake Winnipesaukee 30

Killington | Laconia

Albany | NEW HAMPSHIRE | 31 Canterbury Shaker Village

19 Manchester | 32 Concord

Bellows Falls | 34 Portsmouth

18 Green Mtn National Forest | 33 Manchester | Ogunquit

Bennington | Brattleboro | Lowell | Gloucester

Albany | Williamstown | Greenfield | Leominster | Concord | 3 | 2 Salem

Pittsfield | MASSACHUSETTS | 4 | Cambridge 1 BOSTON

Northampton | Worcester | Logan International | Quincy

8 The Berkshires | Springfield | 7 Sturbridge | Plymouth

CONNECTICUT | Providence 9

14 Litchfield | 13 Hartford | Portsmouth

15 Connecticut River Valley | Norwich | ✈

Lake Candlewood | New Haven | 11 South County Beaches

16 | 17 Connecticut Coast | 12 Block Island | 10 Newport

Bridgeport | RHODE ISLAND

Stamford

New York

View of typical row houses in Boston's Back Bay from John Hancock Tower

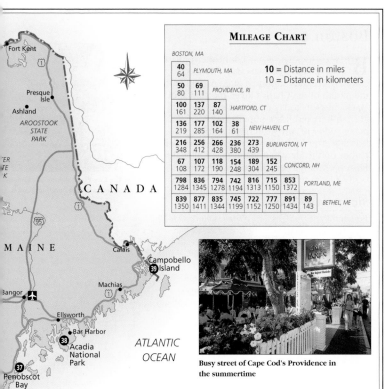

MILEAGE CHART

BOSTON, MA								
40 / 64	PLYMOUTH, MA							**10** = Distance in miles
50 / 80	**69** / 111	PROVIDENCE, RI						**10** = Distance in kilometers
100 / 161	**137** / 220	**87** / 140	HARTFORD, CT					
136 / 219	**177** / 285	**102** / 164	**38** / 61	NEW HAVEN, CT				
216 / 348	**256** / 412	**266** / 428	**236** / 380	**273** / 439	BURLINGTON, VT			
67 / 108	**107** / 172	**118** / 190	**154** / 248	**189** / 304	**152** / 245	CONCORD, NH		
798 / 1284	**836** / 1345	**794** / 1278	**742** / 1194	**816** / 1313	**715** / 1150	**853** / 1372	PORTLAND, ME	
839 / 1350	**877** / 1411	**835** / 1344	**745** / 1199	**722** / 1152	**777** / 1250	**891** / 1434	**89** / 143	BETHEL, ME

Busy street of Cape Cod's Providence in the summertime

SIGHTS AT A GLANCE

Boston ●

BOSTON IS LOCATED ON THE northeastern Atlantic Coast on Massachusetts Bay. Founded in the early 17th century around a large natural harbor at the mouth of the Charles River, the capital of Massachussetts today covers an area of 49 sq miles (127 sq km) and has a population of 556,000. It is a major center of American history, culture, and learning. The central city is focused around the harbor on the Shawmut Peninsula, while Greater Boston encompasses the surrounding area.

The City Place atrium, Massachuset State Transport Building, Boston

SIGHTS AT A GLANCE

SEE ALSO

A   B   C

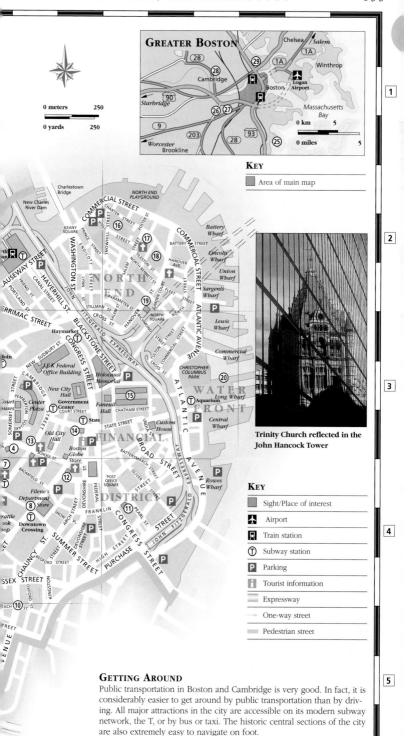

GREATER BOSTON

Chelsea · Salem · Winthrop · Cambridge · Starbridge · Logan Airport · Boston · Massachusetts Bay · Worcester · Brookline

0 km 5
0 miles 5

KEY

Area of main map

Trinity Church reflected in the John Hancock Tower

KEY

Sight/Place of interest

✈ Airport

🚂 Train station

Ⓣ Subway station

P Parking

ℹ Tourist information

Expressway

→ One-way street

Pedestrian street

GETTING AROUND

Public transportation in Boston and Cambridge is very good. In fact, it is considerably easier to get around by public transportation than by driving. All major attractions in the city are accessible on its modern subway network, the T, or by bus or taxi. The historic central sections of the city are also extremely easy to navigate on foot.

Beacon Hill ①

T HE SOUTH SLOPE OF BEACON HILL WAS, from the 1790s to the 1870s, Boston's most sought-after neighborhood, until its wealthy elite decamped to the more exclusive Back Bay. Many of the district's houses were designed by the influential architect Charles Bulfinch (1763–1844) and his disciples, and the south slope evolved as a textbook example of Federal architecture. The finest houses are either on Boston Common or perched on top of the hill, offering fine views. Though the earlier houses were set well back from the street, the economic depression of 1807–12 resulted in row houses being built right out to the street.

Beacon Street
The fine Federal-style mansions here, some with ornate reliefs, overlook the beautiful green expanse of Boston Common.

Louisburg Square
The crowning glory of the Beacon Hill district, this square was developed in the 1830s. Today, it is still Boston's most desirable address.

Charles Street Meeting House was built in the early 19th century to house a congregation of Baptists.

Mount Vernon Street, with its gracious mansions, was described by novelist Henry James in the 1890s as "the most civilized street in America."

PINCKNEY STREET

LOUISBURG SQUARE

MOUNT VERNON STREET

CEDAR STREET

CHARLES STREET

CHESTNUT STREET

SPRUCE STREET

BEACON ST

DE LUCA'S MARKET

"FRESHEST BY FAR SINCE 1905"

Back Bay and South End

0 meters 50

0 yards 50

KEY

– – – Suggested route

STAR SIGHTS

★ **Charles Street**

★ **Nichols House Museum**

★ **Charles Street**
This elegant street is lined with antique stores, fine restaurants, and gourmet groceries. At its top end are two groups of striking Greek Revival row houses.

★ **Nichols House Museum**
This small museum offers an insight into the life and times of Beacon Hill resident Rose Nichols, who lived here from 1885 to 1960.

WALNUT STREET

→ **Massachusetts State House**

Hepzibah Swan Houses
Bulfinch designed these three elegant houses for the daughters of a wealthy Beacon Hill proprietress.

Black Heritage Trail ②

Map C3. 🚶 *tours by National Park Service Rangers, (617) 742-5415.*

In the first US census in 1790, Massachusetts was the only state to record no slaves. During the 1800s, Boston's large free African-American community lived principally on the north slope of Beacon Hill and in the adjacent West End. Free walking tours of several key sites associated with this community, linked by the Black Heritage Trail, are led by the National Park Service Rangers departing from the Robert Gould Shaw Memorial on Boston Common. The sights include safe houses for escaped slaves and the **African Meeting House**, the country's oldest black church. Dedicated in 1806, the building's simple interior once rang with the passionate oratory of abolitionists such as Frederick Douglass and William Lloyd Garrison, who founded the New England Anti-Slavery Society in 1832.

🏛 **African Meeting House**
8 Smith Court. 📞 *(617) 725-0022.*
⊙ *10am–4pm Mon–Sat; Jun–Aug: also 10am–4pm Sun.*
● *public hols.* 🅿 ✔
🆆 *www.afroammuseum.org*

Boston Common & Public Garden ③

Map C4. Ⓣ Park St, Boylston St, Arlington. ⊙ *24 hrs.* **Visitor Center** 146 Tremont St, (617) 426-3115. ⊙ *8:30am–5pm Mon–Fri, 9am–5pm Sat–Sun.* 🆆 *www.bostonusa.com*

The city's most beautiful green space, the 48-acre (19-ha) Boston Common was established in 1634. For two centuries it served as a common pasture, gallows site, and a military camp and drill ground. By the 19th century, it had become a center for open-air civic activity and remains so to this day. At the northeastern edge of the Common is the **Robert Shaw Memorial**, with a magnificent relief depicting the first free

black regiment in the Union Army during the Civil War, and their white colonel, Robert Shaw. In the southeastern corner is the Central Burying Ground, dating from 1756, with graves of British and American casualties from the historic Battle of Bunker Hill in 1775 *(see p149).*

Southwest of the Common is the more formal 24-acre (10-ha) Public Garden, designed in English style in 1869. Amid its beautifully tended lawns and flowerbeds is a superb bronze equestrian statue of George Washington. A path leads from the statue to a serene lagoon, spanned by the miniature, ornamental Lagoon Bridge. Visitors can explore the lagoon on the delightful Swan Boats.

Bronze statue of George Washington in the Public Garden

Boston Athenaeum ④

Map D3. 10 Beacon St. 📞 *(617) 227-0270.* Ⓣ *Park St.* ⊙ *9am–8pm Mon, 9am–5:30pm Tue–Fri; Sep–May: 9am–4pm Sat.*
🆆 *www.bostonathenaeum.org*

Housed in an elegant Palladian-style building, this library's treasures include George Washington's personal library and the theological library given by King William III of England to the King's Chapel *(see p140).* The Athenaeum's collection, first organized in 1807, originally included many fine paintings. These were later donated to the Museum of Fine Arts *(see p146)* when that was set up.

The Freedom Trail ⑤

BOSTON HAS MORE SITES directly related to the American Revolution than any other city. The most important of these sites, as well as some associated with the city's history, have been linked together as "The Freedom Trail." This 2.5-mile (4-km) walking route, marked in red on the sidewalks, starts at Boston Common, weaves through the central city and Old Boston, and ends at Bunker Hill in Charlestown.

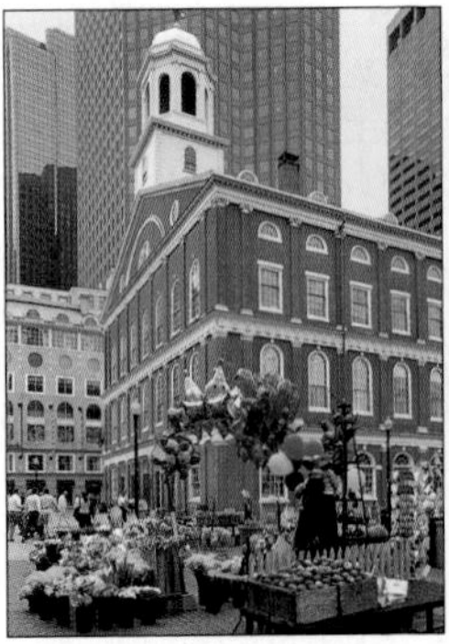

Faneuil Hall, popularly known as the "Cradle of Liberty"

Central City

The Freedom Trail starts at the Visitor Information Center on Boston Common ① *(see pp135)*. This is where angry colonials rallied against their British masters and where the British forces were encamped during the 1775–76 military occupation. Political speakers still expound from their soapboxes here. Walking toward the northwest corner of the Common provides a wonderful view of the Massachusetts State House ② *(see pp138–9)*, located on Beacon Street. It was built as the new center of state governance after the Revolution. Along Park Street, at the end of the Common, is Park Street Church ③ *(see p139)*, built in 1810 and a bulwark of the anti-slavery movement. Adjacent to it, the Granary Burying Ground ④, is the final resting place of patriots John Hancock and Paul Revere. Continuing along Tremont Street you will come to King's Chapel and Burying Ground ⑤ *(see p140)*. The tiny cemetery is Boston's oldest, while King's Chapel was the principal Anglican church in Puritan Boston. The box pew on the right, just inside the front entrance, was reserved for condemned prisoners to hear their last sermons before going to the gallows on Boston Common.

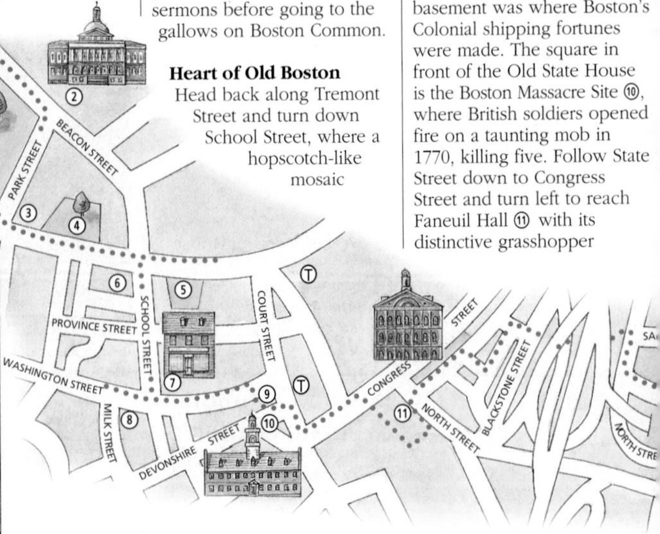

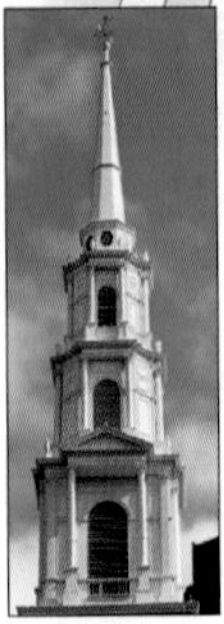

Steeple of Park Street Church

Heart of Old Boston

Head back along Tremont Street and turn down School Street, where a hopscotch-like mosaic embedded in the sidewalk marks the site of the First Public School ⑥, established in 1635. At the bottom of the street is the Boston Globe Store ⑦, a landmark which is more associated with Boston's literary flowering than with the Revolution. To its south on Washington Street is the Old South Meeting House ⑧ *(see p140)*, a graceful, white-spired brick church, modeled on Sir Christopher Wren's English country churches. A few blocks along, the Old State House ⑨ *(see p141)* presides over the head of State Street. The Colonial government building, it also served as the first state legislature, and the merchants' exchange in the basement was where Boston's Colonial shipping fortunes were made. The square in front of the Old State House is the Boston Massacre Site ⑩, where British soldiers opened fire on a taunting mob in 1770, killing five. Follow State Street down to Congress Street and turn left to reach Faneuil Hall ⑪ with its distinctive grasshopper weathervane. Though built primarily as Boston's first central marketplace, it was also known as "Cradle of Liberty." The red stripe of the Freedom Trail points the way to the North End and the Paul Revere House ⑫. This is Boston's oldest house, home to the man known for his "midnight ride" *(see p142)*.

The North End

Following the Freedom Trail through the North End, allow time to try some of the Italian cafés and bakeries along

Hanover Street. Cross through the Paul Revere Mall to reach Old North Church ⑬ *(see p142)*, whose spire is instantly visible over the shoulder of the equestrian statue of Paul Revere. In 1775, two lanterns hung in the belfry signaled the advance of British troops on Lexington and Concord. The crest of Copp's Hill lies close by on Hull Street. Some of Boston's earliest gallows were here, and people would gather below to watch the hangings of heretics and pirates. Much of the hilltop is covered by Copp's Hill Burying Ground ⑭, established in 1660 *(see p142)*.

Charlestown

Cross the iron bridge over the Charles River, which links the North End in Boston with City Square in Charlestown, and turn right, following the Freedom Trail along Water Street to the Charlestown Navy Yard ⑮. Berthed alongside Pier 1 is the USS *Constitution (see p149)*. In the War of 1812, she earned the nickname "Old Ironsides" for the resilience of her live oak hull against cannon fire. The granite obelisk that towers above the Charlestown waterfront is Bunker Hill Monument ⑯ *(see p149)*.

KEY

····· Walk route

[T] Subway station

ℹ Tourist information

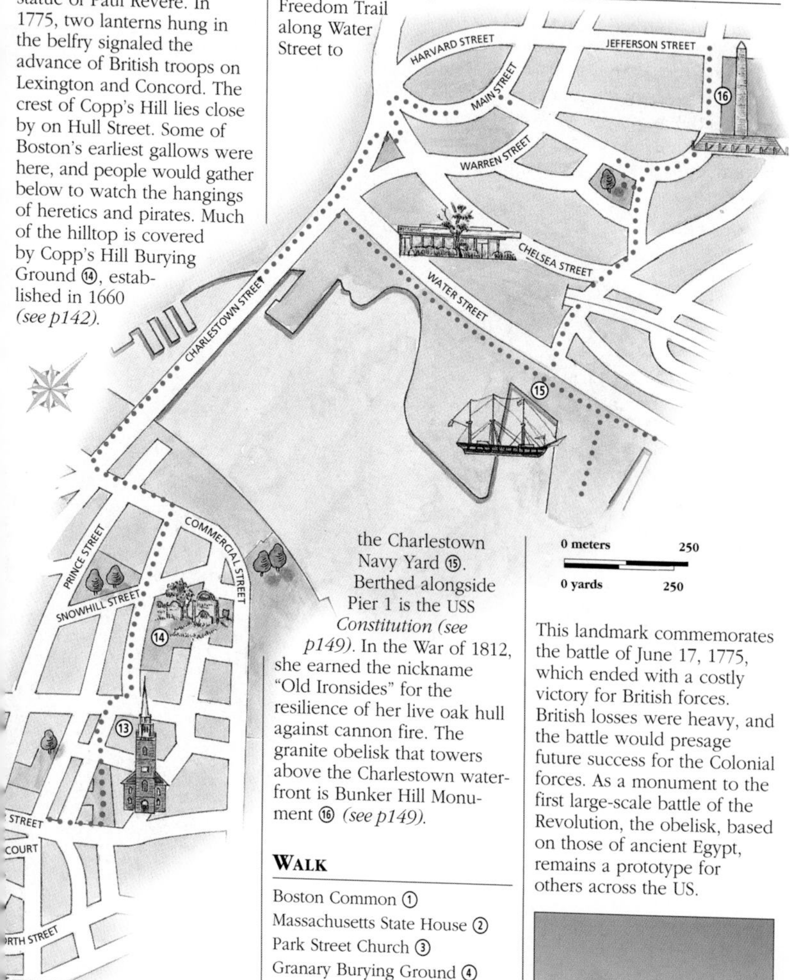

0 meters 250

0 yards 250

This landmark commemorates the battle of June 17, 1775, which ended with a costly victory for British forces. British losses were heavy, and the battle would presage future success for the Colonial forces. As a monument to the first large-scale battle of the Revolution, the obelisk, based on those of ancient Egypt, remains a prototype for others across the US.

WALK

Boston Common ①
Massachusetts State House ②
Park Street Church ③
Granary Burying Ground ④
King's Chapel & Burying Ground ⑤
First Public School ⑥
Boston Globe Store ⑦
Old South Meeting House ⑧
Old State House ⑨
Boston Massacre Site ⑩
Faneuil Hall ⑪
Paul Revere House ⑫
Old North Church ⑬
Copp's Hill Burying Ground ⑭
Charlestown Navy Yard & the USS *Constitution* ⑮
Bunker Hill Monument ⑯

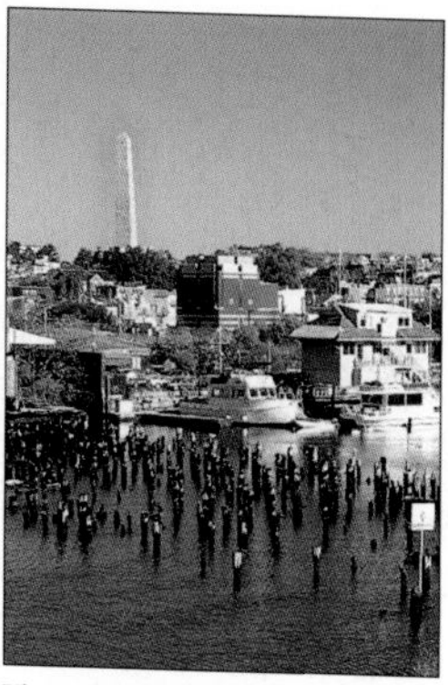

View of Bunker Hill Monument from Charlestown harbor

TIPS FOR WALKERS

Map C4. ***Starting point:*** *Boston Common. Maps available at Boston Common Visitor Center.*
Length: *2.5 miles (4 km).*
Getting there: *Park Street Station ([T] Green and Red lines) to start. State (Orange and Blue lines) and Haymarket (Orange and Green lines). [T] stations can be found on route. Visitors should follow red stripe on sidewalk for the full route.*

Massachusetts State House ⑥

THE CORNERSTONE OF THE Massachusetts State House was laid in 1795 by Paul Revere and Samuel Adams. Completed in 1798, the Charles Bulfinch-designed center of state government served as a model for the US Capitol building in Washington and as an inspiration for many other state capitols. Later additions were made, but the original building remains the archetype of American government buildings. Its gilded dome serves as the zero-mile marker for Massachusetts.

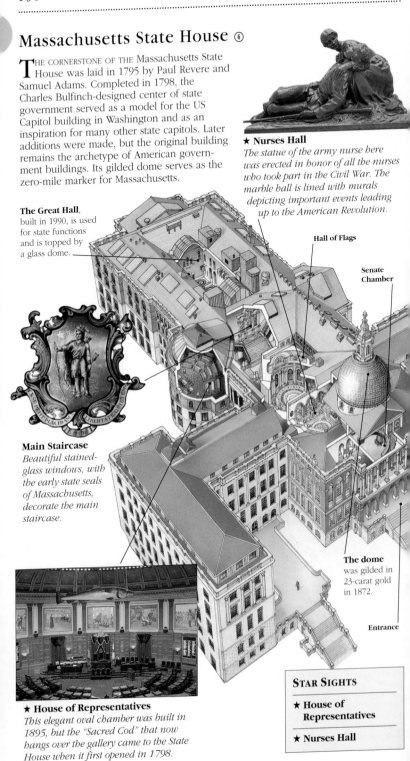

★ Nurses Hall
The statue of the army nurse here was erected in honor of all the nurses who took part in the Civil War. The marble hall is lined with murals depicting important events leading up to the American Revolution.

The Great Hall, built in 1990, is used for state functions and is topped by a glass dome.

Hall of Flags

Senate Chamber

Main Staircase
Beautiful stained-glass windows, with the early state seals of Massachusetts, decorate the main staircase.

The dome was gilded in 23-carat gold in 1872.

Entrance

★ House of Representatives
This elegant oval chamber was built in 1895, but the "Sacred Cod" that now hangs over the gallery came to the State House when it first opened in 1798.

STAR SIGHTS

★ House of Representatives

★ Nurses Hall

Senate Chamber
Situated directly beneath the dome, this chamber features a beautiful sunburst ceiling.

The Wings, added in 1917, are thought by many to sit incongruously with the rest of the structure.

Hall of Flags
Flags carried into battle by regiments from the state of Massachusetts are displayed here beneath a stained-glass skylight, depicting seals of the original 13 colonies.

Park Street Church ⑦

Map D4.1 Park St. **C** *(617) 523-3383.* Ⓣ *Park St.* ☐ *mid-Jun–Aug: 9:30am–3:30pm Tue–Sat; Sep–mid-Jun: by appointment.* ☒ Ⓦ *www.parkstreet.org*

SINCE ITS DEDICATION in 1810, the Park Street Church has been one of Boston's most influential pulpits. In 1829, the firebrand crusader for the abolition of slavery, William Lloyd Garrison, gave his first abolition speech here; and in 1893 the anthem *America the Beautiful* debuted at Sunday service in this church. The church, with its 217-ft (65-m) steeple was designed by the English architect Peter Banner, who actually adapted a design by the earlier English architect, Christopher Wren.

Adjacent to the church, on Tremont Street, is the mid-17th century **Granary Burying Ground**, which was once the site of a grain storage facility. Among those buried in this historic cemetery are three important signatories to the Declaration of Independence – Samuel Adams, John Hancock, and Robert Paine, as well as one of the city's most famous sons, the patriot Paul Revere.

⚰ Old Granary Burying Ground

Tremont St. ☐ *8am–4:30pm daily.*

Downtown Crossing ⑧

Map D4. Washington, Winter, & Summer Sts. Ⓣ *Downtown Crossing.*

THIS LIVELY pedestrian shopping district, crowded with sidewalk stalls and vendors' carts, is dominated by department stores. Among them are the well-known nationwide chain Macy's, and Filene's with its famous Bargain Basement. Another well-known store in the area is Brattle Book Shop, founded in 1825. This bibliophiles' treasure house stocks more than 250,000 rare, used, and out-of-print books and magazines.

Theater District ⑨

Map C4. Ⓣ *Boylston, New England Medical Center.*

BOSTON'S FIRST theater opened in 1793 on Federal Street. Fifty years later, with patronage from the city's elite, Boston had become a major tryout town and boasted several lavish theaters. Many major US premieres were held here, among them Handel's *Messiah*, and Tennessee Williams' *A Streetcar Named Desire*. Among the grandest theaters are the opulent **Colonial Theater**, decorated with frescos and friezes; the 1,650-seat **Shubert Theater**, with its imposing Neo-Classical façade; and the **Wang Center for the Performing Arts**, with a glittering seven-story auditorium.

☷ Colonial Theater

106 Boylston St. **C** *(617) 426-9366.* ☐ *phone to check.* ☒ Ⓦ *www.broadwayinboston.com*

Chinatown ⑩

Map D5. Bounded by Kingston, Kneeland, Washington, & Essex Sts. Ⓣ *Chinatown.*

THIS IS THE third largest Chinatown in the US, after those in San Francisco and New York. Pagoda-topped telephone booths set the tone of the neighborhood, which is full of restaurants, and stores selling garments and Chinese medicine. Boston's Chinese colony was fully established by the turn of the 19th century, and in recent years the area's population has swelled with new arrivals from Korea, Vietnam, and Cambodia.

Typical store and restaurant façades in Boston's Chinatown

Telephone Men and Women at Work, Verizon Building

Verizon Building ⑪

Map E4.185 Franklin St. 🇨 *(617) 743-4747.* Ⓣ *State, Aquarium.* **Museum** ⭘ *24 hours daily.* ♿

THIS IMPRESSIVE Art Deco building, dating to 1947, is renowned for the monumental 160-ft- (49-m-) long mural in its lobby, *Telephone Men and Women at Work*. This remarkable work of art, created by Dean Cornwell, is peopled with 197 life-size figures. At the street level is a small museum which re-creates Alexander Graham Bell's laboratory, where he invented the telephone. A native of Scotland, Bell (1847–1922) moved to Boston in 1871 to teach speech to the deaf, but in his spare time worked on an apparatus for transmitting sound by electric current. The first demonstration of the "telephone" took place in Boston in May 1876. On the building's northern side is the Post Office Square.

Old South Meeting House ⑫

Map D4. 310 Washington St. 🇨 *(617) 482-6439.* Ⓣ *Park St, State, Government Center.* ⭘ *Apr–Oct: 9:30am–5pm daily; Nov–Mar: 10am–4pm daily.* 🎦 ♿ Ⓦ *www.oldsouthmeetinghouse.org*

BUILT FOR Puritan religious services in 1729, this edifice, with a tall octagonal steeple, had Colonial Boston's biggest capacity for town meetings. From 1765 on, it became the venue for large and vociferous crowds, led by a group of merchants called "the Sons of Liberty" to gather in protest against British taxation and the hated Stamp Act. During a protest rally on December 16, 1773, the fiery speechmaker Samuel Adams flashed the signal that led to the Boston Tea Party *(see p143)* at Griffin's Wharf several hours later. The British retaliated by turning Old South into an officers' tavern and a stable for army horses. Today, the Meeting House holds lectures, concerts, and a multimedia show, which relives those raucous days. The shop sells the ubiquitous tins of "Boston Tea Party" tea.

King's Chapel & Burying Ground ⑬

Map D3. 58 Tremont St. 🇨 *(617) 523-1749.* Ⓣ *Park St, State, Government Center.* ⭘ *Jul–Aug: 9am–4pm Mon & Thu–Sat, 1–3pm Sun; Apr–Jun & Sep–Oct: 10am–3pm Mon, Fri & Sat; Nov–Mar: 10am–3pm Sat.* Ⓦ *www.kings-chapel.org*

Alexander Graham Bell

THE FIRST CHAPEL on this site was built in 1689, but when the Governor of New England decided that a larger church was needed, the present granite edifice was begun in 1749. It was constructed around the original wooden chapel, which was then dismantled and heaved out of the windows of its replacement. High ceilings and open arches enhance the sense of spaciousness and light inside the chapel. Its other notable features include a pulpit shaped like a wine glass, dating to 1717, and a huge bell that was re-cast by the foundry of Revolutionary hero Paul Revere *(see p142)*.

The cemetery adjacent to the chapel is Boston's oldest. Among those buried here is Elizabeth Pain, the inspiration for the adultress Hester Prynne in Nathaniel Hawthorne's famous moralistic novel, *The Scarlet Letter*.

The simply decorated interior of King's Chapel on Tremont Street

Old State House ⑭

Map D3. Washington & State Sts.
📞 (617) 720-1713. Ⓣ State.
🕐 9am–5pm daily. 📷 ♿ 🚻
🌐 www.bostonhistory.org

Now dwarfed by the towers of the Financial District, the Old State House was the seat of the British Colonial government between 1713 and 1776. The royal lion and unicorn still decorate each corner of its eastern façade. After independence, the Massachusetts legislature took possession of the building, and it has had many uses since, including a produce market, Masonic Lodge, and Boston City Hall. Its wine cellars now function as a subway station, and the building houses two floors of historic memorabilia of the Bostonian Society.

In 1776, the Declaration of Independence was read from the balcony on the East Façade. A circle of cobblestones below the balcony marks the site of the Boston Massacre. On March 5, 1770, an unruly mob of colonists taunted British guardsmen with insults, rocks, and snowballs. The soldiers opened fire, killing five colonists. After the Boston Tea Party, this was one of the most inflammatory events leading up to the American Revolution *(see p44)*.

Old State House amid the skyscrapers of the Financial District

The tower is a classic example of Colonial style.

A gilded eagle, symbol of America, is on the west façade.

The Central Staircase, with its two spiraling wooden handrails, is a fine example of 18th-century workmanship.

The East Façade still has the royal British lion and unicorn symbol on each corner. It is adorned with a beautiful clock dating to the 1820s.

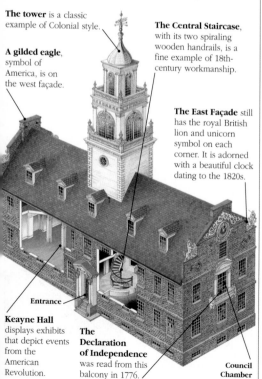

Entrance

Keayne Hall displays exhibits that depict events from the American Revolution.

The Declaration of Independence was read from this balcony in 1776.

Council Chamber

Greek Revival Custom House tower, one of Boston's most striking sights

Quincy Market ⑮

Map E3. Between Chatham & Clinton Sts. 📞 (617) 523-1300. Ⓣ Government Center, State. 🕐 10am–9pm Mon–Sat, noon–6pm Sun. ♿
🌐 www.faneuilhallmarketplace.com

This immensely popular shopping and dining complex attracts nearly 14 million people every year. It was developed from the old buildings of the city's meat, fish, and produce markets, which were beautifully restored in the 1970s. The 535-ft- (163-m-) long Greek Revival-style colonnaded hall is now filled with fast-food stands, and a comedy nightclub is located in the spectacular central rotunda. Completing the ensemble are the twin North and South Market buildings, refurbished to house boutiques, restaurants, and business offices.

A short distance southeast of Quincy Market is the **Custom House** with its Greek Revival tower. When first completed in 1847 this building had a skylit dome. The 495-ft (150m) tower with a four-sided clock was built in 1915 and for much of the 20th century was Boston's only skyscraper. There is a museum of maritime history in the rotunda.

🏛 **Custom House**
3 McKinley Square. 📞 (617) 310-6300. **Museum** 🕐 8am–11pm daily. 🌐 www.marriott.com/vacationclub

Slate tombstones of Boston's early settlers, Copp's Hill Burying Ground

Copp's Hill Burying Ground ⑯

Map E2. Entrances at Charter & Hull Sts. Ⓣ *Government Center, N Station.* ◻ *8am–5pm daily.*

EXISTING SINCE 1659, this is Boston's second oldest cemetery, after the one by King's Chapel *(see p140).* Among those buried here are Robert Newton, the sexton who hung Paul Revere's signal lanterns in the belfry of the Old North Church, influential Colonial period Puritan ministers, as well as hundreds of black slaves and freedmen.

During the British occupation of Boston, King George lll's troops were said to have used the slate headstones for target practice, and pockmarks from their musket balls are still visible. Copp's Hill Terrace, directly across Charter Street, is the site where, in 1919, a 2.3 million-gallon tank of molasses exploded, drowning 21 people in a huge, syrupy tidal wave.

Old North Church ⑰

Map E2.193 Salem St. Ⓒ *(617) 523-6676.* Ⓣ *Haymarket, Aquarium, N Station.* ◻ *daily.* ✝ *9am, 11am & 4pm Sun (also 5pm Jul–Aug).* ♿ ✉ *Jun–Aug: "Behind the Scenes Tour."* ⓦ *www.oldnorth.com*

OFFICIALLY NAMED Christ Episcopal Church, the Old North Church, which dates from 1723, is Boston's oldest surviving religious edifice. It is built of brick in the Georgian style, similar to that of St. Andrew's-by-the-Wardrobe in Blackfriars, London, designed by Sir Christopher Wren. The church was made famous on April 18, 1775, when sexton Robert Newman, aiding Paul Revere, hung a pair of lanterns in the belfry. These were to warn the patriots in Charlestown of the westward departure of British troops, on their way to engage the revolutionaries.

An imposing marble bust of George Washington, dating from 1815, adorns the church interior, which has unusual high-sided box pews. These were designed to enclose footwarmers, which were filled with hot coals or bricks during wintry weather. The tower contains the first set of church bells made in North America, cast in 1745. The top of the bell tower offers panoramic views of the beautiful city.

Paul Revere Mall ⑱

Map E2. Hanover St. Ⓣ *Haymarket, Aquarium.* ♿

THIS BRICK-PAVED plaza, between Hanover and Unity Streets, provides a precious stretch of open space in the crowded neighborhood of the North End, populated largely by people of Italian descent. Laid out in 1933, its focal point is an equestrian statue of Paul Revere (1735–1818). Benches, a fountain, and twin rows of linden trees give the space, much used by local people, a distinctly European feel. South of the Mall is busy Hanover Street, which is lined with Italian eateries.

Paul Revere House ⑲

Map E2.19 N Square. Ⓒ *(617) 523-2338.* Ⓣ *Haymarket, Aquarium.* ◻ *mid-Apr–Oct: 9:30am–5:15pm daily; Nov–mid-Apr: 9:30am–4:15pm daily.* ♿ ⓦ *www.paulreverehouse.org*

BOSTON'S OLDEST surviving clapboard frame house is historically significant, for it was here in 1775 that Paul Revere began his legendary horseback ride to warn his compatriots in Lexington *(see p149)* of the impending arrival of British troops. This historic event was later immortalized by Henry Wadsworth Longfellow *(see p148)* in his epic poem which begins, "Listen, my children, and you shall hear of the midnight ride of Paul Revere."

A versatile gold- and silversmith, and maker of church bells and cannons, Revere lived here from 1770 to 1800. Small leaded casement windows, an overhanging upper story, and nail-studded front door make the house a fine example of 18th-century Early American architecture. Three rooms in the house contain artifacts and furniture made in Revere's workshop. In the courtyard is a large bronze bell cast by Revere, who is known to have made nearly 200 church bells.

Paul Revere House, where Paul Revere began his midnight ride

Waterfront ⑳

Map E3. Atlantic Ave. **New England Aquarium** Central Wharf..
🎫 (617) 973-5200. Ⓣ Aquarium.
◻ Sep–Jun: 9am–5pm Mon–Fri, 9am–6pm Sat & Sun; Jul–Sep: 9am–6pm Mon, Tue, Fri, 9am–8pm Wed & Thu, 9am–7pm Sat & Sun. 🎫
♿ 🎫 📷 💻 🅦 www.neaq.org
Boston Tea Party Ship Congress St Bridge. 🎫 (617) 338-1773. Ⓣ South Station. ◻ Jun–Sep: 9am–6pm daily; Oct–May: 9am–5pm daily. 🎫
🅦 www.historictours.com/boston
Children's Museum 300 Congress St. 🎫 (617) 426-8855. Ⓣ S Station. ◻ mid-Jun–Aug: 10am–5pm Sat–Thu, 10am–9pm Fri; Sep–mid-Jun: 10am–5pm Tue–Sun. 🎫 ♿
🅦 www.bostonkids.org

BOSTON'S WATERFRONT is one of the city's most fascinating areas. Fringed by wharves and warehouses – a reminder of the city's past as a key trading port – its attractions include a famous aquarium and two fine museums.

One of the largest wharves is **Long Wharf**, established in 1710. Once extending 2,000 ft (610 m) into Boston Harbor and lined with shops and warehouses, it provided secure mooring for the largest ships of the time.

Harbor Walk connects Long Wharf with other adjacent wharves, dating from the early 1800s. Most of them have now been converted to fashionable harborside apartments. **Rowes Wharf**, to the south of the waterfront is a particularly fine example of such revitalization. This modern red-brick development, with opulent condominiums and offices, features a large archway that links the city to the harbor.

The waterfront's prime attraction is the **New England Aquarium**, which dominates Central Wharf. Designed in 1969, the aquarium's core encloses a vast four-story ocean tank, which houses a Caribbean coral reef and contains a wide array of marine creatures such as sharks, moray eels, barracudas, and sea turtles, as well as exotic, brightly colored tropical fish. A curving walkway runs around the outside of the tank from the top to the bottom, and provides different viewpoints of the interior at many levels.

Exotic fish, New England Aquarium

A particularly popular section of the aquarium is the Penguin Pool, which runs around the base of the ocean tank, while a recently added west wing has an outdoor tank with a lively colony of harbor seals. In 2001, the Simons IMAX® Theater was opened on the wharf, which presents changing programs of 3-D films on a giant screen. A highlight of the aquarium's programs are the boat trips from Boston Harbor, which take visitors to the whale feeding grounds far offshore. The aquarium also has a gift shop and a café with a beautiful view of the harbor.

Griffin's Wharf, where the Boston Tea Party took place on December 16, 1773, was buried beneath landfill many years ago. But a short distance south of the original site, on Fort Point Channel, the **Boston Tea Party Ship** is anchored. The ship is a Danish-built sailing brig, *Beaver II*, which resembles one of the three original British East India Company ships involved in the Tea Party protest *(see p44)*. Today, modern-day patriots toss imitation bales of tea overboard, re-creating one of the acts of defiance that prompted the British to put the Massachusetts Bay Colony under martial law. A museum on an adjacent pier displays ship models and Tea Party memorabilia.

Overlooking Fort Point Channel is a rejuvenated 19th-century wool warehouse that houses the **Children's Museum**, one of the best in the country. Its many attractions and interactive exhibits include a two-story maze, and a hands-on recyling area with barrels of materials for children to use in self-instructive creative projects. They can also weave fabrics on looms or act in kidstage plays. An international flavor is added by a visit to the silk merchant's house, transplanted from Kyoto in Japan.

View down Long Wharf toward the waterfront and Custom House

Trinity Church ㉑

Bas-relief in Chancel

ROUTINELY VOTED ONE OF America's ten finest buildings, this masterpiece by Henry Hobson Richardson dates from 1877. The church is a beautiful granite and sandstone Romanesque structure, standing on wooden piles driven through mud into bedrock, surmounted by granite pyramids. John LaFarge designed the interior, while some of the windows were designed by Edward Burne-Jones and executed by William Morris.

The Chancel
Seven beautiful windows here show the life of Christ.

★ **North Transept Windows**
Designed by Burne-Jones and executed by William Morris, the three stained-glass windows above the choir relate the story of Christmas.

The Chancel wall behind the altar has a series of gold bas-reliefs, depicting scenes from the Bible.

The Bell Tower was inspired by the Renaissance Cathedral at Salamanca, in central Spain.

★ **West Portico**
The deeply sculpted west portico is modeled after St. Trophime in Arles, France.

The pulpit is covered with carved scenes from the life of Christ as well as portraits of preachers.

North Transept Windows

West Portico

Main Entrance

STAR SIGHTS

★ **North Transept Windows**

★ **West Portico**

View over Back Bay and Charles River from the John Hancock Tower

Copley Square ㉒

Map B5. ⓉⓉ *Copley.*

NAMED AFTER the famous painter John Singleton Copley (*see p147*), Copley Square was a marsh until 1870 and took on its present form only in the late 20th century. Today, this inviting plaza is an open space of trees and fountains, and a hive of civic activity with weekly farmers' markets and concerts in summer. It is surrounded by some of Boston's most striking architecture.

The **John Hancock Tower**, constructed in 1975, anchors the southeastern side of the Square. The tallest building in New England, the 740-ft (226-m) tower's mirrored façade reflects the beautiful Trinity Church and the original (1947) Hancock Building. Unfortunately, the observatory on the 60th floor has been closed following the events of September 11, 2001.

West of the Hancock Tower, across Copley Square, is the Italian palazzo-style **Boston Public Library**, built in 1887–95. A marvel of fine wood and marble, the library has huge bronze doors, and murals by John Singer Sargent in a third-floor gallery. The vast Bates Hall on the second floor of this library is notable for its soaring barrel-vaulted ceiling. Close by, on the corner of Boylston and Dartmouth Streets, is the fabulous Italian Gothic-style **New Old South Church**, built in 1874–75.

🚇 **John Hancock Tower**
200 Clarendon St. ● *to the public.*
🚇 **Boston Public Library**
Copley Square. ▌ *(617) 536-5400.*
◯ *Apr–Sep & Oct–May: 9am–9pm Mon–Thu, 9am–5pm Fri–Sat; Oct–May: 1–5pm Sun.* ● *public hols.*
♿ ✓ Ⓦ *www.bpl.org*

Newbury Street ㉓

Map B5. Ⓣ *Arlington, Copley, Hynes Convention Center/ ICA.*

NEWBURY STREET is a Boston synonym for "stylish." Lined with high-fashion outlets, art galleries, and chic restaurants, this is a great place for people-watching. Churches provide vestiges of a more decorous era. Most notable is the **Church of the Covenant**, which contains the world's largest collection of Louis Comfort Tiffany stained-glass windows and an elaborate Tiffany lantern. At the corner of Newbury and Dartmouth Streets lies the striking Newbury Street Mural, which depicts 72 eminent Bostonians.

🕎 **Church of the Covenant**
67 Newbury St. ▌ *(617) 266-7480.*
◯ *10am Sun.* 📷 ♿ ✓ 🕎
Ⓦ *churchofthecovenant.org*

Commonwealth Avenue ㉔

Map B4. Ⓣ *Arlington, Copley, Hynes Convention Center/ ICA.*

ENVISIONED AS Boston's Champs Elysees, this avenue, 200-ft (61-m) wide, is lined with beautiful townhouses. In the second half of the 19th century, it became an arena for America's leading domestic architects, and a walk along it is like flicking through a catalog of architectural styles. One of the few grand buildings open to the public is the **Boston Center for Adult Education**. Built in 1912, it has a ballroom modeled on the Petit Trianon in Versailles, France.

The Romanesque-style **First Baptist Church**, on the corner of Commonwealth Avenue and Clarendon Street, is one of the most distinctive buildings of the city skyline. Completed in 1872, its freestanding square bell tower, modeled on Italian campaniles, is topped with a decorative frieze by Bartholdi, the sculptor who created the Statue of Liberty. The faces in the frieze, which depict the sacraments, are likenesses of prominent Bostonians of the time, among them Henry Wadsworth Longfellow and Ralph Waldo Emerson.

🚇 **Boston Center for Adult Education**
5 Commonwealth Ave. ▌ *(617) 267-4430.* ◯ *9am–7pm Mon–Thu, 9am–5pm Fri.* ● *Sat–Sun, May 11.*
📷 *for courses.* ♿ ✓
Ⓦ *www.bcae.org*
🕎 **First Baptist Church**
110 Commonwealth Ave.
▌ *(617) 267-3148.* ◯ *for Sun worship.* ♿

Greater Boston

SOUTHWEST OF CENTRAL BOSTON, what were once the marshlands of the Fenway now house two superb art museums – the Museum of Fine Arts and the Isabella Stewart Gardner Museum. West of the city, across the Charles River, is the college town of Cambridge, dominated by Harvard University. To its east is historic Charlestown, which forms a major part of Boston's Freedom Trail *(see pp136–7)*.

The dramatic structure of the John F. Kennedy Library and Museum

John F. Kennedy Library & Museum ㉕

Columbia Point, Dorchester.
📞 *(617) 514-1600.* Ⓣ *JFK/ U Mass.*
🕐 *9am–5pm daily.* ● *Jan 1, Thanksgiving, Dec 25.* 🎫 ♿ 🎥 🎧
🅆 *www.jfklibrary.org*

HOUSED IN A dramatic white concrete and black glass building designed by architect I.M. Pei, this museum chronicles the 1,000 days of the Kennedy presidency. The combination of video and film footage, papers, and memorabilia evoke the euphoria of "Camelot" as well as the numb horror of the assassination with an immediacy that is uncommon in historical museums. Some of the key chambers in the White House, including the Oval Room, are re-created here.

The house at 83 Beals Street in Brookline, where the late president was born in 1917, is now the **John F. Kennedy National Historic Site**. The Kennedy family moved to a larger house in 1921; in 1966 they repurchased this house, furnished it with their belongings circa 1917, and turned it into a memorial.

Isabella Stewart Gardner Museum ㉖

280 The Fenway. 📞 *(617) 566-1401.*
Ⓣ *MFA.* 🕐 *11am–5pm Tue–Sun.*
● *Jan 1, Thanksgiving, Dec 25.* 🎫
🎥 🎧 *call for concert schedule.*
🅆 *www.gardnermuseum.org*

THIS VENETIAN-STYLE palazzo houses a remarkable collection of over 2,500 works of art, including Old Masters and Italian Renaissance pieces. Advised by art scholar Bernard Berenson, the wealthy and strong-willed Isabella Stewart Gardner began collecting art in the late 19th century. Among the works she acquired were masterpieces by Titian, Rembrandt, and Matisse as well as by the American painters James McNeill Whistler and John Singer Sargent. The paintings, sculptures, and tapestries are displayed on three levels around the stunning skylit central courtyard.

Unfortunately, in 1990, 13 of these priceless works were stolen, including a rare Rembrandt seascape, *Storm on the Sea of Galilee*, then conservatively valued in the region of $200 million.

Museum of Fine Arts ㉗

Avenue of the Arts, 465 Huntington Ave. 📞 *(617) 267-9300.* Ⓣ *MFA.*
🕐 *10am–4:45pm Sat–Tue,*
10am–9:45pm Wed–Fri. ● *Jan 1,*
3rd Mon in Apr, Jul 4, Thanksgiving,
Dec 25. 🎫 ♿ 🎥 🎧 **Lectures,**
concerts, & films. 🍴 🖼 🛗
🅆 *www.mfa.org*

THE LARGEST ART museum in New England, and one of the five largest in the US, the Museum of Fine Arts

Central courtyard of the *palazzo*-style Isabella Stewart Gardner Museum

Japanese Temple Room, Museum of Fine Arts

MFA) has a permanent collection of approximately 500,000 objects, ranging from Egyptian artifacts to modern American paintings. Though founded in 1876, the MFA's present Classical-style building dates from 1909, with a west wing designed by I.M. Pei added in 1981. American decorative arts and paintings are on the first floor, and European art is on the second floor, while Classical, Far Eastern, and Egyptian artifacts can be seen on both floors of the museum.

The Museum of Fine Art's excellent collection of ancient **Egyptian and Nubian Art** is unparalleled outside of Africa and derives primarily from the MFA-Harvard University excavations along the Nile, which began in 1905. It also includes a wonderful collection of mummies that is located on the first floor. The adjacent gallery of Ancient Near Eastern Art exhibits Babylonian, Assyrian, and Sumerian reliefs. On the second floor are several monumental sculptures of Nubian kings, dating from the 7th to 6th centuries BC.

The MFA boasts one of America's top holdings of **Classical Art** as well. Among the highlights of this collection are Greek figured vases, carved Etruscan sarcophagi, and Roman portrait busts. Also on display are a series of wall panel paintings unearthed in Pompeii in 1901.

The collections of **Asian Art** are said to be the most extensive under one roof anywhere in the world. They include Indian sculpture and narrative paintings, and exhibitions of Islamic miniature paintings that keep changing.

A beautiful stairway with carved lions leads to the Chinese and Japanese galleries on the second floor. Outstanding exhibits here include scroll and screen paintings. A highlight of the museum is the serene **Japanese Temple Room**, on the first floor, which is known for its exquisite examples of Buddhist art.

Egyptian Mummies

The **European Art** collections date from the 16th to the 20th centuries and begin with Dutch paintings, including several portraits by Rembrandt. The Koch Gallery, with its magnificent wooden coffered ceiling, displays masterpieces by El Greco, Titian, and Rubens.

Boston's 19th-century collectors enriched the MFA with wonderful French art: the museum features several paintings by Pierre François Millet as well as by 19th-century French artists such as Edouard Manet, Pierre-August Renoir, and Edgar Degas. It also has several paintings by Van Gogh, and holds the most important Monet collection outside of Paris. One of the most popular galleries displays *La Japonaise* by Monet and *Dance at Bougival* by Renoir. Examples

of European decorative arts include medieval frescoes, 18th-century French silver, and tableware, ceramics, and glass from the 17th to the early 20th centuries.

The **American Painting Galleries** on the first floor begin with portraits by the Boston artist John Singleton Copley, perhaps America's most talented 18th-century painter. Farther on are lush society portraits by John Singer Sargent, who also embellished the museum's domed rotunda with fine murals. The large and airy Lane Gallery exhibits the works of 20th-century American masters such as Stuart Davis, Jackson Pollock, and Georgia O'Keeffe.

The exhibits in the superb **American Decorative Arts** galleries include silver tea services made by Paul Revere (see p142); 18th-century Boston-style desks, chests, and tall clocks; and reconstructed rooms from a 19th-century mansion, which evoke the well-to-do lifestyle of the Federal era. There is also a gallery of ship models and outstanding examples of contemporary crafts.

In addition to these major collections, the Museum of Fine Arts also has important holdings in the multifarious arts of Africa, Oceania, and the ancient Americas, and collections of musical instruments and manuscripts.

John Singer Sargent's murals on the domed rotunda, MFA

The simple interior of Christ Church in Cambridge

Cambridge ㉘

(T) *Harvard.* 🚌 *1, 69.* ℹ️ **Harvard Square Information Booth** *(617) 497-1630,* **Cambridge Office of Tourism** *(800) 862-5678.* 🏛️ *Sun.* 🎉 *River Festival (late Jun).* 🌐 www.harvard.edu, www.cambridge-usa.org

THOUGH PART OF the Greater Boston metropolitan area, Cambridge is a town in its own right, dominated by two world-famous universities, the **Massachusetts Institute of Technology** (MIT) and **Harvard**. It also has a number of sights associated with the American Revolution.

Among them is the historic house on Brattle Street, now known as the **Longfellow National Historic Site**. Built by Colonial-era merchants loyal to the British Crown during the Revolution, it was seized by American revolutionaries, and served as George Washington's headquarters during the Siege of Boston. From 1843 until his death in 1888 it was also the home of the famous poet Henry Wadsworth Longfellow, who wrote his most famous poems, including *The Song of Hiawatha*, here.

Harvard Square is the area's main shopping and entertainment district, full of cafés, inexpensive restaurants, trendy boutiques, and street performers. Harvard's large student population is much in evidence here, adding to the square's lively character.

Cambridge Common, north of Harvard Square, was set aside as a common pasture and military drill ground in the 1630s. It has served as a center for social, religious, and political activity ever since. The Common was used as an army encampment from 1775 to 1776, and a stone here marks the spot where George Washington took command of the Continental Army on July 3, 1775, beneath the Washington Elm. Today, its tree-shaded lawns and playgrounds are popular with families and students.

Christ Church, a short distance south of the Common, was designed in 1761 by Peter Harrison, the architect of Boston's King's Chapel *(see p140)*. In 1775, it served as a barracks for Continental Army troops, who melted down the organ pipes to cast musket balls. The church was restored for services on New Year's Eve, 1775, when George Washington and his wife were among the worshipers.

The 135-acre (55-ha) campus of the Massachusetts Institute of Technology (MIT), one of the world's leading universities in engineering and the sciences, stretches along the Charles River. Among the masterpieces of modern architecture that dot its campus are Eero Saarinen's Kresge Auditorium and Kresge Chapel, and the Wiesner Building designed by I.M. Pei, which houses a noted collection of avant-garde art in the List Visual Art Center. Art and Science are blended in the MIT Museum, with exhibits such as Harold Edgerton's strobo-scopic flash photographs and the latest holographic art.

An altogether more old-world atmosphere prevails at the campus of Harvard University, with its red-brick, ivy-covered walls. Founded in 1636, Harvard is the oldest university in the US and one of the world's most presti-gious centers of learning. At the heart of the campus, which encompasses more than 400 buildings, is the leafy **Old Harvard Yard**, dotted with student dormito-ries. Its focal point is the statue of its most famous benefactor, the cleric John Harvard. Adjacent to the statue is the imposing Widener Library which, with over 3 million volumes, is the third largest in the US. Another impressive building in the Yard is the Memorial Church, built in 1931, whose steeple is modeled on that of the Old North Church *(see p142)*. Standing out amid Harvard's Georgian-style buildings is the Carpenter Center for Visual Arts, designed by the avant-garde French architect Le Corbusier.

A major draw for visitors to Harvard are its five outstand-ing museums. The **Fogg Art Museum** focuses on master-pieces of European art from the late Middle Ages to the present. Its galleries are orga-nized around a beautiful central courtyard, modeled on

Students strolling through Harvard Yard

a 16th-century church in Montepulciano, Italy. The ground floor galleries and the two-story Warburg Hall display pre-Renaissance Italian art, including massive altarpieces, as well as 17th- and 18th-century Dutch, Flemish, English, and American art. Among the latter are unfinished studies made by John Singleton Copley *(see p147)*. On the second level are pre-Raphaelite paintings and works by John Singer Sargent.

The highlight of the Fogg Museum is its Maurice Wertheim Collection of Impressionist and Post-Impressionist art, also on the second level, with paintings by Renoir, Manet, and Degas. An adjacent gallery has modern American works, such as the minimalist paintings of Frank Stella.

The adjoining **Busch-Reisinger Museum**, entered through the second level of the Fogg Museum, displays the work of 20th-century masters such as Wassily Kandinsky, Paul Klee, and Oskar Kokoschka.

The **Peabody Museum of Archaeology and Ethnology** has impressive collections of Egyptian, North American Indian, and Central American artifacts as well as objects from the South Pacific Islands. Outstanding exhibits include totem carvings by Pacific Northwest tribes, Navajo weavings, and casts of objects unearthed at Chichen Itza in Mexico.

The highlight of the **Harvard Museum of Natural History** is its collection of "glass flowers" – 3,000 botanically correct, exquisite models of 850 plant species in handblown glass, created between 1887 and 1936 by father and son artisans Leopold and Rudolph Blaschka. Don't miss the collections of gems and minerals; the wild animals exhibits are extraordinary.

The **Sackler Museum**, housed in a striking modern building, holds a rich collection of ancient Greek and Roman, Asian, Indian, and Near Eastern art. These include Buddhist and Hindu

Chinese statues from the Sackler Museum's collection

sculptures, Islamic art, and Chinese bronzes, jades, ceramics, and stone statues. The latter are thought to be among the finest works of Chinese art in the West.

🏛 **Fogg Art & Busch-Reisinger Museums**
32 Quincy St. 📞 *(617) 495-9400.*
⬜ *10am–5pm Mon–Sat, 1–5pm Sun.* ⬤ *public hols.* 🈲 🚹 📷
ⓦ *www.artmuseums.harvard.edu*

🏛 **Peabody Museum of Archaeology & Ethnology**
11 Divinity St. 📞 *(617) 496-1027.*
⬜ *9am–5pm daily.* ⬤ *Jan 1, Jul 4, Thanksgiving, Dec 25.* 🈲 🚹 📷
ⓦ *www.peabody.harvard.edu*

🏛 **Harvard Museum of Natural History**
26 Oxford St. 📞 *(617) 495-3045.*
⬜ *9am–5pm daily.* ⬤ *Jul 4, Thanksgiving, Dec 25.* 🈲 🚹 📷
ⓦ *www.hmnh.harvard.edu*

Charlestown ㉙

🚇 *Community College.* 🚍 *93.*
🚢 *from Long Wharf.* 🅐 *Wed.*
🎉 *Jun 24.*

HISTORIC CHARLESTOWN, its picturesque streets lined with Colonial houses, is the site of the infamous battle of Bunker Hill, which took place on June 17, 1775. This was the Revolution's first pitched battle between British and Colonial troops, and though the latter lost, they made a courageous stand, inflicting huge losses on the much larger British force. The **Bunker Hill Monument**, a 221-ft (67-m) granite obelisk, dedicated in 1843, commemorates this event.

Until the Washington Monument was erected in 1885 *(see p204)*, it was the tallest monument in the US. The top of the monument, reached by 294 steps, offers spectacular views of Boston Harbor. At the **Bunker Hill Pavilion**, next to Charlestown Navy Yard, a lively multimedia presentation re-enacts this battle. The show consists of color slides projected on 14 screens, audio effects, and life-sized figures.

Charlestown Navy Yard, established in 1800, is the home of America's most famous warship, the USS *Constitution*. Built in 1797, and nicknamed "Old Ironsides" *(see p137)*, she is the oldest commissioned warship afloat and a veteran of 42 victorious battles at sea. Thoroughly overhauled for the 1997 bicentennial, she is taken out into the harbor on July 4 each year for an annual turnaround that reverses her position at the Navy Yard pier, to insure equal weathering on both sides.

ENVIRONS: The Colonial town of **Lexington**, 16 miles (26 km) northwest of Boston, is the site of the first bloody skirmish between armed colonists, called Minutemen, and British troops. This battle, on April 19, 1775, acted as a catalyst for the Revolutionary War *(see p44)*. The Lexington Battle Green, with its Minute Man statue, is the focal point of the town. Three historic buildings associated with the battle and maintained by the local Historical Society are open to visitors.

Granite obelisk of the Bunker Hill Monument in Charlestown

Massachusetts

O F ALL THE NEW ENGLAND STATES, Massachusetts may have the most diverse mix of natural and man-made attractions. Scenic seascapes and picturesque villages beckon along the eastern seaboard and Cape Cod. Venturing inland, visitors will find historic towns where America's early architecture has been well preserved. In the west, green mountains and valleys, and rich culture characterize the Berkshire Hills.

Salem ❷

🏚 *38,000.* ✈ 🚂 *From Boston's Long Wharf.* 🚌 *2 New Liberty St, (978) 740-1650.* 🎃 *Haunted Halloween (Oct).* 🌐 *www.salem.org*

T HIS COASTAL TOWN, founded in 1626, is best known for the infamous witch trials of 1692, which resulted in the execution of 20 innocent people. A chilling, multi-media re-enactment of the witch-hunt and subsequent trials can be seen at the **Salem Witch Museum**.

In the 18th and 19th centuries, Salem was one of New England's busiest ports, its harbor filled with ships carrying treasures from around the globe. The **Peabody Essex Museum** contains some of the world's deepest holdings of Asian art and artifacts. Many of the museum's exhibits, such as jewelry, porcelain figures, costumes, and scrimshaw objects, were brought back from distant shores by Salem's sea captains. The town's historic waterfront has been preserved as the **Salem Maritime National Historic** Site. It maintains three restored 18th-century wharves and a reconstructed East Indiaman sailing ship built in 1797, the *Friendship*, which is moored at the dock.

🏛 Peabody Essex Museum
East India Sq. 📞 *(800) 745-4054.* 🕐 *check for times.* 🎫 ✓ ♿ 🖥

ENVIRONS: Marblehead, just 4 miles (6 km) from Salem, is a picturesque and historic seaport village. Its hilly twisting lanes are lined with historic buildings, mansions, and cottages, most notable of which are Abbot Hall and the Jeremiah Lee Mansion.

Lowell ❸

🏚 *103,000.* ✈ 🚉 🚌 *9 Central St, Ste 201, (978) 459-6150.*

L OWELL HAS THE distinction of being the country's first industrial city. In the early 19th century, the first cloth mill equipped with a power loom opened here, and the town soon had a number of giant mill complexes. But after the Great Depression *(see p49)* the mills closed down, leaving Lowell a ghost town. Since 1978, many of Lowell's downtown buildings have been restored, and two of its museums trace the history of the town's textile industry. Lowell is also home to the **New England Quilt Museum**, which has a varied collection of displays of beautiful antique as well as contemporary quilts.

Concord's Old Manse, home to 19th-century literary giants

Concord ❹

🏚 *17,750.* ✈ 🚌 *58 Main St, (978) 369-3120.* 🎖 *Battle of Concord Re-enactment (Apr).* 🌐 *www.concordmachamber.org*

T HIS PEACEFUL, prosperous town has an eventful past. It was here that the Battle of Concord took place on April 19, 1775 which, together with the battle at nearby Lexington *(see p149)*, signaled the beginning of the Revolutionary War. The 900-acre (400-ha) **Minute Man National Historic Park** preserves the site of the battle, where a group of ordinary citizens and colonist farmers, known as Minutemen *(see p44)*, fought against British troops, driving them back from the park's North Bridge and chasing them back to Boston.

In the 19th century, Concord blossomed into the literary heart and soul of the country, with many writers establishing homes here. Both Ralph Waldo Emerson and Nathaniel Hawthorne lived briefly in **The Old Manse**; Emerson lived for nearly 50 years, until his death in 1882, at **Emerson House**, where his furniture, books, and memorabilia are on display.

Also in Concord is **Walden Pond**, immortalized in the writings of the essayist Henry David Thoreau (1817–62). In his influential work, *Walden; or Life in the Woods*, Thoreau called for a return to simplicity in everyday life and a respect for nature. Walden is widely considered to be the birthplace of the conserva-

SALEM WITCH TRIALS

In 1692, Salem was swept by a wave of hysteria in which 200 citizens were accused of practicing witchcraft. In all, 150 people were jailed and 19 were hanged as witches, while another man was crushed to death with stones. No one was safe: two dogs were executed on the gallows for being witches. Not surprisingly, when the governor's wife became a suspect, the trials came to an abrupt and officially sanctioned end.

Early accused: Rebecca Nurse

...ionist movement. The pond and its surrounding 333 acres (135 ha) of undeveloped woodland are ideal for walks, swimming, and fishing.

♣ Walden Pond State Reservation
915 Walden St. ☎ *(978) 369-3254.* ○ *call for hours.* 🅿 ✂ ♿

Plymouth ❺

🏨 *52,000.* ✈ 🚌 *to Provincetown (seasonal).* 🛈 *130 Water St, (508) 747-7533, (800) USA-1620.* Ⓦ *www.visit-plymouth.com*

T HE SHIP *Mayflower*, with 102 Pilgrims aboard, sailed into Plymouth Harbor in 1620 and established the first permanent European settlement in New England. Today the town bustles with visitors exploring the sites of America's earliest days, including **Plimoth Plantation**. Plymouth itself is a popular seaside resort, with a 3.5-mile (6-km) beach, offering harbor cruises and fishing excursions. In the fall, the sur-

Mayflower II, replica of the original Pilgrim ship, in Plymouth

rounding bogs turn ruby red as the annual cranberry harvest gets underway.

Most of the historic sights can be accessed on foot by the Pilgrim Path that stretches along the waterfront and downtown areas. A sightseeing trolley also connects points of interest. At the Harbor is **Plymouth Rock**, a boulder marking the spot where the Pilgrims are said to have first stepped ashore. Moored by it is the *Mayflower*

II, a replica of the 17th-century sailing ship that carried the Pilgrims over from England. Many of those who survived the brutal crossing on this small, cramped ship succumbed to illness and malnutrition during their first winter in Plymouth. They are buried across the street on **Coles Hill**, where there is a statue of the Indian chief Massasoit, who became an ally of the survivors. There is a panoramic view of the harbor from here.

The **Pilgrim Hall Museum**, opened in 1824 has the largest existing collection of Pilgrim-era furniture, armor, and decorative arts.

Particularly appealing for children is the **Plymouth National Wax Museum**, which re-creates the Pilgrims' saga through 180 life-size figures in 26 settings.

🛖 Plimoth Plantation
Rte 3A. 🛈 *137 Warren Ave, (508) 746-1622.* ○ *Apr–Nov: 9am–5pm daily.* 🅿 ♿ *limited access to certain parts of site; wheelchairs available on request.* 🅿 Ⓦ *www.plimoth.org*

PLIMOTH PLANTATION
Encircled by a palisade, Plimoth Plantation is a painstakingly accurate re-creation of the Pilgrims' 1627 village, complete with rudimentary thatched dwellings and livestock. Costumed interpreters, portraying personages from the original colony, enhance the period atmosphere.

Storehouse
Provisions were stored here, along with furs and other goods to be shipped to England.

Hopkins House
Stephen Hopkins' wife gave birth to their son Oceanus on the Mayflower.

Vegetable garden

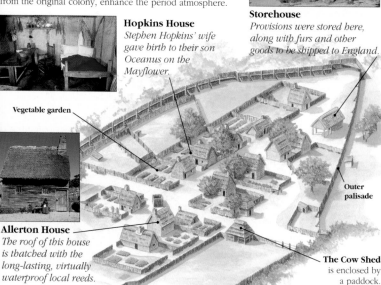

Outer palisade

Allerton House
The roof of this house is thatched with the long-lasting, virtually waterproof local reeds.

The Cow Shed
is enclosed by a paddock.

Cape Cod's Old Harbor Life-Saving Station, built in 1897

Cape Cod **❻**

⊠ ✈ Elm Ave, Hyannis. ⛴ Ocean St, Hyannis; Railroad Ave, Woods Hole. ℹ Jct Rtes 132 & 6, Rte 25, Hyannis, (508) 862-0700, (888) 332-2732. 🗓 Cape Cod Maritime Week (May), Annual Bourne Scallop Festival (Sep).

MORE THAN 13 million people arrive each summer to enjoy the boundless beaches, natural beauty, and quaint Colonial villages of Cape Cod, and the neighboring islands of Martha's Vineyard and Nantucket. A special attraction for visitors are whale-watching cruises, offered from April to mid-October. The Cape, shaped like an upraised arm bent at the elbow, extends some 70 miles (113 km) into the sea.

Cape Cod National Seashore, stretching more than 40 miles (64 km) along the northernmost section of the Cape, from Provincetown to Chatham, is famous for its horseshoe-shaped dunes, white sand beaches, salt marshes, glacial cliffs, and woodlands. Historical structures, such as the **Old Harbor Life-Saving Station** and the 18th-century Atwood Higgins House, are interspersed among the area's beautiful natural features.

One of the most popular destinations on the Cape is **Provincetown**. This picturesque town has a historic past – the Pilgrims first landed here in 1620 and stayed for five weeks before pushing on to the mainland. The 252-ft (77-m) **Pilgrim Monument**, the tallest granite structure in the US, commemorates this event. Today, Provincetown is especially vibrant during the

Pilgrim Monument

summer months, when its population can swell from 3,500 to 80,000. One of the busiest locales is McMillan Wharf, the jumping off point for whale-watching cruises. Since the early 20th century, the town has also had a bustling artists' colony, counting among its famous residents the painters Mark Rothko and Jackson Pollock, and the writers Eugene O'Neill and Tennessee Williams. The work of local artists is also displayed in the Provincetown Art Association and Museum.

Chatham, an attractive, upscale community, offers fine inns, attractive shops, and a popular summer playhouse. Fishing boats stop and unload their catch at the pier, and the surrounding waters offer good opportunities for enthusiastic anglers. The Railroad Museum, housed in an 1887 Victorian train station, has photos, memorabilia, and vintage railroad cars.

Hyannis, the largest village in Cape Cod, is a busy shopping center and the main transportation hub for the region. It is also famous as the summer home of the country's most celebrated political dynasty, the Kennedys. The heavily screened Kennedy compound is best seen from the water aboard a sightseeing cruise.

At its center is the "cottage" that multi-millionaire Joseph Kennedy (1888–1969) bought in 1926, expanding it into a sprawling vacation retreat for his nine children and their families. The Kennedy clan continues to gather here on family occasions. After John F. Kennedy's assassination in 1963, a simple memorial was erected in the town in his honor: a pool and fountain, and a circular wall bearing Kennedy's profile.

One of Hyannis' most popular forms of transportation is the **Cape Cod Central Railroad**, which offers a scenic two-hour round trip to the Cape Cod canal.

Hiking trails, salt marshes, tidal pools, and 12 miles (19 km) of beaches attract visitors to **Falmouth**, with its picturesque village green. It also has the 3.3-mile (5-km) Shining Sea Bike Path, with vistas of beach, harbor, and woodland. The path leads to the world's largest independent marine science research center, the Woods Hole Oceanographic Institute.

Sandwich, the oldest town in the Cape, is straight off a postcard: a church overlooking a picturesque pond, fed by a brook that powers the waterwheel of a Colonial-era gristmill. The church bell, dating to 1675, is said to be the oldest in the US. The town's most unusual attraction is **Heritage Museums & Gardens**, a 75-acre (30-ha) garden and museum housing the eclectic collection of the pharmaceutical tycoon, Josiah K. Lilly Jr. (1893–1966). Exhibits include 37 antique cars, Native American relics, and a 1912 carousel. The gardens are famous for their lovely rhododendrons. Just a 45-minute boatride away from the mainland lies

Popular sightseeing trip on the Cape Cod Central Railroad

Fishing boat moored outside a fishing shack, Martha's Vineyard

Martha's Vineyard. This 108-sq mile (280-sq km) island combines mesmerizing scenic beauty with the charms of a beach resort and abounds in opportunities for outdoor activities. Each town has its own distinctive atmosphere and architectural style.

Most visitors arrive by ferry at the island's commercial hub, Vineyard Haven. On the eastern shore is Edgartown, with the gracious 19th-century homes of the town's wealthy sea captains and merchants. The **Martha's Vineyard Historical Society** is housed in one of them – the Thomas Cooke House (c.1730), filled with antique furniture and ship models. From here, a short ferry ride goes to Chappaquiddick Island, where in 1969, a car driven by Senator Edward Kennedy went off the bridge, killing a woman passenger.

North of Edgartown is Oak Bluff, with its gingerbread cottages, while the Western Shoreline is tranquil and rural with pristine beaches.

Nantucket Island, a 14-mile (22-km) long enclave of tranquility with only one town, remains a largely untamed world of kettle ponds, quiet beaches, cranberry bogs, and fields of wild grapes and blueberries, punctuated by occasional houses. Nantucket was a prosperous center of the whaling industry in the early 1800s, and the mansions of sea captains and merchants reflect those glory days. The **Nantucket Historical Association** (NHA) operates 11 historical buildings in the town, one of which houses a fascinating Whaling Museum. A popular spot, 8 miles (13

km) from town, is Siasconset village, famous for its rose-colored bluffs and lanes with tiny cottages.

🌳 Cape Cod National Seashore
Rte 6, Cape Cod. **ℹ** *Salt Pond Visitor Center, Rte 6, Eastham, (508) 255-3421.* ◯ *year-round.*
Ⓦ *www.nps.gov/caco*
🏛 Heritage Museums & Gardens
67 Grove St, Sandwich. **☎** *(508) 888-3300.* ◯ *mid-May–Oct: 9am–6pm Sat–Wed, 9am–8pm Thu–Fri; Nov–mid-May: call for hours.* 🅿 &
🏛 Martha's Vineyard Historical Society
59 School St, Edgartown. **☎** *(508) 627-4441.* ◯ *mid-Jun–Sep: 10am–5pm Tue–Sat; Oct–mid-Jun: 1–4pm Wed–Fri, 10am–4pm Sat; Jan–Feb: 10am–4pm Sat.* 🅿 & 🚻
🌳 Nantucket Historical Association (NHA)
15 Broad St, Nantucket Island.
☎ *(508) 228-1894.* **Historic buildings** ◯ *call for hours.* 🅿 ✓ & *Whaling Museum only.*

Sturbridge ❼

Old Sturbridge Village Rte 20, Sturbridge. **☎** *(508) 347-3362.* ◯ *Apr–Oct: 9:30am–5pm daily; Jan–mid-Feb: 9:30am–4pm Sat–Sun; mid-Feb–Mar: 9:30am–4pm Tue–Sun.* ● *Dec 25.* 🅿 ✓ &

THIS SMALL TOWN is home to Old **Sturbridge Village**, an open-air museum in the form of an early 19th-century village. At the heart of the museum are about 40 vintage buildings that have been restored and relocated from all over New England. They include the Federal-style Towne House, a meetinghouse, a tavern, and a store, with authentic period settings.

The Berkshires ❽

🧍 🖼 Pittsfield. **ℹ** *Berkshire Common Plaza, Pittsfield, (413) 443-9186, (800) 237-5747.*
Ⓦ *www.berkshire.org*

WOODED HILLS, green valleys, rippling rivers, and waterfalls have long attracted visitors to this western corner of Massachusetts, which is rich in opportunities for outdoor as well as cultural activity. The area is speckled with scenic small towns and villages. **Pittsfield**, in the shadow of Mount Greylock, is famous as the home of Herman Melville (1819–91), where he wrote his masterpiece, *Moby Dick*. **Lenox** has the grand estates of prominent families such as the Carnegies. It also hosts the prestigious Tanglewood Musical Festival every summer. The main street of **Stockbridge** has been immortalized in the paintings of one of America's most beloved illustrators, Norman Rockwell (1894–1978), who lived here for 25 years. His works can be seen in the town's **Norman Rockwell Museum**.

Especially attractive to nature lovers is the **Mount Washington State Forest**, and the Mount Everett State Forest, nearby.

🏛 Norman Rockwell Museum
Rte 183. **☎** *(413) 298-4100 ext 220.* ◯ *May–Oct: 10am–5pm daily; Nov–Apr: 10am–4pm Mon–Fri, 10am–5pm Sat–Sun.* ● *Jan 1, Thanksgiving, Dec 25.* 🅿 ✓ & 🚻 Ⓦ *www.nrm.org*

Bash Bish Falls, Mount Washington State Forest in the Berkshires

Rhode Island

T HE SMALLEST STATE IN AMERICA, Rhode Island is not an island at all but has a shoreline dotted with lovely islets and beaches. Although known as the Ocean State, half of Rhode Island is woodland, ideal for nature walks and camping. The state's two major cities are Providence, the lively capital, and Newport, which has some of New England's most opulent mansions.

Stately buildings along Benefit Street's Mile of History in Providence

Providence ❾

🏙 174,000. ✕ 🚆 *Providence Station, 100 Gaspee St.* 🚌 *1 Bonanza Way.* ⚓ *Point St (to Newport).* ℹ️ *1 W Exchange St, (401) 274-1636 or (800) 233-1636.* 🎭 *Festival of Historic Houses (Jun–Dec); International Film Festival (Aug).* Ⓦ *www.goprovidence.com*

P ERCHED ON seven hills on the banks of Narragansett Bay, Providence is an interesting blend of the historic and the modern. It started life as a farming community, established in 1636 by the clergyman Roger Williams, who was driven from the Massacusetts Bay colony for his outspoken beliefs on religious freedom. It soon became a flourishing seaport, and then evolved into a hub of industry in the 19th century, with immigrants from Europe pouring in to work in its textile mills.

Providence is bisected by the Providence River. On its west bank is the downtown district, revitalized by recent renewal projects, which have restored old buildings, constructed new malls and markets, and developed the waterfront. To the east is tthe campus of Brown University and several historic streets. The most outstanding of these is **Benefit Street's**

Mile of History. This lovely tree-lined street has more than 100 houses ranging in style from Colonial and Federal to Greek Revival and Victorian. Its architectural gems include the **Providence Athenaeum**, a Greek Revival-style library, whose collection dates back to 1753, to the First Unitarian Church. Its 2,500-lb (1,350-kg) bell was one of the largest cast by Paul Revere's foundry. Also on Benefit Street is the Rhode Island School of Design's **RISD Museum of Art**, whose comprehensive collection ranges from Ancient Egyptian to contemporary American art. A short distance to the north, on Main Street, is the **First Baptist Church in America**. Built in 1774–75, it

has an intricately carved wooden interior and a Waterford crystal chandelier.

Founded in 1764, **Brown University** is the seventh-oldest college in the US and one of the prestigious Ivy League schools. Its beautiful campus, a rich blend of Gothic and Beaux Arts styles, is worth exploring. Notable buildings here include the John Hay Library with its collection of memorabilia relating to President Abraham Lincoln, the John Carter Brown Library with a fascinating collection of Americana, and the List Art Center, a striking building designed by Philip Johnson, which features classical and contemporary art.

John Brown House, a Georgian mansion, built in 1786 for a wealthy merchant and shipowner, has been impeccably restored. Its interior is decorated with ornate plaster ornamented ceilings, a grand staircase with twisted balusters, and wallpapers from France. Its 12 rooms are a repository for some of the finest furniture and antiques of that period. Nearby, another house with fine 18th-century furnishings is the 1707 **Governor Stephen Hopkins House**.

One of the newest and brightest additions to downtown Providence is **Waterplace Park and Riverwalk**, a 4-acre (1.6-ha) walkway located at the junction of three rivers – the Moshassock, Providence, and Woonasquatucket. Visitors can also stroll along the park's cobblestone paths, float under

Roger Williams Park and Zoo, a highlight of downtown Providence

footbridges in canoes or gondolas, and enjoy free concerts at the amphitheater during the summer season.

Another successful downtown renewal project is **The Arcade**, an 1828 Greek Revival building that covers an entire block in the city's old financial district. The first indoor shopping mall in the US, this massive three-story stone complex with its high Ionic granite columns, has a skylight extending the entire length of the building, providing light even on rainy days. Restored in 1980, this lively marketplace contains specialty shops, clothing boutiques, and several restaurants.

Downtown Providence is dominated by the imposing **Rhode Island State House** constructed in 1904. Its magnificent white marble dome is topped by a bronze statue called Independent Man, a symbol of Rhode Island's free spirit. Among the displays inside are the original state charter of 1663 and a full-length portrait of President George Washington by Gilbert Stuart.

The city's largest green space is the **Roger Williams Park and Zoo**. Once farmland, this 422-acre (171-ha) park now holds gardens, greenhouses, and ponds, a lake with paddleboats and rowboats, as well as jogging and cycling tracks and a tennis center. Children especially love the carousel rides and train, the planetarium, and the Museum of Natural History. The highlight of the park, however, is the zoo, which has more than 900 animals, including mammals such as zebras, giraffes, and cheetahs. An underwater window allows visitors to look at the penguins and polar bears as they cavort playfully in the water.

Rhode Island State House with its marble dome

🏛 RISD Museum of Art

224 Benefit St. ☎ *(401) 454-6500.* ○ *10am–5pm Tue–Sun, 10am–9pm third Thu of month.* ● *public hols.* $

🏛 John Brown House

52 Power St. ☎ *(401) 331-8575.* ○ *Jan–Feb: 10am–5pm Fri & Sat, noon–4pm Sun; Mar–Dec: 10am–5pm Tue–Sat, noon–4pm Sun.* ● *Mon & public hols.* $ ⚑ 🛍

🏛 Rhode Island State House

82 Smith St. ☎ *(401) 222-2357.* ○ *8:30am–4:30pm Mon–Fri.* ● *public hols.* ⚑ *self-guided, others by appt.* ♿ 🛍 ☕

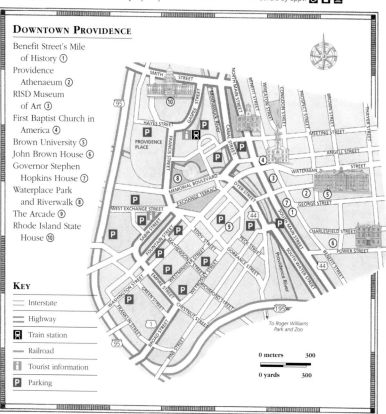

DOWNTOWN PROVIDENCE

Benefit Street's Mile of History 1
Providence Athenaeum 2
RISD Museum of Art 3
First Baptist Church in America 4
Brown University 5
John Brown House 6
Governor Stephen Hopkins House 7
Waterplace Park and Riverwalk 8
The Arcade 9
Rhode Island State House 10

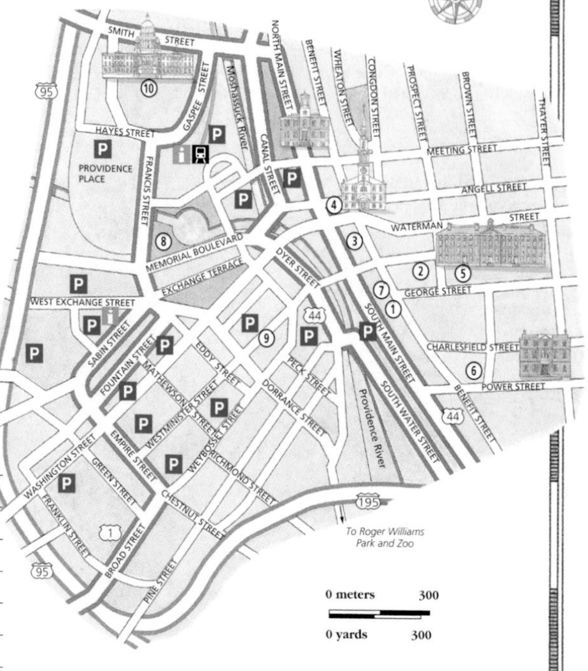
SMITH STREET
GASPEE STREET
Moshassuck River
NORTH MAIN STREET
BENEFIT STREET
WHEATON STREET
CONGDON STREET
PROSPECT STREET
BROWN STREET
THAYER STREET
HAYES STREET
PROVIDENCE PLACE
FRANCIS STREET
CANAL STREET
MEETING STREET
ANGELL STREET
WATERMAN STREET
MEMORIAL BOULEVARD
EXCHANGE TERRACE
DYER STREET
GEORGE STREET
WEST EXCHANGE STREET
SABIN STREET
FOUNTAIN STREET
MATHEWSON STREET
EDDY STREET
PECK STREET
SOUTH MAIN STREET
CHARLESFIELD STREET
POWER STREET
DORRANCE STREET
Providence River
SOUTH WATER STREET
BENEFIT STREET
WESTMINSTER STREET
WEYBOSSET STREET
EMPIRE STREET
WASHINGTON STREET
GREEN STREET
RICHMOND STREET
CHESTNUT STREET
FRANKLIN STREET
BROAD STREET
PINE STREET
To Roger Williams Park and Zoo
95
44
195
1
0 meters 300
0 yards 300

KEY

- Interstate
- Highway
- Train station
- Railroad
- Tourist information
- Parking

Scores of yachts in the harbor at Newport

Newport ⓾

🏛 28,000. ✈ 🚌 Gateway
Center, 23 America's Cup Ave.
🚢 Perrotti Park (to Providence).
ℹ 23 America's Cup Ave, (401)
849-8048. 🎾 Newport Tennis Week
(Jul), JVC Jazz Festival (Aug).
🌐 www.gonewport.com

A CENTER OF trade, culture,
wealth, and military
activity for more than 300
years, Newport is a true sightseeing mecca. The town's
main attractions are its
mansions, most of them
located on Bellevue Avenue
on the southeastern side of
the city. Built between 1748
and 1902, when the rich and
famous flocked here each
summer to beat New York's
heat, these summer "cottage"
retreats of the country's
wealthiest families, such as
the Vanderbilts and the
Astors, are some of America's
grandest private homes.
Modeled on European palaces
and decorated with the finest
artworks, the mansions were
used for only 10 weeks of the
year. **The Breakers** is one of
the finest examples.

Newport is also home to
the oldest synagogue in USA.
Built in 1763 by Sephardic
Jews who had fled Spain and
Portugal in search of religious
tolerance, the **Touro
Synagogue** is an outstanding
example of 18th-century
architecture. It is located just
east of Washington Square
where a number of historic
Colonial buildings have been
preserved. Among them is the
fascinating Museum of
Newport History, housed in
the Brick Market, which was
the center of commerce in
Colonial times. Also on the
Square is the White Horse
Tavern *(see p184)*, which
claims to be the oldest
continuously operating tavern
in America; it was granted its
liquor license in 1673.

Apart from its mansions
and historic sites, Newport
also has numerous outdoor
attractions. South of

THE BREAKERS

The architecture and ostentation of the Gilded Age of the late
1800s reached its pinnacle with The Breakers, the summer home
of the railroad magnate Cornelius Vanderbilt II (1843–99).
Completed in 1895, the four-story, 70-room limestone mansion
was modeled after 16th-century palaces in Turin and Genoa. Its
interior is adorned with marble, stained glass, gilt, and crystal.

The Dining Room,
a two-story room,
has a stunning arched
ceiling and two huge
crystal chandeliers.

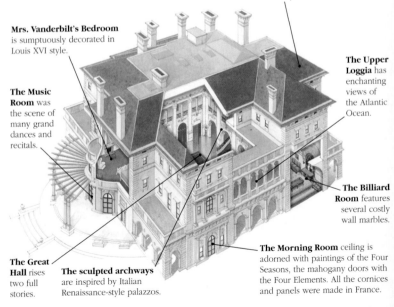

Mrs. Vanderbilt's Bedroom
is sumptuously decorated in
Louis XVI style.

**The Upper
Loggia** has
enchanting
views of
the Atlantic
Ocean.

**The Music
Room** was
the scene of
many grand
dances and
recitals.

**The Billiard
Room** features
several costly
wall marbles.

**The Great
Hall** rises
two full
stories.

The sculpted archways
are inspired by Italian
Renaissance-style palazzos.

The Morning Room ceiling is
adorned with paintings of the Four
Seasons, the mahogany doors with
the Four Elements. All the cornices
and panels were made in France.

The breathtaking Cliff Walk, popular with visitors in Newport

Washington Square is **Fort Adams State Park**, with Fort Adams, built in 1853, as its centerpiece. No longer in use as a garrison, the fort is surrounded with facilities for swimming and other sports. Each year, Newport's famous Jazz Festival is held here. The park also has the Museum of Yachting, as well as a collection of luxury yachts.

Another popular site is the 3.5-mile (5.5-km) long **Cliff Walk**, southwest of downtown. The trail, along the city's ragged cliffs, offers some fine views of the Gilded-Age mansions and has been designated a National Recreation Trail in 1975. The Forty Steps, each named for someone lost at sea, lead to the ocean.

🏛 **The Breakers**
Ochre Point Ave. **(** (401) 847-1000.
◯ mid-Apr–Oct: 10am–5pm daily. Call for winter hours.
⬤ Thanksgiving, Dec 24 & 25.
🎟 every 15 minutes. 🕹 🅰 🅰
Ⓦ www.newportmansions.org
✡ **Touro Synagogue**
85 Touro St. **(** (401) 847-4794.
◯ call for times. 🎟 every half hour.
🕹 Shabbat & all Jewish hols. 🅰 🅰
⚓ **Fort Adams State Park**
Harrison Ave. **(** (401) 847-2400.
◯ sunrise to sunset daily. 🎟 **Museum of Yachting (** (401) 847-1018.
◯ mid-May–Oct: 10am–4pm daily; Nov–mid-May: by appt. 🎟 🕹 🅰

South County Beaches ⓫

Narragansett 🅧 🛈 36 Ocean Rd, (401) 783-7121.
Charlestown 🅧 🚻 🛈 4945 Old Post Rd, (401) 364-3878.

Southwest of Newport, between **Narragansett** and Watch Hill, are some 100 miles (161 km) of pristine white sand beaches and a series of tidal salt ponds. The ponds are big lures for birdwatchers hoping to study the egrets, sandpipers, and herons that swim and wade in the salty marshes. Many of the beaches are free to the public, except for parking fees. **Scarborough State Beach** is excellent for bodysurfing and surfboarding, while the sheltered, cove-protected **Roger Wheeler Memorial Beach** is a favorite for families. **East Matunuck State Beach** is popular with surfers on windy days. The beautiful sandy stretch of **Charlestown Town Beach** has a boat ramp with access to the coastal ponds of the Ninigret National Wildlife Refuge.

Farther west along the coast is **Misquamicut State Beach**. The largest beach in the state, it has gentle surf and an old-time amusement park with rides and many diversions for children.

Block Island ⓬

🅧 ⛴ Point Judith. Ferries carry cars by advance reservations, (401) 783-4613.

Lying just 13 miles (21 km) off the coast, Block Island is a great destination for outdoor enthusiasts who enjoy such activities as swimming, fishing, sailing, bird-watching, canoeing, and horseback riding. Some 30 miles (48 km) of natural trails entice hikers and cyclists to experience the island's natural beauty.

The village of **Old Harbor** is the island's main hub of activity. Victorian houses, hotels, and shops line the streets, and anglers can charter boats to fish for striped bass, bluefish, flounder, and cod. South of the village are the dramatic 200-ft (61-m) high red clay cliffs of **Mohegan Bluffs**, and the Southeast Lighthouse, which was once the most powerful in New England.

A favorite with hikers is **Rodman's Hollow Natural Area**. This glacial depression, well marked with nature trails, is a refuge for hawks and white-tailed deer.

On Block Island's northwestern coast is **Great Salt Pond**, which is completely protected from the ocean. It is an excellent spot for kayaking and fishing. Nearby New Harbor is the island's prime marina and boating center. **Clayhead**, on the island's northeastern coast, offers wonderful views of the Atlantic Ocean,

Plaque to early English pioneers, Settlers Rock, Block Island

and is the starting point for a nature trail that goes all the way north to **Settler's Rock**. A plaque here honors the 16 Englishmen who landed here in 1661. The rock is at the edge of Sachem Pond, a favorite for swimming and kayaking. An 18-mile (29-km) driving tour of Block Island is a comfortable way to take in all these sites.

The dramatic red clay cliffs at Mohegan Bluffs, Block Island

Connecticut

Although compact enough to cross in a few hours, Connecticut has treasures that entice visitors to stay for days. Along its magnificent shoreline are beaches, marinas, and the remarkable maritime museum at Mystic Seaport. Inland, the Connecticut River Valley and the Litchfield Hills are dotted with scenic and historic villages. Hartford, the bustling capital, and New Haven, home of Yale University, are its main cities.

Hartford ⓭

👥 *139,000.* ✈ 🚌 🚆 *1 Union Place.* ℹ *31 Pratt St, 4th floor, (860) 244-8181, (800) 793-4480.*
🎭 *Mark Twain Days (summer).*
[W] www.enjoyhartford.com

Founded in 1636 by a group of English settlers from the Massachusetts Bay Colony, Hartford's golden age was in the 19th century when it became a flourishing center of the insurance industry. It also became a vibrant cultural center, thanks to resident authors such as Mark Twain. In recent years, an ambitious revitalization program has breathed new life into the city.

Dominating the cityscape is the gleaming gold-leaf dome of the **State Capitol**, a Victorian-Gothic building perched on a hilltop. Many of Hartford's attractions are accessible on foot from here. The Capitol overlooks the 40-acre (16-ha) **Bushnell Park**, the creation of Hartford native Frederick Law Olmsted (1822–1903), who also laid out New York's Central Park. There are 100 varieties of trees, and a 1914 carousel with 48 hand-carved horses.

The 1796 **Old State House**, designed by Charles Bulfinch *(see p134)*, is the country's oldest Capitol building. With its grand center hall and staircase, and ornate cupola, it is a superb example of Federal architecture. Nearby, the **Center Church** has five stained-glass windows designed by the US artist Louis Comfort Tiffany (1848–1933). To its south is the **Wadsworth Atheneum**, the oldest continuously operating public art museum in the country. Its collection includes Renaissance, Baroque, and Impressionist art, as well as works by American artists.

West of downtown is the **Mark Twain House**, a picturesque Gothic-style masterpiece with peaked gables, expansive upper balconies, and towering turrets. Legend has it that Twain (1835–1910), once a riverboat captain, designed the house to give it the appearance of one of his beloved Mississippi

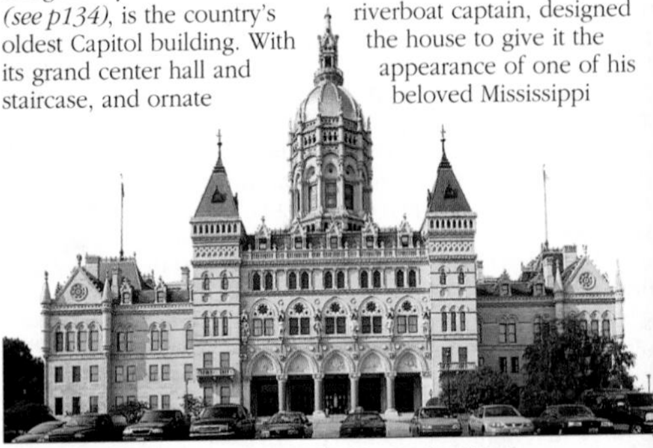

The Connecticut State Capitol, overlooking Bushnell Park

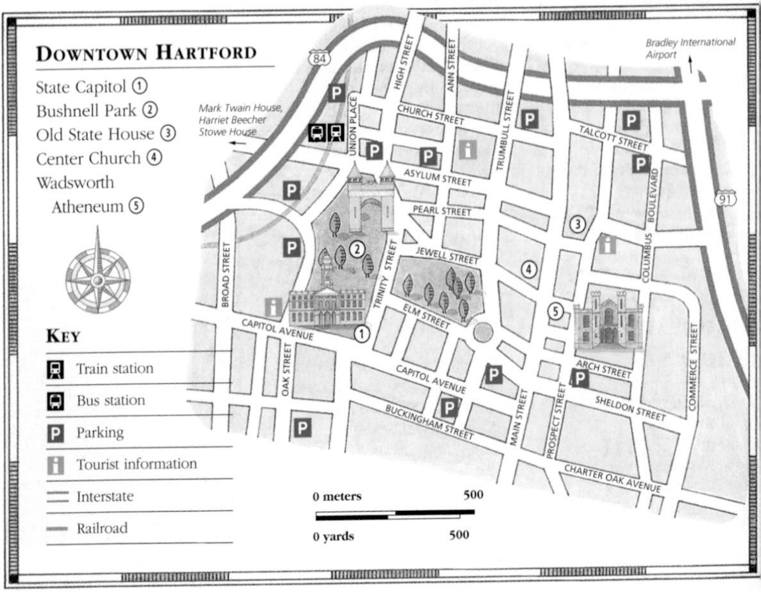

Downtown Hartford
State Capitol ①
Bushnell Park ②
Old State House ③
Center Church ④
Wadsworth Atheneum ⑤
Key
Train station
Bus station
Parking
Tourist information
Interstate
Railroad
0 meters 500
0 yards 500
Mark Twain House, Harriet Beecher Stowe House
Bradley International Airport
84
91
High Street
Ann Street
Union Place
Church Street
Trumbull Street
Talcott Street
Asylum Street
Pearl Street
Jewell Street
Elm Street
Broad Street
Trinity Street
Capitol Avenue
Oak Street
Buckingham Street
Main Street
Prospect Street
Arch Street
Sheldon Street
Charter Oak Avenue
Columbus Boulevard
Commerce Street

The Billiard Room, Mark Twain House, Hartford

steamboats. Of special interest are the library with its ornate wooden fireplace mantel; the tranquil Billiard Room where Twain wrote some of his best known works, including *The Adventures of Tom Sawyer*, and the Master Bedroom with its beautifully carved bed. A new visitor center illuminates Twain's life and work.

Next door is the **Harriet Beecher Stowe House**, where the famous author of the anti-slavery novel, *Uncle Tom's Cabin* (1852), lived until her death in 1896. The house is adorned with gingerbread ornamentation typical of late 19th-century Victorian design, while the elegance of its interior displays Harriet's less well-known talent as a decorator.

♿ Mark Twain House

351 Farmington Ave. 📞 (860) 247-0998 ext 26. ⭘ May–Oct & Dec: 9:30am–5pm Mon–Sat, noon–5pm Sun; Jan–Apr & Nov: 9:30am–4pm Mon & Wed–Sat, noon–4pm Sun. ⬤ Jan 1, Easter Sun, Thanksgiving, Dec 24 & 25. 📷 📷 obligatory. ♿ 1st floor only. 🌐 www.marktwain.org

Litchfield ⑭

🏛 8,850. 🛈 Litchfield Hills Visitors' Bureau, PO Box 968, (860) 567-4506.

Tʜɪs ᴘɪᴄᴛᴜʀᴇsQᴜᴇ and historic town is at the center of the Litchfield Hills region in northwestern Connecticut, which many people consider the most scenic part of the state.

Anchored by the Housatonic River, the bucolic landscape of lovely woods, valleys, lakes, and wildlife offers great opportunities for sports such as canoeing, kayaking, whitewater rafting, tubing, fly-fishing, and hiking. In fall, the brilliant foliage along the region's roads entrances sightseers. Litchfield's many historic houses include the 1784 **Tapping Reeve House** and Law School, the country's first law school. On the outskirts of the town, on Route 202, **Mount Tom State Park** has trails leading to the 1,325-ft (404-m) summit. The lake is ideal for scuba diving, swimming, boating, and fishing.

Connecticut River Valley ⑮

Windsor 🏛 27,800. 🛈 96 Palisado Ave, (800) 248-8283. **Old Lyme** 🏛 6,800. 🛈 470 Bank St, New London, (860) 444-2206, (800) 863-6469.

Tʜᴇ ᴄᴏɴɴᴇᴄᴛɪᴄᴜᴛ River Valley is dotted with picture postcard-perfect little towns and villages. **Windsor**, settled in the early 1630s by Pilgrims from Plymouth (see p151) has a number of historic houses, open to visitors, such as the 1758 John & Sarah Strong House with its fine furnishings. Nearby is the Palisado Green, where nervous settlers built a walled stockade in their 1637 war with the Pequot Indians.

Wethersfield, settled in 1634, stands as a primer of American architecture from the 18th to the 20th centuries. Especially worth visiting is the Webb-Deane-Stevens Museum, which is a trio of dwellings that depict the lifestyles of three different 18th-century Americans – a diplomat, a wealthy merchant, and a leather tanner.

The **Dinosaur State Park**, farther south, preserves some 500 prehistoric dinosaur tracks beneath a geodesic dome. It also has a display of a life-sized model of an 8-ft (2-m) tall Dilophosaurus.

Just outside the town of East Hadham is the bizarre and ostentatious **Gillette Castle**, built in 1919 by the actor William Gillette. This 24-room granite mansion is built like a medieval castle, complete with battlements and turrets, and is rife with oddities such as Gillette's homemade trick locks and furniture set on wheels and tracks.

Picturesque Old Lyme boasts several 18th- and 19th-century houses built for sea captains. It is also renowned for the **Florence Griswold Museum**, housed in an 1817 mansion. Paintings by some of America's leading artists, such as Childe Hassam and Clark Voorhees, adorn the walls of this museum, together with superb works by other artists who lived in art patron Florence Griswold's house and painted on its wall panels to repay her generosity.

♿ Wethersfield

🛈 Greater Hartford Tourism District, 31 Pratt St, Hartford, (860) 244-8181, (800) 793-4480. 🌐 www.enjoyhartford.com

♿ Gillette Castle

67 River Rd off Rte 82, Hadlyme. 📞 (860) 526-2336. ⭘ late May–Columbus Day 10am–5pm daily. 📷 📷 ♿

🏛 Florence Griswold Museum

96 Lyme St, Old Lyme. 📞 (860) 434-5542. ⭘ Jan–Apr: 1–5pm Wed–Sun; May–Dec: 10am–5pm Tue–Sat, 1–5pm Sun. 📷 📷 ♿ 🌐 www.flogris.org

The Harpist by Alphonse Jongers at the Florence Griswold Museum

New Haven

🏃 123, 626. ✈ ℹ *1 Long Wharf Dr, (203) 777-8550.* Ⓦ *www. cityofnewhaven.com* **Yale University** ℹ *Dwight Hall, (203) 432-2300.* ♿ 🎭 *International Festival of Arts and Ideas (Jun).* Ⓦ *www. yale.edu*

FOUNDED IN 1638, New Haven is located on the coast, where three rivers flow into Long Island Sound. Although this has helped make it a major manufacturing center, the city is better known as the home of **Yale University**, one of the world's most prestigious institutions of higher learning. Its alumni include no less than four American presidents, including the Bushes Sr. and Jr, and Bill Clinton. Yale, founded in 1701, has made New Haven a leading center for education, research, and technology, and has enriched its cultural life as well.

The main area of the town is the 16-acre (6-ha) **New Haven Green**, serving as the setting for many of New Haven's activities and festivals. Three beautiful early 19th-century churches are located on the Green, of which the **First Church of Christ** has a Tiffany stained-glass window, regarded as a masterpiece of American Georgian style.

Tiffany stained-glass window, First Church of Christ

Much of the core of downtown New Haven is covered by the Yale University campus, dotted with Georgian and Neo-Gothic buildings, as well as modern structures designed by Eero Saarinen and Philip Johnson. Major landmarks on the campus are the beautiful Gothic-style Memorial Quadrangle and the Harkness Tower, whose carillon rings out at intervals through the day.

Yale's outstanding museums are a prime attraction for visitors. The **Yale Center for British Art**, whose collection was donated by the philanthropist Paul Mellon (1907–99), has the largest collection of British art outside the UK and includes paintings by Gainsborough, Hogarth, and Turner. The treasures of the **Beinecke Rare Book and Manuscript Libraries** include one of the world's few remaining Gutenberg Bibles. The **Yale University Art Gallery**, reflecting the generosity and taste of the Yale alumni, houses works by artists such as Picasso, Van Gogh, Manet, and Monet, while the **Peabody Museum of Natural History** is famous for its collection of dinosaurs.

A must for the musically inclined is the **Yale Collection of Musical**

Entrance to the Peabody Museum of Natural History, Yale University

Instruments. Its stunning exhibits consist of violins and harpsichords dating back centuries. These historical instruments are still played at concerts held here today.

The most popular park in New Haven is the 84-acre (34-ha) Lighthouse Point Park on Long Island Sound. It has nature trails, a picnic grove, a bird sanctuary, as well as a 1840 lighthouse.

🏛 **Yale Center for British Art**
1080 Chapel St. ℹ *(203) 432-2800.* ⧖ *10am–5pm Tue–Sat, noon–5pm Sun.* ● *public hols.* ⧉ ♿ 🛗
🏛 **Beinecke Rare Book & Manuscript Libraries**
121 Wall St. ℹ *(203) 432-0600.* ⧖ *8:30am–5pm Mon–Fri, 10am–5pm Sat.* ● *Sat in Aug & public hols.*
🏛 **Yale University Art Gallery**
1111 Chapel St. ℹ *(203) 432-0600.* ⧖ *10am–5pm Tue–Sat (upto 8pm on Thu), 1–6pm Sun.* ● *public hols.*
⧉ ♿ 🛗

Church spires around New Haven Green, the focal point of the town

The *Charles W. Morgan*, the last wooden whaling ship, in Mystic Seaport

Connecticut Coast ⑰

Mystic 🏛 *2,600.* 🚪 *28 Cottrell St, (860) 572-9578.* **Madison** 🏛 *16,000.* 🚪 *22 Scotland Ave, (203) 245-7394.* **Stamford** *Fairfield County.* 🏛 *117, 083.* 🚪 *(203) 977-6600.*

CONNECTICUT'S magnificent 105-mile (170-km) long shoreline, is scalloped by coves, inlets, and harbors, dotted with beaches, marinas, and state parks. Historic towns and villages also lie along the coast.

One the most popular tourist destinations along the Connecticut Coast is **Mystic Seaport**. This authentic 18th- and 19th-century seafaring village, where nearly every home sports a nautical motif, also has the world's largest maritime museum. Mystic's main attraction is its preservation shipyard and its fleet of antique ships, including the *Charles W. Morgan*, the last wooden whaling ship in the world, built in 1841. Another highlight is the Mystic River Scale Model, with more than 250 detailed buildings. The impressive Mystic Aquarium has a huge gallery of penguins, stingrays, and sharks, while seals and sea lions can be seen cavorting in the outdoor Seal Island.

A short distance west of Mystic Seaport is **New London**. This historic town was torched by British forces during the American Revolution, but remarkably, many of the houses survived. Among them is the Joshua Hempsted House, built in 1678, which is insulated with

seaweed. By the 19th century New London had recovered to become a prosperous center of the whaling industry – the row of colonnaded Greek Revival mansions on Whale Oil Row attest to the affluence of that era.

The resort town of **Madison**, full of antique stores and boutiques, also has several historic homes open for viewing. Among the fascinating artifacts on display at the **Deacon John Grave House** is the family bookkeeping ledger, with entries from 1678 to 1895. Also in Madison is **Hammonasset Beach State Park**, the largest shoreline park in the state, with a 2-mile (3-km) long beach that attracts swimmers, sailors, sunbathers, and divers. Neighboring **Guilford** has a Tudor Gothic-style granite fort. This three-story stronghold, built in 1640 by a group of Puritans settlers to protect themselves against attacks by the local Indians, is the oldest stone dwelling of its kind in New England.

From Guilford's Stony Creek Dock, travelers can cruise to the **Thimble Islands** aboard tour boats that operate in the area, watching seals or taking

The Thimbles, home to seals, whales, and colorful legends

in the glorious fall colors. Many of the 365 islands are little more than large boulders, but some privately owned islands have small communities. Legend has it that the privateer Captain Kidd (1645–1701) hid plundered treasure on Money Island while being pursued by the British fleet.

Coastal Fairfield County, in the southernmost corner of the state, has attractions for every taste. The shoreline is dusted with beaches offering a variety of summer recreation opportunities, while naturalists are drawn to its nature preserves and zoo. The area also has numerous art galleries and museums.

Bridgeport is home to the Beardsley Zoo, the Barnum Museum (named after the circus impresario P.T. Barnum who was the town's mayor), and the Discovery Museum.

The charming town of **Westport** on the banks of the Saugatuck River has the Sherwood Island State Park. **Norwalk** has historic buildings, shops, and cafés along its waterfront, as well as a Maritime Aquarium. **New Canaan**, set in a landscape of woods, streams, and rolling fields, is spectacular in fall. **Stamford** has a unique First Presbyterian Church, shaped like a fish, and a lively downtown area.

Greenwich, blessed with a stunning coastline, is home to an art colony, the Bush-Holley Historic Site. A 44-mile (71-km) drive through Fairfield County gives a good overview of the Connecticut coast.

🏛 **Mystic Seaport**
75 Greenmanville Ave (Rte 7). 📞 *(860) 572-5315.* **Ships & exhibits**
◯ *Apr– Oct: 9am–5pm; Nov–Mar: 10am–4pm.* **Grounds** ◯ *9am–6pm daily.* ● *Dec 25.* 🗐
ⓦ *www.visitmysticseaport.com*

🏛 **Deacon John Grave House**
Madison, 581 Boston Post Rd.
📞 *(203) 245-4798.* ◯ *May–Sep: 10am Wed–Sat.*

🏖 **Hammonasset Beach State Park**
I-95, exit 62. **Park** 📞 *(203) 245-2785.* ◯ *8am–dusk daily.* 🗐 🚻
🏕 **Campground reservations**
📞 *(877) 668-2267.*

Vermont

VERMONT'S VARIED ATTRACTIONS are scattered throughout the state. Historic villages and the natural splendors of the Green Mountain National Forest grace the south, while in the northwest Lake Champlain provides a backdrop for the lively college town of Burlington. Famous ski resorts such as Stowe are perched amid the mountains that run the length of the state. In fall, Vermont's display of leaf colors is spectacular.

Woodward Reservoir in the Green Mountain National Forest

Green Mountain National Forest ⑱

i *Forest Supervisor, Green Mountain National Forest, 231 N Main St, Rutland.* **📞** *(802) 747-6700.*

THIS HUGE SPINE of greenery and mountains runs for 350,000 acres (142,850 ha) – almost the entire length of Vermont – along two-thirds of the Green Mountain Range. The mountains, many of them over 4,000 ft (1,200 m) high, have some of the best ski centers in the US, including Sugarbush and Mount Snow.

The National Forest is divided into northern and southern sectors, and encompasses six wilderness areas, many of them with no roads, electricity, or clearly marked trails. Less primitive areas of the forest, however, have picnic sites, camping grounds, and more than 500 miles (805 km) of hiking paths, including the famous Long and Appalachian Trails. The area's lakes, rivers, and reservoirs offer excellent boating and fishing, and there are designated paths for horseback riders as well as bikers.

In the southwest corner of the Green

Mountain National Forest is **Bennington**, Vermont's third-largest city. An important manufacturing center, Bennington is also home to the small but prestigious Bennington College. Three 19th-century wooden covered bridges (just off Route 67) herald the approach to the town, which was established in 1749. A few decades later, Ethan Allen arrived on the scene to lead the Green Mountain Boys, a citizen's militia that scored several decisive victories against British forces during the Revolutionary War.

The town's most prominent landmark is the 306-ft (93-m) high **Bennington Battle Monument**, a granite obelisk commemorating a 1777 battle, when Colonial forces defeated the British. The monument looms over the Old Bennington Historic District, which has a village green ringed by Federal-style brick buildings. The 1806 First Congregational Church is particularly striking, with its vaulted plaster and wood ceilings. Next to the church is the Old Burying Ground where one of America's most loved poets, Robert Frost, is buried.

A major attraction for

The 1891 Bennington Battle Monument

visitors is the **Bennington Museum and Grandma Moses Gallery**. Apart from an impressive collection of Americana, the museum houses several paintings by famed folk artist Anna Mary "Grandma" Moses, who lived in the Bennington area. A farmer's wife with no formal art training, Grandma Moses (1860–1961) started painting landscapes as a hobby when she was in her mid-70s. "Discovered" by critics in 1940, her distinctive primitive paintings soon won international renown.

🏛 Bennington Museum & Grandma Moses Gallery
W Main St. **📞** *(802) 447-1571.* **◻** *Jun–Oct: 9am–6pm daily; Nov–May: 9am–5pm daily.* **●** *Jan 1, Thanksgiving, Dec 25.* **📷 ♿ 🚻**

Manchester ⑲

👥 *3,860.* **✈** **🚌** **i** *Suite 1, 5046 Main St, (802) 362-2100.*

THIS SCENIC TOWN, ringed by mountains, is a favorite destination for both shoppers and skiers. Manchester Village and Manchester Center are major outlet centers in New England, offering brand-name goods in their designer outlets and factory stores. Visitors also enjoy following the Equinox Skyline Drive, with its panoramic views from the crest of Mount Equinox.

The town has two major ski areas – **Stratton**, with more than 90 trails and a hillside ski village with shops and restaurants, and **Bromley**, a busy, family-oriented ski area.

Manchester has been a vacation resort since the 19th century, and its gracious mansions evoke that era. One of the most elegant is **Hildene**, a 24-room Georgian manor built by Robert Todd Lincoln, son of President Abraham Lincoln. Among its notable features are a 1,000-pipe Aeolian organ and an impeccable formal garden.

⚘ Hildene
Rte 7A. **📞** *(802) 362-1788.* **◻** *mid-May–Oct: 9:30am–4pm daily.* **📷 ✏** *every 30 mins.* **♿** **W** *www.hildene.org*

Killington 20

🏔 *1,000.* ✕ ℹ️ *Rte 4, West Killington, (802) 422-3333 or (800) 621-6867.*

S PORTY TYPES who like outdoor adventure and a lively social life head for this year-round resort. Killington operates the largest ski center in the eastern United States, with 200 runs for alpine skiing and snowboarding spread across seven peaks, including nearby Pico Mountain. It also has superb cross-country ski centers at Mountain Top Inn and Mountain Meadows.

Killington itself is the second highest peak in Vermont, at 4,240 ft (1,295 m). The ski season here lasts eight months, longer than anywhere else in Vermont.

In summer as well as fall a gondola ferries visitors up to the peaks from where, on clear day, there are breathtaking views of five states and distant Canada.

Woodstock 21

🏔 *1,000.* ✕ ℹ️ *18 Central St, (802) 457-3555, (888) 496-6378.*

E VEN IN Vermont, where historic, picturesque villages are commonplace, Woodstock stands out. Founded in 1761, the town is an enclave of renovated brick and clapboard Georgian houses, many of them beautifully restored, thanks to the generosity of philanthropists such as the Rockefeller family, and the railroad magnate Frederick Billings (1823–90), who also financed the planting of 10,000 trees here.

Billings Farm and Museum

The SS *Ticonderoga*, in Shelburne Museum

is still a working entity. The 1890 farmhouse has been restored, and visitors can attend seasonal events such as apple-cider pressing in the fall and plowing competitions in the spring. The museum's exhibits include vintage farm implements, butter churns, and ice cutters.

Woodstock is also home to the **Vermont Raptor Center**, a reserve where injured birds such as owls, falcons, eagles, and other birds of prey are cared for until they can be returned to the wild. The center also offers summer day camps for children.

🏛 **Billings Farm & Museum**
River Rd. 📞 *(802) 457-2355.*
⭘ *May–Oct: 10am–5pm daily.
Call for winter hours.* 🅿️ 🖼 🍴

🦅 **Vermont Raptor Center**
Church Hill Rd. 📞 *(802) 457-2779.*
⭘ *10am–4pm daily.* 🅿️ 🖼 ♿

ENVIRONS: Six miles (10 km) east of town is the stunningly beautiful **Quechee Gorge**. The best view of the chasm is on Route 4, which crosses the gorge via a steel bridge. A short hiking trail leads from the parking lot on the east side to the Ottauquechee River that flows below.

Shelburne Museum & Farms 22

Rte 7, 7 miles (11 km) S of Burlington.
📞 *(802) 985-3346.* ⭘ *Apr–mid May:
1–4pm daily (selected buildings only);
mid-May–mid-Oct: 10am–5pm daily.*
⭘ *mid-Oct–Mar, Thanksgiving,
Dec 25.* 🅿️ ♿ 🍴 🖼 🛍
🌐 *www.shelburnemuseum.org*

E STABLISHED IN 1947 by collector Electra Webb, Shelburne Museum's 37 historic structures and their contents constitute one of America's finest museums. Its eclectic collection, which celebrates three centuries of American ingenuity, includes folk art, antique tools, and circus memorabilia, along with scrimshaw, Native American artifacts, and paintings by artists such as Winslow Homer and Grandma Moses.

Among the relocated or replicated historic buildings on view are a horseshoe-shaped **Circus Building**, housing a 500-ft (152-m) long miniature circus parade, an 1890 **Railroad Station**, and an 1871 Lake Champlain lighthouse. Visitors can explore the SS *Ticonderoga*, a former Lake Champlain steamship, which was rescued from the scrap heap by Webb in 1950. The visitor center is located in the 1901 Round Barn, which also features changing exhibits.

Shelburne is home to a historic 1,400-acre (566-ha) estate, Shelburne Farms, with its beautiful green rolling pastures and woodlands. There are tours of the dairy, and there are also special areas where children can pet and play with the animals.

One of the many beautiful homes in the village of Woodstock

First Unitarian Church, Burlington

Burlington ㉓

🚶 40,700. ✈ 🚊 345 Pine St. 🚢 King St Dock. 🏛 Suite 100, 60 Main St, (802) 863-3489, (877) 686-5253. 🎷 Discover Jazz Festival (Jun). 🌐 www.vermont.org

V ERMONT'S LARGEST city, Burlington is one of the most popular tourist destinations in the state. Half of the population of this lively town is made up of students from the University of Vermont and the city's four colleges. Rich in interesting shops and restaurants as well as grand old mansions and historic landmarks, Burlington is also Vermont's center of commerce and industry. It is scenically located on the shores of Lake Champlain.

The center of Burlington is compact and easy to explore on foot. It includes the historic district, at the core of which is the four-block section known as the **Church Street Marketplace**. The neighborhood has been converted into a pedestrian mall, complete with trendy boutiques, patio restaurants, and crafts shops. Many of them are housed in Queen Anne-style buildings from the late 1800s. The historical attractions in this neighborhood include the 1861 **First Unitarian Church**, the oldest house of worship in Burlington, and the **City Hall**, which marks the southern boundary of the marketplace. This graceful building, built of local brick, marble, and granite, dates to 1928. The City Hall Park is a popular outdoor concert venue, and in summer street performers and musicians add color and action to the area.

On the waterfront is **Battery Park**, the site of a battle between US soldiers and the British Royal Navy in 1812. Today, the park is a peaceful place, from where there are lovely views of Burlington Bay and the backdrop of the Adirondack Mountains on the other side of Lake Champlain. South of the park is the **Burlington Boat House**; here a three-decker cruise ship, *Spirit of Ethan Allen III*, takes visitors on a 90-minute trip, which gives a good historical overview, as the captain narrates tales of the Revolutionary War.

The **Robert Hull Fleming Museum**, on the campus of the University of Vermont, is on a hillside overlooking the city. The artifacts in this elegant 1931 Colonial Revival building range from ancient Mesopotamian objects to European paintings and sculptures and Native American crafts.

Statue in Burlington's Battery Park

🏛 **Robert Hull Fleming Museum**
61 Colchester Ave. ☎ (802) 656-0750. ◻ May–mid-Sep: noon–4pm Tue–Fri; mid-Sep–May: 9am–4pm Tue–Fri; year-round: 1–5pm Sat–Sun. ● public hols. 📷 ♿ 🏪

Lake Champlain ㉔

Vermont-New York border from Whitehall to Alburg. ✈ 🚂 🏛 60 Main St, Burlington, (802) 863-3489, (877) 686-5253.

S OMETIMES CALLED the sixth Great Lake because of its size, Lake Champlain is 120 miles (190 km) long, 12 miles (19 km) wide, and has 500 miles (800 km) of shoreline. Said to be the home of "Champ," a water serpent that could be a distant cousin of the Loch Ness monster, the lake is sprinkled with about 70 islands. At the northern end of the lake is **Isle La Motte**, which has a statue of Samuel de Champlain, the French explorer who discovered and explored much of the surrounding region. On nearby **Grand Isle** is America's oldest log cabin (1783). The lake has its western shore in New York State, and scenic hour-long ferry rides run between Burlington and Port Kent, New York.

Some of Lake Champlain's treasures are underwater, preserved in a marine park

Sailing and boating, popular on beautiful Lake Champlain

where scuba divers can explore shipwrecks resting on sandbars and at the bottom of this clear-water lake.

The **Lake Champlain Maritime Museum** at Basin Harbor gives a complete overview of the region's marine history through fascinating displays of ship models, old divers' suits, and photographs of vintage Lake Champlain steamers.

🏛 **Lake Champlain Maritime Museum**
4472 Basin Harbor Rd, Vergennes.
📞 *(802) 475-2022.* 🕐 *May–mid-Oct: 10am–5pm.* ♿ ♿

Stowe 25

👥 *3,500.* ✈ ℹ *51 Main St, (802) 253-7321, (800) 247-8693.*
🌐 *www.gostowe.com*

THIS MOUNTAIN-RINGED village is the skiing capital of New England and draws hordes of visitors in winter. Mountain Road begins in the village and is lined with chalets, motels, restaurants, and pubs; it leads to the area's highest peak, **Mount Mansfield** (4,393 ft/1,339 m).

In summer, too, there are plenty of outdoor activities on offer. Visitors can hike, rock-climb, fish, canoe, bike, or inline skate along the paved, meandering 5.5-mile (8.5-km) **Stowe Recreational Path**, which winds from the village church across the West Branch River, then through green woodlands.

Stowe's other claim to fame is as the home of the musical Von Trapp family, who were

The Austrian-style Trapp Family Lodge in Stowe

the inspiration behind the 1965 movie *The Sound of Music*. After their daring escape from Austria during World War II, they chose Stowe as their new home. Their **Trapp Family Lodge** is set in a 2,700-acre (1,092-ha) estate. This giant wooden chalet is now one of the most popular hotels in the area *(see p180)*.

Ben & Jerry's Ice Cream Factory 26

Rte 100, Waterbury. 📞 *(802) 244-5641, (866) BJTOURS.*
🕐 *Jun: 9am–5pm daily; Jul–Aug: 9am–8pm daily; Sep–Oct: 9am–6pm daily; Nov–May: 10am–5pm daily.*
♿ ♿ 🍴 🎁

ALTHOUGH Ben Cohen and Jerry Greenfield hail from Long Island, New York, they have done more than any other "flatlanders" to put Vermont's dairy industry on the map. In 1977, these child-hood friends paid $5 for a correspondence course on

making ice cream, and soon parlayed their knowledge into what became an enormously successful ice-cream franchise.

No longer privately owned, the factory uses the richest dairy products to produce their ice cream and frozen yogurt. The Ben & Jerry trademark is the black and white Holstein cow, which embellishes everything on sale in the gift shop.

Tours of the factory start every 15 minutes and run for 30 minutes. Visitors learn all there is to know about making ice cream. They are given a bird's-eye view of the factory floor, and at the end of the tour they get a chance to sample the products and sometimes taste new flavors.

Ben & Jerry's bus, gaily decorated with dairy cows

A ski-lift in Vermont, one of the best skiing areas of the US

SKIING IN NEW ENGLAND

In New England, topnotch slopes and cross-country ski trails are never far away. The best skiing is concentrated in the three northern states. Vermont has the most high-quality peaks, and the world-famous resorts of Killington and Stowe. Two great trails in Vermont for skiers and snowshoers are the Catamount Trail and the Trapp Family Lodge Ski Center. New Hampshire's White Mountains have some of the best downhill, alpine, and cross-country ski trails in the Northeast. In Maine, Sugarloaf/USA and Sunday River are considered the best hills in the state. Downhill ski trails are rated by a standard code: Easier=green circle; More difficult=blue square; Most Difficult=black diamond; and Expert=double diamond. Equipment, and lessons for all levels are available at all the resorts.

New Hampshire

NEW HAMPSHIRE'S NATURAL BEAUTY is evident all over the state. The northern part is rippled by the tall peaks of the White Mountain Range and the spectacular chasm of Franconia Notch. Ponds and lakes, such as the pristine Lake Winnipesaukee, dot central New Hampshire. The main cities – historic Concord and lively Portsmouth, with its scenic Atlantic coastline – nestle amid the tranquil farmlands of the south.

The striking exterior of the Mount Washington Hotel & Resort

Bretton Woods ㉗

🏃 550. ✈ 🛈 (800) 346-3687. ☑

THIS TINY ENCLAVE in the Mount Washington Valley has an unusual claim to fame. In 1944, with the need for currency stability after the economic upheavals of World War II, it hosted the United Nations conference that led to the establishment of the International Monetary Fund and, later, the World Bank.

The setting for this historic meeting was the magnificent Spanish Renaissance-style **Mount Washington Hotel and Resort** (see p180). Opened in 1902, the hotel's sparkling white exterior and crimson roof stand out in contrast to Mount Washington, looming behind it. The hotel has entertained several distin-

guished guests, including the British Prime Minister Winston Churchill, and three US presidents. Surrounded by 17,300 acres (7,000 ha) of parkland, its facilities include a 27-hole golf course. Nearby, Bretton Woods ski area offers alpine skiing and 62 miles (100 km) of cross-country trails.

🏨 Mount Washington Hotel & Resort
Rte 302, Bretton Woods. 📞 (603) 278-1000, (800) 258-0330. ♿ 🛗

ENVIRONS: Dominating the Mount Washington Valley is the 6,288-ft (1,917-m) peak of **Mount Washington**, the highest in the northeastern United States. The peak has the dubious distinction of having the worst weather in the world, and in April 1934 clocked the highest wind ever

recorded on earth: 230 mph (370 kph). On clear days, however, there are panoramic views from the top. There are hiking trails and an auto road to the summit, but the most exciting way up is by the **Mount Washington Cog Railroad**. This steam-powered train chugs the 3.5-mile (5.6-km) route to the top along a heart-stoppingly steep track. Some of the best alpine skiing is in Tuckerman Ravine on Mount Washington.

Franconia Notch ㉘

I-93, Franconia Notch Pkwy. 🛈 (603) 823-8800. Park ◯ daily. **Flume Gorge Visitor Center** 📞 (603) 745-8391. ◯ May–Oct: 9am–5pm daily. 🅿 for Flume Gorge, Visitor Center, & campsites. 🖥 www.flumegorge.com

THIS SPECTACULAR mountain pass, carved between the Kinsman and Franconia ranges, and designated as the Franconia Notch State Park, has some of the state's most stunning natural wonders. Foremost among them was the **Old Man of the Mountain**, a rocky outcrop on the side of a cliff that resembled a man's profile until the nose and forehead crashed down in May 2003. Other attractions compensate for the loss. The trout-filled **Profile Lake** reflects the brilliant colors of fall foliage on the slopes of **Cannon Mountain**. A boardwalk and stairways lead visitors through the **Flume Gorge**, a narrow, chasm whose granite walls tower more than 90 ft (27 m) above the boardwalk, while an aerial tramway speeds

---

FALL FOLIAGE IN NEW ENGLAND

Thousands of visitors head for New England in the fall, to gaze in wonder at the annual changing of leaf colors. The color change is not just a capricious act of Nature. As daylight hours diminish, the leaves of deciduous trees stop producing the green pigment chlorophyll, and other pigments hidden behind the chlorophyll's color now burst into view. More pigments are produced by sugars that remain trapped in the leaves. The result is a riotous display of shades of yellow, orange, crimson, and maroon. The peak period for "leaf-peeping" varies from early October in northern New England to late October in the southern section, but this can differ, depending on the weather (see Fall Foliage Hotlines, p175).

Glorious colors lighting up the New England landscape in fall

Narrow Flume Gorge in Franconia Notch State Park

passengers to the 4,180-ft (1254-m) summit of Cannon Mountain in just 8 minutes.

Robert Frost (1874–1963), one of America's best-loved poets, settled in the Franconia Notch region in 1915. The majestic setting inspired him to pen many of his greatest works here, including the famous poem *Stopping By Woods on a Snowy Evening*.

White Mountain National Forest ㉙

719 Main St, Laconia, (603) 528-8721. **Camping** *(877) 444-6777. Call for availability & reservations.*

NEW HAMPSHIRE'S most beautiful wilderness area, the White Mountain National Forest, sprawls over 770,000 acres (311,600 ha). The area has an abundance of wildlife, including a large population of moose, which can often be seen from the road.

Outdoor activities offered in this region range from bird-watching and rock-climbing to skiing and kayaking. But even less sporty travelers will revel in the spectacular scenery visible from their car – valleys flanked by tall pine forests, waterfalls that tumble over rocky outcrops, and more than 20 summits that soar to over 4,000 ft (1,200 m). An especially scenic stretch of road is the 100-mile (161-km) long **White Mountains Trail** that loops across Mount Washington Valley through Crawford Notch and Franconia Notch. In autumn, brilliant fall foliage colors transform the

rugged countryside into a palette of flaming red maples, golden birch, and maroon northern red oaks, interspersed with evergreens.

Another popular route is the **Kancamagus Highway**, touted by many as the most beautiful road in New England. This 34-mile (55-km) road, which runs through the White Mountain National Forest between Lincoln and Conway, offers exceptional vistas as it climbs 3,000 ft (914 m) through the Kancamagus Pass. The road descends into the Saco Valley and joins up with the trout-filled Swift River. There is easy access for fishermen from the highway to the river, and there are campgrounds and picnic areas along the entire length of the highway. Well-marked trails allow drivers to stretch their legs amid the beautiful scenery – a popular one is the short loop that leads to the lovely Sabbaday Falls.

Kancamagus Hwy

Rte 112 between Lincoln & Conway. *Saco District Ranger Station, 33 Kancamagus Hwy, (603) 447-5448.*

ENVIRONS: Close to the White Mountains is the **Lincoln/ Woodstock** region, whose main attraction is **Clark's Trading Post**. This curious combination of circus acts, amusement park rides, and museums makes a welcome change for children after a leaf-peeping drive. Lincoln is a base camp for both backwoods adventurers and stick-to-the-road sightseers. Nearby **Loon Mountain** is one of the state's premier ski resorts. In summer, it offers activities

such as nature walks, tours of caves, mountain biking, and horseback riding.

Loon Mountain

E of I-93, near Lincoln. (603) 745-6281, (800) 229-5666.

Lake Winnipesaukee ㉚

Lakes Region Association, (800) 605-2537. *www.winnipesaukee.com*

WITH A SHORELINE that meanders for 240 miles (386 km), and a surface area of 72 sq miles (187 sq km), this stunning lake has New Hampshire's largest stretch of waterfront. Ringed by mountains and scattered with 274 islands, Lake Winnipesaukee has sheltered bays, harbors, and resort towns around its shores. The largest and prettiest of these is **Wolfeboro**. Leaving from Weirs Beach, the M/S *Mount Washington* offers the best scenic cruise in all New England. To its north is upscale **Meredith**, with lovely lakeside homes.

North of Meredith is pristine **Squam Lake**, ideal for boating and fishing, where the movie *On Golden Pond* (1981) was filmed. The town of **Center Sandwich** is on Winnipesaukee's north shore. Surrounded by woodland, it is a favorite destination during fall foliage season. On the eastern shore, the Castle in the Clouds mansion crowns the crest of a hill that rises some 750 ft (229 m) above the lake. A 70-mile (113-km) drive around Lake Winnipesaukee takes in all these sights.

Along the Kancamagus Highway, White Mountain National Forest

Canterbury Shaker Village ㉛

288 Shaker Rd, Canterbury. 【 (603)
783-9511, (866) 783-9511.
⬡ May–Oct: 10am–5pm daily; Apr &
Nov–Dec: 10am–4pm Sat & Sun. 🅿
🄫 🍴 🛍 🛗 ⓦ www.shakers.org

F OUNDED IN 1792, this village
was occupied by Shakers
for 200 years. The Shakers
were a sect that broke away
from the Quakers, who fled
to America to escape religious
persecution in Britain in the
mid-18th century. Their belief
in celibacy and strict separa-
tion from the rest of the
world eventually led to their
demise. The 690-acre (280-ha)
site, which has several buildings open to visitors, is punctuated by millponds, nature
trails, and traditional gardens.
Skilled artisans can be seen
re-creating Shaker crafts,
known for their simple
lines and beautiful
workmanship.

**Picturesque buildings at
Canterbury Shaker Village**

The belfry contains a
bell made by the
Revolutionary War hero Paul
Revere.

Dormer rooms were
used for summer
sleeping and as clothes
cupboards.

**Brethren's
Retiring
Room**

**The Sisters'
Retiring Room** was
where women had their
separate sleeping
quarters, each equipped
with plain furniture.

The Dining Room
could hold as many as
60 Shakers per sitting.

The Old Library and Museum
contains 1,500 Shaker books and
documents, and a museum of
Shaker artifacts.

Concord ㉜

🏙 37,500. ✈ 🚌 🚍 🛈 40
Commercial St, (603) 224-2508.

N EW HAMPSHIRE'S capital is
a quiet little town, dom-
inated by its impressive **State
House**. Built in 1819 from
granite and marble, it is one
of the oldest state houses in
America. Another landmark is
the giant glass pyramid of the
**Christa McAuliffe Planetar-
ium**. A Concord schoolteach-
er, McAuliffe (1948–86) was
tragically killed when the
Challenger Space Shuttle *(see
p302)*, launched by NASA on
January 28, 1986, exploded
and crashed 73 seconds after
lift-off. The astronomy and
space exploration exhibits in
the planetarium also include
multi-media shows such as
"Destination Mars."

**🏛 Christa McAuliffe
Planetarium**
3 Institute Dr. 【 (603) 271-7827. ⬡
10am–2pm Mon–Wed, 10am–5pm
Thu–Sat, noon–5pm Sun. ● weekend after Labor Day 🅿 ♿ 🛗

Manchester ㉝

🏙 105,250. ✈ 🚌 🚍 🛈 889 Elm St,
(603) 666-6600. 🎪 (603) 622-7531.

O NCE A MAJOR center of the
textile industry, with its
mills powered by waterpower
from the Merrimack River,
today Manchester is famous
as the home of New Hamp-

**Painting in the Currier Gallery of
Art in Manchester**

shire's premier art museum,
the **Currier Gallery of Art**.
Its collection includes works
by such European masters
as John Constable, Claude
Monet, and Henri Matisse.
The west wing houses the
works of 20th-century
American painters such as
Andrew Wyeth (b.1917) and
Georgia O'Keeffe (1887–

Portsmouth's Market Street, a favorite with tourists

1986), famous for her surrealistic renditions of New Mexico's landscape. Also part of the museum is the Zimmerman House. The single-story home with its elegant exterior was built in 1950 by the pioneering American architect Frank Lloyd Wright. The only indoor mall in the state is the Mall of New Hampshire in Manchester.

🏛 Currier Gallery of Art

201 Myrtle Way. 🌀 *(603) 669-6144.* ◐ *11am–5pm Mon, Wed, Fri, & Sun, 11am–8pm Thu, 10am–5pm Sat.* ▨
▨ ⬥ ⬛ ⬜ ⓦ *www.currier.org*

Portsmouth ❸❹

🧍 *26,000.* ✈ ⬛ *10 Ladd St.*
🛈 *500 Market St or Market Sq, (603) 436-1118.* ◑ *mid-May–Oct: 8:30am–1pm daily.* ▨ *Market Square Day (Jun), Prescott Park Arts Festival (Jul–Aug daily).*
ⓦ *www.portsmouthchamber.org*

GIRDED BY THE Piscataqua River and North and South Mill ponds, Portsmouth is a historic town, compact enough to be explored on foot. Established in 1623, it became a prosperous hub of maritime commerce by the 18th century. It was also a hotbed of revolutionary fervor, and the place where the Colonial naval hero John Paul Jones (1747–92) took command of the warship *Ranger*. During the American Revolution, Jones led several raids along the British coast, for which he was awarded a gold medal by Congress.

A number of Portsmouth's historic buildings, many of which have been turned into boutiques and restaurants, are in the downtown core, especially along **Market Street**. Historic houses and gardens can also be found along the **Portsmouth Harbor Trail**, a walking tour of the Historic District. Especially worth visiting is the elegant 1763 Moffatt-Ladd House on Market Street, one of the earliest examples of the Federal style of architecture. The Wentworth-Gardner House on Mechanic Street, is regarded as one of the finest examples of Georgian architecture in the country. Both houses have beautiful interiors with period furnishings.

A popular destination in summer is Water Country, which has a huge wave pool, a pirate ship, and a man-made lagoon. Interactive exhibits are the highlight of the **Children's Museum of Portsmouth**, where children can fly in the replica of a space shuttle or command a submarine. Visitors can explore the real thing at Albacore Park where a sleek submarine, the USS *Albacore*, is on display. When it was built in 1953, it was the fastest underwater vessel of its kind.

Portsmouth's most popular attraction is **Strawbery Banke**, a 10-acre (4-ha) site near the waterfront located at the very spot at which Portsmouth was founded. This outdoor museum, which can be explored on foot or in authentic horse-drawn carriages, contains more than 40 buildings that depict life from 1695 to 1955. Many buildings are set amid gardens cultivated according to their eras, from early pioneer herb gardens to formal Victorian flower beds. The houses open to the public are furnished in period style and contain interesting collections of decorative arts and ceramics.

The **Jones House**, a 1790 structure, displays artifacts excavated at the site. The elegant 1760s Chase House is furnished with sumptuous pieces from several periods, while the Sherburne House, built in 1695, now serves as an exhibit on 17th-century house design and construction. In the Dinsmore Shop, built in 1800, visitors can watch a cooper making barrels and casks in the traditional way.

Strawbery Banke also has a Colonial Revival Garden, the Aldrich Garden, planted with flowers mentioned in the poetry of Portsmouth native Thomas Bailey Aldrich.

🏛 Children's Museum of Portsmouth

280 Marcy St. 🌀 *(603) 436-3853.* ◐ *mid-Jun–Sep: 10am–5pm Mon–Sat, 1–5pm Sun; Oct–mid-Jun: 10am– 5pm Tue–Sat, 1–5pm Sun.* ▨ ⬥

🏛 Strawbery Banke

Marcy St. 🌀 *(603) 433-1100.* ◐ *check for hours.* ▨ ⬥ *limited access to some buildings.* ⬛ ⬜ ⬜
ⓦ *www.strawberybanke.org*

Inside lavishly furnished Chase House, Strawbery Banke, in Portsmouth

Maine

THE LARGEST STATE in New England, Maine is truly the Great Outdoors. Its most popular attractions are found along the spectacular coastline, beginning in the southeast with its largest and liveliest city, Portland, and the resort towns of the Kennebunks. Farther north, yachts and windjammers ply the waters of Penobscot Bay, while Acadia National Park stands as Maine's coastal jewel. World-class skiing, hiking, and boating opportunities are found inland, at Bethel and Sugarloaf.

Portland 35

👥 65,000. ✈ 🚌 950 Congress St. ⛴ Commercial & Franklin Sts. ℹ 245 Commercial St, (877) 833-1374. 🛒 Wed & Sat. 🎉 Old Port Festival (Jun 4), Victorian Holiday (Nov 24–Dec 23). [W] www.visitportland.com

THIS HISTORIC city has a beautiful location on the crest of a peninsula, with expansive views of Casco Bay and the Calendar Islands. Once a flourishing port, Portland was devastated by no less than four major fires, the last one in 1866. Nevertheless, the city still has a number of sturdy stone Victorian buildings, testifying to its prosperous past.

The West End has fine mansions and a splendid promenade overlooking the water. Portland's liveliest area, however, is around the Old Port, near the harbor. This restored neighborhood's narrow streets are filled with shops, restaurants, and art galleries. Dominating the area is the regal **United States Customs House**, with its gilded ceilings, marble staircases, and chandeliers. It was built after the Civil War (1861–65). From the docks, ships offer cruises to the Calendar Islands, harbor tours, and deep-sea fishing trips.

West of the Old Port, the **Portland Museum of Art**, displays works by the area's most famous artist, Winslow Homer (1836–1910), as well as by European masters such as Gauguin and Picasso. The **Children's Museum of Maine** has three floors of interactive exhibits to keep youngsters amused. The **Maine Narrow Gauge Railroad Co. & Museum** displays vintage locomotives and offers scenic trips along the waterfront.

Several of Portland's fine historic houses are open to visitors. They include the **Wadsworth-Longfellow House** (1785) where poet Henry Wadsworth Longfellow grew up; and the Victoria Mansion with its painted trompe l'oeil walls. Portland's signature landmark is the Portland Head Light at Fort Williams Park. First illuminated in 1791, the lighthouse is surrounded by beach and picnic areas, and the keeper's house is now a museum.

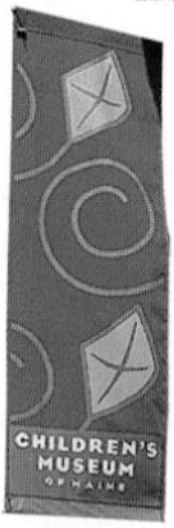
CHILDREN'S MUSEUM OF MAINE

Children's Museum banner

🏛 Portland Museum of Art

7 Congress Sq. ☎ (207) 775-6148. ○ mid-Oct–early May: 10am–5pm Tue, Wed, Sat, & Sun, 10am–9pm Thu & Fri; late May–mid-Oct: 10am–5pm Mon. ● Oct–May: Mon. 🚫📷 ♿

🏛 Children's Museum of Maine

142 Free St. ☎ (207) 828-1234. ○ year-round: 10am–5pm Tue–Sat, noon–5pm Sun; May–Sep: 10am–5pm Mon. ● public hols. 🚫📷 🛍

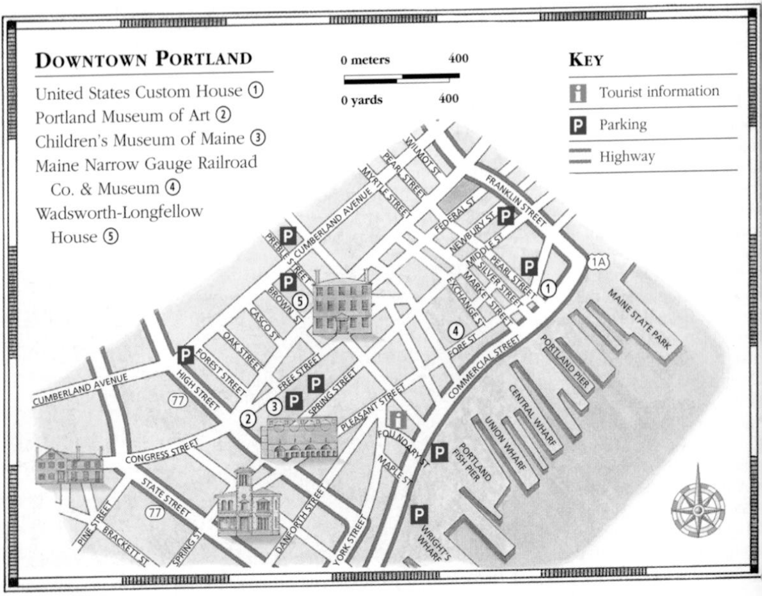
DOWNTOWN PORTLAND
United States Custom House 1
Portland Museum of Art 2
Children's Museum of Maine 3
Maine Narrow Gauge Railroad Co. & Museum 4
Wadsworth-Longfellow House 5
0 meters 400
0 yards 400
KEY
Tourist information
Parking
Highway
WILMOT ST
PEARL STREET
MYRTLE STREET
CUMBERLAND AVENUE
PREBLE STREET
FRANKLIN STREET
FEDERAL ST
NEWBURY ST
MIDDLE ST
PEARL STREET
SILVER STREET
MARKET STREET
EXCHANGE ST
FORE ST
BROWN ST
CASCO ST
OAK STREET
FOREST STREET
HIGH STREET
FREE STREET
SPRING STREET
PLEASANT STREET
COMMERCIAL STREET
FOUNDARY ST
MAPLE ST
CUMBERLAND AVENUE
CONGRESS STREET
STATE STREET
PINE STREET
BRACKETT ST
SPRING ST
DANFORTH STREET
YORK STREET
WRIGHT'S WHARF
PORTLAND FISH PIER
UNION WHARF
CENTRAL WHARF
PORTLAND PIER
MAINE STATE PARK
1A
77

The Kennebunks 36

🏠 ℹ️ *17 Western Ave, Kennebunk,
(207) 967-0857.*

Fɪʀsᴛ ᴀ ᴛʜʀɪᴠɪɴɢ shipbuilding
center and port, then a
summer retreat for the rich,
the Kennebunks are made up
of two villages, Kennebunk
and Kennebunkport.

Kennebunkport's historic
village is graced by several
Federal and Greek Revival
structures, and the striking
1824 **South Congregational
Church**, with its soaring
white steeple. History of a
different sort can be found at
the **Seashore Trolley
Museum**, where some 200
antique streetcars are housed,
including one called "Desire."
Tours of the countryside are
offered aboard one of the
restored trolleys.

The scenic drive along
Route 9 offers views of surf
along rocky Cape Arundel. At
Cape Porpoise, travelers can
sample lobster pulled fresh
from the Atlantic. Kennebunk
is famous for its beaches,
notably **Kennebunk Beach**,
and for one of the most
romantic houses in New
England, the 1826 **Wedding
Cake House**. According to
local lore, George Bourne was
unexpectedly called to sea
before his marriage. Although
a very hastily arranged wedding took place, there was no
time to bake the traditional
wedding cake. So the ship-
builder vowed to his bride
that on his return he would
remodel their home to look
like a wedding cake. Today
the ornate latticework and
gingerbread trim offer proof
that Bourne was a man of his
word. Interesting architectural
walking tours of Kennebunk's
historic area are offered by
the **Brick Store Museum**,
housed in four restored 19th-
century buildings.

🏛 **Seashore Trolley Museum**
195 Log Cabin Rd, Kennebunkport.
📞 *(207) 967-2800.* ⏰ check for
times. ♿ ⚐

🏛 **Brick Store Museum**
17 Main St, Kennebunk. 📞 *(207)
985-4802.* ⏰ *May–Dec: 10am–
4:30pm Tue–Fri, 10am–1pm Sat.*
● *Sun, public hols.* ♿

Boats on the waters of Penobscot Bay's Stonington village, Deer Isle

Penobscot Bay 37

🚢 **Rockland** ℹ️ *1 Harbor Pk, (207)
596-0376.* **Camden** ℹ️ *Commercial
St, Public Landing, (207) 236-4404.*
Searsport ℹ️ *Main & Steamboat,
(207) 548-0173.* **Castine** ℹ️ *Emerson
Hall, Court St, (207) 326-4502.*
Deer Isle ℹ️ *Rte 15 at Eggemoggin
Rd, (207) 348-6124.*

Pᴇɴᴏʙsᴄᴏᴛ ʙᴀʏ is picture-
book Maine, with hills
sloping down into the ocean,
wave-pounded cliffs, sheltered harbors bobbing with
boats, and lobster traps piled
on the docks. Penobscot Bay
is also famous for its islands,
which can be visited on boat
tours from the mainland.

Penobscot Bay's commercial
center is the fishing town of
Rockland, whose biggest
event is the lobster festival
on the first full weekend of
August. A prime attraction
is the Farnsworth Art
Museum, displaying the
works of leading American
painters such as Edward
Hopper and Andrew Wyeth.

A favorite destination for
tourists is **Camden**, with its

Sailboats moored in Penobscot
Bay's Camden Harbor

spired churches, elegant
homes, and shops along the
waterfront. A short distance
from the village is Camden
Hills State Park, which offers
breathtaking views of the bay
from the summit of Mount
Battie. Standing on this point,
the poet Edna St. Vincent
Millay (1892–1950) was
inspired to write her first
volume of poetry. Nearby
Searsport is regarded as the
antiques capital of Maine and
has large and busy fleamarkets
on weekends in the summer.

The more remote eastern
shore leads to serene, perfectly preserved villages such as
Castine and Blue Hill. In
Castine is the historic Fort
George, built by the British in
1799, and witness to the
American Navy's worst defeat
during the Revolutionary War.
Blue Hill is a living postcard,
surrounded by fields of blueberries, and with many of its
clapboard buildings listed on
the National Historic Register.

Deer Isle, reached from the
mainland via a graceful suspension bridge, is actually a
series of small islands linked
by causeways. Island highlights include the scenic
towns of Stonington and Deer
Isle. From Stonington, it is an
8-mile (13-km) boat ride to
the thickly wooded Isle au
Haut, much of which belongs
to Acadia National Park *(see
p172)*. Another unspoiled
haven is Monhegan Island
with its dramatic cliffs and
hiking trails. North Haven
Island is a summer colony,
covered with meadows of
wildflowers. Vinalhaven, with
its granite shoreline and
inland moors, is a perfect
place for a swim or a hike.

Bass Harbor Head, which exemplifies Maine's rock-bound shoreline

Acadia National Park ⑱

🛈 *Hulls Cove Visitor Center, off Rte 3 in Hulls Cove, (207) 288-3338.*
◯ *daily.* 🚌 *Bangor–Bar Harbor.* 🅿️ *at Hulls Cove.* ♿
ⓦ *www.nps.gov/acad/home.htm*

Aɴ ᴜɴsᴘᴏɪʟᴇᴅ paradise, heavily visited in summer, the 35,000-acre (14,164-ha) Acadia National Park covers much of Mount Desert Island, off the southeast Maine coast.

The park's main attraction is the scenic Loop Road, a 27-mile (43-km) drive that climbs and dips with the pink granite mountains of the east coast of the island and takes in its main sights. Among these is the 1,527-ft (465-m) high **Cadillac Mountain**, the highest point on the Atlantic Coast. Hiking trails and an auto road lead to spectacular panoramas at the summit. The road continues south to the idyllic **Sand Beach**, but the icy water discourages many swimmers. Farther south there is a unique natural phenomenon known locally as **Thunder Hole** – when the tide rises during heavy winds, air trapped in this crevice is compressed and then expelled with a resounding boom. The Loop Road continues inland, swinging past Jordan Pond, Bubble Pond, and Eagle Lake.

On the southern shore of the park is the quaint village of **Bass Harbor Head**, where an 1858 lighthouse is perched on the rocky coastline, offering magnificent views of the ocean. The park is home to numerous animals, including woodchucks, white-tailed deer, and red foxes. Visitors who want a closer, more intimate look at the park's flora and fauna can do so on foot, bike, or horseback along the 45 miles (72 km) of old broken-stone carriage roads, which wind through the park.

Cutting through the center of Mount Desert Island is **Somes Sound**, a finger-shaped natural fjord that juts 5 miles (8 km) inland. It separates the quiet village of Southwest Harbor from Northeast Harbor, which is the center of Mount Desert Island's social scene, with its upscale shops and handsome mansions. Southwest Harbor is home to the **Mount Desert Oceanarium**, which features 20 tanks teeming with live coastal sea animals.

The elegant resort town of **Bar Harbor** is a lively tourist center and a good base from which to explore the Acadia National Park. More than 3,000,000 visitors each year pass through Bar Harbor on their way to the wilds of park. Located on Mount Desert Island's northeastern shore, it was the 19th century summer haven for some of America's richest people, including the Astors and the Vanderbilts. In 1947, a fire destroyed a third of the town's lavish homes, thus ending its reign as a high-society enclave. The town's attractions include the **Criterion Theater**, an Art Deco gem that shows both popular and art films, and the **Abbe Museum**, which celebrates Maine's Native American heritage with displays of tools, crafts, art, artifacts, and archaeology. The Wild Gardens of Acadia, with some 300 species of local plants, are located next to the museum.

Bar Harbor Oceanarium, situated 8.5 miles (14 km) northwest of the town, is the place to see harbor seals, explore a salt marsh on Thomas Bay Marsh Walk, or visit the Maine Lobster Museum and take in demonstrations of lobstering.

Acadia Zoo in Trenton, lying across the bridge from Mount Desert Island, is home to some 45 species of animals, including reindeer, wolves, monkeys, and moose.

🛈 **Bar Harbor**
🛈 *93 Cottage St, (207) 288-5103.*

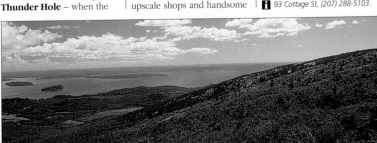

Cadillac Mountain, the highest point on the Atlantic coast, with striking panoramas at the summit

Roosevelt Cottage, built in 1897, on Campobello Island

Campobello Island ㊴

Roosevelt Campobello International Park 🚺 (506) 752-2922. ◯ daily. ⬛ every 15 mins. ♿ 🅆 www.fdr.net

LOCATED ON Campobello Island is the **Roosevelt Campobello International Park**, established in 1964 as a memorial to President Franklin D. Roosevelt *(see p49)*. The island's main settlement of Welshpool was where the future president spent most of his summers until 1921, when he contracted polio. Despite his disability, Roosevelt was elected to four terms, leading the US through the Great Depression and World War II.

The highlight of the 2,800-acre (1,333-ha) park – which actually lies in Canada and is the only international park in the world – is **Roosevelt Cottage**. Built in 1897, this sprawling, 34-room wood-frame summer home displays mementos that had belonged to President F.D. Roosevelt.

At the island's southern tip is **Liberty Point**, where a pair of observation decks perched on the rugged cliffs offer far-ranging views of the Atlantic.

A short distance inland from here is **Lower Duck Pond Bog**, a prime habitat for the great blue heron, killdeer, and the American black duck.

On the island's western shore is **Mulholland Point**, with an 1885 lighthouse and a picnic site offering views of the FDR Memorial Bridge. Other good picnic sites are at Raccoon Beach located on the eastern shore.

Sugarloaf ㊵

🚺 (207) 237-2000, (800) 843-5623.

MAINE'S HIGHEST ski mountain, Sugarloaf is the center of this touristy village packed with hotels, restaurants, and condominiums. Downhill skiers, in particular, are attracted to **Sugarloaf/USA** ski center with its more than 100 trails and a vertical drop of 2,800 ft (870 m). The center also offers cross-country skiing, ice skating, and snowshoeing.

In summer, the emphasis shifts to the resort's 18-hole golf course, boating on the lakes and rivers, and hiking in the nearby Carrabassett Valley. The resort is also famous for its network of more than 50 miles (80 km) of mountain biking trails, through flat as well as steep and challenging terrain.

🅈 **Sugarloaf/USA**
Carrabassett Valley. 🚺 (207) 237-2000, (800) 843-5623. ◯ 8:30am–3:50pm daily. 🈳 📶 ♿ in lodge. 🅿

Bethel ㊶

🚹 2,500. 🚉 🚺 30 Cross St; (207) 824-2282, (800) 442-5826.

A PICTURESQUE historic district, a major ski resort, and proximity to the White Mountains give Bethel year-round appeal. First settled in 1796, the town was a farming and lumbering center until the coming of the railroad in 1851 made it a popular resort. The line-up of classic clapboard mansions on the town green include the Federal-style **Moses Mason House** (c.1813), restored and furnished with period pieces.

There are scenic drives in all directions, taking in unspoiled Colonial hamlets such as Waterford to the south, and beautiful mountain terrain to the north. **Sunday River Ski Resort**, 6 miles (10 km) north of town in Newry, has eight mountains and more than 100 ski trails. **Grafton Notch State Park** has spectacular scenery along its drives and hiking trails. The park's special spots include waterfalls and sweeping views of the scenic surroundings from Table Rock and Old Speck Mountain.

🏛 **Moses Mason House**
10–14 Broad St. 🚺 (207) 824-2908. ◯ Jul–early Sep: 1–4pm Tue–Sun. 🈳 📶 ♿
🅈 **Sunday River Ski Resort**
Off Rte 2 in Newry. 🚺 (207) 824-3000, (800) 5432-SKI. ◯ 9am–4pm Mon–Fri, 8am–4pm Sat–Sun. 🈳
♣ **Grafton Notch State Park**
Rte 26 NW of Newry. 🚺 (207) 824-2912. ◯ mid-May–mid-Oct. 🈳

Screw Auger Falls in Grafton Notch State Park, Bethel

Practical Information

ALTHOUGH PARTICULARLY POPULAR during summer and fall, New England is a four-season vacation destination. The superb skiing facilities attract tourists during winter, which often lasts from mid-November to April. The region offers a wide variety of recreational activities within a relatively small area. On any weekend, vacationers can hike the White Mountains of New Hampshire, swim at Maine's Ogunquit Beach, and take in the Boston Symphony Orchestra. Outside of Boston, where public transportation is excellent, you definitely need a car for sightseeing.

TOURIST INFORMATION

STATE TOURISM offices are great sources of information and are happy to send road maps, brochures, and listings of attractions, accommodations, and events, free of charge. Some places also offer discount vouchers for lodgings, restaurants, and entry fees. Many towns have a visitors' bureau that offers information on local lodgings, events, and restaurants.

PERSONAL SECURITY

NEW ENGLAND'S comparitively low crime rate makes it a safe holiday destination. But it is good to take precautions. Since pickpockets tend to frequent popular tourist sights, use a money belt for cash and documents and keep cameras out of sight. Avoid wearing expensive jewelry and leave your valuables in the hotel safe.

NATURAL HAZARDS

THE VARIETY of outdoor activities in New England often entail risks, which can be minimized with proper precautions. Always be prepared for sudden changes in the weather, especially in higher elevations. Wear protective gear for adventure sports and never try to interfere with wildlife.

GETTING AROUND

MANY BUS companies serve particular sections of New England, making it relatively simple to get from state to state. In Boston and Cambridge, it is easier to get around by public transportation than by driving. Once outside the city you will need a car. In fact, much of New England's charm lies along scenic jaunts down the coast and driving tours during the fall-foliage season.

Several books list the best driving tours of the region. **Yankee** magazine, for instance, offers a complete itinerary of recommended routes, historic stops, and places to eat and stay.

SAFETY FOR DRIVERS

LARGE AREAS of New England are wild, so be prepared for any eventuality. This is doubly true in winter, when sudden blizzards and white-outs caused by blowing snow can leave motorists stranded. In winter, stock salt, a snow brush, an ice scraper, and a small shovel. If you do get stuck in an out-of-the-way place, stay inside your car. Keep the motor running for warmth, but open your window slightly to prevent carbon monoxide buildup. **American Automobile Association (AAA)** and other auto clubs provide roadside assistance.

LAWS

THE LEGAL drinking age in New England is 21, and young people can be asked to produce a proof of age in order to buy alcohol or enter a bar. You can lose your driver's license if caught driving under the influence of alcohol. Cigarettes can be sold only to people 18 years of age or older. Smoking and drinking in public spaces is illegal. Most restaurants have separate areas for smokers.

SPORTS & OUTDOOR ACTIVITIES

WITH MILES OF coastline, mountain ranges, forests, and rivers, the region has much to offer to sports lovers. The choice of camping areas in national forests range from primitive sites to ones with various facilities. Hiking trails crisscross almost the entire region, with the most popular being the New England section of the Appalachian Trail and Vermont's Long Trail. The **Appalachian Trail Conference** runs various information and education programs on the Appalachian

THE CLIMATE OF NEW ENGLAND

New England's weather can vary greatly from year to year. Generally, the short spring is cloudy and wet, with rainy skies and melting snow. Summer can be unpredictable, but is generally dry – July and August are usually the sunniest months. Bright fall days out among the colorful foliage are spectacular – the peak fall-foliage period usually lasts from mid-September to late October. Snow usually starts in December; the temperature can dip to 0° F (–18° C) or lower in winter. In general, it is warmer along the coast and in the southern section of New England.

BOSTON			
°F/C	80/27		
	63/17	63/17	
55/12		46/8	
32°F 39/4			36/2
0°C			20/–7
17 days	20 days	19 days	16 days
3.5 in	2.8 in	3.3 in	3.6 in
month	Apr	Jul	Oct	Jan

Trail. Miles of quiet back roads in the region are a cyclist's paradise. Mountain bikers also have plenty to choose from. Some ski areas let bikers use their lifts and slopes in summer.

New England's Green and White Mountains offer superb rock climbing, hang gliding, and paragliding sites.

Anglers will love New England. Deep-sea fishing is best at Point Judith in Rhode Island. Brook trout and bass are plentiful in the inland streams and lakes, especially in Maine. The state's lattice-work of rivers is ideal for canoeing, kayaking, and whitewater rafting.

Penobscot Bay, Maine, and Newport, Rhode Island, are both considered sailing meccas. For those who want something calmer than the Atlantic Ocean, New England has countless lakes, and boats can be rented at many seaside and lakeside resorts. Whale-watching cruises have become a very popular activity. Take the cruise on a calm day, as choppy water can cause seasickness.

The region's northernmost reaches, with a thick annual blanket of snow, offer great skiing, skating, and snowmo-biling opportunities. Stowe,

located in Vermont, can claim the title of New England's ski capital. The world-famous **Stowe Mountain Resort** offers excellent trails for skiers of all levels.

ENTERTAINMENT

NEW ENGLAND is a traveler's dream as it offers a wide range of entertainment. Free concerts and festivals abound in fall, spring, and summer, and there is no shortage of bars and nightclubs in which to slake, or build, your thirst. Boston's Harvard Square has been famous for four decades for its nightly and weekend scene of street performers. Mellow jazz lounges and smoky blues bars attract a devoted clientele.

Classical music, theater, and dance have long been the mainstays of the region's cultural identity. The larger towns and cities have good symphony orchestras, dance, and drama companies. But the hub of the region's performing arts is Boston. The **Boston Symphony Orchestra (BSO)** and its popular music doppleganger, the Boston Pops, are the city's cherished institutions. The BSO performs a full schedule of concerts at Symphony Hall

from October to April. The Pops move in for perfor-mances in May and June.

Theater is alive and well across New England's six states, but the epicenter of this dynamic world is, again, Boston. The most avant-garde contemporary theater found in Boston is at the **American Repertory Theater (ART)**.

SHOPPING

NEW ENGLAND'S well-known factory outlets offer brand name clothing at huge discounts. Freeport, Maine, has the famous outdoor equipment outlet **L.L. Bean**. **Filene's** in Boston features apparel from some of the best-known American designers and is famed for its bargain basement. The region is an antique hunter's dream, with stores and barns offering a wide array of objects from the past. The Charles Street section of Boston's Beacon Hill is one of the prime antiquing areas. Look for shops run by New Hampshire craftsmen, Vermont-made products, and Maine crafts. Tourists looking for gifts with a regional flavor should sample the maple syrup and maple sugar candy.

DIRECTORY

TOURIST OFFICES

Connecticut
W www.ctbond.org

Greater Boston
W www.bostonusa.com

Maine
W www.visitmaine.com

Massachusetts
W www.massvacation.com

New Hampshire
W www.visitnh.gov

Rhode Island
W www.visitrhodeisland.com

Vermont
W www.1-800-vermont.com

FALL FOLIAGE HOTLINES

Connecticut
C (800) 252-6863.

Maine
C (800) 533-9595.

Massachusetts
C (800) 227-6277.

New Hampshire
C (800) 258-3608.

Rhode Island
C (800) 556-2484.

Vermont
C (800) 828-3239.

ROAD EMERGENCY

American Auto-mobile Assn. (AAA)
C (800) 222-4357.

HIKING

Appalachian Trail Conference
799 Washington St, PO Box 807, Harpers Ferry, WV 25425-0807.
C (304) 535-6331.
W www.appalachiantrail.org

SKIING

Stowe Mountain Resort
5781 Mountain Rd, Stowe, VT 05672.
C (800) 253-4754.
W www.stowe.com

ENTERTAINMENT

American Repertory Theater
64 Brattle St,.
Cambridge, MA.
C (617) 547-8300.

Boston Symphony Orchestra
301 Massachusetts Ave, Boston, MA.
C (617) 266-1492.

SHOPPING

Filene's
426 Washington St, Boston, MA.
C (617) 357-2100.

L.L. Bean
95 Main Street, Freeport, ME.
C (207) 865-4761.

Where to Stay

	CREDIT CARDS	NUMBER OF ROOMS (SUITES)	RECOMMENDED RESTAURANT	CHILDREN'S FACILITIES	GARDEN OR TERRACE

THE INCREDIBLY VARIED ACCOMODATIONS of the New England states are tailored to suit all tastes and budgets. Rustic country inns and B&Bs are plentiful, offering travelers quaint facilities and a more personal touch. Hotels are listed by area and then by price category, with symbols highlighting some of the amenities that may influence your choice of where to stay.

BOSTON, MASSACHUSETTS

BEACON HILL & THE THEATER DISTRICT: *John Jeffries House* $$ 14 David G. Mugar Way. ☎ (617) 367-1866. FAX (617) 742-0313. W www.JohnJeffries.com Rooms are Victorian in style, and while some are tiny, the two-room suites are a bargain. Most of the rooms have kitchenettes. Breakfast is not included. 🏊 ♿ 🔼 🍴 ♿	■	46 (23)		●	
BEACON HILL & THE THEATER DISTRICT: *Tremont Boston* $$$ 275 Tremont St. ☎ (877) 999-3223, (617) 426-1400. FAX (617) 482-6730. W www.wyndham.com The refurbished lobby of this imposing 1925 brick and stone building is decorated with pillars and carved granite. Rooms are simple but have more flair than those in a standard chain hotel. 🏊 ♿ 🔼 🍴 🍽 ♿ P ♿	▨	322			
BEACON HILL & THE THEATER DISTRICT: *Boston Park Plaza* $$$$ 64 Arlington St. ☎ (800) 225-2008, (617) 426-2000. FAX (617) 457-7456. W www.bostonparkplaza.com Opened in 1927, this grand luxury hotel is classically Bostonian. Elegantly appointed, the spacious rooms also have many modern amenities, such as voice mail and dataports. 24 🏊 ♿ 🔼 🍴 🍽 ♿ P ♿	▨	950 (22)			
BEACON HILL & THE THEATER DISTRICT: *Holiday Inn* $$$$ 5 Blossom St. ☎ (800) 465-4329, (617) 742-7630. FAX (617) 482-7630. W www.sixcontinentshotel.com A modern 15-story, business-class chain hotel. On the north side of Beacon Hill near Massachusetts General Hospital, a short walk from the Government Center. 🏊 ♿ 🔼 🍴 ≈ 🍽 ♿ P ♿	▨	303 (2)		●	
BEACON HILL & THE THEATER DISTRICT: *Beacon Hill Hotel* $$$$$ 19 Charles St. ☎ (888) 959-2422. FAX (617) 723-7575. A renovated brick townhouse that blends the charm of Beacon Hill with modern amenities such as flat-screen TV and Internet access. Rooms overlook bustling Charles Street. 🏊 ♿ 🔼 ♿	■	13	■		▨
BEACON HILL & THE THEATER DISTRICT: *Charles Street Inn* $$$$$ 94 Charles St. ☎ (877) 772-8900, (617) 314-8900. FAX (617) 371-0009. W www.charlesstreetinn.com Deluxe boutique hotel in a 1860s townhouse. The Charles Street Inn has sumptuous antiques-filled rooms with fireplaces, whirlpool tubs, and Internet access. 🏊 ♿ 🔼 ♿	■	9			
BEACON HILL & THE THEATER DISTRICT: *Four Seasons* $$$$$ 200 Boylston St. ☎ (800) 332-3442, (617) 338-4400. FAX (617) 423-0154. W www.fourseasons.com The ultimate in service and luxury, and ranked among the top hotels in the city. It has grand reception rooms and sumptuous bedrooms, many overlooking the Public Garden. 24 🏊 ♿ 🔼 🍴 🍽 ♿ P ♿	▨	274 (66)			
OLD BOSTON & THE FINANCIAL DISTRICT: *Harborside Inn* $$$ 185 State St. ☎ (888) 723-7565, (617) 723-7500. FAX (617) 670-2015. W www.hagopianhotels.com The small guest rooms in this old mercantile warehouse have exposed brick walls, period furniture, and wooden floors with Oriental rugs. Near Faneuil Hall, the Harborside Inn is surrounded by the "Big Dig." 🏊 🔼 🍴 ♿ ♿	■	54 (2)			
OLD BOSTON & THE FINANCIAL DISTRICT: *Shawmut Inn* $$$ 280 Friend St. ☎ (800) 350-7784, (617) 720-5544. FAX (617) 723-7784. W www. shawmutinn.com Simply furnished rooms, all with kitchenettes, in a former state office building across the street from North Station. A fine budget choice; suites are a bargain for families. 🏊 ♿ 🔼 ♿ ♿	▨	65 (11)			

	Price categories for a standard double room per night, inclusive of breakfast, service charges, and any additional taxes:		

Price categories for a standard double room per night, inclusive of breakfast, service charges, and any additional taxes:

$ under $100
$$ $100–$150
$$$ $150–$200
$$$$ $200–$250
$$$$$ over $250

CREDIT CARDS
Major credit cards accepted.

NUMBER OF ROOMS
Number of rooms in the hotel (suites shown in parentheses).

RECOMMENDED RESTAURANT
Good restaurant within the hotel.

CHILDREN'S FACILITIES
Hotel has various facilities for young children.

GARDEN OR TERRACE
Hotel has a garden, courtyard, or terrace.

	CREDIT CARDS	NUMBER OF ROOMS (SUITES)	RECOMMENDED RESTAURANT	CHILDREN'S FACILITIES	GARDEN OR TERRACE
OLD BOSTON & THE FINANCIAL DISTRICT: *Fifteen Beacon* $$$$$ 15 Beacon St. (877) 982-3226, (617) 670-1500. FAX (617) 670-2525. www.xvbeacon.com Coolly opulent boutique hotel in a former office building. Chic rooms all have a high-style mix of traditional and contemporary furnishings, with facilities including CD players and fax machines.	■	61 (2)			
OLD BOSTON & THE FINANCIAL DISTRICT: *Le Meridien* $$$$$ 250 Franklin St. (800) 543-4300, (617) 451-1900. FAX (617) 423-2844. www.lemeridienboston.com This deluxe hotel in the heart of the Financial District often offers affordable weekend getaway packages.	■	326 (26)			
OLD BOSTON & THE FINANCIAL DISTRICT: *Omni Parker House* $$$$$ 60 School St. (800) 996-3426, (617) 556-0006. FAX (617) 556-0053. www.omnihotels.com Home of the Parker House Roll and Boston Cream Pie, the traditional, comfortable Omni Parker House has been open and running since 1855.	■	551 (21)			
NORTH END & THE WATERFRONT: *Seaport Hotel* $$$$ One Seaport Lane. (877) 732-7678, (617) 385-4000. FAX (617) 385-4001. www.seaporthotel.com A modern, towering business hotel next to the World Trade Center, every room has an Internet hookup, plus in-room conferencing facilities. Weekend specials are attractive.	■	426 (24)			
BACK BAY & SOUTH END: *Beacon Street Guesthouse* $$ 463 Beacon St. (617) 536-1302. FAX (617) 247-8876. www.463beacon.com The stately five-story Beacon Street Guesthouse is good value for money. Rooms vary, but some have fireplaces and other original features, plus microwaves and refrigerators; most have a private bath. Breakfast not included.	■	20			
BACK BAY & SOUTH END: *The College Club* $$ 44 Commonwealth Ave. (617) 536-9510. FAX (617) 247-8537. www.thecollegeclubofboston.com A hidden gem and excellent value, this Victorian town house near the Public Garden is also home to a private club. The College Club rents six lovely double rooms, and five more austere singles that share bathrooms.	■	12			
BACK BAY & SOUTH END: *Newbury Guesthouse* $$$ 261 Newbury St. (800) 437-7668, (617) 437-7666. FAX (617) 262-4243. www.hagopianhotels.com In Boston's chic shopping neighborhood, this brownstone guesthouse caters to people from all walks of life – business people and fashionable vacationers. Tasteful rooms are furnished with Victorian-style reproductions.	■	32			
BACK BAY & SOUTH END: *Eliot Suite Hotel* $$$$$ 370 Commonwealth Ave. (800) 443-5468, (617) 267-1607. FAX (617) 536-9114. www.eliothotel.com Graciously furnished, all-suite hotel, built in 1925. Rooms have separate sitting rooms, plus business amenities. Home of fine French-American restaurant Clio.	■	95 (95)			
BACK BAY & SOUTH END: *The Lenox* $$$$$ 710 Boylston St. (800) 225-7676, (617) 536-5300. FAX (617) 267-1237. www.lenoxhotel.com This highly regarded and recently refurbished 100-year-old hotel has sumptuously appointed rooms with all manner of luxuries. It is also home to the excellent Azure restaurant.	■	212 (12)			

For key to symbols see back flap

Price categories for a standard double room per night, inclusive of breakfast, service charges, and any additional taxes:

$ under $100
$$ $100–$150
$$$ $150–$200
$$$$ $200–$250
$$$$$ over $250

CREDIT CARDS
Major credit cards accepted.

NUMBER OF ROOMS
Number of rooms in the hotel (suites shown in parentheses).

RECOMMENDED RESTAURANT
Good restaurant within the hotel.

CHILDREN'S FACILITIES
Hotel has various facilities for young children.

GARDEN OR TERRACE
Hotel has a garden, courtyard, or terrace.

	Price	Credit Cards	Number of Rooms (Suites)	Recommended Restaurant	Children's Facilities	Garden or Terrace
GREATER BOSTON: *Constitution Inn* 150 Second Ave, Charlestown. (617) 241-8400. FAX (617) 241-2856. An economy inn run by the armed services, most rooms have two twin beds; although several have queen-sized ones.	$$	■	149 (2)			
GREATER BOSTON: *Harvard Square Hotel* 110 Mt. Auburn St, Cambridge. (800) 458-5886, (617) 864-5200. FAX (617) 864-2409. W www.doubletreehotels.com Its location is the best feature of this refurbished hotel in the heart of Harvard Square. The rooms are basic but comfortable.	$$$	■	73			
GREATER BOSTON: *Hotel@M.I.T. – University Park* 20 Sidney St, Cambridge. (800) 222-8733, (617) 577-0200. FAX (617) 494-8366. W www.hotel@mit.com This contemporary hotel, owned by the Massachusetts Institute of Technology, is filled with state-of-the-art technology such as ergonomically designed furniture, in-room Internet access, and phones with voice mail.	$$$	■	210 (28)			
GREATER BOSTON: *Irving House* 24 Irving St, Cambridge. (877) 547-4600, (617) 547-4600. FAX (617) 576-2814. W www.irvinghouse.com This wooden-framed Victorian house inn has simple rooms (some are rather small), and an attractive terrace. Some of the rooms share baths.	$$$	■	44			

MASSACHUSETTS

	Price	Credit Cards	Number of Rooms (Suites)	Recommended Restaurant	Children's Facilities	Garden or Terrace
CONCORD: *Colonial Inn* 48 Monument Sq. (800) 370-9200, (978) 369-9200. FAX (978) 371-1533. @ colonial@concordscolonialinn.com W www.concordscolonialinn.com This historic place was built in 1716 and has been operating as a hotel since 1889. Beautiful Colonial-style rooms are ornately furnished with period furniture.	$$$	■	56 (7)			
NANTUCKET: *The Nesbitt Inn* 21 Broad St. (508) 228-0156, (508) 228-2446. FAX (508) 228-2446. Located right in town, this Victorian B&B is operated by the exceptionally friendly hosts, Mr. and Mrs. Nesbitt, and is decorated with antiques and Oriental carpets. ○ Mar 1–mid-Dec.	$	■	12			
PLYMOUTH: *Beachside B&B* 159 Ellisville Rd. (888) 738-2337, (508) 888-3692. FAX (508) 888-5978. @ amy@ellisville.com W www.ellisville.com Full breakfasts are served either in the dining room or on the large sundeck. This historic site has a private beach. Swans, deer, and seals can be seen on the grounds in the various seasons.	$$	■	3			
PROVINCETOWN: *The Beaconlight Guesthouse* 12 Winthrop St. (800) 696-9603. FAX (508) 487-9603. W www.beaconlightguesthouse.com A romantic B&B in a sprawling beach house (built around 1900). The Beaconlight Guesthouse is located in a quiet but convenient location for downtown. Children are not allowed.	$$$	■	10			
SALEM: *Hawthorne Hotel* 18 Washington Sq W. (800) SAY-STAY, (978) 744-4080. FAX (978) 745-9842. @ info@hawthornehotel.com W www.hawthornehotel.com This upscale Federal-style hotel located in downtown Salem combines tasteful decoration with modern amenities.	$$$	■	89 (6)			

Rhode Island

BLOCK ISLAND: *1661 Inn and Hotel Manisses* $$$ Spring St. ☎ *(800) 626-4773, (401) 466-2421.* [FAX] *(401) 466-3162.* [W] www.blockislandresorts.com This historic inn, animal farm, and Victorian hotel is a perfect base from which to explore Block Island. No air-conditioning. ● *mid-Oct–Mar.* 👪 🍸 🍴 [P] ♿	■	26			
CHARLESTOWN: *General Stanton Inn* $$ 4115A Old Post Rd, Rte 1A. ☎ *(401) 364-8888.* [FAX] *(401) 364-3333.* One of the oldest continuously run inns in North America, it retains some of the old atmosphere, with fireplaces and brick ovens. 🚭 👪 🍸 [P] ♿	■	16			
NEWPORT: *Beech Tree Inn* $$$$ 34 Rhode Island Ave. ☎ *(800) 748-6565, (401) 847-9794.* [FAX] *(401) 847-6824.* [W] www.beechtreeinn.com This Victorian home boasts rooms with fireplaces and jacuzzis. It is noted for "the biggest breakfast in Newport." 🚭 👪 🍴 [P]	■	8 (2)			
NEWPORT: *Castle Hill Inn and Resort* $$$$$ 590 Ocean Dr. ☎ *(888) 466-1355, (401) 849-3800.* [FAX] *(401) 849-3838.* [W] www.castlehillinn.com This resort with a private beach includes several houses. The restaurant has repeatedly won the *Wine Spectator* Award of Excellence. Limited availability for children under 12. 🚭 👪 🍸 [P] ♿	■	25 (2)			
PROVIDENCE: *C.C. Ledbetter B&B* $$ 326 Benefit St. ☎ *(401) 351-4699.* [FAX] *(401) 351-4699.* @ info@providence-inn.com [W] www.providence-inn.com Located opposite John Brown House, a block from Brown University. The C.C. Ledbetter B&B has charming rooms with traditional handmade quilts. 🚭 [P]	■	10			
PROVIDENCE: *The Westin Providence* $$$$ One West Exchange St. ☎ *(800) WESTIN1, (401) 598-8000.* [FAX] *(401) 598-8200.* [W] www.westinprovidence.com Four-time Pinnacle Award winner. The Agora restaurant was named Best in Hotel Dining by the *Food Network* in 2000. Connected to Providence Place Mall and the Rhode Island Convention Center, the Westin Providence makes a good base for exploring the surroundings. 🚭 👪 ⇅ 🍸 🏊 🏋 🍴 [P] ♿	■	364 (19)			

Connecticut

HARTFORD: *Goodwin Hotel* $$$$ One Haynes St. ☎ *(888) 212-8380, (860) 246-7500.* [FAX] *(860) 247-4576.* [W] www.goodwinhotel.com The historic Goodwin Hotel serves guests with poise and style, but without pretension. The restaurant has been voted Best Hotel Dining by *Connecticut Magazine* for 10 years running. 🚭 👪 ⇅ 🍸 🏋 [P] ♿	■	124 (11)			
LITCHFIELD: *Litchfield Inn* $$$ 432 Bantam Rd. ☎ *(800) 499-3444, (860) 567-4503.* [FAX] *(860) 567-5358.* @ litchfieldinn@compuserve.com [W] www.litchfieldinnct.com A quaint country inn located just west of Litchfield. Features a gigantic chandelier, delicately carved main staircase, and four working fireplaces. Eight luxurious theme rooms. 🚭 👪 ⇅ 🍸 🍴 [P] ♿	■	32			
MYSTIC: *Seaport Motor Inn* $$ Coogan Blvd. ☎ *(877) 523-0993, (860) 536-2621.* [FAX] *(860) 536-4493.* Overlooking Olde Mistick Village and the Mystic Aquarium. The Seaport Motor Inn offers intimate dining steps away at Jamm's Restaurant and adjoining Captain's Lounge. Close to all the major attractions, including beaches and the USS *Nautilus*. 🚭 👪 🏊 [P] ♿	■	118			
MYSTIC: *Steamboat Inn* $$$$ 73 Steamboat Wharf. ☎ *(860) 536-8300.* [FAX] *(860) 536-9528.* @ sbwharf@aol.com [W] www.visitmystic.com/steamboat Spacious rooms are named after famous Mystic ships from the schooner days. All the rooms in this quaint Steamboat Inn have whirlpool baths and antique furnishings. Magnificent views of the river and the dock. 🚭 👪 [P] ♿	■	10 (4)			

For key to symbols see back flap

Price categories for a standard double room per night, inclusive of breakfast, service charges, and any additional taxes: $ under $100 $$ $100–$150 $$$ $150–$200 $$$$ $200–$250 $$$$$ over $250	**CREDIT CARDS** Major credit cards accepted. **NUMBER OF ROOMS** Number of rooms in the hotel (suites shown in parentheses). **RECOMMENDED RESTAURANT** Good restaurant within the hotel. **CHILDREN'S FACILITIES** Hotel has various facilities for young children. **GARDEN OR TERRACE** Hotel has a garden, courtyard, or terrace.	CREDIT CARDS	NUMBER OF ROOMS (SUITES)	RECOMMENDED RESTAURANT	CHILDREN'S FACILITIES	GARDEN OR TERRACE

VERMONT

	CREDIT CARDS	NUMBER OF ROOMS (SUITES)	RECOMMENDED RESTAURANT	CHILDREN'S FACILITIES	GARDEN OR TERRACE
BURLINGTON: *Radisson Hotel* $$$$ 60 Battery St. ((800) 329-7466, (802) 658-6500. FAX (802) 658-4659. w www.radisson.com/burlingtonvt Burlington's most upscale hotel, the Radisson is situated right in the heart of the downtown area. The best rooms have breathtaking views of Lake Champlain.	■	256 (8)			
KILLINGTON: *Mountain Meadows Lodge* $$ 285 Thundering Brook Rd. ((800) 370-4567, (802) 775-1010. @ havefun@mtnmeadowslodge.com w www.mtmeadowslodge.com Vermont's only mountain lodge set on both a lake and the famous Appalachian Trail, it is perfect for outdoor types. It features excellent family services. ● Apr–mid-May.	■	20 (1)			
MANCHESTER: *The Equinox Resort* $$$$$ 3567 Main St. ((802) 362-4747. FAX (802) 362-1595. @ reservations@equinoxresort.com w www.equinoxresort.com This historic 18th-century resort has stunning public spaces and spacious, country-style rooms. The resort also offers outdoor activities such as golf, falconry, fishing, and off-road driving.	■	172 (17)			
RICHMOND: *The Richmond Victorian Inn* $ 191 East Main St. ((888) 242-3362, (802) 434-4410. FAX (802) 434-4411. @ innkeeper@richmondvictorianinn.com w www.richmondvictorianinn.com Located in the foothills of the Green Mountains, this inexpensive inn's six guest rooms are furnished in a country Victorian style with antiques. No televisions or air-conditioning in rooms. Children over 12.	■	6 (1)			
SHELBURNE: *Inn at Shelburne Farms* $$$ 1611 Harbor Rd. ((802) 985-8498. FAX (802) 985-8123. w www.shelburnefarms.org Built in 1897 on a bluff overlooking Lake Champlain, the inn is situated on a 1,400-acre (400-ha) property, landscaped by Frederick Law Olmsted. ● mid-Oct–mid-May.	■	24			
STOWE: *Wood Chip Inn* $$ Mountain Rd. ((800) 676-9181, (802) 253-9080. FAX (802) 253-7873. @ wdchipinn@aol.com w www.gostowe.com/members/woodchip Charming and economical, the inn offers homemade breads and soups in the fall and winter, and afternoon refreshments in the summer.	■	9			
STOWE: *Trapp Family Lodge* $$$$$ 700 Trapp Hill Rd. ((800) 826-7000, (802) 253-8511. FAX (802) 253-5740. @ info@trappfamily.com w www.trappfamily.com World-famous 116-room resort on 2,700-acre (1.092-ha) property. Along with large Austrian-style main lodge, the resort features 100 guesthouses and exquisite cuisine.	■	116 (18)			

NEW HAMPSHIRE

	CREDIT CARDS	NUMBER OF ROOMS (SUITES)	RECOMMENDED RESTAURANT	CHILDREN'S FACILITIES	GARDEN OR TERRACE
BRETTON WOODS: *The Mount Washington Hotel & Resort* $$$$$ Rte 302. ((800) 258-0330, (603) 278-1000. FAX (603) 278-8838. @ hotelinfo@mtwashington.com w www.mtwashington.com Since 1902, this elegant resort has offered quality service in a beautiful setting.	■	191 (6)			
CONCORD: *The Centennial Inn* $$ 96 Pleasant St. ((800) 360-4839, (603) 225-7102. FAX (603) 225-5031. @ centennialinn@totalnetnh.net w www.someplacesdifferent.com Housed in a restored 1876 Victorian mansion, this centrally located inn provides well-furnished rooms and suites.	■	32 (5)			

FRANCONIA: *The Franconia Inn* $$$ ◼ 34
1300 Easton Rd. ▐ *(800) 473-5299, (603) 823-5542.* ﬀ *(603) 823-8078.*   (2)
@ info@franconiainn.com Ⓦ www.franconiainn.com
The Franconia Inn is a cozy historic lodging, surrounded by stunningly
beautiful scenery. This place has enough sports and activities to keep
outdoor enthusiasts satisfied year round. No air-conditioning in any of
the rooms. Television in common room. ● *Apr–mid-May.*
▨ ⌗ ▯ ☂ ♨ ▥ ▯ P

MANCHESTER: *The Highlander Inn* $$ ◼ 88
2 Highlander Way. ▐ *(800) 548-9248, (603) 625-6426.* ﬀ *(603) 625-6466.*   (10)
Ⓦ www.highlanderinn.com
A popular resort for Bostonians since the late 19th century. Its proximity
to the airport is a great convenience for both business and pleasure
travelers. ▨ ⌗ ▯ ☂ ♨ ▯ P ♿

MEREDITH: *Meredith Inn B&B* $$ ◼ 8
2 Waukewan St. ▐ *(603) 279-0000.* ﬀ *(603) 279-4017.*
@ inn1897@meredithinn.com Ⓦ www.meredithinn.com
A restored Victorian home refurbished with all the modern amenities.
Great for fitness enthusiasts – convenient for Lake Winnipesaukee
activities – it is walking distance to the beach on Lake Waukewan. Six
rooms have air-conditioning. ▨ P ♿

PORTSMOUTH: *The Inn at Christian Shore* $$ ◼ 5
335 Maplewood Ave. ▐ *(603) 431-6770.* ﬀ *(603) 431-7743.*
Ⓦ www.portsmouthnh.com/christianshore
The Inn at Christian Shore is a well-preserved late 1800s home furnished
with the unlikely mix of antiques, African art, and contemporary
paintings. The gourmet breakfasts are delicious and offer vast choice.
No children are allowed. ▨ P

PORTSMOUTH: *Sheraton Harborside Portsmouth* $$$ ◼ 200
250 Market St. ▐ *(603) 431-2300.* ﬀ *(603) 433-5649.*   (19)
@ info@sheratonportsmouth.com Ⓦ www.sheratonportsmouth.com
A modern hotel in the historic waterfront district. Close to waterfront
restaurants and shops. Rates vary. ▨ ⌗ ▯ ☂ ♨ ▥ ▯ P ♿

MAINE

BAR HARBOR: *Mira Monte Inn and Suites* $$$ ◼ 16
69 Mount Desert St. ▐ *(800) 553-5109, (207) 288-4263.*   (3)
ﬀ *(207) 288-3115.* @ mburns@miramonte.com Ⓦ www.miramonte.com
Constructed in 1864, this is one of only two B&Bs in town owned by Bar
Harbor natives. All rooms of the Mira Monte Inn and Suites have the
comfort of air-conditioning. ▨ ▯ P ♿

BETHEL: *Bethel Inn and Country Club* $$$$$ ◼ 140
On the Common. ▐ *(800) 654-0125, (207) 824-2175.*   (12)
ﬀ *(207) 824-2233.* @ info@bethelinn.com Ⓦ www.bethelinn.com
A premier Maine resort, the property has its own championship golf
course and a tennis court. Price includes free golf and dinner, except for
townhouse guests. ▨ ⌗ ▯ ☂ ♨ ▥ ▯ P ♿

OGUNQUIT: *The Cliff House* $$$ ◼ 194
Shore Rd. ▐ *(207) 361-1000.* ﬀ *(207) 361-2122.*   (2)
@ info@cliffhouse@maine.com Ⓦ www.cliffhousemaine.com
Oceanside resort with full floor devoted to recreation. It also has a spa.
Cliff house trolley takes guests to spots of interest in the area in July and
August. ● *mid-Dec–Mar.* ▨ ⌗ ▯ ☂ ♨ ▥ ▯ P ♿

PORTLAND: *Inn at St. John* $$ ◼ 40
939 Congress. ▐ *(800) 636-9127, (207) 773-6481.* ﬀ *(207) 756-7629.*
@ theinn@maine.rr.com Ⓦ www.innatstjohn.com
Century-old inn just minutes from Portland's Old Port, Waterfront, and
Arts districts. The Inn at St. John has rooms that are tastefully decorated,
and all are air-conditioned. Some rooms share baths. ▨ ⌗ P ♿

PORTLAND: *Portland Regency Hotel* $$$ ◼ 95
20 Milk St. ▐ *(800) 727-3436, (207) 774-4200.* ﬀ *(207) 775-2150.*   (8)
@ public@the regency.com Ⓦ www.theregency.com
Situated in the heart of the Old Port district, the Portland Regency Hotel
is Portland's premiere hotel. An added bonus in this hotel – fitness center
is free for guests. ▨ ⌗ ▯ ☂ ▥ ▯ P ♿

Where to Eat

NEW ENGLAND'S CUISINE IS A melting pot of different cultures – the English, Irish, and the Italians have each brought their own cuisines as well as adopted native ingredients. The chart below highlights some of the factors that may influence your choice of where to eat. Opening times of restaurants are indicated by a "B" for breakfast, "L" for lunch, and "D" for dinner.

	Credit Cards	Outdoor Tables	Vegetarian	Good Wine List	Late Opening

BOSTON, MASSACHUSETTS

BACK BAY & SOUTH END: *Men Tei Noodle House* ($)
66 Hereford St. (617) 425-0066.
Osaka-style *udon* noodles and an array of great snack foods and entrées for the low-budget visitor. Efficient staff and a mixed, lively clientele make this restaurant well worth a visit. No wine. *L, D.*

			■		

BACK BAY & SOUTH END: *Tapeo* ($$$)
266 Newbury St. (617) 267-4799.
A wonderfully earthy tapas bar right in the middle of pretentious Newbury Street. Regulars are really devoted to the sangria and the tiny dishes, though there is a full menu if you so prefer. *L, D.* P Y ♿

■	●	■	●	

BACK BAY & SOUTH END: *Aujourd'Hui* ($$$$)
200 Boylston St (Four Seasons Hotel). (617) 451-1392.
One of the best dining experiences in Boston, the contemporary cuisine is complemented by a lovely ambience and a view of the Public Garden. There is also an alternative healthy cuisine menu. *B, L, D.*

■		■		

BACK BAY & SOUTH END: *Tremont 647* ($$$$$)
647 Tremont St. (617) 266-4600.
Pushing the boundaries of new and old American food alike, this youthful and unpretentious restaurant enjoys innovation, and it succeeds. Try the sea bass on jasmine rice or the spice-rubbed steak. Sundays' Pajama Brunch is a must, if solely for the cinnamon rolls. *D, Sun Brunch.* P Y ♿ ♿

■	●	■		

BEACON HILL & THEATER DISTRICT: *Legal Seafoods* ($$$)
26 Park Square. (617) 426-4444.
This popular restaurant has many locations throughout the city, all serving the freshest and the best prepared seafood available. Try their raw bar for oysters, then one of their superb entrées, which are delicious. *L, D.* P Y ♿ ♿

■				

BEACON HILL & THEATER DISTRICT: *Locke-Ober* ($$$$$)
3 Winter Place. (617) 542-1340.
New owners have rejuvenated one of America's most legendary restaurants, founded in 1875. Inventive twists enliven European and American classics. Reservations essential. *L, D.* ● Sun. P Y ♿ ♿

■				

GREATER BOSTON: *Mr. Bartley's Burger and Salad Cottage* ($$)
1246 Massachusetts Ave, Cambridge. (617) 354-6559.
A glorious profusion and variety of hamburgers and truly wonderful sweet potato fries to try out in an overwhelmingly chaotic atmosphere. *L, D.* ● Sun. ♿

	●	■		

GREATER BOSTON: *Harvest* ($$$$$)
44 Brattle St, Cambridge. (617) 868-2255.
A favoured haunt of university professors. Modern American cuisine bursting with fresh flavors and local produce. Reservations suggested. *L, D, Sun Brunch.* Y ♿ ♿

■	●	■	●	

GREATER BOSTON: *Olives* ($$$$$)
10 City Square, Charlestown. (617) 242-1999.
Mediterranean-influenced cuisine by local celebrity chef Todd English, served in a bistro-like setting. Perpetually crowded, they do not accept reservations. Dress well to minimize your wait. ● Sun. P Y ♿ ♿

■			●	

NORTH END & THE WATERFRONT: *Rudi's* ($$)
30 Rowes Wharf (Boston Harbor Hotel). (617) 330-7656.
Large delicatessen, where patrons order portions from the serving counter, and seat themselves at café tables. Rudi's also sells pastries and gourmet food gifts. No wine. *B, L, D.* P ♿

■	●	■		

Price categories include a three-course meal for one, a glass of house wine, and all unavoidable extra charges such as sales tax and service.
$ under $20
$$ $20–30
$$$ $30–45
$$$$ $45–60
$$$$$ over $60

CREDIT CARDS
Major credit cards accepted.

OUTDOOR TABLES
Garden, courtyard, or terrace with outside tables.

VEGETARIAN
A good selection of vegetarian dishes available.

GOOD WINE LIST
Extensive list of good wines, both domestic and imported.

LATE OPENING
Full menu or light meals served after 11pm.

	Credit Cards	Outdoor Tables	Vegetarian	Good Wine List	Late Opening
NORTH END & THE WATERFRONT: *Barking Crab* $$$ 88 Sleeper St. ☎ *(617) 426-2722.* Boston's classic shoreside seafood joint, facing the city from across Fort Point Channel. Lobster, steamers, clamrolls, and chowder, served along with paper napkins. *L, D, Sun Brunch (winter only).* ♫ [P] 🍸 🚸 ♿	■	●	■		
NORTH END & THE WATERFRONT: *La Famiglia Giorgio* $$$ 112 Salem St. ☎ *(617) 367-6711.* Huge portions of well-prepared pasta are the order of the day here, and La Famiglia is always ready to help you choose. It's a bargain – you will leave full and happy. *L, D.* 🚸	■		■		
NORTH END & THE WATERFRONT: *Pomodoro* $$$ 319 Hanover St. ☎ *(617) 367-4348.* Crowded, raucous, and aromatic, the small storefront housing Pomodoro brims with patrons at all hours. It is popular for its real Italian dishes, which are always well prepared. Try the monkfish and saffron risotto, which are absolutely delicious. *L, D.* ♿			■		
NORTH END & THE WATERFRONT: *Terramia* $$$ 98 Salem St. ☎ *(617) 523-3112.* Boisterous and mixed clientele line up every night to dine on the trademark gnocchi, prepared daily, as well as on the sublime lobster fritters. Casual, friendly service, and setting. *D.* 🚸	■		■		
OLD BOSTON & THE FINANCIAL DISTRICT: *Durgin-Park* $$$ 340 North Market St (Faneuil Hall Marketplace). ☎ *(617) 227-2038.* A Boston institution, serving all the New England standards that no one else seems to cook anymore – Indian pudding, baked beans, and baked scrod, all of which are dished up by a sharp-tongued staff. *L, D.* ♫ 🍸 🚸	■				
MASSACHUSETTS					
CAPE COD: *Oysterman's Grill & Fish Market* $$ 975 Rte 6, Wellfleet. ☎ *(508) 349-3825.* Seafood restaurant specializes in clams and oysters and other fish and shellfish. The sesame-seared local tuna is a must-have. *L, D.* ● *mid-Oct–April.* 🚭 [T] 🚸 ♿	■	●			
CAPE COD: *Chillingsworth* $$$$$ 2449 Main St (Rte 6A), Brewster. ☎ *(508) 896-3640.* Fine dining served in a 300-year-old house. This place exudes charm, has seamless service, and an elegant French prix-fixe menu. The casual fare available in the Bistro is quite delicious. *L, D, Sun Brunch.* ● *Mon; Dec–mid-May.* [P] 🍸 [T] 🚸 ♿	■				
CONCORD: *Aigo Bistro* $$$$ 84 Thoreau St. ☎ *(978) 371-1333.* Exotic food consisting of superlative Mediterranean and Provençal cuisine. Fine service is the other given in this sophisticated restaurant located upstairs in Concord depot. *D.* ● *Sun, Mon.* [P] 🍸 ♿	■				
MARTHA'S VINEYARD: *Black Dog Tavern* $$$ Beach St Extension, Vineyard Haven. ☎ *(508) 693-9223.* Facing the harbor, this place is a hit with patrons for the little neck clams, grilled bluefish sandwiches, and other fresh seafood. *B, L, D, Sun Brunch.* 🚸 ♿	■				
PLYMOUTH: *Lobster Hut* $$ 25 Town Wharf. ☎ *(508) 746-2270.* Fried clams, fish & chips, and clam chowder are particularly delicious. Huge portions of seafood are notable at this self-serve waterfront spot. *L, D.* ● *Jan.* [P] 🚸 ♿	■	●			

For key to symbols see back flap

						CREDIT CARDS	OUTDOOR TABLES	VEGETARIAN	GOOD WINE LIST	LATE OPENING

Price categories include a three-course meal for one, a glass of house wine, and all unavoidable extra charges such as sales tax and service.
$ under $20
$$ $20–30
$$$ $30–45
$$$$ $45–60
$$$$$ over $60

CREDIT CARDS
Major credit cards accepted.
OUTDOOR TABLES
Garden, courtyard, or terrace with outside tables.
VEGETARIAN
A good selection of vegetarian dishes available.
GOOD WINE LIST
Extensive list of good wines, both domestic and imported.
LATE OPENING
Full menu or light meals served after 11pm.

SALEM: *Lyceum Bar & Grill* $$$$
43 Church St. ((978) 745-7665.
In this historic building, where Alexander Graham Bell gave the first phone demo in 1877, you'll find a good assortment of New American and grilled dishes. L (except Sat), D, Sun Brunch. P 🎵 Y 🚹 &
— *Credit Cards* ■

STURBRIDGE: *Publick House* $$$$
295 Main St. ((508) 347-3313.
In the Sturbridge spirit, this atmospheric 1771 Colonial house with open hearths features Americana, such as lobster pie and prime rib.
B, L, D. P Y 🚹 &
— *Credit Cards* ■

RHODE ISLAND

BLOCK ISLAND: *Finn's Seafood Restaurant* $$$
Water St. ((401) 466-2473.
Its location facing the harbor makes ferry-watching a cinch. The upstairs deck of this popular seafood restaurant looks over the water. Lobster, steamed mussels, clam rolls, and broiled swordfish are all tasty. L, D.
● mid-Oct–mid-May. P Y 🚹 &
— *Credit Cards* ■

NEWPORT: *The Black Pearl* $$$
Bannister's Wharf. ((401) 846-5264.
Justifiably famous for its clam chowder, this landmark blends classic French fare in the sedate Commodore Room with casual dining in the tavern and bar. Try the apple-raisin bread pudding. L, D. ● mid-Jan–mid-Feb. Y &
— *Credit Cards* ■

NEWPORT: *White Horse Tavern* $$$$
26 Marlborough St. ((401) 849-3600.
The oldest operating tavern in America, with low-beamed ceilings, hearth fires, Colonial bric-a-brac, and candlelit dining rooms. Good American food with modern touches. L (except Mon–Tue), D, Sun Brunch. P Y 🚹
— *Credit Cards* ■

PROVIDENCE: *New Rivers* $$$
7 Steeple St. ((401) 751-0350.
Some of the best New American food can be found in this intimate town house. Look for dishes such as five-spice chicken, grilled pork tenderloin, and sweet local scallops. D. ● Sun. P Y 🚹
— *Credit Cards* ■

PROVIDENCE: *Al Forno* $$$$
577 S Main St. ((401) 273-9760.
Wood-fire grilled meats, pizzas from stone floor pizza ovens, and baked pasta dishes are signatures of this popular, informal, no-reservations-taken place. The chef-owners keep inventing new and fabulous dishes using fresh, local ingredients. D. ● Sun–Mon. P Y &
— *Credit Cards* ■

CONNECTICUT

HARTFORD: *Max Downtown* $$$
City Place, 185 Asylum St. ((860) 522-2530.
Smart, modern, bustling, this favorite-with-locals downtown spot features excellent Modern American dishes. Mon–Fri L, D. Y 🚹 &
— *Credit Cards* ■

LITCHFIELD: *West Street Grill* $$$$
43 West St. ((860) 567-3885.
The area's most popular gathering place for big-name New Yorkers who weekend in the vicinity offers pace-setting food in a comfortably casual setting. L, D. ● Mon–Tue in winter. P 🚹
— *Credit Cards* ■

MYSTIC: *Mystic Pizza* $
56 W Main St. ((860) 536-3700.
Immortalized by Julia Roberts' movie, this pizza-and-pasta parlor is a "must-stop" for most Mystic visitors. L, D. P 🚹 &
— *Credit Cards* ■

NEW HAVEN: *Union League Café* $$$
1032 Chapel St. ((203) 562-4299.
This historic building plays second fiddle to superb French food, well prepared. The Union League Café is also known for its impeccable service. *L, D.* ● *Sun.* **P Y &**

NEW HAVEN: *Zinc* $$$
964 Chapel St. ((203) 624-0507.
Stunning minimalist decor suits the vibrant food, a stylish blend of New American with Asian influences, producing unique results. *Tue–Sat L, D.* **Y &**

VERMONT

BURLINGTON: *India House Restaurant* $$
207 Colchester Ave. ((802) 862-7800.
Specializing in traditional North Indian food, with both vegetarian and non-vegetarian choices, the India House offers authentic tandoori cooking. Good choice of beers. *L, D.* **P Å &**

MANCHESTER CENTER: *Up For Breakfast* $
4935 Main St. ((802) 362-4204.
Delicious, nutritious breakfasts, with many varieties of eggs, pancakes, French toast, waffles, fruit plates, and tofu "eggs vegetarian." Choice of coffees, including a maple latte, fresh-squeezed orange or grapefruit juice, or a champagne-and-OJ mimosa. Full champagne menu. *B.* **Å**

STOWE: *Maxwell's at Top Notch* $$$$
000 Mountain Rd. ((800) 451-8686, (802) 253-8585.
The fine dining option at the Top Notch at Stowe Resort and Spa, Maxwell's serves gourmet American cuisine with many health-conscious options, specializing in game and prime aged meats. This is an elegant room with beautiful views from large windows. It has received the Award of Excellence from *Wine Spectator. B, D.* **♫ P Y Y Å &**

NEW HAMPSHIRE

CONCORD: *Cat'n Fiddle* $$$
18 Manchester St. ((603) 228-8911.
This 26-year-old family business is a Concord institution. The traditional American fare includes prime rib, steak, seafood, a huge salad bar, and shish kebabs. The restaurant has a casual setting. Reservations are required on weekends. *L, D.* **P Y Å &**

PORTSMOUTH: *The Blue Mermaid World Grill* $$$
09 The Hill. ((603) 427-2583.
A wonderful selection of internationally flavored dishes that include spiced pork, marinated lamb, and a great choice of seafoods prepared on a wood-burning grill. Beverage list has 12 different margaritas, tropical coolers, martinis, and a good wine list. *L, D, Sun Brunch.* **♫ P Y Å**

PORTSMOUTH: *The Oar House* $$$$
5 Ceres St. ((603) 436-4025.
A museum restaurant in a restored 1803 waterfront warehouse. Both the decor and the mainly seafood menu of the Oar House reflect Portsmouth's maritime heritage. Reservations recommended. *L, D, Sun Brunch.* **P Y Å &**

MAINE

KENNEBUNKPORT: *The Clam Shack* $
Western St. ((207) 967-3321.
This take-out stand is the quintessential seaside experience. The menu consists of some of the best fast-food seafood you'll find in New England, including fried and steamed clams, scallops, and a truly remarkable lobster roll. Known for its fresh-cut onion rings. *L, D.* ● *mid-Oct–mid-May.* **Å &**

PORTLAND: *Back Bay Grill* $$$$
Portland St. ((207) 772-8833.
The Back Bay Grill has a seasonal menu and offers elegant food in a modern setting. A *Wine Spectator* Award of Excellence winner, this restaurant has an enormous selection of wine and is also known for its superb desserts. *D.* ● *Sun.* **&**

Washington, DC & the Capital Region

Washington, DC & the Capital Region at a Glance

WASHINGTON, DC AND the four states that make up the Capital Region lie in the northeastern United States. This area played an important role in America's history – the earliest colonies were established here, and many battles of the Revolutionary War and Civil War were fought on its fields. The region is, therefore, dotted with magnificent historic sites. Washington is one of America's most visited cities and offers a great range of cultural attractions. The surrounding region's rich variety of landscapes includes Virginia's lush, rolling countryside, West Virginia's rugged mountains, Maryland's picturesque bays and harbors, and Delaware's parks, beaches, and opulent country mansions.

New River Gorge National River (see p220), *in West Virginia, runs through dense forests. The dramatic gorge is a perfect whitewater rafting destination.*

Weirton

Wheeling

Morgantown   Cumberla

0 km   50

0 miles   50

Parkersburg

Clarksburg

Weston

Ripley

WEST VIRGINIA
(See pp220–21)

Harrisonbu

Huntington

Monongahela
National Forest

Beckley

Williamson

Laeger

Roanoke

Appomat

Bluefield

Radford

Pulaski

VIRGINIA
(See pp212–19)

Norton

Wytheville

Marion

Martinsville

Blue Ridge Parkway (see p218), *stretching 215 miles (346 km) through Virginia, winds its way along the crest of the Appalachian Mountains all the way to North Carolina. This lovely route is at its best during spring and fall.*

◁ A dramatic nighttime view of the United States Capitol, one of the world's best-known symbols of democracy

Baltimore (see p222) *epitomizes the rich maritime heritage of Maryland. This pleasant port city's redeveloped waterfront features several shops and restaurants, as well as the stunning National Aquarium.*

LOCATOR MAP

MARYLAND
(See pp222–25)

Columbia • Baltimore

ester

New Castle

Dover

Annapolis

DELAWARE
(See pp226–27)

Washington, DC

Rehoboth
Beach

Dale City • Mt. Vernon

Salisbury

ericksburg •

ttesville

Richmond

Williamsburg

Petersburg

Hampton

Virginia Beach

Suffolk

Rehoboth Beach (see p227), *along the Atlantic Ocean in Delaware, is one of the state's liveliest beach resorts, with restaurants and shopping malls, as well as a range of options for endless entertainment.*

Washington, DC (see pp196–211), *the nation's imposing capital, is dominated by the White House, the president's official residence since the 1820s. Millions of visitors take the guided tour of this elegantly decorated mansion, the city's signature landmark.*

WASHINGTON, DC & THE CAPITAL REGION

ENTER OF GOVERNMENT *for the world's most powerful nation, Washington, DC is a stately, Neo-Classical city, with grand avenues and monumental public buildings that reflect the pride and ambitions that course through the corridors of power. Its surrounding region preserves important places where the young nation evolved from a Colonial outpost to an independent country.*

Located midway along the Atlantic Coast, the nation's capital lies at the heart of the East Coast. This was also the heart of the Colonial landscape where the country began, and where many of its most significant events occurred. Besides its rich tapestry of historical events, this region also has one of the country's most beautiful and varied landscapes. Just 30 miles (48 km) east from the White House is Chesapeake Bay, the country's largest and most productive estuary, while to the west are the lush Appalachian hardwood forests. This wide variety of topography and scenery is paralleled by an equally wide range of social and economic situations; the area in and around the nation's capital is home to some of the wealthiest as well as the most deprived citizens in the United States.

HISTORY

The first Europeans to this area were a small band of Spanish explorers and Jesuit priests who tried unsuccessfully to set up a colony around Chesapeake Bay in 1570. They were followed by the English, who in honor of the "Virgin Queen" Elizabeth I, named the entire region between Spanish Florida and French Canada, "Virginia." But, it was not until 1607, under the reign of James I, that Virginia's first successful English settlement, Jamestown, was founded a few miles up the James River on Chesapeake Bay. Despite the initial hardships, the colonists' prospects improved after they learned to cultivate tobacco and corn. By the 1630s, Virginia had become the world's leading producer of tobacco.

Jamestown's eventual success led to the establishment of the Catholic

Natural chimney formations in the Shenandoah Valley at Front Royal, Virginia

◁ **Attractive Colonial townhouses, a typical feature of Georgetown, Washington, DC**

Nighttime view of Lincoln Memorial and Washington Monument with the US Capitol in the distance

colony of Maryland, named in honor of King James's wife, Queen Mary. Governed by Lord Baltimore, the colony attracted Catholics from England as well as Puritan and Quaker settlers from Virginia. Every year, thousands of English immigrants came to the new colonies in search of opportunities impossible back home. By the mid-1660s, both Virginia and Maryland had evolved into England's most profitable New World colonies. In 1664, the English took control of Delaware, founded and settled by the Dutch and the Swedish in the early 1600s. West Virginia, however, did not separate from Virginia until the Civil War.

By the 1670s, a simulataneous rise in taxes and a swift drop in tobacco prices caused widespread suffering and a short-lived rebellion. The situation stabilized in the early 1700s, when some of the tobacco farmers began to reap great fortunes. Much of their success was based on the shift from servant labor to that of African slaves, whose numbers grew from a few hundred in 1650 to over 150,000 in 1750, when blacks made up nearly half the total population.

KEY DATES IN HISTORY

1607 Establishment of the private English colony of Jamestown in Virginia

1624 Virginia becomes a royal colony

1632 King Charles I establishes Maryland

1664 Delaware comes under British rule

1699 Williamsburg becomes Virginia's capital

1774 Virginia's Peyton Randolph leads the first Continental Congress to discuss freedom

1775–81 The Revolutionary War

1791 George Washington obtains land for the capital city

1830 The Baltimore and Ohio Railroad (B&O) is the nation's first long-distance railroad

1846 The Smithsonian Institution is established

1865 Confederate General Robert E. Lee surrenders to the Union at Appomattox

1932 During the Great Depression, a "Bonus Army" of WWI veterans camp around the Capitol to plead for government aid

1935 US Supreme Court building is completed

1963 Martin Luther King Jr. delivers his "I have a Dream" speech before Lincoln Memorial

1989 L. Douglas Wilder is elected governor of Virginia, the first black to hold such high office

1999 Impeachment, trial, and acquittal of President Clinton

Sept 11, 2001 Terrorist attack on the Pentagon

INDEPENDENCE & CIVIL WAR

Frustration over British rule eventually led to calls for independence. Although the Revolutionary War ended at Yorktown, Virginia, in 1781, it was only after the Treaty of Paris that American independence became a reality. Virginia, by far the largest and wealthiest of the American colonies, provided many of the "Founding Fathers," including George Washington, the military leader and first president; Thomas Jefferson, author of the Declaration of Independence and third president; and James Madison, author of the Constitution and two-term president.

n 1791, Washington, empowered by a Congressional act, selected the site for he nation's capital on land incorporated from Maryland and Virginia, a choice determined by its location midway between north and south. This independent federal territory, termed he District of Columbia (DC) was merged with the city of Washington in 1878. When the government moved to Washington in 1800, the US Capitol and he president's home (later renamed he "White House") were still under construction. Both were burned by the British during he War of 1812.

Nothing has been more divisive in the region's history than the issue of slavery. Many residents were slaveholders; others became ardent abolitionists. As racial tensions escalated, war between the North and the South became inevitable. Over the course of the four-year Civil War (1861–65), many significant battles, including General Robert E. Lee's surrender at Appomattox Court House, took place here. The area was also home to the rival capitals – Washington, DC and Richmond, Virginia.

Cycling, a pleasant way to explore Washington, DC

Between the 1880s and the 1930s, Washington, DC evolved into the grand city intended by its planners nearly a century before. Wide avenues were opened up, tawdry railroads were removed from the National Mall, and many grand buildings were constructed to house the expanding bureaucracy. Even so, it wasn't until the mid-1900s, with the advent of air conditioning, that the capital became a year-round, world-class city.

PEOPLE & CULTURE

Washington and the surrounding area reflect less stereotypical aspects of contemporary US. Its residents range from "blue-bloods" with roots reaching back to before the *Mayflower* landed at Plymouth Rock, to more recent immigrants and descendants of African-American slaves. This diversity is often surprising. Some of the most patrician communities are in northern Virginia's anglophile "Hunt Country" and among Annapolis' nautical millionaires. Alongside are outposts of blue-collar industry, and many anachronistic communities, such as the Chesapeake's traditional fisherman ("watermen") villages and the proud holdouts of Appalachian mountain culture, still visible in West Virginia.

Washington itself offers very revealing images of class and character, with its many poor, minority neighborhoods seemingly a world away from the wealthy, mainly white enclave of Georgetown. Even more expressive are the anonymous postwar middle-class suburbs that lie on both sides of the busy "Beltway" surrounding the capital.

From these diverse social strata have emerged many remarkable people. Francis Scott Key composed the national anthem "The Star-Spangled Banner" in Baltimore, while Thurgood Marshall championed Civil Rights as an activist and later as a Supreme Court Justice. Writers include the poet and horror-story creator Edgar Allen Poe, the scholar, editor, and journalist H.L. Mencken, and contemporary novelist Anne Tyler. Singers include Patsy Cline and Ella Fitzgerald, from Virginia, and Baltimore's Billie Holliday and DC native Duke Ellington who made jazz and swing the nation's soundtrack.

ce's surrender at Appomattox Court House

Exploring Washington, DC & the Capital Region

WASHINGTON, DC, the nation's capital, with its magnificent monuments, superb museums, and cosmopolitan flavor, is a favorite destination for tourists. Within easy reach of the capital, the four states of Virginia, West Virginia, Maryland, and Delaware are equally rewarding to explore, offering a varied area of mountains, plains, beaches, and historic towns. Among the region's most popular attractions are the Colonial town of Williamsburg, the scenic splendours of the Shenandoah Valley and the Blue Ridge Parkway, and the unspoiled wilderness of West Virginia. The port city of Baltimore and the tranquil beaches of Delaware also draw many visitors.

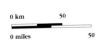
Colorful furled sails on the Maryland coast

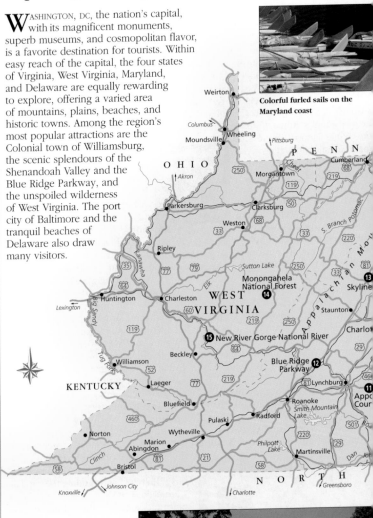

John Brown's Fort, Harpers Ferry National Park in West Virginia

0 km   50

0 miles   50

KEY

- Airport
- Highway
- Major road
- Railroad
- - - State border

SEE ALSO

- **Practical Information** pp228–9
- **Where to Stay** pp230–33
- **Where to Eat** pp234–7

The interior of the Oval Office in the White House, Washington, DC

SIGHTS AT A GLANCE

Washington, DC pp196–211 ❶

Virginia

Alexandria ❷
Mount Vernon pp212–13 ❸
Fredericksburg ❹
Colonial Williamsburg pp214–15 ❺
Jamestown & Yorktown ❻
Norfolk ❼
Richmond ❽
Chincoteague ❾
Charlottesville p217 ❿
Appomattox Court House ⓫
Blue Ridge Parkway ⓬
Skyline Drive p219 ⓭

West Virginia

Monongahela National Forest ⓮
New River Gorge National River ⓯
Harpers Ferry ⓰

Maryland

Antietam National Battlefield ⓱
Frederick ⓲
Baltimore ⓳
Annapolis ⓴
North Bay ㉑
St. Michaels ㉒
Easton ㉓
Crisfield ㉔
Salisbury ㉕
Ocean City ㉖

Delaware

Wilmington ㉗
Winterthur ㉘
Hagley Museum/
  Eleutherian Mills ㉙
Nemours Mansion & Gardens ㉚
New Castle ㉛
Lewes ㉜
Rehoboth Beach ㉝

MILEAGE CHART

WASHINGTON, DC							
7 / 11	*ALEXANDRIA, VA*		**10** = Distance in miles				
107 / 172	**104** / 167	*RICHMOND, VA*	**10** = Distance in kilometers				
68 / 109	**72** / 116	**166** / 267	*HARPERS FERRY, WV*				
46 / 74	**46** / 74	**154** / 248	**67** / 108	*BALTIMORE, MD*			
34 / 55	**40** / 64	**142** / 228	**89** / 143	**31** / 50	*ANNAPOLIS, MD*		
109 / 175	**115** / 185	**223** / 359	**141** / 227	**70** / 113	**98** / 158	*WILMINGTON, DE*	
108 / 174	**121** / 195	**223** / 359	**140** / 225	**69** / 111	**97** / 156	**6** / 10	*NEW CASTLE, DE*

Washington, DC ●

WASHINGTON, DC COVERS an area of 61 sq miles (158 sq km) and has a population of about 600,000. As the capital of the US and the seat of federal government, it is rich in grand monuments. It also has a vibrant cultural life, with superb museums, most of them free, and an array of entertainments. The city is made up of four quadrants, with the US Capitol at the central point. The northwest quadrant contains most of the tourist sights, with other sights and places of interest located round the Capitol and south of the Mall, in the southwest quadrant.

Tourists checking their routes at a tourist information kiosk

GETTING AROUND

Washington's excellent public transportation system is more convenient than driving a car. Traffic is generally heavy, and parking spaces are limited. All the major tourist attractions in the city are accessible on foot, or by Metrorail, Metrobus, or taxi.

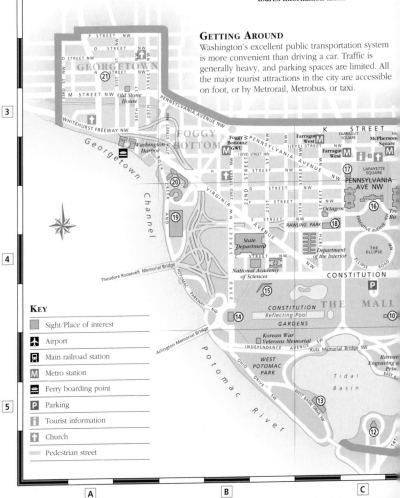

KEY

▮	Sight/Place of interest
✈	Airport
🚉	Main railroad station
Ⓜ	Metro station
⛴	Ferry boarding point
🅿	Parking
ℹ	Tourist information
✝	Church
▬	Pedestrian street

SIGHTS AT A GLANCE

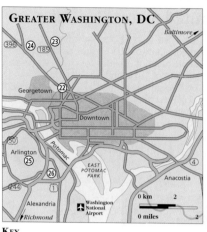

GREATER WASHINGTON, DC

KEY

▢ Area of main map

SEE ALSO

• *Where to Stay* pp230–2

• *Where to Eat* pp234–6

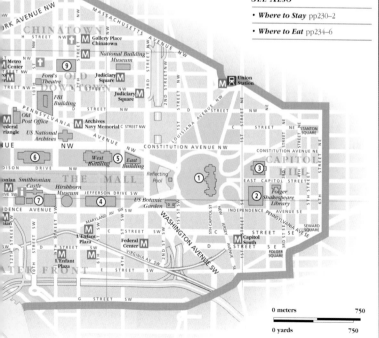

0 meters   750

0 yards   750

United States Capitol ①

ONE OF THE WORLD's best known symbols of democracy, the US Capitol has been the legislative heart of America for over 200 years. The cornerstone of this grand Neo-Classical building was laid by George Washington in 1793, and by 1800 it was occupied, though unfinished. The British burned the Capitol in the War of 1812, and in 1815 work began on its restoration. Many architectural and artistic features, such as Constantino Brumidi's murals and the Statue of Freedom, were added later.

★ The Rotunda
Completed in 1824, the 180-ft (55-m) Rotunda is capped by Apotheosis of Washington, *a fresco by Brumidi.*

US Capitol
The Capitol also marks the center of Washington, DC. The city's four quadrants radiate out from the middle of the building.

The House Chambers

★ National Statuary Hall
The statues of two prominent citizens from each state stand in this hall.

The Hall of Columns is lined with statues of notable Americans.

Library of Congress ②

Map F4. 10 1st St, SE. **C** *(202) 707-5000.* **f** *(202) 707-8000.* **M** *Capitol S.* **🚌** *32, 34, 36, 96.* **○** *10am–5:30pm Mon–Sat.* **●** *federal hols.* **✔ & 11** *For access to reading rooms, visitors must have a user card. The website or information desk can explain how this can be obtained.* **w** *www.loc.gov*

THE LIBRARY OF Congress holds the largest collection of books, manuscripts, microfilms, maps, and music in the world. First established in the US Capitol in 1800, the library was destroyed when the Capitol was burned in 1814. Thomas Jefferson then offered his personal collection as a replacement, and from this seed the collection continued to grow. Since 1897, it has been housed in a grand

Italian Renaissance-style main building, now known as the Thomas Jefferson Building. In front of it is a fountain with a striking bronze statue of the Roman sea god, Neptune.

One of the highlights of this marvel of art and architecture is the **Great Hall** with its splendid marble arches and

The Great Hall, with its splendid marble arches and columns

columns, grand staircases, bronze statues, rich murals, and stained-glass skylights.

Equally impressive is the **Main Reading Room**, where eight huge marble columns, and 10-ft (3-m) high female figures, personifying aspects of human endeavor, dwarf the reading desks. The domed ceiling soars to a height of 160 ft (49 m). There are 10 other reading rooms in the Jefferson Building, notably the African and Asian Reading Rooms.

The staircase landing near the Visitors' Gallery, overlooking the Main Reading Room, is dominated by a beautiful marble mosaic figure of Minerva.

The Library's treasures include one of only three perfect vellum copies of the 15th-century Gutenberg Bible, the first book printed using movable metal type.

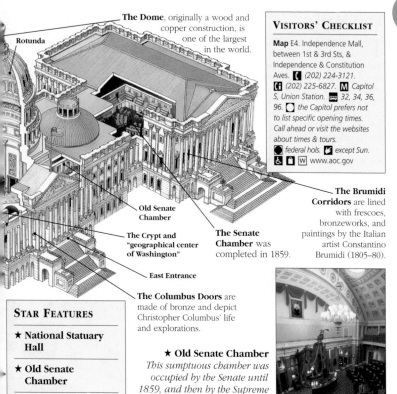

The Dome, originally a wood and copper construction, is one of the largest in the world.

Rotunda

Old Senate Chamber

The Crypt and "geographical center of Washington"

The Senate Chamber was completed in 1859.

East Entrance

The Columbus Doors are made of bronze and depict Christopher Columbus' life and explorations.

The Brumidi Corridors are lined with frescoes, bronzeworks, and paintings by the Italian artist Constantino Brumidi (1805–80).

STAR FEATURES

★ **National Statuary Hall**

★ **Old Senate Chamber**

★ **The Rotunda**

★ **Old Senate Chamber**
This sumptuous chamber was occupied by the Senate until 1859, and then by the Supreme Court for 75 years. It is now used mainly as museum space.

US Supreme Court ③

Map F4. 1st St between E Capitol St & Maryland Ave. 📞 *(202) 479-3000.* Ⓜ *Capitol S.* ⬤ *9am–4:30pm Mon–Fri.* ⬤ *federal hols.* ♿ **Lectures.**

THE JUDICIAL BRANCH of the US government and the highest court in the land, the Supreme Court is the last stop in the disposition of the nation's legal disputes and issues of constitutionality. Groundbreaking cases settled here include *Brown v. Board of Education*, which abolished racial segregation in schools, and *Miranda v. Arizona*, which declared that crime suspects were entitled to a lawyer before they were interrogated.

As recently as 1929, the Supreme Court was still meeting in various sections of the US Capitol. Then, at Chief Justice William Howard Taft's urging, Congress authorized a separate building to be constructed. The result was a magnificent Corinthian edifice designed by Cass Gilbert that opened in 1935. Allegorical

The impressive Neo-Classical façade of the US Supreme Court

sculptures depicting the Contemplation of Justice and the Guardian of the Law stand beside the steps.

The Great Hall that leads to the courtroom is an expanse of marble, lined with columns and the busts of former chief justices. The elegant court chamber itself has a coffered plaster ceiling decorated with gold leaf, and a frieze running around the walls that depicts both real and allegorical legal figures. The exhibit hall has displays on legal systems from around the world and an array of international judges' robes.

Visitors may watch the court in session Monday to Wednesday from October through April. Admission is on a first-come, first-served basis. When the court is not in session, public lectures on the Supreme Court are held every hour in the Courtroom.

The Mall

THIS BOULEVARD, BETWEEN THE Capitol and the
Washington Monument, stretches for 1 mile (1.6 km)
and is the city's cultural heart; the many great museums
of the Smithsonian Institution can be found along this
green strip. At the northeast corner of the Mall is the
National Gallery of Art. Directly opposite is one of the
most popular museums in the world – the National Air
& Space Museum – a soaring construction of glass and
steel. Both the National Museum of American History
and the National Museum of Natural History, on the
north side of the Mall, draw huge numbers of visitors.

★ **National Museum
of Natural History**
*The central Rotunda was
designed in the Neo-Clas-
sical style and opened to the
public in 1910* ⑥

★ **National Museum of
American History**
*From George
Washington's
uniform to this
1940s Tucker
Torpedo, US
history is docu-
mented here* ⑧

Sculpture
Garden

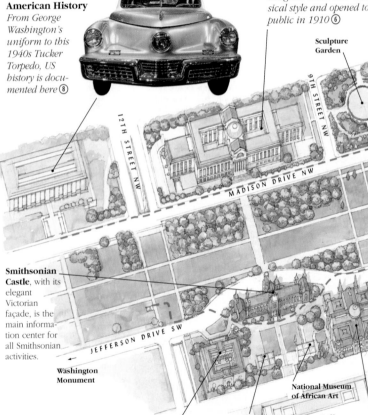

12TH STREET NW

9TH STREET NW

MADISON DRIVE NW

**Smithsonian
Castle**, with its
elegant
Victorian
façade, is the
main informa-
tion center for
all Smithsonian
activities.

JEFFERSON DRIVE SW

**Washington
Monument**

National Museum
of African Art

**National Museum of
African Art**
*Founded in 1965 and
located underground,
this museum houses a
comprehensive
collection of ancient
and modern
African art* ⑦

**Freer Gallery
of Art** displays
masterpieces of
American and
Asian art.

Arthur M. Sackler Gallery
holds an extensive collection
of Asian art, which was
donated to the nation by
New Yorker Arthur Sackler.

Arts & Industries Building, a
masterpiece of Victorian
architecture, was built to contain
exhibits from the Centennial
Exposition in Philadelphia.

0 meters   100

0 yards   100

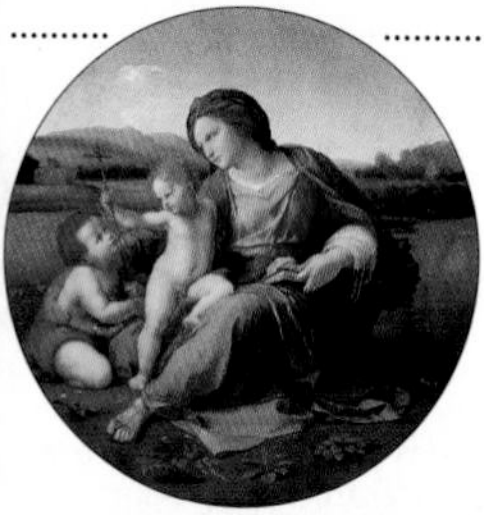

★ **National Gallery of Art**
This gallery's fine collection of art treasures, such as The Alba Madonna *(c.1510) by Raphael, chronicle the history of art from the Middle Ages to the 20th century* 5

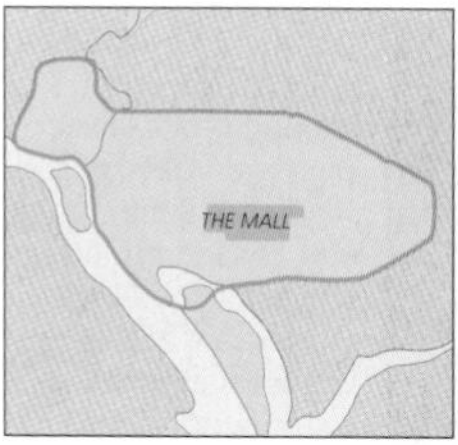
THE MALL

LOCATOR MAP
See Map pp196–97

KEY

– – – Suggested route

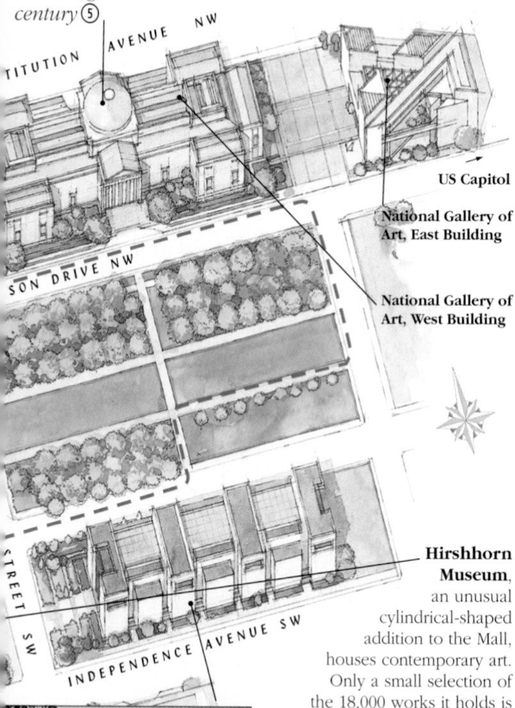
TITUTION AVENUE NW
SON DRIVE NW
STREET SW
INDEPENDENCE AVENUE SW
US Capitol
National Gallery of Art, East Building
National Gallery of Art, West Building

Hirshhorn Museum, an unusual cylindrical-shaped addition to the Mall, houses contemporary art. Only a small selection of the 18,000 works it holds is on display at any one time.

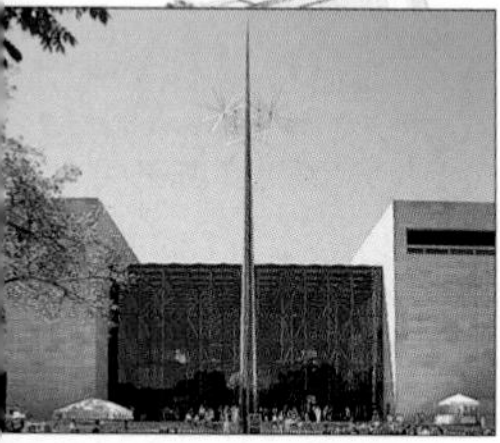

★ **National Air & Space Museum**
The clean, modern design of the National Air & Space Museum echoes the technological marvels on display inside 4

STAR SIGHTS

★ **National Air & Space Museum**

★ **National Gallery of Art**

★ **National Museum of American History**

★ **National Museum of Natural History**

National Air & Space Museum 4

Map D5. 601 Independence Ave, SW. ☎ *(202) 357-2700.* [M] *Smithsonian.* 🚌 *32, 34, 36, 52.* 🕒 *10am–5:30pm daily.* ● *Dec 25.* 🗣 *10:15am, 1pm.* ♿ 🚸 🛍 🍴 [W] www.nasm.si.edu

OPENED on America's Bicentennial on July 1, 1976, the Air & Space Museum is today the most visited site in Washington. The museum's entrance leads into the lofty **Milestones of Flight** gallery, which displays many of the firsts in air and space travel. These include the 1903 Wright *Flyer*, the first powered, heavier-than-air machine to achieve controlled, sustained flight, built by the Wright Brothers; the *Spirit of St. Louis*, in which Charles Lindbergh made the first transatlantic solo flight in 1927; and the *Apollo 11* Command Module, which carried astronauts Buzz Aldrin, Neil Armstrong, and Michael Collins on their historic mission to the moon in 1969. Another gallery that attracts crowds is the **Space Hall**, where exhibits include space suits, a working model of the *Columbia* Space Shuttle, and the Skylab, an orbiting workshop for three-person crews.

An eye-catching exhibit in the **Developments in Flight** gallery is the red Lockheed Vega in which Amelia Earhart became the first woman to make a solo transatlantic flight in 1932. The very popular **World War II Aviation** gallery displays fighter aircrafts from the American, British, German, and Japanese air forces.

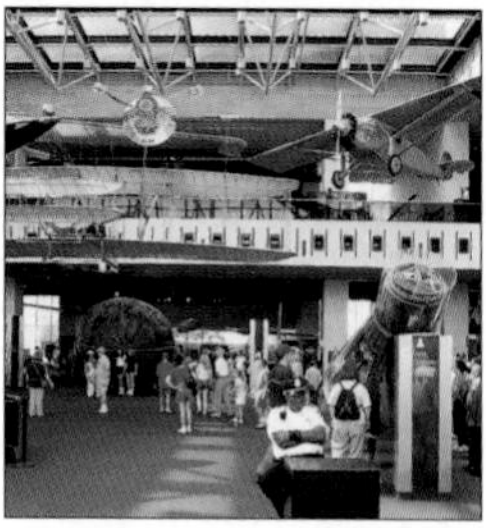

Milestones of Flight gallery in the National Air & Space Museum

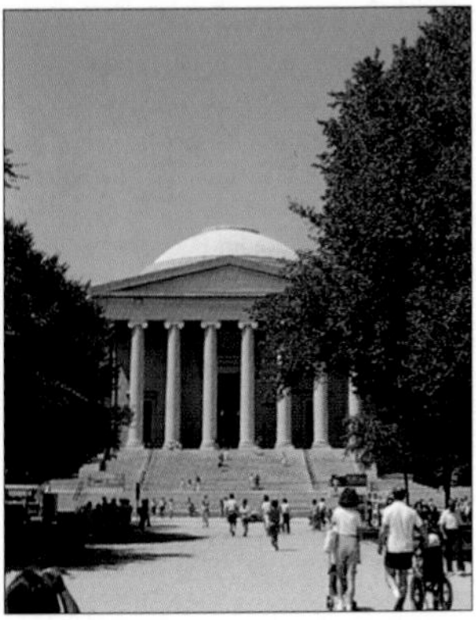

The façade of the National Gallery of Art

National Gallery of Art ⑤

Map E4. **West Building** Constitution Ave between 4th & 7th Sts, NW. **East Building** 4th St between Madison Drive & Constitution Ave, NW. ☎ *(202) 737-4215.* [M] *Archives/Navy Memorial, Judiciary Square, Smithsonian.* 🚌 *32, 34, 36, 70.* 🕒 *10am–5pm Mon–Sat, 11am–6pm Sun.* ● *Jan 1, Dec 25.* 🚶 *call (202) 842-6690.* 🎧 *call (202) 842-6176.* ♿ 🛍 [W] www.nga.gov

One of Washington, DC's top attractions, this superb museum was established when American financier Andrew Mellon bequeathed his collection of European art to form the basis of a National Gallery of Art. Spurred on by his example, other collectors left their art to the proposed museum.

Of the two main buildings, the stately Neo-Classical-style West Building, opened in 1941, features European art from the 13th to the 19th centuries. The modern East Building, completed in 1978, features 20th-century art. An underground concourse, with a cafeteria and shops, joins the two buildings.

Matching wings flank a central rotunda in the **West Building**. West of the rotunda are the galleries displaying Italian, Dutch, Flemish, and Spanish art. The Italian paintings include Madonnas by Giotto, Botticelli, and Raphael; and Leonardo da Vinci's superb portrait of a pensive Florentine girl, Ginevra de Benci. Among other masterpieces on display are works by Rembrandt, Van Dyck, and Rubens, as well as by Goya, El Greco, and Velasquez. Galleries east of the rotunda house an outstanding collection of French Impressionist and Post-Impressionist art. Among its highlights are Monet's *Woman with a Parasol,* Degas' *Four Dancers,* and Toulouse-Lautrec's *Quadrille at the Moulin Rouge.* Portraits by John Singer Sargent and James McNeill Whistler are among the gallery's important collection of American paintings. Adjacent to the West Building is a Sculpture Garden, which is transformed into an ice skating rink in winter.

The huge **East Building** is designed to accommodate large pieces of modern art. Centered in its courtyard is a giant red, blue, and black mobile by Alexander Calder, completed in 1976. Near the entrance is a sculpture by Henry Moore; the atrium displays a 1977 tapestry by Joan Miró.

National Museum of Natural History ⑥

Map D4. Constitution Ave & 10th St, NW. ☎ *(202) 357-2700 (recorded message after museum hours).* [M] *Smithsonian.* 🚌 *32, 34, 36.* 🕒 *10am–5:30pm daily.* ● *Dec 25.* 🚶 *10:30am & 1:30pm Mon–Fri.* 🎧 ♿ 👪 🛍 💻 🍴 [W] www.nmnh.si.edu

Established in 1910, this vast museum's collection of 120 million artifacts includes samples from the world's diverse cultures, as well as fossils and living creatures from land and sea. The museum's entrance leads into the lofty Rotunda, where visitors are greeted by the impressive sight of a massive African Bush elephant. To the right of the Rotunda is one of the most popular areas of the museum, the newly renovated **Dinosaur Hall**, featuring dinosaur skeletons and eggs, and Ice Age mammals, such as the woolly mammoth. Also on the ground floor are galleries displaying objects from Native American, Asian, and Pacific cultures; don't miss the huge Easter Island stone statues. To the left of the Rotunda is an IMAX® Theater and the Discovery Room, where visitors can handle objects such as crocodile heads and elephant tusks.

On the second floor is the **Gems and Minerals** collection, whose highlight is the 45.52-carat Hope Diamond. The largest deep blue diamond in the world and famed for its stunning color and clarity, it once belonged to Louis XVI of France. Also on the second floor is the highly popular **Insect Zoo**, with its giant hissing cockroaches and large leaf-cutter ant colony.

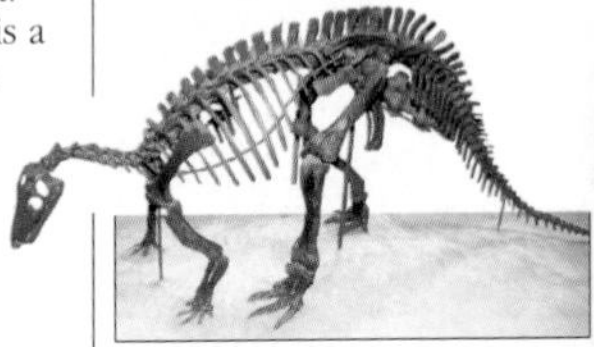

Dinosaur skeleton in the National Museum of Natural History

National Museum of African Art ⑦

Map D5. 950 Independence Ave, SW. ☎ *(202) 357-4600.* [M] *Smithsonian.* 🕒 *10am–5:30pm daily.* ● *Dec 25.* 🚶 ♿ 🛍 🍴 [W] www.si.edu/nmafa

This quiet museum is missed by many visitors, perhaps because much of its exhibition space is underground. The small entrance pavilion at the ground level leads to three subterranean floors where the exhibits are displayed. The 7,000-piece permanent collection includes both modern and ancient art from Africa, although the majority of pieces date from the 19th and 20th centuries. Traditional African bronzes, ceramics, and pottery are on display, as are stunning ivory and gold objects, brightly colored *kente* textiles from Ghana, and photographs.

National Museum of American History ⑧

Map D4. 14th St & Constitution Ave. 📞 *(202) 357-2700 (recorded message outside opening hours).* Ⓜ *Smithsonian–Federal Triangle.* 🚌 *32, 34, 36.* 🕐 *10am–5:30pm daily.* ⬤ *Dec 25.* ♿🚻👶📷🍴 ▢🖼 Ⓦ *www.americanhistory.si.edu*

Ford's *Model T*, in the National Museum of American History

THIS THREE-STORY museum is a collection of artifacts from America's past. The highlight of the first-floor galleries is the 100-year-old Headsville Post Office from West Virginia, which was dismantled and reassembled here in its entirety in 1971 and is still a working post office. Another popular exhibit on this floor is a *Model T* Ford, an engineering landmark that heralded the beginning of the motor age. Visitors can eat at the **Palm Court**, which has a 1900 candy store and an early 20th-century ice-cream parlor.

Dominating the East Wing of the second floor is the **First Ladies** exhibit, which includes First Ladies' gowns worn to the presidents' inaugural balls. Jackie Kennedy's and Nancy Reagan's haute couture gowns are on display here along with Rosalynn Carter's "off the rack" one. Also on the second floor are the largest single exhibit, **America on the Move**, which offers a look at modes of transport from 1876 to the present. It also includes the Star-Spangled Banner that flew over Fort McHenry in 1814 and inspired the Francis Scott Key poem that later became the US national anthem.

Another big draw on the second floor is the **Hands-On History Room**, where everything can be touched by hand. Visitors can try out 19th-century household appliances, or explore and learn what life was like for a slave or a Zuni Indian.

Located on the third floor, the **American Presidency** displays objects that represent the lives and offices of the presidency in 11 themed sections. American popular culture exhibits include the ruby slippers worn by Judy Garland in *The Wizard of Oz*.

Smithsonian American Art Museum & National Portrait Gallery ⑨

Map D4. **Smithsonian American Art Museum** 8th & G Sts NW. 📞 *(202) 357-2700.* Ⓦ *www.americanart. si.edu Closed for renovation.* **National Portrait Gallery** 8th & F Sts NW. 📞 *(202) 357-2700.* Ⓦ *www.npg.si.edu* Ⓜ *Gallery Place–Chinatown.* ♿🚻👶📷🍴 ▢🖼 *Closed for renovation.*

THESE TWO museums are currently closed for major renovations until July 2006. Originally opened in 1968, they are housed in the former US Patent Office, a wonderfully ornate 1836 building. While the galleries are closed, there is a full program of exhibitions and events at the Renwick Gallery *(see p208)*. The Smithsonian American Art Museum contains a wealth of works by American artists, reflecting the history and culture of the country. The highlight of the American folk art collection is an amazing piece of visionary art called *Throne of the Third Heaven of the Nations' Millenium* (c.1950–64), created out of light bulbs, silver and gold foil, and old furniture by a Washington janitor by the name of James Hampton. Among the 19th- and early 20th-century works, the Western landscapes by Thomas Moran stand out. Especially dramatic is his *Cliffs of the Upper Colorado River*, painted in 1882, which captures the vastness of the American West. Another outstanding work from this period is *Achelous and Hercules* by Thomas Hart Benton (1889–1975). In this mythical analogy of early American life, Hercules symbolizes man taming the wild and then enjoying the fruits of his labor. Works by Modernists Jasper Johns, Andy Warhol, and Robert Rauschenberg are among the other treasures of this museum.

The National Portrait Gallery is America's family album, featuring paintings, sculptures, etchings, and photographs of thousands of famous Americans. Assembled here are such diverse works as Gilbert Stuart's famous portrait of George Washington (which features on the one-dollar bill), busts of Dr. Martin Luther King Jr. and the poet T.S. Eliot, and some recently acquired photographs of actress Marilyn Monroe.

***George Washington* by Gilbert Stuart**

Washington Monument ⑩

Map C4. Independence Ave at 17th St, SW. ☎ (202) 426-6841. Ⓜ Smithsonian. 🚌 13, 52. ◯ early Sep–early Apr: 9am–4:30pm; early Apr–early Sep: 9am–11:30pm. ● Dec 25. ♿ 🎧 Interpretive talks. 🖥 www.nps.gov/wamo

Constructed from 36,000 pieces of marble and granite, the 555-ft (170-m) tall Washington Monument is one of the capital's most recognizable landmarks, clearly visible from almost all over the city. Conceived of as a tribute to the first president of the US, its construction began in 1848, but stopped in 1858 when funds ran out. The building work resumed in 1876 after public interest in the project revived – a slight change in the color of the stone indicates the point at which construction stopped and then began again. The original design included a circular colonnade around the monument, but lack of funds prevented its construction.

Recently renovated and cleaned to a gleaming white, the monument has a capstone weighing 3,300 pounds (2,000 kg). It is topped by an aluminum pyramid, and surrounded by 50 flagpoles. Inside the monument are 192 commemorative stones, donated by individuals, states, societies, and nations. There are stunning views across the city from the top.

Washington Monument, which dominates the city skyline

The soaring Hall of Witness in the US Holocaust Memorial Museum

United States Holocaust Memorial Museum ⑪

Map C5. 100 Raoul Wallenburg Place, SW. ☎ (202) 488-0400. Ⓜ Smithsonian. 🚌 13 (Pentagon shuttle). ◯ mid-Jun–Mar: 10am–5:30pm; Apr–mid-Jun: 10am–8pm. ● Dec 25 & Yom Kippur. Time pass required for Permanent Exhibit. Same-day from Pass Desk; advance passes: (800) 400-9373. ♿ 🖥 www.ushmm.org

Opened in 1993, the US Holocaust Memorial Museum bears witness to the systematic persecution and annihilation in Europe of six million Jews and others deemed undesirable by the Third Reich. The museum is meant to be experienced, not just seen. Within the exhibition space, which ranges from the intentionally claustrophobic to the soaringly majestic, are thousands of photographs and artifacts, 53 video monitors, and 30 interactive stations that contain graphic and emotionally disturbing images of violence, forcing visitors to confront the horror of the Holocaust.

Starting from the top, the fourth floor documents the early years of the Nazi regime, with exhibits exposing their ruthless persecution of Jews. The third floor exhibits are devoted to the "Final Solution," the killing of six million "undesirable"

people. Artifacts include a box car that carried prisoners to concentration camps.

On the second floor is the **Hall of Remembrance**, which houses an eternal flame that pays homage to the victims of the Holocaust. The soaring central atrium on the first floor, the **Hall of Witness** features temporary exhibits. On the same floor is a poignant exhibit called **Daniel's Story**, aimed at children. It tells the story of the Holocaust from the point of view of an eight-year-old Jewish boy living in 1930s Germany.

At the Concourse Level is the **Children's Tile Wall**. Over 3,000 tiles, painted by children, constitute this moving memorial to the one-and-a-half million children murdered in the Holocaust.

Jefferson Memorial ⑫

Map C5. S bank of the Tidal Basin. ☎ (202) 426-6841. Ⓜ Smithsonian. ◯ 8am–midnight. ● Dec 25. Interpretive talks. ♿ 🎧 🖥 www.nps.gov/thje/jefm

When this Neo-Classical-style memorial to the third US president, Thomas Jefferson (1743–1826), was completed in 1943, critics gave it the derisive nickname "Jefferson's Muffin." It was dismissed as far too "feminine" for so bold and influential a man who had played a significant part in drafting the Declaration of Independence in 1776. The dome of this round, colonnaded building covers a majestic 19-ft (6-m) statue of Jefferson. The statue was originally cast in plaster since metal was rationed when the building was dedicated in 1943. It was recast in bronze after the end of World War II, and the plaster version is now in the basement of the building. Etched on the walls are Jefferson's words from the Declaration of Independence. Legend says that the architects

Majestic statue of Jefferson

The colonnaded domed Jefferson Memorial, housing the bronze statue

are said to have purposely misquoted and mispelled these words (they claimed because of lack of space).

Jefferson Memorial stands on the banks of the scenic **Tidal Basin**, built in 1897 to catch the overflow from the Potomac River. In the 1920s, hundreds of Japanese cherry trees were planted along its shores, and the sight of the trees in bloom is one of the most photographed in the city. Peak blooming time is for two weeks, between mid-March and mid-April. Rental paddle-boats are available at the Tidal Basin.

Franklin D. Roosevelt Memorial ⑬

Map C5. W Basin Dr, SW. ((202) 426-6841. M Smithsonian. 🚌 13. 🕐 8am–midnight daily. ● Dec 25. 🚹 🚻 **Interpretive programs & talks.** W www.nps.gov/fdrm

THE MEMORIAL to President Franklin D. Roosevelt, opened in 1997, is a mammoth park of four granite open-air rooms, one for each of Roosevelt's terms (see p49). The first room has the visitor center, and a bas-relief of Roosevelt's first inaugural parade. In the second room is a sculpture titled Hunger, recalling the hard times of the Great Depression. A controversial statue of Roosevelt in the third room of this open air park shows the disabled president sitting in a wheelchair hidden by his Navy cape.

Dramatic waterfalls cascade into a series of pools in the fourth room, which also has a statue of Roosevelt's wife,

Eleanor, and a relief of his funeral cortege carved into the granite wall. The water symbolizes the peace that Roosevelt was so eager to achieve before his death.

Lincoln Memorial ⑭

Map B4. Constitution Ave, between French & Bacon Drs. ((202) 426-6841. M Smithsonian. 🕐 8am–midnight daily. ● Dec 25. 🚹 on request. 🚻 🚹 W www.nps.gov/linc

THE LINCOLN MEMORIAL is one of Washington's most awe-inspiring sights, with the seated figure of President Abraham Lincoln in his Neo-Classical "temple," looming over a reflecting pool.

The site chosen for the monument was a swamp, and before building could begin in 1914 it had to be drained. Concrete piers were poured for the foundation so that the building could be anchored in bedrock. As the memorial neared completion, architect Henry Bacon realized that the statue of Lincoln would be dwarfed inside the huge edifice. The original 10-ft (3-m) statue by Daniel Chester French was doubled in size and carved from 28 blocks of

white marble. Engraved on the wall are the words of Lincoln's famous Gettysburg Address (see p106).

In 1963, the memorial was the site of a mammoth gathering of 200,000 people in support of Civil Rights, where Dr. Martin Luther King Jr. made his historic "I have a Dream" speech. A direct result of this speech was the passing by Congress of Civil Rights legislation in 1964.

Vietnam Veterans Memorial ⑮

Map B4. 21st St & Constitution Ave, NW. ((202) 426-6841. M Smithsonian. 🕐 8am–midnight daily. ● Dec 25. 🚹 on request. 🚻 W www.nps.gov/vive

POWERFUL IN ITS symbolism and dramatic in its simplicity, this memorial was designed by Maya Lin, then a 21-year-old student at Yale University, whose design was selected from 1,421 entries. Dedicated in 1982, it consists of two triangular black walls, set into the earth at an angle of 125 degrees, one end pointing to the Lincoln Memorial and the other to the Washington Monument. The walls are inscribed with the names of the Americans who died in the Vietnam War, in chronological order from 1959 to 1975. The site is covered by tokens of remembrance placed by veterans and their families – poems, pictures, toys, and flowers – making this one of the most moving memorials on the Mall. A more conventional memorial was added in 1984 – a statue of three soldiers.

The Lincoln Memorial, one of Washington's most visited monuments

The White House ⑯

THE OFFICIAL RESIDENCE OF the president, the White House was designed by Irish-born architect James Hoban. Known as the Executive Mansion, it was first occupied in 1800 by President John Adams. Burned by the British in 1814, the partially rebuilt edifice was reoccupied in 1817. In 1901, President Theodore Roosevelt renamed the building the White House and ordered the West Wing to be built. The East Wing was added in 1942, completing the building as it is today. Beautifully decorated with period furniture, valuable antiques, and paintings, the White House attracts more than a million and a half visitors every year.

The White House
The official residence of the US president for 200 years, the White House façade is familiar to millions of people around the world.

★ **State Dining Room**
Able to seat as many as 140 people, the State Dining Room was enlarged in 1902. A portrait of President Abraham Lincoln, by George P.A. Healy, hangs above the mantel.

The West Terrace
leads to the West Wing and the Oval Office, the president's official office.

The stonework has been painted over and over to maintain the building's white façade.

★ **Red Room**
One of four reception rooms, the Red Room is furnished in red in the Empire Style (1810–30). The fabrics were woven in the US from French designs.

STAR ROOMS

★ **Red Room**

★ **State Dining Room**

★ **Vermeil Room**

Lincoln Bedroom
President Lincoln used this room as his Cabinet Room, then turned it into a bedroom, furnishing it with Lincoln-era decor. Today it is used as a guest room.

VISITORS' CHECKLIST

Map C4. 1600 Pennsylvania Ave, NW. ⃝ 10–11am Tue–Sat only for groups with Congressional or embassy appointments. Contact Visitor Center for information. ⬤ federal hols & official functions. 🎫 obligatory. W www.nps.gov **White House Visitor Center** 1450 Pennsylvania Ave, NW. ⬤ (202) 208-1631. M Federal Triangle. ⃝ 7:30am–4pm daily. ⬤ Jan 1, Thanksgiving, Dec 25. 🚻 ♿ 🛍 W www.nps.gov/whho

The East Terrace leads to the East Wing.

The East Room is used for large gatherings, such as dances and concerts.

Treaty Room

The Green Room was first used as a guest room before Thomas Jefferson turned it into a dining room.

Blue Room

★ **Vermeil Room**
This yellow room houses seven paintings of First Ladies, including this portrait of Eleanor Roosevelt by Douglas Chandor.

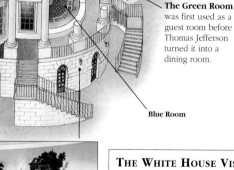

Diplomatic Reception
This room is used to welcome friends and ambassadors. It is elegantly furnished in the Federal Period style (1790–1820).

THE WHITE HOUSE VISITOR CENTER

The Visitor Center has interesting exhibits about the history of the White House as well as royal gifts on display. There are also seasonal lectures by famous speakers on aspects of history in and out of the White House. The center has a monthly Living History program with actors portraying historic figures. The gift shop carries an extensive range, including the annual White House Christmas ornament. Tours of the president's official residence in the White House are extremely limited at this time. Guided tours can be booked only by special arrangement through a member of Congress or an embassy.

Façade of the Visitor Center

The magnificent Renwick Gallery, a fine example of French Empire style

Renwick Gallery ⑰

Map C4. Pennsylvania Ave at 17th St, NW. 🄲 *(202) 357-2700.* Ⓜ *Farragut W.* ◯ *10am–5:30pm daily.* ● *Dec 25.* 🖐 *noon Mon–Fri.* ♿ 🄿 Ⓦ *www.americanart.si.edu*

THIS MAGNIFICENT red-brick building was designed by James Renwick in 1859. It originally housed the art collection of William Wilson Corcoran until it was moved to the current Corcoran Gallery of Art in 1897.

After efforts by First Lady Jacqueline Kennedy saved the building from destruction, it was bought by the Smithsonian. Refurbished and renamed, the Renwick Gallery opened in 1972. It is dedicated primarily to 20th-century American crafts and houses some impressive exhibits in every material including clay, glass, and metal. *Gamefish* (1988) by Larry Fuente is a stunning example of mixed media art.

Corcoran Gallery of Art ⑱

Map C4. 500 17th St, NW. 🄲 *(202) 639-1700.* Ⓜ *Farragut W, Farragut N.* ◯ *10am–5pm daily (until 9pm on Thu except Thanksgiving).* ● *Tue, Dec 25, Jan 1.* 📷 🖐 ♿ 🄿 🄿 Ⓦ *www.corcoran.edu*

A TREASURE TROVE of fine art, this privately funded collection was founded by William Wilson Corcoran, a banker. His collection soon outgrew its original home in the Renwick Gallery and

moved to this massive edifice in 1897. Many of the European works were added in 1925 by art collector and US Senator William A. Clark. The gallery's masterpieces now include 16th-century paintings by Titian, 17th-century works by Rembrandt, and 19th-century Impressionist paintings by Monet and Renoir. It also has the largest collection of paintings by Jean-Baptist Camille Corot outside France, and fine examples of African-American art. Paintings from the 20th century include works by Picasso, John Singer Sargent, and de Kooning. Every Sunday, a gospel brunch takes place in the beautiful atrium, with live music.

Lion Statue, guarding the Corcoran Gallery

The Kennedy Center ⑲

Map B4. New Hampshire Ave & Rock Creek Pkwy, NW. 🄲 *(202) 467-4600, (800) 444-1324.* Ⓜ *Foggy Bottom.* 🚌 *80.* ◯ *10am–9pm daily; 10am–9pm Mon–Sat, noon–9pm Sun & hols (box office).* ◯ *10am–5pm Mon–Fri, 10am–1pm Sat–Sun (call 416-8340).* ♿ Ⓦ *www.kennedy-center.org*

IN 1958, President Eisenhower signed an act to begin fund-raising for a national cultural center that would attract the world's best opera, music, and dance companies to the US capital. His successor, John F.

Kennedy, was also an ardent supporter and fund-raiser for this project but he was assassinated before the completion of the center, which was named in his honor.

Designed by Edward Durrell Stone, the center opened in 1971. The **Grand Foyer**, adorned with a remarkable bronze bust of Kennedy by sculptor Robert Berks, stretches 630 ft (192 m) and provides an impressive entrance to the three main theaters of this vast arts complex. In front of the foyer is the **JFK Terrace**, which runs the length of the center and offers glorious views of the Potomac River.

Of the three huge theaters, the **Eisenhower Theater**, with a bronze bust of Eisenhower, is at one end of the foyer. At the other end is the **Concert Hall**, which seats 2,450 people and is the home of the National Symphony Orchestra. Between them is the sumptuous **Opera House**, hung with an enormous crystal chandelier, and with seating for 2,300 people. The Opera House is flanked by the **Hall of States**, with the flags of each of the 50 American states, and the **Hall of Nations**, with the flags of every country with which the US has diplomatic relations.

The impressive Grand Foyer of the Kennedy Center

Watergate Complex ⑳

Map B3. Virginia Ave between Rock Creek Pkwy & New Hampshire Ave, NW. **M** *Foggy Bottom-GWU.* &

LOCATED NEXT to the Kennedy Center on the banks of the Potomac, the four rounded buildings that make up the Watergate Complex were completed in 1971 and designed to contain apartments, offices, and shops. The Watergate soon became one of Washington's most desirable addresses. In 1972, however, the complex found itself at the center of international news. Burglars, linked to President Nixon, broke into the offices of the Democratic Party headquarters in the complex to bug the telephones there, sparking off a major political scandal. Investigations by *Washington Post* reporters Bob Woodward and Carl Bernstein uncovered the extent of the president's involvement through incriminating tapes and proven bribery. This led to an impeachment hearing, but before Mr. Nixon could be impeached, he resigned. Vice-President Gerald Ford succeeded him.

Georgetown ㉑

Map A3. **Old Stone House** 3051 M St, NW. **[** *(202) 426-6851.* **○** phone ahead. **▭** 30, 32, 34, 36, 38. & **W** www.nps.gov/olst
Georgetown University 37th & O Sts, NW. **[** *(202) 687-5055.* **○** varies. **✔** call 687-3600 for details. & **W** www.georgetown.edu
Dumbarton Oaks 1703 32nd St, NW. **[** *(202) 339-6401.* ▨ ▣ & house only. **W** www.doaks.org

GEORGETOWN developed well before Washington, DC. Native Americans had a settlement here, and by the mid-18th century Georgetown had a substantial population of immigrants from Scotland. With the construction of Washington Harbor and the Chesapeake and Ohio Canal in 1828, it soon grew into a wealthy port.

The picturesque Old Stone House in Georgetown, built in 1765

Today one of Washington, DC's most attractive neighborhoods, Georgetown is lined with elegant townhouses, many of them converted into upscale bars, restaurants, and boutiques. The two main business streets of the area are Wisconsin Avenue and M Street. On the latter is the historic **Old Stone House** (built in 1765), which may be the only building in Washington that predates the American Revolution. N Street, lined with historic buildings, has an array of 18th-century Federal-style mansions, as well as some fine Victorian townhouses. The 1794 Thomas **Beall House** (number 3017), is where Jackie Kennedy lived for a year after JFK's death.

More Federal houses can be seen lining the banks of the **Chesapeake and Ohio Canal**, which was built in 1828 and runs for 184 miles (296 km) from Georgetown to Cumberland, Maryland. The canal, with its ingenious transportation system of locks, aqueducts, and tunnels,

The Riggs National Bank, on Wisconsin Avenue in Georgetown

fell out of use with the arrival of the railroad in the 19th century. It is now a protected national park, offering many recreational facilities. Park rangers in period costume guide tours of the canal in mule-drawn barges, and boating is also popular, especially between Georgetown and Violette's Lock – the first 22 miles (35 km) of the canal. The towpath along the canal is ideal for walks and bike rides.

A major center of activity in this district is **Georgetown University**, founded in 1789. Among the historic buildings on its campus is the Gothic-inspired Healy Building, topped by a fanciful spiral.

Sprawling over 22 acres (9 ha) of land in Georgetown is the historic **Dumbarton Oaks** estate. Its superbly landscaped gardens surround a grand Federal-style brick mansion, which houses a priceless art collection assembled by pharmaceutical heirs Robert and Mildred Bliss.

The historic Dumbarton Oaks Conference, attended by President Franklin Roosevelt and British Prime Minister Winston Churchill, was held in the music room of this house in 1944, laying the groundwork for the establishment of the United Nations.

The Blisses donated the house to Harvard University, and it now houses a library, research institution, and museum, the highlight of which is its superb collection of Byzantine art. A new wing of the house, designed by Philip Johnson, houses pre-Columbian masks, gold jewelry from Central America, frescoes, and Aztec carvings.

Auguste Renoir's masterpiece, *The Luncheon of the Boating Party* (1881)

Phillips Collection ㉒

1600 21st St at Q St, NW.
📞 *(202) 387-2151.* Ⓜ *Dupont Circle.* ○ *10am–5pm Tue–Wed & Fri–Sat, 10am–8:30pm Thu, 12–7pm Sun.* ● *Mon, Jan 1, Jul4, Thanksg., Dec 25.* 🎫 📷 *2pm Wed & Sat.* ♿
🅦 *www.phillipscollection.org*

THIS IS ONE of the finest collections of Impressionist art in the world, and the first museum in the US devoted to modern art of the 19th and 20th centuries. Housed in the beautiful 1897 Georgian Revival mansion of the collection's founders, Marjorie and Duncan Phillips, this museum has a more intimate and personal ambience than the larger Smithsonian art museums.

Among the wonderful selection of Impressionist and Post-Impressionist works on display are *Dancers at the Barre* by Degas, *Self-Portrait* by Cezanne, *Entrance to the Public Gardens at Arles* by Van Gogh, and Renoir's masterpiece, *The Luncheon of the Boating Party* (1881).

Other great paintings in the collection include El Greco's *The Repentant Saint Peter* (1600), *The Blue Room* (1901) by Picasso, Piet Mondrian's *Composition No III* (1921–25), and *Ochre on Red* (1954) by Mark Rothko.

The museum hosts a number of special events, such as gallery talks, film retrospectives, and live jazz concerts. Especially popular are its Sunday afternoon concerts, staged in the Music Room, with performances by classical artists of world renown. These popular concerts are free to anyone who has purchased a ticket for the gallery on that day.

National Zoological Park ㉓

3001 Connecticut Ave, NW. 📞 *(202) 673-4800.* Ⓜ *Cleveland Park, Woodley Park-Zoo.* ○ *May 1–Sep 15: 10am–6pm daily (buildings), 6am– 8pm daily (grounds); Sep 16–Apr 30: 10am–4:30pm daily (buildings), 8am–6pm daily (grounds).* ● *Dec 25.* 🎫 *call (202) 673-4671.* ♿ 🚻 📷
📷 🅦 *www.natzoo.si.edu/*

LOCATED IN a sprawling 163-acre (66-ha) park designed by Frederick Law Olmsted (the landscape designer of New York's Central Park), the National Zoo was established in 1887. Since 1964 it has been part of the Smithsonian Institution, which has developed it as a dynamic "biopark" where animals are

The Komodo dragon, a rare lizard in the National Zoological Park

studied in environments that replicate their natural habitats.

The zoo's most famous residents are a pair of giant pandas, Mei Xiang and Tian Tian, who can be seen playing and roaming around the large trees, pools, and air-conditioned outdoor grottos in the **Giant Panda Exhibit**.

Equally popular with visitors is the **Great Ape House**, which houses lowland gorillas, each weighing around 400 lbs (180 kg), and arboreal orangutans.

The **Reptile Discovery Center** features the rare Komodo dragons, lizards that can grow up to a length of 10 ft (3 m) and weigh up to 200 lbs (90 kg).

In **Amazonia**, which re-creates the lush green Amazonian habitat, visitors can see poison arrow frogs and giant catfish, while the **Prairie Exhibit** houses prairie dogs and bisons.

Other rare creatures include the endangered Golden Lion Tamarins and red wolves.

Washington National Cathedral ㉔

Massachusetts & Wisconsin Aves, NW.
📞 *(202) 537-6200.* ♿ *(202) 364-6616.* 🚌 *32, 34, 36.* ○ *10am–5:30pm Mon–Sat, 12:30–4pm Sun.* 🎫 *group reservations call 537-6207.* 🔓 ♿ 📷 🚻 ✝ *noon Mon–Sat, hourly 8am–11am & 4pm & 6:30pm Sun, 5:30pm Mon–Fri, 4pm Sat & Sun.* 🅦 *www.nationalcathedral.org/*

THE BUILDING of the Church of St. Peter and St. Paul (its official name) was financed entirely by donations. It is the world's sixth largest cathedral, measuring 518 ft (158 m) in length and 301 ft (95 m) from grade to the top of the central tower. It uses building techniques of the Gothic style of architecture, evident in the pointed arches, rib vaulting, stained-glass windows, and exterior flying buttresses. Inside, sculpture, needlework, wrought iron, and wood carving depict the nation's history and biblical scenes.

Above the west entrance is a splendid relief of *The*

Gothic-style architecture of the Washington National Cathedral

Creation by Frederick Hart, which depicts mankind being formed from chaos. The pinnacles on the Cathedral towers are decorated with leaf-shaped ornaments. Above the south entrance is an exquisite stained-glass **Rose Window**, while in the nave another stained-glass window commemorates the *Apollo 11* space flight and contains a sliver of moon rock. The **High Altar** has carvings of 110 figures surrounding the central statue of Christ. The floor in front of the altar has stone from Mount Sinai. By the **Children's Chapel**, built to the scale of a six-year-old, is a statue of Jesus as a boy.

Arlington National Cemetery ㉕

Arlington, VA. [(703) 697-9486. Arlington National Cemetery. Oct–Mar: 8am–5pm daily; Apr–Sep: 8am–6:30pm daily. Dec 25.

A SEA OF simple headstones covers Arlington National Cemetery, marking the graves of around 280,000 American servicemen killed in the nation's major conflicts – from the Revolution to the September 11 terrorist attack. The focus of the cemetery, which sprawls over 612 acres (248

ha) of a hillside, is the **Tomb of the Unknowns**, honoring the thousands whose bodies were never found or identified. Its four vaults are for soldiers from World Wars I and II, Korea, and Vietnam. Each vault held one unidentified soldier until recently, when the Vietnam soldier was identified by DNA analysis and reburied in his hometown. Near it is the **Memorial Amphitheater**, which has hosted many state funerals, and where annual services are held on Memorial Day.

North of the Tomb of the Unknowns, an eternal flame burns at the **Grave of John F. Kennedy**, lit by his wife Jacqueline on the day of his funeral in December 1963. She and their son John Jr. are buried next to the late president, as is his brother Robert F. Kennedy. Close to the Kennedy graves is the imposing **Tomb of Pierre L'Enfant**, the French architect responsible for planning the city of Washington. The cemetery also houses poignant memorials to the victims of the Lockerbie air crash and the *Challenger* Space Shuttle, which exploded seconds after take-off in January 1986.

The Creation, **National Cathedral**

The grand Georgian-Revival mansion at the top of the hill, above the Kennedy graves, is **Arlington House**, which was the home of the Confederate general Robert E. Lee (1807–70). When Lee left his home in 1861 to lead Virginia's armed forces during the Civil

War, the Union confiscated the estate for a military cemetery. The house, now a memorial to the general, is open to visitors.

The Pentagon ㉖

1000 Defense Pentagon, Hwy 1-395, Arlington, VA. [(703) 695-1776. M Pentagon. O tours by appointment only. For details call the above number. W www.defenselink.mil

T HE WORLD'S largest office building, the Pentagon is almost a city in itself. This enormous edifice houses 23,000 people who work for the US Department of Defense, which includes the Army, Navy, and Airforce, and 14 other defense agencies. Despite its enormous size – it has 17.5 miles (28 km) of corridors, and the entire US Capitol could fit into one of its five wedge-shaped sections – the building's efficient design ensures that it takes no more than seven minutes to walk between any two points in the Pentagon. Designed by army engineers, it is built from sand and gravel dredged from the Potomac and molded into concrete. The building was started in September 1941, and completed in January 1943 at a cost of $83 million.

The headquarters of the US military establishment and the ultimate symbol of America's military might, the Pentagon was one of the targets of terrorists who flew a hijacked American Airlines plane into one side of the building on September 11, 2001, killing 189 people. It has now been completely restored.

Uniform rows of headstones in Arlington National Cemetery

Virginia

T**HERE IS ENOUGH HISTORY** and natural beauty in Virginia to satisfy the most avid sightseer. Mount Vernon, the perfectly preserved home of President George Washington, is close to Washington, DC. In eastern Virginia is the old capital, Williamsburg, a living museum of the Colonial era. To its west, the Skyline Drive reveals the spectacular beauty of the Shenandoah National Park and the Blue Ridge Mountains. The state capital, Richmond, retains a charming Old South aura.

Alexandria ❷

🏛 *119,000.* 🚉 *Union Station, 110 Callahan St.* Ⓜ *King Street.* ℹ *Ramsay House Visitor Center, 221 King St (703) 838-4200.* ⓦ *www.funside.com*

O**LD TOWN** Alexandria has kept a special historical flavor, dating back to its incorporation in 1749. Accessible by Metro from Washington, Alexandria is still a busy port, with its lively Market Square. Its tree-lined streets are filled with elegant, historic buildings, among them the 1753 **Carlyle House**, a Georgian

Façade of the elegant Carlyle House, built in 1752, Alexandria

Palladian mansion on Fairfax Street. A guided tour of the house, now beautifully restored, provides fascinating details about 18th-century everday life. On the same street is the **Stabler Leadbeater Apothecary Shop**, established in 1792. When it closed in 1933, the doors were locked with all its contents intact. Now reopened as a museum, the shop's 8,000 original objects include huge mortars and pestles, and jars of herbal remedies.

The **Boyhood Home of Robert E. Lee**, a Federal townhouse where General Lee *(see 193)* lived from the age of 11 until he went to the West Point Military Academy, is currently a private residence and not open to the public. The **Lee-Fendall House Museum** nearby is rich with artifacts from the Revolution to the 1930s Labor Movement. To its south is the 1773 **Christ Church**, a Georgian edifice where George Washington's pew is still preserved with his nameplate as is that of Robert E. Lee.

On Union Street is the **Torpedo Factory Art Center**, displaying the work

Mount Vernon ❸

T**HIS COUNTRY ESTATE** on the Potomac River was George Washington's home for 45 years. The house is furnished as it would have been during Washington's presidency (1789–97), and the 500-acre (202-ha) grounds still retain aspects of the original farm, such as the flower and vegetable gardens, the sheep paddock, and quarters for the slaves who worked the plantation.

The Kitchen, set slightly apart from the main house, has been completely restored.

The Mansion Tour shows visitors the study and dining room, Washington's bedroom, and the bed in which he died.

Overseer's House

The Museum displays belongings of George and Martha Washington.

The Upper Garden
The plants in this colorful garden replicate those grown in Washington's time.

The Slave Quarters housed the estate's slaves. Washington freed all his slaves in his will.

of local artists and craftsmen. From the nearby waterfront, there are boat tours on the Potomac River.

The **Farmers Market** in the center of town dates back to 1749, and George Washington regularly sent produce from his farm at Mount Vernon to be sold here. Today, shoppers can find fresh vegetables and fruit, flowers, baked goods, preserves, and local crafts.

🏛 Carlyle House
21 N Fairfax St. 📞 (703) 549-2997. ⏰ 10am–5pm Tue–Sat, noon–5pm Sun; Nov–Mar: last tour 4pm. ● Mon, Jan 1, Thanksgiving, Dec 25.
🎟 🅿 ♿ 🎁

🏛 Lee-Fendall House Museum
614 Oronoco St. 📞 (703) 548-1789. ⏰ 10am–4pm Tue–Sat, 1–4pm Sun. ● Dec 25–Jan 31 (except 3rd Sun, Lee's birthday celebration).
🎟 🅿 ♿

🏛 Torpedo Factory Art Center
105 N Union St. 📞 (703) 838-4565. ⏰ 10am–5pm daily. ● Jan 1, Easter, Jul 4, Thanksgiving, Dec 25.
🅿 🌐 www.torpedofactory.org

The elegant dining room at Kenmore House, Fredericksburg

Fredericksburg ❹

👥 22,600. 🚗 🚌 ℹ 706 Caroline St, (800) 678-4748. ⏰ 8am–5pm daily (Memorial Day & Labor Day until 7pm). ● Dec 25.
🌐 www.fredericksburgva.net

FREDERICKSBURG'S attractions are its historic downtown district and four Civil War battlefields, including those at Chancellorsville and The Wilderness. The Rising Sun Tavern and Hugh Mercer Apothecary Shop in the old downtown offer living history accounts of life in a town that began as a 50-acre (20-ha) port on the Rappahannock River. **Kenmore Plantation and Gardens**, also in the heart of town, has beautiful rooms and gardens.

The town's visitor center offers horse-and-carriage or trolley tours. The battlefields evoke the Union's long push toward Richmond during the Civil War (see p46).

🏛 Kenmore Plantation & Gardens
1201 Washington Ave. 📞 (540) 373-3381. ⏰ Jan–Feb: 10am–5pm Sat–Sun; Mar–Dec: 10am–5pm daily. ● Thanksgiving, Dec 24–25, 31.
🌐 www.kenmore.org

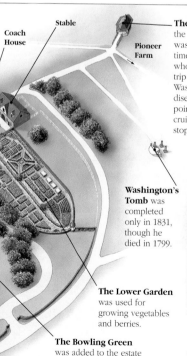

Coach House

Stable

Pioneer Farm

The Wharf is on the same site as it was in Washington's time. Today, visitors who come on day-trip boats from Washington, DC, disembark at this point. Potomac cruise boats also stop off here.

Washington's Tomb was completed only in 1831, though he died in 1799.

The Lower Garden was used for growing vegetables and berries.

The Bowling Green was added to the estate by Washington.

VISITORS' CHECKLIST

S end of George Washington Memorial Pkwy, Fairfax County, VA. 📞 (703) 780-2000. Ⓜ Yellow line to Huntington Station. 🚌 Fairfax Connector bus 101 to Mount Vernon: call (703) 339-7200. **Tour bus services & boat cruises available.** ⏰ Apr–Aug: 8am–5pm; Mar, Sep, Oct: 9am–5pm; Nov–Feb: 9am–4pm. 🎟 🎁 ♿ first floor. 🚻 🅿 🍴 📷
🌐 www.mountvernon.org

The Pioneer Farm
This exhibit demonstrates farming techniques pioneered by Washington. There is also a replica of his unique 16-sided treading barn, created using authentic tools.

Colonial Williamsburg ❺

Colonial couple

A S VIRGINIA'S CAPITAL from 1699 to 1780, Williamsburg was the hub of the loyal British colony. After 1780 the town went into decline. Then in 1926, John D. Rockefeller embarked on a massive restoration project. Today, in the midst of the modern-day city, the 18th-century city has been re-created. People in colonial dress portray the lifestyle of the original townspeople; blacksmiths, silversmiths, cabinet makers, and bakers show off their skills; and horse-drawn carriages pass through the streets, providing visitors with a fascinating insight into America's past.

Courthouse
Built in 1770–71 this was the home of the county court for more than 150 years.

★ **Governor's Palace**
Originally built in 1720 by Governor Alexander Spotswood, the palace has been reconstructed in its full pre-Revolution glory.

Nursery
Costumed living-history interpreters work the land in Colonial Williamsburg using replica tools and the same techniques as the original settlers.

0 meters 200
0 yards 200

STAR SIGHTS
★ **Capitol**
★ **Governor's Palace**
★ **Robertson's Windmill**

★ **Robertson's Windmill**
The windmill has daily demonstrations of the settlers' crafts, such as basket-making and barrel-making. The cart was a traditional means of transporting materials.

Print Office
This store stocks authentic 18th-century foods, including wine, Virginia ham, and peanuts.

VISITORS' CHECKLIST

🚗 🚌 *Corner of Lafayette & N Boundary Sts.* ℹ️ *(757) 253-0192, (800) 368-6511.*
📷 ♿ W *www.colonial williamsburg.com*
W *www.visitwilliamsburg.com*

Milliner
Owned by Margaret Hunter, the milliner shop stocked a wide range of items. Imported clothes for women and children, jewelry, and toys could all be bought here.

Raleigh Tavern
The Raleigh was once an important center for social, political, and commercial gatherings. The building burned in 1859, but this reproduction evokes the original spirit.

NICHOLSON STREET

BOTETOURT ST

DUKE OF GLOUCESTER STREET

★ Capitol
This is a 1945 reconstruction of the original 1705 building. The government resided in the West Wing, while the General Court was in the East Wing.

KEY

- - - Suggested route

Jamestown Settlement, a re-creation of Colonial James Fort

Jamestown & Yorktown ❻

ℹ *York County Public Information Office, (757) 890-3300.*

JAMESTOWN, established in 1607 on the banks of the James River, was the first permanent English settlement in the US. One of the early settlers was John Rolfe, who married Pocahontas, daughter of the Indian chief, Powhatan. But the colony did not last long – disease, famine, and attacks by the Algonquin Indians caused heavy loss of life and in 1699, the colony was abandoned.

Present-day Jamestown Island contains 1,500 acres (607 ha) of marshland and forest. Close to the ruins of the colony, the **Jamestown Settlement** is a re-creation of the original colony, complete with costumed interpreters and replicas of James Fort, an Indian village, and the ships that brought the first successful colonists to Virginia.

On the opposite side of the peninsula, 15 miles (24 km) away, Yorktown was the site of the decisive battle of the American Revolution in 1781. Battlefield tours at **Colonial National Historical Park** explain the siege at Yorktown, which ended with the surrender of the British forces.

🏛 Jamestown Settlement
📞 *(757) 253-4838.* **🕐** *9am–5pm daily.* **●** *Jan 1, Dec 25.* 💶 **♿** **▯**
♣ Colonial National Historical Park
📞 *(757) 898-3400, (757) 229-1733.* **🕐** *9am–5pm daily.* **●** *Dec 25.*
W *www.nps.gov/colo*

Norfolk ❼

🏘 *262,000.* **✈ 🚉 🚌 ℹ** *232 E Main St, (800) 368-3097, (757) 664-6620.* **W** *www.norfolkcvb.com*

A HISTORIC Colonial port, located at the point where Chesapeake Bay meets the Atlantic Ocean, Norfolk is a busy maritime center with the world's largest naval base. The city's logo – a mermaid – is the theme of sculptures and emblems all over Norfolk. The downtown waterfront centers on the massive battleship USS *Wisconsin*, a part of the new **Nauticus National Maritime Center**. The center offers multimedia presentations about naval battles, ships, and deepsea creatures.

Another top attraction is the **Chrysler Museum**, which displays the eclectic personal collection of automobile tycoon Walter Chrysler Jr. The works of art include paintings by Velasquez, Rubens, Degas, Renoir, and modern masters such as Roy Lichtenstein.

Neighboring Virginia Beach is the site of the 18th-century lighthouse at Cape Henry, where the English first landed in 1607. The waterfront is also home to the Virginia Marine Science Museum.

🏛 Nauticus National Maritime Center
📞 *(757) 664-1000.* **🕐** *Apr–Aug: 10am–6pm daily; Sep–Mar: 10am–5pm Tue–Sat, noon–5pm Sun.* **●** *Thanksgiving, Dec 25.* 💶 **♿** **▯** **W** *www.nauticus.org*

Richmond ❽

🏘 *198,300.* **🚉 🚌 ℹ** *550 E Marshall St, (804) 782-2777.* **W** *www.richmondva.org*

THE OLD capital of the Confederacy (*see p47*), Richmond still retains an aura of Old South gentility. Bronze statues of Civil War generals and other heroes line Monument Avenue, while Victorian mansions and brownstones testify to this area's postwar prosperity.

Civil War artifacts, including General Robert E. Lee's coat and sword, are among the exhibits at the **Museum of the Confederacy**. Next door, the White House of the Confederacy is a treasure of the Victorian age.

The graceful Neo-Classical **State Capitol** dominating downtown houses a lifesize sculpture of George Washington by Jean Antoine Houdon. To its west is the serene **Hollywood Cemetery**, the resting place of presidents John Tyler and James Monroe, as well as of 18,000 Confederate soldiers who are buried under a communal pyramid. Palmer Chapel offers superb views of James River and Belle Isle. Farther uptown are two fine museums, the fascinating **Science Museum of Virginia** and the **Virginia Museum of Fine Arts**, which has collections ranging from ancient Egyptian, Indian, and Himalayan art to French Impressionist and modern American masterpieces. The museum's highlight, however, is the priceless Pratt Collection of Imperial Russian Art, which includes five fabulous jeweled Easter eggs made for the Tsar by the jeweler Peter Carl Fabergé.

Statue of Robert E. Lee in Richmond

🏛 Virginia Museum of Fine Arts
2800 Grove Avn at the Blvd. **📞** *(804) 340-1401.* **🕐** *11am–5pm Wed–Sun.* **●** *Mon–Tue, Jan 1, Jul 4, Thanksg., Dec 25.* 💶 *only exhibitions.* **♿** **▯** **▯ W** *www.vmfa.state.va.us*

Chincoteague ❾

🏠 *3,500.* 🛈 *6733 Maddox Blvd,*
(757) 336-6161.

THE MAIN tourist attraction
on Virginia's sparsely
developed Eastern Shore,
Chincoteague draws fishermen, bird-watchers, and
beachcombers. The town itself
is primarily a service center,
with hotels, motels, and
restaurants catering to visitors
bound for the **Chincoteague
National Wildlife Refuge**,
which protects a number of
offshore islands, as well as
coastal marshlands and a 10-
mile (16-km) stretch of
Atlantic Ocean beachfront.

A driving tour loops for
over 3 miles (4.8 km) through
the wildlife preserve, but the
best way to see some of the
numerous egrets, snow geese,
herons, falcons, and other
birds found here is by walking or paddling in a canoe.

**🦌 Chincoteague National
Wildlife Refuge**
📞 *(757) 336-6122.* ⏱ *6am–6pm
daily.* ♿ *limited.*

Charlottesville ❿

🏠 *40,700.* 🚉 🚌 🛈 *Rte 20 S,
(434) 293-6789, (877) 386-1102.*
🌐 *www.charlottesvilletourism.org*

CHARLOTTESVILLE was
Thomas Jefferson's
hometown. It is dominated by
the University of Virginia,
which he founded and
designed, and also by his
home, **Monticello**.

It took Jefferson 40
years to complete
Monticello, which he
began building in 1769.
It is now one of the
most celebrated houses
in the country. The
entrance hall doubled
as a private museum,
and the library held a
collection of around
6,700 books.

The 5,000-acre
(2,023-ha) grounds
include a large ter-
raced vegetable garden where
Jefferson grew and experi-
mented with varieties. The
remains of the slaves' quarters
still stand; nearly 200 slaves
worked the estate's planta-

tions, and recent evidence
suggests that one of them,
Sally Hemmings, bore
Jefferson's child.

The obelisk over Jefferson's
grave in the family cemetery
lauds him as "Father of the
University of Virginia." The
university's Neo-Classical
buildings and grounds are
open to visitors. Vineyards
and wineries surround
Charlottesville. Michie
Tavern *(see p237),*
joined to the Virginia
Wine Museum, has
been restored to its
18th-century appear-
ance and serves typical
Southern cuisine.

Montpelier, on a
2,500-acre (1,012-ha)
site, 25 miles (40
km) to the north,
was the home of
the fourth president,
James Madison.

**The obelisk over
Jefferson's grave**

🏛 Monticello
Route 53, 3 miles (4.8 km) SE of
Charlottesville. 📞 *(434) 984-9822.*
⏱ *Mar–Oct: 8am–5pm; Nov–Feb:
9am–4:30pm.* ⏺ *Dec 25.* 🎫 ⧉
♿ ⧉ 🌐 *www.monticello.org*

MONTICELLO, CHARLOTTESVILLE

*Situated in the leafy foothills of the Blue Ridge
Mountains, this Palladian masterpiece was
built between 1769 and 1809 by
Thomas Jefferson.*

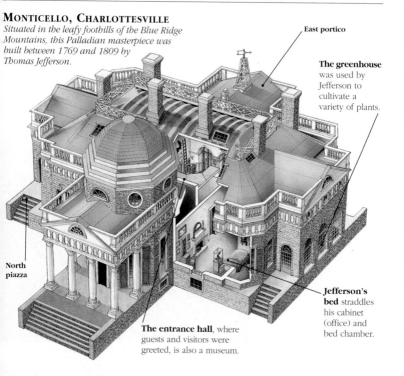

East portico

The greenhouse
was used by
Jefferson to
cultivate a
variety of plants.

**North
piazza**

**Jefferson's
bed** straddles
his cabinet
(office) and
bed chamber.

The entrance hall, where
guests and visitors were
greeted, is also a museum.

A reconstructed building, Appomattox Court House

Appomattox Court House ⓫

ℹ️ (434) 352-2621. ⏰ 9am–5pm daily. ⬤ Jan 1, Thanksgiving, Dec 25. ♨️ ♿

This NATIONAL historic park, located 3 miles (4.8 km) northeast of the town of Appomattox, re-creates the spot where Confederate General Robert E. Lee surrendered to US General Ulysses S. Grant to signal the end of the Civil War *(see p193)*. Today, markers trace the sites of the last skirmishes of the war, and 27 reconstructed and restored buildings replicate the scene where, on April 9, 1865, the two leaders and their armies put an end to that long and destructive war. In the last months of fighting, General Grant had successfully captured the Confederate stronghold at Petersburg, while General Sherman's "March to the Sea" across Georgia surrounded Confederate forces from the South. With the fall of the Confederate capital at Richmond on April 2, General Lee realized that victory was impossible. The terms of surrender were more than generous, since Union leaders hoped to ease reconciliation between the warring sides. When the rebel Confederates laid down their arms, the Northern soldiers saluted their opponents, instead of jeering.

Much of the original setting was destroyed in battle or later dismantled by souvenir hunters. Most of what stands here today was reconstructed by the National Park Service in the 1940s.

Blue Ridge Parkway ⓬

ℹ️ (828) 298-0398.
🌐 www.nps.gov/blri

Stretching for 469 miles (755 km) along the crest of the Appalachian Mountains, the Blue Ridge Parkway *(see p41)* extends from the southern border of Shenandoah National Park all the way to North Carolina, ending finally at Great Smoky Mountains National Park *(see p262)*. Created as a public works project during the "New Deal" era in the depths of the 1930s Great Depression, the scenic route was begun in 1935 but was not completed until 1987. Mileposts along the way, measured from north to south, help travelers discover the points of interest along the route. Some of the highlights along the 215-mile (346-km) portion of the Blue Ridge Parkway in Virginia include a crossing of the James River at milepost 63 and the lakefront lodge in the Peaks of Otter section near milepost 86. The historic **Mabry Mill** at milepost 176 was in use as a backwoods sawmill and blacksmith shop until 1935.

This parkway passes through only one real city, Roanoke, Virginia, and is primarily rural and scenic, with no advertising or commercial traffic allowed. Open all year, the peak travel season is fall.

The picturesque Mabry Mill at milepost 176 of the Blue Ridge Parkway

Skyline Drive ⓭

SKYLINE DRIVE RUNS along the backbone of the Shenandoah National Park's Blue Ridge Mountains. Originally farmland, the government designated the area a national park in 1926. Deer, wild turkey, bears, and bobcats inhabit the park, and wildflowers, azaleas, and mountain laurel are abundant. The park's many hiking trails and its 75 viewpoints offer stunning natural scenery.

North entrance station

Whiteoak Canyon (2)
The Whiteoak Canyon Trail passes six waterfalls on its route.

Pinnacles Overlook (1)
The view of Old Rag Mountain with its outcroppings of granite is spectacular.

Bearfence Mountain (5)
Although it is a bit of a climb up this mountain, partly on rock scramble, it is not too difficult, and the reward is a breathtaking 360-degree view of the surrounding landscape.

Big Meadows (3)
Close to the visitor center, this meadow has been kept in its centuries-old state. It was probably kept clear by fires lit by Indians or by lightning strikes. Herds of deer can easily be seen here.

Rapidan Camp (4)
At the end of Mill Prong Trail, this 164-acre (66-ha) resort was President Hoover's weekend retreat until 1932, when he donated it to the park.

Lewis Mountain (6)
This heavily wooded mountain features quaint cabins, campground, picnic area, camp store, laundry, and showers for campers and hikers on the Appalachian Trail.

KEY

- - - Walk route
- ⁂
- ▬ Lookout point
- Road

0 km 10
0 miles 10

TIPS FOR DRIVERS

Starting points: *North at Front Royal, central at Thornton Gap or Swift Run Gap, south at Rockfish Gap.*
Length: *105 miles (168 km), duration of 4–8 hrs depending on the number of stops.*
When to go: *Mid-October for fall leaf colors; spring and summer for wildflowers.*
What it costs: *Toll charge of $10 per car (valid for 7 days).*

Autumn in Shenandoah National Park

West Virginia

SET ENTIRELY WITHIN THE Appalachian Mountains, this "Mountain State" remains largely forested, despite centuries of aggressive lumbering and mining. The state was part of Virginia until the Civil War, and its early European pioneers were less wealthy and generally very different from the genteel planters of eastern Virginia. As talk of secession grew, western Virginia aligned with the Union. Four years after abolitionist John Brown raided a federal arsenal in Harpers Ferry in a failed attempt to inspire a slave rebellion in 1859, West Virginia was declared a separate state. Today it is known for its woodworking, quilting, and basketry crafts, and traditional Appalachian music and dancing.

Blackwater Falls State Park, in Monongahela National Forest

Monongahela National Forest ⓮

200 Sycamore St, Elkins. ⓒ *(304) 636-1800.* ⓞ *8am–4:45pm Mon–Fri.*

THE EASTERN HALF of the state lies deep within the Allegheny Mountains, a part of the longer Appalachian Range. Much of this rugged terrain is protected as the vast Monongahela National Forest, which encompasses five federally designated wilderness areas and serves as the headwaters for six major river systems. Its landscapes of rhododendron, black cherry, highland bogs, blueberry thickets, and exposed rocks are the habitat for black bear, white-tailed deer, bobcat, otter, mink, and many other species. The forest's trails attracts hikers, horseback riders, and mountain bikers, while in winter, the area is popular for downhill and cross-country skiing.

The small town of **Elkins**, the headquarters of the national forest, makes a convenient base to explore the area. The town's Augusta Heritage Center hosts residential summer programs on traditional folklife and folk arts, as well as bluegrass and old-time mountain music dances and concerts.

Northeast of Elkins, an 8-mile (13-km) stretch of the 124-mile (200-km) Allegheny Trail links two state parks – **Canaan Valley Resort State Park**, a downhill ski resort, and **Blackwater Falls State Park**, a good place for back-country ski touring. Both parks have restaurants and provide facilities for lodging and camping. Farther south, Snowshoe Mountain Resort is the state's largest downhill resort in winter and a mountain biking center from spring to fall (rentals and guided trips are available). The nearby **Cass Scenic Railroad State Park** organizes vintage steam train rides across the mountaintops for panoramic views. Fall foliage rides are the most popular.

Southeast of Elkins, the **Spruce Knob–Seneca Rocks National Recreation Area** draws rockclimbers up the sandstone strata of Seneca Rocks, an hour's drive away. The 75-mile (121-km) Greenbrier River Trail, running parallel to the Virginia border, from White Sulphur Springs in the south all the way to the Cass Scenic Railroad State Park in the north, is a converted "rails-to-trails" rail bed route, which is quite popular for bicycle tours.

🏕 **Spruce Knob-Seneca Rocks National Rec. Area** ⓘ *(304) 567-2827.* ⓞ *May–Oct: 9am–4:30pm daily; Nov–Apr: 9am–4:30 pm Sat–Sun.* ♿
🏕 **Cass Scenic Railroad** Route 66/Main St, Cass. ⓒ *(304) 456-4300.* ♿

New River Gorge National River ⓯

Canyon Rim Visitor Center US Hwy 19, Lansing. ⓒ *(304) 574-2115.* ⓞ *late May–early Sep: 9am–6pm, late Sep–early May: 9am–5pm.* ⓦ *Jan 1, Dec 25.* ♿

THE NEW RIVER courses through a deep gorge in the southeastern corner of the state, drawing rafters for some of the most exciting white-water adventures in eastern US. The National Park Service, located between Fayetteville and Hinton, oversees a stretch that falls 750 ft (225 m) within 50 miles (80 km), with a compact set of

Rock Climber above New River Gorge National River

Overlook at Hawk's Nest State Park, New River Gorge National River

Class V rapids. The modern Canyon Rim Visitor Center and gorge bridge provide easy access to panoramic overlooks and rim hiking trails. The visitor center also distributes comprehensive lists of local rafting outfitters, while the nearby **Hawk's Nest State Park** offers modest lodge rooms and operates an aerial tram down to the river for boat rides during summer. The former mining town of Fayetteville is also a popular base for rafters and outfitters, while the old industrial town of Hinton holds a grittier appeal and is easily accessible to visitors via Amtrak.

🦅 **Hawk's Nest State Park**
Hwy 60, Ansted. 📞 *(304) 658-5212.*
🚡 **Tram Rides, Boat Rides** *Call for seasonal operating days and hours.*

Harpers Ferry 🔟

🏛 *300.* 🚉 🚌 ℹ *NPS Visitor Center, (304) 535-6298.*

Nestled at the confluence of the Potomac and Shenandoah Rivers, where West Virginia meets Virginia and Maryland, is the tiny town of Harpers Ferry. Named after Robert Harper, the Philadelphia builder who constructed a ferry here in 1761, most of the historic downtown area is today the **Harpers Ferry National Historic Park**. It was here in 1859, that Maryland abolitionist John Brown led an ill-fated raid on the federal arsenal. Although his attempt failed, this event ignited the Civil War two years later.

The town looks just as it did in the 19th century, with small clapboard storefronts clinging to steep hillsides that slope down to the rushing rivers. Several historic buildings, including John Brown's Fort and the arsenal, are open to visitors.

The famous Appalachian Trail (see p174), which runs through town, has its head-quarters at the **Appalachian Trail Conference**. The Trail is a 2,000-mile (3,220-km) footpath that stretches along the spine of the Appalachian Mountains from Georgia to Maine. With an Amtrak train station in the heart of downtown, Harpers Ferry is just an hour's ride from Washington, DC, making this remote region accessible for visitors without a car.

🏛 **Appalachian Trail Conference**
Washington & Jackson Sts. 📞 *(304) 535-6331.* ⏱ *9am–5pm Mon–Fri, 9am–4pm Sat–Sun.* ⚫ *Nov–Mar.*

Aerial view of Harpers Ferry, located at the confluence of the Potomac and Shenandoah Rivers

Maryland

MARYLAND HAS AN ABUNDANCE of both natural attractions and historical sites. The rolling farmlands around Antietam in western Maryland are rich in Civil War heritage. Water-related tourism is a mainstay of southern Maryland's Chesapeake Bay, the longest inland shoreline in the US, which attracts sailors, fishermen, and seafood lovers who can indulge in the delicious local specialty – soft-shell blue crabs. The Eastern Shore on the Delmarva Peninsula, dotted with picturesque villages, is also graced by the wild beauty of Assateague and Chincoteague Islands.

Antietam National Battlefield ⑰

Rte 65, 10 miles (16 km) S of Hagerstown. █ (301) 432-5124. ○ Jun–Aug: 8:30am–6pm daily; Sep–May: 8:30am–5pm. ● Jan 1, Thanksgiving, Dec 25. █ █ █ ☒ www.nps.gov/anti

ONE OF THE worst battles of the Civil War was waged here on September 17, 1862, culminating in 23,000 casualties among the Confederate as well as the Union armies.

An observation tower offers a panoramic view of this historic battlefield. Antietam Creek runs peacefully under the Burnside Bridge, where the fighting was severe and much blood was spilled. The whole site has a haunted atmosphere even today. Although the battle did not end in a decisive victory, the horrendous bloodshed at Antietam inspired President Lincoln to issue the Emancipation Proclamation. The visitor center movie recreating the battle should not be missed.

Frederick ⑱

█ 50,000. █ 19 E Church St, (301) 228-2888. ○ 9am–5pm daily. ☒ www.visitfrederick.org

FREDERICK'S HISTORIC center, dating back to the mid-18th century, was renovated in the 1970s and is now a popular tourist attraction.

This charming town is a major antique center and home to hundreds of antique dealers. Its shops, galleries, and eateries are all in 18th- and 19th-century settings, and several historic houses in the town, beautifully restored and furnished with period artifacts, are open to visitors. Francis Scott Key, author of "The Star Spangled Banner," is buried in Mt. Olivet Cemetery. Tourist information is available at the visitor center, which also conducts popular walking tours during the weekends.

Baltimore ⑲

█ 675,500. █ Inner Harbor West Wall, (410) 837-4636, (800) 282-6632. █ █ ☒ www.baltimore.org

THERE IS MUCH to do and see in this pleasant port city of restaurants, antiques, arts, boats, and monuments. A good place to start is the Inner Harbor, the city's redeveloped waterfront, with its harborside complex of shops and restaurants. The centerpiece, and one of Baltimore's most popular attractions, is the stunning **National Aquarium**, whose collection includes many exhibits. The National Aquarium also offers a seal pool, and a delightful dolphin show.

The Harbor is also home to the **Maryland Science Center**, where "do touch" is the rule. It features a number of interactive exhibits, and the Planetarium and IMAX® Theater thrill visitors with images of earth and space.

The **American Visionary Art Museum**, also on the Inner Harbor, houses a collection of extraordinary works by self-taught artists whose materials range from matchsticks to faux pearls.

Uptown is the **Baltimore Museum of Art**, with its famous collection of modern art, including works by Matisse, Picasso, Degas, and Van Gogh. It also has a large collection of pieces by Andy Warhol and two sculpture

The eye-catching architecture of the National Aquarium, Baltimore

gardens featuring works by Rodin and Calder.

Also impressive is the **Walters Art Gallery** on the elegant Mount Vernon Square, lined with Colonial brick townhouses. The gallery's collection includes Greek and Roman classical art, Southeast Asian and Chinese artifacts, Byzantine silver, pre-Columbian carvings, and jeweled objects by Fabergé. There are also paintings by Rubens, Monet, and Manet, and the Victorian artist Alma-Tadema, whose beautiful *Sappho and Alcaeus* (1881) should not be missed.

The lively neighborhood of Little Italy is also definitely worth a visit, not only for its knockout Italian restaurants but also for the games of bocce (Italian lawn bowling), played around Pratt or Stiles Street on warm evenings.

The beautiful formal gardens of the William Paca House, in Annapolis

✗ National Aquarium
501 E Pratt St, Pier 3. ☎ *(410) 576-3800.* ◯ *10am–5pm Mon–Thu, Sat-Sun; 10am–8pm Fri.* ● *Thanksgiving, Dec 25.* ◾ ♿ ♨ ⓦ www.aqua.org

🏛 Maryland Science Center
601 Light St. ☎ *(410) 685-5225.*
◯ *10am–5pm Mon–Fri, 10am–6pm Sat, noon–6pm Sun.*
● *Thanksgiving, Dec 25.* ◾ ♿ ♨
ⓦ www.mdsci.org

🏛 Baltimore Museum of Art
N Charles St & 31st St. ☎ *(410) 396-7100.* ◯ *11am–5pm Wed–Fri, 11am– 6pm Sat-Sun.* ● *Mon, Tue, Jan 1, Jul 4, Thanksgiving, Dec 25.*
◾ *free on Thu.* ♿ ♨ ♨

🏛 Walters Art Museum
600 N Charles St. ☎ *(410) 547-9000.*
◯ *10am–5pm Tue–Sun, 10am–8pm 1st Thu each month.* ● *Mon, Jan 1, Jul 4, Thanksgiving, Dec 24–25.*
◾ *except 10am–1pm Sat.* ♿ ♨

Annapolis ②⓪

👣 *33,300.* ℹ️ *Annapolis & Anne Arundel County Visitors Bureau, 26 West St, (410) 280-0445.* ◯ *9am–5pm daily.* ⓦ www.visit-annapolis.org

THE CAPITAL of Maryland, Annapolis, is regarded as the jewel of Chesapeake Bay. It is defined by the nautical character that comes with the 17 miles (27 km) of shoreline and the longtime presence of the **United States**

Naval Academy. A walk down Main Street leads past the 200-year-old Maryland Inn, shops, and wonderful seafood restaurants that serve local fish, to the City Dock lined with boats. It is then a short walk to the 150-year-old US Naval Academy. Inside the visitor center is the *Freedom 7 Space Capsule* that carried the first American, Alan Shepard, into space. The US Naval Academy Museum in Preble Hall is also worth visiting, especially to see the gallery of detailed ship models.

The **Maryland State House**, completed in 1779, is the oldest state capitol in continuous use. Its Old Senate Chamber is where the Continental Congress (delegates from each of the American colonies) met when Annapolis was briefly the capital of the United States in 1783–84. It was also here that the Treaty of Paris was ratified in 1784, formally ending the Revolutionary War.

Annapolis teems with Colonial-era buildings, most of them still in use. The 1765 **William Paca House**, home of Governor Paca who signed the Declaration of Independence, is a fine Georgian house with an enchanting garden, both of

Tiffany window in the Naval Academy, Annapolis

which have recently been lovingly restored. Another restored mansion worth visiting is the magnificent red brick **Hammond Harwood House**, which boasts exceptionally fine woodcarving. Built in 1774, this masterpiece of Georgian design, a short walk west of the State House on Maryland Avenue, was named after the Hammond and Harwood families. Worth exploring are the Cornhill and Duke of Gloucester Streets, examples of the city's historic residential streets. Many tours are on offer in Annapolis, including bus, boat, and walking tours. It is particularly enjoyable for tourists to view the city from the water by sightseeing boat, schooner, or kayak.

🏛 US Naval Academy
Corner of King George, E of Randall St. ☎ *(410) 293-2108.* ◯ *9:30am–3pm Mon–Sat, 12:30–3pm Sun.*
● *Jan 1, Thanksgiving, Dec 25.* ♿

🏛 Maryland State House
State Circle. ☎ *(410) 974-3400.*
◯ *9am–5pm (call ahead).*
● *Dec 25.* ◾ *11am & 3pm.* ♿

🏛 William Paca House
186 Prince George St. ☎ *(410) 263-5553.* ◯ *Mar–Dec: 10am–5pm Mon–Sat, noon–5pm Sun; Jan–Feb: weekends only.* ● *Thanksgiving, Dec 24–25.* ◾ 🎧

North Bay 21

121 N Union St, Ste. B, Havre de Grace, (800) 597-2649.

At the northern end of Chesapeake Bay, the lovely town of Havre de Grace is home to the Concord Point Lighthouse. Popular with artists and photographers, the lighthouse has been in continuous operation since the mid-1800s. The **Havre de Grace Decoy Museum** exhibits a fine collection of working decoys and chronicles how the craft evolved from a purely practical wildfowl lure into a highly sophisticated form of American folk art.

Across the bay to the east, the lush forests of **Elk Neck State Park** cover the tip of a peninsula crowned by Turkey Point Lighthouse, one of the bay's oldest. The park offers a sandy beach for swimming, boat rentals, miniature golf, and hiking trails.

Northeast of the park across the Elk River is Chesapeake City, where rooftops appear much as they did 100 years ago when the village grew to service the Chesapeake and Delaware Canal. Today, the village is a "boutique town," with fine shops and restaurants. The **C and D Canal Museum** is housed in the canal's original pumphouse. Working models of canal locks, the original steam power plant, and a giant water wheel are on display.

Havre de Grace Decoy Museum
215 Giles St. (410) 939-3739. *11am–4pm daily. public hols.*

Elk Neck State Park
End of Route 272. *(410) 287-5333.*

C&D Canal Museum
End of 2nd St. *(410) 885-5621. 8am–4pm Mon–Sat. Sun, hols.*

St. Michaels 22

1,300. (800) 660-9471. www.stmichaelsmd.org

St. Michaels, founded in 1677, was once a haven for ship builders, privateers, and blockade-runners. Today, the town is a destination for pleasure boaters and yachts flying international colors. B&Bs, a variety of shops, and good restaurants abound.

Chesapeake Bay Maritime Museum is one of Maryland's top cultural attractions. The museum features interactive exhibits on boat building, historic boats, decoys, and various other aspects of Chesapeake Bay life. Several vessels unique to the area are anchored on the property, and the **Hooper Strait Lighthouse**, a fully restored 1879 screwpile wooden structure, is open for exploration.

Chesapeake Bay Maritime Museum
Talbot St, Navy Point. *(410) 745-2916. 9am–5pm (until 6pm in summer, 4pm in winter).* www.cbmm.org

The bay in Blackwater National Wildlife Refuge, Easton

Easton 23

9,400. (410) 822-0065. www.eastonmd.org

A handsome little town, Easton is an interesting combination of unique shops and historic homes. A restored 1820s schoolhouse serves as the premises of the **Academy of the Arts**. Although the emphasis is on Eastern Shore artists, the gallery's permanent collection includes works by famous artists such as James Whistler and Grant Wood.

Once a farm used by muskrat trappers for the fur trade, **Blackwater National Wildlife Refuge** was established in 1933 to provide sanctuary for migrating waterfowl. Geese number 35,000 and ducks exceed 15,000 at the peak of the fall migration. The best time to observe migratory birds is from October through March; however, many song-

Hooper Strait Lighthouse at Chesapeake Bay silhouetted by a pink and violet sunset

birds, reptiles, and mammals can be seen all year round. Blackwater is a haven for endangered species, including the peregrine falcon.

Academy of the Arts
106 South St. ((410) 822-0455. ◯ 10am–4pm Mon–Sat, 10am–9pm Wed. ◻ ◻ www.art-academy.org

Blackwater National Wildlife Refuge
▮ 2145 Key Wallace Dr, Cambridge. ((410) 228-2677. ◯ 8am–4pm Mon–Fri, 9am–5pm Sat–Sun. ◻

Crisfield ㉔

▮ 2,900. ▮▮ ▮ 906 W Main St, Crisfield, (800) 782-3913.

THIS BUSY commercial sea-food port supports a bustling sportfishing industry. From Mid-May through October, the fish are running. The **Governor J. Millard Tawes Historical Museum** is named after a resident who became Maryland's 54th governor. The museum has displays on local history and marine life. It also offers walking tours through a boatyard and a seafood processing plant as well as trolley tours through historic Crisfield to the Ward Brothers Waterfowl carving workshop and the crab-processing shanties of Jenkins Street.

Captain John Smith (1580-1631)

Governor J. Millard Tawes Historical Museum
Somers Cove Marina. ((410) 968-2501. ◯ 9am–5pm daily. ● week of Christmas, week after Christmas. ◻ ◻

ENVIRONS: Accessible only by boat, **Smith Island**, 10 miles (16 km) to the west, was chartered in 1608 by Captain John Smith, founder of the Jamestown settlement *(see p191)*. Ewell, at the north end of the island, is where most of the island's population resides. Some claim that the distinctive local speech is reminiscent of the Eliza-bethan/Cornwall dialect brought here in the 1770s.

Ferris wheel at Trimper's Rides, Ocean City

Salisbury ㉕

▮ 20,600. ▮▮ ▮ 8480 Ocean Hwy, (800) 332-8687.

THE LARGEST CITY on the Eastern Shore, Salisbury is known for its fine antique shops. It developed as a mill community in 1732 and soon became the principal crossroads of the southern Delmarva Peninsula. Salisbury's **Ward Museum of Wildfowl Art** contains the world's premier collection of wildfowl art. Here, wood is carved and painted to resemble wild birds in natural settings. The museum looks at the history of the art, from antique working decoys to contemporary carvings. **Pemberton Historical Park** is the site of Pemberton Hall, built in 1741 for Isaac Handy, a British Army colonel. The grounds are threaded by self-guided nature trails, and the manor house contains a small museum maintained by the local historical society.

Ward Museum of Wildfowl Art
909 S Schumaker Dr. ((410) 742-4988. ◯ 10am–5pm Mon–Sat, noon–5pm Sun. ◻ ◻

A specialist duck decoy maker at work in Crisfield

Ocean City ㉖

▮ 5,100. ▮▮ ▮ 4001 Coastal Hwy, (410) 289-8181.

SOFT BEIGE SAND extends endlessly along the Ocean City peninsula, fronted by miles of hotels. In summer, brightly colored umbrellas provide shade, while at night, the beach boardwalk that stretches from the inlet north past 27th Street is lively with strolling couples, singles, and families.

At the inlet, on the southern border of Ocean City, the **Ocean City Life-Saving Museum**, housed in a decommissioned 1891 Life-saving Station, relates the history of Ocean City and the US Life-saving Service.

North on the broadwalk, **Trimper's Rides** began operating in 1902 with a steam-powered 45-animal carousel. Today, Trimper's includes a 1905 Herschel-Spellman merry-go-round glittering with jewels and fantasy animals, Ferris wheels, bumper rides, mechanized fortune-tellers, and a host of other entertainments.

Ocean City also has many miniature golf courses: visitors can play beneath plaster polar bears, bask in the tropics, or putt around rubber sharks.

Ocean City Life-Saving Museum
Boardwalk at the Inlet. ((410) 289-4991. ◯ May & Oct: 11am–4pm daily; Jun–Sep: 11am–10pm daily; Nov–Apr: 11am–4pm Sat–Sun. ◻ ◻ www.ocmuseum.org

Trimper's Rides
Baltimore & 1st St on the boardwalk. ((410) 289-8617. ◯ mid-May–mid-Sep: 1pm–midnight Mon–Fri, noon–midnight Sat–Sun; mid-Sep–mid-May: limited hours. ◻

Delaware

ALTHOUGH DELAWARE IS THE country's second-smallest state, larger only than tiny Rhode Island, its importance in industry, banking, and technology far exceeds its size. This is mainly due to the laissez faire tax and corporation laws that have attracted several large companies to base their headquarters here. Along with a significant history, stately country homes, and some of the nation's best museums, Delaware's 2,000 square miles (500,000 ha) also boasts more than 20 miles (32 km) of sandy beaches along the Atlantic Ocean.

Detail from *Washington Crossing the Delaware,* **Delaware Art Museum**

Wilmington ㉗

🚶 71,500. 🚌 ℹ️ 100 W 10th St, (800) 422-1181.

THIS FORMER Swedish colony is home to one of the country's finest art museums, the **Delaware Art Museum**, located at Bank One Center till October 2004. Its outstanding collections contain works by American illustrators such as Howard Pyle, and his students N.C. Wyeth and Maxfield Parrish. There are also paintings and sculpture by other 19th- and 20th-century American artists such as Winslow Homer. The galleries feature paintings and decorative arts from the English pre-Raphaelite movement, led by Dante Gabriel Rossetti. The romantic works, second only to those of Victoria and Albert Museum, were bequeathed to the museum in 1935 by the wealthy Wilmington industrialist Samuel Bancroft Jr.

🏛 **Delaware Art Museum**
Located at Bank One Center on the riverfront till Oct 2004. ☎ (302) 571-9590. ⏰ 10am–4pm Tue, Thu, Fri, 10am–9pm Wed, 10am–5pm Sat, 1–5pm Sun. 🎫 ♿ 🌐 www.delart.org

Winterthur ㉘

SR 52. ☎ (800) 448-3883. ⏰ 10am–5pm Tue–Sun. ⬤ Thanksgiving, Dec 25, Jan 1. 🎫 🌐 www.winterthur.org

ORIGINALLY THE home of Evelina du Pont and James Biderman, Winterthur was named after the Biderman ancestral home in Switzerland. Henry du Pont inherited the house in 1927. Du Pont was one of the many post-World War I collectors, whose nationalistic sentiments caused them to take a fresh look at American decorative objects. His collection of American furniture is one of the most important assemblages of early American decorative arts in the world.

Winterthur showcases the du Pont family's fascination with American decorative arts and horticulture. The surrounding 966-acre (391-ha) grounds are landscaped beautifully, with miles of surfaced paths and scenic woodland trails. The part of the museum open to the public consists of two buildings, 175 period rooms, and three exhibition galleries.

Hagley Museum/ Eleutherian Mills ㉙

Rte 141. 🚌 ☎ (302) 658-2400. ⏰ Mar 15–Dec: 9:30am–4:30pm daily; Jan–Mar 14: 9:30am–1:30pm Mon–Fri, 9:30am–4:30pm Sat–Sun. ⬤ Thanksgiving, Dec 25, Jan 1. 🎫 🌐 www.hagley.org

PICTURESQUELY LOCATED on the banks of the Brandywine River, Hagley Yard is the origin of the du Pont fortune in America. Its serene setting is visible in spring when the river banks are ablaze with purple and pink rhododendrons and azaleas.

Eleuthere du Pont acquired the property and established a black powder (explosives) factory here in 1884. Factory buildings, storehouses, drying tables, and the workers' village are open to the public. Facing the river are the Eagle Roll Mill's "mixing rooms," with their 5-ft (1.5-m) thick walls, where powder explosions – 299 blowouts in 20 years – did the least damage. Hagley Museum, at the entryway to the property, explores the history of the sites with exhibits and dioramas.

The modest du Pont family home, **Eleutherian Mills**, dates from 1803. It overlooks the powder works at the far end of the property and contains many original furnishings. This large property is verdant with a variety of native plants, shrubs, and trees.

Boxcar exhibit at Hagley, on the banks of the Brandywine River

The elegant French-style Nemours Mansion, built by Alfred I. du Pont

Nemours Mansion and Gardens ③⓪

1600 Rockland Rd. ((302) 651-6912. ⬛ ◯ May–Nov: tours at 9am, 11am, 1pm & 3pm Tue–Sat; 11am, 1pm & 3pm Sun; Nov 11–Dec 28: limited tours (Christmas tours reservations recommended). ◈ W www.nemoursmansion.org

B UILT BY Alfred I. du Pont in 1909-1910, this Louis XVI-style château is named after the north-central French town that Pierre Samuel du Pont de Nemours, his great-great-grandfather, represented as a member of the French Estates General in 1789. The mansion's 102 rooms are opulently decorated with Oriental rugs, tapestries, and paintings dating from the 15th century. The 300-acre (12-ha) gardens are landscaped in the classic French style.

New Castle ③①

🚶 4,800. ⬛ ℹ PO Box 465, (800) 758-1550. W www.visitnewcastle.com

D ELAWARE'S FORMER capital is today a well-preserved historic site, with restaurants, shops, and residential areas. The **New Castle Courthouse** displays artifacts that illuminate the town's multinational origins; Sweden, Holland, and Britain all have claimed New Castle as their own. Several historic homes lie a short stroll from each other. One, the **Amstel House**, was the home of Governor Van Dyke. The town's most elegant dwelling place in 1738, its most famous guest was George Washington.

🏛 New Castle Courthouse
211 Delaware St. ((302) 323-4453. ◯ 10am–3:30pm Tue–Sat, 1:30–4:30 pm Sun. ◉ Mon, public hols.

Lewes ③②

🚶 2,300. ⬛ ℹ 120 Kings Hwy, (302) 645-8073.

T HE SITE OF Zwaanendael ("Valley of the Swans"), Delaware's original Dutch settlement in 1631, Lewes is a quiet town with a small beach, sophisticated restaurants, residences, and shops. The **Zwaanendael Museum**, built in 1931, is a striking replica of the Town Hall of Hoorn, home of most of the settlers. Its exhibits elaborate on the first encampment as well as the area's other historical aspects.

In 1682, the British Crown granted the colony of Delaware to Englishman William Penn *(see p98)* who established one of the nation's first public lands by setting aside Cape Henlopen for the citizens of Lewes. Besides a bay and ocean beaches, **Cape Henlopen State Park** contains Gordon's Pond Wildlife Area and the Great Dune, which rises 80 ft (24 m) above sea level. The park's varied habitats are home to many birds, reptiles, and mammals, including threatened shorebirds. Attractions include hiking trails, interpretive displays, a pier, camping, and swimming.

🏛 Zwaanendael Museum
Kings Hwy & Savannah Rd. ((302) 645-1148. ◯ 10am–4:30pm Tue–Sat, 1:30–4:30pm Sun. ◉ Mon, hols. ♿

🏞 Cape Henlopen State Park
42 Cape Henlopen Dr. ((302) 645-8983. ⏕

Rehoboth Beach ③③

🚶 1,200. ⬛ ℹ 501 Rehoboth Ave, (302) 227-2233.

U NLIKE OTHER resort towns, Rehoboth Beach was originally a Methodist summer camp. A commercial strip of restaurants and shops stretches along Rehoboth Avenue, meeting sand beaches at Funland on the boardwalk. The Outlets, between Lewes and Rehoboth Beach, feature every major outlet store, taking advantage of the fact that there's absolutely no sales tax in Delaware.

Three miles (5 km) south of the beach, the 2,700-acre (1093-ha) **Delaware Seashore State Park** covers the strip of land between the Atlantic Ocean and Rehoboth Bay. **Millsboro**, west of Rehoboth Bay, is home to the Nanticoke tribe. In mid-September, the tribe holds a public pow-wow to preserve their heritage and explain their beliefs.

South of the park, the 89-ft (27-m) Fenwick Island Lighthouse marks the Delaware-Maryland border. Built in 1852, it was decommissioned during World War II.

🏞 Delaware Seashore State Park
Inlet 850. ((302) 227-2800. ⏕

A Nanticoke Indian at the annual pow-wow, Rehoboth Beach

Practical Information

WASHINGTON, DC AND THE CAPITAL REGION is very rich in museums, cultural events, and entertainment, as well as in scenic sites and outdoor activities around its seashores, rivers, and mountains. This region offers excellent amenities for the large numbers of tourists that it attracts. Spring and fall are the best times to visit, as the summers are hot and humid in much of the region, and the winters cold and damp. However, summer sees the largest number of visitors, so it is best to make reservations for this time of year.

TOURIST INFORMATION

THE CAPITAL REGION is well-equipped to cater to visitors' needs. Visitor information desks at airports and within cities will provide guides and maps, information on guided tours, events, and festivals. Major hotels also have guest services desks. The Smithsonian **Dial-a-Museum** line is a useful resource for finding out about special events in DC's museums. State tourism bureaus are other reliable sources of comprehensive information.

PERSONAL SECURITY

IN RECENT YEARS, Washington has made great efforts to clean up its streets and bring down crime. If you stick to the tourist areas and avoid outlying neighborhoods, you should not run into any trouble. When visiting sights off the beaten track, stay alert and study your map properly before you set off. If you plan to hike alone, always carry a cell phone, and inform someone in advance about your itinerary.

GETTING AROUND

TRAVEL WITHIN DC and the Capital Region is easy. Washington has a comprehensive public transportation system, and all major attractions in the capital are accessible on foot, or by **Metrorail**, **Metrobus**, or taxi. If you decide to drive in DC, be prepared for traffic jams and unexpected route changes. Avoid driving at night if you are unfamiliar with the area.

Several DC-based tour companies offer tours that include Mount Vernon, Williamsburg, and Monticello in Virginia. Baltimore and Annapolis, Maryland's major cities, are connected to DC by rail and bus. Car rental is widely available, but often expensive. Both **Amtrak** trains and **Greyhound** buses are cheaper alternatives, but your choice of destination may be more limited. To explore many of the scenic parts of the Capital Region, it is best to travel by car. Visitors should avoid shortcuts and stay on well-traveled roads.

ETIQUETTE

SMOKING IS prohibited in many buildings, restaurants, and stores in the region. Cigarettes can only be purchased by those over 18 years old; proof of age may be required. The legal age for drinking alcohol in Washington is 21, and you may need a photo identification (ID) as proof of your age in order to purchase alcohol and be allowed into bars. It is illegal to drink alcohol in public parks or to carry an open container of alcohol in your car while driving. Penalties for driving under the influence of alcohol are quite severe, and may even include a jail sentence.

OUTDOOR ACTIVITIES

MARYLAND'S Chesapeake Bay and Eastern Shore offer wonderful opportunities for boating, sailing, and fishing. For outdoor enthusiasts, other highlights of the Capital Region include hiking the **Appalachian Trail** in Virginia and West Virginia, whitewater rafting in West Virginia, and cycling along the picturesque Chesapeake and Ohio Canal Towpath, which runs all the way from Washington to Maryland. There is also a beautiful 16-mile (26-km) biking trail from Washington to Mount Vernon. Delaware's Rehoboth Beach and Seashore State Park are a magnet for those in search of sea and sand.

Among spectator sports, the **Washington Redskins** (football) and the **Baltimore Orioles** (baseball) are hot tickets. If tickets have sold out, it is fun to watch the game along with other enthusiasts at a sports bar.

THE CLIMATE OF DC & CAPITAL REGION

The Capital Region's climate varies greatly. In winter, temperatures can plummet below freezing. During this time, Virginia's Appalachian Mountains are covered with snow, attracting skiers and snowboarders. Summers can be very hot and humid, with almost continuous sunshine. Summer is also the season for the heaviest rainfall, especially between May and August, when the rain comes as a welcome break from the humidity. The rains taper off in September and October, when the weather is pleasantly mild. The region is at its best in spring and fall.

WASHINGTON, DC

°F/C	Apr	Jul	Oct	Jan
		87/31		
	64/18	68/20	67/19	
32°F 44/7			48/9	42/6
0°C				27/–3
☀	14 days	17 days	19 days	18 days
☂	3.1 in	3.5 in	3.2 in	2.7 in
month	Apr	Jul	Oct	Jan

ENTERTAINMENT

VISITORS TO THIS region will never be at a loss for entertainment or cultural events. There are more free activities in DC than in any other American city. The weekend section of Friday's edition of the *Washington Post*, provides listings of free concerts, gallery talks, films, book signings, poetry readings, plays, and concerts.

The **Kennedy Center** in Washington is home to the **Washington Opera Company** and the **National Symphony Orchestra**, two of the capital's crown jewels. It offers a magnificent dance and ballet season as well, featuring the world's finest companies, including the Bolshoi, the American Ballet Theater, and the Dance Theater of Harlem. The center also hosts touring theater companies and many top jazz performers. Other good jazz and blues venues are **Blues Alley** in Georgetown, the **Merriweather Post Pavilion** in Columbia, Maryland, and the **Nissan Pavilion** in Manassas, Virginia.

Film classics and film premieres are shown at the Kennedy Center's American Film Institute and documentaries at the Library of Congress. Many of the capital's museums have regular series of film shows, lectures, and concerts.

Washington holds many seasonal cultural events. In June, there are nightly performances by the **Shakespeare Theatre Free for All** at the Carter Barron Amphitheater. Independence Day celebrations are spectacular along the Mall, with fireworks from the steps of the US Capitol. Labor Day Weekend in September is marked by a free concert by the National Symphony Orchestra on the lawns of Capitol Hill. Tours of the White House are limited at present. Check at the White House Visitor Center for the latest information.

SHOPPING

WASHINGTON, DC as well as Maryland and Virginia are famous for their antique stores. Frederick, Maryland, has the **Emporium at Creekside Antiques**, which houses over 100 antique shops. A great place to shop are the museum shops in DC, which stock an incredibly wide range of products, from African textiles and artwork reproductions to contemporary American crafts. Popular department stores are **Hecht's** in DC and **Nordstrom** in Arlington, Virginia. There are large malls in the Virginia and Maryland suburbs, and at Fashion Center in Pentagon City. Discount hunters should head for the 230 outlets at Potomac Mills, situated 30 miles (48 km) south of DC on I-95, or to Rehoboth Beach in Delaware, with its huge concentration of outlet stores.

Many shops in the Washington, DC area are closed on federal holidays.

DIRECTORY

TOURIST INFORMATION

Delaware
99 King's Hwy, Dover, DE 19901.
☎ (302) 739-4271.
Ⓦ www.visitdelaware.net

Dial-a-Museum
900 Jefferson Dr, SW Washington, DC.
☎ (202) 357-2020.

Maryland
217 E Redwood St, Baltimore, MD 21202.
☎ (800) 634-7386.

Virginia
901 E Byrd St, Richmond, VA 23219.
☎ (800) 847-4882.
Ⓦ www.virginia.org

Washington, DC
1212 New York Ave, NW, suite 600, Washington, DC 20005.
☎ (202) 789-7000.
Ⓦ www.washington.org

West Virginia
☎ (800)-225-5982.
Ⓦ www.callwva.com

TRAVEL

Amtrak
☎ (800) 872-7245.
Ⓦ www.amtrak.com

Greyhound
☎ (800) 229-9424.
Ⓦ www.greyhound.com

Metrorail & Metrobus
600 Fifth St, NW, Washington, DC 20001.
☎ (202) 637-7000, (202) 638-3780.
Ⓦ www.wmata.com

SPORTS & OUTDOOR ACTIVITIES

Baltimore Orioles
Oriole Park at Camden Yards, 333 W Camden St, Baltimore, MD 21201.
☎ (401) 685-9800.

Washington Redskins
FedExField 1600, FedEx Way, Landover, MD 20785.
☎ (301) 276-6050 (ticket office),
(301) 276-6000,
(301) 276-6800,
(703) 726-7000.
Ⓦ www.redskins.com

ENTERTAINMENT

Blues Alley
1073 Wisconsin Ave, NW.
☎ (202) 337-4141.

Kennedy Center
New Hampshire Ave & Rock Creek Pkwy, NW.
☎ (202) 467-4600.
Ⓦ www.kennedycenter.org

Merriweather Post Pavilion
Columbia, MD.
☎ (301) 982-1800,
(703) 218-6500,
(800) 955-5566.

National Symphony Orchestra
☎ (202) 467-4600.

Nissan Pavilion
7800 Cellar Door Dr, Haymarket, VA.
☎ (703)754-6400.

Shakespeare Theatre Free for All
Carter Barron Amphitheater, 16th St & Colorado Ave, NW.
☎ (202) 334-4790.
Ⓦ www.shakespearetheatre.org

SHOPPING

Emporium at Creekside Antiques
112 E Patrick St, Frederick, MD.
☎ (301) 662-7099.

Hecht's Department Store
12th & G St, NW.
☎ (202) 628-6661.

Where to Stay

WASHINGTON OFFERS A WIDE range of accomodations. For a relaxing holiday, you may want to choose a hotel with all the amenities: pool, health club, deluxe restaurant, and room service, though cheaper options are also available. The hotels in Washington, DC tend to be expensive, but there are bargains to be had, especially during the off season and on weekends.

	Credit Cards	Number of Rooms (Suites)	Recommended Restaurant	Children's Facilities	Garden or Terrace
WASHINGTON, DC					
CAPITOL HILL: *Bull Moose Bed-and-Breakfast on Capitol Hill* $ 101 5th St, NE (at A St). ((202) 547-1050, (800) 261-2768. FAX (202) 548-9741. W www.BullMoose-B-and-B.com This historic B&B, five blocks from the Capitol, has original oak woodwork and turreted bedrooms. ⊞	■	9 (1)			
CAPITOL HILL: *Holiday Inn on the Hill* $$$ 415 New Jersey Ave, NW (between D St & E St). ((202) 638-1616, (800) 638-1116. FAX (202) 638-0707. W www.holiday-inn.com/was-onthehill A good choice for both business travelers and families. During the summer there is a play area for children called the Discovery Zone.	■	343 (9)	■	●	■
CAPITOL HILL: *Hyatt Regency Washington* $$$$ 400 New Jersey Ave, NW (at D St). ((202) 737-1234, (800) 233-1234. FAX (202) 942-1512. W www.washingtonregency.hyatt.com Entrance to the Hyatt is through a superbly elegant plant-filled atrium. Children under 18 stay for free.	■	834 (32)	■	●	
CAPITOL HILL: *Phoenix Park Hotel* $$$$ 520 N Capitol St, NW (at F St and N Capitol). ((202) 638-6900, (800) 824-5419. FAX (202) 393-3236. W www.phoenixparkhotel.com The rooms here are furnished in an 18th-century Irish Manor style. Three of the suites have spiral staircases, three have balconies. Irish entertainers perform nightly in the pub.	■	149 (9)	■	●	
THE MALL: *Loews L'Enfant Plaza Hotel* $$$$ 480 L'Enfant Plaza, SW. ((202) 484-1000, (800) 235-6397. FAX (202) 646-5060. W www.loewshotels.com Named after Pierre L'Enfant, architect of the original city plans, this luxury three-star hotel is one of the top properties in DC. Many of the rooms have spectacular views of the city.	■	370 (21)	■	●	■
OLD DOWNTOWN: *Washington International Youth Hostel* $ 1009 11th St, NW (at K St, NW). ((202) 737-2333. FAX (202) 737-1508. W www.hiwashingtondc.org Very inexpensive accommodation for the thrifty young traveler, the dormitory rooms hold up to 12 people.	■	270			
OLD DOWNTOWN: *Hotel Harrington* $$ 436 11th St, NW (at E St NW). ((202) 628-8140. FAX (202) 347-3924. W www.hotel-harrington.com The Harrington is clean and comfortable. Popular with tourists and students, the central location and low prices offset the rather threadbare decor.	■	250		●	
OLD DOWNTOWN: *Willard Inter-Continental Hotel* $$$$$ 1401 Pennsylvania Ave, NW (at 14th St). ((202) 628-9100, (800) 327-0200. FAX (202) 637-7326. W www.washington.interconti.com This famous hotel offers rooms with marble bathrooms. The public areas feature chandeliers and mosaic floors.	■	340 (40)	■		
WHITE HOUSE & FOGGY BOTTOM: *Hotel Lombardy* $$ 2019 Penn. Ave, NW (at I St, NW). ((202) 828-2600, (800) 424-5486. FAX (202) 872-0503. W www.hotellombardy.com A European-style boutique hotel with two restaurants in the building and an accommodating multilingual staff.	■	130 (30)	■		
WHITE HOUSE & FOGGY BOTTOM: *Doubletree Guest Suites* $$$ 801 New Hampshire Ave (at H St NW). ((202) 785-2000, (800) 222-8733. FAX (202) 785-9485. W www.doubletree.com A full kitchen, pull-out beds, and two televisions per suite make this a good choice for families. The staff is friendly and efficient.	■	(105)		●	

	Credit Cards	Number of Rooms (Suites)	Recommended Restaurant	Children's Facilities	Garden or Terrace
Price categories for a standard double room per night, inclusive of breakfast, service charges, and any additional taxes: ⓢ under $100 ⓢⓢ $100–$150 ⓢⓢⓢ $150–$200 ⓢⓢⓢⓢ $200–$250 ⓢⓢⓢⓢⓢ over $250	**CREDIT CARDS** Major credit cards accepted. **NUMBER OF ROOMS** Number of rooms in the hotel (suites shown in parentheses). **RECOMMENDED RESTAURANT** Good restaurant within the hotel. **CHILDREN'S FACILITIES** Hotel has various facilities for young children. **GARDEN OR TERRACE** Hotel has a garden, courtyard, or terrace.				

WHITE HOUSE & FOGGY BOTTOM: *Lincoln Suites Downtown* ⓢⓢⓢ

1823 L St, NW (between 18th St & 19th St). ((202) 223-4320, (800) 424-2970.
FAX (202) 223-8546. W www.lincolnhotels.com
All rooms in this modern, boutique hotel are large studio apartments with full-size kitchens. Continental breakfast is included.

| | ■ | (99) | ■ | | |

WHITE HOUSE & FOGGY BOTTOM: *Wyndham City Center* ⓢⓢⓢⓢ

1143 New Hampshire Ave (between 22nd St & M St). ((202) 775-0800.
FAX (202) 887-9171. W www.wyndham.com
The Wyndham City Center is in a very good location for the busy tourist, close to all amenities and main sights.

| | ■ | 337 (15) | ■ | | |

WHITE HOUSE & FOGGY BOTTOM: *Hay-Adams Hotel* ⓢⓢⓢⓢⓢ

800 16th St, NW (at H St). ((202) 638-6600, (800) 424-5054. FAX (202) 638-2716.
W www.hayadams.com
Italian Renaissance-style property located directly across from the White House. Rooms have antiques and ornamental ceilings.

| | ■ | (143) | ■ | | |

WHITE HOUSE & FOGGY BOTTOM: *St. Regis Washington* ⓢⓢⓢⓢⓢ

923 16th St, NW (at K St). ((202) 638-2626, (800) 562-5661.
W www.stregis.com
A luxury hotel with more character than some of the chain hotels. Dinner in the restaurant makes for a romantic evening.

| | ■ | 181 (14) | ■ | | |

GEORGETOWN: *The Georgetown Inn* ⓢⓢⓢⓢ

1310 Wisconsin Ave, NW (between N St & O St). ((202) 333-8900, (800) 368-5922.
FAX (202) 333-8308. W www.georgetowninn.com
A small, boutique hotel built in the style of historic Georgetown. The large rooms have Colonial-style decor and luxurious bathrooms.

| | ■ | 86 (10) | ■ | | |

GEORGETOWN: *The Latham Hotel* ⓢⓢⓢⓢ

3000 M St, NW (at 30th St). ((202) 726-5000, (800) 368-5922. FAX (202) 337-4250.
A European-style boutique hotel with four poolside bungalows and an excellent French restaurant.

| | ■ | 143 (9) | ■ | | |

GEORGETOWN: *Four Seasons Hotel* ⓢⓢⓢⓢⓢ

2800 Pennsylvania Ave, NW (between M St NW and Rock Creek & Potomac Parkway NW). ((202) 342-0444, (800) 332-2443. FAX (202) 944-2076.
W www.fourseasons.com
A modern exterior belies the old-world elegance of this luxurious hotel, which prides itself on excellent service.

| | ■ | 257 (55) | ■ | ● | |

FARTHER AFIELD: *Brickskeller Inn* ⓢⓢ

1523 22nd St, NW (between P St & Q St NW). ((202) 293-1885. FAX (202) 293-0996.
An old, quaint hotel with an old-fashioned elevator dating from 1950. The restaurant offers over 1,000 kinds of beer from all around the world.

| | ■ | 40 | ■ | | |

FARTHER AFIELD: *The Taft Bridge Inn* ⓢⓢ

2007 Wyoming Ave, NW (at 20th St). ((202) 387-2007.
W www.taftbridgeinn.com
This Georgian-style mansion is within walking distance of Adams-Morgan. Some rooms have a shared bathroom. Breakfast is included.

| | ■ | 12 | ■ | | ■ |

FARTHER AFIELD: *Madera Hotel* ⓢⓢⓢ

1310 New Hampshire Ave, NW (at 13th St). ((202) 296-7600, (800) 368-5691.
FAX (202) 293-2476. W www.hotelmadera.com
A small, simple boutique hotel in a great location near DuPont Circle and the White House. Some suites have kitchenettes.

| | ■ | (82) | ■ | | |

FARTHER AFIELD: *Embassy Square Summerfield Suites by Wyndham* ⓢⓢ

2000 N St, NW (at 20th St). ((202) 659-9000, (800) 424-2999.
W www.embassysquaredc.com This is an all-suite hotel with modern furnishings. Each unit has a kitchenette.

| | ■ | (278) | ■ | | ■ |

For key to symbols see back flap

Price categories for a standard double room per night, inclusive of breakfast, service charges, and any additional taxes: $ under $100 $$ $100–$150 $$$ $150–$200 $$$$ $200–$250 $$$$$ over $250	**CREDIT CARDS** Major credit cards accepted. **NUMBER OF ROOMS** Number of rooms in the hotel (suites shown in parentheses). **RECOMMENDED RESTAURANT** Good restaurant within the hotel. **CHILDREN'S FACILITIES** Hotel has various facilities for young children. **GARDEN OR TERRACE** Hotel has a garden, courtyard, or terrace.	CREDIT CARDS	NUMBER OF ROOMS (SUITES)	RECOMMENDED RESTAURANT / CHILDREN'S FACILITIES / GARDEN OR TERRACE

Listing	Price	Credit Cards	No. of Rooms (Suites)	Rec. Restaurant	Children's Facilities	Garden or Terrace
FARTHER AFIELD: *Swann House* 1808 New Hampshire Ave, NW (between S St & Swann St). ((202) 265-7677. FAX (202) 265-6755. W www.swannhouse.com This B&B, in a Romanesque-style house built in 1883, is within walking distance of Du Pont Circle. ⊞ ≋ ⬗	$$$	■	9 (4)			■
FARTHER AFIELD: *Renaissance Mayflower* 1127 Connecticut Ave, NW (at Desales St). ((202) 347-3000, (800) 468-3571. FAX (202) 466-9083. W www.renaissancehotels.com The Mayflower was built in 1925 and is on the National Register of Historic Places. 24 ⊞ Y ≋ ⬗ P ⬗	$$$$	■	660 (80)			■
FARTHER AFIELD: *Jefferson Hotel* 1200 16th St, NW (at M St). ((202) 347-2200, (800) 235-6397. FAX (202) 331-7982. W www.loewshotels.com Built in 1923, this hotel is part of the America Hotel Historic Association. The rooms are decorated in Federal-style elegance, with antiques and original art. Service is outstanding. 24 ⊞ Y ≋ ⬗ P ⬗	$$$$$	■	100 (35)	■		
FARTHER AFIELD: *Madison Hotel* 1177 15th St, NW (at M St). ((202) 862-1600, (800) 424-8577. FAX (202) 785-1255. W www.themadisonhotel.net The lobby of this hotel is filled with beautiful antiques, including a Louis XVI commode. Though modern on the outside, the hotel specializes in old-world luxury and meticulous service. 24 ⊞ Y ⬗ ⬗ P ⬗	$$$$$	■	311 (32)			

MARYLAND

Listing	Price	Credit Cards	No. of Rooms (Suites)	Rec. Restaurant	Children's Facilities	Garden or Terrace
BALTIMORE: *Ann Street Bed-and-Breakfast* 804 South Ann St. ((410) 342-5883. Originally two 18th-century townhouses, this B&B offers an authentic Colonial atmosphere with open fires and antique furniture.	$$		3 (1)			
BALTIMORE: *Peabody Court, A Clarion Hotel* 612 Cathedral St (between W Centre St & W Monument St). ((410) 727-7101, (800) 292-5500. FAX (410) 789-3312. W www.peabodycourtnbhotels.com A small boutique hotel offering excellent service and located close to the Walters Art Gallery. ⊞ ⬗ ⬗ P ⬗	$$$	■	104 (1)	■		
BALTIMORE: *Renaissance Harborplace Hotel* 202 E Pratt St (between South St & S Calvert St). ((410) 547-1200, (800) 535-1201. FAX (410) 539-5780. W www.renaissancehotels.com Many rooms in this hotel have a view of the harbor. The staff is attentive, and the restaurant serves excellent seafood. 24 ⊞ Y ≋ ⬗ ⬗ P ⬗	$$$$	■	622 (30)			
BERLIN: *Merry Sherwood Plantation* 8909 Worcester Hwy (nr Assateague). ((410) 641-2112, (800) 660-0358. FAX (301) 641-9528. W www.merrysherwood.com This inn is a restored 1850s Italianate Revival-style mansion, set on 21 acres (8.5 ha). The rooms have working fireplaces and Victorian-style furniture. ⊞	$$$	■	8 (1)			■
EASTON: *Tidewater Inn* 101 East Dover St (near Chesapeake Bay). ((410) 822-1300, (800) 237-8775. W www.tidewaterinn.com A charming, historic inn furnished with antiques. The restaurant serves all types of food but the crab cakes are the specialty. ⊞ ≋ P ⬗	$$	■	114 (18)	■		
TILGHMAN ISLAND: *Chesapeake Wood Duck Inn* Gibsontown Rd, at Dogwood Harbor. ((410) 886-2070, (800) 956-2070. FAX (413) 677-7526. An award-winning, waterfront B&B offering great hospitality and innovative cuisine (dinner is available for guests). Recently received 3-diamond AAA and three-star Mobil awards. ⊞	$$$	■	6 (1)			

VIRGINIA

ALEXANDRIA: *Holiday Inn of Old Town* $$$$
480 King St (at S Pitt St). ((703) 549-6080, (800) 465-4329.
W www.axe-oldtown.hiselect.com
A huge, old-fashioned lobby greets guests at this hotel. The refurbished rooms
are Victorian in style.

227
(2)

CHARLOTTESVILLE: *The Boar's Head Inn* $$$
Route 250 West. ((434) 296-2181, (800) 476-1988. FAX (434) 972-6024.
W www.boarsheadinn.com
A luxurious inn, with two lakes on the grounds. Facilities include an 18-
hole golf course, tennis, fishing, biking, and a spa.

160
(11)

COLONIAL WILLIAMSBURG: *Colonial Houses* $$$$
136 East Francis St. (1-800-HISTORY. W www.colonialwilliamsburg.com
Restored 18th-century houses with traditional furnishings and up-to-date
facilities. You can rent one of the 28 independent houses or a room in a
house. The facilities of the nearby Williamsburg Inn are also available.

77

COLONIAL WILLIAMSBURG: *The Williamsburg Inn* $$$$$
136 East Francis St. (1-800-HISTORY. W www.colonialwilliamsburg.com
This famous hotel offers all the luxuries of a modern hotel in a Regency-style
setting. The Regency Room provides fine dining, and afternoon tea is served in
the Terrace Room. Golf, croquet, and tennis are also available.

(62)

FREDERICKSBURG: *Kenmore Inn* $$
1200 Princess Anne St. ((540) 371-7622.
A historic inn with rooms decorated in either Victorian or Colonial style. It has
two dining facilities – formal dining upstairs, and a pub downstairs.

9
(1)

LURAY: *Skyland Resort* $$$
PO Box 727, Luray, VA 22835 (Skyline Drive). ((540) 999-2211, (800) 999-4714.
W www.visitshenandoah.com
The Skyland Resort is on the highest point of a mountain, and most rooms
have a view of the valley below. ● Dec–early Mar.

171
(6)

RICHMOND: *The Berkeley Hotel* $$$
1200 Cary St. ((804) 780-1300. W www.berkeleyhotel.com
A warm welcome is given at this gracious hotel, with its lavish, traditional
furnishings. Situated in the heart of downtown Richmond.

55
(1)

WEST VIRGINIA

CHARLES TOWN: *The Washington House Inn* $$
216 S George St. ((304) 725-7923, (800) 297-6957.
W www.washingtonhouseinnwv.com
This historic three-story brick mansion is located near Harpers Ferry and
Blue Ridge Mountains. Open all year.

7

ELKINS: *Tunnel Mountain B&B* $
Route 1, Box 59-1. ((304) 636-1684, (888) 211-9123.
This three-story stone house is spread across 5 acres (2 ha), at the edge of
the Monongahela National Forest. No kids under 12 permitted.

3

DELAWARE

LEWES: *Sleep Inn & Suites* $$
1595 Hwy 1. ((302) 645-6464, (800) 424-6423.
Fairly close to Rehoboth Beach and the plethora of tax-free outlets in the area,
this inn offers a free Continental breakfast, and free coffee and juice all day.

81

NEW CASTLE: *The Jerry House* $$
130 Delaware St. ((302) 322-2505. W www.jerryhouse.com
This elegant 1860s townhouse is in the heart of New Castle's historic
district, and features tastefully appointed rooms and a mini-museum that
highlights Delaware history.

5

WILMINGTON: *Hotel DuPont* $$$$
11th St & Market. ((302) 594-3100, (800) 441-9019.
W www.hoteldupont.com
Delaware's only four-star hotel provides easy access to Longwood
Gardens and Delaware Art Museum. There are two superb restaurants.

217

For key to symbols see back flap

Where to Eat

A N ECLECTIC CHOICE OF FOOD is on offer across Washington. There are many traditional restaurants that serve classic American dishes, while DC's cosmopolitan population is reflected in the vast number of Ethiopian, Vietnamese, and Italian restaurants. The opening times of some restaurants are indicated by a "B" for breakfast, "L" for lunch, and "D" for dinner.

	CREDIT CARDS	OUTDOOR TABLES	VEGETARIAN	GOOD WINE LIST	LATE OPENING

WASHINGTON, DC

CAPITOL HILL: *America* $
Union Station, 50 Massachusetts Ave, NE. ((202) 682-9555.
The 200-item menu, including all the American classics, is sure to please everybody and makes the choice both easy and inexpensive. **P Y 🚻 ♿**

| | ■ | ● | ■ | ● | |

CAPITOL HILL: *Market Lunch* $
Eastern Market, 225 7th St, SE (at C St). ((202) 547-8444.
Authentic regional food, such as crab cakes and crab sandwiches, are offered here. The cafeteria-style breakfast and lunch are casual but delicious. Expect a long wait on Saturday and Sunday mornings. ● *Mon.* 🚻 ♿

| | | | ● | | |

CAPITOL HILL: *Tunnicliff's* $
222 7th St, SE (opposite Eastern Market). ((202) 544-5680.
The old wooden interior attracts a casual and diverse crowd. The cuisine is American pub-type food. **Y 🚻**

| | ■ | ● | ■ | | ■ |

GEORGETOWN: *Au Pied De Cochon* $
1335 Wisconsin Ave, at Dumbarton St. ((202) 337-6400.
This French café is not noted for its decor or quick service, but it is one of the only restaurants in Georgetown that is open 24 hours a day. Try the eggs Benedict for an early breakfast. **Y**

| | ■ | ● | ■ | ● | ■ |

GEORGETOWN: *Café La Ruche* $
1039 31st St NW (between K St & C&O Canal). ((202) 965-2684.
A typical Parisian bistro with a comfortable atmosphere that is great for chatting with friends. There is a wide range of dishes available, including rainbow trout, crab cakes, mussels niçoise, and soups and salads. ♫

| | ■ | ● | ■ | | |

GEORGETOWN: *Martin's Tavern* $
1264 Wisconsin Ave, NW (at N St). ((202) 333-7370.
Martin's is the oldest family-owned restaurant in DC, and one of the most charming locations for American pub food. **Y 🚻**

| | ■ | ● | ■ | ● | ■ |

GEORGETOWN: *Old Glory All American Barbecue* $
3139 M St, NW (between Wisconsin Ave & 31st St). ((202) 337-3406.
This homey restaurant serves traditional and much-loved American fare, such as spare ribs, hickory-smoked chicken, wood-fried shrimp, and apple crisps. **Y ♫ 🚻 ♿**

| | ■ | ● | ■ | | ■ |

GEORGETOWN: *Zed's Ethiopian Cuisine* $
1201 28th St, NW. ((202) 333-4710.
An Ethiopian restaurant, popular with vegetarians, Zed's is known for its traditional Ethiopian fare – *wats* (red pepper sauces), *alechas* (stews), and *injera* (bread). **Y 🚻**

| | ■ | ● | ■ | ● | |

GEORGETOWN: *Sequoia* $$
Washington Harbor, 3000 K St, NW. ((202) 944-4200.
A trendy restaurant that combines American cuisine with fabulous views of the Potomac and Virginia skyline. **P Y 🚻 ♿**

| | ■ | ● | ■ | ● | ■ |

GEORGETOWN: *Citronelle* $$$$
Latham Hotel, 3000 M St, NW (at 30th St). ((202) 625-2150.
This excellent restaurant serves wonderful food including a variety of sophisticated and exotic French dishes, such as pastry "cigars" stuffed with wild mushrooms, as well as seafood such as potato-crusted halibut.
P Y ♿

| | ■ | | ■ | ● | |

GREATER WASHINGTON: *Ben's Chili Bowl* $
1213 U St, NW (between 12th & 13th Sts). ((202) 667-0909.
A favorite for anyone who loves a good, high-calorie meal. The chili dogs are known nationally. Ben's Chili Bowl also happens to be Bill Cosby's favorite haunt when he visits DC.

| | | | ■ | | |

Price categories include a three-course meal for one, a glass of house wine and all unavoidable extra charges such as sales tax and service.
$ under $20
$$ $20–30
$$$ $30–45
$$$$ $45–60
$$$$$ over $60

CREDIT CARDS
Major credit cards accepted.

OUTDOOR TABLES
Garden, courtyard, or terrace with outside tables.

VEGETARIAN
A good selection of vegetarian dishes available.

GOOD WINE LIST
Extensive list of good wines, both domestic and imported.

LATE OPENING
Full menu or light meals served after 11pm.

	Price	Credit Cards	Outdoor Tables	Vegetarian	Good Wine List	Late Opening
GREATER WASHINGTON: *City Lights of China* 1731 Connecticut Ave, NW (between R & S Sts). ((202) 265-6688. Many people attest that the crowds and waiting in line are worth it. The City Lights of China serves inexpensive and delicious Chinese food. Delivery is available too.	$	■		■		
GREATER WASHINGTON: *Kramerbooks & Afterwords Café* 1517 Connecticut Ave, NW (between Dupont Circle & Q St). ((202) 387-1462. This café serves salads, pasta, as well as exotic Asian-influenced vegetarian dishes. Kramerbooks and Afterwords Café is open 24 hours on weekends.	$	■	●	■	●	■
GREATER WASHINGTON: *Georgetown Seafood Grill* 1200 19th St, NW (between M & N Sts). ((202) 530-4430. High-quality seafood at a moderate price – the crab cakes are said to be the best in town. The service is quick and friendly.	$$	■	●	■	●	
GREATER WASHINGTON: *La Tomate* 1701 Connecticut Ave NW (between R & S Sts). ((202) 667-5505. This Italian restaurant's prime location near Du Pont Circle makes it a summer favorite with the locals for outdoor eating.	$$	■	●	■		
GREATER WASHINGTON: *Pesce* 2016 P St, NW (between 20th & 21st Sts). ((202) 466-3474. The French and Italian menu changes daily but always includes delicious seafood and a fabulous wine list. Great food at a reasonable price.	$$	■			●	
GREATER WASHINGTON: *Nora's* 2132 Florida Ave, NW. ((202) 462-5143. W www.noras.com One of the stalwarts of Washington dining, this restaurant features a varied menu of contemporary American cuisine and organic ingredients.	$$$	■		■	●	
OLD DOWNTOWN: *Full Kee* 509 H St, NW (between 5th & 6th Sts). ((202) 371-2233. The Cantonese noodles and dumplings are excellent. A great place to grab a cheap meal before an MCI Center event.	$			■		
OLD DOWNTOWN: *Hard Rock Café* 999 E St, NW (at 10th St). ((202) 737-7625. All the American classics are available, including a variety of burgers, sandwiches, and salads. Videos, music, and memorabilia make the two floors of this restaurant an exciting, but rather hectic, tourist experience.	$	■		■		
OLD DOWNTOWN: *Old Ebbitt Grill* 675 15th St, NW (between Pennsylvania Ave & G St). ((202) 347-4801. Expect this upbeat American grill to be packed with both locals and tourists – anyone who likes a great meal. Old Ebbitt Grill offers a chance to sample the DC scene as well as quality seafood, pasta, and steaks.	$	■		■	●	■
OLD DOWNTOWN: *Bistro Bis* 15 E St, NW (between N Capitol & New Jersey). ((202) 661-2700. French food with a distinctly American twist, served in a beautiful, cozy dining area. The duck confit and salmon Provençal are recommended.	$$	■	●	■	●	
THE MALL: *Cascade Café* National Gallery of Art, Concourse Level, Constitution Ave, NW (between 4th & 7th Sts). ((202) 216-5966. One of the better options for hungry museum-goers, Cascade Café offers fast and convenient buffet-style food, including salads and great desserts.	$	■		■		

	CREDIT CARDS	OUTDOOR TABLES	VEGETARIAN	GOOD WINE LIST	LATE OPENING

Price categories include a three-course meal for one, a glass of house wine and all unavoidable extra charges such as sales tax and service.
$ under $20
$$ $20–30
$$$ $30–45
$$$$ $45–60
$$$$$ over $60

CREDIT CARDS
Major credit cards accepted.
OUTDOOR TABLES
Garden, courtyard, or terrace with outside tables.
VEGETARIAN
A good selection of vegetarian dishes available.
GOOD WINE LIST
Extensive list of good wines, both domestic and imported.
LATE OPENING
Full menu or light meals served after 11pm.

THE MALL: *Flight Line Café* **$** National Air & Space Museum, Independence Ave (between 4th & 7th Sts). **(** *(202) 357-2700.* The only restaurant in the museum, it offers a range of hamburgers, pizzas, and sandwiches. 🕴 ♿	▪				
THE MALL: *The Palm Court Ice Cream Parlor and Café* **$** National Museum of American History, Constitution Ave, NW (between 12th & 14th Sts). **(** *(202) 357-2700.* A typical American selection of cuisine is offered, but this is a bit more expensive than some of the other Mall eateries. 🕴 ♿	▪				
WHITE HOUSE & FOGGY BOTTOM: *Aroma* **$** 1919 I St, NW (between 19th & 20th Sts). **(** *(202) 833-4700.* This North Indian restaurant is one of the best-kept secrets in Washington. It is casual yet elegant, and the food is excellent. 🍷 ♿	▪		▪		
WHITE HOUSE & FOGGY BOTTOM: *Bombay Club* **$** 815 Connecticut Ave, NW (between H & I Sts). **(** *(202) 659-3727.* Exotic Indian food in a Colonial setting. The attentive service and exclusive clientele provide a glimpse of upper-crust Washington. 🅿 🍷 🎵 ♿	▪	●	▪	●	
WHITE HOUSE & FOGGY BOTTOM: *Hors D'Oeuvrerie* **$** Kennedy Center. **(** *(202) 416-8560.* The Kennedy Center location for light fare, such as salads and wraps. Open after the last show, it is an ideal place to grab a cocktail. 🅿 🍷 🕴 ♿	▪		▪	●	▪
WHITE HOUSE & FOGGY BOTTOM: *Galileo* **$$** 1110 21st St, NW (between L & M Sts). **(** *(202) 293-7191.* The most talked-about Italian restaurant in DC, Galileo is famous for its innovative and elaborate dishes, such as homemade pastas, risottos, and game dishes, as well as its fine selection of wines. 🅿 🍷 🕴 ♿	▪	●	▪	●	
WHITE HOUSE & FOGGY BOTTOM: *Georgia Brown's* **$$** 950 15th St, NW (between I & K Sts). **(** *(202) 393-4499.* Anyone who craves Carolina shrimp, grits (fried, coarse grain), or fried green tomatoes should come here. Southern cooking with style in an inviting but hectic atmosphere. 🅿 🍷 🎵 🕴 ♿	▪	●	▪	●	
WHITE HOUSE & FOGGY BOTTOM: *Kinkead's* **$$** Red Lion Row, 2000 Pennsylvania Ave, NW (bet. 20th & 21st Sts). **(** *(202) 296-7700.* A fantastic seafood restaurant without the price inflation that can come with a big name. Bob Kinkead's creations, such as the pepita-crusted salmon, are wonderfully complemented by the fine wine list. 🅿 🍷 🎵 ♿	▪	●	▪	●	

MARYLAND

ANNAPOLIS: *Middletown Tavern Oyster Bar & Restaurant* **$$** 2 Market Space. **(** *(410) 263-3323.* Located across the street from the harbor, this outdoor restaurant is a perfect spot to soak up the view. The oysters come with beer; also on the menu are crab cakes, seafood, and pasta dishes. 🅿 🍷 🎵 🕴	▪	●	▪	●	▪
BALTIMORE: *Obrycki's Crab House* **$** 1727 E Pratt St. **(** *(410) 732-6399.* A seasonal restaurant that offers superb seafood dining. A favorite of the house is the hard-shell steamed crabs. ● *Dec–Mar.* 🅿 🍷 🕴 ♿	▪		▪	●	▪
CHESAPEAKE BAY: *The Crab Claw* **$$** Navy Point, St. Michaels. **(** *(410) 745-2900.* A seasonal restaurant located right on the harbor, with spectacular views. The fresh seafood dishes are the specialty of the house. ● *Dec–Feb.* 🕴 ♿		●	▪	●	

FREDERICK: *The Red Horse Steak House* $$
996-98 W Patrick St. ((301) 663-3030.
A local institution, famous for the prime ribs, humongous steaks, and fresh
trout. An excellent wine list. *Mon–Fri L, Mon–Sat D, Sun buffet 4pm–9pm.*

OCEAN CITY: *Phillips Crab House* $$
21st St & Philadelphia Ave. ((410) 289-6821.
What's a visit to the Eastern Shore without a visit to Phillips. Fresh crab in
various guises, oysters, clams, and anything fishy. The famous seafood
buffet opens daily at 3:30pm. ◯ *mid-Mar–Oct: daily.* Y

VIRGINIA

ALEXANDRIA: *Gadsby's Tavern* $$
N Royal St, at Cameron St. ((703) 548-1288.
Here the waiters are in Colonial costume, and the decor is in the style of
late 1700s. The menu includes duck, venison, seafood, and pies. 🎵 🏃 &

CHARLOTTESVILLE: *Michie Tavern* $
683 Thomas Jefferson Parkway. ((434) 977-1234. W www.michietavern.com
Casual dining with a Colonial touch – serving staff dress in Colonial
outfits, and the decor is on the rustic side. The traditional Southern fried
chicken is outstanding. *L.* 🏃 &

COLONIAL WILLIAMSBURG: *Chowning's Tavern* $
109 Duke of Gloucester St (at Queen St). (1-800-HISTORY.
This restaurant is a step back into the 18th century. Lunches include full-
fare cafeteria style dishes such as Brunswick stew and ribs; dinners are
light. Gambols (18th-century entertainment) take place nightly. 🎵 🏃 &

COLONIAL WILLIAMSBURG: *The Trellis* $$
403 Duke of Gloucester St. ((757) 229-8610.
Regional cuisine which concentrates on fresh food – the menu changes
every season. Located in the heart of the historic district, it offers an
extensive wine list with more than 20 wines from Virginia. Y 🎵 &

RICHMOND: *Southern Culture* $
2229 W Main St. ((804) 355-6939.
This restaurant serves a variety of regional Southern food, ranging from
Virginia chicken to seafood from the Gulf of Mexico. ● *Mon.* Y 🏃 &

SKYLINE DRIVE: *Inn at Little Washington* $$$$$
Middle St & Main St, Little Washington. ((540) 675-3800.
This five-star and five-diamond restaurant offers regional, eclectic
American cuisine. The 90-minute drive might be discouraging, but the
inviting country house makes it worthwhile. P Y &

WEST VIRGINIA

ELKINS: *Cheat River Inn* $$$
Elkins, WV ((304) 636-6265. W www.cheatriverlodge.com
Riverside dining, prime beef and rainbow trout specialties. Ideal for in
hiking and camping in the Monogahela National Forest. ● *Mon.* Y 🏃

NEW RIVER GORGE: *Hawk's Nest Restaurant* $
US Route 60, Ansted, WV, in the Hawk's Nest State Park. ((304) 658-5215.
Great views of the New River Gorge. This family resturant is popular for
its good home cooking, fine wines, and domestic beers. *B, L, D.*
◯ *7 days: 7am–8:45pm, Sun: deli bar.* ● *Dec 25.* 🏃 &

DELAWARE

NEW CASTLE: *Jessop's Tavern* $$$
114 Delaware St. ((302) 322-6111.
Unique, Colonial decor and tavern fare. Home cooking, authentic with
early American entrees and appetizers. Not commercial at all but a real
atmospheric treat. Nice wooden tables, excellent food. Reservations
recommended. *L, D.* ● *Sun.* P 🏃 &

REHOBOTH BEACH: *The Back Porch Café* $$$
59 Rehoboth Avenue. ((302) 227-3674.
Located in an old beach house, this café specializes in seafood, with a
big wine list and live music on weekends. ◯ *Jun–Sep: L, D daily; May & Oct:
Fri–Sun.* ● *Nov–Apr.* Y 🎵

For key to symbols see back flap

THE SOUTHEAST

The Southeast at a Glance

ALTHOUGH THE FIVE Southeast states – North and South Carolina, Kentucky, Tennessee, and Georgia – share a common history and culture, they are quite distinct from one another. The region covers three different topographical areas. To the east, the low-lying coastal plains along the Atlantic include the historic cities of Savannah, Georgia, and Charleston, South Carolina, bordered by pristine beaches. The central Blue Ridge and Appalachian Mountains hold acres and acres of stunningly scenic wilderness, while in the inland foothills, linked to the Gulf of Mexico by the Mississippi and other broad rivers, are cities such as Louisville, Kentucky, and Tennessee's twin music capitals, Nashville and Memphis. Atlanta is the main commercial center.

Lexington (see p270) *is Kentucky's main horse-breeding center. Visitors are allowed access to most of the stud farms surrounding the city.*

Nashville (see pp264–5) *is Tennessee's state capital as well as the nation's country music capital. The town's revitalized downtown, with its lively restaurants, cafés, and nightclubs, is the center of action, day and night.*

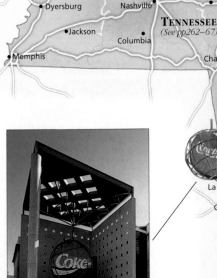

Atlanta (see pp260–61), *Georgia's capital, is the place where Coca-Cola was born in the 1880s. Since then, the drink has become an international favorite. The hard-hitting TV news channel, CNN, is also based in Atlanta.*

Owensboro Elizabethtown Harr

KENTUCKY
(See pp268–71)

Paducah   Somer

Bowling Green

Union City

Dyersburg   Nashville   Cookeville   Oa

Jackson   Columbia   **TENNESSEE**
(See pp262–67)

Memphis   Chattano

Rome

La Gran

Colum

Bainb

◁ **Acres of farmlands stretching across southwestern Georgia**

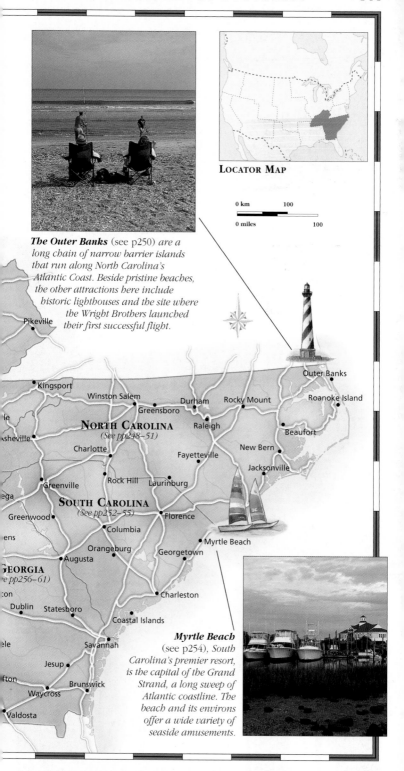

LOCATOR MAP

0 km 100

0 miles 100

The Outer Banks (see p250) *are a long chain of narrow barrier islands that run along North Carolina's Atlantic Coast. Beside pristine beaches, the other attractions here include historic lighthouses and the site where the Wright Brothers launched their first successful flight.*

Pikeville

Outer Banks

Kingsport

Winston Salem Durham Rocky Mount Roanoke Island

Greensboro

NORTH CAROLINA Raleigh
(See pp248–51)

le Asheville Beaufort

Charlotte

Fayetteville New Bern

Jacksonville

Greenville Rock Hill Laurinburg

ega **SOUTH CAROLINA**
(See pp252–55) Florence

Greenwood

ens Columbia Myrtle Beach

Orangeburg
Georgetown

GEORGIA Augusta
e pp256–61)

on

Dublin Statesboro Charleston

ele

Savannah Coastal Islands

Jesup

fton Brunswick

Waycross

Valdosta

Myrtle Beach *(see p254), South Carolina's premier resort, is the capital of the Grand Strand, a long sweep of Atlantic coastline. The beach and its environs offer a wide variety of seaside amusements.*

THE SOUTHEAST

*O*NE OF THE COUNTRY'S *most fascinating regions, the Southeast is home to two of America's most beautiful cities – Charleston and Savannah – as well as some of its most pristine beaches and expanses of primeval forests. Culturally, the region is famous for its vibrant musical traditons, as both country-western and the blues originated in Nashville and Memphis.*

The Southeast's cities reflect the region's proud cultural heritage. Celebrated for their beauty and sophistication, Charleston and Savannah are urban gems, with lushly landscaped parks and gracious homes. Both actively preserve their stately architecture as well as support a fine range of hotels, restaurants, and cultural institutions. Other cities vary greatly. The quiet college town of Durham, North Carolina, rated the "most educated city in America," stands in direct contrast to burgeoning commercial centers such as Atlanta, Georgia, the economic capital of the "New South." Equally engaging are Nashville, the capital of country-western music, and Memphis, the birthplace of the blues.

The region's natural landscape is as memorable. Nearly a thousand miles of Atlantic coastline are formed by a long series of offshore barrier islands, ranging from Cape Hatteras to Cumberland Island on the Florida border. Just inland, and linked to the ocean by several broad rivers, is the heartland of the Colonial-era plantation country. Farther inland are the farmlands of North Carolina, the primary US producer of tobacco products, and the rolling bluegrass fields of Kentucky's verdant Horse Country. At the center lies unforgettable mountain scenery.

HISTORY

Long before the arrival of the first Europeans, the region was home to a highly developed Native American culture, known as the Moundbuilders. Evidence of their large cities can be seen at Georgia's Ocmulgee National Monument. Later Indians, especially the Cherokee who lived in western North Carolina and northern Georgia,

Kentucky Derby, the annual horse-racing event held in Louisville's Churchill Downs

◁ **Colorful, patriotic roofline, South Carolina**

Exhibits in the Civil War Museum, Bardstown, Kentucky

the French and then the English. But it was only in 1670, under Charles II, that the first successful colony, called Carolina, was established near what is today Charleston. Carolina's first settlers came from the congested English colony on Barbados, and it was their agricultural expertise that made the land-owning "planters" the wealthiest in the American colonies. Their wealth, however, was based on slave labor, and thousands of Africans were imported to clear the swamps, dig canals, and harvest the crops. Along the coast where the main crops, rice and indigo, were grown, the white colonists were a small minority, outnumbered four to one by the workers whose labor they exploited.

The great fortunes made in Carolina inspired the creation in 1732 of another colony, Georgia, located to the south. In many ways Georgia was a novel colony, funded by the government rather than private interests and founded with social, rather than commercial, intentions. For the first time in the Americas, slavery was banned, as was drinking alcohol and the presence of lawyers. The new colony, however, faltered and came under the control of Carolina, which introduced the slave-holding practices.

In December 1860, the state of South Carolina declared itself independent from the rest of the country. Though Georgia followed soon after, the other Southeast states remained with the Union. It was only after South Carolina forces attacked the fortress at Fort Sumter near Charleston, on April 12, 1861, did Tennessee and North Carolina join the rebel cause. Ironically, only Kentucky, the birthplace of President Abraham Lincoln and Confederate President Jefferson Davis, remained divided – a true border state.

The impact of the four-year Civil War lasted for another 100 years, as the struggle against the iniquities of slavery gained momentum as the Civil Rights Movement. While primarily a grassroots

were among North America's most civilized tribes. Other tribes included the Creek, Tuscarora, Yamasee, and Catawba, but by the early 1800s, most of the Indians had been decimated by war and disease, or driven westward. Apart from a prominent Cherokee community in the far western corner of North Carolina, very few Indians survive in the region today.

In the early 1500s, explorers from Florida's Spanish colonies ventured here, lured by Indians' tales of great wealth. The Spanish were followed by

KEY DATES IN HISTORY

1587 Sir Walter Raleigh sponsors the establishment of an ill-fated colony at Roanoke in present-day North Carolina

1670 The first permanent English settlement in the Carolina colony is established at Charleston

1729 Carolina divided into North and South

1763 The Anglo-Spanish treaty fixes the Mississippi River as the western extent of the Southeast colonies

1792 Kentucky becomes the 15th US state

1795 The University of North Carolina, the country's first state-sponsored university, opens at Chapel Hill

1838 The government forcibly expels the Cherokees westward on the "Trail of Tears"

1861 Confederates attack on Fort Sumter

1864 General Sherman spares Savannah at the end of his notorious "March to the Sea"

1903 The Ohio-based Wright Brothers make the first successful powered airplane flight at Kitty Hawk, North Carolina

1976 Georgia Governor Jimmy Carter elected 39th president of the United States

1996 Atlanta hosts the centennial Olympics

2002 Jimmy Carter wins the Nobel Peace Prize

Grave of Dr. Martin Luther King Jr. in Atlanta, a pilgrimage site for people from all over the world

campaign, many of the battles were led by Atlanta-born Baptist minister Martin Luther King Jr, who practiced the use of nonviolent direct action to win equality for black people. Though Dr. King was assassinated while participating in a strike by black sanitation workers in Memphis in 1968, the movement for Civil Rights eventually saw his colleague Andrew Young elected to Congress from Georgia. Young was later elected mayor of Atlanta in 1981.

SOCIETY, CULTURE, & THE ARTS

The Southeast has been, and continues to be, a major contributor to American culture. Atlanta gave the world Coca-Cola and CNN, while Kentucky, particularly Colonel Sanders and his Kentucky Fried Chicken, spread the craze for fast food. Kentucky is also well known all over the world for its production of high-quality bourbon whiskey and high-speed horses.

Important though the region's cities are, they are also the conduit through which the outside world reaches into their hinterlands. Nashville's country music, for example, is deeply rooted in Appalachian folkways, while the blues and rock 'n' roll of Memphis emerge from the different ethnic and historical cultures of the broad Mississippi Delta. A roll call of the artists born and bred here spans all musical genres – the Everly Brothers, Bill Monroe, and Loretta Lynn are from Kentucky; John Coltrane, Doc Watson, Thelonius Monk, and Nina Simone hail from North Carolina; the Allman Brothers, James Brown, Otis Redding, and Gladys Knight came from Georgia; while

Tennessee can take credit for Chet Atkins, Tina Turner, and Carl Perkins, and its favorite adopted son, Elvis Presley (1935–77).

This is also true of literature, which witnessed the creativity of such diverse writers as Alice Walker, Thomas Wolfe, Carson McCullers, and James Agee, and characters and settings such as "God's Little Acre" and "Catfish Row" from George Gershwin's opera *Porgy & Bess*. Music, literature, and the arts still dominate Southeastern culture, and numerous events and festivals are celebrated all over the region.

TOURISM

The Appalachain Mountains and their local constituents, the Blue Ridge and Great Smoky Mountains, offer miles of spectacular scenery in near-pristine condition. Much of the mountain landscape is now preserved in a series of local, state, and national parks, and forests. The Great Smoky Mountains National Park, in particular, is one of the country's most popular, drawing millions of visitors each year. Other attractions include the beach resorts that proliferate along the Outer Banks in North Carolina, and Louisville's Kentucky Derby, reputed to be the biggest racing event in the country.

Local band performing in one of the many clubs in downtown Nashville, Tennessee

Exploring the Southeast

DESPITE THE SOUTHEAST's diverse landscape and topography, the region is compact enough to tour in about a week. The coastal cities of Charleston and Savannah, as well as the inland metropolises of Atlanta, Nashville, and Memphis, are well linked by road and short-haul airline flights. The broad crest of mountains that rise up at the center include such prime attractions as the scenic Blue Ridge Parkway and the Great Smoky Mountains National Park. Among the region's other highlights are Georgia's beautiful Golden Isles and Kentucky's spectacular mountain landscapes and bluegrass pasturelands, famous for their thoroughbred horse farms.

SIGHTS AT A GLANCE

North Carolina
Research Triangle Region **1**
Winston-Salem **2**
Blue Ridge Parkway **3**
Asheville **4**
Outer Banks **5**
Roanoke Island **6**
Beaufort **7**

South Carolina
Charleston pp252–3 **8**
Columbia **9**
Myrtle Beach **10**
Georgetown **11**
Coastal Islands **12**

Georgia
Savannah **13**
Golden Isles **14**
Okefenokee Swamp National
　Wildlife Refuge **15**
Americus **16**
Macon **17**
Athens **18**
Dahlonega **19**
Stone Mountain Park **20**
Atlanta pp260–61 **21**

Tennessee
Great Smoky Mountains
　National Park **22**
Chattanooga **23**
Nashville pp264–5 **24**
Memphis pp266–7 **25**

Kentucky
Cumberland Gap National
　Historic Park **26**
Mammoth Cave National Park **27**
Berea **28**
Daniel Boone National Forest **29**
Lexington **30**
Harrodsburg **31**
Hodgenville **32**
Bardstown **33**
Louisville **34**

KEY

✈ Airport

—— Highway

—— Major road

—— Railroad

– – State border

MILEAGE CHART

10 = Distance in miles
10 = Distance in kilometers

ATLANTA, GA							
248 399	SAVANNAH, GA						
208 335	**310** 499	ASHEVILLE, NC					
323 520	**107** 172	**267** 430	CHARLESTON, SC				
249 400	**496** 798	**293** 471	**550** 885	NASHVILLE, TN			
464 746	**712** 1145	**505** 812	**786** 1264	**212** 341	MEMPHIS, TN		
380 611	**583** 938	**283** 455	**540** 869	**212** 341	**422** 679	LEXINGTON, KY	
423 680	**659** 1060	**359** 578	**616** 991	**176** 283	**380** 611	**77** 124	LOUISVILLE, KY

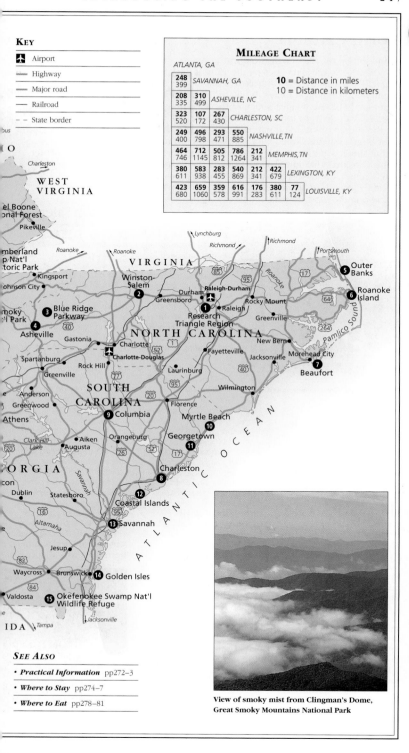

View of smoky mist from Clingman's Dome, Great Smoky Mountains National Park

North Carolina

THE SITE OF THE FIRST English outpost in America in 1585, North Carolina became the 12th of the original 13 states in 1789 – it was also one of the country's 13 original colonies. While the population is increasingly based in cities, much of the state remains covered with fields of tobacco, a crop whose politics are the source of local and national debate. Still, the sight of green fields dotted with plank-wood, tin-roofed drying sheds continues to conjure up a classic image of North Carolina. Though tobacco-growing dominates the state's center, the east is lined by miles of pristine Atlantic Ocean beachfront, and the western mountains are among the most majestic found east of the Rockies.

Façade of North Carolina Museum of History, Raleigh

Research Triangle Region ❶

🏠 1,188,000. ✈ 🚆 🚌 ℹ️ *NC Division of Tourism, 301 N Wilmington St, Raleigh, (919) 733-4171.*

THE STATE CAPITAL of Raleigh forms a regional triangle with the two major university towns of Durham and Chapel Hill. This region is the state's intellectual center, and has spawned the high-technology Research Triangle Park, a corporate campus located between the three cities.

Primarily a business region and gateway, the Triangle provides various urban conveniences and offers some interesting sights. Quiet downtown Raleigh includes a handful of modern state museums located across from the 1840 Greek Revival State Capitol, including the Sports Hall of Fame, the Museum of Natural Sciences, and the **North Carolina Museum of**

History. The latter is well known for a Civil War exhibit describing the state's divided loyalties. A Civil Rights exhibit is also due to open here in 2004. A few miles north toward the airport, the **North Carolina Museum of Art** holds three floors of statuary and paintings. Among these is the 16th-century *Madonna and Child in a Landscape* by the artist Lucas Cranach the Elder, which had been stolen by the Nazis. When this was discovered, the museum returned the painting to its original owner, who in turn, has now loaned it back to the museum.

Of the two university towns, the smaller Chapel Hill, with its wooded **University of North Carolina (UNC)** campus, Morehead Planetarium, art museum, and genteel Carolina Inn with its aristocratic clientele, is by far the quainter of the two. Downtown Durham, wedged between the three-part **Duke University** campus, is home to the Durham Bulls minorleague baseball team. It also hosts the annual September Blues Festival. A major landmark on the West Campus is the superb Neo-Gothic Duke Chapel. Alumni and students of the two universities enjoy the lively rivalry between their respective sports teams – the Duke's Blue Devils and UNC's Tar Heels.

🏛 **North Carolina Museum of History**
5 E Edenton St, Raleigh. 📞 *(919) 715-0200.* 🕐 *9am–5pm Tue–Sat, 1–5pm Sun.* ⚫ *Mon.*

🏛 **North Carolina Museum of Art**
2110 Blue Ridge Rd, Raleigh. 📞 *(919) 839-6262.* 🕐 *9am–5pm Wed–Sat, 10am–5pm Sun.* ⚫ *Mon–Tue.*
♿ 🌐 *www.ncartmuseum.org*

🏢 **UNC Visitor Center**
250 E Franklin St, Chapel Hill.
📞 *(919) 962-1630.* 🕐 *9am–5pm Mon– Fri.* ⚫ *Sat–Sun, public hols.*

Winston-Salem ❷

🏠 *186,000.* ✈ 🚌 ℹ️ *200 Brookstown Ave 27101, (336) 777-3796.*
🌐 *www.visitwinstonsalem.com*

NORTH CAROLINA'S close ties with the tobacco industry are evident in the fact that two major US cigarette brands have been named after this twin city. Moravian immigrants first settled here in 1766. Their descendants celebrate their roots at **Old Salem**, an interesting restoration of a Colonial village, where guides dressed in period costume demonstrate traditional crafts in the church, bakery, tavern, homes, and gardens. They also relate the story of this Protestant sect's journey from Moravia to this region. Gift shops throughout the village offer such Moravian wares as handmade lace and pewter ornaments. The complex is set invitingly on a hill and is compact enough to be covered in an hour or two.

Adjacent to the village is the **Museum of Early Southern Decorative Arts**. Guides take

Actors dressed in period costume, Old Salem Colonial village

A panoramic view of lush vegetation and mountains from the Blue Ridge Parkway

visitors through 24 rooms exhibiting antebellum furnishings and artifacts from across the region. A children's museum is downstairs.

🏛 Old Salem

601 Old Salem Rd. 📞 *(336) 721-7300.* ⏰ *9am–5pm Mon–Sat, 12:30–5pm Sun.* ⬤ *Easter, Thanksgiving, Dec 24–25.* 🎫 ♿ *the museum.*

Blue Ridge Parkway ❸

ℹ️ *(828) 298-0398.*
🌐 *www.nps.gov/blri*

A SCENIC two-lane highway, the Blue Ridge Parkway *(see pp40–41)* runs 469 miles (755 km) south from Virginia along the Blue Ridge Mountain ridge-line. Its most scenic stretches lie in North Carolina, where the road meanders for 250 miles (402 km) past peaks, waterfalls, and the towering, 6,684-ft (2,037-m) Mount Mitchell.

The National Park Service's most popular destination with over 23 million visitors every year, the route has a maximum speed limit of 45 mph (72 km/h), which is strictly enforced. It is most scenic during spring and fall. Some sections close in winter. There are ample opportunities to detour to nearby trails and mountain towns such as Boone and Blowing Rock.

The parkway ends at the entrance to **Great Smoky Mountains National Park**, north of Cherokee *(see p262).* Here, at the reservation of the

Eastern Band of Cherokee Indians, a museum relates the history of the Cherokee people, focusing on the forcible removal of the tribe in 1838 to Oklahoma on the "Trail of Tears." The town of Cherokee itself has a large Indian-run gambling casino.

Asheville ❹

🏙 *69,000.* 🚌 ℹ️ *151 Haywood St, (828) 258-6101.*

P ERCHED ON TOP of a hill, this town's commercial district retains many buildings from its boom years as an early 20th century resort. Downtown Asheville continues to evoke the period of local author, Thomas Wolfe (1900–38), who wrote about his hometown in *Look Homeward Angel.* Today the modest "Dixieland" boardinghouse described in the novel is preserved as the **Thomas Wolfe State Historic Site**.

Biltmore Estate in Asheville, one of the most visited house tours in America

The rest of downtown, said to be among the healthiest in the country, has many health food stores, cafés, bookstores, bluegrass clubs, and music shops, patronized by a non-conformist crowd who still seem to be living in the 1960s.

Asheville is better known for its 250-room, art-studded, **Biltmore Estate** to the south of town. This French Renaissance-style mansion holds a collection of 18th- and 19th-century art and sculpture, and also has the distinction of being the largest residence in America. Beside the main Neo-Classical house, the splendid estate also features a winery, a deluxe inn *(see p274)*, and sprawling gardens designed by Frederick Law Olmsted, who also designed New York's Central Park. Visitors should expect long lines, as the estate attracts huge crowds, making it among the country's most visited house tours, along with the White House and Elvis Presley's "Graceland" *(see p267)*. Whether or not one visits Biltmore, however, Asheville makes a great base for exploring the surrounding mountain region.

🏛 Thomas Wolfe State Historic Site

52 N Market St. 📞 *(828) 253-8304.* ⏰ *9am–5pm Mon–Sat, 1–5pm Sun.* ⬤ *Nov–Mar: Mon.* 🎫 ♿

🏛 Biltmore Estate

Biltmore Ave (Hwy 25). 📞 *(828) 225-1333.* ⏰ *8:30am–5pm daily.* ⬤ *public hols.* 🎫

Cape Hatteras National Seashore, protecting the Outer Banks' northern coast

Outer Banks 5

👥 *32,000.* [i] *1 Visitors Center Rd, Manteo, (800) 446-6262, (252) 473-2138.* [W] www.outerbanks.org

NORTH CAROLINA'S Atlantic coastline is made up of a long chain of narrow barrier islands known as the Outer Banks. Most of the northern coast is protected as part of the **Cape Hatteras National Seashore**, where long stretches of pristine beach, dune, and marsh shelter wild ponies, sea turtles, and many varieties of waterbirds. Offshore, two jet streams that meet in a fury stir up the wild currents, storms, and hurricanes that have earned North Carolina's coast its reputation as "the Graveyard of the Atlantic." The coastline's many historic lighthouses, life-saving stations, and pirate lore are as important a part of the Outer Banks' maritime heritage as is its seafood industry.

Wright Brothers commemorative marker

In the early 20th century, bridges built from the mainland brought in the tourist trade, and now hotels and resort-home developments line the northernmost coast from Corolla all the way to Nags Head. In addition to the sun, surf, and sand, this tourist region offers many historic attractions and family amusements, in the town of **Kill Devil Hills**. The "First in Flight" slogan found on coins and the state's license plates commemorates the Wright Brothers' first historic flight, which took place here. The **Wright Brothers National Memorial** stands at the very site where Orville and Wilbur Wright launched *Flyer*, the first successful experiment in powered flight in 1903. Exhibits here go beyond aviation history to applaud the contributions of dreamers, inventors, and adventurers.

A few minutes drive south at **Jockey Ridge State Park**, hang-gliders participate in a modern version of the Wright Brothers' adventures, while "sandboarders" ride the largest sand dune on the East Coast. "Sandboarding," or running headfirst down the sheer 110-ft (34-m) high sand wall, is a revered local tradition. The dune is also a great spot to watch the sunset. Fewer people venture to the inland side of the island, where a slow kayak ride through the tidal marsh, or a walk through the scenic maritime forest at **Nags Head Woods Preserve**, hold a quieter appeal. Peculiar to barrier islands, these maritime forests, on the rough Atlantic Coast, are lined with banks of sturdy live oaks that protect the lush vegetation from the onslaughts of the water and wind. Follow the signs to the preserve west off Hwy 158 close to the Wright Brothers Memorial.

The drive along the National Seashore is one of the country's most scenic routes, with many opportunities to visit lighthouses and walk along dune and marsh boardwalks. Among the dozens of lighthouses, the 1847 Bodie Island Lighthouse is the only one still in operation. A free ferryride transports cars and passengers between **Hatteras Island** and **Ocracoke Island**. Hatteras's distinctive black-and-white spiral **Cape Hatteras Lighthouse**, built in 1870, is the tallest brick lighthouse in the world at 193 ft (59 m). The scenic village of Ocracoke has a good selection of inns, restaurants, and shops, which makes this remote port an inviting destination for an overnight stay. Visitors can connect with toll mainland ferries (reservations recommended) from here.

🏛 **Wright Brothers National Memorial**
US Hwy 158, milepost 8, Kill Devil Hills. ☎ *(252) 441-7430.* 🕘 *9am–5pm daily.* ● *Dec 25.* 📷 ♿

🌿 **Nags Head Woods Preserve**
701 W Ocean Acres Dr, Kill Devil Hills. ☎ *(252) 441-2525.* 🕘 *dawn–dusk daily.* 📷

🏛 **Cape Hatteras Lighthouse**
Hatteras Is, off Hwy 12, 1 mile (1.6 km) SE of Buxton. ☎ *(252) 995-4474.* 🕘 *9am–5pm daily.* ● *Dec 25.* 📷

☼ **Ocracoke Island**
Ocracoke Car Ferry to Cedar Island or Swan Quarter. ☎ *(800) 293-3779 for fares & schedules (these fluctuate).*

Cape Hatteras Lighthouse, the world's tallest brick lighthouse

The landscaped Elizabethan Gardens on Roanoke Island

Roanoke Island ❻

🛈 *1 Visitors Center Rd, Manteo,
(800) 446-6262, (252) 473-2138.*
Ⓦ *www.outerbanks.org*

A MARSH ISLAND lying between the Outer Banks and the mainland, Roanoke Island was the site of the first English settlement in North America. The first expedition to these shores, sponsored by by Sir Walter Raleigh, was in 1584. In 1587, another ship carrying more than 100 colonists disembarked at the island to create a permanent settlement. But when the next group arrived three years later, all the earlier colonists, including the first English women and children to land in the present-day US, had vanished without a trace. Today, the **Fort Raleigh National Historic Site**, the adjacent **Elizabethan Gardens**, an outdoor drama, and the nearby theme park with a replica of a 16th-century sailing ship as its centerpiece, all relate the mysterious story of this legendary "Lost Colony."

At the northern tip of the island, Fort Raleigh preserves the ruins of the colony's original disembarkation point, and ranger-led tours reveal what little is known about it. The Elizabethan Gardens are ideal for a walk through landscaped paths and lawns. A short drive south, at the port of Manteo, the **Roanoke Island Festival Park** tells the story of the first ship of explorers through tours aboard a re-creation of the *Elizabeth II*, with costumed guides. There is also a museum that relates both the Native and European history of the region.

⛩ Fort Raleigh National Historic Site
US Hwy 64/264, Manteo. 🅲 *(252) 473-5772.* ◗ *9am–5pm daily.*
● *Dec 25.* 🖼 *Elizabethan Gardens only.* Ⓦ *www.nps.gov/fora*

⛩ Roanoke Island Festival Park
Port of Manteo. 🅲 *(252) 475-1506.*
◗ *10am–4pm or 6pm daily (seasonal, call & check).* ● *Jan 1, Thanksgiving, Dec 24–25.* 🖼 ♿

Beaufort ❼

🏘 *4,000.* 🛈 *(252) 726-8148
(Morehead City).*

B EAUFORT'S considerable charms lie in its historic B&B inns, seafood markets, and restaurants. The highlight of this coastal resort's small attractive waterfront is the **North Carolina Maritime Museum**, which interprets the boating, fishing, and pirate history of this coastline. A swashbuckling robot of Edward "Blackbeard" Teach, a notorious pirate who was captured and killed off the Outer Banks in November of 1718, welcomes visitors in the shell room. A popular event is the family-oriented, educational Pirate Day, which is dedicated to pirate lore and has costumes, flag flying, and treasure hunts. Other activities include boat-building and net-making classes, kayaking excursions, and other events. At the docks, private ferries take passengers out to the deserted sands of Lookout Island, preserved from development as the **Cape Lookout National Seashore**. The ecology of Lookout Island is similar to Cape Hatteras, with virgin beaches, marshland, and dunes, all rich in birdlife, but the limited access makes it more remote and less visited. The town at the island's northern tip was abandoned by its last two residents in the 1970s.

🏛 North Carolina Maritime Museum
315 Front St. 🅲 *(252) 728-7317.*
◗ *9am–5pm Mon–Fri, 10am–5pm Sat, 1–5pm Sun.* ● *Jan 1, Thanksgiving, Dec 25.* ♿ Ⓦ *www.ah.dcr. state.nc.us/ sections/ maritime/*

🚢 Cape Lookout National Seashore
3601 Bridge St, Morehead City.
🅲 *(252) 728-2250.*
Ⓦ *www.hikercentral.com/parks/calo*

The waterfront at Salt Marsh and Newport River, Beaufort

South Carolina

AFTER SEPARATING FROM ITS SIBLING North Carolina in 1729, the South Carolina colony spread Upcountry, where Welsh, Irish, and Scottish immigrants established small owner-operated farms, in sharp contrast to the Low-country gentry. By the 1860s, however, the differences between the two had subsided and a unified South Carolina became the first Southern state to declare independence from the Union. Soon after, the first shot of the American Civil War was fired at Fort Sumter. Today, the state's "glory days" of resistance and revolution are re-created at plantations, museums, and monuments. Many visitors, however, head straight for the miles of beaches.

Charleston ❽

🏃 *100,000.* ✈ 🚉 🚌 ℹ *375 Meeting St, (843) 853-8000.* ☞ *Spoleto Festival (late May–early Jun).* Ⓦ *www.charlestoncvb.com/*

ONE OF THE SOUTH'S most beautiful cities and South Carolina's first capital, Charleston is situated on the tip of a peninsula between the Ashley and Cooper Rivers. Named after King Charles II of England, the city was founded in 1670 and soon became a wealthy colony of tobacco, rice, and indigo plantations. The first shot of the Civil War was fired just off the city's harbor, where people gathered to watch the Confederate seige of Fort Sumter. Today, Charleston retains much of its original period architecture and is a popular destination for antebellum house-and-garden tours, horse-and-carriage rides, fine Southern cuisine, and plantation retreats.

The charming 1772 Heyward-Washington House

🏛 Charleston Historic District

Edmondston-Alston House 21 E Battery. 📞 *(843) 722-7171.* ☐ *10am–4:30pm Tue–Sat, 1:30–4:30pm Sun–Mon.* ● *Thanksg., Dec 25.* 🏷
Gibbs Museum of Art 135 Meeting St. 📞 *(843) 722-2706.* ☐ *10am–5pm Tue–Sat, 1–5pm Sun.* 🏷 ♿
The historic district's beautifully preserved architecture evokes the city's Colonial and early American past. The civic and religious buildings here range from styles as varied as Colonial and Georgian, Greek and Gothic Revival, to Italianate and Victorian. Among the highlights are distinctive Charlestonian residences, set perpendicular to the street with grand piazzas running along their lengths. The only high structures are the towering church steeples. Horse-and-carriage rides through tree-lined streets provide a graceful overview.

A trip south from Old City Market to the Battery takes in many highlights along Church Street, including the old magazine, the Gothic French Huguenot Church, and the **Heyward-Washington House**. This 1772 house was built by rice planter Daniel Heyward as a town house for his son and has a splendid collection of Charleston-made furniture. A half-block detour to the east on Chalmers leads to the old slave market, once one of the busiest in the American colonies. At the Battery, the **Edmondston-Alston House** features two floors of an opulent 1825 mansion overlooking the harbor. White Point Gardens Park lies to the south, while in the north, Waterfront Park, with its walk-through fountain, stands across from the popular restaurant row. Visitors can explore the cobblestone alleyways in search of hidden gardens, gargoyles, and harbor views.

To the west of Waterfront Park, the **Gibbs Museum of Art** reveals local history through landscape paintings and portraits of famous South Carolinians from the 18th century to the present day.

⚓ South Carolina Aquarium

100 Aquarium Wharf. 📞 *(843) 577-3474.* ☐ *9am–5pm Mon–Sat, noon–5pm Sun.* ● *public hols.* 🏷 ♿
Picturesquely set overlooking the harbor, Charleston's newest attraction provides an excellent introduction to the indigenous creatures found within the state's aquatic habitats. These range from Appalachian rivers and blackwater swamps, to salt marshes and coral reefs. An IMAX® Theater lies adjacent.

🏛 Fort Sumter Visitor Center

340 Concord St. 📞 *(843) 883-3123.* ☐ *8:30am–5:30pm daily.* ● *Jan 1, Dec 25.* 🏷 *boat tours* .♿
An embarkation point for boat tours to Fort Sumter, the visitor center relates the story of the American Civil War's first battle. The fort, which stands

Civil War cannon lying preserved at Fort Sumter

on an island at the entrance to Charleston harbor, was controlled by Union troops. In April 1861, the Confederate army besieged the fort. When Union troops tried to bring in supplies, the Confederates, who had occupied nearby Fort Johnson, unleashed a 34-hour bombardment. Union forces finally surrendered on April 14, 1861, and the fort remained under Confederate control until 1865. Ironically, General Beauregard, the Confederate leader, was a student of the defending Union commander, Major Robert Anderson, at the US Military Academy at West Point, New York *(see p91)*. Fort Sumter has been preserved unchanged since the end of the war. It is a National Monument and has long been a symbol of Southern independence and pride.

Flowers in bloom at Audubon Swamp Gardens, Magnolia Plantation

🏛 Charleston Museum

360 Meeting St. 📞 *(843) 722-2996.* 🕐 *9am–5pm Mon–Sat, 1–5pm Sun.* ⬤ *public hols.* ♿ 🅦 *www.charlestonmuseum.org*

This museum presents a comprehensive overview of the city's history from pre-Colonial days. Its most distinctive exhibits are in the Native American and Natural History galleries; the former has dug-out canoes and costumed mannequins, and the latter has a number of mounted skeletons of prehistoric animals such as the Cretaceous dinosaur *Thescelosaurus neglectus*.

🏛 Ashley River Plantations

Middleton Place 🚩 550 Ashley River Rd. 📞 *(843) 556-6020.* 🕐 *9am–5pm daily.* ⬤ *Dec 25.* 📷 **Drayton Hall** 3380 Ashley River Rd. 📞 *(843) 769-2600.* 🕐 *9:30am–3pm or 4pm (seasonal).* ⬤ *Jan 1, 1st week Feb, Thanksgiving, Dec 24–25, Dec 31.* 📷 **Magnolia Plantation** Rte 4/Hwy 61. 📞 *(843) 571-1266.* 🕐 *8am–5:30pm daily.* 📷

Within a short drive upriver, three house tours provide a glimpse of Charleston-style country living. Of them, the grandest is **Middleton Place**, with its 1755 mansion located on a bluff overlooking America's oldest landscaped gardens. Closeby, **Drayton Hall** is one of the country's finest examples of Colonial architecture. Built in 1738, the Georgian Palladian mansion has been preserved in its original condition without electricity or plumbing. A daily program on African-American heritage is held here.

Magnolia Plantation has a more modest house, with a petting zoo and a motorized train ride around the property. Prized attractions are the acres of riverfront formal gardens with charming pathways that lead through a profusion of flowers, and **Audubon Swamp Gardens**, a lush tupelo-and-cypress sanctuary.

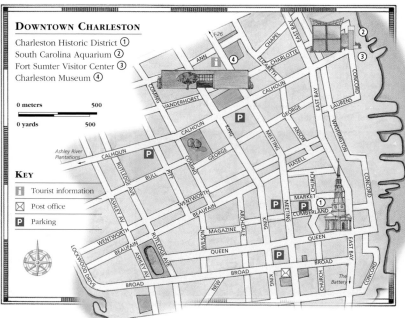

DOWNTOWN CHARLESTON

Charleston Historic District ①
South Carolina Aquarium ②
Fort Sumter Visitor Center ③
Charleston Museum ④

0 meters   500

0 yards   500

Ashley River Plantations

KEY

ℹ Tourist information

✉ Post office

🅿 Parking

Columbia ❾

🏛 *116,000.* 🚆 🚌 **ℹ** *900
Assembly St, (803) 545-0000.*

SITUATED AT THE fall line of
the Congaree River – the
area that marked the limit of
inland navigation – this city
was declared the state capital
over Charleston in 1786.
Although General William T.
Sherman destroyed most of
Columbia during the Civil
War, the **State House** managed to survive intact. Today,
six bronze stars mark the
spots where Union cannon-
balls hit the 1855 copper-
domed building, located in
the center of the quiet downtown on Gervais Street.

On the banks of the river,
the **South Carolina State
Museum** is housed in an
artfully recycled textile mill
built in 1894. Informative
exhibits on the state's natural,
cultural, and industrial history
are displayed on three spacious floors. The adjacent
**South Carolina Confederate
Relic Room and Museum**
maintains a huge collection of
artifacts that trace the military
history of South Carolina's
participation in US wars from
the Civil War onward, as well
as an exhibit on the history
and sometimes controversial
meanings of the Confederate
flag. While Southern tradi-
tionalists proclaim the flag
a symbol of regional pride,
many others see it as a
symbol of white supremacy
that should be abolished.

A 20-minute drive south of
town, the **Congaree Swamp
National Monument** offers

A view of the Grand Strand on Myrtle Beach

visitors a close-up look of the
biodiversity found within a
cypress swamp ecosystem.
The swamp is at its best from
late fall to early spring.

🏛 South Carolina State Museum
301 Gervais St. **ℂ** *(803) 898-4921.*
⬜ *10am–5pm Tue–Sat, 1–5pm Sun.*
● *Mon, Easter, Thanksg., Dec 25.*
🅿 ♿ **ⓦ** www.museum.state.sc.us/

🏛 South Carolina Confederate Relic Room & Museum
301 Gervais St. **ℂ** *(803) 898-8095.*
⬜ *10am–5pm Tue–Sat.* ● *Sun–
Mon, public hols.* ♿

Myrtle Beach ❿

🏛 *23,000.* 🚆 🚌 **ℹ** *1200 N Oak
St, (843) 626-7444.*

THIS POPULAR BEACH is the
center of the "Grand
Strand," a long sweep of the
Atlantic coastline south of the
North Carolina border, which
is dominated by hotels, golf
courses, amusement parks,
and arcades. Its heyday was
in the 1950s, when as a
Spring Break destination,
college students from many

cold northeastern campuses
descended on this beach
town for a weeklong party.
"The Shag," South Carolina's
official state dance, was
invented here and caused a
craze all over the country.
The elite crowd vacations at
exclusive resort communities,
but everyone ventures to the
nearby fishing village of
Murrell's Inlet for seafood.

South of Myrtle Beach two
attractions make a worthwhile
detour. On the inland side of
the coastal Hwy 17, 16 miles
(26 km) south of the beach,
is **Brookgreen Gardens**,
landscaped around 550 works
of statuary by 250 artists. On
the ocean side, **Huntington
Beach State Park** offers
access to an undeveloped
beach and saltmarsh boardwalk, as well as an art studio
that once belonged to Anna
Huntington, the sculptor who
created Brookgreen Gardens
in the 1930s.

🌿 Brookgreen Gardens
US Hwy 17. **ℂ** *(843) 235-6000.*
⬜ *9:30am–5pm daily.* ● *mid-
Nov–Mar: Mon; Dec 25.* 🅿 ♿

Georgetown ⓫

🏛 *10,000.* 🚌 **ℹ** *1001 Front St,
(843) 546-8436.*

SET ALONG THE banks of the
Sampit River, Georgetown
was the center of the state's
lucrative rice trade, producing
almost half the rice grown in
the US in the 1840s. Downtown's **Rice Museum**, housed
in the 1842 Old Market building, explains how the rice
industry influenced almost
every facet of life here. The
museum's new maritime

Civil War arms on display at the South Carolina State Museum, Columbia

gallery features examples of historic local watercraft. The museum leads out to a waterfront park where a wooden boardwalk makes an attractive marsh-side promenade.

The commercial district is reminiscent of a Southern small town in the early-to-mid-1900s, a quiet contrast to the Grand Strand or the bustle of Charleston. About 15 miles (24 km) south of Georgetown, **Hampton Plantation State Park** is an unfurnished 1750 Georgian house undergoing restoration. Visitors can get an inside look at the preservation process through several cutaway displays that reveal the "before, during, and after" stages of restoration.

🏛 **Rice Museum**
Front & Screven Sts. 📞 *(843) 546-7423.* 🕐 *10am–4:30pm Mon–Sat.* ● *public hols.* 📷 ♿
🌐 *www.ricemuseum.com*

Hampton Plantation State Park, Georgetown

🦆 **Hampton Plantation State Park**
US Hwy 17. 📞 *(843) 546-9361.* 🕐 *Memorial Day–Labor Day: 9am–6pm daily (grounds), 11am–4pm daily (house); Labor Day–Memorial Day: 9am–6pm Thu–Mon (grounds), 1–4pm Thu–Mon (house).* 📷 *house.*

Coastal Islands ⑫

ℹ️ *Hilton Head Island Chamber of Commerce, William Hilton Pkwy (Hwy 278), (843) 785-3673.*

E XTENDING FROM Georgetown south to beyond Savannah in Georgia, the remote islands of the Lowcountry are a lush, semi-tropical region with a compelling natural and

cultural history. The shifting sand dunes, dense maritime forests of live oak draped with Spanish moss and muscadine vines, and numerous lagoons and marshes harbor an exotic mix of wildlife including sea turtles, bobcats, alligators, ospreys, and dolphins.

The area's unique African-American history evolved around the common heritage of slaves, brought here from the rice-growing regions of West Africa, to cultivate this crop along the tidal creeks. Isolated on these islands, the Lowcountry Africans were able to perpetuate their cultural traditions over the generations. Today, their "Gullah" heritage remains distinct in the local language, music, cuisine, and folkways.

To the east of Beaufort, two islands preserve the natural and cultural history. Both are accessible by car via Hwy 21, which offers a panoramic view of the Port Royal Sound marsh landscape.

On St. Helena Island, the renowned **Penn Center** is a touchstone of Gullah culture. A former institute established in 1862 by Pennsylvanian abolitionists during the Civil War, the center has a distinguished history from the Civil Rights era. National leaders such as Martin Luther King and groups such as the Southern Christian Leadership Conference met here to advance the Civil Rights Movement. A modest museum located in the old schoolhouse relates numerous events from the center's past through photographs and

other displays. The center also sponsors storytelling programs and an annual festival that celebrates Gullah culture.

Beyond St. Helena, **Hunting Island State Park** on Hunting Island preserves a natural barrier island environment. Its highlights include a pleasant, uncrowded beach, a coastside campground, and a 19th-century lighthouse.

Hilton Head Island, named after the English sea captain William Hilton who explored the island in 1664, is South Carolina's premier beach resort. It is dominated by several deluxe resort complexes, including the Westin Resort, Hyatt Regency, Crowne Plaza, Disney, and of course, the Hilton, providing golf, tennis, and spa facilities. Among the other recreational opportunities are horseback riding, fishing, boating, sailing, and a variety of other water sports.

🏛 **Penn Center**
Martin Luther King Dr, St. Helena. 📞 *(843) 838-2432.* 🕐 *11am–4pm Mon–Sat.* ● *public hols.* 📷 ♿
🦆 **Hunting Island State Park**
Hwy 21. 📞 *(843) 838-2011.* 🕐 *Apr–Oct: 6am–9pm daily; Nov–Mar: 6am–6pm daily.* 📷

Canoeing at the Hilton Head Island Resort, Coastal Islands

A view of the Port Royal Sound marshland at dusk, Coastal Islands

Georgia

THE LAST OF THE 13 original colonies, Georgia was founded by a British general, James Oglethorpe, to stop Spanish expansion up from Florida. While the state initially banned slavery, economic pressures from competing slaveholding colonies led to its introduction. As a result, it grew wealthy from slave labor on rice, indigo, and cotton plantations. Georgia was devastated during the Civil War, when General Sherman's "March to the Sea" set ablaze a swath of land across the state. Led by pragmatic Atlanta *(see pp260–61)*, Georgia was able to overcome the many hardships of its troubled past, and was well positioned to benefit from the economic boom in the late 20th century.

A colorful Halloween display on River Street, Savannah

Savannah ⑬

🏙 251,000. ✈ 🚂 🚌 🛈 *Martin Luther King Jr. Blvd, (912) 944-0460.*

LABELED THE "most beautiful city in America" by the Paris newspaper *Le Monde*, the lushly landscaped parks and gracious homes of Savannah have earned it a reputation for scenic beauty and sophistication. It was established in 1733 on the banks of the Savannah River, 16 miles (26 km) from the Atlantic Ocean. Its founder, James Oglethorpe, laid out a town grid dotted with small squares designed to deter invaders. Today, even after the turmoil of the Revolution and Civil War, his design remains intact, with the squares now serving as scenic parks filled with statues and fountains. The city has one of the largest, and perhaps most beautiful, urban historic districts in the US, which now thrives as the city's downtown

commercial center. Horse-and-carriage tours provide an introduction to historic Savannah, though walking around is the best way to explore the area.

River Street is one of the city's central entertainment districts, lined with seafood restaurants, raucous taverns, and souvenir shops housed in old warehouses constructed of ballast-stones. Water taxis shuttle passengers to the modern Convention Center across the river on Hutchinson Island. Uphill, **Factors Walk** is a stately promenade on top of the bluff. A few blocks in from the river, **City Market** is another lively arts and entertainment district, housed in historic buildings.

Historic house museums throughout Savannah shed light on the city's history, architecture, and culture. Many homes and religious centers are open to tours year-round. Of these, the **Davenport House** on Columbia Square is considered one of the country's finest examples of Federal-style architecture, while nearby, the **Owens-Thomas**

House on Oglethorpe Square is among the finest Regency buildings, built by English architect William Jay in 1816. Other houses can be seen on the popular **Tour of Homes and Gardens**, which is held each spring.

A handful of museums also highlight different aspects of the city's history. The **Telfair Academy of Arts**, at the center of the historic district, displays a fine collection of Impressionist paintings and decorative arts within an 1818 Regency-style mansion. At the western edge of the district, the **Ships of the Sea Maritime Museum** holds ship models of all shapes and sizes within the palatial 1819 Scarborough House. Located just beyond the historic district, the **Ralph Mark Gilbert Civil Rights Museum** has exhibits relating to the city's history. In-depth African-American heritage tours also start at the museum.

Many more attractions await in the surrounding Low-country – the marsh-laden coastal region of Georgia and South Carolina *(see p255)*. A drive out on Hwy 80, east of the **Tybee Island** beach resort (18 miles/29 km east of downtown), passes the **Bonaventure Cemetery**, where singer Johnny Mercer and writer Conrad Aitken are buried. Also located en route is the behemoth brick **Fort Pulaski National Monument**, which rises like a medieval fortress from the vast expanses of cordgrass at the mouth of the Savannah River.

🏛 **Davenport House**
324 E State St. 📞 *(912) 236-8097.* 🕙 *10am–4pm daily.* ⬤ *Jan 1, Mar 17, Jul 4, Thanksgiving, Dec 25.* 📷

Fort Pulaski National Monument, Savannah

Jekyll Island Club Hotel, one of many historic buildings on the Golden Isles

Golden Isles ⑭

68,000 (Glynn County).
4 Glynn Ave, (912) 265-0620.

THE SPANISH called the barrier islands off Georgia's southern coast "the Golden Isles" – possibly after lost treasure or the golden hue of the marshlands in fall – a term that tourism promoters were happy to revive. While they are primarily beach resorts, the islands retain a number of historic sights.

Fort Frederica National Monument, located on St. Simons, along a scenic stretch of the Frederica River that lies adjacent to Christchurch, holds the ruins of a fortified village built by James Oglethorpe in 1736. Another significant site is the marsh off Demere Road, south of Fort Frederica, where the Battle of Bloody Marsh was fought in 1742. This decisive battle between English and Spanish forces determined which Colonial power would control this part of the American continent. Near the island's southern tip, Neptune Park in downtown St. Simons has the historic 1872 **St. Simons Lighthouse**, where visitors can climb to the top. Lying across Bloody Marsh from St. Simons, Sea Island is home to the luxurious Cloister Hotel.

At the turn of the 20th century, **Jekyll Island** was the exclusive preserve of the nation's premier industrialists, such as the Vanderbilts, Goodyears, and Rockefellers. With the advent of World War

II, however, this vulnerable coastal island was deemed unsafe and the families moved elsewhere. Today, the island's historic district comprises the "cottages," as the millionaires' mansions were known, and the elegant Jekyll Island Club. The cottages have been restored and are now open as museums or inns. Among these are the 1892 Indian Mound Cottage, which passed into the hands of William Rockefeller in 1904, and Crane Cottage, which is now part of the **Jekyll Island Club Hotel** (see p276) and features a fine restaurant. Other highlights are a former stable, now a small museum, and Faith Chapel, with its Tiffany windows.

The historic Jekyll River Wharf, next to the Jekyll Island Club Hotel, has a popular seafood restaurant serving raw seafood, mainly fresh oysters. On the ocean side, a selection of franchise motels and restaurants offer family lodging and dining. There is also a campground located at the island's northern tip near "Boneyard Beach," where sun-bleached driftwood gives the beach its name.

St. Simons Lighthouse

🔲 **Fort Frederica National Monument**
Frederica Rd, St. Simons Island.
📞 (912) 638-3639. 🕐 8am–5pm.
● Dec 25. 🎫 ♿

Okefenokee Swamp National Wildlife Refuge ⑮

Hwy 121, Folkston. 🚌 ℹ️ (912) 496-7836. 🕐 sunrise–5:30pm (7:30pm in summer). ● Dec 25. 🎫 ♿ exhibits.

IN THE REMOTE southeastern corner of the state, the Okefenokee Swamp is an exotic, primeval landscape of blackwater and cypress that harbors alligators, softshell turtles, otters, and all kinds of birdlife. The Seminole Indian name "Okefenokee," loosely translated as "trembling earth," characterizes the peat moss hammocks that bubble up from the water as a natural part of swamp ecology. Boat tours provide a close-up view at three sections of the swamp, including the **Okefenokee Swamp Park** near Waycross, and the wildlife refuge headquarters at **Folkston**, which provides details about overnight paddling trips into the swamp. Fargo, near the swamp's western entrance, is the nearest town to the **Stephen C. Foster State Park**, 18 miles (29 km) to the northeast. This section is perched on a peninsula in the deep recesses of the swamp. Camping facilities and cabins are available here.

🔲 **Okefenokee Swamp Park**
Hwy 177, Waycross. 📞 (912) 283-0583. 🕐 9am–5:30pm daily. ●
Thanksg., Dec 25. 🎫 ♿ exhibits only.

Suwanee Canal Recreation Area, Okefenokee Swamp Refuge

Americus 16

🏛 18,000. 🚇 🛈 Windsor Hotel Visitor Center, 123 W Lamar St, (229) 928-6059.

OFF THE BEATEN track in south Georgia, the tidy county seat of Americus lies in a region of diverse attractions. The **Habitat for Humanity**, a worldwide organization offering "self-build" housing for the poor, has its headquarters downtown. In late 2003 the Habitat will open its new Global Village which will include an international marketplace and up to 40 examples of habitat homes built around the world, including Papua New Guinea, Botswana, Ghana, and others.

Located 10 miles (16 km) north of town, Andersonville is the **National Prisoner of War (POW) Museum**. This marks a spot that was a notorious prisoner-of-war camp during the Civil War, which later became a veterans' cemetery. Almost 13,000 of the camp's inmates died from the terrible living conditions. Housed in a structure built to resemble a concentration camp, the museum's disturbing exhibits commemorate American POWs in conflicts from the Civil War through Vietnam to the Gulf and Iraqi Wars.

The local high school in Plains, 10 miles (16 km) west of Americus, is part of the **Jimmy Carter National Historic Site**. It was here that a teacher predicted that her student would become president. Carter proved her right,

Headstones at the Andersonville cemetery near Americus

and the school is now dedicated to the life of the Plains-area peanut farmer's son who became the 39th president in 1976, in the wake of Nixon's resignation *(see p209)*. The former president, recipient of the Nobel Peace Prize in 2002, lives here and teaches Sunday school at the Maranatha Baptist Church when he is in town. An excursion train runs from Cordele in the east through Plains up to Carter's boyhood farm in Archery.

🏛 **Habitat for Humanity**
121 Habitat St at W Lamar St. 📞 (229) 924-6935. ◯ 8am–3pm Mon–Fri, 10am–1pm Sat. ● Sun. 📷 ♿

Macon 17

🏛 107,000. 🚇 🛈 200 Cherry St, (478) 743-3401.

FOUNDED ON THE south bank of the Ocmulgee River in 1823, Mason was laid out in a grid of avenues, which still exist in its historic district downtown. Uphill from here is one of the city's highlights, the Intown Historic District. This area has some of the city's most beautiful homes, a few of which are open to the public. The 1855 **Hay House Museum**, built in the Italian Renaissance style, features period characteristics such as trompe l'oeil marble, a ballroom, and hidden passages. The 1842 House Inn is also located here. Guided architectural tours begin at the visitor center.

The city also has a vibrant musical history and was home to such greats as Little Richard, Otis Redding, and the Allman Brothers. The **Georgia Music Hall of Fame**, located in the historic district, provides an overview of the state's contribution to rhythm-and-blues, rock 'n' roll, gospel, country, and other genres. The nearby **Sports Hall of Fame** celebrates Georgia's athletes, such as Hank Aaron and Ty Cobb. Across the river from downtown, the **Ocmulgee National Monument** marks

Exterior of the Italianate Hay House Museum, Macon

a historic mound complex built around 1100 as the capital of the Creek Confederacy.

🏛 **Hay House Museum**
934 Georgia Ave. 📞 (478) 742-8155. ◯ 10am–4:30pm Mon–Sat, 1–4:30pm Sun. ● public hols. 📷

Athens 18

🏛 80,000. 🚇 🛈 280 E Dougherty St, (706) 353-1820.

HOME TO THE **University of Georgia** (UGA), Athens is well known as the state's intellectual and literary center. It has also gained repute as the originator of alternative music. Local bands such as REM, the B-52s, and Widespread Panic have made it big, and the 40-Watt Club on West Washington Street and the annual Athfest in June continue the tradition.

The city is largely deserted in summer, while in fall it overflows with Georgia Bulldog fans for the home football games. The visitor center provides details about

UGA bulldog mascot

house and garden tours, such as the 1856 structure that now houses the Lyndon House Arts Center and the Founders Memorial Garden in North Campus. The university visitor center directs guests to the art museum, with its 19th- and 20th-century paintings and sculpture, and gives details about sports events and performances on campus.

View from the Amicalola Falls, Amicalola State Park

Dahlonega ⑲

ℹ️ *13 S Park St, (706) 864-3711.*

THE LEGENDARY Blue Ridge Mountain range extends across the state's northeastern corner. With its abundant waterfalls and flowering forests, the region is well known for its cultural heritage of outstanding folk arts such as quilt-making, woodworking, and bluegrass music. The discovery of gold in the main town of Dahlonega in 1828 precipitated the nation's first gold rush, two decades before California's famous "Forty-Niners." The state's **Gold Museum**, housed in the 1836 courthouse in the center of Dahlonega's attractive town square, displays mining equipment, nuggets, and mining lore. The town also offers gold-panning and gold-mine tours as well as a complete set of coins minted in the US Mint that operated here from 1838 to 1861.

🏛 Gold Museum

1 Public Square. 📞 *(706) 864-2257.* 🕐 *9am–5pm Mon–Sat, 10am–5pm Sun.* ⬤ *Jan 1, Thanksgiving, Dec 25.* ♿ ⬤

ENVIRONS: About 18 miles (29 km) from Dahlonega, the **Amicalola Falls State Park** is the gateway to the southern terminus of the 2,144-mile (3,450-km) Appalachian Trail, a hiking route that leads from the top of Springer Mountain in Georgia all the way north to Mount Katahdin, deep in Maine. Less ambitious hikers can head to the park's new Len Foote Hike Inn, which offers ecologically sensitive, comfortably rustic overnight accommodations. The park also features a mountain-top lodge, restaurant, campground, and the Amicalola Falls. East of Dahlonega, along Hwy 441 at the Georgia–South Carolina border, the federally designated "Wild and Scenic" Chatooga River is considered one of the most daring rivers to navigate in eastern US. The book and the film *Deliverance* were based on this region (though the locals don't appreciate being reminded of this notoriety). Visible from high above the river, the Tallulah Gorge features a suspension bridge.

🏕 Amicalola Falls State Park & Lodge

Hwy 52. 📞 *(706) 265-8888.* 🕐 *8am–10pm daily.* ⬤ *Jan 1, Thanksgiving, Dec 25.* ♿ ⬤

Stone Mountain Park ⑳

US Hwy 78. ℹ️ *(770) 498-5600.* 🕐 *6am–midnight (hours vary so call ahead).* ⬤ *Dec 24–25.* ♿ *partial.* 🌐 *www.stonemountainpark.com*

THE CENTERPIECE of this popular park, located about a 30-minute drive east of downtown Atlanta, is a bas-relief carved into the side of a massive granite mountain. The sculpture depicts three Confederate heroes – Jefferson Davis, president of the Confederacy, and generals Robert E. Lee and Stonewall Jackson. Its creator, Gutzon Borglum, began work here in 1924 and later sculpted the faces of four American presidents at Mount Rushmore *(see p447).*

A sky-lift takes visitors up to the summit, and the walk down affords a close-up view of the unusual "monadnock" habitat – it harbors many species of plants that are more commonly associated with the desert than the humid Southeast. The huge lawn, lying between the granite wall and Stone Mountain Park Inn, is the location of various events such as the summer laser light shows and the annual Fourth of July fireworks. Other attractions include an antebellum village, an ice rink, and paddlewheel riverboat rides around the lake. A number of lodging and dining options are also available here.

The centerpiece bas-relief sculpture at Stone Mountain Park

Atlanta ㉑

🏛 400,000. ✈ 🚃 🚌 ℹ️ *Underground Atlanta, (404) 521-6600.*
🌐 www.atlanta.net

Founded as a terminus for two railroad routes in 1837, Atlanta's importance as a transportation hub made it a Union target during the Civil War. After a 75-day siege, General William T. Sherman broke the Confederate defenses and set most of the town ablaze, a history recounted romantically in Margaret Mitchell's *Gone With the Wind*. Today, the city claims to be the "Capital of the New South" and has since been considered more brash and faster paced than its Southern neighbors.

Exploring Atlanta

This cosmopolitan city is home to many industrial giants including Coca-Cola. Its entrepreneurial spirit led to an economic boom that lasted two decades, capped by a successful bid to host the Olympics in 1996. One of the city's landmarks, the **Centennial Olympic Park** downtown, commemorates this event. Yet another is **Turner Field**, where the former boxer Muhammad Ali famously lit the Olympic torch in the stadium. Downtown's attractions, Underground Atlanta, World of Coca-Cola, and the Martin Luther King Jr. Historic Site, are all within a mile of these Olympic landmarks. A short Metro ride north leads to the city's exceptional High Museum in midtown. East of midtown lie the residential neighborhoods of Virginia Highlands and Little Five Points, with their superb specialty restaurants.

🏛 World of Coca-Cola

55 Martin Luther King Jr. Blvd SW.
📞 (404) 676-5151. 🕐 9am–5pm Mon–Sat, noon–6pm Sun. 🈺 ♿
The World of Coca-Cola redefines the factory tour with three floors of dazzling print ads and TV commercials, covering the history of this international beverage company, launched in the 1880s. The admission fee includes all the free Coke one can drink.

The Centennial Olympic Park in downtown Atlanta

🚇 Underground Atlanta

Alabama St at Peachtree. 📞 (404) 523-2311. 🕐 10am–9pm Mon–Sat, noon–6pm Sun. ♿
In the heart of downtown across from the Five Points light railway station, Underground Atlanta is made up of the subterranean streets that were encased under bridges built to bypass the rail yards. Abandoned for decades, the hidden town was reinvented in the 1970s as an underground shopping mall, topped with an above-ground visitor center.

🚇 CNN Studio

Marietta St at Techwood Dr. 📞 (404) 827-2300.
🕐 9am–5pm daily. 🈺
♿ with advance notice.
A 45-minute guided tour of CNN Studio takes visitors through the inner workings of the world's first 24-hour news station, located in a 14-story atrium hotel building. Book in advance for the tour. The lobby gift shop sells merchandise ranging from Atlanta Braves paraphernalia to videos of Desert Storm coverage.

🚇 Martin Luther King Jr. National Historic Site

450 Auburn Ave. 📞 (404) 331-5190.
🕐 9am–5pm or 6pm. ⬤ Dec 25. ♿
Situated in a long reflecting pool beside an eternal flame, the crypt of the Nobel Peace Prize-winner Dr. Martin Luther King Jr. is a pilgrimage site for people from all over the world. The pool lies within the complex of the Center for Nonviolent Social Change, which has a gallery displaying portraits and memorabilia. Also located nearby is the original Ebenezer Baptist Church, where Martin Luther King Jr, his father, and grandfather presided. The Martin Luther King birthplace is down the street to the east, while the National Park Service Visitor Center, housing portraits and exhibits that relate the area's role in the Civil Rights Movement, is right across the street.

This district preserves the heart of the **Sweet Auburn** neighborhood, which was the center of African-American life in the early 1900s.

🏛 Margaret Mitchell House and Museum

990 Peachtree St. 📞 (404) 249-7015. 🕐 9:30am–5pm daily. ⬤ Jan 1, Thanksgiving, Dec 24–25. 🈺 ♿

Margaret Mitchell

Margaret Mitchell (1900–1949) wrote her magnum opus *Gone With the Wind* here in a basement apartment she affectionately called "the Dump." The three-story Tudor Revival house has had a dramatic history. It was abandoned, threatened by urban renewal, and then torched several times by

The reflecting pool, eternal flame, and crypt of Dr. Martin Luther King Jr

High Museum, the art museum of Atlanta

century Asian ceramics and sub-Saharan artifacts. Among the museum's packed calendar of events are blockbuster traveling exhibits, art films, make-art events, and lectures. A satellite gallery located in downtown Atlanta, at Peachtree and John Wesley Dobbs Avenue, is devoted to folk art and photography.

arsonists, once on the eve of the Olympics opening. Various exhibits tell the story of the Georgia-born writer and reveal the extent of house's restoration. Mementos from the famous film, such as Scarlett O'Hara's bonnet, are also on display.

🏛 High Museum

1280 Peachtree St NE. ☎ (404) 733-4444. ◻ 10am–5pm Tue–Sat, noon–5pm Sun. ⬤ public hols. 🖼 ♿

One of the country's best museums, the High Museum lies in the city's premier arts district and is housed behind a colorful Alexander Calder sculpture in a strikingly modern Richard Meier structure. Its extensive permanent collection careens from regional folk art and 19th-century American art to 18th-

🏛 Atlanta History Center

130 W Paces Ferry Rd. ☎ (404) 814-4000. ◻ 10am–5:30pm Mon–Sat, noon–5:30pm Sun. 🖼 ♿

The center contains a museum and two historic houses. The museum is built in the style of a massive railroad depot. Exhibits such as **Fact or Myth?** shed light on antebellum life and the city's African-American community.

Contrasting examples of rural and urban life are presented in the two houses. The Tullie Smith Farm, with its livestock and traditional crafts demonstrations, is a typical mid-1800s farmhouse, while the elegant 1928 Swan House has a grand interior staircase and swan motifs throughout.

🏛 Fernbank Natural History Museum

767 Clifton Rd NE. ☎ (404) 370-0960. ◻ 10am–5pm Mon–Sat, noon–5pm Sun. ⬤ Thanksg., Dec 25. 🖼 ♿

This museum is housed in a striking modern building centered around a skylit four-story atrium. It has natural history exhibits ranging from plate tectonics to bubble science. Of local interest is its coverage of Georgia's diverse ecosystems, including the Appalachian forest, the coastal plain, and a particular favorite, the exotic Okefenokee Swamp habitat (see p257). The museum's IMAX® Theater features frequent "IMAX® and Martinis" nights, and there is also an on-site café. A number of in-town nature trails weave through the forest outside.

🏛 Jimmy Carter Library & Museum

441 Freedom Pkwy. ☎ (404) 331-3942. ◻ 9am–4:45pm Mon–Sat, noon–4:45pm Sun. ⬤ Jan 1, Thanksgiving, Dec 25. 🖼 ♿ ▢

Located on a lushly landscaped hilltop site, the library highlights the humanitarian successes of President Carter's administration (see p258). These include the Camp David accords, Panama Canal treaties, and human-rights and energy policies.

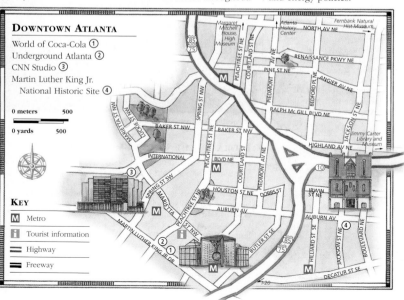

DOWNTOWN ATLANTA

World of Coca-Cola ①
Underground Atlanta ②
CNN Studio ③
Martin Luther King Jr.
  National Historic Site ④

0 meters 500
0 yards 500

KEY

Ⓜ Metro

ℹ Tourist information

Highway

Freeway

Tennessee

Tennessee is made up of three distinct regions. Memphis anchors the western lowlands along the Mississippi River; Nashville, the state capital, heads the central plateau; and the east is dominated by the Appalachian Mountains, with Knoxville as its urban base. With the Cumberland and Tennessee Rivers feeding into the Ohio, then into the Mississippi, the state was well positioned to prosper from the steamboat trade, and later, the railroads. During the Civil War, Chattanooga was the scene of battles, while Memphis and Nashville were occupied by Union forces. Today, Tennessee is known for its tremendous contribution to American roots music, from bluegrass, country, gospel, and blues, to rockabilly, rock 'n' roll, and soul.

Visitors at a preserved log cabin, Cades Cove

Great Smoky Mountains National Park ㉒

🛈 US Hwy 441, Gatlinburg, (865) 436-1200. ○ daily. ♿

The "Smokies," which earn their name from the smoke-like haze that clings to the ridge, hold some of the highest peaks in eastern US and support a diversity of plant life. With more than 10 million visitors each year, this is one of the country's most-visited parks. Established as a national park in 1934, half of it is in Tennessee and the other half in North Carolina. The Tennessee entrance is through Gatlinburg and Hwy 441, which bisects this sprawling park along the Newfound Gap Road and meets up with the Blue Ridge Parkway *(see p249)* on the North Carolina side.

Of the 800 miles (1,287 km) of trails, the most popular is the **Appalachian Trail**, which straddles the state border through the park. Trails to the park's many scenic waterfalls are also popular. The hike to **Mount LeConte** offers panoramic views, and there is even a hike-in lodge that provides rustic overnight accommodations, for which reservations are required. The 6,643-ft (2,025-m) tall **Clingman's Dome**, the state's highest peak, has an observation tower that offers fine views of the surrounding landscape.

At the western end of the Great Smoky Mountains National Park, **Cades Cove** still preserves the historic farm buildings that were erected back in the 1820s. These include structures such as log cabins, barns, and a still operating gristmill. Bicycling, horseback riding, fishing, and whitewater rafting are some of the popular activities available to adventurous tourists in this beautiful park and its surrounding region.

Spectacular view from Clingman's Dome

Sugar Maple

Magnolia

Mountain Laurel

Rhododendron

FLORA OF THE GREAT SMOKY MOUNTAINS

Famed for its incredible biodiversity, the Great Smoky Mountains shelter more than 1,500 species of flowering plants, including some 143 species of trees. The mountains' hardwood forests are made up of sugar maples, yellow birches, and poplars, while its spruce-fir forests are dominated by coniferous red spruce and Frasier fir. The understory consists of dense rhododendron and mountain laurel. Closely interwoven with Appalachian culture, the forest produces honeysuckle vines for basketry and various hardwoods for whittling and musical instruments, in addition to offering wild berries and fruits, medicinal plants (including ginseng), and harboring wild game.

Chattanooga ㉓

🏙 153,000. ✈ 🚆 🛈 2 Broad St, (423) 756-8687.

LOCATED ON THE banks of the Tennessee River along the Georgia border, Chattanooga is surrounded by several high landmasses – the plateaus of Lookout Mountain, Signal Mountain, and Missionary Ridge. Founded as a ferry landing by the Cherokee Indian Chief John Ross in 1815, Chattanooga was later occupied by white settlers after the Cherokees were forced out from here along the tragic "Trail of Tears" to Oklahoma in 1838 (see p46). The railroad leading to Atlanta provided a natural target for the Union Army during the Civil War, and several battles were fought on this dramatic terrain.

Downtown Chattanooga is today a revitalized center surrounding the original site of the ferry landing known as Ross's Landing. Within this compact area are many of the city's most popular attractions such as the Chattanooga Regional History Museum, which covers the area's local history – Native American, Civil War, and cultural; the **Tennessee Aquarium**; the attractive Riverwalk promenade; and the pedestrian-only Walnut Street Bridge that spans the river to Coolidge Park and Carousel.

Former Chickamauga battlefield, with cannons, statuary, and memorials

At the Tennessee Aquarium, visitors can trace the journey of a single drop of water from its origins in the Smoky Mountains through rivers, reservoirs, and deltas, then out into the Gulf of Mexico. Over 9,000 species of fish, amphibians, reptiles, mammals, and birds illustrate the state's varied habitats and ecosystems. An IMAX® Theater lies adjacent.

A short drive south of downtown on East Brow Road, the homespun **Battles for Chattanooga Electric Map** was originally known as "Confederama." It tells the story of local Civil War battles with 5,000 miniature soldiers and a series of tiny lights on large boards which are used to represent the advancing Confederate and Union troops. At the foot of Lookout Mountain, the station at St. Elmo Avenue is the start point for the mile-long **Lookout Mountain Incline Railway**. The train climbs a gradient of 72.7 percent up the side of Lookout Mountain for panoramic views. It was built in the 1890s to bring tourists up to the hotels that were once located on top. The **Chickamauga and Chattanooga National Military Park** of Point Park is a three-block

Lookout Mountain Incline Railway

walk away. The other section of the military park is the Chickamauga battlefield near Fort Oglethorpe across the border in northwest Georgia. The site at Point Park commemorates all the brave Confederate and Union soldiers who fought on the precipitous slopes of this steep plateau in the Battle Above the Clouds in 1863. This battle took place after Union forces were able to reverse an earlier Confederate victory and planted the US flag on the top of Lookout Mountain. At **Ruby Falls**, 3 miles (5 km) away, visitors descend by elevator to the floor of a cave, then walk past stalactites and stalagmites to the 145-ft (44-m) waterfall. A light show transforms the lovely natural surroundings of the falls into a somewhat gaudy display.

On the Georgia side of Lookout Mountain, **Rock City Gardens** has natural limestone rock formations beautified by the Enchanted Trail, a Lover's Leap, and little gnomes peering out from the crevices.

🛪 **Tennessee Aquarium**
1 Broad St. 📞 (423) 265-0695.
🕙 10am–6pm daily. ● Thanksgiving, Dec 25. 📷 ♿
W www.tnaqua.org

🏛 **Chickamauga & Chattanooga National Military Park**
110 Point Park Rd. 📞 (423) 821-7786.
🕙 8am–8pm daily. ● Dec 25. ♿
🏔 **Ruby Falls**
📞 (423) 821-2544.
W www.rubyfalls.com

The Tennessee Aquarium, Chattanooga

Nashville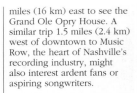

🏛 507,000. ✈ 🚌 ℹ *Broadway at Fifth St, (615) 259-4747.*

BEST KNOWN TODAY as the capital of country music, Nashville is a friendly and fun place to visit. Its musical history dates to 1927, when a radio broadcaster changing from music from the Grand Opera to the more popular Barn Dance show, introduced the upcoming selection as the "Grand Ole Opry." A musical legend was thus born and has flourished ever since. The city, however, has more to it than just music. It was founded as Fort Nashborough on the banks of the Cumberland River in 1779 and was named the state capital of Tennessee in 1843. It is also the financial center of the region and home to Vanderbilt University, one of the country's most prestigious institutions.

Legendary Hank Williams

Exploring Nashville
Nashville's vibrant downtown area is anchored by the new Country Music Hall of Fame. Most of the city's major attractions are within comfortable walking distance, such as the imposing State Capitol at the top of the hill, the historic and beautifully renovated Ryman Auditorium on Fifth Avenue, and the scenic riverfront with its reconstructed fort – a replica of the original outpost. Plenty of restaurants, cafés, and nightclubs lie in the surrounding area, locally known as "the District." Devoted country music fans might want to venture 10 miles (16 km) east to see the Grand Ole Opry House. A similar trip 1.5 miles (2.4 km) west of downtown to Music Row, the heart of Nashville's recording industry, might also interest ardent fans or aspiring songwriters.

🏛 Country Music Hall of Fame & Museum
222 Fifth Ave S. 📞 *(615) 416-2001.*
⏰ *10am–6pm daily.* ● *Jan 1, Thanksgiving, Dec 25.* 🅿
🌐 www.contrymusichalloffame.com
"Spreading the gospel of country music," the Country Music Hall of Fame honors scores of such outstanding musicians as Patsy Cline, Merle Haggard, and Hank Williams in a huge rotunda at a grand new downtown location. In keeping with its exhibits, the building itself has been specially designed to resemble the black and white keys of a giant piano. Inside there is a beloved collection of vintage guitars, costumes, string ties, cowboy boots, well-known lyrics composed on bar napkins, and the celebrated golden Elvis Cadillac. A country music primer explains the academic distinctions between the subgenres of bluegrass, cowboy, Cajun, honky-tonk, and rockabilly.

🎭 Ryman Auditorium
116 Fifth Ave N. 📞 *(615) 458-8700.*
⏰ *9am–4pm.* ● *Thanksgiving, Dec 25.* 🅿 🛗 🌐 www.ryman.com
This landmark auditorium is still an evocative setting for live performances. The Grand Ole Opry was broadcast from here for 31 years, from 1943 to 1974, when it moved to the new Opry House. Daytime tours of the Mother Church of Country Music are available, but the best way to see the 2,000-seat theater is by taking in a show; performers from

Façade of the Ryman Auditorium, a Nashville landmark

B.B. King to the Dixie Chicks and Sheryl Crow are typical of the diverse all-star lineup. Within a few blocks of Ryman Auditorium, the modern Nashville Convention Center, Gaylord Entertainment Center, and nightclubs featuring different kinds of music – country, bluegrass, and blues – can also be found.

🎭 Frist Center
919 Broadway. 📞 *(615) 244-3340.*
⏰ *10am–5:30pm Mon–Sat (until 8pm Thu), 1–5pm Sun.* ● *Jan 1, Thanksgiving, Dec 25.* 🅿 🛗
Downtown's 1934 Art Deco post office has been beautifully restored to house the city's premier arts center. Established in 2001, it has no permanent collection, but displays a wide selection of traveling exhibitions instead.

🏛 Tennessee State Museum
Fifth Ave between Union & Deaderick. 📞 *(615) 741-2692.*
⏰ *10am–5pm Tue– Sat, 1–5pm Sun.* ● *public hols.* 🛗
Although the main focus of this museum is the Civil War, it also covers other aspects of the state's past. Starting with a dugout canoe, exhibits showcase local Native American history, early pioneer life, slavery, the Civil Rights Movement, the river trade, and the Natchez Trace route. There is also a large collection of 19th-century decorative arts, such as European and American antique furnishings. Biographical exhibits shed light on heroes of the state such as President Andrew Jackson and the 19th-century explorer Davy Crockett.

View of Nashville's colorful riverfront

Exterior of the Grand Ole Opry House in Nashville

Grand Ole Opry House

2804 Opryland Dr. (615) 889-3060. 7:30pm Fri, 6:30pm & 9:30pm Sat. Sun–Thu.

Located 10 miles (16 km) east of downtown in a gulch of Opry-themed development called Music Valley, the 4,400-seat modern Opry House continues the "world's longest running radio show" beyond its 75th year. The Who's Who of country music grace the stage of this legendary institution (live broadcast on 650 WSM-AM). The nearby Grand Ole Opry Museum tells the Opry story with wax figurines. A car museum, the Opry mall, and the fabulous Opryland Hotel are part of the complex.

Belle Meade Plantation

5025 Harding Rd. (615) 356-0501. 9am–5pm Mon–Sat, 11am–5pm Sun. Jan 1, Thanksgiving, Dec 25. partial.

A 20-minute drive southwest of downtown, Belle Meade is among the state's best-preserved antebellum estates. The 1853 Greek Revival mansion was once the centerpiece of a 5,300 acre (2144.8 ha) plantation and has been restored to its former splendor. Guides in period costume offer tours of the mansion and outbuildings, including an 1832 slave cabin. A Sunday summer concert series features live performances on the spacious grounds.

The Hermitage

4580 Rachel's Lane. (615) 889-2941. 9am–5pm daily. 3rd week in Jan, Thanksg., Dec 25.

The home of Tennessee's foremost political and military hero, Andrew Jackson, this estate is a 20-minute drive east of downtown. After distinguishing himself as a military leader in the War of 1812, Jackson became the state's single Congressional representative before Tennessee gained statehood. He was elected the seventh president of the United States in 1828 and re-elected in 1832, serving two terms. Most of the contents of the house remain intact from Jackson's time. This famous president and his wife are buried in the garden.

Natchez Trace Parkway

Originally a series of Indian trails, the Natchez Trace Parkway, which links Nashville with Natchez in Mississippi, is today a national historic parkway (see p362). Its northern terminus lies 15 miles (24 km) southwest of town. Here, the contour of the Trace is more rolling and deeply forested than farther down in Mississippi.

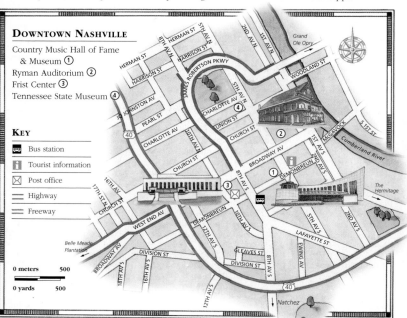

DOWNTOWN NASHVILLE

Country Music Hall of Fame
& Museum ①
Ryman Auditorium ②
Frist Center ③
Tennessee State Museum ④

KEY

Bus station

Tourist information

Post office

Highway

Freeway

0 meters   500

0 yards   500

A neon B.B. King's Blues Club sign on Beale Street

Memphis ㉕

🏃 650,000. ✈ 🚉 🚌 ℹ️ *119 N Riverside Dr, (901) 543-5333.*

MEMPHIS SITS ON the banks of the Mississippi River at Tennessee's southwestern corner, where it meets the states of Arkansas and Mississippi. The city is most closely associated with two very different American icons – Civil Rights leader Dr. Martin Luther King Jr, and the singer Elvis Presley.

Since the early 20th century, Memphis has been synonymous with music. As the birthplace of rock 'n' roll, which originated from blues *(see p361),* the city celebrates this legacy in its many nightclubs and saloons, and out on the streets. Even its festivals revolve around music. Highlights include Elvis's birthday on January 8; "Memphis in May," a month-long series of concerts and cookouts (Memphis is also famous for its barbecue); the W.C. Handy Awards, the blues answer to the Grammys, also in May; Elvis Week or "Tribute Week" around August 16; and the Music and Heritage Festival on Labor Day weekend.

🎸 Beale Street
ℹ️ *(901) 543-5333.*
A thriving commercial center for the city's African-American community, Beale Street's heyday was in the first half of the 20th century. After a period of decline, this historic street has now been resurrected as the heart of a vibrant entertainment district, rivaling New Orleans' Bourbon Street *(see p350)* in popularity. Restaurants, nightclubs, saloons, and shops line a four-block stretch. Many statues also punctuate the strip on either side. There is one of Elvis Presley across from Elvis Presley's Memphis Nightclub, which was established after his death, and one of W.C. Handy stands at the entrance to a plaza where many outdoor festivals take place. A block away, a tiny white shotgun shack that was Handy's home is now a museum to the man who has often been called the "Father of the Blues." At the center of the strip stands the **A. Schwab's Dry Goods Store** at 163 Beale. This shop has been open here since 1876. Many nights Beale Street is closed to traffic, and people come to listen to live music emanating from every door. A short walk from Beale Street, **AutoZone Park** is the new red and green stadium of the Memphis Redbirds baseball franchise. It lies across from the landmark Peabody Hotel at 149 Union Street, where the famous ducks march twice a day to and from the lobby to the fountain where they can be seen frolicking all day *(see p277).*

B.B. King, Rock-N-Soul Museum

🏛 National Civil Rights Museum
450 Mulberry St. ☎ *(901) 521-9699.* ⭕ *9am–5pm Mon–Sat, 1–5pm Sun.* ⬤ *Tue.* 📷 ♿
On April 4, 1968, Dr. Martin Luther King Jr. was tragically assassinated at the downtown Lorraine Motel. Exhibits here chronicle the struggle for racial equality in the United States from "Slavery Time" up until King's death. Across the street, a major exhibit relates the legacy of the Civil Rights Movement from 1968 up until the present.

🏛 Memphis Rock-N-Soul Museum
145 Lt George W Lee Ave. ☎ *(901) 543-0800.* ⭕ *10am–6pm daily.* ⬤ *Dec 25.* 📷 ♿
The intersection between history and race, and its expression in song, is explained with outstanding musical accompaniment at the Memphis Rock-N-Soul Museum. Housed in the new Gibson Guitar factory, this Smithsonian Institution sponsored exhibit examines the blues and country roots of rock 'n' roll with a fascinating movie, as well as displays of old instruments. Here you can see vintage jukeboxes and elaborate stage costumes, along with profiles of artists. A digital audio tour features more than six hours of fabulous music. Music fans may want to travel 10 minutes south to the Stax Museum of American Soul Music, opened in 2003 in the old Stax Records recording studio.

🚠 Mud Island
Via Front & Main Sts. ☎ *(901) 576-7241.* ⭕ *10am–5pm Tue–Sun.* ⬤ *Mon.* 📷 ♿
Reached via monorail, Mud Island holds a museum that tells the story of the Mississippi River with artifacts such as an 1870 steamboat replica. The museum also has many Native American exhibits. The most engaging exhibit in the museum however, is located outside where water courses through a replica of the Mississippi for a five-block-long stretch, ending at a swimming pool shaped like the Gulf of Mexico.

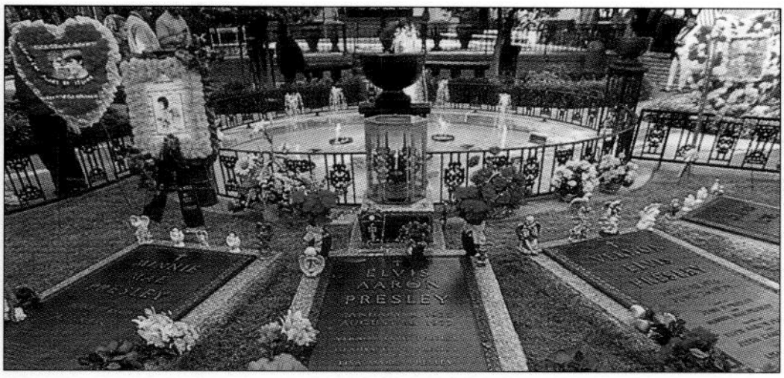

Elvis Presley's grave in his lavish Graceland estate

🏛 Center for Southern Folklore

119 S Main St. ☎ *(901) 525-3655.* 🕐 *11am–7pm Mon–Fri.* ● *Thanksgiving, Dec 25.* ☞ *hourly.* 🎫 *shows.* ♿

A touchstone for all that is authentically Southern, the center offers a great café, folk art gallery, gift shop, and a stage for shows ranging from jug bands to puppetry, with plenty of blues, soul, folk, rock, and gospel in between. It also sponsors the acclaimed Music and Heritage Festival.

🏛 Sun Studio

706 Union Ave. ☎ *(901) 521-0664.* 🕐 *10am–6pm daily.* ● *Thanksgiving, Dec 25.* 🎫 ♿

Famous musicians from all over the world come to record in the legendary studio that launched the careers of Elvis, B.B. King, Johnny Cash, Jerry Lee Lewis, Roy Orbison, and others. Founded in 1954 by Sam Philips, the studio's exhibits include Elvis's original drum set and microphone. Souvenir items with the familiar yellow rooster logo are on sale, and visitors can also make their own souvenir recordings.

🏛 Graceland

3734 Elvis Presley Blvd. ☎ *(901) 332-3322.* 🕐 *9am–5pm Mon–Sat, 10am–4pm Sun.* ● *Jan 1, Thanksgiving, Dec 25.* 🎫 ♿

A 10-minute drive from downtown, Graceland attracts more than 700,000 visitors each year to the estate that Elvis Presley bought as a 22-year-old superstar and called his home until his death in 1977. Starting at the grand visitor complex, guests are taken by van through the metal gates up the drive to the house to view the front rooms, famous Jungle Room den, gallery, racquetball court, and Memorial Gardens, where he is buried. The voice of his widow Priscilla narrates the audio tour. Across the street, additional admission charges are needed to see Elvis's car collection, his two airplanes, and a **Sincerely Elvis** exhibit with home movies and personal effects. The rows of unofficial souvenir shops along **Elvis Presley Boulevard** offer some bizarre but entertaining items, such as Elvis-emblazoned nail clippers, shot glasses, and beach towels.

⛪ Full Gospel Tabernacle Church

787 Hale Rd. ☎ *(901) 396-9192.* ✝ *11am Sun.* 🎫 *donation.*

The Reverend Al Green left a successful recording career in the 1970s (his hits included songs such as "Tired of Being Alone") to pursue his calling. He often presides over Sunday services at his church in Southside Memphis, not far from Graceland. Visitors to the electric gospel service should show respect by wearing decent attire, donating a little, and staying for the entire service.

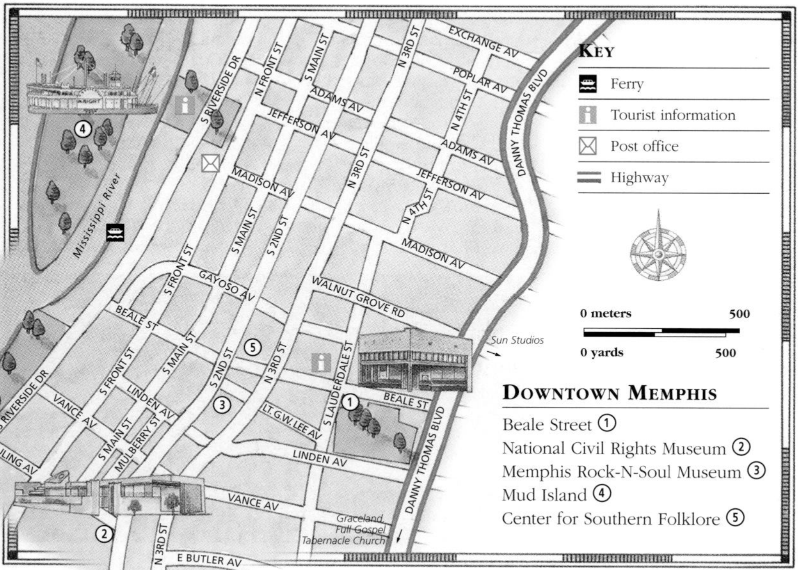
EXCHANGE AV
POPLAR AV
ADAMS AV
JEFFERSON AV
MADISON AV
N FRONT ST
S MAIN ST
N 3RD ST
N 4TH ST
S RIVERSIDE DR
DANNY THOMAS BLVD
S 2ND ST
S FRONT ST
GAYOSO AV
WALNUT GROVE RD
BEALE ST
LINDEN AV
VANCE AV
MULBERRY ST
S LAUDERDALE ST
LT. G.W. LEE AV
E BUTLER AV
Mississippi River
Sun Studios
Graceland Full Gospel Tabernacle Church
KEY
Ferry
Tourist information
Post office
Highway
0 meters 500
0 yards 500
DOWNTOWN MEMPHIS
Beale Street ①
National Civil Rights Museum ②
Memphis Rock-N-Soul Museum ③
Mud Island ④
Center for Southern Folklore ⑤

Kentucky

WITH ITS APPALACHIAN MOUNTAIN landscapes and rolling rural pasturelands, where horses run on acres and acres of bluegrass, Kentucky is easily one of the most picturesque states in the country. The lands west of the mountains were once inhabited by Indian tribes who strenuously opposed the encroachment of white settlers. Today, Kentucky is widely known for its horses, and many thoroughbred stud farms are centered around Lexington. One of the most prestigious horse races, the Kentucky Derby, takes place in Louisville. This state is also famous for its downhome style of country music, and Hwy 23 along its eastern border has been designated the Country Music Highway.

A cannon at Fort McCook, Cumberland Gap National Historic Park

Cumberland Gap National Historic Park ㉖

US Hwy 25 E, Middlesboro. ℹ (606) 248-2817. ◯ 8am–5pm daily. ● Jan 1, Thanksgiving, Dec 25. ♿

SITUATED IN THE southeastern corner where Kentucky meets the states of Virginia and Tennessee, the Cumberland Gap is a natural pass through the Cumberland Mountains, once used by migrating deer and bison. It was first explored by Dr. Thomas Walker in 1750 on behalf of a land company. Some five years later, the legendary fur trapper and explorer Daniel Boone ran his Wilderness Road through the Gap, thus opening the way for some 200,000 pioneers to establish homesteads in the interior wilderness.

This rugged area is thickly forested, and many sights, such as the Sand Cave sandstone overhang and White Rocks sandstone outcrop, are accessible only by hiking trails. The hardwood and softwood forests shelter wild turkeys, white-tailed deer, and many varieties of songbirds.

The Gap was also a strategic point in the Civil War. It was held alternately by Confederate and Union forces, and the fortifications can still be seen throughout the park. Today, a four-lane Interstate Highway and a railroad tunnel run through the Gap. A drive up to **Pinnacle Overlook** leads to a short trail for a view of three states, most dramatic during fall.

Mammoth Cave National Park ㉗

I-65 exit 53. ℹ (270) 758-2328. ◯ Mar–Oct: 8am–6pm daily, Nov–Feb: 8am–5pm. ● Dec 25.

HALFWAY BETWEEN Louisville (see p271) and Nashville (see p264), this park offers guided tours of one of the largest cave systems known, formed by underground rivers that left a dramatic landscape of stalactites and stalagmites. Guests are free to choose from tours with names such as "Historic" or "Wild Cave Tour" (helmets provided). According to experts, evidence suggests that the cave had been inhabited as far back as 4,000 years ago. The Green River runs its course above Mammoth Cave, an area that is crisscrossed by several hiking trails.

Berea ㉘

🏛 9,000. ℹ (800) 598-5263. 🎭 Berea Crafts Festival (Jul).

HOME TO BEREA College, a liberal arts school dedicated to educating disadvantaged Appalachian youth, Berea is known as a highlands crafts center. Typical crafts include woodworking, pottery, and textiles. The town hosts the Kentucky Guild of Artists Fair, the Craftmen's Fair, as well as the Berea Crafts Festival. Year-round, there are public tours of artisans' studios, such as **Churchill Weavers**, founded in 1922.

🏭 Churchill Weavers
100 Churchill Dr. ☎ (859) 986-3127. ◯ 9am–4pm Mon–Fri. ● Dec 25. 🖼

The path leading into the interior of Mammoth Cave

View of dense forest foliage from the Zilpo Road National Scenic Byway, Daniel Boone National Forest

Daniel Boone National Forest ㉙

1700 Bypass Rd, Winchester. **ℹ**
(859) 745-3100. **◯** *8am–4:30pm
daily.* **●** *Jan 1, Thanksg., Dec 25.* **♿**

NAMED AFTER the legendary
pioneer and fur trapper
David Boone, who lived in
Kentucky, this National Forest
protects some of the most
dramatic scenery in Kentucky.
The dense forest provides
shelter to over 35 endangered
species, including red-cockad-
ed woodpeckers, big-eared
bats, and bald eagles. The
**Sheltowee Trace National
Recreation Trail** runs the
entire 260-mile (418-km)
length of the forest, from
Morehead near the Ohio
border in the north to Pickett
State Rustic Park in Tenessee.
Also near Morehead, **Cave
Run Lake** is popular for
boating, and the **Zilpo Road**

National Scenic Byway
offers a good chance to see
the forest's rich variety of
wildlife on a short drive. The
central area east of Stanton
features the **Natural Bridge
State Resort Park**, a naturally
occuring archway surrounded
by rugged terrain, and the
picturesque **Red River
Gorge**, both of which offer
great hiking, canoeing, and
whitewater rafting oppor-
tunities. At the southern end,
**Cumberland Falls State
Resort Park** offers lodging,
camping, and swimming.

**🏕 Cumberland Falls State
Resort Park**
7351 Hwy 90, Corbin. **☎** *(606) 528-
4121.* **◯** *daily.* **♿**

ENVIRONS: Visitors to the
southern portion of the park
might want to detour to
Corbin, off I-75, 50 miles (80
km) north of the state's southern border with Tennessee.

Corbin is notable as the original home of Kentucky Fried
Chicken, where Colonel
Harland Sanders first served
the special recipe that went
on to become a global franchise. The kitchen where the
famous herbs and spices were
first put together is on display,
along with vintage adver-
tisements and KFC artifacts.

**Chairlifts carrying visitors up to
the Natural Bridge**

COUNTRY & BLUEGRASS MUSIC

As the Mississippi Delta is to blues music, so the stretch of eastern
Kentucky (along with West Virginia) is home to the greatest proportion
of country music artists in America. British, Irish, and Scottish immigrants brought Elizabethan ballads, rhythms, and instruments to the
area, which they then forged into a distinctly American style known
as "country." It was characterized by fast fiddling, occasional yodeling,
and laments on the hardscrabble life of the American Southeast. Hwy
23, which runs from Ashland to Pikeville along the state's eastern
border, has been dubbed the "Country Music Highway" to commem-

**Country singer Billy
Ray Cyrus in concert**

orate the vast number of artists who come from here. Along its length,
the route passes by the hometowns of Billy Ray Cyrus, the Judds,
Loretta Lynn, Patty Loveless, and Dwight Yoakum.

Kentucky's vast bluegrass pasturelands defined a particular style of country music known
as "bluegrass." This evolved from the musical style played in the late 1940s by Bill Monroe
and his Bluegrass Boys. The name "bluegrass" stuck, and this acoustic folk style remains
popular in the region today. Traditional bluegrass instruments include the fiddle, guitar,
mandolin, five-string banjo, and bass and dobro guitars.

Thoroughbred race horses grazing in pastures near Lexington

Lexington ③⓪

🏙 226,000. ✈ 🚌 ℹ *301 E Vine St, (859) 233-7299.*

KENTUCKY'S second largest city, Lexington is also the capital of the state's bucolic horse country. The surrounding bluegrass-covered countryside is lined with hundreds of throroughbred stud farms, where many Kentucky Derby winners are bred, reared, and trained. Most farms are open to visitors, who are welcome either on their own with advance reservations or as part of an organized tour. The visitor center supplies lists of farms and tour operators.

About 6 miles (9.6 km) north of town lies the **Kentucky Horse Park**, a state-operated working farm that serves as an equestrian theme park. Here, visitors can watch live shows, ride ponies, sign up for escorted trail rides, take carriage tours, and go swimming and camping. The park's **International**

Museum of the Horse is a monument to the role of the horse in the development of human history. The adjacent **Saddlebred Museum** is named for, and focuses on, America's first registered horse breed. Outside, the Man o' War Memorial marks the grave of the beloved thoroughbred who won several acclaimed races. In town, the 1803 **Mary Todd Lincoln House** preserves the girlhood home of Abraham Lincoln's wife.

🏛 Kentucky Horse Park
4089 Iron Works Pkwy. 📞 (859) 233-4303. ◯ mid-Mar–Oct: 9am– 5pm daily. ● Nov–mid-Mar: Mon– Tue. 🌄 ♿

Harrodsburg ③①

🏙 7,400. ✈ 🚌 ℹ *124 S Main St, (859) 734-2364.*

A LARGE NUMBER of Shaker families from New England relocated in and around Harrodsburg in 1805

and established a farming community renowned for its handicrafts. It grew to a sizeable population of around 500 in 1830 and then, in part due to the Shaker belief in celibacy, it grew less cohesive and became scattered by 1910. The area's premier attraction is the **Shaker Village of Pleasant Hill**, America's finest, largest, and most completely restored Shaker community and living history museum. The architecture and furnishings at the village reflect the spare, utilitarian style that typifies the Shaker values. Artisans demonstrate crafts such as woodworking and weaving. Lodging, dining, and riverboat rides are also available.

🏛 Shaker Village of Pleasant Hill
3501 Lexington Rd. 📞 (859) 734- 5411. ◯ 10am–5pm daily. ● Dec 24–25. 🌄 ♿ partial.

Hodgenville ③②

🏙 2,700. ℹ *72 Lincoln Square, (270) 358-341.*

HODGENVILLE IS the base for the **Abraham Lincoln Birthplace National Historic Site**, located 3 miles (5 km) to its south. The site commemorates the 16th US president's Kentucky roots by preserving his childhood home. Here, 56 steps representing the years of Lincoln's life lead up to a granite-and-marble Memorial Building built around a 19th-century log cabin, where the

Barrel making in the Shaker Village of Pleasant Hill, Harrodsburg

president was born. The site also encompasses a large portion of the original Lincoln family farmland.

🏛 Abraham Lincoln Birthplace National Historic Site
7120 Bardstown Rd (Hwy 31 E). 📞 (502) 549-3741. 🕐 8am–4:45pm or 6:45pm (seasonal). 🔴 Jan 1, Thanksgiving, Dec 25. ♿

The Hodgenville log cabin in which Abraham Lincoln was born

Bardstown 🟤

🚶 6,800. 🛈 107 E Stephen Foster Ave, (502) 348-4877.
🌐 www.visitbardstown.com

THE self-proclaimed "Bourbon Capital of the World," Bardstown is surrounded by the state's largest whiskey distilleries, which have earned Kentucky its legendary reputation as the whiskey-making center of the US. (Bourbon is made from corn, malt, and rye, and is aged in charred white oak barrels.) The most popular distillery, James Beam, known in countless country songs as "Jim Beam," lies 14 miles (22.5 km) west of Bardstown, while a 20-mile (32-km) drive south leads to the famed Maker's Mark distillery,

Stephen Foster statue, My Old Kentucky Home State Park, Bardstown

Kentucky's oldest distillery operating in the same site. However, Bardstown's most popular attraction is **My Old Kentucky Home State Park.** Here, guides lead visitors through the historic mansion that, according to legend, inspired composer Stephen Foster to write "My Old Kentucky Home," the state's beloved anthem. The park also hosts outdoor musicals.

🏛 My Old Kentucky Home State Park
US Hwy 150. 📞 (502) 348-3502. 🕐 Sep–May: 9am–4:45pm; Jun–Aug: 8:30am–6:15pm. 🔴 Jan 1, Thanksgiving, Dec 24–31. ♿

Louisville 🟤

🚶 269,000. ✈ 🚌 🛈 30 Market St, (502) 584-2121.

FOUNDED AT THE falls of the Ohio River in 1788, Louisville (pronounced "Loo-avul") is home to one of the world's most famous horse races, the Kentucky Derby. What Mardi Gras is to New Orleans, or the Masters Tournament is to Augusta, the Derby is to Louisville – it is the event around which all local calendars revolve. Since it first began in 1875, three-year-old horses have run the track at Churchill Downs on the first Saturday in May. Kentucky's high society turns out in spring finery for this social event of the year, with hats and seersucker suits constituting battle uniform. Mint juleps, the Southern concoction of bourbon, ice, sugar, and fresh mint are the unofficial beverage of choice. "My Old Kentucky Home" plays while the horses are led onto the track for an event that lasts less than two minutes. Winners take home the coveted trophy, decorated with lucky silver horseshoes in a "U" shape "so that the luck doesn't spill out." The adjacent **Kentucky Derby Museum** showcases horse-racing history and offers "backside track tours"

Gigantic baseball bat outside the Louisville Slugger Museum

through the Churchill Downs track. A couple of blocks from the historic district on the waterfront, the **Louisville Slugger Museum** produces the worldclass baseball bat in a factory marked by a landmark 120-ft (36-m) high bat.

The **J.B. Speed Art Museum** on South 3rd Street displays a large collection of Renaissance paintings and sculpture. At the Riverfront Plaza on the banks of the Ohio River at Main and Fourth Streets, several paddlewheelers tour the area, and a fountain periodically shoots water 375 ft (114.3 m) into the air. The surrounding historic district's old warehouses have been recast as cafés, galleries, and shops.

Located 2 miles (3.2 km) northeast of downtown, Cave Hill Cemetery is one of the largest and most beautiful in the US. Many Louisvillians go visit the grounds just to feed the ducks, or take in the landscaped lawns. Thirty miles (48.2 km) southwest of Louisville, the exterior of the federal gold bullion repository at **Fort Knox** can be seen.

🏛 Kentucky Derby Museum
704 Central Ave. 📞 (502) 637-1111. 🕐 8am–5pm Mon–Sat, noon–5pm Sun. 🔴 Breeder's cupdays, first Fri–Sat in May, Thanksgiving, Dec 25. ♿

🏛 Louisville Slugger Museum
800 W Main St. 📞 (502) 588-7228. 🕐 9am–5pm Mon–Sat, Apr–Nov: 1–5pm Sun. ♿
🌐 www.sluggermuseum.org

Practical Information

SUCCESSFUL TRAVELING AROUND the Southeast requires a great deal of advance planning, as there is so much to see and do in the vast area. With miles of sandy beaches, picturesque historic cities such as Charleston, the stunning rugged wilderness of the Blue Ridge and Appalachian Mountains, and rolling hills and valleys of the foothills, the Southeast truly has it all. In addition to myriad natural wonders, the region also offers burgeoning commercial centers such as Atlanta, and engaging cultural towns including Memphis, the birthplace of the blues, and Nashville, the commercial and cultural capital of "country-western" music, arts, and entertainment.

TOURIST INFORMATION

EACH OF THE five Southeast states, North Carolina, South Carolina, Kentucky, Tennessee, and Georgia, publishes travel information that can be ordered by phone or via web sites. State "Welcome Centers" located along most major highways greet visitors as soon as they enter each of the Southeast states. Open between 8am and 5pm daily, these centers offer free road maps and a full range of tourist information, covering climate, transportation, attractions, and accommodations. More information is available from a multitude of tourism bureaus across the five states.

NATURAL HAZARDS

THE END OF SUMMER in the Southeast can be very pleasant, but this is also the main hurricane season, and potentially one of the most troubling times for visitors. Hurricane season stretches from August to the end of the year, but since storms form in the Atlantic Ocean near the Equator, emergency alert systems usually give at least a day or two warning before strong winds and heavy rains arrive.

Watch out for tornadoes and thunderstorms in late spring and summer, especially in the south, where they strike suddenly and create flash floods. If a tornado watch or warning is issued, take cover straight away.

GETTING AROUND

LIKE MUCH OF THE US, the Southeast is a region where it can be hard to get around without a car. **Greyhound** buses do serve some larger towns and cities, and visitors can also take **Amtrak** trains to travel around the Southeast. Nevertheless, driving is the best way to get around the region, as public transportation can be limited. Seat belts are required for drivers and front seat passengers in all of the five states. Most states also require seat belts for back seat passengers, and child seats are required for all automobile occupants aged 4 and under. Speed limits vary, but are usually 70 to 75 mph (112 to 120 km/h) on Interstate Highways outside of densely populated urban areas, weather permitting.

ETIQUETTE

COMPARED TO THE rest of the country, Southerners are largely a teatotalling lot. Many of them are Baptists, a religion that frowns on the consumption of alcohol. "Dry" counties can still be found in some rural areas, particularly in the mountains where alcohol cannot be legally served or sold to the public. But exceptions to this tradition are legendary. Makers of "moonshine" a 100-proof home-made whisky typically distilled from corn, gained an outlaw reputation in the days of the Prohibition for evading federal agents by hiding stills deep in the woods and working them by cover of darkness – hence the name "moonshine".

Drinking mint juleps on the day of the Kentucky Derby in Louisville is such a revered local custom that girls start collecting the traditional sterling silver "julep cups" as young as 12 years of age.

FESTIVALS

THE SOUTHEAST states stage a diverse range of annual community, regional, and national festivals. In February, cultural sites all over the Southeast, especially the Martin Luther King Jr. Center for Non-Violent Social Change in Atlanta, celebrate the **Black History Month** with various special programs. In March, Savannah, Georgia, hosts a lively **St. Patrick's Day** celebration, when thousands come together to drink beer, dance, sing, and celebrate

---

THE CLIMATE OF THE SOUTHEAST

The region's states have a mild climate with temperatures rarely dipping below freezing in winter, though summer in the low-lying areas can be very hot. Spring sees azaleas and other blossom in the region's famous gardens. Summer, with its sunny days and warm water along sandy beaches, is the most popular time for travel. The end of summer is the primary hurricane season. In inland areas, leaves change color on mountain hardwood trees in October. In winter, snow can fall across all parts of the region.

ATLANTA

°F/C	Apr	Jul	Oct	Jan
		88/31		
	70/22	69/20	74/23	
	50/10		52/11	54/12
32°F 0°C				36/2
☀	20 days	20 days	20 days	15 days
☔	4.2 in	5 in	3 in	4.7 in
month	Apr	Jul	Oct	Jan

real or imagined Irishness. March and April are also ideal months for enjoying house-and-garden tours and the blossoms of the Southeast's many fruit trees, celebrated in events like the **Cherry Blossom Festival** of Macon, Georgia, where visitors can see more than 200,000 trees line the city streets.

Throughout May, one of the country's largest music and arts festivals takes place in historic Charleston, South Carolina, as part of the **Spoleto Festival USA**.

Summer brings a deluge of outdoor events. Bands, fireworks, and street festivals are the norm for community celebrations of the July 4 Independence Day holiday. One of the largest fireworks displays in the US is staged at Stone Mountain, outside Atlanta. Numerous county and state fairs crop up around this time, as do music festivals such as **Old Time Fiddlers' Jamboree** in Smithville, Tennessee. The end of summer brings **Elvis Week** in Memphis, Tennessee, celebrating the life and times of Elvis Presley with a week-long festival around the anniversary of his death on August 16.

A highlight of autumn is the **Tennessee Fall Home-coming**, an Appalachian-themed crafts, and culture festival that takes place annually at the Museum of Appalachia. At the end of the year, an old-fashioned Christmas is re-created at the living history village of Old Salem, outside Winston-Salem in North Carolina.

SPORTS & OUTDOOR ACTIVITIES

The cities of the Southeast host a wide array of pro-fessional and amateur sports teams, and there are many minor league teams in smaller cities. Especially in basketball and football, hundreds of high-quality and passionately supported sports teams are fielded by public and private colleges and universities. Atlanta has major league teams in all three main American spectator sports, baseball, foot-ball, and basketball, but pro-fessional NFL football is also played in Charlotte, North Carolina, and Nashville, Ten-nessee. At the minor league level, Memphis has an enormous new downtown stadium for their Class AAA baseball team, the Redbirds; Nashville, Charlotte, and Louis-ville also have high-quality Class AAA baseball teams. Baseball season runs from April to September, football from September through January, and basketball from winter through mid-spring.

In other sports, the **Kentucky Derby** in early May draws hundreds of thou-sands of horse-racing fans from all over the world. Golf fans flock to Augusta, Georgia to watch the Masters tournament in April. **NASCAR** stock car races are the region's most popular attractions, drawing more than 200,000 people to weekly races at Atlanta, Bristol, Concord, Rockingham, and Darlington.

Numerous state parks provide opportunities for camping, boating, fishing, and hiking. The coastal states of the Southeast are known to excel in beach activities.

ENTERTAINMENT

The birthplace of the blues, rock 'n' roll, and country-western music, the Southeast is a great place to enjoy live music. Hundreds of events take place all over the region almost every night. Besides the various nightclubs hosting talented musicians, the major entertainment venues of the region include the legendary **Grand Old Opry** in Nashville and **B.B. King's Blues Club** in Memphis.

Where to Stay

O NE OF THE BEST WAYS to sample Southern hospitality is to stay in one of Southeast's many distinctive hotels. Larger cities such as Atlanta offer the widest range of lodging choices, while hideaways can readily be found along the Atlantic shore. National chains, spread throughout the region, offer affordable rooms, designed to be most convenient for motorists.

	CREDIT CARDS	NUMBER OF ROOMS	RECOMMENDED RESTAURANT	CHILDREN'S FACILITIES	GARDEN OR TERRACE

NORTH CAROLINA

ASHEVILLE: *Inn on Biltmore Estate* $\$\$\$\$$
1 Antler Hill Rd. ☎ *(828) 225-1660, (800) 858-4130.*
FAX *(828) 274-6396.* W www.biltmore.com
This seven-story hotel provides luxurious accommodations within the vast Biltmore Estate, with access to nature trails, a winery, restaurants, and the art-filled house museum. ▮ ▮ P ▮ ▮ TV ▮ ▮ ▮

| | ■ | 213 | ■ | | ■ |

BEAUFORT: *Beaufort Inn* $\$\$\$$
101 Ann St. ☎ *(252) 728-2600, (800) 726-0321.* FAX *(252) 728-1864.*
W www.beaufort-inn.com
Overlooking Gallants Channel, the inn makes a good base to explore the compact waterfront area of this quaint coastal town. ▮ P ▮ ▮ TV ▮

| | ■ | 44 | | | |

CHAPEL HILL: *Carolina Inn* $\$\$\$\$\$$
211 Pittsboro St. ☎ *(919) 933-2001.* FAX *(919) 962-3400.*
W www.carolinainn.com
Adjacent to the bucolic University of North Carolina, this genteel historic inn offers a refined faculty club atmosphere. ▮ P ▮ ▮ TV ▮ ▮ ▮

| | ■ | 184 | | | ■ |

DURHAM: *Durham Marriot at the Civic Center* $\$\$\$$
201 Foster St. ☎ *(919) 768-6000.* FAX *(919) 768-6037.*
W www.marriott.com
This eight-story hotel opens onto a fountain plaza next to the Civic Center, near the historic Brightleaf Square district. ▮ ▮ P ▮ ▮ TV ▮

| | ■ | 184 | | | ■ |

MANTEO: *Tranquil House Inn* $\$\$\$\$$
405 Queen Elizabeth St. ☎ *(252) 473-1404.* FAX *(252) 473-1526.*
W www.tranquilinn.com
This inn is set against the marsh overlooking the sails of the re-created ship *Elizabeth II*, part of a popular theme park. ▮ P ▮ ▮ TV ▮

| | ■ | 25 | ■ | | |

NAGS HEAD: *First Colony Inn* $\$\$\$\$\$$
6720 Virginia Dare Trail. ☎ *(252) 441-2343.* FAX *252-441-9234.*
W www.firstcolonyinn.com
Right on the beach, this three-story wooden inn offers a homier alternative to the high-rise hotels lining the shore. ▮ P ▮ ▮ TV ▮ ▮

| | ■ | 26 | | | ■ |

OCRACOKE: *Berkley Manor B&B* $\$\$\$$
PO Box 220. ☎ *(252) 928-5911, (800) 832-1223.*
W www.berkeleymanor.com
Located next to the main ferry landing, this inn set at the heart of the compact village is open from Easter through late October. ▮ ▮ ▮

| | ■ | 12 | | | ■ |

RALEIGH: *Days Inn* $\$$
3901 S. Wilmington St. ☎ *(919) 772-8900.* FAX *(919) 772-1536.*
W www.daysinn.com
A no-frills and affordable lodging on the capitol side of the Raleigh-Durham-Chapel Hill Research Triangle region. ▮ P ▮ ▮ TV ▮ ▮

| | ■ | 103 | | | |

SOUTH CAROLINA

CHARLESTON: *Days Inn Historic District* $\$\$$
155 Meeting St. ☎ *(843) 722-8411.* FAX *(843) 723-5361.*
W www.daysinn.com
Within an inviting two-story courtyard motel, this inn provides extremely affordable lodging in the heart of the historic district. ▮ ▮ ▮ TV ▮ ▮

| | ■ | 124 | | | |

CHARLESTON: *Westin Francis Marion House* $\$\$\$$
387 King St. ☎ *(843) 722-0600.* FAX *(843) 723-4633.*
W www.francismarioncharleston.com
Operating out of a historic building in Charleston's historic district, this inn features an acclaimed restaurant, the Swamp Fox. ▮ ▮ ▮ TV ▮ ▮

| | ■ | 226 | ■ | | |

Price categories for a standard double room per night, inclusive of breakfast, service charges, and any additional taxes:

$ under $100
$$ $100–$150
$$$ $150–$200
$$$$ $200–$250
$$$$$ over $250

CREDIT CARDS
Major credit cards accepted.

NUMBER OF ROOMS
Number of rooms in the hotel.

RECOMMENDED RESTAURANT
Good restaurant within the hotel.

CHILDREN'S FACILITIES
Hotel has various facilities for young children.

GARDEN OR TERRACE
Hotel has a garden, courtyard, or terrace.

	CREDIT CARDS	NUMBER OF ROOMS	RECOMMENDED RESTAURANT	CHILDREN'S FACILITIES	GARDEN OR TERRACE
CHARLESTON: *The Inn at Middleton Place* $$$$ 4300 Ashley River Rd. **C** *(843) 556-0500.* **FAX** *(843) 556-5673.* **W** www.middletonplace.org/inn.htm This striking blond-wood-and-glass inn provides a refined retreat on the bluffs of the Ashley River. Horseback riding and nature walks are among the amenities, and room rates include breakfast. ▮▮▮▮▮ TV ▮▮	▦	54	▦		▦
COLUMBIA: *Adams Mark Hotel* $$$ 1200 Hampton St. **C** *(803) 771-7000.* **FAX** *(803) 254-8307* **W** www.adamsmark.com On Main Street, the capital's premier hotel offers 15 stories of comfortable rooms across the street from the art museum. ▮▮▮ TV ▮▮▮	▦	303	▦		
HILTON HEAD: *Disney's Hilton Head Island Resort* $$$$$ 22 Harbourside Lane. **C** *(843) 341-4100.* **FAX** *(843) 341-4130.* **W** www.dvcmagic.com This all-American family resort features a four-story luxury hotel, complete with a waterslide pool, fishing, and a huge array of fun children's activities. ▮ P ▮▮▮▮ TV ▮▮▮	▦	123	▦	●	▦
MYRTLE BEACH: *Breakers* $$$ 2701 N Ocean Blvd. **C** *(843) 626-5000, (800) 845-0688.* **FAX** *(843) 626-5001.* **W** www.breakers.com Typical of the high-rise hotels that line the Grand Strand, this 19-story beachfront resort offers an exercise room, a restaurant, and a lounge in the heart of the action. ▮ P ▮▮▮▮ TV ▮▮▮	▦	141	▦		▦
MYRTLE BEACH: *Hilton Myrtle Beach Resort* $$$$ 10000 Beach Club Dr. **C** *(843) 449-5000.* **FAX** *(843) 497-0295.* **W** www.hilton.com Offering a stretch of the Grand Strand Atlantic coastline, far removed from the congestion of Myrtle Beach proper, this resort offers pools, restaurants, and an 18-hole golf course. ▮▮▮▮▮ TV ▮▮▮	▦	385	▦		▦

GEORGIA

	CREDIT CARDS	NUMBER OF ROOMS	RECOMMENDED RESTAURANT	CHILDREN'S FACILITIES	GARDEN OR TERRACE
AMERICUS: *Windsor Hotel* $$$ 125 W Lamar St. **C** *(229) 924-1555, (888)-297-9567.* **FAX** *(229) 924-1555.* This rambling Victorian hotel covers an entire city block and comes as a surprise in this rural region. Rooms are plain, despite the hotel's Moorish architecture, three-story atrium, and refined dining room. ▮▮▮ TV ▮	▦	53	▦		
AMICALOLA FALLS: *Amicalola Falls State Park Lodge* $ Hwy 52. **C** *(706) 265-8888.* **W** www.gastateparks.org This modern lodge, with spacious rooms and 14 cabins, overlooks a Blue Ridge Mountain panorama, surrounded by scenic trails. A restaurant offers hearty country meals, ideal after a day on the trails. ▮ P ▮▮▮ TV	▦	57		●	
ATLANTA: *Quality Inn Fairlie Poplar* $$ 89 Luckie St. **C** *(404) 524-7991.* **FAX** *(404) 524-0672.* **W** www.qualityinnatlanta.com This modest, affordable hotel is wonderfully situated in the re-emerging Fairlie-Poplar district downtown. Restaurants, cafes, nightclubs, and the CNN Center are all within a few blocks. P ▮▮▮ TV ▮▮	▦	75			
ATLANTA: *Swissotel* $$$$ 3391 Peachtree Rd, NE. **C** *(404) 365-0065.* **FAX** *(404) 365-8787.* **W** www.swissotel/atlanta.com Overlooking Lenox Mall in the heart of upper Buckhead, the 22-story Swissotel has striking modern architecture stocked with contemporary artwork and Biedermeier-style furnishings. ▮ P ▮▮▮▮ TV ▮	▦	365	▦		▦

For key to symbols see back flap

<table>
<tr><td colspan="2">

Price categories for a standard double room per night, inclusive of breakfast, service charges, and any additional taxes:

$ under $100
$$ $100–$150
$$$ $150–$200
$$$$ $200–$250
$$$$$ over $250

</td>
<td colspan="2">

CREDIT CARDS
Major credit cards accepted:

NUMBER OF ROOMS
Number of rooms in the hotel.

RECOMMENDED RESTAURANT
Good restaurant within the hotel.

CHILDREN'S FACILITIES
Hotel has various facilities for young children.

GARDEN OR TERRACE
Hotel has a garden, courtyard, or terrace.

</td>
</tr>
</table>

		CREDIT CARDS	NUMBER OF ROOMS	RECOMMENDED RESTAURANT	CHILDREN'S FACILITIES	GARDEN OR TERRACE
ATLANTA: *Four Seasons Hotel* 75 14th St. (404) 881-9898, 800-332-3442. FAX (404) 873-4692. www.fourseasons.com Atlanta's hottest new hotel, furnished with all conceivable modern amenities, is known for its impeccable service and the acclaimed Park 75 restaurant.	$$$$	■	244	■		■
DAHLONEGA: *Smith House* 84 S Chestatee St. (706) 867-7000, (800) 852-9577. FAX (706) 864-7564. www.smithhouse.com This 1804 inn was built atop a gold mine, famed as the center of Georgia's 1830's gold rush. Today, the site includes a modern hotel annex. Modest rooms in the original house are the most evocative and comfortable, and only a short walk to the lively town square.	$$	■	18	■		
JEKYLL ISLAND: *Jekyll Island Club Hotel* 371 Riverview Dr. (912) 635-2600, (800) 535-9547. FAX (912) 635-2818. www.jekyllclub.com This historic club was the center of a wealthy vacation community that occupied the island at the turn of the 20th century. It is set in the historic district by the marsh.	$$$	■	157		●	■
MACON: *1842 Inn* 353 College St. (478) 741-1842. FAX (478) 741-1842. www.1842inn.com Offering an amiable setting, this historic inn is ideal for venturing into the state's heartland. The main house is wonderful, and a more modern annex is set across a delightful central courtyard.	$$$	■	19			■
SAVANNAH: *River Street Inn* 124 E Bay St. (912) 234-6400, (800) 253-4229. FAX (912) 234-1478. www.riverstreetinn.com Carved out of a 1853 warehouse, this three-story inn offers small, well-appointed rooms, ideally located for waterfront nightlife.	$$$	■	86			
SAVANNAH: *Kehoe House* 123 Habersham St. (912) 232-1020. FAX (912) 231-0208. www.williamkehoehouse.com Modeled on a European boutique hotel, the refined Kehoe House sits in a square at a quiet corner of the historic district.	$$$$$	■	14			
ST. SIMONS: *King & Prince Hotel* 201 Arnold Rd. (912) 638-3631, (800) 342-0212. FAX (912) 628-7699. www.kingandprince.com Anchoring the East Beach, this rambling beachfront hotel expands from its central building, with an indoor-outdoor pool, dining room, and tavern, to outlying condos, townhouses, and adjacent facilities for this attractive, approachable full-scale resort.	$$$	■	129	■		■

TENNESSEE

		CREDIT CARDS	NUMBER OF ROOMS	RECOMMENDED RESTAURANT	CHILDREN'S FACILITIES	GARDEN OR TERRACE
CHATTANOOGA: *Chattanooga Choo Choo* 1400 Market St. (423) 266-5000. FAX (423) 265-4635. www.choochoo.com Forty-eight rail cars named for the legendary song "Chattanooga Choo-Choo" provide the setting for this chain motel resort, where arcades, fish ponds, and gardens keep families entertained.	$$	■	360	■	●	■
CHATTANOOGA: *Read House* 827 Broad St. (423) 266-4121. FAX (423) 267-6193. www.readhousehotel.com This venerable historic hotel features a 10-story tower, with each floor decorated with illustrations of Civil War battles.	$$	■	136			■

GREAT SMOKIES: *Mt. Leconte Lodge* ⓈⓈⓈ
250 Apple Valley Rd Seiverville 37862. 📞 *(865) 429-5704.*
🆆 www.leconte-lodge.com
This rustic and extremely popular mountain lodge, open in spring and
summer only, provides group lodges and individual cabins for 50 guests.
No electricity, no telephones or TV, and accessible only to hikers able to
make the 5.5-mile (9-km) hike to the lodge. ◯ *late Mar–mid-Nov.*

GATLINBURG: *Buckhorn Inn* ⓈⓈ — 9
2140 Tudor Mountain Rd. 📞 *(865) 436-4668.*
🆆 www.Buckhorninn.com
Overlooking Mount LeConte about a mile outside the national park, the
Buckhorn Inn provides well-appointed rooms in a classic mountain lodge
and cottages. Walk-in stone fireplaces, piano, and rocking chairs on the
porch are important facets of the inn's relaxing atmosphere. 🅿 ⛾ ⚡ ♿

MEMPHIS: *Elvis Presley's Heartbreak Hotel* ⓈⓈ — 128
3677 Elvis Presley Blvd. 📞 *(901) 332-1000.* FAX *(901) 332-2107.*
🆆 www.elvis.com
The 1950s rooms and continuously looping Elvis movies here make the
Heartbreak Hotel the best place to indulge in the full kitschy appeal of a
pilgrimage to Graceland. 🍸 🍴 🅿 ⛾ ⚡ 📺 ♿

MEMPHIS: *Peabody Hotel* ⓈⓈⓈⓈⓈ — 468
149 Union Ave. 📞 *(901) 529-4000.* FAX *(901) 529-3600.*
🆆 www.peabodymemphis.com
One of the most distinguished hotels in the South, the historic Peabody is
also one of the quirkiest. A legion of ducks descend daily from their penthouse lair to cavort in the lobby fountain. 🍸 🍴 🅿 ⛾ ⚡ 📺 ♿ ≋ 🍴

NASHVILLE: *Union Station Hotel* ⓈⓈⓈ — 124
1001 Broadway. 📞 *(615) 726-1001.* FAX *(615) 248-3554.*
🆆 www.wyndham.com
In a stunningly vast old train depot resembling a Gothic cathedral, Union
Station Hotel offers deluxe lodging and dining downtown, a short cab
ride from the lively waterfront district. 🍸 🅿 ⛾ ⚡ 📺 ♿

NASHVILLE: *Opryland Hotel* ⓈⓈⓈ — 2,881
2800 Opryland Dr. 📞 *(615) 889-1000.* FAX *(615) 871-7741.*
🆆 www.oprylandhotelnashville.com
The phenomenal Opryland Hotel more closely resembles a giant lunar
biosphere than any earthy hotel, with breathtaking acreage of gardens,
waterfalls, cafés, shops, and amusements. Even if you're not staying overnight, it has to be seen to be believed. 🍸 🍴 🅿 ⛾ ⚡ 📺 ♿ ≋ 🍴

KENTUCKY

LEXINGTON: *Gratz Park Inn* ⓈⓈ — 44
120 W 2nd St. 📞 *(859) 231-1777.* FAX *(859) 233-7593.*
🆆 www.gratzparkinn.com
Intimate, historic hotel, the Gratz Park Inn features antiques in every
room, exemplary service, and a horse-drawn carriage to take visitors
around town. 🍴 🅿 ⛾ ⚡ 📺

LEXINGTON: *Hyatt Regency* ⓈⓈ — 365
401 W High St. 📞 *(859) 253-1234.* FAX *(859) 233-7974.*
🆆 www.hyatt.com
This comfortable, modern high-rise hotel is ideally located in the heart of
the city. 🍸 🍴 🅿 ⛾ ⚡ 📺 ♿ ≋ 🍴

LOUISVILLE: *Galt House* ⓈⓈ — 650
140 N 4th St. 📞 *(502) 589-5200, (800) 626-1814.* FAX *(502) 589-3444.*
🆆 www.galthouse.com
This modern hotel, with an 18-story interior atrium is located right on the
river. Amazing views can be seen from most rooms and the revolving
rooftop restaurant and cocktail bar. 🍸 🍴 🅿 ⛾ ⚡ 📺 ♿ ≋ 🍴

LOUISVILLE: *Seelbach Hilton Hotel* ⓈⓈⓈ — 321
500 4th Ave. 📞 *(502) 585-3200.* FAX *(502) 585-9239.*
🆆 www.seelbachhilton.com
Opulent hotel, with gold-plated everything and murals in the two-
story lobby depicting scenes from Kentucky history. Built in 1905,
and impeccably maintained ever since, the hotel is now part of the
Hilton chain. 🍸 🍴 🅿 ⛾ ⚡ 📺 ♿

For key to symbols see back flap

Where to Eat

TRADITIONAL SOUTHERN FOOD is affordable across the region. A typical country meal includes meat, bread, and two or three vegetables, washed down by sweet iced tea, and topped off by banana pudding. Innovators are now creating new dishes with local ingredients. In the listings below, opening times are indicated by a "B" for breakfast, "L" for lunch, and "D" for dinner.

	CREDIT CARDS	OUTDOOR TABLES	VEGETARIAN	GOOD WINE LIST	CHILDREN'S FACILITIES

NORTH CAROLINA

ASHEVILLE: *Tupelo Honey* $$
12 College St. (828) 255-4863.
The New South cuisine at Tupelo Honey offers a lighter take on such regional specialties as fried green tomatoes, cheese grits, pimento cheese, chips, and catfish, though the banana pudding is strictly traditional. Open late, till 3am some nights. *B, L, D.* ● *Mon, Jan 1, Thanksgiving, Dec 25.* ▨ ㋹
| | ■ | ● | ■ | ● | ■ |

ASHEVILLE: *Zambra* $$$
85 W Walnut St. (828) 232-1060.
This restaurant is famed for its exotic gypsy cuisine, including salmon herb roll with polenta, succotash, and curry coconut mojo sauce, and for its colorful interior and Moorish style. *L (summer only), D.* ● *Sun, Mon.* ㏐ ▨ ㋹
| | ■ | | ■ | ● | |

BEAUFORT: *Clawson's 1905 Restaurant & Pub* $$
425 Front St. (252) 728-2133.
Within a 1905 grocery store building, Clawson's offers ribs, steaks, and seafood in a setting surrounded by historic photos, displays, and memorabilia. *L.* ● *Sun, Labor Day–Memorial Day.* ▨ ㋹
| | ■ | | | | |

CHAPEL HILL: *Mama Dip's* $
408 W Rosemary St. (919) 942-5837.
Mama Dip's has been serving up such regional favorites as fried chicken, cornbread, and peach cobbler for over 25 years. This casual restaurant offers a buffet as well as table service for a la carte items. *B, L, D.* ● *public hols.* ▨ ㋹
| | ■ | ● | ■ | | |

DURHAM: *Magnolia Grill* $$$$
1002 9th St. (919) 286-3609.
Named by *Gourmet* magazine as one of America's 50 Best Restaurants, Magnolia is noted for Chef Ben Barker and his wife Karen, a pastry chef known for her outstanding dessert repertory. *D.* ● *Sun, Mon, public hols.* ㏐ ▨ ㋹
| | ■ | | ■ | ● | |

MANTEO: *1587 Restaurant* $$$
405 Queen Elizabeth St. (252) 473-1587.
Set within the Tranquil House Inn, 1587 makes the most of its beautiful setting along the small Manteo waterfront and a special-occasion menu of seafood, steaks, and vegetarian entrées. *D.* ● *Dec 25.* ㏐ ▨ ㋹
| | ■ | | ■ | ● | |

NAGS HEAD: *Sam & Omies* $
Milepost 16.5, 7228 Virginia Dave Trail. (252) 441-7366.
Sam and Omies has been a popular local hangout for inexpensive but well-prepared family fare for more than 50 years. *B, L, D.* ●
mid-Dec–Mar. ㏐ ㋹
| | ■ | | | | |

OCRACOKE: *Howard's Pub* $
SR 12 ,1 mile from ferry. (252) 928-4441.
Ocracoke's only year-round restaurant, Howard's Pub offers a raw bar, burgers, and pizza in a casual tavern setting. ● *Sun.* ㏐ ♫ ㋹
| | ■ | ● | ■ | | ■ |

SOUTH CAROLINA

BEAUFORT: *Beaufort Inn Dining Room* $$$
809 Port Republic St. (843) 521-9000.
New Southern cuisine is served in this historic building downtown in the interesting town of Beaufort; tuna and rack of lamb are among the favorite entrées. *D.* ● *Dec 24–25.* ㏐ ▨ ㋹
| | ■ | ● | ■ | ● | |

CHARLESTON: *Blossom Cafe* $$$
171 E Bay St. (843) 722-9200.
A sister restaurant to Magnolia's, Blossom next door features a Tuscan-inspired menu and design, along with flowing fountains and greenery on its spacious sheltered patio. *L, D, Sun brunch.* ● *public hols.* ㏐ ▨ ㋹
| | ■ | ● | ■ | ● | |

		Credit Cards	Outdoor Tables	Vegetarian	Good Wine List	Children's Facilities

Price categories include a three-course meal for one, a glass of house wine, and all unavoidable extra charges such as sales tax and service.
$ under $20
$$ $20–30
$$$ $30–45
$$$$ $45–60
$$$$$ over $60

CREDIT CARDS
Major credit cards accepted.

OUTDOOR TABLES
Garden, courtyard, or terrace with outdoor tables.

VEGETARIAN
A good selection of vegetarian dishes available.

GOOD WINE LIST
Extensive list of good wines, both domestic and imported.

CHILDREN'S FACILITIES
Small portions and/or high chairs available on request.

Restaurant	Price	Credit Cards	Outdoor Tables	Vegetarian	Good Wine List	Children's Facilities
CHARLESTON: *Magnolia's* 185 E Bay St. (843) 722-9200. In a restaurant row on the waterfront, Magnolia's offers contemporary American cuisine, with such regional specialties as crisp and creamy shrimp-and-grits. The casually elegant setting of the place is banked by light wood walls filled with modern artwork. *L, D.* public hols.	$$$	▦		▦	●	
CHARLESTON: *Middleton Place Restaurant* 4300 Ashley River Rd. (843) 556-6020. Within the 1933 guest house on the Middleton Place plantation, the restaurant serves such Low Country plantation fare as okra gumbo, she-crab soup, and Hoppin' John in a comfortably elegant setting overlooking the old rice-mill pond. *L, Tue–Sun D.* public hols.	$$$	▦			●	
CHARLESTON: *McCrady's* 2 Unity Alley. (843) 577-0025. From its obscure little alleyway entrance, McCrady's opens into a spacious set of modern rooms, where they serve French-influenced American cuisine to a sophisticated crowd. *D.* public hols.	$$$$	▦			●	
COLUMBIA: *Maurice's Piggie Park BBQ* 1600 Charleston Hwy. (803) 796-0220. The famous Piggie Park draws truckers, RV campers, and barbecue aficionados from across the region to its big spread devoted to the almighty pig. *L, D.* Thanksgiving, Dec 25.	$	▦	●			▦
COLUMBIA: *Al's Upstairs Italian Restaurant* 304 Meeting St. (803) 794-7404. Seafood, steak, Italian specialties, and such regional items as Oysters Rockefeller are served in this upscale, second-story restaurant downtown. *D.* Sun, Thanksgiving, Dec 25.	$$	▦		▦		
HILTON HEAD: *Charlie's L'Etoile Verte* 1000 Plantation Center. (843) 785-9277. This French bistro is noted for its fish, shellfish, and lamb specialties, along with Cobb salad and homemade desserts, all served in a French country decor. *L, D.* Sun, Mon, public hols.	$$$	▦			●	
MURRELLS INLET: *Oliver's Lodge* 4204 Hwy 17. (843) 651-2963. The oldest restaurant in Murrells Inlet, Oliver's has been serving fresh seafood here since 1910. Right on the waterfront, the restaurant offers a view of the fishing fleet. *D.*	$$	▦	●	▦		

GEORGIA

Restaurant	Price	Credit Cards	Outdoor Tables	Vegetarian	Good Wine List	Children's Facilities
ATHENS: *Last Resort Grill* 174 W. Clayton St. (706) 549-0810. This popular grill in a downtown storefront serves Southern cuisine with Southwestern influences. The salmon-and-grits plate and praline chicken are among the most requested specialties. *L, D.* Sun, public hols.	$$	▦	●	▦	●	
ATLANTA: *Harvest* 853 N Highland Ave NE. (404) 876-8244. Harvest offers light takes on regional cuisine emphasizing fresh vegetables, fish, and pecan-encrusted fare. *L (except Sat), D.* public hols.	$$	▦		▦	●	
ATLANTA: *Mid City Cuisine* Near Pershing Point. (404) 888-8700. In a first floor office building, this restaurant serves fresh organic vegetables, homemade pastas, seafood, and meats. *B, L, D.* Jan 1, Thanksgiving, Dec 25.	$$	▦	●	▦	●	

For key to symbols see back flap

	CREDIT CARDS	OUTDOOR TABLES	VEGETARIAN	GOOD WINE LIST	CHILDREN'S FACILITIES

Price categories include a three-course meal for one, a glass of house wine, and all unavoidable extra charges such as sales tax and service.
(S) under $20
(S)(S) $20–30
(S)(S)(S) $30–45
(S)(S)(S)(S) $45–60
(S)(S)(S)(S)(S) over $60

CREDIT CARDS
Major credit cards accepted.

OUTDOOR TABLES
Garden, courtyard, or terrace with outdoor tables.

VEGETARIAN
A good selection of vegetarian dishes available.

GOOD WINE LIST
Extensive list of good wines, both domestic and imported.

CHILDREN'S FACILITIES
Small portions and/or high chairs available on request.

ATLANTA: *Atlanta Grill* (S)(S)(S) 181 Peachtree St NE. (404) 221-6550. This always-open, elegant restaurant offers balcony seating above Peachtree Street to watch bustling Atlanta go by. *B, L, D.*	■	●	■	●	■
ATLANTA: *Food Studio* (S)(S)(S) 887 W Marietta St NW. (404) 815-6677. Squirreled away in the King Plow Arts Center, Food Studio is the city's most radical restaurant, serving complex fusion dishes in a recycled factory space. *D.* ● *Jan 1, Thanksgiving, Memorial Day, Labor Day, Dec 25.*	■	●	■	●	
ATLANTA: *Seeger's* (S)(S)(S)(S) 111 W Paces Ferry Rd. (404) 846-9779. Internationally recognized as one of the best restaurants in the South, Seeger's offers an eclectic European-influenced menu – prix fixe daily specialties served in a minimalist setting. *D.* ● *Sun, public hols.*	■	●	■	●	
DAHLONEGA: *Rick's* (S)(S) 47 S Park St. (706) 864-9422. Set invitingly in a comfortable clapboard house, a short walk up from the main square, Rick's offers a wide range of entrées from crawfish risotto to meatloaf and burgers. The wine lists offers 200 wines. *L, D, Sun brunch.* ● *Easter, Thanksgiving, Dec 25.*	■	●	■	●	■
MACON: *Len Berg's* (S) Old Post Office Alley. (478) 742-9255. Tucked away in an alley downtown, Len Berg's has been serving traditional Southern lunch plates since 1908. *L.* ● *Sun, public hols.*	■				
SAVANNAH: *Mrs. Wilkes' Boarding House* (S) 107 W Jones St. (912) 232-5997. In the ground floor of a Savannah row house, Mrs. Wilkes has been serving Southern specialties, family-style, for generations. *L.* ● *Sun, public hols.*			■		
SAVANNAH: *Il Pasticcio* (S)(S)(S) 2 E Broughton St. (912) 231-8888. This sophisticated restaurant offers Italian dishes in a smart storefront on the Broughton Street corridor. *D.* ● *Thanksgiving, Dec 24–25.*	■		■	●	
SAVANNAH: *Elizabeth on 37th* (S)(S)(S)(S) 105 E 37th St. (912) 236-5547. Namesake Chef Elizabeth Terry pioneered nouvelle Southern cuisine in this old house in the Victorian district. *D.* ● *Sun, public hols.*	■		■	●	
ST. SIMON'S: *Crabdaddy's* (S)(S) 1217 Ocean Blvd. (912) 634-1129. A crab shack for the polo set, this casual family restaurant serves seafood plates and a variety of other dishes. *D.* ● *public hols.*	■			●	■
TENNESSEE					
CHATTANOOGA: *Dinner on the Diner* (S)(S)(S) 1400 Market St. (423) 266-5000 or (800) 872-2529. In the dining car that is one of 48 train cars constituting the Chattanooga Choo Choo of musical legend, this diner serves family-friendly options that highlight the setting over the cuisine. *D.* ● *Sun, Mon, public hols.*	■				
CHATTANOOGA: *212 Market Restaurant* (S)(S)(S) 212 Market St. (423) 265-1212. Fresh seafood, steak, and homemade bread are the specialties of this appealing restaurant conveniently located right across from the Tennessee Aquarium. *L, D.* ● *Jan 1, Thanksgiving, Dec 25.*	■	●	■	●	■

For key to symbols see back flap

GATLINBURG: *Buckhorn Inn* $$$
2140 Tudor Mountain Rd. 865-436-4668.
Find the finest meals in the area at this fixed price country inn. The daily special might be mountain trout, beef tenderloin, or a mixed grill. Make reservations early in the day. D. ⚏ ᕇ ♪

MEMPHIS: *The Cupboard* $
1400 Union St. (901) 276-8015.
Modestly set in an aging strip mall off the busy connector in midtown, The Cupboard offers traditional meat-and-three dishes, including such favorites as dried catfish and meatloaf. B, L, D (except Sat–Sun). ⚏ ᕇ

MEMPHIS: *Rendezvous* $$
52 S 2nd St. (901) 523-2746.
This landmark alleyway restaurant offers popular spice-rubbed dry rib barbecue in a tavern setting decorated with memorabilia, a short block from the Peabody Hotel. L, D. ● Sun, Mon. ♈ ⚏

MEMPHIS: *Automatic Slim's Tonga Club* $$$
83 S 2nd St. (901) 525-7948.
At the exotically arty Automatic Slim's downtown, the Southwest meets the Caribbean in such dishes as the pork loin with adobo dry rub served over with a exotic mole sauce. There's live music on Friday nights.
L, D. ● Sun, public hols. ♈ ⚏ ᕇ ♪

NASHVILLE: *Monell's* $
1235 Sixth Ave N. (615) 248-4747.
Such traditional favorites as pork chops, Cajun catfish, corn pudding, and apple strudel are served here. (Call and confirm which meals will be served on which days). L, D, Sun brunch. ● Thanksgiving, Dec 25. ⚏ ᕇ

NASHVILLE: *Zanzibar* $$
412 S Main St. (901) 543-9646.
In the arts district south of Beale Street, an artist and gallery owner operates this eclectic bistro for Post-Modern fare accompanied by live jazz Thursday and Friday nights. B, L, D. ● Sun–Tue, public hols. ♈ ⚏ ᕇ ♪

NASHVILLE: *F. Scott's* $$$
2210 Crestmoor Rd. (615) 269-5861.
It's worth the 15-minute drive south of downtown to F. Scott's, where the menu changes every few days. Visitors can also stop for drinks in the jazz bar that features live music nightly. D. ● public hols. ♈ ⚏ ᕇ ♪

NASHVILLE: *Mad Platter* $$$
1239 Sixth Ave N. (615) 242-2563.
North of the Farmers' Market, the Mad Platter offers gourmet cuisine, and the quiet Germantown neighborhood is a nice alternative to the bustling waterfront district of lower Broad. L, D. ● Mon, public hols. ♈ ⚏ ᕇ

KENTUCKY

LEXINGTON: *Ala Lucie* $$$
159 N Limestone. (859) 252-5277.
An offbeat blend of Continental and new American is available at this elegant and romantic dining spot. Try the crab cake taco with avacado.
L (except Sat), D. ● Sun. ♈ ⚏ ♪

LEXINGTON: *Roy & Nadine's* $$$
3735 Harrodsburg Rd. (859) 223-0797.
Settle down into an overstuffed chair and enjoy one of the famous cocktails, while contemplating the eclectic menu of European, Asian, and traditional American dishes. L, D. ♈ ⚏ ᕇ

LOUISVILLE: *Mazzoni's Oyster Café* $
2804 Taylorsville Rd. (502) 451-4436.
In business for over a century, this informal café specializes in oysters that come freshly shucked, cooked in stews, or rolled up in cornmeal batter and fried. The menu includes many fish dishes. L, D. ● Sun. ⚏

LOUISVILLE: *Lilly's* $$$$
1147 Bardstown Rd. (502) 451-0447.
Intimate dining rooms, draped in green and deep purple decor, showcase local seasonal produce in dishes like country ham with morel mush-rooms or rabbit stuffed with lamb sausage. L, D. ● Sun, Mon. ♈ ⚏ ᕇ

A lush, swampy forest in the Everglades, Florida ▷

FLORIDA

FLORIDA

OR THE MAJORITY OF FLORIDA'S *40 million-plus annual visitors, the typical travel poster images of Florida – sun, sea, sand, and Mickey Mouse – are reason enough to jump on the next plane. The Sunshine State deserves its reputation as the perfect family vacation spot, but Florida is much richer in its culture, landscape, and character than its stereotypical image suggests.*

Both climatically and culturally, Florida is a state divided – a bridge between temperate North America and tropical Latin America and the Caribbean. In the north, roads are lined with stately live oak trees and people speak with a southern drawl, while, in the south, shade from the subtropical sun is cast by palm trees, and the inhabitants of Miami are as likely to speak Spanish as English.

For most visitors, Florida's prime attractions lie along the coasts, where the beaches are varied and abundant enough to satisfy every visitor. However, great rewards await those who want to explore farther. The lush forests and rolling hills of the north provide some of the loveliest countryside in the state. Equally exciting are the so-called "wild areas," such as the Everglades, which harbor an extra-ordinary diversity of plant and animal life, and where alligators and snakes are living reminders of the inhospitable place that Florida was not much more than 100 years ago.

HISTORY

At first glance, Florida appears to be a state without history. Yet behind its modern veneer lies a long and rich past, molded by different nationalities and cultures. Until the 16th century, Florida supported a large indigenous population, whose complex political and religious systems demonstrated a high degree of social organization. However, colonization soon decimated the Indians through warfare and disease. In 1513, the Spanish explorer Juan Ponce de León discovered Florida and named it after Pascua Florida, the Feast of the Flowers

Deerfield Beach, a quiet coastal resort within easy reach of Boca Raton

◁ The Marlin Hotel in Miami's South Beach, a classic establishment illuminated in colorful neon

(Easter). For almost 200 years several Spanish conquistadors attempted unsuccessfully to search for gold and colonize the region. Their primary concern was Florida's strategic position. The Gulf Stream carried Spanish galleons laden with gold and treasure from the New World colonies past Florida's coast on their journey back across the Atlantic, and it was thus vital that "La Florida" not fall into enemy hands.

Henry Flagler, 1830–1913

Initially the French troubled the Spanish, but the real threat to their control came in 1742 when English colonists from Georgia defeated them and finally acquired Florida about 20 years later. Though Florida was returned to Spain in 1783, numerous boundary disputes followed. It was only after Andrew Jackson, the ambitious US general, captured Pensacola that the official US occupation took place in 1821. During this period, the plantation system was firmly established in north Florida. The principal cash crop was cotton, for which intensive slave labor was required to work in the fields.

American attempts to subdue the Seminole Indians and take over their land led to over 65 years of conflict. When the Third Seminole War ended in 1858, the Indians retreated to the Everglades, where they still live. Soon after came the Civil War, by the end of which, in 1865, Florida was in ruins. But the state recovered rapidly. Railroad barons, such as Henry Flagler and Henry Plant, built a network of railroads and opulent hotels, which attracted wealthy visitors from the north. Tourism flourished in the early 20th century, and by 1950 it had become Florida's top industry. The launch of the NASA space program at Cape Canaveral in the 1950s also helped boost the state's prosperity.

SOCIETY & CULTURE

The state "where everyone is from somewhere else," Florida has always been a cultural hodgepodge. The earliest inhabitants were the Seminole Indians and the early pioneers of the 1800s, the Cracker farmers, named perhaps from the cracking of their cattle whips or the cracking of corn to make grits. However, both groups are rarely encountered along the affluent, heavily populated coast.

Americans have poured into this land of opportunity since World War II; the twentieth most populous state in the US in 1950, Florida is now ranked fourth. The largest single group to move south has been the retirees, for whom Florida's climate, lifestyle of leisure, and low tax rates, hold great appeal after a life of hard work. While

KEY DATES IN HISTORY

1513 Ponce de León discovers "La Florida"

1563 Pedro Menéndez de Avilés founds St. Augustine after defeating the French

1763 Britain acquires Florida

1783 Britain returns Florida to the Spanish

1785–1821 Spanish-American border disputes

1821 Florida becomes part of the US; Andrew Jackson becomes the first American governor

1835–42 Second Seminole War

1845 Florida becomes the 27th state

1852 Harriet Beecher Stowe publishes the anti-slavery epic, *Uncle Tom's Cabin*

1853 Third Seminole War begins

1886 Henry Flagler starts construction of the Florida East Coast Railway

1958 *Explorer I* is launched after NASA chooses Cape Canaveral as the site of its space program

1959 Over 300,000 Cubans flee to Florida

1980 125,00 Cubans arrive in the Mariel boatlift

1992 Hurricane Andrew devastates south Florida

2000 George W. Bush appointed president after the Florida election debacle

June, 2003 *Spirit*, a rover equipped with eight cameras, heads for Mars from Cape Canaveral

Space shuttle *Discovery* lifts off from the Kennedy Space Center, Cape Canaveral

Mural inside the US Federal Courthouse, Miami

super-rich communities like Palm Beach fit the conservative and staid image that some people still have of Florida, the reality is very different. An increasing number of the new arrivals are young people for whom Florida is a land of opportunity, a place to enjoy the good life. Today, the younger generation has helped turn Miami's South Beach into one of the country's trendiest resorts.

From 1959 on, there has also been massive immigration from Latin America; Dade County in particular has a huge Hispanic community. This ethnic diversity is today celebrated in an endless cycle of exuberant festivals, music, and local food.

ECONOMICS & TOURISM

Economically, Florida is not in bad shape compared with the rest of the country. For most of its history, its main source of revenue has been agriculture – citrus fruits, vegetables, sugar, and cattle, which was originally intro-duced by the Spanish colonists. In fact, Florida produces over 70 percent of the citrus fruits con-sumed in the United States today, while Kissimmee is known as the "cow capital" of the state. High-tech industry is significant as well, and the proximity of Miami to Latin America and the Caribbean has made it the natural route for trade with the region. This prox-imity has also contributed

to the state's flourishing cruise industry. Florida's warm climate has also generated high-profile moneyspinners, such as car racing, and the Daytona International Speedway attracts thousands of visitors every year. Spring baseball training also draws teams and lots of fans south, while the fashion trade brings models by the dozen and plenty of glamour to Miami.

It is tourism, however, that fills the state's coffers. The Walt Disney World Resort may appear to dominate the industry, but Florida makes the most of all its assets. Its superb beaches and the promise of winter sunshine have lured millions of vacationers through the years. Beside beaches and theme parks, there are natural habitats, state-of-the-art musems, and towns, such as St. Augustine and Pensa-cola, that still retain their Spanish Colonial ambience. Conservation is a major issue in Florida today. After decades of intense urban devel-opment, Floridians have finally learned the importance of preserving their rich and varied natural heritage. Great swathes of the natural landscape have already disappeared beneath factories, condos, and cabbage fields, but those involved in industry and agriculture are acting more responsibly, and water use is now strictly monitored. Florida's natural treasures, from its freshwater swamps and hardwood forests to its last remaining panthers, are now protected for posterity.

Beach buggie, Daytona Beach

A vibrant mural in Key West's Bahama Village

Exploring Florida

FROM BEACHES TO theme parks, Florida attracts almost 40 million visitors a year. The principal attractions are Miami and Orlando, but there are other exciting destinations as well, such as St. Augustine and Pensacola, established by Spanish colonialists in the 16th century. For nature lovers, the Everglades is a thrilling experience, while the Keys offer a choice of activities, such as fishing, diving, and snorkeling. An extensive road network links the main towns, so traveling by car in Florida is both quick and enjoyable.

¤

Art Deco motif, popular in Miami

SIGHTS AT A GLANCE

KEY

✈	Airport
⚓	Cruise port
—	Highway
—	Major road
—	Railroad

MILEAGE CHART

MIAMI									
75 / 120	*PALM BEACH*								**10** = Distance in miles
249 / 401	**179** / 288	*ORLANDO*							**10** = Distance in kilometers
318 / 511	**251** / 404	**106** / 171	*ST. AUGUSTINE*						
493 / 794	**448** / 721	**257** / 413	**202** / 327	*TALLAHASSEE*					
711 / 1144	**641** / 1032	**450** / 724	**397** / 639	**196** / 315	*PENSACOLA*				
282 / 454	**213** / 343	**85** / 136	**191** / 307	**279** / 449	**468** / 753	*TAMPA*			
268 / 431	**230** / 370	**106** / 171	**213** / 342	**302** / 486	**490** / 788	**23** / 37	*ST. PETERSBURG*		
233 / 375	**195** / 314	**131** / 212	**237** / 382	**332** / 535	**520** / 837	**362** / 99	**47** / 75	*SARASOTA*	
156 / 252	**232** / 373	**406** / 654	**477** / 768	**680** / 1094	**886** / 1426	**427** / 687	**412** / 663	**377** / 607	*KEY WEST*

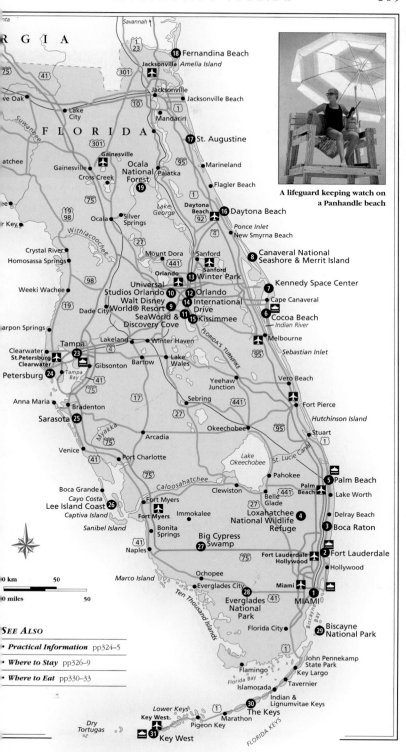

GEORGIA

FLORIDA

Savannah

ve Oak

Lake City

Gainesville

Cross Creek

atchee

ee

r Key

Crystal River

Homosassa Springs

Weeki Wachee

arpon Springs

Clearwater
St.Petersburg
Clearwater

Petersburg

Anna Maria

Sarasota **25**

Venice

Boca Grande
Cayo Costa
Lee Island Coast **26**
Captiva Island

Sanibel Island

Naples

Marco Island

Suwannee

Withlacoochee

Myakka

0 km   50

0 miles   50

SEE ALSO

18 Fernandina Beach
Jacksonville *Amelia Island*

Jacksonville

Jacksonville Beach

Mandarin

17 St. Augustine

Gainesville

Ocala
National
Forest Palatka **19**

Marineland

Flagler Beach

Silver
Springs Ocala

Mount Dora Sanford

Orlando

Universal
Studios Orlando **10** **13** Winter Park
Walt Disney **12** Orlando
World® Resort **9** **14** International
SeaWorld & **11** Drive
Discovery Cove **15** Kissimmee

Lakeland Winter Park

Tampa **23**

Gibsonton

Tampa Bay

Bradenton

Arcadia

Port Charlotte

Fort Myers
Immokalee
Fort Myers
Bonita
Springs

Big Cypress
Swamp **27**

Ochopee

Everglades City
Everglades
National **28**
Park

Florida City

Daytona
Beach **16** Daytona Beach

Ponce Inlet
New Smyrna Beach

8 Canaveral National
Seashore & Merrit Island

Kennedy Space Center **7**

Cape Canaveral

6 Cocoa Beach
Indian River

Melbourne

Sebastian Inlet

Vero Beach

Hutchinson Island

Stuart

Fort Pierce

Yeehaw
Junction

Sebring

Okeechobee

*Lake
Okeechobee*

Pahokee

St. Lucie Canal

Clewiston

Belle
Glade

Palm
Beach **5** Palm Beach

Lake Worth

Loxahatchee **4**
National Wildlife
Refuge

Delray Beach

3 Boca Raton

2 Fort Lauderdale

Fort Lauderdale
Hollywood

Hollywood

Miami

1 MIAMI

Biscayne
Bay

29 Biscayne
National Park

John Pennekamp
State Park

Flamingo Key Largo

Florida Bay Tavernier

Islamorada

Indian &
Lignumvitae Keys

30 The Keys

Lower Keys
Key West

Pigeon Key Marathon

Dry
Tortugas

31 Key West

FLORIDA KEYS

A lifeguard keeping watch on
a Panhandle beach

Lake
George

FLORIDA'S TURNPIKE

Caloosahatchee

Ten Thousand Islands

Miami ❶

A SMALL TRADING POST a century ago, Miami, or Greater Miami, now covers 2,000 sq miles (5,180 sq km) and has a population of two million. The metropolis incorporates many districts and cities and comprises most of Dade County. Miami's top sights are its beaches, especially fun-filled South Beach. Other sights include Little Havana, the heart of the city's Cuban population, and the leafy suburbs of Coral Gables and Coconut Grove.

Miami Beach, a city in its own right, linked by causeways to the mainland

KEY

▢	Sight/Place of interest
▢	Beach area
✈	Airport
Ⓡ	Metrorail station
⛴	Water taxi boarding point
P	Parking
ℹ	Tourist information
	Expressway

Getting Around

Public transportation in Miami is run by the Metro-Dade Transit Agency, which operates the buses, the Metrorail commuter rail network, and downtown's elevated Metromover. A limited Water Taxi service also operates two routes from Bayside Marketplace. However, the best way to get around is by car, while taxis are recommended at night.

See Also

- ***Where to Stay*** p326
- ***Where to Eat*** p330

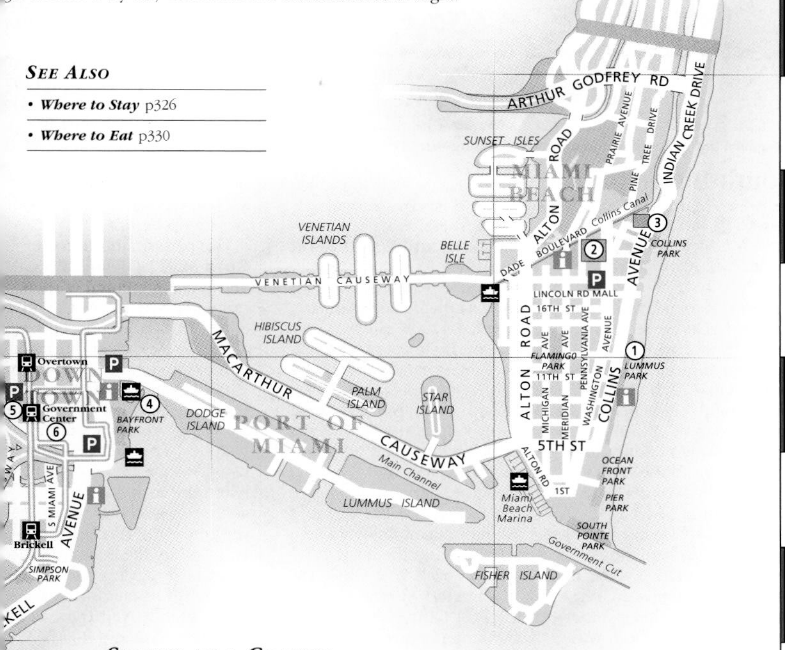

Sights at a Glance

South Beach ①
Holocaust Memorial ②
Bass Museum of Art ③
Biscayne Bay Boat Trips ④
Metro-Dade Cultural Center ⑤
Downtown ⑥
Little Havana ⑦
Coral Gables ⑧
Biltmore Hotel ⑨
Venetian Pool ⑩
Coconut Grove Village ⑪
Vizcaya p297 ⑫

Greater Miami
(see inset map)
North Beaches ⑬
Ancient Spanish Monastery p298 ⑭
Key Biscayne ⑮
Fairchild Tropical Garden ⑯
Miami Metrozoo ⑰
Wings Over Miami ⑱

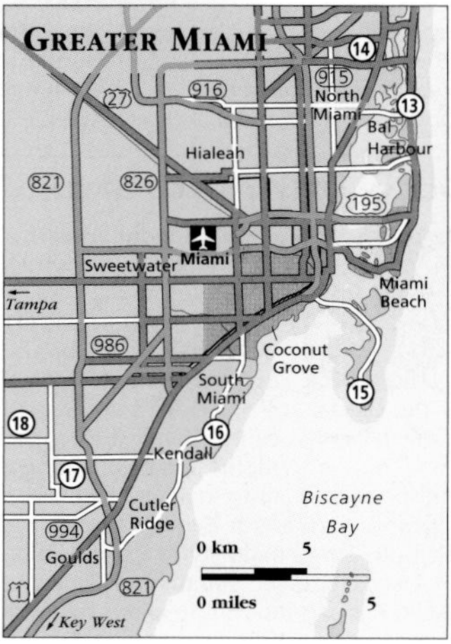

Key

Area of main map

Lifeguard hut in South Beach to match buildings on Ocean Drive

South Beach ①

Map F2. 🚌 *M, S, C, H, G, L, F, M, Night Owl, Airport Owl.* ℹ *1001, Ocean Drive, (305) 672-2014.*

THIS TRENDY DISTRICT, also known as SoBe, extends from 6th to 23rd Streets between Lenox Avenue and Ocean Drive. A hedonistic playground, enlivened by an endless parade of fashion models, body builders, and drag queens, SoBe is also home to the world's largest concentration of well-preserved Art Deco buildings.

The 800-odd buildings along Ocean Drive were, in fact, modest hotels built in the 1930s by architects, the most famous of whom was Henry Hohauser, who used inexpensive materials to create an impression of stylishness. The present use of bright colors, known as Deco Dazzle, was introduced in the 1980s by designer Leonard Horowitz.

Collins and Washington Avenues, too, have their share of Art Deco buildings, such as the classic Marlin Hotel at 1200 Collins Avenue, one of the finest representations of Streamline Moderne. Farther north is the luxury Delano Hotel *(see p326)*, with its striking non-Deco interior of billowing white drapes and original Gaudi and Dali furniture. Other buildings of interest are the 1920s Mediterranean Revival Old City Hall and the austere Miami Beach Post Office on Washington Avenue. Inside the Post Office is a mural showing the arrival of Juan Ponce de León, the Spanish conquistador who discovered Florida in 1513. Also on Washington Avenue is the

Wolfsonian Foundation, built in the 1920s, which has an excellent collection of fine and decorative arts.

Between Washington and Drexel Avenues is **Española Way**, a small, pretty enclave of Mediterranean Revival buildings, where ornate arches, capitals, and balconies adorn salmon-colored, stuccoed frontages. Built from 1922–25, this street is said to be the inspiration for Addison Mizner's Worth Avenue in Palm Beach *(see p301)*. Offbeat art galleries and boutiques line this leafy street, and on weekends craft booths are set up here.

The pedestrian **Lincoln Road Mall** is Miami's up-and-coming cultural corner, dominated by the ArtCenter South Florida. Established in 1984, the ArtCenter has three exhibition areas and a dozen studios that double as work-in-progress and selling space, as well as independent galleries. The galleries are usually open in the evenings when the mall comes alive as theater-goers frequent the restored Art Deco Lincoln and Colony theaters. After a heavy dose of modern art, the stylish restaurants and cafés, such as Van Dyke at 846, along Lincoln Road, offer respite.

The Beach, extending for 10 miles (16 km) up the coast, evolved into a spectacular winter playground

A **flamingo** is etched into glass doors in the Beacon's lobby.

OCEAN DRIVE: DECO STYLE

Deco detail, South Beach

The splendid array of buildings, on Ocean Drive, illustrates Miami's unique interpretation of the Art Deco style, popular all over the world in the 1920s and 30s. Florida's version, often called Tropical Deco, uses motifs such as flamingos, sunbursts, and jaunty nautical features, appropriate to South Beach's seaside location. Three main styles exist: traditional Art Deco, futuristic Streamline Moderne, and Mediterranean Revival, inspired by French, Italian, and Spanish architecture. A spirited preservation campaign, led by Barbara Capitman in the 1970s, made this area the first 20th-century district in the country's National Register of Historic Places.

Beacon *(1936)*
A contemporary color scheme, an example of Horowitz's Deco Dazzle, brightens the abstract decoration above the ground floor windows.

after the bridge connecting the island with the mainland was built in 1913. Much of the sand flanking the beach was imported several decades ago, and it continues to be replenished to counter coastal erosion. The vast stretches of sand are still impressive and draw large crowds of people.

The beach constantly changes atmosphere. Surfers predominate up to 5th Street. The vast beach beyond is an extension of SoBe's lively persona, with colorful lifeguard huts and posing bathers. Alongside runs Lummus Park, where Yiddish is spoken by the mainly Jewish population. Around 21st Street, the clientele is predominantly gay.

The stretch, north of 23rd Street, is sometimes known as **Central Miami Beach**. The most eye-catching sight here is the impressive Fontainebleau Hotel (pronounced "Fountain-blue" locally), with its trompe l'oeil arch. Completed in 1954, this curvaceous structure was architect Morris Lapidus' (1903–2001) interpretation of a modern French château. With its dated grandeur, pool, and waterfall, the hotel was the ideal setting for the 1960s James Bond film classic, *Goldfinger*.

Holocaust Memorial ②

Map F2.1933–45 Meridian Ave. (305) 538-1663. A, FM, G, L, W. 9am–9pm daily. www.holocaustmmb.org

M IAMI BEACH HAS one of the largest populations of Holocaust survivors in the world, hence the great appropriateness of Kenneth Treister's gut-wrenching memorial, finished in 1990. The centerpiece is an enormous bronze arm and hand stretching skyward, representing the final grasp of a dying person. It is stamped with a number from Auschwitz and covered with more than 100 life-size bronze statues of men, women, and children in the throes of the most unbearable grief. Titled *The Sculpture of Love and Anguish*, this is one of the most powerful contemporary sculptures in Florida today. Around the central plaza is a tunnel lined with the names of Europe's concentration camps, a graphic pictorial history of the Holocaust, and a granite wall inscribed with the names of thousands of victims who perished.

The Holocaust Memorial

Coronation of the Virgin (c.1492) by Domenico Ghirlandaio

Bass Museum of Art ③

Map F2. 2121 Park Ave. (305) 673-7530. M, S, C, H, G, L. 10am–5pm Tue–Sat (until 9pm on Thu), 1– 5pm Sun. public hols. (free 2nd Thu of month)

T HIS MAYAN-influenced, 1930s Deco building has a good collection of European paintings, sculpture, and textiles donated in 1964 by the philanthropists John and Johanna Bass. The collection, dating from the 15th to 17th centuries, includes Renais-sance works, paintings from the northern European schools, featuring paintings by Rubens and Dürer, and huge Flemish tapestries. Among the modern works are lithographs by Fernand Léger and Toulouse-Lautrec.

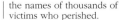

Terra-cotta tiles

A veranda is a prerequisite for most Ocean Drive hotels.

The corners of the building are beautifully rounded.

The terrazzo floor in the bar is a mix of stone chips and mortar – an inexpensive ver-sion of marble that brought style at minimal cost.

Adrian (1934)
Its Mediterranean inspiration and subdued colors make the Adrian stand out from other buildings.

Cardozo (1939)
A late Henry Hohauser work and Barbara Capitman's favorite, this Streamline gem replaces traditional Art Deco details with curved sides and aerodynamic racing stripes.

Biscayne Bay Boat Trips ④

Map D3. Bayside Marketplace. [M] *College/Bayside.* 🚌 *16, 3, C, 95, BM, S, FM, Night Owl.* **Island Queen Cruises** *(305) 379-5119.* **Gondola Tours** *(305) 577-3344.* **Floridian Cruises** *(305) 445-8456.*

A LEISURELY WAY to view the sprinkling of exclusive private island communities around Biscayne Bay is to take one of the many cruises from **Bayside Marketplace**. Tours, such as "Estates of the Rich and Famous" run by Island Queen Cruises, leave regularly and last about 90 minutes.

Biscayne Bay tour boat sign

Tours begin by sailing past Dodge and Lummus islands, where the world's busiest cruise port is situated. This port, which contributes an annual income of more than $5 billion to the local economy, handles more than three million cruise passengers a year.

Near the eastern end of MacArthur Causeway is the US Coastguard's fleet of high-speed craft. Opposite lies the unbridged Fisher Island, separated from South Beach by Government Cut, a water channel dredged in 1905. A restricted beach for African Americans in the 1920s, this is now, ironically, a highly exclusive residential enclave, with homes rarely costing less than $500,000. The tour continues north around the man-made Star, Palm, and Hibiscus islands, where real estate lots were sometimes sold "by the gallon." Among the lavish mansions are the former homes of Frank Sinatra and Al Capone, as well as the present abodes of celebrities such as Gloria Estefan and Julio Iglesias.

Other boat trips include nighttime cruises, deep-sea fishing excursions, and even gondola rides. The Water Taxi also provides a shuttle service along the mainland shore, linking Bayside Marketplace with various hotels. There is also a request service between Bayside and Miami Beach Marina, at the eastern end of MacArthur Causeway.

Bayside Marketplace itself is a fun complex with several shops, bars, and restaurants, including the remarkable-looking Hard Rock Café, complete with a guitar erupting from its roof.

Bayfront Park is nearby. At its center is the Torch of Friendship, commemorating John F. Kennedy, surrounded by the coats of arms of Central and South American countries; a plaque from the city's exiled Cuban community thanks the US for allowing them to settle here.

One of the lavish mansions seen during a Biscayne Bay boat tour

Metro-Dade Cultural Center ⑤

Map D3. 101 West Flagler St. ☎ *(305) 375-3000.* [M] *Government Center.* 🚌 *All buses to Miami Ave.* 🕐 *10am–5pm Tue–Fri (until 9pm on 3rd Thu of month), noon–5pm Sat & Sun.* 📷 ♿ [W] www.miamiartmuseum.org

DESIGNED BY THE celebrated American architect Philip Johnson in 1982, the Metro-Dade Cultural Center is a large complex, with a Mediterranean-style central courtyard and fountains. The complex includes an art gallery, museum, and library. Of these, the most interesting is the Historical Museum of Southern Florida, which concentrates on pre-1945 Miami. Besides displays on the Spanish colonization and Seminole culture, there is a fascinating collection of old photographs. These bring to life Miami's early history, from the hardships endured by the early pioneers to the fun-filled Roaring Twenties.

The Miami Art Museum of Dade County, across the plaza, has a limited permanent collection and many short-term exhibitions, mainly on post-1945 American art.

Metro-Dade Cultural Center, in downtown Miami

Downtown ⑥

Map D3. [M] *various stations.* **US Federal Courthouse** 301 N Miami Ave. ☎ *(954) 356-7451.* [M] *Arena/State Plaza.* 🕐 *8am–5pm Mon–Fri.* ⚫ *public hols.* ♿

WHEN THE development of Miami took off with the arrival of the Florida East Coast Railway in 1896, the early city focused on one square mile (2.5 km) on the banks of the Miami River. Today, this is the site of present downtown and the hub of the city's financial district. Its futuristic skyscrapers are a monument to the banking boom of the 1980s, when the city emerged as a major financial and trade center. The raised track of the Metromover, a driverless shuttle launched in 1986, provides a swift but good overview of the area.

Among the most striking high-rises here are the First Union Financial Center and

View of downtown Miami's skyline from the MacArthur Causeway

the NationsBank, constructed in 1983, and famous for its changing nighttime illuminations. Older structures include the Alfred I. DuPont Building (1938), home of the Florida National Bank, and the Ingraham Building (1927), a Neo-Classical/Renaissance Revival work.

The **US Federal Courthouse**, completed in 1931, is an imposing Neo-Classical building, with a pleasant, very Mediterranean courtyard. It has hosted a number of high-profile trials, including that of Manuel Noriega, the former Panamanian president, in 1990. Its main attraction, however, is the mural on the second floor. Designed by Denman Fink *(see p296)*, it depicts Miami's transformation from a wilderness into a modern city. Entry is often restricted, especially during high-profile cases.

Miami's oldest Catholic parish, **Gesu Church**, built in 1925, is located on Northeast 2nd Street. It is noted for its fine stained-glass windows, which were made in Munich, Germany. The **Freedom Tower**, on Biscayne Boulevard, is loosely modeled on the Giralda in Seville. At first home to the now-defunct *Miami News*, it became the reception center for Cuban exiles in the 1960s. It now stands empty. Burdines department store, founded in 1898, is on Flagler Street.

Freedom Tower (1925)

Little Havana ⑦

Map C3. 🚌 *8 from Downtown, 17, 12, 6.* **Cuban Museum of the Americas** Lowe Art Museum, UM Coral Gables. 📞 *(305) 284-5500.* 🆆 www.lowemuseum.org

As its name suggests, the 3.5 sq miles (9 sq km) area comprising Little Havana has been the surrogate homeland of Cuban immigrants since the 1960s. The atmosphere here, especially on the streets, is vibrant and reflects the Cuban way of life. Spanish is spoken everywhere, while a salsa beat emanates from every other shop, and *bodegas* (canteens) sell Cuban specialties. The main commercial thoroughfare and sentimental heart is **Calle Ocho** (Southwest 8th Street), with its liveliest stretch between 11th and 17th Avenues.

The small but authentic **El Crédito Cigar Factory**, near the corner of Calle Ocho and 11th Avenue, sells boxes of a wide range of cigars. The factory, set up in Havana in

1907, moved to Miami only in 1968. Cigar rollers can be seen at work here. The leaves are grown in the Dominican Republic, reputedly from Cuban tobacco seeds, the world's best.

The district's nationalistic focal point, **Cuban Memorial Boulevard**, as Southwest 13th Avenue is known, is dotted with memorials in honor of Cuban heroes. The most prominent is the Brigade 2506 Memorial's eternal flame commemorating the disastrous Bay of Pigs invasion in 1961. Every April 17, people gather here to remember the Cubans who died in the attempt to overthrow Fidel Castro's regime. Beyond are other memorials to heroes who fought against Cuba's Spanish colonialists in the 1880s.

At intervals, too, along Calle Ocho between 12th and 17th Avenues, are stars on the pavement honoring more recent Latin celebrities such as Julio Iglesias and Gloria Estefan in Little Havana's version of Hollywood's Walk of Fame.

Salsa music album covers

The **Cuban Museum of the Americas** is now located at the University of Miami's Lowe Art Museum in Coral Gables *(see p296)*. Its unique collection includes more than 500 works by Cuban artists, historical and political memorabilia, and Afro-Cuban lore.

Also in this district are the tiny Máximo Gómez Park, or Domino Park, and Woodlawn Cemetery. The Versailles restaurant, nearby, is the Cuban community's cultural and culinary bastion.

A Cuban mural in Little Havana, symbolizing nostalgia for the homeland

Coral Gables ⑧

Map A4. **Lowe Art Museum**
☎ (305) 284-3535. 🚇 Metrorail
(University). 🚌 52, 56, 72. ◐
10am–5pm Tue–Sat, noon–5pm Sun,
noon–7pm Thu. ● Mon, Thanksg.,
Dec 25, Jan 1. 🅿 ♿ **Miracle Mile**
🚇 Metrorail (Douglas Rd), then bus J
or 40, 42, 24 from downtown.

APTLY NAMED the City
Beautiful, Coral Gables is
a separate city within Greater
Miami. In the 1920s, George
Merrick planned this aesthetic
wonderland with Denman
Fink as artistic advisor, Frank
Button as landscaper, and
Phineas Paist as architectural
director. Regulations guaran-
tee that new buildings follow
the same part-Italian, part-
Spanish style advocated by
Merrick. Major landmarks here
include the Spanish Baroque
**Coral Gables Congregation-
al Church**, the district's
first church, the
Spanish Renaissance
Coral Gables City Hall,
and the **Lowe Art
Museum**, located in
the University of
Miami's campus.

Its main shopping
street was named
Miracle Mile (the
walk along one side
and down the other
being the mile in
question) by a developer in
1940. The Colonnade Hotel
was built in 1926 by Merrick
as the headquarters for his real
estate business. Nearby, at
Salzedo Street and Aragon
Avenue, is the Old Police
Station Building, built in 1939.

**Coral Gables
Congregational Church**

South view of the Biltmore Hotel, Coral Gables' most famous landmark

Biltmore Hotel ⑨

Map A4. 1200 Anastasia Ave.
☎ (305) 445-1926. 🚇 Metrorail (S
Miami) then bus 72. ♿ 🅿 Sun free.
🌐 www.biltmorehotel.com

DURING ITS HEYDAY in the
1920s, this hotel (see
p.326) hosted figures such as
Al Capone, Judy Garland, and
the Duke and Duchess of
Windsor. During World War II,
it served as a military hospital
and remained a veterans' hospital until 1968. After a $55-
million restoration in 1986, it
went bankrupt in 1990 but
reopened two years
later. The Biltmore's
most striking
feature is a 315-ft
(96-m) near replica
of Seville Cathe-
dral's La Giralda,
also the model for
Miami's Freedom
Tower (see p295).
Inside is a grand lobby, lined
with Herculean pillars. The
Biltmore has the largest hotel
swimming pool in the US,
where its famous instructor,
Johnny Weismuller – known
for his role as Tarzan – set a
world record in the 1930s.

Venetian Pool ⑩

Map A4. 2701 De Soto Blvd.
☎ (305) 460-5356. 🚇 Metrorail
(S Miami) then bus 72. ◐ mid-Jun–
mid-Aug: 11am–7:30pm Mon–Fri;
Apr–May & Sep–Oct: 11am–5:30pm;
Nov–Mar: 10am– 4:30pm; all year:
10am–4:30pm Sat & Sun. ● Mon
Sep–May, Jan 1, Thanksgiving,
Dec 24–25. 🅿 ♿
🌐 www.venetianpool.com

PERHAPS THE MOST beautiful
swimming pool in the
world, the Venetian Pool was
ingeniously fashioned from a
coral rock quarry in 1923 by
Denman Fink and Phineas
Paist. Pink stucco towers and
vine-covered loggias, candy-
cane Venetian poles, a cobblestone bridge, fountains,
waterfalls, and numerous
caves surround crystal-clear,
spring-fed waters, which are
great for swimming. The pool
was once one of the most
fashionable social spots in
Coral Gables – in the lobby
are a series of photographs of
beauty pageants staged here
during the 1920s. This beautiful public swimming pool is
definitely worth a visit, for a
swim or just a look.

Venetian Pool, ingeniously created in the 1920s out of an old coral rock quarry

Coconut Grove Village ⑪

Map B4. 🚆 *Metrorail (Coconut Grove).* 🚌 *42 from Coral Gables, 48 from downtown, 6, 27, 22.*

Miami's oldest community, Coconut Grove was a fabled hippy hangout in the 1960s. Today, "the village," as it is simply known, is famous for its cafés and restaurants, especially at night or on weekends. This is also the city's most relaxed shopping area with many boutiques and two malls – the outdoor CocoWalk, and the stylish Streets of Mayfair. In contrast are the food stalls of the colorful farmers' market, held every Saturday at McDonald Street and Grand Avenue.

On Grand Avenue, too, are the simple homes of the local Bahamian community, descendants of the Wreckers (*see p323*), who lived here from the mid-1800s. The exuberant Goombay Festival, a party with a parade, great food, and Caribbean music, is held here every June.

In a shady, affluent neighborhood south along Main Highway, is the **Barnacle**,

Coconut Grove Village, a lively area of shops, cafés, and bars

home of Ralph Monroe, a Renaissance man who made his living from ship building and wrecking. At 3400 Devon Road is the picturesque **Plymouth Congregational Church**, built in 1916.

Vizcaya ⑫

Map C4. 3251 S Miami Ave. 📞 *(305) 250-9133.* 🚆 *Metrorail (Vizcaya).* 🚌 *48.* 🕐 *9:30am–5pm, gardens till 5:30pm (last adm: 4:30pm) daily.* ⬤ *Dec 25.* 🏷️ 📷 ♿ *limited.* 🚫 📷 🎁 📷

Florida's grandest residence was completed in 1916 as the winter retreat for millionaire industrialist James Deering. His vision was to replicate a 16th-century Italian estate, but one that had been altered by succeeding generations. As a result, Vizcaya and its opulent rooms come in a blend of styles from Renaissance to Neo-Classical, furnished with the fruits of Deering's shopping sprees around Europe. The formal gardens, a rarity in Florida, beautifully combine Italian and French garden features with tropical foliage.

Statue of Pulcinella

They are dotted with sculptures and quaint buildings, including a Japanese tea house. Deering would always ask of his architect: "Must we be so grand?" fearing that Vizcaya would be too costly to support. After Deering's death in 1925, it proved to be so until it was bought by Dade County in 1952. The house and gardens were opened to public thereafter.

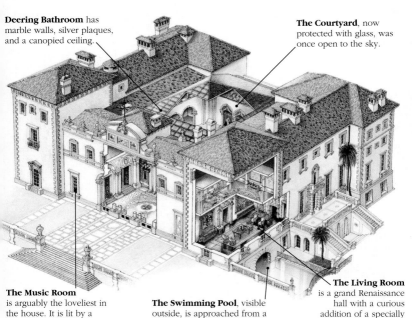

Deering Bathroom has marble walls, silver plaques, and a canopied ceiling.

The Courtyard, now protected with glass, was once open to the sky.

The Music Room is arguably the loveliest in the house. It is lit by a striking chandelier.

The Swimming Pool, visible outside, is approached from a grotto behind the house.

The Living Room is a grand Renaissance hall with a curious addition of a specially made organ.

Greater Miami

THE AREAS NORTH OF MIAMI BEACH and downtown and south of Coral Gables are seldom very scenic, but they are still well worth exploring for the great beaches and family amusements. Many of the area's primary attractions, such as zoos, gardens, and citrus orchards, were badly damaged by Hurricane Andrew, the country's costliest-ever natural disaster, which devastated southern Florida in 1992. Most sights have reopened, although restoration work continues in many cases.

Beach at Haulover Park, under the protective eye of a lifeguard

North Beaches ⑬

Map F4. Collins Ave. 🚌 K, S, or T *from South Beach or downtown.*

THE BARRIER ISLANDS to the north along Collins Avenue are occupied mainly by posh residential areas and inexpensive resorts, popular with package tours. A quiet strip of sand between 79th and 87th Streets separates Miami Beach from **Surfside**, a simple community popular with French Canadians. At 96th Street Surfside merges with **Bal Harbour**, a stylish enclave known for its flashy hotels and one of Miami's swankiest malls, Bal Harbour Shops. To the north is the pleasant **Haulover Park**, with a marina on the creek side and dune-backed sands facing the ocean.

Ancient Spanish Monastery ⑭

Map F4. 16711 W Dixie Hwy, N Miami Beach. 📞 *(305) 945-1462.* 🚌 *H from South Beach, 3 from downtown.* 🕐 *9am–5pm Mon–Fri, 10am–5pm Sat, 1:30–5pm Sun.* ⬤ *public hols.* 🏷 ⚕ Ⓦ *www.spanishmonastery.com*

THESE MONASTERY cloisters have an unusual history. Built in Spain between 1133 and 1141, they were bought in 1925 by newspaper tycoon William Randolph Hearst *(see p688),* who had

their 35,000 stones packed into crates. An outbreak of foot-and-mouth disease led to the crates being opened (to check the packing straw), and the stones were repacked incorrectly. Once in New York, they

remained there until 1952, when it was decided to piece together "the world's largest and most expensive jigsaw puzzle." The cloisters resemble the original, but there is still a pile of unidentified stones in a corner of the gardens.

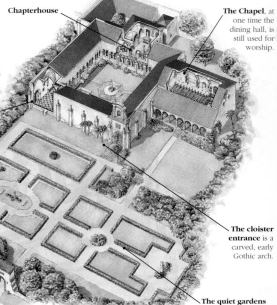

Chapterhouse

The Chapel, at one time the dining hall, is still used for worship.

Statue of Alphonso VII, patron of the monastery

The cloister entrance is a carved, early Gothic arch.

The quiet gardens are a popular spot for wedding photos.

The bell outside the chapel door

The tranquil, palm-fringed lakes of the Fairchild Tropical Garden

Key Biscayne ⑮

Map F5. 7 miles (11 km) SE of downtown. ⬚ B. **Bill Baggs Cape Florida SRA** ☎ (305) 361-5811. ⬚ daily.

THE VIEW OF downtown from Rickenbacker Causeway, connecting the mainland to Virginia Key and Key Biscayne, is one of Miami's best. Views aside, this has some of the city's top beaches. The most impressive is at Crandon Park in the upper half of the **Palms in Fairchild** Key, which is 3 **Tropical Garden** miles (5 km) long and enormously wide, with palm trees and picnic areas. At the southern end, the **Bill Baggs Cape Florida State Recreation Area** has a shorter beach joined to more picnic areas by boardwalks across the dunes.

Fairchild Tropical Garden ⑯

Map F5.10901 Old Cutler Rd. ☎ (305) 667-1651. ⬚ 65 from Coconut Grove. ⬚ 9:30am–4:30pm daily. ● Dec 25. ⬚ ⬚ ⬚
Mattheson Hammock Park ☎ (305) 665-5475. ⬚ 6am–sunset daily. ⬚ www.ftg.org

ESTABLISHED IN 1938, this beautiful tropical garden is also a major botanical research institution. One of world's largest collections of palm trees (550 of the 2,500 known species) stands around a series of man-made lakes. The garden also has an impressive array of cycads – relatives of palms and ferns that bear unusual giant red cones – as well as countless other trees and plants, including a comical-looking sausage tree.

Guides on the 40-minute tram tours describe how plants are used in the manufacture of medicines and perfumes (the flowers of the ylang-ylang tree, for example, are used in Chanel No. 5). The waterfront **Mattheson Hammock Park** is next door to the Fairchild Tropical Garden. Its highlight is the Atoll Pool, an artificial saltwater swimming pool circled by sand and palm trees alongside Biscayne Bay.

Miami Metrozoo ⑰

Map E5. 12400 SW 152nd St, Perrine. ☎ (305) 251-0400. ⬚ Metrorail (Dadeland North) then Zoo Bus. ⬚ 9:30am–5:30pm daily. ⬚ ⬚ www.metro-dade.com/parks

THIS ENORMOUS ZOO is considered one of the country's best. Animals are kept in spacious landscaped habitats, separated from humans by moats. Highlights include lowland gorillas, Malayan sun bears, and white tigers. The Petting Zoo offers elephant rides, and the Wildlife Show demonstrates the agility of the big cats. Take the

20-minute ride on the monorail for an overview, and then visit what you like; or take the monorail to Station 4 and then walk back.

Wings Over Miami ⑱

Map E5.14710 SW 128th St, adjacent to Tamiami Airport. ⬚ (305) 233-5197. ⬚ 10am–5pm daily Thu–Sat. ● public hols. ⬚ ⬚ ⬚ www.wingsovermiami.com

THIS MUSEUM is dedicated to the preservation of old aircraft. Its hangars contain a superb collection of finely preserved examples of aircraft that are still in operation. These include a US F-86 Sabre, a Russian MiG 15, a 1943 AT6D Texan "Old Timer," and a Douglas B-23 Dragon, as well as a wide range of other fascinating exhibits such as a machine-gun turret.

All these planes take to the sky during the Memorial Day weekend celebration. While in February, they are joined by B-17 and B-24 bombers in the Wings of Freedom event.

White tiger in front of a mock Khmer temple at Miami Metrozoo

Fort Lauderdale ➋

🏛 *150,000.* 🚆 🚌 🚍 ⛴ **ℹ**
1850 Eller Dr, Ste 303, (954) 765-4466.

Proclaimed the "Yachting
Capital of the World," Fort
Lauderdale's character is defined by its waterways, which
branch from the New River.
The area around the mouth of
the river is known as the
Isles because of the rows of
peninsulas created when the
canals were dug in the 1920s.
This is the city's prime neighborhood, with sweeping mansions lying behind lush
foliage and luxurious yachts
moored in the waterways.

Millions of visitors head for
the barrier islands lying along
the coast between the
beaches and the
Intracoastal Water-
way. The water-
way crosses **Port
Everglades**, the
world's second
largest cruise port
after Miami.
Riverboat cruises
and water taxis are
also available.

Las Olas Boulevard, the
city's busiest street, is lined
with eateries and boutiques.
The fine **Museum of Art**,
also located here, is best
known for its works by the
CoBrA artists, a group of
20th-century Expressionist
painters from Copenhagen,
Brussels, and Amsterdam.

Downtown is the city's
business and cultural center.
Riverwalk, a 1.5-mile (2.4-
km) stretch along the New
River's north bank, links most
of the city's historical and
cultural landmarks; it starts at

**Peach-pink Mizner Park, one of
Boca Raton's shopping malls**

Stranaham House (1901),
which originally served as a
trading post, post office, and
bank. **Old Fort
Lauderdale** runs
along Southwest
2nd Avenue and
has a few early
1900s buildings,
such as the Old
Fort Lauderdale
Museum of History.
The city has the
liveliest beaches on
the Gold Coast, especially
toward the end of Las Olas
Boulevard, where skaters
cruise past bars and shops.

**Water taxi on the New
River, Fort Lauderdale**

Boca Raton ➌

🏛 *80,000.* 🚌 **ℹ** *1555 Palm Beach
Lakes Blvd, (561) 233-3000.*

Affluent Boca Raton was
originally a sleepy
pineapple-growing settlement
that architect Addison Mizner
(1872–1933) envisaged as the
"greatest resort in the world."
The nucleus of his vision was

the ultra-luxurious Cloister
Inn, finished in 1926, with his
trademark Spanish details.
The hotel is now part of the
exclusive **Boca Raton Resort
and Club** *(see p326)*. Weekly
tours for non-residents are
arranged by the Boca Raton
Historical Society, based at the
Mizner-designed Town Hall.

Just opposite is the open-
air **Mizner Park**, perhaps the
most impressive of Boca
Raton's dazzling malls.
Located in a spectacular
setting within Mizner Park
is the **Boca Raton Museum
of Art**. This museum contains
44,000 sq ft (4,088 sq m)
of space for world-class exhibitions and an impressive
display of contemporary art.

The verdant and historic
Old Floresta district, a mile
(1.6 km) west of the Town
Hall, has 29 Mediterranean-
style houses built by Mizner.

Boca Raton's long, unde-
veloped beach is reached via
beachside parks, such as **Red
Reef Park**, which also has
the informative **Gumbo
Limbo Nature Center**. The
most northerly of the parks,
Spanish River Park is also
the most attractive, with
pleasant picnic areas shaded
by pines and palm trees. It
also has a lovely lagoon on
the Intracoastal Waterway,
next to an observation tower.

🏛 **Boca Raton Museum of
Art**
501 Plaza Rd, Mizner Park.
ℹ *(561) 392-2500.* ⏰ *Tue–Sun.*
⬤ *public hols.* 🅿 **♿**
🆆 *www.bocamuseum.org*

Loxahatchee
National Wildlife
Refuge ➍

10216 Lee Rd. **ℹ** *(561) 734-8303.*
🚌 *Delray Beach.* 🚍 **Refuge**
⏰ *daily.* ⬤ *Dec 25.* 🅿 ♿ 🅿
Visitor Center ⏰ *Nov–Apr: daily;
May–Oct: Wed–Sun.* ⬤ *Dec 25.*

The northernmost part of
the Everglades *(see p321)*,
this 221-sq mile (572-sq km)
refuge is known for its superb
wildlife. The best time to visit
is in winter, when migrating
birds arrive here from the

Cyclists and skaters enjoying the beachfront in Fort Lauderdale

An alleyway along Worth Avenue, Palm Beach's most exclusive street

north. The visitor center, off Route 441, has a display that explains the Everglades' ecology, and there are also two trails. The Cypress Swamp Boardwalk is lined with wax myrtle trees; the longer Marsh Trail is a bird-watcher's paradise, with ibis, herons, and anhingas. Visitors can also spot turtles and alligators. Those with canoes can explore the 5.5-mile (9-km) canoe trail, and there are also numerous nature walks.

Palm Beach ❺

🏛 10,000. ✈ 🚂 🚌 ℹ 45 Cocoanut Row, (561) 655-3282.

Essentially a winter resort for the rich and famous, Palm Beach was created at the end of the 19th century by the railroad baron Henry Flagler. In the 1920s Addison Mizner built luxurious Spanish-style mansions for its residents, a trend that established its unique look and influenced future architectural styles.

Palm Beach's major sights can be viewed in the area between Cocoanut Row and South County Road. Of these, the **Flagler Museum** (formerly Whitehall), Flagler's 55-room winter residence, has a grand marble entrance hall, an Italian Renaissance library, and a Louis XV ballroom. Flagler's private railroad car is on display on the South Lawn.

To the south, the **Society of the Four Arts**, founded in 1936, has two libraries, an exhibition space, and an auditorium for concerts and films. Other interesting buildings include the Town Hall, built in 1926, the Mizner Memorial

Park, and **The Breakers**, a mammoth Italian Renaissance structure and Palm Beach's grandest hotel *(see p327)*.

The epitome of Palm Beach's opulent lifestyle, however, is **Worth Avenue**. Stretching across four blocks from Lake Worth to the Atlantic Ocean, this is the town's best known thoroughfare. It first became fashionable with the construction of the Everglades Club in 1918, a collaborative effort between Mizner and his patron, Paris Singer, heir to the sewing machine fortune. Today, Worth Avenue boasts a spectacular mix of glitzy fashion boutiques, art galleries, and shops.

Picturesque alleyways, reminiscent of the backstreets of Spanish villages, connect with Worth Avenue. These interlinking pedestrian alleys, created by Mizner, are a riot of arches, twisting flights of stairs, cascading bougainvillea, and courtyards. The Esplanade, an open-air mall, is at the eastern end.

The multimillion-dollar mansions of Palm Beach are located in the suburbs. Some were built by Mizner and his imitators in the 1920s, but since then hundreds of other houses have proliferated in styles from Neo-Classical to Art Deco. The most easily visible are on a ridge along South Ocean Boulevard, nicknamed "Mansion Row." The most elaborate residence, Mar-a-Lago (# 1100), is now a top-end private club owned by millionaire Donald Trump.

🏛 Flagler Museum

Cocoanut Row & Whitehall Way. 📞 (561) 655-2833. ⏰ 10am–5pm Tue–Sat, noon–5pm Sun. ⏺ Jan 1, Thanksgiving, Dec 25. 📷 ♿ limited. 🚻 🍴 🅿 🌐 www.flagler.org

Flagler Museum at Palm Beach, formerly Henry Flagler's winter home

Cocoa Beach ➏

🏨 *14,000.* 🚌 *Cocoa.* ℹ️ *400 Fortenberry Rd, (321) 459-2200.*

T HIS LARGE, no-frills resort calls itself the East Coast's surfing capital. Surfing festivals set the tone, along with win-your-weight-in-beer competitions. Motels, restaurants, and gift and souvenir shops characterize the main street. The dazzling **Ron Jon Surf Shop** has surf boards galore (for sale and rent) and a huge T-shirt collection. In front of its flashing towers are sculptures of sports figures.

Kennedy Space Center ➐

Off Rte 405, 6 miles (9.6 km) E of Titusville. 🚗 *(321) 449-4444.* 🚌 *Titusville.* 🕐 *9am–7pm daily.* 🚫 *Dec 25. The center occasionally closes for operational requirements; always call ahead.* ♿ wheelchairs *available at Information Central.* 🍴 🎦 *(321) 867-4636 for schedule of launches.* 🌐 *www.ksc.nasa.gov*

W HEN Cape Canaveral was chosen as the site for NASA's (National Aeronautics and Space Administration) space program in the 1960s, the area came to be known as the Space Coast. The Kennedy Space Center on Merritt Island is the only place in the Western Hemisphere where shuttles carrying humans are launched into space. It was also the site of the historic launch of *Apollo 11* in July 1969, when President John F. Kennedy's dream of landing a man on the moon was realized. The **Visitor Complex**, built in

Rockets on display at the Cape Canaveral Air Station

1967 for astronauts and their families to view space center operations, is a 131-sq mile (340-sq km) facility that includes many attractions. Its highlight, the Galaxy Center, has two **IMAX® Theaters**, which show films on space exploration on screens that are five floors high. Footage from the shuttle missions offer breathtaking views of Earth from space. West of the entrance, the **Rocket Garden** is where visitors can walk through a group of rockets, each representing different stages in space history. **Robot Scouts**, located to the east of Rocket Garden, reveals the latest planetary explorer robots, while **Exploration in the New Millennium** shows visitors what the future holds

for space exploration; guests can even touch a piece of a Mars meteorite. The **Astronaut Encounter** in the same building is where visitors can meet real astronauts.

Guests can also climb aboard **Explorer** – a life-size replica of the Space Shuttle, at Shuttle Plaza in the northeastern corner of the Complex. The **Launch Status Center** alongside, has displays of genuine flight hardware and rocket boosters, as well as exhibits that re-create the shuttle's re-launch, liftoff, and flight procedures. Shuttles were the ingenious alternative to the very expensive, single-use crafts, used in the Apollo missions. Designed in the late 1970s, these re-usable spacecraft are now the backbone of the space program. Close by, the **Astronaut Memorial** honors the astronauts, from the *Apollo 1* to the Space Shuttle *Columbia* missions, who died in the service of space missions.

Close to the entrance of the Complex, an all-glass rotunda leads to the **Hall of Discovery**, which showcases key figures from the early days of rocketry. In the **Mercury Mission Control Room**, visitors view the actual consoles from which the first eight manned missions were

A life-size replica of the space shuttle *Explorer*, Kennedy Space Center

TIMELINE OF SPACE EXPLORATION

1958 First American satellite, the *Explorer 1*, is launched (Jan 31)	**1962** John Glenn orbits the earth in *Mercury* spacecraft	**1975** American *Apollo* and Russian *Soyuz* vehicles dock in orbit (Jul 17)	**1996** *Mars Pathfinder* sent to gather data from the surface of Mars **1981** *Columbia* is the first shuttle in space (Apr 12)		**2001** Dennis Tito pays $20 million to spend one week on board an International Space Center
1950	**1960**	**1970**	**1980**	**1990**	**2000**
1961 On May 5, Alan Shepherd becomes the first American in space. Kennedy commits nation to moon landing		**1969** Neil Armstrong and Buzz Aldrin (*Apollo 11*) walk on the moon (Jul 24)	**1986** The *Challenger* explodes, killing its crew (Jan 28)	**1990** The Hubble telescope is launched (Apr 24)	**2003** Space Shuttle *Columbia* breaks up upon re-entry into the atmosphere (Feb 1)

Launch pads seen on Kennedy Space Center Tours

monitored. Footage and interviews with some of the personnel are the highlights. Next, the **Hall of History** displays some of the authentic Mercury and Gemini spacecraft, which help create some hands-on excitement of early space exploration.

The Center also offers a number of interesting tours. The **Kennedy Space Center (KSC) Bus Tour** leaves frequently from the Visitor Complex and offers an overall tour of three major facilities. Visitors enter secured areas, where guides explain the inner workings of each facility. Each tour takes between two and six hours.

At the tour's first stop – the **LC 39 Observation Gantry** – one can get a bird's-eye view of the launch pads from the 60-ft (18-m) observation tower. Back on the ground, a film and several exhibits tell the story of a shuttle launch. The second facility to visit is the **Apollo/Saturn V Center**, featuring an actual 363-ft (110-m) Saturn V moon rocket, used by the Apollo missions. Visitors can watch the launch of *Apollo 8*, the first manned mission to the moon, in the Firing Room Theater, followed by a film at the Lunar Theater, which shows footage of the moon landing. This is also the only place in the world where guests can dine next to a genuine moon rock, at the Moon Rock Café. At the **International Space Station Center**, the tour's third stop, visitors can peer inside the facility where each space station is readied for launch.

There are three special-interest tours – **Cape Canaveral: Then & Now Tour**, a historic tour of the Mercury, Gemini, and Apollo launch pads; the **NASA Up Close Tour**, an insider's view of the entire space shuttle program; and the **KSC Wildlife Tour**, a tour of the Merritt Island Wildlife Refuge. Special tours to see actual shuttle launches can be arranged by booking at the Visitor Complex. However, missions have been postponed since the *Columbia* disintegrated in 2003; launches will resume at a rate of eight per year once all safety issues have been resolved. Outside the center, prime viewing sites are in Titusville and Cocoa Beach.

ENVIRONS: The **US Astronaut Hall of Fame** at Titusville, 9 miles (14 km) west of KSC, offers exciting opportunities to try out weightlessness and ride flight simulators with G-forces.

Canaveral National Seashore & Merritt Island ❽

🏠 Titusville.
🌐 www.nbbd.com/godo/cns

THESE ADJACENT preserves on the Space Coast share an astounding variety of fauna and a range of habitats including estuaries and hardwood hammocks. Visitors can often

see alligators and the endangered manatee, but the highlight is the rich birdlife.

The **Canaveral National Seashore** has a pristine 24-mile (39-km) stretch of beach. Apollo Beach at the northern end, and Playalinda Beach to the south are fine for sunbathing, but swimming can be hazardous, and there are no lifeguards. The top of Turtle Mound offers splendid views of Mosquito Lagoon (aptly named, so bring repellent in spring and summer).

Route 402 to Playalinda Beach has views of the Kennedy Space Center's launch pads. It also crosses **Merritt Island National Wildlife Refuge**, which covers an area of 220 sq miles (570 sq km). Much of the refuge lies within the Space Center and is out of bounds. Winter is the best season to visit. To view the local wildlife, follow the Black Point Wildlife Drive, which has the 5-mile (8-km) Cruickshank Trail. Be sure to pick up the informative leaflet at the drive's entrance. The Visitors' Information Center has displays on the habitats and wildlife in the refuge. One mile (1.6 km) farther east, the Oak Hammock and Palm Hammock trails have short boardwalks across the marshland for bird-watchers.

🦌 **Canaveral National Seashore**
Rte A1A, 20 miles (32 km) N of Titusville or Rte 402, 10 miles (16 km) E of Titusville. 📞 *(321) 267-1110.*
🕐 daily. 🌑 for shuttle launches. 💳
🦌 **Merritt Island National Wildlife Refuge**
Rte 406, 4 miles (6.5 km) E of Titusville. 📞 *(321) 861-0667.*
🕐 daily. 🌑 for shuttle launches.

SPACE COAST BIRD LIFE

The Space Coast is a bird-watcher's paradise. Its magnificent and abundant birdlife is best viewed early in the morning or shortly before dusk. Between November and March, in particular, the marshes and lagoons teem with migratory ducks and waders, as up to 100,000 birds arrive from colder northern climates. Royal terns, white ibis, black skimmers, brown pelicans, and sandhill cranes are some of the birds that are frequently seen.

Brown pelican

Walt Disney World® Resort ❾

WALT DISNEY WORLD, covering 43 sq miles (69 sq km), is the largest entertainment complex on earth. The main draw is its theme parks: Magic Kingdom, Epcot, Disney-MGM Studios, and Animal Kingdom. A self-sufficient vacation spot, the Resort supplies everything from hotels to golf courses, and each year brings a new wonder – Disney's Animal Kingdom is the biggest new attraction. Peerless in its imagination and attention to detail, the Resort is also a hermetic bubble cocooned from the real world. Everything runs like clockwork, and nothing shatters its illusions of fantasy. Unless you're a confirmed cynic, Walt Disney World Resort will amaze you.

USEFUL NUMBERS

General information
Ⓒ *(407) 824-4321.*

Accommodation information/reservations
Ⓒ *(407) 934-7639.*

Dining reservations
Ⓒ *(407) 939-3463.*
Ⓦ www.disney.go.com

WHEN TO VISIT

THE BUSIEST TIMES of the year are Christmas and Easter, June to August, and the last week in February. At these times, the parks approach capacity – some 90,000 people in the Magic Kingdom alone. Even so, all the rides operate and the parks remain open for much longer. During the off-season, 10,000 visitors a day might visit the Magic Kingdom, and certain attractions may be closed for maintenance. The weather is also a factor – in July and August, hot and humid afternoons are regularly punctuated by thunderstorms. Between October and March, the temperatures and humidity are much more comfortable and permit a more energetic schedule.

LENGTH OF VISIT

WALT DISNEY WORLD offers at least a week of entertainment. To enjoy it to the full, give Magic Kingdom and Epcot two days each, and a day each for Disney-MGM Studios and Animal Kingdom. Keep three nights to see the splendid fireworks displays of Fantasmic!, Fantasy in the Sky, and IllumiNations.

GETTING AROUND

AN EXTENSIVE transportation system handles an average of 200,000 guests each day. Even if you stay outside Walt Disney World Resort, many nearby hotels offer free shuttle services to and from the theme parks. Check when you make your reservation.

The transport hub of Walt Disney World is the **Ticket and Transportation Center** (TTC). Connecting it to the Magic Kingdom are two monorail services. A third monorail links the TTC to Epcot. Ferries run from the TTC to the Magic Kingdom. They also connect the Magic Kingdom and Epcot with resorts in their areas. Buses link everything in Walt Disney World, including direct links to Magic Kingdom. Residents and pass holders can use the entire transportation system for free, while one-day tickets allow holders to use the ferries and monorails between the TTC and Magic Kingdom.

DISABLED TRAVELERS

WHEELCHAIRS CAN be borrowed at the park entrance, and special bypass entrances allow disabled guests to board rides without waiting in line. Staff, however, are not allowed to assist with lifting for safety reasons.

VERY YOUNG CHILDREN

PARENTS WITH pre-school age kids can make use of the unique system known as "switching off," where they can enjoy various rides and attractions one at a time while the other parent stays with the child, without having to line up twice.

The Resort can be exhausting, so it is a good idea to rent a stroller from any park entrance. Take frequent breaks from the excitement and the heat by building in time for snacks or naps.

If you've come with young kids you should focus mainly on the Magic Kingdom.

WALT DISNEY RESORT

KEY

- ☐ Magic Kingdom Resort Area
- ☐ Disney Village Resort Area
- ☐ Epcot Resort Area
- ☐ Studio Resort Area

MAGIC KINGDOM · Discovery Land · Downtown Disney · Ticket and Transportation Center · DISNEY'S ANIMAL KINGDOM · EPCOT · Typhoon Lagoon · DISNEY MGM STUDIOS · Exit 27 · Exit 26B · Exit 25B

0 meters 800
0 yards 800

SAFETY

THE RESORT's first-rate security force means problems are dealt with promptly. Cast members are trained to watch out for unaccompanied children and escort them to lost children centers.

PARKING

VISITORS TO THE Magic Kingdom must park at the TTC and use public transportation; Epcot and Disney-MGM Studios have their own parking lots. Parking is free for Disney Resort residents; others must pay, but only once a day regardless of how many times they move their vehicle.

ADVANTAGES OF STAYING IN THE RESORT

LODGING IN THE resorts and in Walt Disney World Swan and Dolphin (operated independently but Disneyesque in every other respect) are of a very high standard. However, even the lowest-priced places are more expensive than many hotels outside Walt Disney World.

However, a few practical reasons to stay there are:
• Proximity to parks and free use of Disney's transportation.
• Early entry privileges into the parks (up to 90 minutes). Check in advance with each park for details.
• Guaranteed admission to the theme parks even when the parks are otherwise full.
• The possibility of dining with your favorite Disney character in your hotel.
• The delivery of shopping purchases made anywhere within the Resort.
• Note that the hotels close to the Marketplace (which are not run by Disney) offer few of the above mentioned privileges. For information on hotel listings see page 327.

RESORT DINING

VISITORS SHOULD make reservations in advance for any full-service restaurant in Walt Disney World Resort, especially in the theme parks and above all in Epcot. Whether or not you are staying at one of the resorts, reservations for dining can be made 60 days in advance. Some tables are held for same-day reservations, so make your reservation as early in the morning as possible. For restaurant details, see page 331.

MEETING MICKEY

FOR MANY YOUNGSTERS, meeting the Disney characters is the high point of their visit. Apart from seeing them in the parks, you can also meet them in numerous restaurants (usually at breakfast). Each park and many resorts also offer "character dining," but you must book ahead.

INFORMATION

TICKETS & TYPES OF PASSES

YOU CAN BUY one-day, one-park tickets, but if you're staying for over three days consider the following:
Park Hopper Pass: entitles one-day entry to each park on any four or five days.
All-in-One Hopper Pass: offers unlimited access to theme parks, water parks, and Pleasure Island on any five, six, or seven days.
Length of Stay Pass: this useful pass is exclusively for Resort hotel guests; unlimited entry to theme parks, Pleasure Island, water parks, and Disney complex. Prices depend on length of stay.
Annual Pass and Premium Annual Pass: non-Disney guests visiting for over ten days should consider these, which cost little more than a 7-day park hopper. Child pricing applies to ages 3–9.
FastPass allows one to reserve time at 19 popular attractions rather than wait in line. Passes are available at Disney stores, the airport, and the Tourist Information Center on I-Drive (see p313).

BUSIEST DAYS

EACH OF THE theme parks is busiest on certain days:
Magic Kingdom: Monday, Thursday, and Saturday.
Epcot: Tuesday, Friday, and Saturday.
Disney-MGM Studios: Wednesday and Sunday.

OPENING HOURS

WHEN THE theme parks are busiest, opening hours are the longest: 9am to 10/11pm or midnight. In less busy periods, hours are 9am to 6/7/8pm. The parks open early for pass holders and guests at any of the Resort hotels. Call to check details.

THE IDEAL SCHEDULE

TO AVOID THE worst of the crowds and heat, arrive early and visit the popular attractions first. Take a break in the afternoon, when it is hot and parks are busy, and return in the evening to see parades and fireworks.

TOP TIPS

LINES ARE shortest at the start and end of the day, and during parade and meal times. The wait for a show, however, is rarely longer than the show itself.
• Parks fill rapidly after the first hour of opening. Until then, you can often just walk onto rides for which there will be a line later.
• After a thunderstorm, the water parks are often almost empty, even at the busiest times of the year.
• Information regarding timings of shows, parades, and rides, and tips such as the waiting times at various attractions, are usually available at each park. Check at notice boards, Information Centers, and Guest Services.
• During parades, other attractions are quiet.
• Wear a comfortable pair of shoes, as the parks entail a lot of walking.
• There is very little shade, so be sure to wear a hat.

MAGIC KINGDOM

MAGIC KINGDOM is the essential Disney theme park. Disney characters fill its cheerful acres, and seven lands evoke different themes.

It is best to head straight for **Space Mountain**, a superb coaster in Tomorrowland. It shoots around in stygian blackness against projections of asteroids and galaxies, creating superb effects of space travel. The terrifying **ExtraTERRORestrial Alien Encounter** employs amazing special effects which makes you feel as if you are at the mercy of a rampaging alien.

Another popular attraction, **The Timekeeper**, is a 360-degree Circle-Vision screen show, which takes visitors on a whirling trip through time. **Buzz Lightyear's Space Ranger Spin** is a fabulous journey in a two-seater car. It is fitted with laser cannons and a control, so you can shoot at targets with a laser beam.

Fantasyland, dominated by Cinderella's Castle, forms the core of the Magic Kingdom. **The Many Adventures of Winnie the Pooh** uses the latest technology, lighting, and sound effects to create an enchanting experience, while **Peter Pan's Flight** combines the feeling of flying with the delight of perfectly matched music and movement.

The Haunted Mansion in Liberty Square leads visitors through a spook-ridden mansion and graveyard.

Set in the Wild West, Frontierland offers a journey on a runaway train known as **Big Thunder Mountain Railroad**. The fun **Country Bear Jamboree** is an Audio-Animatronics® animal show, and **Splash Mountain** is an exciting flume ride with music and special effects, which ends with a big drop.

Adventureland is a fusion of Africa and the Caribbean. **The Jungle Cruise** goes past an animatronically animated setting of Africa. Another voyage, **Pirates of the Caribbean**, leads you into underground prisons and past 16th-century galleons.

Main Street USA is famous for the **Spectro Magic Parade**, a shimmering fantasy of music, live action, and illuminated floats. In peak season, it takes place at 7pm and again at 9pm. The afternoon parade is best viewed from Frontierland. The evening parade also features **Fantasy in the Sky** – an extravaganza of fireworks and music. Mickey's ToonTown Fair (with numerous attractions for children), is the best place to watch the show.

EPCOT

EPCOT, AN ACRONYM for the Experimental Prototype Community of Tomorrow, was Disney's dream of a technologically advanced community that represented a utopian vision of the future.

The enormous 250-acre (101 ha) park is divided into two halves: **Future World** with an emphasis on entertainment and education; and **World Showcase**, which represents the art, culture, and culinary skills of different countries around the globe. Boats cross the World Showcase Lagoon frequently and are a convenient method of getting here.

Future World's attractions are all corporately sponsored. The unmistakable seven-and-a-half-thousand-ton globe of **Spaceship Earth** is its focal point. It takes visitors past superbly crafted tableaux and Animatronics® scenes portraying future possibilities in technology. Since most people visit here first, there are long lines in the mornings. It is best seen in the afternoon, after tackling "Test Track" and "Honey, I Shrunk the Audience."

Test Track, Epcot's top ride, places visitors in a simulator that moves on tracks at high speeds. You test a prototype sports car, which speeds at over 66 mph (106 km/h) on a raised roadway. Try to visit this ride first thing in the morning.

The Imagination Pavilion is best known for the hilarious "Honey, I Shrunk the Audience," which integrates Disney's unique 3-D film technology with special effects.

The **Wonders of Life** pavilion deals with the human body. **Body Wars**, Epcot's first simulator thrill ride, takes a miniaturized version of you on an adventure inside the human body, while **Cranium Command** is an Animatronics® show about the human brain.

The Living Seas offers Sea Base Alpha, where visitors journey to the "bottom of the ocean" past sharks and dolphins, and watch the sea life through transparent walls.

EATING & DRINKING

The typical fare at **Magic Kingdom** is fast food. However, try the Liberty Tree Tavern or Crystal Palace for quieter dining. Cinderella's Royal Table in the castle has a regal ambience, and Aunt Polly's is great for sandwiches.

The dining at **Epcot** is superb, particularly **World Showcase**, where reservations are required. Recommended are: **Mexico:** the San Angel Inn serves interesting but pricey Mexican cuisine. **Italy:** L'Originale Alfredo di Roma has elegant fare. **Japan:** you can eat communally, either in the Mitsukoshi Teppan Dining Rooms or at the bar of Mitsukoshi Tempura Kiku for sushi and tempura. **France:** the upscale Bistro de Paris (dinner only); Les Chefs de France, an exclusive restaurant with *haute cuisine*; and the terraced Le Cellier Steakhouse for steaks, and crêpes.

At **Disney-MGM Studios**, you can soak up the atmosphere at three of the full-service restaurants. The costly Hollywood Brown Derby replicates Hollywood's Original Brown Derby, where the stars met in the 1930s. Children prefer the Sci-Fi Dine-In Theater Restaurant, where you sit in mini-Cadillacs and watch old sci-fi films. For dining without a reservation, try Hollywood & Vine, which serves pasta, salads, seafood, ribs, and steaks.

World Showcase has architectural masterpieces of 11 different countries, featuring replicas of famous buildings. Each pavilion is staffed by people from the country it represents, selling ethnic products and cuisine. The best live shows are the acrobats at China and the Living Statues at Italy. Highlights include **Wonders of China** – a Circle-Vision film on China's ancient sites; **Maelstrom** in Norway – an exciting trip through fjords; and **Impressions de France** – a film offering a whirlwind tour of France. Do not miss **IllumiNations**, a *son-et-lumière* show with lasers, fire- and waterworks. It is staged near closing time around World Showcase Lagoon.

DISNEY-MGM STUDIOS

DISNEY-MGM STUDIOS opened in 1989, both as a theme park and as a full-fledged working film and TV studio. It combines top-notch shows and rides, based on Disney and Metro-Golden-Mayer films (to which Disney bought the rights), with entertaining tours that allow visitors to glimpse the magic of filmmaking in the working section of the Studios.

At Hollywood Boulevard, Art Deco styled buildings vie with a replica of Mann's Chinese Theater. The best shops are located here: Celebrity 5 & 10 has a range of affordable movie souvenirs, such as clapper boards and Oscars®, and the pricey Sid Cahuenga's One-Of-A-Kind stocks rare film memorabilia such as autographed photos and famous actors' clothes. **The Great Movie Ride** carries visitors past enormous movie sets, where scenes from films are re-created using live action.

Sunset Boulevard is an evocation of the famous Hollywood street in the 1940s. Re-created theaters and storefronts are dominated by the Hollywood Tower Hotel. This lightning-ravaged hotel is the spot for Orlando's scariest ride – **The Twilight Zone Tower of Terror** – in which you are strapped into an elevator for a voyage inspired by the 1950s

TV show *The Twilight Zone*™. Its high point is the ghastly 13-story plunge that everyone knows will come, repeated no fewer than seven times. The **Rock 'n Roller Coaster Starring Aerosmith** accelerates to 60mph (96 km/h) in 2.8 seconds in the dark, and pulls 5G in the first corkscrew.

Animation Courtyard gives visitors a glimpse behind the scenes during the creation of Disney's Audio-Animatronics®. The **Magic of Disney-Animation** tour takes visitors to watch animators at work, while **Playhouse Disney-Live on Stage!** features a collection of Disney Channel characters singing and dancing.

At Mickey Avenue, the entertaining **Disney-MGM Studios Backlot Tour** has a tram ride that takes visitors for a peek at the camera, wardrobe, and lighting departments. It ends in Catastrophe Canyon, in the midst of a flood and explosions. The walking tour demonstrates how special effects are used: battles at sea are re-created using models in a water tank.

New York Street is a clever re-creation of the Big Apple. Its highlight is the spectacular **Jim Henson's Muppet**™ **Vision 3-D**, a slapstick 3-D movie starring the Muppets. Trombones, cars, and rocks launch themselves at you out of the screen – so realistic that children often grasp the air expecting to touch something. Audio-Animatronics® characters and special effects, such as a cannon blowing holes in the walls of the theater, provide the fourth dimension.

Echo Lake offers the sensational **Star Tours** ride, based on the *Star Wars* films. The spaceship – a flight simulator akin to those used to train astronauts, has to cope with a fierce intergalactic battle.

At 5pm, the park holds a parade based on one of Disney's animated films. The evening show, **Fantasmic!** is the finest of its kind in Florida. It combines music, lasers, animation, and over a hundred actors and dancers. Although it seats 10,000 people, you still need to arrive two hours early to get a good seat.

ANIMAL KINGDOM

THIS PARK HAS both real and mythical beasts, spread over seven different "lands."

At Discovery Island, the **Tough to be a Bug** show is a superb 3-D presentation. Camp Minnie-Mickey is where visitors meet Disney characters. The **Festival of the Lion King** show here is superb.

Africa offers the fabulous **Kilimanjaro Safaris**, where you see hippos, rhinos, lions, and elephants roaming freely.

Asia features gibbons, birds, and tigers in a re-creation of Indian ruins. Tapirs and Komodo dragons are found on the **Maharaja Jungle Trek**, the climax of which are the magnificent Bengal tigers that roam the ruins. Dinoland USA has the wild **DINOSAUR** ride, where a motion simulator bucks and weaves, trying to ensnare and avoid dinosaurs. Two new rides, **Primeval Whirl** and **Tricera Top Spin**, attempt to spin visitors dizzy.

THE REST OF WALT DISNEY WORLD® RESORT

WALT DISNEY WORLD offers much more than just its theme parks. There are 22 resorts *(see p327)*, two water parks, a campground, nearly 300 restaurants, a host of nightclubs, a shopping village, and half a dozen golf courses.

Among the waterparks, **Blizzard Beach**, a reconstructed Alpine ski resort, has the tallest speed slide in the world. At **Fort Wilderness Resort and Campground**, activities include horseback riding, fishing, and biking. Jet skiing, rental boats, and fishing gear are also available at the **Marketplace** and at all lakeside resorts. After-dark entertainment revolves around three distinct areas in Downtown Disney: **Pleasure Island** has a range of clubs and discos; The Marketplace is an outdoor mall with lots of shops – The World of Disney sells mountains of merchandise; and **Disney's West Side** has jazz and blues clubs, and the famous Cirque du Soleil.

Universal Studios Orlando ❿

O NCE A SINGLE MOVIE PARK, Universal Studios now boasts two theme parks, an entertainment complex, and the first of its many planned hotels. Together, Universal Studios Park, Islands of Adventure, and Universal CityWalk present a formidable reason to spend time away from Walt Disney World. The parking lot feeds into Universal CityWalk where there is a series of moving walkways to a fork leading to the two separate parks.

Universal Globe marking the entrance to Universal Studios Park

TACKLING THE PARKS

T HE BUSIEST SEASONS are during Christmas and Easter. During the off-season, check with Guest Services for special deals on tickets. Arrive early to combat the long lines for rides (the gates open an hour before opening time). Arrive 15 minutes early for shows to ensure a seat. Children may find most rides too intense; child-friendly attractions are ET Adventure, the Woody Woodpecker Coaster, A Day in the Park with Barney, the Nickelodeon Studios, Jurassic Park Islands, and the Seuss Landing Island.

EATING & SHOPPING

There are plenty of options for dining. The Hard Rock Café is the largest in the world. Lombard's Seafood Grill specializes in fish dishes, while Universal Studios Classic Monsters Café serves Californian and Italian cuisine, and has a great buffet. Most rides and attractions have their own stores. In Hitchcock's 3-D Theater, one can buy a Bates Motel Soap, while Universal Studio Store has everything from fake Oscars to oven mitts with the Universal logo.

UNIVERSAL STUDIOS PARK

T HE ENTRANCE IS known as Front Lot, as it is built to look like the front lot of a 1940s Hollywood film studio. Actors in costumes wander the streets playing characters from *Ghostbusters, Frankenstein*, and legends such as Marilyn Monroe and the Marx Brothers. The shooting schedule posted near the turnstiles has details of shows that are being filmed. Tickets for these are available at the booth located near Guest Services.

A new example of the increasing number of 3-D plus one attractions, **Shrek 4-D** allows visitors to experience 3-D film special effects. The **Nickelodeon Studios** visits the production center of America's most popular TV network, exclusively for young people. Children will definitely enjoy the Slime Geyser outside, which erupts in a shower of green slime every ten minutes or so.

The Backlot area has more than 60 façades, some of which replicate real buildings, others reproduce famous movie settings. There are cutouts of the Guggenheim

Museum and the New York Public Library, as well as Macy's department store, and Louie's Italian Restaurant, where a shootout took place in the original *Godfather* movie. One of the Backlot's attractions, the **Twister** pits visitors against a simulated tornado, which lets them experience the terrifying power of the elements as they stand inside 20 ft (6 m) of the five-floor high funnel of winds.

In the section known as Hollywood, sets of Hollywood Boulevard and Rodeo Drive pay tribute to Hollywood's golden age, from the 1920s to the 50s – featuring the famous Mocambo nightclub, the luxurious Beverly Wilshire Hotel and the top beauty salon, Max Factor. There is even a replica of the Hollywood Walk of Fame, with the names of stars embedded in the sidewalk.

Hollywood's most popular attraction is **Terminator 2: 3-D**, a ride that uses superb robotics and the latest 3-D technology to catapult the audience into the action alongside the star of the *Terminator* films, Arnold Schwarzenegger.

The **Gory, Gruesome & Grotesque Horror Make-Up Show** shows scenes from films such as *The Mummy, The Fly*, and *An American Werewolf in London*, and the automated bloodied masks demonstrate how the special effects are realized.

One of the park's most thrilling rides, **Back to the Future – The Ride** is located at the Expo Center. During

Universal Studios Park's Terminator 2: 3-D, a state-of-the-art attraction

The thrilling river ride in Jurassic Park River Adventure, Jurassic Park Island

the dizzying journey in a time-traveling car, visitors plunge over lava, skim ice fields, and swoop into the mouth of an enormous dinosaur. In the incredibly addictive **Men In Black**, visitors join Will Smith in a simulator, battling aliens with lasers and cannons. In Woody Woodpecker's Kid Zone, the enchanting **ET Adventure** is based on Steven Spielberg's 1982 film. Guests soar off to ET's home planet on a flying bicycle, gliding over a twinkling cityscape, before arriving at a world inhabited by ET look-alikes.

The San Francisco section's big draw is **Earthquake – The Big One**, which demonstrates how earthquakes are simulated. Visitors ride a subway train, set in the movie *Earthquake*, and contend with a tremor of 8.3 on the Richter scale, a descending tidal wave, and a train collision.

Amity, the other half of this section, has the blood-chilling **Jaws** ride, where a giant great white shark lunges at the boat, tearing through the water at terrifying speed.

THE ISLANDS OF ADVENTURE

O NE OF THE world's most technologically advanced theme parks, Islands of Adventure demands a day's visit of its own. The first island visitors encounter is the Marvel Super Hero Island where the theme draws from the Marvel Comics' Super Hero stable of

characters. The **Incredible Hulk Coaster**, probably Florida's best, is a green leviathan that accelerates you to over 40 mph (64 km/h) in two seconds before turning upside down at 100 ft (30 m) above the ground. The **Amazing Adventures of Spider-man**, shows a stunning integration of 3-D technology with motion simulation. Toon Lagoon Island, where cartoons transmute into reality, hosts two wet rides, and the riotous **Toon Lagoons Beach Bash**. Popeye and Bluto are the stars of many rides.

Jurassic Park Island boasts the **Jurassic Park River Adventure**, a cruise where visitors encounter hadrosaurs, Stegosaurs, and others before being diverted due to a raptor breakout. The **Pteranodon Flyers** ride flies pairs of riders over the island on an 80-second trip, while the **Discovery Center** is an interactive natural history exhibit where guests can view the results of mixing DNA from various species, including themselves.

The Lost Continent Island is an island of myth and legend. **The Flying Unicorn** is a pleasant introduction to roller coasting for young children. However, for coaster addicts, **Duelling Dragons** is the ride of choice. Two coasters – Fire and Ice, battle to see who will arrive back first. Stage shows include the Eighth Voyage of Sinbad, and Poseidon's Fury: Escape from the Lost City, with a myriad special effects.

Seuss Landing Island, based on the popular Dr. Seuss children's books, the creation of Theodor Seuss Geisel, caters to children. The **Cat in the Hat** ride serves as an introduction to the characters. There are also a host of innovative rides that captivate younger children.

UNIVERSAL CITYWALK

I NSPIRED BY MANY of popular culture's innovators such as Bob Marley and Motown, Universal CityWalk is a 30-acre (12-ha) entertainment complex of restaurants, nightclubs, and cinemas. Open between 4pm and 2am, its dazzling array of restaurants range from Emeril's (a top TV chef) to the nostalgic Motown Café, and the famous Hard Rock Café. A restaurant known as "Bob Marley – A Tribute to Freedom," is an exact replica of this famous musician's home. Among the many nightclubs are City Jazz and The Groove Dance Club where visitors can watch live musical performances. The complex also has stores and movies, and its stages host concerts, art festivals, and celebrity appearances. A lagoon provides a picturesque setting to sip a cool drink or take a moonlight stroll.

The Hard Rock Café and music venue, Universal CityWalk

SeaWorld & Discovery Cove ⑪

I N SCALE AND SOPHISTICATION, SeaWorld is one
of the world's most impressive marine-life
adventure parks. Established in 1973 to promote
its educational, research, and conservation
programs, the park abounds in fun as well as
entertainment. SeaWorld's answer to the Disney
mouse is Shamu the killer whale, and the
Shamu Adventure Show tops the bill. Next
to SeaWorld is Discovery Cove, a new, all-inclusive park, where guests can swim with rays,
dolphins, and other fascinating sea creatures.

**Dolphin Cove, where everyone can touch
and feed the dolphins**

EXPLORING SEAWORLD

S EAWORLD IS LESS crowded
than Orlando's other theme
parks. Most of the presentations are either walk-through
exhibits or stadium shows.
Arriving 15 minutes early
guarantees a good seat. Show
timings overlap, so guests
cannot leave a show just in
time for another. However, it
is possible to get a seat in the
Clyde and Seamore (Sea Lion
and Otter) show by leaving
the Shamu Stadium while the
performers are taking their
bows. The best time to see
shows such as Wild Artic
and Shark Encounter is while
visitors are busy watching the
stadium events. Young chil-

dren enjoy meeting the actors
in furry suits who play the
parts of Shamu and Crew –
guests can normally find
them near SeaWorld's exit
around closing time. The
400-ft (122-m) Sky Tower
ride offers a superb overview
of the park. For more information, go to Guest Relations
near the exit gate.

EXHIBITS & RIDES

T HREE meticulously land-
scaped habitats are incorporated in **Key West at
SeaWorld**. Dolphin Cove, a
wave pool in the style of
a Caribbean beach, offers
underwater viewing of
bottlenose dolphins
and the chance to
pet and feed them.
Visitors can also
touch one of the
200-odd rays at
Stingray Lagoon,
while Turtle Point
is home to rescued
loggerhead, hawks-
bill, and green sea turtles,
which are too injured to
survive in the wild.

Pacific Point Preserve re-
creates the rugged north
Pacific Coast in the form of a
large, rocky pool. One can
watch harbor seals, South
American fur seals, and noisy
California sea lions basking
on the rocks or gliding
effortlessly through the water.

Most of the other wildlife at
SeaWorld is viewed through
glass. **Manatees: The Last
Generation?** offers a
splendid underwater view
of these irresistibly appealing
herbivores (see p319).

In the fabulous **Penguin
Encounter**, a moving walk-

way leads past a frozen
landscape where a large
colony of penguins demon-
strate their comical waddling
and elegant swimming. The
gawky puffins are also a
delight to watch.

Billed as the world's largest
collection of dangerous sea
creatures, **Shark Encounter**
is very popular. Moray eels,
barracuda, and pufferfish are
the tantalizing appetizers
before a main course of
sharks, whose toothy grins
are a short distance away, as
visitors walk through a glass
tunnel inside their aquarium.

Shamu: Close Up!,
next to the **Shamu
Stadium**, is a re-
search and breeding
facility to study killer
whale behavior – ten
whales have been
born here so far.
Wild Arctic is a
thrilling, hi-tech
ride that simulates
a helicopter flight
through blizzards
and avalanches. Visitors arrive
at Base Station Wild Arctic,
created around an old expedition ship, and encounter
polar bears, harbor seals,
walruses, and beluga whales.

SeaWorld's new **Journey
to Atlantis**, a water coaster
with a mythological twist,
and **Kraken**, a winner of the
annual Orlando roller-coaster
competition, are hot tickets.

SHOWS & TOURS

T HE EXCITEMENT of seeing a
killer whale erupt out of
the water carrying one of the
SeaWorld trainers on its nose
is hard to overstate. In the
park's number one show,

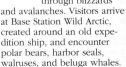
**Shamu, the park's
official mascot**

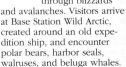

TOP TIPS

• *SeaWorld allows guests to feed
many of the animals, but it
restricts both the type and the
amount of food, which must be
purchased from them. If this is
something you would like to do,
check with guest services as soon
as you enter the park for feeding
times and food availablility.*

• *Build your schedule around the
four main types of presentations:
Shamu Killer Whale, Atlantis
Water Ski, Sea Lion and Otter,
and Whale and Dolphin shows.*

• *Bring a waterproof plastic bag
for your camera as, especially
during the Shamu and Dolphin
shows, people sitting in the first
12 rows often get splashed by
salt water.*

• *Journey to Atlantis is guaranteed
to get you wet, so reserve this
for the hottest part of the day.*

• *SeaWorld's gentle pace means
that visiting after 3pm is a less
crowded experience.*

Shamu Adventure, stunts such as this are supplemented by a giant video screen, providing close-ups of the action. There are five Shamus, which take turns to perform, as well as a Baby Shamu. The show also features the killer whales performing an amazing "underwater ballet."

Key West Dolphin Fest is another remarkable show, based on the speed and agility of bottlenose dolphins and false killer whales. During the show, the mammals play with their trainers and interact with members of the audience. However, the show's highlight is the dolphins' synchronized leaps over a rope.

The **Clyde and Seamore Take Pirate Island** show, held in the Sea Lion and Otter Stadium, features two sea lions (Clyde and Seamore), otters, and walruses in a swashbuckling adventure of lost loot, pirate ships, and hilarity on the high seas.

The Atlantis Water Ski Show is a fantastic waterski extravaganza. The show incorporates speed boats, jet skis, and very impressive waterskiing stunts, including skiing in pyramid formation. The highlight of the show is a competition with superb aquabatics, gymnastics, and high-energy stunts.

Cirque de la Mer is a non-traditional circus, blending dramatic special effects, music, and acrobatics. Another show, **Pets Ahoy**, features talented cats, birds, dogs, and pigs, all of whom have been rescued from animal shelters. **Shamu Rocks America**, held at the Shamu Stadium, features the SeaWorld trainers and killer whales in a nighttime rock 'n' roll show, complete with drenching salt-water waves and dazzling theatrical effects. Other exhibits include **Shamu's Happy Harbor**, a play area for smaller children, **Dolphin Nursery** for new dolphin moms and their calves, and **Caribbean Tide-pool**, which encourages close

Cuddly versions of SeaWorld stars

examination of tropical fish, starfish, sea anemones, and other underwater denizens.

The **SeaWorld Hubbs Research Institute** runs a number of nonprofit "Research, Rescue and Rehabilitation" projects. It has helped thousands of manatees, dolphins, and whales in difficulty – nursing and operating on them. Those that recover fully are released into the wild. Several tours such as The Sharks! tour, offer a glimpse of this work. If interested, inquire at Guest Relations. The **Adventure Express Tour** offers exclusive guided park tours, reserved seats, feeding opportunities, and back door access to rides. The **Laser Fireworks Show**, viewed from the huge lakeside stadium, constitutes a stunning finale to the day.

DISCOVERY COVE

JUST ACROSS THE road from SeaWorld, Discovery Cove is a quiet revolution in Florida's theme parks. With a capacity of only 800 guests a day (the car park is limited to only 50 cars), it offers some unforgettable experiences, the most vaunted of which is an

opportunity to swim with Atlantic bottlenose dolphins.

Discovery Cove has been conceived as a private island. Its five main areas are set within beautifully landscaped grounds with waterfalls, pools, and niches connected by beaches. **Coral Reef** abounds with grottos and a shipwreck, and offers the opportunity to swim alongside threateningly large sharks, separated from visitors by a transparent plexi-glass wall. At the **Aviary**, guests can feed birds, while **Ray Lagoon** offers the chance to snorkel above rays, some of which grow up to a length of 5 ft (1.5 m). The **Dolphin Lagoon** has a 40-minute orientation session, followed by 30 minutes of wading and swimming with these highly intelligent mammals.

It is a good idea to split your party into two for the dolphin experience, to be able to take each other's photographs. Do not bring any sunscreen, as the park has its own "fish friendly" one, the only brand permitted. If you decide not to visit the Dolphin Lagoon, the price of the visit is cut in half. The package price ($199 per person, no child reductions) includes the dolphin experience (children under six cannot participate), all equipment, a free snorkel, a meal, and seven days admission to SeaWorld. Despite the price, the park is very popular, and it is better to book well in advance.

A performing killer whale, one of the star attractions at SeaWorld

Downtown Orlando, dominated by the SunTrust Center

Orlando ⑫

🏠 200,000. ✈ 🚌 🚉 ℹ️ *8723 International Dr, (407) 425-1234.* 🌐 *www.orlandoinfo.com*

ORLANDO WAS JUST a sleepy provincial town until the 1950s. However, its proximity to Cape Canaveral and the theme parks soon transformed it into a burgeoning business center. Downtown, with its glass-sided high-rises, comes to life only at night, when both visitors and locals flock to the many bars and restaurants around Orange Avenue, the town's main street.

During the day, the area around **Lake Eola**, east of Orange Avenue, offers views of the wooden homes of the town's earliest settlers. The residential districts north of downtown have many parks and museums, including the serenely beautiful Harry P. Leu Gardens and **Loch Haven Park**, which houses a trio of museums. The most highly regarded of these is the **Orlando Museum of Art**. Its collections include pre-Columbian artifacts with figurines from Peru, African art, and American paintings from the 19th and 20th centuries. The park is also home to the John and Rita Lowndes Shakespeare Center, which includes the 350-seat Margeson Theater and smaller Goldman Theater. The Center holds the Orlando-UCF Shakespeare Festival.

The **Maitland Art Center**, on Packwood Avenue in the leafy suburb of Maitland, occupies studios designed in the 1930s by artist André Smith as a winter retreat for fellow artists. Set around courtyards and gardens, the buildings show a profusion of Mayan and Aztec motifs. The studios are still used, and exhibitions of contemporary American crafts are held often here.

North of Lake Eola is the town's newest attraction, the **Orlando Science Center**. Covering 207,000 sq feet (19,200 sq m) of floor space, the center's aim is to offer a stimulating environment for experimental science learning. It thus provides a huge range of exciting state-of-the-art interactive exhibits. Among its attractions are the Dr. Philips CineDome, which also functions as a planetarium, its dinosaur fossils collection, and the ShowBiz Science exhibit, which reveals some of tricks and special effects used in movies. Earlier located at Loch Haven Park, the center re-opened here in February 1997.

🌷 **Loch Haven Park**
N Mills Ave at Rollins St. **Orlando Museum of Art** ☎ *(407) 896-4231.* 🕐 *Tue–Sun.* ⬤ *public hols.* 📷 ♿
🏛 **Orlando Science Center**
777 East Princeton St. ☎ *(407) 514-2000.* 🕐 *Tue–Thu.* 📷 🎧 📷 ♿
🌐 *www.osc.org*

Winter Park ⑬

🏠 25,000. 🚌 🚉 ℹ️ *150 N New York Ave, (407) 644-8281.* **Scenic Boat Tour** ☎ *(407) 644-4056.* 📷

GREATER ORLANDO'S most refined neighborhood took off in the 1880s, when wealthy northerners came south and began to build winter retreats here. The **Charles Hosmer Morse Museum of American Art** probably has the finest collection of works by Art Nouveau craftsman, Louis Comfort Tiffany. There are superb examples of his jewelry, lamps, and many of his windows, including the *The Four Seasons* (1899). To the south of Winter Park is **Rollins College**, dotted with 1930s Spanish-style buildings. The finest is the **Knowles Memorial Chapel**, whose main entrance has a relief of a meeting between the Seminole Indians and the Spanish conquistadors. The college's **Cornell Fine Arts Museum's** impressive collection of Italian Renaissance paintings is the oldest in Florida. The **Scenic Boat Tour** explores the nearby lakes, canals, and sprawling mansions.

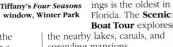

Tiffany's *Four Seasons* window, Winter Park

🏛 **Charles Hosmer Morse Museum of American Art**
445 Park Ave N. ☎ *(407) 645-5311.* 🕐 *Tue–Sun.* ⬤ *public hols.* 📷 ♿
🌐 *www.morsemuseum.org*

Main entrance of Knowles Memorial Chapel, Winter Park

The sinking home of Ripley's Believe It or Not!, International Drive

International Drive ⑭

🚌 Orlando. 🚏 Orlando. ℹ️ Gala Center, 8723 S International Dr, (407) 363-5872.

A STONE'S THROW from Walt Disney World, "I Drive" is a 3-mile (5-km) ribbon of hotels, shops, and theaters. Its most popular attraction is **Wet'n Wild**, known for its big-thrill rides. The Storm and Mach 5 feature terrifying descents down near-vertical slides, and there is also the watery Kid's Playground.

Filled with fantastic objects, illusions, and film footage of strange feats, **Ripley's Believe It or Not!** was created by the American cartoonist, Robert Ripley. It is housed in a building that appears to be falling into one of Florida's sink-holes, which occur due to the erosion of the limestone bedrock. **Titanic – The Exhibition** displays artifacts, movie memorabilia, and re-creations of the ship's rooms and grand staircase. Two blocks from the mall is Orlando's **Official Visitor Information Center**, which has coupons for many attractions, such as discounts on admission and bargain meals.

Kissimmee ⑮

🏃 41,000. 🚌 🚏 ℹ️ 1925 E Irlo Bronson Memorial Hwy, (407) 847-5000.

M EANING "Heaven's Place" in the language of the Calusa Indians, Kissimmee is said to be the cow capital of Florida. In the early 20th century, cows freely roamed the streets of this cattle boom town. Today, the only livestock visitors are likely to encounter are those that appear in the rodeos at **Silver Spur Arena**. Held every February and July, this is the state's oldest and wildest rodeo. Other less extravagant rodeos are held every Friday night at the **Kissimmee Sports Arena**.

Most visitors headed for Walt Disney World often stop at Kissimmee, drawn by the many inexpensive motels, strung along the busy, traffic-ridden US 192. For those who want to linger, Kissimmee's Old Town is a re-created pedestrian street of early 20th-century buildings with several eccentric shops offering psychic readings and tattoos. Near the airport, the **Flying Tigers Warbird Restoration Museum** is another enjoyable experience. Old and damaged World War II aircraft are brought here for repairs. The museum provides guided tours of the hanger, where visitors can learn more about the finer points of airplane reconstruction. For a sizable fee, visitors can even take a spin in a T-6 Navy Trainer.

🏛️ Flying Tigers Warbird Restoration Museum
231 N Hoagland Blvd. 📞 (407) 933-1942. ⏰ daily. 🚫 Dec 25. 💷 ♿
🌐 www.warbirdmuseum.com

ENVIRONS: Orlando's most cultural theme park, **Splendid China**, 24 miles (38 km) west of Kissimmee, is famous for its scaled-down replicas of China's distinctive landmarks. The Great Wall is half-a-mile (1-km) long, made from 6.5 million bricks; the Leshan Grand Buddha Statue, 236 ft (72 m) tall in China, is still splendid in its 35-ft (11-m) version. Beijing's enormous Forbidden City is a minia-turized version of the original; Suzhou Gardens is a full-scale reconstruction of the town of Suzhou as it would have looked 700 years ago. Each of these models is decorated with countless toy people and animals. Splendid China also includes several theaters where displays of traditional Chinese skills such as martial arts, are held. The Chongqing Acrobats are the most popular. In keeping with the theme, the park's restaurants only serve Chinese food.

🎭 Splendid China
3000 Splendid China Blvd, Kissimmee. ℹ️ (407) 396-7111. ⏰ daily. 💷 ♿
🌐 www.floridasplendidchina.com

Beijing's Forbidden City, reduced to more manageable dimensions at Splendid China

Daytona Beach 16

🏃 64,000. ✈ 🚌 ℹ 126 E Orange Ave, (386) 255-0415.
🌐 www.daytonabeach.com

THIS RESORT IS famous for its 23-mile (37-km) beach, lined with a wall of hotels. The old-fashioned boardwalk offers concerts in the bandstand, arcades, and go-karts. During the April Spring Break, nearly 200,000 college students descend on the beach for this ritual party.

This is also one of the few beaches in Florida where cars are allowed on the sands, a hangover from the days when motor enthusiasts, such as Louis Chevrolet and Henry Ford, raced on the beaches. The **Daytona International Speedway** nearby draws huge crowds, especially during the Speedweek in February and the Motorcycle Weeks in March and October (see p28).

Across the Halifax River downtown, the **Halifax Historical Society Museum** occupies a 1910 bank building and displays local history. To the west, the **Museum of Arts and Sciences** has exhibits from 1640 to 1920. **Gamble Place**, run by the museum, is a hunting lodge built in 1907 for James N. Gamble, of Procter & Gamble fame. Museum tours include the Snow White House, built for Gamble's grandchildren.

🏛 Museum of Arts & Sciences
1040 Museum Blvd. 📞 (386) 255-0285. ◯ daily. ● public hols. 📷 ♿

St. Augustine 17

🏃 16,000. 🚌 100 Malaga St, (904) 829-6401. ℹ 10 Castillo Dr, (904) 825-1000. 🎭 Arts & Crafts Spring Festival (Apr). 🌐 www.oldcity.com

AMERICA'S OLDEST continuously occupied European settlement was founded by the Spanish colonist Pedro Menéndez de Avilés on the feast day of St. Augustine in 1565. Today, this town has many attractions for the modern tourist, not least its 43 miles (69 km) of beaches and the fact that it is within easy reach of several golf courses and marinas. St. Augustine burned down in 1702 but was soon rebuilt in the lee of the **Castillo de San Marcos**. This mighty fortress is the largest and most complete Spanish fort in the US. Constructed of coquina, a sedimentary limestone formed by seashells and corals that could withstand the impact of cannonballs, this is a superb example of 17th-century military architecture.

The historic heart of St. Augustine is compact and easy to explore on foot. Horsedrawn carriage tours are popular and depart from Avenida Menendez, north of the Bridge of Lions, which was built across Matanzas Bay in 1926. The 18th-century City Gate is the entrance to the **Old Town**. Its focus is the pedestrian

Cleopatra (c.1890) by Romanelli, Lightner Museum

St. George Street, lined with attractive stone buildings. Some of the main attractions here are the **Spanish Quarter Village**, a museum that recreates an 18th-century garrison town, and **Peña-Peck House**, a fine First Spanish Period home dating to the 1740s. The **Oldest Wooden Schoolhouse**, built from cypress and red cedar wood in the mid-1700s, is also located on this street. The heart of the Spanish settlement is **Plaza de la Constitution**, a leafy square flanked by Government House Museum and the grand Basilica Cathedral. The splendid **Flagler College** started out as the Ponce de Leon Hotel, built by Henry Flagler (see p286) in 1883, a year after he honeymooned in St. Augustine. Its gilded and stuccoed cupola has symbolic motifs representing Spain and Florida, notably the golden mask of the Timucuan Indian sun god and the lamb – a symbol of Spanish knighthood. The other resorts Flagler built here are the Cordoba and Alcazar Hotels. The latter, a three-floor Hispano-Moorish structure, is now the **Lightner Museum**, devoted to the country's Gilded Age. Its exhibits include glass works by Louis Tiffany, and its Grand Ballroom houses an eclectic exhibit of "American Castle" furniture. The lovely **Ximenez-Fatio House** is now a museum run by the National Society of Colonial Dames. It seeks to re-create the genteel boarding house that it was in the 1830s, when invalids and adventurers first visited Florida in order to escape from the harsh northern winters.

🏛 Castillo de San Marcos
1 Castillo Dr. 📞 (904) 829-6506. ◯ 8:45am–4:45pm daily. ● Dec 25. 📷 ♿ limited. call for details. 🌐 www.nps.gov/casa

🏛 Lightner Museum
75 King St. 📞 (904) 824-2874. ◯ daily. ● Dec 25. 📷 ♿ 🌐 www.lightnermuseum.org

Cars cruising the hard-packed sands of Daytona Beach

Fernandina's Beech Street Grill with Chinese Chippendale motifs

Fernandina Beach ⑱

🏠 10,000. 🚉 Jacksonville. ✈ Jacksonville. ℹ 961687 Gateway Blvd Ste 101 G, (904) 261-3248.

THE TOWN OF Fernandina Beach on Amelia Island, just across the St. Mary's River from Georgia, was famous as a pirates' den until the early 1800s. Its harbor attracted a motley crew of foreign adventurers, whose various allegiances earned the island its soubriquet, the "Isle of Eight Flags." Today, Fernandina is better known as a charming Victorian resort and Florida's primary source of sweet Atlantic white shrimp: more than 2 million pounds (900,000 kilos) are harvested by shrimping fleets each year.

Occupying a large section of the town's **Historic District**, the Silk Stocking District was named after the affluence of its original residents. Sea captains and timber barons built homes here in a variety of styles. Queen Anne houses with turrets jostle with graceful Italianate residences and fine Chinese Chippendale structures, such as the **Beech Street Grill**. The weathered buildings on Centre Street once housed chandleries and naval stores. Antique shops and gift shops have now replaced them; the 1878 Palace Saloon, however, still serves a wicked Pirate's Punch at the mahogany bar adorned with hand-carved caryatids. Farther south, the

Amelia Island Museum of History occupies the former jail and offers twice daily, 90-minute guided history tours recounting the island's turbulent past – from the time of its first Indian inhabitants to the early 1900s.

The **Fort Clinch State Park**, at the island's northern tip, has trails, beaches, and campsites, as well as a 19th-century fort built in 1847. Park rangers now dress in Civil War uniforms and perform 19th-century war re-enactments one weekend a month.

🏛 **Amelia Island Museum of History**
📞 (904) 261-7378. ⏰ Mon– Sat. ⏰ public hols. 🏷 ♿ limited. 📷 compulsory; two tours daily.

Ocala National Forest ⑲

⏰ daily. 🏷 campgrounds & swimming areas. ♿ 🏕 **Visitor Center** 3199 NE Co Rd. 📞 (352) 236-0288. **Juniper Springs Canoe Rental** 📞 (352) 625-2808.

BETWEEN OCALA and the St. John's River, the world's largest sand pine forest covers 366,000 acres (148,000 ha) and is crisscrossed by rivers and hiking trails. One of the last refuges of the endangered Florida black bear, it is also home to animals such as deer and otter, and a variety of birds such as bald eagles, barred owls, wild turkey, and several wading birds.

Hiking trails vary from board-walks and short loop trails to the 66-mile (106-km) stretch of the National Scenic Trail. Bass-fishing is popular, and there are swimming holes and campgrounds at the recreation areas of Salt Springs and Alexander Springs.

Canoe rental is widely available; the 7-mile (11-km) canoe run down Juniper Creek from the **Juniper Springs Recreation Area** is one of the finest in Florida. The Salt Springs trail is especially good for bird-watching. There are guides at the main visitor center on the forest's western fringe or at the centers at Salt Springs and Lake Dorr, on Route 19.

ENVIRONS: Silver Springs, on the western border of Ocala National Forest, 29 miles (46 km) west of the Juniper Springs Recreation Area, is the world's largest artesian spring and Florida's oldest tourist attraction. Its famous glass-bottomed boat tours have been running since 1878. Jeep safaris and "Jungle Cruises" also travel through the Florida outback, where the early Tarzan movies starring Johnny Weismuller were filmed. Wild Waters, next to the springs, is a lively water park. The quieter **Silver River State Park**, 2 miles (3 km) southeast, has a lovely walking trail through a hardwood hammock and cypress swamp, leading to a swimming hole in a bend of the crystal clear river.

🌴 **Silver Springs State Park**
7165 NE 7th St, Ocala. 📞 (352) 236-7148. ⏰ daily. 🏷 ♿

Juniper Springs, Ocala National Forest

Tallahassee ⑳

🏛 137,000. ✈ 🚉 918 Railroad
Ave, (800) 872-7245. 🚌 ℹ 106 E
Jefferson, (850) 413-9200. 🎭
Springtime Tallahassee (Mar–Apr).

ENCIRCLED BY rolling hills,
Florida's dignified state
capital is gracious and
uncompromisingly Southern.
Tallahassee grew dramatically
during the plantation era, and
the elegant town houses built
in the 1800s can still be seen
around Park Avenue and
Calhoun Street. The Chamber
of Commerce, on Duval
Street, is housed in the city's
oldest building, a 1830
Classical-Revival mansion,
known as "The Columns."

The **Old Capitol Building**
in downtown Tallahassee has
been beautifully restored to
its 1902 state, with a pristine
white dome and striped
awnings. Once inside, guests
can visit the Supreme Court
chamber and the Senate.
The high-rise **New Capitol
Building** behind it offers a
fabulous view of the city. The
Museum of Florida History
situated on Bronough Street,
covers about 12,000 years of
the region's history.

**The Old and the New Capitol
Buildings, Tallahassee**

ENVIRONS: During the 1820s
and 30s, the area around
Tallahassee was Florida's
most important cotton-
growing region. A tour along
the canopied roads of the old
Cotton Trail takes visitors
past former cotton plantations
and cattle pastures. The
**Goodwood Museum and
Gardens** retains its lovely
1830s mansion; Bradley's
Country Store, set up in
1927, still serves their famous
homemade sausages. Located

15 miles (24 km) south of
Tallahassee, **Wakulla Springs
State Park** has one of the
world's largest freshwater
springs, which pumps 700,000
gal (2.6 million liters) of water
a minute into a large pool.
Here, visitors can swim or
snorkel in its clear waters or
ride in a glass-bottomed boat.
Boat trips on the Wakulla
River are the best way to see
alligators and wading birds.
The elegant Wakulla Springs
Lodge was built in the 1930s.

🏕 **Wakulla Springs State
Park**
550 Wakulla Park Dr, Wakulla
Springs. 📞 (850) 224-5950.
🕐 daily. 🎫 &

Pensacola ㉑

🏛 360,000. ✈ 🚉 980 E Heinburg
St, (850) 433-4966. 🚌 (850) 476-
4800. ℹ 1401 E Gregory St,
(850) 434-1234. 🎭 Fiesta of
Five Flags (Jun).

FLORIDA'S EARLIEST Spanish
settlement, Pensacola was
established by Don Tristan de
Luna, who sailed into Pensacola Bay in 1559. The city
features diverse architectural

The Beaches of the Panhandle

LYING BETWEEN Perdido Key and Panama City Beach are
some of Florida's most beautiful beaches. The brilliant
sand, consisting mainly of quartz, is washed down from the
Appalachian Mountains. One can choose between quiet,
pristine beaches and more lively resorts, with ample opportunities for water sports. The main season is April–July.

Perdido Key ①
Florida's most westerly
shores on Perdido Key
are inaccessible by car
and quieter than most.

Quietwater Beach ②
On Santa Rosa Island, it's not
the Panhandle's finest but is
an easy hop from Pensacola.

Pensacola Beach ③
has miles of pristine sand and a
string of shops, hotels, and bars.
Large crowds gather here on
weekends to sunbathe and swim.

Navarre Beach ④
is quieter than Pensacola but
nevertheless has good facilities,
water sports, and a pier for fishing.

0 km		15

0 miles		10

styles, from Colonial cottages to elegant Classical-Revival homes. Pensacola was wiped out by a hurricane two years after it was established, but it was soon rebuilt, and over the next 300 years the city was occupied by the Spanish, French, English, and the Americans. The 1800s were a period of prosperity ushered in by the timber boom, and much of today's downtown dates from this time.

Pensacola's oldest quarter, the **Historic Pensacola Village**, has a number of museums and houses, built by wealthy pioneers and traders. There are daily tours from Tivoli House on Zaragoza Street. Forming a backdrop to the Museum of Commerce is a cleverly constructed Victorian streetscape, complete with a printer's workshop, a saddlery, and an old-time music store. Florida's earliest church, the Old Christ Church (1832), stands in the leafy Seville Square shaded by oaks and magnolia trees.

The **TT Wentworth Florida State Museum**, set in a Spanish Renaissance Revival building, has an eclectic collection that includes oddities such as a shrunken head from pre-Columbian times and old Coca-Cola bottles.

Farther north, the **North Hill Preservation District** has 19th- and 20th-century houses, built on the sites of British and Spanish forts. Even today, cannonballs are found in local gardens. A very striking home is the McCreary House on North Baylen Street. A Queen Anne home built in 1900, it has a gabled roof and tower. Lying between the two districts, **Palafox Street** is the city's commercial hub.

🏛 TT Wentworth Florida State Museum

330 S Jefferson St. ☎ *(850) 595-5985.* ○ *Mon–Fri.* ● *public hols.* 🚫 ♿

Guides in 19th-century costume in the Historic Pensacola Village

Apalachicola ㉒

👥 *3,000.* 🚌 *Tallahassee.* ℹ *99 Market Street, (850) 653-9419.* [W] www. apalachicolabay.org

A riverside customs station established in 1823, Apalachicola's first 100 years were its finest. It flourished first with the cotton trade, and later with the lumber boom. Today, pines and hardwoods still stand in the **Apalachicola National Forest**. The area offers hiking trails, canoeing opportunities, and campsites. Oystering in the Apalachicola River began in the 1920s. Oyster boats still pull up at the dockside, and Water Street has many places where fresh oysters are available.

A walking map of the old town, available at the Chamber of Commerce, takes in buildings from the cotton era, such as the 1838 Greek Revival Raney House. The **John Gorrie State Museum** houses a model of Gorrie's patent ice-making machine. Designed to cool yellow fever patients, the doctor's 1851 invention was the vanguard of modern refrigeration and air conditioning.

Fort Walton Beach ⑤
A relaxed resort, ideal for family holidays. It is also one of the best beaches for water sports.

Panama City Beach ⑨
Condos and amusement parks line buzzing Panama City Beach, the Panhandle's biggest resort. Water sports facilities are excellent here.

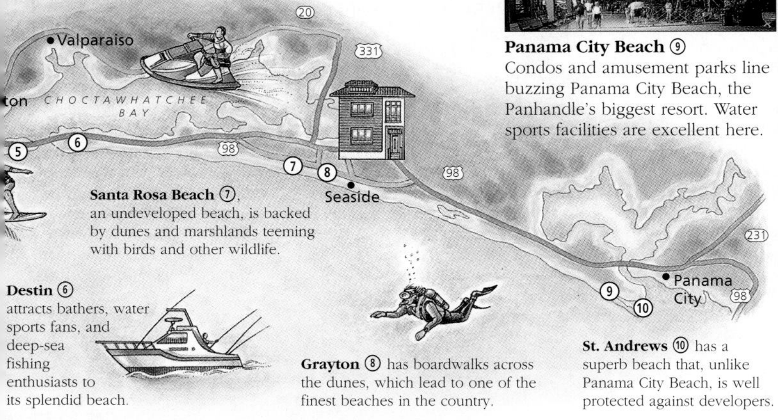

Santa Rosa Beach ⑦, an undeveloped beach, is backed by dunes and marshlands teeming with birds and other wildlife.

Destin ⑥ attracts bathers, water sports fans, and deep-sea fishing enthusiasts to its splendid beach.

Grayton ⑧ has boardwalks across the dunes, which lead to one of the finest beaches in the country.

St. Andrews ⑩ has a superb beach that, unlike Panama City Beach, is well protected against developers.

The high-rise skyline of downtown Tampa on the Gulf Coast

Tampa ㉓

🏛 *300,000.* ✈ 🚉 *601 Nebraska Ave, (800) 872-7245.* 🚌 *610 Polk St, (800) 231-2222.* ⚓ *Channelside Dr, (800) 741-2297.* ℹ *615 Channelside Dr, (813) 223-1111.* 🎭 *Gasparilla Festival (Feb).* 🅦 *www.visittampabay.com*

SITUATED AT THE mouth of the Hillsborough River, Tampa is one of Florida's fastest-growing cities. A perfect harbor, Tampa Bay was a magnet to the Spanish, who arrived here in 1539. However, the city's greatest period of prosperity was in the 1800s, when railroad baron Henry Plant extended his railroad here and made it an important center for trade.

Tampa's downtown area is centered around the partly pedestrian Franklin Street, which has the historic Tampa Theater. To its southeast, on North Ashley Drive, is the **Tampa Museum of Art**. This museum's exhibits range from Greek, Roman, and Etruscan antiquities to 20th-century American art.

The luxurious Tampa Bay Hotel, which houses the **Henry B. Plant Museum**, is the city's premier landmark, its Moorish minarets visible from all over the city. Plant commissioned the building in 1891, and its construction alone cost $3 million. Currently a part of the University of Tampa, the south wing has been preserved as a museum. Its splendidly furnished interior retains the original Wedgwood china, Venetian mirrors, and 18th-century French furniture.

Greek vase, Tampa Museum of Art

The **Florida Aquarium** is on Channelside Drive. It displays a variety of sea creatures such as seabirds, otters, and baby alligators living in tanks that replicate their natural habitats.

Located 3 miles (5 km) east of downtown, **Ybor City** was created by Spaniard Don Vicente Martinez Ybor, when he moved his cigar business from Key West to Tampa in the late 1800s. About 20,000 migrant workers settled here, and the legacy of the cigar boom is still visible on 7th Avenue, with its Spanish tiles and wrought-iron balconies. Today, the area is known for its lively shops, clubs, and restaurants, including the Columbia Restaurant, Florida's oldest establishment.

Northeast of downtown, the **Museum of Science and Industry** features various exhibits including an IMAX® Cinema. The GTE Challenger Learning Center, a living memorial to the Space Shuttle *Challenger*, has simulators and a mission control room.

Nearby is Tampa's biggest attraction – **Busch Gardens**. This theme park incorporates an unusual zoo that re-creates colonial-era Africa. The zoo supports over 2,600 animals, with giraffes and zebras roaming freely over the "Serengeti Plain." Lions and other African animals can be seen on a unique Edge of Africa safari ride.

🎢 Busch Gardens
Busch Blvd, Tampa. 📞 *(813) 987-5082.* ⏰ *9:30am–6pm daily, extended hours for summer & hols.* ♿ 🅗 🅦 *www.buschgardens.com*

St. Petersburg ㉔

🏛 *265,000.* ✈ 🚉 *180 9th St North, (727) 898-1496.* ℹ *100 2nd Ave N, (727) 821-4715.* 🎭 *Festival of the States.* 🅦 *www.stpete.com*

ESTABLISHED IN 1875, "St. Pete," as it is often called, was originally a retired person's mecca. Times have changed however, and extensive renovations have rejuvenated the downtown waterfront area.

The city's claim to fame is the prestigious **Salvador Dali Museum**, which has the largest private collection of the Spanish artist's work in the world, worth more than $350 million. It was opened in 1982, 40 years after the Ohio businessman Reynolds Morse first met Dali and began collecting his works. There are 95 oil paintings, 100 watercolors and drawings, 1,300 graphics, sculptures, and other objects. Spanning the years 1914–70, they range from Dali's early figurative paintings to his first experiments in Surrealism, as well as those mature, large-scale paintings described as his "masterworks."

The city's best-known landmark is **The Pier**, which has a string of shops and restaurants. Close by, the **St. Petersburg Museum of History** focuses on the city's history and has exhibits ranging from mastodon bones and native pottery to a replica of the sea plane that made the world's first flight with a paying passenger in 1914.

The modern Palladian-style **Museum of Fine Arts**, near the bay, is famous for its wide-ranging collection of European, American, and Asian works. Supreme among the French Impressionist paintings are *A Corner of the Woods* (1877) by Cézanne and Monet's classic *Parliament, Effect of Fog, London* (1904).

🏛 Salvador Dali Museum
1000 3rd St S. 📞 *(727) 823-3767.* 🚌 *4, 32, trolley from The Pier.* ⏰ *9:30am–5:30pm Mon–Sat (8pm Thu), noon–5:30pm Sun.* ⏺ *Thanksgiving, Dec 25.* 🎫 🚫 ♿ 🅗 🅦 *www.salvadordalimuseum.org*

South Lido Park Beach on Lido Key, one Sarasota's off-shore islands

ENVIRONS: The Gulf Coast's much advertised "361 days of sunshine a year," lures tourists from all over the world to the beaches between St. Petersburg and Clearwater. Known as the Holiday Isles or the Suncoast, the strip encompasses 28 miles (45 km) of barrier island beaches. St. Pete Beach is the busiest, with excellent water sports facilities; the **Fort de Soto Park** beaches have been ranked among the top 10 in the US. Florida's famous sea cows, or manatees, found all along in the coastal waters, are gentle herbivorous giants that grow to a length of 10 ft (3 m). Once plentiful, today only about 2,500 survive.

Sarasota ㉕

🏠 60,000. ✈ 🚌 575 N Washington Blvd, (941) 955-5735; Amtrak bus, (800) 872-7245. ℹ 655 N Tamiami Trail, (941) 957-1877. 🎪 Circus Festival (Jan). Ⓦ www.sarasotafl.org

Known as Florida's cultural center, Sarasota's affluence is often credited to the millionaire circus owner, John Ringling, who invested much of his fortune, estimated at $200 million, in the area. His legacy is best seen at his house and in his splendid collection of European art, Sarasota's biggest attraction. The **Ringling Museum Complex** comprises the Museum of Art, a colorful Circus Museum, and the Ca' d'Zan – Ringling's winter residence overlooking Sarasota Bay. Ringling had a particular love for Italy, and his fine collection of Italian Baroque paintings are the cornerstone of his collection. The highlight of the Museum of Art is the Rubens Gallery. Also noteworthy are the Astor Rooms, displaying the lavish 19th-century interiors of a New York mansion.

Sarasota has an attractive waterfront setting, and numerous artists and writers have settled here. The restored storefronts in the downtown area around Palm Avenue and Main Street house antique shops, bars, and restaurants.

The nearby barrier islands – Longboat Key, Lido Key, and Siesta Key – have great beaches and excellent tourist accommodations. **South Lido Park Beach** on Lido Key has a lovely woodland trail. The broad **Siesta Key Beach** is always lively, while Turtle Beach is quieter and has the only campsite on these Keys. Longboat Key is well known for its golf courses. Most of the beaches offer excellent water sports facilities.

RINGLING MUSEUM COMPLEX: CA' D'ZAN

The Ca' d'Zan (House of John), modeled after a Venetian palace with Renaissance and Baroque features, is set off by a 200-ft (60-m) marble terrace. Its opulence epitomizes the life of the American super-rich of the early 20th-century.

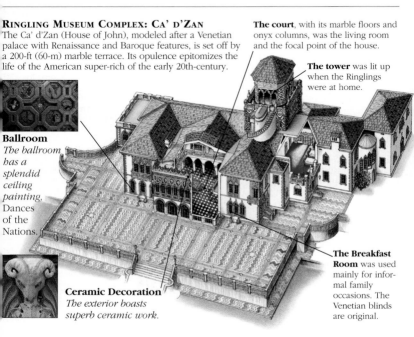

The court, with its marble floors and onyx columns, was the living room and the focal point of the house.

The tower was lit up when the Ringlings were at home.

Ballroom
The ballroom has a splendid ceiling painting, Dances of the Nations.

Ceramic Decoration
The exterior boasts superb ceramic work.

The Breakfast Room was used mainly for informal family occasions. The Venetian blinds are original.

Beachfront cottages on Sanibel Island, Lee Island Coast

Lee Island Coast 26

2275 Cleveland Ave, Fort Myers, (800) 231-2222. 1159 Causeway Rd, Sanibel, (239) 472-1080. **Boat Services** Tropic Star (239) 283-0015; Captiva Cruises (239) 472-5300; North Captiva Island Club Resort (239) 395-1001.

THIS COASTLINE OFFERS an irresistible combination of sandy beaches, beautiful sunsets, and exotic wildlife. Of the two most popular islands, **Sanibel** has manicured gardens and rows of shops and restaurants along Periwinkle Way, the town's hub. Most of the beaches with public access are along Gulf Drive, the best being Turner and Bowman's beaches.

The **Sanibel Captiva Conservation Foundation** on Sanibel-Captiva Road, protects a chunk of the island's wetland. It has 4 miles (6 km) of boardwalk trails and an observation tower, which is a vantage point for viewing birds. The **JN "Ding" Darling National Wildlife Refuge** occupies two-thirds of Sanibel. Its wildlife includes raccoons, alligators, and birds such as roseate spoonbills, bald eagles, and ospreys. The popular scenic "Wildlife Drive" can be covered by bike or car. Paths and canoe trails are lined with red mangrove and sea grape. Canoes and fishing boats are available for rent.

Captiva Island, the other popular island, is less developed. However, visitors can enjoy the ambience of the old-fashioned South Seas Plantation Resort with its busy marina, which is the starting point for boat trips to Cayo Costa Island – a beautiful, untouched barrier island.

Both islands are best known for their shells, and visitors soon get drawn into the shell-collecting culture. Other less developed islands lie close by and can be explored by boat.

JN "Ding" Darling National Wildlife Refuge

Mile Marker 2, Sanibel Captiva Rd. (239) 472-1100. Sat–Thu. public hols.

ENVIRONS: Fort Myers, about 25 miles (40 km) east of the Lee Island Coast, is an old-fashioned city that was put on the map in the 1880s by one of America's most famous inventors, Thomas Alva Edison (1847–1931). The Edison Winter Home is Fort Myers' most enduring attraction. Edison built his estate in 1886, and the house, laboratory, and botanical gardens are much as he left them. The laboratory contains his original equipment and is still lit by carbon filament light bulbs, which have been in constant use since Edison invented them. The museum displays personal items, phonographs, and a 1916 Model T car that was given to Edison by Henry Ford, his great friend. Next door, the Ford Winter Home has a few early Ford cars on display.

The Fort Myers Historical Museum, on Peck Street, is housed in the former railroad station. Interesting exhibits include a model of Fort Myers in the 1900s, and a P-39 bomber that crashed in the 1940s. To the south of the city are a handful of lively beaches.

Big Cypress Swamp 27

Big Cypress National Preserve (239) 695-4111. daily. Dec 25. **Fakahatchee Strand State Preserve** (239) 695-4593. daily. **Corkscrew Swamp Sanctuary** (239) 348-9151. daily.

HOME TO SEVERAL hundred plants and animals including the endangered Florida panther, this vast, wetland basin features islands of slash pine, prairies, and hardwood hammocks. A third of the swamp is covered by cypress trees growing in long, narrow forests or "strands." The Tamiami Trail (US 41) stretches from Tampa to Miami and cuts directly through the swamp.

Big Cypress National Preserve is the swamp's largest protected area. Visitors can stop at the Oasis Visitor Center for information and enjoy the views from US 41. The **Fakahatchee Strand State Preserve** lies to the west. The few remaining specimens of old growth cypresses, some of which are 600 years old, are found at Big Cypress Bend. The country's largest cluster of royal palms are also found here. Route 846 leads to **Corkscrew Swamp Sanctuary**, with its large stand of old growth cypresses. It is famous for its birds and is a winter nesting area for endangered wood storks.

Original equipment in Thomas Edison's laboratory, Fort Myers

Everglades National Park 28

🕒 *daily.* ℹ *all centers open Dec–Apr: 7:30am–5pm daily; check for rest of year.* **Main Visitor Center** 📞 *(305) 242-7700.* 🕒 *all year.* **Gulf Coast Visitor Center** *(Everglades City)* 📞 *(239) 695-3311; boat tours & canoe rental (239) 695-2591.* **Shark Valley Information Center** 📞 *(305) 221-8776; tram tours & cycle rental (305) 221-8455.* **Royal Palm Visitor Center** 📞 *(305) 242-7700.* **Flamingo Visitor Center** 📞 *(239) 695-2945. For canoe, bicycle rental & boat tours, call (239) 695-3101.* ♿ *most boardwalks are accessible.* ⛺ *(800) 365-2267 to book.* Ⓦ *www.nps.gov/ever*

COVERING 1.4 million acres (566,580 ha), the Everglades National Park makes up only a fifth of the world-famous Everglades – low lying wetlands formed from the overspill of Lake Okeechobee. The unique landscape consists of a vast expanse of sawgrass prairie, broken by tree islands, hammocks, and meandering channels. A paradise for wildlife, the park has a wide range of fauna, including 400 species of birds.

The main entrance lies 10 miles (16 km) west of Florida City. Inside are walking trails, most of them elevated boardwalks; some are suitable for bicycles. Boats and canoes can be rented. The best time to visit is during winter. South of the main entrance lies the informative Royal Palm Visitor Center and two boardwalk trails. The popular **Anhinga Trail** attracts wildlife in the dry winter months, and its open site is excellent for photographs. Alligators congregate at the "gator hole" (a pond that is hollowed out by alligators in the dry season to reach the water below) at the head of the trail, and a wide range of fauna, including deer, raccoons, and the splendid anhinga bird, can be spotted. Close by, the **Gumbo Limbo Trail** offers the best chance to explore a tropical hardwood hammock but is ridden with mosquitos. Watch for the pretty bromeliads, non-parasitic members of the pineapple family that grow on other plants, and the trail's namesake, the gumbo-limbo tree with its red bark.

A short distance to the west, **Long Key Pine's** campsite is beautifully situated and is one of the main reasons that people stop here. Several shady trails lead off from it: do not stray from the paths as the limestone bedrock has "solution holes" created by rain, which are deep and difficult to spot.

Shark Valley lies north of Long Key Pine, near the park boundary. The area is best visited by taking a tram tour or a bicycle along the 15-mile (25-km) loop road. A 60-ft (18-m) tower at its end offers great views. The valley is home to the Seminole Indians, who settled here in the 19th-century after being driven into the Everglades by land-hungry Europeans *(see p286)*.

The elevated **Pa-hay-okee Overlook** lies northwest of Long Key Pine. The expanse of sawgrass prairie seen from here is typical of the Everglades landscape. The view from the observation tower is worth the climb: tree islands break the horizon, and a multitude of birds, such as hawks, roseate spoonbills, great blue herons, and snail kites, can be easily spotted.

The **Mahogany Hammock Trail** leads through one of the park's largest hammocks, and it has a variety of fauna and flora. Trails such as West Lake Trail and Snake Bight Trail lie between Mahogany Hammock and **Flamingo** on Florida Bay and are especially rich in birdlife. Flamingo has the park's only hotel and also offers a wide choice of activities such as hiking, fishing, boating, and wildlife viewing. An overnight stay at the campsite is a must, especially for bird-watching. The bays around Flamingo have manatees *(see p319)*, as well as the rare, endangered American crocodile. The Flamingo Visitor Center has information about ranger-led activities: talks, slideshows, and walks through the swamp. Canoeing is the best way to explore the watery trails around Flamingo. These range from short trips to a week-long adventure of the remote Wilderness Waterway, leading past Whitewater Bay along the park's western coast. Northwest of Flamingo, the park's western entrance is marked by the island of Chokoloskee.

Today, the Everglades are under threat. Irrigation canals have disrupted the flow of water from Lake Okeechobee, which could prove disastrous for this delicate ecosystem.

Visitors should follow a few, simple safety tips. Bring insect repellent and protection against the sun. Follow park rules and respect all wildlife. Note that some shrubs and trees are poisonous, as are some caterpillars, spiders, and snakes. Do not wander off the pathways, and drive slowly because animals often venture onto the road.

Park ranger

Boardwalk through swamps in the Everglades National Park

Biscayne National Park ㉙

9700 SW 328th St, Convoy Point.
▢ *Miami.* ▢ ▢ *(305) 230-7275.*
◯ *daily.* ● *Dec 25.* ♿ *limited.*
△ **Boat Tours** ▢ *(305) 230-1100.*
ⓦ *www.nps.gov/bisc*

DENSE MANGROVE swamp
protects the shoreline of
Biscayne National Park,
which incorporates the northernmost islands of the Florida
Keys. Its waters hold the
park's greatest draw – a living
coral reef with myriad forms
and over 200 types of tropical
fish. The barrier islands are
unoccupied, so the coral here
is healthier and the water
even clearer than in the more
popular parks farther south.
Activities include glass-
bottomed boat tours, snorkeling, and diving – all arranged
by the visitor center.

The Keys ㉚

▢ *Miami.*

RUNNING SOUTHWEST off the
tip of the Florida penin-
sula are the Keys, a chain of
fossilized coral islands protected by North America's
only coral reef. Visitors flock
to the resorts here to enjoy
several activities ranging from
fishing to snorkeling.
   From the 1500s, the Keys
lured a succession of settlers,
pirates, and "wreckers." Its
development, however, took
off in the early 1900s, when
rail baron Henry Flagler *(see
p286)* constructed the
Overseas Railroad across the
Keys. It has since been

Bahia Honda's beautiful beach, the finest in the Florida Keys

replaced by the magnificent
Overseas Highway, which
ends at Key West.
   The largest island in the
Upper Keys is **Key Largo**,
named "long island" by
Spanish explorers. One of its
highlights is the *African
Queen*, the boat used
in the eponymous
1951 film, which
makes short pleasure
trips. The island's
greatest draws,
however, are the
diving and snorkeling
opportunities just
offshore in the **John
Pennekamp Coral
Reef State Park**. The
park has a visitor
center, swimming
areas, and woodland trails,
but it is best known for its
fabulous underwater reaches,
which provide a glimpse of
the extraordinary forms of
coral reef life.
   Islamorada, south of Key
Largo, declares itself as the
"Sport Fishing Capital of the
World." Encompassing seven
islands, it is known for its
outstanding big game fishing.
The Whale Harbor Marina on

**Gold ornament
from a treasure
ship**

Upper Matecumbe Key
bristles with impressive deep-
sea charter craft, used to
catch blue-water fish. Fishing
boats, based here, offer half-
day trips, even if visitors are
not expert anglers.
   Long Key Bridge marks
the beginning of the
Middle Keys. The
**Dolphin Research
Center**, a nonprofit
concern on Grassy
Key, conducts the
delightful "Dolphin
Encounter," where one
can swim with these
endearing marine
mammals. It is also a
rest home for sick and
injured dolphins.
   The heavily devel-
oped **Marathon Key** is the
main center of the Middle
Keys. Its primary appeal lies
in fertile fishing grounds, and
enthusiasts can choose from a
range of angling techniques,
including spear-fishing and
line-fishing. Crane Point
Hammock has 64 acres (26
ha) of tropical forest and
mangroves, and several trails,
while the **Museum of Natural History of the Florida
Keys** explains the islands' history, geology, and ecology.
   The Lower Keys are more
rugged and less developed
than the Upper and Middle
Keys. The vegetation is more
wooded and supports a
different flora and fauna.
The most striking change,
however, is in the slow and
languid pace of life.
   After crossing the Seven
Mile Bridge, visitors can head
for the **Bahia Honda State
Park**, which has the finest
beach in the Keys. Brilliant

FISHING IN THE FLORIDA KEYS

**Deep-sea fishing
from a sports boat**

Islamorada, Marathon, and Key West
are the area's major fishing centers, and
small marinas throughout the region
offer boats for rent. There are options
to suit most budgets and abilities, and
one can book places on fishing party
boats or hire guides. Deep-sea fishing,
an exhilarating option, appeals to the
Hemingway spirit of the angler, while
backcountry fishing calls for stealth and
cunning. The numerous bait and tackle
shops rent out gear and sell licenses.

white sand is backed by tropical forest, with unusual species of trees, such as silver palm and yellow satinwood. Canoes, kayaks, and water sports gear are available to rent. The adjacent **Looe Key National Marine Sanctuary** is a spectacular dive location, with abundant marine life.

The second largest island, **Big Pine Key** is the Lower Keys' main residential community and the best place to see the diminutive Key deer. The turning near MM 30 leads to the **Blue Hole**, a flooded quarry whose viewing platform is ideal for watching the deer and other wildlife.

Key Largo

ℹ️ *MM 106, (305) 451-1414, (800) 822-1088.*

John Pennekamp Coral Reef State Park
MM 102.5. 📞 *(305) 451-1202.*
daily. 🦽 *limited.*

Key West ㉛

🏛️ *28,000.* ✈️🚌🛳️ℹ️ *402 Wall St, (305) 294-2587.*

THE SOUTHERNMOST settlement in the US, Key West is a magnet for people who want to leave the rest of America behind. In the 16th century, it became a haven for pirates and "wreckers." "Wrecking," or the salvage of shipwrecks on the Keys' coral reef, was the business that first made Key West rich. It soon became Florida's wealthiest city, and its opportunistic lifestyle attracted a stream of settlers from the Americas, the Caribbean, and Europe; their legacy is visible in the island's unique architecture and cuisine. An influx of writers and a large gay community in recent years have added to Key West's cultural cocktail.

Most of the sights are within a few blocks of **Duval Street**, the main axis of Old Key West. Bylanes, such as Fleming Street, have many fine 19th-century wooden buildings, which contrast with the simple homes erected to house Cuban cigar-workers.

The **Wreckers' Museum** on Duval Street was originally the home of the wreck captain Francis B. Watlington. Built in 1829, its design displays some eccentric maritime influences, such as a hatch used for ventilation in the roof. It is stuffed with nautical bric-a-brac. Farther down, the **San Carlos Institute**, founded in 1871, is a Cuban heritage center. The garden of **Heritage House Museum**, on Caroline Street, has the Robert Frost cottage, named after the famous American poet who frequently stayed here. At the northern edge of the Old Town is **Mallory Square**, which comes to life at sunset, when a variety of performing artists amuse the crowds.

The **Bahama Village** on the western fringe of the Old Town is named after Key West's earliest settlers. It has a lively Caribbean flavor with a number of brightly painted clapboard buildings.

A prime attraction is the Spanish-colonial style **Hemingway Home**, where novelist Ernest Hemingway lived from 1931 to 1940. The room where he penned several of his most famous works, such as *To Have and Have Not* (the only book set in Key West), is above the carriage house. His library, travel mementos, and memorabilia, such as the cigar-maker's chair on which he sat and wrote, are on display.

The **Mel Fisher Maritime Museum** on Green Street, displays fabulous shipwreck treasures such as coins, jewels, and crucifixes. These were salvaged by the late Mel Fisher, who discovered the wrecks of the Spanish galleons *Nuestra Señora de Atocha* and *Santa Margarita*, about 40 miles (64 km) west of Key West, in 1985. Inside were 47 tons of gold and silver bars, and 70 lbs (32 kg) of raw emeralds that sank with the galleons in 1622.

Diver's helmet, Mel Fisher Museum

The **Conch Train** and **the Old Town Trolley Tour** are convenient options for exploring the town.

🏛️ **Hemingway Home**
907 Whitehead St. 📞 *(305) 294-1136.* *daily.* 🦽 *limited.*
🌐 www.hemingwayhome.com

FLORIDA'S CORAL REEF

North America's only live coral reef extends 200 miles (320 km) along the length of the Keys, from Miami to the Dry Tortugas. A complex and delicate ecosystem, it protects these islands from oceanic storms. Coral reefs are created over thousands of years by tiny marine organisms known as polyps and are home to a multitude of plants and sea creatures, including 500 species of fish.

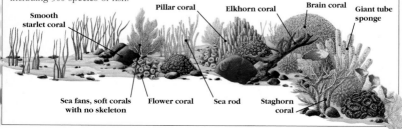

Smooth starlet coral — Pillar coral — Elkhorn coral — Brain coral — Giant tube sponge

Sea fans, soft corals with no skeleton — Flower coral — Sea rod — Staghorn coral

Practical Information

With over 40 million visitors a year, Florida is very well geared for catering to tourists' needs. It is the ultimate family vacation destination. A strong emphasis is placed on entertaining children, and the superb facilities available, make traveling with youngsters a real pleasure. Given its warm climate, Florida is a winter destination for many Americans. The peak season runs from December to April, when the beaches and other attractions are at their busiest. Anyone visiting Walt Disney World or other theme parks should be prepared for long lines during the peak season.

Tourist Information

Most large cities in Florida have a Convention and Visitor's Bureau (CVB), offering a huge array of brochures. Most hotels also have a brochure rack or free "WHERE" magazines that list museums, entertainment, shopping, and dining. To get information before you leave home, call or write for a vacation pack, issued by the Florida Tourism group.

Security & Health

Though crimes against tourists have fallen since the 1990s, it is best to be take precautions in urban areas, especially in Miami. Avoid deserted neighborhoods at night. Carry as little money as possible, and leave valuables at home or check them at the hotel reception desk (it is best not to leave valuables in your hotel room). If attacked, hand over your wallet at once, and do not try to resist. In case of a serious illness or accident, hospitals provide good treatment. Minor ailments can be treated at the 24-hour walk-in clinics. Medical care is expensive, so be sure your insurance documents are up-to-date. In an emergency dial 911, or you can contact **Metro-Dade Police Information**.

Natural Hazards

Hurricanes are infrequent but devastating when they do occur. If a storm is imminent follow the announcements on local television and radio. The **National Hurricane Center** in Miami gives details on impending hurricanes. On beaches, keep an eye on children as riptides are a danger in some places.

The worst climatic hazard is the sun. Use sunscreen, wear hats, and drink plenty of fluids to avoid dehydration.

Alligators are a thrilling sight in the Everglades but they can and do kill, so treat them with respect. Look out for spiders, scorpions, and venomous snakes native to Florida. It is best not to touch unfamiliar vegetation. Wear insect repellent when visiting parks and nature preserves.

Driving in Florida

Driving in florida is a delight because of its excellent road network, inexpensive gasoline, and affordable car rentals. The fastest routes are the six-lane Interstate Highways, referred to as I-10, I-75, and so on. Be warned that local drivers change lanes frequently on expressways, so stick to the right and be alert near exits. Speed limits can vary within a few miles, from 55–70 mph (90–105 km/h) on highways, to 20–30 mph (32–48 km/h) in residential areas, and 15 mph (24 km/h) near schools Speed limits are rigorously enforced, and fines can be as much as $150.

In the event of a serious breakdown, call the emergency number on the rental agreement and the agency will provide a new vehicle. The **American Automobile Association (AAA)** also has its own breakdown service and will assist its members.

Miami has had a bad reputation for crimes against motorists, but be careful in other areas as well. Avoid driving in unfamiliar territory after dark. If you have to refer to a map, stop only when you are in a well-lit area. Ignore any attempt by anyone to stop you from driving.

Etiquette

Dress in florida is mostly casual, but it is illegal for women to go topless on beaches, except in a few places, such as Miami's South Beach. Drinking alcohol on beaches and in other public places is illegal, as is smoking in buses, trains, taxis, and in most public buildings. There are separate areas for smokers in most restaurants and cafés.

The Climate of Florida

With its warm climate, Florida is a year-round destination. Its climatic divide between the temperate north and the subtropical south means that the state has two distinct tourist seaons. In south Florida (including Orlando), the busiest time is when tourists come to enjoy the mild winters. Here the summers can be uncomfortably hot. In the north, the Panhandle attracts most visitors in the summer. Despite this difference, the Sunshine State by and large lives up to its reputation of clear, blue skies and a pleasant climate.

MIAMI			
°F/C	88/31		
80/27	74/23	83/28	75/24
67/19		72/22	61/16
32°F 0°C			
☀ 23 days	22 days	22 days	20 days
☂ 2.9 in	5.7 in	5.6 in	2 in
month	Apr	Jul	Oct	Jan

SPORTS & OUTDOOR ACTIVITIES

FLORIDA'S CLIMATE makes the state a top destination for all sports enthusiasts, from golfers and tennis players to canoeists and deep-sea divers. The best sources of information on outdoor activities are the **Florida Sports Foundation** and the **Department of Environmental Protection (DEP)**.

Water sports of all kinds are well represented, with wonderful beaches on both the Atlantic and Gulf coasts. Most resorts offer the full range from windsurfing to jetskiing. Water-skiing can also be enjoyed on lakes and inland waterways. The state provides ample opportunities for canoeing as well, with the Wilderness Waterway in the Everglades National Park being a favorite run.

Florida has superb diving and snorkeling sports. The country's only living coral reef skirts the state's southeast coast, stretching the length of the Keys. Excellent guided snorkeling trips are available to view the coast's coral and fish. For information on diving, contact the **Keys Association of Dive Operators**.

Fishing off the pier is popular at coastal spots, but the state is best known for its sport fishing. Deep-sea fishing boats can be chartered at seaside resorts; the biggest fleets are in the Panhandle and the Keys. Many rivers and parks offer freshwater fishing. The **Florida Game and Fresh Water Fish Commission** provides details on lcations and licensing costs.

Outdoor adventure tours to wilder areas, such as the Everglades, are organized by some companies, including **Build a Field Trip**.

ENTERTAINMENT

WHETHER YOUR preference is for a Broadway drama, a lavish Las Vegas-style floorshow, or a small cruise, Florida has something for everyone. **Walt Disney World® Resort**, **Universal Orlando** and other attractions offer the best in family entertainment, with theme parks galore to thrill children during the day and dinner shows at night. Here, meals are served, generally themed to the show you are watching. Water parks, throughout Florida, are also big draws.

Lavish road shows are the highest-quality productions in Florida. The state has its own theater groups, orchestras, and opera companies, such as the the **Florida Philharmonic**

Orchestra and the **Florida Grand Opera**. Some of the best places to dance are clubs offering live and varied music. Nightclubs require an ID to prove that you are over 18.

Florida is the world's leading departure point for cruises to the Caribbean. You can also go on mini-cruises, for a day or just an evening, for around $40. Evening cruises usually entail dinner and dancing; casino cruises, operating out of Miami and Port Everglades, are the new rage. Fort Lauderdale and St. Petersburg also have popular tour boats.

SHOPPING

SHOPPING IS ALSO a very popular pastime in Florida, with Miami attracting many overseas shoppers. Although the state has some very upscale stores, often clustered in shopping districts such as the exclusive Worth Avenue on Palm Beach, it is best known for its discount stores. If searching for gifts or souvenirs, the theme parks and seaside tourist centers offer a vast choice. Florida is also famed for its citrus fruit, which you can buy fresh or preserved as colorful candies and jellies. Other buys include seashells, Seminole crafts, Latin music, and hand-rolled cigars.

Where to Stay

FLORIDA HAS A HUGE VARIETY of places to stay suitable for all budgets and tastes – from rustic wooden cabins with minimal facilities to luxurious resort hotels that cater to their guests' every need. In between, visitors can choose from ordinary hotels, more charming B&Bs, convenient motels, or fully equipped apartments.

	CREDIT CARDS	CHILDREN'S FACILITIES	SWIMMING POOL	GOOD RESTAURANT	KITCHEN FACILITIES
MIAMI					
MIAMI BEACH: *Clay Hotel & International Hostel* $$ 1438 Washington Ave, FL 33139. ((305) 534-2988. FAX (305) 673-0346. Booking is essential for this youth hostel, in a lovely Spanish Revival building. Unbeatably cheap for such a prime location. *Beds:* 220.	■				■
MIAMI BEACH: *Brigham Gardens* $$$ 1411 Collins Ave, FL 33139. ((305) 531-1331. FAX (305) 538-9898. W www.brighamgardens.com Two 1930s buildings and a gorgeous garden. The rooms are decorated with a Deco mix of color and art. *Rooms:* 23.	■				■
MIAMI BEACH: *Delano* $$$$$ 1685 Collins Ave, FL 33139. ((305) 672-2000. FAX (305) 673-0888. SoBe's best hotel – where staff dress all in white to match the gorgeous, if stark, rooms. *Rooms:* 208.	■	●	■	●	
MIAMI BEACH: *Fontainebleau Hilton Resort* $$$$$ 4441 Collins Ave, FL 33140. ((305) 538-2000. FAX (305) 673-5351. W www.hilton.com Miami Beach's most prestigious resort has every amenity imaginable, from children's activities to the famous Tropigala floor show. *Rooms:* 1,206.	■	●	■	●	
DOWNTOWN: *Hampton Inn* $$ 2500 Brickell Ave, FL 33129. ((305) 854-2070. FAX (305) 856-5055. W www.hamptoninn.com The Hampton offers easy access to downtown, Coconut Grove, and Coral Gables. Rooms are bright. *Rooms:* 69.	■		■		
CORAL GABLES: *The Biltmore Hotel* $$$$$ 1200 Anastasia Ave, FL 33134. ((305) 445-1926. FAX (305) 913-3159. W www.biltmorehotel.com Rich in history (Al Capone gambled here in the 1920s), the grande dame of Miami's hotels will pamper you with every modern amenity in opulent, antique-filled suites. *Rooms:* 280.	■	●	■	●	
COCONUT GROVE: *Wyndham Grand Bay* $$$$$ 2669 S Bayshore Drive, FL 33133. ((800) 327-2788, (305) 858-9600. FAX (305) 859-2026. W www.wyndham.com Among the world's finest hotels, with crystal chandeliers, designer furnishings, and original art. Pavarotti's suite can be rented when he's not in residence. *Rooms:* 178.	■	●	■	●	
GREATER MIAMI: *Sonesta Beach* $$$$$ 350 Ocean Drive, Key Biscayne, FL 33149. ((305) 361-2021. FAX (305) 361-3096. W www.sonesta.com Stylish but casual, this resort has kids' activities, tennis courts, live music, and tremendous ocean views. *Rooms:* 300.	■	●	■	●	
THE GOLD & TREASURE COASTS					
BOCA RATON: *Boca Raton Resort* $$$$$ 501 E Camino Real, FL 33431. ((561) 395-3000. FAX (561) 447-3183. W www.bocaresort.com The most chic and pretentious place in town, this Spanish-style hotel offers rooms in a choice of décor. *Rooms:* 1,056.	■	●	■	●	
FORT LAUDERDALE: *Holiday Inn Beach* $$$$ 999 Fort Lauderdale Beach Blvd, FL 33304. ((954) 563-5961. FAX (954) 568-3003. W www.holiday-inn.com Located right across from the beach, this hotel offers every amenity, plus a heated pool and a galleria. *Rooms:* 240.	■	●	■	●	

		CREDIT CARDS	CHILDREN'S FACILITIES	SWIMMING POOL	GOOD RESTAURANT	KITCHEN FACILITIES

Price categories for a standard double room per night in high season, including tax and service charges:

- $ under $60
- $$ $60-$100
- $$$ $100-$150
- $$$$ $150-$200
- $$$$$ over $200

CREDIT CARDS
Major credit cards accepted.

CHILDREN'S FACILITIES
Cribs, high chairs, and other facilities for young children.

SWIMMING POOL
The hotel has a swimming pool for use by residents.

GOOD RESTAURANT
Good restaurant, normally also accessible to nonresidents.

KITCHEN FACILITIES
The hotel has some rooms equipped with cooking and other kitchen facilities, usually known as "efficiencies."

PALM BEACH: *Plaza Inn* $$$$
215 Brazilian Ave, FL 33480. **C** *(561) 832-8666.* **FAX** *(561) 835-8776.*
W www.plazainnpalmbeach.com
This Deco gem has four-poster beds, hand-crocheted spreads, and cooked-to-order breakfasts. *Rooms: 50.*

| | ● | ● | |

PALM BEACH: *The Breakers* $$$$$
1 South County Rd, FL 33480. **C** *(561) 655-6611.* **FAX** *(561) 655-8403.*
W www.thebreakers.com
Sumptuous and classy, this "Italian palace" is Palm Beach's finest hotel. It offers excellent children's facilities. *Rooms: 569.*

| | ● | ● | ● | |

ORLANDO & THE SPACE COAST

CAPE CANAVERAL: *Radisson Resort at the Port* $$$
8701 Astronaut Blvd, FL 32920. **C** *(321) 784-0000.* **FAX** *(321) 784-3737.*
W www.radisson.com
Ceiling fans and wicker give this resort a Caribbean feel. Ten minutes' drive from the Kennedy Space Center. *Rooms: 285.*

| | ● | ● | ● | ● |

COCOA BEACH: *Inn at Cocoa Beach* $$$$
4300 Ocean Beach Blvd, FL 32931. **C** *(321) 799-3460.* **FAX** *(321) 784-8632.*
W www.theinnatcocoabeach.com
Patios and balconies give ocean views at this B&B. The decor ranges from modern to traditional. *Rooms: 50.*

| | ● | | ● | |

DOWNTOWN ORLANDO: *Four Points Hotel* $$
151 E Washington St, FL 32801. **C** *(407) 841-3220.* **FAX** *(407) 648-4758.*
W www.fourpoints.com
This downtown hotel offers an included all-you-can-eat breakfast. *Rooms: 250.*

| | ● | | ● | ● |

DOWNTOWN ORLANDO: *The Courtyard at Lake Lucerne* $$$
211 N Lucerne Circle E, FL 32801. **C** *(407) 648-5188.* **FAX** *(407) 246-1368.*
W www.orlandohistoricinn.com
This well-run B&B in a quiet garden beside Lake Lucerne comprises four historic houses. *Rooms: 30.*

| | ● | | ● | ● |

INTERNATIONAL DRIVE: *Holiday Inn Express* $$
6323 International Drive, FL 32819. **C** *(407) 351-4430.* **FAX** *(407) 345-0742.*
Close to Walt Disney World, the Inn is geared to children. They stay and eat for free and enjoy a special "comedy zone." *Rooms: 218.*

| | ● | ● | |

WALT DISNEY WORLD: *Holiday Inn Hotel and Suites Maingate* $$$
5678 W Irlo Bronson Hwy, FL 34746. **C** *(407) 396-4488.* **FAX** *(407) 396-1296.*
Children rule here – there is even a kids' check-in desk. Clowns make up rooms and lead activities at a nearby children's camp. *Rooms: 614.*

| | ● | ● | ● | |

WALT DISNEY WORLD: *Disney's Caribbean Beach Resort* $$$$
900 Cayman Way, FL 32830. **C** *(407) 934-3400.* **FAX** *(407) 934-3288.*
Five cheerful "villages" with attractive rooms are situated around a lake where water birds congregate. *Rooms: 2,112.*

| | ● | ● | ● | |

WALT DISNEY WORLD: *Disney's Beach Club Resort* $$$$$
1800 Epcot Resorts Blvd, FL 32830. **C** *(407) 934-8000.* **FAX** *(407) 354-1866.*
Echoing the style of New England's grand hotels of the 1870s, this lavish resort has exquisite rooms, and one of the best restaurants in the area. *Rooms: 621.*

| | ● | ● | ● | ● |

WALT DISNEY WORLD: *Disney's Wilderness Lodge* $$$$$
901 Timberline Drive, FL 32830. **C** *(407) 938-4300.* **FAX** *(407) 824-3232.*
Wind down at this isolated but romantic "mountain retreat" with wooden floors and crackling fires. *Rooms: 728.*

| | ● | ● | ● | ● |

For key to symbols see back flap

Price categories for a standard double room per night in high season, including tax and service charges:

$ under $60
$$ $60-$100
$$$ $100-$150
$$$$ $150-$200
$$$$$ over $200

CREDIT CARDS
Major credit cards accepted.
CHILDREN'S FACILITIES
Cribs, high chairs, and other facilities for young children.
SWIMMING POOL
The hotel has a swimming pool for use by residents.
GOOD RESTAURANT
Good restaurant, normally also accessible to nonresidents.
KITCHEN FACILITIES
The hotel has some rooms equipped with cooking and other kitchen facilities, usually known as "efficiencies."

	CREDIT CARDS	CHILDREN'S FACILITIES	SWIMMING POOL	GOOD RESTAURANT	KITCHEN FACILITIES
WALT DISNEY WORLD: *Disney's Yacht Club Resort* $$$$$ 1700 Epcot Resorts Blvd, FL 32830. 📞 *(407) 934-7000.* FAX *(407) 934-3450.* Styled like a posh Cape Cod yacht club, with brass fittings and charts on the walls, this lavish resort shares its wide range of facilities with the adjacent Beach Club. 🔲 ⚡ 🌊 🍽 🔒 🅿 🚻 *Rooms: 630.*	▪	●	▪		
WALT DISNEY WORLD: *Walt Disney World Dolphin* $$$$$ 1500 Epcot Resorts Blvd, FL 32830. 📞 *(407) 934-4000.* FAX *(407) 934-4099.* Close to Epcot and architecturally arresting, the urbane Dolphin caters to a business crowd. 🔲 ⚡ 🌊 🍽 🔒 🚻 🅿 *Rooms: 1,510.*	▪	●	▪	●	

<h2 style="background:black;color:white">THE NORTHEAST</h2>

DAYTONA BEACH: *Inn on the Beach* $$ 1615 S Atlantic Ave, FL 32118. 📞 *(386) 255-0921.* FAX *(386) 255-3849.* This budget oceanfront hotel has spacious efficiencies, a sundeck, and both full-sized and kids' swimming pools. ⚡ 🌊 🍽 🚻 *Rooms: 195.*	▪	●	▪		▪
FERNANDINA BEACH: *The Amelia Island Williams House* $$$$ 103 S 9th St, FL 32034. 📞 *(904) 277-2328.* FAX *(904) 321-1325.* Rated one of the South's best B&Bs, this 1856 mansion has exquisite rooms with clawfoot baths. Priceless antiques range from 16th-century Japanese prints to a carpet owned by Napoleon. ⚡ 🌊 🚻 *Rooms: 8.*	▪				
FERNANDINA BEACH: *Amelia Island Plantation* $$$$$ 3000 First Coast Hwy, FL 32034. 📞 *(904) 261-6161.* FAX *(904) 277-5159.* At the southern end of Amelia Island surrounded by live oak trees and huge dunes, this golf resort has spacious rooms, condos, and villas. ⚡ 🌊 🍽 🚻 🔒 *Rooms: 680.*	▪	●	▪		▪
ST. AUGUSTINE: *Kenwood Inn B&B* $$$ 38 Marine St, FL 32084. 📞 *(904) 824-2116.* FAX *(904) 824-1689.* 🆆 www.oldcity.com/kenwood Built in the 1880s, this charming inn in the historic district has a secluded courtyard and rooms decorated with period features. ⚡ 🌊 🚻 *Rooms: 14.*	▪		▪		

<h2 style="background:black;color:white">THE PANHANDLE</h2>

APALACHICOLA: *Coombs House Inn* $$$ 80 6th St, FL 32320. 📞 *(850) 653-9199.* FAX *(850) 653-2785.* 🆆 www.coombshouseinn.com In two 1900s clapboard homes, this B&B offers lovely antiques and full, sumptuous breakfasts. The inn also provides rental bikes for exploring the surroundings. ⚡ 🌊 *Rooms: 18.*	▪				
FORT WALTON BEACH: *The Four Points Hotel* $$$$ 1325 Miracle Strip Parkway, FL 32548. 📞 *(850) 243-8116.* FAX *(850) 244-3064.* 🆆 www.sheraton4pts.com The Four Points Hotel has large, brightly decorated rooms, many with views of the Gulf. Some rooms are right on the beach. ⚡ 🌊 🍽 🔒 🚻 *Rooms: 216.*	▪		▪		
PANAMA CITY BEACH: *Edgewater Beach Resort* $$$$ 11212 Front Beach Rd, FL 32407. 📞 *(800) 874-8686.* FAX *(850) 235-6899.* This lavish seaside resort offers condos with one, two, or three bedrooms. The resort is particularly known for its extensive recreational facilities. ⚡ 🌊 🔒 🚻 *Rooms: 520.*	▪	●	▪	●	▪
PENSACOLA BEACH: *Five Flags Inn* $$ 299 Fort Pickens Rd, FL 32561. 📞 *(850) 932-3586.* FAX *(850) 934-0257.* 🆆 www.fiveflagsinn.com Right on the beach with all rooms overlooking the Gulf, the Five Flags is friendly and well furnished. ⚡ 🌊 *Rooms: 49.*	▪		▪		

TALLAHASSEE: *Radisson Hotel* ⓢⓢⓢ
415 N Monroe St, FL 32301. Ⓒ *(850) 224-6000.* FAX *(850) 222-0335.*
This elegant, cheerful hotel provides complimentary airport transportation
to the downtown area. 🔰 🍴 ⚕ *Rooms: 119.*

TALLAHASSEE: *Ramada Inn North* ⓢⓢⓢ
2900 N Monroe St, FL 32303. Ⓒ *(850) 386-1027.* FAX *(850) 224-0472.*
Ⓦ www.floridaramada.com Just a short drive from downtown, this efficiently run
hotel provides spacious and comfortable rooms. 🔰 🍴 ⚕ ❶ *Rooms: 200.*

THE GULF COAST

FORT MYERS: *Ramada Inn* ⓢⓢⓢ
2500 Edwards Drive, FL 33901. Ⓒ *(800) 833-1620.* FAX *(239) 337-1530.*
Ⓦ www.ramada.com
This fancy high-rise has fine views of the yacht basin and river.
Downtown sights are just a short walk away. 🔰 🔲 🍴 ⚕ *Rooms: 419.*

ST. PETERSBURG: *Beach Park Motel* ⓢⓢ
300 Beach Drive NE, FL 33701. Ⓒ *(800) 657-7687.* FAX *(727) 894-4226.*
Located downtown, with a view of the pier, this motel is ideally placed
for sightseeing. The rooms have small balconies. 🔰 🔲 ❶ *Rooms: 26.*

ST. PETERSBURG: *Renaissance Vinoy Resort* ⓢⓢⓢⓢⓢ
501 5th Ave NE, FL 33701. Ⓒ *(727) 894-1000.* FAX *(727) 822-2785.*
Dating from 1925, this elegantly restored hotel offers lovely bay views.
Most downtown attractions are within walking distance. 24 🔰 🔲 🍴 ⚕
Ⓟ ❶ *Rooms: 360.*

SANIBEL ISLAND: *Island Inn* ⓢⓢⓢⓢ
3111 W Gulf Drive, FL 33957. Ⓒ *(239) 472-1561.* FAX *(239) 472-0051.*
Ⓦ www.islandinnsanibel.com
Built around 100 years ago, this popular inn offers comfy, wicker-filled
cottages and rooms overlooking the Gulf. 🔲 ❶ *Rooms: 57.*

SARASOTA: *Best Western Golden Host Resort* ⓢⓢ
4675 N Tamiami Trail, FL 34234. Ⓒ *(941) 355-5141.* FAX *(941) 355-9286.*
The resort is set in lovely tropical grounds, close to local attractions and
the beach. Breakfast is included. 🔰 🔲 ❶ *Rooms: 80.*

TAMPA: *Days Inn Airport* ⓢⓢ
2522 N Dale Mabry Hwy, FL 33607. Ⓒ *(813) 877-6181.* FAX *(813) 875-6171.*
Located between downtown and the airport, this motel offers
comfortable rooms. Breakfast is included. 🔰 ⚕ 🐾 ❶ *Rooms: 293.*

TAMPA: *Wyndham Harbour Island Hotel* ⓢⓢⓢⓢ
725 S Harbour Island Blvd, FL 33602. Ⓒ *(813) 229-5000.* FAX *(813) 229-5322.*
On an island overlooking the river mouth, this exclusive hotel is linked to
downtown Tampa by the Peoplemover. 🔰 🔲 ⚕ Ⓟ ❶ *Rooms: 300.*

THE EVERGLADES & THE KEYS

KEY LARGO: *Kona Kai* ⓢⓢⓢⓢⓢ
97802 Overseas Hwy, FL 33037. Ⓒ *(305) 852-7200.* FAX *(305) 852-4629.*
Secluded with its own beachfront. It also has a superb collection of
modern European art. 🔰 🔲 Ⓟ ❶ *Rooms: 12.*

KEY WEST: *Key West International Youth Hostel* ⓢ
718 South St, FL 33040. Ⓒ *(305) 296-5719.* FAX *(305) 296-0672.*
At this simple but well-maintained hostel, the cosmopolitan backpacking
crowd have the use of pool tables. Rental bicycles are available to
explore the area. *Beds: 80.*

KEY WEST: *Wicker Guesthouse* ⓢⓢⓢ
913 Duval St, FL 33040. Ⓒ *(305) 296-4275.*
Ⓦ www.wickerhousekw.com
This is a friendly complex of new as well as restored houses in the
historic district and has a wide range of rooms and spacious suites.
🔰 ❶ *Rooms: 18.*

KEY WEST: *Curry Mansion Inn* ⓢⓢⓢⓢⓢ
511 Caroline St, FL 33040. Ⓒ *(305) 294-5349.* FAX *(305) 294-4093.* Ⓦ www.currymansion.com
This historic house, just off Duval Street, is also a museum. Most rooms are in
a lovely annex and very comfortable. 🔰 ⚕ 🐾 ❶ *Rooms: 28.*

For key to symbols see back flap

Where to Eat

The joy of Florida is the abundant fresh produce, from tropical fruit to seafood, which all restaurants use to great effect. Restaurants cater to every palate and budget, from the trendy establishments in Miami to simpler places in the interior, where food tends to be more homey. In the listings below, "L" indicates lunch and "D" stands for dinner.

Miami

Restaurant	Credit Cards	Children's Facilities	Early Bird Specials	Good Regional Cuisine	Bar
Miami Beach: *Nexxt* $ 700 Lincoln Rd. ☎ *(305) 532-6643.* An encyclopedic menu, an eclectic mix, and outside tables in this cafeteria-style eatery make this spot your best bet for a quick, cheap meal.	■				■
Miami Beach: *Joe's Stone Crab* $$$$ 11 Washington Ave. ☎ *(305) 673-0365.* This Miami institution is a must. There's lobster, shrimp, and fish as well as the signature stone crab claws. No reservations are required. ● *Mon L, May–Oct.* [P] [V] 🍷	■	●		●	■
Miami Beach: *The Forge* $$$$$ 432 41st St. ☎ *(305) 538-8533.* Celebrities abound at this Miami Beach landmark. Its glitzy decor has opulent American cuisine to match. ● *L.* [P] [V] 🍷 ⛱ ♫	■			●	■
Miami Beach: *Tuscan Steak* $$$$$ 433 Washington Ave. ☎ *(305) 534-2233.* One of Miami Beach's best. A flashy crowd goes for the giant antipasto, the T-bone with garlic puree, and the pricey drinks. 🍷	■				■
Downtown: *Big Fish* $$$$ 55 SW Miami Ave. ☎ *(305) 373-1770.* An unassuming seafood restaurant on the shore of the Miami River. It offers a great view of the skyline and some of the freshest fish in town. [V] 🚭	■				■
Little Havana: *Casa Juancho* $$$$ 2436 SW 8th St. ☎ *(305) 642-2452.* Deservedly famous for its superlative Spanish cuisine, this restaurant is very popular with Miami's Hispanic community. The decor evokes rural Spain, and troubadors entertain in the evenings. [P] 🍷 ♫	■	●			■
Coral Gables: *Christy's* $$$$ 3101 Ponce de Leon Blvd. ☎ *(305) 446-1400.* A very popular steak house featuring succulent beef and seafood in a club-like setting. A tasty Caesar salad accompanies each entrée. ● *Sat–Sun L.* 🍷	■				■
Coconut Grove: *Señor Frog's* $$$ 3480 Main Hwy. ☎ *(305) 448-0999.* Expect traditional food at this Mexican eatery, where only fresh produce is used. Try the sizzling fajitas and stuffed enchiladas, or one of the unusual savory chocolate *mole* dishes. [V] 🍷 ⛱	■	●			■
Greater Miami: *Chef Allen's* $$$$$ 19088 NE 29th Ave, North Miami Beach. ☎ *(305) 935-2900.* Sleek and chic, this Miami landmark is known for its high quality, daring New Florida cuisine. The activity in the kitchen, framed by a huge picture window, is fascinating. ● *L, Super Bowl.* [P] 🍷	■			●	■

The Gold & Treasure Coasts

Restaurant	Credit Cards	Children's Facilities	Early Bird Specials	Good Regional Cuisine	Bar
Boca Raton: *La Vieille Maison* $$$$$ 770 E Palmetto Park Rd. ☎ *(561) 391-6701.* Built by architect Addison Mizner, this home is now an intimate five-star French restaurant. The restaurant makes a perfect setting for romantic dinners. [P] 🍷 ⛱	■			●	■
Fort Lauderdale: *California Café* $$$$ 2301 SE 17th St Causeway. ☎ *(954) 728-3500.* Sweet potato crusted-salmon is one of the dishes offered at this restaurant, which mixes the flavors of California and Florida. The innovative seasonal menu also includes pizza and pasta dishes. [P] 🍷 ⛱ ♫ *Fri–Sat.*	■	●		●	■

	CREDIT CARDS	CHILDREN'S FACILITIES	EARLY BIRD SPECIALS	GOOD REGIONAL CUISINE	BAR

Price categories include a three-course meal for one, a glass of house wine, and all unavoidable extra charges such as sales tax and service.
ⓢ under $20
ⓢⓢ $20–30
ⓢⓢⓢ $30–45
ⓢⓢⓢⓢ $45–60
ⓢⓢⓢⓢⓢ over $60

CREDIT CARDS
Major credit cards accepted.

CHILDREN'S FACILITIES
Small portions and high chairs available, and there may also be a special children's menu.

EARLY BIRD SPECIALS
Meals offered at a discounted price if you eat early.

GOOD REGIONAL CUISINE
Florida specialties, such as seafood or dishes with Hispanic or Caribbean influence.

Listing	CREDIT CARDS	CHILDREN'S FACILITIES	EARLY BIRD SPECIALS	GOOD REGIONAL CUISINE	BAR
PALM BEACH: *Chuck & Harold's* ⓢⓢ 207 Royal Poinciana Way. ((561) 659-1440. The porch tables are the best for celebrity-spotting while you enjoy dishes such as conch chowder or one of the blackboard specials. 🅿 🍽 🏠 🎵	▣	●	▣	●	▣
PALM BEACH: *Florentine Dining Room* ⓢⓢⓢⓢⓢ Breakers Hotel, 1 S County Rd. ((561) 655-6611. For a truly memorable experience, try the refined setting of this restaurant and the lavish New Florida cuisine served here. 🅿 🍽 🎵	▣	●		●	▣
ORLANDO & THE SPACE COAST					
COCOA BEACH: *The Mango Tree Restaurant* ⓢⓢⓢⓢ 118 N Atlantic Ave. ((321) 799-0513. This gourmet restaurant serves local dishes, with seafood as a specialty. Situated just yards from the Atlantic Ocean, there is a tropical garden with waterfowl, Japanese carp, and lush foliage. ● *Mon.* Ⓥ 🍽 🎙 🏠 🎵	▣	●		●	▣
DOWNTOWN ORLANDO: *O'Boys Barb-Q* ⓢ 924 W Colonial Dr, 32804. ((407) 425-6269. A local favorite with simple decor and stunning slow-smoked barbeque cuisine. They have great all-you-can-eat specials in the evenings. ● *Sun.* 🏠	▣	●		●	
DOWNTOWN ORLANDO: *Le Coq au Vin* ⓢⓢⓢ 4800 S Orange Ave. ((407) 851-6980. Welcoming surroundings and consistently fine rustic French cuisine are a draw at this popular restaurant. ● *Mon, Sat–Sun L, most public hols.* 🍽	▣				
INTERNATIONAL DRIVE: *The Crab House* ⓢⓢⓢ 8291 International Dr. ((407) 352-6140. Choose from no less than nine crab dishes at this informal restaurant. The seafood salad bar is loaded with freshly shucked oysters, shrimp, marinated mussels, and crawfish, and other seafood dishes. 🍽 🏠	▣	●		●	▣
KISSIMMEE: *Pacino's Italian Ristorante* ⓢⓢⓢ 5795 W Hwy 192. ((407) 396-8022. Charbroiled food is the focus of this comfortable and friendly family restaurant. If you prefer, there's a free delivery service to any nearby hotel. 🏠	▣	●			
WALT DISNEY WORLD: *California Grill* ⓢⓢⓢ Disney's Contemporary Resort. ((407) 939-3463. A stylish restaurant with good views and an open-plan kitchen, serving creative West Coast fare. Try the excellent smoked salmon pizza, and pork and polenta. 🅿 🍽	▣	●			
WALT DISNEY WORLD: *Whispering Canyon Café* ⓢⓢ Disney Wilderness Lodge. ((407) 939-3463. Snap on your six-guns and settle in for an all-you-can-eat campfire cookout buffet in a Wild West setting. Also open for frontier-style breakfasts. 🅿 Ⓥ	▣	●			▣
WALT DISNEY WORLD: *Narcoossee's* ⓢⓢⓢ Disney's Grand Floridian Resort. ((407) 824-1400. This restaurant in an octagonal chalet alongside the Seven Seas lagoon serves delicious meat. It is also famed for its superlative fish dishes served with fresh vegetables. ● *L.* 🅿	▣	●			▣
WALT DISNEY WORLD: *Victoria & Albert's* ⓢⓢⓢⓢⓢ Disney's Grand Floridian Resort. ((407) 824-1089. Reservations are a must at this lavish restaurant. The six-course, fixed-price menu is superlative, and you're waited on by a butler and a maid. Ask for the chef's table, the most exclusive one in the house. ● *L.* 🅿 🍽 Ⓥ 🍴 🎵	▣			●	

Price categories include a three-course meal for one, a glass of house wine, and all unavoidable extra charges such as sales tax and service.
$ under $20
$$ $20–30
$$$ $30–45
$$$$ $45–60
$$$$$ over $60

CREDIT CARDS
Major credit cards accepted.

CHILDREN'S FACILITIES
Small portions and high chairs available, and there may also be a special children's menu.

EARLY BIRD SPECIALS
Meals offered at a discounted price if you eat early.

GOOD REGIONAL CUISINE
Florida specialties, such as seafood or dishes with Hispanic or Caribbean influence.

	CREDIT CARDS	CHILDREN'S FACILITIES	EARLY BIRD SPECIALS	GOOD REGIONAL CUISINE	BAR
THE NORTHEAST					
DAYTONA BEACH: *Aunt Catfish's* $$ 4009 Halifax Dr. ((386) 767-4768. This popular eatery on the Intracoastal Waterway is famed for its fried catfish, crab cakes, and clam strips. Also open for Sunday brunch.	▦	●	▦	●	▦
FERNANDINA BEACH: *Florida House Inn* $ 20–22 S 3rd St. ((904) 261-3300. At this lovely gingerbread house (Florida's oldest surviving hotel), diners sit at long trestle tables laden with generous servings of good American home cooking. Always "all-you-can-eat"! ● *Sun, Mon D; Dec 24 D.*	▦				▦
ST. AUGUSTINE: *Raintree* $$$ 102 San Marco Ave. ((904) 824-7211. Occupying one of the street's remaining historic buildings, Raintree is renowned for its award-winning food. Round off a meal of superb seafood or traditional meat dishes with a crêpe at the dessert bar. ● *L, Dec 25.* ♟	▦	●	▦	●	▦
THE PANHANDLE					
APALACHICOLA: *Seafood Grill & Steakhouse* $ 100 Market St. ((850) 653-9510. Located downtown, this friendly grill features a good range of meals. Tuck into the "world's largest" fried fish sandwich, the area's famous oysters, and pick one of the 30 or more beers offered. ● *Sun, public hols.* ♟	▦	●		●	▦
DESTIN: *Marina Café* $$$ 404 E Hwy 98. ((850) 837-7960. A jewel on the Emerald Coast, this restaurant combines excellent service, a spectacular location, and creative, internationally inspired cuisine. Early diners benefit from two-for-one dinners. ● *L, Dec 25, Jan.* ♟ ▦	▦	●	▦	●	▦
FORT WALTON BEACH: *Staff's Seafood Restaurant* $$$ 24 Miracle Strip Pkwy. ((850) 243-3482. Opened in 1913, Staff's has been famed for its fine local recipes ever since. The menu combines fish and seafood dishes with some brilliantly prepared steak, roast beef, and pork dishes. ● *L, public hols, Super Bowl.* ♟ ♫	▦	●		●	▦
PANAMA CITY BEACH: *The Treasure Ship* $$ 3605 S Thomas Dr. ((850) 234-8881. Housed in a replica of a 16th-century galleon, this three-level restaurant combines welcoming surroundings of open-air decks and water views with well-prepared fresh seafood. The grilled tuna, salmon, and mahi steaks are house specialties. ● *Nov–Feb.* ♟ ▦ ♫	▦	●	▦	●	▦
PENSACOLA: *McGuire's Irish Pub* $ 600 E Gregory St. ((850) 433-6789. A visit to Pensacola isn't complete without a stop at McGuire's, where huge portions of steak, pasta, pizza, and pub fare are served. Wash it down with one of their home-brewed beers. ● *Thanksgiving, Dec 25.* ▼ ♟ ♫	▦	●		●	▦
TALLAHASSEE: *Andrew's Capitol Bar & Grille* $$$ 228 South Adams St. ((850) 222-3444. This goumet restaurant is one of three at this address; here the set menu is excellent, and the flavor is Mediterranean dishes. Service is attentive. ● *Sun.* ♟ ♫	▦	●			▦
TALLAHASSEE: *Chez Pierre* $$$ 1215 Thomasville Rd. ((850) 222-0936. Southern hospitality, reasonable rates, and excellent French food make this bistro a local favorite. Chez Pierre is also famed for its desserts, especially delicious pastries. ● *Sun, Dec 25, Jan 1.* ♟ ♫	▦	●			▦

THE GULF COAST

FORT MYERS: *The Veranda* $$$
2122 2nd St. (941) 332-2065.
This charming restaurant housed in a 1902 building offers original culinary creations like artichoke fritters stuffed with blue crab. The décor is Deep South and the service attentive. ● *Sat L, Sun, public hols.* P Y 🖺 ♫

ST. PETERSBURG: *Keystone Club* $$
320 4th St N. (727) 822-6600.
This eatery has an informal atmosphere, is popular with locals, and serves the best prime rib for miles around. ● *L, some public hols.* Y

ST. PETE BEACH: *Hurricane Seafood Restaurant* $$
807 Gulf Way. (727) 360-9558.
Set right on the beach, this restaurant prides itself on its crab cakes and fresh Florida grouper, which comes blackened, grilled, broiled, or in a sandwich. The cocktail deck is especially popular at sunset. Y 🖺 ♫

SANIBEL ISLAND: *Windows On The Water* $$$$
Sundial Beach Resort, 1451 Middle Gulf Drive. (239) 395-6014.
In a beautiful location overlooking the Gulf of Mexico, this rather elegant restaurant features delicious Floribbean cuisine. Y

SARASOTA: *Bart's Bayside* $$
230 Sarasota Quay. (239) 954-3839.
Choose the steak or tasty seafood such as stuffed lobster. Dine indoors or on the terrrace overlooking the bay. P Y 🖺 ♫ *Fri & Sat.*

SARASOTA: *Michael's On East* $$$
1212 East Ave S. (941) 366-0007.
One of Sarasota's premier restaurants, Michael's has innovative regional cuisine and a large selection of microbrewed beers. ● *Sat & Sun L.* P Y

TAMPA: *Bern's Steak House* $$$
1208 S Howard Ave. (813) 251-2421.
A must for meat lovers, Bern's has made steak cuisine a fine art. Each order is prepared to your specificatiions, and accompanied by organic vegetables. It is very popular and reservations are essential. ● *L, Dec 25.* P Y ♫

TAMPA: *Lauro Ristorante Italiano* $$$$
3915 Henderson Blvd. (813) 281-2100.
This restaurant offers delicious traditional Italian food in pleasant surroundings. Good service, moderate prices. ● *Sat–Sun L.* Y

TAMPA: *Mis en Place* $$$$
442 W Kennedy Blvd. (813) 254-5373.
The innovative menu of this busy bistro changes daily but never fails to please. Locals love this place, so reserve ahead. ● *Sat L, Mon, Sun.* Y

THE EVERGLADES & THE KEYS

ISLAMORADA: *Green Turtle Inn* $$
MM 81.5, Overseas Hwy. (305) 664-9031.
This inn has been a Keys tradition since 1947; locals flock to eat the famous turtle chowder and alligator steak. A pianist entertains in the evenings. ● *Mon.* Y ♫

KEY LARGO: *The Fish House Restaurant and Seafood Market* $$
MM 102.4, Overseas Hwy. (305) 451-4665.
It looks like a shack, but this is the place locals depend on for the freshest fish and conch salad. No frills, just good seafood.

KEY WEST: *Blue Heaven* $$$
729 Thomas St. (305) 296-8666.
Housed in a wonderful old Key West building, this friendly restaurant offers delicious seafood in a laid-back atmosphere. The seating at painted wooden tables is basic. ● *Thanksgiving, Dec 25.* V Y 🖺 ♫

KEY WEST: *Pier House Resort* $$$$
Pier House Resort, 1 Duval St. (305) 296-4600.
This exclusive waterfront restaurant, one of the best in the Keys, serves fancy Florida cuisine such as lobster with marinated plantain. Be sure to reserve an outside table for the best sunset views.
● *Mon–Sat L.* Y 🖺 ♫

For key to symbols see back flap

THE DEEP SOUTH

The Deep South at a Glance

COMPRISING THE FOUR STATES OF Louisiana, Arkansas, Mississippi, and Alabama, the Deep South is one of the most distinctive parts of the United States. From the broad plains of the mighty Mississippi River and the bayous of Louisiana's Cajun Country to the hardscrabble forests of Arkansas's Ozark Mountains, the region is both geographically and culturally diverse. While opulent mansions, antebellum homes, and Civil Rights Movement sights are aspects of its past, the Deep South's special charms rest with the people and their natural appreciation of the good things in life. America's two most beloved musical creations – jazz and the blues – were born here, a legacy that is celebrated throughout the region, particularly in New Orleans. This city's universal reputation for nonstop fun is best experienced during Mardi Gras.

0 km   100

0 miles

Fayetteville
Mountain View
Jo
Conway
Little Rock
Hot Springs
Pine Bluff
Mi
ARKANSAS
(See pp358–59)
Camden
El Dorado
Gre
Shreveport
Ruston
Tallulah
LOUISIANA
(See pp344–57)
Natchez
Alexandria
M
De Ridder
H
Bate
Rou
Lafayette
Morgan Cit

Hot Springs (see p358), *Arkansas, is home to the historic Bathhouse Row, where the Buckstaff Bathhouse still offers spa facilities. Former president Bill Clinton spent his youth in this city.*

Lafayette (see p356) is the heart of Louisiana's *Cajun Country, where the descendants of French Canadian immigrants still preserve their language and culture. Much of this local culture can be found in restaurants and nightclubs, at the city's museums and historic parks, as well as out in the surrounding swamps.*

◁ **Two rows of magnificent oak trees lining the drive to Oak Alley, a Lower Mississippi plantation**

LOCATOR MAP

Selma (see p364) *is one of the many towns in Alabama that played a significant role during the Civil Rights Movement in the 1950s and 60s. An important sight here is the National Voting Rights Museum, which tells the story of the successful Selma-to-Montgomery March led by Dr. Martin Luther King Jr. in 1965.*

Corinth
Florence
Huntsville

Oxford

Tupelo
Hamilton
Cullman

Winona

Columbus
Birmingham

MISSISSIPPI
(See pp360–63)

Meridian

Phenix City

Selma
Montgomery

ALABAMA
(See pp364–65)

Laurel

Hattiesburg

Andalusia
Dothan

Mobile

Biloxi

Orleans

The Gulf Coast *(see p363) has traditionally been dominated by the seafood industry. But over the last decade, lavish Las Vegas-style casinos have proliferated along the coast, offering a choice of cuisines as well as different types of entertainment.*

New Orleans *(see pp344–53), the region's cultural capital, is characterized by Colonial architecture, lively bars, and the annual Mardi Gras festivities.*

THE DEEP SOUTH

*W*ITH ITS WARM, SEMITROPICAL CLIMATE *and easy-going temperament, the Deep South is perhaps the most culturally diverse region of the United States. Multiethnic and all-embracing in a friendly, hospitable way, the region offers visitors an unforgettable introduction to Southern charm, as embodied by the pleasure-seeking lifestyle of New Orleans.*

Some 14 million people live in the Deep South, in a region covering about 200,000 sq miles (517,998 sq km), which is similar in size and population density to neighboring Texas. While the four states share a natural appreciation for the good things in life, they are otherwise quite different. Louisiana epitomizes French Catholic culture, whereas Mississippi and Alabama were the heart of the Confederacy during the Civil War. Arkansas differs in its rugged landscape matched by its people's pride in the state's mountain heritage. Most residents of the primarily rural Deep South have family roots reaching deep into history, and a rare continuity exists between past and present.

The rich bottomlands that line the meandering path of the Mississippi River across parts of Mississippi, Arkansas, and Louisiana once yielded the world's largest crops of cotton, and it was here that some of the greatest early American fortunes were made. However, the industry's labor-intensive demands were based on the iniquities of slavery, which has haunted the economy and culture of the Deep South for two centuries.

HISTORY

Some of the region's earliest known inhabitants were the city-based agricultural communities of the Mississippian culture, whose members cultivated extensive fields of corn, beans, and squash, and constructed elaborate mounds for their religious and political rituals. The 3,700-year-old effigy mounds at Poverty Point in northeastern Louisiana, one of North America's oldest, largest, and most significant archaeological remains, dates from this period.

The steamboat *Natchez* leaving Mississippi River port

◁ **Royal Café, a popular Cajun-Creole restaurant in the French Quarter, New Orleans**

Dennis Malone Carter's painting, *The Battle of New Orleans*

When Spanish conquistador Hernando de Soto and his troops first encountered the Mississippian cities, they soon decimated the people and their culture. Thereafter, other more dispersed Indian groups rose to power, most notably the Chickasaw, Choctaw, Quapaw, Creek, and Cherokee tribes. The Creek Indians of central and northern Alabama were perhaps the most successful, numbering some 15,000 at their peak. In the early 1700s, European colonists supported the Creeks, and supplied them with guns and ammunition in exchange for their help in vanquishing the other tribes. A century later, the Creeks themselves were under assault, and by 1810 they had been forced to give up their vast and fertile territory to the incoming Americans. The story of most other Deep South Indians is similar, ending tragically in the 1830s when they were moved to distant Oklahoma. A few, including the Choctaw tribe in central Mississippi, still live on their ancestral lands.

While English-speaking Americans dominate the past and present, the French and Spanish carried out much of the early exploration and settlement. Louisiana and Arkansas were under nominal French control until 1803, while Alabama and Mississippi were part of the Spanish colony of West Florida until 1814. Boundaries and allegiances varied until the US took control, through the Louisiana Purchase of 1803, and by the multiple battles with England, Spain, and their Indian allies.

With the defeat of the British at the Battle of New Orleans in January 1815, the Deep South entered an era of unprecedented growth and prosperity. New Orleans became the fourth-largest US city and the nation's second-busiest port. Steamboats plied the Mississippi River, as chronicled by writer Mark Twain (1835–1910), himself a former steamboat captain.

By the mid-1800s, wealthy individuals from the Carolinas, in particular, introduced the slave-owning, cotton-growing plantation culture that would reap huge fortunes and lead inexorably toward the Civil War. Mississippi, the second state to secede from the US, provided the rebel Confederacy with its president, Jefferson Davis, while Montgomery, Alabama, served as its first capital. The fall of Vicksburg in 1863 effectively ended Confederate control of the Mississippi, and after the war much of the region lay in ruins.

KEY DATES IN HISTORY

1539 Hernando de Soto leads the first European expedition to the Deep South

1699 Fort de Maurepas, near present-day Biloxi, Mississippi, becomes capital of France's Louisiana colony

1723 Louisiana's capital moved to New Orleans

1803 Louisiana Territory purchased from Napoleonic France (the Louisiana Purchase)

1814 Creek and Chickasaw Indians are forced to relinquish their territorial claims

1812 Louisiana becomes a state

1817 Mississippi becomes a state

1819 Alabama becomes a state

1836 Arkansas becomes a state

1863 US forces take control of Vicksburg to end Confederate access to the Mississippi River

1935 Populist Louisiana Governor Huey "Kingfish" Long assassinated in Baton Rouge

1955 Montgomery Bus Boycott

1962 African-American student James Meredith becomes the first nonwhite person to attend classes at the University of Mississippi

1992 Former Arkansas Governor Bill Clinton is elected 42nd president of the United States

2001 Four-time Louisiana Governor Edwin Edwards is sentenced to 10 years in prison for conspiracy and extortion

The post-Civil War economic and social wasteland gave rise to a doctrine of white supremacy and racist violence that plagued the region the following century. It wasn't until the 1950s and 60s, when the dramatic confrontations of the Civil Rights Movement, such as those at Selma, Alabama, in 1965, began to change things for the better.

PEOPLE & THE ECONOMY

The Deep South is remembered for its often troubled history as well as its people's resolute and indomitable spirit to cope with the problems of the past. Despite a large exodus of African Americans to northern US cities after the Civil War, descendants of slaves still form a large percentage of the population, and the slow but steady process of overcoming racial segregation has transformed the region. Today, African Americans are legally entitled to equal treatment, although in reality there remains a distinct gap in opportunities between whites and nonwhites.

Another distinctive component is Louisiana's Cajuns, who live in the watery region north and west of New Orleans. A third very different culture is found in the densely forested mountains of Arkansas and northern Alabama. Long denigrated as "hillbillies" like their figurative cousins in Tennessee, Kentucky, and West Virginia, these mountain people have a fiercely protected independence and self-reliance. Hunting and fishing, both for recreation and sustenance, many still practice traditional crafts and perform the so-called "bluegrass" music derived from the folk music of their Scottish and Irish forebears.

As the cotton-based economy of plantation and Reconstruction days has disappeared, little has emerged to take its place. Thanks to inexpensive imports, the region's once-thriving textile industry has all but disappeared. Except for the steel mills of Birmingham, Alabama, the corridor of petrochemical factories along the Mississippi in Louisiana, or the gambling centers in the Mississippi Delta and along the Gulf of Mexico, the Deep South still suffers from a major lack of industry

and employment opportunities. Success stories include Dillard's department stores and the world-dominating retail might of Wal-Mart, both of which started and still have their corporate headquarters in Arkansas. In contrast, one of the region's economic darlings of the 1990s, the Mississippi-based telecommunications company, WorldCom, crashed into bankruptcy in 2002.

CULTURE & ARTS

If culture and the arts were the most valuable market commodities, the Deep South would be the wealthiest region in the country. The region has been instrumental in creating some of the world's most popular forms of musical, literary, and culinary expression. Jazz, for example, grew from the bubbling melting pot of Creole culture that was New Orleans after the Civil War, while the blues and its offspring rock 'n' roll, emerged from the slave songs of the Mississippi Delta. Writers such as Tennessee Williams and William Faulkner, and novels like Harper Lee's classic *To Kill a Mockingbird*, helped earn the Deep South a place in world literature, while the melange of Cajun, Creole, "Soul Food," and barbecue make it a delicious place to travel.

Statue of William Faulkner in the courthouse square in downtown Oxford, Mississippi

Exploring the Deep South

STRETCHING FROM THE GULF COAST to the Appalachians in the north and the Great Plains in the west, the Deep South region sprawls across some 200,000 sq miles (517,998 sq km). Although large in area, the population is sparse and the transportation facilities limited, with only a few airlines, passenger train services, and inter-city buses connecting the main cities and large towns. As elsewhere in the US, a car is the best way to get around. The main tourist destination, New Orleans, has the region's major airport, while smaller airports serve other Deep South cities.

KEY

✈ Airport

— Highway

— Major road

— Railroad

- - State border

SIGHTS AT A GLANCE

Louisiana
New Orleans pp344–53 **1**
Plantation Alley **2**
Baton Rouge p355
Lafayette **4**
Bayou Teche **5**
Natchitoches **6**
Shreveport **7**

Arkansas
Little Rock **8**
Hot Springs **9**
Mountain View **10**
Eureka Springs **11**

Mississippi
Mississippi Delta **12**
Oxford **13**
Tupelo **14**
Vicksburg National
  Military Park **15**
Jackson **16**
Natchez Trace Parkway **17**
Natchez **18**
Gulf Coast **19**

Alabama
Mobile **20**
Selma **21**
Montgomery **22**
Tuskegee **23**
Birmingham **24**
Huntsville **25**

SEE ALSO

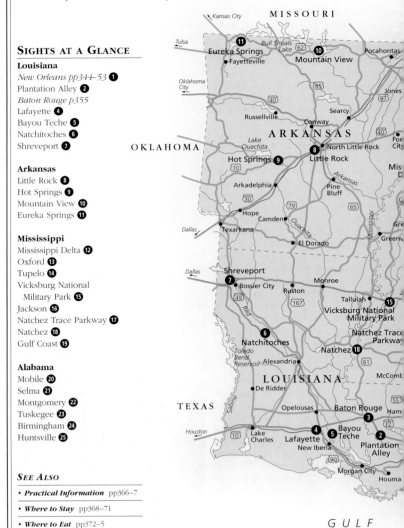

A traditional sternwheeler riverboat cruising the Mississippi River

MILEAGE CHART

NEW ORLEANS, LA						
80 129	**BATON ROUGE, LA**					
443 713	**361** 581	**LITTLE ROCK, AR**				
346 557	**335** 539	**218** 351	**OXFORD, MS**			
190 306	**179** 288	**281** 452	**160** 257	**JACKSON, MS**		
143 230	**201** 323	**525** 845	**344** 553	**189** 304	**MOBILE, AL**	
342 550	**399** 642	**535** 851	**187** 301	**239** 384	**258** 415	**BIRMINGHAM, AL**

10 = Distance in miles
10 = Distance in kilometers

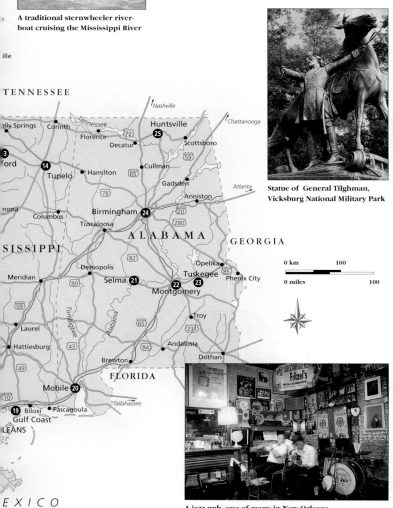

Statue of General Tilghman, Vicksburg National Military Park

A jazz pub, one of many in New Orleans

New Orleans ❶

Located in southeast Louisiana, New Orleans lies between Lake Pontchartrain and a bend in the Mississippi. It covers an area of 199 sq miles (516 sq km) and has a population of nearly 500,000 residents. The city's topmost tourist destination is the French Quarter, where the cultural heritage of its Colonial past is ever present. The legendary Royal and Bourbon Streets are located here, as are Creole-style cottages, lively bars, and markets offering local specialties. Beyond this lie the Central Business District centered along the waterfront, the verdant Garden District, and the area around City Park.

Diners at the popular Acme Oyster House

Sights at a Glance

Old US Mint ①
Old Ursuline Convent ②
French Market ③
Café du Monde ④
Jackson Square ⑤
St. Louis Cathedral, Cabildo, & Presbytère ⑥
New Orleans Historic Voodoo Museum ⑦
St. Louis Cemetery #1 ⑧
Hermann-Grima Historic House ⑨
Bourbon Street ⑩
Royal Street ⑪
Steamboat Natchez ⑫
Custom House ⑬
Aquarium of the Americas ⑭
Ferry to Algiers & Mardi Gras World ⑮
Riverwalk Marketplace ⑯

Greater New Orleans
(see inset map)
Garden District ⑰
City Park ⑱

Royal Street and its well-known LaBranche buildings

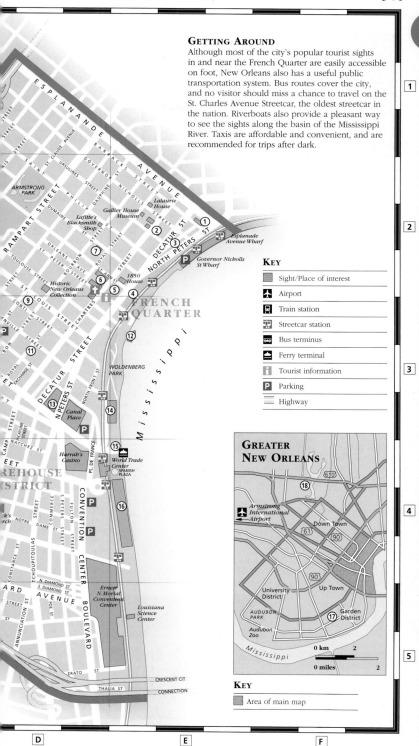

GETTING AROUND

Although most of the city's popular tourist sights in and near the French Quarter are easily accessible on foot, New Orleans also has a useful public transportation system. Bus routes cover the city, and no visitor should miss a chance to travel on the St. Charles Avenue Streetcar, the oldest streetcar in the nation. Riverboats also provide a pleasant way to see the sights along the basin of the Mississippi River. Taxis are affordable and convenient, and are recommended for trips after dark.

KEY

	Sight/Place of interest
	Airport
	Train station
	Streetcar station
	Bus terminus
	Ferry terminal
	Tourist information
P	Parking
	Highway

GREATER NEW ORLEANS

0 km 2
0 miles 2

KEY

Area of main map

Neo-Classical façade of the Old US Mint

admire the splendid pine-and-cypress ceiling, two superb Bavarian stained-glass windows, and a window depicting the Battle of New Orleans, beneath an image of Our Lady of Prompt Succor. The nuns' old kitchen and laundry is now the rectory.

A formal French garden containing a handsome iron gazebo lies in front of the building. It is accessed via the porter's lodge.

Old US Mint ①

Map E2. 400 Esplanade Ave.
(504) 568-6968. Riverfront.
3, 55. 9am–5pm Tue–Sun.
public hols.
www.sm.crt.state.la.us/mintex.htm

THIS GREEK REVIVAL building, built in 1835 by William Strickland, functioned as a mint until 1909, turning out a variety of coinage, including Confederate and Mexican currency. It then became a federal prison and was later used by the Coast Guard. In the late 1970s, it was taken over by the state and converted into a museum to house the **New Orleans Jazz Collection**. The exhibit tells the story of jazz *(see p349)* through a collection of original musical instruments, vintage photographs, and historic documents. Among the instruments displayed are the ebony clarinet George Lewis played on to record "Burgundy Street Blues," and the cornet Louis Armstrong learned to play on. At the entrance are a series of photographs of early bands and musicians, as well as a steamboat scale model.

The building also houses the **History of the Old US Mint Exhibition**, which displays gold and silver coins formerly minted here. The carefully restored façade is embellished with some of the city's most beautiful wrought-iron balconies and railings.

Old Ursuline Convent ②

Map E2. 1100 Chartres St. (504) 529-3040. Riverfront. 3, 55.
10am–3pm Tue–Fri, 11:15am–2pm Sat–Sun (guided tours only).

THE OLDEST BUILDING in the Mississippi Valley, the Old Ursuline Convent was built in 1752, some 25 years after the Ursuline Sisters first arrived in New Orleans. With its steep-pitched roof punctuated by a row of dormers and tall chimneys, it is a typical French Colonial structure and one of the few to remain from that period. In the 1820s, the nuns moved to new quarters, and the convent became the first official residence for the bishops and archbishops of New Orleans, and the home of the arch-diocesan archives. Later, it became part of a parish.

Photograph, New Orleans Jazz Collection

The current chapel, now known as Our Lady of Victory, was consecrated in 1845. Inside, visitors can

Old Ursuline Convent, dating from 1752

French Market ③

Map E2. N Peters St, from St. Ann to Barracks St. Riverfront. 3, 5, 48. Shops: 9am–7pm daily; Farmers Market: 24 hours daily.
www.frenchmarket.org

A NEW ORLEANS institution since 1791, this area served as a trading place for Native Americans much before European settlement. Officially the French Market is five blocks between St. Ann and Barracks Streets, beginning roughly at Café du Monde and ending at the Old Mint museum. In daily use, the term "French Market" usually denotes the open air markets from St. Philip to Barracks, which stock many New Orleans specialties. The Farmers Market (beginning at Ursulines Street) is a shadow of its former vigorous self but even today shoppers can find fresh Louisiana produce here. Strawberries in the spring and the pecans in the fall are especially prized.

The majority of the space is now given over to the **Flea Market** – all kinds of items, ranging from jewelry and pottery to African arts and crafts, can be bought at the stalls and tables around the French Market buildings. The Flea Market stands on the site of the notorious neigh-borhood around Gallatin Street, which was once inhabited by crimi-nals, prostitutes, and visiting sailors.

Café du Monde ④

Map E2. 1039 Decatur. ☎ *(504) 587-0833.* 🚋 *Riverfront.* 🚌 *3, 5, 55.* 🕒 *24 hours daily.* ♿ ☕ 🛍 [W] www.cafedumonde.com

EVERYONE WHO visits New Orleans stops here for a plate of sugar-dusted *beignets* (square French donuts) accompanied by plain *café au lait* or the famous chicory-flavored version. These are the only items offered at this 100-year old coffee house, where visitors can relax at a table under the arcade and listen to the street musicians, or simply watch people as they go by.

During the mid-19th century there were 500 similar coffee houses in the French Quarter. Coffee was one of the city's most important commodities, and the coffee trade helped the economy recover after the Civil War, when New Orleans vied with New York City to control coffee imports. Chicory-flavored coffee was conceived during the Civil War, when the root was used to stretch the coffee supply.

Taking a break at Café du Monde with coffee and *beignets*

Jackson Square ⑤

Map E2. 🚋 *Riverfront.* 🚌 *3, 5, 55.*

ONCE LITTLE MORE than a muddy field called the Place d' Armes where troops were drilled, criminals were placed in the stocks, and executions were carried out, this square lies in the heart of the French Quarter. It was renamed in honor of General Andrew Jackson *(see p265)* who defeated the British at the Battle of New Orleans in 1815.

Jazz band playing in Jackson Square

The gardens and pathways, as they exist today, were laid out in 1848, when the beautification of the square took place under the patronage of Baroness Micaela Pontalba, then one of the city's most colorful personalities. Under her auspices, the Pelanne brothers designed the handsome wrought-iron fence that encloses the square. At the center stands a statue of General Jackson astride a rearing horse, sculpted by Clark Mills for $30,000. The inscription "The Union must and shall be preserved," on the plinth was added by Union General Benjamin "Beast" Butler, when he occupied the city during the Civil War.

Today, the square is a lively meeting place, where artists exhibit their works and jazz musicians entertain visitors throughout the week.

A developer like her philanthropist father Don Andreés Almonester y Rojas *(see p348)*, the baroness also commissioned the **Pontalba Buildings**, flanking the uptown and downtown sides of Jackson Square. Built at a cost of over $300,000, they were considered the best and the largest apartments of their kind at that time. These elegant apartment buildings are based on plans the baroness brought back from Paris after she separated from her husband. The design of the initials A and P (for Almonester and Pontalba) in the cast-iron railings of the balconies and galleries is attributed to one of the baroness's sons, an artist.

The **1850 House**, in the lower Pontalba building, displays opulent decorations that re-create the middle-class lifestyles of the antebellum era. Opposite Jackson Square is Le Petit Théâtre du Vieux Carré, established in 1916 by a small group of actors called the Drawing Room Players. Behind it, at 632 St. Peter Street, is the apartment where Tennessee Williams wrote his famous play *A Streetcar Named Desire*.

🏛 1850 House

523 St. Ann St. ☎ *(504) 568-6968.* 🕒 *9am–5pm Tue–Sun.* ● *public hols.* 💲 📷 [W] www.lsm.crt.state.la.us

NEW ORLEANS IRONWORK

The shadows cast by New Orleans ironwork add a romantic touch to the city. Wrought iron, which came first, was fashioned by hand into beautiful shapes by German, Irish, and African-American artisans. Cast iron, on the other hand, was poured into wooden molds and allowed to set. As a result, the latter has a somewhat solid, fixed appearance, unlike wrought iron, which is handmade and has a more fluid aspect. Both kinds of ironwork can be seen throughout the city, particularly in the French Quarter and the Garden District, where balconies, fences, window grilles, and gates are adorned with decorative motifs such as abstracts, cherubs, fruit, flowers, and animals.

Ironwork on the Pontalba Buildings

St. Louis Cathedral

St. Louis Cathedral, Cabildo, & Presbytère ⑥

Map D2. Jackson Square. **(** (504) 525-9585 (St. Louis Cathedral), (504) 568-6968 (Cabildo & Presbytère). 🚊 St. Charles Ave. 🚌 3, 5, 55, 81. ⏱ 9am–5pm daily (St. Louis Cathedral); 9am–5pm Tue–Sun (Cabildo & Presbytère). 🕆 St. Louis Cathedral, regular services throughout the day. ♿ 📷 🏛 Ⓦ www.saintlouiscathedral.org

T HIS COMPLEX of buildings comprises the cathedral, Cabildo, and Presbytère. St. Louis Cathedral stands on the site of two earlier churches that were destroyed. The current building, begun in 1789, was dedicated as a cathedral in 1794. Inside are superb murals and a carved-wood Baroque main altar.

The Cabildo, designed by Guilberto Guillemard, was built and financed in 1795 by Don Andrés Almoneŝter y Rojas. It served as a capitol for the legislative assembly of the Spanish Colonial government and subsequently as the City Hall. From 1853 to 1911 it housed the state Supreme Court. The Louisiana Purchase (see p340) was signed in the Sala Capitular in 1803.

The Casa Curial, or Presbytère, was built between 1794 and 1813, and used as a courthouse until 1911. It now houses the Mardi Gras Museum, featuring colorful objects and memorabilia.

New Orleans Historic Voodoo Museum ⑦

Map D2. 724 Dumaine St. **(** (504) 523-7685. 🚌 3, 5, 55. ⏱ 10am–8pm daily. 📷 📹 🏛

R ITUAL OBJECTS, charms, and spirit portraits are displayed in this small museum, devoted to the origin and development of voodoo. A cult-religion, voodoo is an amalgam of West Indian fetish worship and Roman Catholic saint-worship. Its most famous practitioner was the mulatto hairdresser, Marie Laveau, who performed her ritual celebrations in public along Bayou St. John. Citizens consulted her for charms, amulets, and magical *gris-gris* powders (dried frog, dried lizard, and many more), which were believed to help accomplish any purpose, from evicting a neighbor to inspiring love.

A beseeching angel, St. Louis Cemetery #1

The museum displays some of her alleged possessions. The cramped rooms are filled with altars, including one dedicated to the "alligator man," which is considered a very powerful image. There is also a coiled live python in a box (the serpent is believed to be the earthly form of the voodoo god and the source of the religion's power). A detailed documentary video, in a room off the back courtyard, explains what voodoo is and its role in the New Orleans community.

St. Louis Cemetery #1 ⑧

Map D2. Basin St between St. Louis & Conti. **(** (504) 596-3050. 🚌 46, 48, 52, 57. ⏱ 9am–3pm Mon–Sat, 9am–noon Sun. ♿ 📹

T HE CITY'S OLDEST surviving cemetery was established in 1789. This fascinating place, with its rows of mausoleums, is the resting place of many legendary local residents. The most famous of all is probably Marie Laveau. Crowds visit her tomb, marking it with an "X" (symbolically requesting that she grant a particular wish). By 1829, St. Louis Cemetery #1 was filled, mostly with victims of yellow fever, and the nearby **St. Louis Cemetery #2** was established as an extension. Many of the city's 19th-century Creole aristocracy are buried here in ornate mausoleums.

However, the cemeteries should not be visited alone, as they are in secluded areas where muggers and pickpockets operate. It is advisable for visitors to join guided tours, given by the **Save Our Cemeteries** organization and by **New Orleans Tours, Inc.** Both provide plenty of excellent local information.

📹 **New Orleans Tour Inc.**
((888) 486-8687.
Ⓦ www.bigeasy.com
📹 **Save Our Cemeteries**
((888) 721-7493.

VOODOO WORSHIP

Voodoo arrived in New Orleans from Africa, via the Caribbean, where it originated as a form of ancestor worship among the West African tribes, who were brought to North America as slaves. During the slave uprising in Saint Dominigue in 1793, many of the planters from Haiti fled to New Orleans, bringing their slaves (and voodoo) with them. Marie Laveau (c.1794–1881), the voodoo queen, used Catholic elements such as prayer, incense, and saints in her rituals, which she opened to the public for an admission fee. The voodoo calendar's high point was the celebration she held along Bayou St. John on St. John's Eve.

Portrait of Marie Laveau

New Orleans Jazz

Blue Lu Barker

JAZZ IS AMERICA'S original contribution to world culture. It evolved slowly and almost imperceptibly from a number of sources – from the music played at balls, parades, dances, and funerals, and New Orleans' unique blend of cultures. Its musical inspirations included African work chants and spirituals, as well as European and American folk influences – the entire mélange of music that was played in 19th-century New Orleans.

Trumpeter Oscar "Papa" Celestin, the founder of the Tuxedo Brass Band in 1911, also composed "Down by the Riverside."

Kid Ory's trombone, which he played while performing with King Oliver and others, is displayed at the Old US Mint.

STORYVILLE JAZZ SALON

The 38-block area bounded by Iberville, Basin, Robertson, and St. Louis Streets, was the city's legal red-light district from 1897 to 1917. Known as Storyville, many early jazz artists, including Jelly Roll Morton, King Oliver, and Edward "Kid" Ory, entertained at the bordellos, playing behind screens.

Riverboat Jazz Bands came into being after Storyville was closed down in 1917. New Orleans' best musicians either performed on boats or migrated to northern cities. Pianist Fate Marable's band included Louis Armstrong, who played the cornet.

Congo Square was where slaves gathered every Sunday to celebrate their one day off by playing music and dancing.

Louis Armstrong, the internationally famous jazz trumpeter, began singing on the streets of New Orleans. He played with Kid Ory before leaving the city in 1923 to join King Oliver's band in Chicago.

Master bedroom at the Hermann-Grima Historic House

Hermann-Grima Historic House ⑨

Map D3. 820 St. Louis St. 📞 *(504) 525-5661.* 🚌 *3.* ◷ *10am–3:30pm Mon–Fri.* ● *public hols.* 📷 📹 ♿ 🌐 *www.gnofn.org/~hggh*

THIS GABLED BRICK house is one of the French Quarter's few examples of American Creole-style architecture. It was built in 1831 by William Brand for Samuel Hermann, a German-Jewish merchant who lost his fortune in 1837 and sold the house to Judge Felix Grima. It features a central doorway with a fanlight and marble steps; another window with a fanlight graces the second floor. Inside, the floors and doors are made of cypress. The three-story service quarters are in a building off the parterre behind the house. They contain a kitchen with a rare four-burner wood-fired stove with a beehive oven.

Bourbon Street ⑩

Map D3. 🚌 *3, 55, 89.*

TODAY BOURBON Street, rather than Basin Street, is synonymous with sin. This legendary street, named after the French royal family of Bourbon, is lined with bars that offer vats of such lethal concoctions as Brain Freeze, Nuclear Kamikaze, and Sex on the Bayou, most often to the accompaniment of blasting rock or blues. Other places offer everything from peep shows, topless dancers, and strip joints, to drag shows and gay action. During Mardi Gras, the sidewalks and overhanging balconies are jammed with crowds and drinking revelers.

Some of the most famous establishments near this lively street include **Pat O'Brien's** (St. Peter Street), which is well-known for its rum-based "Hurricane" cocktail, **Preservation Hall** (St. Peter Street), a top-quality jazz venue, and **Arnaud's** (Bienville Street),

Fire fountain at Pat O'Brien's, near Bourbon Street

a restaurant that is a true New Orleans classic. Galatoire's, close to Arnaud's, is another premier New Orleans restaurant *(see p373).* **Lafitte's Blacksmith Shop**, at 941 Bourbon Street, is considered one of the finest bars in New Orleans. Constructed sometime before 1772, it is a good example of the brick-between-posts French-style building, in which soft local bricks are supported by cypress timbers and protected by plaster. Inside, several small fireplaces warm the place on cool evenings, and there is also a small patio containing a sculpture of Adam and Eve, created by an artist as payment for his bar bill.

Despite its name, there is no concrete evidence that the pirate brothers, Jean and Pierre Lafitte, operated a smithy here as a front for their smuggling activities. They were also prominent slave traffickers, selling "black ivory" to Louisiana's prominent slave-holding families. The brothers earned local gratitude by warning the Americans of the planned British attack on New Orleans in 1815, and they fought bravely in the ensuing battle.

Just up from Lafitte's is the oldest gay bar in the country, **Lafitte's in Exile**. It is so called because, until the early 1950s, gays frequented the old Lafitte's; when the bar changed hands, its new owner refused to renew the lease, and its gay patrons established their new quarters here. It has remained a popular alternative ever since.

A VIEW OF ROYAL STREET

The pride of the French Quarter, Royal Street is lined with beautiful buildings that have been carefully restored. Today, they are occupied by elegant stores and restaurants.

Brennan's (#417)
Built around 1802 for a Spanish merchant, this building became a bank, and then a restaurant in 1954. Its balcony seal is made of cast iron.

Antoine Peychaud's Pharmacy (#437)
An antique shop offering a range of fine objects is now housed in the pharmacy where the cocktail was born.

Louisiana State Bank (#403)

Moss Antiques

Lafitte's Blacksmith Shop, Bourbon Street

Royal Street ⑪

Map D3. *St. Charles Ave.* *3, 5, 55, 81, 82.*

ANTIQUE SHOPS filled with beautiful, often French, objects line Royal Street, undoubtedly the most fetching street in the French Quarter. In the early colony, this was the city's financial center and its main and most fashionable street. Today, many of the antique stores occupy handsome landmarks. Their merchandise includes crystal chandeliers, massive inlaid armoires, and ormolu furnishings – treasures associated with an opulent Southern lifestyle.

The **Historic New Orleans Collection**, born of one couple's interest in the Battle of New Orleans (1815), is housed in a complex of houses built for Jean François Merieult and his wife in 1792. The collectors were General and Mrs. L. Kemper Williams, who lived in the residence at the rear of the courtyard from the 1940s to the 60s.

The museum's 10 galleries display historical artifacts, ranging from maps and paintings to furnishings and decorative objects. The Empire Gallery displays tables, chests, and sofas, alongside portraits of such native New Orleanians as Madame Auguste de Gas, mother of artist Edgar Degas. The museum's other galleries include the Plantation Gallery, the Louisiana Purchase Gallery, the Victorian Gallery, and the Spanish Colonial Gallery.

Farther away are **Gallier House Museum**, an attractive 19th-century residence that combines Creole and American architectural elements, and the lovely **Lalaurie House**, associated with ghosts. Also on Royal Street is **Rumors**, a gift shop that sells Mardi Gras souvenirs all year long – masks, beads, krewe costumes, and posters are all available for sale here.

Historic New Orleans Collection

533 Royal St. *(504) 523-4662.* *10am–4:30pm Tue–Sat.*

Artifacts from the Historic New Orleans Collection on Royal Street

Steamboat *Natchez*, offering regular two-hour cruises

Steamboat Natchez ⑫

Map E3. Woldenberg Riverfront park wharf. *(504) 586-8777.* *Riverfront.* *45, 87.* *Harbor Jazz Cruises: 11:30am & 2:30pm daily; Dinner Jazz Cruise: 7pm daily.* www.steamboatnatchez.com

A REMINDER OF THE old days of river travel, the Steamboat *Natchez* is typical of the steamboats that traveled the length of the Mississippi, taking three to five days to get from Louisville, Kentucky *(see p271)*, to New Orleans. The boatmen, notorious brawlers in search of women and liquor at the end of a trip, established New Orleans' reputation as the "City of Sin." In their heyday, from 1830 to 1860, some 30 steamboats lined up at the levee. The era ended by the close of the 19th century as railroads and highways replaced them. Today, daily cruises offer visitors a glimpse into a forgotten lifestyle.

St. Anthony's Garden
This beautiful garden stands at the back of St. Louis Cathedral. Its serenity hides the fact that it was a staging ground for duels in the 18th century.

The LaBranche Buildings (#700)
Embellished with fine oak-leaf ironwork, these buildings were constructed in 1835 for sugar planter Jean Baptiste LaBranche.

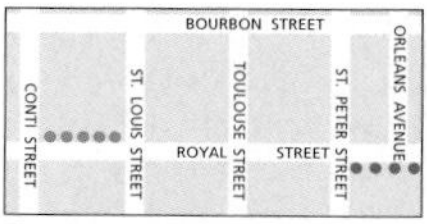

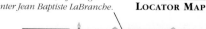

LOCATOR MAP

Custom House ⑬

Map D3. 423 Canal St. 🚋 *3, 41.*
⚫ *closed to the public.*

PERHAPS THE MOST important Federal-style structure in the South, this Quincy granite building took 33 years (from 1848 to 1881) to complete. Inside, the Marble Hall is a dramatic space under a ground-glass ceiling with a decorative stained-glass border and a skylight above. Juno and Mercury embellish the capitals of the 14 marble columns, each 41 ft (12.5 m) high, which support the structure. The floor is made of a combination of black and white marble. Over the years the building has served as the post office, an armory, and a Union prison.

Aquarium of the Americas ⑭

Map E3. Canal St at Mississippi River.
☎ *(504) 581-4629.* 🚋 *Riverfront.*
🚌 *3, 5, 55, 57.* ⚪ *9:30am–7pm Fri–Sat, 9:30am–6pm Sun (9:30am–7pm daily in summer).* ⚫ *Dec 25 & Mardi Gras.* 🎥 📷 ⚡ 🚻 🏪

FOCUSING ON the waters around New Orleans, from the Mississippi and the swamps to the Gulf of Mexico and the Caribbean, this complex features some 560 species of marine life. Highlights include a tank containing a Caribbean reef, and a replica of an oil rig. Other tanks contain species that illustrate everything there is to know about life beneath

Under the sea at the Aquarium of the Americas

Entrance to the Riverwalk Marketplace

the ocean, including how fish communicate and how they camouflage themselves. The complex also includes The Entergy IMAX® Theater. Daily riverboat cruises can also be taken from here.

Ferry to Algiers & Mardi Gras World ⑮

Map E4. Take the ferry at the end of Canal St. In Algiers take the shuttle.
🚋 *Riverfront.* 🚌 *55, 57.* ⚪ *9am–5pm daily.* 🎥 🏪 ✏ **Blaine Kern's Mardi Gras World** 233 Newton St, Algiers. ☎ *(504) 361-7821.*
⚪ *9:30am–5pm daily.*
W *www.mardigrasworld.com*

A FERRY TAKES visitors across the Mississippi to Algiers and the fascinating Blaine Kern's Mardi Gras World. Blaine Kern is often called "Mr. Mardi Gras" because many of the massive floats are constructed here in his warehouse.

The tour begins with coffee and the traditional King Cake. A short film shows the floats and the stages of their production, from the original drawings and molds to the end result. Visitors can try on some of the flamboyant costumes worn by Krewe members in past parades. Visitors can also wander through the warehouses and view huge decorative figures made of fiberglass or Styrofoam overlaid with papier-mâché. The cost of making the floats is usually borne by each Krewe and can range from anywhere between $300 and $3,000.

Riverwalk Marketplace ⑯

Map E4. 1 Poydras St. ☎ *(504) 522-1555.* 🚋 *Riverfront.* 🚌 *3, 55, 57, 65.* 🍴 🏪 ⚡
W *www.riverwalkmarketplace.com*

THIS MASSIVE riverside shopping mall, designed by the same company that developed Boston's Faneuil Hall *(see p136)*, contains more than 140 stores, most of which are brand-name favorites such as Eddie Bauer, Banana Republic, and the Museum Company. The top floor is devoted to a food court, while a highlight of the ground floor is the Creole Delicacies Gourmet Shop, which offers a two-hour course in cooking. In addition to plentiful shopping opportunities, the mall has an outdoor walkway that runs along the Mississippi River, giving visitors one of the best views of the river and river traffic in the city. International and other cruise ships dock alongside the marketplace, the most notable being those operated by the Delta Queen Steamboat Company, which was established in 1890. Several information plaques attached to railings along the walkway describe everything from the types of boats plying the river to the seagulls that drift up from the Gulf of Mexico.

The **Spanish Plaza**, near the entrance, has a fountain in the center. Surrounding it is a circular mosaic bench, depicting the coats of arms of the city's Spanish immigrants.

St. Charles Avenue Streetcar, a New Orleans landmark

Garden District ⑰

Between Jackson & Louisiana Aves, & St. Charles Ave & Magazine St. 🚋 *St. Charles.* 🚌 *11, 14, 27.*

WHEN THE Americans arrived in New Orleans after the Louisiana Purchase in 1803, they settled upriver from the French Quarter. This area is referred to as the Garden District because of the lush gardens planted with magnolia, camellia, azalea, and jasmine. A residential neighborhood, it is filled with large mansions built by wealthy city planters and merchants. Some of the grand residences here are the Robinson House and Colonel Short's Villa, which has a handsome cast-iron cornstalk fence.

A romantic New Orleans experience is to take a ride on the slow-moving **St. Charles Avenue Streetcar.** The last of the sort that featured in Tennessee Williams' *A Streetcar Named Desire,* it travels 6.5 miles (10.5 km) from Canal Street to Carrollton Avenue. Along the way it passes many famous landmarks. The most

prominent are Lee Circle with its memorial to Confederate general Robert E. Lee, the Gothic Revival Christ Church, Touro Synagogue, the Latter Public Library, and Loyola and Tulane Universities.

Just off St. Charles Avenue is one of the loveliest urban parks in the country. The 340-acre (137-ha) Audubon Park was originally the sugar plantation of Jean Etienne Boré, who developed the commercially successful sugar granulation process. It was also the location of the 1884 World Exposition. The **Audubon Zoo** occupies 58 acres (23 ha) of the park's grounds. Beautifully landscaped, the zoo opened in 1938 but was completely redesigned in the 1980s. Today, the animals live in open paddocks that replicate their natural habitats. The Louisana Swamp, where white alligators bask along the banks or float in the muddy lagoon, is one of the most engaging exhibits. Don't miss the flamingo gardens or the lush Jaguar Jungle.

Evocative statue in the City Park's New Orleans Botanical Gardens

City Park ⑱

🚌 45, 46, 48, 87, 90. **New Orleans Museum of Art** 📞 *(504) 488-2631.* 🕐 *10am–5pm Tue–Sun.* ● *public hols.* 🖼️ 🚻 🅦 *www.noma.org*

THE FIFTH LARGEST urban park in the US, the 1,500-acre (607-ha) City Park is a New Orleans institution, where visitors can relax and enjoy the semitropical Louisiana weather. The **New Orleans Botanical Gardens** and the prestigious **New Orleans Museum of Art** share this space with moss-draped live oaks, lagoons for boating and fishing, and the championship Bayou Oaks Golf Course.

Housed in an impressive Beaux Arts building, the museum has an astonishingly varied collection. Originally the Delgado Museum of Art, it was founded in 1910 when Isaac Delgado, a millionaire bachelor, donated the original $150,000 to construct an art museum in City Park. In 1971 it was renamed the New Orleans Museum of Art in deference to some of its later benefactors. Prize exhibits include a Faberge egg (1896) and Picasso's *Woman in an Armchair* (1960). The New Orleans Botanical Garden was created in the 1930s. Then, it was primarily a rose garden, but today there are also spring and perennial gardens, featuring camellias, azaleas, and magnolias, as well as tropical plants and trees. Several statues by Mexican artist Enrique Alferez stand among the live oaks and other flora.

Colorful costume for the Mardi Gras parade

MARDI GRAS

Culminating on the day before Ash Wednesday – Mardi Gras – the Carnival festivities in New Orleans are celebrated with lavish masked balls, presented by groups of citizens known as "Krewes." Although most balls are private, many Krewes also put on parades, with ornate costumes and colorful floats. Many Carnival traditions began with the Krewe of Rex. The symbolic purple, green, and gold colors used for masks, banners, and other decorations are derived from the original costume worn by Rex, the King of Mardi Gras, in the 1872 parade. The tradition of throwing souvenir doubloons (coins), beads, and dolls from the floats to the crowds began in 1881.

Louisiana

Old Plantation water pump

Renowned for its exotic landscape of bayous and swamps, antebellum plantation homes, jazz, and fine food, Louisiana is a state richly steeped in history and tradition. Its predominant French heritage is the legacy of the French settlers who named the colony for Louis XIV. Both France and Spain colonized Louisiana before the United States finally acquired the territory through the Louisiana Purchase of 1803. Louisiana became a state in 1812 and in the following decades played a strategic role in the Civil War and the painful struggle for Civil Rights. Today, the state preserves both its Colonial history as well as its distinct Creole and Cajun heritage. Highlights include the beautiful plantations along the Mississippi and the cultural delights of Cajun Country.

Plantation Alley ❷

Hwy 18 from New Orleans, which joins Hwy 1. ℹ️ New Orleans Convention & Visitors' Bureau, (800) 672-6124; the bureau maintains a list of tour operators.

Before the Civil War, the Mississippi River was lined with plantations producing first indigo, then cotton, rice, and sugar. At the time, this was one of the nation's wealthiest regions and home to two-thirds of America's millionaires. Of the 350 opulent estates that once flourished here, around 40 remain. Of these about a dozen are open to the public on a stretch of the Great River Road *(see pp40–41)* between New Orleans and Baton Rouge, known as "Plantation Alley."

Today, large neighboring petrochemical plants have replaced sugar cane and cotton as the mainstay of the riverside economy. High levees, reinforced by the Army Corps of Engineers after the flood of 1927, block the river from the road. The tradition since the 1880s has been to light bonfires atop them each Christmas Eve, to illuminate the way for Santa Claus.

Oak Alley Plantation in Vacherie, is 40 miles (64 km) west from New Orleans airport. An arcade of 28 arching live oaks, planted some 300 years ago, leads to this striking 1839 house. The picture of the Greek Revival mansion down the long arcade seems the archetypal Hollywood image. Both the recently refurbished house and garden have been used as a location for several movies, including *Interview with the Vampire* (1994). The mansion offers five B&B cottages for overnight stay. To its east, **Laura Plantation** has an 1805 Creole house constructed of cypress,

designed by Senegalese builders. The plantation slaves are thought to be the source of various Senegalese folk tales, including the famous *Br'er Rabbit* stories translated into English by Joel Chandler Harris.

A 15-minute drive from New Orleans, **Destrehan Plantation**, built in 1787, is the oldest documented plantation home in the Lower Mississippi Valley. The French Colonial-style home features demonstrations of indigo dyeing and other crafts like bousillage construction, a method using a mixture of clay and Spanish moss. San Francisco Plantation, near Garyville, is a 40-minute drive away from New Orleans. Built in 1856, under centuries-old spreading live oak trees, this galleried home in the Creole open-suite style is listed as a National Historic Landmark. Viewed from some vantage points, the design of the home resembles that of a riverboat.

Closest to Baton Rouge and the area's largest plantation home, the palatial 1860 **Nottoway Mansion** occupies an area of 53,000 sq ft (4,924 sq m), and comprises 65 rooms, 165 doors, and 200 windows. Completed in 1859, its largest room happens to be the Grand White Ballroom, where the owner, John Hampden Randolph, celebrated his daughters' weddings.

In addition to guided house tours, several plantations now operate restaurants and comfortable B&B inns. The region is best explored by car, although there are many bus tours available.

🏠 **Oak Alley Plantation**
3645 Hwy 18 Vacherie. **(** *(225) 265-2151.* ◯ *9am–5pm daily.* ⬤ *Jan 1, Thanksgiving, Dec 25.* 🎫 ♿

🏠 **Laura Plantation**
2247 Hwy 18. **(** *(225) 265-7690.* ◯ *9am–5pm daily.* ⬤ *Jan 1, Mardi Gras, Easter, Thanksg., Dec 25.* 🎫 ♿

🏠 **Destrehan Plantation**
13034 River Road, Destrehan. **(** *(985) 764-9315.* ◯ *9am–4pm daily.* ⬤ *public hols.* 🎫

🏠 **Nottoway Mansion**
White Castle. **(** *(225) 545-2730.* ◯ *9am–5pm daily.* ⬤ *Dec 25.* 🎫 ♿

The Grand White Ballroom, Nottoway Mansion, in Plantation Alley

Louisiana Old State Capitol, Baton Rouge

Baton Rouge ❸

🏠 470,000. ✈ 🚌 1253 Florida Blvd, (225) 383-3811. 🚉 730 North Blvd, (800) 517-0843. 🎪 Greater Baton Rouge State Fair (mid-Oct). 🌐 www.visitbatonrouge.com

ESTABLISHED BY THE French in 1699 to control access to the Mississippi, Baton Rouge ("Red Stick") was named for the spikes hung with bloody fish heads that marked the boundary between two Native American territories. The capital of Louisiana since 1849, this city is a favored tourist destination.

North of downtown, the **State Capitol** was built in 1932 under the tireless direction of ex-governor and US Senator Huey Long

(1893–1935), who persuaded legislators to approve the $5 million construction budget. Ironically, Long was assassinated in the building in 1935. This 34-story structure, the country's tallest capitol, offers superb city views from its 27th-floor observation deck. To the south, the autocratic senator's penchant for lavish buildings is further reflected in the **Old Governor's Mansion**, built in 1930 and modeled on the White House. Today, this restored Greek Revival structure displays such memorabilia of past governors as Jimmie Davis's guitar and Huey Long's pajamas. The ornate 1849 Gothic Revival **Louisiana Old State Capitol**, to the southwest, holds interactive exhibits on the state's tumultuous political history. Outside, an observation plaza overlooks the river, where the massive World War II-era destroyer, USS *Kidd*, offers

public tours. Farther south, visitors can get a feel of the antebellum era firsthand at the 1791 **Magnolia Mound Plantation**, a 16-acre (6-ha) French-Creole style home and working plantation.

A short, 10-minute drive southwest from downtown leads to the attractive, tree-shaded **Louisiana State University** campus and the **LSU Rural Life Museum**, maintained by the university. Unlike the grand plantation restorations, this museum, with its simple artifacts, reveals how the common owner-operated farming families lived in the 19th century. On view are a grist mill, cockfighting spurs, and pirogues (shallow canoes used to ply the bayous).

Statue in the new State Capitol

🏛 **Louisiana Old State Capitol**
100 N Blvd. 📞 (225) 342-0500. 🕐 10am–4pm Tue–Sat, noon–4pm Sun. ⬤ Mon, public hols. ♿

🏛 **LSU Rural Life Museum**
I-10 exit 160, at 4650 Essen Ln. 📞 (225) 765-2437. 🕐 8:30am–5pm daily. ⬤ Jan 1, Easter, Thanksgiving, Dec 24–25. 🎟 ♿
🌐 www.rurallife.lsu.edu

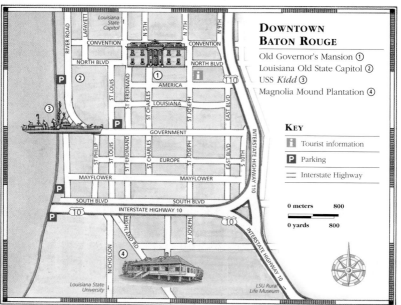

DOWNTOWN BATON ROUGE

Old Governor's Mansion ①
Louisiana Old State Capitol ②
USS *Kidd* ③
Magnolia Mound Plantation ④

KEY

🛈 Tourist information

🅿 Parking

🟰 Interstate Highway

| 0 meters | 800 |
| 0 yards | 800 |

Cathedral of St. John the Baptist, Lafayette

Lafayette ❹

👥 *94,500.* 🚌 🚆 ℹ *1400 Evangeline Thruway, (337) 232-3808.* [W] www.cityoflafayette.com

THE UNOFFICIAL "Capital of French Louisiana" is an entertaining introduction to the world of bayous, alligators, superb cuisine, and lilting Cajun accents. When the first Acadians arrived here in 1764, they settled along the bayous and prairies west of New Orleans, working as farmers to make a living from the swamps and marshes.

Lafayette evolved from a small settlement, set up in the 1821 around a church, now the towering **Cathedral of St. John the Baptist**, near the Vermilion River. Today, the town is the heart of Cajun Country, distinguished by its unique cultural heritage.

Lafayette's living history museum, **Vermilionville** (the original name of the town), evokes 19th-century Acadiana with its characteristic French-influenced architecture. The buildings here are constructed of bousillage *(see p354)*, and have high-pitched roofs. Both Vermilionville and nearby **Jean Lafitte National Historic Park Acadian Cultural Center** feature exhibits as well as demonstrations on the skills needed to survive in 18th- and 19th-century Louisiana. These include the netmaking that was vital for a life dependent on harvesting food from the bayou, and woodcraft that built plows and the shallow-draft wooden pirogue. The National Park Service, which operates the Jean Lafitte National Historic Park, also maintains other Acadian cultural centers in the wetlands region in Thibodaux (100 miles/160 km to the southeast), and in the prairie region in Eunice that lies about 30 miles (48 km) to the northwest.

🏛 Vermilionville
300 Fisher Rd. ☎ *(337) 233-4077.*
🕐 *10am–4pm Tue–Sun.*
● *Mon, Jan 1, Martin Luther King Jr. Day, Thanksgiving, Dec 24–25, & Dec 31.* 📷 ♿

🏛 Jean Lafitte National Historic Park Acadian Cultural Center
501 Fisher Rd. ☎ *(337) 232-0789.*
🕐 *8am–5pm daily.* ● *Dec 25.* ♿

Bayou Teche ❺

Hwy 31 runs from Breaux Bridge to New Iberia. ℹ *2704 Hwy 14, (337) 365-1540.*

BAYOU TECHE (pronounced "Tesh") meanders north-to-south alongside a scenic route between Lafayette and the Atchafalaya Swamp. Stretching between Breaux Bridge and New Iberia, the 25-mile (40-km) length of Hwy 31, with its lush vegetation and beautiful moss-draped oaks, offers a true flavor of the region.

In downtown **Breaux Bridge**, a tiny drawbridge over Bayou Teche proclaims the town "the Crawfish Capital of the World." The town also hosts the annual Crawfish Festival in May. At **Lake Martin**, the Nature Conservancy's Cypress Island Preserve offers an opportunity to see swamp wildlife from a hiking trail and boat tours. The preserve has the world's largest white ibis rookery.

Farther south, in **St. Martinville**, the famous Evangeline Oak marks the spot where Evangeline and her lover Gabriel were supposed to be reunited. Both their tragic tale and the Acadian saga are narrated in *Evangeline*, Henry Wadsworth Longfellow's 1847 poem. Nearby, St. Martin de Tours Church dates back to the town's founding in 1765. An adjacent museum displays carnival costumes.

Just outside town, the evocative **Longfellow-Evangeline State Historic Site** offers tours of an 18th-century sugar plantation house. Bayou Teche flows through the town of **New Iberia**, famous for its grand plantation home – the 1834 Shadows-on-the-Teche, which is now a museum.

A detour to Avery Island leads to the **McIlhenny Tabasco Company**, a popular stop for gourmands (a guide presents information

Shadows-on-the-Teche plantation house in New Iberia, Bayou Teche

The Fort St. Jean Baptiste reconstruction in Natchitoches

about the company's history and manufacturing, although visitors can no longer tour the factory). The adjacent **Jungle Gardens** is a natural swamp.

Longfellow-Evangeline State Commemorative Area
1200 N Main St, St. Martinville. (318) 394-3754. ☐ 9am–5pm daily. ● Jan 1, Thanksgiving, Dec 25. ☒ W www.ohwy.com/la/l/lonevasa.htm

McIlhenny Tabasco Company
Avery Island. (337) 365-8173. ☐ 9am–4pm daily. ● public hols. ☒

Natchitoches ❻

🏛 17,000. ✈ ⓘ 781 Front St, (318) 352-8072, (800) 259-1714.

The OLDEST permanent settlement in Louisiana, Natchitoches ("Nack-a-tish") was founded on the banks of the Cane River by the French in 1714. The town's compact 33-block riverfront district retains much of its 18th-century Creole architecture, with elaborate ironwork and spiral staircases. South of downtown, **Fort St. Jean Baptiste** re-creates the 1732 frontier outpost designed to deter Spanish expansion eastward from Texas.

The surrounding Cane River Country features several plantation house tours. Of these, **Melrose Plantation** was visited by such writers as John Steinbeck and William Faulkner. The **Bayou Folk Museum** takes visitors into the house of the famed author Kate Chopin, whose daring 19th-century novel, *The Awakenings*, although initially banned, was later widely acclaimed.

Melrose Plantation
LA 119. (318) 379-0055. ☐ noon–4pm daily. ● public hols. ☒

Bayou Folk Museum
LA 1, Cloutierville. (318) 379-2233. ☐ 10am–5pm Mon–Sat, 1–5pm Sun. ● public hols. ☒ ☒

Shreveport ❼

🏛 198,500. ✈ ⓘ 629 Spring St, (318) 222-9391.

Situated near the Texas border, Shreveport was founded on the Red River in 1839. Agriculture and river transport trade were mainstays of the local economy until the turn of the 20th century, when the discovery of oil made the city a boom town. Shreveport declined after the oil industry moved offshore. Today, however, the town is rapidly changing and has a friendly atmosphere with a number of cultural activities. The **Louisiana State Museum** illustrates the state's history through murals and exhibits, while the annual Louisiana State Fair, held here in late October or early November, attracts more than 300,000 visitors.

ENVIRONS: About 165 miles (265 km) from Shreveport in the far northeastern corner of Louisiana state is one of the most significant archaeological sites located in the eastern part of the country. **Poverty Point National Monument** *(see p339)* in Epps retains the burial and temple mounds built by the Mississippian civilization that flourished in the Lower Mississippi basin from around 1000 BC to AD 1000. Visitors can reach this national monument through Hwy 577.

Poverty Point National Monument
Hwy 577. (888) 926-5492. ☐ 9am–5pm daily. ● Dec 25. ☒

Exterior of Louisiana State Museum in Shreveport

THE ACADIANS – CAJUN COUNTRY

The Acadians, or "Cajuns," were originally French immigrants who had founded a colony in Nova Scotia, Canada, in 1604, naming it l'Acadie after the legendary Greek paradise, Arcadia. Exiled by the British in 1755, they finally settled along the isolated bayous of Louisiana, where they developed a rich French-influenced culture, deeply rooted in its music and cuisine. Acadian culture is best seen in the region's many festivals. Of these the Courir de Mardi Gras, literally "the race," is a distinctly Cajun version of the Mardi Gras *(see p353).* Colorfully dressed and masked horseback riders ride from house to house, ostensibly collecting ingredients for a community gumbo. They then triumphantly parade through the town, before gathering together for food, drink, music, and frivolity. "Acadiana" is a 22-parish region comprising the wetlands area near New Orleans, the prairies north of Lafayette, **Acadian dress** and the remote southwestern coast.

Arkansas

APTLY KNOWN AS THE "Natural State," Arkansas abounds in mountains, valleys, dense woodlands, and fertile plains. Its two mountain ranges, the Ozark and the Ouachita, are separated by the Arkansas River, which flows through the state capital, Little Rock. The birthplace of former president Bill Clinton, the state actively promotes sights associated with him, including his birthplace, Hope, his boyhood home in Hot Springs, and Little Rock, where he served as governor and waged his campaign for presidency. This former frontier state remains largely wild even today, with vast areas of natural beauty, famous for adventure sports.

Display in the Central High Museum, Little Rock

Little Rock ❽

🏛 183,133. ✈ 🚌 🚐 🛈 615 E Capitol Ave, (501) 370-3290.

FOUNDED ON the Arkansas River, near a boulder for which it is named, Little Rock was another modest-sized Southern state capital until native son Bill Clinton was elected 42nd US president in 1993. As a result, executive attention has helped revitalize the city. A new center for much activity is Little Rock River Market District, lined with lively clubs, restaurants, cafés, and shops. Adjacent to the district is the site for the new William J. Clinton Presidential Center, slated to open in November 2004. The **Old State House State History Museum**, just west of Main Street, is where Clinton announced his candidacy in 1992 and 1996. The 1833 Doric structure features state history exhibits.

In 1957, the contentious desegregation of Little Rock Central High School catapulted the city to the forefront of the national struggle for Civil Rights. Despite the Supreme Court ban, the governor refused to integrate the school, forcing President Eisenhower to send in the 101st Airborne Division to protect the "Little Rock Nine" (the first nine black students) as they entered the school amid the protests of local segregationists. Today, Central High School is a national historic site and the only operating school to be thus designated. **Central High Museum and Visitor Center** documents this story.

🏛 **Central High Museum & Visitor Center**
2125 W, 14th St. 🎧 *(501) 374-1957.* 🕐 *10am–4pm Mon–Sat, 1–4pm Sun.* ⬤ *Jan 1, Thanksgiving, Dec 25.* ♿
🏛 **Old State House State History Museum**
300 W Markham St. 🎧 *(501) 324-9685.* 🕐 *9am–5pm Mon–Sat, 1–5pm Sun.* ⬤ *Jan 1, Thanksg., Dec 25.* ♿

Hot Springs ❾

🏃 *35,750.* 🚌 🛈 *Bathhouse Row, (501) 321-2277.*

IN ITS HEYDAY in the early 20th century, this was a popular resort for people seeking restorative cures from the thermal springs flowing from the southwestern slope of Hot Springs Mountain. The area became the first US federal reserve park in 1832 and a national park in 1921. The original "Bathhouse Row" is now a National Historic

Exterior of the Spanish-style Fordyce Bathhouse, the visitor center for Hot Springs National Park

Landmark District within **Hot Springs National Park**. The visitor center is housed in the opulent Spanish Renaissance-style 1915 Fordyce Bathhouse. Only the **Buckstaff Bathhouse** today remains in operation, offering spa facilities. Hotels, such as the Arlington Resort Hotel *(see p370)*, also offer full bathing facilities.

At the Row's south end, the city visitor center distributes maps to sights associated with President Clinton, who spent his childhood in the city. Hot Springs High School, where Clinton graduated in 1964, is now an apartment building with a "cultural campus" that has exhibits from Clinton's teenage years. Visitors can also tour sights such as Clinton's church and his favorite hamburger joint.

A scenic drive to the summit of Hot Springs Mountain leads to an observation tower offering panoramic views of the Ouachita Mountains, the city, and the forests and lakes that surround it.

⚜ Hot Springs National Park

Reserve and Central Aves. 🅲 ⁻501) 624-2701. ◯ 9am–5pm daily. ● Jan 1, Thanksgiving, Dec 25. ⚐

⚜ Buckstaff Bathhouse

509 Central Ave, Bathhouse Row. 🅲 (501) 623-3208. ◯ 7am–noon Mon–Sat, 1:30–3pm Mon–Fri. ● Jan 1, Jul 4, Thanksg., Dec 25. ⚐ ⚐

Mountain View ⑩

🏠 2,876. 🛈 (870) 269-3851.

N ESTLING DEEP in the hills and valleys of the remote Ozark Mountains, the secluded hamlet of Mountain View is a haven for outdoor enthusiasts. A short drive to the north is the **Ozark Folk Center State Park**. The park celebrates the Ozark Mountain region's cultural heritage with living history exhibits, crafts demonstrations, festivals, and traditional music performances held at the state park theater. It also offers hiking trails, a lodge open year round, a lively restaurant, and swimming pool. The nearby Wild and Scenic" **Buffalo**

Steeply inclined streets of the Victorian commercial area, Eureka Springs

National River is highly popular for float fishing and canoeing; many local outfitters organize guided canoe trips of the river. The National Forest Service maintains several campgrounds in the area.

⚜ Ozark Folk Center State Park

Spur 382. 🅲 (870) 269-3851. ◯ check for times. ⚐ ⚐ Ⓦ www.ozarkfolkcenter.com

ENVIRONS: About 15 miles (24 km) northwest of Mountain View, via Hwy 14, lie **Blanchard Springs Caverns**, which feature an extensive collection of limestone cave formations and an underground stream open for public tours. The ever-changing crystalline formations in these "living" caves are the result of minerals deposited by dripping water. Exploring the magnificent caves can be difficult because of the damp air and cramped conditions. However, both the two main routes, the half-mile (1-km) Dripstone Trail as well as the 1.2-mile (2-km) Discovery Trail, offer an unforgettable experience of life underground. A visitor center features exhibits and videos that describe the caves and their long process of creation.

⚜ Blanchard Springs Caverns

Hwy 14. 🅲 (870) 757-2211. ◯ mid-Apr–Oct: 9am–5pm daily; Oct–Apr: 9:30am–4pm Wed–Sun. ● Jan 1, Jul 4, Thanksg., Dec 25. ⚐

Eureka Springs ⑪

🏠 2,278. 🛈 35 N Main St, (479) 253-7333, (888) 387-3520.

T HE WORLD'S second-largest statue of Jesus, the seven-story-high "**Christ of the Ozarks**," towers above the former resort town of Eureka Springs. After nearly a century of decline, the town has benefited by its development as a sort of Christian theme park and romantic getaway, and by the establishment of country music performances in the style of Nashville's Grand Ole Opry *(see p264)* held at the Hoe-Down and Pine Mountain Jamboree.

For almost 30 years running, the Great Passion Play has been performed at the city's **Sacred Arts Center**. This outdoor drama depicts the days leading up to the death of Jesus Christ.

Christ of the Ozarks, Eureka Springs

The religious tone of the town is perpetuated in the **Bible Museum** with its collection of more than 6,000 Bible editions in 625 languages. Eureka Springs Historic Gardens and a scenic railroad are the town's other attractions. Many visitors also tour the well-preserved Victorian buildings and savor the magic of the town's forested mountain setting.

⚜ Sacred Arts Center

Passion Play Rd. 🅲 (800) 882-7529. ◯ Oct–Apr. Attraction & performance times vary. ● Mon. ⚐ ⚐

Mississippi

THE BIRTHPLACE OF Tennessee Williams, Elvis Presley, B.B. King, and Oprah Winfrey, Mississippi is a complex state best known for blues music, antebellum plantation homes, and a lamentable Civil Rights history. The endless horizon of cotton fields, most often associated with Mississippi, can be found in the northwest Delta region, while in the northeastern corner is the hardscrabble hill area around Tupelo. The state capital, Jackson, sits in the central plain and is the urban center of this largely rural state. Today, Mississippi offers such contrasting diversions as glittering Las Vegas-style casinos, excellent Vietnamese seafood restaurants, and ferry rides to deserted beaches.

Mississippi Delta **⑫**

🏛 20,000 (Clarksdale). 🚌 🚉 Greenwood. **ℹ** 1540 DeSoto Ave, Hwy 49, Clarksdale, (662) 627-7337.

THE MISSISSIPPI DELTA, a vast, alluvial basin, cleared of its once-thick forests, and blanketed with cotton fields, is the birthplace of blues music. The **Delta Blues Museum** in downtown Clarksdale is the touchstone for music lovers from around the world. Located in a renovated 1916 freight depot, this museum is a virtual repository of blues music, with personal belongings, photographs, instruments, and videos of such resident legends as Robert Johnson, Howlin' Wolf, and Muddy Waters. Exhibits include the wooden "Muddywood" guitar created by Z.Z. Top with planks from the original House of Blues, the birthplace of Muddy Waters. The Sunflower River Blues and Gospel Festival is held outside the museum each August. The Delta's creative legacy extends beyond music. The annual Tennessee Williams festival celebrates the work of the famous playwright who spent his childhood in Clarksdale.

About 55 miles (88 km) south of Clarksdale, the **Cottonlandia Museum** in Greenwood documents the history of the Delta with a special emphasis on cotton, the industry that fueled the culture and economy of the region. A 24-mile (38-km) drive south brings visitors to Greenville, the largest town in the Delta. The visitor center of this major riverport occupies a riverboat docked at the foot of the bridge. The Mississippi Delta Blues Festival is held in town every September. Other sights include the tiny museum in Leland honoring Jim Henson, the creator of the Muppets; Belzoni, said to be the "Catfish capital of the World," located in the county that has the most farm-raised catfish; and Indianola, the hometown of B.B. King.

Catfish farm sign

🏛 **Delta Blues Museum**
1 Blues Alley, Clarksdale. **☎** (800) 626- 3764. ⬤ Mar–Oct: 9am–5pm Mon–Sat; Nov–Feb: 10am–5pm Mon–Sat. ⬤ Sun, Jan 1, Thanksgiving, Dec 25. 🎟 🚻 **w** www.deltabluesmuseum. org

🏛 **Cottonlandia Museum**
Hwy 82 W, Greenwood. **☎** (662) 453-0925. ⬤ 9am–5pm Mon–Fri. ⬤ Sun, Jan 1, Thanksgiving, Dec. 25. 🎟 🚻

Ventress Hall, University of Mississippi campus, Oxford

Oxford **⑬**

🏛 10,000. 🚉 **ℹ** (662) 234-4680. **w** www.touroxfordms.com

HOME TO THE stately 1848 University of Mississippi, fondly known as "Ole Miss," the appealing college town of Oxford is the state's intellectual and cultural center. The local literary landmark is the secluded 1840 **Rowan Oak**, home of William Faulkner, one of the most influential writers of the time and pioneer of the Southern Gothic literature movement. The plot outline of A Fable, the book the Nobel Prize-winning author was working on at his death, can be seen inscribed on the walls. A Faulkner statue stands in downtown's classic courthouse square, surrounded by sophisticated galleries, restaurants, cafés, and live music venues.

The University of Mississippi campus houses the **University Museums**. In addition to classical Greek and Roman antiquities, the

One of the many riverboat casinos in the Mississippi Delta

adjacent museums hold a small but dynamic collection of Southern folk art.

⚏ Rowan Oak
Old Taylor Rd. ◖ *(662) 234-3284.* ◯ *10am–noon & 2–4pm Tue–Sat, 2–4pm Sun.* ◯ *university hols.* ♿

⚏ University Museums
University Ave at Fifth St. ◖ *(662) 915-7073.* ◯ *10am–4:30pm Tue–Sat, 1–4 pm Sun.* ◯ *public hols & a few university hols.* ♿

Tupelo ⓮

⚏ *31,000.* ▮ *322 University Dr, (662) 841-6521.* ⓦ *www.tupelo.net*

AN HOUR'S DRIVE west from Oxford, Tupelo is the birthplace of Elvis Presley, one of the world's most enduring cultural icons. Here, in a modest, two-room shotgun shack on the eastern fringe of town, the King of Rock 'n' roll was born in 1935, along with his stillborn twin Jesse. Elvis lived in Tupelo until age 13, when the family was forced by financial constraints to move to Memphis *(see p266).* Today the **Elvis Presley Birthplace**, refurbished to look as it did in 1935, is a pilgrimage site for Elvis fans the world over. An adjacent museum holds a unique private collection of Elvis memorabilia. A chapel, which overlooks the birthplace, features Elvis' own bible.

The new Tupelo Automobile Museum, the first of its kind in the state, displays more than 100 restored cars and includes a replica of a vintage garage.

Tupelo offers all the basic necessities for lodging and dining, and serves as a pit stop for the famous Natchez Trace Parkway *(see p362).*

⚏ Elvis Presley Birthplace
306 Elvis Presley Dr. ◖ *(662) 841-1245.* ◯ *9am–5pm Mon–Sat, 1–5pm Sun.* ◯ *Thanksgiving, Dec 25.* ▨ ♿ ⓦ *www.ci.tupelo.ms.us/ attractions.html*

Vicksburg National Military Park ⓯

3201 Clay St. ▮ *(662) 636-0583.* ◯ *8am–5pm daily.* ◯ *Dec 25.* ▨ ♿ ⓦ *www.nps.gov/vick/index*

THE VICKSBURG National Military Park, established in 1899, commemorates one of the most tragic sieges in Civil War history *(see p47).* Its strategic location, high on the bluffs overlooking the Mississippi River, made Vicksburg the target of Union forces, which wanted to gain control of the vital river corridor and cut the Confederacy in half. On March 29, 1863, the Union Army surrounded the city. After a 47-day siege, the Confederates surrendered on July 4, 1863, giving the North undisputed control of the river and sounding the death knell of the Confederacy. The impact of defeat was so severe that Vicksburg's citizens refused to recognize the Fourth of July holiday until the mid-20th century.

The campaign's story is retold in statuary headstones, earthworks, and artifacts at the park. Guided tours bring the landscape to life, where re-enactments of the Civil War are held in May and July.

Grave markers in Vicksburg National Military Park

Statue of young Elvis at Tupelo, his birthplace

BLUES MUSIC

The sound at the root of all contemporary popular music heard around the world springs from the large, flat, alluvial basin called the Mississippi Delta. Here African rhythms, work chants, and spirituals evolved into a distinctive style of music known as the blues. When Alabama musician W.C. Handy came through the Delta in 1903, he declared it "the weirdest music I ever heard," and carried the sound up to Memphis, where he recorded the Memphis Blues. Along with the Great Migration of African Americans from the rural South to the industrial North in the early 1900s, the blues reached Chicago, where such famous artists as Muddy Waters electrifed the sound. Rock 'n' roll is said to be born from this sound.

Muddy Waters figure in Delta Blues Museum

Old gas station at the Mississippi Agriculture and Forestry Museum

Jackson ⓰

🏙 202,000. ✈ 🚉 🚌 🛈 201 S President St, (601) 960-1891.

FOUNDED on a bluff above the Pearl River, Mississippi's capital city was named after popular national hero General Andrew Jackson *(see p265)*. During the Civil War, the city was torched on three separate occasions by Union General William Tecumseh Sherman, earning it the nickname "Chimneyville." The few buildings that survive are treasured landmarks today. Of these, the old 1883 Capitol, now the **State Historical Museum**, presents an overview of the state's Civil Rights history, juxtaposing stark black-and-white video footage of violent clashes between the police and protesters, with plainspoken commentary. Upstairs, the museum features revolving exhibits on such topics as author Eudora Welty, a Jackson resident, or "Pride of the Fleet" about the battleship USS *Mississippi*. A small, 20th-century room elaborates on the impact of the cotton and lumber industries on the state's economy, ecology, and society.

Yet, the city itself is the best historical exhibit. With its railroad trestles, smoky coffee shops, and franchise-free main street, downtown Jackson appears like a movie set from the 1950s. The **Mississippi State Capitol**, built in 1903, resembles the US Capitol in Washington, DC, and houses the legislative, judicial, and executive branches of the

state government. Jackson is also home to the **Mississippi Agriculture and Forestry Museum**, a very appealing family attraction that celebrates the state's rural heritage. Among its exhibits are an 1850s homestead, complete with livestock and gardens, and a 1930s small-town Main Street with a general store selling penny candy. The Chimneyville Crafts Gallery, a handicraft store on the grounds, displays and sells folk arts, including Choctaw crafts. The expansive site also has a lively cafeteria and produce stand. The adjacent Sports Hall of Fame honors the state's beloved athletes and college teams with enjoyable interactive exhibits.

Other sights in Jackson include the local zoo, botanical gardens, the Mississippi Museum of Natural Science, and the Mississippi Museum of Art, which displays the state's largest art collection. All these attractions, plus the city's growing reputation as a blues venue, make Jackson a pleasant stop for visitors coming through the Natchez Trace Parkway.

🏛 **State Historical Museum**
Old Capitol, 100 S State St. 📞 *(601) 359-6920.* ◯ *9am–5pm daily.* ● *public hols.*
🏛 **Mississippi Agriculture & Forestry Museum**
1150 Lakeland Dr. 📞 *(800) 844-8687.* ◯ *9am–5pm Mon–Sat.* ● *Sun.* 🅿 ♿

Natchez Trace Parkway ⓱

Visitor Center Mount Locust.
📞 *(662) 680-4027.* ◯ *8:30am–5pm daily.* W *www.nps.gov/natr*

ESTABLISHED AS a national historic parkway in 1934, this 450-mile (724-km) highway linking Natchez with Nashville, Tennessee *(see p264–5)*, was originally a buffalo trail. Later, it evolved into a footpath and played a vital role in the development of the country's midsection by linking the Ohio River Valley and the Gulf of Mexico. Pioneers used the route to transport their crops and produce downriver by barge to Natchez, where they sold both their goods and barges for scrap lumber, and then returned north on foot.

Today, the Natchez Trace Parkway *(see pp40–41)* is a scenic, year-round destination. No commercial traffic is permitted in this haven for hikers, motorists, and cyclists, and the speed limit is a leisurely 50 mph (80 km/h).

Natchez Parkway sign

The parkway preserves several historical sites, such as **Emerald Mound**. Situated near Natchez, it dates from AD 1400 and is the second largest Native American ceremonial mound in the country. A detour west, along Hwy 552, leads to the "**Ruins of**

Natchez Trace Parkway, a historic wooded trail

Windsor," where a ghostly set of 23 towering Corinthian columns serves as a poignant reminder of a mansion that burned down in 1890. The **Mount Locust** visitor center, located 15 miles (24 km) northeast of Natchez in a restored 1783 inn, distributes maps detailing various sights along the route.

Natchez ⑱

🚶 20,000. 🚐 🚢 🛈 640 S Canal St, (601) 442-5880.

BEST KNOWN for its fine antebellum architecture, Natchez is an attractive little town on the bluffs above Mississippi River. Many of its historic buildings lie within easy walking distance of the compact downtown district. Some of these gems include the oldest house in town, the 1798 **House on Ellicott's Hill**; the stately and palatial **Stanton Hall** (1857); the unfinished **Longwood** (1860), whose construction was interrupted by the Civil War; and **Rosalie**, an 1829 brick mansion atop the bluff that served as Union headquarters during the Civil War.

Many house museums are open all year, but many more can be seen during the **Natchez Pilgrimage** held in April, October, and December (see p28). A short drive east of downtown is **Melrose Plantation**, the country's most intact antebellum estate.

Maintained by the National Park Service, it displays African-American history in slave quarters alongside the 1845 Greek Revival mansion. At the south end of town, a mile (1.6 km) off Hwy 61, is the Grand Village of the Natchez Indians, with Indian mounds, replicas of huts, nature trails, and a museum.

🏛 **House on Ellicott's Hill**
Jefferson & Canal Sts. 🕻 (601) 442-2011. 🕐 9am–4:30pm daily. ⬤ Dec 25. 🏷 ♿
🎭 **Natchez Pilgrimage Tour**
🕻 (601) 446-6631, (800) 647-6742.

Gulf Coast ⑲

🚶 87,000 (Biloxi & Gulfport). 🚆 🚌 🛈 Hwy 90, Biloxi Town Green, (228) 896-6699. 🖥 www.gulfcoast.org

LINGERING French influences and a maritime heritage combine to make the scenic Gulf of Mexico coastline unlike the rest of Mississippi. In 1699, two Québcois brothers, Pierre le Moyne, Sieur d'Iberville, and Jean Baptiste le Moyne, Sieur de Bienville, reached what is now Ocean Springs, to set up France's first permanent settlement in the South. In 1704, the French government sponsored the transport of 20 young women as prospective brides for the male colonists. Armed with their trousseaux in state-issued suitcases or "cassettes," the "cassette girls" were housed on Ship Island.

Fishing schooners lining the waterfront on the Gulf Coast

After the Americans gained control of the coast, they built **Fort Massachusetts** in the mid-1800s on Ship Island. During the Civil War, the Union used the fort to house POWs, including a troop of African-American Confederates from Louisiana.

In August 1965, Hurricane Camille, one of the worst storms to hit mainland US, split Ship Island into two – West Ship and East Ship (although it is still referred to locally in the singular). Today, both are part of the **Gulf Islands National Seashore**. A ferry transports passengers to the beach and for tours of the historic fort. Boating is a popular recreation – visitors can take boat and kayak trips to deserted islands, or fishing charters on traditional shrimp boats.

The **Maritime and Seafood Industry Museum**, at Point Cadet in Biloxi, holds elaborate displays on the industry that dominated the local economy until gambling was legalized in the 1990s. Now, huge Vegas-style casinos line the coast.

🏝 **Gulf Islands National Seashore**
3500 Park Rd, Ocean Springs. 🕻 (228) 875-9057. 🖥 www.nps.gov/guis
🏛 **Maritime & Seafood Industry Museum**
115 1st St. 🛈 (228) 435-6320. 🕐 9am–4:30pm Mon–Sat, noon–4pm Sun. ⬤ Jan 1, Thanksg., Dec 25. 🏷 ♿ 🖥 www.maritimemuseum.org

Longwood, the octagonal, domed house, in Natchez

Alabama

Alabama slopes from the Cumberland Plateau in the northeast, across forested ridges and fertile plains to the Gulf of Mexico at Mobile Bay. The first European presence was established by the French along the coast in the early 1700s. During the next 100 years, settlement increased as overland immigrants from Tennessee and Georgia moved here, ousting the Choctaw, Cherokee, and Creek Indians from their ancestral lands. With progress, cotton fed the port of Mobile, and the steel industry drove Birmingham's economy. Today, the state is known for its diverse landscape, its antebellum architecture, and, most importantly, its Civil Rights history.

Reconstructed Fort Conde, Mobile

Mobile 20

🏛 201,200. ☒ 🚊 🚌 ⓘ
1 S Water St, (251) 208-2000.

This beautiful port city was founded as a French colony in 1702. Later it served as a strategic Confederate port until the final days of the Civil War. Today, the city retains both its French and Southern flavor and is best known for its **Mardi Gras Cottage Museum**, which includes memorabilia dating from the early 1800s.

At the head of Mobile Bay is **Fort Conde**, a partially reconstructed fort built by the French. Moored nearby is the World War II battleship, USS *Alabama*. A scenic loop drive around the bay leads to two other historic forts, Fort Morgan to the east, and Fort Gaines on Dauphin Island. Both are havens for birdlife.

🏛 Fort Conde
150 Royal St. 📞 (208) 208-7569.
🕐 8am–5pm daily. ● public hols,
Mardi Gras. ♿

Selma 21

🏛 20,700. 🚌 ⓘ 513 Lauderdale St,
(334) 875-7241.

Situated on a bluff high above the Alabama River, this city was the site of one the most notorious scenes in Civil Rights history. On March 7, 1965, a day that became known as "Bloody Sunday," 600 Civil Rights protesters heading toward Montgomery, the capital, violently clashed with the police at Edmund Pettus Bridge. A few weeks

Display inside the Voting Rights Museum in Selma

later, however, Dr. Martin Luther King Jr. led a successful march to the State Capitol steps. The **National Voting Rights Museum** encapsulates the story, and an annual re-enactment pays tribute to the event.

Before the Civil Rights era, Selma's place in history was assured as the "Arsenal of the Confederacy." It produced weapons, cannons, and ironclad ships. Much of the city was destroyed during the war, but the townscape along the river remained intact. The city's 1891 cherry-red train depot holds exhibits on all aspects of local history.

🏛 National Voting Rights Museum
1012 Water Ave. 📞 (334) 418-0800.
🕐 8:30am–5pm Mon–Fri, 10am–3pm Sat. ♿ 🌐 www.voterights.org

Montgomery 22

🏛 203,900. 🚌 ⓘ 300 Water St,
(334) 262-0013.

Alabama's capital city since 1846, Montgomery was also the Confederacy's first capital during the Civil War. In 1861, Jefferson Davis was sworn in as the Confederate president on the steps of the Greek Revival State Capitol. Across the street, the **First White House of the Confederacy** is now a museum related to those times.

The city also played a pivotal role during the Civil Rights Movement. The segregation of the city's transportation system led to an act of defiance by Rosa Parks, when she refused to surrender her bus seat to a white man. In 1956, the young Dr. Martin Luther King Jr. supported the year-long Montgomery Bus Boycott, which ultimately brought about the desegregation of the city's public transportation system. Its success was significant as it not only strengthened the movement, but also saw the rise of King as the campaign's leader. The city's landmark **Civil Rights Memorial**, designed by Vietnam Veterans Memorial artist Maya Lin

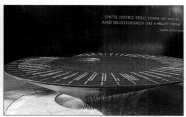

Montgomery's Civil Rights Memorial Fountain

(see p205), honors 40 martyrs who sacrificed their lives in the fight for racial equality.

Montgomery is also associated with two major figures of 20th-century arts. Local girl Zelda Fitzgerald and her husband, writer F. Scott Fitzgerald, lived here in 1931, while he was writing *Tender is the Night*. Their house is now a museum. In 1958, country singer Hank Williams played his final concert in the city three days before his death. Williams is buried in Oakwood Cemetery, and a statue of the singer stands downtown.

🏛 **First White House of the Confederacy**
644 Washington Ave. 📞 *(334) 242-1861.* ⏰ *8am–4:30pm Mon–Fri.* 🚫 *Sat–Sun, state hols.*

Tuskegee ㉓

🚶 *11,534.* 🚉 ℹ️ *121 Main St, (334) 727-6619.*

FORMER SLAVE Booker T. Washington founded the Tuskegee Normal and Industrial Institute here in 1881 to improve educational opportunities for African Americans. The school evolved into

Tuskegee University, best known for agriculturist George Washington Carver's innovations that revolutionized agricultural growth in the region. The "Tuskegee Airmen," the group of African American pilots who distinguished themselves in World War II, also graduated from the institute, now part of the Tuskegee Institute National Historic Site.

Birmingham ㉔

🚶 *245,600.* ✈ 🚉 🚌
ℹ️ *2200 9th Ave N, 319, (205) 458-8000.*

THE LARGEST city in Alabama, Birmingham was once the region's foremost producer of steel. Celebrating the city's industrial past is **Sloss Furnaces National Historic Landmark**, a museum housed in an old steel mill, and a 55-ft (17-m) high iron statue of Vulcan, the Roman god of fire, on the summit of Red Mountain, the source of the iron ore. Today, the city's attractions are typical of a modern Southern city – antebellum houses, botanical gardens, and the acclaimed **Birmingham Museum of Art**, with its fine collection of Wedgwood. Yet, the most moving landmarks are those that relate to the city's African-American history. These can be seen within walking

Dr. Martin Luther King Jr.

distance of the central downtown district's visitor center, where maps as well as guided neighborhood tours are available.

The **Birmingham Civil Rights Institute** uses vintage film footage to explain the city's Civil Rights Movement. Among the exhibits is the door of the cell in which Dr. Martin Luther King Jr. wrote his famous "Letter from a Birmingham Jail," arguing that individuals have the right to disobey unjust laws. Down the street, the restored Sixteenth Street Baptist Church stands as a memorial to four black girls killed by a Ku Klux Klan bomb in 1963. To its southeast, in the historic **Carver Theatre**, the Alabama Jazz Hall of Fame hosts live music performances and celebrates the achievements of such artists as Dinah Washington, Nat King Cole, W.C. Handy, and Duke Ellington. At the north end of town, the **Alabama Sports Hall of Fame** honors beloved native African-American athletes such as Joe Louis and Jesse Owens.

🏛 **Birmingham Civil Rights Institute**
520, 16th St N. 📞 *(205) 328-9696.* ⏰ *10am–5pm Tue–Sat, 1–5pm Sun.* 🚫 *public hols.* 🎟 *(Sun free).* ♿

Huntsville ㉕

🚶 *160,000.* 🚉 ℹ️ *700 Monroe St, (256) 533-5723.*

SET IN a curving valley in northern Alabama, the cotton market town of Huntsville developed into a space and military research and development, and manufacturing center after World War II. Home to the NASA-Marshall Space Flight Center, the city's main attraction is the US Space and Rocket Center and the mission control tours. Exhibits include Apollo capsules and a life-size space shuttle. A camp here also teaches children about space exploration.

George Washington Carver Museum, Tuskegee University

Practical Information

ADVANCE PLANNING IS NECESSARY for a successful tour around the Deep South, simply because there is so much to see and do. New Orleans, the region's largest city, is packed with entertainment and music venues, clubs, hotels, and restaurants, while many small towns and the expansive and diverse areas between them often double as low-key resort areas, catering to city-dwellers in need of a change of pace. Depending upon the time, visitors can explore significant historical sights, appreciate stunning scenery, gaze at the well-manicured gardens of former plantation homes, take in a local celebration, or simply relax alongside a lazy river.

TOURIST INFORMATION

EACH OF THE Deep South states publishes a wide variety of informative travel guides, which may be ordered by telephone or accessed via web sites. As soon as visitors enter Louisiana, Mississippi, Alabama, or Arkansas, they may check in one of a dozen official "Welcome Centers" along major highways. Staffed by helpful volunteers and open from 8am to 5pm daily, these centers offer free road maps and a full range of tourist information. Such information is also available from the multitude of local and regional tourism bureaus across all four states.

NATURAL HAZARDS

THE DEEP SOUTH is prone to hurricanes and occasional tornadoes from early June to November each year. However, hurricanes are detected well in advance, and

if planning a visit, visitors should follow the storm forecasts for the Gulf and Caribbean. The **National Hurricane Center** in Miami also provides information on impending hurricanes. When a Hurricane Warning is posted in the area you are visiting, either cancel your trip or evacuate the area. There are tried and tested emergency procedures, so follow the broadcasts on radio and television, or ask hotel staff for help.

The biggest hazard is the sun. Use high-factor sunscreen and wear a hat. Also, drink plenty of fluids to avoid getting dehydrated. Biting and stinging insects, especially mosquitoes, are a nuisance between April and November, so remember to carry insect repellent.

GETTING AROUND

LIKE MUCH OF the US, the Deep South is a region where it can be difficult to get around without a car. Seat

belts are mandatory for drivers and front-seat passengers in all Deep South states. Most states also require seat belts for back-seat passengers. All automobile occupants under the age of four require child safety seats.

Public transportation options are limited. **Greyhound** buses only serve some larger towns and cities, while **Amtrak** runs two train routes – north–south across the Mississippi Delta between Memphis and New Orleans, and east–west, connecting New Orleans with Mobile and Birmingham. However, an unusual way to get around the Deep South is to board a replica Mississippi riverboat. The **Delta Queen Steamboat Company** offers tours along "Old Muddy," from New Orleans up to Baton Rouge, Natchez and other cities.

ETIQUETTE

THE OLD-WORLD traditions of the Deep South hospitality and courtesy, especially toward women, are legendary. Addressing people politely, with a "sir" or "ma'am" will be much appreciated, and will help social interaction.

Check for non-smoking signs as smoking is prohibited in most public buildings, including stores and restaurants. Although the laws for drinking alcohol vary from state to state, the legal age is 21. Only in New Orleans is it permissible to drink on the streets, though only in plastic containers called "go cups."

FESTIVALS

THE DEEP SOUTH states stage a diverse range of annual community, regional, and national festivals. The nation's biggest party, and one of the world's most colorful and lively annual events, is the 10-day long series of celebrations leading up to **Mardi Gras**, French for "Fat Tuesday." The carnival parades, music, drinking, and dancing are at their liveliest at New Orleans, though smaller but no less energetic celebrations are also held in several

---

THE CLIMATE OF THE DEEP SOUTH

The climate across this region does not vary much from state to state, although seasonal differences are distinct. Winter is rather wet, while the summer heat and humidity can be sweltering. By September the weather is fine again, though late summer storms or hurricanes can put a damper on travel. Spring and autumn are the ideal times to plan an extended trip. Spring flowers, such as magnolia blossoms, set the tone for the early months of the year.

NEW ORLEANS

°F/C

	Apr	Jul	Oct	Jan
high °F/°C	77/25	90/32 76/24	79/26	62/17
low °F/°C	61/16		64/18	47/8
daylight	14 days	19 days	18 days	20 days
rainfall	4.5 in	6.1 in	3 in	5 in
month	Apr	Jul	Oct	Jan

32°F 0°C

other Deep South towns, including Mobile, Alabama.

Spring is a fine time to be in Mississippi, especially if you can time your trip to enjoy the *"Gone With the Wind"*-like re-creations of the **Natchez Pilgrimage**, a month-long celebration of the antebellum "Old South." Many of the city's historic homes are open to the public, and several pageants and performances take place.

Summer brings a profusion of outdoor events, and fireworks, bands, and street festivals are the norm for community celebrations of the July 4 Independence Day holiday. Numerous county and state fairs take place in the countryside in July and August, as do a number of music festivals such as the **B.B. King Indiana Bayou Festival** in Indianola Mississippi, the first of many blues-themed festivals that take place in and around the Mississippi Delta. Later in the summer comes the grand **Mississippi Delta Blues** and Heritage Festival, held in September in Greenville, Mississippi. In October, the historic homes of Natchez and Vicksburg are again opened to the public during the **Fall Pilgrimage**. During this time, lucky visitors may sample freshly-made, sugary pralines, sold by vendors.

SPORTS & OUTDOOR ACTIVITIES

THE TOWNS AND cities of the Deep South are not large enough to support top-tier professional sports teams, but they field dozens of minor league teams and hundreds of high-quality sports teams of various public and private colleges and universities. New Orleans has the New Orleans Saints football team and the New Orleans Hornets basketball team, both of which play in the **Superdome**, one of the world's largest indoor sports arenas. The main events of the college sporting seasons are football and basketball games between regional rivals, including Louisiana State University Tigers, the University of Alabama's Crimson Tide, and the Rebels of the University of Mississippi. Baseball season runs from April to September, football from September through January, and basketball from winter through mid-spring.

Although both fishing and boating are also prominent, fishing is by far the more popular of the two sports. Lake fishing for bass or crappie is available in many state parks, while Arkansas streams offer trout fishing. Deep-sea fishing for grouper, tarpon, or snapper, or by net for the shrimp, can be arranged from Gulf of Mexico ports such as Biloxi, Mississippi, Mobile, Alabama, or Grand Island, Louisiana. Visitors should check with the various state Fish and Game departments to see which permits are required.

ENTERTAINMENT

THE BIRTHPLACE of jazz and a melting pot of American music, New Orleans is a showcase for all types of performances. Local newspapers such as the *Times-Picayune* or the weekly *New Orleans Magazine* carry detailed listings of the events and activities. A major venue for music in New Orleans is the historic **Preservation Hall**, where traditonal "Dixieland" jazz may be heard most nights. A huge range of nightclubs in the tourist-dominated French Quarter as well as in the uptown area offer live musical entertainment. For traditional Cajun music, head to Lafayette and the roadhouse restaurant, **Prejean's**, the most reliable of the music venues in the region.

Many other cities also host popular musical events. Blues festivals take place all over Mississippi and Arkansas during summer. A wonderful place to listen to the blues is **Ground Zero Blues Club**, in Clarksdale, Mississippi.

DIRECTORY

TOURIST OFFICES

Alabama
C (888) 365-6946.
W www.touralabama.org

Arkansas
C (800) 226-6632.
W www.arkansas.com

Louisiana
C (888) 784-7328.
W www.louisianatravel.com

Mississippi
C (800) 657-3700.
W www.visitmississippi.org

NATURAL HAZARDS

National Hurricane Center, Miami
C (305) 229-4483.

TRAVEL

Amtrak
C (800) 872-7245.

Greyhound
C (800) 231-2222.

RIVER CRUISES

Delta Queen Steamboat Co.
Robin St Wharf, 1380 Port of New Orleans Place.
C (800) 543-1949.

FESTIVALS

Mardi Gras, New Orleans
C (800) 672-6124.

B.B. King Indiana Bayou Festival
C (662) 887-4454.

SPORTS

Superdome
C (504) 587-3808.
W www.superdome.com

DEPARTMENTS OF FISH & GAME

Arkansas
C (501) 223-6300.

Alabama
C (334) 242-3465.

Louisiana
C (225) 765-2800.

Mississippi
C (601) 432-2400.

ENTERTAINMENT

Preservation Hall
C (504) 522-2841.

Prejean's
C (337) 896-3247.

Ground Zero Blues Club
C (662) 621-9009.
W www.groundzerobluesclub.com

Where to Stay

In the Deep South region, New Orleans has the greatest selection and variety of accommodations, with many historic and architecturally distinctive properties. Beyond New Orleans, the bayou country around Lafayette and the Mississippi town of Natchez also offer historic lodgings. Casino hotels along the Mississippi River and Gulf Coast generally offer low room rates.

Louisiana

	Credit Cards	Number of Rooms	Recommended Restaurant	Children's Facilities	Garden or Terrace
Baton Rouge: *Courtyard Acadian Center* $$$ 2421 S Acadian Thruway. ☎ *(225) 924-6400, (800) 321-2211.* FAX *(225) 923-3041.* [W] www.marriott.com/btrch Close to downtown Baton Rouge, this chain motel is comfortable, convenient, and hosts many business travelers. 🍸 🅿 ❄ 🚭 📺 ♿ 🏊 🏋	■	149	■		■
Baton Rouge: *Radisson Hotel* $$$ 4728 Constitution Ave. ☎ *(225) 925-2244, (800) 333-3333.* FAX *(225) 930-0140.* [W] www.radisson.com A comfortable hotel conveniently located near Louisiana State University, casinos, and the Government Center. 🍸 🅿 ❄ 🚭 📺 ♿ 🏊 🏋	■	294	■		
Bayou Teche, New Iberia: *Comfort Suites New Iberia* $$ 2817 Hwy 14. ☎ *(337) 367-0855.* FAX *(337) 367-0845.* [W] www.comfortsuites.com Conveniently close to Jefferson Island, Avery Island, and Jungle Gardens, this hotel offers large, comfortable suites. 🅿 ❄ 🚭 📺 ♿ 🏊 🏋	■	78			
Bayou Teche, St. Martinville: *Bienvenue House* $$$ 421 N Main St. ☎ *(337) 394-9100.* [W] www.bienvenuehouse.com In one of the loveliest towns in South Louisiana, this antebellum house has porch swings, gardens, and Foti's is just across the square for some of the best food in Louisiana. 🅿 ❄ 🚭 📺 ♿	■	4			■
Lafayette: *Courtyard Lafayette Airport* $$ 214 E Kaliste Saloom Rd. ☎ *(337) 232-5005, (800) 321-2211.* FAX *(337) 231-0049.* [W] www.courtyard.com/LFTCYI Close to Acadian Mall, restaurants, the university, and dance halls, the Courtyard offers spacious rooms. 🅿 ❄ 🚭 📺 ♿ 🏊 🏋	■	90	■		■
Lafayette: *Bois des Chenes B&B Inn* $$$ 338 N Sterling St. ☎ *(337) 233-7816.* FAX *(337) 233-7816.* [W] http://members.aol.com/boisdchene/bois1.htm This former 1820s sugar and cattle plantation has suites with antique furniture and ambience galore. The owner will arrange trips through the Atchafalaya Swamp for nature lovers. Reservations essential. ❄ 🚭 📺 ♿	■	5			■
Natchitoches: *Comfort Inn* $$ 5362 Hwy 6 at I-49. ☎ *(318) 352-7500, (800) 228-5150.* FAX *(318) 352-7500.* [W] www.comfortinn.com This chain motel offers furnished rooms, complete with microwave ovens and refrigerators, and a free Continental breakfast. 🅿 ❄ 🚭 📺 ♿ 🏊	■	59	■		
New Orleans (French Quarter): *St. Louis Hotel* $$$ 730 Bienville St. ☎ *(504) 581-7300, (888) 508-3980.* FAX *(504) 524-8995.* [W] www.stlouishotel.com This small, centrally located hotel, has all the amenities. The elegant, Louis XVI restaurant is one of the best in the city. 🍸 🛎 🅿 ❄ 🚭 📺 ♿	■	81	■	●	
New Orleans (French Quarter): *Cornstalk Hotel* $$$$ 915 Royal St. ☎ *(504) 523-1515.* FAX *(504) 522-5558.* [W] www.travelguides.com/bb/cornstalk A great place to stay in Victorian splendor and comfort. The second-floor gallery is perfect for morning coffee and people-watching. ❄ 📺 🏋	■	14			
New Orleans (French Quarter): *Hotel St. Pierre* $$$$ 911 Burgundy St. ☎ *(504) 524-4401, (800) 225-4040.* FAX *(504) 524-6800.* [W] www.hotelstpierre.com A lovely hotel with French-style cottages, it serves Continental-style breakfast in your room or by the pool. 🅿 ❄ 🚭 📺 ♿ 🏊	■	74			

Price categories for a standard double room per night, inclusive of breakfast, service charges, and any additional taxes:

$ under $100
$$ $100–$150
$$$ $150–$200
$$$$ $200–$250
$$$$$ over $250

CREDIT CARDS
Major credit cards accepted.

NUMBER OF ROOMS
Number of rooms in the hotel.

RECOMMENDED RESTAURANT
Good restaurant within the hotel.

CHILDREN'S FACILITIES
Hotel has various facilities for young children.

GARDEN OR TERRACE
Hotel has a garden, courtyard, or terrace.

	CREDIT CARDS	NUMBER OF ROOMS	RECOMMENDED RESTAURANT	CHILDREN'S FACILITIES	GARDEN OR TERRACE
NEW ORLEANS (FRENCH QUARTER): *Le Richelieu* $$$$ 1234 Chartres St. (504) 529-2492, (800) 535-9653. FAX (504) 524-8179. www.lerichelieuhotel.com The luxurious guest rooms and deluxe suites in this hotel are decorated in traditional style.	▦	86	▦		▦
NEW ORLEANS (FRENCH QUARTER): *Monteleone Hotel* $$$$$ 214 Royal St. (504) 523-3341, (800) 535-9595. FAX (504) 528-1019. www.hotelmonteleone.com This is the oldest, largest, and most charming hotel in New Orleans. The Carousel Bar in the lobby is world famous.	▦	597	▦		▦
NEW ORLEANS (FRENCH QUARTER): *Ritz Carlton Hotel* $$$$$ 921 Canal St. (504) 524-1331, (800) 241-3333. FAX (504) 524-7233. www.ritzcarlton.com This luxurious hotel, housed in two of Crescent City's restored landmarks, the Maison Blanche and the Kress Building, preserves many of the original late 19th century design elements.	▦	452	▦	●	▦
NEW ORLEANS (FRENCH QUARTER): *Royal Sonesta* $$$$$ 300 Bourbon St. (504) 586-0300, (800) 766-3782. FAX (504) 586-0335. www.royalsonestano.com Pink marble and beveled glass doors highlight the lobby of this timelessly elegant, luxurious, and expensive hotel.	▦	500	▦	●	▦
NEW ORLEANS (CENTRAL BUSINESS DISTRICT): *Lafayette Hotel* $$$ 600 St. Charles Ave. (504) 524-4441, (888) 856-4706. FAX (504) 523-7327. www.thelafayettehotel.com This charming hotel with marble baths and wrought-iron balconies, makes a good getaway from the noise of the Quarter.	▦	44	▦		
NEW ORLEANS (CENTRAL BUSINESS DISTRICT): *Le Pavillon Hotel* $$$$ 833 Poydras St. (504) 581-3111, (800) 535-9095. FAX (504) 529-4415. www.lepavillon.com This 1907 hotel has the most spectacular lobby in New Orleans. Reasonably priced, it offers upscale amenities.	▦	226	▦	●	
NEW ORLEANS (CENTRAL BUSINESS DISTRICT): *Fairmont Hotel* $$$$$ 123 Baronne St. (504) 529-7111, (800) 441-1414. FAX (504) 529-4764. www.fairmont.com Once the famous Roosevelt Hotel, the Sazerac Bar and extravagant lobby still speak of the 1930s at this hotel. Every conceivable luxury is offered here, including in-room computer hook-ups.	▦	700	▦	●	
NEW ORLEANS (CENTRAL BUSINESS DISTRICT): *Windsor Court Hotel* $$$$$ 300 Gravier St. (504) 523-6000, (800) 262-2662. FAX (504) 596-4513. www.windsorcourthotel.com This may be the best hotel in New Orleans in terms of service and amenities. The corridors in the lobby level hold original Renaissance and Baroque art.	▦	324	▦		
NEW ORLEANS (GARDEN DISTRICT): *Hampton Inn* $$$ 3626 St. Charles Ave. (504) 899-9990, (800) 426-7866. FAX (504) 899-9908. www.hamptoninn.com This Garden District chain hotel is located right on the St. Charles Avenue streetcar line. The rooms strike a balance between the elegance of old New Orleans and the comfort of modern facilities.	▦	100		●	
NEW ORLEANS (GARDEN DISTRICT): *1891 Castle Inn* $$$$ 1539 4th St. (504) 897-0540, (888) 826-0540. FAX (504) 895-2231. www.castleinnofneworleans.com The rooms in this large, converted house boast ornate mirrors and carved wooden furniture, including some fantastic four-poster beds.	▦	9			

For key to symbols see back flap

Price categories for a standard double room per night, inclusive of breakfast, service charges, and any additional taxes:

$ under $100
$$ $100–$150
$$$ $150–$200
$$$$ $200–$250
$$$$$ over $250

CREDIT CARDS
Major credit cards accepted:

NUMBER OF ROOMS
Number of rooms in the hotel.

RECOMMENDED RESTAURANT
Good restaurant within the hotel.

CHILDREN'S FACILITIES
Hotel has various facilities for young children.

GARDEN OR TERRACE
Hotel has a garden, courtyard, or terrace.

		Price	Credit Cards	Number of Rooms	Recommended Restaurant	Children's Facilities	Garden or Terrace

ARKANSAS

EUREKA SPRINGS: *Crescent Hotel & Spa* — $$$ — Credit Cards ■, 60, Recommended Restaurant ■, Garden or Terrace ■
75 Prospect Ave. (479) 253-9766, (888) 522-9766. FAX (479) 253-5296.
www.crescent-hotel.com
One of the "Historic Hotels of America," this luxurious hotel offers a full-service spa and swimming pool among its many deluxe amenities.

HOT SPRINGS: *Arlington Resort Hotel* — $$ — Credit Cards ■, 481, Recommended Restaurant ■, Children's Facilities ●
239 Central Ave. (501) 623-7771, (800) 643-1502. FAX (501) 623-2243.
www.arlingtonhotel.com
Guests have been coming to the Arlington Hotel and Spa since 1907 to partake of its healing waters. It is the only spa on historic Bathhouse Row that offers overnight accommodations.

LITTLE ROCK: *Comfort Inn* — $$ — Credit Cards ■, 70
300 Markham Center Dr. (501) 227-0120, (877) 550-7666. FAX (501) 227-0120.
www.choicehotels.com
Four miles from downtown, this reliable chain motel is convenient for drivers who prefer to skirt the downtown area.

LITTLE ROCK: *Capital Hotel* — $$$$ — Credit Cards ■, 126, Recommended Restaurant ■
111 Markham St. (501) 374-7474, (800) 766-7666. FAX (501) 370-7091.
www.thecapitalhotel.com
The elegant Capital Hotel was built in the 19th century and features two restaurants, including the acclaimed Ashleys.

MOUNTAIN VIEW: *Ozark Folk Center Dry Creek Lodge* — $$ — Credit Cards ■, 60, Recommended Restaurant ■, Children's Facilities ●
Hwy 382. (870) 269-3871. FAX (870) 269-2909.
www.ozarkfolkcenter@arkansas.com
The State Park Service operates this modern lodge at the engaging Ozark Folk Center, where there is a restaurant and a truckload of amusing family activities.

MISSISSIPPI

BILOXI: *Grand Casino Biloxi Hotel* — $$ — Credit Cards ■, 1000, Recommended Restaurant ■, Children's Facilities ●, Garden or Terrace ■
265 Beach Blvd. (228) 436-2946. FAX (228) 435-8901.
www.grandcasinos.com
The Grand Casino mimics Vegas style with accommodations that are large, bright, and stimulating, yet affordable. It is right on the scenic inlet, and the local museum is across the street.

CLARKSDALE: *Hampton Inn* — $$ — Credit Cards ■, 93, Recommended Restaurant ■
710 State St. (601) 627-9292. FAX (601) 624-4763.
www.hamptoninn.com
This motor lodge, offering the fanciest accommodations in Clarkesdale, is relatively new and slightly more upscale than others. It serves complimentary Continental breakfast to guests.

JACKSON: *Best Value Inn & Suites* — $$ — Credit Cards ■, 133, Recommended Restaurant ■
5035 I-55 N. (601) 982-1011.
This no-frills motel, right off the Interstate might be all that Natchez Trace through-travelers are looking for. The attached restaurant offers excellent fare.

JACKSON: *Edison Walthall Hotel* — $$ — Credit Cards ■, 208, Recommended Restaurant ■
225 E Capitol St. (601) 948-6161, (800) 932-6161. FAX (601) 948-0088.
www.edisonwalthallhotel.com
This institution is where Mississippi powerbrokers have gathered for generations to conduct the business of state. Rooms are more modest and motel-like, unlike the fancy lobby.

NATCHEZ: *Radisson Natchez Eola Hotel* $$$ 132
110 N Pearl St. ((601) 445-6000, (866) 445-3652. FAX (601) 446-5310.
W www.natchezeolahotel.com
A downtown hotel since the 1930s, the restored Natchez Eola is within
easy walking distance of several museums, attractions, restaurants, shops,
and the riverfront. Carriage tours start outside. ▯ P ▤ ▥ TV ▱

NATCHEZ: *Monmouth Plantation Inn* $$$$ 30
36 Melrose Ave. ((601) 442-5852, (800) 828-4531. FAX (601) 446-7762.
W www.monmouthplantation.com
Rated among the country's top romantic hotels, Monmouth sits on a hill
outside town near the Natchez Trace. The luxurious antebellum inn is
furnished with antiques, and breakfast is provided. ▯ P ▤ ▥ TV ▱

OXFORD: *Downtown Inn* $$ 123
400 N Lamar Blvd. ((662) 234-3031, (800) 606-1497. FAX (662) 234-2834.
W www.downtowninnoxford.com
Located in a quiet residential area, this motel is a minute away from
restaurants, shops, and nightclubs, and a 15-minute walk from the
University of Mississippi and Faulkner's Rowan Oak house museum.
▯ ▯ P ▤ ▥ TV ▱ ▨

OXFORD: *Oliver Britt House Inn* $$ 5
512 Van Buren Ave. ((662) 234-8043. FAX (662) 236-2816.
W www.travelguides.com
This modest guest house is centrally located between the town square
and the university. Reasonably priced for the area, the rooms are quiet
and comfortable. ▤ ▥ TV

ALABAMA

BIRMINGHAM: *Pickwick Hotel* $$$ 63
1023 S 20th St. ((205) 933-9555, (800) 255-7304. FAX (205) 933-6918.
W www.pickwick.com
This small 1920s building, which retains its Art Deco styling, is within
walking distance of some of the best restaurants, clubs, and shops.
Continental breakfast and nightly wine and cheese are served in the
lobby pub. ▯ ▯ P ▤ ▥ TV ▱

BIRMINGHAM: *Tutwiler Wyndham Hotel* $$$ 147
2021 Park Place N. ((205) 322-2100. FAX (205) 325-1183.
W www.wyndham.com
Birmingham's 1913 grande dame hotel, the Tutwiler offers spacious,
elegant rooms near downtown attractions. Includes a pleasant bar and
restaurant. ▯ ▯ P ▤ ▥ TV ▱

HUNTSVILLE: *Huntsville Marriott* $$$ 290
5 Tranquility Base. ((256) 830-2222. FAX (256) 895-9528.
W www.marriott.com
A popular choice, adjacent to the US Space Center, the Huntsville
Marriott offers attractive and comfortable rooms and suites, furnished
with all sorts of amenities. ▯ ▯ P ▤ ▥ TV ▱ ▨ ▥

MOBILE: *Radisson Admiral Semmes Hotel* $$$ 170
600 S Beltline Hwy. ((251) 432-8000, (800) 333-3333. FAX (251) 405-594.
W www.radisson.com
Built in the 1940s, this historic hotel offers free Continental breakfast with
its spacious rooms. Guests can also use its well-equipped gym and
swimming pool. ▯ ▯ P ▤ ▥ TV ▱ ▨ ▥

MONTGOMERY: *Holiday Inn Hotel and Suites* $$ 172
120 Madison Ave. ((334) 264-2231, (800) 214-8378. FAX (334) 263-3179.
W www.holiday-inn.com
A few blocks from the Capitol and Old Alabama Town, the spacious
rooms of this elegant, well-located hotel open onto an attractive atrium.
The restaurant serves excellent meals. ▯ P ▤ ▥ TV ▱ ▨

SELMA: *St. James Hotel* $$ 42
1200 Water Ave. ((334) 872-3234. FAX (334) 872-0332.
W www.stjameshotelselma.com
The St. James began operating in the steamboat era, accommodating
passengers en route up the Alabama River. The lovely historic hotel
retains its original grill work and many architectural flourishes. It also has
a restaurant and a few shops. ▯ P ▤ ▥ TV ▱

For key to symbols see back flap

Where to Eat

THE ENTIRE DEEP SOUTH REGION IS known for its outstanding and distinctive cuisine. Chefs in New Orleans enjoy the same celebrity status as film stars do in Los Angeles. Creole and Cajun delicacies make the most of fresh local seafood. Opening times for restaurants are indicated by a "B" for breakfast, "L" for lunch, and "D" for dinner.

	CREDIT CARDS	OUTDOOR TABLES	VEGETARIAN	GOOD WINE LIST	REGIONAL CUISINE
LOUISIANA					
BATON ROUGE: *Don's Seafood & Steak House* $$$ 6823 Airline Hwy. (225) 357-0601. This institution since 1934 has dishes prepared with the freshest seafood and meats. Try Don's in Lafayette, too. *L, D.* ● *Thanksg., Dec 25.*	■			●	■
BATON ROUGE: *Juban's* $$$ 3739 Perkins Rd. (225) 346-8422. With progressive Creole cuisine, this restaurant has a charming courtyard bar. *L, D.* ● *Sun, public hols.*	■	●			■
BAYOU TECHE, ST. MARTINVILLE: *Foti's Oyster Bar/Restaurant* $ 108 S Main St. (337) 394-3058. No frills, but this is where you will find the very best fried seafood, boiled crawfish, and raw or fried oysters. Try the fresh-brewed Cajun coffee. *L, D.* ● *Sun, public hols.*	■				■
BAYOU TECHE, NEW IBERIA: *Clementine's* $$$ 113 E Main St. (337) 560-1007. Classic south Louisiana cooking offering seafood, salad bar, and a wide selection of cocktails. *L, D.* ● *Sun, public hols.* *Fri & Sat.*	■			●	■
LAFAYETTE: *Café Vermilionville* $$$ 1304 W Pinhook Rd. (337) 237-0100. Housed in a 19th-century Acadian inn, this elegant restaurant offers French and Cajun seafood dishes. The soft-shelled crabs, snapper Acadian, and the andouille gumbo are superb. *L, D.* ● *Sun, Dec 25.*	■			●	
LAFAYETTE: *Prejean's* $$$ 3480 US Hwy 167 N. (337) 896-3247. A favorite with locals, this restaurant offers great Cajun rack of elk and American buffalo au poivre, along with an authentic atmosphere and live Cajun music. *L, D.* ● *public hols.*	■	●			■
NACHITOCHES: *The Landing* $$ 530 Front St. (318) 352-1579. The Landing serves some of the city's best seafood, including crawfish etouffée and blackened alligator, in an elegant setting in the historic district. *L, D.* ● *Mon, Thanksgiving, Dec 25.*	■	●	■		■
NEW ORLEANS (FRENCH QUARTER): *Acme Oyster House* $ 724 Iberville St. (504) 522-5973. Although there are mixed opinions about the look of the place, most maintain that the lack of decor is part of its charm, and it is still one of the best places in town for raw oysters and crawfish.	■				■
NEW ORLEANS (FRENCH QUARTER): *Café du Monde* $ 800 Decatur St. (504) 587-0833. Sit and watch the world go by from this historic 24-hour open-air coffee shop, offering mouth-watering *beignets* and *café au lait* (see p347).		●			
NEW ORLEANS (FRENCH QUARTER): *Old Dog, New Trick Café* $ 517 Frenchman St. (504) 943-6368. This health-food haven offers some of the best vegetarian dishes in the city, including delicious Cajun specialties. *L, D.* ● *public hols.*	■		■		
NEW ORLEANS (FRENCH QUARTER): *Antoine's* $$ 713 St. Louis St. (504) 581-4422. Antoine's offers over 130 dishes on its vintage French-Creole menu. Although it is a bit faded, the classic elegance and excellent cuisine never go out of style. *L, D.* ● *Sun.*			■	●	■

Price categories include a three-course meal for one, a glass of house wine, and all unavoidable extra charges such as sales tax and service.
$ under $20
$$ $20–30
$$$ $30–45
$$$$ $45–60
$$$$$ over $60

Credit Cards
Major credit cards accepted.

Outdoor Tables
Garden, courtyard, or terrace with outside tables.

Vegetarian
A good selection of vegetarian dishes available.

Good Wine List
Extensive list of good wines, both domestic and imported.

Regional Cuisine
A good selection of regional specialties available.

New Orleans (French Quarter): *Arnaud's* $$$
813 Bienville St. ☎ *(504) 523-5433.*
The lovely atmosphere makes this elegant 19th-century French Quarter classic one of the great old New Orleans restaurants. The famous shrimp remoulade alone is worth the trip. *L, D.* 🍸 ♫ 👔

New Orleans (French Quarter): *Bayona* $$$
430 Dauphine St. ☎ *(504) 525-4455.*
"New World" is the label Chef Susan Spicer applies to her cooking style. Imaginative dishes are served in an early 19th-century Creole cottage on this quiet French Quarter street. *L, D.* ● *Sun.* 🍸

New Orleans (French Quarter): *Bacco* $$$$
310 Chartres St ☎ *(504) 522-2426.*
A local favorite, the stylish Bacco serves delicious wood-fired pizza and every kind of seafood. *L, D.* 🍸

New Orleans (French Quarter): *Galatoire's* $$$$
209 Bourbon St. ☎ *(504) 525-2021.*
This restaurant epitomizes the old-style French-Creole bistro. A lengthy menu filled with standard-setting sauces, glistening brass chandeliers, bentwood chairs, and white tablecloths add to its timeless atmosphere. *L, D.* ● *Mon.* 🍸 👔

New Orleans (French Quarter): *K-Paul's Louisiana Kitchen* $$$$
416 Chartres St. ☎ *(504) 524-7394.*
Chef Paul Prudhomme started the Cajun craze in this rustic café. Its inventive gumbos and fresh seafood are mouthwatering. Prices are steep at dinner but moderate at lunch. *L, D.* ● *Sun.* 🍸

New Orleans (Marigny): *Siam Café* $
435 Esplanade Ave ☎ *(504) 949-1750.*
Surrounded by the sights, sounds, and aromas of Thailand, Siam offers authentic Thai food, from vegetarian dishes to such specialties as Bangkok beef in oyster sauce. *L, D.*

New Orleans (Marigny): *Feelings Café* $$
2600 Chartres St. ☎ *(504) 945-2222.*
Away from the bustle of the Quarter, with a beautiful piano and intimate, romantic atmosphere, this café offers updated renditions of Creole favorites such as chicken Clemenceau. *L, D.* 🍸 ♫ *Fri & Sat.*

New Orleans (Central Business District): *Mother's* $
401 Poydras St. ☎ *(504) 523-9656.*
Since 1938 locals have lined up for great po' boys, red beans and rice, and ham biscuits. Service is cafeteria-style, and you can't beat the prices. *L, D.*

New Orleans (Central Business District): *Herbsaint* $$
701 St. Charles St. ☎ *(504) 524-4114.*
The Louisiana-inspired French cooking in this chic restaurant produces ever-changing gumbo, prime ribeye, and gorgeous desserts. A must for any visiting gourmand. *L, D.* 🍸

New Orleans (Central Business District): *Palace Café* $$
605 Canal St. ☎ *(504) 523-1661.*
Colorfully crafted from a multistory building that was once the city's oldest music store, the Palace offers imaginative contemporary Creole dishes like crab chops and rabbit ravioli in piquant sauce. *L, D.* 🍸

New Orleans (Central Business District): *Emeril's* $$$$
800 Tchoupitoulas St. ☎ *(504) 528-9393.*
Chef Emeril Lagasse's fantastic contemporary Louisiana cuisine makes this avant-garde restaurant a special treat. *L, D.* ● *Sun.* 🍸 👔

	Credit Cards	Outdoor Tables	Vegetarian	Good Wine List	Regional Cuisine
Arnaud's	■		■	●	■
Bayona	■	●	■	●	■
Bacco	■	●	■	●	
Galatoire's	■		■	●	■
K-Paul's Louisiana Kitchen	■		■	●	■
Siam Café	■		■		
Feelings Café	■	●			■
Mother's	■		■		■
Herbsaint	■			●	■
Palace Café	■			●	■
Emeril's	■		■	●	■

	CREDIT CARDS	OUTDOOR TABLES	VEGETARIAN	GOOD WINE LIST	REGIONAL CUISINE

Price categories include a three-course meal for one, a glass of house wine, and all unavoidable extra charges such as sales tax and service.
$ under $20
$$ $20–30
$$$ $30–45
$$$$ $45–60
$$$$$ over $60

CREDIT CARDS
Major credit cards accepted.
OUTDOOR TABLES
Garden, courtyard, or terrace with outside tables.
VEGETARIAN
A good selection of vegetarian dishes available.
GOOD WINE LIST
Extensive list of good wines, both domestic and imported.
REGIONAL CUISINE
A good selection of regional specialties available.

NEW ORLEANS (GARDEN DISTRICT): *Jamila's Café* $$ 7808 Maple St. (504) 866-4366. A romantic restaurant in the university area, where you can coo over the couscous and other North African dishes. Among the better ethnic restaurants in New Orleans. L, D. ● Mon.	■		■		
NEW ORLEANS (GARDEN DISTRICT): *Commander's Palace* $$$$ 1403 Washington Ave. (504) 899-8221. No restaurant captures New Orleans' gastronomic heritage and celebratory spirit as well as this one in a stately Garden District mansion. This restaurant is considered to be one of the best in the US. L, D. ▮ ♫ ▮	■	●	■	●	■
NEW ORLEANS (UPTOWN): *Brigtsen's* $$$ 723 Dante St. (504) 861-7610. The ever-changing menus at Brigtsen's add up to some of the best Creole/Cajun cooking you will find anywhere in the US. Lucky are the customers who can get one of the two tables in an enclosed sunroom out front. L, D. ● Sun, Mon.	■			●	■
NEW ORLEANS (MIDCITY): *Mandina's* $$ 3800 Canal Street. (504) 482-9179. This classic Creole seafood restaurant with an old-fashion bar offers large portions of good food, especially great oyster and shrimp po' boys and tasty trout *amandine*. L, D. ▮ -					■

ARKANSAS

EUREKA SPRINGS: *1905 Basin Park Restaurant* $$ 12 Spring St. (479) 253-7837. This restaurant offers casual dining overlooking the city's historic Spring Street and Basin Park shopping district. The menu is eclectic, including traditional American and Mexican dishes. L, D. ▮ ⓑ ♫	■	●	■		
HOT SPRINGS: *McClard's BBQ* $ 505 Albert Pike. (501) 623-9665. w http://mcclards.com A local Bill Clinton landmark, McClard's has been in business since 1928 and is considered Arkansas's premier house of barbecue. L, D. ● Sun–Mon, Thanksgiving, Dec 15–Jan 15, one week in late Jul. ♦ ⚹ ⓑ					■
HOT SPRINGS: *Faded Rose* $$ 210 Central Ave. (501) 624-3200. New Orleans-style specialties, such as gumbo, Creole shrimp, po' boys, and steaks are served in this historic building dating back to 1889. L, D. ● Thanksgiving, Dec 25. ▮ ⚹ ⓑ	■				■
LITTLE ROCK: *Doe's Eat Place* $$ 1023 W Markham St. (501) 376-1195. Occupying a worn corner storefront at the fringe of downtown, this landmark dive is a favorite with capital politicos. Doe's serves tamales, gumbo, and "pillowy" sirloin steaks up to six pounds. L, D. ● Sun. ▮ ⓑ	■				■
LITTLE ROCK: *Ashley's* $$$ 111 W Markham St. (501) 374-7474. Within the Capital Hotel, Ashley's is widely considered the best restaurant in town, specializing in steaks and seafood. L, D. ● Sun. ▮ ⚹ ⓑ	■			●	■
MOUNTAIN VIEW: *Bar None Bar-B-Q & Steakhouse* $ 803 W Main St. (870) 269-2200. w www.barnonebar-b-q.com The family-friendly restaurant specializes in dishes such as dry-rubbed ribs and hickory BBQ, as well as a variety of steaks. L, D. ● Mon–Tue, public hols. ♦	■	●			■

MISSISSIPPI

CLARKSDALE: *Madidi*
164 Delta Ave. (662) 627-7770. $$
Co-owned by actor and local resident Morgan Freeman, this restaurant offers French-influenced cuisine, such as herb-encrusted rack of lamb, in a restored brick storefront downtown. *L, D.* ● Sun.

GULFPORT/BILOXI: *Mary Mahoney's Old French House*
116 Rue Magnolia & Water St. (228) 374-0163. $$
If you can tear yourself away from the casino buffets, Mary Mahoney's offers Southern hospitality and traditional dishes in a historic 1737 house appointed in period decor. *L, D.* ● Sun, Dec 24–25.

JACKSON: *Palette Restaurant*
201 E Pascagoula St. (601) 960-1515. $
On the second floor of the Mississippi Museum of Art Café, this inviting café offers light lunches of soups, salads, sandwiches, and pastas, with a tempting selection of desserts. *L.* ● Sat, Sun.

NATCHEZ: *Cock of the Walk*
200 N. Broadway. (601) 446-8920. $$
This restaurant offers a crowd-pleasing, wide menu selection in an old train station at the top of the bluff above the Mississippi River. *L, D.*

NATCHEZ: *Monmouth Plantation Inn*
36 Melrose Ave. (601) 442-5852, (800) 828-4531. $$$
Monmouth offers plantation fare in a richly appointed antebellum mansion, and also provides overnight accommodations. *L, D.* ● Mon.

OXFORD: *Bottletree Bakery*
923 Van Buren Ave. (662) 236-5000. $
This welcoming town bakery offers European-style breads and pastries, specialty coffees, and light lunches in a folk-arty, laid-back café environment. *B, L.* ● Mon.

OXFORD: *City Grocery*
152 Courthouse Square. (662) 232-8080. $$
This hardwood-floored, exposed-brick restaurant is famous for its signature shrimp-and-grits. *L, D.* ● Sun, major hols.

ALABAMA

BIRMINGHAM METRO AREA, BESSEMER: *Bob Sykes Bar-B-Que*
1724 N 9th Ave. (205) 426-1400. $
A short drive from Birmingham on I-20 W, Bob Sykes is a culinary landmark serving delicious barbecue. *L, D.* ● Sun, Thanksgiving, Dec 25, Jan 1.

BIRMINGHAM: *Bombay Café*
2839 7th Ave S. (205) 322-1930. $$
Bombay Café offers seafood, lamb, and children's dishes in the former 1920s Arondale Theater downtown. *D.* ● Sun, public hols.

HUNTSVILLE: *Fogcutter*
3805 University Dr NW. (256) 539-2121. $
Fogcutter specializes in steak and seafood in a family restaurant with a nautical decor. *L, D.* ● public hols.

MOBILE: *The Pillars*
1757 Government St. (334) 478-6341. $$$
In an elegantly appointed Victorian mansion, The Pillars offers Italian pasta and a Continental menu, including fresh Gulf seafoods, Angus beef, homemade breads, and tempting desserts. *D.* ● Sun, public hols.

MONTGOMERY: *Vintage Year*
405 Cloverdale Rd. (334) 264-8463. $$
One of the best spots in town for a nice dinner, it offers a wide range of entrées, including chicken and seafood. *D.* ● Sun, Mon, public hols.

SELMA: *Major Grumble's*
1300 Water Ave. (334) 872-2006. $$
Set at the bluff above the Alabama River, Major Grumble's serves Southern catfish, charbroiled chicken, steaks, and seafood in a former cotton warehouse dating from 1850. *L, D.* ● Sun, public hols.

For key to symbols see back flap

The Great Lakes at a Glance

SPREADING BETWEEN THE Colonial-era landscapes of the East Coast and the wide open spaces of the Wild West, this region stakes a strong claim to being the most "American" part of the US. Home to more than one in five Americans, the Great Lakes is energetic and surprisingly varied. With its bustling big cities and sleepy small towns, idyllic rural scenes and sublime waterfront wilderness, industrial might and broad swaths of pristine natural beauty, the attractions here are as varied as the six states of Illinois, Ohio, Michigan, Indiana, Wisconsin, and Minnesota that form the center of America's heartland.

0 km   100

0 miles   100

Crookston

Grand Rapids

Apostle Island

MINNESOTA
(See pp416–21)

Willmar

Minneapolis-St.Paul

WISC
(See pp

Rochester

La Crosse

Ma

Voyageurs National Park (see p421) *in Minnesota covers endless stretches of watery wilderness near the Canadian border. The park, with its lakes, bogs, and islands, is now a prime outdoor destination.*

R

Wisconsin's (see pp412–15) *natural wonders attract hikers, bikers, and campers who explore the state's glacial moraines, lakes, and valleys through well-marked trails.*

Roc

ILL
(See pp

Sp

Springfield (see p399) *is the capital of Illinois, a state characterized by vast expanses of rich, flat farmland. Abraham Lincoln, who lived here for 31 years (1830–61), delivered his famous "House Divided" speech in 1858 at the Old State Capitol.*

Car

◁ **Aerial view of Chicago's magnificent high-rises, towering above Lake Shore Drive**

Chicago (see pp386–97), *the region's largest city, is located on the southwestern edge of Lake Michigan. One of the world's most celebrated centers of architectural innovation, the city has attracted many of North America's most influential architects. The most significant of these was Frank Lloyd Wright.*

LOCATOR MAP

Detroit *(see p408–409), still known as the Motor City, is also Michigan's main city and commerical center. Downtown's Hart Plaza, at the riverfront, is the site of the city's lively summer festivals.*

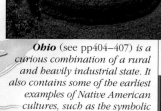

Lake Huron

Lake Superior

Lake Michigan

MICHIGAN
(See pp408–11)

Saginaw

Grand Rapids

Flint

Lansing

Ann Arbor

Detroit

Lake Erie

Cleveland

South Bend

Toledo

Sandusky

Fort Wayne

OHIO
(See pp404–07)

Canton

Lafayette

Columbus

Indianapolis

Dayton

Bloomington

Cincinnati

INDIANA
(See pp400–403)

Ohio *(see pp404–407) is a curious combination of a rural and heavily industrial state. It also contains some of the earliest examples of Native American cultures, such as the symbolic earthen Serpent Mound.*

Indianapolis' *(see p402) Monument Circle is the dominant feature of downtown. The city's many excellent museums adds to its status as Indiana's state capital.*

THE GREAT LAKES

URROUNDING THE WORLD'S *largest bodies of fresh water, the Great Lakes region is a land of epic proportions. From the towering skyscrapers of Chicago, Illinois, and the factories of Detroit, Michigan, to the seemingly endless plains of Indiana, the bountiful pastures of Wisconsin, and Minnesota's watery wilderness, this is one of the most exciting destinations in the country.*

Spreading west from the original American colonies to beyond the Mississippi River, the Great Lakes region formed the first frontier of the early United States. The lakes themselves – Ontario, Erie, Huron, Michigan, and Superior – were a conduit for trade and exploration, and a key to the region's development. Plentiful harvests from the fertile soils, lumber from the forests, and ore from the region's mines all came together to support the growth of such cities as Chicago, Cleveland, Detroit, and Minneapolis. From the mid-19th century on, immigrants from all over the country and around the world came here to work on farms and in factories, thus establishing the diverse cultures and traditions that still flavor

Great Lakes life. While industry and agriculture have given way to the service economy, the region's history and heritage have now become important tourist attractions, enhancing the natural beauty of its many lakes, rivers, forests, and mountains.

HISTORY

Long before the United States was founded, the region surrounding the Great Lakes was home to some of the most developed and powerful Native American cultures. Evidence of one of the most significant archaeological remnants in North America can be found in southern Ohio and Illinois, where the enigmatic Moundbuilder culture constructed the largest cities north of Mexico. Of these, the most

A 1920s photograph showing parked automobiles at Detroit's Cadillac Square

◁ Stacked icicle formations in the Sawtooth Mountain Range along Lake Superior's northern shore, Minnesota

impressive is at Cahokia. Farther north, spanning the international border between the US and Canada – which runs right through the center of the Great Lakes – Native Americans were grouped together into many distinct though related tribes. The Huron and Ojibwe in the north, and the Fox, Shawnee, and Menominee in the south and west had developed intricate trade

Replica of Christopher Columbus's ship *Santa Maria* in Columbus, Ohio

and cultural relationships. However, after some 100 years of European contact, large Native populations had been decimated through disease and internecine warfare.

Initially, early European exploration of this part of the New World was dominated by the French. Traveling from their colony at Quebec, the first French explorers were rapidly followed by fur trading "voyageurs" who bartered tools and weapons for beaver pelts. At the same time, French Jesuit

missionaries began to establish commercial, military, and religious outposts at Sault Sainte Marie in 1668 and at Detroit in 1701. Until the mid-1700s, religion and the fur trade remained the main points of contact between Indians and Europeans.

The pace of settlement accelerated after the end of the Seven Year's War in Europe in 1763, and the Americans and British acquired territorial control of the region. Within a few decades Ohio, Indiana, and Illinois had changed from isolated frontier territories to states. Following the completion of the Erie Canal in 1825, and improved transportation on the lakes, settlers were able to reach the previously distant lands of Michigan and Wisconsin. In 1858, Minnesota became the last of the Great Lakes states to join the nation.

IMMIGRANTS & INDUSTRY

The opening up of the Great Lakes region to settlement coincided with a major influx of immigrants. From the 1840s on, immigration increased tenfold as more than 200,000 people, mostly Irish and Germans fleeing the potato famine and political unrest respectively, came to America every

KEY DATES IN HISTORY

1620 Etienne Brule is the first European to explore present-day Michigan and Wisconsin

1673 Jesuit missionary Jacques Marquette and explorer Louis Jolliet cross the northern Great Lakes and descend the Mississippi River

1750 The population of Detroit, the only large Great Lakes settlement, numbers 600

1763 France surrenders its Great Lakes territorial claims to Great Britain

1783 The US acquires the region from Britain, forms the Northwest Territory

1803 Ohio is the first to become a state

1903 Henry Ford establishes the Ford Motor Company in Detroit

1936 A factory strike leads General Motors to accept the United Auto Workers union as the sole bargaining agent for its workers

1968 Chicago police attack anti-Vietnam War protestors at the Democratic National Convention

1995 Heat wave kills more than 500 people in Chicago

2000 Former World Wrestling Federation champion Jesse "The Body" Ventura is elected Governor of Minnesota

2003 Ohio celebrates its bicentennial

Historical Museum, Winona on the Mississippi

year. Many settled in ethnic enclaves in rapidly growing cities such as Chicago, Detroit, Cincinnati, and Cleveland, where some three-quarters of residents were either foreign-born or first-generation Americans.

Large numbers of other immigrants set up wheat and dairy farms on recently cleared forests, or found work in other resource-based industries. Copper mining in Michigan's Upper Peninsula, for example, produced more than 75 percent of the nation's supplies between 1850 and 1900. With a total value of nearly $10 billion, this mining boom was 10 times more lucrative than the legendary California Gold Rush of 1849. Another major industry was food processing. Meat-packing, which was concentrated on the huge stockyards of Chicago and Minneapolis, relied on the railroads to transport millions of cattle and pigs from across the Midwest. The Great Lakes also came to dominate grain processing, and some of the nation's largest companies, including the world-famous Kellogg's and General Mills, are still based here.

The early 20th century witnessed the largest and most enduring industrial boom, mainly because of the mutually dependent growth of the steel and automobile industries, both largely based in the Great Lakes region. Dearborn and Detroit, headquarters of Ford Motor Company as well as other smaller companies that evolved into the giant General Motors, emerged as the "Motor City." Despite competition from other countries, the Great Lakes automobile industry flourished and in turn supported a network of other industries, such as the iron mines in Minnesota, steel mills in Indiana, and rubber plants in Ohio.

POLITICS & CULTURE

The success of the industries may have reaped huge fortunes for its owners, but the workers' conditions were often dire. This exploitation led to a number of violent battles, particularly around Chicago, such as the riots in Haymarket Square in 1886 and the bitter strike against the Pullman Palace Car company in 1894. The growth of unions gave workers some semblance of political power, which in turn supported a number of left-leaning social movements. The Great Lakes in general, and Minnesota and Wisconsin in particular, were early strongholds of the Populist and Progressive movements, which in the early 1900s proposed such now-accepted innovations as the eight-hour workday and graduated rates of income tax.

This social awareness also influenced art and literature. One of the region's most famous works of art, Diego Rivera's massive mural on the walls of the Detroit Institute of Art, depicts workers struggling under the demands of industrialization. The region's great literary works include Hamlin Garland's depictions of life on the Wisconsin frontier, Sherwood Anderson's *Winesburg, Ohio*, the vivid exposés of Sinclair Lewis, and the stories of St. Paul native F. Scott Fitzgerald.

A view of Detroit's gleaming skyscrapers, including the Renaissance Center, from across the Detroit River

Exploring the Great Lakes

ENCOMPASSING LARGE CITIES as well as endless stretches of pastoral farmland and places of natural beauty, the Great Lakes covers a vast area that is best explored by car. While the major towns and cities are linked by both Interstate Highways and Amtrak trains, public transportation is otherwise limited, particularly across the lakes themselves. Chicago is the region's largest and most cosmopolitan city; other cities include Indianapolis, Detroit, Cleveland, Cincinnati, Milwaukee, and Minnesota's twin cities of Minneapolis & St. Paul.

SEE ALSO

- *Practical Information* pp422–3
- *Where to Stay* pp424–7
- *Where to Eat* pp428–31

Visitors near Old Mission Lighthouse, Lake Michigan Shore, Michigan

SIGHTS AT A GLANCE

Illinois
Chicago pp386–97 **1**
Rockford **2**
Galena **3**
Springfield **4**
Southern Illinois **5**

Indiana
New Harmony **6**
Bloomington **7**
Indiana Dunes
  National Lakeshore **8**
South Bend **9**
Shipshewana **10**
Fort Wayne **11**
Indianapolis **12**
Columbus **13**
Ohio River Valley **14**

Ohio
Cincinnati **15**
Dayton **16**

Serpent Mound **17**
Hopewell Culture
  National Historic Park **18**
Columbus **19**
Berlin **20**
Cleveland **21**
Lake Erie Islands **22**
Sandusky **23**
Toledo **24**

Michigan
Detroit pp408–409 **25**
Ann Arbor **26**
Lansing **27**
Grand Rapids **28**
Lake Michigan Shore **29**
Mackinac Island **30**
Upper Peninsula **31**

Wisconsin
Milwaukee **32**
Door County **33**

Wisconsin Dells **34**
Baraboo **35**
Madison **36**
Spring Green **37**
La Crosse **38**
Apostle Islands **39**

Minnesota
Minneapolis &
  St. Paul pp416–17 **40**
Mississippi River Towns **41**
Rochester **42**
Pipestone National
  Monument **43**
Brainerd Lakes Area **44**
Duluth **45**
Iron Range **46**
Boundary Waters Canoe
  Area Wilderness **47**
Voyageurs National
  Park **48**

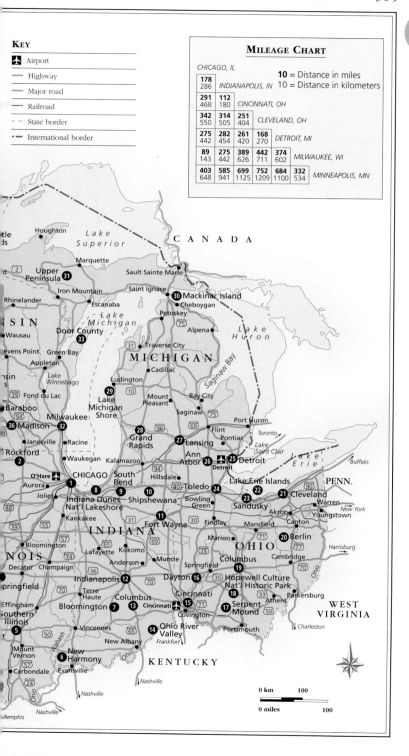

KEY

✈ Airport
— Highway
— Major road
— Railroad
- - State border
·-·- International border

MILEAGE CHART

CHICAGO, IL						
178			**10** = Distance in miles			
286	INDIANAPOLIS, IN		**10** = Distance in kilometers			
291	**112**					
468	**180**	CINCINNATI, OH				
342	**314**	**251**				
550	**505**	**404**	CLEVELAND, OH			
275	**282**	**261**	**168**			
442	**454**	**420**	**270**	DETROIT, MI		
89	**275**	**389**	**442**	**374**		
143	**442**	**626**	**711**	**602**	MILWAUKEE, WI	
403	**585**	**699**	**752**	**684**	**332**	
648	**941**	**1125**	**1209**	**1100**	**534**	MINNEAPOLIS, MN

0 km — 100

0 miles — 100

Chicago ❶

CHICAGO, A CITY OF ALMOST 3 million people, covers 228 sq miles (591 sq km) of the US's Midwest. Situated at the southwest edge of the vast Lake Michigan, the city claims 29 miles (47 km) of lakefront. Despite burning to the ground in 1871 and witnessing terrible social unrest, the city soon rebuilt itself to emerge as the financial capital of the Midwest. Today, this third largest city in the US is world famous for its innovative architecture, its vibrant cultural and educational institutions, and for its colorful and turbulent political history and significance as the national transportation hub.

Sights at a Glance

Chicago Historical Society ①
Newberry Library ②
Magnificent Mile ③
John Hancock Center ④
Navy Pier ⑤
Chicago Children's Museum ⑥
Museum of Broadcast Communications ⑦
Art Institute of Chicago ⑧
Sears Tower ⑨
The Loop pp390–91 ⑩
South Loop ⑪
Museum Campus ⑫

South Side
(see inset map)
Museum of Science & Industry ⑬
University of Chicago ⑭
DuSable Museum of African American History ⑮

Greater Chicago
(see inset map)
Lincoln Park Zoo ⑯
Oak Park pp396–7 ⑰

Getting Around

Although Chicago is a sprawling Midwestern metropolis, many of the city's sights and main cultural centers are located downtown, making the city a walker's dream. The city's public transportation is inexpensive and efficient. The train system, known as the "L" for elevated, is the easiest way to get around. Buses crisscross the city, but the system is complicated and best left to regular commuters. Taxis are affordable, convenient, and readily available.

Key

- Sight/Place of interest
- ✈ Airport
- 🚆 Metro train station
- [M] CTA train station
- [i] Tourist information
- [P] Parking
- Railroad line
- Expressway

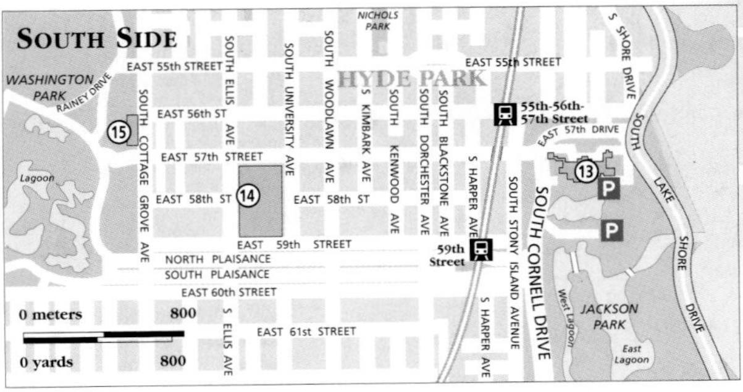

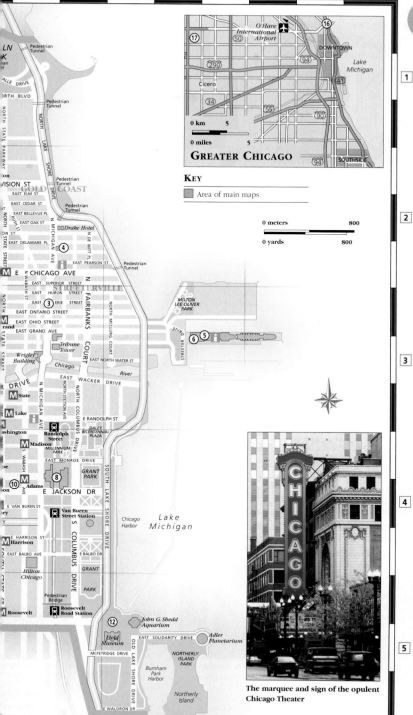

O'Hare
International
Airport

17

50

290

Cicero

34

DOWNTOWN

94

41

55

90

Lake
Michigan

94

SOUTHSIDE

16

GREATER CHICAGO

0 km 5

0 miles 5

KEY

Area of main maps

0 meters 800

0 yards 800

1

2

3

4

5

LN
K

Pedestrian
Tunnel

ALLE DRIVE

NORTH BLVD

NORTH LAKE SHORE DRIVE

Pedestrian
Tunnel

NORTH STATE PARKWAY

VISION ST

GOLD COAST

EAST ELM ST

EAST CEDAR ST

EAST BELLEVUE PL

EAST OAK ST

N RUSH ST

N MICHIGAN AVE

N DE WITT PL

Drake Hotel

4

Pedestrian
Tunnel

EAST DELAWARE PL

i

EAST PEARSON ST

Pedestrian
Tunnel

M E CHICAGO AVE

N WABASH ST

EAST SUPERIOR STREET

STREETERVILLE

EAST HURON STREET

N FAIRBANKS COURT

N ERIE STREET

3

EAST ERIE STREET

M

EAST ONTARIO STREET

Grand

EAST OHIO STREET

N MCCLURG COURT

EAST GRAND AVE

Tribune
Tower

STREETER DRIVE

MILTON
LEE OLIVER
PARK

6 5 i

Wrigley
Building

EAST NORTH WATER ST

Chicago River

DRIVE

EAST WACKER DRIVE

M State

N MICHIGAN AVE

N STETSON AVE

N COLUMBUS DRIVE

M Lake

M

E RANDOLPH ST

DALEY
BICENTENNIAL
PLAZA

ashington

Randolph
Street

S

Madison

MILLENNIUM
PARK

EAST MONROE DRIVE

GRANT
PARK

S WABASH AVE

be

10 M Adams

8

E JACKSON DR

on

E VAN BUREN ST

Van Buren
Street Station

SOUTH LAKE SHORE DRIVE

Lake
Michigan

M Harrison

E HARRISON ST

EAST BALBO AVE

Chicago
Harbor

E BALBO DR

Hilton
Chicago

COLUMBUS DRIVE

GRANT

PARK

Pedestrian
Bridge

M Roosevelt

Roosevelt
Road Station

OLD LAKE SHORE DRIVE

12

John G. Sbedd
Aquarium

Field
Museum

EAST SOLIDARITY DRIVE

Adler
Planetarium

MCFETRIDGE DRIVE

NORTHERLY
ISLAND
PARK

Burnham
Park
Harbor

Northerly
Island

E WALDRON DR

The marquee and sign of the opulent
Chicago Theater

D E F

Original Neo-Georgian entrance to the Chicago Historical Society

Chicago Historical Society ①

Map D1. 1601 N Clark St. **【** *(312) 642-4600.* **M** *Clark/Division then bus 22, 36.* **🚌** *11, 151, 156.* **◐** *9:30am–4:30pm Mon–Sat; noon–5pm Sun.* **◐** *Jan 1, Thanksg., Dec 25.* **🎫** *(free Mon).* **♿ 【** *(call for times).* **🅿** *Concerts, lectures.* **ⓦ** *www.chicagohistory.org*

THE CITY'S oldest cultural institution, the 1856 Chicago Historical Society is a major museum and research center, with a library open for public research. It traces the history of Chicago and Illinois, from its first explorers through the development of the city to the major events in modern-day Chicago. Miniature dioramas depict great events such as the the Great Fire of 1871, the Chicago River during the Civil War, and the bustling LaSalle Street in the mid-1860s.

The American Wing holds one of only 23 copies of the Declaration of Independence, and a 1789 copy of the American Constitution, first printed in a Philadelphia newspaper. The building itself is fascinating with its two faces – the original 1932 Neo-Georgian structure, and a 1988 addition with a three-story, glass-and-steel atrium entrance.

Newberry Library ②

Map D2. 60 W Walton St. **【** *(312) 943-9090.* **M** *Chicago (red line).* **◐** *hours for lobby, book rooms, & exhibits vary. Call ahead.* **◐** *public hols.* **♿ 【** *3pm Thu; 10:30am Sat.* **🅿** *Exhibits, lectures, concerts.*

FOUNDED IN 1887 by banker Walter Newberry, this independent research library for the humanities was designed by Henry Ives Cobb, master architect of the Richardsonian Romanesque style.

The superb collection includes cartography, Native American history, Renaissance studies, and such rarities as a 1481 edition of Dante's *Divine Comedy*, and first editions of Milton's *Paradise Regained* and the King James Version of the Bible.

Magnificent Mile ③

Michigan Ave, between E Walton Pl & E Kinzie St.

THE MAGNIFICENT MILE, a stretch of Michigan Avenue north of the Chicago River, is the city's most fashionable street. Almost completely destroyed in the 1871 fire, the street grew into Chicago's premier shopping district after the opening of the Michigan Avenue Bridge in 1920. Exclusive shops line the wide boulevard, while modern retail outlets and skyscrapers rub shoulders with historic buildings.

To the north lies the Gothic Revival-style **Fourth Presbyterian Church**. Its exposed buttresses, stone spire, and recessed main window reflect the influences of medieval European churches.

To its right are two historic castellated structures, the **Water Tower** and the **Pumping Station**, among the few buildings that survived the 1871 fire. The tower, originally housing a standpipe, is now home to a photography gallery and a theater. The station still fulfills its original purpose of pumping water and houses a Visitor

Open-air skywalk topping the John Hancock Center

ARCHITECTURE IN CHICAGO

Chicago is world famous as a center of architectural innovation, a city where architects have pushed the boundaries of creativity. This reputation had its beginnings in the tragic fire of 1871. Working on a blank slate, architects rose to the challenge of reshaping a devastated city. It was in Chicago that the world's first skyscraper was built, and here that Frank Lloyd Wright developed his Prairie School of architecture.

Gothic Revival style, represented by the Water Tower, drew from medieval European architecture.

Italianate design style was inspired by Renaissance palaces and villas of northern Italy. The elegant Drake Hotel exemplifies this style.

Richardsonian Romanesque style – typified by rough-cut stone, round arches, and recessed windows – can be seen in the Newberry Library.

Information Center (163 E Pearson St) and café. Across the street, **Water Tower Place** contains eight floors of upscale boutiques and restaurants. Other "vertical shopping malls" on the street include Chicago Place and City Place. Nearby, the **Terra Museum of American Art** is noted for its superb collection of American Impressionist paintings.

In the south, the Gothic-style **Tribune Tower**, office of the *Chicago Tribune*, holds rock fragments from world-famous sites, such as St. Peter's Basilica in Rome, the Forbidden City in Beijing, and even a 3.3-billion-year-old piece of moon rock embedded in its exterior walls. At the southern end of the street is the two-part **Wrigley Building**. This white terra-cotta structure, one of Chicago's most beloved, features a giant four-sided clock and a quiet courtyard, which is open to the public.

John Hancock Center ④

Map D2. 875 N Michigan Ave. **Observatory** ☎ *(312) 751-3681.* [M] *Chicago (red line).* 🕐 *9am–11pm daily.* 🎫 *to observatory (children under 5 free).* ♿ 🍴 🍸 [P]

AFFECTIONATELY called "Big John" by Chicagoans, the 100-story, cross-braced steel John Hancock Center stands out in the Chicago skyline. The tapering obelisk tower's major attraction is the Hancock Observatory on the 94th floor. Here, 1,127 ft (344 m) above the Magnificent Mile, an open-air (screened) skywalk offers spectacular views of the city. The elevator ride to the top at 20 miles (32 km) is one of the fastest in the US.

Designed by architect Bruce Graham of Skidmore Owings and Merrill and engineer Fazlur R. Khan, the center houses offices, condominiums, and shops in 2.8 million sq ft (0.26 million sq m) of space. The ground-level plaza has a fountain and cafés.

Navy Pier ⑤

Map D2. 600 E Grand Ave. ☎ *(800) 595-7437.* 🚌 *29, 56, 65, 66, 120, 121, 124.* 🕐 *10am; closing times vary by day & season.* ● *Thanksgiving, Dec 25.* ♿ 🍴 ☕ 🍸 [P] [i] ***Lake cruises.*** [W] www.navypier.com

NAVY PIER is a bustling recreational and cultural center. Designed by Charles S. Frost, the 3,000-ft (915-m) long and 400-ft (120-m) wide pier was the largest in the world when built in 1916. Over 20,000 timber piles were used in its construction.

The giant Ferris wheel, Navy Pier Park

Originally a municipal wharf, the pier was used for naval training during World War II. After a four-year renovation, Navy Pier opened in its present incarnation in 1995. Navy Pier Park has a 150-ft (45-m) Ferris wheel, an old-fashioned carousel, an outdoor amphitheater, ice skating, miniature golf, and an IMAX® 3D Theater. The Smith Museum features stained glass.

Chicago Children's Museum ⑥

Map E3. 700 E Grand Ave. ☎ *(312) 527-1000.* 🚌 *29, 56, 65, 66.* 🕐 *10am–5pm Tue–Sun; Memorial Day–Labor Day.* ● *Thanksg., Dec 25.* 🎫 *(free 5–8pm Thu).* ♿ 🛍 [P] ***Special activities daily.***

CHICAGO Children's Museum, focusing on activating the intellectual and creative potential of children ages 1 to 12, is an activity center for the whole family. All exhibits are hands-on: kids can build a fort, be part of a TV crew, make a flying machine, or channel water with dams and locks. The Dinosaur Expedition gallery has a reproduction of a huge *Suchomimus* skeleton. Children can dig for bones in an excavation pit, or simply slide, climb, and jump around.

***Queen Anne** style, once a popular design for Chicago residences, is exemplified by row houses in Crilly Court.*

***Chicago School**, developed here, led to an engineering and aesthetic revolution with commercial skyscrapers like the Reliance building.*

***Neo-Classical** style has classical Greco-Roman elements, as seen in the Chicago Cultural Center.*

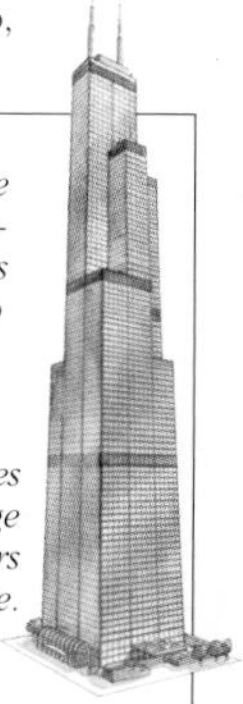

***International Style** stresses severe geometry and large expanses of glass. Sears Tower is a fine example.*

***Post-Modern** architecture, an eclectic style without strict rules, is seen in the Harold Washington Library Center.*

Museum of Broadcast Communications ⑦

Map D3. The museum is shifting to its new premises at State & Kinzie. Call for details. **📞** *(312) 629-6000, 629-6016 (for tours).* **Ⓜ** *Washington (red line).* **🕐** *10am–4:30pm Mon–Sat; noon–5pm Sun.* **⦿** *public hols.* **♿** **📷 🎟 ⓦ** *www.museum.tv*

The Neo-Classical façade of the Art Institute of Chicago

FOUNDED IN 1987 and housed in the Chicago Cultural Center, this museum is one of the only three broadcast museums in the US. Permanent displays and special exhibitions examine popular culture through the sights and sounds of TV and radio. A TV studio offers visitors the opportunity to anchor the "news" and take home a souvenir videotape.

The Sportscaster Café shows replays of famous moments in sports history, and the Radio Hall of Fame features taped voices, such as Jack Benny and Bing Crosby from radio's golden age. The museum's collection

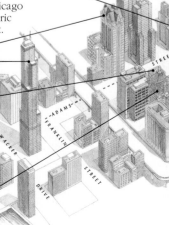

"His Master's Voice" dog and early NBC microphone

of media icons include Charlie McCarthy, Garfield Goose, and Dirty Dragon. Exhibits also include vintage and contemporary TV sets and radios, as well as "the camera that changed America," the one used to televise the Kennedy/Nixon debate (1960) that marked a turning point in the relationship between TV and politics. In the museum's research center guests can, for a fee, hear from a collection of over 50,000 hours of radio programming, or view thousands of TV broadcasts and commercials. A gift shop sells postcards, books, and broadcast memorabilia.

The Art Institute of Chicago ⑧

Map D4.111 S Michigan Ave. **📞** *(312) 443-3600.* **Ⓜ** *Adams.* **🚌** *3, 6, 7, 126, 145, 147.* **Ⓡ** *Van Buren St.* **🕐** *10:30am–4:30pm Mon, Wed–Fri; 10:30am–8pm Tue; 10am–5pm Sat; noon–5pm Sun.* **⦿** *Thanksg., Dec 25.* **💳** *(children under 6 free; free Tue; separate adm to some exhibits).* **♿** *via Columbus Dr entrance.* **📷 🍴 🎟 📷** *at Monroe St.* **Exhibits, lectures, films.** **ⓦ** *www.artic.edu*

THE EXTENSIVE collections at the Art Institute of Chicago represent nearly 5,000 years of creativity through paintings, sculptures, textiles, photographs, cultural objects, and decorative arti-

The Loop ⑩

THE LOOP GETS ITS NAME from the elevated track system that circles the center of downtown. Screeching trains and a steady stream of people add to its bustle. In the canyon vistas, through the historic buildings and modern edifices, you can catch glimpses of the bridges spanning the Chicago River. The renovation of warehouses and historic theaters is helping to enliven the Loop at night.

190 South LaSalle Street (1987), designed by Philip Johnson, has a white-marble lobby with a gold-leafed, vaulted ceiling.

The Rookery, designed by Burnham and Root in 1888, typifies the Richardsonian Romanesque style.

Chicago Board of Trade occupies a 45-story Art Deco building, a statue of Ceres atop its roof. The frenetic action inside can be observed from a viewers' gallery.

Marquette Building, an early skyscraper (1895), was designed by William Holabird and Martin Roche, central Chicago School figures and architects of more than 80 buildings in the Loop.

Sears Tower

facts from around the world. Founded by civic leaders and art patrons in 1879 as The Chicago Academy of Fine Arts, the museum became The Art Institute of Chicago in 1882. Outgrowing two homes as wealthy patrons donated their art collections, it finally settled in this Neo-Classical structure. Today, the complex combines modern additions in the original structure made by Shepley, Rutan, and Coolidge.

The museum's holdings span from 3rd millennium BC Egyptian and Chinese artifacts to modern and contemporary American and European art. Though best known for its world famous Impressionist and Post-Impressionist collection with such masterpieces as Paul Cézanne's *The Basket of Apples* (c.1895), Henri de Toulouse-Lautrec's *At the Moulin Rouge* (1895), and Claude Monet's six versions of a wheat field, the museum represents almost every major artistic movement of the 19th and 20th centuries. Particularly strong are examples of Cubism, Surrealism, and German Expressionism.

The 35,000-strong exquisite Asian collection is also note-worthy for its illuminated Persian manuscripts, Japanese woodblock prints, and Indian and Chinese historic artifacts.

Sears Tower ⑨

Map C4. 233 S Wacker Dr. 📞 *(312) 875-9696.* Ⓜ *Quincy.* ⭕ *May–Sep: 10am–10pm daily; Oct–Apr: 10am–8pm daily; last adm 30 min before closing.* 🎫 ⬠ 🍴 🎁 🅿
🌐 www.sears-tower.com

View of the Sears Tower and Skydeck, looking northeast

AT A HEIGHT of 1,450 ft (442 m) the Sears Tower is one of the world's tallest buildings. Boasting the highest occupied floor and the highest height to the rooftop, it was designed by Bruce Graham, of Skidmore Owings and Merrill, and engineer Fazlur Khan. Over 110 concrete caissons, anchored in bedrock, support the tower's 222,500 tons.

Today, the tower contains 3.5 million sq ft (0.3 million sq m) of office space, more than 100 elevators, and almost enough telephone cable to circle the Earth twice. The elevator to the glass-enclosed 103rd-floor Skydeck travels at 1,600 ft (490 m) per minute, and offers stunning views.

Nearby, the 12-story **Rookery** building, the world's tallest when it opened in 1888, is one of the city's most photographed edifices. Its dark redbrick façade with terra-cotta trim gives way to a two-tiered court, remodeled in 1907 by Frank Lloyd Wright, who covered the iron columns and staircases with white marble, inlaid with gold leaf.

🏛 **The Rookery**
209 S LaSalle St. 📞 *(312) 553-6150.* ⭕ *9am–8pm Mon–Fri; 9am–3pm Sat.* ⬤ *public hols.* ♿

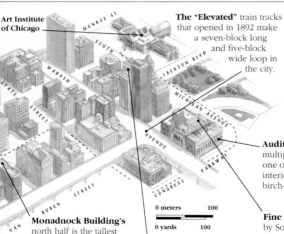

Art Institute of Chicago

MONROE ST
SOUTH
WABASH
STATE STREET
JACKSON BLVD
MICHIGAN AVENUE
AVENUE
PARKWAY
CONGRESS
BUREN STREET
VAN

The **"Elevated"** train tracks that opened in 1892 make a seven-block long and five-block wide loop in the city.

Monadnock Building's north half is the tallest building ever constructed entirely of masonry.

Federal Center is a three-building office complex designed around a central plaza by Ludwig Mies van der Rohe.

Santa Fe Center, a classic Chicago School building, with an elegant two-story atrium, houses the Chicago Architecture Foundation.

0 meters 100
0 yards 100

DOWNTOWN CORE

LOCATOR MAP

Auditorium Building, an 1889 multipurpose skyscraper, features one of Adler and Sullivan's best interiors in its seventh-floor, birch-paneled recital hall.

Fine Arts Building, designed by Solon S. Beman in 1885, was originally a wagon carriage showroom. It once also housed Frank Lloyd Wright's studio.

KEY

- - - Suggested route

Rowe Building, Printing House Row District

South Loop ⑪

Map D4. **M** *Harrison, Roosevelt.*
🚌 *via State St & Dearborn St buses (near South Side: Michigan Ave bus 3).*

LOCATED A SHORT walk south of the downtown core, the South Loop has changed dramatically in recent decades, from a run-down industrial district to a residential and retail neighborhood. The South Loop developed as an industrial area in the late 1800s, but after World War II, manufacturers left and the area declined. In the 1970s, with the conversion of the district's derelict warehouses to fashionable lofts, businesses sprang up as Chicagoans took advantage of the area's proximity to downtown.

This transformation is most evident in the two blocks of the **Printing House Row Historic District**, which by the 1890s had earned Chicago the title of the printing capital of the US. By the 1970s, with the closing of the nearby Dearborn Station, manufacturers withdrew and the area fell into decline. Many of the massive buildings erected for the printing trade remain today. Their conversion into stylish condominiums and office lofts has led to the revitalization of the neighborhood and an influx of commercial activity.

The Second Franklin Building has ornamental tilework illustrating the history of printing over its entranceway, while the Rowe Building houses a bookstore specializing in local authors and travel literature. The adjacent Richardsonian Romanesque-style **Dearborn Station Galleria**, Chicago's oldest surviving passenger train station building, has also been converted into a shopping mall. Its square clock tower is a landmark. Dominating the South Loop, on South Street, is the world's largest public library building, the **Chicago Public Library, Harold Washington Library Center**, holding close to 2 million books and periodicals on its 90 miles (145 km) of shelving. This Post-Modern giant pays tribute to many of Chicago's historic buildings, through its varied architectural features. Artwork is displayed throughout the building, including work by Cheyenne artist Heap of Birds. The library also showcases exhibits relating to Chicago's history.

To the east, the **Museum of Contemporary Photography** focuses on American photography produced since 1959, with selections from its 5,000-strong collection and temporary exhibitions. Next to it, the **Spertus Museum** with its world-famous collection of Judaic art, highlights decorative objects and religious artifacts that span 5,000 years of Jewish history. Highlights include ornate Torah arks and scrolls from around the world. Decorative candelabras and Hanukkah lamps include 18th-century eastern European examples and modern Israeli designs.

Judaic art showcased in the Spertus Museum

A computer in the deeply moving Zell Holocaust Memorial room lists the names of people lost by Chicago families in the Holocaust; it takes a full day to read the list. Shoes and a spoon from Auschwitz and a prisoner's outfit are likewise haunting reminders of this horrific period of history.

The hands-on archeological exhibit at the ARTiFACT Center, allows kids to excavate artifacts in a 32-ft (10-m) long re-created dig site. The museum also houses the Asher Library, the largest public Jewish library in the central US, with more than 100,000 books and 1,000 Jewish films on video and DVD.

A short walk east leads to **South Michigan Avenue**, one of Chicago's finest streets. Featuring a spectacular row of historic buildings, it is an excellent place to window shop and admire the varied architectural styles for which the city is famous. Farther along the street lies the opulent Hilton Chicago. Decorated in French Renaissance style, this 25-story hotel – with 3,000 rooms, a rooftop golf course, and a 1,200-seat theater – was the largest in the world when it opened in 1927. Across the street Buddy Guy's Legends presents big-names and local blues acts. Owner and blues legend Buddy Guy can often be found among the club's many patrons.

🏛 Chicago Public Library, Harold Washington Library Center
400 S State St. **📞** *(312) 747-4300.*
M *Library.* **◯** *9am–7pm Mon–Thu, 9am–5pm Fri–Sat, 1–5pm Sun.*
● *public hols.* **♿** *call (312) 747-4136.* 🎫 💻 🎦 *Exhibits, lectures, films.* **W** *www.chipublib.org*

🏛 Spertus Museum
618 S Michigan Ave. **📞** *(312) 322-1747.* **M** *Harrison.* **◯** *10am–5pm Sun–Wed, 10am–7pm Thu, 10am–3pm Fri.* **●** *Sat, public & Jewish hols.*
🎫 *(free Fri).* **♿** 🎦 *Concerts, lectures, films.*
W *www.spertus.edu*

Museum Campus ⑫

Map E5. S Lake Shore Dr.
M Roosevelt then free trolley. 🚌 12, 146. 🚆 Roosevelt then free trolley.

THE MUSEUM CAMPUS is a vast lakefront park connecting three world-famous natural science museums, thus providing educational and recreational opportunities for all. This 57-acre (23-ha) extension of Burnham Park was created by the relocation of Lake Shore Drive in 1996.

Located in the southwest part of the lush green campus is the Daniel Burnham-designed Neo-Classical structure housing the **Field Museum**. This great natural history museum holds an encyclopedic collection of zoological, geological, and anthropological objects from around the world. Founded in 1894 (with funding from Marshall Field) to house objects from the 1893 World's Columbian Exposition, the museum now holds over 20 million objects.

Particular strengths of the museum include such dinosaur fossils as "Sue" – the most complete *Tyrannosaurus rex* skeleton ever found, Native Indian and Ancient Egyptian artifacts, and extensive displays on mammals and birds.

Exhibits on prehistoric life include the bones of an 18-year-old Cro-Magnon woman and a model of a 15,000-year-old Ukranian shelter, made of 300 bones from 13 mammoths. Among the major crowd pleasers is Underground Adventure – a subterranean

The moumental Neo-Classical entrance to Field Museum

exhibit where visitors can walk through worm tunnels, meet giant bugs, and feel reduced to insect size.

A short walk northeast along terraced gardens leads to the **John G. Shedd Aquarium**, housing nearly 8,000 saltwater and freshwater animals, representing 650 species of fish, birds, reptiles, amphibians, invertebrates, and mammals. Named for its benefactor, a prominent Chicago businessman, the aquarium opened in 1930 in a Neo-Classical building. The Oceanarium has a magnificent curved wall of glass facing Lake Michigan, whose water flows into its tank. This marine-mammal pavilion showcases beluga whales and dolphins. The aquarium's exhibits can be viewed from many viewpoints, some under water.

Farther east, the Museum Campus houses the **Adler Planetarium and Astronomy Museum** featuring one of the world's finest astronomical collections, with artifacts dating as far back as 12th-century Persia. It also has the world's first virtual-reality theater. Spectacular sky shows complement displays on navigation and space exploration. State-of-the-art technology enables visitors to explore exhibits hands-on. Funded by businessman Max

Xochpilli, Aztec God of Flowers, Field Museum

Aquatic motifs adorning John G. Shedd Aquarium, Museum Campus

Adler, this 12-sided, Art Deco structure was designed by Ernest Grunsfeld in 1930 and is now a historical landmark.

🏛 **Field Museum**
1400 S Lake Shore Dr. 📧 (312) 922-9410. ⏰ 9am–5pm daily. ⬤ Jan 1, Dec 25. 🎟 (free Sep–Feb: Mon–Tue). ♿ via west entrance. 📷 11am, 1pm. 🍴 🛍 **P** **Lectures, films, events.** [W] www.fieldmuseum.org

🏛 **John G. Shedd Aquarium**
1200 S Lake Shore Dr. 📧 (312) 939-2438. ⏰ Memorial Day–Labor Day: 9am–6pm daily (Jun–Aug: 9am–10pm Thu, Oceanarium 9am–8pm Thu); Labor Day–Memorial Day: 9am–5pm Mon–Fri; 9am–6pm Sat, Sun, public hols. ⬤ Jan 1, Dec 25. 🎟 (free Sep– Feb: Mon & Tue; except special exhibits). ♿ 📷 🎁 🍴 🛍 **P** **Lectures.** [W] www.shedd.org

🏛 **Adler Planetarium & Astronomy Museum**
1300 S Lake Shore Dr. 📧 (312) 922-7827. ⏰ 9:30am–4:30pm daily (5–10pm 1st Fri of each month). ⬤ Thanksgiving, Dec 25. 🎟 (free Sep–Feb: Mon & Tue, but separate adm to theaters still applies). ♿ 📷 🛍 🍴 **P** **Lectures, films, light shows.** [W] www.adlerplanetarium.org

---

OLD MONEY

Chicago has a beautiful sound because Chicago means money – so the late actress Ruth Gordon reputedly said. By the beginning of the 20th century the city was home to 200 millionaires. One of the most prominent was dry-goods merchant and real-estate mogul Potter Palmer who, with his socialite wife Bertha Honoré, had an enormous impact on the city's cultural and economic life. In 1882, Palmer built an opulent home at North Lake Shore Drive. Perhaps no feature of the mansion epitomized the family's wealth as much as the doors: there were no outside handles, as the doors were always opened from inside, by servants. Department-store owner Marshall Field was less ostentatious. Although he rode in a carriage to work, he stopped short of his store to walk the last few blocks so people would not see his mode of transport. Likewise, he asked the architect of his $2-million, 25-room mansion not to include any frills.

Potter Palmer

View of the Museum of Science and Industry from across Columbia Basin

Museum of Science & Industry ⑬

Map B5. 57th St & S Lake Shore Dr.
 (773) 684-1414, (800) 468-6674.
 Garfield then eastbound bus 55.
 1, 6, 10. 55th-56th-57th St, 59th St. 9:30am–4pm Mon–Fri, 9:30am–5:30pm Sat, Sun, public hols.
 Dec 25. (free Jan–Feb, mid-Aug–mid-Dec: Mon & Tue; Jun: 1st Mon & Tue).
Films. www.msichicago.org

THE MUSEUM of Science and Industry celebrates scientific and technological accomplishments, with an emphasis on achievements of the 20th and 21st centuries. With its collection of over 800 exhibits and 2,000 interactive displays, the museum makes the exploration of science and technology an accesssible experience.

Though best known for its exhibits on space exploration and transportation, the 350,000 sq ft (32,500 sq m) of exhibition space in the museum has more than enough to keep visitors of all ages engaged for a full day.

The **Henry Crown Space Center** features the Apollo 8 Command Module, the first manned spacecraft to circle the moon, in 1968, a replica of NASA's Apollo Lunar Module Trainer, and a 6.5-oz (185-gm) piece of moon rock. A 20-minute movie simulates the experience of blasting off in a space shuttle, complete with shaking seats, allowing viewers to feel like astronauts, if only briefly.

The transportation section features outstanding examples of transport from train and plane to automobile. In **All Aboard the Silver Streak** visitors can climb aboard a record-breaking 1930s train that revolutionized industrial design. One of the most popular exhibits, **Take Flight** explores the inner workings of a 727 jetliner, cantilevered to the museum's balcony, and simulates a seven-minute San Francisco-to-Chicago flight.

Visitors can walk through a 16-ft (5-m) tall replica of the human heart, seeing it from the perspective of a blood cell, and calculate the number of times their heart has beaten since birth, or look inside the human body in a detailed exhibit on anatomy. **AIDS: The War Within** is the world's first permanent museum exhibit on AIDS and HIV. It explores the nine stages of the AIDS virus and the efforts of scientists to control it.

A few exhibits fall outside the museum's defined focus but prove to be enduring crowd pleasers, such as **Circus**. Roland Weber, a railroad worker, spent 33 years carving and casting the 22,000 figures that come to life in this tiny, animated circus.

University of Chicago ⑭

Map A5. Bounded by 56th & 59th Sts, Ellis & Woodlawn Aves. Garfield (green line) then bus 55. 59th.

THE UNIVERSITY OF Chicago, was founded in 1891 with the endowment of John D. Rockefeller, on land donated by Marshall Field (see p393). Today, this outstanding private university has the greatest number of Nobel laureates among faculty, alumni, and researchers of any US university. It is particularly lauded in

---

FROM PLASTER TO STONE

Originally built as the Palace of Fine Arts for the 1893 World's Fair, this structure later became the first home of the Field Museum of Natural History. Based on Classical Revival style, this plaster-clad building was designed by Charles B. Atwood. After the Field Museum moved out, the building sat in a state of disrepair until the mid-1920s, when Julius Rosenwald, chairman of Sears Roebuck and

Co., campaigned to save it, launching a million-dollar reconstruction program. Exterior plaster was replaced with 28,000 tons of limestone and marble in an 11-year renovation. The Museum of Science and Industry opened in 1933, in time for the Century of Progress World's Exposition.

The original building during the 1893 World's Columbian Exposition

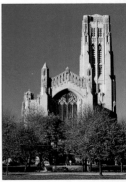

The Rockefeller Memorial Chapel, University of Chicago

The Robie House, a masterpiece of the Prairie School of architecture

the fields of economics and physics. Henry Ives Cobb designed 18 of the university's limestone buildings and developed its cloistered quadrangle plan (along the lines of Cambridge and Oxford), before the Boston firm Shepley Rutan and Coolidge took over as the main architects in 1901. Now the campus features designs from more than 70 architects.

The north entrance houses the ornamental Cobb Gate, a gargoyled ceremonial gateway donated by Henry Cobb in 1900. Across the street, the Regenstein Library holds rare book and manuscript collections, along with millions of other volumes.

Situated at the northern end of the campus is the light-filled, intimate **Smart Museum of Art**. Named after its benefactors, David and Alfred Smart, the museum holds more than 8,000 objects, including antiquities and Old Master prints, Asian paintings, calligraphies, and ceramics, spanning five centuries of Western and Eastern civilizations. The museum's café, with tall windows overlooking the tranquil sculpture garden, is a great spot for a quiet lunch. Outside the museum, sculptor Henry Moore's *Nuclear Energy*, marks the spot where, in 1942, a team of scientists led by Enrico Fermi ushered in the atomic age

with the first controlled nuclear reaction.

In the southeast of the vast campus lies the **Oriental Institute Museum**, the exhibition arm of the university's Oriental Institute, whose scholars have excavated in virtually every region of the Near East since 1919. Highlights of the museum's collections include a rare reconstruction of an Assyrian palace (c.721–705 BC) and a 17-ft (5-m) sculpture of King Tutankhamen, the tallest ancient Egyptian statue in the Western Hemisphere (c.1334–25 BC). Opposite the museum, the massive Gothic-style **Rockefeller Memorial Chapel**, topped with a 207-ft (63-m) carillon tower, is the tallest building on campus. John D. Rockefeller had requested that this limestone-and-brick structure representing religion be the university's most dominant feature. Two blocks north lies Frank Lloyd Wright's world-famous **Robie House** (1906–1909). Designed for Frederick Robie, a bicycle and motorbike manufacturer, the home is one of Wright's last Prairie School houses: Wright left both his family and his Oak Park practice during its three-year construction. The exterior design of the house perfectly captures the prairie landscape of flat, open fields. The roof's sweeping planes embody the house's aesthetic

Statue of King Tutankhamen, Oriental Institute Museum

of bold rectilinear simplicity. Steel beams support the overhanging roof. Also bold but simple, the interior is furnished with Wright-designed furniture. The house is an organic whole, underscored by the harmonious interplay between the exterior and interior and is admired by architects worldwide.

🏛 **Oriental Institute Museum**
1155 E 58th St. 📞 (773) 702-9514. ⭕ 10am–4pm Tue & Thu–Sat, 10am–8:30pm Wed, noon–4pm Sun. ⬤ public hols. ♿ 📷 **Special events.**

🏛 **Robie House**
5757 S Woodlawn Ave. 📞 (773) 834-1847. ⭕ daily. ⬤ Jan 1, Thanksgiving, Dec 25. 💷 (children under 7 free). 📷 mandatory: 11am, 1pm, 3pm Mon–Fri; every 30 min between 11am–3:30pm on weekends. 🔲 www.wrightplus.org

DuSable Museum of African American History ⑮

Map A5. 740 E 56th Pl. 📞 (773) 947-0600. Ⓜ Garfield (green line) then bus 55. 🚌 4, 10. ⭕ 10am–5pm Mon–Sat, noon–5pm Sun & public hols. ⬤ Jan 1, Thanksgiving, Dec 25. 💷 (children under 6 free; free on Sun). ♿ 📷 book in advance. 🔲 🅿 **Lectures, films.**

FOUNDED in 1961 to preserve and interpret the diverse historical experiences and achievements of African Americans, the DuSable Museum highlights the accomplishments of the ordinary and extraordinary alike.

The museum's permanent exhibit, **Songs of My People**, brings together diverse images by Black photojournalists of African-American lives. Other exhibits include memorabilia from the life and political career of Chicago's first Black mayor, Harold Washington, and **Distorted Images: Made in USA?**, an exhibit focusing on contrived and demeaning images of African Americans. **Africa Speaks** presents handcrafted functional art from Africa, and fascinating ritual masks from closed West African societies.

Greater Chicago

V ISITORS EAGER TO DISCOVER more of Chicago will not be disappointed by the rich mix of historical sights, recreational activities, and picturesque suburbs that the city's outlying areas have to offer. For lovers of architecture, Oak Park is a must-see for its Frank Lloyd Wright designs. Other Chicago neighborhoods, such as Wicker Park and Lakeview are ideal day-trip destinations. The vast expanse of Lincoln Park offers a respite from the bustle of the city in its lush gardens, flowering plants, and a zoo, famed for its naturalistic animal habitats.

A lowland gorilla at the zoo's Lester E. Fisher Great Ape House

Lincoln Park Zoo ⑯

2200 N Cannon Dr. 📞 *(312) 742-2000.* Ⓜ *Clark/Division.* 🚌 *22, 36, 135, 136, 145, 146, 147, 151.* ◯ *8am–6pm daily (May–Sep: 8am–7pm Sat, Sun & hols).* ♿ 🍴 🐾 🅿 *on N Cannon Dr.* **Workshops** 📞 *(312) 742-2053.* **Special events** 📞 *(312) 742-2283.* 🆆 *www.lpzoo.com*

L OCATED IN THE heart of Lincoln Park, this zoo is easily accessible from downtown. Established in 1868 with the gift of two swans from New York's Central Park, Lincoln Park Zoo is the country's oldest free public zoo. Today, more than 1,000 mammals, reptiles, and birds from around the world live here in realistic habitats. A world leader in wildlife conservation, the zoo shelters such animals as the threatened Grevy's zebra from Africa and the endangered Bactrian camel from Mongolia, as well as rare gazelles, deer, antelopes, and alpacas in its 11 outdoor habitats. A 1912 historic building houses rare cats, including Siberian tigers. The zoo's large collection of lowland gorillas bears testimony to a successful breeding program. A working farm with cows, horses, pigs, and chickens, is popular with kids for the daily milking and horse-grooming demonstrations.

Lincoln Park, Chicago's largest, offers walking and biking paths that wind along paddle-boating ponds, lagoons, and sandy beaches. The stunning Lincoln Park Conservatory houses exotic plants and tropical trees.

Frank Lloyd Wright's Home and Studio, Oak Park

Oak Park ⑰

Bounded by North Ave, Roosevelt Rd, Austin Blvd, & Harlem Ave. 🛈 *(708) 848-1500.* Ⓜ *Oak Park (green line); Harlem/Lake (green line).* 🚉 *Oak Park (Union Pacific/ West line).* **Visitor Center** *158 N Forest Ave.* ◯ *10am–4pm daily.* ● *Jan 1, Thanksg., Dec 25.* 🎫 🎟 **Frank Lloyd Wright Preservation Trust** *931 Chicago Ave.* 📞 *(708) 848-1976.* 🎫 🆆 *www.wrightplus.org*

F RANK LLOYD Wright moved to Oak Park in 1889, at the age of 22. During the next 20 years here, he created many groundbreaking buildings as his legendary Prairie School style evolved. This tranquil community is now home to 25 Wright buildings – the largest grouping of his work anywhere. The best place to feast on Wright's achievement is the superbly restored **Frank Lloyd Wright Home and Studio**, designed by

Pink flamingos in the Waterfowl Lagoon at Lincoln Park Zoo

Unity Temple, Frank Lloyd Wright's "little jewel," Oak Park

Wright in 1889. This was also where he developed his influential architectural style.

Nearby are two private homes that reveal Wright's versatility. The 1902 **Arthur Heurtley House** is typically Prairie style, with its row of windows spanning the low roofline, and a simple but elegant entrance arch. The 1895 **Moore-Dugal House** across the street, is a hybrid of styles, rich with Tudor Revival and Gothic elements.

At the southern end of Oak Park is the masterful **Pleasant Home**, a 30-room Prairie-style mansion designed in 1897 by George W. Maher. The house holds extraordinary art glass – designed panels of leaded glass. It also includes intricate woodwork, and decorative motifs, and a display on the area's history.

Wright was especially proud of **Unity Temple**, his design for the Unitarian Universalist Congregation. He called this church one of his most important designs, his first expression of an "entirely new architecture." It was built between 1906 and 1908, using a then-unusual technique of poured reinforced concrete, in part because of a budget of only $45,000. Unity Temple is a masterpiece of powerful simplicity wedded with functional ornamentation.

Oak Park is also famous as the birthplace of the famed American writer Ernest Hemingway (1899–1960), who lived here until the age of 20. Although Hemingway *(see p323)* rejected the conservative mindset of this Chicago suburb saying it was full of "wide lawns and narrow minds," Oak Park continues to pride itself on its literary association. The **Ernest Hemingway Birthplace**, a grand Victorian home decorated with turn-of-the-20th-century furnishings, has displays on this Nobel Prize-winner's life. The **Ernest Hemingway Museum**, features several artifacts from Hemingway's early life, including a childhood diary.

The Victorian house in which Ernest Hemingway was born

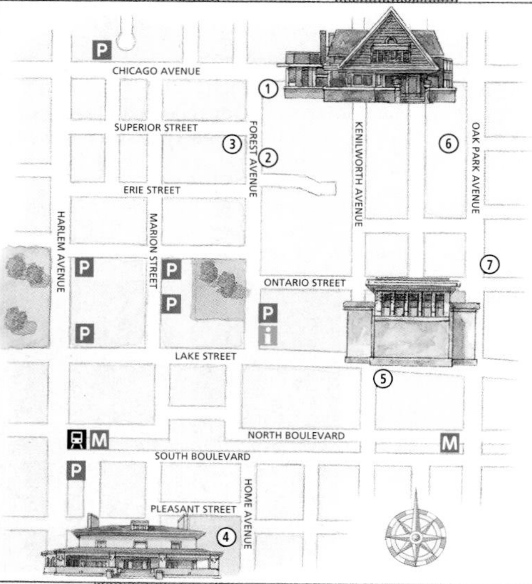

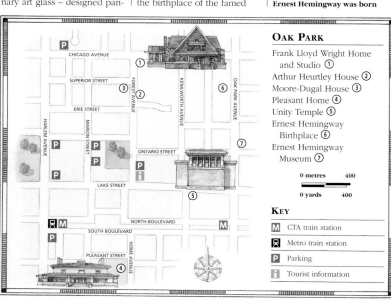

OAK PARK

Frank Lloyd Wright Home and Studio ①
Arthur Heurtley House ②
Moore-Dugal House ③
Pleasant Home ④
Unity Temple ⑤
Ernest Hemingway Birthplace ⑥
Ernest Hemingway Museum ⑦

0 metres 400

0 yards 400

KEY

[M] CTA train station

🚆 Metro train station

[P] Parking

[i] Tourist information

Illinois

E XCEPT FOR THE DENSELY populated area around Chicago *(see pp386–97)*, Illinois is a predominantly rural state. Large expanses of rich, flat farmland are dotted with the occasional small agricultural community or county seat. Known as the "Land of Lincoln," most of the sites related to the president are concentrated in Springfield, the heart of the state. Some rather unusual and picturesque scenery can be found in the hilly "Driftless Region" along the Mississippi in the northwest, and in the rugged "Illinois Ozarks" in the southeast.

Statue of Sac hero Black Hawk, southwest of Rockford

Rockford ❷

🏠 *139,400.* ✈ 🚌 🛈 *211 N Main St, (800) 521-0849.*
🌐 *www.gorockford.com*

D UBBED THE Forest City in the late 1800s, Rockford today has beautiful public and private gardens and miles of parkland along the Rock River, which bisects the city. Of its two most-visited gardens, the **Klehm Arboretum and Botanic Garden** contains 150 acres (61 ha) of plants. The other, the **Sinnissippi Gardens**, runs south along the Rock River's east bank. Its features include an aviary, lagoon, and recreation path. The path offers views of downtown's historic buildings, including the restored Coronado Theater, a gilded 1927 Moorish movie palace.

On the town's east side, the **Midway Village and Museum Center** is both a living history center and local history museum. Exhibits tell the story of ethnic groups who flocked to the city's factories. The grounds have been turned into a 19th-century village, with restored buildings from the area.

The growth of Rockford followed the tragic 1830s Blackhawk War between the Sac Indians of northern Illinois and the US Army, determined to displace the tribes from their farmlands. After the Sacs lost, they were relocated to Iowa. A stone statue of the Sac warrior Chief Blackhawk is located 27 miles (43 km) southwest of Rockford.

🌺 Klehm Arboretum & Botanic Garden

2701 Clifton Ave. 📞 *(888) 419-0782.*
🕐 *9am–4pm daily.* 🚫 ♿
🌐 *www.klehm.org*

🌺 Sinnissippi Gardens

1300 N 2nd St. 📞 *(815) 987-8858.*
🕐 *9am–4pm daily.* ● *Thanksgiving, Dec 25.* ♿ 🌐 *www.rockfordparks.- org/sinnissi.htm*

Galena ❸

🏠 *3,600.* ✈ 🚌 🛈 *720 Park St, (815) 777-3557.* 🌐 *www.galena.org*

P ERCHED ON a bluff overlooking the Galena River near its confluence with the Mississippi, this immaculately preserved town is a relaxing tourist destination with 19th-century homes, historical landmarks, and antique shops. Its status as the shipping center for the region's many lead mines made Galena the busiest Mississippi River Valley port between St. Louis and St. Paul in the 1840s. The town's population peaked at 15,000 during the Civil War, when the elite erected many magnificent homes in a wide variety of ornate styles.

Many of Galena's historic homes are now open to visitors. **The Belvedere Mansion**, built in 1857 by a local steamboat owner, is a 22-room Italianate structure with a varied collection of period furnishings and some quaint recent additions, including the draperies from the *Gone with the Wind* movie set. Civil War general and US president Ulysses S. Grant lived quietly in Galena, between the signature events of his military career and time in the White House. His small, Federal-style 1860 home contains many of Grant's original possessions and furnishings.

The **Galena/Jo Daviess County History Museum**, located in an old Illinois Central Railroad depot, chronicles Galena's lead mining and Civil War shipping days. **Vinegar Hill Lead Mine**, 6 miles (10 km) north of town, provides regular 30-minute tours of the 19th-century mine.

🏛 The Belvedere Mansion

1008 Park Ave. 📞 *(815) 777-0747.*
🕐 *May 31–last weekend in Oct: 11am–4pm.* 🚫 🌐 *www.galena.org/ historic.cfm*

🏛 Galena/Jo Daviess County History Museum

211 S Bench St. 📞 *(815) 777-9129.*
🕐 *9am–4:30pm daily.* ● *Jan 1, Easter, Thanksgiving, Dec 24–25, 31.* 🚫 ♿
🌐 *www.galenahistorymuseum.org*

A view of Galena with its historic landmarks

Cozy Dog Drive-in, a popular Route 66 café

Springfield ❹

🏛 105,400. ✈ 🚉 🚌
ℹ️ 109 N 7th St, (800) 545-7300.
W www.visitspringfieldillinois.com

T HE STATE CAPITAL since 1837, Springfield gained fame as the adopted hometown of 16th US president, Abraham Lincoln, who lived here for 24 years before assuming the presidency in 1861. The four-block **Lincoln Home National Historic Site** is a pedestrian-only historic district, with restored 19th-century homes, gaslights, and wooden sidewalks surrounding the neat frame house where Lincoln and his wife, Mary, lived for 16 years.

An on-site visitor center provides details about the city's other Lincoln-related attractions, including his law office, tomb, and the 1853 **Old State Capitol**. It was here that he delivered his famous 1858 "House Divided" speech, outlining the sectional differences that would soon plunge the nation into the Civil War. Lincoln's political career began in 1834, when he was elected to the Illinois General Assembly while working as postmaster in the nearby community of New Salem, now a living history museum.

The town's other attraction is the elegant **Dana-Thomas House**, a 1904 Prairie-style home designed by Frank Lloyd Wright (see p396). It contains much of Wright's original white oak furniture, light fixtures, art-glass doors, windows, and light panels. Many Wright experts consider this to be the best-preserved of the houses designed by the famous architect.

Springfield is also rich in Route 66 lore (see pp40–41). The old road follows a clearly marked path through the city, leading to the southside **Cozy Dog Drive-in**, a legendary Route 66 eatery, which claims to have invented the corndog. The café's Route 66 Museum and its trademark "cozy dogs," still available at rock-bottom prices, make it a popular tourist destination.

🏛 Lincoln Home National Historic Site
8th & Jackson Sts. 📞 (217) 492-4241. ⊙ 8:30 am–5pm daily (extended spring, summer & fall hours). ● Jan 1, Thanksgiving, Dec 25. & W www.nps.gov/liho
🏛 Old State Capitol
5th & Adams Sts, Springfield. ⊙ Mar–Oct: 9am–5pm daily; Nov–Feb: 9am–4pm daily. ● public hols. & W www.state.il.us/HPA/hs/Capitol.htm

Southern Illinois ❺

🚌 ℹ️ 501 W DeYoung St, Marion, (618) 998-9397.
W www.adventureillinois.com

I N SOUTHERN Illinois, flat farm-lands give way to rolling hills and forests along the Mississippi and Ohio Rivers. This terrain provided strategic vantage points from which Native Americans and, later, French traders and missionaries could monitor river traffic.

Near the confluence of the Mississippi, Missouri, and Illinois Rivers (90 miles/145 km southwest of Springfield) are the remains of the largest prehistoric Native American city north of Mexico. The **Cahokia Mounds State Historic and World Heritage Site** contains more than 100 earthen mounds dating from 1050–1250, when 15,000 people of the Mississippian culture are estimated to have occupied the city. The flat-topped Monks Mound covers 14 acres (6 ha) and rises, in four terraces, to a height of 100 ft (30 m), providing sweeping views of the nearby river valleys and the Gateway Arch (see p454), about 12 miles (19 km) away in downtown St. Louis. The site's interpretive center recounts the fascinating story of these mounds, which were mysteriously abandoned by around 1500.

Further evidence of Native American habitation is abundant in the rugged, unglaciated "Illinois Ozarks," or "Little Egypt" region, where the Ohio River separates the state from Kentucky. The forested ridges and hollows of the sprawling **Shawnee National Forest** can be viewed most dramatically at the Garden of the Gods, a rocky outcropping marked by sandstone towers, boulders, and strangely shaped rocks.

🏛 Cahokia Mounds State Historic Site
30 Ramey Dr, Collinsville. 📞 (618) 346-5160. ⊙ 8am–sunset daily. **Visitor Center** ⊙ 9am–5pm. ● public hols. &
W www.cahokiamounds.com

Grass-covered mounds in the Cahokia Mounds State Historic Site

Indiana

UNLIKE THE OTHER STATES of the Great Lakes region, Indiana has only a short, 45-mile (72-km) stretch of shoreline along Lake Michigan. As a result, the state's history has centered on its extensive river systems – the Maumee/Wabash in the north, and the Ohio in the south – and the development of the railroads and highways that linked Indiana to key Midwestern and Eastern markets. Indiana today is an engaging place to explore by car, especially along its hilly Ohio River backroads and Amish-country scenic lanes.

New Harmony ❻

🏠 800. ℹ️ Atheneum, North & Arthur Sts, (800) 231-2168.

AMERICA'S TWO most successful utopian communities flourished in this neat village on the eastern banks of the Wabash River. The first, the Harmonie Society, was founded by a Pennsylvania-based German Lutheran separatist group in 1814. The sect followed a doctrine of perfectionism and celibacy in anticipation of the second coming of Christ, focusing on the development of profitable agricultural and manufacturing enterprises.

In 1825, the Harmonists returned to Pennsylvania, after selling the town and the surrounding lands to Scottish textile magnate Robert Owen. The latter, too, sought to create an ideal society based on free education and the abolition of social classes and personal property ownership. The colony failed after two years, but Owen's sons, David and Robert, pursued their father's ideas and later established the Smithsonian Institution in Washington, DC.

The tree-lined town is now a State Historic Site with 25 well-preserved Harmonist buildings, an inn, and many beautiful manicured gardens. These include the reconstructed Labyrinth, a maze-like set of hedges arranged in concentric circles around a stone temple that stands at the center.

🏛 Historic New Harmony
410 Main St. 📞 (812) 682-4488.
⭕ Mar–Dec daily, call for times.
📷 ♿ 🆆 www.newharmony.org

Monroe County Courthouse, Bloomington, a Beaux Arts building

Bloomington ❼

🏠 60,600. ✈ 🚌 ℹ️ 2855 N Walnut St, (800) 800-0037.
🆆 www.visitbloomington.com

SURROUNDED BY rugged limestone outcrops, this city is home to the leafy Indiana University campus. Quarrying of the limestone deposits fueled Bloomington's 19th-century growth, the results of which can still be seen in the city's magnificent public buildings. A prime example is the 1906 Beaux Arts **Monroe County Courthouse**, at the center of the Courthouse Square Historic District located downtown.

On the campus are a variety of historic buildings and outdoor spaces. The 1941 Auditorium displays 20 panels of Thomas Hart Benton's controversial 1933 mural,

The Social and Industrial History of Indiana, which ironically relates several key events of the state's history. The **Indiana University Art Center** was designed by architect I.M. Pei. It includes works by Henri Matisse, Claude Monet, Auguste Rodin, and Andy Warhol, as well as Picasso's 1934 *L'Atelier (The Studio)* and Stuart Davis's 1938 *Swing Landscape*, a mural inspired by the 1920s jazz age.

🏛 Indiana University Art Center
1133 7th St. 📞 (812) 855-5445.
⭕ 10am–5pm Tue–Sat, noon–5pm Sun. ⚫ public hols. ♿
🆆 www.indiana.edu/~iuam

Indiana Dunes National Lakeshore ❽

ℹ️ Dorothy Buell Memorial Visitor Center, 1100 N Mineral Springs Rd, Porter. 📞 (219) 926-7561.
⭕ Jun–Aug: 8am–6pm daily; Sep–May: 8am–5pm daily. ⚫ Jan 1, Thanksgiving, Dec 25. 📷 ♿
🆆 www.nps.gov/indu

ONE OF THE nation's most diverse groups of ecosystems is contained within the 15,000-acre (6,070-ha) Indiana Dunes National Lakeshore. Only a 30-minute drive from downtown Chicago, this stunning refuge is located along the 25-mile (40-km) stretch of the Lake Michigan shore. Its ecosystems include bogs, swamps, marshes, glacial moraines, prairies, forests, oak savannas, and dunes linked by scenic roads and a network of hiking and biking trails. Home to a dizzying variety of native plant

Deer at the Indiana Dunes National Lakeshore

species, the park is also known as a bird-watcher's paradise as herons, cardinals, kingfishers, and towhees are frequently spotted here.

South Bend ⑨

🏛 107,789. ✈ 🚉 🚌 ℹ 401 E Colfax Ave, (800) 828-7881.
🌐 www.livethelegends.com

SOUTH BEND is widely known today as the home of the Roman Catholic **University of Notre Dame**. The 10,800-student institution was established in 1842 by Father Edward Sorin, a priest from the Congregation of the Holy Cross.

While religion is still important, the students and countless alumni are equally passionate about the Notre Dame "Fighting Irish" football team, one of the most successful in college football history. In fact, one of the most famous sculptures at the art-filled campus is a large mural of Christ known as *The Word of Life* that students call "Touchdown Jesus."

The **College Football Hall of Fame** relates the history of such legends as coaches Knute Rockne and Ara Parseghian, and players George Gipp, Paul Hornung, and Joe Montana. Extensive displays are enlivened by a playful exhibit on cheerleaders, bands, and mascots. A 360-degree theater literally surrounds visitors with its range of historical film and video highlights.

South of downtown, the **Studebaker National Museum** contains the horse-drawn carriages and early automobiles manufactured by the town's now-defunct Studebaker corporation. The collection includes the carriage in which President Lincoln rode to Ford's Theatre the night he was assassinated in Washington, DC, and a 1909 backward-forward automobile that shuttled US senators between their offices and the Capitol.

"Touchdown Jesus" mural at Notre Dame, South Bend

🏛 College Football Hall of Fame

111 S St Joseph. 📞 (800) 440-3263.
🕐 10am–5pm. ⬤ Jan 1, Thanksgiving, Dec 25. 📷 ♿
🌐 www.collegefootball.org

Shipshewana ⑩

🏛 525. 🚌 ℹ 440 1/2 S Van Buren St, (800) 254-8090.
🌐 www.backroads.org

THIS SMALL VILLAGE, nestled in the rolling farmlands of northeastern Indiana, has one of the world's largest Amish communities *(see p109)*. The town's **Menno-Hof Mennonite Anabaptist Interpretive Center** provides a detailed background on the European Anabaptist movement, which gave rise to the Mennonite, Hutterite, and Amish sects. Religious persecution in the 19th century led to the large-scale immigration of Anabaptists to the US and Canada. Exhibits at the center re-create this dark period. The town also has the Midwest's largest open-air flea market.

Local Amish farmers, with their distinctive black hats, white shirts, and black suits, riding horse-drawn buggies, are frequent sights in Shipshewana and the surrounding villages of Bristol, Elkhart, Goshen, Middlebury, Nappanee, and Wakarusa. Tourists come to the villages in search of furniture, dairy, baked goods, and quilts.

Amish horse-drawn carriage

🏛 Menno-Hof Mennonite Anabaptist Interpretive Center

Rte 5. 📞 (260) 768-4117.
🕐 Apr–Dec: 10am–5pm Mon–Sat, noon–4pm Tue–Fri; Jan–Mar: 10am–5pm Sat. ⬤ Jan 1, Thanksgiving, Dec 25. 📷 ♿
🌐 www.mennohof.org

Fort Wayne ⑪

🏛 230,000. ✈ 🚌 ℹ 1021 S Calhoun St, (800) 767-7752.
🌐 www.visitfortwayne.com

FORT WAYNE'S location at the confluence of the St. Mary's, St. Joseph, and Maumee Rivers made it a strategic site for the Native Americans, French fur traders, British armies, and American settlers who sought to control the access to the Great Lakes. The city's prosperity during the railroad era is exemplified in the fascinating downtown Allen County Courthouse, constructed in 1902.

Although Abraham Lincoln had no personal connection with Fort Wayne, the city boasts one of the nation's finest collections of Lincoln memorabilia. Besides displays on the president's life and achievements, the **Lincoln Museum** has the distinction of possessing more than 300 original Lincoln documents.

🏛 Lincoln Museum

200 E Berry St. 📞 (260) 455-3864.
🕐 10am–5pm Tue–Sat, 1–5pm Sun.
⬤ Mon, Jan 1, Easter, Thanksgiving, Dec 25. 📷 ♿
🌐 www.thelincolnmuseum.org

A view of the Allen County Courthouse in Fort Wayne

A view of the architecture of modern Indianapolis

Indianapolis ⑫

🏛 860, 500. ✈ 🚌 🚆 ℹ 201 S
Capitol Ave, (800) 958-4639.
ⓦ www.indy.org

K NOWN AS "The Crossroads
of America," Indianapolis
is much more than a transportation hub where multiple
railroads and Interstate Highways intersect. The city's
many parks and monuments,
and vibrant in-town neighborhoods make it one of the
region's most surprising and
satisfying destinations.

Selected as the state capital
in 1820, Indianapolis was laid
out on the banks of the
shallow White River, with a
network of wide boulevards
radiating outward from the
central **Monument Circle**.
Today, this is downtown's
main gathering point, dominated by the towering 1901
Beaux Arts obelisk, the Soldiers' and Sailors' Monument.

The city's first-rate museums
and lively arts and theater
scenes are complemented
by an active interest in sports.
Every Memorial Day, the
world's largest, single-day
sporting event – the Indianapolis 500 auto race – fills the
**Indianapolis Motor Speed-
way** with nearly 400,000 fans.
Built in 1909 as a 2.5-mile
(4-km) test track for the city's
then-burgeoning automotive
industry, the speedway
played host to the first Indy
500 in 1911. The race was the
brainchild of Indianapolis
auto parts manufacturer Carl
Fisher, who later gained fame
as the tireless promoter of the
Lincoln Hwy (now US 30),
the nation's first transcontinental highway, from New

York to San Francisco. The
track's Hall of Fame displays
more than 75 racing cars and
other Indy 500 memorabilia,
in addition to examples of the
Stutz, Cole, Marmon, National, and Duesenberg automobiles built in the city before
the industry centralized in
Detroit. Visitors can also take
a guided test drive around
the famous track.

The five-story **Children's
Museum of Indianapolis**,
which opened in 1976, has
been consistently rated as one
of the country's best. The
museum's 10 galleries and
over 100,000 artifacts are
displayed in a manner that
encourages hands-on,
interactive exploration of the
sciences, history, world
cultures, and the arts. Among
the many highlights here are
an authentic Indy 500 race
car, a restored carousel, and
a dinosaur discovery exhibit,
where children work along
side practicing paleontologists
to excavate ancient fossils.

The **Indiana State
Museum** relocated in early

**Display in the Indianapolis Motor
Speedway Hall of Fame**

2002 to a brand-new facility
west of downtown in White
River State Park, a 250-acre
(101-ha) urban oasis. The
spacious new building is
constructed of locally sourced
materials, including Indiana
limestone, sandstone, brick,
steel, extruded aluminum,
and glass. Focusing on
Indiana's natural and cultural
history, the museum displays
extensive exhibits on sports
and the early days of radio in
this predominantly rural state.

Lockerbie Square District,
northeast of downtown, is the
city's oldest surviving 19th-
century immigrant neighborhood. Immortalized in the
poetry of resident James
Whitcomb Riley (1849–1916),
the square has attracted
recent attention for the
dogged efforts to preserve its
modest workers' cottages and
restore its cobblestone streets
and period street lights.
Riley's 1872 brick Italianate
home is now a museum,
displaying many of the
writer's books, furniture,
and personal items.

Situated on the grounds of
the Oldfields estate of local
pharmaceutical pioneer, J.K.
Lilly Jr, 5 miles (8 km) north
of downtown, the **Indi-
anapolis Museum of Art**
houses a wide-ranging
collection of American,
European, Asian, and African
art. Among the museum's
more acclaimed holdings are
Winslow Homer's *The Boat
Builders*, Edward Hopper's
Hotel Lobby, Georgia
O'Keeffe's *Jimson Weed*, and
many of Paul Gauguin's
works from his 1886 visit to
the French artists' colony of
Pont-Aven.

The restored Oldfields-Lilly
house and superb gardens,
designed by Percival Gal-
lagher of the famed Olmsted
Brothers landscape architecture firm, have been carefully
restored to their original 1920s
grandeur. The house and
gardens are open for tours.

The **Eiteljorg Museum of
American Indians and
Western Art**, west of
downtown, has one of the
most impressive collections of
Native American and Western
American art in the US.

George Carlson's *The Greeting* (1989) outside Eiteljorg Museum

Established in 1989 by Harrison Eiteljorg, a successful Indianapolis businessman and art collector, the museum is housed in a Southwest-inspired adobe building, in deference to Eiteljorg's large collection of works from the early 20th-century Taos Society of Artists *(see p544)*, who incorporated Native American, Western American, and Hispanic themes into their work.

On view are paintings by such celebrated artists as Georgia O'Keeffe, Frederic Remington, and Charles M. Russell, whose *Indians Crossing the Plains* is a famous depiction of vanishing Native American culture on the late 19th-century Great Plains. Many Native American artifacts are also displayed.

🏛 Indianapolis Motor Speedway
Hall of Fame, 4790 W 16th St.
🄲 *(317) 492-6784.* ☐ *9am–5pm daily.* ⬤ *Dec 25.* 🄰 🄳
🅆 www.brickyard.com

🏛 Indianapolis Museum of Art
1200 W 38th St. 🄲 *(317) 923-1331.*
☐ *10am–5pm Tue–Sat, 5–8:30pm Thu, noon–5pm Sun.* ⬤ *Jan 1, Thanksgiving, Dec 25.* 🄰 🄳
🅆 www.ima-art.org

🏛 Eiteljorg Museum of American Indians & Western Art
500 W Washington St. 🄲 *(317) 636-9378.* ☐ *Sep–Jun: 10am–5pm Mon–Sat, noon–5pm Sun; Jul–Aug: 10am–5pm Tue–Sat, noon–5pm Sun.*
⬤ *Sep–May: Mon, Jan 1, Thanksgiving, Dec 24–25.* 🄰 🄳
🅆 www.eiteljorg.org

Columbus ⑬

🏯 *39,000.* 🚌 🛈 *506 5th St, (800) 468-6564.* 🅆 www.columbus.in.us

ONE OF THE world's most concentrated collections of modern architecture can be found in this small southern Indiana city. From 1942 on, after the completion of architect Eliel Saarinen's **First Christian Church,** Columbus garnered international attention for the more than 60 churches, schools, banks, and commercial and public buildings constructed here. Today, the city's commitment to high-quality design has resulted in Columbus being ranked sixth on the American Institute of Architects list of cities marked by innovation in architecture and design.

A philanthropic foundation endowed by the city's largest employer, Cummins Engine, attracted some of the world's most distinguished architects. Among those who left their stamp on the city environment are Robert Trent Jones, Richard Meier, Robert Venturi, Alexander Girard, and I.M. Pei, whose 1969 Cleo Rodgers Memorial Library is at 536 5th Street. The **Columbus Architecture Tours** allow visitors to catch a glimpse of these architectural delights.

🏛 Columbus Architecture Tours
506 5th St. 🄲 *(800) 468-6564.*
☐ *Mar–Nov 30: Mon–Sat.*
⬤ *Sun, Dec–Feb.* 🄼 *call for tour times.* 🄰 🄳

Ohio River Valley ⑭

🛈 *301 E Main St, (800) 559-2956.*
🅆 www.visitmadison.org

FROM INDIANA'S eastern border with Ohio, Routes 56 and 156 follow the serpentine Ohio River for nearly 80 miles (129 km) as it winds lazily through the river towns of Rising Sun, Patriot, Florence, and Vevey. These highways are the best way to explore both the river valley and the southern hill country.

The antebellum river port of **Madison,** 90 miles (145 km) southeast of Indianapolis, is one of the best-preserved towns on the river. Many of its residential and commercial buildings have benefited from a generous grant from the National Trust for Historic Preservation. The town's architectural charms include the Greek Revival **Lanier Mansion,** built in 1844 for railroad magnate James Lanier, and the Shrewsbury-Windle House, an 1849 riverboat entrepreneur's home featuring an elegant, free-standing circular staircase. Downtown is the restored 19th-century office of progressive frontier physician Dr. William D. Hutchings.

🏛 Lanier Mansion State Historic Site
511 W 1st St Madison. 🄲 *(812) 265-3526.* ☐ *Apr–Dec: 9am–5pm Tue–Sat, 1–5pm Sun; Jan–Mar: group tours by appointment only.*
⬤ *public hols, except Memorial Day, Jul 4, Labor Day.*

Exterior of Eliel Saarinen's First Christian Church (1942), Columbus

Ohio

O HIO IS A STUDY IN CONTRASTS. As one of the nation's largest agricultural producers, the state is dotted with picturesque farmland, small towns steeped in history, and more recently settled Amish areas where horse-drawn buggies and barns are a thing of the present. Ohio also contains several of the country's most urbanized industrial centers along the Ohio River – the state's southern and eastern border – and in port cities that lie along the shores of Lake Erie.

Art Deco façade of the Union Terminal, Cincinnati

Cincinnati **⑮**

🏛 *331, 285.* ✈ 🚉 🚌 ℹ *300 W 6th St, (800) 246-2987.*
W www.cincyusa.com

B UILT ON A series of steep hills overlooking the Ohio River, Cincinnati was once called "Porkopolis" for its rank slaughterhouses and belching factories. Later, its winding side streets and stunning views from the hilltop Mount Adams neighborhood inspired British prime minister Winston Churchill to call it "the most beautiful of America's inland cities." The city is today a vibrant corporate center with a revitalized riverfront entertainment and parks district.

Cincinnati's location at the intersection of the Erie Canal and the Miami and Ohio Rivers, and its strategic perch on the border of the slave-holding South and the industrializing North made it a heterogeneous cultural and commercial crossroads. Many prominent locals, including writer Harriet Beecher Stowe, whose home is now a state historic site, strongly supported the anti-slavery movement. The recently opened (summer 2004) **National Underground Railroad Freedom Center**, focuses on the city's one-time heroic past.

Cincinnati's most celebrated landmark is the 1867 stone and steel suspension bridge, built by Brooklyn Bridge engineer John A. Roebling to link this city with Covington, Kentucky, across the Ohio River. Another landmark is the vaulting 1933 Art Deco **Union Terminal**, west of downtown. The refurbished terminal now houses a complex of superb museums such as the Cincinnati History Museum and its re-creation of the 1850s waterfront, which is complete with a paddlewheeler.

On the eastern part of town, the **Cincinnati Art Museum** overlooks Eden Park. The museum's extensive collections include Roman, Greek, Egyptian, Asian, and African artifacts. Among its exhibits of contemporary art is a specially commissioned portrait by Andy Warhol of the controversial Cincinnati Reds baseball great, Pete Rose.

🏛 The Cincinnati Art Museum
953 Eden Park Dr. 📞 *(513) 721-5204.* ⏱ *11am–5pm Tue–Sat, 5–9pm Wed, noon–6pm Sun.* ● *Thanksgiving, Dec 25.* 🎟 🚹
W www.cincinnatiartmuseum.org

Dayton **⑯**

🏛 *201,134.* ✈ 🚌 ℹ *1 Chamber Plaza, Suite A, (800) 221-8235.*
W www.daytoncvb.com

T HIS PLEASANT city on the Great Miami River is known as the "Birthplace of Aviation." It was here that aviation pioneers, Wilbur and Orville Wright *(see p250)*, carried out much of their research and experimentation, which led to their successful flight in 1903 in Kitty Hawk, North Carolina. Five miles northeast lies the new Dayton Aviation Heritage Center at the spot where the brothers tested their second and third aircraft in 1904 and 1905. The **Carillon Historical Park** contains the Wright *Flyer III* aircraft – the first capable of executing a turn. Over 300 aircraft and missiles from the post-Wright aviation era are also displayed at the **United States Air Force Museum** that lies nearby.

Overlooking the Great Miami River, the Italian Renaissance-style **Dayton Art Institute** features a large collection of European and American paintings, such as Claude Monet's *Waterlilies* and Edward Hopper's *High Noon*.

🚌 Carillon Historical Park
1000 Carillon Blvd. 📞 *(937) 293-2841.* ⏱ *Apr–Oct: 9:30am–5pm Tue–Sat, noon–5pm Sun & public hols.* 🎟 🚹 W www.carillonpark.org

🏛 Dayton Art Institute
456 Belmonte Park N. 📞 *(800) 296-4426.* ⏱ *10am–4pm daily, 10am–8 pm Thu.*
W www.daytonartinstitute.org

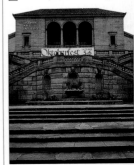

Italian Renaissance-style Dayton Art Institute, Dayton

The 1,348-ft (411-m) Serpent Mound

Serpent Mound ⑰

3850 Rte 73, Peebles. 【 (800) 752-2757. 【 Memorial Day–Labor Day: 10am–8pm daily; Labor Day–Memorial Day: 10am–4pm daily. ● Jan 1, Thanksgiving, Dec 25. 🎫 ♿

THE LARGEST serpent-shaped effigy mound in the US, the 1,348-ft (411-m) long Serpent Mound overlooks Brush Creek in the Ohio River Valley. Although its exact age is unknown, research suggests that the mound was constructed between 800 BC and AD 400 by the ancient Adena people, Ohio's earliest farming Native American community.

The 5-ft (1.5-m) high, 20-ft (6-m) wide mound appears to represent an uncoiling serpent, with a tightly coiled tail at one end and a mouth-like opening, swallowing an oval-shaped egg, at the other. An on-site museum describes the mound's history and its protection under an 1888 law, the first in the US to safeguard important archeological sites.

Hopewell Culture National Historic Park ⑱

16062 Rte 104, Chillocothe. 【 (740) 774-1125. ◐ 8:30am–5pm daily. ● Jan 1, Thanksgiving, Dec 25. 🎫 ♿ W www.nps.gov

LOCATED IN THE Scioto River Valley, this 120-acre (48-ha) park preserves 23 Native American burial mounds built by the Hopewell tribes who lived here from 200 BC to AD 500. The Hopewell culture, which emerged from the Adena culture, covers a broad network of beliefs and practices among different Native groups spread over eastern US. As characteristic of the culture, the mounds are arranged in geometric shapes, ringed by an earthen wall. A visitor center provides an in-depth look at the social and economic life of the long-vanished Hopewell peoples, based on the archeological work conducted here.

Columbus ⑲

🏛 632,900. ✈ 🚉 🚌 🛈 90 N High St, (614) 221-6623, (800) 354-2657. W www.visitcolumbus.org

OHIO'S CAPITAL since 1816, Columbus has grown from a sleepy, swampy lowland site on the east bank of the Scioto River to become a bustling cultural, political, and economic center. Today, the city supports a thriving arts scene, with a superb symphony and ballet, in addition to revitalized historic neighborhoods and entertainment districts. Downtown's central feature is the Greek-Revival style **Ohio Statehouse**. Built between 1839 and 1861, the structure is surmounted by a large drum-shaped cupola marked by a 29-ft (9-m) wide skylight.

The **Ohio Historical Center** is the best place to begin the exploration of Columbus. Its interactive displays trace Ohio's evolution from an 18th century frontier outpost to its current urban and industrial status. Permanent exhibits detail the origin of the city's fine public architecture and parklands, dating from its 1890s fascination with the City Beautiful Movement.

The **Franklin Park Conservatory and Botanical Garden**, built in 1895, has a bonsai and sculpture garden. It also has indoor simulations of exotic climates, and a Pacific Island water garden.

🏛 **Ohio Historical Center**
1982 Velma Ave. 【 (614) 297-2300. ◐ 9am–5pm Tue–Sat, noon–5pm Sun; call for special Dec hours. ● Jan 1, Thanksgiving, Dec 25. 🎫 ♿

� **Franklin Park Conservatory & Botanical Garden**
1777 E Broad St. 【 (614) 645-8733. ◐ 10am–5pm Tue–Sun, 10am–8pm 1st Wed. ● Jan 1, Thanksgiving, Dec 25. 🎫 ♿

Berlin ⑳

🏛 3,100. 🚌 🛈 35 N Monroe St, Millersburg, (330) 674-3975.

MUCH OF Ohio's large Amish population is concentrated in Holmes County in the north-central part of the state, about 90 miles (145 km) northeast of Columbus. Lying just outside Berlin village, **Schrock's Amish Farm** provides a good overview of the reclusive Amish, who have maintained

Amish quilt patterns on display

their simplified 19th-century way of life. The farm has a multimedia visitor center and offers a tour of a working farm, complete with freshly baked goods and buggy rides.

Visitors are requested to drive carefully along the rural backroads and busier thoroughfares, out of respect for the dark-attired Amish farmers and their slow-moving, horse-drawn carriages.

Schrock's Amish Farm
4363 SR 39. 【 (330) 893-2951. ◐ Apr–Oct:10am–5pm Mon–Fri, 10am–6pm Sat. 🎫 ♿

Sculpture in Franklin Park Conservatory and Botanical Garden

View of the Cleveland skyline from The Flats, the city's nightlife zone

Cleveland ㉑

🏠 505,600. ✈ 🚇 🚌
🛈 Terminal Tower, Suite 3100,
50 Public Square, (800) 321-1001.
🌐 www.travelcleveland.com

Hard-working Cleveland has re-invented itself and is now a role model for other Great Lakes cities seeking to revitalize their urban cores while celebrating their industrial pasts. Founded in 1796 by speculator Moses Cleaveland, the city evolved from a frontier town into a bustling commercial port in 1832, when the Ohio and Erie Canal linked Cleveland to the Ohio River.

Cleveland's steel industry was born after the Civil War, when railroads linked the city with Minnesota's Iron Range and the coalfields of western Pennsylvania. The industry thrived in the early 1900s, catering to the Detroit automobile industry's demand for easily transported steel. After World War II, however, the city's fortunes faded as industries moved away, leaving behind vast polluted landscapes and scores of unemployed workers.

Cleveland's "Rust Belt" image is today a thing of the past. The city now encompasses 19,000 acres (7,689 ha) of pristine parkland, while its downtown riverfront industrial zone is a bustling entertainment district, **The Flats**.

A signature feature since 1927, the 52-story Beaux Arts **Terminal Tower**, was designed as a "city within a city." It made maximum use of vertical space, squeezing an office building, railroad station, and hotel into its confines. The 42nd-floor observation deck offers grand views of the city and, on a clear day, one can see the Canadian shoreline.

The 1995 **Rock and Roll Hall of Fame and Museum** on the Lake Erie waterfront in downtown, put Cleveland at center stage of the nation's entertainment scene. The massive 150,000-sq-ft (13,935-sq-m) I.M. Pei-designed Hall traces the development of the musical genre, beginning with its roots in the Mississippi Delta blues (see pp360–61) and Appalachian string bands. On display are memorabilia ranging from Chuck Berry's Gibson electric guitar to a Cub Scout shirt worn by Jim Morrison. To its west, the **Great Lakes Science Center** uses interactive exhibits to stimulate public interest in the fragile ecosystem of the Great Lakes region.

Cleveland's principal cultural attractions lie about 4 miles (6 km) east of downtown, around University Circle. Surrounding this expanse of parkland near the Case Western Reserve University campus are a series of early 20th-century buildings that now contain several fine museums. Among them is the **Cleveland Museum of Art**, with its superb collection of ancient Egyptian relics and pre-Columbian artifacts. Its European painting collection includes such masterpieces as Renoir's *Mother and Child* and Van Gogh's *Landscape with Wheelbarrow*. Facing this museum, the city's popular **Botanical Garden** features 4 acres (1.6 ha) of outdoor gardens, as well as a Japanese garden and a peace garden.

🏛 Rock and Roll Hall of Fame & Museum
1 Key Plaza. 📞 (216) 515-1945.
◯ Jun–Sep: 10am–5:30pm Mon–Tue, Thu–Fri & Sun, 5,30–9pm Wed & Sat; Oct–May: 10am–5:30pm Mon–Tue & Thu–Sun, 5:30–9pm Wed. ● Thanksg., Dec 25. 🎟 ♿
🌐 www.rockhall.com

🏛 Cleveland Museum of Art
11150 East Blvd. 📞 (216) 421-7340.
◯ 10am–5pm Tue, Thu & Sat–Sun, 5–9pm Wed & Fri. ● Mon, Jan 1, Jul 4, Thanksgiving, Dec 25. ♿
🌐 www.clevelandart.org

ENVIRONS: Located 25 miles (40 km) west of Cleveland, **Oberlin** is home to Oberlin College, one of the first to admit African-American and female students. The Allen Memorial Art Museum on campus displays American, Asian, and European art.

The steel manufacturing center **Canton** 60 miles (96 km) south of Cleveland, is famed for the Pro Football Hall of Fame.

The Rock and Roll Hall of Fame and Museum in downtown Cleveland

Perry's Victory Memorial at Put-in-Bay, Lake Erie Islands

Lake Erie Islands ㉒

🏕 ⓘ *770 SE Catawba Rd, Port Clinton, (800) 441-1271.*
ⓦ *www.lake-erie.com*

LOCATED JUST offshore from the Marblehead Peninsula separating Sandusky Bay from Lake Erie, the Lake Erie Islands are a prime summer tourist destination. The islands include the bucolic, peaceful Kelleys Island and the rowdier South Bass Island, with the village of Put-in-Bay as its lively nightlife center.

Home of the Erie, Ottawa, and Huron Indian tribes until the 19th century, the Lake Erie Islands rose to national prominence during the War of 1812. On September 10, 1813, US Navy Commodore Oliver Hazard Perry defeated the more heavily fortified British fleet in the pivotal Battle of Lake Erie, fought off South Bass Island. A new visitor center and a 352-ft (107-m) granite column at Put-in-Bay, **Perry's Victory and International Peace Memorial**, commemorates his victory and his famous message to US General William Henry Harrison: "We have met the enemy and they are ours."

Kelleys Island State Park has the fascinating Glacial Grooves, a series of deep limestone grooves caused by the movement of a heavy glacial wall. These grooves have been protected from quarrying since 1923.

Short ferry rides from nearby Sandusky, Port Clinton, and Marblehead are available. The Marblehead Lighthouse, built in 1821, is a popular regional icon.

♛ Perry's Victory & International Peace Memorial
93 Delaware Ave, Put-in-Bay, S Bass Island. ⓘ *(419) 285-2184.* ○ *mid-Jun–Sep: 10am–7pm daily; mid-Apr–mid-Jun & Sep–Oct: 10am–5pm; by appointment rest of year.* 🅟 ♿
ⓦ *www.nps.gov/pevi*

♣ Kelleys Island State Park
Kelleys Island. ⓘ *(419) 797-4530.* ○ *Apr–Nov: sunrise–sunset.* ♿
ⓦ *www.dnr.state.oh.us/parks/lakeerie.htm*

Sandusky ㉓

🏕 *29,800.* 🚇 🚌 ⛴ ⓘ *4424 Milan Rd, Sandusky, (800) 255-3743.*
ⓦ *www.visitohio.com*

SANDUSKY WAS once one of the Great Lakes' largest coal-shipping ports. Today, its ferry terminal provides easy access to many of the Lake Erie Islands. The city is, however, best known for the 364-acre (147-ha) **Cedar Point Amusement Park**, one of the busiest summer tourist spots in the Midwest. The park claims to have the world's largest collection of roller coasters, ranging from rickety old wooden ones to the high-speed Magnum, Millennium Force, and Top Thrill Dragster. Cedar Point also includes a water park, the children-centered Camp Snoopy, an ice show, and a sandy Lake Erie beach.

🎢 Cedar Point Amusement Park
One Cedar Point Dr. ⓘ *(800) 237-8386.* ○ *early May–Labor Day: 10am–sunset daily; Labor Day–end of Oct: 10am–sunset Sat–Sun.* 🅟 ♿
ⓦ *www.cedarpoint.com*

Toledo ㉔

🏕 *332,900.* ✈ 🚇 🚌 ⓘ *401 Jefferson Ave, (800) 243-4667.*
ⓦ *www.toledoohionow.com*

ONE OF THE world's leading glass manufacturing centers and the third busiest Great Lakes port, Toledo occupies a Maumee River site steeped in history. The 1794 Battle of Fallen Timbers that took place nearby opened northwestern Ohio and Indiana to white settlement. The area was also a strategic one during the War of 1812. The reconstructed Fort Meigs, about 10 miles (16 km) south of Toledo in Perrysburg, commemorates the stockade that withstood two British and Native American sieges in 1813.

Today, the city is famed for the **Toledo Museum of Art**, a Neo-Classical marble structure in the historic Old West End founded by local glass tycoon Edward Drummond Libbey. In addition to Egyptian, Greek, Roman, and medieval exhibits, the museum features one of the world's largest collections of ornamental glass. Some of the best pieces are an oversized punch bowl crafted by Libbey's firm, and *Vitrano*, a colorful 1969 glass sculpture by Dominick Labino. Adjoining the main gallery is a sand castle-like structure by architect Frank Gehry. The building is now used for fine art classes at the School of Art and Design.

🏛 Toledo Museum of Art
2445 Monroe St. ⓘ *(419) 255-8000.* ○ *10am–4pm Tue–Sat, 4–10pm Fri, 11am–5pm Sun.* ● *public hols.* 🅟 ♿
ⓦ *www.toledo-museum.org*

A roller-coaster ride at Cedar Point Amusement Park, Sandusky

Michigan

THIS INLAND STATE HAS A rich maritime history. Michigan's principal land mass, the so-called Lower Peninsula, is a mitten-shaped area surrounded by the four Great Lakes – Michigan, Superior, Huron, and Erie. This landmass contains the largest cities, including Detroit, and accounts for most of Michigan's industry and population. In the 19th century, the Lower Peninsula, with its wind-blown dunes and rolling cherry orchards, was a prime destination. The rugged Upper Peninsula to the northwest only became part of the state in 1834. More recently, the Upper Peninsula's fine scenic views have also made it a popular tourist getaway.

Crowds enjoying the annual jazz festival in Detroit's Hart Plaza

Detroit ㉕

🏙 951,270. ✈ 🚃 🚌
ℹ 211 W Fort St, (800) 338-7648.
ⓦ www.visitdetroit.com

KNOWN TODAY AS the "Motor City," Detroit (meaning "the Strait" in French) was founded in 1701 by the French fur trader Antoine de la Mothe Cadillac. The city has since evolved from a shipbuilding center into a leading manufacturer of railroad equipment, cars, and bicycles. Its massive industrial growth, however, took place after Henry Ford began manufacturing automobiles in Detroit in 1896. By the 1920s, most American automobile manufacturers – Ford, General Motors, Pontiac, and Chrysler – had moved their headquarters and production facilities to the city.

The automobile industry still dominates Detroit. A confusing web of highways fan out from the city's revitalized downtown. The city's present focal point is the huge riverfront **Renaissance Center**, General Motors' current headquarters. Nearby, **Hart Plaza** hosts summer riverfront festivals, including the Ford Detroit International Jazz Festival. Directly across, the 25-ft (8-m) Big Fist outdoor sculpture on Woodward Avenue, is a tribute to the local African-American boxer Joe Louis, known as "The Brown Bomber." East of downtown is the lively Greek neighborhood and restaurant district centered on Monroe Avenue. Northwest of downtown is the former General Motors Building, designed by Albert Kahn in 1922.

🏛 Charles H. Wright Museum of African American History

315 E Warren St. 📞 (313) 494- 5800. ⏱ 9:30am–5pm Wed–Sat, 1–5pm Sun. ⬤ public hols. ✍ ♿ ⓦ www.maah-detroit.org
Built in 1997, this center commemorates the contributions made by Detroit's large African-American population

to the city's commercial and cultural progress. It depicts the Middle Passage of enslaved Africans across the Atlantic, the Underground Railroad, the Civil Rights Movement, and other milestones in African-American history. The two main highlights are the door from the Birmingham, Alabama, jailhouse where Dr. Martin Luther King Jr. was imprisoned in the 1960s, and the flight suit worn by Mae Jemison, the first African-American NASA pilot, on her historic 1992 voyage on the Space Shuttle *Endeavour*.

🏛 The Detroit Institute of Arts

5200 Woodward Ave, Detroit Cultural Center. 📞 (313) 833-7900. ⏱ 10am–4pm Wed–Thu, 10am–9pm Fri, 10am–5pm Sat–Sun. ⬤ Mon–Tue. ✍ ⓦ www.dia.org
The museum's centerpiece is a monumental 27-panel mural by Mexico City artist Diego Rivera. His controversial *Detroit Industry* depicts the automobile manufacturing process in a stark way, reflecting the artist's Leftist views of the relationship between management and labor.

The museum's outstanding collections range from pre-Columbian, Native American, and African art to 17th-century Dutch and Flemish paintings. It has a large selection of 19th-century American paintings.

🏛 Detroit Historical Museum

Detroit Historical Museums & Society 5401 Woodward Ave. 📞 (313) 833-1805. ⏱ 9:30am–5pm Tue–Fri, 10am–5pm Sat–Sun. ✍ ♿ ⓦ www.detroithistorical.org
The recently renovated "Streets of Old Detroit" display as well as a permanent exhibit on Detroit's automotive heritage are the main features of this museum. Located in

Nymph and Eros, The Detroit Institute of Arts

the Detroit Cultural Corridor near Wayne State University, this museum is also the base of the Detroit Historical Society, which operates a series of sites across the city.

The society's **Historic Fort Wayne and Tuskegee Airmen Museum**, along the Detroit River on the city's southwest side, incorporates many of the surviving buildings from Fort Wayne, the last military bastion to defend the city. The society also operates the **Dossin Great Lakes Museum** in Belle Isle Park in the Detroit River. The focus here is the maritime history of the Great Lakes.

Exterior of Henry Ford Museum in Dearborn, a suburb of Detroit

�🏛 Motown Historical Museum

2648 W Grand Blvd. 📞 *(313) 875-2264.* 🕐 *10am–5pm Tue–Sat, noon–5pm Sun–Mon.* ⬤ *public hols.* 📷

During the early 1960s, the Motown record label revolutionized American popular music with its trademark "Motown Sound," which is a melodic blend of pop, soul, and rhythm and blues. The creative genius of label founder Berry Gordy Jr. and his stable of talented artists such as Marvin Gaye, Smokey

Robinson, Stevie Wonder, the Temptations, and Diana Ross and the Supremes are honored in this museum, housed in the original brick building where hit records such as "Heard It Through the Grapevine" and "Baby Love" were produced. The renovated building, called Hitsville USA by Gordy, has a good display of a wide range of old photographs, instruments, and recording equipment, including the original "Studio A" where the classic sounds were first created. Displays narrate the story of Motown as the singlemost successful independent African-American-controlled record label in the history of the country. Today this label is owned by the PolyGram Corporation.

ENVIRONS: The suburb of Dearborn, 8 miles (13 km) west of Detroit, is home to **The Henry Ford Museum and Greenfield Village**, one of the nation's most impressive collections of Americana. Within the complex is the Henry Ford Museum, which displays a range of vintage cars. The open-air Greenfield Village, on the other hand, exhibits Ford's eclectic collection of historical artifacts. These include diverse objects: a cot used by George Washington during the Revolutionary War; the chair in which Abraham Lincoln was shot; inventor Thomas Edison's laboratory; and the Dayton home and bicycle shop of aviation pioneers Orville and Wilbur Wright.

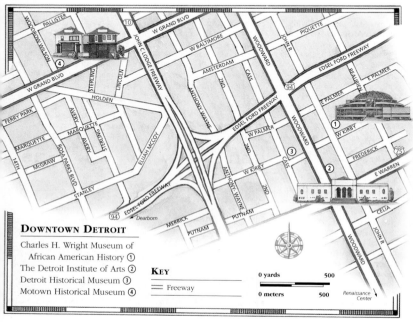

DOWNTOWN DETROIT

Charles H. Wright Museum of African American History ①
The Detroit Institute of Arts ②
Detroit Historical Museum ③
Motown Historical Museum ④

KEY

═ Freeway

0 yards   500

0 meters   500

Renaissance Center

University of Michigan campus, Ann Arbor

Ann Arbor ㉖

🏛 114, 000. ✕ 🚉 🚌
ℹ 120 W Huron St, (800) 888-9487.
🅦 www.annarbor.org

A PICTURESQUE, midsized city, with a vibrant pedestrian-friendly downtown, Ann Arbor is a bastion of laid-back liberalism and environmental activism on the western fringe of conservative Detroit. The city's independent streak springs from the professors and students affiliated with the **University of Michigan**, the city's largest employer.

Music, film, and art festivals are a year-round tradition. One of the nation's largest outdoor art fairs is held in the city. This annual July event attracts more than 1,000 artists and 500,000 art fans and dealers. Ann Arbor is also home to many new and used bookstores, including **Border's Books**, a global chain that began in 1973. Its downtown Liberty Street store is still the city's focal point.

The 2,800-acre (1,133-ha) Gothic central campus of the University of Michigan straddles Washtenaw Avenue, southeast of downtown. The **Kelsey Museum of Archaeology**, on the main campus, houses a variety of Greek, Roman, Egyptian, and Near Eastern artifacts from university-sponsored excavations over the past century.

Lansing ㉗

🏛 119,128. ✕ 🚉 🚌
ℹ 1223 Turner St, (888) 252-6746.

A GOVERNMENT and industrial center, this city benefits from its proximity to the Michigan State University in adjacent East Lansing. Selected as the state capital in 1847, the subsequent arrival of railroads in 1871 and the completion of the downtown statehouse in 1879 fueled the city's growth. The **Michigan Historical Museum** recounts the construction of the Second Renaissance Revival-style State Capitol and traces the state's history from the prehistoric era to the present through various interactive exhibits.

Lansing's status as a major automotive manufacturing center is linked to the business founded by Ransom E. Olds, who began building prototype vehicles here in 1885. He later produced the Curved Dash Olds, considered by many to have been the world's first mass-produced automobile. The **R.E. Olds Transportation Museum** has the distinction of showcasing an original 1901 Curved Dash Olds Runabout and a variety of classic Oldsmobiles from the 1930s and 1940s. General Motors now owns the Oldsmobile brand, and produces over 400,000 vehicles every year.

Exhibit from the Olds Museum

🏛 **R.E. Olds Transportation Museum**
240 Museum Dr. 📞 (517) 372-0422.
📷 ♿ ◷ 10am–5pm Tue–Sat, noon–5pm Sun. ● public hols.

Grand Rapids ㉘

🏛 197,800. ✕ 🚉 🚌 ℹ 134 Monroe Center NW, (877) 847-4847.
🅦 www.visitgrandrapids.org

G RAND RAPIDS owes its reputation as a major furniture manufacturing center to the Grand River that flows through the heart of the city. The water-powered lumber mills that were set up along its banks in the 19th century formed the foundation for the growth of fine furniture makers such as Herman Miller and Steelcase.

East of downtown is the fashionable **Heritage Hill Neighborhood**, where several of the city's industrial moguls once lived. Now a historic district, this area has many Tudor, Victorian, Italianate, and Spanish-style mansions. The stately 1895 **Voigt House Victorian Museum**, with its grand period furnishings, is now a museum, and the 1909 **Meyer May House** is one of Frank Lloyd Wright's last Prairie-style family homes.

Also in town is the **Gerald R. Ford Museum**. It traces the career of the 38th president, who grew up in Grand Rapids, where his father ran a paint and varnish company. The museum includes a holographic tour of the White House and a replica of the Oval Office.

🏛 **Voigt House Victorian Museum**
115 College Ave SE. 📞 (616) 456-4600. ◷ 11am–3pm Tue, 1–3pm 2nd & 4th Sun of month. 📷 ♿
🅦 www.grmuseum.org/voigt

Frank Lloyd Wright's 1909 Meyer May House in Grand Rapids

Hikers at Sleeping Bear Dunes Lakeshore, Lake Michigan Shore

Lake Michigan Shore ㉙

☒ ⛟ ℹ *950 28th St SE, Grand Rapids, (800) 442-2084.*

A MAJOR tourist destination since wealthy Chicagoans first came here in the late 1800s, Lake Michigan Shore is lined with sandy beaches, 19th-century resorts, working ports, and more than 25 scenic lighthouses. The resort town of South Haven makes an ideal base to explore the shore. In addition to its many recreational and dining attractions, the town's excellent **Michigan Maritime Museum** narrates the history of fishing, shipping, and ship-building on the Great Lakes.

Located 200 miles (322 km) to the north on US 31, **Sleeping Bear Dunes National Lakeshore** incorporates many ecosystems and its signature sand dunes, which tower some 460 ft (140 m) above the lakefront beaches and an inland lake. The park's ghost forest of sand-buried trees can be explored through hiking trails or a 7-mile (11-km) drive.

The busy resort of **Traverse City**, 25 miles (40 km) north of Sleeping Bear Dunes, is a convenient base to visit the picturesque Old Mission Peninsula. A short trip toward the north along Route 37 provides beautiful views of green rolling hills, cherry orchards, and the lake. At its tip stands the Old Mission Point Lighthouse, built in 1870. The white wooden

structure sits exactly on the 45th parallel, which is halfway between the Equator and the North Pole.

⛵ Sleeping Bear Dunes National Lakeshore
9922 Front St, Empire. ☏ *(213) 326-5154.* ⬯ *Park: year-round. Visitor Center: Jun–Sep: 9am–6pm daily; Oct–May: 9am–4pm daily.* ⬤ *Jan 1, Thanksgiving, Dec 25.* ⬯ ♿
w *www.nps.gov/slbe*

🏛 Michigan Maritime Museum
260 Dyckman Ave, South Haven. ☏ *(800) 747-3810.* ⬯ *Memorial Day–Labor Day:10am–5pm Mon–Sat, noon–5pm Sun.* ⬤ *Tue, Sep–May.* ⬯ ♿

Mackinac Island ㉚

🚶 *500.* ☒ ⛟ ℹ *Main St, (800) 454 5227.*
w *www.mackinacisland.org*

THE LIMESTONE OUTCROP of Mackinac Island, covering 6 sq miles (16 sq km), sits in the middle of the Straits of Mackinac, separating the Lower and Upper Peninsulas. Ferries that depart regularly from Mackinaw City and St. Ignace on the mainland are the only way to reach the island, where no cars are permitted. The principal landmark here is the 1887 **Grand Hotel** *(see p425)*, a classic Gilded Age summer resort that has the world's longest front porch at 660 ft (201 m). Fort Mackinac, overlooking the harbor, is in the **Mackinac Island State Park**. This restored fort commemorates the island's 18th-

century past as a French, British, and American military outpost through a variety of demonstrations as well as multimedia shows.

Upper Peninsula ㉛

☒ ⛟ ℹ *Iron Mountain, (800) 562-7134.* w *www.uptravel.com*
Soo Locks Boat Tours *Dock #1, 1157 E Portage Ave, Sault Ste. Marie.* ☏ *(800) 432-6301.* ⬯ *May 12–Oct 15; call for tour schedule.* ⬯ ♿
w *www.soolocks.com*

THE SPARSELY populated wilderness of the 384-mile (618-km) wide Upper Peninsula is dotted with old lumber, mining, and fishing towns, and some of Michigan's most striking natural attractions. Also called the "UP," this region was first explored by 17th-century French adventurers, one of whom, Etienne Brule, established Michigan's oldest community, **Sault Sainte Marie**, on its northeastern tip.

One of its most popular attractions, **Pictured Rocks National Lakeshore**, stretches along Lake Superior. Although accessible by car from Hwy 28, this 40-mile (64-km) stretch of beaches and bluffs can be viewed more dramatically on guided cruises, departing from Munising.

For more rugged scenery, head west to **Porcupine Mountains Wilderness State Park** along Lake Superior. It is known for its old-growth forests, lakes, rivers, and a 90-mile (145-km) network of hiking trails.

Canon at the British Landing, Mackinac Island State Park

Wisconsin

M OST AMERICANS ASSOCIATE Wisconsin either with cheese – because of its advertised nickname of "America's Dairyland" – or with beer, from Milwaukee's many historic breweries. While both images are accurate, this predominantly agricultural state is also famed as the Midwest's premier vacation destination. Wisconsin's recreational jewels range from the gorgeous Apostle Islands on its northern Lake Superior coast to 85 carefully maintained state parks that allow hikers and bikers to explore glacial moraines, rugged lakeside cliffs, broad rivers, dense forests, and lush green valleys.

Façade of the 1892 Pabst Mansion in Milwaukee

Milwaukee ❸❷

🏙 590,500. ✈ ▦ 🚌 ℹ 101 W Wisconsin Ave, (800) 554-1448. 🎪 Summerfest. 🌐 www.milwaukee.org

L IKE CHICAGO, its more famous neighbor 90 miles (145 km) to the south, this manufacturing and brewing center grew up on a swampy Lake Michigan marshland. Treaties signed with local Indian tribes opened the area to white settlement in the 1830s. The city's strong German ambience dates to the arrival of "Forty-Eighters," the revolutionaries who fled Germany after an aborted attempt to overthrow the monarchy in 1848. By the 1870s, Milwaukee had as many as six daily German-language newspapers.

Pabst, Blatz, Schlitz, and Miller were the beers that "made Milwaukee famous." This tradition took such strong root in the city that even the local baseball team came to be called the Brewers. Milwaukee's wealthy beer barons were active philan-thropists, investing in the arts, architecture, and social causes. The city's spectacular Lake Michigan shoreline hosts a long schedule of festivals, the most popular being Sum-merfest, an 11-day culinary and musical extravaganza that takes place in late June and early July.

The **Milwaukee County Historical Society** is located in the heart of downtown. Housed in a stately Beaux Arts bank building, the insti-tution provides an excellent introduction to the city's economic, political, and social history. Its permanent displays explore the impact of the German immigrants on Milwaukee's active socialist movement, while revolving exhibits take a look at the city's multicultural heritage.

To its southwest, the 150,000-square-ft (13,935-m) **Milwaukee Public Museum** is part science museum, part local and cultural history center. Its interactive, child-targeted science holdings include the world's largest dinosaur skull and a glass-enclosed tropical butterfly garden. Here, visitors can walk amid more than 300 free-flying moths and butterflies. The museum's pre-Columbian and Native American exhibits paint a vivid and honest portrait of the culture and fate of the continent's Native Americans, while the "Streets of Old Milwaukee" provides a fascinating glimpse of this metropolitan melting pot.

Captain Frederick Pabst, a successful Milwaukee brewer, amassed a fortune with his popular Pabst Blue Label beer brand and real estate invest-ments. The cornerstone of his empire, the 1892 Flemish Renaissance Revival-style **Pabst Mansion**, lies at the west end of the city's grand Wisconsin Avenue. At that time the 37-room palace was considered one of the world's most technologically sophisticated houses, as it was equipped with full electrical service, a heating system, and nine bathrooms. Much of the original ornate woodwork, furniture, and artwork has been restored by a historical trust that purchased the home in 1978.

Located in the city's Historic Third Ward warehouse dis-trict, south of downtown, the **William F. Eisner Museum of Advertising and Design** critically assesses the impact of advertising on culture and society. It is one of the few museums in the country dedicated to this subject. Revolving exhibits focus on

Spectacular new entrance of the Milwaukee Art Museum

topics as diverse as the marketing of US presidents, the use of sports heroes to market beers, and the legendary Burma-Shave advertising campaigns. The precursor to billboards on America's earliest highways, the signs for one of the world's first brushless shaving creams were often humorous jingles placed at intervals along the road. Each revealed one line of a four-part rhyme, while the fifth and final sign concluded with the simple tagline "Burma Shave."

Eastward, the lakefront **Milwaukee Art Museum** was established in 1888 and holds a 20,000-piece collection, renovated galleries, and massive new reception hall, designed by Spanish architect Santiago Calatrava. This pavilion has a grand, winglike sunshade to complement the museum's windswept setting. Its signature collections are its Frank Lloyd Wright decorative arts holdings and the modern and contemporary galleries, which include Mark Rothko's *Green, Red, Blue* and Picasso's *The Cock of the Liberation*. The recently added Asian and African art augment the museum's already existing collection of Haitian folk art.

The Miller Brewing Company, the only major brewer still in operation in the city, is at the town's western edge. This firm, which produces the top-selling Miller beers, opened in 1855, when immigrant brewer Frederick Miller purchased the floundering Plank Road Brewery. Today, it is the second-largest brewer in the US, after the St. Louis-based Anheuser-Busch *(see p455)*. The **Miller Brewing Company Tour** takes visitors on a tour of its brewery and the nearby Caves Museum, where beer was naturally cooled deep inside Milwaukee's bluffs. Complimentary Miller beverages, including water and sodas for children under legal drinking age, are offered at the end of the tour.

Milwaukee's other major sight is the Annunciation Greek Orthodox Church, one of Frank Lloyd Wright's last commissions. Designed in 1956, it was opened in 1961, two years after Wright's death.

🏛 **William F. Eisner Museum of Advertising & Design**
208 N Water St. 📞 *(414) 847-3290.* ⏱ *11am–5pm Wed–Fri, 5–8pm Thu, noon–5pm Sat, 1–5pm Sun.* 🚫 ♿ W www.eisnermuseum.org

🏛 **Milwaukee Art Museum**
700 N Art Museum Dr. 📞 *(414) 224-3200.* ⏱ *10am–5pm Tue–Sun, 5–8pm Thu.* 🚫 ♿ W www.mam.org

🏭 **Miller Brewing Company Tour**
4251 W State St. 📞 *(414) 224-3220.* ⏱ *10am–5pm daily; 10am–8pm Thu; call (414) 931-2337 for free guided tours Mon–Sat.* ♿ W www.millerbrewing.com

Door County ㉝

✈ 🚌 ℹ *1015 Green Bay Rd, Sturgeon Bay, (920) 743-4456.* W www.doorcountyvacations.com

STRETCHING LIKE the spout of a teapot, between Green Bay and Lake Michigan, the Door Peninsula is a rugged New England-like expanse of rolling hills, lakeside cliffs, and pretty port villages. The county comprises the northern two-thirds of the peninsula and derives its name from the French-Canadian voyageurs' sobriquet for the treacherous shipping channel off the peninsula's northern point – Porte des Morts, or "Death's Door." The area's fishing and shipping heritage is on display at the **Door County Maritime Museum**, in downtown Sturgeon Bay, the county's largest port and southernmost city. A few miles north is **The Farm**, a traditional Wisconsin dairy farm and petting zoo, replete with an array of animals – cows, goats, pigs, chickens, horses, and barn cats.

A view of Eagle Bluff Lighthouse, Door County

The peninsula's 250-mile (402-km) shoreline is lined with more than a dozen county parks and five magnificent state parks. The largest of these is the 3,776-acre (1,528-ha) **Peninsula State Park**, between the picturesque communities of Fish Creek and Ephraim on the northwestern coast. After traversing the park's miles of hiking and biking trails and visiting the restored Eagle Bluff Lighthouse, visitors can take in a performance by the Peninsula Players, the nation's oldest resident summer stock theater company.

Washington Island, 6 miles (10 km) across the Porte des Morts Straits to the northeast of Newport State Park, can be reached, year-round, via a short ferry ride. The island was home to the Potawatomi Indians until a hardy group of Icelandic immigrants arrived in the 19th century. The latter's descendants continue to farm the island's fertile soil and to welcome day-trippers who come in search of peace, quiet, and splendid lake views.

🏛 **Door County Maritime Museum**
120 N Madison Ave, Sturgeon Bay. 📞 *(920) 743-5958.* ⏱ *Jun–Sep: 9am–6pm; Oct–May: 10am–5pm.* ⏺ *public hols.* 🚫 ♿ W www.dcmm.org

🌿 **Peninsula State Park**
9462 Shore Rd, Fish Creek. 📞 *(920) 868-3258.* ⏱ *6am–11pm daily.* 🚫 ♿ W www.dnr.state.wi.us

Sign of the Miller Brewing Company

Guided boat tour along the Wisconsin River

Wisconsin Dells ❸❹

🏠 4,000. 🚉 701 Superior St, (800) 223-3557. 🌐 www.wisdells.com

WISCONSIN DELLS has one of the most spectacular locations along the Wisconsin River as it winds through an awe-inspiring, 15-mile (24-km) stretch of deep sandstone canyons. The area's natural beauty and a variety of attractions, such as miniature golf, and amusement and water parks, make it a prime summer vacation destination. Among the highlights are the guided **Dells Boat Tours**, which offer excursions past the storied cliffs through the Upper and Lower Dells.

The region owes much of its popularity to photographer H.H. Bennett, whose late-19th-century photographs of the Wisconsin River's rugged landscapes became famous throughout America. The Wisconsin Historical Society operates the **H.H. Bennett Studio and History Center**, displaying examples of Bennett's portrait and landscape photography.

🎣 Dells Boat Tours
Upper & Lower Dells Docks.
📞 (608) 254-8555. 🕐 Apr–Oct: 9am–6pm daily. 🅿️ ♿
🌐 www.dellsboats.com

🏛 H.H. Bennett Studio & History Center
215 Broadway, Wisconsin Dells.
📞 (608) 253-3523. 🕐 May–Sep: 10am–5pm daily; Sep 15–Oct 31: 10am–5pm Sat–Sun. 🅿️ ♿
🌐 www.wisconsinhistory.org/sites/bennett

Baraboo ❸❺

🏠 9,200. 🚉 600 W Chestnut St, (800) 227-2266.

THIS TINY TOWN was the winter base of the Ringling Brothers Circus (see p319) from 1884 until 1918. Thereafter, the troupe merged with its popular rival Barnum and Bailey to create the Ringling Brothers, Barnum and Bailey Circus, the largest in the United States. The **Circus World Museum**, located on the original Ringling wintering grounds, celebrates the town's heritage with live performances, music, parades, calliope concerts, and demonstrations from the early 20th century heyday of the traveling circus. The museum also contains one of the world's largest collections of carved and painted circus wagons.

Circus World Museum, Baraboo

🏛 Circus World Museum
550 Water St. 📞 (866) 693-1500.
🕐 mid-May–Aug: 9am–6pm; Sep–mid-May:10am–4pm. 🔴 Jan 1, Easter, Thanksgiving, Dec 24–25, 31.
🅿️ ♿

Madison ❸❻

🏠 208,054. ✈️ 🚉 🚌 🚉 615 E Washington Ave, (800) 373-6376.
🌐 www.visitmadison.com

NESTLED ON a narrow isthmus of land between Lake Mendota and Lake Monona, Madison is one of the country's most attractively situated capital cities. Established as the territorial capital in 1836, it became the state capital and home of the lakeside University of Wisconsin campus when Wisconsin achieved statehood, in 1848.

The majestic, 200-ft (60-m) dome of the **Wisconsin State Capitol** rises above the city's beautiful downtown. Among its key interior features are a rotunda encircled by marble Corinthian columns and an exquisite four-panel, glass mosaic symbolizing the themes of liberty and justice.

Madison is considered one of the nation's best places to live and work. The University of Wisconsin and the city's liberal political leanings have drawn scores of artists, environmentalists, and health-food devotees to the area. As a result, downtown features a variety of bookshops, galleries, and restaurants that are vegetarian-friendly. A network of biking and walking trails provides access to the shimmering lakes around the city of Madison. The **Monona Terrace Community and Convention Center**, completed in 1997 from plans proposed by Frank Lloyd Wright (see p396), has a tranquil rooftop garden that provides panoramic views of downtown and Lake Monona. It includes a memorial to soul singer Otis Redding, who died in a plane crash on the lake in 1967.

🚩 Monona Terrace Community & Convention Center
2 blocks E of Capitol Square.
📞 (608) 261-4000. 🕐 8am–6pm daily. 🅿️ 1 pm daily. ♿
🌐 www.mononaterrace.com

Wisconsin State Capitol
Capitol Square. 📞 (608) 266-0382.
🕐 8am–4pm daily. 🅿️ 9am, 10am, 11am, 1pm, 2pm, 3pm Mon–Sat; 1pm, 2pm, 3pm Sun. 🅿️ ♿

Majestic dome of the Wisconsin State Capitol, Madison

Taliesin, architect Frank Lloyd Wright's sprawling estate in Spring Green

Spring Green 🟡

🏛 *1,300.* 🚌 🛈 *150 E Jefferson St,
(800) 588-2042.*
🅦 *www.springgreen.com*

THIS HANDSOME farming community lies just north of the Wisconsin River, surrounded by undulating hills. In 1911, architect Frank Lloyd Wright, who spent his childhood in nearby Richland Center, built **Taliesin** ("Shining Brow" in Welsh) on a bluff overlooking the river. The 600-acre (240-ha) estate was Wright's home until his death in 1959 and included a school where his disciples were instructed in his Prairie-style design philosophy. Today, the Taliesin Fellowship runs the school and an architectural firm on the grounds. Guided tours lead visitors through Wright's eclectic home and its courtyards and gardens.

About 9 miles (14 km) north of Spring Green is the **House on the Rock**. This sprawling resort complex has a home built on top of a 60-ft (18-m) chimney rock formation. The house, constructed in the 1940s by eccentric architect Alex Jordan, is the focal point for a rambling museum exhibiting Jordan's vast collection of Americana.

🏛 **Taliesin**
5607 County Rd C, Spring Green.
📞 *(608) 588-7900.* 🕐 *May–Oct: 8:30am –5:30pm daily.* 🅿 🚻

🏛 **House on the Rock**
5754 Hwy 23. 📞 *(608) 935-3639.*
🕐 *Mar–Memorial Day: 9am–6pm; Memorial Day–Labor Day: 9am–7pm; Labor Day–Oct: 9am–6pm; Nov–Jan: 9am–5pm.* 🅿 🚻

La Crosse 🟡

🏛 *51,000.* ✈ 🚉 🚌 🛈 *410 Veterans Memorial Dr, (800) 658-9424.* 🅦 *www.explorelacrosse.com*

FOUNDED AS A trading post in 1842, La Crosse emerged as a key railroad junction after the Civil War. The city's well-preserved downtown district, and tree-lined neighborhoods around the University of Wisconsin-La Crosse campus, add to its charm. It also makes a fine base for exploring the Mississippi River towns along the Great River Road Scenic Byway *(see p41)* as it passes through the state.

East of downtown, **Grandad Bluff**, 600 ft (180 m) above the city, offers superb views of La Crosse and the

Sailor mannequins for sale at Bayfield

Grandad Bluff, an observation point east of downtown La Crosse

Mississippi River Valley. Two restored paddlewheel steamboats offer great views of the river. A good alternative may be **Perrot State Park**, 30 miles (48 km) north of La Crosse. In Trempeleau, south of the park entrance, stands the Trempeleau Hotel *(see p427)*, the town's only building to have survived a fire that took place in 1888.

Apostle Islands 🟡

🚌 *Ashland.* 🛈 *Ashland County (800) 284-9484, Bayfield County (800) 472-6338.*
🅦 *www.travelbayfieldcounty.com*

OFF THE STATE'S northeastern Lake Superior coast lie a group of 22 islands, the remains of retreating glaciers from the last Ice Age. They were named the Apostle Islands by 17th-century French missionaries, who incorrectly assumed that the archipelago included only 12 islands. Today, 21 islands form part of the **Apostle Islands National Lakeshore**. The old-growth forests here provide the habitat for resident bald eagles and black bears, while vast stretches of sand beaches with sea caves, carved by the wind and lake into craggy, brownstone cliffs, make the Apostle Islands a fairly popular destination for those interested in eco-tourism.

A local cruise service from **Bayfield**, on the mainland, ferries visitors to the islands, many of which hold historic lighthouses, such as the 1881 Sand Island Light Station, with its octagonal tower built from locally quarried sandstone. The 22-chain archipelago also offers the area's best sea kayaking. Various outfitters in Bayfield rent kayaks and provide guided charter tours.

🚣 **Apostle Islands National Lakeshore**
415 Washington Ave, Bayfield.
📞 *(715) 779-3397.* 🕐 *8am–6pm daily.* 🅿 🚻 🅦 *www.nps.gov/apis*

Minnesota

MINNESOTA HAS BEEN seductively nicknamed "The Land of 10,000 Lakes." While beautiful lakes have added to the state's appeal as an affordable outdoors destination, it was the meandering rivers that actually shaped Minnesota's history as an important trading and agricultural hub. Many of these rivers, streams, and lakes have now been preserved and offer a rare solitude and natural splendor in vast stretches of its watery wilderness.

Minneapolis & St. Paul [40]

Minneapolis 👥 *368,400.* ✈ 🚆 🚌 ℹ *33 S 6th St, (800) 445-7412.* [W] www.minneapolis.org
St. Paul 👥 *287,150.* ✈ 🚆 🚌 ℹ *175 W Kellogg Blvd, (800) 627-6101.* [W] www.stpaulcvb.org

THE TWIN CITIES, separated by the Mississippi, are a study in contrasts. Flamboyant Minneapolis, with its modern skyscrapers, is an urbane, commercial center where most of the state's corporate headquarters, museums, and high-end retail stores are located. St. Paul, the state capital, is more sedate, but has a colorful history, well-preserved downtown, and some architectural and cultural attractions.

Exploring Minneapolis

Downtown revolves around the pedestrian **Nicolett Mall**, which hosts various cultural events, including the Minnesota Orchestra's annual summer MusicFest. The **Uptown** neighborhood, on the southwest, revolves around the Chain of Lakes, with its network of biking and jogging trails. The country's largest enclosed shopping mall, the **Mall of America**, is in the southern suburb of Bloomington.

🏛 Walker Art Center

The Loop, Hennepin Ave & Vineland Pl. ☎ *(612) 375-7622.* 🕐 *10am–5pm Tue–Wed & Fri–Sat, 5–9pm Thu, 11am–5pm Sun.* ● *public hols.* 🗣 ♿
The performing, visual, and media arts are the focus of the exhibits at the Twin Cities' most complete contemporary art resource. Among the highlights of the Walker's permanent and revolving exhibits are the minimalist work of sculptor Donald Judd, including the restored 1971 *Untitled,* a group of six, large-scale aluminium cubes, and painter Edward Hopper's *Office at Night* (1940). The

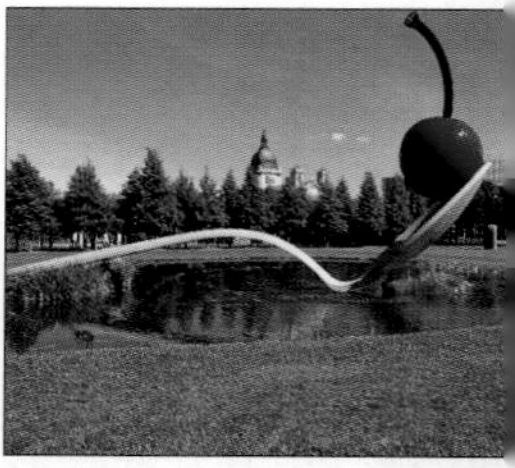

***Spoonbridge and Cherry* at the Walker Art Center**

Center also presents dance, theatrical, performance art, and musical productions, and also conducts community outreach programs.

🏛 Minneapolis Institute of Arts

2400 3rd Ave S. ☎ *(612) 870-3131.* 🕐 *10am–5pm Tue–Wed & Fri–Sat, 5–9pm Thu, noon–5pm Sun.* ● *Jul 4, Thanksg., Dec 25.* 🗣 ♿
Established in 1915, this is one of the region's largest and most highly regarded museums. Its traditional collection includes a wide range of Greek and Roman statuary, Italian and Dutch Renaissance paintings, as well as American works by John Singleton Copley, Benjamin West, Georgia O'Keeffe, and regionalist Grant Wood.

The **Ulrich Architecture and Design Gallery** houses an astonishing collection of Prairie School furniture, architectural fragments, art-glass windows, and silver.

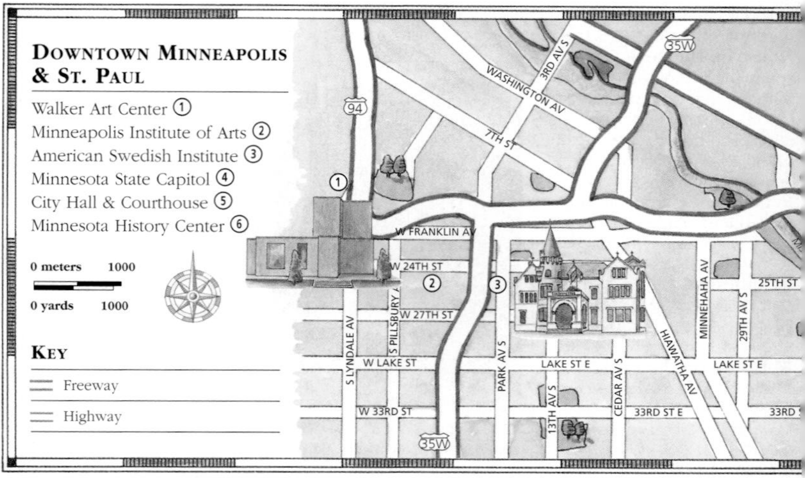
DOWNTOWN MINNEAPOLIS & ST. PAUL
Walker Art Center 1
Minneapolis Institute of Arts 2
American Swedish Institute 3
Minnesota State Capitol 4
City Hall & Courthouse 5
Minnesota History Center 6
0 meters 1000
0 yards 1000
KEY
Freeway
Highway
35W
94
WASHINGTON AV
3RD AV S
7TH ST
W FRANKLIN AV
W 24TH ST
W 27TH ST
S PILLSBURY AV
S LYNDALE AV
W LAKE ST
W 33RD ST
PARK AV S
13TH AV S
CEDAR AV S
LAKE ST E
33RD ST E
HIAWATHA AV
MINNEHAHA AV
29TH AV S
25TH ST
LAKE ST E
33RD

🏛 American Swedish Institute

2600 Park Ave. **☎** (612) 871-4907. ◐ noon–4pm Tue & Thu–Sat, 4–8pm Wed, 1–5pm Sun. ● public hols. 📷 ♿

Housed in a grand 1907 Romanesque mansion, this institute chronicles the contributions of Swedish-Americans to the state's history and culture. Guided tours of the house, built by Swedish newspaper publisher Swan Turnblad, allow visitors to view his collection of Swedish-American *kakelugnar* (porcelain tile stoves), woodcarvings, textiles, and immigration artifacts. A revolving exhibit traces the journey of Swedes to the Twin Cities and explores the popular culture of early 20th-century Swedish-American districts.

Exploring St. Paul

Founded in 1841 on the site of Pig's Eye, the notorious French-Canadian trading post, St. Paul flourished as the busiest river port on the Upper Mississippi. By the late 19th century, the new state capital had emerged as a railroad hub, powered by the completion of the railroad between St. Paul and Seattle in 1893. The stately Romanesque, Queen Anne, and Jacobean mansions along **Summit Avenue** date from those prosperous days.

Downtown centers on the Art Deco City Hall and Courthouse on Kellogg Boulevard and St. Peter Street. The popular Minnesota Public Radio program, *A Prairie Home Companion*, is recorded live on many Saturday evenings at the **Fitzgerald Theater**, a beautifully restored 1910 vaudeville and movie palace at Exchange and Wabasha Streets. The city also hosts the Minnesota State Fair in late August and early September.

🏛 Minnesota State Capitol

75 Constitution Ave. **🏛** (651) 296-2881. ◐ 9am–5pm Mon–Fri, 10am–4pm Sat, 1–4pm Sun. ● Jan 1, Mar 31, Nov 23, Dec 25. ♿

Designed by Cass Gilbert, architect of the US Supreme Court *(see p199)*, the Minnesota State Capitol is a monumental domed Beaux Arts structure. It features the sculpture, *Progress of the State*, a group of gold-leafed copper and steel statues in the front.

The sculpture *Progress of the State*, Minnesota State Capitol

🏛 City Hall & Courthouse

15 W Kellogg Blvd. **☎** (651) 266-8500. ◐ 8am–4:30pm Mon–Fri. ♿

This Art Deco masterpiece, painstakingly restored from 1990 to 1993, is built of Indiana limestone and black Wisconsin granite. Its three-story base steps back to the central tower, making the structure appear to soar above the surrounding downtown. No detail was spared in the building's construction, with every light fixture, elevator door, railing, mailbox, door handle, and lock specially crafted in the ornate style of Art Deco.

🏛 Minnesota History Center

345 W Kellogg Blvd. **☎** (800) 657-3773. ◐ 10am–8pm Tue, 10am–5pm Wed–Sat, noon–5pm Sun. ● public hols. 📷 ♿

A treasure trove of interactive exhibits that chronicles the state's 19th century history is housed in this granite and limestone building. Exhibits such as a huge boxcar, giant grain elevator, lifelike meat-packing plant, and a replica of a 1930s dairy farm – complete with two full-size model cows with milking instructions – help visitors relive history from the point of view of a farmer or factory worker. The center's pop culture highlight, **Sounds Good to Me: Music in Minnesota**, showcases the music that originated here.

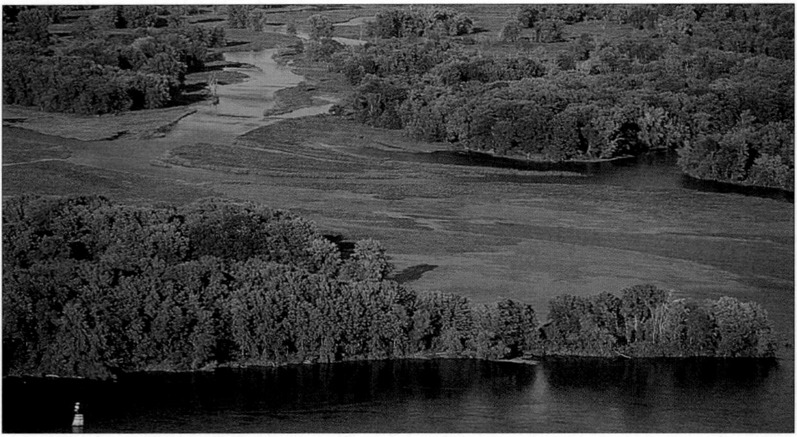

View of the Mississippi River from the Great River Bluffs State Park, southeast of the river town Winona

Mississippi River Towns 41

(651) 385-5934.

THE MISSISSIPPI RIVER courses 572 miles (921 km) through Minnesota. It originates in the north-central part of the state and continues until its confluence with the St. Croix River near Hastings. South of the confluence, it widens and picks up speed, rushing through deep, fog-laden valleys along the Minnesota-Wisconsin border. The Great River Road Scenic Byway *(see p41)*, or US 61, hugs the river's west bank, revealing breathtaking views of attractive towns and parks.

The 15,100-person, 19th-century town of **Red Wing** was built on the site of a Dakota Sioux farming village. Today, the town is known primarily as the headquarters of the Red Wing Shoe Company, the popular work boot manufacturer, established in 1905. A downtown museum showcases its manufacturing process. The restored 1904 Sheldon Theater presents a musical history of the city.

About 10 miles (16 km) southeast of Red Wing is **Frontenac State Park**, one of the premier bird-watching sites along the river, where over 260 species pause on their journeys north and south every year. Bald eagles and warblers flock to the diverse habitats of Lake Pepin, the widest stretch of the river.

Picturesque **Winona**, 65 miles (105 km) southeast of Red Wing, is located on an island in the river. It prospered in the 19th century as a steamboat refueling stop, mill town, and wheat-shipping depot.

The beautiful **Great River Bluffs State Park**, about 20 miles (32 km) southeast of Winona, occupies one of the river's most scenic stretches. The park features half-dome bluffs and sheer rock cliffs.

Rochester 42

90,000. Centerpiece-Galleria 111 S Broadway St 301, (800) 634-8277.

THE PRIMARY attraction in this southeastern Minnesota city is the **Mayo Clinic**, founded by the physician brothers Will and Charles Mayo in the early 1900s. They initiated the first collaborative medical practice, integrating the findings of a group of medical specialists to more effectively diagnose and treat serious illnesses. With an 18,000-strong staff, the clinic now treats over 240,000 patients.

Mayo Clinic
200 1st St SW. *(651) 284-2450.*
tours at 10am Mon & Fri, 1:30pm Tue & Thu.
www.mayoclinic.org

Pipestone National Monument 43

4,600. 117 8th Ave SE, (507) 825-3316.
www.nps.gov/pipe

PIPESTONE SITS in the state's southwestern corner. The name derives from Dakota Sioux Indians who lived here for generations, quarrying the region's soft red quartzite to craft elegant ceremonial pipes. The stone catlinite has been named in honor of artist George Catlin, who depicted this place in his 1838 masterpiece, *Pipestone Quarry*.

Indian craftsmen continue the tradition in the remains of the quarries. The pipes are then sold at the adjoining Upper Midwest Indian Cultural Center.

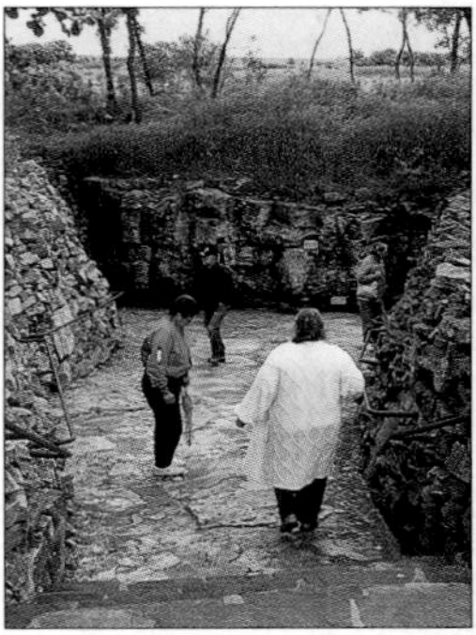

Visitors negotiating a trail through Pipestone's quarries

Brainerd Lakes Area 44

65,000. *124 N 6th St, Brainerd, (800) 450-2838.*
www.explorebrainerdlakes.com

FOUNDED BY the Northern Pacific Railroad in 1871, the Upper Mississippi River city of Brainerd was carved out of a dense forest, felled to meet the demands of the state's lumber boom. The area's heritage as a hard-working railroad and lumber town is personified in the flannel-shirted, bearded character of Paul Bunyan, the mythical Herculean Minnesota woodsman, and his massive pet, Babe, the Blue Ox. His name seems to appear at every turn; the Paul Bunyan Trail bike route, and Paul Bunyan Scenic Byway back-roads auto tour are the more tasteful examples.

Crow Wing State Park, located 9 miles (14 km) south of Brainerd, offers canoe tours of the placid Crow Wing and Mississippi River waters.

Brainerd is also the gateway to north-central Minnesota's lake region, where the state's trademark lodge-resorts were first developed on the shores of more than 500 fresh-water lakes. **Mille Lacs Lake**, 40 miles (64 km) southeast of Brainerd, is bordered by beautiful state parks and the Mille Lacs Band of Ojibwe tribal reservation. The Minnesota Historical Society collaborated with the tribe to develop the Mille Lacs Indian Museum, on the lake's southwest shore.

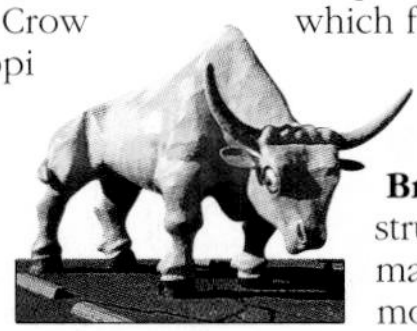

Babe, the Blue Ox

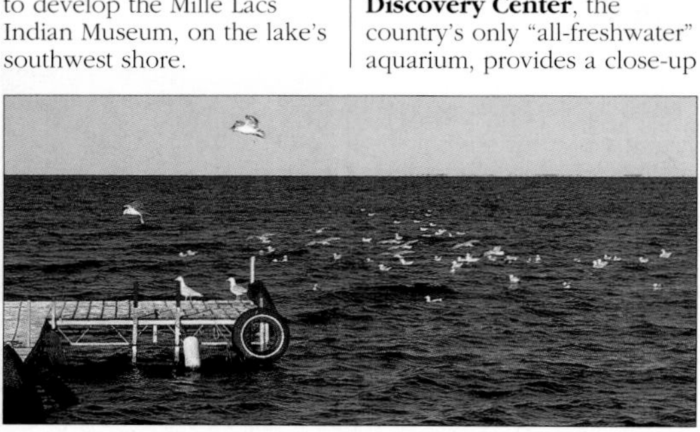

Mille Lacs Lake, Minnesota's second largest lake, southeast of Brainerd

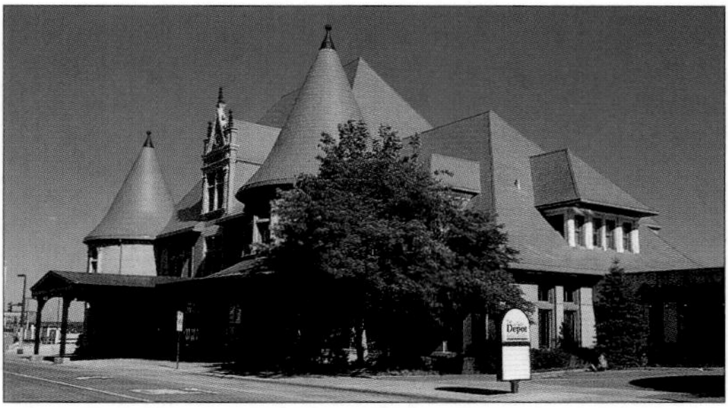

The restored railroad Depot, the centerpiece of downtown Duluth

Duluth 45

87,000. *100 Lake Place Dr, (800) 438-5884.*

MINNESOTA'S THIRD largest city, Duluth is one of the Midwest's most enjoyable destinations. Clinging to the sides of the 800-ft (240-m) high granite slopes that ring its lively downtown, this city successfully juxtaposes numerous nature preserves with operating industries, which fuel its bustling port. Its most striking feature is the **Aerial Lift Bridge**, a huge steel structure linking the mainland to the mouth of the Duluth harbor with a 385-ft (115-m) span. The bridge can raise at the rate of 138 ft (41 m) a minute to allow hulking freighters to pass into the harbor. One of these massive ships, the docked 610-ft (186-m) SS *William A. Irwin*, is now a museum.

The **Great Lakes Aquarium and Freshwater Discovery Center**, the country's only "all-freshwater" aquarium, provides a close-up view of the bridge in action. In Canal Park, next to the bridge, the **Lake Superior Maritime Visitor Center** details the shipping history of the Upper Great Lakes. It also relates the US Army Corps of Engineers' feat of constructing the Aerial Lift Bridge in 1930.

The centerpiece of the redbrick-paved streets of Duluth's attractive downtown is the 1892 **Depot**, or **St. Louis County Heritage and Arts Center**. The restored brownstone railroad depot houses four superb museums, including the Duluth Art Institute, Duluth Children's Museum, and Lake Superior Railroad Museum. Depot Square, a re-creation of early 20th-century Duluth, features the waiting room where US immigration officials processed many of the state's Scandinavian and German immigrants.

The **North Shore Scenic Railroad** offers sightseeing trips from the depot in period trains. The excursions head north along the shore of Lake Superior, yielding spectacular views of waterfalls and cliffs plunging down to the shoreline. Motorists can also experience this magical trip on the North Shore Scenic Drive, a section of old Hwy 61 that runs along the lakeshore from Duluth all the way to the Canadian border.

The Depot/St. Louis County Heritage & Arts Center

506 W Michigan St. *(888) 733-5833.* *Jun–Sep: 9:30am–6pm daily; Oct–May: 10am–5pm Mon–Sat, 1–5pm Sun.*
www.duluthdepot.org

A view of Mesabi, one of the three ranges that comprise the Iron Range

Iron Range ⑯

🎫 ℹ️ *10–2nd Ave W, Chisholm,
(800) 422-0806.*

WHEN IRON ORE was discovered in northeast-ern Minnesota in the 1880s, waves of immigrant workers came to boomtowns that grew up along three ranges – the Vermilion, Mesabi, and Cuyana. These ranges collectively came to be known as the Iron Range district. By the 1960s, the mines' productivity diminished and many were shut down, decimating local communities and leaving behind empty mining pits. But in the past two decades, a growing tourist interest in the mining era has revitalized the Iron Range district.

About 225 miles (362 km) north of Minneapolis, the **Soudan Underground Mine** is Minnesota's oldest and deepest iron mine. It opened in 1884, closed in 1962, and is now part of a 1,300-acre (520-ha) state park. Visitors can go a half-mile (1 km) underground into the heart of the mine that also holds an operating atomic physics lab.

The Iron Range city of Chisholm, 45 miles (72 km) southwest of Soudan, is home to the **Ironworld Discovery Center**. The center presents a glitzier, theme-park version of the Iron Range story with living history interpreters and trolley rides. Its highlight is the Minnesota CCC History Museum, commemorating the achievements of the state's Civilian Conservation Corps,

Statue outside Ironworld

a Depression-era program that put 84,000 young men to work on soil and forest conservation projects.

⛏ Soudan Underground Mine

1379 Stuntz Bay Rd, Soudan. 📞
🕐 Jun–Sep: 10am–4pm. 🅿️ 🔔

🎭 Ironworld Discovery Center

Hwy 169 W, Chisholm. 📞 (800) 372-6437. 🕐 May–Sep: 9:30am–5pm.
🅿️ 🔔 🌐 www.ironworld.com

Boundary Waters Canoe Area Wilderness ⑰

☒ 🎫 ℹ️ *1600 E Sheridan St, Ely,
(800) 777-7281.* 🌐 www.ely.org

THE LARGEST wilderness preserve east of the Rocky Mountains, the Boundary Waters Canoe Area Wilderness stretches for almost 200 miles (322 km) along the Canadian border in the state's northeastern corner. One of country's most unspoiled natural regions, this vast area attracts adventurers seeking an escape from civilization. The region is also one of the world's largest canoeing and fishing destinations, with more than 1,200 miles (1,932 km) of canoe routes which snake through 1,000 streams and lakes in the dense Superior National Forest.

To preserve the area's unique appeal, there is a limit on the number of campers as well as restrictions on the use of motorized watercraft. The

area has no roads, and campers have to carry their equipment from lake to lake via portage methods perfected by the Ojibwe Indians. Still, visitors throng to the area either to canoe in waters teeming with northern pike or to spot rare Canadian lynx or wolverine.

Most camping parties begin their exploration at Ely, 240 miles (386 km) north of Minneapolis. One of the park's far-western entry points, Ely has more canoe-trip outfitters per capita than any other town in the world. It also has the **Dorothy Molter Museum**, a memorial to the wilderness area's last human resident, who ran a resort here and died in 1986. The **International Wolf Center** in town promotes the survival of the region's once-threatened wolf population through interactive exhibits and close views of the resident gray and Arctic wolf.

Visitors can also take the 63-mile (101-km) Gunflint Trail, a scenic auto road into the northeastern corner of the Boundary Waters area. Motorists are encouraged to fill up the tank, pack food and water, and drive carefully to avoid moose.

🏛 Dorothy Molter Museum

2002 E Sheridan St. 📞 (218) 365-4451. 🕐 Memorial Day–Labor Day: 10am–5:30pm Mon–Sat, noon–5:30pm Sun; May: weekends.
🅿️ 🔔 🌐 www.canoecountry.com/dorothy

🐺 International Wolf Center

1396 Hwy 169 Ely. 📞 (800) 359-6437. 🕐 May–Oct: 9am–5pm daily; Nov–May first week: 9am–5pm Sat & Sun. 🅿️ 🔔 🌐 www.wolf.org

Kayakers on Moose Lake, near Ely, Boundary Waters Wilderness

Voyageurs National Park 48

📋 3131 Highway 53, International Falls, (218) 283-9821. ✗ 🚐
W www.nps.gov/voya

Pelicans on one of the numerous lakes of Voyageurs National Park

THE WATERY Rainy Lake borderlands west of Superior National Forest contain the old Voyageur Highway, an old network of lakes, streams, and portage routes used by Native Americans and French-Canadian trappers to move furs from the Minnesota and Northern Ontario forests across the Great Lakes to Montreal. The route was taken over by the British after the French and Indian War, and extended as far west as the Canadian province of Alberta.

Today, 218,000 acres (87,200 ha) of this largely empty Canadian Shield wilderness are preserved in the Voyageurs National Park, a water-based park with 30 lakes and countless bogs, swamps, beaver ponds, and islands – habitat of large packs of Eastern timber wolves.

Rainy Lake, the finest fishing lake in the park, abounds in walleye, pike, and bass. The Rainy Lake Visitor Center, near International Falls, 295 miles

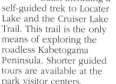

Lithograph of a fur trapper's cabin

(475 km) north of Minneapolis and 160 miles (258 km) west of Duluth, is one of three staffed access points to the park and the only one open year-round. The center features interactive exhibits concerning the fur trade and provides information about naturalist-guided tours. Although most vistors traverse the park's vast area using boat (motorized watercrafts are permitted here) and canoe, hikers can take advantage of a network of hiking trails, including a self-guided trek to Locater Lake and the Cruiser Lake Trail. This trail is the only means of exploring the roadless Kabetogama Peninsula. Shorter guided tours are available at the park visitor centers.

For those people keen on boating, the border city of International Falls is the home base for stocking up on supplies or arranging a boat or canoe rental. The town's Boise Paper Solutions houses what the company claims to be the "largest, fastest paper machine in the world." In winter, the Voyageurs National Park offers opportunities for snowmobiling, ice fishing, and cross-country skiing.

WOLVES

Voyageurs National Park is one of the largest wolf sanctuaries in the US. The animals that roam here are gray wolves, one of three species of wolves in the world. Wolves live in packs, dominated by two adult parents, their offspring of the past 2–3 years, and several un-related members. Contrary to folklore, wolves tend to shy away from humans.

Gray Wolf

Aerial view of the many islets in wild, spectacular Voyageurs National Park

Practical Information

Traveling around the Great Lakes states requires a lot of planning, since there is so much to see and do in such a wide area. From the towering skyscrapers of bustling big cities such as Chicago to the idyllic pastures of Wisconsin, the attractions here are as varied as the six states that form the Great Lakes region. With its rolling hills, endless farmlands, and sublime waterfront wilderness, America's heartland abounds in pristine wonders that offer a wide choice of outdoor pursuits.

TOURIST INFORMATION

Each of the Great Lakes states houses a state Welcome Center that offers a full range of tourist information, as well as clean restrooms and free coffee. Most airports have information desks stocked with free brochures and maps. All the larger cities and many smaller towns have Convention & Visitors' Bureaus or Chambers of Commerce, with free directories of attractions, accommodations, and events.

NATURAL HAZARDS

Winters in the northern parts of Michigan, Minnesota, and Wisconsin can be very cold, with blizzards and snowstorms. Visitors should dress warmly and pack a small snow shovel, gloves, and a hat when traversing this region between November and April. Ice and snow can make driving extremely treacherous.

GETTING AROUND

Most major cities in the region have public bus systems, which provide limited service around town for a reasonable fare. Light rail, subway, and commuter train services only run in Chicago and Cleveland. A new public rail transit system is under construction in the Twin Cities, serving Minneapolis, St. Paul, and the surrounding metro area. It should open in 2004.

However, driving is the best way to get around this region. Seat belts are a must for drivers, front seat passengers, and back seat passengers. Child seats are mandatory for occupants aged four and under. Helmets are compulsory for motorcyclists under the age of 18 in all of the Great Lakes states, except Illinois, which has no restrictions regarding helmet usage. Speed limits vary, but are usually 70–75 mph (113–121 km/hour) on Interstate Highways outside urban areas.

ETIQUETTE

Residents of the Great Lakes are friendly and polite – especially in Minnesota, where the phrase, "you bet," epitomizes the helpful attitude of the state's hearty residents. Visitors to the Amish communities in Indiana and Ohio will be impressed by the shy, reserved manner of the traditional Amish inhabitants, whose simple, black outfits and horse-driven buggies are common sights on the roads.

FESTIVALS

The Great Lakes states stage a diverse range of annual, community, regional, state, and cultural festivals. As an expression of Chicago's strong Irish heritage, the city actually dyes the Chicago River green as part of its boisterous **St. Patrick's Day Parade**. The Mexican-American population residing in the region celebrates **Cinco de Mayo** (early May) festivals in many of the Great Lakes cities; it is celebrated in a big way especially in Chicago. Summer brings a deluge of outdoor events, starting on Memorial Day weekend with the Indianapolis 500 auto race. Fireworks and street festivals are the norm for various county and state fairs that crop up in July and August. The Minnesota State Fair (August), held in St. Paul is one of the largest summer events, along with the immensely popular Milwaukee **Summerfest**.

SPORTS

The Great Lakes region harbors a wide array of professional and amateur sports teams, with major pro baseball, football, and basketball franchises operating in nearly all of the major cities. The onset of spring signals the beginning of the baseball season, with fans flocking to historic **Wrigley Field**, home of the Chicago Cubs. Ohio boasts some of the region's best minor league parks in Toledo, Akron, and Dayton. This region also loves its

---

THE CLIMATE OF THE GREAT LAKES

Weather in most of the Great Lakes states is fairly consistent. Temperatures tend to be cooler in the northern states of Michigan, Wisconsin, and Minnesota where cold, snowy winters lure residents to ski. The southern regions of Ohio, Indiana, and Illinois witness a more temperate climate. Summer months are ideal for touring the lakeside areas in Ohio, Wisconsin, Michigan, and Minnesota. Cooler temperatures and fall colors make Sep–Oct ideal for an extended trip to Chicago and scenic drives through the rugged forests of Michigan's Upper Peninsula.

CHICAGO

°F/C	Apr	Jul	Oct	Jan
high	59/15	86/30	65/18	33/1
low	40/4	66/19	46/8	19/–7
sun	15 days	20 days	17 days	14 days
rain	3.6 in	3.6 in	2.6 in	1.7 in

32°F / 0°C

football. The gregarious fans of the Chicago Bears and Cleveland Browns pro teams go head-to-head with the Wisconsin "Cheeseheads," who strip to the waist in the freezing cold to cheer on the Green Bay Packers. The region's universities compete in the **Big Ten** conference that draws over 100,000 fans.

Winter brings basketball and hockey to the frozen region, with four NHL hockey teams, and many minor league teams active in arenas across the region.

OUTDOOR ACTIVITIES

R ELATIVELY SHORT summers and long winters do not deter Great Lakes residents from enjoying the outdoors. On the contrary, the region's climate seems to encourage a more passionate pursuit of recreational activities, with mountain biking and cycling enthusiasts thronging paths and trails from April through early November. Northern Minnesota and Wisconsin are favorite canoe and kayak destinations, while sail and motorboats are omnipresent on all of the Great Lakes throughout summer. Many fishing enthusiasts look forward to ice fishing in winter.

Skiing and snowmobiling are also extremely popular outdoor winter pursuits in the region.

Some of the region's best outdoors outfitters are located at Ely, entrance to the Boundary Waters Area Canoe Wilderness, and in Bayfield, gateway to the Apostle Islands National Lakeshore. For a list of outfitters in these locations, contact the **Ely Chamber of Commerce** or the **Bayfield Chamber**.

ENTERTAINMENT

M OST OF THE region's most famous live music and theatrical venues are in Chicago. **Buddy Guy's Legends** and the **Checkerboard** are the best places to hear authentic electric Chicago blues. The **House of Blues** hosts a wide range of blues and alternative rock acts. Comedy fans flock to Chicago's **Second City**, training ground for *Saturday Night Live* cast members, and to St. Paul's **Fitzgerald Theater**, home base for Minnesota humorist Garrison Keillor's long-running *A Prairie Home Companion* comedy and radio program. The summertime **Big Top Chautauqua**,

situated near the Apostle Islands, holds similar, old-time comic and musical shows. Visitors can also check out rides at the region's largest amusement parks: **Cedar Point** in Sandusky and **Paramount Kings Island** in Cincinnati.

SHOPPING

T HE REGION's premier retail destination is Chicago's "Magnificent Mile." This dense stretch of Michigan Avenue north of the Chicago River holds some the nation's premier specialty shops, augmenting the classic **Marshall Field's** department store on State Street in the heart of the Loop. Another popular shopping destination is the pedestrian **Nicollet Mall** in Minneapolis. This pleasantly designed downtown district is far removed from the Twin Cities' busiest retail attraction, the 500-store **Mall of America**, the country's largest indoor shopping mall. Tourists can also travel to the Amish communities in northern Indiana. **Shipshewana** has a busy flea market, where quilts, rugs, and baked goods can be bought at fairly reasonable prices.

Where to Stay

Most great lakes cities offer a range of chain hotels and motels to visitors. While larger centers such as Chicago, St. Paul, Cincinnati, and Indianapolis have historic boutique hotels and bed-and-breakfast inns, the remote northwoods areas of Minnesota, Wisconsin, and Michigan's Upper Peninsula harbor a choice of relaxing lakeside lodge and cabin resorts.

	CREDIT CARDS	NUMBER OF ROOMS	RECOMMENDED RESTAURANT	CHILDREN'S FACILITIES	GARDEN OR TERRACE

ILLINOIS

CHICAGO: *Days Inn Lincoln Park North* ⓈⓈ
644 W Diversey Pkwy, Lincoln Park. 【 (773) 525-7010, (888) 576-3297. FAX (773) 525-6998.
Ⓦ www.lpndaysinn.com
This winner of the Days Inn Chairman's Award for consistent quality has been recently remodeled. 🍽 🛏 P 🚗 💱 TV 🌿 🍴
| | ■ | 133 | | ● | |

CHICAGO: *Hotel Burnham* ⓈⓈⓈ
1 W Washington St. 【 (312) 782-1111, (877) 294-9712. FAX (312) 782-0899.
Ⓦ www.burnhamhotel.com
Originally designed by Daniel Burnham in 1895, the remodeled steel-and-glass Reliance Building is just minutes away from the theater district. This Kimpton hotel is pet-friendly. 🍽 🛏 P 🚗 💱 TV & 🍴
| | ■ | 122 | ■ | ● | |

CHICAGO: *House of Blues Hotel* ⓈⓈⓈ
333 N Dearborn St. 【 (312) 245-0333, (877) 569-3742. FAX (312) 923-2444.
Ⓦ www.loewshotels.com
The creatively furnished rooms of this musically themed, River North hotel, sport stereo systems and an in-room blues CD collection. 🍽 🛏 P 🚗 💱 TV & 🍴
| | ■ | 360 | ■ | ● | |

CHICAGO: *Renaissance Chicago Hotel* ⓈⓈⓈ
1 W Wacker Dr. 【 (312) 372-7200, (800) 228-9290. FAX (312) 795-3474.
Ⓦ www.renaissancehotels.com
Friendly service and richly appointed rooms overlooking the river. The fee for Club Level, which includes complimentary breakfast and evening hors d'oeuvres, is well worth the fare. 🍽 🛏 P 🚗 💱 TV 🌿 🍴
| | ■ | 553 | ■ | ● | |

CHICAGO: *Tremont Hotel* ⓈⓈⓈ
100 E Chestnut St. 【 (312) 751-1900, (800) 621-8133. FAX (312) 751-8691.
Ⓦ www.tremonthotel.com Located just off Michigan Avenue, this European-style hotel offers cozy, comfortable lodgings. The lobby, with its carved-wood ceiling, has an English-country atmosphere. 🍽 P 🚗 💱 TV 🍴
| | ■ | 130 | | ● | |

CHICAGO: *Ritz-Carlton Chicago* ⓈⓈⓈⓈ
160 E Pearson St. 【 (312) 266-1000, (800) 621-6906. FAX (312) 266-4238.
Ⓦ www.fourseasons.com
Located above Water Tower Place, the Ritz-Carlton (owned by the Four Seasons chain) provides unparalleled service. 🍽 🛏 P 🚗 💱 TV 🌿 🍴
| | ■ | 435 | ■ | ● | |

CHICAGO: *The Silversmith* ⓈⓈⓈⓈ
10 S Wabash Ave. 【 (312) 372-7696, (800) 227-6963. FAX (312) 372-7320.
Ⓦ www.silversmith.crowneplaza.com
This Arts-and-Crafts-style hotel, housed in a historic building, has pleasant rooms with high windows and ceilings. 🍽 🛏 P 🚗 💱 TV 🍴
| | ■ | 143 | ■ | ● | |

CHICAGO: *The Drake* ⓈⓈⓈⓈⓈ
140 E Walton St. 【 (312) 787-2200, (800) 553-7253. FAX (312) 787-2549.
Ⓦ www.hilton.com
This ornate, 1920 Gold Coast classic offers great views of Lake Michigan and the intimate Coq d'Or piano bar. 🍽 🛏 P 🚗 💱 TV & 🍴
| | ■ | 537 | ■ | ● | |

GALENA: *DeSoto House Hotel* ⓈⓈⓈ
230 S Main St. 【 (815) 777-0090. FAX (815) 777-9529.
Ⓦ www.desotohouse.com
Built in 1855, this smartly renovated period hotel provides easy access to the Galena Historic District's shops and restaurants. 🛏 P 🚗 💱 TV &
| | ■ | 55 | ■ | ● | |

OAK PARK: *Carleton of Oak Park Hotel* ⓈⓈ
1110 Pleasant St, Oak Park. 【 (708) 848-5000, (888) 227-5386. FAX (708) 848-0537.
Ⓦ www.carletonhotel.com
The hotel offers pleasant accommodations just minutes away from specialty shops and boutiques. 🍽 P 🚗 💱 TV 🌿 🍴
| | ■ | 154 | ■ | ● | |

Price categories for a standard double room per night, inclusive of breakfast, service charges, and any additional taxes:

Ⓢ under $100
ⓈⓈ $100–$150
ⓈⓈⓈ $150–$200
ⓈⓈⓈⓈ $200–$250
ⓈⓈⓈⓈⓈ over $250

CREDIT CARDS
Major credit cards accepted.

NUMBER OF ROOMS
Number of rooms in the hotel.

RECOMMENDED RESTAURANT
Good restaurant within the hotel.

CHILDREN'S FACILITIES
Hotel has various facilities for young children.

GARDEN OR TERRACE
Hotel has a garden, courtyard, or terrace.

	CREDIT CARDS	NUMBER OF ROOMS	RECOMMENDED RESTAURANT	CHILDREN'S FACILITIES	GARDEN OR TERRACE
INDIANA					
COLUMBUS: *The Columbus Inn Bed & Breakfast* ⓈⓈⓈ 445 5th St. ☏ *(812) 378-4289.* FAX *(812) 378-4289.* W www.thecolumbusinn.com This 1895 Romanesque-style inn was built as the Columbus City Hall. Its renovated rooms and downtown location make it a favorite for tourists seeking architecturally significant accommodations. ▣ P ▣ ▣ TV	▣	34			
INDIANAPOLIS: *The Canterbury Hotel* ⓈⓈⓈⓈ 123 S Illinois St. ☏ *(317) 634-3000, (800) 538-8186.* FAX *(317) 685-2519.* W www.canterburyhotel.com This European-style boutique hotel offers fine service and plush quarters in a beautifully restored downtown building. ▣ P ▣ ▣ TV ▣ ▣	▣	99			
MADISON: *Hillside Inn* ⓈⓈ 831 E Main St. ☏ *(812) 265-3221.* FAX *(812) 265-2453.* W www.hillsidemadison.com Offering panoramic views of the Ohio River and downtown historic district, this newly renovated property was the site of the 1958 film *Some Came Running*, starring Frank Sinatra, Dean Martin, and Shirley MacLaine. ▣ P ▣ ▣ TV ▣	▣	30			▣
NEW HARMONY: *The New Harmony Inn* Ⓢ 504 North St. ☏ *(812) 682-4491, (800) 782-8605.* FAX *(812) 682-3423.* W www.newharmonyinn.com Built in the simple Harmonist style, The New Harmony Inn has a restorative ambience, complete with an enclosed swimming pool. ▣ P ▣ ▣ TV ▣ ▣	▣	90	▣		
MICHIGAN					
DETROIT: *The Atheneum Suite Hotel* ⓈⓈⓈⓈ 1000 Brush Ave. ☏ *(313) 962-2323, (800) 772-2323.* FAX *(313) 962-2424.* W www.atheneumsuites.com Downtown Detroit's only all-suite luxury hotel provides convenient access to the Renaissance Center office complex. ▣ ▣ P ▣ ▣ TV ▣ ▣	▣	174	▣		
GRAND RAPIDS: *Amway Grand Plaza Hotel* ⓈⓈⓈ 187 Monroe Ave NW. ☏ *(616) 774-2000, (800) 253-3590.* FAX *(616) 458-6641.* W www.amwaygrand.com Designed in 1913 by the architects of New York's Grand Central Terminal, this hotel features a gold-leafed lobby ceiling. ▣ ▣ P ▣ ▣ TV ▣ ▣ ▣	▣	682	▣		
MACKINAC ISLAND: *The Grand Hotel* ⓈⓈⓈⓈⓈ 1 Grand Ave. ☏ *(906) 847-3331, (800) 334-7263.* FAX *(906) 847-3259.* W www.grandhotel.com A fine summer resort, this 1887 hotel provides picturesque lake views, and guest rooms filled with elegant antiques. ▣ ▣ P ▣ ▣ TV ▣ ▣ ▣	▣	381	▣	●	▣
SOUTH HAVEN: *Carriage House at the Harbor Bed & Breakfast* ⓈⓈⓈ 118 Woodman St. ☏ *(269) 639-2161.* FAX *(269) 639-2308.* W www.carriagehouseharbor.com Well-appointed accommodations and scenic Lake Michigan views are the trademark of this inn, housed in a Victorian mansion. ▣ P ▣ ▣ TV	▣	11	▣		
TRAVERSE CITY: *Bayshore Resort* Ⓢ 833 E Front St. ☏ *(231) 935-4400, (800) 634-4401.* FAX *(231) 935-0262.* W www.bayshore-resort.com This smoke-free, Victorian-style beachside resort offers sweeping views of West Grand Traverse Bay, as well as on-site sailboat, parasail, and jet-ski rentals. ▣ ▣ P ▣ ▣ TV ▣ ▣ ▣	▣	120		●	▣

For key to symbols see back flap

Price categories for a standard double room per night, inclusive of breakfast, service charges, and any additional taxes:

$ under $100
$$ $100–$150
$$$ $150–$200
$$$$ $200–$250
$$$$$ over $250

CREDIT CARDS
Major credit cards accepted:

NUMBER OF ROOMS
Number of rooms in the hotel.

RECOMMENDED RESTAURANT
Good restaurant within the hotel.

CHILDREN'S FACILITIES
Hotel has various facilities for young children.

GARDEN OR TERRACE
Hotel has a garden, courtyard, or terrace.

		CREDIT CARDS	NUMBER OF ROOMS	RECOMMENDED RESTAURANT	CHILDREN'S FACILITIES	GARDEN OR TERRACE
MINNESOTA						
DULUTH: *Fitger's Inn* $$$ 600 E Superior St. (218) 722-8826, (800) 726-2982. FAX (218) 722-8826. www.fitgers.com Breathtaking Lake Superior views and graciously appointed rooms are among the many charms of this downtown hotel, located in a restored 1880s brewery building.		■	62	■		■
ELY: *Grand Ely Lodge Resort and Conference Center* $$$ 400 N Pioneer Rd. (218) 365-6565. FAX (218) 365-2840. www.grandelylodge.com This commodious, northwoods lodge is perched on the shores of the secluded Shagawa Lake. Guests can explore the surrounding wilderness on foot, by bike, or by boat.		■	61	■	●	■
ELY: *Burntside Lodge* $$$ 2755 Burntside Lodge Rd. (218) 365-3894. FAX (218) 365-3459. www.burntside.com This serene resort located at the water's edge on the spring-fed Burntside Lake, features sandy beaches, a Finnish sauna, and an excellent restaurant.		■	21	■	●	■
GRAND MARAIS: *Gunflint Lodge* $$$$ 143 S Gunflint Lake. (218) 388-2294, (800) 328-3325. FAX (218) 388-9429. www.gunflint.com This Lake Superior lodge features lakeside cabins with fireplace, saunas and hot tubs, and provides guided fishing tours, nature hikes, and horseback rides through the Boundary Waters region.		■	23	■	●	■
LAKE KABETOGAMA (VOYAGEURS NATIONAL PARK): *Kettle Falls Hotel* $ 10502 Gamma Rd. (218) 875-2070. www.kettlefallshotel.com Constructed by a timber baron in 1910, this remote lakeside inn can only be reached by boat or float plane, with free shuttle boats departing daily from nearby towns.		■	12	■		■
MINNEAPOLIS: *Marquette Hotel* $$$ 710 Marquette Ave. (612) 333-4545, (800) 328-4782. FAX (612) 288-2188. www.marquettehotel.com This boutique-style, downtown hotel is conveniently located near Nicolett Mall's many shops and restaurants.		■	277	■		■
MINNEAPOLIS: *Minneapolis Grand Hotel* $$$$$ 615 2nd Ave S. (612) 288-8888, (866) 843-4726. FAX (612) 373-0407. www.grandhotelminneapolis.com Every room is unique in this upscale, downtown hotel, which also features an exceptional two-story fitness center and spa.		■	140	■		
RED WING: *St. James Hotel* $$$$ 406 Main St. (800) 252-1875. FAX (651) 388-5226. www.st-james-hotel.com Each guest room is named after a different Mississippi River steamboat in this elegant 1875 hotel, which offers spectacular Sunday-brunch river views from the top-floor Summit Room.		■	61	■		■
ST. PAUL: *St. Paul Hotel* $$$$$ 350 Market St. (651) 292-9292. FAX (651) 228-9506. www.stpaulhotel.com From the lobby's Gustav Klimt paintings to the plushly furnished guest rooms, this stately 1910 Italian Renaissance hotel is a destination unto itself in downtown St. Paul.		■	254	■		

OHIO

CINCINNATI: *The Cincinnatian Hotel* $$$$
601 Vine St. (513) 381-3000, (800) 876-2100. FAX (513) 651-0256.
W www.cincinnatianhotel.com
Artfully renovated and attired, this hotel has been consistently ranked as
the city's premier luxury hotel. 🍸 🛏 P 🛌 ⚡ TV 🔧 ♿ 🍴

146

CLEVELAND: *Renaissance Cleveland Hotel* $$$
24 Public Sq. (216) 696-5600, (888) 236-2427. FAX (216) 696-0432.
W www.renaissancehotels.com
This historic, upscale downtown hotel is connected via an indoor
walkway to The Avenue shops and Jacobs Field, home of the Cleveland
Indians baseball team. 🍸 🛏 P 🛌 ⚡ TV 🔧 ♿ 🍴

441

COLUMBUS: *The Lofts Hotel* $$$$
55 E Nationwide Blvd. (614) 461-2663, (800) 735-6387. FAX (614) 461-2630.
W www.55lofts.com
This 1882 commercial building, now offers loft-style guest rooms with
luxurious beds and high-speed Internet access. 🛏 P 🛌 ⚡ TV ♿ 🍴

44

TOLEDO: *Mansion View Inn* $$
2035 Collingwood Ave. (419) 244-5676. FAX (419) 244-9268.
W www.bbhost.com/mansionview
This elegant, 11,000-sq-ft (1,022-sq-m) Victorian mansion offers cozy suites
within walking distance of the Toledo Museum of Art. 🛏 P 🛌 ⚡ ♿

4

WISCONSIN

BAYFIELD: *Old Rittenhouse Inn* $$$
301 Rittenhouse Ave. (715) 779-5111, (800) 779 2129. FAX (715) 779-5887.
W www.rittenhouseinn.com
This Lake Superior inn holds a superb restaurant and rooms with fireplaces
in two Victorian-style homes and a guest cottage. 🍸 🛏 P 🛌 ⚡ ♿

23

MADISON: *Mansion Hill Inn* $$$
424 N Pinckney St. (608) 255-3999, (800) 798-9070. FAX (608) 255-2217.
W www.mansionhillinn.com
Perched on a ridge along Lake Mendota, this elegant inn was built in
1857 as a private residence. The lush grounds include a Victorian garden
with a beautiful fountain. P 🛌 TV ⚡

11

MILWAUKEE: *Hotel Metro* $$$$
411 E Mason St. (414) 272-1937, (877) 638-7620. FAX (414) 223-1158.
W www.hotelmetro.com
Milwaukee's only historic boutique hotel features enormous guest suites
and one of the city's liveliest lounges. 🍸 🛏 P 🛌 ⚡ ♿ 🍴

64

MILWAUKEE: *Pfister Hotel* $$$$$
424 E Wisconsin Ave. (414) 273-8222, (800) 558-8222.
W www.pfister-hotel.com
This grand downtown hotel was built in 1893 by a successful Milwaukee
merchant. Renovated to its original opulence, the Pfister offers excellent
service and luxurious accomodations. 🍸 🛏 P 🛌 ⚡ TV ♿ 🍴

307

SISTER BAY: *Country House Resort* $$$
715 N Highland Rd. (920) 854-4551, (800) 424-0041. FAX (920) 854-9809.
W www.country-house.com
This cedar-framed, native stone 1907 building overlooks the Green Bay
shoreline, just south of the peaceful village of Sister Bay. The plush
penthouse suite includes a fireplace and whirlpool. 🛏 P 🛌 ⚡ 🏊

46 ●

STURGEON BAY: *Glidden Lodge Beach Resort* $$$$
4676 Glidden Dr. (920) 746-3900, (888) 281-1127. FAX (920) 746-3905.
W www.gliddenlodge.com
Every condominium unit in this secluded, upscale, and trendsetting resort
has a well-appointed kitchen, private patio, and sweeping views of Lake
Michigan. 🍸 🛏 P 🛌 ⚡ TV ♿ 🏊 🍴

31

TREMPELEAU: *Trempeleau Hotel* $
150 Main St. (608) 534-6898. FAX (608) 534-6054.
W www.greatriver.com/oldhotel.htm
This laid-back 1871 inn features a vegetarian-friendly restaurant and
comfortable rooms with views of the Mississippi River. 🍸 ⚡

11

For key to symbols see back flap

Where to Eat

ALTHOUGH FAMILY-STYLE DINING establishments are legion in all the Great Lakes states, nearly every sizable community contains a variety of fine-dining alternatives to the traditional meat-and-potatoes Midwestern fare. Very few Great Lakes restaurants require formal dining attire. Opening times are indicated by a "B" for breakfast, "L" for lunch, and "D" for dinner.

	CREDIT CARDS	OUTDOOR TABLES	VEGETARIAN	GOOD WINE LIST	CHILDREN'S FACILITIES

ILLINOIS

CHICAGO: *Ed Debevic's* $
640 N Wells St, Chicago. ☎ *(312) 664-1707.*
The menu, from meatloaf to milkshakes, is painted on the wall outside,
Inside, a disc jockey spins 1950s tunes while costumed wait staff sing,
dance, and dish out sassy attitude with the fries. *L, D.* 🍷 ✈ ♿

CHICAGO: *Heaven on Seven* $
Garland Building, 111 N Wabash Ave (7th Fl). ☎ *(312) 263-6443.*
A spicy tingle in your mouth on your first bite is an indication that you're
in for real Cajun cooking here. That, and the 1,165 bottles of hot sauces
on the wall. The gumbo is truly heavenly. *L, D on 3rd Fri of the month.*
● *Sun.* ✈ ♿ ♫

CHICAGO: *Star of Siam* $
11 E Illinois St. ☎ *(312) 670-0100.*
This sunny, open-concept River North Thai restaurant features spicy curries
and Phad Thai – with many vegetarian options – in a contemporary, stylish
setting. *L, D.*

CHICAGO: *Carson's "The Place for Ribs"* $$
612 N Wells St. ☎ *(312) 280-9200.*
Famous nationwide for its ribs, Carson's also offers outstanding Greek
chicken, and pork chops. Seating is ample and comfortable, and the
service excellent.

CHICAGO: *La Cantina Enoteca* $$
71 W Monroe St. ☎ *(312) 332-7005.*
This cozy spot is the first in a trilogy of Italian restaurants at this location
known as Italian Village. The kitchen specializes in fresh seafood and
hearty traditional Italian dishes. Not wheelchair accessible. ● *Sun L.*

CHICAGO: *The Berghoff* $$
17 W Adams St. ☎ *(312) 427-3170.* 🌐 www.berghoff.com
A Loop institution since 1898, this former corner saloon dishes out hearty
portions of German favorites such as bratwurst, schnitzel, and sauerkraut,
washed down with The Berghoff's house beer. *L, D.* ● *Sun.* 🍷 ✈ ♿

CHICAGO: *North Pond* $$$
2610 N Cannon Dr, Lincoln Park. ☎ *(773) 477-5845.*
Both the regional American cuisine inspired by local produce, and the
decor, reflect the philosophy of the Arts and Crafts movement – simplicity
and respect for quality craftsmanship. Excellent weekend brunch. ● *Mon.*

CHICAGO: *Topolobampo* $$$$
445 N Clark St. ☎ *(312) 661-1434.*
Some of the most innovative Mexican food is served at Topolobampo,
one of the country's most highly ranked restaurants and its casual
Frontera Grill sister restaurant. The restaurant offers various facilties for
young children. *L, D.* ● *Sun, Mon.* 🍷 ✈ ♿

GALENA: *Perry Street Brasserie* $$$$
124 N Commerce St. ☎ *(815) 777-3773.*
Organically grown ingredients, international cuisine, and rich desserts are the
hallmarks of this historic brasserie. The chocolate desserts are strongly
recommended. *D.* ● *Sun, Mon.* 🍷 ✈ ♿

ROCKFORD: *Paragon on State* $$$
205 W State St. ☎ *(815) 963-1660.*
A hip, sophisticated interior augments some of the state's finest gourmet
cuisine, along with an impressive wine list in this bustling downtown
establishment. *L Tue–Fri, D Tue–Sat.* ● *Sun, Mon.* 🍷 ✈ ♿

Price categories include a three-course meal for one, a glass of house wine, and all unavoidable extra charges such as sales tax and service: $ under $20 $$ $20–30 $$$ $30–45 $$$$ $45–60 $$$$$ over $60	**CREDIT CARDS** Major credit cards accepted. **OUTDOOR TABLES** Garden, courtyard, or terrace with outside tables. **VEGETARIAN** A good selection of vegetarian dishes available. **GOOD WINE LIST** Extensive list of good wines, both domestic and imported. **CHILDREN'S FACILITIES** Various facilities for young children.	CREDIT CARDS	OUTDOOR TABLES	VEGETARIAN	GOOD WINE LIST	CHILDREN'S FACILITIES

INDIANA

BLOOMINGTON: *Michael's Uptown Café* — $$
102 E Kirkwood Ave. ((812) 339-0900.
This downtown bistro serves a dizzying array of Cuban, Creole, and Cajun creations alongside adventurous continental fare. The persimmon pudding is a house specialty. *B, L, D.*

Credit Cards	Outdoor Tables	Vegetarian	Good Wine List	Children's Facilities
■	●	■	●	■

BLOOMINGTON: *Scholar's Inn Gourmet Café & Wine Bar* — $$$
717 N College Ave. ((812) 332-1892.
A 19th-century brick mansion houses one of the state's top restaurants, offering award-winning steak, poultry, seafood, and vegetarian entrées. The cuisine is immaculately matched by an excellent wine list. *L, D.* ● *Mon.*

Credit Cards	Outdoor Tables	Vegetarian	Good Wine List	Children's Facilities
■	●	■	●	■

FORT WAYNE: *Park Place Grill* — $$$
200 E Main St. ((260) 420-7275.
Known for its casually elegant atmosphere and choice of fine steaks, the Park Place Grill also features a wide variety of fresh seafood dishes, including filet of escalore and Thai-blackened mahi. *L, D.* ● *Sun.*

Credit Cards	Outdoor Tables	Vegetarian	Good Wine List	Children's Facilities
■		■	●	

INDIANAPOLIS: *Dunaway's Palazzo Ossigeno* — $$$$
351 S East St. ((317) 638-7663.
Located in the historic Indiana Oxygen building, Dunaway's features a fireside dining room and a summer-only rooftop view. The superb crab cakes, risotto-encrusted salmon, and roasted pork loin are highly recommended. *L, D.* ● *Sun.*

Credit Cards	Outdoor Tables	Vegetarian	Good Wine List	Children's Facilities
■	●	■	●	

INDIANAPOLIS: *St. Elmo Steak House* — $$$$
127 S Illinois St. ((800) 637-1811. W www.stelmos.com
This New York-style steakhouse has been an Indianapolis fixture since 1902. Its 20,000-bottle wine cellar and photo gallery of celebrity visitors enhance a selection of succulent steaks, chops, seafood, and chicken. *L, D.*

Credit Cards	Outdoor Tables	Vegetarian	Good Wine List	Children's Facilities
■		■	●	

SOUTH BEND: *LaSalle Grill* — $$$$
115 W Colfax Ave. ((574) 288-1155. (800) 382-9323.
This bustling urban establishment specializes in grilled steaks, seafood, lamb, and pork chops, served in a comfortable dining room in an historic downtown office building. *D.* ● *Sun.*

Credit Cards	Outdoor Tables	Vegetarian	Good Wine List	Children's Facilities
■		■	●	

MICHIGAN

ANN ARBOR: *The Earle* — $$$$
121 W Washington St. ((734) 994-0211.
Fresh French and Italian cuisine has made this romantic bistro Ann Arbor's premier downtown dining establishment. A piano bar and live weekend jazz combos complement the exquisite cuisine.
D. ● *May–Sep: Sun.*

Credit Cards	Outdoor Tables	Vegetarian	Good Wine List	Children's Facilities
■		■	●	

DETROIT: *Cyprus Taverna* — $$$
579 Monroe Ave. ((313) 961-1550.
A cozy atmosphere and a rich range of gourmet Greek dishes – including keftedakia lamb and beef meatball appetizer – have made this one of Greektown's most popular restaurants. The exotic entrées on the menu are equally matched by some excellent wines. *L, D.*

Credit Cards	Outdoor Tables	Vegetarian	Good Wine List	Children's Facilities
■		■	●	

FARMINGTON HILLS: *Tribute* — $$$$$
31425 W 12 Mile Rd. ((248) 848-9393.
One of *Gourmet* magazine's top 50 US restaurants, the Tribute achieves an innovative synthesis of European and regional American cuisine in a bold, colorful dining space. *L, D.*

Credit Cards	Outdoor Tables	Vegetarian	Good Wine List	Children's Facilities
■			●	

Price categories include a three-course meal for one, a glass of house wine, and all unavoidable extra charges such as sales tax and service:
$ under $20
$$ $20–30
$$$ $30–45
$$$$ $45–60
$$$$$ over $60

CREDIT CARDS
Major credit cards accepted.

OUTDOOR TABLES
Garden, courtyard, or terrace with outside tables.

VEGETARIAN
A good selection of vegetarian dishes available.

GOOD WINE LIST
Extensive list of good wines, both domestic and imported.

CHILDREN'S FACILITIES
Various facilities for young children.

	Price	Credit Cards	Outdoor Tables	Vegetarian	Good Wine List	Children's Facilities
GRAND RAPIDS: *The Sierra Room* 25 Ionia SW. ((616) 459-1764. A fusion of Asian, American, French, and Southwestern ingredients make eating at the downtown Sierra Room, one of western Michigan's most sophisticated dining experiences. L, D. ● Sun. 🍸 ⚡ & 🎵	$$$	■		■	●	■
MARQUETTE: *Vierling Restaurant and Brewery* 119 S Front St. ((906) 228-3533. This renovated 1883 saloon now houses a festive brewpub, featuring an ample selection of microbrewed beers alongside regional specialties such as Lake Superior whitefish, served in the traditional, Cajun, or picatta style. L, D. 🍸 ⚡ &	$$	■		■	●	

MINNESOTA

	Price	Credit Cards	Outdoor Tables	Vegetarian	Good Wine List	Children's Facilities
DULUTH: *Bennett's on the Lake* 600 E Superior St. ((218) 722-2829. Located in the historic Fitger's Brewery building overlooking Lake Superior, this romantic hideaway's specialties include honey-drizzled, pan-fried lake trout and a seared Isle Royale whitefish. The wine list is excellent. 🍸 ⚡ &	$$$	■		■	●	■
ELY: *The Dining Room at Blue Heron* 827 Kawishiwi Trail. ((218) 365-4720. Tucked away in an intimate B&B of the same name, the Blue Heron features such unique creations as pecan-crusted walleye, Korean bulgogi beef, and Honduran Mayan pork medallions. D. ● Mon, Tue. 🍸 ⚡ &	$$$	■		■	●	
MINNEAPOLIS: *Nye's Polonaise Room* 112 E Hennepin Ave. ((612) 379-2021. A lively piano bar and even livelier polka band provide the perfect backdrop for this no-nonsense, Polish supper club's hearty pierogi, cabbage rolls, sausage, and sauerkraut. L, D. ● Sun. 🍸 ⚡ & 🎵	$$	■		■	●	
MINNEAPOLIS: *Goodfellow's* 40 S 7th St. ((612) 332-4800. Tender cuts of beef, spicy Southwestern chicken, and a delicate mushroom ravioli are among the signature dishes at this elegant, downtown Minneapolis favorite. L, D. ● Sun. 🍸 ⚡ &	$$$$	■		■	●	■
ROCHESTER: *Broadstreet Café & Bar* 300 1st Avenue NW. ((507) 281-2451. Housed in a renovated historic warehouse, this luxurious and spacious bistro specializes in French and American *haute* cuisine. L, D. 🍸 ⚡ &	$$$	■		■	●	■
ST. PAUL: *Mickey's Dining Car* 36 W 7th St. ((612) 222-5633. Built in 1937, this classic streamlined diner serves some of the Twin Cities' best breakfast food, burgers and milkshakes, alongside its time-tested mulligan stew. L, D. ⚡ &	$	■				
ST. PAUL: *Pazzaluna Urban Trattoria and Bar* 360 St Peter St. ((651) 223-7000. Hand-painted tiles, plush seating and marble floors set the mood for this trendy, downtown St. Paul restaurant's superb antipasto, shiitake ravioli, and gourmet pizzas. D. ● Sun. 🍸 ⚡ &	$$$$	■		■	●	

OHIO

CINCINNATI: *The Celestial* $$$
1071 Celestial St. *(513) 241-4455.*
A stunning hilltop view, cozy fireplace, and sophisticated jazz combo create the perfect mood for this Mount Adams establishment's French-influenced cuisine and excellent wine list. *L, D.* ● *Sun.*

CLEVELAND: *Blue Point Grille* $$$
700 W St Clair. *(216) 875-7827.*
An elegant Warehouse District space houses one of Cleveland's most innovative seafood restaurants. Honduran tilapia and sea bass with red curry coconut sauce augment the more traditional grouper, swordfish, and salmon offerings. *D.* ● *Sun.*

CLEVELAND: *Il Circo Zibibbo* $$$
1300 W 9th St. *(216) 575-0699.*
Hand-blown glass, intimate lighting, and a colorful decor combine with unlikely combinations of Italian ingredients for one of Cleveland's more memorable downtown dining experiences. *D.*

COLUMBUS: *Alana's* $$$
2333 N High St. *(614) 294-6783.*
A creamy vegan risotto, artichoke-mashed potatoes, and a multiple-course "degustation" delight are among the many unexpected delights at this remarkable University District find. *D.* ● *Sun, Mon.*

TOLEDO: *Tony Packo's Café* $
1902 Front St. *(419) 691-6054.*
Made famous by M.A.S.H. TV star Jamie Farr, Tony Packo's serves spicy Hungarian hot dogs, with live Dixieland jazz on weekends. Don't miss the gallery of celebrity-autographed buns. *L, D.*

WISCONSIN

MADISON: *Café Continental* $$$
108 King St. *(608) 251-4880.*
Intimate lighting, textured walls, and a funky zinc bar complete the Parisian atmosphere of this downtown favorite, known locally for its pastas, gourmet pizzas, and continental cuisine. *L, D.*

MADISON: *Quivey's Grove* $$$
6261 Nesbitt Rd. *(608) 273-4900.*
Located in a renovated 1855 stable structure, Quivey's Grove specializes in comfort food – perch, trout, meatloaf, portobella mushrooms – prepared with fresh, native Wisconsin ingredients and served with regional beers and wines. *L, D.* ● *Sun.*

MILWAUKEE: *Coquette Café* $$
316 N Milwaukee Ave. *(414) 291-2655.* W www.coquettecafe.com
Housed in a former bank, this delightful Third Ward bistro's French and Mediterranean offerings include a crisp Alsatian pizza, sweet potato gnocchi, and fennel-puréed potatoes. *L, D.* ● *Sun.*

MILWAUKEE: *Mader's Restaurant* $$$
1037 N Old World Third St. *(414) 271-3377.* W www.maders.com
This landmark downtown restaurant serves German fare such as pork shank and schnitzel, as well as steaks, seafood, and a special children's menu. Housed in a 1913 brick building, it includes an art gallery and store featuring art prints, beer steins, and Lladró figurines. *L, D.*

SISTER BAY: *Sister Bay Café* $$
611 N Bayshore Dr. *(920) 854-2429.*
This friendly, unassuming café dishes out hearty doses of traditional Swedish cuisine in a casual, small town setting. Don't miss the chilled meatballs or the Rodgrod Med Flode pudding for dessert. High chairs or special items for children can be requested. *B, L, D.*

SPRING GREEN: *Spring Green Café* $
137 S Albany St. *(608) 588-7070.*
Housed in a converted cheese warehouse, this spunky café features home-style health food and ethnic cuisine, as well as an adjoining store selling gourmet groceries and natural products. The restaurant offers good facilities for young children. *B, L.*

For key to symbols see back flap

THE GREAT PLAINS

The Great Plains at a Glance

Centering on the midway longitude, the 100th meridian – which divides the United States roughly into East and West – this region is the essence of Middle America. Stretching from Canada to Texas, and sloping gradually from the foot of the Rocky Mountains to the floodplain of the Mississippi River, the Great Plains covers seven states, from North and South Dakota across Iowa, Nebraska, Missouri, Kansas, and Oklahoma. This largely rural and agricultural region is a place of small towns, wide open spaces, and distant horizons. Museums, historic sights, and entertainment options can be found in cities such as Tulsa, St. Louis, Kansas City, and Oklahoma City.

Williston   Minot

NORTH DAKOTA
(See pp442–43)

Jam

Bismarck

Bowman

Mobridge

Al

SOUTH DAKOTA   Pierre
(See pp444–47)

Hot Springs

Chadron   Valentine

Scotts Bluff   **NEBRASKA**
(See pp448–51)

North Platte

Ogallala   Ke

Colby

Hays

KANSAS
(See pp458–59)

Dodge City

Clinton

De

Theodore Roosevelt National Park
(see p443), *in North Dakota, was created in 1947 as a memorial in the president's honor. Today, herds of buffalo can frequently be seen roaming the park's stark but beautiful badlands.*

Black Hills
(see pp446–7), *South Dakota's main attraction, has six Native American reservations, as well as Mount Rushmore, with its giant, sculpted heads of four US presidents.*

Scotts Bluff (see p450) *is a major landmark on the Nebraska portion of the Oregon Trail. Vast, grassy expanses of open range still contain reminders of 19th-century overland routes, along which pioneer settlers traveled westward. The Oregon Trail from Independence, Missouri, followed the North Platte River as it headed northwest across the Rocky Mountains.*

◁ **Endless expanse of cornfields, a common sight in rural Iowa**

Des Moines (see p452) *is the state capital of Iowa, one of the country's largest agricultural producers, with a rich stock of hard-working farming communities. Iowa's green river valleys and lush cornfields encapsulate an idyllic image of a nearly vanished rural America.*

LOCATOR MAP

St. Louis (see pp454–5) *is one of Missouri's largest and most cosmopolitan cities. Its location on the route leading west made St. Louis an active commercial and cultural crossroads, a role symbolized by the Gateway Arch.*

0 km   100

0 miles   100

Spencer

Dubuque

Davenport

Iowa City

Des Moines

Omaha

IOWA
(See pp452–53)

Quincy

St. Joseph

MISSOURI
(See pp454–57)

hattan

Topeka   Kansas City

Columbia

Jefferson City

St. Louis

hita

rkansas City   Springfield

Poplar Bluff

Tulsa   OKLA.
66

oma   Muskogee

OKLAHOMA
(See pp460–61)

dmore

Wichita (see p459), *Kansas, was once a cattle drive destination, where cowboys stopped to let off steam. The town's colorful past is displayed at the Old Cowtown Museum. Dodge City is the state's other Old West town.*

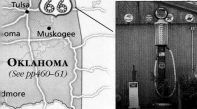

Oklahoma (see pp460–61) *boasts more miles of the original Old Route 66 highway than any other state. This historic road, famous as the "mother road" in John Steinbeck's* The Grapes of Wrath, *has also been celebrated in blues and jazz. Old gas pumps, signboards, and other exhibits can be seen at some Route 66 museums, especially in Clinton.*

THE GREAT PLAINS

FROM AN AIRPLANE, *the Great Plains looks like a repeated pattern of rectangular fields and arrow-straight highways, prompting urban Americans to dub it "fly-over country." This predominately rural and agricultural region, which stretches clear across the center of the country, embodies the all-American ideals of independence and hard-working self-sufficiency.*

The Great Plains are deeply rooted, both literally and figuratively, at the center of the American psyche. Though city-dwellers on both the East and West coasts may deride the region's general lack of sophistication, its residents' obvious pride in traditional values and old-fashioned lifestyles explains why this area is still the ideal location for all that is essentially American.

In fiction and film, the region has spawned such all-American creations as Mark Twain's *Huckleberry Finn*, Dorothy in *The Wizard of Oz*, the pioneer family of *Little House on the Prairie*, and the homespun sentimentality of *Field of Dreams* and *The Bridges of Madison County*.

Its rural reaches, with their vast expanses of fertile farmlands, form the basis of the Great Plains identity. Larger cities, such as Tulsa, St. Louis, Kansas City, and Oklahoma City, hold the bulk of the population as well as the museums, historic sights, and a wide range of hotels and resturants. Visitors can get a better sense of the region's culture by spending some time in bucolic, smaller towns.

HISTORY

Throughout the 17th and 18th centuries, French traders and fur trappers explored the region, coming into contact with the diverse Native American tribes who lived here. These tribes varied from the sedentary, agriculture-based cultures of the Caddo and Mandan people to the Pawnee, Osage, and Comanche Indians, whose livelihoods depended on hunting migratory herds of bison (or buffalo). As Europeans settled along the East Coast, other tribes relocated westward to the Great Plains. The most tragic mass migration to this region took place in 1838, when the

Herd of bison roaming the grasslands of Custer State Park, South Dakota

◁ **Eroded sandstone forms at Theodore Roosevelt National Park, North Dakota**

Lewis and Clark expedition mural at the Lewis & Clark Interpretive Center, Washburn, North Dakota

Cherokee Nation was forced to relinquish all lands east of the Mississippi River. In exchange, they were granted land for "as long as the grass grows and the waters run," in what was then known as Indian Territory (present-day Oklahoma). More than 4,000 people died from hunger, disease, and exposure on the long journey, dubbed the "Trail of Tears," from North Carolina to Oklahoma. Native American influence on the region is hard to quantify, but its heritage survives in numerous place names, including those of each state – Iowa, Missouri, Oklahoma, Kansas, Nebraska, and the Dakotas.

Among the first Americans to explore the Great Plains were the legendary Lewis and Clark, whose expedition to the Pacific Ocean and back took almost three years, from 1803 to 1806. Remarkable as their journey was, the later expedition of the German Prince Maximilian made perhaps the most enduring contribution to the region's lore. Maximilian's journals, as well as artist Karl Bodmer's drawings and paintings of Indians, were published in Germany in 1838, and finally put the Great Plains on the international map.

Both expeditions embarked from St. Louis, the region's oldest city founded as a distant French fur-trading frontier outpost. By the mid-19th century, Kansas City had joined St. Louis as an outpost for pioneers crossing the Great Plains on the legendary Santa Fe, California, and Oregon Trails.

After the Civil War, a series of transcontinental railroads followed many of the same routes, cutting down on travel time and transportation costs. The railroads, however, sliced across the migration routes for the bison herds

KEY DATES IN HISTORY

1738-43 French fur trader Pierre Gaultier du Varennes, Sieur de la Verendrye, explores the northern Great Plains

1764 St. Louis established

1803 The US buys much of the region from France as part of the Louisiana Purchase

1833 German artist Karl Bodmer documents Native American lifestyles

1882 "Buffalo Bill" stages the world's first rodeo in North Platte, Nebraska

1890 Massacre of 300 Sioux Indians by the US Army at Wounded Knee on Pine Ridge Reservation, South Dakota

1907 Hollywood actor John Wayne is born in Winterset, Iowa

1930-37 Extended drought and sustained winds create the Dust Bowl

1941 Mount Rushmore completed

1993 Disastrous springtime floods in Iowa and across the Great Plains

1995 The Federal Building in downtown Oklahoma City is destroyed by a truck bomb

2000 White supremacist Timothy McVeigh is executed for his role in the Oklahoma City bombing

whose numbers dwindled from millions to near extinction. As the railroads opened up the land, the Indians were forced onto reservations, while homesteading settlers took their place. These family-run farms, growing wheat, corn, cattle, and pigs, are still emblematic of the region, though many farms are now operated on an industrial scale by absentee landlords. The high point of agriculture was the World War I era, when farm prices were high and mechanization had yet to replace horse-drawn plows and other labor-intensive methods. The economic low point came soon afterward, when a sudden postwar drop in prices and a decade of drought turned the region into the "Dust Bowl," forcing some 200,000 farmers and their families to move west to California, a saga movingly documented in John Steinbeck's *The Grapes of Wrath*.

GEOLOGY & CLIMATE

The land is what defines life in the Great Plains. Some 500 million years ago, a deep inland sea laid the foundation of layers of sedimentary rock, with their rich array of ancient fossils as well as the fossil fuels that industries rely on today. Above this solid rock, a series of Ice Age glaciers, scraping their way south from Canada, deposited the pulverized soil that makes the eastern half of the Great Plains – and Iowa in particular – some of the world's most fertile farmland. Exceptions to the typically horizontal landscape are found at its fringes. The rugged Ozark Mountains lie in southern Missouri and Oklahoma, while in western South Dakota, the densely forested, gold-bearing granite peaks of the Black Hills rise high above the eroded sandstone of Badlands National Park.

While the underlying geology may make for uneventful scenery, the climate is anything but mild. The Great Plains experiences some of the nation's most extreme weather, particularly its fierce tornados. These powerful windstorms form with little warning in late spring and are most frequent along the "Tornado Alley," which runs through eastern Kansas and Oklahoma. The region also frequently suffers from flood-inducing rains and thunderstorms, scorching summer heat and humidity, and frigid winter blizzards.

PEOPLE & CULTURE

The Great Plains is, by and large, conservative, with patriotism and religion the dominating cultural values. Yet it also is a region of varied cultural and political traditions. In the 19th century, Kansas was one of the prime anti-slavery battlegrounds, but at the turn of the 21st century the state insisted that biblical ideas of creationism be taught in school science classes.

Ethnically, however, the population is surprisingly diverse. Many of the original immigrants were lured here from similar terrain in Europe, notably the steppes of eastern Europe, by promises of land ownership. A significant number were adherents of nonconformist religions, such as the Mennonites who came from German-speaking regions of Russia to settle in central Kansas and the Dakotas. Their past explains the presence of the many German-style pastry shops in what may seem like quintessentially American small towns.

Native Americans also play an increasingly visible role in the region's identity, thanks both to burgeoning casinos operated by the various tribes and to a growing respect for their culture and heritage. Oklahoma, for example, has one of the country's largest Native American populations, numbering nearly 10 percent of the state's 3 million inhabitants.

Prairie dog, Badlands

Pine Ridge Indian Reservation in South Dakota

Exploring the Great Plains

THE GREAT PLAINS DRAWS VISITORS in search of a taste of wholesome America. Its singular attraction is the countryside with its wide-open, seemingly endless spaces, where visitors can travel for miles without seeing more than a few railroad tracks, a set of power lines, or perhaps an occasional windmill or grain elevator. For those who want to explore farther, the Great Plains' highlights include the magnificent, sculpted monument of Mount Rushmore, the eerie landscape of Badlands National Park, and historic frontier outposts such as St. Louis and Kansas City, two of the region's largest cities. A car is essential to make the most of a visit to the Great Plains.

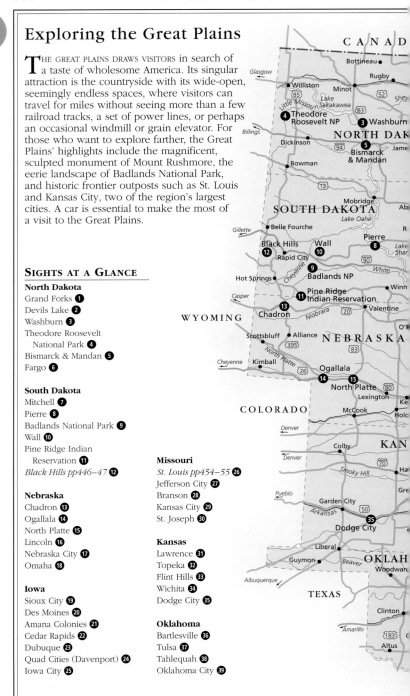

SIGHTS AT A GLANCE

North Dakota
Grand Forks **1**
Devils Lake **2**
Washburn **3**
Theodore Roosevelt
   National Park **4**
Bismarck & Mandan **5**
Fargo **6**

South Dakota
Mitchell **7**
Pierre **8**
Badlands National Park **9**
Wall **10**
Pine Ridge Indian
   Reservation **11**
Black Hills pp446–47 **12**

Nebraska
Chadron **13**
Ogallala **14**
North Platte **15**
Lincoln **16**
Nebraska City **17**
Omaha **18**

Iowa
Sioux City **19**
Des Moines **20**
Amana Colonies **21**
Cedar Rapids **22**
Dubuque **23**
Quad Cities (Davenport) **24**
Iowa City **25**

Missouri
St. Louis pp454–55 **26**
Jefferson City **27**
Branson **28**
Kansas City **29**
St. Joseph **30**

Kansas
Lawrence **31**
Topeka **32**
Flint Hills **33**
Wichita **34**
Dodge City **35**

Oklahoma
Bartlesville **36**
Tulsa **37**
Tahlequah **38**
Oklahoma City **39**

KEY

✈ Airport

〰 Highway

— Major road

— Railroad

- - State border

•—• International border

MILEAGE CHART

BISMARCK, ND

10 = Distance in miles
10 = Distance in kilometers

351 562	*RAPID CITY, SD*					
606 970	**524** 838	*OMAHA, NE*				
709 1134	**626** 1002	**135** 216	*DES MOINES, IA*			
1039 1662	**955** 1528	**435** 696	**433** 693	*ST. LOUIS, MO*		
786 1258	**706** 1130	**183** 293	**193** 309	**248** 397	*KANSAS CITY, MO*	
1034 1654	**706** 1130	**365** 584	**410** 656	**442** 707	**202** 323	*WICHITA, KS*
1122 1795	**924** 1478	**520** 832	**564** 902	**516** 826	**354** 566	**161** 258 *OKLAHOMA CITY, OK*

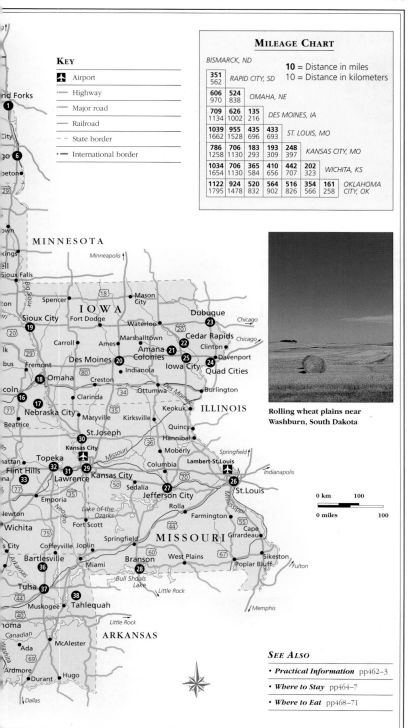

Rolling wheat plains near Washburn, South Dakota

0 km 100

0 miles 100

SEE ALSO

- *Practical Information* pp462–3

- *Where to Stay* pp464–7

- *Where to Eat* pp468–71

North Dakota

Fort Lincoln State Park

A STATE OF UNEXPECTED VARIETY, North Dakota's vast blue skies, tiny farming communities, and endless wheat fields along its eastern half can lull visitors into a state of quiet contemplation. Toward the west, North Dakota's drier, more rugged Missouri Plateau contains the stark badlands of Theodore Roosevelt National Park and more than a dozen historic sites visited by Lewis and Clark *(see p570)* on their 1803–06 expedition up the Missouri River. The explorers spent 146 days in North Dakota on their outbound and return journeys. Vast tracts of undeveloped areas along the river north of the pleasant capital city of Bismarck still look much like they did in the early 19th century.

Grand Forks ❶

49,400. ✈ 🚉 🚌 ℹ 4251 Gateway Dr, (800) 866-4566.
www.visitgrandforks.com

LOCATED AT THE junction of the Red and Red Lake Rivers, the city attracted international attention in 1997, when the Red River flooded downtown, destroying many historic structures and inflicting huge damage. Massive clean-up, water control, and reconstruction efforts have helped Grand Forks overcome much of the flood's disastrous effects.

The **Empire Arts Center**, housed in the restored 1919 Empire Theatre, is now downtown's vibrant performing arts center. The University of North Dakota campus, 2 miles (3 km) west of downtown, is home to the **North Dakota Museum of Art**, with its good collection of contemporary art.

🏛 **Empire Arts Center**
415 Demers Ave. 🅲 (701) 746-5500.
◯ call for times. 🅿 ♿
www.empireartscenter.org

Devils Lake ❷

7,800. 🚉 🚌 ℹ US 2 E, PO Box 879, (800) 233-8048.
www.devilslakend.com

THE PRIMARY recreational attraction in northeastern North Dakota is the 120,000-acre (48,600-ha) glacial Devils Lake, 90 miles (150 km) west of Grand Forks. With miles of shoreline and no natural outlet, the lake is an excellent spot for fishing and boating. Many of the area's residents, however, face an uncertain future, as the lake's ever-rising waters have forced them to relocate their homes.

Fort Totten State Historic Site, 14 miles (22 km) to the south, is one of the best-preserved United States Army bases from the post-Civil War era. The restored buildings around the parade ground contain period furniture.

🚩 **Fort Totten State Historic Site**
Rte 57. 🅲 (701) 766-4441.
◯ 8am–5pm daily. 🅿 ♿ www.state.nd.us/hist/totten/totten.htm

Washburn ❸

1,500. ℹ c/o McLean County Historical Society, 610 Main Ave, (701) 462-3526.
www.rootsweb.com/~ndmclean

THE KEY ATTRACTION in the area surrounding this sleepy Missouri River town is the **Lewis and Clark Interpretive Center**. A stunning view of the Missouri River Valley greets visitors, who can also don buffalo robes, listen to Native American music, and view exhibits tracing the river's shifting course over the past 200 years.

The newly constructed museum is an ideal starting point for a tour of the sites associated with Lewis and Clark's historic expedition. About 2 miles (3 km) north of the visitor center is the reconstructed **Fort Mandan**. It was near here that Lewis and Clark's 44-man Corps of Discovery wintered between 1804 and 1805.

The **Knife River Indian Village National Historic Site**, 20 miles (32 km) west of Washburn, contains the remains of the largest villages of the interrelated Mandan, Hidatsa, and Arikara tribes. Among these are a restored 50ft x 12-ft (15m x 12-m) earth lodge. The French trapper Charbonneau, and his Native American wife, Sacagawea, joined the Lewis and Clark expedition near this spot in 1804.

🚩 **Lewis & Clark Interpretive Center**
US 83 & Rte 200A. 🅲 (877) 462-8535. ◯ Jun–Sep: 9am–7pm; Oct–May: 9am–5pm. 🅿 ♿
www.fortmandan.com

The reconstructed, high-stockaded façade of Fort Mandan, near Washburn

The Painted Canyon, Theodore Roosevelt National Park

Theodore Roosevelt National Park ❹

Medora. 🚹 (701) 623-4466.
🕐 8am–4:30pm daily. 🚫 Jan 1,
Thanksgiving, Dec 25. 🎫 🚻
🅦 www.nps.gov/thro

THE TINY WESTERN North
Dakota town of Medora is
the gateway to the Theodore
Roosevelt National Park and
the remote, beautiful North
Dakota badlands. The bill
that created this park as a
memorial to Roosevelt was
signed on April 25, 1947, by
President Truman. On Nov-
ember 10, 1978, the area was
given national park status by
virtue of another bill signed
by President Carter.

The Theodore Roosevelt
National Park is a sprawling
one, covering over 70,000
acres (28,328 ha) of land. It is
divided into two pockets – the
North and South Units – about
70 miles (112 km) apart. The
butte-studded South Unit has
the phantasmagoric **Painted
Canyon** and can be explored
on horseback or seen from an
overlook from a 36-mile (58-
km) self-guided auto tour. The
North Unit features a
dramatic, oxbow bend in the
Little Missouri River. Its
moonlike landscape is dotted
with mushroom-shaped stone
formations and windswept
grasslands. Unlike the much-
visited South Unit, this pocket
lies in very isolated country.
However, a 14-mile (22-km)
auto route through this
rugged landscape provides
access to a nature trail and
numerous scenic overlooks.

Bismarck & Mandan ❺

🏃 65,000. ✈ 🚌 🛈 1600 Burnt
Boat Dr, Bismarck, (800) 767-3555.
🅦 www.bismarckmandancvb.com

RIVERBOAT TRAFFIC, railroads,
and the government were
instrumental in the development of the state capital of
Bismarck, founded in 1872 on
the east bank of the Missouri
River. The 19-story, Art Deco
North Dakota State Capitol
dominates the city's leafy,
low-slung skyline. Known as
the "Skyscraper of the
Prairies," the 1933 structure is
visible for miles in every
direction, mainly because of
its location on top of a small
rise north of downtown. The
**North Dakota Heritage
Center**, abutting the Capitol,
provides a fascinating introduction to the state's Native
American heritage and territorial settlement. It also traces
the story of the Capitol's
design and construction.

The shipping and ware-
housing center of Mandan lies
just across the Missouri. To
the south of downtown is
**Fort Abraham Lincoln State
Park**, which contains On-a-
Slant Indian Village, the
excavated remains of a 17th-
century Mandan Native
American community, and
several other reconstructed
buildings. The fort was the
last base for reckless George
Armstrong Custer, who led
the 7th Calvary from here to
their disastrous defeat at the
Battle of Little Bighorn (see
p581) in 1876.

🏛 **North Dakota Heritage
Center**
Capitol Mall, Bismarck. 🚹 (701) 328-
2666. 🕐 8am–5pm Mon–Fri, 9am–
5pm Sat, 11am–5pm Sun. 🚻
🏛 **Fort Abraham Lincoln
State Park**
4480 Fort Lincoln Rd. 🚹 (701) 663-
9571. 🕐 May 1–Memorial Day:
9am–5pm daily; Memorial Day–Labor
Day: 9am–7pm; Labor Day–Sep 30:
9am–5pm. 🎫 🚻

Fargo ❻

🏃 90,600. ✈ 🚊 🚌 🛈 2001 44th
St SW, (800) 235-7654.
🅦 www.fargomoorhead.org

A GRAIN PROCESSING center,
Fargo lies directly across
the Red River from its sister
city, Moorhead, Minnesota.
Fargo's historic downtown
includes the renovated 1926
Fargo Theatre, an Art
Moderne structure that still
presents art and period films
as well as live performances.
Southwest of the theater is
the superb **Plains Art
Museum**, housed in a
restored 1904 International
Harvester Company ware-
house. This museum has the
state's largest public art
collection, with works by the
region's Native American and
folk artists. The **Roger Maris
Baseball Museum**, in the
West Acres Shopping Center,
celebrates the achievements
of Fargo's most famous native
son, who hit 61 home runs in
1961, setting a record for
most home runs in a season.

🎭 **Fargo Theatre**
314 Broadway. 🚹 (701) 239-8385.
🕐 call for schedule. 🎫 🚻

**Exterior of the historic Fargo
Theatre, Fargo**

South Dakota

Pine Ridge Reservation

Rivers, hills, buttes, rolling prairies, and badlands are South Dakota's defining geographical features. The Missouri River bisects the state from north to south, with the corn and soybean fields of the flatter eastern plains giving way to shortgrass prairie and rocky badlands as one heads west on the state's main east–west corridor, I-90. Culturally, the state is dominated by the heritage of the Dakota, Lakota, and Nakota Sioux tribes, who roamed and hunted the buffalo-rich area until they were moved onto reservations in the late 1800s. Over 60,000 Native Americans still reside here.

Exterior of the South Dakota State Capitol in Pierre

Mitchell ❼

🏙 13,800. 🚂 ℹ️ 601 Main St, (866) 273-7676. 🌐 www.cornpalace.com

Located in the fertile James River Valley, Mitchell is the state's corn, grain, and cattle center. The city's claim to fame is the well-known **Corn Palace**, a Moorish auditorium that was built in 1921 to house the city's Corn Belt Exposition. Colorful domes, minarets, and kiosks are the only permanent design features on the ever-changing façade of the palace. Every year, local artists use more than 3,000 bushels of corn and grasses to create new murals, which depict agricultural scenes from South Dakota. This tradition dates back to 1892, when the Corn Real Estate Association constructed the first palace to showcase the area's crops, in an endeavor to lure settlers.

🏛 **Corn Palace**
⏱ May: 8am–5pm daily; Jun–Aug: 8am–9pm daily; Sep: 8am–5pm daily; Oct–Apr: 8am–5pm Mon–Fri. ♿

Mural at the Corn Palace, Mitchell

Pierre ❽

🏙 12,900. ✈️ 🚂 ℹ️ 800 W Dakota Ave, (800) 962-2034.
🌐 www.pierrechamber.com

The second smallest capital in the US, Pierre lies in the Missouri River Valley, and forms a leafy oasis in the shortgrass, largely treeless plains of central South Dakota. The 1910 **South Dakota State Capitol** has a grand marble staircase and overlooks a lake visited each spring and fall by thousands of migratory birds. In 2004, Pierre hosted a bicentennial commemoration of the famed Lewis and Clark expedition.

The excellent **South Dakota Cultural Heritage Center** is built into the side of a Missouri River bluff, covered with shortgrass prairie. Its exhibits trace the history of South Dakota's Sioux tribes and also provide information on the diverse ethnic backgrounds of the state's homesteading white settlers. On display is a lead plate that was buried in a nearby river bluff in 1743 by the French-sponsored Verendrye expedition to mark the site as French territory. The **Verendrye Museum**, across the river in Fort Pierre, focuses on French trading and exploration activities.

Badlands National Park ❾

ℹ️ Ben Reifel Visitor Center, Rte 240, S of I-90 exit 131. 📞 (605) 433-5361. ⏱ Jun–Aug: 7am–8pm; Sep–Oct: 8am–6pm; Nov–May: 9am–4pm. 🅿️ ♿ 🌐 www.nps.gov/badl

South Dakota State Capitol
500 E Capitol Ave. 📞 (605) 773-3765. ⏱ 8am–10pm daily.

South Dakota Cultural Heritage Center
900 Governors Dr. 📞 (605) 773-3458. ⏱ 9am–4:30pm Mon–Fri, 1–4:30pm Sat–Sun. ⏺ Jan 1, Thanksgiving, Dec 25. 🅿️ ♿

The eerie desolation of Badlands National Park is an awe-inspiring sight for travelers unprepared for such a stark, rugged landscape after miles of gentle, rolling South Dakota prairie. Formed over 14 million years ago from silt and sediment washing down from the Black Hills (see pp446–7), the badlands were sculpted into their present craggy form by harsh sun and powerful winds.

Some of the region's most dramatically eroded buttes, pinnacles, and spires are contained in this 244,000-acre (98,744-ha) park. The **Ben Reifel Visitor Center** is the gateway to several self-guided hiking tours and the 30-mile (48-km) Badlands Loop Road (Route 240). The scenic drive follows the northern rim of the 450-ft (137-m) high Badlands Wall escarpment and leads to several overlooks and trails that provide breathtaking vistas of the eroded

View of the eroded gullies from Changing Scenes Overlook in Badlands National Park

gullies below. The road loops back north to I-90 near **Sage Creek Wilderness Area**, where golden eagles, hawks, and various songbirds gather in a vast expanse of steep grasslands, festooned each summer with wildflowers. The park-managed buffalo herd can be seen grazing on large stretches of prairie.

Wall Drug Store, a shopping and entertainment complex

Wall ⑩

🏞 800. 🚌 ℹ 503 Main St, (888) 852-9255. W www.wall-badlands.com

WALL HAS DONE a thriving tourist trade since 1936, when local pharmacist Ted Hustead put up signs along the highway offering free ice water. This primitive roadside advertising tactic soon grew into a statewide slew of billboards, which still line I-90 all the way across South Dakota. Hustead's small-town pharmacy, **Wall Drug**, is now a sprawling Wild West shopping and entertainment complex. Along with Western and Native American

souvenirs are interactive exhibits of cowboys, homesteaders, gunfighters, and medicine-show hucksters.

The sprawling **Buffalo Gap National Grasslands** lies south and west of Wall. Its visitor center describes the ecological and cultural history of the grasslands. Various exhibits outline the various habitats and illustrate the astonishing biodiversity of the shortgrass, mixed-grass, and tallgrass prairies, which once covered most of the region.

🚻 Wall Drug
510 Main St. 🄲 *(605) 279-2175.*
⬜ *6:30am–7pm daily (extended summer hours).*
Ⓦ *www.walldrug.com*
🏞 Buffalo Gap National Grasslands
ℹ *708 Main St, (605) 279-2125.*
⬜ *Memorial Day: 8am–6pm daily; Labor Day–Memorial Day: 8am–4:30pm Mon–Fri.* ♿

Pine Ridge Indian Reservation ⑪

ℹ *Oglala Sioux Tribe, Pine Ridge, (605) 867-6075.*

HOME TO THE Oglala Sioux tribe, the Pine Ridge Reservation is the nation's second-largest Native American reservation. The reservation lands abut the South Dakota–Nebraska border and extend west into the badlands region. The Oglala and their chief, Red Cloud, were relocated here in 1876. On December 29, 1890, the US

Army's 7th Cavalry massacred about 300 Lakota men, women, and children at **Wounded Knee**. This was the last in a series of misunderstandings concerning the ceremonial Ghost Dance, which the tribe believed would reunite them with their ancestors, bring the buffalo back, and help them regain their lost lands. A lone stone monument, about 10 miles (16 km) east of the village of Pine Ridge, marks the site.

The **Red Cloud Heritage Center**, on the Red Cloud Indian School campus near Pine Ridge, contains the gravesite of Chief Red Cloud. It also displays a range of Native American artifacts.

🚻 Red Cloud Heritage Center
4.5 miles (7 km) N of Pine Ridge Village on Hwy 18. 🄲 *(605) 867-5491.* ⬜ *8am–5pm Mon–Fri.*
⬤ *public hols.* ♿
Ⓦ *www.redcloudschool.org*

The Red Cloud Heritage Center at the Pine Ridge Indian Reservation

Black Hills ⑫

KNOWN TO THE LAKOTA SIOUX as Paha Sapa, these majestic hills were a mysterious, sacred place where Native Americans would retreat to seek guidance from the Great Spirit. In 1874, George Armstrong Custer's *(see p581)* expedition discovered evidence of gold deposits in the thickly forested, oddly shaped granite hills. A series of misleading treaties followed, forcing the Sioux to relinquish their land, as miners, speculators, and settlers rushed into these once-sacred hills to stake their claims. Today, the Black Hills harbor some of the state's most visited attractions, particularly Mount Rushmore National Memorial. The 125-mile x 65-mile (201-km x 105-km) area is linked by US 385 and US 16, which meanders from Rapid City, the main center in the area, to Wyoming.

LOCATOR MAP

☐ *Black Hills* ☐ *Area illustrated*

Crazy Horse Memorial

When complete, the statue of the great Sioux warrior, Crazy Horse, will be the world's largest sculpture. At present only the nine-story high face has been finished.

Jewel Cave
National Monument

Jewel Cave National Monument

The underground attractions in the third-longest cave in the world are more varied than those at Wind Cave. Tough spelunking (cave exploring) tours allow participants into some of the more astounding areas. A simpler paved route offers a broad overview.

Deadwood

The restored downtown re-creates Deadwood's past as a wild, lawless gold mining town. Gunfighter Wild Bill Hickock was shot here in 1876, and Calamity Jane also left her mark here. Today, visitors try their luck in the historic gaming halls.

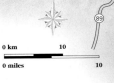

| 0 km | 10 |
| 0 miles | 10 |

KEY

— Custer State Park boundary

— Wind Cave NP boundary

═ Major road

Mount Rushmore National Memorial

An American icon since its completion in 1941, the giant, sculpted heads of presidents George Washington, Thomas Jefferson, Abraham Lincoln, and Theodore Roosevelt took 14 years to create. Sculptor Gutzon Borglum's studio, tools, and models are preserved on site.

Custer State Park

This 73,000-acre (29,542 ha) park is one of the region's most pristine natural habitats, with towering rock formations such as the Needles Eye, a spire rising 30–40 ft (9–12 m) high.

Wind Cave National Park

This park contains the world's sixth-longest limestone cavern, its underground labyrinth studded with strange, popcorn-like forma-tions. Guided tours include a historical candlelight tour, and the Natural Entrance tour.

The Mammoth Site

Discovered in 1974, this site displays the world's largest concentration of Columbian mammoth fossils. Originally a spring-fed sinkhole where animals were trapped and preserved, only 30 percent of the 26,000-year-old site has been explored so far.

Nebraska

Indian tepee, Chadron

NEBRASKA'S VAST, grassy expanses of open range, and ruts from old overland routes, epitomize the geography and history of the Great Plains. The modern I-80 freeway stretches westward in the shadow of the wide Platte River Valley, the historic Oregon, Mormon, and Pony Express Trails, and the original Lincoln Hwy (now US 30). Farther north, the sparsely settled central Nebraska Sandhills contain some of the nation's largest expanses of unbroken, mixed-grass prairie, while the Panhandle in the northwest is studded with rocky outcrops and jagged canyons. The state's two largest cities, Omaha and Lincoln, are in the southeast.

Chadron ⓭

🏛 5,600. ✈ 🛈 706 W 3rd St, (800) 603-2937. 🌐 www.chadron.com

CHADRON IS THE ideal base to tour the Pine Ridge and Sandhills regions as well as explore aspects of the state's fascinating past. About 3 miles (5 km) east of town is the **Museum of the Fur Trade**. Built on the grounds of an 1833–49 American Fur Company post, the museum traces the history of the complex North American fur trade and its effect on Native American communities. One of its main features is a reconstructed trading post built into the sides of a low hill.

The area's key historical attraction is **Fort Robinson State Park**, just west of Crawford, which itself is 23 miles (37 km) west of Chadron. The park occupies the parade grounds, barracks, and officers' quarters of the US Army's Fort Robinson. The fort was built in 1874 to protect the nearby Red Cloud Indian Agency, where Sioux

chief Red Cloud and his followers moved to before being relocated at Pine Ridge *(see p445)*. In 1877, the great Oglala Sioux chief, Crazy Horse *(see p446)*, and 900 of his tribe surrendered and set up camp outside of the fort. In a series of tragic events, Crazy Horse was killed while federal troops attempted to imprison him. A restored blockhouse commemorates the site where he fell.

The excellent Fort Robinson Museum details the fort's other lives as an experimental cattle ranch and a training ground for the army's World War II canine corps. The fort's restored quarters provide accommodation for visitors, while horseback trails lead through the surrounding lonesome buttes and grassy plains. The park also harbors a large herd of longhorn cattle and more than 400 bison.

Chadron State Park, 8 miles (13 km) south of Chadron, is a quieter, more scenic alternative, with ample campgrounds and cabin facilities. Hiking and biking trails

from the park crisscross the spine of the 230-mile (370-km) long Pine Ridge escarpment. Hikers and mountain bikers seeking more challenging routes can follow the 25-mile (40-km) Pine Ridge Trail, a steep, meandering route through patches of meadows and thick stands of ponderosa pine. The trail is part of the Pine Ridge National Recreation Area, a craggy portion of the vast Nebraska National Forest, which runs along the brow of the escarpment, south of US 20, between Chadron and Crawford.

🏰 **Fort Robinson State Park**
US 20, 3 miles (5 km) W of Crawford.
📞 (308) 665-32900. ◯ daily. ♿
🌐 ngpc.state.ne.us/parks/frob.html

Martin Bay in Lake McConaughy State Recreation Area, near Ogallala

Ogallala ⓮

🏛 5,100. 🚌 🛈 204 E A St, (800) 658-4390. 🌐 www.visitogallala.com

LOCATED ON THE South Platte River near the junction of I-80, US 26, and Route 92, Ogallala is the gateway to the Panhandle part of the Oregon Trail tour *(see p450)*. The city gained a rowdy reputation as the "Gomorrah of the Plains" soon after its founding in 1867, when the arrival of the railroad drew herds of cattle and hordes of Texas cowboys. Most modern visitors now come seeking camping, boating, hunting, and fishing supplies for their exploration of **Lake McConaughy State Recreation Area**, about 9 miles (14 km) to the north.

A refreshing oasis in the middle of the dry Panhandle

Restored officers' quarters in Fort Robinson State Park, Chadron

plains, Lake McConaughy is the state's largest reservoir. Known locally as "Big Mac," its cool waters are a prime breeding ground for rainbow trout, catfish, walleye, and white bass. The north shore is lined with fine sand beaches, while the marshes, woodlands, and grasslands on the lake's western end attract a wide variety of waterfowl. Loons, ducks, mergansers, and western grebes frequent Big Mac, making it one of the richest birding spots in the Great Plains region.

🦆 Lake McConaughy State Recreation Area
1475 Hwy 61 N. 📞 (308) 284-8800. ⏰ Memorial Day–Labor Day: 8am–8pm daily. ♿ Visitor center only. 🌐 ngpc.state.ne.us/parks/bigmac.html

North Platte 🄖

🏙 25,000. ✈ 🚂 ℹ 219 S Dewey, (800) 955-4528.
🌐 www.northplatte-tourism.com

NOW ONE OF the country's major railroad centers, North Platte was the late-19th-century home of the famed William "Buffalo Bill" Cody (see p582). The comfortable ranch house he built on the outskirts of town was the base of operations for his traveling Wild West show until 1902, when he founded Cody in Wyoming. Cody's home is now part of the **Buffalo Bill Ranch State Historical Park** that includes a horse barn and log cabin from one of his previous ranches. The nearby **Lincoln County Historical Museum** exhibits a replica of the famous North Platte Canteen,

which served countless pots of coffee and quantities of snacks to the military troops who passed through the town during World War II.

🎪 Buffalo Bill Ranch State Historical Park
2921 Scouts Rest Ranch Rd. 📞 (308) 535-8035. ⏰ Apr–Memorial Day: 10am–4pm Mon–Fri; Memorial –Labor Day: 9am–5pm daily; Labor Day–Oct: 10am–4pm Mon–Fri. ● Oct–Apr. 🎥 ♿
🌐 www.ngpc.state.ne.us/parks

🏛 Lincoln County Historical Museum
2403 Buffalo Bill Ave. 📞 (308) 534-5640. ⏰ Jun–Labor Day: 9am–8pm Mon–Sat, 1–8pm Sun; Labor Day–Sep 30: 9am–5pm Mon–Sat, 1–5pm Sun. 🎥 ♿
🌐 www.npcanteen.tripod.com/canteen/lchm.html

Cody's house in North Platte's Buffalo Bill Ranch State Historical Park

Lincoln 🄗

🏙 235,000. ✈ 🚂 🚌 ℹ 201 N 7th St, (800) 423-8212.
🌐 www.lincoln.org

STATE CAPITAL and Nebraska's second-largest city, Lincoln is also home to the University of Nebraska, whose Cornhuskers football team is so

Bronze statue surmounting the Nebraska State Capitol in Lincoln

popular that it has sold out every home game at the 77,000-seat Memorial Stadium since 1962. The city's principal landmark, however, is the 400-ft (120-m) Indiana limestone tower of the **Nebraska State Capitol**. Completed in 1932, the "Tower of the Plains" is surmounted by a bronze statue of a man sowing grain and visible for miles around. Intricate murals and ornate ceilings adorn the interior. The building houses the nation's only unicameral legislature, a vestige of cost-saving measures introduced by the state during the Great Depression of the 1930s.

The state's political history is related alongside its rich Native American heritage in the excellent **Museum of Nebraska History**, located on 15th and P Streets. The **University of Nebraska State Museum**, in the down-town campus, has a wide-ranging collection of elephant fossils and Native American artifacts. In the nearby historic Haymarket District, several 19th-century warehouses have been converted into bars, restaurants, and shops.

🏛 Museum of Nebraska History
15th & P Sts. 📞 (402) 471-4754. ⏰ 9:30am–4:30pm Mon–Fri, 1–4:30pm Sat & Sun. ● public hols. ♿ 🌐 www.nebraskahistory.org

🏛 University of Nebraska State Museum
Morrill Hall, 14th & Vine Sts.
📞 (402) 472-2642. ⏰ 9:30am–4:30pm Mon–Sat, 1:30–4:30pm Sun. ● Jan 1, Thanksgiving, Dec 25. ♿ 🌐 www.museum.unl.edu

A colorful billboard in a parking lot welcoming visitors to North Platte

The Oregon Trail

Founded by trader William Sublette in 1830, this formidable 2,000-mile (3,200-km) trail was the main wagon route between Independence, Missouri *(see p457)* in the east and Oregon to the west. The original route curved northwest after crossing the Missouri River near present-day Kansas City, passing through northeastern Kansas and southeastern Nebraska on the way to the Platte River. Between 1841 and 1866, a staggering 500,000 settlers bound for the fertile farmlands of Oregon and the goldfields of northern California passed through Nebraska, following the northern banks of the Platte, past a string of army forts to Ogallala. As the trail veered northwest, away from the flat landscape of the Platte River Valley and up into the craggy Panhandle plateau along the North Platte River, pioneers were awestruck by the massive rock formations that signaled the Rockies to the west.

Trail marker, North Platte

Locator Map
The Oregon Trail

The Oregon Trail in Nebraska

More than 428 miles (689 km) of the original Oregon Trail passed through the flat grasslands of Nebraska before it turned northwestards. Today, most of the old routes are easily accessible, with historic markers guiding travelers on I-80, along the Platte River, or Route 92 and US 26, which follows the trail's northwestern ascent of the North Platte. This undated illustration by William H. Jackson depicts the first covered wagon caravan, led by Smith-Jackson-Sublette, consisting of ten wagons drawn by five mules each, heading for Wind River Valley near present-day Lander in Wyoming.

Chimney Rock, *east of the town of Scottsbluff, rises 500 ft (152 m) above the mixed-grass plains. This was one of the more frequently noted sights in travelers' diaries and sketchbooks.*

Scotts Bluff National Monument *has a well-staffed visitor center, which runs various interpretive and living history programs. These include an excellent overview of the Oregon Trail history as well as exhibits on the Mormon Trail. Visitors can hike to the summit of the 800-ft (244-m) sandstone outcropping and walk along still-visible Oregon Trail ruts.*

Morton's mansion at Arbor Lodge State Historical Park, Nebraska City

Nebraska City ⓱

🏠 7,200. ℹ️ 806 1st Ave, (800) 514-9113. 🅦 www.nebraskacity.com

SEDATE, TREE-LINED Nebraska City's origins were as a rowdy Missouri River way station, where families and adventurers bound for the Oregon Trail mingled with trappers, traders, and riverboat employees. Today, the city is best known as the birthplace of Arbor Day, established by Nebraska politician and newspaper editor Julius Sterling Morton (1832–1902). When he was Secretary of Agriculture under President Grover Cleveland, Morton introduced a resolution to make April 10 a state holiday to encourage farmers in Nebraska to plant trees as protection from high plains winds and soil erosion. Later, the date was changed to April 22, Morton's birthday. Arbor Day is still commemorated throughout the United States, although the date varies from state to state.

The city is also well known as the home of **Arbor Day Farm**, a 260-acre (105-ha) experimental farm, conference center, and forestry research center. Scenic hiking trails and guided tours offer casual explorations of the farm's apple orchards, windbreak arboretum, and a renewable energy plant.

The **Arbor Lodge State Historical Park** contains Morton's Georgian Revival mansion, greenhouse, and grounds. The park includes tours of the formal Italian garden and 52-room mansion, completed in 1902, and a carriage house with a stagecoach once driven by Wild West impresario Buffalo Bill *(see p582)*.

🚜 Arbor Day Farm
100 Arbor Ave. 📞 *(402) 873-9347.* ⭕ *9am–5pm Mon–Sat, noon–5pm Sun.* ⬤ *Jan 1, Thanksgiving, Dec 25.* ♿ 🅦 www.adflcc.com

Omaha ⓲

🏠 335,700. ✈️ 🚌 ℹ️ 1001 Farnam St, Ste 200, (402) 444-4660. 🅦 www.visitomaha.com

OMAHA EVOLVED from a rough-and-tumble Missouri River town and outfitting post into a major railroad terminus with the construction of the transcontinental railroad in 1868 *(see p571)*. The restored Old Market warehouse district just south of downtown preserves the city's historical roots. Its old commercial buildings and cobblestone streets are now home to some of the region's best restaurants, bookstores, and antique shops. A few blocks south, the city's landmark 1931 Art Deco Union Station has been refurbished and converted into the **Durham Western Heritage Museum**. This splendid local history museum features displays on Omaha's railroad and transportation heritage.

Just west of downtown is the pink marble **Joslyn Art Museum**, a Smithsonian affiliate and the crown jewel of Omaha's cultural attractions. The museum features 19th and 20th century European and American art. It also is a treasure trove of Western American art, with paintings, sculpture, and photographs by George Catlin, Frederic Remington, George Caleb Bingham, and Edward S. Curtis. The centerpiece of its Western collection are the watercolors and prints by Swiss artist Karl Bodmer *(see p438)*, who documented life on the upper Plains when he traveled across North America with German naturalist, Prince Maximilian of Wied, in 1833.

North of downtown, the **Great Plains Black History Museum** relates the rarely told story of African-American migration and settlement on the Great Plains, beginning with the Exoduster group of freed slaves that left Reconstruction-ravaged Tennessee in the 1870s to homestead in Kansas. The **Mormon Trail Center**, about 5 miles (8 km) to the north, commemorates the 1846-48 migration of Mormons from the Midwest to Utah *(see p519)*. Located on the pioneers' late-19th-century Winter Quarters campsite, an informative visitor center provides background on the religious persecution that led to the migration. It also displays a reconstructed Mormon Trail handcart and wagon.

🏛 Durham Western Heritage Museum
801 S 10th St. 📞 *(402) 444-5071.* ⭕ *10am–5pm Tue–Sat, 1–5pm Sun.* 📷 ♿ 🅦 www.dwhm.org

🏛 Joslyn Art Museum
2200 Dodge St. 📞 *(402) 342-3300.* ⭕ *10am–4pm Tue–Sat, noon–4pm Sun.* 📷 ♿ 🅦 www.josyln.org

Art Deco façade of Omaha's Durham Western Heritage Museum

Iowa

Stretching from the Mississippi on its eastern border to the Missouri River on the west, Iowa offers seemingly endless vistas of rolling hills, lush cornfields, old-fashioned barns, and clapboard, country churches. It is one of the nation's largest agricultural producers, with a rich stock of tidy, hard-working farming communities. These are the images that make the state a perfect setting for Hollywood movies seeking to capture a nearly vanished rural America. Iowa also has a handful of lively cities, including the state capital Des Moines, with its excellent art and history museums.

Sioux City ⑲

🏙 85,000. ✈ 🚌 ℹ 801 4th St, (800) 593-2228.
ⓦ www.siouxcitytourism.com

A busy railroad center and Missouri River port, Sioux City sits on the northern cusp of Iowa's green, shaggy Loess Hills. This unique ecosystem is comprehensively explained at the **Dorothy Pecaut Nature Center** in Stone State Park, about 3 miles (5 km) north of the city. The northern tip of the 200-mile (320-km) Loess Hills Scenic Byway, which traverses the hills, can be accessed from the park. The park also has one of the state's few surviving stands of tallgrass prairie and a network of bike and hiking trails.

Just south of downtown, the **Floyd Monument** standing on a loess bluff marks the 1804 burial of Sargent Charles Floyd, who was a member of Lewis and Clark's *(see p570)* Corps of Discovery. Floyd was the first and only member to die on the transcontinental journey of the three-year long expedition. The city's newest attraction, the **Lewis & Clark Interpretative Center**, opened along the riverfront in September 2002.

🏛 **Dorothy Pecaut Nature Center**
4500 Sioux River Rd. 📞 (712) 258-0838. ◷ 9am–5pm Tue–Sat, 1–5pm Sun. ⬤ public hols. ♿

Des Moines ⑳

🏙 199,005. ✈ 🚌 ℹ 405 6th Ave, (800) 451-2625.
ⓦ www.seedesmoines.com

The state capital draws its name from French voyageurs who explored the Raccoon and Des Moines River Valleys, calling the latter *La Rivière des Moinesk*, "River of the Monks." The city is now an important agricultural and entertainment center and home of the massive Iowa State Fair, which lures more than a million visitors every August.

Dominating the area east of downtown is the gold-leafed central dome of the **Iowa State Capitol**. Nearby is the **Iowa Historical Building**, with its displays on the state's Native American, geological, and cultural history. West of the Capitol, the Eliel Saarinen-designed **Des Moines Art Center** exhibits an impressive collection of paintings by Henri Matisse, Jasper Johns, Andy Warhol, and Georgia O'Keeffe. The center's modern sculpture gallery was designed by I.M. Pei.

Floyd Monument

🏛 **Des Moines Art Center**
4700 Grand Ave.
📞 (515) 277-4405.
◷ 11am–4pm Tue–Sat, 11am–9pm Thu, noon–4pm Sun. ♿
ⓦ www.desmoinesartcenter.org

Environs: Winterset, located about 35 miles (56 km) to the south, is the attractive seat of

Madison County and birthplace of Hollywood Western star John Wayne. The four-room house where the actor grew up is a much-visited museum today. The local Chamber of Commerce provides a map of the five covered bridges that inspired author Robert Waller's famous 1992 novel, *The Bridges of Madison County*.

A typical family home in the Amana Colonies

Amana Colonies ㉑

ℹ 39 38th Ave, Amana, (800) 579-2294. ⓦ www.amanacolonies.com

The seven Amana Colonies, along the Iowa River were settled in the 1850s by the Inspirationists, a mainly German religious sect. The colonists prospered, building a profitable woolen mill and a series of communal kitchens, shops, and factories. In 1932, residents voted to end their communal lifestyle, setting up a profit-sharing society instead.

One of the community businesses has since evolved into the Amana appliance manufacturer, while the 1857 Amana Woolen Mill is the state's only woolen mill still in operation. The **Museums of the Amana Heritage Society** commemorate the success of the colonies' enterprises and its unique history in five separate museums.

🏛 **Museums of the Amana Heritage Society**
📞 (319) 622-3567. ◷ May–Oct: 10am–5pm Mon–Sat, noon–5pm Sun.
📷 ♿ ⓦ www.amanaheritage.org

Cedar Rapids 22

108,800. ☒ ▦ ℹ️ 119 1st Ave SE, (800) 735-5557.
☒ www.cedar-rapids.com

THIS TOWN'S downtown straddles the Cedar River. The Iowa artist Grant Wood lived in Cedar Rapids for much of his adult life and developed a Regionalist style that celebrated the people and landscapes of his home state. The **Cedar Rapids Museum of Art** has one of the country's largest collection of Wood's paintings, including the well-known *Young Corn*.

The recently renovated History Center details the area's early history, while the **National Czech and Slovak Museum** celebrates the city's large Czechoslovak immigrant population. Czech Village, a corridor along 16th Avenue SW, is still lined with shops selling kolaches, babovkas, and other Czech delicacies.

Dubuque 23

57,500. ☒ ▦ ℹ️ 300 Main St, (800) 798-8844.
☒ www.dubuquechamber.com

IOWA'S OLDEST CITY was established in 1788 by a French voyageur, Julian Dubuque. During the 19th century, the city's noveau riche constructed luxurious homes atop the bluffs ringing the city. These citizens rode to and from downtown, 189 ft (57 m) below, via the **Fenelon**

View of Dubuque from the Fenelon Place Elevator

Place Elevator, an incline railway that is a major tourist attraction today.

The city's main attraction is the **Mississippi River Museum**, a riverfront complex with exhibits on the mighty river's history and ecology. A series of aquariums replicate the habitat and ecosystem of the country's different rivers.

Quad Cities (Davenport) 24

102,000. ☒ ▦ ℹ️ 2021 River Dr, Moline, Il, (800) 747-7800.
☒ www.visitquadcities.com

DAVENPORT IS ONE of the four Mississippi River communities that comprise the sprawling 400,000-person "Quad Cities" area on both sides of the Iowa and Illinois border. It is the only city not blocked off from the river by flood control walls. The excellent **Davenport**

Museum of Art west of downtown has one of the better collections of early-20th-century American Regionalist paintings. It displays works by Missouri's Thomas Hart Benton and Kansas-born John Steuart Curry, as well as the only painted self-portrait of Grant Wood. The **Putnam Museum** charts the early history of the Mississippi River Valley and includes an aquarium. Its newest addition is the IMAX® Theater at the Putnam.

🏛 **Davenport Museum of Art**
1737 W 12th St. 📞 (563) 326-7804. ◻ 10am–4:30pm Tue–Sat, 4:30–8pm Thu, 1–4:30pm Sun. ● public hols. ♿ ☒ www.art-dma.org

Iowa City 25

62,220. ▦ ℹ️ 408 1st Ave, Coralville, (800) 283-6592.
☒ www.icccvb.org

EASYGOING Iowa City is home to the 1,900-acre (769-ha) University of Iowa campus and the school's noteworthy American Writers' Workshop. The town served as the territorial and state capital until 1857 and the Old Capitol, now the **Old Capitol Museum**, is on campus.

About 10 miles (16 km) east of Iowa City is the **Herbert Hoover National Historic Site**. The president's boyhood cottage has been restored, along with a number of buildings constructed by the local Quaker community.

Boats sailing below a bridge that spans the mighty Mississippi River, Davenport

Missouri

THE MISSOURI RIVER AND THE I-70 Interstate Highway bisect the state of Missouri, linking its two largest cities – St. Louis and Kansas City – and providing quick access to the centrally located state capital of Jefferson City. In the southwestern corner of Missouri, the rugged Ozark Mountain region is veined with beautiful streams and rivers, making the area a popular camping and canoeing destination.

Gateway Arch, symbol of the city of St. Louis

St. Louis ❷❻

🏛 348,189. ✈ 🚋 🚌 ℹ 308 Washington Ave, (314) 241-1764.
🆆 www.explorestlouis.com

LOCATED JUST south of the point where the Missouri empties into the Mississippi River, St. Louis has been one of the country's most active crossroads. Founded by a French fur trader in 1764, this frontier city became a part of the US as a result of the Louisiana Purchase in 1803. It soon established itself as the "Gateway to the West," as steamboats chugged up the Missouri River into territories opened up by the Lewis and Clark expedition.

Scott trial plaque in the Old Courthouse

🏛 Gateway Arch-Jefferson National Expansion Memorial

Memorial Dr & Market St. ℃ (314) 655-1600. ◯ 6am–11pm daily. ● Jan 1, Thanksgiving, Dec 25. 🈁 ⅗
Old Courthouse 11 N 4th St.
℃ (314) 655-1700. ◯ 8am–4:30pm daily. ● Jan 1, Thanksgiving, Dec 25.
⅗ 🆆 www.nps.gov/jeff
Museum of Westward Expansion
℃ (314) 655-1600. ◯ Jun–Sep: 8am–10pm; Oct–May: 9am–6pm.
⅗ 🆆 www.stlouisarch.com
Completed in 1965 on the site of fur trader Pierre Laclede's original 1764 settlement, Eero Saarinen's 630-ft (192-m) tall **Gateway Arch** symbolizes the city's role as a commercial and cultural gateway between the settled eastern US and the wide-open lands to the west. The excellent **Museum of Westward Expansion** at the base of the arch features several detailed exhibits on the 1803–1806 expedition by the explorers Lewis and Clark (see p570) and other 19th-century expeditions. The museum also includes two movie theaters. Elevator-like tram rides transport visitors to the top of the arch, where picturesque views of the surrounding city and Illinois farmlands make the cramped quarters well worth the one-hour round trip.

The stately, domed **Old Courthouse** (1839–62) is one of the oldest buildings in the city of St. Louis. This Greek Revival structure was the site of two of the initial trials in the landmark Dred Scott case, which resulted in an 1857 decision by the US Supreme Court stating that African Americans were not citizens of the country and had no rights under the laws of the US. The decision overturned an earlier suit by Scott, an African-American slave who had returned to St. Louis with his owners after nine years in free states, to win his freedom. It also deepened the sectional and racial differences that finally erupted in the American Civil War that lasted for four years (from 1861 to 1865) and went on to claim many thousands of lives.

A museum that stands within the Old Courthouse recounts the events of the famous Dred Scott trial for the benefit of visitors and depicts what life must have been like for ordinary people living in 18th-century St. Louis under the yoke of French and Spanish rule.

🚋 Laclede's Landing

Morgan St & Lucas St between I-70 & the Mississippi River.
℃ (314) 241-5875. ◯ area open year-round; individual restaurant and club hours vary. ⅗
🆆 www.ladedeslanding.org
This vibrant restaurant and entertainment district consists of several blocks of restored 19th-century cotton, tobacco, and food warehouses that lie along the riverfront. The popular restaurants and blues clubs are known to attract large crowds, especially during the annual Big Muddy Blues Festival during the Labor Day weekend. The tall, six-story, cast-iron Raeder Place Building located on 719-727 N 1st Street), was built in 1873 and is one of the best-preserved warehouses in St. Louis. The 1874 Eads Bridge defines the Landing's southern boundary.

Raeder Building in Laclede's Landing area

Brick exterior of Anheuser-Busch Brewery

🏛 Forest Park

St. Louis Art Museum 1 Fine Arts Dr. 📞 *(314) 721-0072.* ⏰ *10am–5pm Tue–Thu & Sat–Sun, 10am–9pm Fri.* ⬤ *Jan 1, Thanksgiving, Dec 25.* ♿ 🌐 www.slam.org

Missouri History Museum Jefferson Memorial Bldg. 📞 *(314) 746-4599.* ⏰ *10am–6pm Wed–Mon, 10pm–8pm Tue.* ♿ 🌐 www.mohistory.org

Designed in 1876 by German-trained landscape architect Maximilian Kern, this 1,300-acre (526-ha) park is one of the nation's largest urban green spaces. The 1904 World's Fair, known officially as the Louisiana Purchase Exposition, was held on the grounds, drawing nearly 20 million visitors. After the fair, nearly all the grand Beaux Arts structures designed by Cass Gilbert were demolished. The only exception, the Palace of Fine Arts, is now home to the **St. Louis Art Museum**. Its sweeping collection of American art includes paintings by Missourians George Caleb Bingham and Thomas Hart Benton, and artists Georgia O'Keeffe, Winslow Homer, and Andy Warhol. The **Missouri History Museum** sits on the site of the main entrance to the 1904 fair. The Beaux Arts building houses impressive exhibits depicting the multicultural history of St. Louis. Its holdings include an original Louisiana Purchase transfer document, a replica of aviator Charles Lindberg's 1927 *Spirit of St. Louis* airplane (re-opening in May 2004), and extensive displays on the World's Fair. An interactive arts gallery explores the city's rich musical history.

🏛 Anheuser-Busch Brewery

1127 Pestalozzi St. 📞 *(314) 577-2626.* ⏰ *Jun–Aug: 9am–5pm Mon–Sat, 11:30am–5pm Sun; Sep–May: 9am–4pm Mon–Sat, 11:30am–4pm Sun.* ♿ 🌐 www.budweisertours.com

The world's largest brewery, Anheuser-Busch, was founded in 1860 by entrepreneurial German immigrants. Its famous trademark Budweiser lager brand is still very popular. The complex contains many of the company's 19th-century brick structures. Tours include a visit to the famous Clydesdale horse stables.

🏛 Missouri Botanical Garden

4344 Shaw Blvd. 📞 *(800) 642-8842, (314) 577-9400.* ⏰ *9am–5pm Sun–Tue & Thu–Fri, 7am–7pm Wed & Sat.* ⬤ *Dec 25.* ♿ 🌐 www.mobot.org

This garden was created in 1859 by a wealthy St. Louis businessman on the grounds of his estate. The grounds contain an English garden, a Japanese garden, as well as a scented garden for the visually impaired. The geodesic domed Climatron® has exotic birds and over 1,200 species of tropical plants, including banana trees, orchids, and epiphytes.

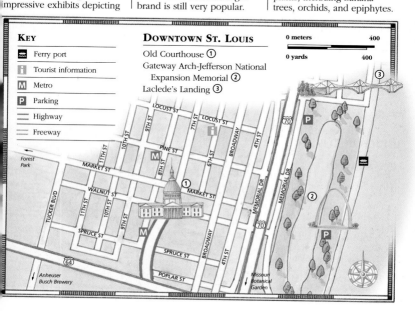

KEY

🚢	Ferry port
ℹ	Tourist information
Ⓜ	Metro
🅿	Parking
═	Highway
═	Freeway

DOWNTOWN ST. LOUIS

Old Courthouse ①
Gateway Arch-Jefferson National Expansion Memorial ②
Laclede's Landing ③

0 meters   400
0 yards   400

The Classic Revival Missouri State Capitol, Jefferson City

Jefferson City ㉗

🏃 40,000. ✈ 🚃 🚌
ℹ 213 Adams St, (800) 769-4183.

SOON AFTER ITS founding as the state capital in 1821, Jefferson City grew into a busy Missouri River port. The **Jefferson Landing State Historic Site** preserves many structures from its original waterfront, including the 1839 Lohman Building. The Classic Revival **Missouri State Capitol**, completed in 1924, now houses the Missouri State Museum and a mural by Thomas Hart Benton. His bold 1935 *A Social History of the State of the Missouri* was criticized by Missouri's conservative power brokers for its stark depiction of the state's widespread poverty and seamier underclass.

🏛 Jefferson Landing State Historic Site

📞 (573) 751-2854. ☐ 10am–4pm Tue–Sat. ⬤ Jan 1, Thanksgiving, Dec 25. ⛨

Branson ㉘

🏃 6,000. ℹ PO Box 1897, (800) 214-3661.
🌐 www.explorebranson.com

THIS SLEEPY Ozark Mountain resort was radically transformed over the past 40 years, thanks to the phenomenal success of several family-oriented tourist attractions. A musical pageant revolving around the Ozarks-based novel, *The Shepherd of the Hills*, was one of the area's first big hits. It is still staged every night in a picturesque, outdoor arena attached to a working, mountain farm.

The **Silver Dollar City** amusement park features high-tech roller coasters and water rides in a 19th-century Ozark pioneer setting, about 9 miles (14 km) west of town. The area's biggest draws are Branson's nightly music programs, presented at more than 30 alcohol-free performance venues crowded together on the "The Strip" (Route 76 W).

🏛 Shepherd of the Hills Homestead

5586 W Hwy 76, 2 miles W of Branson. 📞 (800) 653-6288. ☐ May–Oct: 9am–5pm. 🚫 ⛨
🌐 www.oldmatt.com

Kansas City ㉙

🏃 435,100. ✈ 🚃 🚌 ℹ 1100 Main St, (800) 767-7700.
🌐 www.visitkc.com

A DELIGHTFUL study in contrasts, Kansas City is rife with imagery associated with the Wild West. This vibrant city now contains beautifully landscaped parks and boulevards, sophisticated museums, fine public architecture, and high-end urban retail districts.

On the bluffs overlooking the Missouri River, just north of downtown, the **City Market** sits on the site of the town's original Westport Landing business district. The riverfront's 19th-century brick and cast-iron warehouses were converted into loft apartments and restaurants in the 1970s. Today, the 1930s City Market building houses an eclectic collection of shops, farmers' markets, retail outlets, and the Arabia Steamboat Museum, which displays artifacts salvaged from a 1856 wreck.

Northeast of the City Market, the **Kansas City Museum** is housed in a 50-room mansion in one of the city's most exclusive 19th-century neighborhoods. Its collections trace the city's evolution from a fur trading post into a powerful railroad and agricultural center. Exhibits include a replica of fur trader François Choteau's original 1821 Westport Landing post and a 1910 corner drugstore with a working soda fountain.

The newly minted "**Crossroads District**" refers to the area stretching south of downtown to Penn Valley Park and Crown Center, roughly bounded on the east and west by Main Street and Broadway. The city's two most prominent architectural landmarks, **Union Station** and **Liberty Memorial** are located here. The magnificent Beaux Arts Union Station, built in 1914, was one of the country's busiest and most glamorous railroad terminals. It rose to national prominence in 1933 when outlaw Pretty Boy Floyd gunned down an accomplice and several police officers in what became known as the Union Station Massacre. Renovated after years of neglect, the station

Kansas City skyline with Union Station in the foreground

Sprawling lawn of the Nelson-Atkins Art Museum, Kansas City

now a local history museum, children's science museum, and restaurant complex.

The recently restored 217-ft (66-m) Liberty Memorial overlooks the old train depot on the grassy bluffs of Penn Valley Park. It houses the nation's only World War I museum. The "Torch of Liberty" observation tower offers a sweeping view of the city. To its south, the **Hallmark Visitors Center** presents the history of Hallmark, the well-known greeting card company.

Southeast of downtown, the **18th & Vine Heritage District** commemorates the city's rich African-American heritage. In the 1930s, all-night jazz clubs showcased the innovative riffs of local musicians such as Count Basie, Lester Young, and Charlie Parker. This was Kansas City's heyday, when under the free-wheeling "rule" of Tom Pendergast, a local concrete contractor, it was known as a "wide-open" town that stayed awake all night. Refurbished to form the backdrop for Robert Altman's 1996 film *Kansas City*, the district's premier attractions include the **American Jazz Museum**, which re-creates the city's swinging jazz era, and the **Negro Leagues Baseball Museum**, which honors talented African-American baseball players who toiled in low-paid obscurity for all-black teams in the US, Canada, and Latin America. In 1945, Kansas City Monarchs shortstop Jackie Robinson broke the color barrier by signing with the all-white Brooklyn Dodgers in the National League.

Once an outfitting post for travelers on the Santa Fe and Oregon Trails, the village of **Westport** became part of Kansas City in 1899. In the retail district along Westport Road, shops and restaurants now occupy some of the city's oldest buildings, such as Kelly's Westport Inn, an 1837 tavern. Several blocks south of Westport, the **Country Club Plaza**, the nation's first planned suburban shopping district, was designed in 1922. To its east, the **Nelson-Atkins Art Museum** has a stellar collection of paintings by Missouri's George Caleb Bingham and Thomas Hart Benton. The outdoor sculpture garden features 13 exclusive works by British artist Henry Moore.

Mural at the American Jazz Museum

🏛 **American Jazz Museum**
1616 E 18th St. 📞 *(816) 474-8463.*
⭘ *9am–6pm Tue–Sat, noon–6pm Sun.* ⬤ *public hols.* 📷 ♿
ⓦ *www.americanjazzmuseum.com*

🏛 **Nelson-Atkins Art Museum**
45th St & Oak St. 📞 *(816) 751-1278.*
⭘ *10am–4pm Tue–Fri, 10am–5pm Sat, noon–5pm Sun.* 📷 ♿ ⓦ *www.nelson-atkins.org*

🏛 **Kansas City Museum**
3218 Gladstone Blvd. 📞 *(816) 483-8300.* ⭘ *9:30am–6pm Mon–Sat, noon–4:30pm Sun.* ⬤ *Jan 1, Thanksgiving, Dec 25.* 📷 ♿

ENVIRONS: The suburb of **Independence**, 15 miles (24 km) east of downtown Kansas City, has one of the country's best westward expansion museums, the National Frontier Trails Center. It was also the home of Harry S. Truman, 33rd US president. His simple downtown home is now a national historic site.

St. Joseph ㉚

🏞 *72,000.* 🚉 ℹ *109 S 4th St, (800) 785-0360.* ⓦ *www.stjomo.com*

LIKE MANY Missouri River communities, St. Joseph grew from a fur trading post into a wagon train outfitting center. Its position as the nation's westernmost railroad terminal instigated local entrepreneurs to launch the Pony Express in the mid-1800s. This service sought to deliver mail from St. Joseph to Sacramento – a 1,966-mile (3,214-km) trip – in less than 10 days. Informative displays in the **Pony Express Museum** relate the story of this short-lived enterprise, while the Patee House Museum preserves an 1858 hotel that served as the headquarters of the Express. On its grounds is the house where the notorious Missouri outlaw, Jesse James, was killed by one of his former gang members in 1882.

🚇 **Pony Express Museum**
914 Penn St. 📞 *(800) 530-5930.*
⭘ *9am–5pm Mon–Sat, 1–5pm Sun.* ⬤ *Jan 1, Thanksg., Dec 24–25 & 31.* 📷 ♿ ⓦ *www.ponyexpress.org*

Bronze statue of a Pony Express rider, St. Joseph

Kansas

F OR MOST AMERICANS, Kansas conjures up images of rolling wheat fields, flatlands, sunflowers, and scenes from the 1939 film *The Wizard of Oz*. The real Kansas, however, is infinitely more interesting, both historically and geographically. Reminders of the state's turbulent 19th-century history as an Indian resettlement territory, anti-slavery battleground, and cattle drive destination can be seen frequently as one traverses the principal Interstate Highways, I-70 and I-35, and the meandering backroads. Kansas is also home to two of the country's few remaining stands of unbroken, tallgrass prairie, preserved in the undulating Flint Hills, just south of the lovely Kansas State University town of Manhattan.

Entrance to the Kansas Natural History Museum, Lawrence

Lawrence ❸

🏙 65,600. 🚐 🚹 *734 Vermont Ave,* *(888) 529-5267.* 🔳 *www.visitlawrence.com*

F OUNDED BY New England abolitionists in 1854, Lawrence's strong "free state" leanings made it a target for Missouri's pro-slavery "border ruffians," only 40 miles (64 km) to the east. The attractive, downtown retail district is lined with 19th-century stone and brick commercial buildings, reminders of the city's massive reconstruction drive after a destructive 1863 raid led by Confederate guerrilla William Quantrill.

A restored 1889 railroad depot houses the **Lawrence Visitor Information Center**, which relates key episodes in the city's history and provides information about the University of Kansas campus, just southwest of downtown. Situated astride a hill, known locally as Mount Oread, the campus includes the **Kansas**

Natural History Museum and the **Spencer Museum of Art**. Its broad sampling of American and contemporary art makes this is one of the finest university art museums in the United States.

🏛 **Spencer Museum of Art** 1301 Mississippi St. 🔳 *(785) 864-3560.* 🔲 *10am–5pm Tue–Sat,* *5–9pm Thu, noon–5pm Sun.* ⬤ *public hols.* ♿

Topeka ❸

🏘 125,000. ✈ 🚌 🚹 *1275 SW Topeka Blvd, (800) 235-1030.* 🔳 *www.topekacvb.org*

A QUIET GOVERNMENT center, Topeka's most significant historical attraction is Kansas Regionalist painter John Steuart Curry's mural in the **Kansas State Capitol**. His mural, *The Settlement of Kansas*, depicts abolitionist John Brown in a dramatic confrontation with pro-slavery forces that threatened to make Kansas a slave state in the 1850s. More background on this tense period and the state's settlement can be found at the superb **Kansas History Center**, to the city's west.

🏛 **Kansas History Center** 6425 SW 6th Ave. 🔳 *(785) 272-8681.* 🔲 *9am–5pm Tue–Sat, 1–5pm Sun.* ⬤ *public hols.* 🔳 *www. khs.org/places/ khcenter.htm*

Flint Hills ❸

✈ 🚌 🚹 *Manhattan CVB, 501 Poyntz Ave, (800) 759-0134.* 🔳 *www.manhattancvb.org*

T HE SHAGGY, rolling Flint Hills are among Kansas' most spectacular natural features. The best way to explore the area is to drive along the scenic 85-mile (137-km) stretch of Route 177, running south from the university town of **Manhattan**, across I-70, and down to Cassody at I-35. About 6 miles (10 km) southeast of Manhattan is **Konza Prairie**, the country's largest remaining parcel of virgin tallgrass prairie. The 8,600-acre (3,482-ha) preserve contains a variety of spectacular hiking trails that wind up and down the chert-studded hills, providing awe-inspiring views of the surrounding landscape.

Route 177 intersects US 56 at **Council Grove** (40 miles/ 64 km south of Manhattan). The town takes its name from a huge oak tree, the Council Oak, which commemorates the spot where the Kansa and Osage tribes agreed to allow the old Santa Fe Trail to pass through their ancestral lands. The **Kaw Mission School**, now a state historic site, was set up by the Methodists from 1851 to 1854 in an attempt to "westernize" male children from the Kaw (also known as Kansa or Kanza) tribe. This experiment did not succeed. The site now displays artifacts from the Mission school.

The red-roofed Chase County Courthouse, Cottonwood Falls, Flint Hills

Hikers at the Tallgrass Prairie National Preserve, Flint Hills

The **Tallgrass Prairie National Preserve**, 20 miles (32 km) south of Council Grove, protects what remains of an 11,000-acre (4451-ha) 19th-century cattle ranch. A hiking trail leads visitors from the ranch's Second Empire main house through large stands of native prairie. The ranching community of **Cottonwood Falls**, located about 3 miles (5 km) south on Route 177, contains another impressive Second Empire structure. Built in 1873, the red-roofed, limestone **Chase County Courthouse** is the oldest still in use in Kansas.

🏛 **Konza Prairie**
McDowell Creek Rd. ☎ (785) 587-0441. ☐ sunrise–sunset daily.
W www.ksu.edu/konza
🏞 **Tallgrass Prairie National Preserve**
Hwy 177, 2 miles (3 km) N of Strong City. ☎ (620) 273-8494. ☐ 9am–4pm daily.
W www.parktrust.org/zbar.html

Wichita ❸

🏙 304,000. ✈ 🚉 🚌 🛈 100 S Main St, (800) 288-9424.
W www.visitwichita.com

WICHITA DEVELOPED in 1865 as a lawless railhead town, where cowboys driving cattle north from Texas on the Chisholm Trail *(see p481)* would stop to let off steam in the city's rowdy saloons and brothels. Those early cattle hands would not recognize today's Wichita, which has grown into a busy aircraft

manufacturing and oil refining center. The town's colorful past is recreated at the **Old Cowtown Museum**. The original jail and period houses, as well as stores and saloons from surrounding rural communities are on display here. To its southeast is the **Mid-America All-Indian Center**, which depicts the 19th-century Great Plains lifestyles of the Kiowa, Cheyenne, and Lakota tribes. The main feature in this center is a reconstructed village featuring a winter lodge built of local materials such as grasses and wood.

Artifact, Indian Center Museum, Wichita

🏛 **Old Cowtown Museum**
1871 Sim Park Dr. ☎ (316) 264-0671.
☐ Apr–Oct: 10am–5pm Mon–Sat, noon–5pm Sun. 🦽 ⚟
W www.old-cowtown.org
🏛 **Mid-America All-Indian Center**
650 N Seneca St.
☎ (316) 262-5221. ☐ 10am–5pm Tue–Sat, Apr–Dec: 1–5pm Sun.
● public hols. 🦽 ⚟
W www.theindiancenter.com

Dodge City ❸

🏙 21,100. ✈ 🚌 🛈 400 W Wyatt Earp Blvd, (800) 653-9378.
W www.visitdodgecity.org

THE WILD WEST'S two most colorful characters, lawmen Wyatt Earp and Bat Masterson, earned their tough reputations in Dodge City during its brief but boisterous heyday. Between 1872 and 1884, the town flourished as a High Plains buffalo-hunting, cattle-driving, and railroad center. The **Boot Hill Museum** re-creates the infamous Front Street strip of saloons and burlesque houses that earned Dodge City the sobriquet of "Hell on the Plains." On the museum grounds is Boot Hill cemetery, where many gunfight victims were buried.

Before hordes of cowboys and gun-toting buffalo hunters came to town, Dodge City was just another stop on the Santa Fe Trail. Ruts from the old wagon trail can still be seen 9 miles (14 km) west of Dodge City along US 50 and at the **Fort Larned National Historic Site**, 55 miles (88 km) east of Dodge City. The site contains several restored original sandstone structures from the US Army fort that protected travelers along the Santa Fe Trail from 1859 to 1878.

🎩 **Boot Hill Museum**
Front St & 5th Sts. ☎ (620) 227-8188. ☐ Jun–Aug: 8am–8pm daily, Sep–May: 9am–5pm Mon–Fri, 1–5pm Sun. ● Jan 1, Thanksgiving, Dec 25.
🦽 ⚟ W www.boothill.org

Fort Larned National Historic Site, east of Dodge City

Oklahoma

Delaware tribe mask

BORDERED BY SIX STATES, Oklahoma is a cultural, geographical, and historical crossroads, where jagged mountain ranges and High Plains mesas merge with forests, flatland wheat fields, and vast grassy ranges. The state has the nation's largest Native American population – more than 250,000 people representing 67 tribes – as a result of forced 19th-century migrations to the region, then known as the Indian Territory. Several "land runs" between 1889 and 1895 brought a huge influx of white and African-American settlers to this area, which joined the US in 1907 after oil was discovered.

Praying Hands at Oral Roberts University, Tulsa

Bartlesville ㊱

🏃 34,300. ✈ 🚌 🚌 ℹ *201 SW Keeler, (800) 364-8708.*
🅦 www.bartlesville.com

THE STATE'S first commercial oil well was drilled here in 1897, kicking off a large-scale oil boom. A replica of the original well, the Nellie Johnstone #1, now stands as a memorial in a downtown park. Today, the city's largest employer is still the Conoco-Phillips company, founded in 1917 as Phillips Petroleum, by two speculators from Iowa.

ENVIRONS: Frank Phillips's extensive 3,600-acre (1456-ha) rural estate, **Woolaroc Ranch**, is located 12 miles (19 km) southwest of Bartlesville. The picturesque ranch includes a superb Western art collection, the Native American Heritage Center, and a wildlife preserve. About 45 miles (72 km) northwest of Bartlesville (by way of Pawhuska) is the Nature Conservancy's **Tallgrass Prairie Preserve**.

In this vast expanse of rolling prairie, a herd of bison graze among stands of big bluestem grasses, coneflowers, and blazing star wildflowers.

✵ Woolaroc Ranch
Rte 123, 12 miles (19 km) SW of Bartlesville. 📞 *(918) 336-0307.*
🕙 *Jun–Sep: 10am–5pm daily; Oct–May: 10am–5pm Tue–Sun.*
⬤ *Thanksgiving, Dec 25.* 🎟 ♿
🅦 www.woolaroc.org

Tulsa ㊲

🏃 367,300. ✈ 🚌 🚌 ℹ *Williams Center Tower 2, 2 W 7th St, (800) 558-3311.* 🅦 www.visittulsa.com

ORIGINALLY a railroad town, Tulsa prospered after the discovery of oil in 1901. Fortunes were made literally overnight, leading to the construction of Art Deco commercial buildings, roads, and bridges across the Arkansas River. Although Tulsa is still a major oil center, it also contains numerous man-made lakes, parks, and Arkansas River bike trails. Its top

attraction is the **Thomas Gilcrease Institute**, a comprehensive art museum founded by a wealthy local oilman. Its collection includes a wide range of Native and Western American paintings by such well known artists as George Catlin and Frederic Remington. The city's most popular roadside sight is the Prayer Tower Visitor Center at Tulsa's **Oral Roberts University**. The 200-ft (60-m) glass and steel tower includes an 80-ft (24-m) pair of hands folded in prayer.

🏛 Thomas Gilcrease Institute
1400 N Gilcrease Museum Rd, off US 64. 📞 *(918) 596-2700.*
🕙 *10am–4pm Tue–Sun.* ⬤ *Mon & Dec 25.* 🎟 ♿
🅦 www.gilcrease.org

Tahlequah ㊳

🏃 10,400. 🚌 ℹ *123 E Delaware St, (800) 456-4860.*
🅦 www.okchamber.com

THE CAPITAL OF the Cherokee Nation, Tahlequah lies in the eastern Oklahoma Ozark Mountain foothills, the tribe's home since 1839. The city preserves several late 19th-century buildings, including the prison and the Cherokee National Capitol Building.
Of primary interest here is the **Cherokee Heritage Center**. Its attractions include a village dating from the 1875–90 Indian Territory era and a re-creation of a 17th-century settlement from the tribe's ancestral lands in the

Carriage on display at Woolaroc Ranch Museum, near Bartlesville

Earth lodges in the Cherokee Heritage Center, Tahlequah

Appalachian Mountains. Exhibits at the Cherokee National Museum chronicle the tribe's forced march along the "Trail of Tears" from North Carolina to Oklahoma in the 1830s *(see p438)*. This tragic event is also dramatized every year in June.

🎭 Cherokee Heritage Center

US 62, 3 miles (5 km) S of Tahlequah. (888) 999-6007. 10am–5pm Mon–Sat, 1–5pm Sun. public hols. www.cherokeeheritage.org

Oklahoma City 39

444,700. 189 W Sheridan, (800) 225-5652. www.visitokc.com

OKLAHOMA CITY was built and founded in a single day, April 22, 1889, as part of the first Oklahoma Territory land rush. Over 10,000 land claims were filed on that day, creating a city out of thin air. The city became the state capital in 1910 and saw its first oil strike in 1928. Today, there are more than 2,000 still-active oil wells, including one on the grounds of the Oklahoma State Capitol, within the city limits.

The **Oklahoma State Museum of History** chronicles the state's intimate relationship with oil, as well as its pre-settlement history. The **National Cowboy Museum** contains one of the country's most comprehensive collections of Western art. Among its exhibits are works by such artists as Charles Russell, and Albert Bierstadt. It also features a giant statue of the famed Wild West figure Buffalo Bill and a collection of Western actor John Wayne memorabilia. On a more somber note, the city has paid homage to the 168 people killed in the tragic 1995 Federal Building bombing incident *(see p438)* with the dignified **Oklahoma City National Memorial**. The 3.3-acre (1.3-ha) downtown memorial includes a museum, a reflecting pool, and a 60-year-old American elm tree.

🏛 National Cowboy Museum

1700 NE 63rd St. (405) 478-2250. 9am–5pm daily. Jan 1, Thanksgiving, Dec 25. www.nationalcowboymuseum.com

🏛 Oklahoma State Museum of History

2100 Lincoln Blvd. (405) 521-2491. 8am–5pm Mon–Sat. public hols. www.ok-history.mus.ok.us

The reflecting pool at the Oklahoma City National Memorial

OLD ROUTE 66: THE HISTORIC "MOTHER ROAD"

Route 66 has been immortalized as the "mother road" traveled by the migrant Oklahoma family in author John Steinbeck's 1939 novel, *The Grapes of Wrath*, as they fled the drought-stricken Dust Bowl on the way to California. This historic highway, charted in 1926, was the first to link Chicago to Los Angeles. Old Route 66 heads southwest from the state's northeastern corner to its western border with Texas, meandering along the original two-lane alignment much of the way, frequently within sight of the modern interstates, I-44 and I-40 that parallel its original route. West of Oklahoma City, the route runs alongside I-40, with several sections of old road veering off the Interstate. The **Oklahoma Route 66 Museum** in Clinton sits across from a Best Western Motel where Elvis Presley slept on four separate occasions. The recently renovated museum has one of the country's best Route 66 collections. The **National Route 66 Museum** in Elk City (30 miles/48 km west of Clinton) sports a smaller but equally engaging array of exhibits, including a pickup truck modeled after the one used in director John Ford's 1940 film adaptation of *The Grapes of Wrath*. Other sights along the route include the **Totem Pole Park** (about 4 miles/6 km east of Foyil), and the **Will Rogers Memorial Museum** at Claremore (27 miles/43 km east of Tulsa). Oklahoma's favorite son, humorist Will Rogers, was born in a log cabin in nearby Oologah. The museum relates the life story of this colorful actor and newspaper columnist, and screens several of his films.

Totem Pole Park

Practical Information

U P-TO-DATE INFORMATION is essential when planning an itinerary across the Great Plains, where cities and attractions are often separated by miles and miles of rolling prairie. A region of small towns, wide-open spaces, and distant horizons, the beautiful landscape of the Great Plains draws visitors searching for a taste of wholesome Americana. The best time to plan a trip is from mid-April through late October, but bear in mind that many of the historical sights are open only from Memorial Day (end May) to Labor Day (end August).

TOURIST INFORMATION

TRAVELERS ENTERING the Great Plains via a principal Interstate Highway are greeted with signs advertising a state "Welcome Center." These centers provide a full range of tourist information, as well as clean restrooms and free coffee. Most of the region's major airports and train stations have information desks stocked with free brochures and maps. All of the larger cities and smaller towns operate Convention & Visitors' Bureaus, which provide free directories of events, attractions, accommodations, and restaurants, both in print and online.

NATURAL HAZARDS

TORNADOES USUALLY occur during summer, particularly in the eastern portions of Kansas and Oklahoma, called "Tornado Alley." In the event of a tornado warning, travelers should first seek shelter in the basement of a solidly constructed building and then tune into a local radio station for additional information.

GETTING AROUND

MOST OF THE major cities in the Great Plains have public bus systems that provide affordable but limited service. However, the convenient St. Louis Metrorail system is the only public rail transit system in the region.

DRIVING IN THE GREAT PLAINS

DRIVING IS THE best way to explore the region, since most sights are usually situated far away from each other. Thus certain precautions are necessary to ensure a safe journey. Seat belts are a must for drivers and front-seat passengers in all the states. Most states also require seat belts for back-seat passengers. Child seats are also mandatory, but age restrictions may vary from one state to another. Motorcyclists are required to wear helmets in all of the states except Iowa, which has no restrictions.

Speed limits vary but are usually between 70–75 mph (112–120 km/h) on Interstate Highways, which are located outside crowded urban areas. Radar detectors are permitted in all the states.

ETIQUETTE

GREAT PLAINS residents tend to be friendly and polite. Drivers on the empty back roads usually acknowledge an oncoming car or truck by raising one or two fingers off of the steering wheel in a modified version of a wave. The polite response is to offer the same in return.

FESTIVALS

THE GREAT PLAINS states stage a wide range of annual community, regional, and state festivals. The largest of the region's many fairs is the **Iowa State Fair**, held in August in Des Moines, while one of the country's friendliest Independence Day celebrations takes place in historic Independence, Missouri. All through summer, Native Americans in South Dakota hold several traditional "pow-wow" get-togethers. Other summertime events are the historical productions staged by the Great Plains Chautauqua Society.

Musical festivals also abound in the region, with summer blues festivals in Kansas City, St. Louis, and Lincoln vying for top billing. The Walnut Valley bluegrass festival in Winfield, Kansas, and **Woody Guthrie Free Folk Festival** in his hometown Okemah, Oklahoma, are also very popular. Polka music, beer, and German food end the festival season at Missouri's **Oktoberfest**, in the Missouri River community of Hermann.

SPORTS

MISSOURI HAS a monopoly on professional sports teams in the region, with Kansas City and St. Louis operating the region's only pro baseball (Kansas City

THE CLIMATE OF THE GREAT PLAINS

This is a region of extremes, with hot summers and cold winters, especially in North and South Dakota. The southern states – Kansas, Missouri, and Oklahoma – have a more temperate climate, with milder winters. With its cooler nights and sunny days, June is perfect for touring the region's historic sites. Wildflowers are most colorful in May and September, while October's changing colors make it ideal for scenic drives through the wooded Ozark Mountains.

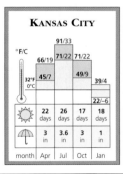

KANSAS CITY

°F/C				
		91/33		
	66/19	71/22	71/22	
32°F 45/7			49/9	
0°C				39/4
				22/–6
☀	22 days	26 days	17 days	18 days
☂	3 in	3.6 in	3 in	1 in
month	Apr	Jul	Oct	Jan

Royals and St. Louis Cardinals) and football (Kansas City Chiefs and St. Louis Rams) franchises. Many of the states have minor league baseball teams as well, providing travelers with opportunities to watch up-and-coming players in cozier settings. Iowa is a mecca for minor league fans, with A-level teams in Burlington, Cedar Rapids, Clinton, and Davenport, and the AAA affiliate of the Chicago Cubs in Des Moines.

College football and basketball are also very popular, particularly in the southern Plains states. The annual **Kansas–Kansas State** football game is the seasonal climax to one of college football's most colorful intrastate rivalries.

OUTDOOR ACTIVITIES

IN DEFIANCE of the stereotypical image of the Great Plains as flat and devoid of topography, hikers, cyclists, and mountain bikers flock to the region's hilly areas. Nebraska's Pine Ridge country, South Dakota's Badlands and Black Hills, and the Kansas Flint Hills are havens for campers and hikers. The 200-mile (320-km) **Katy Trail** bike path winds along the Missouri River for much of its route. Iowa's seven-day 500-mile **RAGBRAI** cycling event is one of the world's largest, while the August motorcycle rally and race in Sturgis, draws thousands of participants and spectators. Fishing and boating enthusiasts can choose from a range of mainly man-made lakes, such as Nebraska's Lake McConaughy. Streams and rivers in the Missouri Ozarks near Branson provide opportunities to fish and canoe. Visitors should contact the state tourist offices for lists of outfitters for a particular region.

ENTERTAINMENT

THE BUSIEST live music and theatrical venues in the Great Plains are in Kansas City and St. Louis, with an array of clubs and theaters sprinkled in cities such as Tulsa, Lawrence, Lincoln, Omaha, Grand Forks, and Des Moines. The region's most spectacular outdoor performance venues include **The Muny** in Forest Park in St. Louis, Kansas City's **Starlight Theater**, in the city's bucolic Swope Park; and North Dakota's **Medora Musical**, featuring live Wild West musical programs on summer nights against the backdrop of the Theodore Roosevelt National Park badlands. A dizzying array of rides and activities awaits those who are more adventurous at the region's largest amusement parks, Kansas City's Worlds of Fun and Six Flags St. Louis.

SHOPPING

THE REGION's premier retail destination is Kansas City's elegantly designed **Country Club Plaza**. This 1920s urban shopping district has several higher-end specialty shops and department stores. A popular suburban shopping destination is the upscale **Galleria** mall in Clayton.

Iowa's Amana Colonies offer some of the best locally made products at the **Amana Woolen Mill** and **Millstream Brewing Company**. The best place to visit for Native American crafts and other merchandise is South Dakota. The **Native American Educational and Cultural Center** at the Crazy Horse Memorial in the Black Hills, and the **Red Cloud Heritage Center** on the Pine Ridge Reservation offer a wide selection of handmade rugs, apparel, and other items. For Wild West souvenirs, travelers should visit **Wall Drug**, in Wall, located in South Dakota, for the widest selection.

DIRECTORY

TOURIST OFFICES

Iowa
(888) 472-6035.
www.traveliowa.com

Kansas
(800) 252-6727.
www.travelks.org

Missouri
(800) 877-1234.
www.missouritourism.org

Nebraska
(800) 228-4307.
www.visitnebraska.org

North Dakota
(800) 435-5663.

Oklahoma
(800) 652-6552,
(405)521-2406.
www.travelok.com

South Dakota
(605) 773-3301.
www.state.sd. us

ROAD CONDITIONS

Iowa
(800) 288-1047.

Kansas
(800) 585-7623.

Missouri
(800) 222-6400.

Nebraska
(402) 479-4512.

North Dakota
(701) 328-7623.

Oklahoma
(405) 425-2385.

South Dakota
(866) 697-3511.

FESTIVALS

Woody Guthrie Free Folk Festival
Okemah Industrial Park,
Okemah, OK.
(918) 623-2440.

ENTERTAINMENT

The Muny
Forest Park, St. Louis,
MO.
(314) 361-1900.

Starlight Theater
4600 Starlight Rd, KC, MO.
(800) 776-1730.
www.kcstarlight.com

Medora Musical
Burning Hills
Amphitheater, Medora, ND
(800) 633-6721.
www.medora.com

SHOPPING

Amana Woolen Mill
800 48th Ave, Amana, IA.
(800) 222-6430.
www. amana
woolenmill.com

Red Cloud Heritage Center
US 18, Pine Ridge, SD.
(605) 867-5491.

Where to Stay

THIS REGION'S UNIQUE NATURAL features and vibrant cities make it worth one's while to seek out interesting places to stay. There are a variety of historic hotels, chain hotels, and luxurious bed-and-breakfast inns in larger centers, while guest ranches, mountain lodges, and state park cabins provide comfortable accommodations in spectacular natural settings.

	CREDIT CARDS	NUMBER OF ROOMS	RESTAURANT	CHILDREN'S FACILITIES	GARDEN OR TERRACE

NORTH DAKOTA

MANDAN: *Fort Abraham Lincoln State Park* 4480 Fort Lincoln Rd, Mandan. █ (701) 667-6340. FAX (701) 667-6349. W www.state.nd.us/ndparks//Parks/FLSP.htm Relax in the historical shadows of Lewis & Clark in clean, simply furnished cabins overlooking a beautiful, unspoiled section of the Missouri River. P	$	2		●	
MEDORA: *Dahkotah Lodge* West River Rd, 20 miles S of Medora. █ (701) 623-4897. FAX (701) 623-4878. W www.dahkotahlodge.com Guests can take part in trail rides and annual livestock branding in this ranch that stands on the edge of the North Dakota badlands. P ⊟ ⚡ ⛄ █	$$	8	▣	●	▣

SOUTH DAKOTA

BADLANDS NATIONAL PARK: *Cedar Pass Lodge* 1 Cedar Pass Lodge. █ (605) 433-5460. FAX (605) 433-5560. These rustic cabins are conveniently located in the heart of Badlands National Park, providing convenient access for hikers and motorists eager to explore the park. ⛄ P ⊟ ⚡	$$	22	▣		
CUSTER: *State Game Lodge* HC 83, US 16A. █ (605) 255-4541. FAX (605) 255-4706. W www.custerresorts.com Built in 1920, this stately stone-and-wood lodge overlooks a picturesque Black Hills valley. The structure served as President Calvin Coolidge's "Summer White House" in 1927. ▾ ⛄ P ⊟ TV ⚡ ⛶	$$$	66	▣		▣
CUSTER: *Sylvan Lake Lodge & Resort* At Hwy 89-87 Junction. █ (605) 574-2561. FAX (605) 574-4943. W www.custerresorts.com This deluxe Black Hills mountain resort features a rustic lodge with cozily furnished guest rooms, as well as private cabins with fireplaces and kitchenettes. ▾ ⛄ P ⊟ TV ⚡ ⛶	$$$	66	▣		▣
DEADWOOD: *Bullock Hotel* 633 Main St. █ (800) 336-1876. FAX (605) 578-1382. W www.bullockhotel.com The popular 1895 sandstone Bullock Hotel has been impeccably restored with wet bars and jacuzzi tubs in its spacious guest rooms. ▾ ⛄ P ⊟ TV ⚡ ⛶	$$$	28	▣		
INTERIOR: *Circle View Guest Ranch* 20055 E Hwy 44. █ (605) 433-5582. FAX (605) 433-5581. W www.circleviewranch.com On the edge of Badlands National Park and the Pine Ridge Reservation, this guest ranch provides comfortable, affordable accommodations with easy access to hiking trails through the rugged badlands. P ⊟ ⚡	$$	7	▣		▣
PIERRE: *Governor's Inn* 700 W Sioux Ave. █ (605) 224-4200. FAX (605) 224-4200. W www.govinn.com Located just minutes from the State Capitol and downtown Pierre, the rooms in this remodeled hotel are furnished with microwaves and refrigerators. Guests are served Continental breakfast. ⛄ P ⊟ TV ⚡ ⛶ ⛲ █	$$	82	▣		
RAPID CITY: *Alex Johnson Hotel* 523 6th St. █ (605) 342-1210. FAX (605) 342-7436. W www.alexjohnson.com Known in its heyday as "The Showplace of the West," this downtown, 1928 Rapid City gem is ornately decorated with Native American motifs and artwork, and Germanic Tudor designs. ▾ ⛄ P ⊟ TV ⚡ ⛶ ⛲ █	$$	143	▣		

<table>
<tr><td colspan="2">

Price categories for a standard double room per night, inclusive of service charges, and any additional taxes:

(S) under $50
$(S)(S)$ $50–$100
$(S)(S)(S)$ $100–$150
$(S)(S)(S)(S)$ $150–$200
$(S)(S)(S)(S)(S)$ over $200

</td><td colspan="2">

CREDIT CARDS
Major credit cards accepted.
RESTAURANT
Hotel restaurant or dining room usually open to nonresidents unless otherwise stated.
CHILDREN'S FACILITIES
Cribs and a baby-sitting service available. Some hotel restaurants have children's portions and high chairs.
GARDEN OR TERRACE
Hotels with a garden, courtyard, or terrace.

</td></tr>
</table>

	CREDIT CARDS	NUMBER OF ROOMS	RESTAURANT	CHILDREN'S FACILITIES	GARDEN OR TERRACE

NEBRASKA

CHADRON: *Olde Main Street Inn* $(S)(S)$
115 Main St. 📞 *(308) 432-3380.*
🔲 www.chadron.com/memberpages/oldemain
This 1890s hotel offers a rustic High Plains saloon, home-cooked meals, and convenient access to the downtown business district. 🍽 🛏 🚗 ⚡

| | ▩ | 9 | ▩ | | |

CRAWFORD: *Fort Robinson State Park* (S)
US 20, 3 miles (5 km) W of Crawford. 📞 *(308) 665-2900.* FAX *(308) 665-2906.*
🔲 www.ngpc.state.ne.us
Housed in a historic US Army fort, the horseback rides, cookouts, and hiking trails make this stay an essential Great Plains' experience.
P 🚗 ⚡ ▦

| | ▩ | 22 | | | |

LINCOLN: *Cornhusker Hotel* $(S)(S)(S)$
333 S 13th St. 📞 *(402) 474-7474, (800) 793-7474.* FAX *(402) 474-1847.*
🔲 www.thecornhusker.com
This deluxe urban hotel provides convenient access to the historic Haymarket District, downtown museums, shops, and the University of Nebraska campus. 🍽 🛏 P 🚗 TV ⚡ ♿ ▦ 🍴

| | ▩ | 290 | ▩ | | |

NEBRASKA CITY: *Lied Lodge & Conference Center/At Arbor Day Farm* $(S)(S)(S)$
2700 Sylvan Rd. 📞 *(402) 873-8733.* FAX *(402) 873-4999.*
🔲 www.liedlodge.org
This hotel offers a good restaurant, wooden beam construction and scenic views of the surrounding parks and orchards. 🛏 P 🚗 TV ⚡ ♿ 🍴 ▦

| | ▩ | 144 | ▩ | | ▩ |

OMAHA: *Best Western Redick Plaza Hotel* $(S)(S)$
1504 Harney St. 📞 *(402) 342-1500, (888) 342-5339.* FAX *(402) 342-2401.*
🔲 www.redickplazahotel.com
This Art Deco hotel offers downtown accommodations within walking distance of the antique shops, bookstores, and restaurants of the lively Old Market warehouse district. 🍽 🛏 P 🚗 TV ⚡ ♿ 🍴

| | ▩ | 89 | ▩ | | |

SCOTTS BLUFF: *Barn Anew B&B* $(S)(S)$
170549 County Rd. 📞 *(308) 632-8647.* FAX *(308) 632-5518.*
🔲 www.nabb1.com/sco8647.htm
Located on the old Oregon Trail, in the shadow of Scotts Bluff National Monument, this renovated 1907 barn provides relaxing accomodations on the site of an original Nebraska homestead. 🛏 P 🚗 ⚡

| | ▩ | 4 | | | ▩ |

IOWA

AMANA COLONIES: *Die Heimat Country Inn B&B* (S)
4434 V St, Homestead #10. 📞 *(319) 622-3937.*
🔲 www.dheimat.com
Sleep in an authentic canopy bed in this historic 1850s former stagecoach stop and communal kitchen in the heart of Homestead village. Keeping with Amana traditions, the rooms are simply decorated with Amana walnut and cherry furniture. 🛏 P 🚗 ⚡

| | ▩ | 18 | | | ▩ |

DES MOINES: *Hotel Fort Des Moines* $(S)(S)(S)$
1000 Walnut St. 📞 *(515) 243-1161.* FAX *(515) 243-4317.*
🔲 www.hotelfortdesmoines.com
This stately 1919 downtown hotel has hosted John F. Kennedy, Elvis Presley, and Elizabeth Taylor. 🍽 🛏 P 🚗 TV ⚡ ♿ ▦ 🍴

| | ▩ | 240 | ▩ | | |

DUBUQUE: *The Redstone Inn & Suites* $(S)(S)(S)$
504 Bluff St. 📞 *(563) 582-1894.* FAX *(563) 582-1893.*
🔲 www.theredstoneinn.com
This 1894 private residence and tavern has been convererted into an inn. The Redstone Inn overlooks downtown Dubuque and the Mississippi River. 🛏 🚗 P TV ⚡

| | ▩ | 15 | ▩ | | |

Price categories for a standard double room per night, inclusive of service charges, and any additional taxes:

$ under $50
$$ $50–$100
$$$ $100–$150
$$$$ $150–$200
$$$$$ over $200

CREDIT CARDS
Major credit cards accepted.
RESTAURANT
Hotel restaurant or dining room usually open to nonresidents unless otherwise stated.
CHILDREN'S FACILITIES
Cribs and a baby-sitting service available. Some hotel restaurants have children's portions and high chairs.
GARDEN OR TERRACE
Hotels with a garden, courtyard, or terrace.

	CREDIT CARDS	NUMBER OF ROOMS	RESTAURANT	CHILDREN'S FACILITIES	GARDEN OR TERRACE
MISSOURI					
KANSAS CITY: *Quarterage Inn* $$$ 560 Westport Rd. ((816) 931-0001. FAX (816) 931-8891. W www.quarteragehotel.com In the heart of Old Westport, this inn offers reasonably priced accommodations in one of the city's most central locations.	■	123			
KANSAS CITY: *Raphael Hotel* $$$ 325 Ward Pkwy. ((816) 756-3800. FAX (816) 802-2131. W www.raphaelkc.com Built in 1927 as an upscale apartment house, the Raphael was intended to complement the adjacent Country Club Plaza shops. This Spanish-influenced boutique hotel provides excellent service and European-style accommodations.	■	123	■		
KANSAS CITY: *Southmoreland on the Plaza* $$$$ 116 E 46th St. ((816) 531-7979. FAX (816) 531-2407. W www.southmoreland.com An elegant, discreet urban oasis, this inn serves wine and hors d'oeuvres every night in the lobby.	■	13			■
KANSAS CITY: *Hotel Phillips* $$$$ 106 W 12th St. ((816) 221-7000. FAX (816) 221-3477. W www.hotelphillips.com Recently renovated, this 1931 Art Deco hotel combines historic ambience and modern convenience in the heart of Kansas City's bustling downtown business district.	■	217	■		
ST. LOUIS: *Napolean's Retreat B&B* $$$ 1815 Lafayette Ave. ((314) 772-6979. FAX (314) 772-7675. W www.napoleonsretreat.com Overlooking the lovely Lafayette Square park, this 1880 Victorian B&B offers deluxe accommodations in an elegant, refined atmosphere just minutes from downtown St. Louis.	■	5			■
ST. LOUIS: *Seven Gables Inn* $$$ 26 N Meremac. ((314) 863-8400. FAX (314) 863-8846. W www.sevengablesinn.com This Prince Tudor-style inn features sophisticated lodging, excellent service, and three top-notch restaurants.	■	32	■		
ST. LOUIS: *WS on Washington* $$$$ 400 Washington Ave. ((314) 231-1100. FAX (314) 231-1199. W www.wshotels.com Strikingly furnished suites and a top-notch spa and fitness center are among the features of this luxury hotel in the vibrant, downtown warehouse and loft district.	■	78	■		
KANSAS					
COTTONWOOD FALLS: *1874 Stonehouse B&B* $$ Mulberry Hill, Rte 1, Flint Hills. ((620) 273-8481. FAX (620) 273-8481. W www.stonehousebandb.com Plush guest rooms and a relaxing tallgrass prairie and Cottonwood River nature trail make this 19th-century farmhouse inn the premier lodging destination in the Flint Hills.	■	4			■
COTTONWOOD FALLS: *Grand Central Hotel* $$$$ 215 Broadway. ((620) 273-6763. FAX (620) 273-8381. W www.grandcentralhotel.com Built in 1884 and renovated in 1995, the historic Wild West Grand Central Hotel is noted for its plush, oversized guest rooms.	■	10	■		

COUNCIL GROVE: *Cottage House Hotel & Motel* $$$
25 N Neosho. ☎ (620) 767-6828. [FAX] (620) 767-6414.
[W] www.cotthouse.com
Located on the Santa Fe Trail, this historic lodging establishment features period furnishings and unique guest rooms, including an ornate turret room and private honeymoon cottage. 🛎 [P] 🚗 [TV] 🚭

■	40			

LAWRENCE: *Eldridge Hotel* $$
7th & Massachusetts St. ☎ (785) 749-5011. [FAX] (785) 749-4512.
[W] www.eldridgehotel.com
A tastefully renovated hotel built in 1926 lies just a short distance away from downtown Lawrence's sophisticated restaurants and shopping area. 🛎 [P] 🚗 [TV] 🚭 ♿

■	48	■		

LAWRENCE: *Circle S Ranch & Country Inn* $$$$
3325 Circle S Ln. ☎ (785) 843-4124. [FAX] (785) 843-4474.
[W] www.circlesranch.com
Just minutes north of downtown Lawrence, this luxurious retreat offers sweeping views and imaginatively themed guest rooms – including the Cowboy Room and its longhorn headboard and bucket-shaped shower head. 🛎 [P] 🚗 🚭 ♿

■	12	■		■

TOPEKA: *Senate Luxury Suites* $$$
900 SW Tyler. ☎ (785) 233-5050. [FAX] (785) 233-1614.
[W] www.senatesuites.com
Built in 1928 and recently refurbished, this downtown Victorian hotel offers individually decorated suites, each with ornate woodwork and private balconies. 🛎 [P] 🚗 [TV] 🚭 🏋 ♿

■	52			

TOPEKA: *Capitol Plaza Hotel* $$$
1717 SW Topeka Blvd. ☎ (785) 431-7200. [FAX] (785) 431-7206.
[W] www.jqhhotels.com
An elegant, 5,000 sq-foot (465 sq-m) ballroom, lush garden atrium, and heated indoor pool make the Capitol Plaza Hotel Topeka's premier business and luxury hotel. 🍸 🛎 [P] 🚗 [TV] 🚭 ♿ 🏊 🏋

■	224	■		

WICHITA: *Hotel at Old Town* $$$
830 E 1st St. ☎ (316) 267-4800. [FAX] (316) 267-4840.
[W] www.hotelatoldtown.com
Built in 1906, this former warehouse structure now houses a deluxe suites hotel in the heart of Wichita's Old Town neighborhood. Each suite features a fully equipped kitchen and CD player. 🍸 🛎 [P] 🚗 [TV] 🚭 ♿ 🏋

■	115			

WICHITA: *Inn at the Park* $$$
3751 E Douglas. ☎ (316) 652-0500. [FAX] (316) 652-0525.
[W] www.innatthepark.com
This romantic getaway in the heart of Wichita's stately, early 20th century neighborhood provides elite accomodations for business travelers and vacationers seeking to unwind in an opulent mansion. 🛎 [P] 🚗 [TV] 🚭

■	12			■

OKLAHOMA

BARTLESVILLE: *Hotel Phillips* $$
821 S Johnstone. ☎ (918) 336-5600. [FAX] (918) 336-0350.
[W] www.hotelphillips66.com
A favorite haunt of petroleum executives, Hotel Phillips offers large, comfortable rooms and the very good Grill 66 restaurant, right in downtown Bartlesville. 🍸 🛎 [P] 🚗 [TV] 🚭 ♿

■	157	■		

CLINTON: *Best Western Tradewinds Courtyard Inn* $
2128 Gary Blvd. ☎ (580) 323-2610. [FAX] (580) 323-4655.
[W] www.bestwestern.com
Elvis Presley fans can rent a suite where "The King" stayed several times during his visits here in the 1960s. The suite contains original furnishings from Presley's last visit – including the bed and vanity.
[P] 🚗 [TV] 🚭 ♿ 🏊

■	76	■		

TULSA: *Hotel Ambassador* $$$
1324 S Main St. ☎ (918) 587-8200. [FAX] (918) 587-8208.
[W] www.hotelambassador-tulsa.com
This upscale 1929 hotel is known to be favored by Tulsa's swashbuckling oil barons and has been lovingly renovated, with beautiful marble-topped vanities and stone tile baths in luxurious rooms. 🍸 🛎 [P] 🚗 [TV] 🚭 ♿ 🏋

■	55	■		

For key to symbols see back flap

| | | | | | | Credit Cards | Outdoor Tables | Vegetarian | Good Wine List | Regional Cuisine |

Price categories include a three-course meal for one, a glass of house wine, and all unavoidable extra charges such as sales tax and service.
- $ under $25
- $$ $25–35
- $$$ $35–50
- $$$$ $50–70
- $$$$$ over $70

CREDIT CARDS
Major credit cards accepted.

OUTDOOR TABLES
Garden, courtyard, or terrace with outside tables.

VEGETARIAN
A good selection of vegetarian dishes available.

GOOD WINE LIST
Extensive list of good wines, both domestic and imported.

REGIONAL CUISINE
The menu contains some regional specialties.

Restaurant	Credit Cards	Outdoor Tables	Vegetarian	Good Wine List	Regional Cuisine
DUBUQUE: *Elizabeth's Tollbridge Inn* $$ 2800 Rhomberg Ave. (563) 556-5566. Succulent prime rib, shrimp scampi, and panoramic views are the hallmarks of this downtown restaurant, which is built into the Mississippi River bluffs on the site of an old tollbridge. *L (only on Sat & Sun) D.*	■		■	●	■
IOWA CITY: *Devotay* $$ 117 N Linn St. (319) 354-1001. This cozy downtown tapas restaurant offers a full range of cold and hot tapas, sandwiches, and other entrées. *L, D.*	■		■	●	■

MISSOURI

Restaurant	Credit Cards	Outdoor Tables	Vegetarian	Good Wine List	Regional Cuisine
KANSAS CITY: *Bluebird Bistro* $$$ 1700 Summit St. (816) 221-7559. This colorful West Side bistro has expanded its wide-ranging vegetarian menu to include a succulent range of meat dishes, including organic beef tenderloin, bison, and free-range chicken. *L, D.* ● *Sun.*	■		■	●	■
KANSAS CITY: *Garozzo's Ristorante* $$$ 526 Harrison St. (816) 221-2455. Garozzo's Ristorante offers an authentic Italian dining experience, complete with intimate lighting, wisecracking waiters, homemade pastas, excellent tiramisu, and a hearty wine list. *L, D.* ● *Sun.*	■		■	●	■
KANSAS CITY: *Hereford House Restaurant* $$$$ 2 E 20th St. (816) 842-1080. This classic 1950s steak house offers thick Kansas City steaks with oven-roasted tilapia, cedar-planked salmon, and mouthwatering Caesar salads. *L, D.*	■			●	
ST. LOUIS: *Cunetto House of Pasta* $$$ 5453 Magnolia Ave. (314) 781-1135. Located in the Italian neighborhood known as The Hill, Cunetto offers a dizzying array of pastas and entrées, as well as a hearty toasted ravioli appetizer. *L, D.* ● *Sun.*	■		■		■
ST. LOUIS: *Café Balaban* $$$$ 405 N Euclid Ave. (314) 361-8085. Since 1972, this Central West End institution has served a wide range of entrées, ranging from its signature beef Wellington to glazed salmon, jerk chicken, and bison carpaccio. *L, D.*	■		■	●	■
ST. LOUIS: *Sidney Street Café* $$$$ 2000 Sidney St. (314) 771-5777. Exposed brick, hardwood floors, and intimate lighting provide a romantic backdrop for this cozy restaurant's trademark staples, including steak wasabi, Tuscan sea bass, and Asian salmon. *D.* ● *Sun, Mon.*	■		■	●	■

KANSAS

Restaurant	Credit Cards	Outdoor Tables	Vegetarian	Good Wine List	Regional Cuisine
COTTONWOOD FALLS: *Grand Central Hotel Grill* $$$ 215 Broadway. (316) 273-6763. Located on the first floor of a restored 1884 hotel, this bustling gem serves up a wide range of tender steaks in addition to vegetarian-friendly pastas and entrées. *L, D.* ● *Sun.*	■		■	●	■
COUNCIL GROVE: *Hays House Restaurant Tavern* $ 112 W Main St. (620) 767-5911. Built in 1857 on the old Santa Fe Trail, the oldest continuously operating restaurant west of the Mississippi is famous for its pan-fried chicken, cranberry-strawberry pie, and handmade ice cream. ● *Sun, Mon.* *B, L, D.*	■				■

LAWRENCE: *Teller's* $$
746 Massachusetts St. (785) 843-4111.
Housed in a former bank building, this comfortable downtown Lawrence favorite specializes in imaginatively prepared Italian cuisine, using fresh, locally grown produce. *L, D.*

LAWRENCE: *Pachamama's* $$$
2161 Quail Creek Dr. (785) 841-0990. www.pachamamas.com
This eclectic, upscale-casual establishment tucked away on the southwest side of town features an evolving array of regional, Asian, and Italian delights, with at least one flavorful vegetarian special every evening. *D.*

MANHATTAN: *Harry's Uptown Supper Club* $$$
418 Poyntz Ave. (785) 537-1300.
This beautifully designed, high-ceilinged restaurant serves pastas and exceptionally prepared American dishes on the first floor of downtown Manhattan's stately Wareham Hotel. *D.* Sun.

TOPEKA: *New City Café* $$
4005 S, Gage Center Dr. (785) 271-8646.
One of Topeka's true finds, New City Café offers a constantly changing set of salads, internationally inspired entrées, and homemade desserts for a casually elegant dining experience. *L, D.* Sun.

WICHITA: *Tanya's Soup Kitchen* $$
725 E Douglas. (316) 267-5349.
This intimate, quirky downtown restaurant has built a loyal following with its delicious gourmet soups and a varied mix of sandwiches and salads. *L, D.* Sun.

OKLAHOMA

CATOOSA: *Molly's Landing* $$
3700 N Hwy 66. (918) 266-7853.
This Route 66 roadside tradition features thick steaks and homemade breads and desserts, in a rustic log cabin furnished with leather, rawhide chairs, and Wild West decor. *L, D.* Sun.

OKLAHOMA CITY: *Bricktown Brewery Restaurant & Pub* $$
1 N Oklahoma. (405) 232-2739. www.bricktownbrewery.com
A former warehouse and candy factory, this busy brewpub features handcrafted beers, live music, and a variety of regional dishes, including BBQ ribs and chicken-fried steak. *L, D.*

OKLAHOMA CITY: *Iguana Lounge* $$$
6714 N Western Ave. (405) 840-3474.
Mexican haute cuisine is this creatively designed Oklahoma City restaurant's specialty. A wide range of salsas, fresh peppers, and smoked meats are served with premium tequilas and excellent margaritas. *L, D.*

OKLAHOMA CITY: *The Coach House* $$$$
6437 Avondale Dr. (405) 842-1000.
World-renowned Chef Kurt Fleischfresser prepares a delicious variety of contemporary American dishes, including a roasted rack of pork with huckleberry sauce, at this elegant, fine-dining restaurant. *L, D.* Sun.

TULSA: *Casa Bonita* $
2120 S Sheridan. (918) 836-6464.
This restaurant entices over 10,000 patrons a week to experience its strolling mariachi musicians and out-of-this-world decor, which includes an erupting volcano, 30-foot (9-m) waterfall, and Victorian carousel. *L, D.*

TULSA: *Garlic Rose* $$$
3509 S Peoria. (918) 746-4900.
Located in the heart of Tulsa's Brookside restaurant and retail district, the Garlic Rose offers succulent pastas and Italian main courses in a lively in-town setting. *L, D.* Mon.

TULSA: *The Chalkboard* $$$
1324 S Main St. (918) 582-1964.
Housed in the historic Hotel Ambassador, The Chalkboard's flavorful Italian, American, and regional creations, along with its romantic atmosphere, make this one of Tulsa's long-standing favorites. *B, L, D.*

For key to symbols see back flap

TEXAS

TEXAS

B Y ALMOST ANY STANDARD *Texas is big. Stretching nearly 1,000 miles (1,600 km) across, and even longer north to south, it is by far the largest of the "Lower 48" states and also among the most populous, with 20 million residents. While its size has inspired a love of all things large, its past as an independent nation has given Texans a sense of pride and spirit of freedom, as is evident by the state flag that still carries the Lone Star, emblem of the Republic.*

The huge scale of Texas seems to have encouraged a culture of exaggeration, and according to residents, everything about the state is bigger, better, and brasher than anywhere else. The horns on the emblematic longhorn cattle, the great fortunes made from the state's supplies of oil, and even the one-time role of the Dallas Cowboys football team as "America's Team" – almost every aspect of life is imbued with a sense of superiority. Whether this is deserved or not is a matter of opinion, but contradiction is not what many Texans want to hear. As signs and songs all over the state say: "Don't Mess With Texas."

Dome of Texas State Capitol, Austin

HISTORY

In Texas, history begins at the Alamo, a former Spanish mission and Mexican fort. "Remember the Alamo" was the battle cry of the Texas war of independence from Mexico. In December 1835, a band of rebellious American settlers commandeered the fort. Two months later, the vanquished Mexican army retaliated by attacking the fort for 13 days until all the 189 Americans inside were killed. Despite this setback, the freelance Americans under General Samual Houston defeated the Mexicans in 1836 and declared the independent Republic of Texas. The Republic, which included parts of what are now New Mexico, Oklahoma, Colorado, and Wyoming, was annexed by the US in 1845. This move ignited the Mexican War, and after two years of sporadic fighting Mexico was forced to accept the loss of Texas, and the rest of the West, in 1848.

Plaque depicting a scene from the Texas War of Independence, the Alamo complex, San Antonio

◁ **Cowboy boots on display at M.L. Leddy's Boots and Saddlery in San Angelo, southwest of Abilene**

Sculpture of longhorn cattle outside the Dallas Convention Center

The second half of the 19th century was the heyday of the great cattle drives of the Wild West. Huge herds of Texas longhorn cattle, descendants of animals introduced by the Spanish colonists centuries before, roamed the open range. Rounded up and driven by cowboys to towns such as Fort Worth and Dallas, these cattle were loaded onto trains and shipped to different markets located in the eastern US. After working on the range for weeks at a time, the cowboys' arrival into town was often heralded by a frenzy of gunplay and general debauchery.

KEY DATES IN HISTORY

1519 Spanish explorer Alonso Alvarez de Pineda sets foot in what is now Texas

1528 Cabeza de Vaca and a black African slave spend six years traveling across Texas

1685 Rene-Robert Cavelier, Sieur de la Salle, establishes a short-lived French colony on the Gulf of Mexico at Matagorda Bay

1716 Spain establishes Catholic missions in southern Texas

1822 American immigrant Stephen F. Austin establishes a settlement along the Brazos River

1836 Battle of the Alamo; Texas becomes a Republic

1845 Texas becomes a state

1870 Texas readmitted to the Union

1900 Hurricane hits Galveston, killing 6,000

1901 Oil is discovered at Spindletop

1962 NASA's "Mission Control" in Houston

1963 President John F. Kennedy assassinated in Dallas; Texas native Vice President Lyndon B. Johnson assumes leadership

1986 Crude oil prices fall, damaging economy

2001 Texas Governor George W. Bush is named as 43rd president, despite losing the popular vote

ECONOMY & CULTURE

Though Texas has one of the nation's most diversified economies, historically it has been dependent upon two main industries, oil and agriculture. Since the discovery of oil in the early 1900s, the state has remained the center of the US petroleum industry, producing one-third of the nation's output and controlling most of the vast quantities imported from overseas. In fact, it is hard to think of Texas without reference to the oil industry, thanks to images of gushers, "Texas Tea," and the machinations of the Ewing family on the 1980s TV show *Dallas*.

Agriculture, too, is very important. The livestock industry is still big business, so identified with its "cowboy culture" roots that boots, jeans, and a Stetson hat seem to be the official state costume. However, Texas also produces other crops such as cotton and citrus. The state's high-tech industry is led by Texas Instruments and Austin-based Dell Computer, while the huge military presence supports a major aeronautical engineering industry, particularly at NASA's "Mission Control" in Houston.

These frequently booming and often busting industries have created many fortunes. Texan wealth supports not only glitzy shops and fancy restaurants but has also endowed several excellent museums in Houston, Fort Worth, and other cities. However, the most authentic images of Texas are not of urban sophistication but of the down-home informality and vast open spaces of its rural reaches. Perhaps the best way to find its heart is to follow a dusty country road, stopping for coffee in a small-town café, with its parking lot full of pickup trucks, or watching the sun set over the ever-distant horizon.

Cowboys relaxing on a Texas ranch at sunset

Exploring Texas

Texas is so large that it is a challenge to see all of it. Public transportation is negligible in this fossil-fueled state, where driving is an essential part of life. Many visitors fly between the main cities of Dallas, Austin, and Houston, and then rent a car to get around. About 90 percent of the state's 20 million residents live in the cities, which are equipped with restaurants, hotels, and visitor attractions. Out in the countryside, where the "real" Texas lives, facilities are few and far between. Even in the more popular areas such as the Hill Country outside Austin, hotels and restaurants tend to be basic, and distances are so great that travel time can take up a large portion of the day.

NEW MEXICO

SIGHTS AT A GLANCE

KEY

✈ Airport

— Highway

— Major road

— Railroad

- - State border

·— International border

MEXICO

Sparkling glass office towers, dominating the Dallas skyline

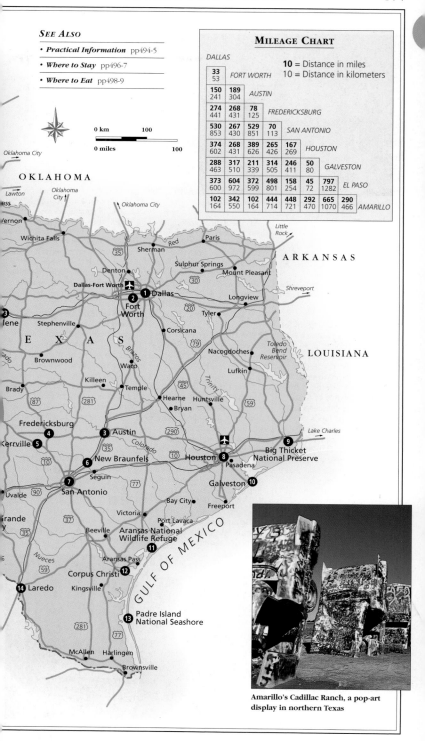

See Also

- ***Practical Information*** pp494-5
- ***Where to Stay*** pp496-7
- ***Where to Eat*** pp498-9

Mileage Chart

10 = Distance in miles
10 = Distance in kilometers

	Dallas	Fort Worth	Austin	Fredericksburg	San Antonio	Houston	Galveston	El Paso
Fort Worth	**33** 53							
Austin	**150** 241	**189** 304						
Fredericksburg	**274** 441	**268** 431	**78** 125					
San Antonio	**530** 853	**267** 430	**529** 851	**70** 113				
Houston	**374** 602	**268** 431	**389** 626	**265** 426	**167** 269			
Galveston	**288** 463	**317** 510	**211** 339	**314** 505	**246** 411	**50** 80		
El Paso	**373** 600	**604** 972	**372** 599	**498** 801	**158** 254	**45** 72	**797** 1282	
Amarillo	**102** 164	**342** 550	**102** 164	**444** 714	**448** 721	**292** 470	**665** 1070	**290** 466

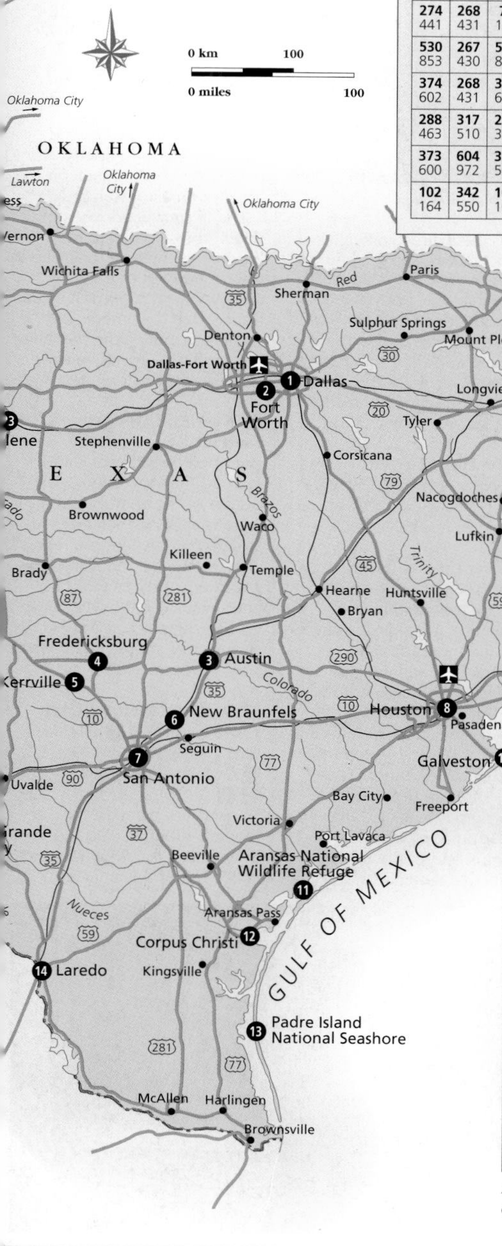

0 km 100
0 miles 100
Oklahoma City
OKLAHOMA
Lawton
Oklahoma City
Oklahoma City
Wichita Falls
Sherman
Red
Paris
Little Rock
ARKANSAS
Sulphur Springs
Mount Pleasant
Denton
Dallas-Fort Worth
1 Dallas
2 Fort Worth
Shreveport
Longview
Tyler
Stephenville
Corsicana
T E X A S
Brownwood
Brazos
Waco
Nacogdoches
Toledo Bend Reservoir
LOUISIANA
Lufkin
Killeen
Temple
Brady
Trinity
Hearne
Bryan
Huntsville
Fredericksburg 4
Kerrville 5
3 Austin
Colorado
Lake Charles
9 Big Thicket National Preserve
Houston 8
Pasadena
6 New Braunfels
Seguin
7 San Antonio
Uvalde
Galveston 10
Bay City
Freeport
Victoria
Port Lavaca
Beeville
Aransas National Wildlife Refuge 11
Nueces
Aransas Pass
Corpus Christi 12
GULF OF MEXICO
14 Laredo
Kingsville
13 Padre Island National Seashore
McAllen
Harlingen
Brownsville

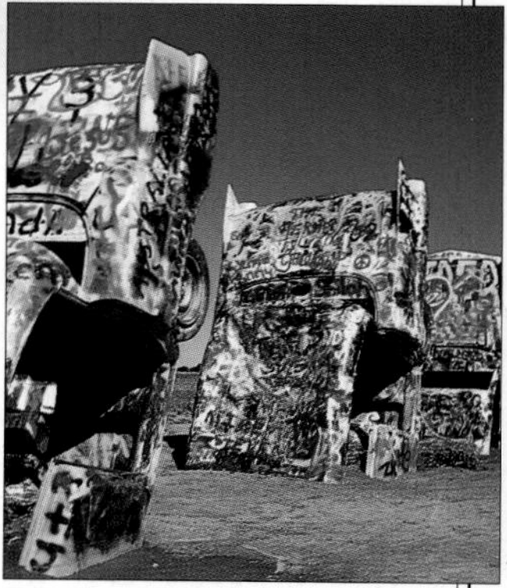

Amarillo's Cadillac Ranch, a pop-art display in northern Texas

View of Dallas from the Reunion Tower Observation area

Dallas ❶

🏙 *1,100,000.* ✈ 🚉 *Union Station, 400 S Houston St.* 🚌 *Greyhound Lines, 205 S Lamar St.* ℹ *100 S Houston St, (214) 571-1300.* 🎭 *Cotton Bowl Parade (Jan 1); Dallas Blooms (Mar 15–Apr 20); Texas State Fair (Sep–Oct).*

WHEN MOST PEOPLE think of Texas, they think of Dallas, even though it is neither the state capital nor the biggest city. Located in the northeastern corner of the state, this is where the cotton fields and oil wells of East Texas meet the wide-open West Texas rangelands. With a forest of sparkling glass office towers dominating the downtown area, Dallas is the commercial and financial center of the "Lone Star" state, a role it has played since its days as the junction between the two main southwestern railroads. This fast-growing metropolis devoted to business has a huge concentration of technology firms, corporate headquarters, and wholesale markets. Infamous as the place where President Kennedy was assassinated, Dallas is nonetheless an energetic, enjoyable city, home to many prestigious museums, restaurants, and cultural venues.

Dallas is a sprawling city, merging into neighboring Fort Worth *(see pp480–81)*. The nation's eighth-largest city features a lively downtown, where most of the visitor attractions are located. A square-mile grid of streets centering on Main Street

holds the main commercial district that is also the home of some of the country's best museums. The lively West End and hip Deep Ellum districts lie at the edges of downtown. Walking in Dallas is an option, but a car, a cab, or the new DART trams can help make the most of a visitor's time.

🏛 Reunion Tower

300 Reunion Blvd E. 📞 *(214) 651-1234.* 🕙 *10am–10pm Mon–Thu, 10am–noon Fri, 9am–noon Sat.* 🚫 ♿

Looking over Dallas from the western edge of downtown, this 50-story landmark is topped by a geodesic sphere containing a restaurant, a cocktail bar, and an observation area. Although not the city's tallest building, a title held by the 72-story Bank of America Tower located on Main Street, Reunion Tower does offer an unforgettable panoramic view of Dallas and its surrounding suburbs, and remains one of the city's most distinctive landmarks.

🏛 Sixth Floor Museum

411 Elm St. 📞 *(214) 747-6660.* 🕙 *9am–6pm daily.* ⏺ *Thanksgiving, Dec 25.* 🚫 ♿

At the west end of downtown Dallas, this private museum meticulously re-creates the context while describing the controversial events of November 22, 1963, when President Kennedy was assassinated. Located in the former warehouse from which Lee Harvey Oswald shot and killed Kennedy, the exhibition concentrates on the life and times of Kennedy.

The corner window from which the shots were fired has been rebuilt to look like it did on the day of the assassination. A portion of the floor space documents the many conspiracy theories that question the official version of the president's murder.

🏛 West End Historic District

Bounded by highways and railroad tracks, this compact district of the century-old warehouses has been revitalized as the city's prime recreation center. At the north end, a former candy factory has been resurrected as the West End Marketplace, a four-story complex of shops, nightclubs, and movie theaters.

🏛 Dallas Museum of Art

1717 N Harwood St. 📞 *(214) 922-1200.* 🕙 *11am–5pm Tue–Sun.* ⏺ *Jan 1, Thanksgiving, Dec 25.* 🚫 ♿

Housed in an expansive modern building north of downtown, the wide-ranging collection of this museum

Modernist façade of the Dallas Museum of Art

gives a fine overview of art history. The main galleries are arranged by continent, with works shown in chronological order. Noteworthy among these is the Art of the Americas gallery, displaying treasures from ancient Maya and Inca civilizations through paintings by such American artists as Frederic Church and Thomas Hart Benton, with a special focus on Texas-made art of the Wild West.

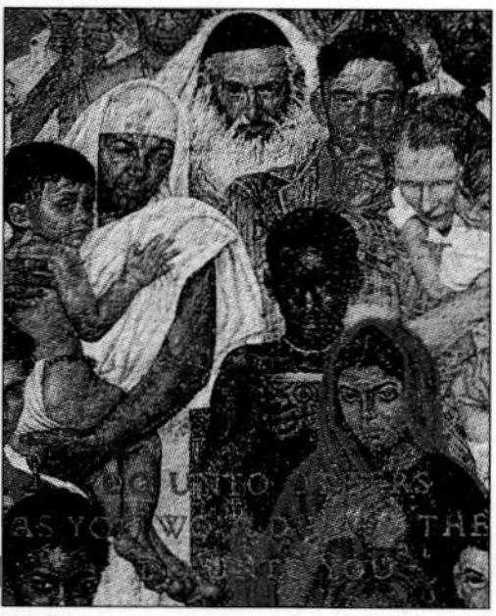

Mosaic mural in downtown's Thanks-giving Square

The European Sculpture and Painting gallery traces the evolution of art from Greek and Roman antiquities through the Renaissance, ending with a fine display of Modernist paintings. The world's most extensive collection of works by influential Dutch artist Piet Mondrian (1872–1944) is also on display.

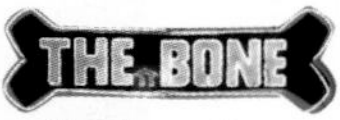
THE BONE

Sign from a Deep Ellum nightclub

Thanks-giving Square

Pacific Ave. ☎ *(214) 969-1977.*

A peaceful and quiet oasis in bustling downtown, this pocket-sized park is packed with waterfalls, gardens, a belltower, and a chapel. A small museum traces the history of the American custom of Thanksgiving and expresses gratitude for life in all its myriad forms.

Fair Park

First Ave. ☎ *(214) 421-9600.*

This 277-acre (111-ha) exhibition center is the site of the annual Texas State Fair. It hosts the famous annual Cotton Bowl football game as well as many concerts and theater festivals. Alongside an aquarium, a natural history museum, and an African-American history museum, a highlight here is the Hall of State, a huge Art Deco repository of exhibits tracing all things Texan with customary bravado.

Deep Ellum

Main & Commerce Sts. ☎ *(214) 748-4332.*

Long known as Deep Ellum (a corruption of Elm Street), this is one of the centers of historic Dallas. During Prohibition *(see p49)* the neighborhood flourished as secret "speakeasy," with nightclubs providing alcohol and entertainment. Seminal jazz and blues musicians have performed here over the years. Today, the neighborhood is a combination of industrial premises, stylish restaurants, and avant-garde nightclubs.

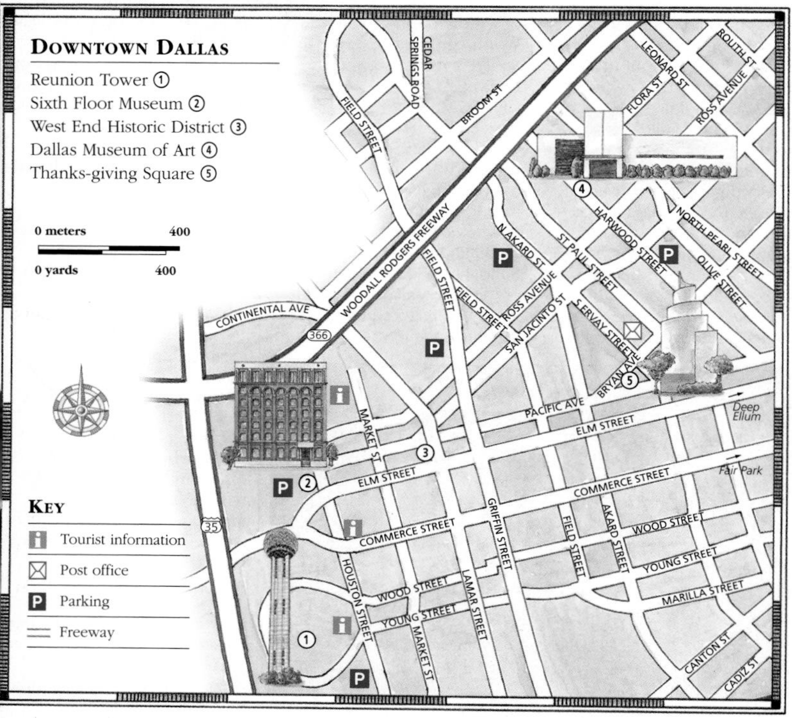
DOWNTOWN DALLAS
Reunion Tower 1
Sixth Floor Museum 2
West End Historic District 3
Dallas Museum of Art 4
Thanks-giving Square 5
0 meters 400
0 yards 400
KEY
Tourist information
Post office
Parking
Freeway
CEDAR SPRINGS ROAD
FIELD STREET
BROOM ST
LEONARD ST
FLORA ST
ROUTH ST
ROSS AVENUE
HARWOOD STREET
NORTH PEARL STREET
OLIVE STREET
N AKARD ST
ST PAUL STREET
WOODALL RODGERS FREEWAY
CONTINENTAL AVE
366
SAN JACINTO ST
S ERVAY STREET
BRYAN AVE
PACIFIC AVE
ELM STREET
Deep Ellum
MARKET ST
COMMERCE STREET
Fair Park
GRIFFIN STREET
AKARD STREET
WOOD STREET
YOUNG STREET
MARILLA STREET
HOUSTON STREET
LAMAR STREET
CANTON ST
CADIZ ST
35

Fort Worth ❷

🏛 *492,000.* ✈ 🚌 *Greyhound Lines, 901 Commerce St.* ℹ *415 Throckmorton St, (817) 336-8791.* 🎫 *Fort Worth Stock Show & Rodeo (late Jan–early Feb); Van Cliburn International Piano Competition (Jun).* 🌐 *www.fortworthgov.org*

U NLIKE ITS FLASHY neighbor, Dallas, 25 miles (40 km) to the east, Fort Worth is smaller, much calmer, and more down-to-earth. In many ways it is also truer to its Texas roots. Founded in 1849 as a US Army outpost, Fort Worth boomed after the Civil War, when Chisholm Trail cattle drives made the city one of the country's largest livestock markets. Although cowboy culture lives on in the Stockyards District and the Amon Carter Museum, Fort Worth is also a capital of "high" culture, with some of the nation's finest performing arts spaces and organizations.

Fort Worth has three main areas of interest. Downtown Fort Worth revolves around Sundance Square, comprising more than a dozen blocks of historic buildings at the center of the city. To the north is the Stockyards District, where the Wild West culture is alive and well. About 2 miles (3 km) to the west, the Fort Worth Cultural District has some of the country's best museums. These are centered around the landmark Kimbell Art Museum, which along with the Amon Carter Museum traces the highpoints of European and American art. Other museums include the

The Water Gardens, designed by the architect Philip Johnson

excellent Modern Art Museum, and the Museum of Science and History, which also houses a planetarium.

While walking is enjoyable in and around downtown, a car is essential to get around the rest of city.

🏛 Sundance Square
ℹ *(817) 255-5700.*
The heart of downtown Fort Worth, Sundance Square's name is a reminder of the city's Wild West past, when Chisholm Trail cattle drives used to come right through town, and cowboys and outlaws such as Butch Cassidy and the Sundance Kid frequented the city's many saloons. Filled with well-restored commercial buildings dating from the turn

Advertisement for Western wear in the Stockyards District

of the 20th century, the brick-paved streets of Sundance Square are now lined with theaters, shops, and restaurants. The city's symphony, ballet, and opera companies are all housed here. An important museum in this area is the **Sid Richardson Collection of Western Art** on Main Street. Housed in a replica of an 1895 building, the museum exhibits 60 paintings of the famed artists Frederic Remington and Charles M. Russell. Also on Main Street is the trompe l'oeil mural of the Chisholm Trail by Richard Haas.

🎋 Water Gardens
Houston & Commerce Sts.
ℹ *(817) 871-7275.*
Located on the site of Fort Worth's historic red-light district of Wild West saloons, this 5-acre (2-ha) park features a variety of waterfalls, cascades, streams, and fountains. Constructed in concrete and designed by architect Philip Johnson, the Water Gardens provide a welcome relief on hot summer days.

🏛 Fort Worth Stockyards National Historic District
ℹ *(817) 626-7921.*
With its cobblestoned streets, raised wooden sidewalks, and streetlights designed to resemble old-fashioned gas lights, this small but engaging 10-block neighborhood is located 2 miles (3 km) north of downtown. Known as the Stockyards District, it developed alongside the sprawling Fort Worth Stockyards, where each day more than a million head of cattle were sold and shipped to markets in the eastern United States. Though the stockyards ceased to be commercially viable many years ago, the complex preserves the old wooden pens and holds daily livestock auctions.

Today, the neighborhood offers a glimpse of what life in Texas was like a century

View of Stockyards District with its many saloons

Longhorn cattle being led through Stockyards National Historic District

ago. A number of lively cowboy-themed saloons and honky-tonk nightclubs, many featuring live music, are also located here. The oldest and most atmospheric of these is the White Elephant Saloon. Also nearby are the Longhorn Saloon and **Billy Bob's Texas** (see p495). Said to be the largest nightclub in the world, Billy Bob's Texas is housed in a huge building and boasts 42 bar areas. Live bull-riding demonstrations also take place here on weekend nights. The district includes a small museum and a steam train. Other attractions include weekend rodeos and a daily parade of longhorn cattle down Exchange Avenue. Today, this is an up-and-coming area, where trendy bars and cafés spring up almost every day.

Sign for Billy Bob's Texas nightclub

🏛 Kimbell Art Museum

3333 Camp Bowie Blvd. 🄲 (817) 332-8451. ◯ 10am–5pm Tue–Thur, noon–8pm Fri, 10am–5pm Sat. ⬤ Jan 1, Jul 4, Thanksgiving, Dec 25. 📷 exhibitions only. ♿

One of the most unforgettable museums and art collections in the United States, the Kimbell Museum is an architectural masterpiece, designed by Louis Kahn in 1971 as a series of vaulted roofs that seem to hover in mid-air. The gallery spaces are bathed in natural light, showing off the varied beauty of the diverse collections, which include pre-Columbian Mayan pottery, and jewelry, as well as rare ancient Asian bronzes. Paintings on display range from Renaissance and Baroque masterpieces by Rubens, Rembrandt, Tiepolo, and Tintoretto to a world-class collection of Post-Impressionist and early Modernist paintings by such celebrated masters as Cezanne, Picasso, and others.

🏛 Amon Carter Museum

3501 Camp Bowie Blvd. 🄲 (817) 738-1933. ◯ 10am–5pm Wed, Fri & Sat, 10am–8pm Thu, noon–5pm Sun. ⬤ Jan 1, Jul 4, Thanksg., Dec 25. ♿ 🅆 www.cartermuseum.org

Along with the Kimbell Art Museum across the street, the Amon Carter Museum anchors Fort Worth's much-vaunted Cultural District, which is located 2.5 miles (4 km) west of downtown. In contrast to its neighbor, however, the Amon Carter Museum concentrates entirely on American art of the Wild West, housing seminal paintings, drawings, and sculptures by Thomas Moran, Frederic Remington, Charlie Russell, and Georgia O'Keeffe among others. Said to be one of the foremost collections of cowboy art, the Amon Carter Museum also has the distinction of possessing the world's most extensive library. It has more than 100,000 photographs documenting the discovery, exploration, and settlement of the country's western frontier.

The Amon Carter Museum, which features cowboy art

COWBOYS

The romanticized image of the cowboy, as portrayed by Hollywood Westerns, was far removed from reality. During the 1880s, the demand for beef in the East and Midwest led to the Texas cattle trails, which linked the open ranges with railroads. Of these, the most famous was the Chisholm Trail to Abilene, Kansas. Cowboys traveled across the country on trail drives that were often fraught with danger. These poorly paid young men mostly rode the flanks of a herd to prevent cattle from wandering off. Those at the rear faced even more difficult conditions: Indian attacks, choking dust, long hours, and outlaw hustlers. From this tough life emerged the myth of the cowboy, celebrated in films, literature, music, and fashion. The first cowboy star was Buffalo Bill (see p582). Since then, the rugged roles played by John Wayne and Clint Eastwood fashioned popular perceptions of cowboys and life in the Wild West.

Magazine cover depicting cowboy in action, 1913

Exterior of the Texas State Capitol in Austin

Austin ❸

🏙 575,000. ✈ 🚊 🚌 ℹ *201 E 2nd St; (512) 478-0098, (800) 926-2282.* 🌐 *www.ci.austin.tx.us*

THE CAPITAL CITY of Texas, Austin is also home to a thriving high-tech industry as well as the state's main university. However, it is best known for hosting one of the liveliest popular music scenes in the country since the 1960s. Musicians as diverse as Janis Joplin and Willie Nelson achieved prominence in Austin, and the city still abounds in live music venues, concert halls, and nightclubs that host scores of young musicians aspiring to fame.

Nightclub sign, Austin

Showcasing the Texan love of all things large, the **Texas State Capitol**, in the heart of downtown, is the largest such structure in the US. Built in 1888, it has 500 rooms covering some 8.5 acres (3.5 ha) of floor space. With its over 300-ft (92-m) high pink granite dome dominating the downtown skyline, the building is taller than the US Capitol in Washington *(see pp198–9)*. In the rotunda beneath the dome, the floor contains the official seals of the six nations – Spain, France, Mexico, the Republic of Texas, the Confederacy, and the US – whose flags have all flown over Texas.

North of the Capitol complex, the expansive campus of the **University of Texas** spreads east from Guadalupe Street. Centering on a landmark tower, the campus holds a number of museums and libraries. The **Blanton Museum of Art** has over 13,000 works of art, from the Renaissance to Abstract Expressionism, many of which were donated by novelist James Michener. The **Lyndon Baines Johnson Presidential Library**, at the northeast edge of the campus, is a repository for all official documents of the Texas-born Johnson (1908–73), who served as US senator, vice-president, and US president following the assassination of John F. Kennedy *(see p478)*. Videotapes trace the Civil Rights Movement, the Vietnam War, and other key events of his tumultuous career. A 7/8th scale reproduction of his Oval Office is displayed on the top floor of this monumental building.

🏛 **Texas State Capitol**
11th St & Congress Ave. 🅲 *(512) 463-0063.* ⭕ *7am–10pm Mon–Fri, 9am–8pm Sat–Sun.* ⬤ *Jan 1, Easter, Thanksgiving, Dec 24–25.* ♿

🏛 **Blanton Museum of Art**
23rd & San Jacinto Sts. ℹ *(512) 471-7324.* ⭕ *9am–5pm Mon–Fri, 1–5pm Sat–Sun.* ⬤ *public hols.* ♿

Fredericksburg ❹

🏙 *8,400.* ℹ *302 E Austin St, (830) 997-6523.*

ONE OF THE loveliest small towns in Texas, and centerpiece of the rolling Hill Country that spreads over 25,000 sq miles (64,749 sq km) west of Austin, Fredericksburg was first settled by German immigrants in 1846. The town's strong Germanic heritage is kept alive by a number of biergartens and Bavarian-style buildings such as the reconstructed Vereinskirche (community or union church) in the Marktplatz, off Main Street.

The town is also home to the **National Museum of the Pacific War**, which traces the history of US military activities in the South Pacific during World War II. The museum is housed in the steamboat-shaped Nimitz Hotel. The hotel was built in the 1850s by the family of US Admiral Chester Nimitz, the commander-in-chief of US forces, who was born in Fredericksburg. It operated as a hotel until the early 1960s and opened as a museum in 1967. The museum has been greatly expanded since, but the appearance of the old hotel has been preserved. The tranquil Japanese Peace Garden, gifted by the Japanese government, is at the back.

Located midway between Fredericksburg and Austin, the boyhood home of the Vietnam War-era, 36th US president has been preserved as the **Lyndon B. Johnson**

Tank display in the National Museum of the Pacific War, Fredericksburg

National Historical Park.
Other features of the park,
which includes some sites
spread out over the surrounding area, are Johnson's one-
room rural school, the ranch
that served as his "Texas
White House," and his grave.

**National Museum of the
Pacific War**
340 E Main St. ☎ *(830) 997-4379.*
○ *10am–5pm daily.* ● *Dec 25.*
⬛ ⬛ ⬛

**Lyndon B. Johnson
National Historical Park**
US 290 in Johnson City. ☎ *(830)
868-7128.* ○ *8:45am–5pm daily.*
● *Jan 1, Thanksg., Dec 25.* ⬛ ⬛

Kerrville ❺

⬛ *21,000.* 🚌 ⬛ *2108 Sidney
Baker St, (830) 792-3535.*
⬛ *www.kerrvilletx.com*

German-style architecture in New Braunfels

A PICTURESQUE RESORT and
retirement community
located in the rugged hills
above the Guadalupe River,
Kerrville is one of the largest
towns in the Texas Hill
Country. This friendly town is
famous for the 18-day folk
music festival it hosts annually at the Quiet Valley Ranch
just south of town, starting
Thursday before Memorial
Day. While the festival now
attracts singers and fans from
all over the world, it still
retains the homey, intimate
atmosphere of the early years.
  Another highlight in town
is the **National Center for
American Western Art**,
which showcases contem-
porary painting and sculpture
depicting the working life of
cowboys. The many galleries

within the museum display
everything from illustrations
made for Western novels to
more workaday aspects of
cowboy life such as saddles
and spurs.

**National Center for
American Western Art**
1550 Bandera Hwy. ☎ *(830) 896-
2553.* ○ *9am–5pm Mon–Sat,
1–5pm Sun.* ● *Jan 1, Easter,
Thanksgiving, Dec 25.* ⬛ ⬛
⬛ *www.caamuseum.com*

New Braunfels ❻

⬛ *28,000.* ⬛ *390 S Seguin St,
(830) 625-2385.*
⬛ *www.nbcham.org*

A POPULAR DAY-TRIP from San
Antonio (*see pp484–5*),
New Braunfels was one of
many towns settled by
German immigrants in the
tumultuous 1840s, when
Texas was an independent
republic offering land grants
to Anglo-Saxon settlers. The
German heritage still thrives
in local architecture, cuisine,

language, and festivals. Many
historic and restored German-
style buildings can be seen
across the town. However,
German influence is most
evident in the numerous
annual festivals celebrated
here, such as the sausage and
beer festivals and the Polka
Festival, all of which help
preserve the town's strong
German roots.
  Built on the site that the
town's aristocratic founder
Prince Carl of Solms-
Braunfels, Germany, chose
for his castle (it was never
built), the **Sophienburg-New
Braunsells Archives and
Museum of History** docu-
ments the town's history.
Exhibits include several local
artifacts and re-creations of
pioneers' homes and shops,
an early bakery, a doctor's
office, and a pharmacy.

**Sophienburg-New
Braunsells Archives &
Museum of History**
401 W Coll St. ☎ *(830) 629-1572.*
○ *10am–5pm Mon–Sat, 1–5pm Sun.*
● *public hols.* ⬛ ⬛

A gallery inside Kerrville's National Center for American Western Art, displaying paintings and
sculptures exemplifying the life of cowboys.

San Antonio ●

Detail, Alamo Memorial

THE MOST HISTORIC CITY in Texas, San Antonio is also the most popular, both for its pivotal historic role and its natural beauty. Once home to the Comanche Indians, the riverside site drew the attention of Spanish missionaries, who founded Mission San Antonio de Valero in 1718. Later converted into a military outpost and renamed the Alamo, it was the site of the most heroic episode of the Texan revolution. Predominantly Hispanic and Mexican in character, San Antonio balances a thriving economy with a careful preservation of its past. Most of the historic sites lie within a block of the pedestrian-friendly Riverwalk in the downtown core.

Hertzberg Circus Museum

Hertzberg Circus Museum

★ **Riverwalk (Paseo del Rio)**
This tree-shaded path along the San Antonio River was built as a flood-control project during the Depression-era New Deal. Now a horseshoe-shaped, open-air promenade lined with shops, Riverwalk is a peaceful oasis in the middle of the city.

★ **La Villita**
It was in this early 19th-century "little village," that the Mexicans officially surrendered to the Republic of Texas. The quaint village of stone and adobe buildings now houses craft workshops.

MISSIONS NATIONAL HISTORICAL PARK

Mission San Jose

This 819-acre (331-ha) historic park preserves four Spanish frontier missions, which, along with the Alamo, formed the northern edge of Spain's North American colonies in the 18th century. Still in use as Catholic parish churches, the former missions such as Missions San Jose, San Juan, Espada, and Concepcion spread south from downtown San Antonio along the 9-mile (14-km) "Mission Trail." The finest of the group, Mission San Jose, is known for the intricately carved stonework of the Rose Window adjacent to the sacristy.

0 meters   200

0 yards   200

Buckhorn Saloon & Museum

This intriguing museum is crowded with Wild West exhibits and stuffed animals from around the world.

★ **The Alamo**

*"Remember the Alamo" was the battle
cry that inspired Texans during their
war for independence against Mexico
(1835–36). The secularized mission was
the site of a long, bloody siege that took
the lives of 189 Americans, shortly after
which the Texas Republic was born.*

Rivercenter Mall

**Tower of
the Americas**

**HemisFair
Park**

Institute of Texas Cultures

*On the grounds of
HemisFair Park, this
expansive museum
chronicles the past and
present of 27 distinct
ethnic and cultural groups
prominent in Texas.*

STAR SIGHTS

★ **La Villita**

★ **Riverwalk**

★ **The Alamo**

Houston

🏛 *1,800,000.* ✈ 🚉 *902 Washington Ave.* 🚌 *Greyhound Lines, 2121 S Main St.* ℹ *901 Bagby St, (713) 437-5200.* 🎭 *Houston Livestock Show (late Feb–early Mar); Art Car Parade (May); Thanksgiving Day Parade (Nov).* 🌐 *www.houston-guide.com*

A CITY OF constant change and great diversity, the story of Houston is a typical Texas success story. Founded in 1836 in what was then a swamp, the city was named in honor of Texas hero General Sam Houston *(see p474)* and served as capital of the Texas Republic until 1839. A center for shipping cotton, Houston's fortunes faded after the Civil War, but it developed into a major port following the construction of a shipping channel to the Gulf of Mexico. The discovery of oil turned the city into a major petrochemical producer, and in recent years it has grown into the biggest city in Texas and the fourth-largest in the US. Free enterprise rules Houston, the home of the now-defunct Enron, but a long tradition of community pride has also endowed the city with some of the world's finest art museums.

A huge, sprawling city that has grown to cover over 600 sq miles (1554 sq km), Houston is a thoroughly confusing place, lacking in an overall plan. The absence of zoning codes or any real visual order, the frequent changes in street names and directions, and the lack of public transportation and often heavy road traffic, can make matters worse.

In short, to see Houston visitors should be prepared to

Expansive gardens surrounding Ima Hogg's mansion, Bayou Bend

drive, and to get lost more than once. The main attractions for visitors lie southwest of downtown, on and around the Rice University campus.

🏛 Menil Collection

1515 Sul Ross. ☎ *(713) 525-9400.* ◯ *11am–7pm Wed–Sun.* ● *Jan 1, Easter, Jul 4, Thanksgiving, Dec 25.* ♿
One of the world's better assemblies of painting and sculpture, this collection was endowed by the family of Houston philanthropist Dominque de Menil, who died in 1997. It is housed in a striking modern building designed by Italian architect Renzo Piano, one of the designers of the Pompidou Center in Paris. The most extensive display here is of Surrealist paintings, notably by Rene Magritte and Max Ernst. The museum also has a world-class collection of Cubist painting by Picasso and Braque in particular, as well as a full survey of 20th-century American paintings by Jackson Pollock, Jasper Johns, Robert Rauschenberg, and Cy Twombly. Separate galleries display ancient and medieval art of the Mediterranean. Also on view is a

show of works by Native peoples of Africa, the South Pacific, and the Pacific Northwest region of North America.

A short walk east from the main museum stands the ecumenical **Rothko Chapel**, a spare concrete space designed around a series of large, dark-colored abstract paintings by the American artist Mark Rothko. Commissioned by the de Menil family and completed by architect Philip Johnson in 1971, the chapel is open during museum hours. Two blocks to its south lies the Menil-sponsored **Byzantine Fresco Chapel Museum**, a detailed replica of a 13th-century Eastern Orthodox chapel, which displays the only Byzantine frescos on view in the Western Hemisphere.

🏛 Museum of Fine Arts

1001 Bissonnet St. ☎ *(713) 639-7300.* ◯ *check for times.* ● *Jan 1, Thanksgiving, Dec 25.* 🎟 ♿
The oldest art museum in Texas, and one of the largest in the US, the collections here range from Greek and Roman antiquities to Wild West sculptures by Frederic Remington. The striking new Beck Building has European art of the late 19th and early 20th century, with a survey of works by Manet, Pisarro, Renoir, and other masters.

✿ Bayou Bend

1 Wescott St. ☎ *(713) 639-7750.* ◯ *10–11:30am, 1–2.45pm Tue–Fri, 10–11:15am Sat.* ● *Jan 1, Thanksgiving, Dec 25.* 🎟 🎥 ♿
The largest public gardens in Houston surround the pink stucco mansion of oil heiress Ima Hogg (1882–1975), who survived her somewhat unfortunate name to become one

A view of downtown Houston and Memorial Park

Neon signs light up the lively Montrose District

of Houston's greatest benefactors. The wealthy philanthrope was not only famous as a patron of the arts but was also passionately concerned with the well-being of the city. Now run by the Museum of Fine Arts, her home displays a collection of decorative arts, highlighted by a sugar bowl crafted by Colonial hero Paul Revere *(see p142)*, and 5,000 pieces of furniture, ceramics, and textiles. Also on display are portraits by early American artists John Singleton Copley and Charles Willson Peale.

🚻 Montrose District

"Montrose" is a catch name for the lively collection of countercultural-flavored galleries, shops, nightclubs, cafés, and restaurants that can be found along Montrose Street and its intersection with Westheimer Road. Apart from the shopping malls and downtown business district, Montrose District is one of the few walkable neighborhoods in Houston and is especially popular on weekend nights.

🚻 Space Center Houston

1601 Nasa Rd 1. ☎ *(281) 244-2100.* ⏰ *times vary. Call to check.* ● *Dec 25.* ♿ ♿ ✔

Adjacent to the Johnson Space Center, the mission control for all manned US explorations of space since 1965, this visitor-friendly attraction traces the full story of the Space Race. Hands-on exhibits let visitors try on space helmets, touch moon rocks, or peer into actual spaceships such as those from the Mercury, Gemini, and Apollo programs. Computer simulations let visitors fly the space shuttle or land on the moon. But the major attraction of the Space Center is the tour of the still-in-use mission control facilities, where the historic missions to the moon and back were guided.

🚻 San Jacinto Battleground

Hwy 134, 21 miles (34 km) SE of downtown. ☎ *(281) 479-2431.* ⏰ *8am–9pm daily.* ♿ ♿

The vast plains of Texas can be seen for miles from the foot of this 605-ft (184-m) tall monument, claimed to be one of the tallest in the world. It marks the site of the final battle for the independence of the Texas Republic in 1836. The slim shaft is topped by a massive "Lone Star." A museum at the base traces the history and culture of the state, while an adjacent theater hosts a popular 42-projector, multi-image slide show called "Texas Forever!! The Battle of San Jacinto."

San Jacinto tower

DOWNTOWN HOUSTON

Menil Collection ①
Museum of Fine Arts ②
Bayou Bend ③
Montrose District ④

KEY

⊠ Post Office

═ Freeway

CHILTON RD
W CLAY ST
W CLAY ST
W GRAY ST
W GRAY ST
INWOOD DR
INWOOD DR
VERMONT ST
VERMONT ST
VERMONT ST
WILLARD ST
SAN FELIPE RD
FAIRVIEW
FAIRVIEW ST
FAIRVIEW ST
FAIRVIEW ST
WESTHEIMER
WESTHEIMER
REBA DRIVE
KIPLING
KIPLING
W ALABAMA
W ALABAMA
BRANARD ST
BRANARD ST
RICHMOND AV
SOUTHWEST FWY
SOUTHWEST FWY
MONTROSE BLVD
TAFT ST
TAFT ST
STANFORD ST
STANFORD ST
SHEPHERD DR
KIRBY DR
WOODHEAD ST
WINDROP ST
WAUGH DR
MAIN ST
SAN JACINTO
Space Centre Houston

0 meters   250
0 yards   250

Dense cypress swamp in the Big Thicket National Preserve

Big Thicket National Preserve ⑨

Junction of US 69 & Hwy 420, 7 miles (11 km) N of Kountze. **[** (409) 246-2337. **◯** 9am–5pm daily. **●** Jan 1, Dec 25. **[&] [W]** www.nps.gov/bith

MAINTAINING A unique mixture of mountains, plains, swamps, and forests, the Big Thicket National Preserve protects 15 distinct biologically diverse areas (nine land units and six water corridors) encompassing over 97,000 acres (39,255 ha) along the Texas–Louisiana border.

Although much of the preserve is relatively inaccessible, the area once served as a hideout for runaway slaves and outlaws. Today, it is best known for housing a wide range of plants and animals. A series of short hiking trails offer close-up views of dense groves of resident oaks, cactus, carnivorous "pitcher plants," and millions of mosquitoes.

Galveston ⑩

[60,000. **✈ ⊞ ℹ** 2428 Seawall Blvd, (409) 763-4311.

THOUGH comparatively smaller than other Texas cities, Galveston rivals the rest of the state for historical significance and character. Originally a notorious hideout for slave-trading Gulf Coast pirate Jean Lafitte *(see p350)*, Galveston was burned to the ground by US forces in 1821. But by the 1890s the port had grown to be the largest and wealthiest city in Texas. The economy soon declined following a devastating hurricane in 1900, which killed as many as 6,000 people. The subsequent rise of Houston also contributed to Galveston's fading fortunes.

In recent years, many of the city's grand Victorian mansions and 19th-century storefronts have been restored to their original glory. Many exuberantly designed buildings from that period survive in the Strand National Historic Landmark District, near the waterfront. The superbly restored **Ashton Villa** offers a glimpse of an era of wealth and prosperity as well as disaster and change.

Often hailed as one of the state's best resorts on the Gulf of Mexico, the charming island city features more than 30 miles (48 km) of pristine, sandy

Bird-watching in Aransas

beaches. Visitors can also indulge in the family-friendly fun of **Moody Gardens**, with its waterpark pools, a 10-story Rainforest Pyramid offering an incredible tropical environment, and a series of massive aquariums showcasing life from the world's oceans.

⊞ Ashton Villa
2328 Broadway. **[** (409) 762-3933. **◯** 10am–4pm Mon–Sat, noon–4pm Sun. **●** Thanksgiving, Dec 25. **[&]**
● Moody Gardens
1 Hope Blvd. **[** (409) 744-4673. **◯** Apr–Oct: 10am–9pm daily; Nov–Mar: 10am–6pm Sun–Thu, 10am–9pm Fri–Sat. **●** Dec 25. **[&] [&]**

Aransas National Wildlife Refuge ⑪

Hwy 239. 65 miles (105 km) NE of Corpus Christi. **[** (361) 286-3559. **◯** dawn–dusk. **●** Dec 25. **[&]**

WHILE SUN worshipers flock to the Gulf Coast beaches throughout winter, birds and bird-watchers congregate slightly inland at the 70,000-acre (28,328-ha) Aransas National Wildlife Refuge. Established in 1937 to protect the vanishing wildlife of coastal Texas, Aransas is today home to alligators, armadillo, boars, javelinas, coyotes, white-tailed deer, and many other species of wildlife. The most famous visitors here are the endangered whooping cranes, the tallest birds native to North

Pyramid-shaped greenhouse in Moody Gardens, Galveston

Padre Island National Seashore – a popular vacation destination

America. Standing 5 ft (1.5 m) tall, with white bodies, black-tipped wings, and red heads, the cranes migrate here from Canada between November and March, making the salt-water marshes their winter feeding grounds.

Ringed by tidal marshes and broken by long, narrow ponds, Aransas is an ever-changing land that is still being shaped by the turquoise blue waters of San Antonio Bay and the storms of the Gulf of Mexico. Grass-lands, live oaks, and red bay thickets that cover deep, sandy soils provide spectac-ular background scenery.

Corpus Christi ⑫

🏙 *325,000.* ✈ 🚆 🛈 *1201 N Shoreline, (361) 881-1888.*

THE DEEPEST commercial port in Texas and an extensive US military pres-ence have made Corpus Christi one of the fastest-growing cities in the state. Its military importance is marked by the famous 910-ft (277-m) long aircraft carrier, the USS *Lexington,* moored along the 2-mile (3-km) downtown waterfront. To its south, the **Texas State Aquarium** explores the sea life of the Gulf of Mexico with whales, rays, and sharks, and re-creations of reefs similar to those that have grown around the Gulf's many offshore oil rigs. Texas river otters and the Kemp's Ridley sea turtle are also found here.

"Corpus," as residents call the city, looks out across the harbor to **Mustang Island State Park**, where over 5 miles (8 km) of sandy beach stretch along the Gulf of Mexico. At the park's north end, modern condominium resorts detract from the natural scene, overshadowing the historic community of Port Aransas at the island's northern tip.

🍴 Texas State Aquarium
2710 N Shoreline Blvd. 📞 *(361) 881-1200.* 🕐 *May–Sep: 9am–6pm Mon–Sat, 10am–6pm Sun; Oct–Apr: 9am–5pm.* ⬤ *Thanksg., Dec 25.* 🈚 🏬

Padre Island National Seashore ⑬

🛈 *Malaquite Visitor Center, (361) 949-8068.* 🅰 🕸 *www.nps.gov/pais*

BORDERED BY a pair of tourist resorts at its north and south ends, Padre Island is a slender sandbar that

stretches for more than 110 miles (177 km) between Corpus Christi and the Mexican border. The central 65 miles (105 km) have been preserved as the Padre Island National Seashore, which, with few roads and no commercial development, is among the longest wild stretches of coastline in the country. The park is open throughout the year for camp-ing, beachcombing, surfing, swimming, hiking, fishing, and various other activities. Coyotes and other native wild animals still roam the heart of the island.

This is one of the nation's most popular vacation spots. It receives an average of 800,000 visitors per year, especially during the Spring Break, when university students from colder climes in the northern Midwest flock here to unwind and party. South Padre Island marks the southern end of the Gulf Coast of Texas.

A view of the Corpus Christi waterfront

Republic of the Rio Grande Museum, San Augustin Plaza, Laredo

Laredo ⓮

🚶 *200,000.* 🚌 **ℹ** *501 San Augustin St, (956) 795-2200.*

LOCATED ON THE north bank of the legendary Rio Grande (or Rio Bravo, as it is known in Mexico), Laredo is often referred to as the "Gateway to Mexico." It operates two international bridges to Mexico and is hence one of the principal US ports of entry into Mexico.

Located north of the Rio Grande, the original center of Laredo has been well preserved around the historic San Augustin Plaza. Here, the intriguing **Republic of the Rio Grande Museum** is housed in a building that once served as the Capitol of the short-lived independent republic that in 1840 included southern Texas and the three northernmost states of Mexico. The museum traces Laredo's role under six different national flags.

ⅯⅡ Republic of the Rio Grande Museum
1005 Zaragoza St. **ℂ** *(956) 727-3480.* ⏰ *9am–4pm Tue–Sat, 1–4pm Sun.* ● *public hols.* 🈹 ⚟ 🅰

Rio Grande Valley ⓯

ℹ *FM 1015 Expressway 83, Welasco, (956) 968-3141.*

STRETCHING ALONG the Rio Grande for 200 miles (322 km) between Laredo and the Gulf of Mexico, the Rio Grande Valley is a bustling corridor of agricultural,

commercial, and retirement communities all jumbled together in a complicated sprawl. Linked by east-west US 83, which becomes increasingly busy as it gets closer to the Gulf, the valley feels very different from the rest of Texas, thanks in part to the lush, temperate climate softened by moisture-laden breezes. Numerous roadside stands sell bags of grapefruits and bunches of red chili peppers, while convoys of trucks lumber past between warehouses and factories on both sides of the river.

The region's story from border banditry to bilateral trade is traced with permanent and changing exhibits at the **Rio Grande Valley Museum**, while numerous parks try to protect the region's varied natural heritage. The 525-acre (212-ha) **Sabal Palm Sanctuary** preserves the last stand of the stumpy native Sabal palm trees, which once lined the river for miles upstream.

ⅯⅡ Rio Grande Valley Museum
24–25 Boxwood & Raintree Sts, Harlingen. **ℂ** *(956) 430-8500.* ⏰ *10am–4pm Wed–Sat, 1–4pm Sun.* 🈹 🅰 ⚟ *by appointment.*
🏃 Sabal Palm Sanctuary
International Blvd, 6 miles (10 km) SE of Brownsville. **ℂ** *(956) 541-8034.* ⏰ *7am–5pm daily.* ● *Jan 1, Thanksgiving, Dec 25.* 🈹 🅰

Big Bend National Park ⓰

ℹ *Panther Junction, (915) 477-1158.* 🈹 **ⓦ** *www.nps.gov/bibe*

ONE OF THE wildest and most isolated corners of the US, this diverse park covers 801,000 acres (324,154 ha) of southwest Texas. The name "Big Bend" comes from the 90-degree turn, from east to north, made by the Rio Grande as it carves its way toward the Gulf of Mexico through the volcanic rock of the San Vicente and Sierra del Carmen Mountains. Ranging from 1,500-ft (457-m) deep river canyons along the Rio Grande to the pine-forested Chisos Mountains, Big Bend offers a complete experience of the rivers, mountains, canyons, and deserts that define the American Southwest. These contrasts in topography have created

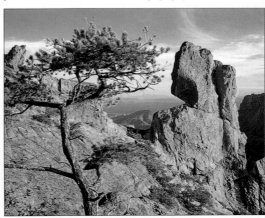

Fascinating rock formations at Big Bend National Park

a unique diversity of plant and animal habitats. Coyotes, roadrunners, and javelinas roam freely amid blossoms of spring wildflowers and cacti.

Fort Davis **17**

600. Town Square, (915) 426-3015.

SITUATED IN THE scenic Davis Mountains at a height of 4,900 ft (1,494 m), Fort Davis is a popular destination for visitors seeking relief from a typical Texas summer. A key site during the Indian Wars of the 19th century, it was originally established in 1854 as a US Army fort along the main road between El Paso and San Antonio (see pp484–5). Today, it has been preserved as the **Fort Davis National**

Guide dressed as an 1880s cavalry soldier in Fort Davis

Historic Site. In summer, costumed interpreters help visitors on self-guided tours through some of the site's restored structures.

The area's high altitude and isolation from large cities has also made it a fine location for astronomical research. Located atop the 6,791-ft (2,070-m) Mount Locke, 17 miles (27 km) northwest of town, the **McDonald Observatory** gives visitors the opportunity to see stars and planets. The Hobby-Eberle spectroscope here has a 430-inch (1,092-cm) mirror, the world's largest.

Fort Davis National Historic Site
Hwy 17. (915) 426-3224. 8am–5pm daily. Dec 25.

McDonald Observatory
Hwy 118. (915) 426-3640. Sep–Apr: 9am–5pm daily; May–Aug: 8–11pm Tue, Fri, Sat. Jan 1, Thanksgiving, Dec 25.

El Paso **18**

560,000. 1 Civic Center Plaza, (915) 534-0600.

LOCATED ON THE northern bank of the Rio Grande, at one of the river's safest natural crossing places, El Paso has long been part of

Catholic Ysleta Mission in El Paso

the largest and liveliest international community along the US–Mexico border. In 1598, Spanish explorer Juan de Onate crossed the river from Mexico and named the place "El Paso del Rio del Norte." It took another 80 years before the city was established with a trio of Catholic missions at Ysleta, Socorro, and San Elizario. Still in operation, the missions are among the oldest communities in Texas.

The story of the varying course of the Rio Grande, which frequently shifted its course (and the international border) until a concrete channel was built in 1963, is detailed in a museum at the **Chamizal National Memorial**, a 55-acre (22-ha) park on the US side. Outside, a 1.8 mile (2.9 km) walking trail circles the park.

Chamizal National Memorial
800 S San Marcial St. (915) 532-7273. 8am–5pm daily. Jan 1, Thanksgiving, Dec 25.

VISITING MEXICO

A short, easy walk over the "International Bridge" from San Augustin Plaza, Laredo, leads visitors across the border in the typical Mexican border town of Nuevo Laredo. This trip gives visitors a deeper appreciation of the interdependence of these two very different yet increasingly similar countries. There is so much shared culture that, in the border areas at least, the differences between the US and Mexico are less striking than the similarities. Thanks mainly to the "Mexicanization" of the American side, where the population is more than 80 percent Latino, the food, music, and language is much the same. Nuevo Laredo, Juarez, and other Mexican cities are far larger and busier than their American counterparts, with a huge array of shops, restaurants, and bars offering a taste of Mexico. Elsewhere, along the more than 1,000-mile (1,609-km) border, dozens of small towns and villages are less frenetic, letting visitors sample a taco while soaking up some south-of-the-border ambience. For US citizens, a trip across the border requires little more than proof of identity. For non-citizens, however, it is vital to confirm their legal status and ensure that they can return to the US. For all travelers, it is far easier and usually quicker to cross the border on foot.

"International Bridge" across the river to Nuevo Laredo, Mexico

Towering El Capitan in Guadalupe Mountains

Guadalupe Mountains National Park ⑲

US 62/180, (915) 828-3251.
www.nps.gov/gumo

AN ALMOST road-free region on the Texas–New Mexico border, this national park covers 85,000 acres (34,398 ha) of rugged mountains that make up portions of the world's most extensive Permian limestone fossil reef, El Capitan, and the 8,749-ft (2,667-m) Guadalupe Peak, the highest point in Texas. Formed as part of the same prehistoric limestone that makes up the nearby (and more popular) Carlsbad Caverns National Park (see p552), the Guadalupe Mountains reward visitors with lofty peaks, spectacular views, unusual flora and fauna, and a colorful record of the past.

A short trail from the visitor center leads to the remains of a stone wall and foundations of a former frontier stagecoach station. This was built as part of the **Butterfield Trail**, which first established a link between St. Louis and California in 1858.

A few miles northeast of the visitor center, a forest of hardwood trees lines the trail of **McKittrick Canyon**. Here lies the site's most famous attraction, the spectacular red-and-orange foliage in October

and November. The hiking trails between the canyon walls that shelter a perennial stream are also very popular.

Lubbock ⑳

195,000. ✈ 🚌
ℹ 1301 Broadway, (806) 747-5232.

HOME TO 30,000 sports-crazy students at Texas Tech University, Lubbock is a cattle-ranching and cotton-growing city that is perhaps best known for its musical progeny. Local musicians including Roy Orbison, Joe Ely, Waylon Jennings, and Tanya Tucker are all honored in Lubbock's guitar-shaped **Buddy Holly Center**, a musical Hall of Fame named for the city's favorite son, Charles Hardin Holley. A statue of Buddy Holly, one of rock 'n' roll's most enduring icons, stands along 8th Street and Avenue Q.

Other aspects of Lubbock history are covered in the Texas Tech University's **Ranching Heritage Center**, an outdoor assembly of historic structures collected from all over Texas. On display are more than 30 original ranch buildings, from cowboy huts to stately overseers' mansions.

🏛 **Buddy Holly Center**
1801 Ave G. 📞 (806) 767-2686.
🕐 10am–6pm Tue–Fri, 11am–6pm Sat. ● Jan 1, Easter, Jul 4, Thanksgiving, Dec 25. 🎫 🚻

🚌 **Ranching Heritage Center**
3121 4th St. 📞 (806) 742-0498.
🕐 10am–5pm Mon–Sat, 1–5pm Sun.
● Jan 1, Thanksg., Dec 24–25. 🚻

Canyon ㉑

12,000. 🚌 ℹ 1518 5th Ave, (806) 655-7815.

TAKING ITS NAME from the beautifully sculpted geology of nearby Palo Duro Canyon, this medium-sized Texas town is also home to the largest and best-known historical museum in the state. **The Panhandle-Plains Historical Museum**, housed in a stately 1930s complex on the campus of West Texas A&M University, holds over three million exhibits tracing the history of north-central Texas. Flint arrowheads from the Alibates quarry, north of Amarillo, highlight the culture of the region's prehistoric people, while geology and paleontology come together in exhibits exploring prehistoric dinosaurs and their relation to the region's prime industry, petroleum. The story of another great Texas tradition, cattle ranching, is explored through the life of Wild West rancher Charles Goodnight, who owned a

---

BUDDY HOLLY (1936–59)

Singer, instrumentalist, and songwriter, Buddy Holly was one of the first major rock 'n' roll music performers. Deeply influenced by local blues and country music, he began to sing in country groups while still in high school. By the mid-1950s, Holly was playing in small clubs throughout the Southwest. Drawn increasingly to rock music as exemplified by Elvis Presley, he recorded both alone and as lead performer with the Crickets. The group's energetic style, combining elements of country music and a strong background rhythm, together with Holly's unique hiccoughing vocals, quickly made them a success. Songs such as "Maybe Baby" and Holly's solo hit "Peggy Sue" became run-away hits. Holly's phenomenal career came to an abrupt end in 1959 when he died in a plane crash in Iowa.

Buddy Holly's statue, Lubbock

View of Palo Duro Canyon, the "Grand Canyon of Texas"

500,000-acre (202,344-ha) ranch, and later led the fight to save native bison from extinction. Goodnight's home is now preserved in the enjoyable "Pioneer Town," located behind the museum.

About 12 miles (19 km) east of town, **Palo Duro Canyon State Park** protects the 60-mile (97-km) long, 1,100-ft (335-m) deep red and yellow sandstone gorge also known as the "Grand Canyon of Texas." A number of scenic drives and hiking routes run between the rim and the canyon floor, offering views of such geological oddities as the 300-ft (91-m) tall stone "Lighthouse." Palo Duro is also home to a wide variety of flora and fauna, including spring wildflowers, mule deer, and wild turkeys. In summer, one of the canyon's 600-ft (183-m) cliffs forms the back-

drop for the pageantry of *Texas*, a popular play on the history of the state.

🏛 Panhandle-Plains Historical Museum

2503 4th Ave. 📞 (806) 651-2244. ⬜ Jun–Aug: 9am–6pm Mon–Sat, 1–6pm Sun; Sep–May: 9am–5pm Mon–Sat, 1–6pm Sun. ⬤ Jan 1, Thanksgiving, Dec 24–25. 🏷 ♿

🌿 Palo Duro Canyon State Park

Hwy 217. 📞 (806) 488-2227. ⬜ 8am–10pm daily. 🏷 ♿ ⛺

Amarillo ㉒

🏠 176,000. ℹ 4th & Buchanan Sts, (806) 374-1497.
🌐 www.ci.amarillo.tx.us

THE COMMERCIAL HEART of the sprawling Texas Panhandle region, and a key center for agriculture as well as oil, natural gas, and nuclear power industries, Amarillo was first settled in 1887 along the Santa Fe Railroad. The city later thrived thanks to its location along the legendary Route 66 (see p40). The route is now immortalized by **Cadillac Ranch**, a Pop Art work created from 10 classic Cadillac cars planted nose-down in a pasture west of downtown. Another more typically Texas experience is the **Amarillo Livestock Auction**, where modern-day cowboys buy and sell their cattle.

🚜 Cadillac Ranch

S side of I-40 between Hope Rd & Arnot Rd exits. ⬜ 24 hours. ♿

Abilene ㉓

🏠 110,000. 🚌 ℹ 1101 N 1st St, (915) 676-2556.

ALTHOUGH named for the notorious Wild West town in Kansas, Abilene evolved from a frontier settlement to a solid, stable community. Also known as the "Buckle of the Bible Belt," thanks to its predominantly Christian colleges where 8,000 students study, Abilene's past is kept alive at **Buffalo Gap Historical Village**, 14 miles (23 km) southwest of downtown. Founded in 1878, Buffalo Gap maintains over a dozen old buildings such as a courthouse, a train station, and a schoolhouse. Exhibits include Paleo-Indian artifacts and a frontier weapons collection.

🚜 Buffalo Gap Historical Village

Hwy 89. 📞 (915) 572-3365. ⬜ Mar 15–Nov 15: 10am–6pm Mon–Sat, noon–6pm Sun; Nov 16–Mar 14: 10am–5pm Fri–Sun. ⬤ Thanksgiving, Dec 25. 🏷 ♿

A sculpturally implanted Cadillac car at Cadillac Ranch, Amarillo

Cowboy in Buffalo Gap Historical Village, Abilene

Practical Information

I N A STATE AS VAST AS TEXAS, it helps greatly that
information for travelers is readily accessible. Images
of oil and cattle ranches immediately spring to mind,
and while this is true for much of the state, Texas has
much variety to offer. Stretching for nearly 800 miles
(1,287 km) from east to west, the state offers everything
from bayous and forests to prairies, bare windswept
plains, and beautiful beaches. The dynamic, bustling
big cities of Dallas and Houston are a contrast to the
laid-back charm of the capital city of Austin with its
lush riverside parks, and historic San Antonio with its
predominantly Hispanic cultural ambience.

TOURIST INFORMATION

A LONG MOST major highways
in Texas, there are
"Welcome Centers," operated
by the **Travel Division** of
the Texas Department of
Transportation. Open between
8am and 5pm daily, these
centers offer a full range of
tourist information, including
details of weather and road
conditions, attractions and
accommodations. Texas also
publishes a magazine called
Texas Monthly with travel
stories and photographic
essays on the wonders of the
"Lone Star" state.

Most airports have information desks, and all major
towns and cities have tourist-
oriented Visitors' Bureaus or
Chambers of Commerce.

NATURAL HAZARDS

T EXAS HAS ITS fair share of
natural hazards. Winter
blizzards block roads and
strand drivers under heavy
snows, while in spring, torren-
tial rains that occur along with
tornadoes and severe thunderstorms flood towns and cities
located along streams and
rivers. The most dangerous
hazards are hurricanes, which
can strike the Gulf Coast from
June till December. Hurricane
winds reach speeds of 75 to
150 mph (121 to 241 km/hr) or
more, but even more dangerous than the high winds is the
storm surge, a dome of ocean
water that can cause severe
flooding along coastal rivers
and bays. Fortunately, sophisticated warning systems are in
place to give visitors plenty of
time to get out of harm's way.
Radio and TV stations broadcast storm watches and evacu-
ation warnings.

GETTING AROUND

P UBLIC TRANSPORTATION is
almost negligible in this
state, although a few
Greyhound routes cover
some major cities. A single
Amtrak route also shuttles
along the southern part of the
state. There is an excellent
network of airports across the
state, and many visitors fly
between the major cities, and
then rent a car to get around
the surrounding region.

Driving is essential in
Texas and the low price of
gas makes it a cheap and
convenient option. Seat belts
are required for drivers and
front seat passengers, as
well as back seat passengers
under 15 years of age. Child
seats are mandatory for all
occupants aged 2 and under.
Motorcyclists under 21 years
of age must wear helmets,
while riders over 21 years.
must have proof of health
insurance before they ride
without a helmet. Radar
detectors are permitted.

Speed limits for vehicles
vary in Texas, with a statewide maximum of 70 mph
(113 km/hour) allowed on
Interstate Highways during
daylight hours.

ANNUAL EVENTS & FESTIVALS

O NE OF THE BEST ways for
visitors to get a feel for
Texas is to take part in one
of the state's huge range of
annual events and festivals.
Soon after the New Year sets
in, the annual cleaning of
the Riverwalk Canal in San
Antonio launches the Mud
Week, a 10-day festival of arts
and entertainment. In March,
Austin hosts the youthful
South by Southwest festival
of popular music.

But the festival season
really gets going in summer,
starting at the end of May
with the nationally acclaimed
Kerrville Folk Festival.
Many other local festivals,
fairs and events take place in
towns all over the state,
winding up with the massive
Texas State Fair. This is one
of the largest state fairs in
the country, and is held in
October in Dallas' extensive
Fair Park. In addition to the
national holidays, Texas also
celebrates Confederate Heroes
Day (Jan 19), Emancipation
Day (June 19), and Lyndon
Johnson's Birthday (Aug 27).

THE CLIMATE OF TEXAS

Despite its generally mild climate, weather across the vast
state tends to vary greatly.
Spring is ideal for travel,
when the days are cool and
wildflowers are in full bloom.
Summer can be very hot and
humid, with severe rains
often causing floods along
rivers and in low-lying areas.
October is also good for travel, as temperatures are mild
and the skies clear. In winter,
snow storms blow down
from the Great Plains, and
hurricanes hit the Gulf Coast.

DALLAS

°F/C	Apr	Jul	Oct	Jan
high	75/24	95/35	79/26	57/14
low	55/13	75/24	56/13	36/2
	32°F / 0°C			
sun	21 days	25 days	23 days	21 days
rain	3.5 in	2.3 in	3.5 in	1.8 in
month	Apr	Jul	Oct	Jan

SPORTS

SPRINGTIME IN Texas is synonymous with baseball, which is played at a variety of levels all over the state. Major league baseball is represented here by the Houston Astros and the Texas Rangers, both of whom play in state-of-the-art stadiums, though the Astros no longer play in the Astrodome – once the world's largest indoor space. Tickets for major league baseball games, however, can be expensive and hard to come by. In any case, a better sense of the game and its importance to Texas can be experienced by attending a Texas League baseball game, which may not be as slick, but is often more fun. Played in smaller arenas in front of a close-knit crowd of enthusiastic fans, the main Texas League teams include the El Paso Diablos and the San Antonio Missions.

As summer fades into fall, the American football season begins. A number of intense intrastate rivalries, such as that between the University of Texas and Texas A&M University, enliven the college football season. At the professional National Football League (NFL) level, the pride of Texas is the Dallas Cowboys, self-proclaimed "America's Team." The New Year kicks off in Dallas with the Cotton Bowl, a championship football game played between two of the top universities in the country.

Winter is also basketball season, and games are played at all levels throughout the state. At the professional National Basketball Association level, Texas has the Houston Rockets, the Dallas Mavericks, and the San Antonio Spurs.

OUTDOOR ACTIVITIES

VISITORS CAN participate in a vast range of outdoor activities all over Texas. From golf to fishing, river rafting to cycling, Texas has something for everyone at all levels and abilities. There are golf courses all over the state, most of them open to the public. Fishing, in a variety of freshwater lakes and in the Gulf of Mexico, is regulated by the **Texas Parks Department**. River rafting along the Rio Grande through **Big Bend National Park** draws people from all over the world, so advance reservations are essential. Biking is also a popular activity, and bicycles can easily be rented from shops in most Texas towns.

ENTERTAINMENT

LOCATED IN Fort Worth's lively Stockyard District, **Billy Bob's**, the world's largest honky-tonk, is just one of hundreds of nightclubs and performance venues all over this music-loving state. More upscale and refined music can also be enjoyed, thanks to the many orchestras in Texas. Fort Worth has one of the finest music venues, the **Bass Performance Hall**, home to the city's symphony, opera, and ballet.

SHOPPING

VISITORS WANTING to bring home a souvenir of Texas should try cowboy boots. Western wear shops all over the state may have the perfect pair, but some visitors may wish to take advantage of the discounts offered close to the source at El Paso-based **Tony Lama's**, one of the country's largest and most famous boot makers. For more upscale needs, nothing beats **Neiman-Marcus**, one of the nation's most exclusive department stores, which started in Dallas and is still in business downtown. The sales tax in Texas is 6.25 percent, and cities and counties may impose an additional tax of 2 percent.

DIRECTORY

TOURIST INFORMATION

Travel Division
Dept. of Transportation,
PO Box 149248,
Austin, TX 78714.
((512) 486-5800.
Road Conditions
((800) 452-9292.

NATURAL HAZARDS

National Hurricane Center
((305) 229-4470.

GETTING AROUND

Amtrak
((800) 872-7245.

Greyhound
((800) 231-2222.

ANNUAL EVENTS & FESTIVALS

Kerrville Folk Festival
W www.kerrville-music.com

Texas State Fair
W www.bigtex.com

SPORTS

Dallas Cowboys
((972) 556-9900.

Dallas Mavericks
((214) 748-1808.

El Paso Diablos
((915) 755-2000.

Houston Astros
((713) 799-9555.

Houston Rockets
((713) 627-3865.

San Antonio Missions
((210) 675-7275.

San Antonio Spurs
((210) 554-7787.

Texas Rangers
((817) 273-5100.

OUTDOOR ACTIVITIES

Big Bend Nat'l Park
((915) 477-2251.

Texas Parks Dept.
((512) 389-4800.

ENTERTAINMENT

Bass Performance Hall
525 Commerce St,
Fort Worth.
((817) 212-4200.

Billy Bob's
Texas Rodeo Plaza,
Fort Worth.
((817) 624-7117.

SHOPPING

Neiman-Marcus
1618 Main St, Dallas.
((214) 741-6911.
W www.neimanmarcus.com

Tony Lama Boots
7156 E Gateway, El Paso.
((915) 772-4327.

Where to Stay

Travelers to Texas can choose from a wide variety of places to stay, from anonymous highway motels to atmospheric lodgings in historic buildings. Larger cities such as San Antonio and Dallas offer the best range of options. The Gulf Coast has many beach resorts, and there are also unique rural accommodations, many of which pay homage to the state's ranching traditions.

	CREDIT CARDS	NUMBER OF ROOMS	RECOMMENDED RESTAURANT	CHILDREN'S FACILITIES	GARDEN OR TERRACE
AMARILLO: *Big Texan Motel* $$	■	54	■		
AUSTIN: *Carrington's Bluff* $$	■	8		●	■
AUSTIN: *Driskill Hotel* $$$	■	188	■		■
BIG BEND NATIONAL PARK: *Chisos Mountains Lodge* $	■	72			■
DALLAS: *Adolphus Hotel* $$$$	■	433	■	●	
DALLAS: *The Mansion on Turtle Creek* $$$$$	■	141			■
EL PASO: *Camino Real Hotel* $$$	■	359	■	●	■
FORT DAVIS: *Historic Prude Ranch* $$	■	41	■	●	■
FORT DAVIS: *Indian Lodge* $$	■	39	■	●	■
FORT WORTH: *Stockyards Hotel* $$$	■	52		●	

AMARILLO: *Big Texan Motel* $$
7701 E I-40. ☎ *(806) 372-5000, (800) 657-7177.* FAX *(806) 371-0099.*
W www.bigtexan.com
Part of the famous "Big Texan" steak house restaurant complex, this standard highway motel, with all the modern amenities, is designed to look like a Wild West town. 🛏 🗲 TV P 🍷 ≋

AUSTIN: *Carrington's Bluff* $$
1900 David St. ☎ *(512) 479-0638.* FAX *(512) 478-2009.*
W www.carringtonsbluff.com
A charming B&B inn, Carrington's Bluff lies within walking distance of downtown and the university campus. 🛏 🗲 TV P 🔢

AUSTIN: *Driskill Hotel* $$$
604 Brazos St. ☎ *(512) 474-5911.* FAX *(512) 474-2214.* W www.driskillhotel.com
This distinctive, 1886 landmark features stylized heads of longhorn steers amid an opulent Neo-Classical decor. 🛏 🗲 TV P 🍷 🔢

BIG BEND NATIONAL PARK: *Chisos Mountains Lodge* $
☎ *(915) 477-2291.* W www.chisosmountainslodge.com
A large, modern motel with a few historic stone cottages and excellent views, this complex offers the only indoor accommodations in the park. Advance reservations are essential. 🛏 🗲 P

DALLAS: *Adolphus Hotel* $$$$
1321 Commerce St. ☎ *(214) 742-8200.* FAX *(214) 651-3561.*
W www.hoteladolphus.com
Built by beer baron Adolphus Busch in 1912, this opulent hotel has since become a Baroque-style showcase. 🛏 🗲 TV P 🔢 🍷 ♿ 🎬

DALLAS: *The Mansion on Turtle Creek* $$$$$
2821 Turtle Creek Blvd. ☎ *(214) 559-2100.* FAX: *(214) 528-4187.*
W www.mansiononturtlecreek.com
This Marriott-affiliated property has spacious and tastefully appointed rooms, furnished with all modern amenities.
🛏 🗲 TV P 🔢 🍷 ♿ ≋ 🎬

EL PASO: *Camino Real Hotel* $$$
101 S El Paso St. ☎ *(915) 534-3000.* FAX: *(915) 534-3024.*
W www.caminoreal.com
A downtown landmark, this grand hotel's elegant dining area features a huge Tiffany stained-glass dome. 🛏 🗲 TV P 🔢 🍷 ≋ 🎵

FORT DAVIS: *Historic Prude Ranch* $$
Hwy-118. ☎ *(915) 426-3202, (800) 458-6232.* FAX *(915) 426-4401.*
W www.prude-ranch.com
The most popular "dude ranch" in Texas, this hotel offers a wide range of activities to its guests including horseback riding, bird-watching, swimming, and taking part in ranching activities. 🛏 🗲 P 🔢 ≋

FORT DAVIS: *Indian Lodge* $$
P O Box 1707, Fort Davis 79734. ☎ *(915) 426-3254.*
W www.tpwd.state.tx.us/park/indian
Backed by the rugged foothills of Davis Mountain State Park, this historic 1930s lodge has an evocative ambience. Advance reservations are essential. 🛏 🗲 TV P 🔢 ≋ ♿

FORT WORTH: *Stockyards Hotel* $$$
109 E Exchange Av. ☎ *(817) 625-6427.* FAX *(817) 624-2571.*
W www.stockyardshotel.com
This stylish hotel in the heart of the lively Stockyards District is a historic landmark. Room 305, where bank robbers Bonnie and Clyde stayed in 1933, is now the "Bonnie and Clyde Suite." 🛏 TV P 🍷

	Price categories	for a standard double room per night, inclusive of breakfast, service charges, and any additional taxes:		

Price categories for a standard double room per night, inclusive of breakfast, service charges, and any additional taxes:

Ⓢ under $100
ⓈⓈ $100–$150
ⓈⓈⓈ $150–$200
ⓈⓈⓈⓈ $200–$250
ⓈⓈⓈⓈⓈ over $250

CREDIT CARDS
Major credit cards accepted.

NUMBER OF ROOMS
Number of rooms in the hotel.

RECOMMENDED RESTAURANT
Good restaurant within the hotel.

CHILDREN'S FACILITIES
Hotel has various facilities for young children.

GARDEN OR TERRACE
Hotel has a garden, courtyard, or terrace.

		CREDIT CARDS	NUMBER OF ROOMS	RECOMMENDED RESTAURANT	CHILDREN'S FACILITIES	GARDEN OR TERRACE
FORT WORTH: *Etta's Place* ⓈⓈⓈ 200 W 3rd St. 【 (817) 255-5760. FAX (817) 878-2560. W www.ettas-place.com This comfortable and atmospheric B&B inn has a large library, a music room, and a rooftop terrace. 🔲 🔲 TV 🔲		▦	9			▦
FREDERICKSBURG: *Creekside Inn* ⓈⓈ 304 S Washington St. 【 (830) 997-6316. FAX (830) 997-9864. This small B&B inn lies just south of Main Street in the heart of the historic Hill Country town. 🔲 🔲 TV P		▦	7			▦
GALVESTON: *Tremont House* ⓈⓈⓈ 12300 Mechanic St. 【 (409) 763-0300. FAX (409) 763-0300. W www.galveston.com/thetremonthouse A modern hotel in a Victorian-era building, Tremont House's rooftop terrace overlooks the Gulf Coast and Galveston harbor. 🔲 🔲 TV P 🔲 Y 🔲 🔲		▦	117	▦	●	
HARLINGEN: *La Quinta Inn* Ⓢ 1002 S Expressway 83. 【 (956) 428-6888. FAX (956) 425-5840. W www.laquinta.com A comfortable motel with great service, La Quinta is conveniently located in the heart of the Rio Grande Valley. 🔲 🔲 TV P 🔲 🔲 🔲		▦	130			
HOUSTON: *Lovett Inn* ⓈⓈ 501 Lovett Blvd. 【 (713) 522-5224. FAX (713) 528-6708. W www.lovettinn.com Located on a tree-lined street near Montrose District, this friendly inn is known for its genteel Southern hospitality. 🔲 🔲 TV P 🔲 🔲		▦	13		●	
HOUSTON: *Warwick Hotel* ⓈⓈⓈ 5701 Main St. 【 (713) 526-1991. FAX (713) 526-0359. W www.warwickhotelhouston.com Within walking distance of the Museum of Fine Arts, this well-restored 1920s hotel feels like a luxury resort. 🔲 🔲 TV P 🔲 Y 🔲 🔲 🔲		▦	308			
LAREDO: *La Posada Hotel* ⓈⓈⓈ 1000 Zaragoza St. 【 (956) 722-1701, (800) 444-2099. FAX (956) 722-4758. W www.laposadahotel-laredo.com Built in 1916, this adobe-style building with all modern conveniences offers a very pleasant overnight stay. 🔲 🔲 TV P 🔲 Y 🔲 🔲 🔲		▦	208			
LUBBOCK: *La Quinta Inn* Ⓢ 601 Avenue Q. 【 (806) 763-9441. FAX: (806) 747-9325. W www.laquinta.com Located along the musical "Walk of Fame," across from the statue of Buddy Holly, this inn is a convenient base for enjoying the city. 🔲 🔲 TV P 🔲 🔲 🔲		▦	137		●	
MARATHON: *Gage Hotel* ⓈⓈⓈ 102 W US-90. 【 (915) 386-4205, (800) 884-4243. FAX (915) 386-4510. W www.gagehotel.com Each room in this low-key but distinctive 1920s hotel has period furniture and many accoutrements of cowboy life. 🔲 P 🔲 Y 🔲 🔲 🔲		▦	43			
SAN ANTONIO: *Hampton Inn Riverwalk* ⓈⓈ 414 Bowie St. 【 (210) 225-8500. FAX (210) 225-8526. W www.hamptoninn.com Located in downtown San Antonio, this family-friendly lodge has large rooms and a free breakfast buffet. 🔲 🔲 TV P 🔲 🔲 🔲		▦	169		●	
SAN ANTONIO: *Menger Hotel* ⓈⓈⓈⓈ 204 Alamo Plaza. 【 (210) 223-4361. FAX (210) 228-0022. W www.historicmenger.com Built in an unbeatable location, this 1859 hotel offers four-star facilities with a deep sense of Texas heritage. 🔲 🔲 TV P 🔲 Y 🔲 🔲		▦	315	▦	●	▦

For key to symbols see back flap

Where to Eat

THE BEST PLACES TO EAT in Texas are those that offer variations within the state's traditional cuisines. "Tex-Mex" is the predominant food style, mixing Mexican dishes with large quantites of Texas beef. Beef also features prominently in the steakhouses and barbecue restaurants. Opening times of restaurants are indicated by a "B" for breakfast, "L" for lunch, and "D" for dinner.

	Credit Cards	Outdoor Tables	Vegetarian	Good Wine List	Children's Facilities
ABILENE: *Perini Ranch* $$ Hwy-89 in Buffalo Gap. (915) 572-3339. One of many contenders for "Best Steakhouse in Texas," Perini's draws customers with juicy steaks. *L, D.* ● *Mon, Tue.*	■	●	■	●	■
AMARILLO: *Golden Light Café* $ 2908 W 6th St. (806) 374-9237. For some of the best burgers, crispiest fries, coldest beers, and coolest live music along historic Route 66, stop at this place – in business since 1946. *L, D.*	■	●	■		■
AMARILLO: *Big Texan Steak Ranch* $ 7701 E I-40. (806) 372-6000. The Big Texan offers a unique test of appetites – if you can eat an entire 72-oz steak, plus accompaniments, within an hour, the meal is free. (If you don't eat enough to finish, and nine out of ten people don't, the price is around $60). *L, D.*	■				■
AUSTIN: *Hoover's Cooking* $ 2002 E Manor Rd. (512) 479-5006. Described as "Texas Comfort Food," the offerings in this boisterous east Austin barn range from okra and black-eyed peas to smoky ribs, chicken, and sausage links. The place also serves great desserts. *L, D.*	■		■		■
AUSTIN: *Threadgill's* $ 6416 N Lamar Blvd. (512) 451-5440. All-American diner food with a Texas twist is served in a reincarnation of one of Austin's landmark nightclubs – a former gas station. The huge collection of neon signs alone is well worth a visit. *L, D.*	■		■		■
CORPUS CHRISTI: *City Diner* $$ 622 N Water St. (361) 883-1609. This friendly, retro-1950s diner offers fresh Gulf Coast seafood and a delectable array of seasonal shellfish. *B, L, D.*	■				
CORPUS CHRISTI: *Republic of Texas Steakhouse* $$$ 900 N Shoreline. (361) 887-1600. With a staggering view of the Gulf Coast, thanks to its position atop the 20-story Omni Hotel, this wonderfully cozy restaurant serves Texas-style steak, chicken, and seafood. *D.* ● *Sun.*	■			●	
DALLAS: *Gennie's Bishop Grill* $ 321 N Bishop Ave. (214) 946-1752. Line up in this 1970s cafeteria to load your plate with an array of fresh vegetables, cornbread muffins, and delicious garlic chicken. But save room for dessert, as the pies are fantastic. *L, D.*	■		■		
DALLAS: *Deep Ellum Café* $$ 2706 Elm St. (214) 741-9012. Popular and stylish, this "New American" bistro in the heart of the artsy Deep Ellum district serves up a variety of freshly prepared Mexican and Southern-style comfort food. *L, D.*	■	●	■	●	■
DALLAS: *Zodiac Restaurant* $$ 1618 Main St. (214) 573-5800. Take a break from shopping and enjoy a soup, sandwich, or salad at this delectable café, located on the sixth floor of the legendary Neiman-Marcus department store. ● *Sun.*	■		■	●	■
DALLAS: *Mansion on Turtle Creek Restaurant* $$$$ 2821 Turtle Creek Blvd. (214) 559-2100. This top-rated, elegant restaurant specializes in gourmet versions of traditional Texas and Southwestern food. (optional)	■			●	

Price categories include a three-course meal for one, a glass of house wine, and all unavoidable extra charges such as sales tax and service.
$ under $25
$$ $25–35
$$$ $35–50
$$$$ $50–70
$$$$$ over $70

CREDIT CARDS
Major credit cards accepted.
OUTDOOR TABLES
Garden, courtyard, or terrace with outside tables.
VEGETARIAN
A good selection of vegetarian dishes available.
GOOD WINE LIST
Extensive list of good wines, both domestic and imported.
CHILDREN'S FACILITIES
Various facilities for young children.

	Price	Credit Cards	Outdoor Tables	Vegetarian	Good Wine List	Children's Facilities
EL PASO: *H&H Coffee Shop* 701 E Yandell Ave. (915) 533-1144. Although basic, the fare here has drawn admiration from such culinary lights as the *Gourmet* magazine and Julia Child. B, L. ● Sun.	$			■		■
EL PASO: *Forti's Mexican Elder* 321 Chelsea St. (915) 772-0066. One of the oldest and largest "Tex-Mex" restaurants, this hacienda-style place serves fine food enlivened by the strolling bands of mariachi musicians. L, D. ● Thanksgiving, Dec 25.	$$	■	●	■		■
FORT WORTH: *Joe T. Garcia's* 2201 N Commerce St. (817) 626-4356. This large Mexican restaurant offers all the usual favorites – tacos, enchiladas, and fajitas. L, D.	$			■		■
FORT WORTH: *Cattleman's Steak House* 2458 N Main St. (817) 624-3945. With walls covered in life-size portraits of beloved bovine breeds, and a selection of sirloin, rib eye, strip, and filet steaks ready to be grilled over a charcoal fire, there's no doubt that beef is the draw here. L, D.	$$$	■		■		
FREDERICKSBURG: *Altdorf Biergarten* 301 W Main St. (830) 997-7865. For a taste of the German heritage that animates this Hill Country town, it is hard to beat this massive *biergarten*, with its sausages, schnitzels, and sauerkraut. L, D.	$$	■	●	■		
GALVESTON: *Gaido's* 3700 Seawall Blvd. (409) 762-9625. Located right on the Gulf of Mexico, this family-run landmark has been serving fresh-caught fish and shrimp for generations. L, D.	$$$	■	●	■		
HOUSTON: *Boulevard Bistrot* 4319 Montrose Blvd. (713) 524-6922. Located in the trendy Montrose District, this stylish bistro serves a variety of meat, fish, and chicken dishes. L, D, Sun Brunch.	$$	■		■	●	
HOUSTON: *Americas* 1800 Post Oak Blvd. (713) 961-1492. One of the city's most popular restaurants, Americas looks like a rain-forest and specializes in Carribean cuisine. Try the Gulf Coast snapper paired with a fresh corn on the cob. L, D. ● Sun.	$$$	■		■	●	
LUBBOCK: *Stella's* 4646 50th St. (806) 755-9299. Boar's head cold cuts and corned beef are favorites at Stella's deli counter, while Italian and American dishes are served in the main room.	$$	■	●	■		■
MARATHON: *Café Cenizo* 101 W US-90. (915) 386-4437. This atmospheric place in the middle of the lonesome West Texas cattle country offers eclectic versions of Texas fare.	$$$	■		■		
SAN ANTONIO: *Mi Tierra Café* 218 Produce Row. (210) 225-1262. Well-prepared "Tex-Mex" food is served at this café 24-hours a day. Strolling "travatore" musicians add to the experience.	$	■		■		
SAN ANTONIO: *Boudro's* 1421 E Commerce St. (210) 224-8484. This waterfront restaurant mixes Texas beef with Mexican and Louisiana Cajun specialties. L, D.	$$$	■	●	■	●	■

For key to symbols see back flap

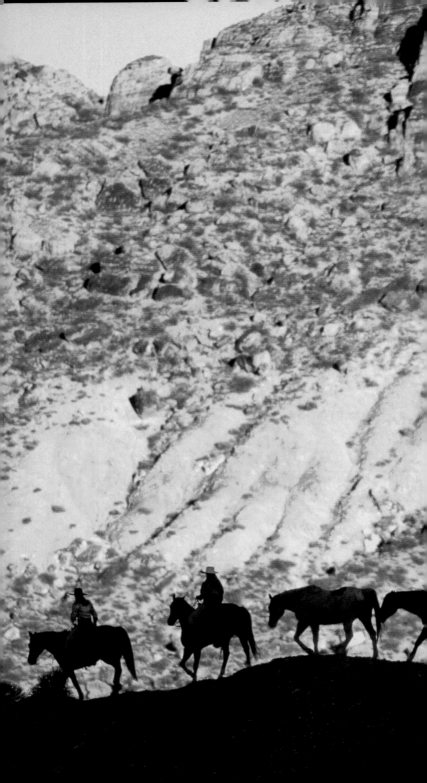

THE SOUTHWEST

The Southwest at a Glance

A MERICA'S SOUTHWEST IS MADE UP of the states of Nevada, Utah, Arizona, and New Mexico. It also includes the Four Corners area, the only place in the US where four states – parts of Utah, Arizona, New Mexico, and Colorado – meet at a central point. The region boasts spectacular landscapes, dominated by desert, deep canyons, and high mesas. Equally fascinating is its multicultural heritage, influenced by Native American, Hispanic, and Anglo-American settlers. Today, this region offers visitors a range of sights, most of which are concentrated in the cities of Phoenix, Tucson, Albuquerque, and Las Vegas.

Hopi-made coiled basket made of willow or yucca leaves

Las Vegas (see pp510–15) *in Nevada draws more than 37 million visitors each year. Its unique attractions are its fantastic, palace-like hotels and casinos with their promise of million-dollar jackpots.*

NEVADA
(See pp510–17)

Winnemucca

Elko

Austin

Carson City

Hawthorne

Tonopah

Las Vegas

Kingman

Blythe

Yuma

Brigham City

Log

Salt Lake C

UTAH
(See pp518–27)

Nep

Delta

Capitol
Nationa

Grand Cany

Flag

ARIZONA
(See pp528–43)

Wickenburg

Phoer

Tucs

N

*The **Grand Canyon** (see pp536–9) in Arizona is the second most-visited national park in the country. This is, however, one of the many natural wonders in a state well-known for its stunning landscapes of pristine deserts, forested hills, and fertile meadows.*

0 km   100

0 miles   100

◁ **Horseback riders negotiating a steep trail along a canyon, southern Utah**

Cacti and dried chilies adorning a flower shop, Tucson

LOCATOR MAP

Arches National Park (see pp520-21) *is just one of the many geological wonders in Utah, a state with the highest concentration of national parks in the United States. The dramatic and unpromising landscape of Utah also became the spiritual and worldly base of the Mormons. Salt Lake City, the state capital, is located northwest of the park.*

nlands
al Park

Shiprock

nent

Raton

Taos

Clayton

ow

Santa Fe

Grants

Tucumcari

Albuquerque

NEW MEXICO

Vaughn

Clovis

(See pp544–53)

Johns

Socorro

Roswell

Silver City

Tularosa

Hobbs

Deming

El Paso

glas

New Mexico (see pp544–53) *is one of the Southwest's most popular destinations. Its scenic beauty and rich cultural heritage have lured generations of artists, who have made Santa Fe and Taos vibrant creative centers. Albuquerque, the largest city, has many fine museums.*

THE SOUTHWEST

DISTINGUISHED BY ITS DRAMATIC LANDSCAPE, *the Southwest is a land of twisting canyons, cactus-studded deserts, and rugged mountains. For more than 15,000 years, the region was inhabited by Native Americans, but by the 20th century Anglo-American traditions had mingled with those of the Hispanic and Native peoples to create the region's multicultural heritage.*

The states of Nevada, Utah, Arizona, and New Mexico make up America's Southwest. Perceptions of this region are influenced by the landscape – the red sandstone mesas of Monument Valley, the tall saguaro cacti of Arizona's Sonoran Desert, the staggering scale of the Grand Canyon, and New Mexico's adobe architecture. At its heart is its defining geological feature – the Colorado Plateau – a rock tableland rising more than 12,000 ft (3,660 m) above sea level and covering a vast area of around 130,000 sq miles (336,700 sq km). The plateau was created by the same geological upheavals that formed the Rocky Mountains. Subsequent erosion by wind, water, and sand molded both hard and soft rock to form the mesas, canyons, and mountains. Many of these natural wonders have been preserved as national parks.

The region's main city, Las Vegas, has been synonymous with glamor and entertainment ever since Nevada legalized gambling in 1931. Mobster Bugsy Siegel opened the first luxury hotel, the Flamingo, in 1946, and soon there was a proliferation of casinos. Some of the biggest names in show business, such as Frank Sinatra and Elvis Presley, as well as eccentric millionaire Howard Hughes, have all contributed to Vegas's image as the fun city of limos, showgirls, and glitzy lifestyles. This city of megaresorts and casinos is as popular for its wedding chapels, where more than 100,000 couples get married each year.

HISTORY

The first Native American people were a society of hunters who inhabited the region between 10,000 and 8,000 BC. The introduction of new farming techniques and crops, especially corn from Mexico, saw the start of settled farming communities in around 800 BC. By AD 500 an agrarian society

The desert floor dotted with sagebrush and ponderosa pines, Monument Valley, Arizona

◁ **Sparkling neon stars of the Riviera Hotel in Las Vegas, Nevada** was well established, and large villages or pueblos began to develop. By 700 the three main cultures in the region were the Hohokam, the Mogollon, and the Ancestral Puebloan. Ancestral Puebloan people constructed elaborate dwellings that grew into large cities such as Chaco Canyon. However, in the 12th and 13th centuries, these settlements were mysteriously abandoned. It is thought that the people migrated to the Pueblo Indian settlements along the Rio Grande Valley and northwest New Mexico, where their descendants still live. The 15th century saw the arrival of the Navajo, who were hunters, and the fierce Apache warriors from Canada.

Ancient pottery bowl

In the 1500s, the Spanish quest for wealth, particularly gold, led to the establishment of a permanent colony called New Mexico, which included all of the present-day states of New Mexico and Arizona, as well as parts of Colorado, Utah, Nevada, and California. Mexican independence from Spain was declared in 1821, paving the way for Anglo-American traders. The first

Anglos (non-Spanish people of European descent) in the Southwest were "mountain men" or fur trappers, who helped open up the trade routes to the west. With the establishment of the Old Spanish and the Santa Fe Trails, this remote region became more accessible.

The US government's vigorous expansion led to conflict with Mexico, and the region became a part of the United States in 1848. Soon, the settlers began to forcibly acquire Native land, and more than 8,000 Navajo were made to march "The Long Walk" to a reservation in New Mexico in 1864. Resentment against the Anglos instigated the Indian Wars, which finally ended with the surrender of Apache leader Geronimo in 1886.

At the same time, rich lodes of gold, silver, and copper were discovered in Arizona, and mining camps such as Bisbee and Tombstone became boomtowns. This was the Wild West of mining prospectors, ranch cowboys, and notorious outlaws, such as Billy the Kid, whose exploits form part of American folklore

KEY DATES IN HISTORY

800 BC Corn brought from Mexico

AD 800 Chaco Canyon under construction

1400 Migrations of the Navajo and Apache

1540–42 Francisco Vasquez de Coronado leads the search for gold in New Mexico

1610 Santa Fe established as capital of New Mexico

1680 The Pueblo revolt against the Spanish

1821 Santa Fe Trail opened

1848 Treaty of Guadalupe-Hidalgo cedes Mexican territory to the US

1868 Navajo reservation founded in Four Corners region

1869 The coming of the railroad

1912 New Mexico and Arizona become 47th and 48th states of the United States

1931–36 Hoover Dam constructed in Arizona

1945 First atomic bomb tested in New Mexico

1974 Central Arizona Project begins to extract water from the Colorado River

1996 President Clinton signs Navajo-Hopi Land Dispute Settlement Act

2000 Forest fires devastate large parts of northern New Mexico and Arizona

SOCIETY & CULTURE

The Southwest is a crossroads of the three great cultures that shaped America – Native American, Hispanic, and Anglo-American. The Spanish language is prominent, not only in bilingual New Mexico but also in Arizona. A host of Native American languages are also spoken, reflecting the far longer history of the region's Native inhabitants. The Hopi and other Pueblo peoples trace their ancestry back to the Ancestral Puebloan peoples, while the Navajo occupy the country's largest reservation, stretching across the northern ends of both Arizona and New Mexico. The Apache and many other tribes have land here as well. Today, Native populations have a hand in governing their own lands, and many have diversified their business interests to regenerate their economy and are involved in tourism, running casinos, and the production of such crafts as pottery and rugs.

A colorful Navajo rug

A trinity of religious activity is dominant in the Southwest. The most visible is Roman Catholicism, which was introduced in the 16th century by the Spanish colonists. It is today the main religion, although several Protestant denominations exist as well. Utah's residents, however, are predominantly Mormon. Native American spiritual beliefs are complex, as each tribe has its own practices.

One of the region's most famous attributes is the quality of light found in the hills of northern New Mexico. Georgia O'Keeffe's paintings of the local landscape in the 1940s helped to make the area around Santa Fe a mecca for artists. Today, the city has the country's second largest art trade. The smaller resort town of Taos is also famous for its resident painters and sculptors. Santa Fe, as well as Phoenix, Tucson, and Albuquerque also offer opera, ballet, classical music, and major theatrical productions. The Pheonix Symphony and New Mexico Symphony Orchestra, based in Albuquerque, are best known for their concerts, while jazz and country music can be heard in almost every city and major town.

FLAGSTAFF ROUTE 66

Route 66 Flagstaff sign

ECONOMICS & TOURISM

Today, New Mexico and Arizona are the country's fifth and sixth largest states. Despite the fact that the region's population is increasing, it remains one of the least populated in the United States. The cities of Phoenix, Tucson, Santa Fe, and Albuquerque account for around 60 percent of the region's population. Such intense urbanization has put tremendous pressure on the region's resources, particularly water, which has become one of the Southwest's most pressing issues.

The legacy of the two World Wars changed the Southwest's economic course. In the 1940s, New Mexico's sparsely populated and remote desert area of Los Alamos was chosen as the location for the top secret Manhattan Project, which developed the world's first atomic bomb. Since then, the region has been a major center for national defense research and development of nuclear weapon technology, as well as for research into space travel, with both state and federal governments as major employers. Today, other research projects, including biotechnology, especially the Genome Project (which maps all human genes) and computer technology, attract scientists to the Southwest.

Tourism is another of the region's principal employers. Vast wilderness areas and a warm climate make outdoor leisure popular in the Southwest. Its national parks, established in the early 1900s, draw ever-increasing numbers of tourists each year as well. There are also miles of hiking trails, rivers for whitewater rafting, lakes for water sports, ski resorts, and some of the nation's finest golf courses. One of the best ways to experience the landscape is on a trail ride, while armchair cowboys can attend that great Southwestern event – the rodeo.

The Southwest is as much a state of mind as it is a geographical region. The attractions of the landscape and a romantic sense of the past combine to conjure up the idealized legends of the "Wild West." For many visitors, the Southwest offers the chance to indulge that bit of cowboy in their souls.

Horseback riding, a popular pastime in the Sonoran Desert near Tucson, Arizona

Exploring the Southwest

THE FOUR STATES OF THE Southwest encompass many natural wonders, such as the Grand Canyon and Monument Valley in Arizona, and Zion National Park in Utah. Beyond the scenic are the pueblo villages along the Rio Grande in New Mexico and the glitter of Las Vegas, Nevada's fastest growing city. Above all, the region conjures up images of the Wild West, as portrayed by Hollywood and preserved by the myths around old mining towns, such as Bisbee and Tombstone.

Chili wreath, Santa Fe

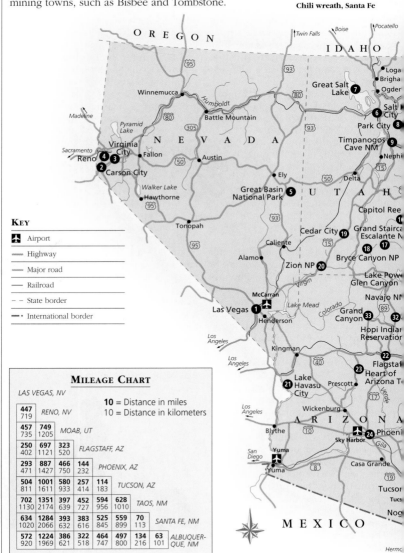

KEY

✈ Airport

— Highway

— Major road

— Railroad

– – State border

—·— International border

MILEAGE CHART

10 = Distance in miles
10 = Distance in kilometers

LAS VEGAS, NV								
447 719	RENO, NV							
457 735	**749** 1205	MOAB, UT						
250 402	**697** 1121	**323** 520	FLAGSTAFF, AZ					
293 471	**887** 1427	**466** 750	**144** 232	PHOENIX, AZ				
504 811	**1001** 1611	**580** 933	**257** 414	**114** 183	TUCSON, AZ			
702 1130	**1351** 2174	**397** 639	**452** 727	**594** 956	**628** 1010	TAOS, NM		
634 1020	**1284** 2066	**393** 632	**383** 616	**525** 845	**559** 899	**70** 113	SANTA FE, NM	
572 920	**1224** 1969	**386** 621	**322** 518	**464** 747	**497** 800	**134** 216	**63** 101	ALBUQUER-QUE, NM

SIGHTS AT A GLANCE

Nevada
Las Vegas pp510–15 ❶
Carson City ❷
Virginia City ❸
Reno ❹
Great Basin National Park ❺

Utah
Salt Lake City ❻
Great Salt Lake ❼
Park City ❽
Timpanogos Cave National Monument ❾
Arches National Park pp520–21 ❿
Moab ⓫
Canyonlands National Park p522 ⓬
Green River ⓭
Hovenweep National Monument ⓮
Lake Powell & Glen Canyon
   National Recreation Area ⓯
Capitol Reef National Park ⓰
Grand Staircase–Escalante
   National Monument ⓱
Bryce Canyon National Park pp526–7 ⓲
Cedar City ⓳
Zion National Park p525 ⓴

Arizona
Lake Havasu City ㉑
Flagstaff ㉒
Heart of Arizona Tour p529 ㉓
Phoenix pp530–31 ㉔
Tucson ㉕
Nogales ㉖
Bisbee ㉗
Amerind Foundation ㉘
Petrified Forest National Park ㉙
Window Rock ㉚
Hopi Indian Reservation ㉛
Tuba City ㉜
Grand Canyon pp536–9 ㉝
Navajo National Monument ㉞
Monument Valley pp540–41 ㉟
*Canyon de Chelly National
   Monument pp542–3* ㊱

New Mexico
Chaco Culture National Historical Park ㊲
Taos ㊳
Northern Pueblos Tour p545 ㊴
Santa Fe pp546–7 ㊵
Albuquerque pp548–50 ㊶
Roswell ㊷
Carlsbad Caverns National Park ㊸
White Sands National Monument ㊹
Gila Cliff Dwellings National Monument ㊺

SEE ALSO

- *Practical Information* pp554–5
- *Where to Stay* pp556–9
- *Where to Eat* pp560–63

Mummy Cave Overlook in Canyon de Chelly, Arizona

Las Vegas ❶

THE HEART OF LAS VEGAS, Nevada's most famous city, lies along Las Vegas Boulevard, a sparkling vista of neon known simply as "the Strip." The southern stretch of this 3.5-mile (6-km) long street that runs northeast through the city is home to a cluster of lavishly themed hotels, with their own shops, restaurants, and gaming casinos. They lure almost 37 million visitors every year, making Vegas the entertainment capital of the world. When the lights come on in the evening, these new megaresorts become a fantasyland with riotous design and architecture, such as that of the Luxor's striking pyramid with its sphinx. The exotically themed Aladdin Hotel is evidence of the city's ability to reinvent itself quickly – it took only two years to build.

A dazzling nighttime view of the Strip

New York New York
A replica of the Statue of Liberty forms part of the façade of this hotel, which is composed of a host of such Manhattan landmarks as the Empire State Building.

Luxor
The hotel's Egyptian features include a reproduction of Tutankhamun's tomb in the King Tut Museum.

The Boardwalk Casino
is a Holiday Inn hotel and features a roller coaster facing the Strip.

Mandalay Bay's
interior, with its palm trees and bamboo, re-creates a 19th-century tropical paradise.

Excalibur's towers are a kitsch fantasy of medieval England.

TROPICANA AVE

LAS VEGAS BLVD

Showcase Mall is a striking building, with its giant neon Coca-Cola bottle. A huge games arcade makes the mall very popular with families.

Tropicana
This casino was rebuilt in the late 1970s with a stunning Art Nouveau-style stained-glass ceiling and glass lamps.

MGM Grand Hotel
The largest hotel in the US with more than 5,000 rooms, the Grand displays a 45-ft (15-m) high statue of Leo, symbol of the Hollywood film studio, MGM.

Caesars Palace

Reproduction Roman statuary adorns the grounds of Caesars Palace. One of the Strip's oldest and most glamorous hotels, Caesars was built in 1966. Inside, the lavish Forum Shops mall features moving statues.

Imperial Palace
A pagoda fronts this Asian-themed hotel, famous for its classic car collection, which is open to all visitors.

Bellagio

Built in 1998, this luxury resort's elegant lobby is hung with sculpted glass flowers, designed by glass artist Dale Chihuly (see p628).

Paris, with its half-scale replica of the Eiffel Tower, is a $760-million resort modeled on the French capital.

W DUNES RD

THE STRIP

FLAMINGO ROAD

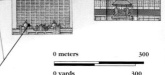

| 0 meters | 300 |
| 0 yards | 300 |

Aladdin Hotel
Opened in 1963, Aladdin's reputation as one of the glitziest Strip hotels was sealed when Elvis Presley married Priscilla here in 1967. The old building was imploded in 1998, and a new Arabian Nights-themed resort opened in 2000.

Flamingo Hilton
The flaming pink and orange neon flower of the Flamingo hotel's façade is a famous Strip icon. New York City Gangster Bugsy Seigel created the hotel and casino in 1946. He was killed, just a year later, by fellow investors.

Las Vegas (The Strip Continued)

THE LEGALIZATION OF GAMBLING in Nevada paved the way for Las Vegas' casino-based growth. The first casino resort, the El Rancho Vegas Hotel-Casino, opened in 1941 and was located on the northern section of the Strip. A building boom followed in the 1950s, resulting in a plethora of resorts. The Sands, Desert Inn, Sahara, and Stardust hotels began the process that transformed the Strip into a high-rise adult theme park. Although many of these north Strip resorts remain, they are now unrecognizable, thanks to million-dollar rebuilding programs.

Roulette is very popular in Vegas – gambling was legalized in Nevada in 1931

Treasure Island
Treasure Island's skull and crossbones sign lures passers-by to the battling pirate ship show, held each evening on the hotel's Strip-side lagoon.

The Fashion Show Mall is currently the largest shopping destination in Vegas, with more than 200 stores, an entertainment complex, and a food court serving both fast and fresh food.

The Mirage is both stylish and tacky – its beautiful, Strip-facing gardens feature an "erupting" volcano.

SPRING MOUNTAIN RD

LAS VEGAS BLVD

SANDS AVE

0 meters 300

0 yards 300

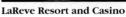

LaReve Resort and Casino
This new hotel and golf course, formerly the Desert Inn, is currently being rebuilt and is scheduled to open in April 2005.

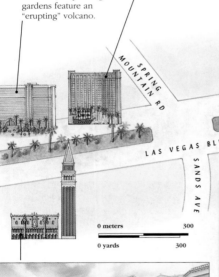

Venetian
One of the world's most luxurious hotels, this has mock canals flowing through its shopping area. Madame Tussaud's Wax Museum is located inside the hotel.

Stardust

This famous sign, with its twinkling neon colors, is a noted Strip landmark. Originally made in 1968, today's hotel sign was altered in 1991.

Stratosphere Tower

An observation deck at the top of this 1,149-ft (350-m) tower offers fine views of the city and the ring of mountains that rise from the desert.

Circus Circus

Lucky the Clown beckons visitors to this resort, which offers circus acts and traditional carnival games on the mezzanine floor above the casino.

La Concha Motel

is a rare remnant of stylish old Vegas. It was built in 1961.

The Candlelight Wedding Chapel

is located next to the Algiers Hotel. It is possible to get married here at any time of the day or night.

Neon lights at the Riviera Hotel

LAS VEGAS NEON

The twinkling, flashing neon sign remains the dominant icon of Las Vegas, even though several of the new themed megaresorts here have opted for a more understated look. Neon is a gas discovered by British chemist Sir William Ramsey in 1898. But it was a French inventor, Georges Claude, who, in 1910, discovered that an electric current passed through a glass tube of neon emitted a powerful, shimmering light. In the 1940s and 50s the craft of neon sign-making was elevated to the status of an art form in Las Vegas.

Algiers Hotel

Built in 1953, this is the oldest intact hotel left on the Strip. Despite extensive redecoration, it retains the low-rise motel style of Vegas's original resorts, with its pink and blue exterior and elegant neon.

Exploring Las Vegas

Rising like a mirage out of Nevada's beautiful southern desert, Las Vegas is a fascinating wonderland that promises fun to all its visitors. Beyond the allure of the Strip are the glittering malls and museums in the downtown area. For those who can tear themselves away from the city, the surrounding canyons, mountains, deserts, and parks offer a wealth of natural beauty and outdoor pleasures. Apart from tourism and gaming, Las Vegas is also famous for wedding chapels that offer a wide range of customized ceremonies.

⛫ Liberace Museum

1775 E Tropicana Ave. 📞 *(702) 798-5595.* ⏰ *10am–5pm Mon–Sat; 1–5pm Sun.* 🅿 ♿
🌐 *www.liberace.org*

This museum, founded in 1979, celebrates the life and work of one of Las Vegas's best-loved performers, Liberace (1919–87). It displays 18 of his 39 pianos, his lavish costumes, trademark capes, and stage jewelry. The costumes worn at his final 1986 performance took six seamstresses, wearing protective sunglasses against the glare of the stones, several months to make. The customized cars include a rare Rolls Royce covered with mirror tiles, in which the flamboyant artist would arrive at his show. Collections of objects from around the world include a piano-shaped ring, set with 260 diamonds.

🎰 Fremont Street Experience

Light Shows ⏰ *6pm–midnight daily.* ♿ 🌐 *www.vegasexperience.com*
Binion's Horseshoe 128 E Fremont St. 📞 *(702) 382-1600.* ⏰ *24 hours.* ♿ 🌐 *www.binions.com*
Four Queens 202 E Fremont St. 📞 *(702) 385-4011.* ⏰ *24 hours.* ♿ 🌐 *www.fourqueens.com*

Known as "Glitter Gulch," Fremont Street was where the first casinos with neon signs and illuminated icons were located. However, during the 1980s and 1990s as the Strip became more glamorous, this street went into decline. To reverse the process, an ambitious $70-million project was initiated by the city in 1994 to revitalize the area.

The street is now a colorful, bustling pedestrian mall, covered by a vast steel canopy, from which seven spectacular sound-and-light shows are projected every night. Alongside the shows, many of the neon façades belonging to some of the city's oldest and best-loved casinos remain.

Established by Dallas bootlegger and gambler Benny Binion, the landmark **Binion's Horseshoe** retains an old-style Vegas atmosphere. Although it hosts the annual World Series of Poker competition, it continues to attract many locals with its popular, low-stakes games.

Another historic casino along the Street is **Four Queens**. Named for the owner's four daughters, the casino has chandeliers and gilt mirrors, reminscent of 19th-century New Orleans. Four Queens also claims to have the largest slot machine in the world.

⛫ Lied Discovery Children's Museum

833 Las Vegas Blvd. 📞 *(702) 382-3445.* ⏰ *10am–5pm Tue–Sun.* 🌑 *Mon (except school hols), Jan 1, Thanksgiving, Dec 25.* 🅿 ♿ 🌐 *www.ldcm.org*

A conical, concrete teepee forms part of this striking museum devoted to interactive exhibits. Children can stand inside a gigantic bubble, freeze their shadows on a wall, or even work in the in-house television studio.

⛫ The Las Vegas Natural History Museum

900 Las Vegas Blvd. 📞 *(702) 384-3466.* ⏰ *9am–4pm daily.* 🌑 *Jan 1, Thanksgiving, Dec 25.* 🅿 ♿ 🌐 *www.lvnhm.org*

A popular choice with families who need a break from the Strip resorts, this museum has an appealing range of exhibits. Dioramas re-create the African savanna, complete with leopards, cheetahs, and antelopes. The marine exhibit offers a chance to view live sharks and eels at close quarters. Animatronic dinosaurs and the hands-on discovery room, where visitors can dig fossils and operate a robotic baby dinosaur, are popular with children.

Façade of Binion's Horseshoe

🏞 Boulder City & Hoover Dam

🏚 *12,500.* ✈ 🚌 📞 *(702) 597-5970.* 🅿 ♿

Named after Herbert Hoover, the 31st president, the historic Hoover Dam lies about 30 miles (48 km) east of Las Vegas. Before its construction, the Colorado River frequently flooded acres of farmland in Mexico and southern California. After much consideration, the dam was built between 1931 and 1935 across the Colorado River's Black Canyon. Hailed as an engineering marvel, it gave this desert region a reliable water supply and provided inexpensive electricity to Nevada, Arizona, and California. This colossus of

An animatronic *Tyrannosaurus rex* in roaring form at the Las Vegas Natural History Museum

View of the Hoover Dam

concrete is today a huge tourist attraction. Guided tours take visitors into the depths of the dam. The top of the visitor center offers superb views of the dam.

Just 8 miles (13 km) west of the dam, Boulder City was built to house the dam's construction workers. With its neat yards and suburban streets, it is one of Nevada's most attractive well-ordered towns. Several of its 1930s buildings remain, including the historic Boulder Dam Hotel, which houses the Hoover Dam Museum.

Hoover Dam sign

Lake Mead National Recreation Area

Las Vegas. (702) 293-8906, (702) 293-8990. 8:30am–4:30pm daily. Jan 1, Thanksgiving, Dec 25. limited. www.nps.gov/lame

After the completion of Hoover Dam, the waters of

the Colorado River filled the deep canyons, which once towered above the river, to create Lake Mead. This huge reservoir is the largest man-made body of water in the US. Its 700-mile (1,130-km) shoreline is home to forests, canyons, and flower-rich meadows. Dotted with beaches, marinas, and camp-grounds, the reservoir area offers water sports such as sailing, waterskiing, swimming, and fishing. Striped bass and rainbow trout are popular catches.

Valley of Fire State Park

Las Vegas. (702) 397-2088. partial. www.state.nv.us/stparks

Lost City Museum of Archaeology
721 S Moapa Valley Blvd, Overton. (702) 397-2193. 8:30am–4:30pm daily. public hols.

This spectacularly scenic state park is in a remote desert location some 60 miles (97 km) northeast of Las Vegas. It derives its name from the red sandstone formations that began as huge, shifting sand dunes about 150 million years ago. The extreme summer temperatures mean that spring or fall are the best times to explore the wilderness. Of the four well-maintained trails, the Petro-glyph Canyon Trail is an easy half-mile (0.8 km) loop, which takes in several fine prehistoric Ancestral Puebloan rock carvings. One of

the most famous depicts an *atlatl*, a notched stick used to add speed and distance to a thrown spear. Ancestral Puebloan people settled in the nearby town of Overton along Muddy River, around 300 BC. They left some 1,500 years later, perhaps because of a long drought. Archaeologists have discovered hundreds of prehistoric artifacts in the area, many of which are housed in Overton's **Lost City Museum of Archaeology**, just outside the town. Its large collection includes pottery, beads, woven baskets, and delicate turquoise jewelry, which was a local specialty.

Red Rock Canyon

Las Vegas. (702) 363-1921. 8am–5pm daily. public hols. limited. www.redrockcanyon.blm.gov

From downtown Las Vegas it is a short, 10-mile (16-km) drive west to the low hills and steep gullies of the Red Rock Canyon National Con-servation Area. Here, baked by the summer sun, a gnarled escarpment rises out of the desert, its gray limestone and red sandstone the geological residue of an ancient ocean and the huge sand dunes that succeeded it. The canyon is easily explored on a 13-mile (21-km) long scenic road that loops off Hwy 159 providing a good overview and great picnic spots, but the best way to explore these steep winding canyons is on foot. Watch for the bighorn sheep and desert tortoises when hiking.

Extraordinary rock formations in the Valley of Fire State Park

Nevada

Nevada was known as the "Silver State" mainly because of the immense wealth that came out of the late 19th-century silver mines of the Comstock Lode, east of Reno. Today, it is synonymous with adult fun, thanks to the presence of the world's largest gambling and entertainment mecca at glittering Las Vegas (see pp510–15). Away from its few cities, Nevada is mostly uninhabited desert, with ridge after ridge of rugged mountains dividing the endless sagebrush plains.

Façade of the impressive State Capitol in Carson City

Carson City ❷

🏃 42,000. 🚌 | 1900 S Carson St, (775) 687-7410.
ⓦ www.visitcarsoncity.com

The state capital and third largest city in Nevada, Carson City was named in honor of the Wild West explorer Kit Carson. Nestled at the base of the eastern escarpment of the Sierra Nevada, the city was founded in 1858, a year before the discovery of the Comstock Lode mines. It still retains a few old-fashioned casinos in its downtown core.

The excellent **Nevada State Museum**, across the street from the impressive State Capitol, is housed inside the 1870 US Mint building, where coins were made from Comstock silver. The museum holds a full-scale replica of a working mine, as well as displays on the natural history of Nevada and the Great Basin.

On the south side of Carson City, the **Nevada State Railroad Museum** preserves 60 steam engines and freight cars

from the old Virginia & Truckee Railroad, which carried ore from the Comstock Lode between 1869 and the 1930s. Later used in Hollywood films, the trains also offer excursions on summer weekends.

🏛 **Nevada State Museum**
600 N Carson St. | (775) 687-4810.
◻ 8:30am–4:30pm daily. ● Jan 1, Thanksgiving, Dec 25. 🗎 ♿
🏛 **Nevada State Railroad Museum**
2180 S Carson St. | (775) 687-6953.
◻ 8:30am–4:30pm daily. ● Jan 1, Thanksgiving, Dec 25. 🗎 ♿.

Virginia City ❸

🏃 1,500. ℹ 131 S C St, (775) 847-0311. ⓦ www.vcnevada.com

Prospectors following the gold deposits up the slopes of Mount Davidson discovered one of the world's richest strikes, the Comstock Lode, in 1859. Almost overnight, the bustling camp of Virginia City grew into the largest settlement between Chicago and San Francisco. It had over 100

Old timers in a Wild West-themed saloon in Virginia City

saloons and 25,000 residents, among whom was a journalist from Missouri who later became famous under the pseudonym Mark Twain.

Over the next 20 years, tons of gold and silver were mined here, but by the turn of the 20th century the town had begun to fade. However, the popular 1960s TV show *Bonanza* has given the city a new lease on life as one of Nevada's most enjoyable destinations. A National Historic Landmark, the city is located at an elevation of 6,220 ft (1,896 m); its steep streets offer fine views of the surrounding mountains. The old main street, **C Street** is packed with historic sites dotted alongside Wild West-themed saloons and souvenir shops. Up the hill along B Street, the elegant **Castle** is the state's best-preserved mansion. It still retains its original furnishings, giving visitors a glimpse of the wealth that flowed through the city in the 1860s.

The city's main historical museum fills the old **Fourth Ward School**, the Victorian Gothic landmark at the south end of C Street. It showcases the city's lively history with exhibits ranging from mining tools to Mark Twain, who began his career at the city's *Territorial Enterprise*. An intact classroom is preserved as it was in 1936, when the last class graduated.

🏚 **The Castle**
70 B St. | (775) 847-0275.
◻ late May–Oct: 11am–5pm daily.
● Nov–late May. 🗎 ♿ limited
🏚 **Fourth Ward School**
C St. | (775) 847-0975. ◻ mid-May–Oct: 10am–5pm daily.
● Nov–late May. 🗎 ♿

Reno ❹

🏃 135,000. ✈ 🚆 🚌 ℹ 4590 S Virginia St, (775) 827-7366.
ⓦ www.renolaketahoe.com

Self-proclaimed "The Biggest Little City in the World," Reno was Nevada's main gambling destination until it was surpassed by glitzy Las Vegas in the 1950s. The city

Archway over Virginia Street in downtown Reno

also achieved national prominence in the 1930s as a center for quick divorces. Although smaller than Las Vegas, Reno has a similar array of 24-hour-a-day casino-fueled fun. At the **Liberty Belle Saloon and Restaurant** south of downtown, visitors can see the first slot machine, the seductive device that led to the gambling mania. Exhibits here tell the complete story of automated gambling, starting with the invention of the three-reel slot machine by the immigrant Charlie Fey in San Francisco in 1885. More than 75 old slot and fortune-telling machines, as well as penny arcade games are on view.

For automobile fans, the **National Automobile Museum**, on the south bank of the Truckee River, has one of the country's most extensive car collections. From early classics to 1960s hot rods, the museum – styled like a late-1940s Chrysler – showcases the cars in stage-set "streets" that provide evocative period backgrounds.

🏛 **Liberty Belle Saloon & Restaurant**
4250 S. Virginia St. 🎧 (775) 825-1776.
⬜ 11am–9pm Mon–Fri, 4pm–10pm Sat–Sun. ● Thanksg., Dec 25. 🔗

🏛 **National Automobile Museum**
10 S Lake St. 🎧 (775) 333-9300.
⬜ 9:30am–5:30pm Mon–Sat, 10am–4pm Sun. ● Thanksgiving, Dec 25.
🖼 🔗 🖥 www.automuseum.org

ENVIRONS: West of Reno, the startling beauty of **Lake Tahoe** (see p718) greets visitors at the Nevada/California border.

Surrounded by summer resorts and winter ski areas, this is one of the most popular destinations in western US.

Great Basin National Park ❺

ℹ 100 Great Basin Hwy, Baker, (775) 234-7331. ⬜ 8am–5pm daily (extended summer hours). ● Jan 1, Thanksgiving, Dec 25. 🖼 🔗 limited. 🖥 www.nps.gov/grba

TRAVELERS DRIVING along the "Loneliest Road in America" are beckoned by the towering silhouette of the 13,063-ft (3,982-m) Wheeler Peak which stands at the center of Great Basin National Park. Below the peak lies the park's centerpiece, the **Lehman Caves**, discovered when homesteader Absalom Lehman stumbled upon their small entrance in 1885. Their fantastic limestone formations, including thousands of stalactites and shields, can be seen on various guided tours that take place at intervals all through the day.

Tours start from the park visitor center, which offers hiking and camping details, along with exhibits on Great Basin's wildlife. The well-maintained **Wheeler Peak Scenic Drive** starts near the visitor center and passes through all the major Great Basin climate zones while climbing from 6,500 ft (1,982 m) to over 10,000 ft (3,048 m) in 12 steep miles (19 km). Great Basin National Park's remote location has made it one of the least-visited national parks in the country, so hikers and campers can find immense solitude among the limestone caves, alpine forests, ancient bristlecone pines, and glacial lakes.

Picturesque Wheeler Peak at Great Basin National Park

THE LONELIEST ROAD IN AMERICA

One of the country's most compelling drives, the Nevada portion of transcontinental US 50, stretching between Lake Tahoe in the west and Great Basin National Park on the Utah border, traverses over 400 miles (644 km) of corrugated country. Early explorers mapped this region, Pony Express riders raced across it, and the long-distance Lincoln Highway finally tamed it. But US 50 has long played second fiddle to busy I-80, the more popular route across the state. The Nevada Commission on Tourism now sponsors a tongue-in-cheek promotion where travelers on US 50 can get a certificate saying "I Survived the Loneliest Road in America."

Sign on US 50 highway

Utah

B EST KNOWN AS world headquarters for the Mormon Church, Utah is also home to some of the most remarkable landscapes in the US. The inhospitably rugged sandstone canyons of the Colorado Plateau, which covers the southern half of the state, have been preserved within a series of unforgettably beautiful national parks, forests, and monuments. The towering snow-capped peaks of the Wasatch Mountains in the northern half of the state, a haven for skiers worldwide, played host to the 2000 Winter Olympics. West of the mountains sits the Mormon-dominated state capital Salt Lake City, Utah's only major city, bordered by its namesake lake.

Visitors enjoying the view from the Great Salt Lake shore

Salt Lake City ❻

🏃 175,000. ⊠ 🚆 🚌 🛈 90 South West Temple St, (801) 521-2822.

P LEASANT AND FRIENDLY Salt Lake City makes a great stopover for weary travelers between Denver and San Francisco. Although its name derives from the undrinkable alkaline Great Salt Lake that spreads to the west, the city actually has abundant fresh water, thanks to the rain and snowmelt of the Wasatch Range, which rises to the east. Founded and controlled by the Mormons since 1847, the city spreads for miles and miles along the base of the snowcapped peaks.

Apart from its spectacular natural setting, Salt Lake City is known as the spiritual base of the Mormon church, which has its worldwide headquarters in Temple Square downtown. Here, the six spires of the main Mormon temple and the famous oblong auditorium of the **Mormon Tabernacle**, built in 1867, stand side by side. The temple is open only to confirmed Mormon believers, though the Tabernacle offers pipe organ recitals and guided tours that show off its amazing acoustics.

To the west of Temple Square, the amazing **Family History Library** holds records of Mormon family trees dating back to the mid-16th century. Eastward, the 1850 Beehive House has been preserved as it was when Mormon leader Brigham Young lived here. At its entrance stands the stately 76-ft (23-m) Eagle Gate, capped by a 4,000-pound eagle with an impressive wingspan of 20 ft (6 m). To the north, the domed **Utah State Capitol**, modeled after the US Capitol, features a series of exhibits on Utah's history.

⛪ Mormon Tabernacle

Temple Square. 🎫 (801) 240-2534. ◯ 9am–9pm daily. ● Jan 1, Thanksgiving, Dec 25. 🕭

🏛 Family History Library

35 NW Temple St. 🎫 (801) 240-2331 ◯ 7:30am–5pm Mon, 7:30am–10pm Tues–Sat. ● Sun, Jul 4, Dec 25–26. 🕭

Great Salt Lake ❼

Great Salt Lake State Park, I-80 exit 104. 🛈 (801) 250-1898. ◯ 8am–5pm daily. 🕭 limited.

T HE LARGEST salt lake in North America, the Great Salt Lake is a shallow remnant of the prehistoric Lake Bonneville. Depending on the weather, the lake covers an area ranging from 1,000 sq miles (2,590 sq km) to 2,500 sq miles (6,477 sq km). The salt flats stretching west from the lake to the Nevada border are so hard and expansive that they have long been used as a proving ground for automobile racers.

Apart from some algae and microscopic brine shrimp, the lake itself supports almost no life. However, the **Antelope Island State Park**, located in the middle of the lake, is home to resident herds of bighorn sheep, mule deer, bison, and its namesake, the pronghorn antelope. Access to the island, lying about 40 miles (64 km) northwest of Salt Lake City, is by way of a 7-mile (11-km) long causeway. Visitors can camp or swim along the shore or take guided lake cruises.

West from Salt Lake City, toward the lake's south shore, the **Great Salt Lake State Park** offers a broad, sandy beach with a marina and observation deck.

🦌 Antelope Island State Park

I-15 exit 335. 🎫 (801) 773-2941. ◯ 7am onward, hours vary. 🎫 🕭 limited.

View of "Eagle Gate" looking toward the Utah State Capitol

Park City ❽

🏠 4,500. ℹ️ 1910 Prospector Ave,
(435) 649-6104.
W www.parkcityinfo.com

A N HOUR's drive east from
downtown Salt Lake City,
through the Wasatch Mountains, leads to this popular
resort. The city started life in
the 1860s as a silver mining
camp and still retains several
turn-of-20th-century buildings
along its photogenic Main
Street. In recent years, it has
become world-famous as the
home of the prestigious
Sundance Film Festival.
Founded by actor and director Robert Redford in 1981,
the annual festival focuses on
independent and documentary films and has become
America's foremost venue for
innovative cinema. The festival's popularity is linked to
Park City's excellent skiing
facilities, showcased in the
2000 Winter Olympics. A
sense of the town's history

can be obtained at **Park City
Museum** in the old City Hall.

🏛 **Park City Museum**
528 Main St. 📞 (435) 649-6104.
🕐 May & Nov: 11am–5pm Mon–Sat,
noon–6pm Sun; rest of the year:
10am–7pm Mon–Sat, noon–6pm Sun.
⬤ Jan 1, Thanksgiving, Dec 25.
♿ limited.

Timpanogos Cave National Monument ❾

Rte 3, American Fork. 📞 (801)
756-5238. 🕐 mid-May–mid-Oct:
7am–5:30pm daily ⬤ Nov–mid-May
🚫 W www.nps.gov/tica

O NE OF THE the most
popular destinations
around Salt Lake City, the
Timpanogos Cave National
Monument lies deep beneath
the 11,750-ft (3,581-m) summit of Mount Timpanogos.
The site preserves a trio of
massive limestone caverns

**Scenic view along Alpine Loop
following Highway 92**

stretching nearly 1,800 ft (549
m) deep into the mountain.
Reached by way of a steep,
1.5 mile (2 km) uphill hike
from the visitor center, and
linked by man-made tunnels,
the three caves are very cool
(43° F/6° C), very damp, and
full of spectacular limestone
formations. Electric lights
showcase the sundry stalactites, stalagmites, crystalline
helictites, and other water-sculpted formations, all of
which are still being formed.
Only a limited number of
people are allowed inside, so
visitors should come early in
the day or during the week to
avoid the worst crowds.
    Timpanogos Cave is one
of the many highlights of
the drive along the 40-mile
(64-km) **Alpine Loop**, which
follows Highway 92 around
the landmark mountain. Many
campgrounds, picnic spots,
scenic views, and hiking trails
can be enjoyed by trekkers
along the way.

Historic houses lining Main Street in Park City

THE MORMONS

The Church of Jesus Christ of Latter Day Saints, a large Christian
denomination, was founded by Joseph Smith (1805–44), a farm
worker from New York State. In 1820 Smith claimed to have seen
visions of the Angel Moroni, who led him to a set of golden tablets,
which he translated and later published as the *Book of Mormon*, thus
establishing the Mormon Church. Although this new faith grew rapidly, it attracted hostility because of its political and economic beliefs,
and the practice of polygamy. Seeking refuge, the Mormons moved
to Illinois in 1839, where Smith was killed by an angry mob. Leadership passed to Brigham Young, who led the members on an arduous journey west, in the hope of escaping persecution and setting
up a safe haven in the unpromising landscape of Salt Lake Valley.
The pioneers traveled across bleak prairies and mountains in primitive
wagons, braving the fierce weather. Young's followers finally established successful farming
communities across Utah's wilderness. Today, Mormons form 70 percent of Utah's population.

**Portrait of Brigham
Young (1801–77)**

Arches National Park ❿

Wildflowers in the park

Aᴿᴄʜᴇs ɴᴀᴛɪᴏɴᴀʟ ᴘᴀʀᴋ has the the highest concentration of natural sandstone arches in the world. More than 80 of these natural wonders have formed over millions of years. The park "floats" on a salt bed, which once liquefied under the pressure exerted by the rock above it. About 300 million years ago, this salt layer bulged upward, cracking the sandstone above. Over time the cracks eroded, leaving long "fins" of rock. As these fins eroded, the hard overhead rock formed arches, which range today from the solid looking Turret Arch to the graceful Delicate and Landscape Arches.

Devil's Garden
This area contains several of the park's most beautiful arches, including Landscape Arch, a slender curve of sandstone more than 300 ft (91 m) long, which is thought to be the longest natural arch in the world.

Sunset Watch at Delicate Arch
A natural amphitheater surrounds the arch, creating seating from which vistas of the La Sal Mountains are framed.

Tʜᴇ Wɪɴᴅᴏᴡs Sᴇᴄᴛɪᴏɴ

In the park's Windows Section, a one-mile loop trail leads to Turret Arch, then the North and South Windows Arches, located side by side. With excellent viewing spots available, many visitors photograph the North and South arches framed by the sandstone Turner Arch, as seen here.

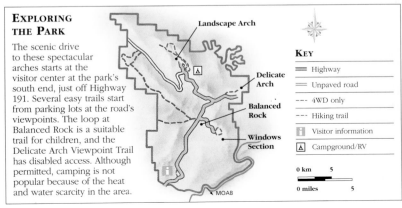

Exᴘʟᴏʀɪɴɢ ᴛʜᴇ Pᴀʀᴋ

The scenic drive to these spectacular arches starts at the visitor center at the park's south end, just off Highway 191. Several easy trails start from parking lots at the road's viewpoints. The loop at Balanced Rock is a suitable trail for children, and the Delicate Arch Viewpoint Trail has disabled access. Although permitted, camping is not popular because of the heat and water scarcity in the area.

Landscape Arch

Delicate Arch

Balanced Rock

Windows Section

MOAB

Kᴇʏ

═══ Highway

═══ Unpaved road

--- 4WD only

--- Hiking trail

ℹ Visitor information

🅰 Campground/RV

0 km   5

0 miles   5

Delicate Arch
The most celebrated of all the arches here, and a state symbol, Delicate Arch appears on many Utah license plates. It is reached by a moderate 45-minute walk over sandstone.

Arches are formed through a process that takes millions of years; today's arches continue to erode and will eventually collapse.

Balanced Rock
This precariously balanced boulder atop a sandstone spire is one of the park's landmarks. Good views are available from the trail as well as the scenic road route.

Western-style, timber-clad gift store on Main Street, Moab

Moab ⓫

🏨 6500. ℹ️ Main & Center Sts, (435) 259-8825.
🚾 www.discovermoab.com

A TOWN OF DRAMATIC ups and downs, Moab is currently riding its second great boom of the last 50 years. Once a quiet Mormon settlement, the discovery in 1952 of several major uranium deposits outside town made Moab one of America's wealthiest communities. When the uranium market declined in the 1970s, the town was saved by tourism and its proximity to Arches and Canyonlands National Parks. Many movies, including some John Wayne Westerns and the Indiana Jones classics were shot here.

Today, Moab is a top destination for lovers of the outdoors. Mountain bikers come here for the challenging ride from Moab Rim, reached by Moab Skyway, a scenic tram ride offering panoramic views of the area. Numerous hiking trails and 4WD routes take in some of this region's fabulous landscapes. Moab is also a major center for whitewater rafting on the Colorado River.
Matheson Wetlands Preserve off Kane Creek Boulevard has 2 miles (3 km) of hiking trails along a riverside wetland, home to birds and indigenous wildlife.

🦅 Matheson Wetlands Preserve
Off Kane Creek Blvd. 📞 (435) 259-4629. 🕐 9am–dusk daily. 📷

Park Avenue and the Courthouse Towers
The large, rock monoliths known as Courthouse Towers bear an uncanny resemblance to city skyscrapers. They can be seen from Park Avenue, an easy, short trail.

Canyonlands National Park ⑫

MILLIONS OF YEARS AGO, the Colorado and Green Rivers cut winding paths deep into rock, creating a labyrinth of rocky canyons that form the heart of this stunning wilderness. At its center, the rivers' confluence divides the park's 527 sq miles (1,365 sq km) into three districts – the Needles, the Maze, and the grassy plateau of the Island in the Sky. Established as a national park in 1964, Canyonlands is growing in popularity. Most wilderness travel here requires a permit.

VISITORS' CHECKLIST

🔖 2282 South West Resource Blvd, Moab, (435) 719-2313. 🕐 visitor center: 8am–4:30pm daily (longer during spring & fall). ● Jan 1, Thanksgiving, Dec 25. 🚫
♿ 🚻 📷 🅰
🌐 www.nps.gov/cany

Mesa Arch
An easy and rewarding 500-yard (455-m) trail leads to Mesa Arch, a long, low curve of stone that perfectly frames the snowcapped La Sal Mountains in the distance.

KEY

▬	Highway
═	4WD only
	Hiking route
🅰	Campground/RV
🏕	Picnic area
🛈	Visitor information
—	National Park boundary
⚜	Viewpoint

Horseshoe Canyon
contains 6,000-year-old petroglyphs, said to be some of the oldest in existence.

Upheaval Dome Overlook

Grand View Point Overlook

Maze Overlook

Green River

Colorado River

White Rim Road
is a 100-mile (160-km) trail accessed via the exhilarating Shafer Road, a 4WD track down a steep cliff.

Needles District
The most interesting features in this remote district are the hundreds of red rock spires, or needles, for which it was named.

The Maze
canyons, where outlaw Butch Cassidy hid out in the late 1800s, offer a challenge to skilled hikers.

Island in the Sky
Easy access by car makes this the most visited district of the park. A popular stop here is the Grandview Overlook, which offers panoramic views of the rocky canyons of the Green and Colorado Rivers.

0 km 5
0 miles 5

The deep crevices of the canyons in the wide valley around Green River

Green River ⑬

🏠 *1,000.* ℹ️ *885 E Main St, (435) 564-3526.* ⏰ *Apr–Oct: 8am–8pm; Nov–Mar: 8am–5pm daily.*

LOCATED IN A broad, bowl-shaped valley, the town grew around a ford of the wild Green River in the 19th and early 20th centuries. Today, it is a launching spot for whitewater rafting on the Green and Colorado Rivers.

American geologist and ethnologist John Wesley Powell (1834–1902) began his exploration of the Colorado River and Grand Canyon from here in 1871. The **John Wesley Powell River History Museum** at Green River has 20,000 sq ft (1,860 sq m) of displays tracing the history of the area's exploration.

🏛 **John Wesley Powell River History Museum**
885 E Main St. 📞 *(435) 564-3427.* ⏰ *Apr–Oct: 8am–8pm daily; Nov–Mar: 8am–5pm daily.* ⬤ *public hols.* 📷 🎥

Hovenweep National Monument ⑭

E of Hwy 191. 📞 *(970) 562-4282.* ⏰ *8am–5pm daily.* ⬤ *Jan 1, Thanksgiving, Dec 25.* 📷 🎥 🅿️
🌐 *www.nps.gov/hove*

THE SIX SEPARATE sets of ruins at this Ancestral Puebloan site were discovered by W.D. Huntington, leader of a Mormon expedition, in 1854. The culture at Hovenweep, a Ute word meaning "Deserted Valley," reached its peak between 1200 and 1275. Little

is known of the Utes beyond the clues found in the round, square, and D-shaped towers, and pottery and tools that they left behind.

Researchers have speculated that the towers might have been built as defensive fortifications, astronomical observatories, storage silos, or as religious structures for the entire community.

Lake Powell & Glen Canyon National Recreation Area ⑮

2 miles (3 km) N of Page on Hwy 98, off Hwy 160. ❌ ℹ️ *Carl Hayden Visitor Center, (928) 608-6404.* ⏰ *Apr–Oct: 8am–7pm daily; Nov–Mar: 8am–5pm daily.* ♿ *visitor center only.* 📷 🖥 🍴 🅿️ 🅰️ *Page & Wahweap only.* 🌐 *www.nps.gov/glca, www.lakepowell.com*

THE GLEN CANYON National Recreation Area (NRA), established in 1972, covers more than one million acres of dramatic desert and canyon country around the 185-mile (298-km) long Lake Powell, named after John Wesley Powell. The lake was created by damming the Colorado River and its tributaries to supply electricity to the region's growing population.

The construction of the Glen Canyon Dam, completed in 1963, was controversial from the start. The spirited campaign, led by the environmentalist Sierra Club, continues to argue for the restoration of Glen Canyon, believing that ancient ecosystems are being ruined. Pro-dam advocates, however, firmly believe in its ability to store water, generate power, and provide recreation.

The "Y"-shaped recreation area follows the San Juan River east almost to the town of Mexican Hat, and heads northeast along the Colorado toward Canyonlands National Park. Within the area is the **Antelope Canyon**, a famously deep "slot" canyon. Other highlights include Lees Ferry, a 19th-century Mormon settlement that now offers tourist facilities, and the **Rainbow Bridge National Monument**. Rising 309 ft (94 m), this is the largest natural bridge in the world.

Today, the lake is busy with water sports enthusiasts and houseboat parties, exploring the myriad sandstone side canyons. Glen Canyon is also one of the most popular hiking, biking, and 4WD destinations in the country.

Rose-colored sandstone of Antelope Canyon, in Glen Canyon NRA

Capitol Reef National Park ⓖ

10 miles (16 km) E of Torrey,
Hwy 24. ⓘ (435) 425-3791.
◯ 8am–4:30pm daily. ● Dec 25.
🚫 ♿ 📷 🅰
ⓦ www.nps.gov/care

Covering 378 square miles (980 sq km), this spectacular park encloses a 100-mile (160-km) long, colorful wall of rock that was thrust up by the earth 65 million years ago. The strata that buckled upward folded back on itself, trapping water in the process. Around 100 years ago, prospectors crossing the desert were forced to stop at this wind-carved Waterpocket Fold. They likened the rock barrier to an ocean reef and thought its round white domes looked just like the US Capitol building, hence the park's name.

An adventurous drive along the partly unpaved Notom-Bullfrog Road provides a good overview of the area. Cars can negotiate the road in dry weather, but extra gas and water are essential. Capitol Gorge, to the north, can be reached via a scenic route, extending about 10 miles (16 km) into the heart of the park. Guided walking tours are available during summer, but be aware that only experienced hikers should attempt to explore the back country here.

To the north lies the 1908 **Gifford Farmhouse**. Now a cultural center, it is dedicated to the 1880s Mormon settlement that once flourished here. Fremont Canyon, on its right, features the famous Fremont Petroglyphs, created by the Ancestral Puebloans between 700 and 1250. Farther north, is the Cathedral Valley, named for the rock monoliths that tower over the desert.

Grand Staircase-Escalante National Monument ⓗ

ⓘ 755 W Main St, Escalante, (435) 826-5499. ◯ Apr–Oct: 7am–6pm daily; Nov–Mar: 8am–5pm Mon–Fri.
ⓦ www.ut.blm.gov/monument

Established by President Clinton in 1996, this monument encompasses 1.9 million acres (769,000 ha) of pristine rock canyons, mountains, and high desert plateaus. It was named for its four 12-million-year-old cliff faces that rise in tiered steps across the Colorado Plateau. To preserve its wild state, no new roads, facilities, or campgrounds are being built here. This vast untamed area is best explored on scenic drives combined with daylong hikes.

Vintage wagon outside Cedar City's museum

About 9 miles (14 km) south of Highway 12 stands **Kodachrome Basin State Park**, a distinctive landscape noted for its 67 free-standing sand pipes or rock chimneys, formed millions of years ago as geyser vents.

♣ Kodachrome Basin State Park

ⓘ (435) 679-8562; (800) 322-3770.
◯ dawn–dusk daily. 🚫 📷 🅰

Bryce Canyon National Park ⓘ

See pp526–7.

Cedar City ⓙ

🏘 15,750. ✈ 🚆
ⓘ 286 N Main St, (435) 586-5124.

Founded by Mormons in 1851, Cedar City developed as a center for mining and smelting iron. The Iron Mission State Park and Museum offers a glimpse of this pioneering spirit and features a large collection of early vehicles. The town offers a choice of hotels within an hour's drive of Zion National Park. Cedar City is popular for its annual Shakespeare Festival, staged in a replica of London's Globe Theatre. East of town, the spectacular **Cedar Breaks National Monument** features limestone cliffs and a lake topped by a deep green forest. In winter, the area is a popular skiing resort.

⛰ Cedar Breaks National Monument

ⓘ (435) 586-9451. ◯ daily.
Visitor Center ◯ Jun–Labor Day: 8am–6pm daily; Labor Day–mid-Oct: 9am–5:30pm daily. 🚫
ⓦ www.nps.gov/cebr

Fishing in the lake at Cedar Breaks National Monument, near Cedar City

Zion National Park ❷⓿

Wild-flowers

A T THE HEART OF THIS beautiful national park lies Zion Canyon, perhaps the most popular of all of Utah's natural wonders. It was carved by the powerful waters of the Virgin River and then widened, sculpted, and reshaped by wind, rain, and ice. Its majestic walls rise up to 2,000 ft (600 m) and are shaped into jagged peaks and formations in shades of red and white. Wild meadows and luxuriant foliage along the river account for the area's abundant wildlife. The park shuttle is the only way into the canyon. A number of short walks, beginning at the shuttle stops, follow marked trails to the tough 16-mile (26-km) hike through the canyon and involves wading through the river.

The spectacular Zion–Mt. Carmel Highway

ZION CANYON

The Virgin River meanders quietly through banks of wildflowers, cotton-wood, oak, and willow trees, which grow beneath the sloping walls of the canyon. Be aware that sudden summer rainstorms may cause floods, so visitors are advised to check conditions first.

EXPLORING ZION CANYON

A guided trail takes visitors along the 6-mile (10-km) scenic road that follows the Virgin River into an ever-narrowing canyon. In summer a shuttle bus operates along the Zion Canyon Scenic Drive and from the Information Center to the turn of Springdale.

KEY

═══	Highway
---	Hiking trail
🚶	Ranger station
🅰	Campground / RV

0 meters 500
0 yards 500

Hiking

Numerous guided walking and hiking tours of Zion's geology and history leave daily from the visitor center. Emerald Pools Trail and Canyon Overlook Trail are particularly popular trails.

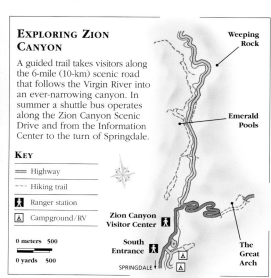

Weeping Rock

Emerald Pools

The Great Arch

Zion Canyon Visitor Center 🚶

South Entrance 🚶

SPRINGDALE

Arizona

OFTEN REFERRED TO AS the Grand Canyon State after its most famous sight, Arizona offers a range of stunning natural beauty. Its southwest corner features the hostile but eerily beautiful Sonoran Desert, bordered by the state's economic hub, Phoenix, and the city of Tucson. To the north, the landscape changes, rising through high desert plateaus, toward canyons and mountains, the romanticized "Wild West" of cowboy films. Here, the city of Flagstaff and the picturesque towns of Sedona and Jerome attract thousands of visitors. Over 25 percent of Arizona is Native American reservation land. The state also houses several Ancient Puebloan ruins.

London Bridge spanning a man-made waterway in Lake Havasu City

Lake Havasu City ㉑

🏚 45,000. ✈ 🚌 ℹ️ *314 London Bridge Rd, (928) 453-3444.*
🆆 *www.golakehavasu.com*

CALIFORNIA businessman Robert McCulloch founded Lake Havasu City in 1964. The resort city he built on the Colorado River was popular with the landlocked citizens of Arizona. His real brainwave, however, came four years later when he bought London Bridge and painstakingly transported it stone-bystone from England to Lake Havasu. Some mocked McCulloch, suggesting that he had thought he was buying London's Gothic Tower Bridge, not this more ordinary one. There was more hilarity when it appeared that there was nothing in Havasu City for the bridge to span. Undaunted, McCulloch simply created the waterway he needed by digging a channel to divert water from Lake Havasu. The bridge and its adjoining mock-Tudor village complex have since become one of Arizona's most popular tourist attractions.

Flagstaff ㉒

🏚 58,000. ✈ 🚌 *Amtrak Flagstaff Station, 1 E Rte 66.* 🚌 *Flagstaff bus station, 399 S Malpais Lane.*
ℹ️ *Amtrak depot, 1 E Rte 66, (928) 774-9541.* 🕐 *8am–5pm daily.* ⬤ *public hols.* 🎭 *Flagstaff Festival of the Arts (early Jul–mid-Aug).*

NESTLING AMONG the pine forests of northern Arizona's San Francisco Peaks, Flagstaff is one of the region's most attractive towns. Its historic downtown, an attractive ensemble of red-brick buildings housing bars and restaurants, dates from the 1890s, when the town developed as a lumber center.

Flagstaff's lively café society owes much to the students of the **Northern Arizona University**, home to two campus art galleries. The Beasley Gallery holds temporary exhibitions and student work, while the Old Main Art Museum and Gallery has the permanent Weiss collection, which includes works by the Mexican artist Diego Rivera.

Situated on Mars Hill is the 1894 **Lowell Observatory**, named for its benefactor, Percival Lowell, a member of one of Boston's wealthiest families. Lowell wanted to look for life on Mars and although he did not succeed, the observatory earned repute with its documented evidence of an expanding universe, along with the discovery of Pluto by astronomer Clyde Tombaugh.

A few miles northwest of downtown, set picturesquely in a pine forest, is the **Museum of Northern Arizona**. It holds one of the Southwest's most comprehensive collections of Southwestern archaeological artifacts, as well as fine art and natural science exhibits. The museum presents an excellent overview of Anasazi history and contemporary Navajo, Hopi, and Pai cultures.

The collections are arranged in a series of galleries around a central courtyard. The Archaeology Gallery provides a fine introduction to the region's historic cultures. The award-winning anthropology exhibition in the Ethnology Gallery documents 12,000 years of Hopi, Zuni, Navajo, and Pai tribal cultures on the Colorado Plateau. The museum shop sells Native American arts and crafts. A section has exhibits that focus on the variety of plants and animals found on the Colorado Plateau through the ages.

🏛 **Museum of Northern Arizona**
3101 N Fort Valley Rd. 📞 *(928) 774-5213.* 🕐 *9am–5pm daily.*
⬤ *public hols.* 💷 ♿ 🅿 🛍 🛒
🆆 *www.musnaz.org*

Native American exhibits, Museum of Northern Arizona in Flagstaff

Heart of Arizona Tour ㉓

THE VERDE RIVER passes through the wooded hills and fertile meadows of central Arizona, before opening into a wide, green valley between Flagstaff and Phoenix. The heart of Arizona is full of charming towns such as Sedona, hidden away among stunning scenery, and the former mining town of Jerome. Over the hills lies Prescott, once the state capital and now a busy, likable little town with a center full of dignified Victorian buildings. The area's ancient history can be seen in its two beautiful pueblo ruins, Montezuma Castle and Tuzigoot.

Tips for Drivers

Recommended route: *From Sedona, take Hwy 89A to Tuzigoot, Jerome, & Prescott. Hwy 69 runs east from Prescott to Interstate Hwy 17, which connects to Camp Verde, Fort Verde, & Montezuma Castle.*
Tour length: *85 miles (137 km).*
When to go: *Spring & fall are delightful; summer is very hot.*

Sedona ①
Set among dramatic red rock hills, Sedona is a popular resort, known for its New Age stores and galleries as well as for its friendly ambience.

Key

Tour route
Other road

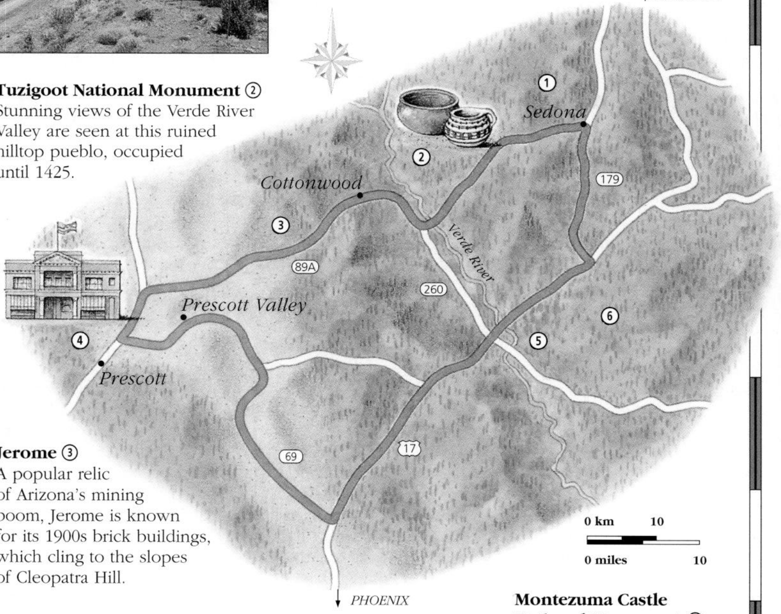

FLAGSTAFF
1
Sedona
2
179
Cottonwood
3
Verde River
89A
260
Prescott Valley
4
Prescott
5
6
69
17
0 km 10
0 miles 10
PHOENIX

Tuzigoot National Monument ②
Stunning views of the Verde River Valley are seen at this ruined hilltop pueblo, occupied until 1425.

Jerome ③
A popular relic of Arizona's mining boom, Jerome is known for its 1900s brick buildings, which cling to the slopes of Cleopatra Hill.

MATTS
SALOON
112

Prescott ④
This cool hilltop town is set among the rugged peaks and lush woods of Prescott National Forest, making it a popular center for many outdoor activities.

Montezuma Castle National Monument ⑥
The Ancestral Puebloan ruins here date from the 1100s and occupy one of the loveliest sites in the Southwest.

Camp Verde ⑤
A highlight of this little town is Fort Verde. Built by the US Army in 1865, this stone fort is manned by costumed guides.

Phoenix ㉔

🏙 *1,300,000 (city only).* ✈
🚌 *Greyhound Bus, 2115 E Buckeye Rd.* ℹ *50 North 2nd St, (602) 254-6500.* ⛳ *The PGA's Phoenix Golf Open (Jan).*

S TRETCHING ACROSS the entire Salt River Valley, Arizona's capital, Phoenix, started out as a farming town in the 1860s and soon developed into the economic hub of the state. As it grew, it gradually absorbed the surrounding towns of Scottsdale, Mesa, and Tempe, and now has over a million people within the city and almost three million in Metro-politan Phoenix. Downtown Phoenix has many historic attractions while the metropolitan area, famed for its design studio Taliesin West, is also popular with tourists for its spas and resorts during the warm winter months.

Exploring Downtown Phoenix
Downtown, where the city began in the 19th century, covers a few blocks east and west of Central Avenue and north and south of Wash-ington Street. Washington Street houses the copper-domed **Arizona State Capitol Museum**, originally the state legislature. Among the exhibits are a series of sepia photographs docu-menting the city's political history. To its west is the **Arizona Mining and Mineral Museum** that traces

Arizona's colorful mining history, which made millionaires of some and destitutes of many. Exhibits include photographs, historic tools, and quarried rocks.

More glimpses of the city's history can be seen in the attractive restored Victorian houses on the tree-lined **Heritage Square**, some of which have been converted into tearooms and small museums. Visitors can get a better impression of the city's early history at the inventive **Phoenix Museum of History** across the street. It features unusual artifacts, such as a steam-powered bicycle, and re-creates the city's first jail.

Cash register at the Museum of History

In between these historic attractions stands the ultra-modern **Arizona Science Center**, with over 300 interactive science exhibits offering virtual reality trips through the human body.

A short drive north of downtown leads to the highly acclaimed **Phoenix Art Museum**, renowned for its stimulating temporary exhibi-tions. The museum's second floor houses works by 18th- and 19th-century American artists, particularly those painters connected with the Southwest. Among the exhibits are works by Georgia O'Keeffe and Gilbert Stewart, whose celebrated *Portrait of George Washington* (1796) is seen on every dollar bill.

The **Heard Museum**, farther north, was founded in 1929 by Dwight Heard, a wealthy rancher and newspaper tycoon, whose wife, Maie,

amassed an extraordinary collection of Native Southwestern American art. The museum exhibits over 30,000 works, but its star attraction is the display of more than 500 dolls. Apart from dolls, the award-winning Katsina Doll Collection displays Native American pottery, jewelry, and textiles. Other interesting galleries are the Sandra Day O'Connor Gallery, which documents the museum's history and showcases the Heard family's early collection, and the Freeman Gallery, with its interactive hands-on display, which shows how artists interpret their environment through art.

🏛 Heard Museum
2301 North Central Ave.
📞 *(602) 252-8840.* ℹ *(602) 252-8848.* ⏰ *9:30am–5pm daily.* ● *public hols.* ♿ 🅿 🛗 🍴 🛍
🌐 *www.heard.org*

ENVIRONS: About 12 miles (19 km) northeast of downtown lies the former town of **Scottsdale**, founded in the late 19th century. Replete with air-conditioned malls, designer stores, hotels, cafés, and restaurants, it is also famous for its world-class golf courses. Scottsdale's quiet, tree-lined streets and desert setting attracted the visionary architect Frank Lloyd Wright (*see p396*) to establish his winter studio **Taliesin West** here in 1937. The 600-acre (240-ha) complex is now an architecture school and a working design studio. The muted tones of its low-

The 1900 façade of the Arizona State Capitol Building, Phoenix

Taliesin West façade, designed to blend with the desert landscape

Key

[P]	Parking
ℹ	Visitor information

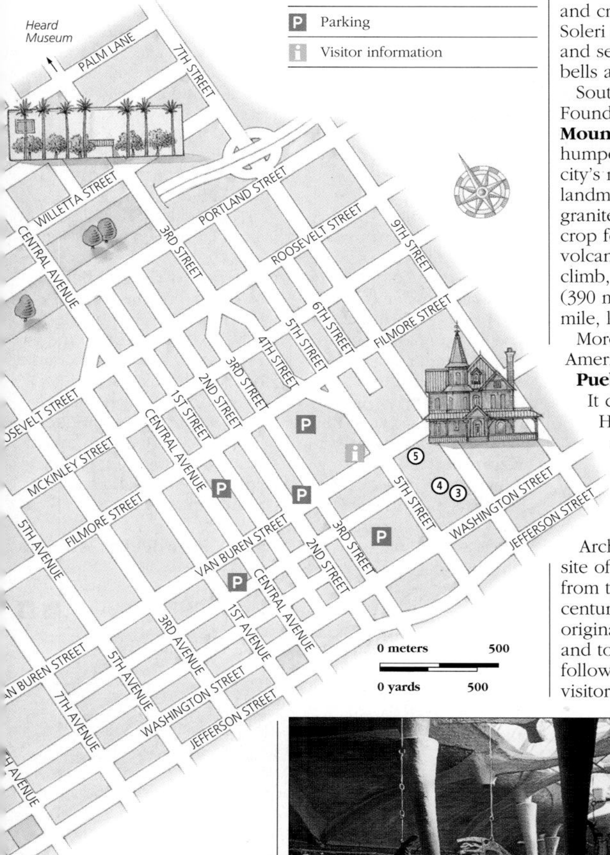

lying buildings and use of local stone for irregular walls reflects Wright's enthusiasm for the desert setting.

The **Cosanti Foundation**, 4 miles (6 km) west of Taliesin West, was established by the Italian architect and student of Wright, Paolo Soleri (b.1919), to further his study of what he termed "arcology": a combination of architecture and ecology to create new urban habitats. Today, the site consists of simple, low structures, housing studios, a gallery, and craft workshops, where Soleri and his workers make and sell their trademark wind-bells and cast bronzes.

South of the Cosanti Foundation is the **Camelback Mountain**, named for its humped shape. One of the city's most distinctive landmarks, the mountain is a granite and sandstone out-crop formed by prehistoric volcanic forces. A steep climb, covering 1,300 ft (390 m) in the space of a mile, leads to the summit.

More glimpses of the Native American past can be at the **Pueblo Grande Museum.** It displays an ancient Hohokam ruin, as well as artifacts such as cooking utensils and pottery. Many of these pieces come from the adjacent Archaeological Park, the site of a Hohokam settlement from the 8th to the 14th centuries. The site was originally excavated in 1887, and today has an easy-to-follow path, which guides visitors through the ruins.

Sights at a Glance

Arizona State Capitol Museum [1]
Arizona Mining and Mineral Museum [2]
Heritage Square [3]
Arizona Science Center [4]
Phoenix Museum of History [5]
Phoenix Art Museum [6]

Innovative design of the Cosanti Foundation gift shop, Scottsdale

Tucson ㉕

🏛 *750,000.* ✈ 🚉 *Amtrak Station,
400 E Toole Ave.* 🚌 *Greyhound
Lines, 2 S 4th Ave.* ℹ *110 S Church
Ave, (520) 624-1817, (800) 638-
8350.* 🎭 *La Fiesta de los Vaqueros
(late Feb); Tucson Folk Music Festival
(May).* 🌐 *www.visittucson.org*

T HE SECOND largest city in
Arizona, Tucson (pro-
nounced too-sahn) is located
on the northern boundary of
the Sonoran Desert, in a basin
surrounded by five mountain
ranges. The town's Colonial
past dates to the 1770s, when
strong resistance from the
local Tohono O'odham
and Pima Native tribes
forced the Spanish to
move their regional
fortress, or presidio,
from nearby Tubac
to Tucson.

The city's main
sights are clustered
around the Uni-
versity of Arizona
campus and the
historic downtown
area. The **Barrio**
and **El Presidio**
historic districts are located
here. El Presidio occupies the
area where the original
Spanish fortress was built.
Today, many of the historic
buildings have been con-
verted into restaurants, shops,
and offices. Five of El
Presidio's oldest dwellings,
including the J. Knox Corbett
House, are located in the
Historic Block. They form a
part of the **Tucson Museum**

**Stained-glass window
in the Cathedral**

of Art, with its excellent
collection of pre-Columbian
artifacts, and exhibitions of
contemporary American and
European work. Southeast of
the museum, the Pima County
Courthouse, built in 1927, is
a fine example of Spanish
Colonial Revival Style.

The **St. Augustine
Cathedral**, with its imposing
sandstone façade, is southwest of El Presidio. Begun
in 1896, the cathedral is
modeled after the Spanish
Colonial style of the Cathedral
of Querétaro in central
Mexico. The Barrio Historic
District, farther south, was
once a business district.
Today, its quiet
streets are lined with
brightly painted
adobe houses. On
nearby Main Street
is the "wishing
shrine" of El
Tiradito, where a
young man was
killed as a conse-
quence of a lovers'
triangle. The locals
believe that if a
candle lit here
burns through a night, their
wishes will come true.

The University of Arizona
campus houses several museums. The most notable is the
Arizona State Museum,
renowned for its collections
of artifacts covering 2,000
years of Native history.
Beyond downtown,
Metropolitan Tucson extends
into the surrounding
mountain ranges. **Mount**

Lemmon (9,157 ft/2,790 m),
the highest peak, is to the
north, while to the west is
one part of the Saguaro
National Park (the other is to
the east), where vistas of the
tall saguaro cacti can be seen.

About 14 miles (22 km)
west of the university, lies the
fascinating **Arizona-Sonora
Desert Museum**. Covering
more than 21 acres (8.5 ha),
it includes a botanical garden,
zoo, and natural history
museum with displays
describing the history, geology, and flora and fauna of
the Sonoran Desert.

Nearby is the **Old Tucson
Studios**, a Wild West theme
park originally built as a set
for a Western movie in 1939.
Some of Hollywood's most
famous Westerns, such as
Gunfight at the OK Corral
(1957) and *Rio Bravo* (1958)
were filmed here.

The Southwest's oldest
and best preserved Mission
church lies south of Tucson.
The **San Xavier del Bac
Mission**, completed in 1797
by Franciscan missionaries,
is built of adobe brick and is
considered the finest example
of Spanish Colonial architecture in the US. Its highlights
include an ornate Baroque
façade decorated with carved
figures of saints, a glorious
painted ceiling, and a spectacular main altar.

San Xavier del Bac Mission
1950 W San Xavier Rd, 10 miles
(16 km) S of Tucson on I-19. 📞 *(520)
294-2624.* 🕐 *8am–5pm daily.* ♿ 📷

SOUTHWEST ARCHITECTURE

The Southwest has been witness to a
range of architecture styles from
Ancestral Puebloan adobe to Spanish
Colonial, and 19th- and early 20th-
century Mission and Pueblo Revival.
Colonizers brought their own forms
that mingled with the Native, creating a
unique plethora of multicultural styles.

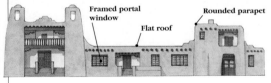

Canale (water pipe)   **Adobe bricks**

This adobe home *in El Rancho de las Golondrinas
Museum in Santa Fe is made of adobe (sun-baked bricks
that are a mixture of mud, sand, and straw), cemented
with similar material, and replastered with mud.*

**Framed portal
window**

Flat roof   **Rounded parapet**

***The Santa Fe Museum of Fine
Arts*** *was the city's first building
in Pueblo Revival style, with
adobe walls, rounded parapets,
framed portal windows, and
pueblo-style multitiered stories.*

Statue of Virgin Mary at the San Xavier del Bac Mission, Tucson

Nogales ㉖

🏠 19,500. ⛲ 🚇 ℹ️ 123 W Kino Park, (520) 287-3685.

THE BIRTHPLACE of jazz star Charles Mingus, Nogales is really two towns that straddle the US border with Mexico. It is a busy port of entry, handling huge amounts of freight, including 75 percent of all winter fruit and vegetables sold in North America. The town attracts large numbers of visitors in search of bargains at shopping districts on both sides of the border. There is a profound contrast between the quiet, ordered streets of the US side, and the ramshackle houses and bustling, large-scale street market across the border.

Mexican pottery from Nogales

Visas are required only for visitors traveling beyond town limits. US citizens should carry a passport or birth certificate for identification, while foreign nationals should carry their passport and make sure that their visa status enables them to re-enter the US.

Bisbee ㉗

🏠 6,500. ⛲ ℹ️ 31 Subway St, (520) 432-5421.

THE DISCOVERY of copper here in the 1880s sparked a mining rush, and by the turn of the century Bisbee was the largest city between St. Louis and San Francisco. Today, this is one of the Southwest's most atmospheric mining towns. Victorian buildings such as the landmark Copper Queen Hotel still dominate the historic town center, while attractive clusters of houses cling to the sides of the surrounding mountains. Visitors can tour the mines that once flourished here. The Bisbee Mining and Historical Museum illustrates the realities of mining and frontier life.

ENVIRONS: Some 25 miles (40 km) north of Bisbee is **Tombstone**, one of the wildest towns in the West. Founded by a prospector in 1877, its name derives from the warning he received that "all you'll find out there is your tombstone." Instead, the silver he found led to a silver rush. Today, Tombstone is a living legend, famous as the site of the 1881 gunfight at OK Corral between the Earp brothers and the Clanton gang. The OK Corral is now a museum, where the infamous gunfight is re-enacted. The old seat of justice, Tombstone Courthouse, is a historic site.

Amerind Foundation ㉘

📞 (520) 586-3666. ☐ Oct–May: 10am–4pm daily. ● Jun–Sep: Mon & Tue; public hols. 🅿️ 🔤 www.amerind.org

THE AMERIND Foundation is one of the country's most important private archaeological and ethnological museums. The name Amerind is a contraction of "American Indian," and this collection depicts all aspects of Native American life through thousands of artifacts of different cultures. The displays include Inuit masks, Cree tools, and sculpted effigy figures from Mexico's Casas Grandes.

The adjacent Amerind Art Gallery has a fine collection of Western art by such artists as William Leigh and Frederic Remington. The delightful pink buildings, designed in the Spanish Colonial Revival style, are also interesting.

Moorish-style dome

Ornate wooden carvings

Iron grille work

Red-tiled roof

White plaster

J. Knox Corbett House in Tucson was designed in the 20th-century Mission Revival style by the Chicago architect David Holmes in 1906. It is characterized by white stucco walls, flat roofs, courtyards, and minimal ornamentation.

San Xavier del Bac Mission is a fine example of the Baroque tradition of Spanish Colonial churches. The style saw a resurgence in the 20th century as Spanish Colonial Revival, with red-tiled roofs, ornamental terra-cotta, iron grille work, and white walls.

Petrified Forest National Park ❷⁹

Off I-40. ☎ *(928) 524-6228.*
⬤ *summer: 7am–7pm; winter:*
8am–5pm. ⬤ *Dec 25.* 🏞
ⓦ *www.nps.gov/pefo*

THIS FOSSILIZED prehistoric forest is one of Arizona's most unusual attractions. Millions of years ago, rivers swept trees downstream into a vast swamp that once covered this whole area. Groundwater transported silica dioxide into downed timber, eventually turning it into the quartz stone logs seen today, with colored crystals preserving the shape and structure of the trees.

Running the entire length of the forest is the famous Painted Desert. This is an area of colored bands of sand and rock that change from blues to reds throughout the day as the shifting light catches the different mineral deposits.

A 28-mile (45-km) scenic road starting at the visitor center travels the length of the park. There are nine overlooks along the way, including Kachina Point, where the Painted Wilderness trailhead is located. A permit is required to camp in the wilderness area. Near the south end of the road is the fine **Rainbow Forest Museum**.

🏛 **Rainbow Forest Museum**
Off Hwy 180 (S entrance). ☎ *(928) 524-3138.* ⬤ *8:15am–5pm daily.* 🏞

Eroded sandstone opening of Window Rock, near Highway 12

Window Rock ❸⁰

🏘 *4,500.* 🚍 🛈 *Hwy 264, (928) 871-6436.*

WINDOW ROCK is the capital of the Navajo Nation, the largest Native American reservation in the Southwest. The town is named for the natural arch found in the sandstone cliffs located about a mile north of the main strip on Highway 12.

The **Navajo Nation Museum** located in Window Rock is one of the largest Native American museums in the country. Opened in 1997, the huge *hogan*-shaped building houses displays that cover the history of the Ancestral Puebloans and the Navajo.

🏛 **Navajo Nation Museum**
Hwy 264 & Post Office Loop Rd, *(928) 871-7941.* ⬤ *8am–5pm Mon, 8am–8pm Tue–Fri, 9am–5pm Sat.*

Hopi Indian Reservation ❸¹

🏘 *10,000.* 🛈 *Hwy 264, Second Mesa, (928) 734-2401.* ⬤ *May–Sep: 6am–9pm daily; Oct–Apr: 7am–8pm daily.*

BELIEVED TO be direct descendants of the Ancestral Puebloans, the Hopi Indians have lived in and cultivated this harsh and barren reservation area for almost a thousand years. They worship through the *kachina*, the living spirits of plants and animals, believed to visit the tribe during the growing season. Most Hopi villages are located on or near one of three mesas (flat-topped elevations), named First, Second, and Third Mesa. Artisans of each mesa specialize in particular crafts.

Visitors can take a guided walking tour of the impressive pueblo, **Walpi**, on the

Historic pueblo town of Walpi on First Mesa at the Hopi Indian Reservation

Ancestral Puebloan ruins of Keet Seel at the Navajo National Monument

First Mesa. Inhabited in the 12th century, it was built to be easily defended against possible Spanish or Navajo attacks. It straddles a dramatic knife-edge of rock, extending from the tip of the First Mesa. In places, Walpi is less than 100 ft (33m) wide with a drop of several hundred feet on both sides. The Walpi tour includes several stops where visitors can purchase *kachina* figurines, distinctive hand-crafted pottery, rugs, and baskets, or sample the Hopi *piki* bread. A wider range of Hopi arts and crafts are available in the galleries and stores of the Second Mesa. The Hopi Cultural Center here has a restaurant and the only hotel for miles around, as well as a museum that has an excellent collection of photographs depicting various aspects of Hopi life.

Kachina doll

On the Third Mesa, Old Oraibi pueblo, thought to have been founded in the 12th century, is fascinating because of claims that it is the oldest continually occupied human settlement in North America.

🏠 **Walpi**
ℹ️ *(928) 737-2262.* 🚶 **Walking Tours** *9:30am–4pm daily.*

Tuba City ⓷②

🏛️ *17,300.* ℹ️ *Tuba City Trading Post, (928) 283-5441.*

NAMED FOR TUUVI, a Hopi Indian who converted to the Mormon faith, Tuba City is best known for the 65-million-year-old dinosaur tracks found just off the main highway, 5 miles (8 km) southwest of the town. This is also the largest community in the western section of the Navajo Reservation and is a good spot from which to explore both the Navajo National Monument and the Hopi Reservation.

Grand Canyon ⓷③

See pp536–9.

Navajo National Monument ⓷④

📞 *(928) 672-2700.* 🕐 *8am–5pm daily.* 🚫 *Jan 1, Thanksgiving, Dec 25.* 🅿️ 🅰️ 🖥️ *www.nps.gov/nava*

ALTHOUGH NAMED because of its location on the Navajo Reservation, this monument is actually known for its Ancestral Puebloan ruins. The most accessible ruin here is the beautifully preserved, 135-room pueblo of Betatakin, which fills a vast, curved niche in the cliffs of Tsegi Canyon. An easy, 1-mile (1.6-km) trail from the visitor center, along piñon pines and juniper trees, leads to an overlook, which provides a captivating view of Betatakin. For a closer look at these ancient houses, visitors can take the daily six-hour hiking tours held from late May to early September.

A more demanding 17-mile (27-km) hike leads to **Keet Seel**, a more impressive ruin. Only a limited number of permits to visit the ruin are issued each day. This hike requires overnight camping at a campsite with the most basic facilities. Keet Seel was a larger and more successful community than Betatakin. Construction began in about 1250, but the site is thought to have been abandoned by 1300.

The Keet Seel ruins at the Navajo National Monument

Grand Canyon ⊛

ONE OF THE WORLD'S GREAT natural wonders, the Grand Canyon is an instantly recognizable symbol of the Southwest. Running through Grand Canyon National Park *(see pp538–9)*, it is 217 miles (349 km) long, about 4 to 18 miles (6 to 29 km) wide, and over 5,000 ft (1,500 m) deep. It was formed over a period of six million years by the Colorado River, whose fast-flowing waters sliced their way through the Colorado Plateau, which includes the gorge, most of northern Arizona, and the Four Corners region. The plateau's geological vagaries have defined the river's course, and exposed vast cliffs are ringed by rocks of different color, variegated hues of limestone, sandstone, and shale. By any standard, the canyon, with its vast scale, is spectacular. But its special beauty is in the ever-shifting patterns of light and shadow and the colors of the rock, bleached white at midday, but bathed in red and ocher at sunset.

Mule Trip Convoy
A mule ride is a popular method of exploring the canyon's narrow trails.

Havasu Canyon
Since 1300 Havasu Canyon has been home to the Havasupai Indians. A population of around 500 Indians lives on the Havasupai Reservation, making a living from the tourist trade.

Grandview Point
At 7,400 ft (2,250 m), this is one of the highest places on the South Rim, the canyon's southern edge. It is one of the stops along the breathtaking Desert View Drive (see p538). The point is thought to be the spot from where the Spaniards had their first glimpse of the canyon in 1540.

North Rim

The North Rim receives roughly one-tenth the number of visitors of the South Rim. While less accessible, it is a more peaceful destination offering a sense of unexplored wilderness. Hikes include the North Kaibab Trail, a steep descent down to Phantom Ranch, the only lodge on the canyon floor.

Bright Angel Trail

Used by both Native Americans and early settlers, the Bright Angel Trail follows a natural route along one of the canyon's enormous fault lines. It is an appealing option for day-hikers; unlike some other trails in the area, it offers plenty of shade and several seasonal water sources.

YAVAPAI POINT AT THE SOUTH RIM

Situated 5 miles (8 km) north of the canyon's South Entrance, along a stretch of the Rim Trail, is Yavapai Point. Its observation station offers superb views, and a viewing panel identifies several of the central canyon's landmarks.

HOW THE CANYON WAS FORMED

While the Colorado River, which changed course four million years ago, accounts for the canyon's depth, its width and formations are the work of even greater forces. Wind rushing through the canyon erodes the limestone and sandstone a few grains at a time, and rain pouring over the rim cuts deep side canyons through the softer rock. Perhaps the greatest force is ice. Water from rain and snowmelt works into cracks in the rock. When frozen, it expands, forcing the rock away from the canyon walls. Soft layers erode quickly into sloped faces, while harder rock resists erosion, leaving sheer vertical faces.

Cracks formed by water erosion

Exploring Grand Canyon National Park

Bell near Hermits Rest

A WORLD HERITAGE SITE, Grand Canyon National Park covers 1,904 sq miles (4,930 sq km), and consists of the canyon itself, which starts where the Paria River empties into the Colorado, and stretches from Lees Ferry to Lake Mead *(see p515)*. The park has two main entrances, on the North and South Rims of the canyon. Its main roads, Hermit Road and Desert View Drive, both accessible from the south entrance, overlook the canyon. Visitors can also enter the park from the north, although this route (Hwy 67) is closed during winter. Walking trails along the North and South Rims offer staggering views but to experience the canyon at its most fascinating, the trails that head down toward the canyon floor should be explored. The Bright Angel Trail on the South Rim and the North Kaibab Trail on the North Rim descend to the canyon floor and are tough hikes involving an overnight stop.

Adobe, Pueblo-style architecture of Hopi House, Grand Canyon Village

🏠 Grand Canyon Village

Grand Canyon National Park.
📞 *(928) 638-7888.* ♿ *partial.*
Grand Canyon Village has its roots in the late 19th century. The extensive building of visitor accommodations started after the Santa Fe Railroad opened a branch line here from Williams in 1901, although some hotels had been built in the late 1890s. The Fred Harvey Company constructed a clutch of well-designed, attractive buildings. The most prominent is the El Tovar Hotel *(see p562).* Opened in 1905, it is named after Spanish explorers who reached the gorge in 1540. The Hopi House also opened in 1905 – a rendition of a traditional Hopi dwelling, where locals could sell their craftwork as souvenirs. It was built by Hopi craftsmen and

designed by Mary E.J. Colter, an ex-schoolteacher and architect, who drew on Southwestern influences, mixing both Native American and Hispanic styles. She is responsible for many of the historic structures that now grace the South Rim, including the 1914 Lookout Studio and Hermits Rest, and the rustic 1922 Phantom Ranch *(see p562)* on the canyon floor.

Today, Grand Canyon Village has a wide range of hotels, restaurants, and stores. It can be surprisingly easy to get lost here since the buildings are spread out and discreetly placed among wooded areas. The village

is the starting point for most of the mule trips through the canyon. It is also the terminus for the Grand Canyon Railway, restored steam trains that make the 64-mile (103-km) journey from Williams.

The South Rim

Most of the Grand Canyon's 4.3 million annual visitors come to the South Rim, since, unlike the North Rim, it is open year-round and is easily accessible along Highway 180/64 from Flagstaff *(see p528)* and Williams. **Hermit Road** and **Desert View Drive** (Hwy 64) start at Grand Canyon Village and encompass a selection of the choicest views of the gorge. Hermit Drive is closed to private vehicles from March to November each year, but Desert View Drive is open all year.

From the village, Hermit Road meanders along the South Rim, extending for 8 miles (13 km). Its first viewpoint is **Trailview Overlook**, which provides an overview of the canyon and the winding course of the Bright Angel Trail. Moving on, **Maricopa Point** offers especially panoramic views of the canyon but not of the Colorado River, which is more apparent from nearby **Hopi Point**. At the end of Hermit Road lies **Hermits Rest**, where a gift shop, decorated in rustic style, is located in yet another Mary Colter-designed building. The longer Desert View Drive runs in the opposite direction, and covers 26 miles (42 km). It winds for 12 miles (20 km) before reaching **Grandview Point**, where the Spaniards are believed to have had their first glimpse of the canyon in

The interior of the Hermits Rest gift store with crafts for sale lining the walls

Desert View's stone Watchtower on Desert View Drive

The numbers of visitors touring Grand Canyon's South Rim increased dramatically in the 1990s, and a summer visit to the canyon became an extremely busy, traffic-congested experience. In 1995, the federal government announced plans to develop a transportation system here, involving a light rail and bus service, as well as extended off-site parking. Decreasing visitor numbers in recent years have prompted a review of these plans.

South Rim entrance to the park

1540. Ten miles (16 km) farther on lie the pueblo remains of Tusayan Ruin, where there is a small museum with exhibits on Ancestral Puebloan life. The road finally ends at the stunning overlook of **Desert View**. The Watchtower here was Colter's most fanciful creation, its upper floor decorated with early 20th-century Hopi murals.

Just east of Grand Canyon Village is **Yavapai Point** from where it is possible to see Phantom Ranch. This is the only roofed accommodation available on the canyon floor, across the Colorado River.

The North Rim
Standing at about 8,000 ft (2,400 m), the North Rim is higher, cooler, and greener than the South Rim, with dense forests of ponderosa pine, aspen, and Douglas fir. Visitors are most likely to spot wildlife on the North Rim. Mule deer, Kaibab squirrel, and wild turkey are among the most common sights. The North Rim is reached via Highway 67, off Highway 89A, ending at **Grand Canyon Lodge** (see p558) where there are visitor services, a campground, a gas station, restaurant, and a general store. Nearby there is a national park information center, which offers maps of the area. The North Rim and all its facilities are closed between October and May, when it is often snowed in. The North Rim is twice as far from the

river as the South Rim, and the canyon really stretches out from the overlooks giving a sense of its 10-mile (16-km) width. There are about 30 miles (45 km) of scenic roads along the North Rim as well as hiking trails to high viewpoints or down to the canyon floor (particularly the North Kaibab Trail that links to the South Rim's Bright Angel Trail).

The picturesque **Cape Royal Drive** starts north of Grand Canyon Lodge and travels 23 miles (37 km) to Cape Royal on the Walhalla Plateau. From here, several famous buttes and peaks can be seen, including Wotans Throne and Vishnu Temple. There are also several short, easy walking trails around Cape Royal, along the top. A 3-mile (5-km) detour leads to **Point Imperial**, the highest point on the canyon rim, while along the way the **Vista Encantada** has delightful views and picnic tables overlooking the gorge.

Mule deer on the canyon's North Rim

The Bright Angel Trail
This is the most popular of all Grand Canyon hiking trails. The Bright Angel trailhead is at Grand Canyon Village on the South Rim. The trail begins near the Kolb Studio at the western end of the village. It then switches dramatically down the side of the canyon for 9 miles (13 km). The trail crosses the river over a suspension bridge, ending a little farther on at Phantom Ranch. There are two rest-houses and a fully equipped camp-ground along the way. It is not advisable to attempt the whole trip in one day. Many walk from the South Rim to one of the rest stops and then return up to the rim. Temperatures at the bottom of the canyon can reach 110°F (43°C) or higher during the summer. Day-hikers should therefore carry a quart (just under a liter) of water per person per hour for summer hiking. Carrying a first-aid kit is also recommended.

Hikers taking a break on the South Rim's Bright Angel Trail

Monument Valley ㉟

FROM SCENIC HIGHWAY 163, which crosses the border of Utah and Arizona, it is possible to see the famous buttes and mesas of Monument Valley. These ancient rocks, soaring upward from a seemingly boundless desert, have come to symbolize the American West, since they have been used as a backdrop for countless movies and TV shows.

The area's visitor center sits within the boundary of Monument Valley Tribal Park, but many of the valley's spectacular rock formations and other sites are found just outside the park boundary.

Guided Tours
A row of kiosks at the visitor center offer Navajo-guided 4WD tours of the valley. The marketing tactics can be aggressive, but the tours offer an excellent way to see places in the park that are otherwise inaccessible.

Three Sisters
One of several distinctive pinnacle rock formations at the valley, the closest view of the Three Sisters can be seen from John Ford's Point, and is one of the most photographed sights here.

Art & Ruins
Petroglyphs such as this deer can be seen on Navajo-guided tours of rock art sites, which are dotted around the valley's ancient ruins.

Left Mitten

MONUMENT VALLEY
Monument Valley is not really a valley. The tops of the mesas mark what was once a flat plain. Millions of years ago, this plain was cracked by upheavals within the earth. The cracks widened and eroded, leaving the formations rising from the desert floor.

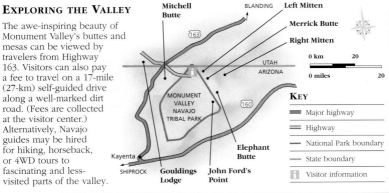

EXPLORING THE VALLEY

The awe-inspiring beauty of Monument Valley's buttes and mesas can be viewed by travelers from Highway 163. Visitors can also pay a fee to travel on a 17-mile (27-km) self-guided drive along a well-marked dirt road. (Fees are collected at the visitor center.) Alternatively, Navajo guides may be hired for hiking, horseback, or 4WD tours to fascinating and less-visited parts of the valley.

Mitchell Butte
BLANDING
Left Mitten
Merrick Butte
Right Mitten
163
UTAH
ARIZONA
0 km   20
0 miles   20
MONUMENT VALLEY NAVAJO TRIBAL PARK
160
Kayenta
SHIPROCK   Gouldings Lodge   John Ford's Point
Elephant Butte

KEY

Major highway

Highway

National Park boundary

State boundary

Visitor information

John Ford's Point

The most popular stop along the valley drive is John Ford's Point, which is said to be the film director's favorite view of the valley. Various stands offer a range of Navajo crafts. A nearby native hogan (Navajo dwelling) serves as a gift shop where Navajo weavers demonstrate their craft.

VISITORS' CHECKLIST

🛈 PO Box 360289, Monument Valley, (435) 727-5870. 🕐 May–Sep: 8am–7pm daily; Oct–Apr: 8am–5pm daily; Thanksgiving: 8am–noon. ● Dec 25. 📷 🛗 visitor center only. 🗎 📷 🍴 ⛺

Right Mitten

Merrick Butte

Navajo Weaver

Navajo women are usually considered to be the finest weavers in the Southwest. One rug can take months to complete and sell for thousands of dollars. Using the natural colors of the land, the weavers often add a "spirit line" to their work to prevent their spirit being "trapped" within the rug.

THE WILD WEST

Romanticized in cowboy movies, the "Wild West" conjures up images of tough men herding cattle across the country before living it up in a saloon. But frontier life was far from romantic. Settlers arriving in this wilderness were caught up in a first-come first-served battle for land and wealth, fighting Native Americans and each other for land. The rugged life of the mining prospectors and ranch cowboys helped to create the idea of the American West. Today, visitors can still see former mining towns such as Bisbee or enjoy re-enacted gunfights on the streets of Tombstone *(see p533)*, the site of one of the Wild West's most famous tales. In the late 19th-century, however, such survival skills as good shooting often co-existed with a kill-or-be-killed ethos. Guided trail rides, offered at many dude ranches, are a great way to explore the contemporary Wild West.

Guided trail rides, conducted to explore the Wild West

Canyon de Chelly National Monument 🕏

Flowering cactus

THE AWESOME thousand-foot cliffs of the Canyon de Chelly boast of a long and eventful history of human habitation. Archaeologists have found evidence of four periods of Native culture, starting with the Basketmaker people around AD 300, followed by the Great Pueblo Builders, who created the cliff dwellings in the 12th century. They were succeeded by the Hopi, who lived here seasonally for around 300 years, taking advantage of the canyon's fertile soil. Today, the canyon is the cultural and geographic heart of the Navajo Nation, where Navajo farmers still live tending the sheep, introduced by the Spanish, and women weave rugs at outdoor looms. Pronounced "d'Shay," de Chelly is a Spanish corruption of the Native name *tsegi*, meaning rock canyon.

Yucca House Ruin
Perched on the mesa top, this ruin of an Ancestral Puebloan house sits in a rock hollow, precariously overhanging a sheer drop to the valley floor.

Canyon Vegetation
Within the canyon, cottonwood and oak trees line the river washes; the land itself is a fertile oasis of meadows, alfalfa and corn fields, and fruit orchards.

Stone and adobe cliff dwellings were home to the Ancestral Puebloans from the 12th to the 14th centuries and were built to face south toward the sun, with cooler areas within.

Navajo Fortress
This imposing rock tower was the site of a three-month siege in 1863, when a group of Navajos reached the summit via pole ladders. They were trying to escape a US government patrol led by Kit Carson (see p544) to settle the Navajo raids. Carson's persistence finally led them to surrender and they were marched to a camp in New Mexico.

Hiking in the Canyon
Canyon de Chelly is a popular destination for hikers, but apart from the White House Ruins Trail, visitors can enter the canyons only with a Navajo guide.

The pale walls of the White House cliff drop 550 ft (160 m) to the canyon floor.

***Hogan* Interior**
The hogan is the center of Navajo family life. Made of horizontal logs, a smoke hole in the center provides contact with the sky, while the dirt floor gives contact with the earth. A door faces east to greet the rising sun.

WHITE HOUSE RUINS

This group of rooms, tucked into a tiny hollow in the cliff, seem barely touched by time. The dwellings were originally situated above a larger pueblo, much of which has now disappeared. It is the only site within the canyon that can be visited without a Navajo guide, reached via a steep 2.5-mile (5-km) round-trip trail that winds to the canyon floor and offers magnificent views.

MASSACRE CAVE

The canyon's darkest hour was in 1805, when a Spanish force under Lieutenant Antonio Narbona entered the area. The Spanish wanted to subdue the Navajo, claiming they were raiding their settlements. While some Navajo fled by climbing to the canyon rim, others took refuge in a cave high in the cliffs. The Spanish fired into the cave, and Narbona boasted that he had killed 115 Navajo including 90 warriors. Navajo accounts are different, claiming that most of the warriors were absent (probably hunting) and those killed were mostly women, children, and the elderly. The only Spanish fatality came when a Spaniard attempting to climb into the cave was attacked by a Navajo woman and both plunged over the cliff, gaining the Navajo name "Two Fell Over." The Anglo name is "Massacre Cave."

Pictograph on a canyon wall showing invading Spanish soldiers

New Mexico

NEW MEXICO'S RICH CULTURAL HERITAGE and unique mix of Native American, Hispanic, and Anglo American people make it a fascinating place to visit. The forested peaks of the Rocky Mountains offer ski resorts in winter and cool retreats in summer. Northern New Mexico, with its soft colors and vivid desert landscapes, has attracted generations of artists to the creative centers of Santa Fe and Taos. In the vast, wild south visitors can explore ancient Native ruins at Bandelier National Monument and the fascinating cave systems of Carlsbad Caverns.

Fajada Butte in Chaco Culture National Historical Park

Chaco Culture National Historical Park 🟢

3 miles (5 km) SE of Nageezi off US 550. ⓘ (505) 786-7014 (ext 221). ○ May–Sep: 8am–6pm daily; Sep–May: 8am–5pm daily. ● public hols. 🈂 ♿ ✔ Ⓦ www.nps.gov/chcu

ONE OF THE Southwest's most impressive cultural sites, Chaco Canyon reflects the sophistication of the Ancestral Puebloan civilization that existed here. With its six "great houses" (pueblos containing hundreds of rooms) and many lesser sites, the canyon was once the political, religious, and cultural center for settlements that spread across much of the Four Corners.

Visitors can access the site via a 16-mile (26-km) dirt road that is affected by flash floods in wet weather. A paved loop road in the site passes several of Chaco's highlights. The major stop is **Pueblo Bonito**, the largest of the "great houses," a D-shaped, four-story structure with more than 600 rooms, and 40 *kivas*, round, pit-like rooms used for religious

ceremonies. Begun around AD 850, it was built in stages over the course of 300 years. **Casa Riconada**, the largest religious chamber at Chaco, measuring 62 ft (19m) in diameter, lies to the southeast.

A short trail from Pueblo Bonito leads to another great house, **Chetro Ketl**, covering 3 acres (2 ha). The masonry used to build the later portions of this structure is among the most sophisticated found in any Ancestral Puebloan site. A two-hour hike northward leads to **Pueblo Alto**, built atop the mesa at the junction of many ancient Chacoan roads.

Finely wrought stonework at Chaco Canyon

Taos 🟢

🏨 6,000. 🚌 Greyhound, Taos Bus Center, Hwy 68. ⓘ 1139 Paseo del Pueblo Sur (505) 758-3873, (800) 732-8267.

THE CITY OF TAOS, home to Indians for around 1,000 years, is now a vibrant artistic center. In 1898, artists Ernest Blumenschein and Bert Phillips stopped here to repair a wagon wheel and never left. In 1915 they established the Taos Society of Artists, which continues to promote the work of local artists. Some of these are exhibited at the **Harwood Foundation Museum**, located in a tranquil, 19th-century adobe compound. More works by the society's artists are housed in the **Blumenschein Home and Museum**, nearby.

The tree-lined, old Spanish **Plaza** at the heart of Taos makes for a pleasant stroll. To its east is the **Kit Carson Home and Museum**. A fur trapper and soldier, Carson's (1809–68) remarkable life is the focus of this museum.

A few miles north of the town center, Taos' main street, Paseo del Pueblo Norte, leads to the **Millicent Roger Museum**, with its brilliant collection of Native arts and crafts, and black-on-black pottery of Puebloan artist Maria Martinez. This road leads to the dramatic Rio Grande Gorge Bridge, the country's second-highest suspension bridge, built in 1965. It offers awesome views of the gorge and the surrounding stark, sweeping plateau.

Taos Pueblo is north of the city. It features two multistory communal adobe houses still inhabited by villagers, making it one of the oldest communities in the country.

The Hacienda Martinez (*see p551*) at **Rancho de Taos**, south of the city, is a well-preserved Spanish Colonial house with thick adobe walls and heavy gates. The 18th-century adobe church of San Francisco de Asis, was often painted by Georgia O'Keeffe, the most distinguished member of the Taos Society of Artists.

Northern Pueblos Tour [39]

Redware pottery

THE FERTILE VALLEY of the Rio Grande between Santa Fe and Taos is home to eight pueblos of the 19 Native American pueblos in New Mexico. Although geographically close, each pueblo has its own government and traditions, and many offer attractions to visitors. Nambe gives stunning views of the surrounding mountains, mesas, and high desert. San Idelfonso is famous for its fine pottery, and other villages produce handcrafted jewelry or rugs.

Tips for Drivers

Starting point: *Tesuque Pueblo, N of Santa Fe on Hwy 84.*
Length: *45 miles (70 km). Local roads leading to pueblos are often dirt tracks, so allow extra time.*
Note: *Visitors are welcome, but respect their laws & etiquette* (see p554). ℹ *Indian Pueblo Cultural Center, (505) 843-7270.*
[W] www.indianpueblo.org

Santa Clara Pueblo [5]
This small pueblo is known for its artisans and their work. As in many pueblos, it contains a number of craft shops and small studios, often run by the Native artisans themselves.

Puye Cliff Dwellings [6]
Now deserted, this site contains over 700 rooms, complete with stone carvings, which were home to Native peoples until 1500.

San Juan Pueblo [7]
Declared the first capital of New Mexico in 1598, this village is now a center for the visual arts and has an arts cooperative.

San Ildefonso Pueblo [4]
Occupied since AD 1300, this pueblo is best known for its etched black pottery, the proceeds of which saved its people from the Depression of the 1930s.

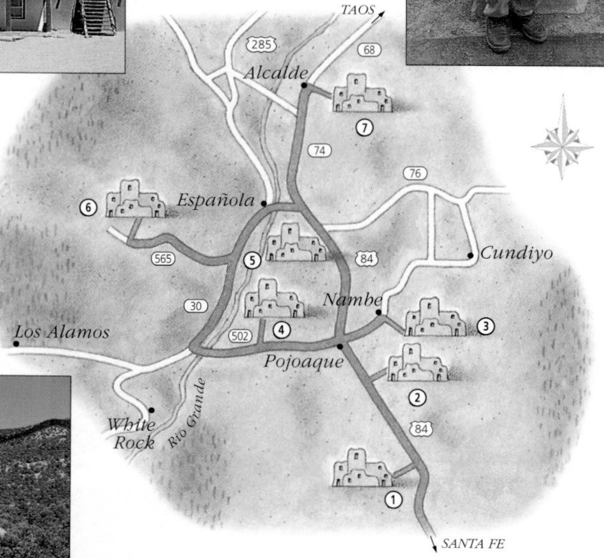
TAOS
285
68
Alcalde
7
74
76
6
Española
565
5
84
Cundiyo
30
Nambe
3
4
502
Los Alamos
Pojoaque
2
White Rock
Rio Grande
84
1
SANTA FE

Nambe Pueblo [3]
Set in a beautiful fertile valley, this village is bordered by a lakeside hiking trail with waterfall views and a buffalo ranch.

Pojoaque Pueblo [2]
The new Peoh Cultural Center and Museum here is an excellent introduction to the pueblo way of life in these small communities.

Tesuque Pueblo [1]
The Tewa people here have concentrated on farming and pottery-making for centuries.

0 km 10
0 miles 10

Key

Tour route
Other road

Santa Fe ❹

THE OLDEST STATE CAPITAL in North America, Santa Fe was founded by the Spanish conquistador Don Pedro de Peralta, who established a colony here in 1610. This colony was abandoned in 1680 after the Pueblo Revolt, but was later recaptured. When Mexico gained independence in 1821, traders and settlers from Missouri poured into the area via the Santa Fe Trail. Perched on a high plateau, this beautiful city is surrounded by mountains. Its heart, since its founding, is the central Plaza, and there is no better place to begin exploring the city. Today, it houses a Native American market under the portal of the Palace of the Governors, and the square is lined with shops, cafés, and several galleries.

★ Museum of Fine Arts
Built of adobe in 1917, this museum focuses on the paintings and sculpture of Southwestern artists.

★ Palace of the Governors
This single-story adobe building, built in 1600, was the seat of regional government for 300 years. Now part of the Museum of New Mexico, it houses displays on the city's history.

SHERIDAN

LINCOLN

PALACE AVENUE

BURRO ALLEY

W SAN FRANCISCO STREET

PLAZA

DON GASPAR AVENUE

GALISTEO STREET

WATER STREET

```
0 meters        100
0 yards         100
```

KEY

--- Suggested route

Original Trading Post sells Hispanic art, antiques, and Native American crafts.

STAR SIGHTS
★ **Museum of Fine Arts**
★ **Palace of the Governors**

The Plaza
The obelisk at the center of this main square commemorates Santa Fe's war veterans. The Plaza is lined with old Colonial buildings, including the Palace of Governors.

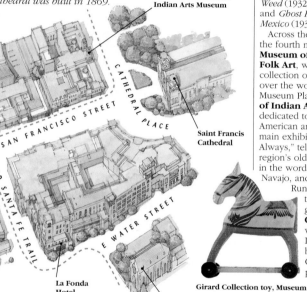

Saint Francis Cathedral
This colorful, carved wooden statue of the Virgin stands in a side chapel belonging to the original 17th-century church on which the present cathedral was built in 1869.

Institute of American
Indian Arts Museum

Saint Francis
Cathedral

La Fonda
Hotel

Girard Collection toy, Museum
of International Folk Art

Loretto Chapel
Built in Gothic style by French architects in the 1870s, the Loretto Chapel was modeled on the Sainte-Chappelle in Paris. Its elegant spiral staircase has no nails or center support, and its perfect craftsmanship is all that keeps it aloft.

Exploring Santa Fe

This city's rich history and beautiful architecture have made it one of the country's most popular destinations. It is famous for its adobe buildings, art galleries, and the Museum of New Mexico's four museums. In addition to the Palace of the Governors and Museum of Fine Arts, there is the **Georgia O'Keeffe Museum**, northwest of the Plaza. This has the world's largest collection of O'Keeffe's works, including several of her best-loved paintings such as *Jimson Weed* (1932), *Purple Hills II*, and *Ghost Ranch, New Mexico* (1934).

Across the Santa Fe River is the fourth museum, the **Museum of International Folk Art**, with its stunning collection of folk art from all over the world. Alongside, on Museum Plaza, the **Museum of Indian Art and Culture** is dedicated to traditional Native American arts and culture. Its main exhibit, "Here, Now and Always," tells the story of the region's oldest communities, in the words of Pueblo, Navajo, and Apache people.

Running parallel to the river, the gallery-lined **Canyon Road** was originally an Indian track between the Rio Grande and Pecos pueblo. To its west, on the Old Santa Fe Trail, is the **San Miguel Mission**, built in 1610. To the northwest, the 1795 **Santuario de Guadelupe**, dedicated to the Virgin of Guadelupe, patron saint of Mexican and Pueblo peoples, marked the end of Camino Real, the main trade route from Mexico. About 15 miles (24 km) south of Santa Fe, **El Rancho de las Golondrinas**, now a living history museum, was a historic stopping-off point on the Camino Real.

🏛 Museum of International Folk Art
706 Camino Lejo. **(** (505) 476-1200. **○** 10am–5pm Tue–Sun. **●** public hols. ⚑ ♿ 🔲 🚻

Albuquerque ⓐ

🏛 580,000. ✈ 🚉 🚌 🛈 401 2nd St NW, (505) 842-9918, (800) 284-2283.

Occupied by Native peoples from 1100 to 1300, Albuquerque's first inhabitants were a small group of Colonial pioneers who settled by the Rio Grande in the wake of late 16th-century Spanish explorers. In 1706, a band of 18 families won formal approval for their town from the Spanish crown by naming the city after the Spanish Duke of Alburquerque, (the first "r" in the name was later dropped). Albuquerque's Old Town, today, still has many original adobe buildings dating from the 1790s, while

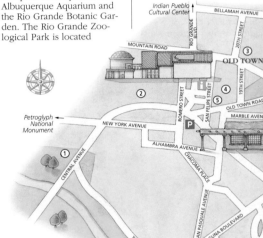

Modern sculpture

downtown, to its east, is much more contemporary. Many of the city's shops, museums, and high-tech industries are located here.

Exploring Albuquerque
Dominating the historic Old Town is the Plaza, which was the center of Albuquerque for over 200 years. Today, this charming square is a pleasant open space where both locals and visitors relax on benches, surrounded by lovely adobe buildings. Opposite is the imposing **San Felipe de Neri Church**. Completed in 1793, this was the city's first civic structure. Despite many renovations, the church retains its original adobe walls. The nearby streets are lined with museums, colorful craft shops, and restaurants,

such as the Church Street Café *(see p563)*. Said to occupy the oldest house in the city, this café serves excellent New Mexican cuisine. Beyond is a craft store, the Agape Pueblo Pottery, which stocks a wide selection of hand-crafted pueblo pottery.

🦎 Albuquerque BioPark
2601 Central Ave NW. ☎ (505) 764-6200. ◑ 9am–5pm daily. ● Thanksgiving, Dec 25. 🎫 &

The park encompasses the Albuquerque Aquarium and the Rio Grande Botanic Garden. The Rio Grande Zoological Park is located

San Felipe de Neri Church, at the north end of Old Town Plaza

nearby. The botanic garden occupies 10 acres (4 ha) of woodland along the Rio Grande and has a wide variety of rare plants and gardens.

The aquarium focuses on the marine life of the Rio Grande, one of America's great rivers, and features a fascinating walk-through eel cave containing moray eels. There is also an impressive 285,000-gallon (1,078,842-liter), floor-to-ceiling shark tank.

🏛 Turquoise Museum
2107 Central Ave NW. ☎ (505) 247-8650. ◑ 9:30am–5pm Mon–Sat. ● Thanksgiving, Dec 25. 🎫 &

The fascinating displays in this museum focus on consumer education, helping visitors to judge the quality of turquoise gemstones. The entrance is a replica mine tunnel that leads to the "vault," which contains an unsurpassed collection of rare and varied turquoise specimens from around the world.

Glasshouse at Rio Grande Botanic Garden, Albuquerque BioPark

New Mexico Museum of Natural History & Science

1801 Mountain Rd NW. **(** *(505) 841-2800.* ☐ *9am–5pm daily.* ● *Jan & Sep: Mon, public hols.* 🖼 ⚫ W *www.nmnaturalhistory.org*

This entertaining museum has a series of interactive exhibits. Visitors can stand inside a simulated live volcano or explore an ice cave. The "Evolator" is a ride through 38 million years of the region's evolution using the latest video technology. Replica dinosaurs, a state-of-the-art planetarium, and a large-screen film theater are all highly popular with children.

Albuquerque Museum of Art & History

2000 Mountain Rd NW. **(** *(505) 242-4600.* ☐ *9am–5pm Tue–Sun.* ● *public hols.* ⚫ W *www. cabq.gov/museum*

This excellent museum depicts four centuries of history in the middle of Rio Grande Valley. The well-chosen artifacts are expertly arranged for maximum impact. Exhibits focus on the Spanish Colonial period (1598–1821) and include a reconstructed 18th-century house and chapel. From March to December, the museum organizes walking tours of the Old Town.

Colorful tiles decorating the Art Deco-style façade of the KiMo Theater

American International Rattlesnake Museum

202 San Felipe Ave N. **(** *(505) 242-6569.* ☐ *10am–6pm daily.* ● *public hols.* ⚫ W *www.rattlesnakes.com*

This animal conservation museum explains the life cycles and ecological importance of some of Earth's most misunderstood creatures. It contains the world's largest collection of live rattlesnakes, including natives of North, Central, and South America. The snakes are displayed in glass tanks that simulate their natural habitat as closely as possible and are accompanied by explanatory notices suitable for both adults and children. The museum also features other much-maligned venomous animals such as tarantulas and the Gila monster lizard.

KiMo Theater

423 Central Ave NW. **(** *(505) 848-1370.* ☐ *call for program.* 🖼 ⚫ W *www.cabq.gov/rimo*

Built in 1927, the KiMo Theater was one of many entertainment venues constructed in the city during the 1920s and 30s. The building's distinctive design was inspired by that of the nearby Native American pueblos and created a fusion of Pueblo Revival and Art Deco styles. Today, the KiMo Theater presents an eclectic range of musical and theatrical performances.

Rio Grande Zoological Park

903, 10th St SW **(** *(505) 764-6200.* ☐ *9am–5pm daily.* ● *Thanksgiving, Dec 25.* 🖼 ⚫

The Rio Grande Zoo forms part of the Albuquerque Bio-Park. The zoo is noted for its imaginative layout with enclosures designed to simulate the animals' natural habitats, including the African savanna. Among the most popular species here are lowland gorillas and white Bengal tigers.

(Map labels)

MARQUETTE AVENUE
TIJERAS AVENUE
CENTRAL AVENUE (ROUTE 66)
PARK AVENUE
GOLD STREET
SILVER ST.
LEAD AVENUE
COAL AVENUE
IRON STREET
STOVER AVENUE
ATLANTIC DRIVE
DOWNTOWN
10TH STREET
8TH STREET
7TH STREET
6TH STREET
COPPER AVENUE
CENTRAL AVENUE (ROUTE 66)
GOLD STREET
SILVER ST.
LEAD AVENUE
COAL AVENUE
IRON STREET

University of New Mexico

National Atomic Museum

0 meters 500
0 yards 500

SIGHTS AT A GLANCE

KEY

🚌 Bus station

P Parking

ℹ Visitor information

Indian Pueblo Cultural Center courtyard

Albuquerque: Farther Afield

New Mexico's largest city, Albuquerque, has grown to fill the valley that stretches westward from the foothills of the Manzano and Sandia Mountains and across the banks of the Rio Grande. The coming of the railroad during the 1880s brought increasing numbers of settlers and greater prosperity. Today, the best way to explore the city is by car. The major sights, including the historic Old Town *(see p548)*, are all located near highway exits. Two Interstate Highways cross the center of the city. I-25 travels north to south across downtown, while I-40 cuts west to east. At the eastern end of this lies the University of New Mexico campus with its museums and galleries.

⬛ Indian Pueblo Cultural Center

2401 12th St NW. **⬛** *(505) 843-7270.* ⬛ ⬛ *daily.* ⬛ *Jan 1, Thanksgiving, Dec 25.* ⬛ ⬛ ⬛ ⬛ ⬛
⬛ www.indianpueblo.org
This impressive museum and cultural center is run by the 19 Indian pueblos that lie along the Rio Grande around Albuquerque and Santa Fe. It traces the Puebloan peoples' complex history and varied culture through their oral history and presents it from their viewpoint.

The building is designed to resemble the layout of a pueblo dwelling, and is set around the Puebloan Central Courtyard. This large courtyard, with its red adobe walls decorated with murals and

hung chilies, emulates the layout of a Pueblo dwelling. Each weekend exuberant dance performances are held here. The center also contains a restaurant serving Pueblo Indian cooking, and an excellent group of gift shops offering high-quality pottery, jewelry, and other crafts from each pueblo.

⬛ University of New Mexico & Art Museum

ℹ *1700 Las Lomas Rd NE, (505) 277-1989.* **⬛** www.unm.edu **University Art Museum ⬛** *(505) 277-4001.* ⬛ *9am–4pm Tue–Fri, 11am–4pm Sat, 1–4pm Sun.* ⬛ *Mon, Sat.*
⬛ Maxwell Museum of Anthropology ⬛ *(505) 277-5963.* ⬛ *9am–4pm Tue–Fri, 10am–4pm Sat.* ⬛ *Mon, Sun.*
The campus of New Mexico's largest university (UNM) is known for its Pueblo Revival-style architecture and its museums. The
University Art Museum has one of the state's largest fine arts collection, including paintings and sculpture by Old Masters, and other works from the 17th to the 20th centuries.

The **Maxwell Museum of Anthropology**, one of the finest of its kind in the US, emphasizes the culture of the Southwest, with an important collection of art and artifacts. The museum also has traveling exhibits on regional and international themes, as well as a permanent exhibition entitled "Ancestors," which traces human development.

Horse at Museum of Anthropology, UNM

⬛ National Atomic Museum

1905 Mountain Rd NW. **⬛** *(505) 245-2137.* ⬛ *daily.* ⬛ *public hols.*
⬛ ⬛ **⬛** www.atomicmuseum.com
This museum recently relocated from Kirkland Air Force Base to near Old Town Albuquerque. Its displays are devoted to the history of nuclear weapons and atomic energy in the US, from the time when Los Alamos was chosen as the location of the Manhattan Project *(see p507)*. This top-secret project resulted in the world's first nuclear explosion in 1945.

Artifacts range from Einstein's letter to President Roosevelt suggesting the possibility of an atom bomb to the casings of bombs themselves. There are replicas of Little Boy and Fat Man, the bombs dropped on Hiroshima and Nagasaki in 1945.

⬛ Petroglyph National Monument

ℹ *4735 Unser Blvd NW, (505) 899-0205.* ⬛ *8am–5pm daily.*
⬛ *public hols.* ⬛ ⬛ *limited.*
⬛ www.nps.gov/petr
This site, on the western outskirts of Albuquerque, was established in 1990 to preserve nearly 20,000 images carved into rock along the 17-mile (27-km) West Mesa escarpment. The earliest date back to 1,000 BC, but the most prolific period is thought to be between 1300 and 1680.

The pictures range from human figures such as musicians and dancers to animals, including snakes, birds, and insects. Spirals and other geometric symbols are common, as are hands, feet, and animal tracks. The meanings of some petroglyphs have been lost over time, but others have great cultural significance to today's Puebloan population.

Hundreds of petroglyphs are accessible along Boca Negra Canyon, 2 miles (3 km) north of the park visitor center, where three trails wind past them. Visitors should not touch the petroglyphs; they are easily damaged.

Hispanic Culture in New Mexico

THE HEART OF Hispanic culture in the Southwest is found in New Mexico. Here, the Hispanic population, descendants of the original Spanish colonizers of the 16th century, outnumbers that of the Anglo-Americans. The Spanish introduced sheep and horses to the region, as well as bringing Catholicism with its saints' festivals and colorful church decorations.

Chili *ristras*, garlands of dried red chilies

Centuries of mixing with both the Southwest's Native and Anglo cultures have also influenced every aspect of modern Hispanic society, from language and cooking to festivals and the arts. Contemporary New Mexican residents bear the Hispanic surnames of their ancestors, and speak English with a Spanish accent. Even English speakers pepper their speech with Spanish terms.

SPANISH INFLUENCE

The restored El Rancho de las Golondrinas *(see p547)* is today a living museum, centered on the hacienda, pioneered in the Southwest by Spanish colonists. In a hacienda, a large number of rooms (approximately 20) would be set around one or two courtyards, reflecting the extended family style of living favored by the Spanish.

Wells were located in the middle of the main courtyard to be easily accessible.

Adobe beehive ovens *(bornos)* were introduced by the Spanish for baking bread. They were originally of Moorish design.

Hacienda Martínez (see p544) *was built south of Taos in 1804 by Don Antonio Martínez, an early mayor of the town. It is one of the few Spanish haciendas to be preserved in more or less its original form. Today, it is open to visitors who can watch local artisans demonstrating a variety of traditional folk arts.*

Navajo rug

Carved wooden *bulto* of St. Joseph

CRAFTS

Navajo rugs are considered a Native handicraft, but their designs also show signs of Moorish patterns brought by colonizers from Spain. Other folk art forms include artistic pottery, intricate silverwork, and carved wooden figures known as *bultos*, which combine religious beliefs and artistic expression.

Corn, the region's staple food since pre-Columbian times, is used to make tortilla chips, which are served with guacamole (avocado dip).

Roswell ④

🏠 50,000. ℹ️ 426 N Main St, (505) 624-7704. 🕐 8:30am–5:30pm Mon–Fri, 10am–3pm Sat & Sun. 🌐 www.roswellcvb.com

THIS SMALL ranching town is a byword for aliens and UFOs since the night of July 4, 1947, when an unidentified airborne object crashlanded here. Jim Ragsdale, camping nearby, later claimed in 1995 to have seen a flash and a craft, hurtling through the trees and the bodies of four "little people," with skin like snakeskin. The US Air Force issued a statement that a flying saucer had been recovered, and despite a denial later on, the story caught people's imagination.

Witnesses were allegedly sworn to secrecy, fueling rumors of a cover-up and alien conspiracy theories to this day. The **International UFO Museum and Research Center** features a collection of newspaper clippings and photographs of the crash site, and a film with over 400 interviews of various people connected to the incident.

Roswell's Alien Zone symbol

Roswell's **Museum and Art Center** houses a large collection of artifacts on the history of the American West. The fascinating Robert H. Goddard Collection details 11 years of experiments by the famous rocket scientist.

Limestone columns in the Big Room at Carlsbad Caverns

Carlsbad Caverns National Park ④

3225 National Parks Hwy, Carlsbad. ✈️ to Carlsbad. 🚌 to White's City. ☎️ (505) 785-2232, (800) 967-2283 (tour reservations). 🕐 May–Aug: 8:30am– 5pm daily; Sep–mid-May: 8:30am–3:30pm (Natural Entrance). Call for last entry times. ● Dec 25. 📷 ♿ partial. 🌐 www.nps.gov/cave

LOCATED IN THE state's remote southeastern corner, this park protects one of the world's largest cave systems. Geological forces carved out this complex of chambers, and their decorations began to be formed around 500,000 years ago when dripping water deposited drops of the crystalized mineral calcite. Native pictographs near the Natural Entrance indicate that they had been visited by Native peoples, but it was cowboy Jim White who brought them to national attention in 1901. Concrete trails and electric lights have been laid out through this underground gallery of limestone caves. From the visitor center, elevators drop 750 ft (229 m) down to the **Big Room**. This space can also be reached via the **Natural Entrance Route**, which involves a half-hour walk over a steep, paved trail.

A self-guided tour leads to the Big Room, 25 stories high and 8.2 acres (3.3 ha) in area, festooned with stalagmites, stalactites, and flowstone formations. The adjoining ranger-led **King's Palace Tour** takes in the deepest cave open to the public, 830 ft (250 m) below ground. To its right, a paved section serves as the popular **Underground Lunchroom**, a diner and souvenir shop.

The caverns' recesses are the summer abode of almost a million free-tailed bats. They emerge at dusk to cross the desert in search of food.

White Sands National Monument ④

☎️ (505) 679-2599. 🕐 daily. ● Dec 25. 📷 ♿ 🌐 www.nps.gov/whsa

THE GLISTENING dunes of the White Sands National Monument rise up from the Tularosa Basin at the northern end of the Chihuahuan Desert. It is the world's largest gypsum

---

DESERT FLORA AND FAUNA

Desert scorpion

Most of the Southwest is covered by four deserts, yet it is not an arid wasteland. The Sonoran Desert, with its rich array of flora and fauna, is famed for its saguaro cactus. The climatic extremes of the Chihuahuan Desert support hardy agaves and coyotes. The cooler Great Basin is home to many grasses and desert animals. The winter rain in the Mojave Desert results in a spectacular display of wildflowers in spring.

Prickly pear cacti *flower in spring and are among the largest of the many types of cacti that flourish in the Sonoran Desert.*

Bighorn sheep *are shy, elusive creatures and are not easily spotted. Now a protected species, they are being gradually reintroduced throughout the desert areas.*

Soaptree yucca plant in the White Sands National Monument

dune field, covering around 300 sq miles (800 sq km). Gypsum is a water soluble mineral, rarely found as sand. But here, with no drainage outlet to the sea, the sediment washed by the rain into the basin becomes trapped. As the rain evaporates, dry lakes form and strong winds blow the gypsum up into the vast fields of rippling dunes.

Visitors can explore White Sands by car on the Dunes Drive, a 16-mile (26-km) loop. Four clearly marked trails lead from points along the way, including the wheelchair-accessible Interdune Boardwalk. Year-round ranger-led walks introduce visitors to the dunes' flora and fauna. Only plants that grow quickly enough not to be buried survive, such as the hardy soaptree yucca. Most of the animals are nocturnal and include foxes, coyotes, and porcupines.

The park is surrounded by the White Sands Missile Range, a military testing site. For safety, the park and the road leading to it (Hwy 70) may close for up to two hours when testing is underway. The **White Sands Missile Range Museum** displays many of the missiles tested here, as well as the V-2 rockets used in World War II.

Gila Cliff Dwellings National Monument [45]

☎ *(505) 536-9461.* 🕒 *late May–early Sep: 8am–6pm daily; mid-Sep–mid-May: 9am–4pm daily.* ⛔ *Jan 1, Dec 25.* ♿

THE GILA (pronounced hee-la) Cliff Dwellings are one of the most remote archaeological sites in the Southwest, situated among the piñon, juniper, and ponderosa evergreens of the Gila National Forest. The dwellings occupy five natural caves in the side of a sandstone bluff high above the Gila River.

Hunter-gatherers and farmers called the Tularosa Mogollon established their 40-room village here in the late 13th century. The Mimbres Mogollon people, famous for their abstract black-and-white pottery designs on hand-coiled earthenware, also lived in this area. The cliff dwellers hunted the local wildlife, including whitetail and mule deer. They probably farmed the fields alongside the Gila River, growing corn and squash. A granary still holds a dessicated reserve of tiny corn. The ruins are accessed by a 1-mile (1.6-km) round-trip hike from the footbridge crossing the Gila River's West Fork. Allow two hours to navigate the 40-mile (64-km) road to the site from Silver City as it winds and climbs through the mountains and canyons of the forest.

The Joshua tree *was named by Mormons who saw the upraised arms of Joshua in its branches.*

Yucca plants *have been gathered for centuries and have many uses: their fruit can be eaten, and the roots make shampoo.*

The javelina *is a strange pig-like mammal that wanders the Chihuahuan and Sonoran Deserts in small packs.*

Golden eagles *can be seen high in the sky in daytime as they hunt for prey across the Great Basin Desert.*

Practical Information

DOTTED WITH DRAMATIC rock formations, canyons, ancient sites, and wild deserts, the Southwest offers visitors a range of outdoor pleasures. The cities feature superb museums, good dining, and accommodations, along with a laid-back culture. A major draw for visitors are the casinos of Las Vegas. The Southwest is a year-round destination. The high-lying areas of Arizona, New Mexico, and Utah have cold, snowy winters, making them popular for skiing, while the states' southern areas offer warm and sunny winters. But the less-crowded and milder spring and fall are the ideal seasons to visit.

TOURIST INFORMATION

EACH STATE and major towns and cities have departments of tourism. Many of the Southwest's attractions on Indian reservation lands are managed by Native American tribal councils. For advice on these contact the local **Bureau of Indian Affairs** or the **Navajo Tourism Department**.

PERSONAL SECURITY

MOST TOURIST AREAS in the Southwest are friendly and unthreatening, but it is wise to be cautious. Find out which parts of town are unsafe at night. Never carry too much cash, and lock your valuables in the hotel safe.

NATURAL HAZARDS

RAPID WEATHER changes in the Southwest often present dangerous situations. In parts of southern Utah and Arizona, sudden summer storms can cause flash floods. Visitors often underestimate the dry heat of the region's summers. Hikers must carry at least a gallon (4 liters) of drinking water per person for each day of walking.

The Southwest's wilderness harbors venomous creatures such as scorpions, snakes, and the Gila monster lizard; but it is unlikely you will be bitten if you avoid their habitats. Insect bites may hurt but are rarely fatal to adults. But, if bitten, seek medical help.

GETTING AROUND

THOUGH SLOWER than car and plane travel, trains and buses are enjoyable means of exploring the region. Visitors can take special railroad trips to enjoy some of the Southwest's most delightful scenery. The Grand Canyon Railway's diesel and steam rail trips from Williams to Grand Canyon feature packages that include Western entertainments.

Long-distance buses are the least expensive mode of travel. A bus tour is often the most convenient way of seeing both major city sights and some of the more remote scenery of the Southwest. In major cities, local bus routes cover most attractions. Taxis are also an efficient way of traveling around cities.

DRIVING IN THE SOUTHWEST

A CAR IS OFTEN the only means of reaching remote areas. There are car rental agencies all over the region, but it is best to arrange a fly-drive deal for cities such as Las Vegas. Pay attention to road signs especially in remote areas where they may issue warnings about local hazards. Check your route to see if a Four-Wheel Drive (4WD) vehicle is required. Most backcountry areas now have roads that can carry conventional cars, but a 4WD is essential in some wild areas. When traveling between remote destinations, inform someone of your plans. Be wary of seasonal dangers such as flash floods in Utah's canyonlands. Carry plenty of food and water, and a cell phone as a precaution. If your vehicle breaks down, stay with it since it offers protection from the elements, and telephone for help.

ETIQUETTE

DRESS IN THE Southwest is informal, practical, and dependent on the climate. Some of the region's most famous sights are located on reservation land. Visitors are welcome but must be sensitive as to what may cause offense. It is illegal to bring alcohol onto reservations – even a bottle visible in a locked car will land you in trouble. Ask before photographing anything, especially ceremonial dances or Native homes, and bear in mind that a fee may be requested. Do not wander off marked trails, as this is forbidden.

THE CLIMATE OF THE SOUTHWEST

The weather in this region ranges from the heat of the desert to the ice and snow of the mountains. Temperatures usually vary with altitude. As a result the higher elevations in the north, especially Utah, northern Arizona, and New Mexico, experience cold, snowy winters. The southern areas, on the other hand, have mild, sunny winters and hot, dry summers. Summer temperatures in the desert often reach more than 100°F (38°C), but can drop to almost 30°F (10°C) after sunset. Except for violent summer storms, rainfall is scarce in the Southwest.

LAS VEGAS

°F/C	Apr	Jul	Oct	Jan
	81/27	103/40	84/29	
32°F 0°C	45/7	68/20	47/8	60/16
				29/–2
	26 days	27 days	26 days	24 days
	0.3 in	0.5 in	0.3 in	0.7 in
month	Apr	Jul	Oct	Jan

OUTDOOR ACTIVITIES

WITH THOUSANDS of miles of rock canyons, spectacular deserts, and snow-capped peaks, the Southwest is a magnet for climbers, hikers, mountain bikers, 4WD drivers, and skiers. All national parks have well-marked trails and ranger-led hikes, focusing on the local flora, fauna, and geology.

Utah considers itself the world's mountain bike capital, and Moab is a pilgrimage site for such bikers. **Poison Spider Bicycles** sells and repairs bikes as well as runs Nichols Tours, which leads groups through wilderness areas.

The Green, San Juan, and Colorado Rivers are ideal for whitewater rafting. A thrilling 12–20 day rafting trip along the Colorado River through the Grand Canyon is offered by many outfitters, including **Canyon Explorations**. Water sports, such as powerboating, jetskiing, and fishing, are popular in the artificial lakes.

Air tours are a good option for time-restricted travelers who wish to see the remote attractions. **Slickrock Air Guides of Moab** offer three-hour tours that cover Canyon-lands, Lake Powell, Capitol Reef National Park, and the Grand Canyon's North Rim. However, helicopter tours of the Grand Canyon have a reputation for bad safety.

Arizona's 275 golf courses make the Southwest a golfer's paradise. Scottsdale, considered America's premier golf spot, is famous for its **Boulders Resort**. The ski season runs from November to April. Utah has some of the best skiing in the region, while New Mexico's **Taos Ski Valley** includes world-class slopes.

ENTERTAINMENT

THE SOUTHWEST'S blend of cultures has made the region a lively center for arts and entertainment. The cities of Phoenix, Santa Fe, Tucson, and Albuquerque offer opera, ballet, classical music, and theatrical productions. The small resort towns of Sedona and Taos, famed for their resident artists, regularly host touring productions and theater and musical shows. Most cities and major towns have a lively nightlife that includes country music, jazz, and rock as well as dinner theater and standup comedy.

The Southwest is a mecca for Western-style entertainment such as rodeo contests. Historic frontier towns such as Tombstone also stage mock gunfights. Check with the **Tombstone Visitor Center** for details. For sports fans, there are major league and college football, baseball, and basketball games.

GAMBLING IN LAS VEGAS

DESPITE ITS GROWING fame as the entertainment capital of the world, Las Vegas is popular mainly for its casinos. They can seem daunting at first, but with a basic understanding of the rules, most games are relatively easy. Some hotels have gaming guides on their in-house TV channels, and many casinos give free lessons at the tables. If you are winning, it is customary to tip the dealers.

SHOPPING

THE SOUTHWEST'S exciting range of Indian, Hispanic, and Anglo-American products make shopping a cultural adventure. Native crafts, including rugs and jewelry, can be bought in reservation posts or Pueblo stores.

Santa Fe is famous for its galleries selling Georgia O'Keeffe-inspired landscapes, contemporary art, and bronze cowboy sculptures.

Across the region, specialty grocery stores stock local products such as hot chili sauces and blue corn chips.

The big cities offer a choice of air-conditioned malls. The biggest concentration is in Phoenix, and its **Metrocenter Mall** is the region's largest. Las Vegas' fantasy themed malls make shopping one of its many attractions.

Where to Stay

THE SOUTHWEST HAS A LONG HISTORY of hospitality that is reflected in the wide variety of accommodations on offer. There is a wealth of options for visitors, ranging from luxurious five-star resorts to simple rustic lodges. Las Vegas hotels are noted for their themes and size. Across the region prices tend to vary according to the season.

Nevada	Number of Rooms	Restaurant	Children's Facilities	Garden or Terrace	Swimming Pool
DOWNTOWN LAS VEGAS: *Binion's Horseshoe* $ 128 E Fremont St, NV 89101. ☎ *(702) 382-1600* [FAX] *(702) 384-1574.* [W] www.binions.com Known for hosting the world series poker championship, all rooms have been remodeled in shades of pink. 🛁 [TV] ♿ [P] 💳	366	●	■		■
DOWNTOWN LAS VEGAS: *Four Queens Hotel & Casino* $$ 202 E Fremont St, NV 89109. ☎ *(800) 634-6045.* [FAX] *(702) 387-5160.* [W] www.fourqueens.com With its impressive, glittering façade this hotel retains the glamorous atmospere of Old Las Vegas. 🛁 [24] [TV] ♿ [P] 💳	690	●			■
LAS VEGAS – THE STRIP: *Tropicana* $$$ 3801 Las Vegas Blvd S, NV 89109. ☎ *(800) 634-4000.* [FAX] *(702) 739-2492.* [W] www.tropicanalv.com Noted for the lush gardens and waterfalls around its delightful pool area, the Tropicana is a popular Vegas institution. 🛁 [24] [TV] ♿ [P] 🏋 💳	1,874	●		●	■
LAS VEGAS – THE STRIP: *Caesars Palace* $$$$ 3570 Las Vegas Blvd S, NV 89109. ☎ *(800) 634-6001.* [FAX] *(702) 9671-3890* [W] www.caesars.com This Vegas institution is world-famous for its luxurious rooms, all with marble bathrooms. 🛁 [24] [TV] ♿ [P] 🏋 💳	2,454	●		●	■
LAS VEGAS – THE STRIP: *Treasure Island* $$$$ 3300 Las Vegas Blvd S, NV 89109. ☎ *(800) 288-7206.* [FAX] *(702) 894-7446.* [W] www.treasureisland.com This hotel is a popular choice with families because of its pirate theme. 🛁 [24] [TV] ♿ [P] 🏋 💳	2,885	●			■
LAS VEGAS – THE STRIP: *Venetian* $$$$ 3355 Las Vegas Blvd S, NV 89109. ☎ *(888) 283-6423.* [FAX] *(702) 414-4805.* [W] www.venetian.com All rooms are luxury suites with a minibar, two TVs, fax, and three telephone lines, set among palatial splendor. 🛁 [24] [TV] ♿ [P] 🏋 💳	3,036	●		●	■
LAS VEGAS – THE STRIP: *Bellagio* $$$$$ 3600 Las Vegas Blvd S, NV 89109. ☎ *(888) 987-6667.* [FAX] *(702) 693-8546.* [W] www.bellagiolasvegas.com The rooms in this highly sophisticated resort are decorated with imported Carrara marble bathrooms and silk furnishings. 🛁 [24] [TV] ♿ [P] 🏋 💳	3,000	●	■	●	■
CARSON CITY: *Best Western Piñon Plaza Resort* $$ 2171 Hwy 50E, NV 89701. ☎ *(775) 885-9000, (887) 519-5567* [W] www.pinonplaza.com This hotel in Nevada's capital city is popular for its delightful pool area and spa, as well as its full-service casino/resort. 🛁 [TV] ♿ [P] 🏋 💳	148	●	■	●	■
GREAT BASIN NATIONAL PARK: *Hotel Nevada* $$ 501 Aultman St, Ely, NV 89301. ☎ *(775) 289-6665, (888) 406-3055* [W] www.hotelnevada.com Located in downtown Ely, this landmark hotel was built in 1929. It has a full-service casino-resort, and a restaurant that serves breakfast, lunch, and dinner 24-hours a day. 🛁 [P] 💳	65	●			
RENO: *Peppermill Reno* $$ 2707 S Virginia St, NV 89502. ☎ *(775) 826-2121, (800) 282-2444* [W] www.peppermillreno.com This high-rise resort is located close to the airport, shopping, downtown, and Lake Tahoe. Housing seven restaurants, this totally full-service casino-resort offers everything from a barber to a spa to business facilities to pools, and outdoor activities. 🛁 [24] [TV] ♿ [P] 🏋 💳	1,070	●		●	■

Price categories for a standard double room per night, inclusive of service charges and any additional taxes:
- Ⓢ under $50
- ⓈⓈ $50–100
- ⓈⓈⓈ $100–150
- ⓈⓈⓈⓈ $150–200
- ⓈⓈⓈⓈⓈ over $200

RESTAURANT
Hotel restaurant or dining room usually open to nonresidents unless otherwise stated.

CHILDREN'S FACILITIES
Cribs and a baby-sitting service available. Some hotel restaurants have children's portions and high chairs.

GARDEN OR TERRACE
Hotels with a garden, courtyard, or terrace.

SWIMMING POOL
Hotel with an indoor or outdoor swimming pool.

		NUMBER OF ROOMS	RESTAURANT	CHILDREN'S FACILITIES	GARDEN OR TERRACE	SWIMMING POOL
UTAH						
BRYCE CANYON: *Bryce Canyon Lodge* ⓈⓈⓈ Bryce Canyon National Park, UT 84717. Ⓒ *(435) 834-5361.* FAX *(303) 297-3175.* Ⓦ www.brycecanyonlodge.com This Western classic, just 100 yds (30 m) from the canyon rim, has elegant period decor, rooms with Southwestern themes, and fireplaces. ● *Nov 1–Mar 31.* 🛏 Ⓟ 🌳		115	●		●	
CEDAR CITY: *Crystal Inn Cedar City* ⓈⓈ 1575 W 200 North, UT 84720. Ⓒ *(888) 787-6661.* FAX *(435) 586 1010.* Ⓦ www.crystalinns.com Fully renovated and redecorated in 2002, this is still one of Cedar City's best hotels. 🛏 📺 Ⓟ 🍽 🌳		100		▪		▪
DINOSAUR NATIONAL PARK: *Best Western Dinosaur Inn* ⓈⓈ 251 E Main St, Vernal, UT 84078. Ⓒ *435-789-2662, (800) 780-7234* Ⓦ www.bestwestern.com A reasonably priced, comfortable inn located near Dinosaur National Park, with its own pool and a restaurant. 🛏 📺 Ⓟ 🌳		60		▪		▪
ESCALANTE: *Prospector Inn* ⓈⓈ 380 W Main St, UT 84726. Ⓒ *(435) 826-4653.* FAX *(435) 826-4285.* Ⓦ www.prospectorinn.com This is one of Escalante's nicer family hotels. The spacious rooms are comfortable, and all have two beds. 🛏 📺 Ⓟ ♿ 🌳		50	●			
MOAB: *The Landmark Motel* ⓈⓈ 168 N Main St, UT 84532. Ⓒ *(800) 441-6147.* FAX *(435) 259-5556.* Ⓦ www.landmarkinnmoab.com A downtown Colonial building with spacious rooms. A bargain for large families. 🛏 📺 Ⓟ 🌳		36		▪		▪
SALT LAKE CITY: *Carlton Hotel* 140 E S Temple, UT 84111. Ⓒ *(801) 355-3418, (800) 633-3500.* This family-run hotel is near the Mormon temple and genealogical library and caters mainly to genealogists. 🛏 ♿ 🍽 🌳		40	●			
TORREY: *Wonderland Inn* ⓈⓈ 875 E Hwy 24, UT 84775. Ⓒ *(877) 854-0184.* FAX *(435) 425-3212.* Ⓦ www.capitolreefwonderland.com A bright, cheerful property with pleasant rooms located close to Capitol Reef National Park. 🛏 📺 Ⓟ 🌳		50	●		●	▪
ZION NATIONAL PARK: *Zion Lodge* ⓈⓈⓈ Springdale, UT 84767. Ⓒ *(435) 772-3213.* FAX *(435) 772-2001.* Ⓦ www.zionlodge.com A spacious lodge in Zion National Park, offering comfortable rooms and cabins surrounded by natural beauty. 🛏 Ⓟ		121	●	▪	●	
ARIZONA						
BISBEE: *Copper Queen Hotel* ⓈⓈⓈ 11 Howell Ave, AZ 85603. Ⓒ *(800) 247-5829.* FAX *(520) 432-4298.* Ⓦ www.copperqueen.com A late 19th-century hotel, decorated in the period style. A comprehensive list of sightings of various resident ghosts is also available! 🛏 📺 ♿ Ⓟ 🌳		47	●		●	▪
CHINLE: *Thunderbird Lodge* ⓈⓈⓈ Canyon De Chelly, AZ 86503. Ⓒ *(800) 679-2473.* FAX *(928) 674-5844.* Ⓦ www.tbirdlodge.com This lodge is part of the excellent complex that lies at the mouth of the scenic and beautiful Canyon de Chelly. Rooms are tastefully decorated. 🛏 📺 ♿ Ⓟ 🌳		72	●			

		NUMBER OF ROOMS	RESTAURANT	CHILDREN'S FACILITIES	GARDEN OR TERRACE	SWIMMING POOL

Price categories for a standard double room per night, inclusive of service charges and any additional taxes:
$ under $50
$$ $50–100
$$$ $100–150
$$$$ $150–200
$$$$$ over $200

RESTAURANT
Hotel restaurant or dining room usually open to nonresidents unless otherwise stated.

CHILDREN'S FACILITIES
Cribs and a baby-sitting service available. Some hotel restaurants have children's portions and high chairs.

GARDEN OR TERRACE
Hotels with a garden, courtyard, or terrace.

SWIMMING POOL
Hotel with an indoor or outdoor swimming pool.

	Rooms	Rest	Child	Garden	Pool
FLAGSTAFF: *Hotel Weatherford* $ 23 N Leroux St, AZ 86001. **(** *(928) 779-1919.* **FAX** *(928) 773-8951.* The 1890s Weatherford is one of Flagstaff's most distinctive hotels. Its better rooms are decorated with antiques. 🛏 **P** 🌿	8	●			
FLAGSTAFF: *Hotel Monte Vista* $$ 100 San Fransisco St, AZ 86001. **(** *(928) 779-6971.* **FAX** *(928) 779-2904.* Many of the rooms in this unique 1920s hotel are named after some of the most famous guests who stayed here, such as Bob Hope. 🛏 📺 **P** 🌿	46				
GRAND CANYON: *Bright Angel Lodge* $$ Grand Canyon South Rim, AZ 86023. **(** *(303) 297-2757.* **FAX** *(303) 297-3175.* **W** www.grandcanyonlodges.com Popular with hikers, Bright Angel offers frugal rooms in its 1930s lodge as well as appealing log cabins. 🛏 **P** 🌿	89	●		●	
GRAND CANYON (NORTH RIM): *Grand Canyon Lodge* $$ Bright Angel Point, Grand Canyon, AZ 86052. **(** *(303) 297-2757.* **FAX** *(303) 297-3175.* **W** www.grandcanyonlodges.com The only hotel on the canyon's North Rim, this lodge has cabins and motel-style rooms. ● *Oct–May.* 🛏 ♿ **P** 🌿	207	●			
GRAND CANYON VILLAGE: *Maswik Lodge* $$$ Grand Canyon South Rim, AZ 86023. **(** *(303) 297-2757.* **FAX** *(303) 297-3175.* **W** www.grandcanyonlodges.com Popular with families, this lodge is located at the west end of the village close to the South Rim. 🛏 📺 ♿ **P** 🌿	278	●	◼	●	
GREEN VALLEY: *Best Western Green Valley* $$$ 111 S La Cañada, AZ 85614 **(** *(800) 344-1441.* **FAX** *(520) 625-0215.* This hotel serves as a great base for exploring San Xavier Mission and Madera Canyon. It features a heated pool and spa. 🛏 📺 **P** 🌿	108	●		●	◼
JEROME: *Ghost City Inn* $$$ 541 N Main St, AZ 86331. **(** *(928) 634-4678.* **W** www.ghostcityinn.com In a handsome Victorian villa, this well-maintained inn has tastefully decorated bedrooms and fabulous views. 🛏 📺 **P** 🌿	6			●	
LAKE HAVASU CITY: *Ramada Inn* $ 271 S Lake Havasu Ave, AZ 86403. **(** *(928) 855-1111.* **FAX** *(928) 855-6228.* Recently revamped, this stylish hotel offers spacious elegant rooms and is a short walk from London Bridge. 🛏 📺 ♿ **P** 🌿	170	●	◼		◼
MONUMENT VALLEY: *Gouldings Lodge* $$$$ Off Hwy 163, UT 84536. **(** *(800) 874-0902.* **FAX** *(435) 727-3344.* **W** www.gouldings.com This inn has hosted movie stars and directors from almost every film made here. Rooms offer superb views of Monument Valley. 🛏 📺 **P** 🌿	62	●			◼
PHOENIX: *Pointe At South Mountain Resort* $$$$ 7777 S Pointe Parkway, AZ 85044. **(** *(602) 438-9000.* **FAX** *(602) 659-6350.* **W** www.pointesouthmtn.com In the hills south of Phoenix, this resort offers every amenity, including golf and four restaurants. 🛏 📺 ♿ **P** 🍴 🌿	640	●	◼	●	◼
SCOTTSDALE: *Scottsdale Princess* $$$$$ 7575 E Princess Dr, AZ 85255. **(** *(480) 585-4848.* **FAX** *(480) 585-0091.* **W** www.fairmont.com A first-rate resort-hotel in a handsome setting with all amenities and several award-winning restaurants. 🛏 24 📺 ♿ **P** 🍴 🌿	651	●	◼	●	◼

SECOND MESA, HOPI RESERVATION: *Hopi Cultural Center Hotel* $$ 33
Rte 264, AZ 86043. ((928) 734-2401. FAX (928) 734-6651.
W www.hopionline.com
This renovated hotel with an adobe look and pastel interior is the best
accommodation for miles around. 🛏 TV P 🗐

SEDONA: *Star Motel* $$ 11
295 Jordan Rd, AZ 86336. ((928) 282-3641.
Conveniently located in the center of Sedona, this unassuming
motel offers some of the most reasonably priced rooms in town.
🛏 TV P 🗐

TUCSON: *Hacienda del Sol Guest Ranch Resort* $$$$ 30
5601 N Hacienda del Sol Rd, AZ 85718. ((800) 728-6514. FAX (520) 299-5554.
W www.haciendadelsol.com
Overlooking desert landscape, this luxury retreat in the hills above town
has been popular since the 1940s, when such stars as Katherine Hepburn
used to visit. 🛏 TV & P 🗐

WINDOW ROCK: *Navajo Nation Inn* $$ 56
48 W Hwy 264, AZ 86515. ((800) 662-6189. FAX (928) 871-5466.
This attractive, comfortable hotel is one of the reservation's showpieces.
Rooms are immaculately clean. 🛏 TV P 🗐

NEW MEXICO

ALBUQUERQUE: *Albuquerque Doubletree Hotel* $$$ 295
201 Marquette Ave, NW, NM 87102. ((888) 223-4113. FAX (505) 247-7025.
W www.doubletreehotels.com
Very comfortable, friendly, well-appointed hotel in the heart of
downtown. 🛏 TV & P 📺 🗐

ALBUQUERQUE: *Albuquerque Hilton* $$$ 263
1901 University Blvd, NE, NM 87102. ((800) 274-6835. FAX (505) 880-1196.
W www.hilton. com
Resort-like facility in the heart of downtown, with courtyard gardens, and
in- and outdoor pools. 🛏 TV & P 📺 🗐

ALBUQUERQUE: *Casas de Sueños* $$$$ 22
310 Rio Grande Blvd, SW, NM 87104. ((505) 247-4560. FAX (505) 842-8493.
W www.casasdesuenos.com
This "House of Dreams" was a 1930s artists' colony. Charming cottages
surround a lovely courtyard. 🛏 TV & P 🗐

CHAMA: *The Gandy Dancer Bed & Breakfast* $$$ 7
299 Maple Ave, NM 87520. ((505) 756-2191. FAX (505) 756-2649.
W www.gandydancerbb.com
One block from the Cumbres and Toltec Scenic Railroad, this delightful
B&B is in a Victorian mansion. 🛏 TV P 🗐

SANTA FE: *El Rey Inn* $$ 86
1862 Cerrillos Rd, NM 87505. ((800) 521-1349. FAX (505) 989-9249.
W www.elreyinnsantafe.com
Set among lush gardens, this pleasant hotel has rooms decorated in
Southwestern style. 🛏 TV & P 🗐

SANTA FE: *Inn of the Turquoise Bear* $$$ 10
342 E Buena Vista St, NM 87505. ((800) 396-4104. FAX (505) 988-4225.
W www.turquoisebear.com
B&B in an adobe villa set in acres of gardens, rock terraces, and tall
pines. Great rooms and delicious breakfast. 🛏 TV & P 🗐

SANTA FE: *La Fonda Hotel* $$$$ 167
100 E San Francisco, NM 87501. ((800) 523-5002. FAX (523) 982-6367.
W www.lafondasantafe.com
A Santa Fe landmark, this newly renovated 1920s hotel stands on the site
of an original 1610 adobe. 🛏 TV & P 🗐

TAOS: *Taos Inn* $$$ 36
125 Paseo del Pueblo Norte, NM 87571. ((888) 461-8267. FAX (505) 758-5776.
W www.taosinn.com
This historic inn just north of the Plaza has rooms in adobe buildings
dating from the 1800s, decorated with Mexican tiles, locally made
furniture, and hand-woven bedspreads. 🛏 TV & P 🗐

Where to Eat

THE SOUTHWEST OFFERS a top-class regional cuisine, as well as a diverse range of other eating experiences, especially in the larger cities. Mexican food is often best at local restaurants in New Mexico and Arizona, while Utah favors American fare. Hotel restaurants often serve the best food in small towns. "L" indicates lunch and "D" indicates dinner in the listings below.

		CREDIT CARDS	OUTDOOR TABLES	VEGETARIAN	BAR AREA	CHILDREN'S FACILITIES
NEVADA						
DOWNTOWN LAS VEGAS: *California Pizza Kitchen* $$ At the Mirage, 3500 Las Vegas Blvd S, NV 89109. ((702) 791-7111. California Pizza Kitchen features an enormous range of gourmet woodfired pizzas, as well as a choice of pastas, salads, and delicious desserts. ♿		■		■	●	
DOWNTOWN LAS VEGAS: *The Steakhouse* $$$$ At Binion's Horseshoe, 128 E Fremont St, NV 89101. ((702) 382-1600. Classic American steakhouse fare includes prime rib as well as seafood at reasonable prices in this venerable Las Vegas casino. ● *L.* ♿		■			●	
LAS VEGAS – THE STRIP: *Coyote Café* $$$ MGM Grand, 3799 Las Vegas Blvd S, NV 89109. ((702) 891-7349. With its Southwestern decor, this popular place offers regional fusion cook- ing with an exciting mix of Native American, Mexican, and Cajun flavors. Reservations required in the grill room but not the café. ♿ ♻		■		■	●	
LAS VEGAS – THE STRIP: *Rosewood Grille* $$$ 3339 Las Vegas Blvd S, NV 89109. ((702) 792-5965. This is one of Las Vegas' landmark restaurants, famous for its good seafood, especially the Maine lobsters, and extensive wine list. ♿ ♻		■			●	
LAS VEGAS – THE STRIP: *Top of the World* $$$ Stratosphere Tower, 2000 Las Vegas Blvd S NV89104. ((702) 380-7711. Panoramic views are available from this restaurant 833 ft (255 m) above the Strip. The menu is European with great meat, steak, and seafood. ♿ ♻		■			●	
LAS VEGAS – THE STRIP: *Trattoria del Lupo* $$$ At Mandalay Bay, 3950 Las Vegas Blvd S, NV 89109. ((702) 740-5522. Owned by famous chef, Wolfgang Puck, who is credited with combining classic Italian cooking with contemporary California cuisine. ♿		■	●	■	●	
LAS VEGAS – THE STRIP: *Emeril's New Orleans Fish House* $$$$ At MGM Grand, 3799 Las Vegas Blvd S, NV 89109. ((702) 891-7374. One of the most popular restaurants in Las Vegas, noted for its unique fusion of Creole and Cajun cooking. Some great snacks are available at the Seafood Bar. ♿		■		■	●	
LAS VEGAS – THE STRIP: *Spago* $$$$ At Caesars Palace, 3570 Las Vegas Blvd S, NV 89109. ((702) 369-6300. Spago's contemporary interior echoes its famous sister restaurant in Los Angeles. Fusion cooking mixes Asian and American dishes with Italian styles in such dishes as fried salmon on soba noodles. ♿ ♻		■	●	■	●	
CARSON CITY: *The Steak House* $ Best Western Piñon Plaza Resort, NV 89701. ((775) 885-9000. Steaks, seafood, and pasta are the specialties at this popular restaurant, which has a full bar. Also try the wild game dishes such as venison and buffalo. ♻			●	■	●	■
CARSON CITY: *Red's Old 395 Grill* $$ 395 Grill 1055 S Carson St, NV 89701. ((775) 887-0395. Popular with locals for all kinds and sizes of steaks and seafood specials. It has a full bar that serves wine. ♻			●	■	●	■
GREAT BASIN NATIONAL PARK (BAKER): *The Border Inn Restaurant* $ Hwys 50 & 6, Baker, NV 89311. ((775) 234-7300. Good American food – hearty steaks, chicken, and burgers – is the specialty at this lively, 24-hour restaurant, near the Great Basin National Park. ♻		■				■

Price categories include a three-course meal for one, a glass of house wine, and all unavoidable extra charges such as sales tax and service.
- $ under $20
- $$ $20–30
- $$$ $30–45
- $$$$ $45–60
- $$$$$ over $60

CREDIT CARDS
Major credit cards accepted.

OUTDOOR TABLES
Garden, courtyard, or terrace with outside tables.

VEGETARIAN
A good selection of vegetarian dishes available.

BAR AREA
There is a bar area or cocktail bar within the restaurant, available for drinks and/or bar snacks.

CHILDREN'S FACILITIES
Small portions and/or high chairs available on request.

UTAH

	Price	Credit Cards	Outdoor Tables	Vegetarian	Bar Area	Children's Facilities
BRYCE CANYON NATIONAL PARK: B-Bar-D Covered Wagon Company 1089 W. Main St, UT 84764. ((435) 834-5202. A family oriented theater experience starting with a wagon ride, followed by a chuckwagon dinner and country music. ● Sun, Nov–mid-May.	$$	■	●			
BRYCE CANYON NATIONAL PARK: Bryce Canyon Lodge Bryce Canyon National Park, UT 84717. ((435) 834-5361. This is the best fine dining establishment in the area, serving Continental cuisine in an elegant setting. It serves meals that are traditional and well done. ● Nov 1–Mar 31.	$$	■	●	■		■
CEDAR CITY: Rusty's Ranch House 2275 E Hwy 14, UT 84720. ((435) 586-3839. This barn surrounded by mountain views houses a comfortably elegant country steakhouse specializing in hearty meals like slow-roasted baby back ribs and broiled salmon with garlic, basil, and butter. ● L; Sun.	$$	■		■		■
MOAB: Eddie McStiff's 57 S Main St, UT 84532. ((435) 259-2337. Pizza, pasta, and McStiff's own award-winning beer are the specialties here. Another favorite is skewered steak and chicken satay.	$	■	●		●	■
MOAB: Center Café 60 N 100 W, UT 84532. ((435) 259-4295. International cuisine featuring specialties such as pan-seared lamb loin with roasted garlic flan. Specials can include exotic, tasty dishes featuring ostrich or bison.	$$	■	●			
SALT LAKE CITY: Lion House Pantry 63 E South Temple, UT 84150. ((801) 363-5466. Housed in the historic Brigham Young house (1856), this restaurant serves authentic Mormon cuisine in cafeteria style.	$	■	●	■	●	
SALT LAKE CITY: Market Street Grill 48 Market St, UT 84101. ((801) 322-4668. This popular place serves steaks, seafood, and a great hearty breakfast in an informal setting.	$$$				●	
TORREY: Capitol Reef Café 360 W Main St, UT 84775. ((435) 425-3271. Located near Capitol Reef National Park, this unusual find features locally farmed smoked or grilled trout, stir fries, vegetarian entrées, and a host of imaginative dishes. It serves delicious homemade soups and salads.	$$	■		■		■
ZION NATIONAL PARK: Zion Lodge Zion National Park, UT 84767. ((435) 772-3213. Better than average tourist fare, with a very good breakfast buffet and dinners that include steak and trout.	$$	■	●		●	■

ARIZONA

	Price	Credit Cards	Outdoor Tables	Vegetarian	Bar Area	Children's Facilities
CHINLE: Thunderbird Lodge Canyon De Chelly, AZ 86503. ((928) 674-5841. Cafeteria-style place serving large portions of classic American diner food from breakfast through dinner. Excellent value and tasty.	$	■				
FLAGSTAFF: Charly's Pub & Grill 23 N Leroux, AZ 86001. ((928) 779-1919. This fast-moving restaurant is a popular spot, serving an enticing range of burgers and sandwiches, as well as Mexican specialties.	$$	■		■	●	

For key to symbols see back flap

Price categories include a three-course meal for one, a glass of house wine, and all unavoidable extra charges such as sales tax and service.
$ under $20
$$ $20–30
$$$ $30–45
$$$$ $45–60
$$$$$ over $60

CREDIT CARDS
Major credit cards accepted.

OUTDOOR TABLES
Garden, courtyard, or terrace with outside tables.

VEGETARIAN
A good selection of vegetarian dishes available.

BAR AREA
There is a bar area or cocktail bar within the restaurant, available for drinks and/or bar snacks.

CHILDREN'S FACILITIES
Small portions and/or high chairs available on request.

Restaurant	Credit Cards	Outdoor Tables	Vegetarian	Bar Area	Children's Facilities
FLAGSTAFF: *Cottage Place Restaurant* $$$ 126 W Cottage Ave, AZ 86001. (928) 774-8431. One of Flagstaff's best eating places with an imaginative menu that includes vegetarian dishes and a good selection of seafood and meats.	■		■		
GRAND CANYON: *Bright Angel Restaurant* $ Bright Angel Lodge, AZ 86023. (928) 638-2631. A bustling café-restaurant that serves light meals and salad as well as full meals. Reservations are not accepted, so you may have to line up.	■		■		■
GRAND CANYON: *Phantom Ranch* $$ Grand Canyon, AZ 86023. (928) 638-2631. Situated on the canyon floor and accessible only by hiking or mule trail, Phantom Ranch has a canteen providing meals by advance reservation only. The house specialty is the "Hiker's Stew."	■	●	■		
GRAND CANYON VILLAGE: *El Tovar Hotel* $$$ Grand Canyon South Rim, AZ 86023. (928) 297-2757. El Tovar has a large dining room overlooking the South Rim of the Grand Canyon. The menu is wide-ranging and portions are large. Reservations for dinner are essential.	■		■	●	
JEROME: *English Kitchen* $ 119 Jerome Ave, AZ 86331. (928) 634-2132. This café serves standard but well-prepared breakfast and lunch in premises that once served as an opium den in Jerome's wild past.	■	●	■		
JEROME: *Flatiron Café* $ 416 N Main St, AZ 86331. (928) 634-2733. Great salads are a specialty of this amiable café in the center of Jerome. Also try the tasty scrambled eggs at breakfast. ● D.	■	●	■		
LAKE HAVASU CITY: *London Arms Pub & Playhouse* $$ 422 English Village, AZ 86403. (928) 855-8782. Styled as an authentic English pub, the London Arms offers fine dining and live theater with views of the London Bridge.	■	●	■	●	■
PHOENIX: *Ed Debevic's* $ 2102 E Highland Ave, AZ 85016. (602) 956-2760. Good food and fun are the hallmarks of this lively diner, which features many 1950s accoutrements, including a mini-jukebox on most tables.	■	●	■	●	■
PHOENIX: *Aunt Chilada's at Squaw Peak* $$ 27330N Dreamy Draw Dr, AZ 85020. (602) 944-1286. Mexican food is the specialty of this popular restaurant, which occupies an imaginatively modernized, 19th-century general store.	■	●	■	●	■
PHOENIX: *Vincent's on Camelback* $$$$$ 3930 E Camelback Rd, AZ 85251. (602) 224-0225. This classy restaurant offers an imaginative menu that blends French and Southwestern cuisine. Advance reservations are recommended. ● mid-May–Sep: Mon & Sun.	■		●	■	
SCOTTSDALE: *The Squash Blossom* $$$ Hyatt Regency at Gainey Ranch, 7500 E Doubletree Ranch Rd, AZ 85258. (480) 991-3388. The emphasis of this excellent café is on Southwest cuisine.	■	●	■	●	■
SECOND MESA, HOPI RESERVATION: *Hopi Cultural Center Restaurant* $ Rte 264, AZ 86043. (928) 734-2401. Traditional dishes like Hopi stew can be interesting, although standard Mexican and American fare is also served. ● Thanksgiving, Dec 25.	■				■

SEDONA: *Shugrue's Hillside Grill* $$$
Hillside Courtyard, 671 Hwy 179, AZ 86336. *(928) 282-5300.*
Arguably the best steaks in town can be enjoyed at this brisk, modern restaurant. The service is excellent – both efficient and courteous. &

TUBA CITY: *Hogan Restaurant* $
PO Box 247, AZ 86045. *(928) 283-5260.*
Located next to the Quality Inn, Hogan's offers a full Mexican/American menu, which is a cut above average diner fare. &

TUCSON: *El Charro Café* $
311 N Court Ave, AZ 85701. *(520) 622-1922.*
Tucson's oldest Mexican restaurant is critically acclaimed as serving some of the best traditional Mexican food in the country. Try the famous *carne seca* (sun-dried beef), a Tucson specialty. &

TUCSON: *Janos* $$$$
Westin La Paloma, 3770 E Sunrise Dr, AZ 85718. *(520) 615-6100.*
One of Tucson's most elegant restaurants, Janos blends French cooking techniques with Southwestern ingredients. The menu changes seasonally and the extensive wine list is chosen to match. ● *Sun, public hols.* &

TOMBSTONE: *Big Nose Kate's* $
417 E Allen St, AZ 85638 *(520) 457-3107.*
This restaurant has a great old-fashioned saloon atmosphere, with an original cowboy bar and loads of Western memorabilia. &

WINDOW ROCK: *Navajo Nation Inn Dining Room* $
48 West Hwy 264, AZ 86515. *(928) 871-4108.*
This is where the Navajo businessmen and politicians eat. Traditional dishes are served in a room decorated with Native art. ● *Sat & Sun D.* &

NEW MEXICO

ALBUQUERQUE: *Church Street Café* $
2111 Church St NW, NM 87124. *(505) 247-8522.*
Located in the Old Town just behind San Felipe de Neri church, this atmospheric restaurant is found in one of the oldest buildings in the state. Highly acclaimed for its authentic Hispanic fare. &

ALBUQUERQUE: *Monte Vista Fire Station* $$$
3201 Central Ave NE, NM 87106. *(505) 255-2424.*
Now a National Historic Site, this Art Deco Pueblo Revival building was once a fire station. A local favorite, it serves creative Southwestern food. &

ALBUQUERQUE: *The Artichoke Café* $$$
424 Central Ave SE, NM 87102. *(505) 243-0200.*
This relaxed but stylish downtown restaurant serves French-American bistro fare. You can eat outside in good weather. ● *Sat & Sun L.* &

CARLSBAD: *The Flume* $$
1829 S Canal St, NM 88220. *(505) 887-2851.*
This casual restaurant is one of the best in Carlsbad. It is famous for its prime rib, but steaks, chicken, and seafood are also served. &

SANTA FE: *Dave's Not Here* $
1115 Hickox St, NM 87501. *(505) 983-7060.*
A popular eatery featuring good-sized portions of New Mexican favorites, including *chili rellenos* (stuffed chilies) and tacos, for around $5. &

SANTA FE: *Maria's New Mexican Kitchen* $
555 W Cordova Rd, NM 87501. *(505) 983-7929.*
This very busy local restaurant serves authentic old Sante Fe-style cooking. Margaritas are a specialty of the house. &

SANTA FE: *Old House Restaurant* $$$$
309 W San Francisco St, NM 87501. *(505) 988-4455.*
This is in the Eldorado Hotel and is one of Sante Fe's finest restaurants. Specialties include pepper-crusted salmon. &

TAOS: *Doc Martin's Restaurant* $$$
125 Paseo del Pueblo Norte, NM 87571. *(505) 758-1977.*
Located in the historic Taos Inn, dating from 1600, this perennial favorite serves New American and northern New Mexican cuisine. &

For key to symbols see back flap

THE ROCKIES

The Rockies at a Glance

THE FOUR STATES OF Montana, Idaho, Wyoming, and Colorado form the heart of the Rockies, the mountain range that dominates the landscape of North America. This beautiful but sparsely populated region encompasses a wealth of natural wonders such as the geysers of Wyoming's Yellowstone National Park, the varied landscapes of Montana's Glacier National Park, and the cliff dwellings of Colorado's Mesa Verde National Park. Colorado is also celebrated as the skiing capital of the United States. The area's human history lends itself to superlatives as much as the land does. Throughout the Rockies there are tangible signs of such legendary 19th-century Native Americans and cowboys as Sitting Bull and "Buffalo Bill" Cody.

IDAHO
(See pp574–77)

Coeur d'Alene (see p574) *in Idaho is located along Lake Coeur d'Alene. This popular vacation destination is famous for its unique floating golf green on the 14th hole.*

Sun Valley (see p576), *in southern Idaho, is one of the oldest and most exclusive winter resorts in the country. Its picturesque environs also offer many recreational options.*

Yellowstone National Park
(see pp584–5) *is perhaps one of the country's most visited parks. The highlights of this wild wonderland are the hot springs, particularly Old Faithful Geyser and its steaming plume.*

◁ **Mountain summit reflected in the placid waters of Lake Josephine, Glacier National Park, Montana**

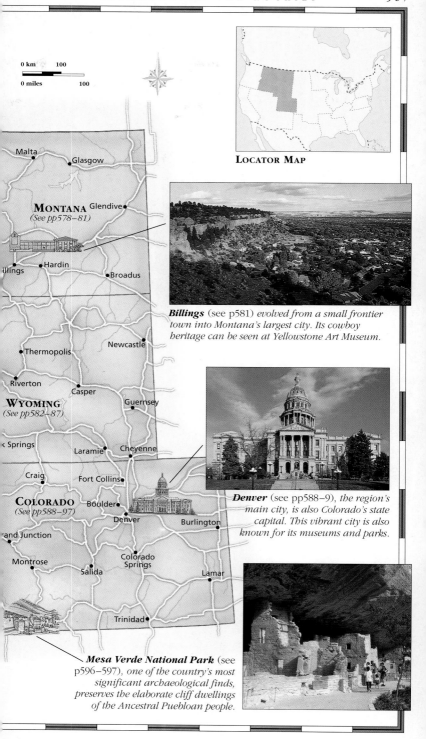

LOCATOR MAP

0 km   100
0 miles   100

Malta
Glasgow

MONTANA Glendive
(See pp578–81)

illings   Hardin
Broadus

Billings (see p581) *evolved from a small frontier town into Montana's largest city. Its cowboy heritage can be seen at Yellowstone Art Museum.*

Thermopolis
Newcastle

Riverton
Casper

WYOMING
(See pp582–87)   Guernsey

Springs   Laramie   Cheyenne

Craig   Fort Collins

COLORADO   Boulder
(See pp588–97)
Denver   Burlington

Denver (see pp588–9), *the region's main city, is also Colorado's state capital. This vibrant city is also known for its museums and parks.*

and Junction
Colorado
Montrose   Springs
Salida   Lamar

Trinidad

Mesa Verde National Park (see *p596–597*), *one of the country's most significant archaeological finds, preserves the elaborate cliff dwellings of the Ancestral Puebloan people.*

THE ROCKIES

O NE OF THE WORLD'S GREAT OUTDOOR REGIONS, *the Rockies offer a variety of experiences not found anywhere else. The sheer scale of the landscape is breathtaking, and words can hardly express the thrill of seeing firsthand the broad expanses of the Wyoming plains, Idaho's deep river canyons, the towering peaks of Colorado, or the rugged vastness of Montana.*

The underlying geology of the Rocky Mountains is ancient, with some of the country's oldest rocks forming the highly stratified Precambrian peaks and valleys of Glacier National Park. The rest of the range is varied, with mineral-rich granite batholiths sharing space with the vast red-rock mesas of the Colorado Plateau. Evidence of volcanic activity, forming and reforming the landscape from deep beneath the surface, is also omnipresent, most prominently in Idaho's Craters of the Moon National Monument, and most famously in the geysers, mudpots, and hot springs of Yellowstone National Park in Wyoming.

This region has also been shaped by some of North America's mightiest rivers. Beside the terrifying whitewater rapids of the Snake and other tumultuous rivers, the Rockies form the headwaters of many major western rivers, including the Colorado, the Missouri, the Columbia, and the Rio Grande. These rivers and their many tributaries offer some of the finest fishing in the world. Wildflowers are abundant, especially in the alpine meadows, while the dense forests are the habitat of a wide range of wildlife. Moose, elk, and bald eagles are spotted frequently along trails and roads, and the backwoods areas hold some of the nation's last wild populations of carnivores, including mountain lions, wolves, and massive grizzly bears.

HISTORY

The history of the Rockies is as wild and larger-than-life as the land itself. From the late 18th century, intrepid "mountain men" – French-Canadian and American fur trappers – traveled throughout the Rockies, trapping beavers and other animals for their valuable skins. After the Louisiana Purchase in 1803, the fledgling country acquired control of the Rockies, and the first official American

Pool along the Firehole Lake Drive, Yellowstone National Park, Wyoming

◁ **Cross-country skiing at Steamboat Springs, one of Colorado's popular ski resorts** presence was established between 1803 and 1806 by explorers Meriwether Lewis and William Clark. These daring men were accompanied by a "Corps of Discovery" made up of 29 soldiers and fur trappers, and joined by the legendary Indian guide Sacagawea and her baby son. They followed the Missouri upstream from the frontier outpost of St. Louis, traveling by boat and later by foot across Montana and Idaho on an epic 5,000-mile (8,047-km) journey to the Pacific Ocean and back. Also in 1806, Zebulon Pike led an expedition to Colorado, following the Arkansas River and spotting the majestic mountain that bears his name.

Lewis & Clark National Historic Trail Interpretive Center, Great Falls, Montana

These explorers' published accounts, describing the sublime landscape and its wealth of wildlife, attracted increasing numbers of trappers and hunters, and by the 1830s several commercial outposts had been established, usually at the confluence of major rivers. Their routes across what had once been seen as an impenetrable barrier slowly but surely paved the way for transcontinental travelers. By the mid-1800s, thousands of pioneers following the Oregon Trail and other routes crossed the Rocky Mountains, bound for the Pacific Northwest, the California gold fields, and the Mormon lands in Utah. As a result, conflicts between immigrants and Native Americans increased dramatically. In the mountains, the Nez Percé and other small tribes lived comparatively peaceful and sedentary lives, while east of the mountains were migratory bands of Plains Indians, including such diverse and often rival tribes as the Sioux, Cheyenne, Crow, Arapahoe, and Shoshone. Most of these eastern tribes were themselves recent arrivals. Living in mobile encampments of tepees, they had mastered the art of riding horses and hunting buffalo. As cowboys and ranchers moved into the rich grazing lands, some 50 million native bison were all but eradicated, and the tribes whose entire culture was based on these mighty herds came under desperate threat.

By the beginning of the 20th century, all the tribes had been contained into small reservations, far from their previous homelands. Ironically, one of the country's greatest Native American cultural repositories is in Wyoming's Buffalo Bill Historical Center, a memorial to the man who, as buffalo hunter and Indian fighter, contributed greatly to their destruction.

KEY DATES IN HISTORY

1200 Ancestral Pueblo Indians abandon their cliff dwellings at Mesa Verde, Colorado

1700–1800 French-Canadian fur trappers explore the Rockies

1803 The US acquires much of this region through the Louisiana Purchase

1803 The Lewis and Clark expedition begins

1806 Zebulon Pike explores the Arkansas River in southern Colorado

1843 The Oregon Trail is opened

1858 Gold is discovered outside Denver

1869 Wyoming gives women the vote

1872 US Congress establishes the world's first national park at Yellowstone

1876 Battle of Little Bighorn

1915 The Lincoln Highway, the first transcontinental route from New York City to San Francisco, runs across southern Wyoming

1951 Warren Air Force Base in Cheyenne is declared the base of operations for all US Intercontinental Ballistic Missiles (ICBMs)

1988 Forest fires across the Rockies cause serious damage to Yellowstone National Park

2003 Memorial commemorating the Native American victory at the Battle of Little Bighorn is dedicated at the site of the battle in Montana

Tepees, Buffalo Bill Historical Center, Wyoming

The former silver-mining town of Wallace, near Coeur d'Alene, Idaho

PROGRESS & DEVELOPMENT

The first transcontinental railroad crossed southern Wyoming in the late 1860s, followed in the 1870s and 1880s by other railroads, such as the Northern Pacific and Great Northern. Carrying cattle to eastern markets, and bringing weapons and supplies to the Wild West, it was these railroads that actually consolidated American settlement.

The search for and discovery of valuable minerals, mainly gold, silver, and copper, was another primary impetus to settlement. Because of the region's expansive forests, the lumber industry, too, had been an economic mainstay since pioneer times, and over the previous century oil and coal deposits have been the source underlying numerous booms and busts, especially in Colorado and Wyoming.

TOURISM & THE ECONOMY

Natural resource-based industries are still active all over the Rockies, though the main economic force today is tourism. These four states contain the highest mountains, the densest forests, the wildest rivers, and the most rugged canyons in the "Lower 48" states. Consequently, the Rockies is a magical place offering sublime scenery as well as a wide variety of attractions, such as historic train rides, summer "dude ranches," and historic sites. Many places also feature music festivals, Plains Indian pow-wows, or theatrical re-creations of Wild West shootouts.

This is also the best place to appreciate the great outdoors. Intrepid guides offer unforgettable trips such as whitewater rafting or fly-fishing for trout. The proliferation of ski resorts has also added to the state's tourism potential. When gold was discovered outside Denver in 1850, several mining camps sprang up at such evocatively named places as Silverton and Cripple Creek in Colorado and "Last Chance Gulch," now Helena, Montana. Many of these erstwhile mining centers are now deluxe winter resorts, such as Crested Butte, Telluride, and Aspen in Colorado, and Idaho's Sun Valley.

Neon sign for the Cowboy Bar, Jackson, Wyoming

Exploring the Rockies

THE SHEER VASTNESS OF THE Rocky Mountains landscape and the relative shortness of the tourism season means that visitors need to plan well ahead. Many attractions on this 1,000-mile (1,609-km) long swath of mountains are on such high elevations that they are inaccessible during the long winter, with snow blocking roads from late October until June. The heavy snowfalls, however, enhance the region's phenomenal winter sports, and Denver, the main city, is a prime starting point for most visitors. Driving is the best way to explore the area, because public transportation is limited, and the national parks and most of the other attractions are far away.

KEY

✈ Airport

━ Highway

━ Major road

━ Railroad

– – State border

▪▪▪ International border

SIGHTS AT A GLANCE

Idaho
Coeur d'Alene **1**
Hells Canyon National Recreation Area **2**
Salmon **3**
Sawtooth National Recreation Area **4**
Boise **5**
Sun Valley **6**
Three Island Crossing State Park **7**
Bruneau Dunes State Park **8**
Twin Falls **9**
Craters of the Moon National Monument **10**
Idaho Falls **11**

Montana
Big Hole National Battlefield **12**
Missoula **13**
Flathead Valley **14**
Glacier National Park p579 **15**
Great Falls **16**
Helena **17**
Butte **18**
Bozeman **19**
Billings **20**
Little Bighorn Battlefield National Monument **21**

Wyoming
Cody **22**
Yellowstone National Park pp584–5 **23**
Jackson **24**
Grand Teton National Park p583 **25**
Bighorn Mountains **26**
Devil's Tower National Monument **27**
Casper **28**
Guernsey **29**
Laramie **30**
Cheyenne **31**

Colorado
Denver pp588–9 **32**
Boulder **33**
Golden **34**
Idaho Springs & Georgetown **35**
Rocky Mountain National Park **36**
Manitou Springs **37**
Colorado Springs **38**
Cripple Creek **39**
Cañon City **40**
Colorado Ski Resorts pp594–5 **41**
Great Sand Dunes National Monument & Preserve **42**
Durango **43**
Mesa Verde National Park **44**
Ouray **45**
Black Canyon of the Gunnison National Park **46**
Colorado National Monument **47**

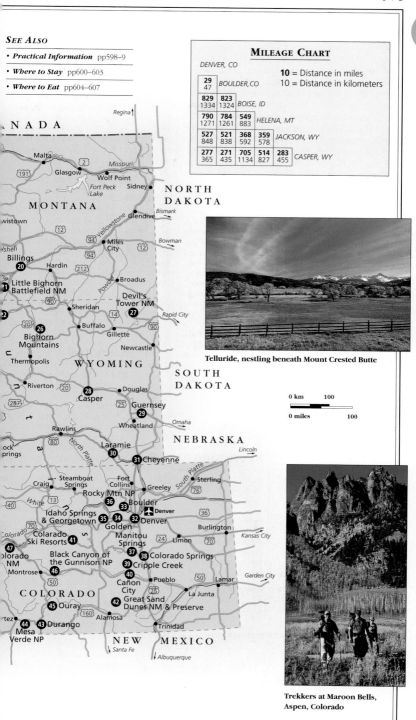

MILEAGE CHART					
DENVER, CO					
29 / 47	BOULDER, CO		**10** = Distance in miles		
829 / 1334	**823** / 1324	BOISE, ID	10 = Distance in kilometers		
790 / 1271	**784** / 1261	**549** / 883	HELENA, MT		
527 / 848	**521** / 838	**368** / 592	**359** / 578	JACKSON, WY	
277 / 365	**271** / 435	**705** / 1134	**514** / 827	**283** / 455	CASPER, WY

CANADA

Regina

Malta Missouri Glasgow Wolf Point Fort Peck Lake Sidney

MONTANA Glendive Bismark

NORTH DAKOTA

Lewistown

Billings **20** Miles City Bowman

Hardin

Little Bighorn Battlefield NM **21** Broadus Devil's Tower NM **27** Rapid City

Sheridan

Buffalo **26** Gillette Newcastle

Bighorn Mountains

Thermopolis

WYOMING

SOUTH DAKOTA

Riverton Casper **28** Douglas Guernsey **29** Wheatland Omaha

Rawlins North Platte Laramie **30** Cheyenne **31** Lincoln

NEBRASKA

Rock Springs

Craig Steamboat Springs Fort Collins Greeley Sterling South Platte

Rocky Mtn NP **36** Boulder **33** Denver **32**

Idaho Springs & Georgetown **35** **34** Golden Burlington

Colorado Ski Resorts **41** Manitou Springs Limon Kansas City

Black Canyon of the Gunnison NP **47** Colorado Springs **38**

Montrose **46** Cripple Creek **39** **37** Garden City

COLORADO Cañon City **40** Pueblo Lamar

Ouray **45** Great Sand Dunes NM & Preserve **42** La Junta

Durango **43** **44** Alamosa Trinidad

Mesa Verde NP

NEW MEXICO

Santa Fe Albuquerque

Telluride, nestling beneath Mount Crested Butte

0 km   100

0 miles   100

Trekkers at Maroon Bells,
Aspen, Colorado

Idaho

ONE OF THE COUNTRY'S LEAST populous states, Idaho has vast tracts of unexplored wilderness – remote mountain ranges, dense forests, frozen lakes, and deep river gorges. It is an ideal vacation spot for adventure sports enthusiasts, offering abundant opportunities for hiking, mountain biking, and whitewater rafting. To the north lie resorts such as Coeur d'Alene; the center has the majestic Sawtooth Mountains; while the south consists mainly of cultivated fields, prompting automobile license plates in the state to declare Idaho's pride in its primary product, "Famous Potatoes."

Coeur d'Alene ❶

🏔 25,000. ✈ 🚌 ℹ️ *1621 N 3rd St, (208) 664-3194.*
🆆 *www.coeurdalene.org*

A MAJOR VACATION destination, Coeur d'Alene was founded in the 1870s as a US Army outpost. Its present "four star" status refers to the luxury available at the town's world-famous **Coeur d'Alene Resort** *(see p600).* Located along the shore of the beautiful Lake Coeur d'Alene, this exclusive resort is well known for its unique floating golf green on the 14th hole. On the resort's east side, the 120-acre (49-ha) **Tubbs Hill Park** is a nature preserve with hiking trails, dense pine forests, and great views. Lake Coeur d'Alene is also home to one of the country's largest populations of ospreys and bald eagles, which can be seen frequently during the winter months diving for salmon in the waters of Wolf Lodge Bay.

A century ago, Coeur d'Alene was a busy service center for the prosperous silver mines in mountains east of the lake. A number of Victorian-era towns still stand

in the former mining districts, and museums and mine tours offer a glimpse into this lost world. The town of Wallace, 52 miles (84 km) east, offers the **Sierra Silver Mine Tour**, which guides visitors through the workings of an 1890s silver mine.

Kayaking, Hells Canyon

🦆 **Tubbs Hill Park**
710 E Mullan Ave. 📞 *(208) 769-2252.* ⏰ *dawn–dusk daily.*
🚋 **Sierra Silver Mine Tour**
420 5th St, Wallace. 📞 *(208) 752-5151.* ⏰ *July–Aug: 9am–6pm daily; May–Jun & Sep: 9am–4pm.* 🅿️ ♿

Hells Canyon National Recreation Area ❷

PO Box 832, Riggins. 📞 *(208) 628-3916.* 🆆 *www.tcfn.org/tctour/parks/ HellsCanyonNRA.html*

THE DEEPEST RIVER gorge in North America, Hells Canyon was carved from the craggy granite of the Seven Devils Mountains by the Snake River. Over a mile (1.6 km) deep and straddling the three-state border where Idaho, Washington, and Oregon meet, the canyon and its surroundings are now a recreational area that includes some 215,000 acres (87,008 ha) of wilderness where no motor vehicles are permitted. Nearly 100 miles (161 km) of undeveloped and turbulent whitewater draws kayakers, rafters, and other thrillseekers. Hells Canyon lies downstream from Hells Canyon Dam. The main visitor center is on the Oregon *(see pp640–41)* side of the dam, while in Idaho, the best introduction to the area is from Riggins, located deep in a canyon on the banks of the Salmon River, which joins the Snake River farther downstream. Riggins also has many outfitters who provide rental gear.

Salmon ❸

🏔 2,954. ℹ️ *200 Main St, (208) 756-2100.* 🆆 *www.salmonidaho.com*

SITUATED ALONG THE banks of the wild and scenic Salmon River, this was an important point along the Lewis and Clark Trail *(see p570).* Essentially a supply town and resort center, Salmon makes a fine base for exploring the surrounding region. Among the activities offered are raft trips, kayaking, skiing, horseback riding, mountain biking, and snowmobiling. It is also possible to hike along parts of the legendary route that the explorers Lewis and Clark followed in the early 1800s while traveling from Illinois to find a navigable water route to the Pacific Ocean.

The main highway, scenic US 93, winds along the main stream of the Salmon River, while smaller roads follow tributaries into the wild. At the hamlet of North Fork, the Salmon River Road turns west from the highway, heading downstream along the impassable rapids that Lewis and Clark aptly dubbed the "River of No Return."

A view of the scenic Lake Coeur d'Alene, near the resort

A view of the Sawtooth Mountains, from the shores of Redfish Lake

Sawtooth National Recreation Area ❹

Hwy 75. 🄸 *(208) 727-5013.* **Camp-ground.** ⬜ *year-round.* ♿ ✔

THIS SUPERB destination for hiking and camping encompasses 765,000 acres (309,586 ha) of rivers, mountain meadows, forests, and jagged peaks of the Sawtooth Range. For visitors driving up Hwy 75 from Sun Valley *(see p576)*, the best introduction to the area is at the 8,701-ft (2,652-m) high **Galena Summit**, where a spectacular panorama looks north over the Salmon River.

At an elevation of 6,200 ft (1,890 m), surrounded by the Sawtooth Mountains, the tiny hamlet of **Stanley** (population 75), has one of the most beautiful settings of any town in the US. The unpaved streets and wood-fronted frontier-style buildings make visitors feel like they have, at last, arrived in the Wild West, despite the fact that the glitzy resort of Sun Valley is barely an hour away to the south. Another attraction is **Redfish Lake**, 10 miles (16 km) south of Stanley, where rustic Red-fish Lake Lodge is found near the foot of Mount Heyburn.

Boise ❺

🄸 *185,787.* ✈ 🚍 🄸 *2676 Vista Ave, (208) 385-0362.*

FRENCH TRAPPERS in the 19th-century named this outpost "Boise," meaning wooded. Even today, this homespun, slow-paced city presents a picture-postcard image of America. Locals and visitors walk, ride bicycles, or enjoy an afternoon picnic on the grass in the vast Greenbelt parkland that adjoins the Boise River in the heart of downtown.

Boise is also the state capital and the largest city in rural Idaho. Its focal point is the domed **State Capitol**, which was completed in 1920 after 15 years of construction. The building's main distinc-tion is that it is the only US capitol to be heated by natu-rally occurring geothermal water. It was built of sand-stone blocks quarried by inmates at the **Old Idaho Penitentiary**, 2 miles (3 km) east of the capitol.

Now open to visitors, the state penitentiary was in use from 1870 to 1970. Apart from the prison, the grounds also house a series of museums dedicated to such subjects as transportation, the uses of electricity, and mining.

The city's historic center is three blocks south of the capitol. Here a dozen late-Victorian commercial build-ings have been restored and house a lively set of coffee houses, bars, restaurants, and boutiques. Boise's oldest building, completed in 1864, now houses the **Basque Museum and Cultural Center**, which traces the presence of Basque sheep-herders in Boise and across western US, and is also known for celebrating Basque culture with frequent events. A cluster of museums and cultural centers lie in **Julia Davis Park**, a 40-acre (16-ha) green area that straddles the Boise River at the heart of the Greenbelt.

A 15-minute drive by car away from the city is the **Peregrine Funds World Center for Birds of Prey**. One of the most successful organizations for breeding as well as studying raptors, the world center has been instru-mental in recovering endan-gered populations of peregrine falcons in the US, a species that was nearly wiped out by lethal pesticides in the 1970s. Visitors also have the rare opportunity to see a variety of birds including eagles, condors, and falcons while enjoying a hilltop view of the surrounding sagebrush plains.

🄫 **Peregrine Funds World Center for Birds of Prey**
5666 Flying Hawk Lane. 🄲 *(208) 362-8687.* ⬜ *Mar–Oct: 9am–5pm daily; Nov–Feb: 10am–4pm daily.* ⬤ *Jan 1, Thanksgiving, Dec 25.*

The beautiful exterior of the Idaho State Capitol in Boise

Skaters outside Sun Valley Lodge, Sun Valley

Sun Valley ❻

⊠ ℹ *411 N Main St, Ketchum, (208)
726-3423.* Ⓦ *www.visitsunvalley.com*

DEVELOPED IN the late 1930s
by the Union Pacific Railroad baron Averell Harriman,
Sun Valley is one of the oldest
and highest-profile winter
resorts in the US. The construction of the Tyrolean-style
Sun Valley Lodge *(see p600)*
and the adjacent ski area was
completed in 1936, after
which Harriman was inspired
to invite Hollywood movie
stars and other members of
the glitterati to enjoy his
facilities. Sun Valley's fame
was thus ensured by the
presence of celebrities such
as Errol Flynn, Gary Cooper,
Clark Gable, and Ernest
Hemingway. Since then, the
Olympic-quality skiing on the
well-groomed slopes of the
9,151-ft (2,789-m) Bald
Mountain has continued to
draw an exclusive clientele
during the season between
November and April. The
resort also commissioned the
world's first ski-lift.

Before the 1930s, however,
the area was a mining and
sheep-ranching center,
based in the adjacent town
of Ketchum. This town still
retains many of its rugged
frontier characteristics,
despite the influx of multimillion-dollar vacation
homes. The region's
history is on view
in the **Ketchum
Sun Valley
Museum**.
The town also
offers a variety of
accommodations.

Although most visitors never
stray beyond Sun Valley and
Ketchum, the surrounding
landscape is filled with other
recreational options. Bicyclists
can follow the 20-mile (32-
km) **Wood River Trail**, along
the old Union Pacific Railroad
right-of-way. The Wood River
is also a prime trout-fishing
stream, while to the north, the
majestic Sawtooth National
Recreation Area *(see p575)*
offers pristine hiking and
camping country.

🏛 **Ketchum Sun Valley
Museum**
180 1st St E. Ⓒ *(208) 726-8118.*
◯ *May–Oct: 11am–4pm daily.* ♿

Three Island
Crossing State
Park ❼

Off I-84, Glenns Ferry Exit. ℹ *Glenns
Ferry, (208) 366-2394.* **Campground.**
Ⓦ *www.idahoparks.org/parks/
threeisland.html*

ONE OF THE most evocative
sights along the historic
Oregon Trail *(see p450)* is the
famous Three Islands
Crossing, which provided
one of the few safe places
for emigrants to cross the
dangerous Snake River. The
ford was in use until 1869,
when Gus Glenn construct-
ed a ferry 2 miles (3 km)
upstream. Not all attempts
at crossing, however,
were successful.
Depending on the
time of year and
the level of the
water, it some-
times proved fatal

**The Hemingway
Memorial, Sun Valley**

to the pioneers in the
westward-bound wagons.
Some pioneers balked at the
dangers involved and did not
attempt the crossing. Instead,
they would continue along
the river's barren south bank
before rejoining the main trail
west of Boise.

Today, the park offers a
campground and numerous
picnic areas. Visitors can still
experience the dangers of the
1800s if they visit the park in
mid-August, when the ford
crossing is re-created by history enthusiasts wearing
period costumes and driving
replica wagons.

Bruneau Dunes
State Park ❽

Off I-84, Hwy 78. Ⓒ *Mountain
Home, (208) 366-7919.* **Campground.** ♿

IMMEDIATELY south of the
Snake River, at the foot of
the high-desert Owyhee
Mountains, a surprising sight
arises from the surrounding
sagebush plains. Some of the
largest sand dunes in North
America, the Bruneau Dunes
rise to heights of nearly 500 ft
(152 m). They are protected
from the destructive impacts
of cars, motorcycles, and
dune buggies within one of
Idaho's largest state parks.

A visitor center explains
how these quartz and feldspar
sand dunes were formed,
and why they are not blown
away. The reason for this phenomenon is simple: prevailing
winds blow from opposite
directions for roughly equal
amounts of time, which keep
the dunes fairly stable. There
are also specimens of local
wildlife on display, including
a short-eared owl. A small
astronomical observatory is
often open to the public.

The park encompasses a
variety of habitats such as
marsh, prairie, and desert.
Wildlife includes snakes and
lizards, and birds such as owls
and eagles. A few small lakes
lie at the foot of the dunes
where visitors can go fishing
in canoes or rubber rafts.
Other activities offered are
camping and horseback riding.

Snake River Gorge, Twin Falls

Twin Falls ❾

🏞 34,164. 🚌 ℹ 858 N Blue Lakes Blvd, (208) 733-3974.
ⓦ www.twinfallschambers.com

THE FALLS FOR which the city was named have been diminished by dams and irrigation, but Twin Falls is still home to a splendid waterfall. Called the "Niagara of the West," the 212-ft (65-m) high and 1,000-ft (305-m) wide **Shoshone Falls** is an impressive sight, especially in spring when the water flows are at their peak.

Located 5 miles (8 km) northeast of the city, the falls are framed by the deep **Snake River Gorge**, famous for the ill-fated attempt by motorcycle daredevil Evel Knievel to leap across it in 1974. He survived, but with many injuries. The city stretches along the level plains to the south of the gorge, and is the center for potato-growing farms and cattle ranches.

Craters of the Moon National Monument ❿

US 20. ℂ (208) 527-3257.
🅿 (Campground only).
ⓦ www.nps.gov/crmo

SPRAWLED ACROSS 83 sq miles (215 sq km) in central Idaho, the Craters of the Moon National Monument showcases one of the most extraordinary landscapes in the country. The most accessible section can be explored via the numerous short trails that lead through rippling, jagged, lava fields, strewn with cones and craters. They range from 15,000 to 2,000 years of age. The fields were formed by molten lava, which seeped out from gaps in the earth's crust over a period of 13,000 years. Despite their forbidding, blackened appearance, the lava fields harbor more than 50 species of mammals, 170 species of birds, and millions of resplendent wildflowers, which bloom in summer each year. Numerous caves and lava tubes also run beneath the surface.

The name "Craters of the Moon" was coined in the 1920s, when the monument was established. The visitor center near the entrance recounts the park's geological and natural history. Visitors can also improve their Hawaiian lava vocabulary, learning the scientific terms for sharp lava (*a'a*), layered lava (*kipukas*), and smooth lava (*pa'hoe'hoe*).

In the 1960s, astronauts from the *Apollo 14* space mission visited the monument to learn more about volcanic geology that was similar to that of the moon.

Camping is also available in the park during the summer, and the main loop road draws crowds of cross-country skiers during winter.

Idaho Falls ⓫

I-15. ⌧ 🚌 ℂ (208) 523-1010.

SET ALONG THE banks of the Snake River, with Wyoming's Grand Teton Mountains rising to the east, Idaho Falls is a charming and predominantly agricultural city with a large Mormon population (*see p519*). Dominated by the towering Mormon temple, the city has a vast "Greenbelt" area where people can jog and inline skate. Although the Idaho Falls, which lent their name to the city, have now been dammed, they still provide a scenic setting to the parkland.

The main attraction here is the **Idaho National Engineering and Environmental Laboratory** (INEEL), located 50 miles (80 km) west of the city. Established in 1949 to design, build, and test nuclear reactors for military and civilian purposes, the 890-sq-mile (2,305-sq-km) site now holds the largest concentration of nuclear reactors in the world. The world's first reactor, the EBR-1, was built here in 1951 and is now open for viewing. On July 17, 1955, INEEL was the site of the world's first peaceful use of atomic power, when INEEL engineers sent 2,000 kilowatts (2 megawatts) of electricity to light up the nearby town of Arco.

Idaho National Engineering & Environmental Lab
Hwy 20/26. ℂ (208) 526-0050, (800) 708-2680. ⃝ May–Sep: 8am–4pm daily. ⬤ Jul 4. ♿

Blackened volcanic cones, Craters of the Moon National Monument

Montana

THE NORTHERNMOST OF THE Rocky Mountain states, Montana abounds in tall, rugged mountains, snowcapped peaks, lush valleys, and seemingly endless plains stretching beneath its trademark "big sky." The sheer scale and majesty of its wide open spaces and the larger-than-life character of its inhabitants, past and present, prompted Nobel Prize-winning novelist John Steinbeck to write "Montana seems to me to be what a small boy would think Texas is like from hearing Texans. Of all the states it is my favorite and my love."

Big Hole National Battlefield, surrounded by mountains

Big Hole National Battlefield ⑫

Hwy 43 near Wisdom. 〖 *(406) 689-3155.* ◯ *May–Sep: 8:30am–6pm; Oct–Apr: 9am–5pm daily.* ● *Jan 1, Thanksgiving, Dec 25.* ⟩⟨ *(free in winter).* ♿

LOCATED NEAR the Idaho border at an altitude of some 7,000 ft (2,134 m) in the Bitterroot Mountains, this battlefield site sits at the head of the lush Big Hole Valley, famed for its cattle ranches and trout-fishing opportunities. This serene pastoral scene is far removed from the suffering experienced here on August 9, 1877. On that day, the flight north by 750 Nez Perce Indians, mostly women and children, was cut short by a surprise attack by US Army soldiers and civilian volunteers, leading to the death of nearly 100 Indians. The tribe continued their journey toward Canada, traveling another 1,500 miles (2,414 km) before finally surrendering in October, just 30 miles (48 km) short of the Canadian border.

Missoula ⑬

🏙 *58,000.* ✈ ➡ 🚉 *825 E Front St, (406) 543-6623.*

NESTLING IN the Rocky Mountains of western Montana, Missoula is still dependent upon traditional Montana industries, such as timber and transportation. This lively city is also home to the University of Montana.

Surrounded by acres of magnificent wilderness, this picturesque city formed the backdrop of the book and subsequent movie *A River Runs Through It*. The city also houses the **Smokejumpers Base Aerial Fire Depot**, a national center for fighting forest fires in the Rockies. Exhibits explore fire-fighting techniques and equipment, and depending on the time of the year (summer is forest-fire season), guests are able to tour the airplanes and meet fire-fighters.

To the south, the Bitterroot Valley has ranches and small towns, hemmed in by a pair of towering mountain ranges.

🚒 Smokejumpers Base Aerial Fire Depot
W Broadway. 〖 *(406) 329-4934.* ◯ *May–Sep: 8:30am–5pm daily; Sep–May: by appointment.* ⟩

Flathead Valley ⑭

ℹ *Bigfork Chamber of Commerce, 8155, Hwy 35, (406) 837-5886.* **Salish & Kootenai Tribal Council** 〖 *(406) 675-2700.*

MOST OF THE valley's land, which stretches between the 40-mile (64-km) long and 15-mile (24-km) wide Flathead Lake and Missoula, is part of the Flathead Indian Reservation. Since 1855 this has been home to descendants of the region's Salish, Kootenai, and Pend D'Oreille Indian tribes. In summer, communities such as Elmo and Arlee celebrate Native traditions in numerous pow-wows, which are traditional gatherings featuring rodeo competitions, craft demonstrations, and sales.

The **People's Center** in Pablo traces the history of the Flathead region from a Native American perspective. To the west, some 18,500 acres (7,487 ha) of rolling ranch-land were set aside in 1908 as the National Bison Range, housing bison, deer, bighorn sheep, and pronghorn.

The largest natural freshwater lake west of the Mississippi River, Flathead Lake is a deep-blue jewel at the western foot of the Rocky Mountains. Cherry orchards and towns like Bigfork line Hwy 35 on the lake's eastern shore, while to the west the busier US 93 hugs the water for more than 35 miles (56 km). Visitors can rent bikes, or take kayaks and guided boat tours into the scenic lake.

🏛 People's Center
US 93 in Pablo. 〖 *(406) 675-0160.* ◯ *9am–5pm Mon–Fri, 10am–6pm Sat–Sun.* ♿

Flathead Lake, nestling at the foot of the Rocky Mountains

Glacier National Park ⑮

North of W Glacier. 🛈 *(406) 888-7800.* 🚫♿✉⚠
Ⓦ www.nps.gov/glac

S PREADING NEARLY a million
acres (404,690 ha) over the
northern Rocky Mountains,
Glacier National Park holds
some of the world's most
sublime scenery. With elevations ranging from 3,200 ft
(975 m) along the Flathead
River to summits topping
10,000 ft (3,048 m), the park
contains a wide variety of
landscapes. Alongside four
dozen glaciers (which gave
the park its name) and
millennia-old limestone cliffs,
there are many lakes, waterfalls, and abundant wildlife,
including moose, wolves, and
bears. The flora ranges from
high grassy plains to alpine
tundra. In July, the park's
higher altitudes are ablaze
with meadows of blue
gentians, yellow lillies, pink
heathers, and feathery white
Bear Grass.

Hiking, a popular activity in Glacier National Park

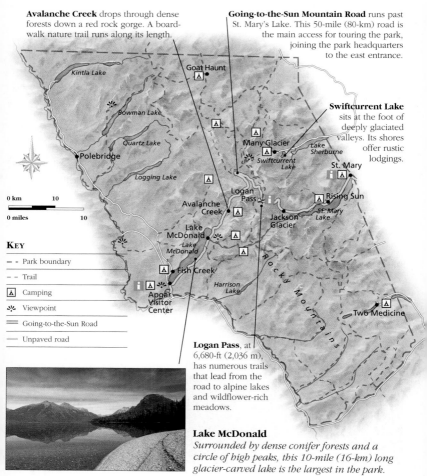

Avalanche Creek drops through dense
forests down a red rock gorge. A boardwalk nature trail runs along its length.

Going-to-the-Sun Mountain Road runs past
St. Mary's Lake. This 50-mile (80-km) road is
the main access for touring the park,
joining the park headquarters
to the east entrance.

Swiftcurrent Lake
sits at the foot of
deeply glaciated
valleys. Its shores
offer rustic
lodgings.

KEY

- – Park boundary
- - - Trail
- 🅰 Camping
- 🌿 Viewpoint
- ═══ Going-to-the-Sun Road
- ══ Unpaved road

Logan Pass, at
6,680-ft (2,036 m),
has numerous trails
that lead from the
road to alpine lakes
and wildflower-rich
meadows.

Lake McDonald
*Surrounded by dense conifer forests and a
circle of high peaks, this 10-mile (16-km) long
glacier-carved lake is the largest in the park.*

Great Falls ⑯

🏛 56,000. ✈ 🚌 ℹ 710
1st Ave, (406) 761-5036.
🌐 www.greatfallsonline.net

NESTLING picturesquely between the majestic Rocky Mountains to the west and Little Belt Mountains to the east, this rural city owes its name to its location along the Missouri River. As the river cuts through the city, it drops over 500 ft (152 m) in a series of rapids and five breathtaking waterfalls, first noted by explorers Lewis and Clark *(see p570)* in 1805.

The city is best known for its two excellent museums. One, the **Charles M. Russell Museum**, traces the history of the American West, focusing on the life and work of resident cowboy and prolific Wild West artist "Charlie" Russell, who gave the city much of its cultural flavor. His home and log cabin studio are adjacent to the expansive museum.

On a bluff overlooking the Missouri River, 2 miles (3 km) northeast of downtown, is the **Lewis and Clark National Historic Trail Interpretive Center**. This museum details the epic explorations of the Corps of Discovery, the cross-country expedition led by Meriwether Lewis and William Clark from 1803 to 1806.

For 45 miles (72 km) downstream from the center, the Missouri River runs as a "Wild and Scenic" river on one of its virgin stretches, a route paralleled by a bike trail and driving tour along US 87. The route ends at Fort Benton, historic head of navigation on the Missouri River.

🏛 **Charles M. Russell Museum**
400 13th St. 📞 (406) 727-8787. 🕐 May–Sep: 9am–6pm Mon–Sat, noon–5pm Sun; Oct–Apr: 10am–5pm Tue–Sat, 1–5pm Sun. ● Jan 1, Easter, Thanksgiving, Dec 25. 📷 ♿
🏛 **Lewis & Clark National Historic Trail Interpretive Center**
📞 (406) 727-8733. 🕐 Jun–Sep: 9am–6pm daily; Oct–May: 9am–5pm Tue–Sat, noon–5pm Sun. ● Jan 1, Thanksgiving, Dec 25. 📷 ♿

Helena ⑰

🏛 45,000. ✈ 🚌 ℹ 225 Cruse Ave, (406) 442-4120.

THE STATE capital, Helena makes a fine base for exploring Montana. Originally known as "Last Chance Gulch," Helena was founded as a gold-mining camp in the 1860s. Fortunately much of the wealth generated here remained, as is evident from the number of mansions built by mining millionaires. Many of these exuberantly designed Victorian-era homes have been converted into B&B inns. The centerpiece of Helena is the copper-domed **Montana State Capitol**, decorated with several fine historical murals, including one of explorers Lewis and Clark painted by Charlie Russell. A statue on the grounds portrays Helena resident Jeanette Rankin, who in 1917 was the first woman to be elected to the United States Congress.

Statue of Jeanette Rankin, Montana State Capitol

Butte ⑱

🏛 34,000. ✈ 🚌 ℹ 1000 George St, (406) 723-3177, (800) 735-6814.

LOCATED IN THE heart of the Rocky Mountains, Butte is named for the prominent conical hill, Big Butte, which guards its northwest corner. That Butte has some of the world's richest mineral reserves is evident by the extensive signs of the gold, silver, and copper mining industry that thrived here from the 1870s through the first half of the 20th century. Glimpses of Butte's multiethnic, immigrant culture are also visible in such events as the St. Patrick's Day celebration by the town's Irish Catholic population. Of Butte's many fine museums, the **World Museum of Mining** occupies the site of an early gold mine. Its superb collection of mineral specimens, mining machinery, and mementos of the town's proud industrial heritage, also includes displays on Butte's leading role in the development of mineworkers' unions. Outside, some 30 historic buildings dating from 1880 to 1910 re-create an early mining camp, complete with a church, a schoolhouse, bordellos, and boarding houses.

Sites such as the **Granite Mountain Mine Memorial** commemorate the 168 men killed in a 1917 mine disaster. High above the city, the 90-ft (27-m) statue of "Our Lady of the Rockies" stands as a proud symbol of Butte's strength and endurance.

🏛 **World Museum of Mining**
Park St. 📞 (406) 723-7211. 🕐 9am–5:30pm daily. 📷 ♿

Lewis and Clark National Historic Trail Interpretive Center, Great Falls

Exterior of the Museum of the Rockies, Bozeman

Bozeman ⑲

🏃 32,000. ✈ 🚌 ℹ 2000 Commerce Way, (406) 586-5421.

Situated in the heart of the Gallatin Valley, Bozeman lies in the middle of a sacred Sioux Indian hunting ground, which is now the state's most productive agricultural region. Founded in the 1860s, the city is one of the few Montana towns where the economy and history are not based on mining or railroads. Its present prominence is due mainly to the Montana State University. Established in 1893, it is the state's largest university and houses the **Museum of the Rockies**. The museum takes visitors through four billion years of Earth's history, delving into everything from displays of dinosaurs and dinosaur eggs unearthed in Montana Plains, to pioneer history, Indian artifacts, and Western art. A planetarium presents astronomy and laser light shows.

Downtown's tree-lined streets are pleasant to stroll through. Visitors can also learn about local history at the **Gallatin Pioneer Museum**, housed in the former county jail.

Bozeman is also a base for various activities based in the surrounding countryside. The headwaters of the Missouri River, the longest river in the US, are formed by the confluence of the Jefferson, Madison, and Gallatin Rivers, which come together 40 miles (64 km) northwest of Bozeman. All three smaller rivers are famous for fishing and whitewater rafting.

🏛 **Museum of the Rockies**
600 W Kagy Blvd on the Montana State University Campus. 📞 (406) 994-2251. ◻ May–Sep: 8am–8pm daily; Oct–Apr: 9am–5pm Mon–Sat, 12:30–5pm Sun. ● Thanksgiving, Dec 25. 🎫 ♿

🏛 **Gallatin Pioneer Museum**
317 W Main St. 📞 (406) 522-8122. ◻ May–Sep: 10am–4:30pm Mon–Sat; Oct–Apr: 11am–4pm Tue–Sat. ● public hols. ♿

Billings ⑳

🏃 110,000. ✈ 🚌 ℹ 815 S 27th St, (406) 252-4016. 🌐 www.billingschamber.com

Founded by the Northern Pacific Railroad in 1882, and now Montana's largest city, Billings was named after the railroad company's president. In just a few months, Billings grew into a bustling community of 2,000 people. Visitors can get a feel of the town's frontier days, and of Montana's proud cowboy traditions, from the Wild West paintings and sculptures displayed in the **Yellowstone Art Gallery**. The gallery is located in the old county jail.

However, the most striking feature of Billings is the Rimrocks, a 400-ft (122-m) high sandstone wall that runs the length of the city along the Yellowstone River.

Outside the city the scenery is even more spectacular, especially along the Beartooth Highway that runs southwest toward Yellowstone National Park (see pp584–5). The 65-mile (105-km) section of highway between Red Lodge

and the Wyoming border has been rated among the country's most breathtaking driving routes.

🏛 **Yellowstone Art Museum**
401 N 27th St. 📞 (406) 256-6804. ◻ 10am–5pm Tue–Sat (until 8pm on Thu), noon–5pm Sun. ● public hols. 🎫 ♿

Little Bighorn Battlefield National Monument ㉑

Exit 510 off I-90 Hwy 212, Crow Agency. ℹ (406) 638-2621. 🌐 www.nps.gov/libi

Located on the Crow Indian Reservation, this battlefield preserves the site of a key moment in American history, known as "Custer's Last Stand." In June 1876, the impetuous US Army Lieutenant Colonel George Armstrong Custer (see p446) led his troop of 210 soldiers of the 7th Cavalry in an attack on a large Indian encampment along the Little Bighorn River. Almost immediately they were surrounded by more than 2,000 combined Sioux and Cheyenne Indian warriors under the leadership of legendary Chief Sitting Bull. Custer's soldiers were wiped out. A sandstone marker stands above the soldiers' mass grave, and a small museum describes the disastrous battle.

Memorial to Custer's Last Stand, Little Bighorn Battlefield

Wyoming

THE WYOMING STATE INSIGNIA, an image of a cowboy waving his Stetson hat while riding on the back of a bucking horse, says it all. This is classic cowboy country, a land of wide-open grasslands stretching for miles in every direction, where fewer than a half-million people inhabit an area of nearly 100,000 sq miles (260,000 sq km). For visitors, the main draws of Wyoming lie in its northwestern corner, where the twin spectacles of Yellowstone and Grand Teton National Parks attract some three million visitors annually.

Buffalo Bill Historical Center, Cody

Cody ㉒

🏠 9,000. ℹ️ 836 Sheridan Ave, (307) 587-2297.

CODY WAS FOUNDED by Wild West impresario "Buffalo Bill" Cody in 1896. Long the symbol of the American West, the city maintains its frontier look and is home to two museums that document this unique era. The smaller of these is **Trail Town**, a home-spun collection of artifacts and buildings assembled on the original site of Cody. One highlight here is a log cabin reputedly used as a hideout by outlaws Butch Cassidy and the Sundance Kid.

Cody's main attraction, however, is the **Buffalo Bill Historical Center**, a 240,000-sq-ft (22,300-sq-m) complex of galleries that trace the natural, cultural, and military history of the Wild West. It holds more than 500 weapons, a superb collection of Western art, and Plains Indians arti-facts, as well as a museum on Buffalo Bill himself.

In keeping with Buffalo Bill's pursuit of public spec-tacle, Cody's other great attraction is the **Cody Night Rodeo**, the nation's

longest-running rodeo, held daily between late June and August.

🏛 Buffalo Bill Historical Center

720 Sheridan Ave. 📞 (307) 587-4771. 🕐 Jun–Sep 15: 7am–8pm; Sep 16–Oct: 8am–5pm; Nov–Mar: 10am–3pm Tue–Sun. ⬤ Jan 1, Thanksgiving, Dec 25. 🅿 ♿

Yellowstone National Park ㉓

See pp584–5.

Jackson ㉔

🏠 9,000. ✈ 🚌 ℹ️ 532 N Cache St, (307) 733-3316.

A POPULAR STOP since the days of the fur-trapping moun-tain men, Jackson is perhaps Wyoming's most visited city. Located at the southern entrance to Grand Teton and Yellowstone National Parks, much of its natural beauty is giving way to vacation homes and ski resorts. But Jackson retains its Wild West ambience despite the boutiques and art galleries that surround its tree-lined central square, and the congested summer traffic.

Alongside the national parks, dude ranches, and Wild West re-enactments, the main attraction is wildlife. The 25,000-acre (10,120-ha) **National Elk Refuge**, stretch-ing between Jackson and the Grand Teton National Park, is home to some 7,500 native elk that congregate here in winter. Its entrance lies one mile (1.6 km) northeast of Jackson. Guided tours on horse-drawn sleighs are offered daily between November and April. In summer, the main gondola at Jackson Hole Ski Area (rated as one of the country's most challenging) lifts sight-seers over 4,000 ft (1,219 m) to the top of Rendevous Peak for a grand panorama.

🦌 National Elk Refuge

E Broadway at Elk Refuge Rd. 📞 (307) 733-9212. 🕐 8am–5pm daily. ⬤ Thanksgiving, Dec 25. 🅿 sleigh rides.

BUFFALO BILL

One of the most colorful Wild West figures, William Frederick Cody (1846–1917) started out as a teenage rider for the Pony Express. He then served as US Army scout during the Indian Wars. When the war ended in 1865, he began supplying buffalo meat to workers of the transcontinental railroad, earning himself the nick-name "Buffalo Bill." Cody was the model for a series of newspaper stories and "dime novels" written by Ned Buntline. The real-life Buffalo Bill soon parlayed his credentials into world-wide fame and fortune. Star of a spectacular circus in which historical scenes were acted out by cowboys and Indians, including such figures as Chief Sitting Bull, Cody toured the world between 1883 and World War I. Despite his fortune, by 1913 he was bankrupt, and died four years later in Denver (see pp588–9).

Statue of Buffalo Bill

Grand Teton National Park [25]

Moose. [i] *Grand Teton National Park Headquarters, (307) 739-3600.*
[W] www.nps.gov/grte

THE YOUNGEST peaks in the Rockies, the Grand Tetons are among the sharpest and most dramatic mountains in the world. Their silver granite peaks rise over a mile above the lush Snake River Valley of Jackson Hole, all of which has been protected within the boundaries of the 485-sq-mile (1,256-sq-km) Grand Teton National Park. There are miles of hiking trails that lead to numerous glaciers and lakes. Wildlife, such as elk, bison, and bears, abound. In summer, kayakers and rafters float the Snake River, while powerboats and canoes take more leisurely cruises on Jackson and Jenny Lakes. In winter, all hiking trails are open to skiers who make their way through the wilderness.

A view of the Grand Teton summits and fall colors

Jenny Lake
The popular Jenny Lake lies at the base of the 13,770-ft (4,197-m) Grand Teton. Trails lead along forested shores to quiet beaches, with the mountains reflecting in the distance.

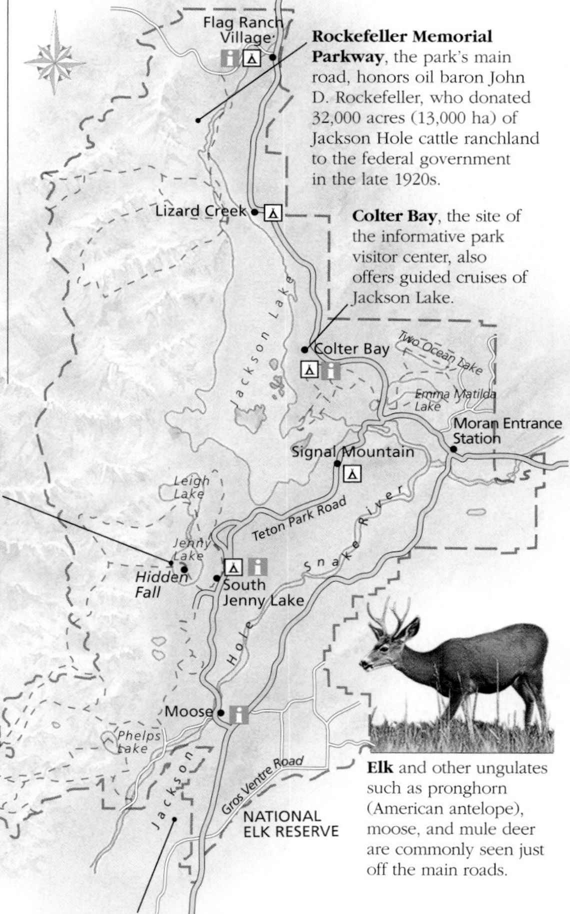

Rockefeller Memorial Parkway, the park's main road, honors oil baron John D. Rockefeller, who donated 32,000 acres (13,000 ha) of Jackson Hole cattle ranchland to the federal government in the late 1920s.

Colter Bay, the site of the informative park visitor center, also offers guided cruises of Jackson Lake.

Elk and other ungulates such as pronghorn (American antelope), moose, and mule deer are commonly seen just off the main roads.

0 km 10

0 miles 10

KEY

- Park boundary
- Trail
- [Δ] Camping
- Major road
- Unpaved road

Jackson Hole
Frontier fur trappers referred to a large valley ringed by mountains as a "hole." This valley of the Snake River runs between the Grand Teton and Gros Ventre Mountains, upstream from Jackson.

Yellowstone National Park ㉓

Official park sign

Oꜰ THE marvels of the world, and the country's oldest national park, this wild wonderland spreads across the three states of Wyoming, Montana, and Idaho. Its heart is a volcanic plateau at an average elevation of 8,000 ft (2,438 m), housing over 10,000 hot springs and geysers – more than half of the world's total. Alongside the spectacular shows of geothermal activity, it has dense forests, towering peaks, deep river canyons, and enough outdoor recreation to last a lifetime. The 175-mile (282-km) Grand Loop Road does a full circuit of the main sights. Lodging is often booked solid, so visitors should reserve in advance.

An elk crossing the road in the park

★ Mammoth Hot Springs

Hundreds of geothermal springs bubble up in Yellowstone, forming colored pools of boiling hot, mineral-rich water. The mineral content drapes delicate curtains of marble-like travertine over the cascading terraces of stone.

Grand Prismatic Spring

The 370-ft (113-m) wide Grand Prismatic Spring lies close to Old Faithful. The rainbow-colored hot spring, lining the bank of the Firehole River, is one of the world's largest.

★ Old Faithful Geyser

Named for its precise 90-minute eruption cycle, Old Faithful is the park's icon. Its steaming plume shoots as high as 120–180 ft (36–55 m) and lasts 2 to 5 minutes. Visitors line up on the wooden boardwalk to watch it spurt nearly 8,400 gallons (31,797 liters) of water per eruption.

Bison

With over 3,000 bison, Yellowstone has the world's largest herd. They roam freely across the park, often even disrupting traffic. Despite their docile appearance, bison can be dangerous, so visitors should avoid contact with them or any other wild animal.

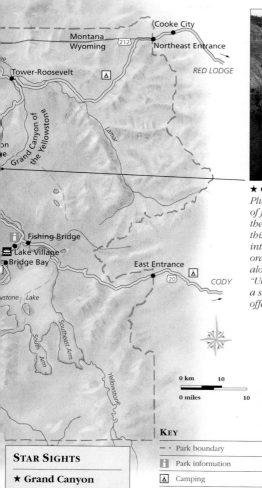

★ Grand Canyon

Plunging 500 ft (152 m) in a pair of falls – Upper and Lower Falls – the Yellowstone River has carved this 20-mile (32-km) long canyon into the mineral-rich yellow and orange rhyolite rock. Many trails along its rim offer splendid vistas. "Uncle Tom's Trail" drops down a steep staircase on to a platform, offering a close-up view of the falls.

Bears

Bears are plentiful in the park. Black bears are the most common, and more than 200 grizzlies inhabit its wilder reaches. Most animals avoid contact with humans, and rangers advise that humans should avoid any contact with bears.

KEY

- – – Park boundary
- 🛈 Park information
- 🅰 Camping
- ⛴ Ferry
- 🎣 Geyser
- ══ Major road
- — State border

STAR SIGHTS

★ **Grand Canyon**

★ **Mammoth Hot Springs**

★ **Old Faithful Geyser**

The Medicine Wheel on Medicine Mountain, the Bighorn Scenic Byway (US 14)

Bighorn Mountains ㉖

Bighorn National Forest ▮ (307) 674-2600.

STANDING AT the western edge of the historic plains of the Powder River Basin, the Bighorn Mountains were named for the bighorn sheep that were once abundant here. Crowned by the 13,175-ft (4,016-m) Cloud Peak, the mountains are crossed by a pair of very scenic highways, US 16 in the south (the old Yellowstone Trail) and US 14 in the north, which divides into two forks. The northern-most section of US 14 climbs past one of the country's most enigmatic archaeological sites, the **Medicine Wheel**, an 80-ft (24-m) diameter stone circle, which is located 27 miles (43 km) east of Lovell. This ancient circle is held sacred by Native Sioux and Cheyenne Indians, and offers a vast panorama from its 10,000-ft (3,048-m) elevation.

Devil's Tower National Monument ㉗

▮ (307) 467-5283. ▯
▥ www.nps.gov/deto/home.htm

RISING OVER 1,200 ft (366 m) above the surrounding plains, Devil's Tower is a flat-topped volcanic plug that looks like a giant tree stump. Featured in the 1977 Steven Spielberg movie *Close*

Encounters of the Third Kind, this geological landmark is located in Wyoming's north-eastern corner, looming over the banks of the Belle Fourche River. Set aside as a national monument by President Theodore Roosevelt in 1906, Devil's Tower (also known as Bear's Lodge) is a sacred site of worship for many Native Americans. The rolling hills of this 1,347-acre (545-ha) park are covered with pine forests, deciduous wood-lands, and prairie grasslands, and abound in deer, prairie dogs, and other wildlife. The site's vertical rock walls and scenic trails are a magnet for rock-climbers and hikers.

Casper ㉘

▨ 50,000. ▤ ▮ 330 S Center St, (307) 234-5362.
▥ www.casperwyoming.info

LOCATED IN the heart of Wyoming, Casper has been the center of the state's large petroleum industry

since 1890. Surrounded by miles of broad, flat plains, this large, busy city grew up around the 1860s Fort Caspar, now a historical site and museum, known as the **Fort Caspar Museum**. Many of the fort buildings have been reconstructed at the point where the historic Oregon Trail *(see p450)* crossed the North Platte River, west of downtown. The museum features a variety of cultural and natural history exhibits pertaining to central Wyoming.

North and west of Casper lie miles of arid badlands, including such sites as the legendary "Hole in the Wall," where outlaws such as Butch Cassidy had hideouts. More accessible to visitors is the weirdly eroded forest of figures known as "Hell's Half Acre," located 35 miles (56 km) west of town on the south side of US 20.

🏛 **Fort Caspar Museum**
Hwy 220. ▮ (307) 235-8462.
▢ check for times. ▯

A view of the exterior of Fort Caspar Museum, Casper

Guernsey ㉙

🏛 1,300. ℹ 91 S Wyoming St, (307) 836-2715.

SET ALONG THE banks of the North Platte River, this is a small town whose size belies a wealth of historical interest. Just south of town are two of the most palpable reminders of the pioneer migrations westward along the Oregon Trail. The **Oregon Trail Ruts State Historic Site** preserves a set of 4–6-ft (1–1.8-m) deep gouges carved by wagon wheels into the soft riverside sandstone. A mile south, the Register Cliff has been inscribed with the names of hundreds of explorers, fur trappers, and Oregon Trail pioneers who crossed the area in the mid-1800s.

Evocative as these sights are, Guernsey's most important historic spot is the **Fort Laramie National Historic Site**, a reconstruction of a fur-trapping and US cavalry outpost. Between its founding in the 1830s and its abandonment in 1890s, the fort was a prime point of contact between Europeans, Americans, and Native Americans. Many of the buildings have been restored, and costumed interpreters act out roles from the fort's history.

🏚 **Fort Laramie National Historic Site**
US 26. ☎ (307) 837-2221.
◻ May–Sep: 8am–7pm daily; Oct–Apr: 8am–4:30pm daily. ● Jan 1, Thanksgiving, Dec 25. 🅿 ♿

Laramie ㉚

🏛 27,000. 🚏 🚌 ℹ 800 S 3rd St, (307) 745-7339.

HOME TO THE main state university campus, the small city of Laramie exudes an infectious youthful vitality, which is rare in other Wyoming cities. Located east of downtown at an elevation of 7,200 ft (2,195 m), the University of Wyoming is the highest college in the country. The campus is dominated by the strikingly modern **American Heritage**

Center, an art museum and library documenting Wyoming history and culture. The town also housed Wyoming's first prison, now restored to its 1880s condition, when Butch Cassidy and other outlaws served time here. Located west of downtown, the old prison is now the centerpiece of the **Wyoming Territorial Park**, which also includes a re-creation of a frontier town.

The area around Laramie is rich historically and scenically. The 50-mile (80-km) stretch of the Lincoln Highway between Laramie and Cheyenne preserves part of the first transcontinental road in the US. To the west of Laramie, Hwy 130 follows the Snowy Range Scenic Byway through the beautiful Medicine Bow Mountains.

🏛 **American Heritage Center**
22nd St & Willett Dr. ☎ (307) 766-2570. ◻ Mon–Fri: 8am–5pm; Sat: 11am–5pm. ● public hols. ♿
🌿 **Wyoming Territorial Park**
975 Snowy Range Rd. ☎ (307) 745-6161. ◻ May–Sep:10am–5pm daily. 🅿 ♿

Cheyenne ㉛

🏛 55,000. ✈ 🚏 🚌 ℹ 301 W 16 St, (307) 638-3388.

FOUNDED IN 1867 as a US Army fort along the newly constructed Union Pacific Railroad, Cheyenne later

Statue of cowboy, Old West Museum, Cheyenne

matured from a typical Wild West town into Wyoming's state capital and the largest city in the area.

The 10-day Cheyenne Frontier Days festival, held every summer, brings to life the old days with parades, Indian pow-wows, horse races, and the world's largest outdoor rodeo. Visitors can also get a sense of Cheyenne heritage at the **Frontier Days Old West Museum**, which displays hundreds of antique saddles and wagons, such as the historic Deadwood Stage. During the 1870s and 1880s, this coach made a three-day trip between Cheyenne and the gold mines at Deadwood in South Dakota (see p446). Downtown Cheyenne features two landmark buildings – the 1917 State Capitol and the former Union Pacific Depot, an elaborate Romanesque-style structure that has been restored to its original 1886 splendor. The western edge of Cheyenne features Warren Air Force Base, the primary command center of the US arsenal of nuclear-tipped intercontinental ballistic missiles, which are known as ICBMs.

🏛 **Frontier Days Old West Museum**
Frontier Park on N Carey Ave.
☎ (307) 778-7290.
◻ 8:30am–5:30pm Mon–Fri, 9am–5pm Sat-Sun. ● public hols. 🅿 ♿

The prison in Wyoming Territorial Park, Laramie

Colorado

THE NAME "COLORADO" dates back to the 16th century, when Spanish explorers first used the moniker in reference to the red rock formations that skirt the Front Range of the Rocky Mountains. Over 400 years later, the term conjures images of majestic peaks and snow-clad ski slopes, with good reason. Colorado is the most mountainous state in the US, with 54 summits that measure more than 14,000 ft (4,267 m) above sea level. Officially a state since 1876, during the past century Colorado has evolved from a sparsely inhabited mining and trapping country to become the most populous business center for the Rocky Mountain region.

Denver skyline with the Rockies forming a backdrop

Denver 32

🧗 554,000. ✈ 🚉 🚌 ℹ 918 16th St. 🛈 (303) 892-1505.

FOUNDED AT THE junction of the Platte River and Cherry Creek as a supply base for miners in 1858, Denver's mild climate attracted settlers. Soon after, it emerged as the region's primary trade and population center, and eventually became the state capital in 1876.

In the new millennium, abundant parklands, a vibrant downtown, and a number of well-known museums define this growing city. Denver is set picturesquely at the foot-hills of the Rocky Mountains.

♣ Civic Center Park

Between Colfax Ave & 14th Ave Pkwy, Broadway & Bannock St.
Colorado History Museum 1300 Broadway. 🛈 303) 866-3682. ◯ 10am–4:30pm Mon–Sat, noon–4:30pm Sun. 🈳 🅿 🆒 www.coloradohistory.org
Denver Art Museum 100 W 14th Ave Pkwy. 🛈 (720) 865-5000. ◯ 10am–5pm Tue–Sat (until 9pm Wed), noon–5pm Sun. 🈳 🆒 www.denverartmuseum.org
The geographical, cultural, and political heart of Denver, the Civic Center Park is dominated by the gold-domed Colorado State Capitol on its eastern border. This ornate structure houses the state legislature and governor's office. To the south stands the **Colorado History Museum**, where a comprehensive, wall-mounted timeline traces the state's history. Rotating exhibits also focus on varied aspects of Colorado's past. Continuing clockwise around the park is the tiled, seven-story high **Denver Art Museum**. This is one of the city's best museums and has impressive collections of both Western as well as Native American objects. Finally, a block west of the park is the **Denver Mint**, one of four mints in the country, which presses more than ten billion coins in a year.

⛩ Molly Brown House

1340 Pennsylvania St. 🛈 (303) 832-4092. ◯ 10am–4pm Tue–Sat, noon–4pm Sun (& Mon during Jun–Aug). 🈳
This restored mansion, now a museum, was the home of "The Unsinkable Molly Brown," so-called for her survival of the *Titanic* in 1912. Margaret Tobin Brown was a flamboyant and persistent woman whose life story exemplifies the boom-and-bust backdrop that is Colorado history. Born in 1867 in Hannibal, Missouri, she came west to the boom-town of Leadville, Colorado, in 1886, where she married a well-known mining man, J.J. Brown. When the silver market collapsed, J.J. persevered until he laid claim to one of Colorado's richest veins of gold in 1893. The couple then moved to Denver, where they lived in luxury, despite not being accepted by the city's elite. Her courageous rescue efforts during the sinking of the *Titanic* made her a national celebrity. With this came the society approval that had previously eluded her. However, she died in New York in 1932, penniless and alone. Later, in the 1960s, she was immortalized on stage and screen.

⛩ Larimer Square & Lower Downtown (LoDo)

Larimer Square Larimer St between 14th & 15th Sts. ℹ (303) 685-8143. 🆒 🆆 www.larimersquare.com
LoDo District Bordered by Market & Wynkoop St. ℹ (303) 628-5428. 🆒
The birthplace of Denver, Larimer Square remains a commercial and cultural hub for the city. Lying adjacent to Confluence Park, where the Platte River and Cherry Creek meet, this was the site where white settlers first set up camp. The square bustles with activity both day and night, mainly because of its many boutiques, galleries, bars, and restaurants.

After a disastrous fire in 1863, wooden structures were prohibited. As a result, red-brick Victorian architecture dominates both the square and the neighboring Lower Downtown area (nicknamed

Larimer Square, the birthplace of Denver

"LoDo"). Centered on Union Station, LoDo experienced a renaissance of sorts in the 1990s, thanks to the arrival of the city's professional baseball team and their Coors Field stadium. Today, this is a favorite club-hopping district, well known for its smoky jazz joints, dance clubs, and famous microbreweries.

🍁 City Park

Between 17th & 26th Avenues from York St to Colorado Blvd. ☎ *(303) 964-2500.* ○ *24 hours daily.* ♿
Denver Zoo 2300 Steele St. ☎ *(303) 376-4800.* ○ *Apr–Sep: 9am–6pm daily; Oct–Mar: 10am–5pm daily.* ♿ 🖐 [W] www.denverzoo.org
Denver Museum of Nature & Science 2001 Colorado Blvd. ☎ *(303) 370-8339.* ○ *9am–5pm daily.* ● *Dec 25.* 🖐 ♿ [W] www.dmns.org

About 2 miles (3 km) east of downtown is Denver's largest park, which offers a wide range of activities. It has a well-stocked fishing lake, running trails, a golf course, shady picnic areas, and sports fields. The park also contains the city's two most popular attractions – the **Denver Zoo** and the **Denver Museum of Nature and Science**. The zoo, the seventh largest in the country, is noted especially for its innovative animal habitats, which include the world's largest indoor Komodo dragon exhibit. The Denver Museum of Nature and Science, on the eastern edge of the City Park, features a wide range of exhibits.

🏛 Black American West Museum & Heritage Center

3091 California St. ☎ *(303) 292-2566.* ○ *May–Sep: 10am–5pm Mon–Fri, noon–5pm Sat & Sun; Oct–Apr: 10am–2pm Wed–Fri, noon–5pm Sat & Sun.* ● *Jan 1, Easter, Thanksgiving, Dec 25.* 🖐 ♿

A hidden gem in the Five Points neighborhood, this fascinating museum is housed in a Victorian home, previously the abode of Justina Ford. In 1902 she became Denver's first female African-American doctor. The museum's founder, Paul Stewart, opened the museum in 1971 to commemorate Ford's life and to educate people about the African-American contribution to the American West. The museum's collection includes letters, photographs, and assorted memorabilia that effectively re-create the incredible stories of African Americans in pioneer times.

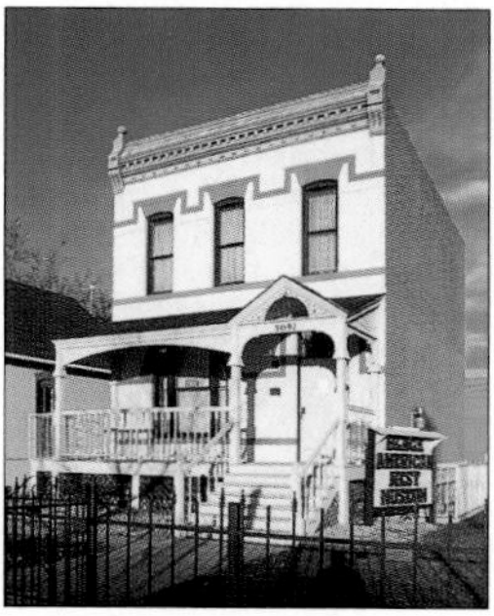

Black American West Museum and Heritage Center

🏛 Museo de las Americas

861 Santa Fe Dr. ☎ *(303) 571-4401.* ○ *10am–5pm Tue–Sat.* ● *Jan 1, July 4, Thanksgiving, Dec 25.* 🖐 ♿

Founded in the early 1990s, the Museo de las Americas is a touchstone for Denver's sizable Hispanic population. The first such museum in the region, it relates Mexican and Latin American history, as well as offers fascinating glimpses of their artistic and cultural traditions. The permanent collections are dedicated to the pre-Colombian Aztec as well as the Colonial period. Among the exhibits on display are a replica of an Aztec Sun Stone and a wall-size mural of the Aztec metropolis Tenochtitlán.

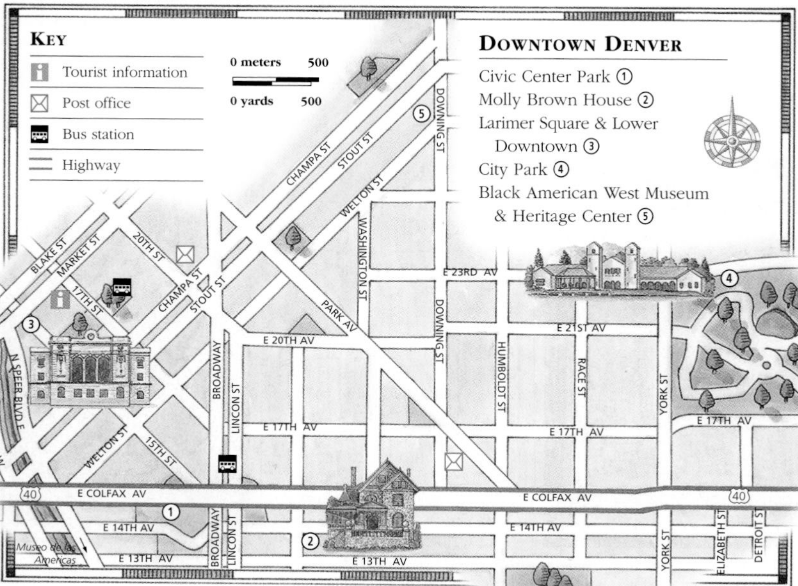
KEY
Tourist information
Post office
Bus station
Highway
0 meters 500
0 yards 500
DOWNTOWN DENVER
Civic Center Park ①
Molly Brown House ②
Larimer Square & Lower Downtown ③
City Park ④
Black American West Museum & Heritage Center ⑤
BLAKE ST
MARKET ST
17TH ST
20TH ST
CHAMPA ST
STOUT ST
WELTON ST
15TH ST
N SPEER BLVD E
N SPEER BLVD W
BROADWAY
LINCOLN ST
DOWNING ST
WASHINGTON ST
PARK AV
HUMBOLDT ST
RACE ST
YORK ST
ELIZABETH ST
DETROIT ST
E 23RD AV
E 21ST AV
E 20TH AV
E 17TH AV
E COLFAX AV
E 14TH AV
E 13TH AV
40
Museo de las Americas

The attractive University of Colorado, Boulder

Boulder ❸

🏃 95,000. ✈ 🚌 🚊 ℹ️ *2440 Pearl St, (303) 442-2911.*

A N IDYLLIC college town set at the foot of the Rockies, Boulder is best known for its bohemian culture, liberal politics, and thriving high-tech industry. The city was founded in 1858 as a commercial hub for the miners and farmers who settled nearby. After Colorado gained statehood, the **University of Colorado** (CU) was established here, at an altitude of 5,400 ft (1,646 m). Since then, the attractive Victorian-era campus and its coinciding vibrant culture have defined Boulder, attracting intellectuals, radicals, and individualists.

Northwest of the campus, the pedestrian-only Pearl Street Mall, lined with lively restaurants, bars, and shops,

is the stage for many street performers. Nearby, the Hill District forms the center of Boulder's energetic nightlife and music scene. The I.M. Pei-designed **National Center for Atmospheric Research** is to the southeast. The center also features an art gallery and is a start-off point for some lovely nature trails.

West of Boulder, the jagged and forested crags of the Rockies provide a scenic backdrop to the city below. The nearby Flatiron Range, Eldorado Canyon, and Indian Peaks Wilderness Area are popular with climbers, hikers, and backpackers.

🏛 National Center for Atmospheric Research
1850 Table Mesa Dr. 📞 *(303) 497-1174.* ⬜ *8am–5pm Mon–Fri, 9am–4pm Sat–Sun.* 🚫 ♿
🏃 Indian Peaks Wilderness Area
70 miles (113 km) W of Boulder, US Forest Service. 📞 *(303) 444-6600.* ⬜ *24 hours daily.* ♿

Golden ❸

🏃 18,000. ✈ 🚌 ℹ️ *1010 Washington Ave, (303) 279-3113, (800) 590-3113.*

G OLDEN'S HISTORY as an early nexus of trade and politics remains visible today. Its origins date to the early 1840s, when hunter Rufus Sage, one of the first Anglos to camp in this area, spotted flakes of gold in the waters of Clear Creek. His findings led to an influx of Easterners in the 1850s, and by the 1860s the city emerged as a regional

railroad hub and was declared the capital of the newly formed Colorado Territory. The original Territorial Capitol in the Loveland Building, which forms the center of downtown, dates from that period.

Golden's past is also visible at the impeccably restored **Astor House Museum.** Several rooms here re-create the 1867–1908 era when it served as a boarding house. The Old Armory nearby is the largest cobblestone building in the US. The 3-acre (1.2-ha) **Clear Creek History Park** houses many historic structures such as a 1876 schoolhouse. The town is also home to **Coors Brewery** where visitors can glimpse the malting, brewing, and packaging processes and sample the famous beer.

The gravesite and museum of William "Buffalo Bill" Cody *(see p582)* overlooks the city on Lookout Mountain. An observation deck here offers beautiful panoramic views.

🏛 Astor House Museum
822 12th St. 📞 *(303) 278-3557.* ⬜ *May–Sep: 10am–4pm Mon–Sat, noon–4pm Sun; Oct–Apr 10am–3pm Mon–Sat.* ⬤ *Jan 1, Jul 4, Nov 27, Dec 24–25.* ♿
ⓦ *www.astorhousemuseum.org*
🏛 Clear Creek History Park
11th St between Arapahoe & Cheyenne St. 📞 *(303) 277-2337.* ⬜ *summer: 10am–4pm Wed–Sat, 1–4pm Sun; winter & Tue: by appointment only.* ♿ ⓦ *www.clearcreekhistorypark.org*

Cobblestone exterior of the armory, near Astor House, Golden

Cycling across Boulder Canyon, minutes from downtown Boulder

Idaho Springs & Georgetown ㉟

🏚 *2,000.* 🚌 🛈 *2060 Miner St,
(303) 567-4382.*

Sɪᴛᴜᴀᴛᴇᴅ ᴡɪᴛʜɪɴ an hour's drive from downtown Denver, the well-preserved 1860s mining towns of Idaho Springs and Georgetown are best known for their unblemished Victorian architecture, stunning mountains, and some excellent museums.

Idaho Springs was founded in 1859 and quickly emerged as a mining center when the surrounding streams and mountains were found to be exceptional sources of gold. The town's mining history is traced through exhibits that include equipment, payroll records, receipts, and photographs at the **Argo Gold Mine, Mill, and Museum**.

Georgetown, another mining town set up during the mid-19th century Gold Rush, is 15 miles (24 km) west of Idaho Springs. It is a vision of Victorian elegance tucked into an alpine valley 8,500 ft (2,591 m) above sea level. The main attraction here is the **Georgetown Loop Railroad**, a twisting 3.5-mile (5.6-km) rail line. Hailed as one of the most spectacular narrow-gauge rides, the loop railroad travels between the towns of Georgetown and Silver Plume, both rich in mining and railroad history.

South from Idaho Springs, summer drivers can wind their way up the highest road in the United States. The Mount Evans Scenic Byway

Victorian architecture in downtown Georgetown

follows Hwy 103 and Hwy 5 through the Pike National Forest toward the 14,264-ft (4,347-m) high summit of Mount Evans.

🏛 Argo Gold Mine, Mill, & Museum

Just W of Idaho Springs, S of I-70, exit from 241A. ☎ *(303) 567-2421.* ◯ *mid-Apr–mid-Oct: 9am–6pm daily.* 🚫 ♿
🖥 *www.historicargotours. com*

Georgetown Loop Railroad

1106 Rose St. ☎ *(303) 569-2403.* ◯ *late May–early Sep: 9am–4pm.* 🚫
♿ ♿ 🖥 *www.georgetownloop.com*

Rocky Mountain National Park ㊱

1000 US Hwy 36. ☎ *(970) 586-1206.* ◯ *24 hours daily. (Trail Ridge Road closed between Nov–May).* 🚫
♿ 🅰 🖥 *www.nps.gov/romo*

Tʜɪs ɴᴀᴛɪᴏɴᴀʟ ᴘᴀʀᴋ offers some of the most spectacular mountain views in the United States. Established in 1915, the park spreads across 416 sq miles (1,077 sq km)

and includes 114 named peaks that measure more than 10,000 ft (3,048 m). The tallest of these, Longs Peak, is 14,255 ft (4,345 m) high. Snaking through the alpine scenery is the Continental Divide, which separates the western part of the US from the east, and where snowmelt flows down and eventually empties into the Atlantic and Pacific Oceans. Almost 150 lakes originate here, some occupying pastoral, forested settings, while others are perched on almost inaccessible shelves, high in the wilderness.

The majority of the two million annual visitors to the park drive 50 miles (80 km) on **Trail Ridge Road**, a spectacular stretch of highway that showcases the park's brilliant panoramas. After leaving the resort environment of Estes Park, the road climbs to its highest point of 12,183 ft (3,713 km) near the center of the park, before descending into a scenic valley north of the small town of Grand Lake. The tundra in the park's high country is an island of arctic vegetation surrounded by plants of lower latitudes. Wildlife watchers are likely to see elk, moose, black bear, and bighorn sheep.

Popular summer activities within the park include hiking, biking, backpacking, and fishing, while winter attracts snowshoers and skiers. Although there are no hotels inside the park, there are five fee-based campgrounds and numerous accommodations in both Estes Park and Grand Lake.

A view of the myriad peaks from the pinnacle of Trail Ridge Road, Rocky Mountain National Park

Pikes Peak Cog Railway atop the mountain, Manitou Springs

Manitou Springs ㊲

🚶 5,500. 🚌 ℹ️ 354 Manitou Ave, (800) 642-2567.
🌐 www.manitousprings.org

THIS CHARMING Victorian community attracts weekend visitors who come to explore its art galleries, shops, and restaurants. A product of the Gold Rush of the 1850s, it later became a popular spa town because of the natural mineral springs found here. Manitou (meaning "Full of Spirit" in Native Algonquian) is one of the largest national historic districts in the country. It is famous for two attractions that predate it by centuries, the **Cave of the Winds**, an impressive limestone cavern (now with light shows and tours) and the **Manitou Springs Cliff Dwellings**, dating from 1100 to 1300.

Clocktower, Manitou Springs

Manitou Springs is also the gateway to Pikes Peak (see p570). The **Pikes Peak Cog Railway**, a historic train that climbs to the summit of the 14,110-ft (4,300-m) mountain, has its depot here.

🏞 Cave of the Winds
US 24, exit 141. 📞 (719) 685-5444.
🕐 May–Sep: 9am–9pm daily; Oct–Apr: 10am–5pm daily. 📷 📹
🌐 www.caveofthewinds.com

🏛 Pikes Peak Cog Railway
515 Ruxton Ave. 📞 (719) 685-5401.
🕐 Apr–Oct: several departures daily; Nov–Dec: limited schedule. ● Jan–Mar. 📷 ♿ 🌐 www.cograilway.com

🏞 Manitou Springs Cliff Dwellings
3 Kreg Lane. 📞 (800) 354-7791.
🕐 check for times. 📷 ♿ 📹
🌐 www.cliffdwellingsmuseum.com

Colorado Springs ㊳

🚶 380,000. ✈ 🚌 🚆 ℹ️ 104 S Cascade Ave, (719) 635-7506.

ESTABLISHED BY railroad baron William Jackson Palmer in 1871, Colorado Springs nestles below the looming beauty of Pikes Peak. The first resort town in the western US, it was initially nicknamed "Little London" because of the scores of English tourists that it attracted.

The **Garden of the Gods** on the west side of town lures hikers and climbers with its awe-inspiring red sandstone formations, rife with arches, overhangs, stately walls, and precarious balancing rocks. One of the most recognizable – and most photographed – formations is Kissing Camels, so named for its resemblance to a pair of lip-locked dromedaries. Also located here is the Rock Ledge Ranch Historic Site, a preserved ranch that dates to the 1880s. The Italian Renaissance-style **Broadmoor Resort** (see p603) on Lake Circle, initially opened in 1918, epitomizes this era.

In the 1950s, Colorado Springs was chosen to be the home of the prestigious **US Air Force Academy** and the National Missile Defense Headquarters (NORAD). The latter is situated on the city's southwestern fringe, deep within the bomb-proof Cheyenne Mountain.

Culturally more conservative than Denver (see pp588–9), modern-day Colorado Springs is one of the fastest-growing cities in the US, with rows of houses extending into the foothills to the west, and the vast plains to the east. However, the town continues to retain many aspects of its past. The spirit of the Wild West remains alive even today at the **Pro Rodeo Hall of Fame**, which documents the origins of rodeo as well as the stories of prominent American rodeo stars through the ages. The **Colorado Springs Pioneers Museum** presents the area's history in the restored 1903 El Paso County Courthouse.

🏞 Garden of the Gods
1805 North 30th St. 📞 (719) 634-6666. 🕐 9am–5pm daily; extended hours in summer. ● Jan 1, Thanksgiving, Dec 25. ♿ only for Rock Ledge Ranch Historic Site. ♿ 📹

🏨 Broadmoor Resort
1 Lake Circle. 📞 (719) 634-7711.
🕐 daily, but can vary. Call ahead to check. ♿ 🌐 www.broadmoor.com

🏛 Pro Rodeo Hall of Fame
1805 North 30th St. 📞 (719) 528-4764. 🕐 9am–5pm daily. ● Jan 1, Easter, Thanksgiving, Dec 25. 📷 ♿
🌐 www.prorodeo.com

🏛 Colorado Springs Pioneers Museum
215 S Tejon St. 📞 (719) 385-5990.
🕐 Nov–Apr: 10am–5pm Tue–Sat; May–Oct: above mentioned hrs plus 1–5pm Sun. ♿ 🌐 www.cspm.org

Kissing Camels formations, Garden of the Gods in Colorado Springs

The magnificent view over the Royal Gorge Bridge and Park located in Cañon City

Cripple Creek 39

🏛 1,200. ℹ 5th St & 337 E Bennett Ave, (719) 689-3315.

KNOWN AS "Poverty Gulch" before a gold strike in 1890 transformed it, this is one of the best-preserved 19th-century mining towns in the entire state. The fascinating **Mollie Kathleen Gold Mine** is the best place to explore the town's mining history. Discovered by Mollie Kathleen Gortner in 1891, this gold mine on the southwest face of Pikes Peak is the country's only vertical-shaft mine that offers tours. Even though mining operations ended in 1961, gold veins are still visible on its walls.

The town is anomalous, as the surrounding area is still mined for gold though mining has ceased in most other Colorado boomtowns. Its quaint charm has faded after low-stakes gambling was legalized here in 1990. This,

however, is tempered by the fact that most of the casinos are housed in atmospheric storefronts that resemble the sets of a Hollywood Western.

🏛 Mollie Kathleen Gold Mine

N Colorado Hwy 67. 🚗 (719) 689-2466. ⏱ Apr–early Nov: 8am–6pm; early Nov–Mar: 10am–4pm Fri–Sun. ♿ 🅿 🆆 www.goldminetours.com

Cañon City 40

🏛 16,000. ℹ 403 Royal Gorge Blvd, (719) 275-2331, (800) 876-7922.

A COLORFUL place, blessed with clear skies, sunshine, and spectacular scenery, Cañon City, surprisingly, is also the "Prison Capital of Colorado." It acquired this title in 1876, after it chose to house the state prison instead of the state university. Today, prisons remain a key component of the regional economy. The **Museum of Colorado Prisons**, housed in a former correctional facility, was established in 1871.

Just 12 miles (19 km) west of the city stands the well-known **Royal Gorge Bridge and Park**. Etched into the granite bedrock for three million years by the Arkansas River, this beautiful, breath-taking gorge is over 1,000 ft (305 m) from rim to river at its deepest, but only 40 ft (12 m) wide at its base. Traversed by the world's highest suspension bridge and 12 miles (19 km) of fabulous railroad – the **Royal Gorge Route Railroad** – the park also attracts whitewater rafters to the challenging stretch of the river raging and foaming below.

🏛 Museum of Colorado Prisons

1st & Macon St. 🚗 (719) 269-3015. ⏱ May–Sep: 8:30am–6pm daily; Oct–Apr: 10am–5pm Fri–Sun. ♿ 🆆 www.prisonmuseum.org

🍂 Royal Gorge Bridge & Park

US Hwy 50. 🚗 (719) 275-7507, (800) 333-5597. ⏱ 10am–7pm daily. ♿ 🆆 www.royalgorgebridge.com **Royal Gorge Route Railroad** 🚗 (303) 569-1041. ⏱ mid-May–early Oct: 9am–3pm daily. ⬤ Oct–mid-May. ♿

Interior of Mollie Kathleen Gold Mine, Cripple Creek

WHITEWATER RAFTING IN COLORADO

The best way to enjoy the pristine Colorado wilderness is to take a whitewater rafting trip on the Arkansas River. The picturesque towns of Salida and nearby Buena Vista, 26 miles (42 km) to the north, are hubs for outfitters who offer guided river trips. With about 100 rafting companies in operation, this is the most intensively rafted river in the US. The Colorado River Outfitters Association (303-280-2554), is one of the best sources of information on rafting trips.

Rafting on the Arkansas River, Colorado

Colorado Ski Resorts ④

ONE OF COLORADO'S MOST enduring symbols is of pristine white mountains dotted with skiers. The state's recreational ski industry dates to 1935 when Berthoud Pass, northwest of Denver, became the destination ski resort for pioneering skiers. As the sport's economic potential developed after World War II, many old mining towns emerged as popular ski resort towns. Today the state is undoubtedly the country's skiing capital, with more than 24 resorts. In recent years, other winter sports, such as snowboarding, have become very popular, and most ski mountains now allow snowboarders.

Aspen, *a favorite of the rich and famous, has more than 200 different runs on three striking mountains. It developed when the Aspen Skiing Company opened its first lift in 1947. Sleek restaurants and boutiques housed behind Victorian-era storefronts complement the splendid ski terrain. Aspen also has a vibrant art and culture scene.*
Max altitude: *11,675 ft (3,559 m)*
Geared to: *all levels*
Ski level: 🎿 16% 🎿 61% 🎿 23%

Steamboat Springs, *the cowboy cousin to the conservative luxury of Aspen, wears its rambunctious Western spirit as a badge of honor. It has some of the state's best snow (a dry, feathery powder), a 3,668-ft (1,118-m) vertical drop, and a total of 142 runs.*
Max altitude: *10,564 ft (3,220 m)*
Geared to: *all levels*
Ski level: 🎿 13% 🎿 56% 🎿 31%

Snowmass, just a 30-minute drive from Aspen, is a complete resort in itself. Larger than all three of Aspen's ski areas combined, it has plenty of wide-open runs.

Crested Butte draws serious skiers to its unparalleled expert terrain. The town sits at the base of Mount Crested Butte, with a vertical drop of 2,775 ft (846 m) and 824 acres (333 ha) for "extreme" skiing.

0 km 50
0 miles 50

Steamb
Spring
⑷
Mount Werr
(10,564 ft/3,22
Pyramid Pea
(11,611 ft/3
⑺⓪
Aspen
(11,210 ft/3,
Snowmass ●
Snowmass Mt. △
(14,092 ft/4,295 m)
Maroon Peak
(14,156 ft/4,315
Crested Butte ●
Kebler Pass
(10,007 ft/3,050 m)
Crested
(12,16 ft
⒀
Montrose ●
Cerro Summit
(7,958 ft/2,426 m)
⑸⓪
⑸⑸⓪
Sneffels Peak
△ (14,150 ft/4,313 m)
△ Palmyra Peak
(13,319 ft/4,060 m)
Telluride ●
Red Mt. Pass
(11,018 ft/3,358 m)

Telluride, *a former mining community, opened as a ski resort in 1971. The nearby valley was once a hideout for outlaw Butch Cassidy. The town is also known for its bohemian politics, a lively nightlife, and trails that lead to such scenic areas as Bridal Veil Falls.*
Max altitude: *12,255 ft (3,736 m)*
Geared to: *all levels*
Ski level: 🎿 22% 🎿 38% 🎿 40%

Winter Park, Colorado's oldest full-service ski resort, is linked to Denver by the Ski Train – 67 miles (108 km) of track that connect the slopes with LoDo's Union Station. The resort's three ski mountains offer downhill terrain for every skill level, and there are also numerous cross-country trails nearby.
Max altitude: *12,060 ft (3,676 m)*
Geared to: *experts*
Ski level: 9% 21% 70%

Keystone, with its 12-hour ski day, is now famous for being Colorado's best night-skiing resort. Open eight months a year, it has three ski mountains and offers a variety of activities such as snowboarding, ice skating, sleigh rides, and indoor tennis.

Copper Mountain offers some of the most advanced skiing and snowboarding terrain in Colorado, as well as areas for novice and intermediate skiers. Once maligned, the newly re-designed village now brims with shops, bars, and restaurants.

Leadville, at an elevation of 10,152 ft (3,094 m), is the highest town in the US. This boom-and-bust mining town was once the site of the richest mines in the country – its story is told at the National Mining Hall of Fame and Museum. Today, it has a small, crowd-free ski resort.

Map labels:
Park View Mt. (12,296 ft/3,748 m)
Winter Park
Berthoud Pass (11,315 ft/3,449 m)
Keystone
Breckenridge
Copper Mt. (12,440 ft/3,792 m)
Mt. Elbert (14,433 ft/4,399 m)
nd Pass (3,658 m)

SKI RESORTS & COMPANIES

Aspen Skiing Company (Aspen-Snowmass)
(800) 525-6220, (800) 308-6935. Dec–mid-Apr: 9am–4pm daily.
www.aspensnowmass.com

Breckenridge Ski Resort
(970) 453-5000. late Oct–May: 8:30am–4pm daily.
www.breckenridge.com

Keystone (800) 427-8308. mid-Oct–Apr: 8:30am– 8:30pm daily.
www.keystoneresort.com

Steamboat Ski Corp.
(970) 879-6111. mid-Nov–mid-Apr: 8:30am–4pm daily.
www.steamboat.com

Telluride Ski Company
(800) 801-4832. late Nov–mid-Apr: 8:30am–4pm daily. www.telski.com

Vail Mountain (800) 404-3535, (970) 476-5601. mid-Nov–Apr: 8:30am–4pm daily. www.vail.com **Winter Park** (970) 726-5514. mid-Nov–late Apr: 8:30am–4pm daily. www.skiwinterpark. com **Ski Train** (303) 296-4754. *See also pp598–9.*

Breckenridge boasts an interesting history, recreation facilities including ice skating (above), and nightlife. The resort is spread across four peaks on the west side of town.
Max altitude: *12,998 ft (3,962 m)*
Geared to: *all levels*
Ski level: 13% 32% 55%

Vail, the largest single-mountain ski resort in the US, attracts skiers and snowboarders alike. The domain of Native tribes until the 1870s mining boom, the town actually developed when Vail Mountain opened to skiers in 1962. It has over 2,000 trails and a 3,450-ft (1,052-m) vertical drop.
Max altitude: *11,570 ft (3,527 m)*
Geared to: *all levels*
Ski level: 18% 29% 53%

KEY

▬	Major road
=	Minor road
	Good for beginners
	Good for intermediate skiiers
	Good for advanced skiiers
△	Peak
)(	Pass

Great Sand Dunes National Monument & Preserve

Great Sand Dunes National Monument & Preserve ④

11500 Colorado Hwy 150, NE of Alamosa. **(** *(719) 378-2312.* **○** *24 hrs daily.* 📷 ♿ △ **W** *www.nps.gov/grsa*

N AMED AFTER North America's tallest sand dunes, this unique place will soon become Colorado's newest national park, following the resolution of a long legal battle over water rights in 2002. The dunes sit at the foot of the gnarled Sangre de Cristo Mountains, their sand long since carried to this scenic spot by melting glaciers and the Rio Grande River. This unusual ecosystem is home to several equally unusual animals and insects, such as a species of kangaroo rat that never drinks water, and the Great Sand Dunes tiger beetle.

The park has a campground and a mix of long and short trails. Many visitors scale the dunes, which sometimes measure up to 700 ft (213 m).

Durango ④

(*16,000.* ✈ ➡ **i** *111 South Camino del Rio, (800) 525-8855, (970) 247-0312.*

O NCE DESCRIBED by American humorist Will Rogers as "out of the way and glad of it," Durango was established in the Animas River Valley in 1881 as a rail

station for the mines in the nearby San Juan Mountains. After the mining boom ended, Durango emerged as a major tourism center and cultural symbol of the West. This modern city is today a model of historic preservation, with late-19th-century saloons and hotels lining Main Avenue, and elegant mansions from the same era on Third Street. One thing, however, has changed – diehard mountain bikers, entrepreneurs, and artists have replaced the rugged miners.

Many visitors take a day trip on the **Durango & Silverton Narrow Gauge Railroad**. A fully functional 1882 steam engine, it follows a scenic 50-mile (80-km) journey, traveling from the valley floor to rock ledges en route to the erstwhile mining town of Silverton. Durango's other prime attraction is the great outdoors of the **San Juan National Forest**, where mountain biking is the top sport. Other popular activities are hiking, horseback riding, backpacking, rock-climbing, and river rafting.

🏛 **Durango & Silverton Narrow Gauge Railroad & Museum**
479 Main Ave. **(** *(970) 247-2733.* **○** *May–Oct: 7:30am–7pm daily; Nov–Apr: 9am–5pm daily.* 📷 ♿ **W** *www.durangotrain.com*
🍂 **San Juan National Forest**
15 Burnett Court. **(** *(970) 247-4874.* **○** *24 hrs daily.*

Mesa Verde National Park ④

East of Cortez via US Hwy 160. **(** *(970) 529-4465.* **○** *8am–5pm daily, open after 5pm till sunset in summer.* 📷 ♿ △ 🚻 **W** *www.nps.gov/meve*

W HEN IT WAS established in 1906, Mesa Verde became the first archaeological site in the US to receive national park status. Tucked into the recesses of canyon walls, the park's defining features are 500 fascinating cliff dwellings last inhabited by the indigenous Puebloan people before they abandoned them in 1300. The dwellings range from small houses to the 200-room **Cliff Palace** and are some of the most significant archaeological finds in the US.

Park rangers lead tours between April and November to some of the most important dwellings, including Cliff Palace. Visitors can also explore several structures on their own, including the well-preserved Spruce Tree House, and Square Tower House, the park's tallest ruin. The **Chapin Mesa Museum** displays a fascinating collection of pottery and other artifacts, which were used by the Puebloan people in their daily life.

There are also 18 miles (29 km) of hiking trails within the

Durango & Silverton Narrow Gauge Railroad

park. One of them, the **Petroglyph Loop Trail**, offers visitors a chance to view ancient rock art. Camping and wildlife viewing (including foxes, mountain lions, and elk) are among the other activities. In winter, cross-country skiing and snowshoeing are popular.

🏛 Chapin Mesa Museum
Limited hours. Call park for details.

Square Tower House, Mesa Verde National Park

Ouray 45

🏠 800. 🛈 *Adjacent to Ouray Hot Springs Pool on North US Hwy 550, (970) 325-4746, (800) 228-1876.*

Nicknamed the "Switzerland of America" for its resemblance to a village in the Alps, Ouray is located 80 miles (128 km) north of Durango. It was named after the Ute chief whose people hunted in the area before gold and silver prospectors established the town in 1876. Today the entire town is listed on the National Register of Historic Places, a testament to the number of well-maintained 19th-century structures still in existence. Two natural wonders – the massive geothermal-powered **Ouray Hot Springs Pool**, and the stunning **Box Canyon Falls**, which cascades 285 ft (87 m) down a natural cliff-side chute – are easily accessible from the town center.

Ouray is also on the **San Juan Skyway**, a 236-mile (380-km) loop that includes the "Million Dollar Highway" to Silverton. Its surrounding

wild-lands lure rock- and ice-climbers, four-wheel-drive enthusiasts, and other outdoors adventurers.

Ouray Hot Springs Pool
US Hwy 550, at the northern end of Ouray. 🎟 *(970) 325-7073.* ⏰ *May–Sep: 10am–10pm daily; Oct–Apr: noon–9pm daily.* 🗐

Box Canyon Falls & Park
S of Ouray via US Hwy 550. 🎟 *(970) 325-4464.* ⏰ *May 15–Oct 15: 8am–8pm daily.* ● *Oct 16–May 14.* 🗐

Black Canyon of the Gunnison National Park 46

E of Montrose via US Hwy 50.
🎟 *(970) 641-2337.* ⏰ *24 hrs daily.*
🗐 ♿ 🌐 www.nps.gov/blca

Though not as vast as Arizona's Grand Canyon (*see pp536–9*), the Black Canyon is strikingly deep with steep sides. The canyon was created by the Gunnison River as it slowly sliced through solid stone for two million years. Its north and south rims have completely different ecosystems and are separated by a crevice 2,400 ft (732 m) at its deepest point and just 40 ft (12 m) at its narrowest point.

The **South Rim Road** meanders for about 7 miles (11 km) past several overlooks, including a fantastic vista of a multihued rock face known as Painted Wall, which is twice the height of New York's Empire State

Building (*see p73*). Although the park's northern edge is more isolated, it has a campground and offers magnificent sunset views.

Climbing is a popular sport in the park, as is hiking, camping, and fishing. Among the many trails is one particularly difficult one that descends to the canyon's floor.

The park's varied and abundant wildlife includes a variety of birds such as the peregrine falcons who nest on the canyon's sheer walls. Wildcats and bears also roam the vast park.

Colorado National Monument 47

W of Grand Junction via I-70 or 7 miles (11 km) S of Fruita on US Hwy 340. 🎟 *(970) 858-3617.* ⏰ *24 hrs daily.* 🗐 ♿ 🌐 www.nps.gov/colm

Carved by wind and water over the last 225 million years, this immense 20,500-acre (8,296-ha) national monument has been molded into an eerie high desert landscape of spectacular canyons, and red sandstone arches. A driving tour on the 22-mile (35-km) **Rim Rock Drive** offers several splendid panoramas, while numerous trails lead visitors right into the heart of the landscape. The park's two geological highlights are the incredible sandstone arches of Rattlesnake Canyon, and Miracle Rock, which is considered to be the largest balanced rock in the world.

The eerie high desert landscape of Colorado National Monument

Practical Information

EXPLORING THE FOUR Rocky Mountain states requires some advance planning, simply because of the sheer size and diversity of the region's landscape. The boundaries of this mountainous region stretch from the Canadian border in the north to New Mexico in the south. To the west, the area is bordered by the plateaus and basins of the Intermontane region. The breath-taking scenery, rugged terrain, scanty resources, and sparse population of the Rockies are spread across elevations that range from under 1,000 ft (305 m) to over 14,000 ft (4,267 m) above sea level.

TOURIST INFORMATION

TRAVELERS ENTERING the Rocky Mountain states via an Interstate Highway are greeted with signs advertising a state "Welcome Center." These centers provide a full range of tourist information as well as clean restrooms and free coffee. Denver's International Airport (DIA), and most of the region's other major airports and train stations have information desks, stocked with free brochures and maps. Most larger cities and smaller towns operate **Convention & Visitors Bureaus** or **Chambers of Commerce**, which provide free travel information.

NATURAL HAZARDS

THE SHORT SUMMERS of the Rockies region are warm and glorious, but can bring sudden thunderstorms, especially in the mountains. Rock slides, bugs, and wild-life are other hazards.

Elevation across the four states can vary from under 1,000 ft (305 m) to over 14,000 ft (4,267 m) above sea level. At higher elevations, in areas such as Yellowstone National Park, roads may be closed by snow between late October and early June. The Interstate Highways and access routes to the region's many ski areas are kept open all year round.

Winters are long and often bitterly cold with heavy win-ter and spring snows, and travelers should take sensible precautions. Drivers should make sure that they possess, and know how to install, snow chains or other traction devices, which are required by law. Be especially careful while driving on icy surfaces, which are treacherous.

In remote areas, hikers should be prepared for all weather conditions in winter as well as summer. Carry basic emergency supplies, including food and water, and extra clothing in case the weather changes for the worse.

GETTING AROUND

FOR VISITORS coming from the East or West Coast, Denver is a prime starting point. Smaller regional cities through-out the Rockies have airports, such as the Missoula, (MT) County International Airport. Other than organized bus tours, public transportation is limited. Denver has city buses, a light-rail system, and free shuttle buses. Having a car is essential in this region since most national parks and other sights are located at great distances from the major cities.

Seat belts are required for drivers and front seat passen-gers in all four states. Child seats are compulsory for all passengers aged eight and under. Helmets are required for all motorcyclists under the age of 18.

Speed limits vary but are usually 70–75 mph (112–120 km/hr) on Interstate High-ways outside the populated urban areas. Radar detectors are permitted in the entire Rocky Mountain region.

ETIQUETTE

VISITORS TO THIS part of the West should wear clothing appropriate to the weather. Guests at dude ranches, ski areas, and other vacation spots need to dress com-fortably, depending on the outdoor sport they pursue.

Some of the region's most famous sights are located on Native American reservation land. Visitors are welcome but must be sensitive as to what may cause offense. It is illegal to bring alcohol onto reserva-tions, and taking photographs may not be allowed.

FESTIVALS

SUMMER IN THE ROCKIES brings a deluge of outdoor events, including community and state fairs, in addition to regional and national music, and art festivals. Fireworks, bands, and festivals abound for the July 4th celebrations, while the region's strong Native American heritage is also cele-brated with a number of pow-wows in July and August on

THE CLIMATE OF THE ROCKIES

Weather across the Rocky Mountain region is marked by long, snowy winters, short springs and fall, and hot summers. The main factor determining weather is eleva-tion – temperatures are cooler and snowfalls heavier the higher you go. Visitors should be prepared for winter condi-tions at any time of year. Yet, months like October offer crisp days, ideal for scenic drives through the mountains when you can enjoy the fall colors of the aspens.

DENVER

°F/C	Apr	Jul	Oct	Jan
high	60/15	85/30	65/18	43/6
low	35/2	60/15	37/3	16/–8
☀	20 days	21 days	22 days	22 days
☂	1.7 in	2 in	1 in	0.5 in
month	Apr	Jul	Oct	Jan

32°F / 0°C

selected reservations. Music and various cultural events, such as the ever popular **Telluride Bluegrass Festival**, the world-famous **Aspen Music Festival & School** (970-925-3254), and the **Big Sky Arts Festival** take place throughout the summer months.

SPORTS

THE ROCKY MOUNTAIN states all offer a wide variety of sports throughout the year. Denver is home to many of the region's professional teams. The **Colorado Rockies** play baseball all summer at the old-fashioned Coors Field downtown. The **Denver Broncos** play professional football in the fall, and winter sees the **Denver Nuggets** on the basketball court. Many of the region's universities and colleges play seasonal games, often with heated regional rivalries, and if you're lucky, you can take in a local summer softball game.

One spectator sport characteristic of the Rockies is the rodeo, and many national competitions are held here. Events such as bull- and bronco-riding, calf roping, and steer wrestling showcase a cowboy's skill. Cheyenne, Wyoming, hosts the "World's Largest Outdoor Rodeo" when more than 250,000 fans flock

here during **Frontier Days** at the end of July (800-227-6336). Dude ranches often offer special rodeos for guests.

OUTDOOR ACTIVITIES

THE MOST POPULAR outdoor activity is downhill skiing, which draws many participants and billions of dollars to the region's world-class resorts. Colorado has many of the biggest and most highly regarded resorts in the United.States, but there is also excellent skiing at Idaho's Sun Valley, Wyoming's Jackson Hole, and at smaller resorts throughout the region. Snowboarding is also popular, and cross-country skiing can be enjoyed in the stunning landscape of the region's many parks and forests. The ski season is from December to March, but many resorts are open until May or June depending on the weather.

Montana is home to such famous trout-fishing spots as the Madison and Yellowstone Rivers, while Idaho, Wyoming, and Colorado all offer excellent fly-fishing. Licenses are required, and catch-and-release is encouraged. Visitors can contact the **Montana Fish & Wildlife Department** or the **Idaho Fish & Game Department** for details.

Other popular warm-weather activities include hiking, mountain biking, and rafting.

Rafting the Snake River through Grand Teton National Park is extremely popular, as is the wilder Salmon River in Idaho. The **Colorado River Outfitters Association** is one of the best sources of information on guided river-rafting trips. **Lewis & Clark Trail Adventures** lead whitewater raft trips through miles of Idaho rivers. **Snow King Ski Resort** near Jackson, Wyoming also offers historical hiking and rafting trips. Bicycle and motorcycle riding is gaining as much popularity as hiking, fishing, and skiing. **Open Road Bicycles** in Missoula, Montana, rents bikes for a day or by the week (406-549-2453). They will also help outfit and plan trips.

ENTERTAINMENT

THE SKI RESORTS and dude ranches in the area offer evening entertainment from cabaret and local theater productions to first-run movies. However, many evenings at these resorts are spent in hot tubs, relaxing around the bar, or at in-house casinos. College towns, such as Bozeman and Missoula, Montana, have many of the amenities that the back-country lacks: good bookstores, brew pubs, museums, and events that appeal to both urban and cowboy culture.

DIRECTORY

TOURIST INFORMATION

Colorado
PO Box 3524 Englewood, CO 80155.
℡ (800) 265-6723.
W www.colorado.com

Idaho
700 W State St Boise.
℡ (208) 334-2470,
(800) 635-7820.
W www.visitid.org

Montana
301 S Park Ave Helena.
℡ (406) 841-2870.
W www.visitmt.com
W www.visitmt.gov

Wyoming
I-25 at College Dr, Cheyenne.
℡ (800) 225-5996.
W www.wyomingtourism.org

ROAD CONDITIONS

Idaho
℡ (208) 336-6600.

Montana
℡ (800) 226-7623.
W www.mdt.state.mt.us/travinfo

FESTIVALS

Colorado State Fair
℡ (719) 561-8484.
W www.coloradosfair.com

Idaho State Fair
℡ (208) 785-2480.
W www.idaho-state-fair.com

Montana State Fair
℡ (406) 727-8900.
W www.mtexpopark.com

Telluride Bluegrass Festival
℡ (800) 624-2422.
W www.bluegrass.com

Wyoming State Fair
℡ (307) 358-2398.
W www.wystatefair.com

SPORTS

Colorado Rapids
℡ (303) 299-1570.

Colorado Rockies
℡ (303) 292-0200.

Denver Broncos
℡ (303) 949-9000.

Denver Nuggets
℡ (303) 405-1100.

FISHING

Idaho Fish & Game Dept.
600 S Walnut St Boise,
ID 83707.
℡ (208) 334-3700.

Montana Fish & Wildlife Dept.
1420 E 6th Ave Helena,
MT 59620.
℡ (406) 444-2535.

Where to Stay

Places to stay in the Rocky Mountains region are as varied as the landscape. In towns, visitors can choose from historic hotels and quaint B&B inns, but in rural areas the choice is usually limited to highway motels. Most national parks have large rustic lodges, and there are also several "dude ranches" where guests can play cowboy while enjoying luxurious all-inclusive accommodations.

	CREDIT CARDS	NUMBER OF ROOMS	RECOMMENDED RESTAURANT	CHILDREN'S FACILITIES	GARDEN OR TERRACE
IDAHO					
BOISE: *Owyhee Plaza Hotel* $$ 1109 Main St. 【 (208) 343-4611. FAX (208) 336-3860. W www.owyheeplaza.com Located downtown, this grand old-fashioned hotel has character to spare plus full services and modern conveniences. ▭ TV ⚡ P ♿ ≋	●	100	▪	●	
BOISE: *Idaho Heritage Inn* $$$ 109 W Idaho St. 【 (800) 626-4773. FAX (208) 343-2325. W www.idheritageinn.com Within walking distance of the State Capitol and the historic downtown area, this inn was built for Governor Chase Clark in 1904. It retains its period character but has all modern facilities. ▭ ⚡ P	●	6		●	▪
COEUR D'ALENE: *Coeur d'Alene Resort* $$$$$ PO Box 7200, 115 South 2nd St. 【 (208) 765-4000, (800) 688-5253. FAX (208) 664-7276. W www.cdaresort.com/ Located on the lovely Lake Coeur d'Alene, this deluxe golf, ski, and spa resort is famous for its floating golf green, and offers a range of activities such as lake cruises, jet skiing, and parasailing. ▭ TV ⚡ P ♿ ≋	●	338	▪	●	▪
IDAHO FALLS: *Best Western Driftwood Inn* $$ 575 River Parkway. 【 (208) 523-2242, (800) 939-2242. FAX (208) 523-0316. W www.bwdriftwoodinn.com Located within walking distance of the Snake River and downtown Idaho Falls, this inn is a comfortable base for exploring eastern Idaho. ▭ ⚡ P ♿	●	74		●	▪
KETCHUM: *Best Western Tyrolean Lodge* $$ 260 Cottonwood St. 【 (208) 726-5336, (800) 333-7912. FAX (208) 726-2081. W www.bestwestern.com Located at the south end of town, off the main highway, this comfortable motel is convenient for visits to the Sun Valley region. ▭ TV ⚡ P ≋	●	56			
RIGGINS: *Salmon Rapids Lodge* $$$ 1010 S Main St. 【 (208) 628-2743, (877) 957-2743. FAX (208) 628-3834. W www.salmonrapids.com Located at the confluence of the Salmon and Little Salmon Rivers, this hotel is ideal for rafters and visitors to Hells Canyon. ▭ TV ⚡ P ♿ ≋	●	55	▪		
SALMON: *Twin Peaks Ranch* $$$$$ Twin Peaks. 【 (208) 894-2290, (800) 659-4899. FAX (208) 894-2429. W www.twinpeaksranch.com Located on 3,000 acres (1,214 ha) in the rugged mountains above the Salmon River, this guest ranch offers deluxe accommodations and a range of outdoor activities, from fly-fishing to horseback riding. ▭ ⚡ P ≋	●	24	▪		▪
STANLEY: *Salmon River Lodge* $ Hwy-75. 【 (208) 774-3422. W www.mywildidaho.com Across the river from the main highway, this quiet, peaceful, 8-acre (3 ha) resort offers four individual cabins, many with kitchens. ▭ ⚡ P	●	4		●	▪
STANLEY: *Redfish Lake Lodge* $$$ Hwy-75. 【 (208) 774-3536. FAX (208) 774-3546. W www.redfishlake.com An old-fashioned, unpretentious lodge with two dozen rustic log cabins fronting a beautiful lake, and surrounded by dense forests and sublime mountains. The ideal Idaho experience. ⚡ P	●	40	▪	●	▪
SUN VALLEY: *Sun Valley Lodge* $$$$$ Sun Valley. 【 (208) 622-2151, (800) 786-8259. FAX (208) 622-2030. W www.sunvalley.com Rustic luxury is the hallmark of this deluxe lodge, built as the centerpiece of the country's most exclusive downhill ski resort. ▭ TV ⚡ P ♿ ≋	●	150	▪	●	▪

<table>
<tr><td colspan="2">

Price categories for a standard double room per night, inclusive of breakfast, service charges, and any additional taxes:

$ under $100
$$ $100–$150
$$$ $150–$200
$$$$ $200–$250
$$$$$ over $250
</td><td colspan="2">

CREDIT CARDS
Major credit cards accepted.

NUMBER OF ROOMS
Number of rooms in the hotel.

RECOMMENDED RESTAURANT
Good restaurant within the hotel.

CHILDREN'S FACILITIES
Hotel has various facilities for young children.

GARDEN OR TERRACE
Hotel has a garden, courtyard, or terrace.
</td></tr>
</table>

	CREDIT CARDS	NUMBER OF ROOMS	RECOMMENDED RESTAURANT	CHILDREN'S FACILITIES	GARDEN OR TERRACE

MONTANA

BUTTE: *Copper King Mansion*　　$　●　5　　●　▦
219 W Granite St. ⓒ *(406) 782-7580.* Ⓦ *www.copperkingmansion.com*
This 1884 mansion is packed with so much opulent Victoriana that it doubles as a museum. 🍽 P

FLATHEAD VALLEY: *Best Western KwaTaqNuk Resort*　　$$　●　112　▦　　▦
303 E US-93, Polson. ⓒ *(406) 883-3636.* ℻ *(406) 883-5392.* Ⓦ *www.kwataqnuk.com*
Located on the shores of Flathead Lake, this large modern hotel (whose Salish Indian name means "Where the Water Leaves the Lake") is part of a resort and casino complex run by the local Indian tribes. 🛏 TV 🍽 ♿ 〰

GLACIER NATIONAL PARK: *Lake McDonald Lodge*　　$$　●　100　▦　●　▦
Lake McDonald. ⓒ *(406) 888-5431, (406) 892-2525.* ℻ *(406) 892-1375.*
Ⓦ *www.lakemcdonaldlodge.com*
The most intimate of the park lodges, the Lake McDonald Lodge features a huge fireplace in the lobby and grand views over sublime Lake McDonald. 🛏 🍽 P ♿

GLACIER NATIONAL PARK: *Glacier Park Lodge*　　$$$　●　151　　●　▦
US-2, East Glacier Park. ⓒ *(406) 226-5600, (406) 892-2525.* ℻ *(406) 892-1375.*
Ⓦ *www.glacierparkinc.com*
Built by the Great Northern Railroad in 1913, this rustic landmark is remarkable for the massive 50-ft (15-m) high Douglas fir trees supporting the roof over the spacious lobby. 🍽 P ♿ 〰

GLACIER NATIONAL PARK: *Izaak Walton Inn*　　$$$　●　33　▦　　▦
US-2, Essex. ⓒ *(406) 888-5700.* ℻ *(406) 888-5200.* Ⓦ *www.izaakwaltoninn.com*
Built as a lodging house for railroad crews in the early 1900s, this inn has traditional rooms and a few cabooses for train enthusiasts. In winter, the inn is a mecca for cross-country skiers. 🛏 🍽 P

GLACIER NATIONAL PARK: *Many Glacier Hotel*　　$$$　●　215　▦　　▦
Many Glacier. ⓒ *(406) 732-4411, (406) 892-2525.* ℻ *(406) 732-5522.*
Ⓦ *www.glacierparkinc.com*
The largest and most stunningly sited of the park's lodges, it overlooks Swiftcurrent Lake against a backdrop of glaciated peaks. 🍽 P ♿

GREAT FALLS: *Best Western Heritage Inn*　　$$　●　239　▦　　▦
1700 Fox Farm Rd. ⓒ *(406) 761-1900, (800) 548-8256.* ℻ *(406) 761-0136.*
Ⓦ *www.bestwestern.com/heritageinngreatfalls*
This large, comfortable motel features a large indoor pool and an atrium garden, perfect for those long Montana winters. 〰 🛏 TV 🍽 P

GREAT FALLS: *Pine Butte Guest Ranch*　　$$$　●　10　▦　　▦
HC 58 Box 34C. ⓒ *(406) 466-2158.* ℻ *(406) 466-5462.*
Ⓦ *http://nature.org/wherewework/states/montana/travel/*
This 1930s dude ranch, now operated by the Nature Conservancy, lets visitors hike mountain trails, ride horses, or just read a good book by the heated pool. The hotel requires a minimum one-week stay. 〰 🛏 🍽 P

HELENA: *Sanders Bed & Breakfast*　　$$　●　7　　　▦
328 N Ewing St. ⓒ *(406) 442-3309.* ℻ *(406) 443-2361.* Ⓦ *www.sandersbb.com*
Built in 1875 by Montana's first US senator, this lavish home is filled with period furnishings but has been thoroughly outfitted with modern conveniences. 🛏 TV 🍽

MISSOULA: *Goldsmith's Inn*　　$$　●　7　▦　●　▦
809 E Front St. ⓒ *(406) 728-1585.* ℻ *(406) 543-0045.*
Ⓦ *www.missoulabedandbreakfast.com*
Located on the banks of Clark Fork River, within walking distance of downtown, this 1911 home offers the best in comfort. 🛏 TV 🍽 P

For key to symbols see back flap

Price categories for a standard double room per night, inclusive of breakfast, service charges, and any additional taxes:	CREDIT CARDS / NUMBER OF ROOMS / RECOMMENDED RESTAURANT / CHILDREN'S FACILITIES / GARDEN OR TERRACE
Price categories for a standard double room per night, inclusive of breakfast, service charges, and any additional taxes: $ under \$100 $$ \$100–\$150 $$$ \$150–\$200 $$$$ \$200–\$250 $$$$$ over \$250	**CREDIT CARDS** Major credit cards accepted. **NUMBER OF ROOMS** Number of rooms in the hotel. **RECOMMENDED RESTAURANT** Good restaurant within the hotel. **CHILDREN'S FACILITIES** Hotel has various facilities for young children. **GARDEN OR TERRACE** Hotel has a garden, courtyard, or terrace.

	CREDIT CARDS	NUMBER OF ROOMS	RECOMMENDED RESTAURANT	CHILDREN'S FACILITIES	GARDEN OR TERRACE
WYOMING					
BIGHORN MOUNTAINS: *Tensleep Preserve* $ 1095B Rd 56, Ten Sleep. **C** *(307) 366-2671.* **W** www.tncwyoming.org/where/tensleep.shtml This Nature Conservancy guest ranch offers luxurious tent cabins. Meals are served on the deck overlooking canyons and pine-forested uplands in the foothills of the Bighorn Mountains. Book in advance. ● *Oct–Apr.*	●	12	■	●	■
CHEYENNE: *Nagle Warren Inn* $$ 222 E 17th St. **C** *(307) 637-3333, (800) 811-2610.* **FAX** *(307) 638-6879.* **W** www.naglewarrenmansion.com This late-Victorian stone mansion offers contemporary luxury and historic ambience within walking distance of downtown. ■ ■ TV ■	●	12		●	■
CODY: *Hotel Irma* $ 1192 Sheridan Ave. **C** *(307) 587-4221, (800) 745-4762.* **FAX** *(307) 587-1775.* **W** www.irmahotel.com Built in 1902 by Wild West impresario "Buffalo Bill" Cody, and named for his daughter, this unpretentious hotel is a historic landmark. The cherry-wood bar in its restaurant was a gift from England's Queen Victoria. ■ **P**	●	40	■	●	
GRAND TETON NATIONAL PARK: *Flagg Ranch Resort* $$ US-89, Moran Junction. **C** *(307) 543-2861, (800) 443-2311.* **FAX** *(307) 543-2356.* **W** www.flaggranch.com Located in a beautiful setting midway between Grand Teton and Yellowstone National Parks, this hotel is open year-round. ■ ■ ■ **P** ■	●	92	■	●	■
GRAND TETON NATIONAL PARK: *Jenny Lake Lodge* $$$$$ Jenny Lake. **C** *(307) 733-4647, (800) 628-9988.* **FAX** *(307) 543-3358.* **W** www.gtlc.com A romantic retreat in the heart of the park, this deluxe inn has a rustic ambience but luxurious amenities. ■ ■ **P** ■	●	37	■	●	■
JACKSON: *Wort Hotel* $$$$ 50 N Glenwood St. **C** *(307) 733-2190.* **FAX** *(307) 733-2067.* **W** www.worthotel.com Located at the heart of downtown, the Wort lets you sample the Wild West flair of Jackson, while savoring all creature comforts. ■ ■ ■ **P** TV ■	●	60	■	●	
LARAMIE: *Vee-Bar Guest Ranch* $$$$$ 2091 Hwy-130, Centennial. **C** *(307) 745-7036, (800) 483-3227.* **FAX** *(307) 745-7433.* **W** www.ranchweb.com/veebar With log cabins set along a rushing stream, this "dude ranch" in the Medicine Bow Mountains is one of the country's most popular. ■ ■ **P**	●	9	■		■
YELLOWSTONE NATIONAL PARK: *Bill Cody Ranch* $$ US-20, Wapiti. **C** *(307) 587-2097.* **FAX** *(307) 587-6272.* **W** www.billcodyranch.com Located at the east entrance to Yellowstone, this rustic lodge offers several private cabins and a full range of "Wild West" activities. ■ ■ **P**	●	14	■	●	■
YELLOWSTONE NATIONAL PARK: *Old Faithful Inn* $$ Old Faithful. **C** *(307) 344-7311.* **FAX** *(307) 344-7456.* **W** www.travelyellowstone.com Built in 1903–04, now with a modern annex, this hotel has an unbeatable location near Old Faithful geyser. The rustic lobby and dining room ceiling soaring nearly 100 ft (31 m) overhead is spectacular. ■ **P** ■	●	327	■	●	■
YELLOWSTONE NATIONAL PARK: *Lake Yellowstone Hotel* $$$ Lake Yellowstone. **C** *307) 344-7311.* **FAX** *(307) 344-7456.* **W** www.travelyellowstone.com A romantic retreat in the heart of the park, this deluxe inn has a rustic ambience but luxurious amenities. ■ ■ **P** ■	●	300	■	●	■

COLORADO

ASPEN: *Hotel Jerome* $$$$$ 91
330 E Main St. **C** *(970) 920-1000.* **FAX** *(970) 925-2784.* **W** www.hoteljerome.com
Built at the height of Colorado's silver boom, this downtown landmark
exudes luxury in its rooms and amenities. 🛏 📺 ⚡ 🍴 ♒ P ♿

BOULDER: *Hotel Boulderado* $$$$ 160
2115 13th St. **C** *(303) 442-4344.* **FAX** *(303) 442-4378.* **W** www.boulderado.com
Opened in 1909, Boulder's oldest and best hotel retains a level of
Victorian grandeur along with its many modern amenities. 🛏 ⚡ P ♿

COLORADO SPRINGS: *Broadmoor* $$$$$ 700
1 Lake Ave. **C** *(719) 634-7711.* **FAX** *(719) 577-5700.* **W** www.broadmoor.com
Located near Cheyenne Lake, this hotel offers superb rooms, a full-service
spa, three golf courses, and fine restaurants. 🛏 📺 ⚡ 🍴 ♒ P ♿

DENVER: *Queen Anne B&B* $$ 14
2147-51 Tremont Pl. **C** *(303) 296-6666.* **FAX** *(303) 296-2151.* **W** www.queenannebnb.com
A romantic getaway, Denver's best B&B features a pair of Victorian man-
sions. Rates include breakfast and complimentary wine. 🛏 ⚡ P ♿

DENVER: *Brown Palace Hotel* $$$ 241
321 17th St. **C** *(303) 297-3111.* **FAX** *(303) 321-5900.* **W** www.brownpalace.com
Located in downtown Denver, this hotel is best known for its nine-story
atrium lobby and lavish presidential suites. 🛏 📺 ⚡ P ♿

DENVER: *Adam's Mark Hotel* $$$$ 1,225
1550 Court Pl. **C** *(303) 893-3333.* **FAX** *(303) 626-2542.* **W** www.equinoxresort.com
This 18th-century resort offers spacious, country-style rooms, and activities such as golf, falconry, and off-road driving. 🛏 ♒ 📺 ⚡ P ♿

DURANGO: *Strater Hotel* $$$$ 93
699 Main Ave. **C** *(970) 247-4431.* **FAX** *(970) 259-2208.* **W** www.strater.com
One of the few Colorado hotels to have been open continuously since
the 1880s, the Strater retains a historic ambience but offers all modern
conveniences. 🛏 📺 ⚡ P

ESTES PARK (ROCKY MOUNTAIN NATIONAL PARK): *Stanley Hotel* $$$$$ 135
333 Wonderview Ave. **C** *(970) 586-3371.* **FAX** *(970) 586-4964.*
W www.stanleyhotel.com
Opened by steam engine pioneer F.O. Stanley in 1909, the hotel combines
stately elegance with spectacular mountain views. 🛏 📺 ⚡ ♒ P ♿

MANITOU SPRINGS: *Cliff House* $$$$$ 55
306 Canon Ave. **C** *(719) 685-3000.* **FAX** *(719) 685-3913.*
W www.thecliffhouse.com
One of the state's oldest hotels, the Cliff House is a fine example of Rocky
Mountain Victorian architecture in a splendid setting. 🛏 📺 ⚡ P ♿

MESA VERDE NATIONAL PARK: *Far View Lodge* $$ 150
Mile Marker 15, Mesa Verde. **C** *(970) 529-4422.* **FAX** *(970) 529-4411.*
W www.visitmesaverde.com
The only indoors accommodation in Mesa Verde National Park, this lodge
offers standard rooms with amazing views, as well as immediate access
to the park and its stunning cliff dwellings. 🛏 ⚡ P ♿

STEAMBOAT SPRINGS: *Sheraton Steamboat Resort* $$$$ 325
2200 Village Inn Ct. **C** *(970) 879-2220.* **FAX** *(970) 879-7686.* **W** www.steamboat-sheraton.com
This full-service resort offers a nice mix of hotel rooms and larger condo-
minium units, as well as a shopping arcade, a top-rated golf course, and
seven rooftop spas with splendid mountain views. 🛏 📺 ⚡ 🍴 ♒ P ♿

TELLURIDE: *New Sheridan Hotel* $$$ 32
231 W Colorado Ave. **C** *(970) 728-4351.* **FAX** *(970) 728-5024.*
W www.newsheridan.com
Rebuilt after an 1891 fire, this hotel has the comforts of a B&B and the ski-
oriented amenities common to Telluride's larger resorts. 🛏 📺 ⚡ P ♿

VAIL: *Vail Cascade* $$$$$ 399
1300 Westhaven Dr. **C** *(970) 476-7111.* **FAX** *(970) 479-7020.*
W www.vailcascade.com
One of the most complete ski-oriented lodgings in Colorado, this four-
season resort has a spa and full range of amenities. 🛏 📺 ⚡ ♒ P ♿

Where to Eat

RESTAURANTS IN THE Rockies reflect the rugged character of the region and are often decorated to evoke the region's Wild West heritage. Most eateries are unpretentious and tend to close by 9pm, but in cities they often aspire to cosmopolitan sophistication. Opening times are indicated by a "B" for breakfast, "L" for lunch, and "D" for dinner.

	CREDIT CARDS	OUTDOOR TABLES	VEGETARIAN	GOOD WINE LIST	CHILDREN'S FACILITIES
IDAHO					
BOISE: *Guido's Original New York Pizza* $ 235 N 5th St. ((208) 345-9011. Rated as the best pizza place in Boise, Guido's is a great little restaurant to eat cheaply and take in the pulse of this youthful, energetic city at the same time. *L, D.* ⏚ ♿			▪		▪
BOISE: *Doughty's Bistro* $$$ 195 N 8th Street. Housed in a stately former bank building, Doughty's Bistro is a semi-formal restaurant that specializes in variations on traditional dishes, such as a chicken parmigiana with a goat cheese ragout. *D.* ● *Sun, Mon.* ⏚ ♿ ▵	▪		▪	●	▪
COEUR D'ALENE: *Iron Horse Bar & Grill* $$ 407 Sherman Ave. ((208) 667-7314. Historic photos and artifacts from Idaho's mining and railroad heritage set the stage for the Iron Horse Bar & Grill, with its range of hamburgers, steaks, and fish. *B, L, D.* ⏚ ♿ ▵ ♫	▪	●	▪		▪
COEUR D'ALENE: *Moon's Saloon* $$ 204 N 2nd St. Adjacent to the local brewery, this lively café has a full range of "pub grub": sausages, soups, salads, and pizzas. *B, L, D.* ⏚ ♿ ▵ ♫	▪		▪	●	▪
COEUR D'ALENE: *Cedars Floating Restaurant* $$ N-1 Marina Dr. ((208) 664-2922. Its hard to imagine a better view than one you get from your table here. Cedars offers a huge menu featuring fresh and deep-sea fish from all over the world. There is also a floating deck with boat parking available for visitors. *D.* ⏚ ♿ ▵	▪	●	▪	●	▪
IDAHO FALLS: *Rutabaga's* $$$ 415 River Parkway. ((208) 529-3990. An unexpected treat for visitors, this small Idaho Falls restaurant has been serving adventurous food for more than a decade, mixing various influences from all over the world. *L (Fri only), D daily, Sun (only brunch).* ⏚ ♿ ▵	▪	●	▪	●	
KETCHUM: *Sawtooth Club* $$ 231 N Main St. ((208) 726-5233. Steaks and seafood, grilled over a mesquite fire, are the stars of the menu here. *D.* ⏚ ♿ ▵	▪	●		●	▪
SUN VALLEY: *The Ram Restaurant* $$$$ Sun Valley Village. ((208) 622-2225. After a grueling day on the resort's challenging ski slopes, treat yourself to a delicious meal of French bistro fare. The Ram Restaurant's sample dishes include duck liver and poached pear paté, a cassoulet of smoked bacon and potatoes, as well as a range of seafood and beef specialties. *D.* ⏚ ♿ ▵ ♫	▪		▪	●	▪
TWIN FALLS: *Buffalo Café* $ 218 W 4th Ave. ((208) 734-0271. Start the day with an enormous, stomach-stretching breakfast at this tiny, ever-popular café. Don't forget to try their signature dish – the Buffalo Chip – which is a hefty omelet of eggs, bacon, cheese, and fried potatoes. *B, L.* ⏚ ♿			▪		▪
TWIN FALLS: *Rock Creek* $$ 200 W Addison Ave. ((208) 734-4154. For good steak or seafood, and the state's largest salad bar, come to this long-standing local favorite. *D.* ⏚ ♿ ▵	▪			●	

<table>
<tr><td colspan="2">

Price categories include a three-course meal for one, a glass of house wine and all unavoidable extra charges such as sales tax and service.
- $ under $25
- $$ $25–35
- $$$ $35–50
- $$$$ $50–70
- $$$$$ over $70

</td><td>

CREDIT CARDS
Major credit cards accepted.

OUTDOOR TABLES
Garden, courtyard, or terrace with outside tables.

VEGETARIAN
A good selection of vegetarian dishes available.

GOOD WINE LIST
Extensive list of good wines, both domestic and imported.

CHILDREN'S FACILITIES
Restaurant has various facilities for young children.

</td></tr>
</table>

	CREDIT CARDS	OUTDOOR TABLES	VEGETARIAN	GOOD WINE LIST	CHILDREN'S FACILITIES
MONTANA					
BIGFORK: *Swan River Café* $$ 360 Grand Ave. ((406) 837-2220. This friendly local favorite serves a wide array of seafood, fresh fish, and steaks. Their popular Sunday night buffet includes shrimp appetizers, prime rib, salmon, salads, vegetables, and desserts. *B, L, D.*	■	●	■	●	
BIGFORK: *Bigfork Inn* $$$$ 604 Electric Ave. ((406) 837-6680. One of the main proponents of regional Rocky Mountain cuisine, this long-standing favorite is famous for wild game, venison, and duck served with a local cherry-and-blackcurrant sauce. *D.* ♪ *(Fri & Sat only).*	■		■	●	■
BILLINGS: *Walkers Grill* $$ 301 N 27th St. ((406) 245-9291. Modern decor in a historic setting, Walker's Grill offers local meat and fish dishes along with pizzas and pastas. *D.* ● *Sun.* ♪ *(Fri & Sat only).*	■		■		■
BOZEMAN: *Mackenzie River Pizza Company* $$ 232 E Main Street. ((406) 587-0055. Excellent pizza and a wide range of local micro-brewed beers, in the heart of downtown Bozeman. *L, D.*	■		■		
BUTTE: *Matt's Place* $ Corner of Rowe Rd & Montana St. ((406) 782-8049. One of the original "drive-ins" in the Rockies, this Butte landmark has been serving burgers and milk shakes since the 1930s. An all-American classic. *L, D.*					■
BUTTE: *Uptown Café* $ 47 E Broadway. ((406) 723-4735. Informal bistro serving upscale but not expensively priced fish, meat, and pasta dishes. *L, D.*			■	●	
GLACIER NATIONAL PARK: *Izaak Walton Inn* $ US-2 in Essex. ((406) 888-5700. Built for railroad workers, this unpretentious dining room serves big portions of inexpensive, hearty food with a railroad theme. *B, L, D.*			■		■
GLACIER NATIONAL PARK: *Lake McDonald Lodge* $$$ Going-to-the-Sun Rd. ((406) 888-5431. The meals served in this rustic hunting lodge setting are as memorable as the scenery outside. *B, L, D.*			■		■
GREAT FALLS: *Dante's Creative Cuisine* $$ 1325 8th Ave N. ((406) 453-9599. Located in a former iron foundry, this innovative restaurant offers a wide range of Italian-inspired pastas and salads. *L, D.*	■		■	●	■
HELENA: *The Stonehouse* $$$ 120 Reeder's Alley. ((406) 449-2552. Get a taste of frontier life at this rustic restaurant, housed in an 1890s miners' boarding house. Famed for steak and seafood. *D.*	■			●	■
MISSOULA: *The Shack* $ 222 W Main St. ((406) 549-9903. In business since the 1950s, this bustling place draws workers, students, and families for breakfast omelets and other filling fare. *B, L, D.*	■		■		■
MISSOULA: *Guy's Lolo Creek Steakhouse* $$ 6600 W US-12. ((406) 273-2622. Located in the southern foothills of Missoula, this massive log cabin serves excellent steaks and fresh fish grilled over an open fire. *D.*	■			●	■

For key to symbols see back flap

	Credit Cards	Outdoor Tables	Vegetarian	Good Wine List	Children's Facilities

Price categories include a three-course meal for one, a glass of house wine and all unavoidable extra charges such as sales tax and service.
Ⓢ under $25
ⓈⓈ $25–35
ⓈⓈⓈ $35–50
ⓈⓈⓈⓈ $50–70
ⓈⓈⓈⓈⓈ over $70

CREDIT CARDS
Major credit cards accepted.
OUTDOOR TABLES
Garden, courtyard, or terrace with outside tables.
VEGETARIAN
A good selection of vegetarian dishes available.
GOOD WINE LIST
Extensive list of good wines, both domestic and imported.
CHILDREN'S FACILITIES
Restaurant has various facilities for young children.

WYOMING

		CC	OT	V	GW	CF
BIGHORN MOUNTAINS: *Colonel Bozeman's* ⓈⓈ 655 E Hart St, Buffalo. (307) 684-5555. Located in the historic cowboy town of Buffalo, this friendly restaurant serves local specialties like buffalo steaks in a room full of Wild West memorabilia. *L, D.*		■	●			■
CASPER: *Poor Boy's Steakhouse* ⓈⓈ 739 N Center St. (307) 237-8325. Popular, family-friendly American-style restaurant, with checkered tablecloths and large portions of steak, chicken, and fish. *L, D.*		■				
CODY: *Cassie's Supper Club* Ⓢ 214 Yellowstone Ave. (307) 527-5500. Steaks and hamburgers are the favorite foods at this friendly, unpretentious restaurant. Late at night, Cassie's turns into Cody's most popular dance hall. *L, D.*		■				
GRAND TETON NATIONAL PARK: *Dornan's Chuck Wagon* Ⓢ 100 Moose Rd. (307) 733-2415. Open since 1948, and located near the park's main visitor center in Moose, this family restaurant is unique, to say the least. Eating inside tepees, or at tables along the Snake River, visitors can enjoy pancake breakfasts, lunchtime picnics, or chuckwagon barbecue buffets at dinner. *B, L, D.* ● *Oct–May.*		■	●			■
GRAND TETON NATIONAL PARK: *Jenny Lake Lodge Dining Room* ⓈⓈⓈⓈⓈ Inner Park Rd. (307) 733-4647. Set amid pine trees near a wildflower meadow, this exclusive restaurant serves some of the finest cuisine in the Rockies. *B, L, D.* ● *Oct–May.*		■		■	●	
JACKSON: *Jedediah's Original House of Sourdough* Ⓢ 135 E Broadway. (307) 733-5671. Located in a historic log cabin, this informal favorite is usually surrounded by lines of hungry patrons waiting for their pancake breakfasts. Lunch and dinner choices include steaks and fresh-caught trout. *B, L, D (only between Jun–Aug).*		■				■
JACKSON: *Granary Restaurant* ⓈⓈⓈ 1800 Spirit Dance Rd. (307) 733-8833. Set atop Gros Ventre Butte in the luxurious Spring Creek Ranch resort, this fine restaurant has a view of the Grand Tetons that complements the array of fresh fish and meat dishes on the menu. *B, L, D.*		■		■		■
YELLOWSTONE NATIONAL PARK: *Old Faithful Inn Dining Room* ⓈⓈⓈ Old Faithful Bypass. (307) 545-4999. Served in a massive room with a 50-ft (15-m) fireplace and a soaring timber ceiling, the food here is secondary to the setting, which is an architectural landmark of the Rockies. *B, L, D.* ● *mid-Oct–mid-May.*		■		■		■

COLORADO

		CC	OT	V	GW	CF
BOULDER: *John's Restaurant* ⓈⓈⓈ 2328 Pearl St. (303) 444-5232. John's is a testament to owner-chef John Bizzarro's culinary skill. The menu blends classical Mediterranean traditions with those of the Far East and the Southwest. *D.* ● *Sun, Mon.*		■		■	●	
BOULDER: *Flagstaff House* ⓈⓈⓈⓈⓈ 1138 Flagstaff Rd. (303) 442-4640. Long considered one of the area's most romantic restaurants, Flagstaff House has an excellent Continental menu to match. *D.*		■	●	■	●	■

For key to symbols see back flap

BRECKENRIDGE (SUMMIT COUNTY): *Café Alpine* $$$$
106 E Adams Ave. (970) 453-8218.
The popular Café Alpine eatery features a tapas bar and terrific wine list. The restaurant's eclectic menu offers everything from Jamaican-style Gulf shrimp to stuffed rainbow trout with spicy Southwestern sauce. L (Summer only), D.

COLORADO SPRINGS: *Blue Star* $$
1645 S Tejon St. (719) 632-1086.
A hip restaurant and bar, the Blue Star restaurant serves an eclectic menu with a variety of Mediterranean, Asian, and Southwestern dishes. L (Mon–Fri), D. (Mon only).

DENVER: *Tosh's Hacienda* $
3090 Downing St. (303) 295-1861.
A longtime standout Mexican restaurant, Tosh's Hacienda has staked its reputation since it opened in the 1940s on its zesty family recipes, which include a top-notch enchilada and relleno. The restaurant also serves succulent margaritas as accompaniment. Brunch (11am onwards), L, D.

DENVER: *Wynkoop Brewing Company* $$
1634 18th St. (303) 297-2700.
The Wynkoop is the city's best and oldest microbrewery, housed in a redbrick structure. It offers its patrons pub fare, steaks, poultry, and seafood alongside its standout beers. L, D. (Sun only).

DENVER: *Buckhorn Exchange* $$$
1000 Osage St. (303) 534-9505.
In proud possession of Denver's first liquor license, this 1893 restaurant appointed with taxidermy of all descriptions, now serves gargantuan steaks as well as elk, buffalo, and other game dishes. L (Mon–Fri), D. (Wed–Sat).

DENVER: *The Fort* $$$
19192 Colorado Hwy 8. (303) 697-4771.
Housed in a replica of a historic Colorado fort, this restaurant specializes in wild game and offers excellent cuisine, service, and atmophere. D. (occasionally).

DURANGO: *Randy's* $$
152 College Dr. (970) 247-9083.
Durango's most intimate restaurant, Randy's features an attractive cherry-wood bar, and serves beef and fresh seafood with attractive presentations. The restaurant is known for its delicious prime rib dinners. D.

ESTES PARK (ROCKY MOUNTAIN NATIONAL PARK): *Dunraven Inn* $$
2470 Colorado Hwy 66. (970) 586-6409.
This Italian restaurant, decorated with reproductions of Leonardo Da Vinci's *Mona Lisa*, serves pasta and steak dishes to a boisterous clientele. D.

MANITOU SPRINGS: *Briarhurst Manor* $$$$
404 Manitou Ave. (719) 685-1864.
Housed in the 1876 manor built by the founder of Manitou Springs, the Briarhurst is a landmark restaurant that is known for its wide selection of beef, poultry, seafood, and game, as well as its innovative sauces.
D. Jan–Mar: Mon, Tue.

SNOWMASS: *Krabloonik* $$$$
4250 Divide Rd. (970) 923-3953.
Located in a charming log building, Krabloonik is known for its house-smoked game and its homemade soups and breads. The proprietors also operate dogsled trips in winter from an onsite kennel. D (Summer); L & D (Winter). (Visitors must call in advance if they require wheelchair access).

VAIL: *Sweet Basil* $$$
193 E Gore Creek Dr. (970) 476-0125.
One of Vail's culinary trendsetters since it opened in 1977, Sweet Basil infuses Pacific Rim touches in contemporary cuisine. The saffron linguine with scallops, shrimp, and lobster is a perennial favorite. L, D.

Space Needle, dominating the Seattle skyline ▷

THE PACIFIC
NORTHWEST

summer, they moved up the mountain slopes to pick berries and dig roots. This tranquil existence was abruptly disturbed with the arrival of European traders and settlers.

The quest to discover the Northwest Passage – a quick ocean route linking Europe with the Far East – lured early European explorers to this region in the 16th century. The first was Spanish explorer Juan Rodriguez, who sailed from Mexico to southern Oregon in 1543. He was followed by Britain's Sir Francis Drake, who ventured as far north as the Strait of Juan de Fuca in 1592.

Britain's next major expedition was in the 1770s, when Captain James Cook, accompanied by George Vancouver and Peter Puget, sailed up the coasts of Oregon and Washington. In 1791, Vancouver and Puget also charted what is now Puget Sound in Washington. Their explorations coincided with those of an American fur trader from the East Coast, Captain Robert Gray, who discovered the Columbia River in 1792,

Portland, City of Roses

naming it after his ship. Soon, other American vessels arrived in search of animal pelts and other bounty.

The battle to control the Pacific Northwest was waged by the British and Americans with trade, not gunfire. The 1803–06 Lewis and Clark expedition opened up the region to American fur traders, who were determined to wrest this very lucrative trade from the British. At that time, the dominant player was Britain's Hudson Bay Company (HBC), which continued to more or less rule the region until the middle of the 19th century.

Between 1843 and 1860, thousands of American settlers migrated westward on the 2,000-mile (3,218-km) Oregon Trail. As a result, America and Britain divided the region in 1846, using the 49th parallel as the new boundary between British Columbia to the north and Oregon to the south. Oregon, which included the present-day states of Oregon, Washington, and Idaho, became a US territory two years later. In 1852, this territory was further divided into Washington and Oregon.

Those who profited least from the division of spoils were the Native peoples. Diseases had already decimated many tribes, but now, those who survived were removed from their lands and moved to reservations.

PEOPLE & POLITICS

Nearly ten million people call the Pacific Northwest region their home. The nationwide spurt in growth of the Hispanic population in the 1990s is visible in this region as well. Hispanics,

---

KEY DATES IN HISTORY

1543 Spanish explorer Juan Rodriguez Cabrillo sails to the coast of southern Oregon

1765 Robert Rogers maps the vast territory he refers to as Oregon

1792 Robert Gray crosses the Columbia River

1829 Oregon City is the first town west of the Rocky Mountains

1846 US acquires Oregon and Washington

1848 Oregon Territory established

1851 Portland is incorporated

1852 Washington Territory is formed

1859 Oregon becomes 33rd state

1865 Seattle is incorporated

1897 Klondike Gold Rush brings prosperity to Seattle

1889 Washington becomes 42nd state

1905 Portland hosts World's Fair with Lewis & Clark Exposition

1916 Boeing Air Company founded in Seattle

1949 Seattle earthquake

1980 Mt. St. Helens erupts in Washington

1995 Amazon.com launched from Seattle

2002 Seahawks stadium opens in Seattle

Romantic interpretation of the Oregon Trail's westward trek, painted c.1904

Snowboarding at Mount Hood, Oregon

today, constitute the largest ethnic group in the state of Oregon, representing 8 percent of the state's population. Hispanics also form 7.5 percent of Washington's local population. Native Americans have a significant presence here as well, having recovered from the decline that took place after European settlement. Many of the tribes continue to live in traditional communities, preserving their cultural identities.

Portland and Seattle are among the continent's fastest-growing cities. Though both tend to be liberal in their politics, other areas in the Pacific Northwest region remain conservative. Even so, a unique political climate has emerged in the area. Oregonians are the first in the US to have approved assisted suicide for the terminally ill, while Washingtonians have the distinction of electing the country's first Asian-American governor. Culturally, the region has cultivated a rich tradition of excellence in the arts, sciences, public services, and creative entrepreneurship. Some of the region's best creative talents include Dale Chihuly (b. 1941), one of the world's leading glass sculpturists, rock legend Jimi Hendrix (1942–70), Matt Groening (b. 1954), creator of the popular TV show *The Simpsons*, and Linus Pauling (1901–94), winner of two Noble Prizes, for chemistry in 1954 and peace in 1962.

ECONOMY & INDUSTRY

In recent years, the region's economy had undergone great changes. While traditional industries such as fishing, mining, and logging struggle for survival, those based on services and technology flourish. Since the 1980s, when Bill Gates, the founder of Mircosoft, the world's foremost computer software company, established his headquarters in Seattle, there has been a proliferation of high-tech companies. Some 3,000

software and e-commerce businesses operate in the Seattle area alone. Jeff Bezos, another Seattle-based entrepreneur, set up Amazon.com, the world's largest online retailer. Among the other major companies with interests here are computer industry giants Intel, Epson, and Hewlett-Packard, the aerospace leader Boeing, which operates several plants in western Washington, and the sportswear chain Nike. Starbucks, the coffee house that first opened in Seattle's Pike Place Market in the 1970s, now has coffee bars all over the world.

Amid this economic transformation, one industry has done consistently well. Increasingly, tourists are spending healthy sums to enjoy what the locals have long considered their greatest resource – the Pacific Northwest's natural beauty. The region not only offers great opportunities for some of the world's finest adventure sports such as whitewater rafting, kayaking, hiking, skiing, and rockclimbing, but for those who prefer more placid pastimes, the opportunities for sitting next to a mountain stream, or strolling along a remote beach are seemingly endless.

Neon sign at Seattle's Pike Place Market

Portlanders relaxing at one of the city's local cafés and wine bars

Exploring the Pacific Northwest

T HE PACIFIC NORTHWEST, comprising Oregon and Washington, is a region of great natural beauty. Its lofty mountains, deep canyons, crystal clear lakes, mighty rivers, and rugged shoreline offer visitors a chance to enjoy a wide range of outdoor activities. Equally alluring are its two principal cities – Portland and Seattle, with their excellent museums and vibrant cultural scene. Both cities are well-connected by air, road, and rail. However, the best way to explore the region, especially remote areas, such as Oregon's Hell Canyon and Washington's Olympic Peninsula, is by car.

The Space Needle, dominating the Seattle skyline

SIGHTS AT A GLANCE

Washington
Seattle pp616–19 **1**
Olympic Peninsula **2**
Port Townsend **3**
Bellingham **4**
San Juan Islands pp622–3 **5**
North Cascades Highway **6**
Lake Chelan **7**
Leavenworth **8**
Spokane **9**
Walla Walla **10**
Yakima Valley **11**
Maryhill **12**
Mount Rainier National Park pp626–7 **13**
Tacoma **14**
Olympia **15**
Mount St. Helens National Volcanic Monument **16**
Fort Vancouver **17**

Oregon
Portland pp630–31 **18**
Columbia River Gorge **19**

Mount Hood **20**
Astoria **21**
Oregon Coast **22**
Salem **23**
Eugene **24**
Madras & Warm Springs **25**
Sisters **26**
Bend **27**
Newberry National Volcanic Monument **28**
Crater Lake National Park pp636–7 **29**
Oregon Caves National Monument **30**
Ashland **31**
Steens Mountain **32**
Malheur National Wildlife Refuge **33**
John Day Fossil Beds National Monument **34**
Pendleton **35**
Wallowa Mountains **36**
Hell's Canyon National Recreation Area pp640–41 **37**

Vancouver
Belling
San Juan Islands **5**
Mou
Anacortes Verr
Port Townsend **3**
Port Angeles
Olympic Peninsula **2**
Ev
Bremerton Sea **1**
Seattle-Tacoma **14**
Aberdeen
Olympia **15** Tacom
Centralia Mt. Rainier
Mt. St. He
Astoria **21** Longview
Oregon Coast Colu
Ri
22 Gc
Fort Vancouver **17** Vancouver
Portland **18** Mt.
Portland Hood
McMinnville
Salem **23**
Albany Madras & V
Sp
Corvallis
Eugene **24** Springfield
Be
Coos Bay Newberry Na
Volcanic Mon
Roseburg
Crater La
National
Grants Pass
Medford
Oregon Caves NM **30** **31** Ashland
CALIFORNIA
Sacramento

0 km 100
0 miles 100

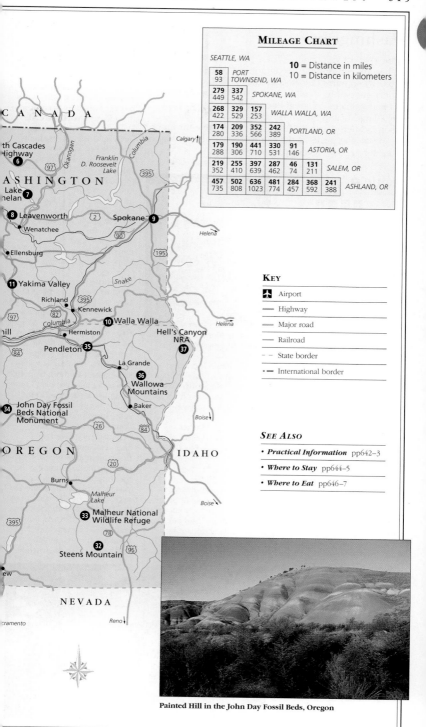

MILEAGE CHART

SEATTLE, WA

10 = Distance in miles
10 = Distance in kilometers

58	PORT						
93	TOWNSEND, WA						
279	**337**	SPOKANE, WA					
449	542						
268	**329**	**157**	WALLA WALLA, WA				
422	529	253					
174	**209**	**352**	**242**	PORTLAND, OR			
280	336	566	389				
179	**190**	**441**	**330**	**91**	ASTORIA, OR		
288	306	710	531	146			
219	**255**	**397**	**287**	**46**	**131**	SALEM, OR	
352	410	639	462	74	211		
457	**502**	**636**	**481**	**284**	**368**	**241**	ASHLAND, OR
735	808	1023	774	457	592	388	

CANADA

th Cascades
Highway
6

Franklin
D. Roosevelt
Lake

Calgary↑

ASHINGTON

Lake
helan **7**

8 Leavenworth
• Wenatchee

(2)

Spokane **9**

Helena

• Ellensburg

(90)

(195)

11 Yakima Valley

Snake

Richland **(395)**
Kennewick

(97)

Columbia **(82)**

10 Walla Walla

Helena

ill

Hermiston

Hell's Canyon
NRA
37

Pendleton **35**

La Grande •

(84)

36
Wallowa
Mountains

34
John Day Fossil
Beds National
Monument

• Baker

Boise↓

(26)

(84)

O R E G O N

(20)

IDAHO

Burns •

Malheur
Lake

Boise ↓

(395)

33 Malheur National
Wildlife Refuge

(78)

32
Steens Mountain

(95)

ew

N E V A D A

Reno↓

cramento

KEY

✈ Airport

— Highway

— Major road

— Railroad

- - State border

•– International border

SEE ALSO

• *Practical Information* pp642–3

• *Where to Stay* pp644–5

• *Where to Eat* pp646–7

Painted Hill in the John Day Fossil Beds, Oregon

Washington

THE ONLY US STATE named for a president, Washington has an extraordinary geographical diversity within its 68,139 sq miles (176,466 sq km) of land. Of its three distinct geographic regions, the coastal Olympic Peninsula is dominated by great tracts of forest. Most of the state's largest cities are in the damp, green western region, scattered around Puget Sound. A drive through the spectacular peaks of the North Cascades takes visitors to the sunny, dry eastern part of the state.

Seattle ❶

🏛 534,700. ✈ 🚉 🚌 🛈 800 Convention Place, Galleria Level, (206) 461-5840. 🌐 www.cityofseattle.net

NESTLED BETWEEN Puget Sound and Lake Washington, with Mount Rainier in the background, Seattle has a spectacular setting. The home of Microsoft and Boeing, the city's growth since the Klondike Gold Rush of 1897 (see p737) has been vigorous. Its prime geographic location, enviable lifestyle, and flourishing film and music scene make Seattle one of America's most attractive cities.

🏛 Pioneer Square

Bounded by Alaskan & Yester Ways, 2nd Ave & S King St. 🚌 15, 18, 21, 22, 56. Ⓜ Occidental Park. **Klondike National Historical Park** 117 S Main St. 🅲 (206) 553-7220. ◯ 9am–5pm daily. ⬤ Jan 1, Thanksg., Dec 25. 🚻
Seattle's first downtown and later a decrepit skid row, Pioneer Square is now a revitalized business neighborhood and National Historic District with a thriving art scene. Many of its buildings were constructed in the years between the two pivotal events in Seattle's history – the Great Fire of 1889 and the Klondike Gold Rush of 1897–98. The handsome Pioneer Building on 1st Avenue, for instance, was completed three years after the fire.
The story of Seattle's role in the Gold Rush is told in the **Klondike National Historical Park** on South Main Street. A Seattle institution, the **Elliott Bay Book Company** nearby, occupies the site of the city's first hospital and stocks around

A display in Klondike Gold Rush National Historical Park

150,000 titles. Opened in 1914, Seattle's first skyscraper, the terra-cotta **Smith Tower**, offers superb views from its wraparound observation deck.

🏛 Pike Place Market

Bounded by Pike & Virginia Sts, from 1st to Western Aves. 🅲 (206) 682-7453. 🚌 15, 18. ◯ 8am–9pm Mon–Sat, 11am–5pm Sun; may vary. ⬤ public hols. 🚻 🌐
🌐 www.pikeplacemarket.org
Said to be the soul of Seattle, Pike Place Market is known as much for its colorful personality as for its abundant local produce. Established in 1907, the country's oldest continu-

ously operating farmers' market is now a historic district bustling with farmers, artists, and street performers. Rachel, an enormous piggy bank, stands at the main entrance to the market, whose heart is the **Main Arcade** and the adjacent **North Arcade**. Here, low counters display fresh fruit, vegetables, herbs, and flowers grown by local farmers. Shoppers get to "meet the producer," as promised by the market's signature green sign. Attractions include the Pike Place Starbucks, birthplace of the omnipresent chain, and **Pike Place Fish**, the market's best-known seafood vendor. Here, fish-flinging fishmongers are a long-standing tradition.

🐟 Seattle Aquarium

Pier 59 off Alaskan Way. 🅲 (206) 386-4320. 🚌 15, 18, 21, 22, 56. 🚋 Pike. ◯ Memorial Day–Labor Day: 10am–7pm daily; Labor Day–Memorial Day:10am–5pm daily. 🚻 🎦 🌐 www.seattleaquarium.org
One of the country's top aquariums, the Seattle Aquarium showcases more than 400 species of animals, plants, and mammals indigenous to the Pacific Northwest. A highlight is the huge underwater glass dome, filled with sharks, octopus, and other Puget Sound creatures. The world's first aquarium-based salmon ladder – the fish jumping up the rungs to the maturing pond – explains the entire life cycle of the Pacific salmon. In the **Discovery Lab**, children can touch starfish and hermit crabs and examine live plankton through a high-resolution video microscope.

Pike Place Fish in Pike Place Market, which offers both fish and fun

🏛 Odyssey Maritime Discovery Center

Bell St Pier 66, 2205 Alaskan Way. ☎ *(206) 374-4000.* 🚌 *15, 18, 21, 22, 56.* 🚝 *Bell.* 🕐 *10am–5pm Tue–Sat, noon–5pm Sun.* ● *Mon, Jan 1, day before Thanksgiving, Thanksgiving, Dec 24–25.* 💵 ♿ 🛍 [P] *Exhibits, lectures, films.*
[W] www.ody.org

Located on Seattle's historic working waterfront, the Odyssey is the country's first maritime discovery center. It uses interactive exhibits and short films to explain how the maritime and fisheries industries contribute to the well-being of the region. In **Sharing the Sound**, visitors can paddle kayaks through virtual waters, dock a small tanker, and learn about Puget Sound. Interactive exhibits in the **Harvesting the Sea** gallery invite visitors to experience the lives of crabbers and salmon fishermen. While the hands-on exhibits are geared primarily toward children, people of all ages enjoy this cleverly designed museum.

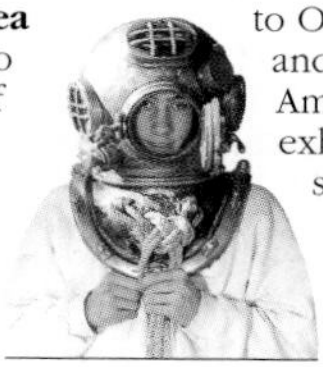

Inside Odyssey Maritime Discovery Center

🏛 Seattle Art Museum

100 University St. ☎ *(206) 654-3100.* 🚌 *174.* 🕐 *10am–5pm Tue–Wed & Fri–Sun, 10am–9pm Thu.* ● *Mon (except some hols), Jan 1, Thanksg., Dec 25.* 💵 *(free 1st Thu of month).* 🚫 ♿ 🚩 🎧 ☕ 🛍
[W] www. seattleartmuseum.org
Benaroya Hall 200 University St. ☎ *(206) 215-4700.* 🚌 *174.* 🚩 *noon & 1pm Tue & Fri.* 🚫 ♿ ☕ 🛍 [W] www.benaroyahall.com

At the entrance of the Seattle Art Museum stands the giant *Hammering Man*, a 48-ft (15-m) animated steel sculpture created as a tribute to workers. The bold limestone-and-sandstone museum building is as impressive. Its permanent collection includes 23,000 objects ranging from ancient Egyptian reliefs and wooden African sculptures to Old Master paintings and contemporary American art. Traveling exhibits are on the second floor. Also part of the museum are the Seattle Asian Art Museum in Volunteer Park in Capitol Hill *(see p618)*, and the

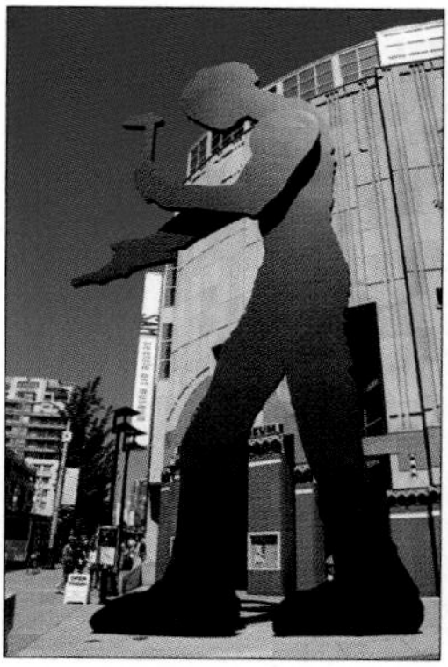

The *Hammering Man* sculpture at the entrance of Seattle Art Museum

Olympic Sculpture Park, slated for completion in 2004, on Seattle's waterfront.

Across the street, **Benaroya Hall**, home of the Seattle Symphony, occupies an entire city block. Of its two performing halls, Taper Auditorium, acclaimed for its fine acoustics, has 2,500 seats. The multilevel Grand Lobby, dramatic at night when lit, offers stunning views of the city skyline. Benaroya Hall has some excellent tours and an impressive private art collection.

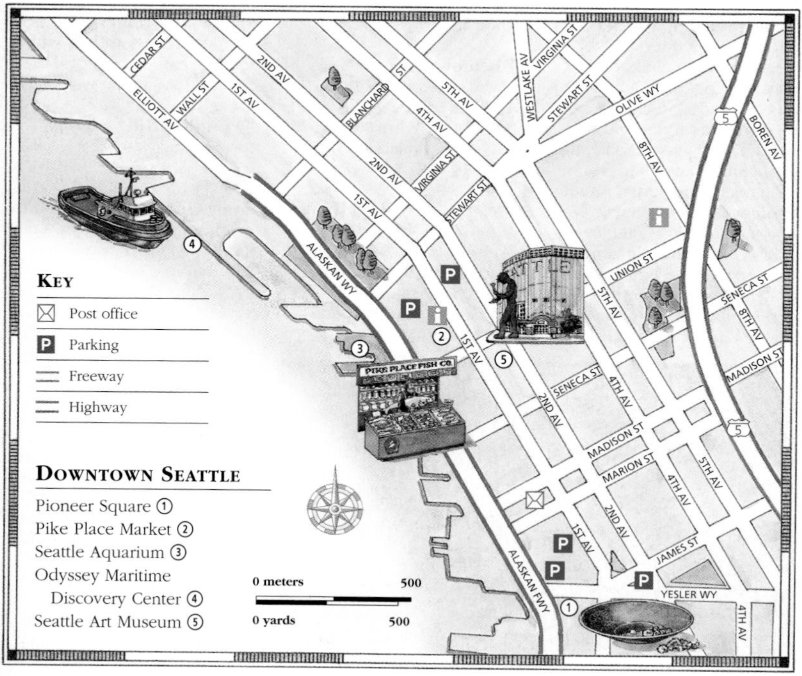
CEDAR ST
ELLIOTT AV
WALL ST
1ST AV
2ND AV
BLANCHARD ST
5TH AV
4TH AV
WESTLAKE AV
VIRGINIA ST
STEWART ST
OLIVE WY
5
BOREN AV
8TH AV
ALASKAN WY
UNION ST
SENECA ST
MADISON ST
MARION ST
JAMES ST
YESLER WY
ALASKAN FWY
PIKE PLACE FISH CO.
KEY
Post office
Parking
Freeway
Highway
DOWNTOWN SEATTLE
Pioneer Square ①
Pike Place Market ②
Seattle Aquarium ③
Odyssey Maritime Discovery Center ④
Seattle Art Museum ⑤
0 meters 500
0 yards 500

Seattle: Beyond Downtown

This extensive city offers plenty of opportunities for exploration and recreation. Immediately north of downtown are the prime cultural venues of Seattle Center, while to its northeast is the prominent Capitol Hill. Farther afield are the lively University District, Woodland Park Zoo, and the characterful neighborhoods of Fremont and Ballard.

⊞ Seattle Center

Bounded by Denny Way & 1st Ave N, Mercer & Broad Sts. ℹ *(206) 684-7200.* 🚌 *Seattle Center.* 🚍 *2, 3, 4, 16, 19, 24, 33.* Ⓦ www.seattlecenter.com
Space Needle 400 Broad St. 📞 *(206) 905-2100.* ⭕ *check for times.* ♿ 🍴 Ⓦ www.spaceneedle.com
Experience Music Project 325 5th Ave N. 📞 *(206) 367-5483.* ⭕ *check for times.* ● *Thanksgiving, Dec 25.* 📷 🚫 ♿ 🎧 🍴 ⛴ Ⓦ www.emplive.com

The proud legacy of the city's second World's Fair in 1962, this 74-acre (30-ha) urban park contains several innovative structures, cultural venues, and excellent museums. Among the most striking is the **Space Needle**. Supported by three curved steel legs, the needle's glass-enclosed tophouse features an observation deck and a revolving restaurant. At the base of the Space Needle, the exuberant Frank Gehry-designed **Experience Music Project** celebrates music with rare memorabilia, interactive exhibits, and live performance space. The Jimi Hendrix Gallery here has been recently revamped. Also in the Seattle Center, the **Pacific**

Space Needle, Seattle's best-known landmark and prime tourist attraction

Science Center features six buildings of white pre-cast concrete surrounding five arches that soar over reflecting pools and fountains. Its hands-on science and math exhibits are especially appealing to kids.

The center is best reached by the **Seattle Monorail**. It covers the 1.2-mile (2-km) distance between the downtown station (5th Avenue at Pine Street) and the Seattle Center in 90 seconds.

⊞ Belltown

Bounded by Denny Way, Virginia St, Elliot Ave, & Broad St. 🚍 *15, 18, 21, 22, 56.* **Austin A. Bell Building** 2326 1st Ave. **Virginia Inn** 1937 1st Ave. 📞 *(206) 728-1937.* ⭕ *11:30am–midnight Sun–Thu, 11:30am–2am Fri–Sat.* ♿ 🍴 ⛴

South of the Seattle Center lies trendy Belltown. With its broad avenues lined with hip clubs, chic restaurants, and eclectic shops, it has been compared to Manhattan's Upper West Side. Earlier an unremarkable area filled with labor union halls, car lots, and sailors' taverns, its identity began to change in the 1970s when artists, attracted by cheap rents and abundant studio space, moved in. Belltown experienced a building boom during the software explosion of the 1990s and now bears little resemblance to its early days. The handsome four-story brick **Austin A. Bell Building** is one of the few remaining original structures. Commissioned in 1888 by Austin Americus Bell, the wealthy son of Seattle pioneer William M. Bell, for whom Belltown is named, it is listed on the National Register of Historic Places. The building now houses pricey condominiums, a coffee shop, and an upscale restaurant. The brick-and-tile **Virginia Inn** *(see p646),* on the southern boundary of Belltown, is another historic building. A popular watering hole for more than a century, it is now Seattle's hottest art bar, with rotating exhibits by local artists adorning the walls.

⊞ Capitol Hill

Bounded by Montlake Blvds E & NE, E Pike & E Madison Sts, 23rd Ave E & I-5. 🚍 *7, 9, 10.*

Lively Capitol Hill is a colorful neighborhood where no one blinks at spiked purple hair and multiple body piercings. Broadway, the district's major avenue, is lined with shops and ethnic restaurants. Bronze footsteps, to teach passersby the tango and fox trot, are embedded in the sidewalk of Broadway.

While people-watching is a major source of entertainment, Capitol Hill also features two vintage movie houses: the **Egyptian** on East Pine Street, and the **Harvard Exit** on East Roy Street. The hill is also home to **St. Mark's Episcopal Cathedral** on 10th Avenue Street, known for its magnificent Flentrop organ, consisting of 3,944 pipes.

The Experience Music Project building, in Seattle Center

Richard Beyer's aluminium sculpture in Fremont

🏛 Fremont

Bounded by N 50th St, Lake Washington Ship Canal, Stone Way Ave N, & 8th Ave NW. 🚌 26, 28.

This funky district declared itself an "artists' republic" in the 1960s, one consisting of students, artists, and bohemians attracted here by low rents. By the late 1990s, its character began to change, after a high-tech firm set up office here. However, Fremont has managed to hold on to cherished traditions, such as the Summer Solstice Parade and an outdoor film series.

Public art is a fixture of Fremont. A 13.5-ft (4-m) tall statue of Lenin towers above pedestrians at Fremont Place, and a 15-ft (4.5-m) tall Volkswagen-eating troll lurks under the north end of the Aurora Bridge. On 34th Street, sculptor Richard Beyer's *People Waiting for the Interurban* is regularly clothed by locals. The dog's face in the sculpture is modeled after an honorary mayor, with whom the artist had a dispute.

🏛 University District

Bounded by NE 55th St, Portage Bay, Montlake Blvd NE, & I-5. 🛈 4014 University Way NE, (206) 543-9198. 🚌 7, 25, 43, 70, 71, 72, 73. ◯ 8am–5pm Mon–Fri. **Washington Park Arboretum** 2300 Arboretum Dr E. ☎ (206) 543-8800. **Visitor Center** ◯ 10am–4pm. **Grounds** ◑ 7am–dusk. 🖼 to Japanese Garden. ♿ ◻ 🖵 www.depts. washington.edu/wpa

The hub of the energetic U-District is the University of Washington, the premier institute of higher learning in the Northwest. Located on the site of the 1909 World's Fair,

the lovely 693-acre (280-ha) parklike campus is home to more than 35,000 students and 218 buildings in a mix of architectural styles. Just inside the main campus entrance is the **Burke Museum of Natural History and Culture**, featuring dinosaur fossils and Northwest Native art. On the western edge of the campus sits the **Henry Art Gallery**, the first public art museum in the state. The university's main avenue **University Way Northeast**, just west of the campus, is lined with bookstores, pubs, and inexpensive restaurants. University Village, east of the campus, offers an upscale shopping and dining experience.

A must-see is the **Washington Park Arboretum**, a 230-acre (93-ha) garden and living plant museum, with 4,600 species. Its Japanese Garden has carp-filled ponds and an authentic teahouse that is open for ceremonies once a month.

🦙 Woodland Park Zoo

5500 Phinney Ave N. ☎ (206) 684-4800. 🚌 5. ◯ check for times. 🅿 🖼 ◻ 🖵 www.zoo.org

Designed in 1909, this is one of the oldest zoos on the West Coast and a major Seattle attraction. The nearly 300 animal species residing at the 92-acre (37-ha) zoo are grouped together in ecosystems rather than by species, in habitats designed to resemble their natural habitats.

A visitor center at the main entrance provides maps and other information, such as animal feeding times. Among the excellent naturalistic habitats are the **Elephant Forest** – with its enormous elephant pool and Thai logging camp replica – and the **Trail of Vines**, which includes the first open-forested canopy for orangutans to be created within a zoo. The **Family Farm** features a popular petting zoo; a recent addition here is the Bug World exhibit. Indigenous North American animals can be viewed in their natural habitats along the **Northern Trail**.

🏛 Ballard

Bounded by Salmon Bay, Shilshole Bay, & Phinney Ridge. 🚌 15, 17, 18. **Hiram M. Chittenden Locks** 3015 NW 54th St. ☎ (206) 783-7059. **Grounds** ◯ 7am–9pm daily. **Visitor Center** ◯ check for times. ♿ 🖼 2pm Thu–Mon (Dec–Feb by arrangement only).

Located in northwest Seattle, Ballard's distinct Scandinavian accent dates to its settlement by Scandinavian fishermen and loggers in 1853. At the turn of the 19th century, Ballard was a mill town, producing an impressive three million wooden shingles a day. North of the shingle mills, **Ballard Avenue** was the commercial center of this area and is now a historic district, which features a wide array of ethnic cafés and lively music clubs.

Historic belltower in Ballard

The area's Scandinavian heritage is celebrated at the annual Norwegian Constitution Day Parade on May 17, at the excellent **Nordic Heritage Museum** on Northwest 67th Street.

Located at the west end of Ballard, the **Hiram M. Chittenden Locks** allow boats to travel between saltwater Puget Sound and freshwater Lake Union and Lake Washington. Its grounds include 7 acres (3 ha) of botanical gardens.

The Olympic Peninsula ❷

Olympic National Park Headquarters ℹ️ *3002 Mt Angeles Rd, 1 mile S of Port Angeles, (360) 452-0330.*
🌐 *www.nps.gov/olym/home.htm*

Bordered by the Pacific Ocean, the Strait of Juan de Fuca, and Puget Sound, Washington's Olympic Peninsula is an extraordinary piece of land. Its coastline, etched with bays and inlets, is peppered with majestic sea stacks – portions of wave-eroded headlands that remain as offshore mounds. Some of the country's most pristine mountains, beaches, and forestlands can be found in this remote region.

Sitting on the northwest tip of the peninsula, historic **Port Townsend** is known for its Victorian architecture and vibrant arts community. To its south, **Port Gamble**, a former logging town on the Kitsap Peninsula, has retained its original New England Victorian-style homes, country store, and church. The 1982 movie, *An Officer and a Gentleman*, was filmed here.

The centerpiece of the peninsula is the sprawling **Olympic National Park** *(p34)*, a UNESCO biosphere reserve and World Heritage Site. Encompassing 923,000 acres (373,540 ha), this biologically diverse park is a treasure-trove of snowcapped mountain peaks, lakes, water-

The peninsula's Lake Crescent Lodge

falls, rivers, and rainforests. Running through the center of the park are the jagged, glacier-covered Olympic Mountains. With its West Peak rising to a height of 7,965 ft (2,428 m), the three-peaked Mount Olympus is the highest mountain in the range.

The park headquarters are located in Port Angeles, a working port town. Sitting in the rain shadow of the Olympic Mountains, Sequim (pronounced "Squim") features an elk viewing site and the Olympic Game Farm, home to endangered animals. Southwest of Sequim, **Hurricane Ridge** offers panoramic views of the Olympic Mountains, the Strait of Juan de Fuca, and Vancouver Island from its 5,230-ft (1,594-m) high summit. In spring, the ridge is covered with wildflowers.

To the west, is the picturesque Lake Crescent area. Trout fishing is the main draw in this 625-ft (190-m) deep freshwater lake whose crystal clear waters also make it a favorite with divers. The

historic resort, **Lake Crescent Lodge** *(see p644)*, located on the lake's southern shore, is a lovely place to stay. Farther west, the 4-mile (6.5-km) long **Rialto Beach** offers superb views of the Pacific Coast, with its tide pools, sea stacks, rocky islands, and the Hole in the Wall, a tunnel carved by waves into a cliff.

The coastline receives the highest rainfall in the state. As a result, rainforests carpet much of the region. The **Hoh Rainforest**, with its annual rainfall of 14 ft (4 m), is a magical place, lush with Sitka spruce, Douglas fir, yew, and red cedar, draped with moss. Ancient trees here tower to nearly 300 ft (91 m) in height, and even the ferns grow taller than the hikers. Rainforests also surround the shores of Lake Quinalt. Snowcapped mountains encircle this glacial lake, which attracts fishermen and swimmers alike.

Wildlife is plentiful in the Olympic Peninsula – deer and bear abound, and the Olympic National Park has the country's largest herd of Roosevelt elk. The peninsula offers a wide range of outdoor recreation activities; among the most popular pursuits are fly- and deep-sea fishing, kayaking, whitewater rafting, mountain biking, hiking, and bird-watching. Skiing and snowshoeing are popular winter activities.

The majestic Olympic Mountains in Olympic National Park

Point Wilson Lighthouse, in Port Townsend's Fort Worden State Park

Port Townsend ❸

👥 8,000. 🚢 from Keystone on Whidbey Island & from Edmonds. ℹ 2437 E Sims Way, (888) 365-6978. 🆆 www.ptguide.com

THIS SEAPORT, a National Historic Landmark, is one of only three seaports on the National Registry. A building boom in the late 1800s left the town with several grand Victorian mansions, which now form the cornerstone of its thriving tourism industry.

Downtown's Romanesque **Jefferson County Courthouse** with its 124-ft (38-m) tall clock tower, is claimed to be the jewel of Port Townsend's Victorian architecture. Farther away, the old City Hall is now the **Jefferson County Historical Society**, home to the city council, as well as an excellent museum. Other famous buildings include the Ann Starrett Mansion and the Rothschild House.

The **Fire Bell Tower**, on the bluff overlooking downtown, was built to summon the town's voluntary fire fighters. The tower now heads the country's list of the Ten Most Endangered Historic Treasures. **Point Wilson Lighthouse**, in Fort Worden State Park, first lit in 1879, is still in operation.

Port Townsend is also an excellent base from which to make whale-watching, kayaking, and cycling day-trips.

Jefferson County Courthouse

1322 Washington St. ☎ (360) 385-1100. ⬜ 8am–5pm Mon–Fri. ● public hols. ♿

Bellingham ❹

👥 61,500. ✈ ℹ 904 Potter St, (360) 671-3990. 🆆 www.bellingham.org

OVERLOOKING Bellingham Bay and many of the San Juan Islands (see pp622–3), this town consists of four original towns – Whatcom, Sehome, Bellingham, and Fairhaven – consolidated into a single entity in 1904. The town's historic architecture includes Old Whatcom County Courthouse on East Street, the first brick building north of San Francisco, built in 1858, and the majestic City Hall. Built in 1892 in the Victorian Second Empire style, the City Hall is now the heart of the **Whatcom Museum of History and Art**. This four-building campus includes a children's museum. Among the highlights here are exhibits on the Northwest Coast Native Americans and the birds of the Pacific Northwest.

Tower of Bellingham's former City Hall

The downtown area has several restaurants, art galleries, and specialty shops. South of downtown, the historic Fairhaven district is an artsy enclave of Victorian buildings housing galleries, restaurants, and bookstores.

Just up the hill from downtown sits the campus of **Western Washington University**, with its famous collection of outdoor sculptures, including artworks by noted American artists Richard Serra, Mark di Suvero, and Richard Beyer.

From Bellingham's ports, passenger ferries leave for whale-watch cruises and tours to Vancouver Island and the San Juan Islands. Near the city are several waterfront parks, hiking and biking trails, and recreational areas. South of the city, Chuckanut Drive (Hwy 11) is a scenic 21-mile (34-km) loop. Some 55 miles (88.5 km) east of Bellingham is the 10,778-ft (3,285-m) high Mount Baker, popular for skiing and snowboarding.

🏛 Whatcom Museum of History & Art

121 Prospect St. ☎ (360) 676-6981. ⬜ noon–5pm Tue–Sun. **Children's Museum** Tue–Wed, 10am–5pm Thu–Sat, noon–5pm Sun. 🅿 to Children's Museum. ♿ 🚻

🏛 Western Washington University

ℹ S College Dr & College Way. ☎ (360) 650-3424. **Visitor Center** ⬜ mid-Sep–mid-Jun: 7am–8pm Mon–Fri; mid-Jun–mid-Sep: 7am–5pm Mon–Fri. ● public hols. ♿ 🆆 www.wwu.edu

Crab traps on a boat ready to set out from Bellingham Harbor

San Juan Islands ❺

A Washington State ferry sailing from the mainland to the islands

SCATTERED BETWEEN the Washington mainland and Vancouver Island, the San Juan archipelago consists of over 700 islands, 172 of them named. Ferries sail from Anacortes to the four largest islands – Lopez, Shaw, Orcas, and San Juan. Affectionately called "Slopez" because of its laid-back nature, Lopez's gently rolling roads, numerous stopping points, and friendly drivers make it a popular destination for cycling. Horseshoe-shaped Orcas, the hilliest island in the chain, offers breathtaking views from atop 2,409-ft (734-m) Mount Constitution. The best destination for walk-on passengers, San Juan Island is home to Friday Harbor, the largest town in the archipelago. The nationally renowned Whale Museum is located here. Primarily residential, Shaw Island does not offer any visitor facilities.

Sailboats in the Channel
Sailors love the many harbors and good winds in the San Juan Channel.

VICTORIA

Roche Harbor

SAN JUAN

SAN JUAN ISLAND

Lime Kiln Point State Park

SEATTLE

★ Roche Harbor
A charming seaside village, Roche Harbor features a marina, Victorian gardens, a chapel, and the historic Hotel de Haro, built in 1886.

0 km 2
0 miles 2

STAR SIGHTS

★ Deer Harbor

★ Friday Harbor

★ Lopez

★ Roche Harbor

Lime Kiln Point State Park
This state park, with its picturesque lighthouse, is the only park in the country dedicated to whale-watching.

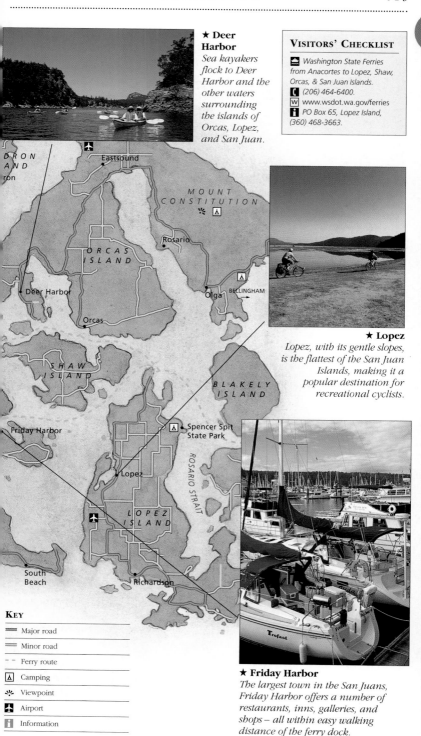

★ Deer Harbor
Sea kayakers flock to Deer Harbor and the other waters surrounding the islands of Orcas, Lopez, and San Juan.

VISITORS' CHECKLIST

Washington State Ferries from Anacortes to Lopez, Shaw, Orcas, & San Juan Islands.
(206) 464-6400.
www.wsdot.wa.gov/ferries
PO Box 65, Lopez Island, (360) 468-3663.

★ Lopez
Lopez, with its gentle slopes, is the flattest of the San Juan Islands, making it a popular destination for recreational cyclists.

★ Friday Harbor
The largest town in the San Juans, Friday Harbor offers a number of restaurants, inns, galleries, and shops – all within easy walking distance of the ferry dock.

KEY

═══	Major road
──	Minor road
– – –	Ferry route
🏕	Camping
✷	Viewpoint
✈	Airport
🛈	Information

Turquoise-colored Diablo Lake in North Cascades National Park

North Cascades Highway ❻

State Rte 20.

THE SCENIC North Cascades Highway is the northernmost mountain pass route in Washington. It is the 132-mile (213-km) section of Highway 20 between Winthrop in the east and I-5 to the west. Bisecting the **North Cascades National Park**, it offers access to the many wonders of this breathtakingly beautiful ecosystem of jagged snowcapped peaks, forested valleys, and cascading waterfalls. The entire route is open from mid-April to mid-October.

The road follows the Skagit River, passing Gorge Creek Falls, Lake Diablo, and Ruby Creek. Along the way, the Ross Lake Overview is an ideal spot to view the scenic lake. At 5,477 ft (1,669 m), **Washington Pass Overlook** provides heart-pounding vistas of the steep pass up Liberty Bell Mountain. A dominant feature of the park, **Mount Shuksan** at the height of 9,131 ft (2,783 m), is one of the state's highest mountains.

The heavily glaciated park is home to a variety of animals – bald eagles, gray wolves, and bears. Many hiking trails link the highway to the quiet town of Stehekin at the northernmost tip of Lake Chelan.

North Cascades National Park
ℹ️ SR 20, near milepost 120 & Newhalem, (206) 386-4495.
Ⓦ www.ncascades.org

Lake Chelan ❼

ℹ️ 102 E Johnson Ave, (509) 682-3503. Ⓦ www.lakechelan.com

MAGNIFICENT Lake Chelan, in the remote northwest end of the Cascades, claims the distinction of being the country's third-deepest lake, reaching 1,500 ft (457 m) at its deepest point. Fed by 27 glaciers and 59 streams, the lake, which is less than 2 miles (3 km) wide, stretches for 55 miles (89 km). In summer, it buzzes with activity – boating, fishing, snorkeling, water-skiing, and wind surfing. The resort town of **Chelan** at the southeastern end of the lake has been a popular summer vacation destination for generations of Western Washingtonians seeking the sunny, dry weather on the eastern side of the state. Basking in the rain shadow of the Cascade Mountains, the town enjoys 300 days of sunshine each year. The town's vintage **Ruby Theatre** on East Woodin Avenue is one of the oldest continuously running movie theaters in the Northwest. Chelan's other highlights are the murals on buildings, which depict the history of the Lake Chelan Valley.

About 9 miles (14 km) from downtown Chelan is the town of **Manson**, whose main attraction is the Scenic Loop Trail. It offers easy exploration of

Sign welcoming visitors to Lake Chelan

the nearby orchards and hilly countryside. Farther north, the lakeside town of **Stehekin** can be reached by ferry.

Leavenworth ❽

📷 2,200. ℹ️ 220 9th St, (509) 548-5807. 🚐 Ⓦ www.leavenworth.org

ONCE A LOGGING town, Leavenworth, at the foot of the Cascade Mountains in central Washington, is now a quaint little Bavarian-style town seemingly straight out of a fairy tale. This theme was consciously developed in the 1960s to help revitalize the town and, today, every commercial building in town, Starbucks and McDonald's included, looks as though it belongs in the Alps.

The town now bustles with festivals, art shows, and summer theater productions, attracting more than a million visitors each year. Among its popular festivals are Fasching, a classic Bavarian carnival held in February; Maifest, with its 16th-century costumes, maypole dances, and jousting; and Oktoberfest *(see p30)*, the traditional celebration of German food, beer, and music. Teeming with Bavarian specialty shops and restaurants, the town also has the fascinating **Leavenworth Nutcracker Museum**, which showcases 4,500 nutcrackers from 38 countries, some dating back 500 years.

🏛 Leavenworth Nutcracker Museum
735 Front St. 📞 (509) 548-4573. ⏱ May–Oct: 2–5pm daily; Nov–Apr: 2–5pm Sat–Sun. 🈲 📷 for groups by appt.

A traditional horse-drawn 13-barrel beer wagon in Leavenworth

Spokane 9

🏘 195,000. ✈ ℹ 201 W Main Ave, (509) 776-5263.
W www.visitspokane.com

WASHINGTON's second largest city, this is the Inland Northwest's commercial and cultural center. The city was rebuilt in brick and terra-cotta after a disastrous fire in 1889 – its many handsome buildings are reminders of that building boom.

Spokane is the smallest city to host a world's fair (Expo '74). The fair site is now the sprawling **Riverfront Park**, a 100-acre (40-ha) expanse in the heart of the city. Of the town's two museum's, the **Northwest Museum of Arts & Culture** showcases regional history, while **Campbell House** (1898) nearby is an interactive museum. Other attractions are an IMAX® Theater and a 1909 carousel. A 37-mile (60-km) trail connects the city with Riverside State Park, located 6 miles (10 km) to the northwest.

🏛 Northwest Museum of Arts & Culture

2316 W 1st Ave. 📞 (509) 456-3931. ◷ 11am–5pm daily (until 8pm Wed & Fri). ● public hols. 🎫 ♿ 🖥 📷
W www.northwestmuseum.org

Walla Walla 10

🏘 30,000. ℹ 29 E Sumac St, (509) 525-0850. W www.wallawalla.org

LOCATED IN THE southeast corner of the state, Walla Walla is a green oasis in the midst of an arid landscape. The town features several National Register buildings,

lovely parks, and a wealth of public art. The attractive campus of **Whitman College**, one of the nation's top-rated liberal arts colleges, is three blocks from downtown.

A popular destination for wine connoisseurs, the Walla Walla Valley has more than 35 wineries – several right in the heart of downtown. Among the town's other claims to fame are its delicious sweet Walla Walla onions and its annual Hot Air Balloon Stampede, a rally of some 45 pilots, held in May. The stampede also features live music, arts-and-crafts booths, and various events.

Fort Walla Walla Museum, on Myra Road, consisting of original and replica pioneer buildings, gives a historical perspective of the area. The **Whitman Mission National Historic Site**, about 7 miles (11 km) west of town, is a memorial to pioneer missionaries Marcus and Narcissa Whitman who were massacred by Cayuse Indians. On weekends, the Living History Company honors the area's history through music and dance.

🏛 Fort Walla Walla Museum

755 Myra Rd. 📞 (509) 525-7703. ◷ Apr–Oct: 10am–5pm daily. ♿ (call ahead). 📷 by arrangement. W www.fortwallawallamuseum.org

🏛 Whitman Mission National Historic Site

Hwy 12. 📞 (509) 522-6360. ◷ Jun–Sep: 8am–6pm daily; Oct–May: 8am–4:30pm daily. ● Jan 1, Thanksgiving, Dec 25. 🎫 ♿ (except Monument Hill).
W www.nps.gov/whmi

Yakima Valley 11

ℹ 10 N 8th St, Yakima, (509) 575-3010. W www.visityakima.com

WITH ITS RICH volcanic soil, abundance of irrigation water, and 300 days of annual sunshine, the Yakima Valley is the fifth largest producer of fruits and vegetables in the US, and home to more than 30 regional wineries. Yakima, the valley's largest community and commercial hub, serves as an good base to visit the valley's award-winning wineries. The **Washington's Fruit Place Visitor Center** offers free fruit samples and an overview of the state's fruit industry.

Grapes from Yakima Valley

ℹ Washington's Fruit Place Visitor Center

105 S 18th St. 📞 (509) 576-3090. ◷ year round: 10am–5pm Mon–Fri; May–Dec: also 10am–4pm Sat. ♿

Maryhill 12

🏘 100. ℹ Klickitat County Visitor Information Center, (509) 773-4395.

A REMOTE SAGEBRUSH bluff overlooking the Columbia River is where entrepreneur Sam Hill chose to build his palatial residence. In 1907, he purchased 7,000 acres (2,833 ha) here, with the vision of creating a utopian colony for Quaker farmers. He called the community Maryhill, in honor of his daughter, Mary. The ideal community did not materialize, and Hill turned his unfinished mansion into a museum. The treasures of the **Maryhill Museum of Art** include the throne and gold coronation gown of his friend Queen Marie of Romania, 87 sculptures and drawings by Auguste Rodin, and an impressive collection of Native American art. The beautifully landscaped grounds include a picnic area.

🏛 Maryhill Museum of Art

35 Maryhill Museum Dr, Goldendale. 📞 (509) 773-3733. ◷ Mar 15–Nov

Balloons over Walla Walla during the annual Hot Air Balloon Stampede

The modern stainless steel exterior of the Tacoma Museum of Glass

Tacoma ⑭

195,000. ✈ ℹ 747 Market St,
(253) 627-2836.
W www.cityoftacoma.org

WASHINGTON'S third-largest
city, located south of
Seattle, Tacoma was founded
as a sawmill town in the
1860s. It prospered with the
arrival of the railroad in the
late 1880s, becoming a major
shipping port for important
commodities such as
lumber, coal, and
grain. Many of the
Pacific Northwest's
railroad, timber,
and shipping
barons settled in
Tacoma's Stadium
District. This
historic area, with
its stately turn-of-the-20th-
century mansions, is named
for the French château-style
Stadium High School, also
known as the "Castle."

The undisputed star of the
city's revitalized waterfront is
the striking **Museum of
Glass**. The 75,000-sq-ft
(6,968-sq-m) landmark
building showcases contemporary art, with a focus
on glass. A dramatic 90-ft
(37-m) metal-encased cone
houses a spacious glass-
blowing studio.

The stunning Chihuly
Bridge of Glass serves as a
pedestrian walkway linking
the museum to downtown
Tacoma and the innovative
**Washington State History
Museum**. The museum fea-
tures interactive exhibits,
high-tech displays, and
theatrical storytelling by

Sign denoting the old
town of Tacoma

actors in period costume,
who relate stories of the
state's past history.

The 50,000-sq-ft (4,645-sq-
m), stainless-steel-wrapped
Tacoma Art Museum was
designed to be a dynamic
cultural center and a show-
piece for the city. Its growing
collection of works, from the
18th century to the present
day, include a large assembly
of Pacific Northwest art,
European Impressionist
pieces, Japanese wood-
block prints, and
Tacoma artist Dale
Chihuly's *(see
p613)* glassworks.
In keeping with its
vision of creating
a place that "builds
community through
art," the museum's
facilities include the Bill and
Melinda Gates Resource
Center, providing visitors with
access to a range of state-of-
the-art research equipment.
Children of all ages can also
make use of the in-house,
interactive art-making studio,
ArtWORKS.

Tacoma's most popular
attraction is **Point
Defiance Park**, ranked
among the 20 largest
urban parks in the US.
Encompassing 700
acres (285 ha), its
grounds include

Fort Nisqually, the first European settlement on Puget
Sound and a major fur-trading
establishment. Also in the
park are seven specialty gardens, a scenic drive, hiking
and biking trails, beaches, a
boat marina, and a picnic area.

Highlighting a Pacific Rim
theme, the **Point Defiance
Zoo and Aquarium** on Pearl
Street features more than
5,000 animals. A vantage
point at the park's west end
offers superb views of Mount
Rainier *(see p626–7)*, Puget
Sound, and the Tacoma
Narrows Bridge, famous as
one of the longest suspension
bridges in the world.

The fishing village of **Gig
Harbor**, 11 miles (17 km)
south of Tacoma, has shops
and restaurants that reflect the
Scandinavian and Croatian
heritage of its 6,500 inhabitants.

🏛 Museum of Glass

1801 E Dock St. ℂ (253) 284-4750,
(866) 468-7386. ◯ 10am–5pm
Tue–Wed & Fri–Sat, 10am–8pm Thu,
noon–5pm Sun. ● Mon, Jan 1,
Thanksgiving, Dec 25. 🎫 👍 🖥 📷
W www.museumofglass.org

🏛 Washington State
History Museum

1911 Pacific Ave. ℂ (888) 238-4373.
◯ 10am–5pm Tue–Wed & Fri,
10am–8pm Thu, 10am–5pm Sat,
noon–5pm Sun. ● public hols. 🎫
👍 📷 for groups. W www.wshs.org

Olympia ⑮

43,000. ℹ 103 14th Ave SW,
(360) 586-3460.
W www.olympiachamber.com

NAMED FOR ITS magnificent
view of the Olympic
Mountains, Washington's
state capital is located at
the southern tip of
Puget Sound. The
city's **State Capitol
Campus** is domi-
nated by the 28-story
Legislative

The Romanesque Legislative Building on the State Capitol Campus, Olympia

Building (the Capitol), whose 287-ft (87-m) brick-and-sandstone dome is one of the tallest masonry domes in the world. One of the most impressive in the nation, the campus encompasses superb buildings, several fountains, and monuments. Its land-scaped grounds were designed in 1928 by the Olmsted Brothers, sons of Frederick Olmsted, one of the creators of New York City's Central Park (see p78).

The **State Capital Museum** provides a historical perspective of Washington's early pioneer settlements, through its collections of early photographs and documents. The **State Archives**, with its historical records and artifacts, is another institution related to the state's past. Visitors can access such unique treasures as documents from the Canwell Committee, which blacklisted suspected Communists during the 1950s (see p50).

Tree-lined streets, old homes, a picturesque water-front, and a thriving cultural community all contribute to Olympia's charm. Tucked among downtown's historic buildings are several shops, restaurants, and galleries. Within walking distance are attractions such as the lively **Olympia Farmers Market,** offering local produce, sea-food, and crafts, along with dining and entertainment.

Percival Landing, a 1.5-mile (2.5-km) boardwalk along Budd Inlet, offers views of the Olympic Mountains, the Capitol dome, Puget Sound, and ships in port.

🏛 **State Capitol Campus**
ℹ 409 13th Ave SW, (360) 586-8687. ● Jan 1, Thanksgiving, Dec 25. **Legislative Building** ● until Jan 2005 for renovation. 🚫 Campus: hourly 10am–3pm daily; Temple of Justice: 8am–5pm Mon–Fri.
🏛 **State Capital Museum**
211 W 21st Ave. ☏ (360) 753-2580. ● 10am–4pm Tue–Fri; noon–4pm Sat. ● public hols. 🚫 ♿
ᴡ www.wshs.org
🏛 **State Archives**
1129 Washington St SE.
☏ (360) 753-1801.
● 8:30am–4:30pm Mon–Fri. ♿

Mount St. Helens and the surrounding area after the 1980 explosion

Mount St. Helens National Volcanic Monument ⓰

☏ (360) 449-7800. 🚫 🚻 🅿
ᴡ www.fs.fed.us/gpnf/mshnvm

ON THE MORNING of May 18, 1980, Mount St. Helens literally exploded. Triggered by a powerful earthquake, the peak erupted, spewing one cubic mile (4.17 cubic km) of rock into the air and causing the largest recorded avalanche in history. In the blink of an eye, the mountain lost 1,314 ft (400 m), and 234 sq miles (606 sq km) of forestlands were destroyed. The eruption also claimed 57 human lives and those of millions of animals and fish.

The 110,000-acre (44,000-ha) monument was created in 1982 to allow the environment to recover naturally while encouraging research, recreation, and education. Roads and trails allow visitors to explore this fascinating region by car and foot. On the mountain's west side, Hwy 504 leads to five visitor centers, which document the disaster and recovery efforts. Mount St. Helens National Volcanic Monument Visitor Center, at milepost 5, features interpretative exhibits of the mountain's history. The visitor center at Hoffstadt Bluffs, at milepost 27, gives visitors their first full view of Mount St. Helens and offers helicopter tours into the blast zone from May to September. **Johnson Ridge Observa-tory**, at the end of the road, offers panoramic views.

Fort Vancouver ⓱

☏ (360) 696-7655. ● Mar–Oct: 9am–5pm daily; Nov–Feb: 9am–4pm daily. ● Thanksgiving, Dec 24–25, & 31. 🚫 ♿ partial. 🚫
ᴡ www.nps.gov/fova

BETWEEN 1825 and 1849, Fort Vancouver was an important trading outpost for the British-based Hudson's Bay Company, the giant fur-trading organization. Located close to major tributaries and natural resources, it was the center of political and com-mercial activities in the Pacific Northwest during these years. During the 1830s and 1840s, the fort also provided essen-tial supplies to settlers.

A National Historic Site, Fort Vancouver features accurate reconstructions of nine of the original buildings, including the jail, fur store, and wash house, all on their original sites. Guided tours and re-enactments offer a window into the fort's past. Over a million artifacts have been excavated from this site.

The three-story bastion, dating from 1845, at Fort Vancouver

Oregon

Oregon is best known for its many scenic wonders – snowcapped mountains, flowing rivers, verdant forests, and desert vistas are just some of the attractions in this incredibly diverse state. This rugged landscape was first settled by pioneers who migrated along the Oregon Trail *(see p450)*. Today, the state is known not only for its scenic beauty but also for its cosmopolitan pleasures. Portlanders are eager to claim their city as one of the most sophisticated and cultured anywhere.

Evening view of the Portland skyline and the Willamette River

Portland ⓲

🏃 *536,240.* ✈ 🚉 🚌 🚊 ℹ *26 SW Salmon St, (503) 222-2223.*

Known as the City of Roses, Portland was founded in 1843, on the west bank of the Willamette River. It grew into a major port, but later, with the arrival of the railroad and decline in river trade, the city center moved inland. This area, with its steel-framed buildings, is now the city's downtown, while Old Town encompasses the former port and riverfront quarter. Portland's beautiful parks and gardens and well-preserved historic landmarks are a tribute to foresight and successful urban planning.

🏛 Pioneer Courthouse Square

SW Broadway & Yamhill St. ℂ *(503) 223-1613.* 🚊 **Pioneer Courthouse** 701 SW 6th Ave. ℂ *(503) 326-2115.* ◯ *9am–5pm Mon–Fri.* ● *weekends & public hols.* ♿
This one-block, brick-paved pedestrian square, in eastern downtown, is the heart of Portland, where Portlanders gather for free lunchtime concerts, flower shows, and other events, or simply for a chance to sit and enjoy their beautiful city. Underground spaces next to the square

accomodate offices and businesses, which include the Portland Visitors Association Information Center, a coffee shop, and a branch of Powell's City of Books, a well-known store that specializes in travel books.
Opposite is the **Pioneer Courthouse**, the first federal building to be built in the Pacific Northwest region. The US Court of Appeals and a US post office branch are housed here. Its octagonal tower has been a fixture of the Portland skyline from 1873.

🌿 South Park Blocks

Bounded by SW Salmon St & I-405, SW Park & SW 9th Aves. **Oregon Historical Society** 1200 SW Park Ave. ℂ *(503) 222-1741.* ◯ *10am–5pm Tue–Sat, until 8pm Thu.* ● *public hols.* 🎫 ♿ 🛒 🖥 www.ohs.org **Portland Art Museum** 1219 SW Park Ave. ℂ *(503) 226-2811.* ◯ *10am–5pm Tue–Wed & Sat, 10am–8pm Thu–Fri, noon–5pm Sun.* ● *Dec 25.* 🎫 ♿ 🛒 🖥 www.pam.org
A green ribbon of elm-shaded lawns laid out by frontier businessman and legislator Daniel Lownsdale in 1852, the so-called South Park Blocks is a 12-block stretch running through the central city. Among its distinctive features are statuary and some 40 ornamental fountains. South

Park Blocks is also the venue for a colorful local market, held every Saturday, where farmers sell their wares to locals and visitors alike.
The **Oregon Historical Society** to the south of the park has huge murals on its façades that depict scenes from the Lewis and Clarke expedition *(see p570)* and other significant moments in the state's history. On display in the galleries, which extend through three buildings, are paintings, photographs, maps, and historical documents that make this museum the largest repository of Oregon's historical artifacts.
The **Portland Art Museum**, opposite South Park Blocks in Southwest Park Avenue, is the oldest museum in the Pacific Northwest. Its sizable collection of European works, includes paintings by Picasso, Van Gogh, and Monet, and sculpture by Rodin and Brancusi. Its new Grand Ronde Center for Native American Art displays masks, jewelry, and totem poles created by the indigenous peoples of North America.

🍂 Governor Tom McCall Waterfront Park

Bounded by SW Clay & NW Glisan Sts, SW Naito Pkwy & Willamette River.
Buried beneath an expressway from the 1940s to the 1970s, this 1.5-mile- (2.5-km-) long stretch of Willamette River waterfront was reclaimed and transformed into a park. Named after Tom McCall, Oregon's environmentally minded governor from 1967 to 1975, the park is now a frequently used riverside

The Saturday Farmers Market in South Park Blocks

Main gateway to Portland's Saturday Market

Saturday Market, America's largest handicrafts bazaar. Chinatown Gate, a five-tiered, dragon-festooned gateway leads to Chinatown, home to the city's many Asian immigrants, who first arrived in Portland more than 135 years ago. The neighborhood's tranquil **Classical Chinese Garden** is a 15th century Ming-style walled enclave, with waterways and pavilions.

promenade and the venue for many local festivals, including the annual Rose Festival, held between May and June.

One of its most popular attractions is **Salmon Street Springs**, a fountain whose 100 jets splash water directly onto the pavement, providing relief on a hot day. Another highlight is the **Battleship Oregon Memorial**, at its southern end. Built in 1956, the memorial honors an 1893 US Navy ship. A time capsule sealed in its base in 1976 is to be opened in 2076.

RiverPlace Marina at the southwest end of Tom McCall Park offers many amenities including restaurants, one of the city's higher-end hotels – the RiverPlace Hotel *(see p645)*, upscale shops, sloping lawns, riverside walks, and a large marina.

🚩 Old Town & Chinatown
Bounded by SW Naito Pkwy & NW Glisan St, NW 3rd Ave & SW Pine St.
Elegant brick façades and quiet streets belie Old Town's raucous, 19th-century frontier-town past. A National Historic Landmark today, this riverfront district once drew dockworkers, shipbuilders, and traders from all over the world during its heyday as a major port and the city's commercial center. Old Town is now a trendy, colorful neighborhood, especially during weekends, when vendors gather for the **Portland**

🏛 American Advertising Museum
211 NW 5th Ave. 📞 *(503) 226-0000.*
🕐 *noon–5pm Wed–Sun.*
● *public hols.* ♿ 🅿
🌐 www.admuseum.org
This fascinating museum is devoted entirely to advertising, or the art of persuasion, as it is also called. Displays trace the subtleties and excesses of this art from 1700 to the present day – from quaint broadsides to Burma Shave roadside signs *(see p413)* as well as MTV-inspired video clips.

🚩 Pearl District
W Burnside to NW Lovejoy Sts, from NW 8th to NW 15th Aves. **Portland Streetcar** East- & southbound on NW Lovejoy St & 11th Ave, north- & westbound on 10th Ave & NW Northrup St. 🕐 *every 15 mins, 5:30am–11pm Mon–Thu, 5:30am–1am Fri, 7:30am–1am Sat, 7:30am–11pm Sun.*
Often called Portland's "newest" neighborhood, Pearl District actually occupies an old industrial district on the north side of Burnside Street. Many former warehouses and factories have been refurbished to house chic galleries, designer shops, design studios, clubs, cafés, restaurants, and breweries. A good time to visit Pearl District is during a First Thursday event, which takes place the first Thursday of every month. At

this time, the many art galleries in the area remain open for longer.

A quaint way to travel between Pearl District and Nob Hill, a gracious, late-19th-century neighborhood, is to take the **Portland Streetcar**. These low-slung Czech-built trams are not only a convenient way to get around but are also free within the city center.

🌿 Washington Park
SW Park Pl. 📞 *(503) 823-2223.*
🕐 *24 hrs daily (not all sights).*
🎟 *to some exhibits.* 🅿
🌐 www.parks.ci.portland.or.us
Washington Park, a popular outdoor playground, is surrounded by the city on all its sides. Its attractions include the Hoyt Arboretum, which has more than 8,000 trees and shrubs, the Japanese Garden, the International Rose Test Garden, and the popular **Oregon Zoo**, which has the largest number of elephants bred in captivity.

🏛 Oregon Museum of Science and Industry
1945 SE Water Ave.
📞 *(503) 797-4000.*
🕐 *Sep 4–Jun 14: 9:30am–5:30pm Tue–Sun; Jun 15–Labor Day: 9:30am–7pm daily.*
● *public hols.* 🎟 ♿ 🅿
of submarine. 🅿 🅿
🌐 www.omsi.edu
Sign at Oregon Zoo

Eastbank Esplanade
Bounded by Willamette River & I-5, Steel & Hawthorne Bridges.
East of the river, the Oregon Museum of Science and Industry (OMSI) is a top US science museum. A favorite among the hundreds of interactive exhibits is the earthquake simulator, in which visitors are shaken and rattled while learning about the tectonic plates that still shift beneath Portland.

Nearby, the **Eastbank Esplanade** is a pedestrian and bicycle path following the east bank of the Willamette River. A 1,200-ft (365-m) section floats on water, while a cantilevered portion is suspended above one of the city's original commercial piers, providing unobstructed river views.

Columbia River Gorge and the Cascade Mountains

Columbia River Gorge ⑲

ℹ️ *775 Summer St NE, Salem, (800) 547-7842.*

THIS MAGNIFICENT fir- and maple-covered river canyon cuts through the Cascade Mountains, forming a boundary between the states of Washington and Oregon. The best way to explore the area is to take the **Historic Columbia River Highway**. Blasted out of narrow cliffs, this road was designed to maximize viewing pleasure while minimizing environmental damage as much as possible. Along the route are the spectacular **Multnomah Falls**, tumbling 620 ft (186 m) in two picturesque cascades, and the cosy, rustic Timberline Lodge dating from the 1930s *(see p645)*.

Mount Hood ⑳

ℹ️ *775 Summer St NE, Salem, (800) 547-7842.*

THE SPECTACULAR snow-covered peak of Mount Hood, the tallest of Oregon's Cascade peaks, rises south of the Columbia River Gorge. Home to year-round skiing and snowboarding, the valleys below are famous for their produce of apples, apricots, pears, and peaches. The **Mount Hood Loop** is a good way to explore the area; the highest point on the loop,

known as **Barlow Pass**, is so steep that at one time, wagons had to be lowered down the hillsides with ropes. The Hood River Valley offers blossoming fruit trees in season and lovely views of the majestic Mount Hood throughout the year. **Hood River**, a riverside town called the "Windsurfing Capital of the World," also offers great opportunities for other sports such as mountain biking.

Astoria ㉑

🏃 *10,000.* ℹ️ *111 W Marine Dr.* 📞 *(800) 875-6807.* 🌐 *www.oldoregon.com*

THE OLDEST American settlement west of the Rocky Mountains, Astoria was established when John Jacob Astor sent fur traders around Cape Horn to establish a trading post at the mouth of the Columbia River in 1811. Earlier, explorers Lewis and Clark *(see p570)* spent the winter of 1805–1806 at a crude stockade near Astoria, making moccasins, preserving fish, and recording in their journals accounts of bear attacks and the almost continual rain. The stockade has since been rebuilt at Fort Clatsop National Memorial.

Astoria Column

These days, the town is a bustling port; its old Victorian homes climb a hillside above the river. One such home, the stately **Captain George Flavel House Museum**, retains the cupola from which the captain and his wife once watched river traffic. An even better view can be enjoyed from atop the 164-step spiral staircase of the **Astoria Column**, encircled with friezes paying homage to the history of the Pacific Northwest.

The town honors its seafaring past at the **Columbia River Maritime Museum**, where riverside galleries house fishing dories as well as Native American dugout canoes and other river-oriented artifacts. The lightship *Columbia*, berthed in front, once guided ships across the treacherous area at the mouth of the river.

🚍 **Captain George Flavel House Museum**
441 8th St. 📞 *(503) 325-2203.* 🕐 *10am–5pm daily.* 🔴 *Jan 1, Thanksgiving, Dec 24–25.* ♿

🏛 **Columbia River Maritime Museum**
1792 Marine Dr. 📞 *(503) 325-2323.* 🕐 *9:30am–5pm daily.* 🔴 *Thanksgiving, Dec 25.* ♿ 📷 🌐 *www.crmm.org*

The majestic peak of Mount Hood as seen from Hood River Valley

Sea stacks rise off Bandon coast, with houses in the background

Oregon Coast ㉒

i *PO Box 74, 137 NE 1st St, Newport, Oregon 97365, (541) 265-2188.*
W *www.visittheoregoncoast.com*

Hundreds of miles of pristine beaches make the Oregon Coast one of the the state's best-loved tourist destinations. The developed northern part has some of Oregon's most popular resorts, while the southern part is more wild and rugged. The coast is ideal for a range of recreational activities such as driving, cycling, hiking, camping, shell-fishing, and whale- or bird-watching.

Oregon's favorite beach town, **Cannon Beach**, south of Astoria, retains a quiet charm. Haystack Rock, one of the tallest coastal monoliths in the world, towers 235 ft (72 m) above a long beach and tidal pools. Ecola State Park, at the beach's north end, carpets Tillamook Head, a basalt headland, with verdant forests. Viewpoints look across raging surf to Tillamook Rock Lighthouse, which was built in 1880.

Picturesque house on Hemlock Street, Cannon Beach

Nature is the main attraction along the 35-mile (56-km) **Three Capes Scenic Route**, farther south. The rocks below Cape Meares State Scenic Viewpoint and Cape Meares Lighthouse are home to one of the largest colonies of nesting seabirds in North America. The Cape Lookout State Park is a good place to spot migrating gray whales. The Oregon State Parks Association provides detailed information about the sights along this stunning route.

The **Cape Perpetua Scenic Area** has the highest viewpoint on the coast. A road ascends to the top at 800 ft (240 m), and an easy hike along the Giant Spruce Trail leads to a majestic, 500-year-old Sitka spruce. From Cape Perpetua, Hwy 101 leads to Heceta Head State Park, with its ocean views – birds nest on rocks and sea lions and gray whales swim offshore. Rising high above the surf, the Heceta Head Lighthouse was first lit in 1894. Steller's sea lions inhabit the Sea Lion Caves, the only wild sea lion rookery on the North American mainland.

The massive sand dunes of the **Oregon Dunes National Recreation Area** stretch south from Florence for 40 miles (64 km). Towering sand formations, lakes, pine forests, grasslands, and open beaches attract a variety of recreation

Dune buggy, Oregon Dunes National Recreation Area

enthusiasts. Boardwalks make it easy to enjoy stunning vistas from Oregon Dunes Overlook, about 20 miles (32 km) south of Florence, while the mile-long Umpqua Scenic Dunes Trail, 30 miles (48 km) south of Florence, skirts the tallest dunes.

Bandon, near the mouth of the Coquille River, is so small and weathered that it is difficult to imagine that it was once a major port. Craggy rock formations rise from the ocean just off the beach. These wind-sculpted shapes include Face Rock, allegedly an Indian maiden who was frozen into stone by an evil spirit. A wild landscape of dunes and sea grass can be seen at the Bullards Beach State Park, which lies across the marshy, bird-filled Coquille Estuary.

⚓ Three Capes Scenic Route
Oregon State Parks Association
C *(800) 551-6949.*
W *www.oregonstateparks.org*
⚓ Cape Perpetua Scenic Area
Interpretive Center **C** *(541) 547-3289.* ☐ *Memorial Day–Labor Day: 9am–5pm daily; Labor Day–Memorial Day: 9am–4pm Sat–Sun.* ● *public hols.* 🅰 🅿
⚓ Oregon Dunes National Recreation Area
i *855 Highway Ave, Reedsport.*
C *(541) 271-3611.* ☐ *dawn–dusk daily.* 🅰 **W** *www.fs.fed.us/r6/ siuslaw/oregondunes*

Local arts and crafts on display at the Saturday Market in Eugene

Salem ㉓

🏠 121,000. ℹ️ 1313 Mill St SE, (503) 581-4325. 🌐 www.scva.org

O NCE A THRIVING trading and lumber port on the Willamette River, Salem became the capital of the Oregon Territory in 1851.

At the edge of Bush's Pasture Park stand **Asahel Bush House**, an 1878 home with a conservatory said to be the first greenhouse west of the Mississippi River, and the historic **Deepwood Estate**. The **Mission Mill Museum** preserves some of the state's earliest structures. These include the 1841 home of Jason Lee, who helped found Salem, and the Kay Woolen Mill, where waterwheels from the 1890s are still intact.

Asahel Bush House, Salem

The state's history is also in evidence around the **Oregon State Capitol**. A gilded pioneer stands atop the rotunda, marble sculptures of Lewis and Clark *(see 570)* flank the entrance, and the murals inside depict Captain Robert Gray's discovery of the Columbia River *(see p612)*.

Waller Hall, built in 1867, houses the **Hallie Ford Museum of Art** with its outstanding collection of 20th-century Native American basketry and paintings.

🏛 Mission Mill Museum
1314 Mill St SE. ℹ️ (503) 585-7012. ⭕ 10am–5pm Mon–Sat. ⬤ major hols. 🈺 ✔

Eugene ㉔

🏠 130,000. ℹ️ 115 W 8th Ave, (541) 484-5307. 🌐 www.eugene.com

T HE UNIVERSITY of Oregon brings culture and distinction to Eugene, which straddles the banks of the Willamette River at the south end of the river valley. The glass-and-timber **Hult Center for the Performing Arts**, is regarded as one of the best-designed performing arts complexes in the world. The **University of Oregon Museum of Natural History** counts among its holdings some ancient shoes – a pair of sagebrush sandals dating from as early as 9500 BC.

Local artisans sell their wares at the **Saturday Market**, in downtown Park Blocks. The **Fifth Street Public Market**, an assemblage of shops and restaurants in a converted feed mill, bustles with locals and university students.

Madras & Warm Springs ㉕

Madras ℹ️ 274 SW 4th St, (541) 475-2350.
🌐 http://madrasor.areaguides.net
Warm Springs ℹ️ 1233 Veterans St, (541) 553-3333.
🌐 www.warmsprings.com

M ADRAS IS A desert ranching town surrounded by rimrock and vast tracts of wilderness recreation lands. **Crooked River National Grassland** provides endless vistas as well as fishing and rafting opportunities on two US National Wild and Scenic Rivers – the Deschutes and the Crooked – that weave through thousands of acres of juniper and sage brush. **Cove Palisades State Park** surrounds the deep waters of Lake Billy Chinook, a popular destination for boaters.

The Treaty of 1855 between the US government and the Wasco, Walla Walla, and Paiute tribes established lands for the tribes located on the 640,000-acre (256,000-ha) Warm Springs Reservation in central Oregon. Today, these Confederated Tribes preserve their cultural heritage at the **Museum at Warm Springs** with a stunningly beautiful collection of basketry and beadwork, haunting historic photographs, and videotapes of tribal ceremonies. The tribes also manage a casino and a resort, where a large pool is heated by hot springs.

🏛 Museum at Warm Springs
Hwy 26, Warm Springs. 🅲 (503) 553-3331. ⭕ 10am–5pm daily. 🈺
📷 🌐 www.ctws.org/museum

Swimming pool fed by hot springs at the Warm Springs Reservation resort

Galloping horses near Sisters, the peaks of the Three Sisters Mountains visible in the distance

Sisters 26

900. 164 N Elm St, (541) 549-0251.
www.sisterschamber.com

THIS WILD-WEST style ranching town is surrounded by lush pine forests, alpine meadows, and rushing streams. The peaks of the Three Sisters, each above 10,000 ft (3,000 m), rise majestically in the background.

ENVIRONS: The McKenzie Pass climbs from Sisters to a 1-mile (1.6-km) summit amid a massive lava flow. The **Dee Wright Observatory** provides panoramic views of more than a dozen Cascade Mountain peaks, buttes, and sweeping lava fields.

Dee Wright Observatory
Hwy 242, 15 miles (24 km) west of Sisters. mid-Jun–Oct: dawn–dusk daily. Oct–mid-Jun.

Bend's High Desert Museum, which showcases life in the region

Bend 27

50,650. 63085 N Hwy 97, (541) 382-8048.
www.bendchamber.org

BUSY BEND, once a sleepy lumber town, is alluringly close to the ski slopes, lakes, streams, and many other natural attractions. While unsightly development is quickly replacing the juniper-

and sage-covered grazing lands on the outskirts, the old brick business district retains its small-town charm. Drake Park is a grassy downtown retreat on both banks of the Deschutes River, and **Pilot Butte State Scenic Viewpoint**, atop a volcanic cinder cone that rises near the center of town, overlooks the High Desert and snow-capped Cascade peaks.

The **High Desert Museum** celebrates life in the rugged terrain that covers much of central and eastern Oregon. Walk-through dioramas use dramatic lighting and sound effects in authentic re-creations of Native American dwellings. A trail leads to replicas of a settler's cabin and a sawmill, and to natural habitats, including a trout stream and an aviary full of hawks and other raptors.

High Desert Museum
59800 S Hwy 97. (541) 382-4754. 9am–5pm daily. Jan 1, Thanksgiving, Dec 25.
www.highdesert.org

ENVIRONS: The best way to explore the magnificent South Cascades Mountains is to take the **Cascade Lakes Highway**, a 95-mile (153-km) long loop, starting from Bend. Southward, the route passes Lava Butte, which offers fine mountain views. Also located along the highway is Elk Lake, popular for sailing, fishing, and windsurfing. Another interesting sight is Mount Bachelor, 12 miles (20 km) west of Bend. It offers some of the best skiing and snowboarding in the region. An enormous, 45-sq-mile (117-sq-km) lava flow – Devil's Garden – lies northwest of Mount Bachelor. Astronauts used it to train on foot and in moon buggies for their historic 1969 moonwalk.

Newberry National Volcanic Monument 28

Apr–Oct: dawn–dusk daily.
www.fs.fed.us Lava Lands Visitor Center, 11 miles S of Bend on US 97, (541) 593-2421.

ENCOMPASSING EERIE and bleak landscapes of black lava, as well as sparkling mountain lakes, waterfalls, hemlock forests, and snow-capped peaks, the Newberry National Volcanic Monument occupies an area of 55,000 acres (22,000 ha). Exhibits at the **Lava Lands Visitor Center** explain how the volcano has been built by thousands of eruptions which, seismic activity suggests, may begin again. Other exhibits here highlight central Oregon's cultural history.

At Lava River Cave, a passage extends for almost one mile (0.8 km) into a lava tube, through which molten lava once flowed. The Lava Cast Forest has a trail that transverses a forest of hollow molds, formed by hot, molten lava that created casts around the tree trunks.

A jagged outcrop at the Newberry National Volcanic Monument

Steens Mountain ❷

Steens Mountain Loop Rd (for 58 miles/93.5 km), starting North Loop Rd in Frenchglen. ⓘ *PO Box 1645, Medford, Oregon 97501, (800) 448-4856.*

Scenery does not get much grander than it does here on this 9,700-ft (2,910-m) mountain in southeastern Oregon. The west slope rises gradually from sagebrush country, while the eastern slope drops more steeply. Antelope, bighorn sheep, and wild horses roam gorges and alpine tundra carpeted with wildflowers; eagles and falcons soar overhead.

The **Steens Mountain Loop Road** traverses this remarkable landscape. Lovely, marsh-fringed Lily Lake, on the west side of the Warner Mountains, is slowly silting up. However, it is popular with anglers because of its trout-fishing opportunities. The nearby Donner and Blitzen River was named "Thunder and Lightning" by an army officer attempting to cross it during a thunderstorm in 1864. Kiger Gorge to the east affords views of four immense gorges scooped out from the mountainside by massive glaciers. **East Rim Viewpoint** is a full mile (1.6 km) above the alkali flats of the Alvord Desert. Sitting in the mountain's rain shadow, this desert receives a mere 6 inches (15 cm) of rain a year.

Resting mule deer in the Malheur National Wildlife Refuge

Malheur National Wildlife Refuge ❸

ⓘ *(541) 493-2612.* **Refuge & Museum** ◯ *dawn–dusk daily.* ● *public hols.* **Visitor Center** ◯ *7am–4:30pm Mon–Thu, 7am–3:30pm Fri (some weekends in spring & summer).* ● *public hols.* ♿

One of the nation's largest wildlife refuges, Malheur spreads across 186,500 acres (74,600 ha) of the Blitzen Valley floor. More than 320 species of birds and 58 species of mammals are found here. Sandhill cranes, tundra swans, snowy white egrets, white-faced ibis, pronghorn antelope, mule deer, and redband trout are among the most numerous of the refuge's denizens.

Spring and fall are the best times to view birds, which alight in the refuge on their annual migrations up and down the Pacific Flyway, a major north–south route for migrating North American waterfowl. A small museum houses specimens of birds commonly seen in the refuge.

Environs: From the refuge, the 69-mile (110.5-km) **Diamond Loop National Back Country Byway** heads into sage-covered hills and red rimrock canyons. Along the route are Diamond Craters, a volcanic landscape; the Round Barn, a distinctive 19th-century structure; and Diamond, a small, poplar-shaded ranch town.

🗻 **Diamond Loop National Back Country Byway** ⓘ *28910 Hwy 20 W, Hines, (541) 573-4400.*

John Day Fossil Beds National Monument ❹

ⓘ *Hwy 19, 40 miles (64 km) W of John Day.* ⓘ *(541) 987-2333.* ◯ *dawn–dusk daily.* **Visitor Center (Sheep Rock Unit)** *Mar–Memorial Day & Labor Day–Thanksgiving: 9am–5pm daily; Memorial Day–Labor Day: 9am–6pm daily; Thanksgiving–Feb: 9am–5pm Mon–Fri.* ● *public hols.* ⓦ *www.nps.gov/joda*

Prehistoric fossil beds litter the John Day Fossil Beds National Monument, where sedimentary rocks preserve the plants and animals that flourished in jungles and

View of the Steens Mountain from the East Rim Viewpoint, above the alkali flats of the desolate Alvord Desert

Formations at John Day Fossil Beds National Monument's Sheep Rock unit

savannas for 40 million years, between the extinction of the dinosaurs and the start of the most recent Ice Age. The monument's 14,000 acres (5,600 ha) comprise three units – Sheep Rock, Painted Hills, and Clarno. At all three, trails provide opportunities for the close-up observation of the fossil beds. Painted Hills presents the most dramatic landscapes – volcanic rock formations in vivid hues of red, pink, bronze, tan, and black. Clarno contains some of the oldest formations, dating back 54 million years and including some of the finest fossil plant remains on earth. At Sheep Rock, the visitor center displays many important finds from the beds.

Pendleton ㉟

🏔 *17,000.* ℹ️ *501 S Main St, (541) 276-7411.*

PENDLETON'S OUTSIZED reputation for raucous cowboys and lawless cattle rustlers is matched by the fact that it is eastern Oregon's largest town. But visitors may be disappointed to learn that these colorful days belong to the past. However, cowboy lore comes alive during the Pendleton Round-Up each September, when rodeo stunt performers and some 50,000 spectators crowd into town. Previous rodeos are honored in the photographs and other memorabilia at the **Round-Up Hall of Fame**.
   The town's biggest business, the **Pendleton Woolen Mills**, is known for its warm clothing and blankets, particularly its

"legendary" blankets whose designs are a tribute to Native American tribes. The mill wove its first Indian trade blanket in 1895.
   The **Pendleton Underground Tours** begin in a subterranean labyrinth of opium dens, gaming rooms, and Prohibition-era drinking establishments and include stops at a bordello and the cramped 19th-century living quarters of Chinese laborers.
   The **Tamástslikt Cultural Institute** commemorates local history by displaying recreations of historic structures, exhibits of war bonnets, and other artifacts.

🎫 **Pendleton Woolen Mills**
1307 SE Court Pl. ☎ *(541) 276-6911.* **Salesroom** ⬜ *May–Dec: 8am–5pm Mon–Sat, 11am–3pm Sun; Jan–Apr: 8am–5pm Mon–Sat.* ⬤ *Jan 1, Dec 25.* 🎥 *9am, 11am, 1:30pm, 3pm Mon–Fri.* 🅿️
🌐 *www.pendleton-usa.com*
🏛 **Round-Up Hall of Fame**
1205 SW Court Ave. ☎ *(541) 276-2553.* ⬜ *May–Sep: 10am–5pm Mon–Sat; Oct–Apr: by appointment.* ⬤ *public hols.*

A rodeo rider at the popular Pendleton Round-Up

Wallowa Mountains ㊱

Elkhorn Drive National Scenic Byway (for 83 miles/134 km), starting Baker City.

THE WALLOWA Mountains form a 10,000-ft (3,050-m) high, 40-mile (64-km) long wall of granite in northeastern Oregon. Driving through the region takes in some of the finest scenery in the state.
   The best way to explore the Wallowa Mountains is to take the **Elkhorn Drive National Scenic Byway**, a two-lane paved road, which begins from Baker City. Nestled between the Wallowa Mountains and the Elkhorn Range, the town has some lovely downtown blocks and fine Victorian houses. Farther north, the National Historic Oregon Trail Interpretive Center displays replicas of

Wallowa Lake

pioneer scenes. Surrounded by dense wilderness, the sleepy town of **Joseph** lies to the east of the Wallowa Mountains. Named after Chief Joseph, leader of the Nez Percé peoples, Joseph is a popular destination for recreation enthusiasts and artisans. One of Joseph's main attractions is the **Manuel Nez Percé Crossing Museum**, with its fine collection of local bronzes, blankets, and baskets; Wallowa County Museum is devoted to Chief Joseph's famous retreat.
   The crystal-clear waters of the **Wallowa Lake** sparkle at the foot of the Wallowa Mountains. The Wallowa Lake Lodge, a log building dating from the 1920s, still provides accommodations and meals. The popular Wallowa Lake Tramway whisks riders up to the summit of Mount Howard to enjoy spectacular views of the sparkling lake below and majestic peaks rising up.

🏛 **Manuel Nez Percé Crossing Museum**
400 N Main St, Joseph. ☎ *(541) 432-7235.* ⬜ *Jun–Oct: 8am–5pm daily; Nov–May: 10am–4pm daily.* ♿

Practical Information

THE STUNNING SCENERY OF THE Pacific Northwest attracts visitors from around the world. Booming tourism – and in more recent years, ecotourism – has spawned a vast network of facilities and services: internationally acclaimed restaurants and accommodations abound, and efficient transportation by air, land, and water takes travelers virtually anywhere they want to go. The peak tourist season extends from mid-May through September. Winter is also a great time to visit the region as it is ideal for skiing and other snow sports.

TOURIST INFORMATION

MAPS AND information about sights, events, accommodations, and tours are available free of charge from **Washington State Tourism** and the **Oregon Tourism Commission**. These agencies also provide either free reservations services for a wide range of accommodations or referrals to these services. Most Pacific Northwest communities operate visitor centers or tourism booths, offering information about local activities, lodgings, and restaurants.

PERSONAL SECURITY

THE PACIFIC NORTHWEST prides itself on its safe cities and its welcoming attitude toward visitors. Street crime is rare, and the police are a visible presence in all major cities. However, it is wise to be careful and find out which parts of town are less safe than others. Your hotel or a tourist information center will provide information about which areas are best to stay away from. In the country, wildlife and natural dangers can be avoided by heeding local warnings and advice.

In an emergency, call 911 for the fire department, police, or an ambulance; if you are not in a major city, dial 0. The call can be placed from any phone free of charge. Hospitals are listed in phone books, and each has an emergency room that can be accessed 24 hours a day.

NATURAL HAZARDS

BEFORE HEADING out on a hike or going camping, check in with the forest service for information on the conditions in the surrounding area and recommended safety precautions. Skiers and snowboarders should always heed warning signs and stay on groomed runs.

Insects can be annoying while hiking or camping – blackflies in the spring or mosquitoes in the summer.

Ticks, which can be carriers of Lyme disease, are found in dry, wooded areas. Protect yourself by using tick repellant and wear long trousers, long sleeves, and socks. In case of a rash or flu-like symptoms, contact a doctor immediately.

On the beach, heed the red tide warnings that alert shellfish collectors to contamination. When camping, beware of cougars, wolves, coyotes, and bears. Be advised that leaving any food or garbage out will attract dangerous wildlife.

Potential safety hazards for drivers include gravel roads, which may become very slippery with rain, heavy snowfalls, black ice, and fog. To be safe, always carry a spare tire, and salt or sand in winter, also a flashlight, jumper cables, blankets, water, emergency food, and a shovel. Always carry a cell phone.

GETTING AROUND

VISITORS TO the Pacific Northwest have a wide range of transportation options. **United Airlines** offers flights to the major cities of the Pacific Northwest, while **Alaska Airlines** and **Horizon Airlines** fly to these and regional destinations.

Although the bus may be the slowest way of getting to the Pacific Northwest, it is probably the most economical. **Greyhound** has bus routes throughout the region; **Gray Line**, **Maverick**, and **Pacific Coach Lines** offer sightseeing tours. Discounts are available for children, students, and senior citizens. The train is a good way to get to the Pacific Northwest and to travel within it. **Amtrak** offers daily service to Oregon and Washington from the Midwest and California and has daily runs between Seattle, Portland, and Eugene. **American Orient Express Railway** offers scenic trips in the Pacific Northwest aboard luxury cars.

Driving is by far the best mode of transport in the region, especially to enjoy the spectacular beauty of more

---

THE CLIMATE OF THE PACIFIC NORTHWEST

Rain is a distinctive presence in only half the Pacific Northwest – the part west of the mountains that divide the region. The weather in this western, coastal region remains mild throughout the year, and snow is rare in all but the higher elevations. The mountains see heavy winter snowfall, much to the delight of skiers. East of the mountains, the summers are hot, dry, and sunny, and winters more severe than west of the mountains.

SEATTLE

°F/C			
	72/22		
58/14	54/12	59/15	
32°F 43/6		47/8	45/7
0°C			36/2
☀ 16 days	20 days	13 days	9 days
☂ 2.5 in	0.8 in	3.2 in	5.3 in
month Apr	Jul	Oct	Jan

remote areas. Remember to tune into local television and radio news channels for regular reports on traffic and road conditions, particularly during the winter.

ETIQUETTE

DRESS IN THE Pacific Northwest tends to be casual, practical, and dependent on the weather. Stricter clothing requirements apply in theaters, high-end restaurants, and other more formal places. Designated beaches allow topless and nude sunbathing. The legal drinking age is 21. Smoking in public places is prohibited.

LAWS

THE SEATTLE and Portland Police Departments are a visible presence, either on foot, bicycle, or squad car. There are also neighborhood security teams made up of citizen volunteers, which patrol on foot. Outside the metropolitan areas, there are county police and sheriff's offices to assist you.

It is illegal and insensitive to comment on or joke about bombs, guns, and terrorism in places such as airports. Drunk driving is also taken seriously; remember that open alcohol containers in a car are illegal. Narcotics users can face criminal charges and severe penalties.

SPORTS & OUTDOOR ACTIVITIES

THE DRAMATICALLY varied terrain and beautiful landscape of the Pacific Northwest make this the ideal region for a wide variety of outdoor activities. Both Washington and Oregon provide great conditions for adventure sports such as hang gliding and paragliding. Whitewater rafting is also popular, especially in the waters of the Cascades Range. Skiing and snowboarding are other popular activities.

For those interested in more placid pastimes, the **Oregon Department of Fish and Wildlife** or the **Washington Department of Fish and Wildlife**, provide information on freshwater fishing.

One of the most exciting ways to explore the scenic Pacific Northwest is by foot. Visitor centers and the **American Hiking Society** provide information about hiking; and the **Pacific Northwest Trail Association** offers details about the beautiful 1,200-mile (1,931-km) trail, which runs from the Continental Divide to the Pacific Ocean.

In summer, the region's many beaches are ideal for relaxing and offer refreshing waters to swim in. The coasts are also a delight for bird-watchers who can catch sight of gulls, sandpipers, plovers,

and ducks. Canoeing and kayaking provide environmentally friendly ways of seeing the region's beautiful waters and abundant marine life. Washington's Puget Sound and San Juan Islands are the most popular destinations for sea kayaking, while Olympic National Park is the hot spot for canoeists. In Oregon, the Columbia River provides stretches of calmer water for paddling.

Cycling and inline skating are inexpensive ways of traveling. Several companies offer long-distance cycling tours in the region; **Bicycle Adventures** offers tours through the two states.

SHOPPING

DOWNTOWN DISTRICTS in the Pacific Northwest provide everything from luxury goods offered by exclusive stores to flea market bargains. Outdoor gear manufactured by world-famous local companies such as REI are popular with tourists interested in adventure sports. Other items to shop for are antiques, books, and music from both the chain stores and independents, first-class wines (Pinot Noirs, Chardonnays, Rieslings, and dessert wines), and smoked Pacific salmon. Native American jewelry, carvings, paintings, and other handicrafts are also available throughout the region.

DIRECTORY

TOURIST INFORMATION

Oregon Tourism Commission
775 Summer St NE,
Salem, OR 97301-1282.
((503) 986-0000,
(800) 547-7842.
W www.traveloregon.
com

Washington State Tourism
P.O. Box 42500.
Olympia, WA 98504-2500.
((360) 725-5052.
W www.tourism.wa.gov

TRAVEL

Alaska Airlines
((800) 252-7522.

Horizon Airlines
((800) 547-9308.

United Airlines
((888) 864-8331.

Gray Line
(In Portland:
(800) 422-7042.
In Seattle:
(800) 426-7532.

Greyhound
((800) 229-9424.
W www.greyhound.com

American Orient Express Railway
((888) 759-3944.

Amtrak
((800) 872-7245.

FRESHWATER FISHING

Oregon Dept of Fish and Wildlife
((503) 872-5268.
W www.dfw.state.or.us

Washington Dept of Fish & Wildlife
((360) 902-2200.
W www.wa.gov/wdfw

HIKING

American Hiking Society
((301) 565-6704.
W www.american
hiking.org

Pacific Northwest Trail Association
((877) 854-9415.
W www.pnt.org

BIRD-WATCHING

Malheur National Wildlife Refuge
((541) 493-2612.
W pacific.fws.gov/
malheur

Where to Stay

WHETHER YOU ARE LOOKING for a relaxing oceanside inn, a small B&B, a low-key hostel, a convenient motel, or a perfectly appointed hotel in the heart of the city, the Pacific Northwest offers accommodations to suit every taste and budget. In addition, rustic lodges and guest ranches, usually near scenic areas, provide lodgings and unforgettable outdoor experiences.

		CREDIT CARDS	NUMBER OF ROOMS	RESTAURANT	CHILDREN'S FACILITIES	GARDEN OR TERRACE
WASHINGTON						
CHELAN: *Campbell's Resort* 104 W Wooden Ave. 【 (509) 682-2561, (800) 553-8225. FAX (509) 682-2177. W www.campbellsresort.com Enjoying a prime beachfront location, this long-time local favorite offers a host of on-site facilities including a spa and a beach bar. Rooms are spacious and unfussy; a few have kitchens. 🛏 TV 🍸 🔧 ≋	$$	▣	175	▣	●	▣
LEAVENWORTH: *Pine River Ranch* 19668 Hwy 207. 【 (800) 669-3877. FAX (509) 763-2073. W www.prranch.com Experience a down-home feel at this small B&B set in the Cascade Mountains, where a full breakfast is delivered each morning.	$$	▣	6			▣
PORT ANGELES: *Lake Crescent Lodge* 416 Lake Crescent Rd. 【 (360) 928-3211. FAX (360) 928-3253. W www.lakecrescentlodge.com Set on the shores of a fjord, this lodge makes a fine base for exploring Olympic National Park's northern areas. ● *Nov–Mar.* 🍸 ⅙	$$$	▣	52	▣	●	▣
PORT TOWNSEND: *Manresa Castle Hotel & Inn* 7th & Sheridan St. 【 (360) 385-5750, (800) 732-1281. FAX (360) 385-5883. W www.manresacastle.com Built for the city's first mayor, the Manresa Castle has been a hotel since the 1960s. The restaurant-lounge has been beautifully restored. 🛏 TV 🍸	$$	▣	40	▣		
QUINAULT: *Lake Quinault Lodge* PO Box 7, Quinault. 【 (360) 288-2900, (800) 562-6672. FAX (360) 288-2901. W www.visitlakequinault.com Styled along the lines of a grand park lodge, this 1926 property offers rooms retaining their original charm, without intrusive modern amenities; only a few rooms have TVs. 🛏 🍸 ≋ ⅙	$$$	▣	92	▣		▣
SEATTLE: *Ace Hotel* 2423 1st Ave, Seattle. 【 (206) 448-4721. FAX (206) 374-0745. W www.theacehotel.com Groovy, minimalist decor and friendly service are the hallmarks of this modern hotel in Belltown. The hotel and its Cyclops Bar are popular with visiting musicians and artists. Most rooms share bathrooms.	$$	▣	24		●	
SEATTLE: *Pensione Nichols* 1923 1st Ave. 【 (206) 441-7125, (800) 440-7125. FAX (206) 441-7125. W www.seattle-bed-breakfast.com Located near Pike Place Market, two suites in this B&B offer amenities such as kitchen, private bathroom, and balcony; the other rooms share bathrooms. TV	$$	▣	12			
SEATTLE: *MarQueen Hotel* 600 Queen Anne Ave N. 【 (206) 282-7407, (888)-3076. FAX (206) 283-1499. W www.marqueen.com This quaint brick hotel close to the Seattle Center is small but classic. Each spacious room has a kitchenette and is richly appointed with hardwood floors, area rugs, and upscale amenities. 🛏 TV 🍴 ⅙	$$$	▣	56		●	
WALLA WALLA: *Best Western Walla Walla Suites Inn* 7 E Oak St. 【 (509) 525-4700. FAX (509) 525-2457. W www.bestwestern.com This modern, comfortable all-suites inn is handy for nearby wineries and restaurants, with rooms that are well appointed. 🛏 TV 🔧 ≋ 🍴 ⅙	$	▣	78		●	
YAKIMA: *Birchfield Manor Country Inn* 2018 Birchfield Rd. 【 (509) 452-1960, (800) 375-3420. FAX (509) 452-2334. W www.birchfieldmanor.com This quaint inn offers accomodations in the original manor house and the guest cottage, in a gracious pastoral setting. All rooms have private baths; some with jacuzzis and fireplaces. 🛏 ≋ ⅙	$$$	▣	11		●	▣

		CREDIT CARDS	NUMBER OF ROOMS	RESTAURANT	CHILDREN'S FACILITIES	GARDEN OR TERRACE

Price categories for a standard double room per night, including tax and service charges. (Prices may fluctuate depending on arrival date and availability.)

Ⓢ under $100
ⓈⓈ $100–$150
ⓈⓈⓈ $150–$200
ⓈⓈⓈⓈ over $200

CREDIT CARDS
Major credit cards accepted.

RESTAURANT
Hotel restaurant or dining room also open to nonresidents.

CHILDREN'S FACILITIES
Child cots and a baby-sitting service available. Some hotel restaurants provide children's portions and highchairs.

GARDEN OR TERRACE
Hotels with a garden, courtyard, or terrace.

OREGON

ASTORIA: *Rose River Inn Bed and Breakfast* ⓈⓈ 1510 Franklin Ave. ☎ (503) 325-7175, (888) 876-0028. FAX (503) 325-7188. W www.roseriverinn.com Simply furnished with European antiques and art, this lovely B&B is run by a hospitable Finn, Kati, who also offers massage treatments. Enjoy Finnish goodies with your morning coffee. 🔲	▦	4		●	▦
BEND: *Mount Bachelor Village Resort* ⓈⓈⓈ 19717 Mt Bachelor Dr. ☎ (800) 452-9846. FAX (541) 388-7401. W www.mtbachelorvillage.com Myriad activities are accessible from this upscale, full-service resort: on-site tennis courts and spa; hiking, running, and biking trails; skiing at Mount Bachelor. Choose from a selection of well-appointed condominiums. 🔲 📺 ▮ 🔧 🏊 🍴 ♿	▦	130	▦	●	▦
COLUMBIA RIVER GORGE: *Timberline Lodge* ⓈⓈⓈ Timberline, Mount Hood. ☎ (503) 622-7979, (800) 547-1406. FAX (503) 622-0710. W www.timberlinelodge.com This celebrated 1930s-era lodge, set midway up Mount Hood, was built using local stone and rough-hewn timber, adding greatly to its rustic ambience. Highlights include the handsome main staircase with animal carvings, and the atrium's huge rock fireplace. ▮ 🏊 ♿	▦	70	▦	●	▦
CRATER LAKE NATIONAL PARK: *Crater Lake Lodge* ⓈⓈⓈ 565 Rim Village Dr. ☎ (541) 830-8700. FAX (541) 830-8514. W www.craterlakelodges.com This splendid 1915 lodge sits poised to take in spectacular lake views. Its magnificent Great Hall, detailed with Art Deco flourishes, is a reminder of a bygone era. The rooms are fully refurbished, some with old-fashioned claw-foot bathtubs. ● Nov–mid-May. 🔲 ▮ ♿	▦	71	▦	●	▦
PORTLAND: HEATHMAN HOTEL ⓈⓈⓈ 1001 SW Broadway. ☎ (503) 241-4100, (800) 551-0011. FAX (503) 790-7110. W www.heathmanhotel.com The award-winning Heathman Restaurant is a major draw, but guests also appreciate the comforts offered by this stylish hotel with a distinct European flavor. On display are the great city views and works by local artisans in each well-appointed room. 🔲 📺 ▮ ♿	▦	150	▦	●	
PORTLAND: *Embassy Suites* ⓈⓈⓈⓈ 319 SW Pine St. ☎ (503) 279-9000, (800) 362-2779. FAX (503) 497-9051. W www.embassysuites.citysearch.com Centrally located, this family- and business-friendly hotel provides spacious rooms and the convenience of many on-site amenities, including a day spa. 🔲 📺 ▮ 🔧 🏊 🍴 ♿	▦	276	▦	●	
PORTLAND: *Governor Hotel* ⓈⓈⓈⓈ 611 SW 10th Ave. ☎ (503) 224-3400, (800) 554-3456. FAX (503) 241-2122. W www.govhotel.com This stately hotel is adorned with local Native art and murals depicting the Lewis and Clark expedition era. Some of its elegantly furnished rooms feature fireplaces and balconies. Complimentary wine receptions Monday to Thurday evenings. 🔲 📺 ▮ 🔧 🏊 🍴 ♿	▦	100	▦		
PORTLAND: *RiverPlace Hotel* ⓈⓈⓈⓈ 1510 SW Harbor Way, Portland. ☎ (800) 227-1333. FAX (503) 295-6190. W www.riverplacehotel.com This lovely European-style hotel has light wood furnishings inside, and a beautifully manicured garden outside. Room decor is soft and intimate. Complimentary on-site spa services. 🔲 📺 ▮ 🔧 🍴 ♿	▦	84	▦	●	▦

For key to symbols see back flap

Where to Eat

KNOWN FOR ITS VAST RANGE of local seafood, the Pacific Northwest also boasts a large number of coffee bars. Seattle and Portland are in the midst of a culinary revolution – small restaurants popping up on every block with a variety of fare ranging from wildberry pancakes to pumpkin soup. "B" indicates breakfast, "L" lunch, and "D" dinner in the listings below.

	CREDIT CARDS	VEGETARIAN	OUTDOOR SEATING	CHILDREN'S FACILITIES	LATE OPENING

WASHINGTON

BELLINGHAM: *Pepper Sisters* — $$$
1055 N State St. (*(360) 671-3414.*
Centrally located in a historic commercial building, this cheerful bistro presents imaginative Southwestern fare, such as cilantro grilled salmon and spicy eggplant *tostada.* D. ● *Mon.*
| | ■ | ● | | | |

LEAVENWORTH: *Echo Bistro* — $$$
911 Commercial St. (*(509) 548-9685.*
This cheery restaurant, located in a turn-of-the-19th-century home, is popular for its mixed grill items and handmade German sausage. A good selection of German brews is served in the large outdoor *biergarten.*
| | ■ | ● | ■ | ● | |

PORT TOWNSEND: *Sentosa Sushi* — $$
218 Polk St. (*(360) 385-2378.*
A great place to dine on a variety of sushi and Pan-Asian noodle dishes in a funky but relaxing setting. Some vegan menu choices also offered.
| | ■ | ● | | | |

SEATTLE: *Jack's Fish Spot* — $
1514 Pike Place. (*(206) 467-0514.*
This no-nonsense eatery is a must-try for some of the best fish-and-chips and chowder in the city. Open until 5pm.
| | | ● | ■ | ● | |

SEATTLE: *Virginia Inn and Tavern* — $$
1937 1st Ave. (*(206) 728-1937.*
This local centenarian, an atmospheric spot for dining on tasty fare, such as tapenade and chicken gumbo, is also a popular watering hole.
| | ■ | ● | ■ | | ■ |

SEATTLE: *Elliott's Oyster House* — $$$
1201 Alaskan Way. (*(206) 623-4340.*
This convivial seafood house on the waterfront has an interior distinguished by teak, copper, and rough-hewn timber. Locals and tourists alike sit at the 21-foot (7-m) bar for local brews and raw oysters on the half shell.
| | ■ | ● | ■ | ● | |

SEATTLE: *Peso's* — $$$
605 Queen Anne Ave N. (*(206) 283-9353.*
This popular Mexican restaurant, decorated in kitsch style, fills up on weekends. The food packs a spicy punch, and is consistently good. Highlights include the meat dishes and the award-winning margaritas.
| | ■ | ● | | ● | ■ |

SPOKANE: *Paprika* — $$$$
1228 S Grand Blvd. (*(509) 455-7545.*
Paprika prides itself on its creative, seasonally changing menu, with highlight dishes such as braised rabbit with chestnuts. The artwork displayed here was created by the restaurant's sous-chef. ● *Sun, Mon.*
| | ■ | ● | ● | | |

TACOMA: *El Gaucho* — $$$$
2119 Pacific Ave. (*(253) 272-1510.*
This stylish steakhouse attracts a sophisticated crowd, with a menu that features sirloin steaks and seafood dishes. The cigar lounge is popular for martinis and after-dinner drinks. ♫
| | ■ | ● | | | ■ |

WALLA WALLA: *Merchants LTD* — $$
21 E Main St. (*(509) 525-0900.*
A great spot for healthy and hearty breakfasts and lunches, this eatery covers the space of three red-brick storefronts along Main Street. It also has a bakery and a gourmet groceries section. ● *Sun.*
| | ■ | ● | ■ | ● | |

YAKIMA: *Birchfield Manor Restaurant* — $$$$
2018 Birchfield Rd. (*(509) 452-1960.*
This charming Victorian inn prides itself on the fine French country cuisine offered in the cozy dining room. Its European-trained chef presents six main dishes with well-considered wine choices.
| | ■ | ● | | ● | |

Price categories for a three-course meal and a glass of house wine, including taxes and service:
- $ under $25
- $ $ $25–$35
- $ $ $ $35–$50
- $ $ $ $ $50–$70
- $ $ $ $ $ over $70

CREDIT CARDS
Major credit cards accepted.

VEGETARIAN
A selection of vegetarian dishes available.

OUTDOOR SEATING
Garden, terrace, or courtyard with outside seating available.

CHILDREN'S FACILITIES
Children's menu or portions; highchairs available.

LATE OPENING
Full meals or light menu served after 11pm.

OREGON

Restaurant	Price	Credit Cards	Vegetarian	Outdoor Seating	Children's Facilities	Late Opening
ASTORIA: *Wet Dog Café and Brew Pub* 144 11th St. (503) 325-6975. A friendly and casual place on the Columbia River waterfront to grab burgers, sandwiches, and other hearty American fare. On weekends, the brew pub becomes a popular spot featuring live music. ♫	$ $	■	●	■		
ASTORIA: *Baked Alaska* 1 12th St. (503) 325-7414. The nautical decor suggests the mood for fresh seafood and assorted game meats served at this pier-side restaurant. Great views of the Columbia River can be enjoyed by visitors from the floor-to-ceiling windows in the airy dining room.	$ $ $ $	■	●	■	●	
BEND: *Merenda Restaurant and Wine Bar* 900 NW Wall St. (541) 330-2304. Rustic French and Italian dishes, grilled on a wood fire, are the specialties at this charming restaurant, popular for its stellar list of spirits and local wines – 65 selections by the glass. ♫	$ $ $	■	●		●	
EUGENE: *Oregon Electric Station Restaurant and Lounge* 27 E 5th Ave. (541) 485-4444. Located inside a 1912 train depot, this charming red-brick restaurant serves top-notch steak, fish, and pasta entrées and offers a lengthy wine list. Guests can dine in antique train cars, or *al fresco* on the front patio.	$ $ $ $	■	●	■	●	
PORTLAND: *Fong Chong* 301 NW 4th Ave. (503) 220-0235. This Chinatown restaurant makes up for its well-worn interior by serving what is arguably the city's best *dim sum*.	$	■	●		●	
PORTLAND: *Good Dog/Bad Dog* 708 SW Alder St. (503) 222-3410. This fun and funky hangout, with photos of four-legged stars adorning the walls, has all types of low-fat hot dogs, including the Oregon Smokey, a local favorite made with blackstrap molasses.	$	■	●			
PORTLAND: *San Felipe Taqueria* 6221 SE Milwaukie Ave, Portland. (503) 235-8158. A favorite lunch spot with locals, this unassuming *taqueria* (no-fuss eatery serving mainly burritos, tacos, etc) offers tasty Mexican fare. The *gorditas* (puck-shaped tarts filled with a choice of meats) and *tortas* (Mexican sandwiches) are particularly good. ● *Sun, Mon.*	$	■	●		●	
PORTLAND: *Oritalia* 750 SW Alder St. (503) 295-0680. Oritalia offers a menu full of Mediterranean-Asian fusion options, such as tuna tartare and curried Thai beef, which work well together. The eclectic decor, with huge tentacled chandeliers, adds to the exotic ambience.	$ $ $	■	●			■
PORTLAND: *Heathman Restaurant and Bar* 1001 SW Broadway. (503) 790-7752. This award-winning, special-occasion restaurant features a menu of Pacific Northwest cuisine, which changes seasonally. Standout dishes include the *foie gras* cappucino and tuna Rossini. Live jazz Wednesday to Saturday. ♫	$ $ $ $ $	■	●			
SALEM: *Roadhouse Grill and Saloon* 481 Lancaster Dr NE. (503) 375-0942. It must be the mix of well-presented American classics such as steaks, chops, and grilled chicken, plus the live musical entertainment nightly that keep patrons, both locals and tourists, coming back to this easy-going restaurant. ♫	$ $ $	■	●		●	

For key to symbols see back flap

CALIFORNIA

California at a Glance

SITUATED ON THE Pacific Coast, California is 800 miles (1,300 km) long and 250 miles (400 km) wide, covering an area of 158,710 sq miles (411,060 sq km). An area of startling contrasts, the scorching deserts and snowcapped mountains of the south lead to the vast wilderness areas of the north. Los Angeles and San Francisco are the state's two major cities, and the state capital is Sacramento.

Sacramento (see p717) *in Gold Country is California's capital city. Its primary landmark is the California State Capitol, completed in 1874. In the old city, along the river, are many historic buildings built for the gold miners of 1849.*

Napa Valley (see p712), *a long, sliver of land, lies in the heart of Northern California's Wine Country. Hundreds of wineries dot the entire length of the valley; most offer tours and wine tastings.*

San Francisco's (see pp694–711) *Golden Gate Bridge connects the city with Marin County. This famous landmark was opened in 1937.*

Santa Barbara (see p686), *on the Central Coast, is a repository of the region's Spanish heritage. Its legendary mission, referred to as the "Queen of Missions," was built four years after the city was established as an important garrison in 1782.*

◁ **Rocks and crashing surf at Big Sur, Central Coast**

651

Yosemite National Park (see p718) *in the High Sierras is an unforgettable wilderness of forests, alpine meadows, breathtaking waterfalls, and imposing granite rocks. The giant sequoia trees here were California's first tourist attraction.*

LOCATOR MAP

0 km   100

0 miles   100

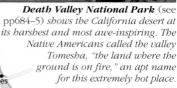

Death Valley National Park (see *pp684–5*) *shows the California desert at its harshest and most awe-inspiring. The Native Americans called the valley Tomesha, "the land where the ground is on fire," an apt name for this extremely hot place.*

Los Angeles (see *pp658–77*) *is a city dominated by wealth, fame, and glamor, as perceived by Hollywood. Its popular beaches along the Pacific Ocean attract more than 30 million people a year.*

San Diego (see p678) *was the site of the first Spanish mission. Today, it is a major commerical and military port, where air-craft carriers, cruise ships, fishing boats, and pleasure craft are a common sight.*

CALIFORNIA

IMPRESSIVE FOR BOTH ITS SIZE *and its sway over modern culture, California symbolizes the United States' diversity and sense of prosperity. Here can be found towering forests, high mountain peaks, deserts within half a day's drive of ocean beaches, and two of the world's foremost cities, San Francisco and Los Angeles.*

Perceptions of California vary so greatly that some people now joke that there are two states. The first is geographic – California is the Union's third-largest state (after Alaska and Texas). It claims some high mountain peaks such as Mount Whitney as well as the country's lowest expanse of dry land – Death Valley. Roughly one in every eight Americans is a Californian, making this the most populous of the 50 states, represented by the largest Congressional delegation.

State Seal

The other California is a realm of romance, formed by flickering celluloid images. Think "California" and pictures are immediately conjured up of bikini-clad beachcombers, middle-class suburban families in sprawling ranch houses, and glamorous film stars emerging from limousines before hordes of autograph seekers. These stereotypes are perpetuated by the tourism and entertainment media, especially Hollywood. The earlier Spanish legends had glorified Califorina as exotic, while the later Gold Rush elevated it to a land of fortune and opportunity. Whatever the truth may be, such were the eulogies that created California's colorful and seductive image.

HISTORY

Although the Spanish first "discovered" California in 1542, they colonized the area only in the 18th century. Their rule was enforced through three institutions – the mission (church), the presidio (fort), and the pueblo (town). Of these the mission was the most influential, and Franciscan friars set up 21 missions at

Window-shopping along Ocean Avenue, Carmel's most exclusive street

◁ **The Los Angeles skyline with snowy Mount Baldy in the background, a view from Baldwin Hills**

approximately 30-mile (48-km) intervals along El Camino Real ("the Royal Road") from San Diego to Sonoma. Still, the territory remained remote until 1848 when Mexico ceded California to the US, and gold was found in the Sierra Nevada foothills. The Gold Rush of 1849 drew hordes of prospectors, known as "Forty-Niners" after the year of their arrival. The discovery of silver deposits in the western Sierras, as well as the completion of the transcontinental railroad in 1869, brought greater prosperity. But along with the changes came racial tensions, ignited by the influx of Chinese immigrants, who were brought to help build the railroad. Immigrants have since contributed to the state's cultural richness as well as its overpopulation and social tensions.

On April 18, 1906, San Francisco was struck by the country's worst ever earthquake, and many believed that

The popular Third Street Promenade, Santa Monica

California's heyday was over. However, the state's subsequent revival was linked to Hollywood's lucrative film industry. Movies and the new medium of television made California the symbol of America's postwar resurgence – suddenly everybody wanted the prosperous middle-class existence they believed was common here. At the same time racial discrimination and violence persisted, state schools lacked funds, and Hollywood found itself attacked by politicians as a hotbed of Marxist Communism.

Since the 1960s, however, California has been the birthplace of some of the country's most significant social movements. The University of California at Berkeley was home to the Free Speech Movement, and Haight Ashbury in San Francisco was the mecca for "hippies." Today, Silicon Valley is a leading center of the computer industry, and many world-class high-tech firms are based here. Yet, despite progress and prosperity, California is still earthquake prone.

KEY DATES IN HISTORY

1542 Spanish explorer Juan Rodríguez Cabrilho discovers California

1769 The first mission is set up at San Diego

1776 New presidio set up in San Francisco

1781 Pueblo of Los Angeles founded

1848 US annexes California. Gold discovered

1853 Levi Strauss lands in the Bay Area and begins selling his canvas trousers

1854 Sacramento becomes the state capital

1869 Transcontinental railroad completed

1891 Stanford University opens

1893 San Andreas Fault discovered

1906 Earthquake strikes San Francisco

1911 *The Law of the Range* is the first film made in Hollywood

1929 Actor Douglas Fairbanks Sr. hosts the first Academy Awards presentation

1945 UN Charter signed in San Francisco

1968 Senator Robert F. Kennedy assassinated

1978 Apple Computer's first personal computer

1984 Los Angeles hosts its second Olympics

1992 Statewide racial riots

2001 Energy crisis; rolling blackouts conserve electricity

SOCIETY & POLITICS

If the US as a whole is a melting pot of people, California is an ethnic microcosm. It receives the highest number of immigrants (more than 200,000 every year), and its racial makeup is the nation's most diverse. The percentage of whites and African Americans is lower than the national average, but the Asian population is more than triple the national level. Hispanics too, account for more than a quarter of all Californians. This ethnic cocktail is most visible in such cities as San Diego, Los Angeles, and San Francisco. Population growth has inevitably disturbed the balance between rural and urban sectors. Since the 1950s, farmlands have declined as the need for housing has arisen. Today, the fast-expanding job markets are in the service industries and in the Silicon Valley.

Most visitors usually come to see California's two main cities – San Francisco and Los Angeles. In the north and south of the state respectively, they define the opposing sides of its character. San Francisco is more compact, and prides itself on its nonconformity and open-mindedness. It has evolved into a pro-labor hotbed, with a history of activism (the Bay Area led the anti-Vietnam War movement). It also has one of the world's largest concentrations of gays and lesbians. Los Angeles, in contrast, is a sprawling city without a focal point, where illusions of wealth, fame, and glamor have created a dimensionless image of bright lights and conservative politics. The conflicting power that the two cities exert on the politics of the state and the nation explains why California may appear a little schizophrenic.

CULTURE & THE ARTS

For most people, California's contributions to culture are Hollywood blockbusters or televised sitcoms. But another creativity reveals itself through its history of landscape painting, portraiture, and 20th-century avant-garde art. Modern artists such as John McLaughlin and Elmer Bischoff, and such pioneers of photographic art as Imogen Cunningham and Ansel Adams, have all achieved international recognition. British artist David Hockney lived here for many years, capturing the state's sun-soaked image on canvas. California is also home to some of the world's finest art museums, including the Los Angeles County Museum of Art, the San Francisco Museum of Modern Art, and the J. Paul Getty Museum. The Bay Area's Victorian architecture has always been a major tourist attraction,

and visiting designers Frank Lloyd Wright and Daniel Burnham have left their mark here as well. Recent influential architects include residents Frank Gehry and Joe Esherick.

Over the years, California has been home to scores of successful writers, including Nobel Prize-winner John Steinbeck and Beat authors Jack Kerouac and Allen Ginsburg. The tradition continues with Amy Tan (*The Joy Luck Club*), and detective novelist Sue Grafton, among others. Pop music also plays a major role, for this is where the Beach Boys, Janis Joplin, the Grateful Dead, and the Red Hot Chili Peppers launched their careers.

Beat writer Jack Kerouac

Californians love to eat out, and chefs Wolfgang Puck and Alice Waters have achieved fame promoting "California cuisine" – a blend of local ingredients and Asian techniques. This, combined with a selection of world-class local wines, is proof that Californians take good care of their palates. They are generally body-conscious and frequent gyms, or participate enthusiastically in sports and a wide range of activities. Luckily, surrounded by some of the nation's most beautiful countryside and the gentlest climate, they don't have to go far to enjoy a satisfying outdoor experience.

San Francisco's cable car, a good way to get around

Exploring California

BEYOND LOS ANGELES and San Francisco are other interesting towns and sights to visit. Highlights include San Diego and the Death Valley National Park in the south, and Monterey, Sacramento, and the Yosemite National Park in the north. Most visitors arrive at airports in Los Angeles and San Francisco. Both cities are linked to the rest of the state by an extensive road and rail network.

Shelter Island yacht harbor in San Diego Bay

SIGHTS AT A GLANCE

Map labels:
O R E G O N
Crescent City
Yreka
Lava Beds National Monument ㉜
Klamath
Mount Shasta ㉛
Redwood National Park ㉙
Dunsmuir
Arcata
Weaverville ㉚
Eureka ㉘
Redding
Lassen Vol National P ㉝
Scotia
Humboldt Redwoods State Park ㉗
Leggett
Paradise
Chico
Nevada Cit ㉞
Mendocino ㉖
Ukiah
Grass Valle ㉟
Russian River Valley ㉔
Marshall Discove State P ㊱
Fort Ross State Historic Park ㉕
Davis
Rutherford
Highw ㊳
Bodega
Santa Rosa
Sacramento ㊲
Sonoma Valley ㉒
Napa Valley ㉓
Columbia St Historic P
SAN FRANCISCO
Oakland
Modesto
San Francisco ㉑
San Jose
Santa Cruz ⓴
Monterey ⓳
Pinnac Natio Monur
Carmel ⓲
Big Sur ⓱
Hearst Castle ⓰
San Miguel
San Simeon
Morro Bay
San Luis Obispo
Pismo Bea
Lompoc Val

SEE ALSO

• *Practical Information* pp720–21

• *Where to Stay* pp722–5

• *Where to Eat* pp726–9

0 km   100
0 miles   100

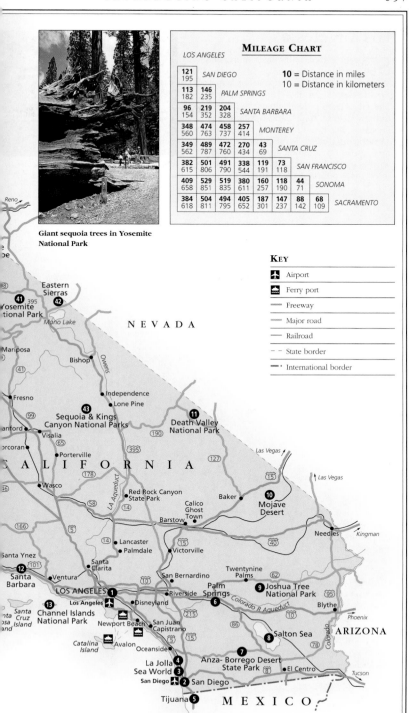

Giant sequoia trees in Yosemite National Park

MILEAGE CHART

LOS ANGELES

121 195	SAN DIEGO			10 = Distance in miles			
113 182	**146** 235	PALM SPRINGS		10 = Distance in kilometers			
96 154	**219** 352	**204** 328	SANTA BARBARA				
348 560	**474** 763	**458** 737	**257** 414	MONTEREY			
349 562	**489** 787	**472** 760	**270** 434	**43** 69	SANTA CRUZ		
382 615	**501** 806	**491** 790	**338** 544	**119** 191	**73** 118	SAN FRANCISCO	
409 658	**529** 851	**519** 835	**380** 652	**160** 257	**118** 190	**44** 71	SONOMA
384 618	**504** 811	**494** 795	**405** 652	**187** 301	**147** 237	**88** 142	**68** 109	SACRAMENTO

KEY

✈ Airport

⛴ Ferry port

— Freeway

— Major road

— Railroad

- - State border

-- · International border

Reno

Eastern Sierras

41 42 395
Yosemite National Park

Mono Lake

NEVADA

Mariposa

Bishop

Owens

Fresno

Independence
Lone Pine

43
Sequoia & Kings Canyon National Parks

11
Death Valley National Park

anford Visalia

rcoran Porterville

Las Vegas

C A L I F O R N I A

Wasco

Red Rock Canyon State Park

Calico Ghost Town

Barstow

Baker

10
Mojave Desert

Las Vegas

Needles Kingman

Santa Ynez

Lancaster
Palmdale

Victorville

San Bernardino

Twentynine Palms

62

9 Joshua Tree National Park

12
Santa Barbara

Ventura

Santa Clarita

LOS ANGELES 1

Riverside

Palm Springs

6

Blythe

Phoenix

13
Channel Islands National Park

Los Angeles ✈

Disneyland

Newport Beach

San Juan Capistrano

215

86

8 Salton Sea

ARIZONA

nta Cruz osa sland Island

Catalina Island

Avalon

Oceanside

7
Anza- Borrego Desert State Park

El Centro

Tucson

La Jolla
Sea World 4
3

San Diego ✈ 2 San Diego

Tijuana 5

M E X I C O

Los Angeles ❶

Sitting in a broad, flat basin, surrounded by beaches, mountains, and deserts, the 467-sq-mile (1,200-sq-km) city of Los Angeles has a population of 3.7 million. The city's celluloid self-image, with its palm trees, shopping malls, and opulent lifestyles, has been idealized as the ultimate "American Dream." While known for its museums and galleries, it is still the fantasy worlds of Hollywood and Disneyland that draw most people to Los Angeles.

Waterskiing, a popular activity along the south Los Angeles coastline

Sights at a Glance

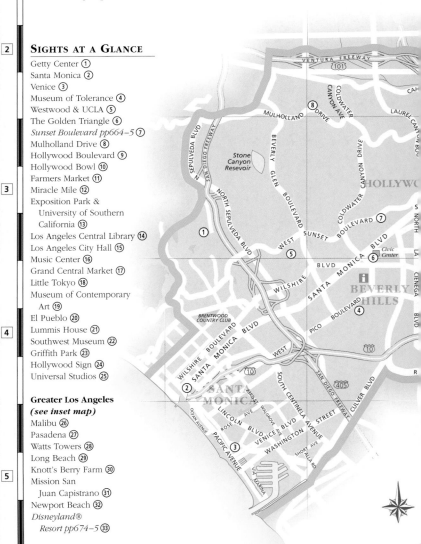

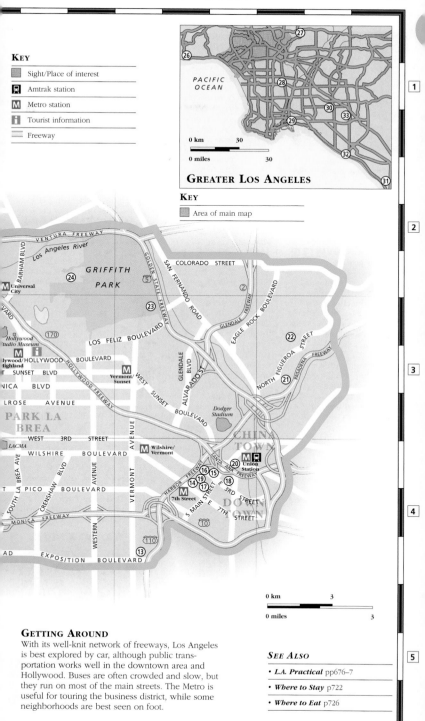

KEY

- Sight/Place of interest
- Amtrak station
- M Metro station
- i Tourist information
- Freeway

0 km 30
0 miles 30

GREATER LOS ANGELES

KEY

- Area of main map

VENTURA FREEWAY

Los Angeles River

BARHAM BLVD

GRIFFITH PARK

M Universal City

COLORADO STREET

GOLDEN STATE FREEWAY

SAN FERNANDO ROAD

EAGLE ROCK BOULEVARD

GLENDALE FREEWAY

NORTH FIGUEROA STREET

PASADENA FREEWAY

Hollywood Studio Museum

LOS FELIZ BOULEVARD

lywood/HOLLYWOOD BOULEVARD
Highland

SUNSET BLVD

NICA BLVD

Vermont/ Sunset

WEST SUNSET BOULEVARD

GLENDALE BLVD

ALVARADO ST

LROSE AVENUE

PARK LA BREA

WEST 3RD STREET

LACMA

WILSHIRE BOULEVARD

SOUTH LA BREA AVE

CRENSHAW BLVD

PICO BOULEVARD

Wilshire/ Vermont

VERMONT AVENUE

AVENUE

Dodger Stadium

CHINA TOWN

Union Station

HARBOR FREEWAY

SANTA ANA FREEWAY

7th Street

S MAIN STREET

3RD STREET

DOWN TOWN

7TH STREET

MONICA FREEWAY

WESTERN

EXPOSITION BOULEVARD

0 km 3
0 miles 3

0 km 30

GETTING AROUND

With its well-knit network of freeways, Los Angeles is best explored by car, although public transportation works well in the downtown area and Hollywood. Buses are often crowded and slow, but they run on most of the main streets. The Metro is useful for touring the business district, while some neighborhoods are best seen on foot.

SEE ALSO

- *L.A. Practical* pp676–7
- *Where to Stay* p722
- *Where to Eat* p726

Adoration of the Magi (c.1495–1505)
by Andrea Mantegna, Getty Museum

Getty Center ①

Map B3. 1200 Getty Center Dr.
📞 *(310) 440-7300.* ⏰ *10am–6pm*
Tue–Thu & Sun,10am–9pm Fri–Sat.
No parking reservations needed
Sat–Sun. ⬤ *public hols.* ♿ 🅿 🏛
📷 ⓦ *www.getty.edu*

Situated amid the untamed
beauty of the Santa
Monica Mountains in the
Sepulveda Pass, the Getty
Center holds a commanding
physical and cultural position
in the area. Opened in 1997,
the 110-acre (45-ha) complex
houses not only the Getty
Museum but also the center's
research, conservation, and
grant programs, dedicated to
art and cultural heritage.

J. Paul Getty (1892–1976)
made his fortune in the oil
business and became an
ardent collector of art. He
amassed a remarkable
collection of European art
works, focusing on pre-20th-
century artistic movements,
from the Renaissance to Post-
Impressionism. A bold
collector, Getty enjoyed the
pursuit of an object almost
more than the possession of
it. He wanted his collection to
be open to the public free of
charge. His original home, the
Getty Villa in Malibu, was the
site of the first Getty Museum.
The villa, now undergoing
remodeling, will house Greek
and Roman antiquities when
it reopens in fall 2005.

Since Getty's death, the
Trust has purchased works of
the highest quality to complement the existing collection.
New departments such as
manuscripts and drawing
have also been added.

From below, the center may
look like a fortress, but once
inside, the scale is
intimate, with foun-
tains, walkways,
courtyards, and
niches. An electric
tram brings visitors
from the parking lot
to the complex. The
museum has a tall,
airy foyer that opens
onto a central court-
yard. Facing this
courtyard are the
five two-story pavil-
ions that feature the
varied art collections. European paintings in the museum
date from the 13th to the late
19th centuries and include
masterpieces such as Andrea
Mantegna's *Adoration of the
Magi* (c.1495–1505), Rem-
brandt's *The Abduction of
Europa* (1632), Paul Cézanne's
Still Life with Apples (1900),
and Vincent Van Gogh's
Irises (1889). The last was
painted by the artist
when he was in
the asylum at St-
Remy. The Getty's
collection of
sculpture contains
fine examples of
Baroque and Neo-
Classical works,
including François
Girardon's *Pluto
Abducting Proserpine*
(c.1693–1710) and statues –
Venus, Juno, and *Minerva*
(1773) – by Joseph Nollekens.

The museum's photography
department features works of
many of the pioneers of
photography, such as Louis-
Jacques-Mande Daguerre
(inventor of the daguerreo-
types) and William Henry Fox
Talbott (the first to make
prints from negatives).

Decorative arts were Getty's
first love as a collector, after
he rented a New York penthouse furnished with 18th-
century French and English
antiques. The museum holds
a superb collection of ornate
French furniture and decorative arts, with coffers,
chandeliers, wall-lights, and
tapestries, dating from the
reign of Louis XIV to the
Napoleonic era (1643–1815).

The museum traces the
development of handwritten
and illuminated manuscripts
from the sixth to the 16th
century, and holds an impressive collection of masterpieces
from different historical periods such as the Byzantine,
Ottoman, Romanesque,
Gothic, and the Renaissance.

Santa Monica ②

Map B4. 🚶 *90,000.* 🛫 🚌
ℹ *1400 Ocean Ave, (310) 393-7593.*
📷 *Santa Monica Festival (Apr).*

With its fresh sea breezes,
mild climate, and
friendly streets, Santa Monica
has been the star of the Los
Angeles coastline since the
1890s, when trolleys linked it
to the city, and beach parties
became the rage. In the early
days, it lived a dual life as a
sleepy coastal town and the
headquarters for offshore
gambling ships. In the
1920s and 30s,
movie stars such
as Cary Grant and
Mary Pickford bought
land here, creating "the
Gold Coast." Following the
success of the television
series *Baywatch*, the
popular beach and pier
gained worldwide
fame. But the city,
perched on a high
yellow cliff
overlooking Santa Monica
Bay, is also noted for its
restaurants, shopping areas,
and vibrant arts scene. Lush
parks dot the city's landscape,
with none quite as beautiful
as **Palisades Park**, on the
bluff overlooking the ocean.
Stretching 1.5 miles (2.5 km)

**Street entertainer
playing guitar**

**Tall palm trees lining the road in
Palisades Park, Santa Monica**

The Chiat Day Mojo Advertising Agency, designed by Frank Gehry

along the cliff's edge, this narrow, well-manicured park is one of the best spots to watch the sun set. For the quintessential California experience, take a walk or jog along the paths, with the ocean as a backdrop and the towering palms overhead. At the northern end, the aptly named Inspiration Point has great views of the bay, stretching from Malibu to Palos Verdes.

Inland, between Wilshire Boulevard and Broadway, is **Third Street Promenade**. Once a decaying shopping street, this boulevard has undergone a major face-lift and is now one of the liveliest places in Los Angeles. Its three pedestrian blocks are lined with shops, cafés, bookstores, and theaters. At night the mood is especially festive, with street performers entertaining visitors with music, dance, and magic tricks.

Santa Monica's other important shopping area is Main Street, which runs south toward Venice. It abounds in a wide range of shops, restaurants, and galleries. Many examples of public art are displayed along the street, such as Paul Conrad's *Chain Reaction*, a stainless-steel and copper-link chain statement against nuclear war. The Frank Gehry-designed **Chiat Day Mojo Advertising Agency** building, shaped like a pair of binoculars, dominates the street. Main Street also features the California Heritage Museum, which has the distinction of showcasing various periods in the state's history.

Northeast of the beach, the 1908 **Santa Monica Pier** is the West Coast's oldest

amusement pier, with bumper cars, roller coasters, and a giant Ferris wheel. There is also the 1922 carousel that featured in Paul Newman's 1973 film, *The Sting*. **Bergamot Station** is a large, sprawling 5.5-acre (2-ha) arts complex that stands on the site of an abandoned trolley station. The crude buildings are constructed out of aluminum siding, but with an added touch of elegant high-tech styling. More than 20 galleries display the latest in contemporary as well as radical art. The Santa Monica Museum of Art, within the Bergamot Station, focuses on the work of contemporary artists, particularly those who are involved in performance and multimedia art.

🚋 Santa Monica Pier
Colorado & Ocean Aves. [(310) 458-8900, 260-8744 Pacific Park information.] daily. **Carousel**] May–Sep: 10am–5pm Tue–Sun; Oct–Apr: 10am–5pm Sat–Sun. [(310) 395-4248.

🏛 Bergamot Station
2525 Michigan Ave. [(310) 829-5854.] 10am–5pm Tue–Fri, 11am–5pm Sat. ● Sun, public hols.

Man-made canal in Venice

Venice ③

Map B5. ℹ *2904 Washington Blvd, Suite 100, (310) 396-7016.*
W www.venice.net

FOUNDED BY tobacco tycoon Abbot Kinney, as a US version of Venice (Italy), this lively beach town was a swampland little more than 100 years ago. Hoping to spark a cultural renaissance in California, Kinney built a system of canals, and imported gondolas to punt along the waterways. Today, only a few of the original canals remain, the rest having been filled in. The best place to see the canals is on **Dell Avenue**, where old bridges, boats, and ducks grace the waterways.

However, the town is best known for the bustling, circus atmosphere of its beach. On the boardwalk during weekends, men and women whiz past on bicycles and skates, while a zany array of jugglers, acrobats, and one-man bands captivate the crowds. Muscle Beach, where Arnold Schwarzenegger used to work out, still attracts body builders.

RAYMOND CHANDLER

American novelist Raymond Chandler (1888–1959) set several of his works in Santa Monica, a city that he loathed and thinly disguised as sleazy Bay City in *Farewell, My Lovely*. Corruption, vice, and the city's offshore gambling circuit of the 1920s and 1930s are well documented in his portrayal of Santa Monica. His novels, such as *The Big Sleep, The High Window, and The Long Goodbye*, depicting the dark side of L.A., were made into films. A leading figure of the so-called hard-boiled school of detective writing of the period, Chandler's famous detective Philip Marlowe epitomized a tough, unsentimental point of view.

Raymond Chandler

Museum of Tolerance ④

Map C4. 9786 W Pico Blvd. ☎ *(310) 553-8403.* ○ *11:30am–4pm Mon–Thu, 11:30am–1pm Fri, 11am–5pm Sun.* ● *Sat, Jan 1, Thanksgiving, Dec 25, & all major Jewish hols.* 🎟 ♿ 🛍 [W] www.wiesenthal.com/mot

Dedicated to the promotion of respect and understanding among all people, this museum focuses on the history of racism and prejudice in the United States, and on the European Holocaust experience.

The museum tour begins in the **Tolerancenter**, where visitors are challenged to confront racism and bigotry through interactive exhibits. A computerized wall map locates more than 250 known racist groups in the US, while a 16-screen video wall depicts the 1960s Civil Rights struggle in the country. Interactive videos also pose questions of responsible citizenship and social justice. They offer footage and interviews of the 1992 L.A. race riots, in which 26 people were killed and 3,000 homes destroyed. In the **Whisper Gallery** visitors actually hear racial and sexual taunts so that they can experience these themselves. The Holocaust section has a re-creation of the Wannsee Conference, in which Third Reich leaders decide on the "The Final Solution of the Jewish Question," outlined right down to its harrowing implementation in a reproduced gas chamber. Some of the exhibits may not be suitable for children under the age of 10.

Entrance to UCLA at the Armand Hammer Museum of Art

Westwood & UCLA ⑤

Map B4. 🚌 **UCLA Campus** [i] *(310) 825-4321.* **Westwood Village** [i] *10779 W Pico Blvd, Westside, (310) 475-8806.*

With its wide range of academic departments and professional schools, boasting a strength of over 35,000 students, the 419-acre-(170-ha) University of California Los Angeles (UCLA) is a city within a city. The original campus was designed in 1925 to resemble the Romanesque towns of Europe. But as the university expanded, more modern architecture was favored. The disappointing mix of bland structures that resulted is redeemed by the beautiful landscaped grounds. The four red-brick buildings that make up the **Royce Quadrangle** are the oldest on UCLA's campus. Built in the Italian Romanesque style, Royce, Kinsey, and Haines Halls and Powell Library far surpass the other buildings at UCLA in beauty.

Exhibition on racial prejudice at the Museum of Tolerance

Since it was first developed in 1928, Westwood Village with its pleasant, pedestrian-friendly streets has been one of the most successful shopping districts in Southern California. It remains the most densely packed movie-theater district in the US, with some theaters offering sneak previews of the latest films. South of Westwood, the **Armand Hammer Museum of Art and Culture** holds the art collection of businessman Armand Hammer (1899–1990). The Hammer collection includes a variety of Impressionist and Post-Impressionist works by such artists as Claude Monet, Camille Pissarro, and Vincent Van Gogh. Southeast of the museum, the tranquil **Westwood Memorial Park** marks the final resting place of several celebrities such as Dean Martin, Peter Lorre, Natalie Wood, and most famously, Marilyn Monroe.

Tucked away in a shady canyon northeast of Westwood, the serene **Mildred E. Mathias Botanical Garden** contains a wide variety of plants – almost 4,000 rare and native species that include subtropical and tropical varieties.

Farther north, UCLA's **Fowler Museum of Cultural History** holds exhibitions that focus on the prehistoric, historic, and contemporary societies of Africa, Asia, the Americas, and Oceania. The collection consisting of 750,000 artifacts makes it one of the nation's leading university museums.

🏛 Armand Hammer Museum of Art & Culture

10899 Wilshire Blvd. ☎ *(310) 443-7000.* ○ *11am–7pm Tue, Wed, Fri, Sat; 11am–9pm Thu; 11am–5pm Sun.* ● *Jul 4, Thanksgiving, Dec 25.* 🎟 *(free 11am–9pm Thu).* ♿ ☕ 🛍 [W] www.hammer.ucla.edu

🏛 Fowler Museum of Cultural History

☎ *(310) 825-4361.* ○ *noon–5pm Wed–Sun (until 8pm Thu).* ● *public hols.* 🎟 *(free Thu).* 🛍

The Golden Triangle ⑥

Map C4.

THE AREA BORDERED by Santa Monica Boulevard, Wilshire Boulevard, and North Crescent Drive is the business district of Beverly Hills, known as the "Golden Triangle." The shops, restaurants, and art galleries lining the streets are some of the most luxurious in the world. Cutting through the middle is **Rodeo Drive**, one of the most celebrated shopping streets. It derives its name from El Rancho Rodeo de las Aguas ("the Ranch of the Gathering of Waters"), the name of an early Spanish land grant that included Beverly Hills. Today, Rodeo Drive's wide, tree-lined sidewalks house Italian designer boutiques and the best names in fashion, such as Gucci and Christian Dior, world-class jewelers, and many leading L.A. retailers. The place is also a prime area for celebrity-spotting.

Next to it, on Wilshire Boulevard, the cream of American department stores offer a heady mix of style and opulence. Around the corner, **2 Rodeo**, developed in 1990 as a mock-European shopping street, is one of the most expensive retail centers ever built.

At the eastern end of the Golden Triangle lies the MGM Building. Built in 1920, it was the headquarters of the newly formed Metro-Goldwyn-Mayer film studios.

Façade of the Beverly Hills Civic Center in Los Angeles

To the north are the beautifully manicured Beverly Gardens and the elegant **Beverly Hills Civic Center**, with its landmark Spanish Colonial **City Hall**. Designed in 1932 by local firm Koerner and Gage, the hall's majestic tower, capped by a tiled cupola, has now become a symbol of the European-inspired city of Beverly Hills. In 1990, architect Charles Moore linked the building to a new Civic Center by a series of pedestrianized courtyards. On the upper levels, balconies and arcaded corridors continue the Spanish Colonial theme. The modern section houses a beautiful public library as well as the local fire and police stations. Billboards are banned in the area, and a height restriction of three stories is imposed on any new buildings, leaving City Hall to dominate the skyline.

The latest addition to the Golden Triangle, the **Museum of Television and Radio** on North Beverly Drive, holds a collection of 75,000 television and radio

programs and offers a comprehensive history of broadcasting. Visitors can watch and listen to news and a collection of entertainment and sports programs from the earliest days of radio and television to the present. Pop music fans can see footage of the early Beatles or of a young Elvis Presley making his television debut, while sports enthusiasts can relive classic Olympic competitions. The museum also hosts exhibitions, seminars, and screenings on specialized topics and selected actors or directors.

North of Golden Triangle, above Sunset Boulevard (see pp664–5), lie the palatial estates, the famed **Hollywood Actors' Homes** that have made Beverly Hills the symbol of success for those in the entertainment industry. When, in 1920, Mary Pickford and Douglas Fairbanks Sr. built their mansion, **Pickfair**, at the top of Summit Drive, everyone else followed – and stayed. Sunset Boulevard divides the haves from the have-nots: people who live south of it may be rich, but those who live to the north of the road are considered to be the super-rich. Houses come in almost every architectural style; some are ostentatious, others surprisingly modest. They can be toured along a 5-mile (8-km) drive, maps for which are available from street vendors. Visitors must remember that film stars' homes are private residences; please do not tresspass.

Cushion on display in the Gucci boutique

🚇 **Beverly Hills Civic Center**
455 N Rexford Dr. 📞 (310) 285-1000. 🕐 7:30am–5:30pm Mon–Thu, 8am–5pm Fri. ● public hols. ♿
🏛 **Museum of Television & Radio**
465 N Beverly Dr. 📞 (310) 786-1000. 🕐 noon–5pm Wed–Sun (until 9pm Thu). ● public hols.
🚇 **2 Rodeo**
268 N Rodeo Dr. 📞 (310) 247-7040. 🌐 www.2rodeo.com

Faye Dunaway's house at No. 714 Palm Drive, Beverly Hills

Sunset Boulevard ⑦

SUNSET BOULEVARD HAS BEEN associated with the movies since the 1920s, when it was a dirt track linking the burgeoning Hollywood studios with the hillside homes of the screen stars. Its liveliest and most historically rich stretch, Sunset Strip, is filled with restaurants, luxury hotels, and nightclubs. Once a magnet for gamblers and bootleggers, this 1.5-mile (2.4-km) stretch held famous nightclubs such as Ciro's and Mocambo – where legend says Margarita Cansino met studio boss Harry Cohen, who renamed her Rita Hayworth. While the Strip remains at the center of L.A.'s nightlife, the other section of the Boulevard, the Old Studio District, once the hub of the film industry, is now a mostly run-down, decrepit area frequented by drug dealers and prostitutes.

A view of Sunset Strip from Crescent Heights

The Rainbow Bar & Grill, formerly the Villa Nova, has walls lined with wine casks and gold records. Vincente Minnelli proposed to Judy Garland here and, eight years later in 1953, Marilyn Monroe met Joe DiMaggio here on a blind date.

The Comedy Store, *a world-famous spot for stand-up comedy, occupies the site of the 1940s' nightclub Ciro's.*

The Roxy
This trendy nightclub stands on the site of the old Club Largo.

Sunset Plaza

CLARK ST   LARRABEE ST   HORN AVE   N LA CIENEGA BLVD

HAMMOND ST   HILLDALE ST   SAN VICENTE BLVD   HOLLOWAY DRIVE

The Viper Room is a popular live music club, part-owned by Johnny Depp. In 1993 actor River Phoenix, having taken a lethal cocktail of drugs, collapsed and died on the sidewalk outside.

The Original Spago was celebrity Chef Wolfgang Puck's first restaurant. Many Oscar night parties were hosted here by legendary Hollywood agent Irving "Swifty" Lazar, in the 1970s and 80s.

Sunset Plaza
Lined with chic stores and cafés, this area is best explored on foot.

Hyatt Hotel
Visiting rock stars regularly frequent this hotel. Jim Morrison stayed here when he played with The Doors at the nearby Whisky A Go Go.

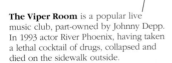

Argyle Hotel
An apartment complex in Hollywood's heyday, this Art Deco high-rise was once home to luminaries such as Jean Harlow and Clark Gable.

Chateau Marmont
The hotel was modeled on a Loire Valley château. When it opened in 1929, it attracted actors such as Errol Flynn and Greta Garbo. Among today's regulars are Christopher Walken and Winona Ryder.

A & M Records
was built by Charlie Chaplin as homes for workers at his studio.

The Trocadero
nightclub had Nat "King" Cole as its pianist in its heyday. Only three steps remain of the old building.

Directors' Guild of America
This is one of the many offices on the Strip connected with the film industry.

The Roxbury Club, west of the Chateau Marmont hotel, is popular with the stars of teenage TV shows. It stands on the site of the 1940s Players Club, owned by movie director Preston Sturges.

Schwab's
Now a Virgin Megastore, this former drugstore was a popular meeting place for film stars and columnists. Facing it, the legendary Garden of Allah apartment complex once held such residents as Scott Fitzgerald and Dorothy Parker.

The House of Blues
This tin-roofed blues bar has been transported from Clarksdale, Mississippi. It is part-owned by the actor Dan Ackroyd, who co-starred with John Belushi in the 1980 cult movie The Blues Brothers.

Billboards
Huge billboards, handpainted by Hollywood's finest artists to promote new films or personalities, are landmark symbols of Sunset Strip.

Mulholland Drive ⑧

Map C2. Off Hwys 1 & 27, from Hollywood Fwy to Leo Carrillo State Beach. 🅸 23805 Stuart Ranch Rd, Ste 100, (310) 456-9025.

MULHOLLAND DRIVE, one of the most famous roads in Los Angeles, runs for nearly 50 miles (80 km) from north Hollywood to the Malibu Coast. As it winds along the ridge of the Santa Monica Mountains, the route has spectacular views of the city and the San Fernando Valley.

The road was named for William Mulholland (1855–1935), who designed a series of aqueducts to channel water into Los Angeles. He oversaw the completion of Mulholland Drive in 1924.

Hollywood Boulevard ⑨

Map D3.

ONE OF THE most famous streets in the world, Hollywood Boulevard's name is still redolent with glamor. Despite its recent run-down look, many of its landmark sights retain the original appeal and charisma.

Perhaps the only pavement in the city to be cleaned six times a week, the **Walk of Fame** is set with more than 2,000 celebrated marble stars. Since 1960, luminaries from the worlds of film, radio, television, theater, and music have been immortalized on the boulevard and on Vine Street. However, stardom does not come easily: each personality must be spon-

Façade of the well-known Mann's Chinese Theatre

sored and approved by the Chamber of Commerce, and pay a $7,500 installation fee.

The famed **Mann's Chinese Theatre** on the north side of the boulevard has changed little since its opening in 1927, with the premiere of Cecil B. de Mille's *King of Kings*. The theater's creator, Sid Grauman, is also credited with one of Hollywood's longest-running publicity stunts: its famed autograph patio with hand- and footprints of stars. Legend has it that the custom began when silent screen star Norma Talmadge accidentally stepped on the wet cement. Grauman then invited her, along with Mary Pickford and Douglas Fairbanks Sr. to legitimately leave their imprints. Across the road stands the **Clarion Hotel Hollywood Roosevelt**, frequented by famous figures such as Marilyn Monroe, Clark Gable, and Ernest Hemingway. It was the locale of the first Academy Awards ceremony in 1929. Nearby, the restored **El Capitan Theater** was the venue for

many movie openings. Neon lights draw visitors to this theater that now has premiers of Disney animations. To its west, **Ripley's Believe It or Not!**® is devoted to the bizarre. Farther along, **Frederick's of Hollywood** is the flagship store of Fredrick Mellinger's famous mail-order lingerie business launched in 1946. Its Celebrity Lingerie Hall of Fame includes Marilyn Monroe's bra from the film *Let's Make Love* (1960), Tony Curtis's black lace bra from *Some Like It Hot* (1959), and Madonna's black bustier.

MARILYN MONROE

Star in Walk of Fame

🎬 **Walk of Fame**
🅸 6541 Hollywood Blvd, (323) 461-2804. 🆔 (323) 469-8311.
🎬 **Mann's Chinese Theatre**
6925 Hollywood Blvd. 📞 (323) 461-3331. 🆔 (323) 464-8111. 🕐 daily. 🎫 ♿ 🆆 www.mannmoviefone.com

Hollywood Bowl ⑩

Map D3. 2301 N Highland Ave. 📞 (323) 850-2000. 🕐 late Jun–late Sep. 🎫 ♿ Box office 🕐 10am–6pm Tue–Sun. 🆆 www.hollywoodbowl.com

SITUATED IN A natural amphitheater that was once revered by the Cahuenga Pass Gabrielino Indians, the 60-acre (24-ha) Hollywood Bowl has now become sacred to Angelenos. The summer home of the L.A. Philharmonic since 1922, the site attracts thousands of people on warm evenings to listen to the orchestra.

Much altered over the years, the shell-shaped stage was first designed in 1929 by Lloyd Wright, son of architect

---

THE RISE OF HOLLYWOOD

In 1887, prohibitionist Harvey Henderson Wilcox and his wife, Daeida, set up a sober, Christian community in an L.A. suburb and called it Hollywood. Ironically, over the next several decades the movie business with all its decadence came to replace their Utopia. The takeover started in 1913 with the filming of Cecil B. de Mille's *The Squaw Man*. Silent film stars such as Charlie Chaplin and Mary Pickford were succeeded by icons of a more glamorous Hollywood, such as Errol Flynn and Mae West. Wall Street bankers soon realized their potential and invested heavily in the film industry.

Oscar statuette

Frank Lloyd Wright. Rumor says that material for the building was taken from the set of Douglas Fairbanks Sr's movie *Robin Hood*.

The Edmund D. Edelman Hollywood Bowl Museum explores the site's rich history through videos, old programs and posters, and memorabilia of the artists who have come here, from violinist Jascha Heifetz to the Beatles.

Hollywood Bowl, nestling in the Hollywood Hills

Farmers Market ⑪

Map D3. 6333 W 3rd St. 📞 *(323) 933-9211.* ⏰ *9am–9pm Mon–Fri, 9am–8pm Sat, 10am–7pm Sun.* ● *Jan 1, Thanksgiving, Dec 25.* ♿ 🅦 *www.farmersmarketla.com*

DURING the Great Depression in 1934 a group of farmers began selling their produce directly to the public in a field at the edge of town. Since then, Farmers Market has been a favorite meeting place for Angelenos. Bustling with stalls and shops selling everything from fresh produce to antiques and T-shirts, the market also has some of the best cafés and restaurants in the city.

Miracle Mile ⑫

Map D4. Wilshire Blvd between La Brea & Fairfax Aves. 🛈 *685 S Figueroa St, (213) 689-8822; 6541 Hollywood Blvd, (213) 689-8822.*

DEVELOPER A.W. Ross bought 18 acres (7.2 ha) of land along Wilshire Boulevard in 1920 and built an upscale shopping district, with wide streets meant for cars and Art Deco buildings, earning it the name "Miracle Mile." Today,

dotted with grocery stores, this stretch is a shadow of its former self. The western end of the Miracle Mile has fared better. With its five museums, including the **Los Angeles County Museum of Art** (LACMA), the area is now known as Museum Row.

The largest encyclopedic art museum west of Chicago, LACMA offers a comprehensive survey of the history of world art, with a collection of over 100,000 objects dating from the prehistoric to contemporary times. Collections include pre-Columbian stone objects, Islamic art, and a wide selection of European and American decorative arts, paintings, and sculpture. Especially impressive are its collection of scrolls and ceramics from the Far East.

Nearby, the **George C. Page Museum** showcases over one million fossils discovered at the La Brea Tar Pits. The tar, formed some 42,000 years ago, entrapped and killed animals who came here to drink water. Their bones were then fossilized. For centuries the tar was used by the Native Americans, Mexicans, and Spanish to waterproof baskets and roofs. In 1906, geologists discovered the largest collection of fossils of mammals, birds, reptiles, plants, and insects from the Pleistocene Epoch ever found in one place. The only human skeleton found in the pits is that of the "La Brea Woman." A hologram changes her from a skeleton to a fully fleshed person and back again. The **Peterson Automotive**

Los Angeles County Museum of Art (LACMA), Miracle Mile

Museum traces the evolution of the nation's car culture with detailed displays of vintage cars, old showrooms, and cars of filmstars, such as Rita Hayworth's 1953 Cadillac and Clark Gable's Mercedes-Benz. Its other exhibits include a 1920s garage; an opulent 1930s car showroom; and a 1950s drive-in restaurant. Farther along, the **Craft and Folk Art Museum**, houses more than 3,000 folk art and craft objects from around the world. These range from objects as diverse as 19th-century American quilts to contemporary furniture and African masks.

African mask at the Craft Museum

🏛 **LACMA**
5905 Wilshire Blvd. 📞 *(323) 857-6000.* ⏰ *noon–8pm Mon–Tue & Thu (until 9pm Fri), 11am–8pm Sat–Sun.* ● *Wed, Thanksgiving, Dec 25.* 🎟 *(free 2nd Tue of month).* ♿ 🛈 📷 📷 🅦 *www.lacma.org*

🏛 **George C. Page Museum of La Brea Discoveries**
5801 Wilshire Blvd. 📞 *(323) 934-7243.* ⏰ *9:30am–5pm daily.* ● *Jan 1, Jul 4, Thanksgiving, Dec 25.* 🎟 *(free first Tue of month).* ♿ 📷 🛈

Model of La Brea Tar Pits in the George C. Page Museum

Exposition Park & University of Southern California ⑬

Map E4. 🚇 *DASH Shuttle C from Business District.* 🚌 *81.* **Natural History Museum of L.A. County** 📞 *(213) 763-3466.* **L.A. Memorial Coliseum** 📞 *(213) 748-6136.* **University of Southern California** 📞 *(213) 740-5371.* 🔲 *www.usc.edu*

Located southwest of downtown, Exposition Park began life in the 1880s as an area of open-air markets, carnivals, and horse-racing. By the end of the century, the district was rife with drinking, gambling, and prostitution. When Judge William Miller Bowen's Sunday school pupils began skipping church to enjoy local temptations, he pushed for the transformation of the area into a cultural landmark that today includes three museums. The **Natural History Museum of Los Angeles County**, at the heart of the park, displays a variety of specimens and artifacts, alongside an insect zoo and a hands-on Discovery Center. A short drive southeast leads to the **California Museum of Science and History**, with its interactive exhibits aiming to make science accessible to all.

Farther east lies the **California Afro-American Museum** that is a record of Afro-American achievements in various fields. The park is also home to the **Los Angeles Memorial Coliseum**, which was the site of the 1932 and 1984 Olympics, and was also home to the University's Trojan football team. Across

Natural History Museum at Exposition Park

Rotunda of Los Angeles City Hall

the street, stands the 152-acre (62-ha) **University of Southern California** that houses about 28,000 students.

Los Angeles Central Library ⑭

Map E4. *630 W 5th St.* 📞 *(213) 228-7000.* 🕐 *10am–8pm Mon–Thu, 10am–6pm Fri–Sat, 1–5pm Sun.* ⬤ *public hols.* ♿ 🔲 *www.lapl.org*

Built in 1926, this civic treasure was struck by an arson attack in 1986. Seven years later, after a $213.9 million renovation program sympathetic to the original architecture, the library's capacity was doubled to more than 2.1 million books.

The original building combines Beaux Arts grandeur with Byzantine, Egyptian, and Roman architectural elements. The library is also a popular venue for prose and poetry readings, and concerts.

The **First Interstate World Center** across the street is a 73-story office block designed by I.M. Pei. At 1,017 ft (310 m), it is the tallest building in the city.

Los Angeles City Hall ⑮

Map E4. *200 N Spring St.* 📞 *(213) 485-2121.* 🕐 *8am–5pm Mon–Fri.* ⬤ *public hols.* ♿ *from Main St.* 📷 *advance reservations required.*

When it was built in 1928, sand from every county in California and water from each of the state's 21 missions was added to the City Hall's mortar. The tower of this 28-

story structure is still one of L.A.'s most familiar landmarks. It served as the Daily Planet building in the television series *Superman.* Inside, the rotunda has a inlaid-tile dome and great acoustics. The **Los Angeles Children's Museum** across the street is guided by the principle that children learn best by doing. Some 20 hands-on activities are linked by a series of ramps. Called the Discovery Maze, the system was designed by architect Frank Gehry.

Music Center ⑯

Map E4. *135 N Grand Ave.* 📞 *(213) 972-7211.* 📷 ♿ **Dorothy Chandler Pavilion box office** 🕐 *noon–6pm Tue–Sat, noon–4pm Sun.* **Mark Taper Forum & Ahmanson Theater box offices** 🕐 *noon–8pm Tue–Sun.* 🔲 *www.musiccenter.org*

This performing arts complex is situated at the northern end of Bunker Hill. The Dorothy Chandler Pavilion is named after the wife of the former publisher of the *Los Angeles Times.* It is home to the L.A. Music Center Opera, the L.A. Master Chorale, and, from fall to spring, the L.A. Philharmonic. The Ahmanson Theater has movable walls to adjust the auditorium size, and it stages Broadway plays. The Mark Taper Forum has won almost every theatrical prize in the US. It presents first-class plays such as Tony Kushner's *Angels in America.* The Walt Disney Concert Hall opened here in October 2003; it is the new home of the L.A. Philharmonic Master Chorale.

Music Center Plaza and Fountain

Grand Central Market ⑰

Map E4. 317 S Broadway.
📞 (213) 624-2378. ⏰ 9am–6pm
daily. ● Jan 1, Thanksgiving,
Dec 25. ♿

ANGELENOS have been
coming to this vibrant
indoor bazaar since 1917.
Today, over 40 stallholders
operate inside the marketplace, selling fruit, vegetables,
meat, and herbs. The market's
Latin American clientele come
here to buy exotic products
from their home countries,
such as fresh Nogales cacti
and beans from El Salvador.

Billed as the "shortest railway in the world," the adjacent **Angels Flight** funicular
transported riders between
Hill Street and Bunker Hill for
almost 70 years. By 1969,
Bunker Hill had degenerated,
and the city dismantled the
funicular, promising to
reinstall it once the area had
been redeveloped. It fulfilled
that vow in 1996, some 27
years later.

🚋 **Angels Flight**
Between Grand, Hill, 3rd & 4th Sts.
📞 (213) 626-1901. Closed for the
foreseeable future.

Little Tokyo ⑱

Map F4. ℹ 244 S San Pedro St,
(213) 628-2725.

SITUATED SOUTHEAST of the
City Hall, Little Tokyo
attracts more than 200,000
visitors to its Japanese markets
and temples. The first Japan-
ese settled here in 1884.
Today, the heart of the area
is the Japanese American
Cultural and Community
Center, from which cultural
activities are organized.
Nearby, the Japanese Village
Plaza is a lively place to shop.
Housed in a former Buddhist
Temple, the **Japanese
American National Museum**
traces the history of Japanese-
American life in the US.

To its east, on Central
Avenue the **Geffen
Contemporary at MOCA**,
once an old police garage,

**Japanese American Art Museum,
Little Tokyo**

was used as an exhibition
space for MOCA. Redesigned
by Frank Gehry, the ware-
house is a permanent fixture
of the L.A. arts scene, hosting
exhibitions often including
highlights from MOCA.

🏛 **Japanese American
National Museum**
369 E 1st St. 📞 (213) 625-0414.
⏰ 10am–5pm Tue–Sun (until 8pm
Thu). ● Jan 1, Thanksgiving, Dec 25.
📷 ♿ 🎥 W www.janm.org

Museum of Contemporary Art ⑲

Map E4. 250 S Grand Ave.
📞 (213) 621-2766. ⏰ 11am–5pm
Tue–Sun (until 8pm Thu). ● Jan 1,
Jul 4, Thanksgiving, Dec 25. 📷 (free
5–8pm Thu). ♿ W www.moca.org

RATED AS ONE of the ten
best works of architecture
in the United States, the
Museum of Contemporary
Art (MOCA), designed by
Japanese architect Arata
Isozaki, presents an intriguing
combination of pyramids,
cylinders, and cubes.

It holds a respectable
selection of post-1940 art,
including Pop Art and
Abstract Expressionist works
by artists as diverse as Mark
Rothko, Robert Rauschenberg,
and Claes Oldenburg.

El Pueblo ⑳

Map F4. Downtown L.A.
between N Main St & Olvera St &
N Alamenda St.

THE OLDEST PART of the city,
El Pueblo de la Reina de
Los Angeles was founded in
1781 by Felipe de Neve, the
Spanish governor of Cali-
fornia. Today, El Pueblo is a
State Historic Monument,
housing some of the city's
oldest buildings, such as the
Old Plaza Church and the
Avila Adobe, the city's oldest
existing house, furnished as
it would have been in the
1840s. Olvera Street, preserved as a Mexican marketplace in the 1920s, abounds
in shops selling colorful
Mexican dresses, leather
sandals, *piñatas* (clay or
paper-mâché animals), and
snacks like *churros*, a
Spanish-Mexican fried bread.
During festivals, such as the
Blessing of the Animals,
Cinco de Mayo (see p28),
and the Mexican indepen-
dence Day fiesta (September
13–15), El Pueblo is ablaze
with color and sound.

Nearby, the 1939 grand
passenger terminal, **Union
Station**, is a blend of Spanish
Mission, Moorish, and Streamline Moderne architectural
styles. Stars of 1940s films
were photographed here.
Recently it has been the
location for several movies,
such as Sydney Pollack's
The Way We Were (1973).

The distinctive façade of Union Station, El Pueblo

Lummis House ㉑

Map F3. 200 E Ave 43. ☎ *(323)* 222-0546. ○ *8:30am–5pm Mon–Fri.* ♿ ▢ *Donation.*

Aᴌꜱᴏ ᴋɴᴏᴡɴ as "El Alisal," Spanish for "Place of the Sycamore," this house was the home of journalist, photographer, artist, and historian Charles Fletcher Lummis (1859–1928). The structure, which Lummis built with his own hands, displays various design elements – Native American, Mission Revival, and Arts and Crafts – revealing the dominant influences in his life.

Today, Lummis House is the headquarters of the Historical Society of Southern California. It exhibits Native American artifacts from the owner's collection, and its impressive interiors include a grand Art Nouveau fireplace.

The garden, originally planted with vegetables and fruit trees, was redesigned in 1985. It now grows drought-tolerant and native southern California plant species.

Restored interior of the 19th-century Lummis House

Southwest Museum ㉒

Map F3. 234 Museum Dr. ☎ *(323) 221-2164.* ○ *10am–5pm Tue–Sun.* ● *Jan 1, Easter Sun, Thanksgiving, Dec 25.* 🎟 ▢ ⓦ *www. southwestmuseum.org*

Wɪᴛʜ ᴏɴᴇ ᴏꜰ the nation's richest collections of Native American art and artifacts, this museum was the brainchild of Charles Fletcher

Mission Revival-style Southwest Museum

Lummis, who donated many of his personal holdings to start the collection. During his cross-country trek from Ohio to L.A. in the late 19th century, Lummis spent a long time in the Southwest, becoming one of the first whites to appreciate the history and culture of Native Americans.

The museum displays tribal artifacts from prehistoric times to the present day, providing an excellent overview of Native American heritage. The collection of 11,000 baskets is particularly impressive. Tepees, storytelling, and workshops help to involve children at the museum.

Set atop Mount Washington, the Mission Revival building offers excellent views of downtown L.A. to the south.

Sequoyah Indian relief

Griffith Park ㉓

Map E3. 🚌 96. ○ *6am–10pm daily.* ℹ *4730 Crystal Springs Dr, (213) 485-5027.* ♿ 🅿 ▢ 🍴 ▣ ⓦ www.laparks.org

Gʀɪꜰꜰɪᴛʜ ᴘᴀʀᴋ is a 4,000-acre (1,600-ha) wilderness of rugged hills, forested valleys, and green meadows in the center of L.A. The land was donated to the city in 1896 by Colonel Griffith J. Griffith, a Welshman who emigrated to the US in 1865 and made a fortune speculating in mining. Today, people come to Griffith Park to escape from the city crowds, visit the sights, picnic, hike, or go horseback riding.

The **Griffith Observatory**, currently closed for renovation until late 2005, is located on Mount Hollywood, and commands stunning views of the L.A. basin below. Inside, the Hall of Science explains important scientific concepts with exhibits such as the Foucault Pendulum, demonstrating the earth's rotation. Visitors are taken on a journey through space and time, as some 9,000 stars and planets are projected onto the ceiling at the Planetarium Theater. On the roof, the Zeiss Telescope is open to the public on clear nights.

Northeast of the observatory lies the **Greek Theater**. Styled after an ancient Greek amphitheater, this open-air music venue has excellent acoustics. On summer nights, more than 6,000 people sit under the stars and enjoy popular and classical music performances. Farther north, in the hills just off Griffith Park Drive, is a 1926 merry-go-round. Adults and children can still ride on its 66 horses and listen to its giant band organ.

A short drive north leads to the 113-acre (46-ha) hilly compound of **Los Angeles Zoo**, housing more than 1,200 mammals, reptiles, and birds living in simulations of their natural habitats. Many newborn creatures can be seen in the Animal Nursery, including some from the zoo's respected breeding program for rare and endangered species. The zoo also hosts several animal shows, aimed at a young audience.

Opposite the zoo, the **Autry Museum of Western Heritage** explores the many

View of the Griffith Observatory on Mount Hollywood, Griffith Park

cultures that have shaped the American West. Exhibits include a replica of a 19th-century Mexican-American ranch from Arizona. Founded by the film star Gene Autry, "the Singing Cowboy," the museum also houses a superb collection of movie and television memorabilia.

At the northwestern end of the park, **Travel Town** presents an outdoor collection of vintage trains and cars. Children and adults can climb aboard freight cars and railroad carriages, or ride on a small train. To its east, on Zoo Drive, miniature steam trains take people on rides during weekends.

🚌 Griffith Observatory

2800 Observatory Rd. 📞 *(323) 664-1181.* 🎟 *Planetarium.* ♿ *limited.* 🌐 www.griffithobs.org
Currently closed for renovation until late 2005.

Hollywood Sign ㉔

Map D2. Mount Cahuenga, above Hollywood. 🛈 *Hollywood Visitors Information Center, 6541 Hollywood Blvd, (213) 689-8822.*

THE HOLLYWOOD SIGN is an internationally recognized symbol of the movie business. Set high up in the Hollywood Hills, it is now a protected historic site. Though visible for miles from many parts of Los Angeles, it is not possible for the public to reach the sign itself, since there is no legitimate trail leading up to the tall 45-ft (13-m) letters.

Erected in 1923, it originally advertised the Hollywoodland housing development of the former *L.A. Times* publisher Harry Chandler. The "land" was removed in 1949. Nearly 30 years later, donors pledged $27,000 per letter for a new sign. It has been the scene of one suicide – that of disappointed would-be actress Peg Entwhistle, who jumped off the "H" in 1932 – and numerous prank spellings, such as "Hollyweed," acknowledging the more lenient marijuana laws of the 1970s; and "UCLA" during a football game.

Universal Studios ㉕

Map D2. 100 Universal City Plaza, Universal City. 📞 *1-800-UNIVERSAL.* 🚌 *424.* 🕐 *Jun–Sep: 8am–10pm daily; Oct–May: 9am–7pm daily.* ● *Thanksgiving, Dec 25.* 🎟 ♿ 📷 🍴 🖥 w www.universalstudioshollywood.com

SPREAD OVER 415 acres (168 ha), the world's largest working movie and television studio and theme park, Universal Studios Hollywood started out as a poultry farm. In 1915, Carl Laemmle bought a chicken ranch on this site and moved his film studio here from Hollywood. He charged visitors 25 cents to see films being made, and guests could also buy fresh eggs. With the advent of the "talkies" in 1927, the sets needed quiet and the visits stopped.

In 1964, Universal Studios Hollywood launched its **Studio Tour** tram ride, a behind-the-scenes view of Hollywood movie making. Boarded from the Entertainment Center, which has the new **Spiderman Rocks!** show with dazzling pyrotechnics and stunts, the Studio Tour takes guests through movie sets in trams, outfitted with state-of-the-art audio and video systems. Celebrity hosts, such as actor Jason Alexander and director Ron Howard, narrate the inner workings of the real Hollywood. Passengers experience an earthquake, encounter King Kong and Jaws, and survive a collapsing bridge, a

Jurassic Park sign

flash flood, and an avalanche. If they are lucky, visitors can even see a film being made.

Another popular attraction is **CityWalk Promenade**, designed by architect Jon Jerde. With its festive assortment of façades for the shops, restaurants, bars, and theaters, Universal's CityWalk is being hailed as the entertainment mecca of Southern California. It is also one of the prime areas for visitors to buy Hollywood memorabilia. Universal's Entertainment Center and the lower portions of the studio lots give an insight into the special effects and stunts used to make a film, and offer some of the park's most spectacular thrill rides. The audience becomes part of the wild jetskiing in the sea water spectacular, **WaterWorld**, they are terrified by monsters at the **Terminator 2:3D** show, and panicked in the heat of the blazing inferno in a re-creation of the final scene of the fire-fighting film *Backdraft*. The ride **Jurassic Park**, literally recaptures the thrill of the movie, while **Shrek 4-D**, reunites the talents of Eddie Murphy, Mike Myers, and Cameron Diaz in an all-new animated saga based on the Oscar-winning film *Shrek*. Another new blockbuster ride, **The Mummy Returns – Chamber of Doom**, takes visitors through hair-raising adventures in the labyrinth of the mummy's tomb, past Egyptian burial chambers and waterfalls of scorpions.

Terrifying the audience at the Terminator 2:3D show, Universal Studios

Greater Los Angeles

Mausoleum at Huntington, designed by John Russell Pope

F ROM THE FREEWAYS, it is hard to appreciate the many treasures that lie within Los Angeles's sprawl. But a short drive beyond the central sights to nearby areas can be surprisingly rewarding. Upscale Pasadena with its delightful old town has some excellent museums and galleries. Farther south, Orange County offers visitors a wide range of attractions, from sandy beaches to cultural sites and museums. For visitors seeking family fun and roller-coaster thrills, there are the homey Knott's Berry Farm, and the fantasy kingdom of Disneyland.

Malibu ㉖

Malibu Colony 🚻 ℹ️ *(310) 456-5737.* **Malibu Lagoon State Beach** 🅿️ *(818) 880-0367.* ⏰ *8am–sunset daily.* 📷 ♿ **Adamson House** 🅿️ *(310) 456-8432.* ⏰ *11am–3pm Wed–Sat.* **Malibu Creek State Park** 🅿️ *(818) 880-0350; for camp bookings (800) 444-7275.* ⏰ *8am–sunset.* 📷

T WENTY MILES NORTH of Santa Monica Bay, the Rancho Topanga Malibu Sequit was bought in 1887 by Fredrick and May Rindge. The Rindge family fought with the state for many years to keep their property secluded. Eventually failing, they had to sell much of Malibu to film stars such as Bing Crosby and Gary Cooper. Today the **Malibu Colony** is a private, gated compound still favored by people from the entertainment industry.

A few miles east, the **Malibu Lagoon State Beach**, the largest village of Chumash people in the 16th century, is now a natural preserve and bird refuge. To its east, Surfrider County Beach is considered by many to be the surfing capital of the world.

Nearby, the Spanish Colonial **Adamson House** with vivid tiles and opulent decor, houses a museum showcasing the history of Malibu.

To the north, the 10,000-acre (4,000-ha) **Malibu Creek State Park** features forests, meadows, waterfalls, picnic areas, and hiking trails. Much of the park was owned by 20th Century Fox until 1974. *M*A*S*H*, *Butch Cassidy and the Sundance Kid*, and *Tarzan* were all filmed here.

Pasadena ㉗

🏛️ *135,000.* 🚌 *79 from downtown.* ℹ️ *171 S Los Robles Ave, (626) 795-9311.* 🎭 *Tournament of Roses Parade (Jan 1); Pasadena Spring Art Festival (mid-Apr).* 🌐 *www.pasadenacal.com*

W ITH THE completion of the Santa Fe Railroad in 1887, wealthy people from the East Coast, along with artists and bohemians, settled in Pasadena to savor the warm winters of Southern California. This mix of creativity and wealth has resulted in a city with a splendid cultural legacy.

The historic district of **Old Town Pasadena**, at the heart of the city, underwent a recent face-lift ushering in a spate of upscale shops, restaurants, and cafés in restored historic buildings. The highlights of the area include the **Norton Simon Museum** featuring one of the finest collections of Old Masters and Impressionist paintings in the country.

To the north, local architects Charles and Henry Greene's sprawling **Gamble House** is considered a consummate craftsman bungalow by many.

A few miles east of Old Town, opulent San Marino is home to the **Huntington Library, Art Collections, and Botanical Gardens**. Once the estate of railroad tycoon Henry E. Huntington (1850–1927), the Beaux Arts mansion holds one of the most important libraries and collections of 18th-century British and French art in world. Rare books in the library's collection include priceless objects such as a Gutenberg bible, a Chaucer manuscript, and Benjamin Franklin's handwritten autobiography. The botanical gardens are made up of 15 theme areas: the most popular are the Desert, Japanese, and Shakespearean Gardens.

🏛️ **Huntington Library, Art Collections, & Botanical Gardens**
1151 Oxford Rd. 🅿️ *(626) 405-2100.* ⏰ *Jun–Aug: 10:30am–4:30pm Tue–Sun; Sep–May: noon–4:30pm Tue–Fri, 10:30am–4:30pm Sat–Sun.* ⚫ *public hols.* 📷 ♿ 🏬 🍴 📖 🌐 *www.huntington.org*

Watts Towers ㉘

1727 E 107th St, Watts. 🅿️ *(213) 847-4646.* ⏰ *10am–4pm Tue–Sat, noon–4pm Sun.* 📷 *Towers only.* 🅿️ *Arts Center only.* 📷

W ATTS TOWERS embodies the perseverance and vision of Italian folk artist Simon Rodia. Between 1921 and 1954, the tile-worker sculpted steel rods and pipes

View across Malibu Lagoon to the Santa Monica Mountains

into a huge skeletal framework, adorning it with shells, tiles, and broken glass. He never gave a reason for building the towers and, upon finishing, deeded the land to a neighbor and left L.A. The towers, standing 100 ft (30 m) at their tallest, are now a State Historic Site. Next to the monument, the Watts Towers Arts Center is well known for holding temporary exhibitions of work by African-American artists. It also hosts workshops for artists of all ages.

The *Queen Mary*, Long Beach's most famous hotel

Long Beach ㉙

M *Metro Blue Line from downtown Los Angeles.*

WITH PALM TREES and ocean as a backdrop, downtown Long Beach is a mixture of carefully restored buildings and modern glass high-rises. At its heart, **Pine Avenue**, lined with stores, cafés, and restaurants, retains the early Midwestern charm that gave the city its nickname, "Iowa by the Sea."

Along the ocean, the restaurants and shops in Shoreline Village offer views of the ocean liner *Queen Mary (see p722)*. The Cunard flagship from 1930s to the 1960s, this luxury liner was converted into a troopship during World War II. It carried more than 80,000 soldiers during its wartime career. At the end of the war, it transported more

than 22,000 war brides and children to the US during "Operation Diaper." It was permanently docked for use as a hotel and tourist attraction in 1967. Today, visitors can view part of the original Engine Room, examples of the different accommodations, and an exhibition on the war years.

Nearby, the **Aquarium of the Pacific** is one of the largest aquariums in the United States. It holds 550 species in 17 major habitats, offering visitors a fascinating exploration of marine flora and fauna from the Pacific Ocean's three distinct regions: Southern California/Baja; the Tropical Pacific, and the Northern Pacific.

🚢 **Queen Mary**
Pier J, 1126 Queens Hwy. 📞 *(562) 435-3511.* ⏰ *10am–6pm daily.* 📷 ♿ 🅿 W *www.queenmary.com*
🏛 **Aquarium of the Pacific**
100 Aquarium Way. 📞 *(562) 590-3100.* ⏰ *9am–6pm daily.* ● *Dec 25, weekend of the Toyota Grand Prix.* 📷 ♿ 🅿 🅿
W *www.aquariumofpacific.org*

Knott's Berry Farm ㉚

8039 Beach Blvd, Buena Park. 📞 *(714) 827-1776.* 📠 *(714) 220-5200.* 🚌 *29, 38, 42.* ⏰ *hours vary per season & day. Call to verify park hours.* ● *Dec 25.* 📷 ♿ 🅿 🍴 🛒
W *www.knotts.com*

LOCATED IN Buena Vista in Orange County, Knott's Berry Farm has grown from a 1920s boysenberry farm to a 21st-century multi-day entertainment complex. Offering more than 165 different rides and attractions, its main charm lies in its emphasis on authenticity. The **Old West Ghost Town**, in the heart of the park, has original ghost town buildings. America's very first theme park, Knott's offers six themed areas, dozens of live-action stages, thrill rides, shopping, and dining, as well as a full-fledged resort.

Cloisters framing Mission San Juan Capistrano's central courtyard

Mission San Juan Capistrano ㉛

Camino Capistrano & Ortega Hwy. 📞 *(949) 234-1300.* ⏰ *8:30am–5pm daily.* ● *Good Fri pm, Thanksg., Dec 25.* 📷 ♿ 🅿 🅿 🎭 *Swallow Festival (Mar).* W *www.missionsjc.com*

THIS "Jewel of the Missions" was founded in 1776, and its chapel is the only surviving building in California where Fr. Junípero Serra preached. One of the largest in the chain, the mission was built as a self-sufficient community. Its Great Stone Church was destroyed by an earthquake in 1812, leaving a rambling complex of adobe and brick buildings. A recent restoration program re-creates the mission's former glory.

Newport Beach ㉜

Hwy 1, S from Los Angeles.

FAMOUS FOR ITS million-dollar homes and lifestyles to match, Newport Beach has a 3-mile (5-km) stretch of wide sand and two piers along Orange County's coast. Fresh fish, caught by the historic Dory fishing fleet, is sold beside Newport Pier at the northern end of the beach. Farther inland, the coastal wetland of **Upper Newport Bay Ecological Preserve** is a refuge for wildlife and migratory birds. It also offers a bike path, fishing, and guided tours on foot and by kayak.

Statues of cowboys on a Ghost Town bench

Disneyland® Resort ㉝

DISNEY'S "MAGIC KINGDOM" in Anaheim is not only the top tourist attraction in California, it is part of the American Dream. Now encompassing the original Disneyland Park, Disney's California Adventure, Downtown Disney, plus three enormous hotels, the Resort has become the model for theme parks around the globe. Visitors to "The Happiest Place on Earth" find fantasy, thrill rides, glittering shows, and shopping in a brightly orchestrated land of lines, fireworks, and Mickey Mouse, which is as American as apple pie.

Exploring the Resort

Spread over 85 acres (34 ha), the original Disneyland Park is divided into eight theme areas or "lands." Transportation around the park is provided by Disneyland Railroad and monorail. Disney's newest venture, Disney's California Adventure Park, is smaller than Disneyland Park and can easily be covered on foot. With three theme areas, it is more suited to teenagers, as the attractions may be too intense for toddlers. At the heart of the Resort, Downtown Disney, is a lively area full of restaurants, shops, and entertainment venues.

It takes at least three days to explore the theme parks. Both parks stay open late during the peak seasons. The **Fireworks Show** in Disneyland and in Downtown Disney are fantastic.

DISNEYLAND PARK

MAIN STREET USA is a colorful street lined with historic buildings. Central Plaza is the venue for the daily "Parade of the Stars," featuring Disney characters and scenes from Disney's most famous movies. Guests can meet with famous Disney characters and will find ample opportunities for photographs. City Hall offers maps, dining, and entertainment schedules, while the Main Street Cinema screens early Disney silent films. There is also a large selection of shops and eateries.

Visions of the future inspire the rides in Tomorrowland, where sights change regularly to keep one step ahead of real-life technology. One of the first attractions in 1955 was **Autopia**, that has since been updated and now takes visitors on a ride into a parallel universe. **Star Tours** was redesigned in collaboration with the *Star Wars* genius George Lucas. Its fabulous use of flight-simulator technology makes it one of the park's most realistic rides. Visitors board a StarSpeeder spaceship and are transported through outer space strewn with starships, comets, and asteroids. **Space Mountain** is a Disneyland favorite that offers a high speed roller-coaster ride, 118 ft (36 m) above the ground. Conducted almost entirely in darkness, the ride has sudden meteoric flashes and celestial showers, and is not suitable for very young children.

The colorful architecture of cartoons comes to life in Mickey's Toontown – a three-dimensional cartoon world where all Disney's favorite animated characters reside. The most popular residences are Mickey's house and Minnie's cottage. Most of the attractions are geared toward kids from age three up.

Chip 'n Dale Treehouse, a mini-roller coaster; Goofy's Bounce House; and a floating bumper-boat ride offer gentle thrills. **Roger Rabbit's Car Toon Spin** is the favorite. Its spinning cars take visitors on a madcap drive through a surreal cartoon world.

Fantasyland, dominated by the pink and gold towers of **Sleeping Beauty's Castle** and a replica of the **Matterhorn**, is a shrine to children's dreams. Nursery heroes such as Peter Pan and Snow White provide the themes for gentle fairytale rides. The historic **Matterhorn Bobsleds** offers "icy" roller-coaster rides down the slopes of a replica of Switzerland's famous peak. Bobsleds climb to its summit, then drop into a high-speed descent, passing glacier caves and waterfalls as they go. **It's a Small World** creates a Utopian vision of global harmony, with almost 300 singing-and-dancing Audio-Animatronics® dolls dressed in national costumes.

Inspired by the Wild West, Frontierland features a skirt-lifting song and dance on the **Golden Horseshoe Jamboree**. Every weekend night, the skies above Frontierland are lit up with the spectacular **Fantasmic!** fireworks show, complete with sound effects and live performers. Thrill-seekers should not miss the **Big Mountain Thunder Railroad** roller-coaster ride, where a runaway train speeds through the cavernous interior of Big Thunder Mountain, narrowly escaping boulders and waterfalls.

TICKETS & TIPS

Each theme park (except for Downtown Disney) has a separate admission ticket that covers all the rides and shows, and includes a park map and schedule of events. Parking is extra, as are certain shows, food, and arcades. Multi-day tickets for three to four days and Annual Passports allow unlimited admission and access to attractions. A Fastpass lets guests obtain a voucher with a computer-assigned boarding time for specific attractions or rides. This eliminates waiting in long lines. Guests can also save time at the front gate by buying tickets in advance.at any Disney store or online at www.disney.com. To help plan your day, there is updated information on showtimes, waiting times, and ride closures at the information board at the end of Main Street opposite the Plaza Pavillion.

Critter Country is built in a rustic style, based on the rugged American Northwest. It is home to **Splash Mountain**, one of Disneyland's most popular attractions. This watery ride in hollowed-out logs features singing characters from the 1946 film *Song of the South* such as Brer Rabbit and Brer Fox, and ends in a plummet down a steep waterfall.

The charming New Orleans Square is modeled on the French Quarter in New Orleans as it was during the city's heyday in the 19th century. Quaint wrought-iron balconies adorn buildings housing French-style shops. One of its top attractions, **Haunted Mansion**, promises "999 ghosts and ghouls," and some visitors are so familiar with its introductory commentary that they join in as they descend into its spooky world of mischievous spirits and grave-diggers. The ethereal figures, including a talking woman's head in a crystal ball, are extremely realistic. Another favorite, **Pirates of the Caribbean** provides a floating ride through a yo-ho-ho world of ruffians who have the gifts of song, dance, and heavy drinking with the use of Audio-Animatronics®. This technique, which brings models to life using electronic impulses to control sounds and actions, was perfected at Disneyland. **The Disney Gallery** shows visitors the art behind the world of Disney, and some of the original artworks and designs for Disney's elaborate projects are on display here.

The exotic atmosphere in Adventureland offers dark, humid waterways lined with tropical plants. This is the smallest, but perhaps most adventuresome, "land" in the park. The **Enchanted Tiki Room** showcases mechanical singing birds in a zany, musical romp through the tropics. Inspired by the 1982 film trilogy, the **Indiana Jones**™ **Adventure** sets off on a jeep-style drive through the Temple of the Forbidden Eye. Theatrical props and scenery, a realistic soundtrack, superb film images, and the sensation of a roller coaster make this the ultimate experience in Disneyland. The safari-style **Jungle Cruise** boat ride leads visitors through a jungle full of rampant apes and blood-thirsty headhunters, accompanied by a real-life captain.

DOWNTOWN DISNEY

LOCATED BETWEEN the entrances to Disneyland Park and Disney's California Adventure, Downtown Disney® is a garden paradise, offering visitors some 300,000 sq ft (27,870 sq m) of innovative restaurants, shops, and entertainment venues. The fact that this area has no admission fee makes Downtown Disney® one of the more popular – but crowded – spaces. A 12-screen AMC Theatre®, ESPN Zone™, and a LEGO Imagination Center® are its top attractions. The snack shops, restaurants, vast range of retail and specialty shops, and a travel center create a total Disney experience.

DISNEY'S CALIFORNIA ADVENTURE

THE NEWEST STAR in Anaheim is Disney's California Adventure, lying adjacent to Disneyland. It is divided into three "lands," each offering themed experiences that celebrate the California dream. The emphasis is on adults and older teens, but there are still plenty of rides available for all ages.

Hollywood Pictures Backlot offers a tongue-in-cheek view of the motion picture industry. The two blocks of façades and fakery give the visitor a Disney-eye view of Hollywood. The **Hyperion Theater** features staged live musical shows, and at Jim Henson's **Muppet*Vision 3-D** visitors can see Miss Piggy, Kermit, and all the lovable Muppet characters in a tribute to movie making. Golden State features California's topography and agriculture. The star ride is **Soarin' Over California**, a simulated hang-glider ride that portrays the beauties of California's landscape on a huge wrap-around screen. Guests can feel the wind currents and smell the scent of orange blossoms as they soar 40 feet (12 m) high. **Bountiful Valley** features healthy snacks and a 3-D film starring Flik from *A Bug's Life*. Smell-o-Vision and touchy-feelies make this a completely buggy experience for all.

Considerably lower key than the thrills in the original park, Paradise Pier is the place where roller coasters, Ferris wheels, and parachute rides rule. **California Screamin'**, the giant **Sun Wheel**, and **King Triton's Carousel** are reminiscent of seaside recreation parks as they used to be years ago.

Los Angeles Practical Information

LOS ANGELES OFFERS a wealth of entertainment and outdoor pleasures to its visitors. At the center of the film industry, L.A. dominated the world stage for most of the 20th century. It is therefore not surprising that L.A. sees itself as the "Entertainment Capital of the World." But the glamor of the movies is just one aspect of the city that manufactures the American Dream. This year-long vacation spot is also famous for its long beaches, mountain ranges, and some of the world's best museums.

TOURIST INFORMATION

THE MAIN BRANCH of the **Los Angeles Convention and Visitors' Bureau** is in downtown L.A., and it offers multilingual assistance. Its visitors' guide, *Destination Los Angeles*, gives listings of restaurants, coffee houses, hotels, shops, and other attractions. There is also a 24-hour events hotline. The city's two other main information centers are the **Hollywood Visitors' Information Center** and the **Beverly Hills Visitors' Bureau**. Various publications can help sift through the city's entertainment riches. The *L.A. Weekly* – a free paper available at bars, clubs, and corner markets across Los Angeles – has the most comprehensive entertainment and arts listings.

GETTING AROUND

THE SPRAWLING 467 sq miles (1,200 sq km) city of Los Angeles may seem a bit daunting to navigate. The most cost-effective method of getting around is by car. A network of freeways provides a convenient, if crowded, means of traveling in the area. It is advisable to avoid the freeways during rush hours (8am to 9:30am and 4am to 6:30pm). Some freeways are busy regardless of the hour, and it can be less stressful to take one of the city's major streets. When parking, read the posted signs for limitations, and carry plenty of quarters for the parking meters. At nights, it is safer to valet park.

Although the city is spread out, many of its districts are pedestrian-friendly. Third Street Promenade and the beach in Santa Monica are best explored on foot. Other such areas include Old Pasadena, downtown, and the Golden Triangle in Beverly Hills. Visitors should avoid walking at night unless the street is well lit and populated.

Greater Los Angeles is served by the **Metropolitan Transportation Authority (MTA)**. Bus stops display an MTA sign, and buses run on the main thoroughfares. The **DASH** shuttle provides travel within small areas, such as downtown and Hollywood, for a quarter. Bus tickets are sold at most grocery stores.

L.A.'s growing subway system, the **Metro**, serves parts of the city well. It is made up of three lines, red, blue, and green, which serve different areas. The Green Line is useful for the airport.

Other ways to get around include the somewhat expensive taxis, which have to be called by phone. Two reliable taxi companies are **Yellow Cab** and the Independent Cab Co. Visitors can also rent a limousine for a luxurious alternative. Private bus lines, such as **L.A. Tours**, offer package tours of the city.

OUTDOOR ACTIVITIES

EACH YEAR MORE than 30 million people visit the beaches around Los Angeles, making them the most popular vacation destinations on the West Coast. The Malibu headland, from Point Dume to Malibu Lagoon, alternates between rocky shorelines and beaches. Farther along, the shoreline becomes a long sandy strand leading to the renowned beaches of Santa Monica and Venice. Inland, the pristine and rugged terrain of the Santa Monica Mountains offer plenty of hiking trails with panoramic views of the Pacific Ocean. L.A.'s beaches are a great natural resource and offer great swimming and volleyball opportunities. The waters off the Malibu Pier and Topanga State Beach are considered to be the best for surfing.

Griffith Park offers miles of hiking trails, opportunities for horseback riding, and cycling. But the best place for cyclists is the coastal bike path that runs for 25 miles (40 km) along Santa Monica Bay (bicycles are not allowed on the freeways). Bicycles can be rented from **Sea Mist Skate Rentals** (Santa Monica Pier) and at the local pizza stands (Santa Monica Beach). Sports include baseball at the famed Dodger Stadium, and college football at Pasadena's Rose Bowl. Basketball and ice hockey, at the Great Western Forum, are popular draws, as are horse racing at the Hollywood Park Racetrack and polo at the Will Rogers State Historic Park.

ENTERTAINMENT

LOS ANGELES's large and successful artistic community guarantees that there is always plenty to do in the city, although only small areas tend to be lively after dark.

Most visitors don't spend a lot of time seeing movies in Los Angeles, even though all the current releases and countless classics are always being shown. The movie palaces themselves, however, draw the crowds, with Mann's Chinese and El Capitan theaters on Hollywood Boulevard being the best known. Multiplexes, such as those in **Universal City** and the Beverly Center, offer state-of-the-art facilities.

Stage productions are also plentiful and diverse, with L.A. putting up over a 1,000 professional plays each year. Pantages in Hollywood is a leading venue for touring Broadway musicals. Housed in beautiful Mediterranean-style theaters, the **Pasadena Playhouse** and the **Geffen**

Playhouse both put on new works as well as old favorites.

The city has a well-respected symphony orchestra, the L.A. Philharmonic, and an opera company, the **L.A. Opera**. In the summer there are outdoor concerts in places such as the Hollywood Bowl.

Naked ambition and unbridled youth fuel the rock clubs that line Sunset Strip. The venerable **Whiskey a Go Go** and **The Roxy** compete with relative newcomers such as the Viper Room and the Key Club. L.A.'s jazz scene is exemplified by cozy joints such as **The Baked Potato**. Whether it's house or hiphop at The Century Club, or hipster big beats at The Garage, the L.A. club scene runs all types of dance music. With its large gay population, West Hollywood has several discos. A current favorite is **The Factory**.

Many of L.A.'s television and film studios offer behind-the-scenes tours as well as tickets to tapings of popular shows. In the high-tech **CBS-TV** studios, soap operas, such as *The Bold and the Beautiful*, and game shows are taped

before live audiences. The popular **Warner Bros** tour is probably the truest look at modern-day filmmaking.

Most of the areas within L.A. have local festivals, particularly in the summer, which feature food, live music, arts, and crafts.

SHOPPING

WHATEVER MONEY can buy can be found in Los Angeles, from Cartier necklaces to everyday items. While indoor shopping malls are the norm for much of the US, L.A.'s temperate climate allows for a range of pleasant outdoor alternatives. Melrose Avenue and Santa Monica's Third Street Promenade are both young, lively areas, while upscale Rodeo Drive is probably the most famous. One of the more pleasant shopping areas in L.A. is Old Pasadena, which has a range of unique shops in late 19th-century buildings.

L.A.'s favorite and best known department stores are **Bloomingdales** and **Macy's**, and Nordstrom's popular shoe department draws

cutomers especially in January and June during its half-price sales.

Fashion styles are casual in L.A. but couture clothes are available in Beverly Hills. Todd Oldham and Tyler Trafficante are two of the hottest women's fashion labels in town, while Bernini and Mark Michaels have some of the best fashions for men.

Antique shops are centered around Melrose Place, close to Melrose Avenue, while some of L.A.'s leading art galleries are located at Bergamot Station.

Hollywood memorabilia is on sale as well. Two good shops are Fantasies Come True and **Larry Edmund's Cinema Bookshop**. There is a selection of Latin American arts and crafts, popular in Los Angeles, at The Folk Tree.

The California fresh produce and wines have representation in L.A. Grand Central Market, and Farmers Market overflows with a wide range of fresh fruit and vegetables. Trader Joe's, cited as one of the finest reasons to live in the city, sells a vast array of gourmet foods and wines.

DIRECTORY

TOURIST OFFICES

Beverly Hills
((310) 248-1015.

Hollywood
((323) 461-9520.

Los Angeles Visitors' Bureau
((213) 689-8822.

PUBLIC TRANSPORTATION

DASH
((800) 266-6883.

L.A. Tours
((323) 460-6490.

MTA
((800) 266-6883.
W www.mta.net

Yellow Cab
((800) 200-1085.

CYCLING

Sea Mist Skate Rentals
1619 Ocean Front Walk, Santa Monica, CA 90401.
((310) 395-7076.

CINEMAS

Cineplex Odeon Universal City Cinemas
Universal City, CA 91608.
((818) 508-0588.

THEATERS

Geffen Playhouse
10886 Le Conte Ave.
((310) 208-5454.
W www.geffenplayhouse.com

Pasadena Playhouse
39 S El Molino Ave, Pasadena, CA 91101.
((626) 356-7529.

OPERA

L.A. Opera
135 N Grand Ave.
((213) 972-8001.

ROCK, JAZZ, BLUES, & CLUBS

Baked Potato
3787 Cahuenga Blvd W, Studio City, CA 91105.
((818) 980-1615.

Key Club
9041 W Sunset Blvd.
((310) 274-5800.

The Factory
652 N La Peer Dr.
((310) 659-4551.

The Roxy
9009 W Sunset Blvd.
((310) 276-2222.

Whiskey a Go Go
8901 W Sunset Blvd.
((310) 652-4202.

STUDIO TOURS

CBS-TV
7800 Beverly Blvd.
((323) 575-2624.

Warner Bros
4000 Warner Blvd, Burbank.
((818) 954-1744.

SHOPPING

Bloomingdales
Beverly Center, 8500 Beverly Blvd.
((310) 360-2700.
W www.bloomingdales.com

Larry Edmund's Cinema Bookshop
6644 Hollywood Blvd.
((323) 463-3273.
W www.larryedmunds.com

Macy's
8500 Beverly Blvd.
((310) 854-6655.
W www.macys.com

San Diego County

S AN DIEGO'S CHARACTER has always been determined by the sea. Its magnificent natural harbor attracted the Spanish as well as gold prospectors and whalers. The US Navy arrived in 1904, and today San Diego has become one of the largest military establishments in the world. Extending to the Mexican border, its coastline has 70 miles (112 km) of stunning beaches, rocky cliffs, coves, and seaside resorts, with plentiful opportunities for leisure activities.

The Gaslamp Quarter, the star of downtown San Diego

San Diego ❷

🏙 1,500,000.　✈ 🚉 1050 Kettner Blvd.　🚌 120 W Broadway.　ℹ Horton Plaza, 1st & F Sts, (619) 236-1212.　🎭 Street Scene Festival (Sep).

T HE MUSEUMS and art venues of **Balboa Park** (see pp 680–81) are the prime cultural attractions of San Diego, California's second largest city. San Diego's growth as a modern city began with the waterfront development initiated by San Francisco businessman, Alonzo Horton, in the 1870s. He also designed the plan of the **Gaslamp Quarter**, which is now the centerpiece of downtown, and the best place to shop and dine. The wealth of period buildings ranges from a pie bakery to ornate offices and grand Victorian hotels. The district is particularly attractive at night, when it is illuminated by graceful gaslamps. Close by is **Horton Plaza**, an innovatively designed shopping center built in 1985.

At the western end of Broadway is the **Santa Fe Depot**, a Spanish Colonial-style railroad station dating from 1915. The towering America Plaza houses the **Museum of Contemporary Art**, whose galleries display work by new artists and selections from its large permanent collection.

The promenades and piers of the **Embarcadero** waterfront pathway lead to the Maritime Museum and its three historic ships. Of these, the highlight is the *Star of India*, an 1863 merchantman. To the south is Broadway Pier, where visitors can take a harbor excursion.

North of downtown is **Old Town**, site of the original Spanish settlement near the San Diego River. Today, more than 20 historic buildings have been restored to form the Old Town San Diego State Historic Park. The Plaza, at its center, was where parades and fiestas once took place. The old Spanish presido and mission is now part of Presido Park. Crowning the hill the **Junípero Serra Museum** is named after the founder of California's missions (see p692). On display are archaeological finds as well as exhibits on San Diego's successive Native American, Spanish, Mexican, and American communities.

To the west of Old Town is the **Point Loma Peninsula**, at the southern tip of which is the Cabrillo National Monument, named after the city's discoverer, Juan Rodríguez Cabrillo; his statue overlooks the Bay. Between December and March, the nearby Whale Overlook is a popular spot to watch gray whales on their annual migration south.

The peninsula of Coronado has the city's most exclusive boutiques and hotels. The **Hotel del Coronado**, or "Del," opened in 1888 and is a lovely Victorian seaside hotel (see p722). Its guest list reads like a Who's Who of 20th-century US history, including Presidents Franklin D. Roosevelt and Bill Clinton, and film star Marilyn Monroe. It has been the setting for several films, including *Some Like It Hot*, the 1959 classic starring Marilyn Monroe, Jack Lemmon, and Tony Curtis. The Coronado Ferry ride is enchanting at dusk, when the sun's last rays illuminates the skyscrapers of downtown.

🏛 **Junípero Serra Museum**
2727 Presidio Dr.　📞 (858) 297-3258.　◯ 10am–4:30pm Fri–Sun.　⬤ Dec 25. 🎟

Impressive turrets and gables of the Hotel del Coronado, San Diego

Sea World ❸

500 Sea World Dr. 📞 *(619) 226-3901.* 🚌 *9.* ⭘ *daily.* 🅿 ♿ ▣
▣ www.seaworld.com

S AN DIEGO'S Sea World
covers 150 acres (60 ha) of
Mission Bay. The ride up the
Skytower, a 320-ft (98-m) column, offers splendid views.
Another fabulous ride is the
100-ft (30-m) Bayside Skyride,
where gondola cars make an
enormous loop over the
waters of Mission Bay.

The stars of Sea World are
the performing whales and
dolphins. One performance
reveals the intelligence of
dolphins and pilot whales,
while another demonstrates
the virtuosity of killer whales.
Other attractions include the
shark and otter pools, and
opportunities to feed killer
whales and seals. Shamu's
Happy Harbor is an aquatic
adventure park for children.

Sea World's staff are devoted to animal rescue and rehabilitation, and run educational
and conservation programs.

La Jolla ❹

🚶 *32,000.* 🚌 *from San Diego.*
ℹ *1055 Wall St, Suite 110, (858)
454-1444.*

S ET AMID CLIFFS and coves,
La Jolla is an elegant
coastal resort. Its streets are
lined with gourmet choco-
latiers and jewelers, and
visitors come to enjoy the art
galleries and the restaurants

Killer whales performing acrobatic feats for the crowd at Sea World

that promise a "Mediterranean"
view. The town is home to
the University of California at
San Diego and the **Salk
Institute for Biological
Studies**, founded by Dr. Jonas
Salk, who developed the polio
vaccine. The Scripps Institution
of Oceanography has the
Birch Aquarium at Scripps.
It provides an insight into the
world of oceanography. The
**Museum of Contemporary
Art** occupies a prime ocean-
front location. A companion
to the gallery in San Diego,
it displays works of post-1950
art and houses a bookstore
and café.

Tijuana, Mexico ❺

Mexico. 🚇 *San Diego Trolley to San
Ysidro, then bus or walk.* **Tourist
Office** *Ave Revolución y Calle.*
📞 *(011-52-66) 88-05-55.* ⭘ *daily.*

T HE INTERNATIONAL border
crossing at Tijuana is one
of the busiest in the world.
Thousands of Americans

come here every year, for the
inexpensive shopping and
exuberant nightlife – Mexican
laws permit anyone over 18
to drink alcohol.

The futuristic **Centro
Cultural Tijuana**, built on
the banks of the Tijuana River
in 1982, has an OMNIMAX
theater, which screens films
on Mexico. Exhibitions on
Mexican themes are also held
here. The open-air Mexitlán
rooftop exhibition re-creates
the country's architectural
treasures in miniature.

The best shopping is in the
quiet bazaars located on both
sides of the lively Avenida
Revolución. Painted pottery,
leather boots, silver jewelry,
and tequila are some favorite
buys. Visitors rarely need to
change money, as US dollars
and major credit cards are
accepted widely. The Tourist
Office provides maps and has
an English-speaking staff.

🏛 **Centro Cultural Tijuana**
Paseo de los Héroes. 📞 *(011-52-66)
84-11-11.* ⭘ *daily.* 🅿

The beautiful rocky shoreline of La Jolla Cove

The Deserts

National park sign

THE SEARING DESERTS of Southern California have a haunting beauty all their own, with jagged canyons, steep hills, and carpets of wildflowers in spring. At the heart of the Low Desert is Palm Springs, the region's most sought-after resort, with hotels and golf courses. The stark Joshua Tree National Park lies to the east. Farther north, the Mojave Desert is the state's greatest secret, all too often missed by visitors. Its main draw, Death Valley National Park, has some of the highest temperatures in the Western Hemisphere.

Sculpture Garden in the Palm Springs Desert Museum

Palm Springs ⑥

🏔 42,000. ✕ 🚉 Indio. 🚌 3111 N Indian Ave. 🛈 2781 N Palm Canyon Drive, (800) 347-7746, (760) 778-8418. 🎬 Palm Springs International Film Festival (early–mid-Jan).
🌐 www.palm–springs.com

THE LARGEST OF the desert cities, Palm Springs was first sighted in 1853 when a survey party came across a grove of palm trees surrounding a freshwater spring pool in the Coachella Valley. The first hotel was constructed in 1886, and by the turn of the century, Palm Springs was a thriving health spa. Soon after, it became a fashionable winter resort for the rich and famous. Today, its population doubles each winter, when visitors come to enjoy the relaxing, outdoor lifestyle. First-class hotels such as the Marriot and Givenchy abound, and a number of celebrities live here. The area around Palm Springs has numerous

resort cities, such as Rancho Mirage, Indian Wells, and La Quinta, and more than 80 luxury golf courses.

Downtown's two main shopping streets are Palm Canyon and Indian Canyon Drives; both are lined with restaurants, boutiques, and art galleries. The **Village Green Heritage Center**, in the heart of the shopping area, has a few historic buildings, including Ruddy's 1930s General Store Museum, a replica of the original, with authentic packaged goods ranging from licorice to patent medicines. The Agua Caliente Cultural Museum displays the heritage of the area's Cahuilla people.

The state-of-the-art **Oasis Water Resort** has 13 water-slides, including a 70-ft (20-m) free-fall slide. An enormous wave-action pool creates 4-ft (1.2-m) high waves suitable for surfing and boogie boarding. The resort also has a hotel, heated spas, health clubs, and restaurants.

The **Palm Springs Aerial Tramway** covers a 2.5-mile (4-km) trip via cable car, which ascends 5,900 ft (1,790 m) over spectacular scenery to the Mountain Station in the Mount San Jacinto Wilderness State Park. Visitors travel through five distinct ecosystems, ranging from desert to alpine forest, where the weather becomes icy cold. At the top, there are 54 miles (85 km) of hiking trails, a ski center, campsites, and a cafeteria. Observation decks offer terrific views of the Coachella Valley, Palm

Springs, and the San Bernardino Mountains to the north. On a clear day, it is possible to see the Salton Sea, 50 miles (80 km) away.

The **Palm Springs Desert Museum** focuses on art, natural science, and the performing arts. The galleries contain paintings from the 19th century to the present day, as well as Native American artifacts and natural history exhibits. Modern sculpture adorns the gardens. About 5 miles (8 km) south of Palm Springs are the **Indian Canyons**, four spectacular natural palm oases, set in rocky gorges. Clustered along streams fed by mountain springs, Murray, Tahquitz, Andreas, and Palm Canyons are located on the land of the Agua Caliente Cahuilla people. Rock art and other traces of these early inhabitants can still be seen. Palm and Andreas Canyons have many trails that are popular for either hiking or driving.

🚡 Palm Springs Aerial Tramway
Tramway Rd. 🆑 (760) 325-1391.
◯ daily. 🌐

Anza-Borrego Desert State Park ⑦

🚌 Escondido. **Visitor Center**
🆑 (760) 767-4205. ◯ Jun–Sep: Sat & Sun; Oct–May: daily.
🌐 www.anzaborregostatepark.org

DURING THE Gold Rush of 1849 *(see p654)*, tens of thousands of miners passed through the Anza-Borrego

Oasis Water Resort in Palm Springs

Desert. Today, this former gateway to San Diego County is a remote and pristine park, offering an insight into the unique desert environment, with its steep ravines and rocky badlands.

The visitor center is in **Borrego Springs**, the park's only significant town. Nearby, the Palm Canyon Nature Trail leads to an oasis where endangered bighorn sheep can often be seen. From the **Box Canyon Historical Monument**, lying southwest of the visitor center, there are views of the old road once used by miners en route to the goldfields, which lay 500 miles (800 km) to the north.

The desert bursts into bloom between March and May. Cacti and desert flowers such as desert poppies and dune primroses produce a riot of color.

Much of the park, including its campsites, is accessible via the 100 miles (160 km) of roads. Four-wheel drive vehicles are recommended, however, for the 500 miles (800 km) of unsurfaced roads.

Salton Sea ❽

🚗 Mecca. 🚉 Indio. **Visitor Center** 📞 (760) 393-3052. ⏰ daily.

THE SALTON SEA was created by accident in 1905 when the Colorado River flooded and flowed into a newly dug irrigation canal leading to the Imperial Valley. By the time the flow was stemmed two years later, a 35-mile (55-km) inland sea had formed in the Salton Sink, 230 ft (70 m) below sea level.

Despite the high salinity, saltwater game fish live here, with 10-lb (4.5-kg) orange-mouth corvina being caught regularly. Waterskiing, wind-surfing, and boating are other popular activities. The area off Mecca Beach has the best spots for swimming. The adjoining marshlands are a refuge for migrating birds such as geese, blue herons, and egrets. On the eastern side, there are hiking trails and camp sites within the State Recreation Area.

Spiny-leaved Joshua trees in Joshua Tree National Park's western half

Joshua Tree National Park ❾

🚌 Desert Stage Lines from Palm Springs to Twenty-nine Palms.
🏛 **Oasis Visitors' Center** 74485 National Park Dr, Twenty-nine Palms. 📞 (760) 367-5500. ⏰ 8am–4:30pm daily. ⬤ Dec 25.

THE JOSHUA TREE National Park was established to protect the unique Joshua tree. The tree was named by early Mormon travelers, who saw the upraised arms of the biblical Joshua in its twisted branches. The species can grow up to 30 ft (9 m) and live for about 1,000 years.

The 630,800-acre (255,300-ha) park, with its formations of pink and gray rocks, abandoned mines, and oases, is a climber's and hiker's paradise. A popular trail begins close to the **Oasis Visitors' Center**. South of here, the gigantic boulders in **Hidden Valley** form corrals, which were hideouts for cattle rustlers in the days of the Wild West. Farther south, **Key's View** offers sweeping vistas of the valley, desert, and mountains. Close to Key's View, the **Lost Horse Mine** was the historic mine where over $270,000 in gold was extracted in its first decade of operation.

A variety of animals, which have specially adapted to this environment, thrive here. The kangaroo rat gets its food and water from seeds alone, and the jackrabbit has a coat of muted fur to camouflage it from predators such as the coyote, bobcat, and eagle.

Mojave Desert ❿

🚉 Barstow. 🚻 ℹ 831 Barstow Rd, (760) 252-6000.

LYING AT AN altitude of 2,000 ft (600 m), the Mojave or High Desert was the gateway to California for traders in the 19th century. **Barstow**, the largest town, is a stop-over between L.A. and Las Vegas. In the 1870s, gold and silver were discovered in this area, and towns such as Calico sprang up. They were soon abandoned and became ghost towns when the mines became exhausted. Many of Calico's buildings are intact, and visitors can even take a ride in a mine train. To the west, Edwards Air Force Base is famous for its space shuttle landings. The **Red Rock Canyon State Park** nearby has red sandstone and pink volcanic rock, while the **Mitchell Caverns** have limestone formations. Northern Mojave is dominated by the **Death Valley National Park** (see pp684–5).

Rock formations in the Mitchell Caverns, Mojave Desert

Death Valley National Park ⓫

THE NATIVE AMERICANS CALLED the valley Tomesha, "the land where the ground is on fire," an apt name for Death Valley, which has the highest mean temperature on earth – the highest ever recorded was 134° F (57° C) in the shade in 1913. This is a land of wrenching extremes, a sunken trough in the earth's crust that reaches the lowest point in the Western Hemisphere. The park stretches 140 miles (225 km) and is guarded on two sides by some of the highest mountains on the continent. Its unique landscape includes delicate rock formations, polished canyons, and burning salt flats. Although always inhospitable, it is one of the most popular tourist destinations in California.

Dante's View, taking in jagged peaks and the entire valley floor

Exploring Death Valley National Park

Death Valley was once an insurmountable barrier to miners and emigrants. Today, it is accessible by car, and visitors can take short walks from the roads to spectacular viewpoints. The best time to visit is between October and April, when temperatures average 65° F (18° C). Avoid the period between May and September, when the ground temperatures can exceed a searing 100° F (38° C).

There is a surprising amount of plant life, and for a few weeks each year wild-flowers appear amid the rocks. An array of animals such as foxes and tortoises have evolved to survive in this harsh climate.

Furnace Creek, with its visitors' complex, is located in the heart of Death Valley. Millennia of winter floods have carved a gateway into the Valley through the eastern hills. The springs here are some of the desert's few freshwater sources and are thought to have saved the lives of hundreds of gold prospectors crossing the desert. Today, the same springs make Furnace Creek a desert oasis shaded by date palms. There are a variety of restaurants and motels, and the **Death Valley Museum and Visitor Center** has exhibits and slide shows explaining the area's natural and human history. In winter, ranger programs and guided walks are available. The world's lowest golf course, lying at 214 ft (65 m) below sea level, and the 1920s Furnace Creek Inn *(see p723)*, which runs bus tours in winter, are also located here.

On Hwy 190, close to the visitor center, the eerie ruins of the **Harmony Borax Works** can still be seen. Borax was discovered here in 1873, but mining did not begin until the 1880s, when crystallized borate compounds were taken to be purified. They were then loaded onto wagons and hauled 165 miles (265 km) to Mojave Station. Used for producing heat-resistant glass, borax is commonly used today as an ingredient in detergents. The Borax Museum has exhibits of mining tools and transport machinery used at the 19th-century refinery.

Salt Creek, lying near the Borax Museum, supports the hardy pupfish. Endemic to Death Valley, the pupfish can live in water almost four times as salty as the sea and can withstand temperatures of up to 111° F (44° C). The fish attract other wildlife, including great blue herons. Walk-ways allow visitors to explore this unique site.

Some of the Valley's most breathtaking natural features lie south of Furnace Creek. About 3 miles (5 km) south, on Hwy 178, a short hike leads into **Golden Canyon**. The mustard-colored walls after which the canyon was named, are best seen in the afternoon sun. Native Americans used the red clay at the mouth of the canyon for face paint. The layers of rock were originally horizontal, but geological activity has now tilted them to an angle of 45°. The roads are often in bad condition due to flash floods. **Zabriskie Point** offers great views of the mud hills of Golden Canyon. Made famous by Antonioni's eponymous 1960s film, the point was named after a general manager of the Valley's borax operations.

Dante's View lies 5,475 ft (1,650 m) above sea level at Death Valley's southern end. Its name was inspired by Dante's *Inferno*. The best time

Multicolored hills of the Artist's Palette

Salt formations at the Devil's Golf Course

VISITORS' CHECKLIST

**Death Valley Museum
& Visitor Center** Rte 190,
Furnace Creek. ☎ (760) 786-
2331. ☐ daily. ⬤ Jan 1,
Thanksgiving, Dec 25. ☒
Emergency For Park Rangers,
call up 911 or (760) 786-2331.
ⓦ www.nps.gov/deva

to see the view, which takes in the entire floor of Death's Valley, is in the morning.
Badwater, to the west, is the lowest point in the Western Hemisphere. It lies 282 ft (85 m) below sea level and is one of the world's hottest places. The air can reach 120° F (49° C), and as the ground temperature is 50 percent higher than the air temperature, it really is possible to fry an egg on the ground. The water here is not poisonous, but it is unpalatable, filled with sodium chloride and sulfates. In spite of the extreme conditions, Badwater is home to several species of insect and to the endangered Death Valley snail.

Devil's Golf Course is an expanse of salt pinnacles, located 12 miles (19 km) south of Furnace Creek, off Hwy 178. Until about 2,000 years ago, a succession of lakes covered the area. When the last lake evaporated, it left behind alternating layers of salt and gravel, some 1,000 ft (305 m) deep and covering 200 sq miles (520 sq km). The ground is 95 percent salt, and visitors can actually hear the salt expand and contract with the continual change of temperature. New salt crystals (identified by their whiter hue) continue to form. The multicolored hills known as the **Artist's Palette** are to the north. Created by mineral deposits and volcanic ash, their hues are at their most intense in the late afternoon.

Located northwest of the visitor center, the village of **Stovepipe Wells**, founded in 1926, was the valley's first

resort. According to legend, a lumberjack traveling west struck water here and stayed on. An old stovepipe, similar to the ones that were used to form the walls of wells, marks the site, which is the Valley's second-largest outpost.

A walk along the 14 sq miles (36 sq km) of undulating **Sand Dunes**, north of Stovepipe Wells, is one of the greatest experiences of Death Valley. Shifting winds blow the sand into the classic crescent dune shape. Mesquite trees dot the lower dunes. A variety of wildlife feeds on the seeds of these trees, such as kangaroo rats and lizards. Among the region's other, mainly nocturnal, creatures are animals that are as diverse

as the rattlesnake, the chuckwalla lizard, and the coyote.

Northern Death Valley has the 3,000-year-old **Ubehebe Crater**, where few tourists venture, despite the beauty of the landscape. This is only one of the dozen volcanic craters in the Mojave area; it is 900 yds (800 m) wide and 500 ft (150 m) deep.

East of the crater, lies the Moorish-style **Scotty's Castle**. It was commissioned by Albert Johnson at a cost of $2.4 million in 1922, and covers about 30,000 sq ft (2,800 sq m). "Death Valley Scotty," a friend of Johnson's, lived here until his death in 1948. In 1970 it was bought by the National Park Service which gives guided tours.

Scotty's Castle
Hwy 267. ☎ (760) 786-2392. **Castle**
☐ daily. ☒ ☑ **Grounds** ☐ daily.

DEATH VALLEY SCOTTY

Walter Scott, would-be miner, beloved charlatan, and sometime performer in Buffalo Bill's Wild West Show, liked to tell visitors that his wealth lay in a secret gold mine. That "mine" was, in fact, his friend Albert Johnson, a Chicago insurance executive, who paid for the castle where Scott lived and received visitors. Built in the 1920s by European craftsmen and Native American labor, the castle has a Moorish feel. Scott never owned the building, and Johnson paid all his bills. "He repays me in laughs," said Johnson. Although Johnson died in 1948, Scott was allowed to remain here until his death in 1954. The edifice is still known as Scotty's Castle.

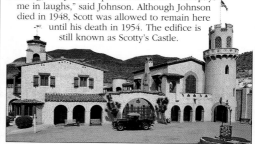

The grandiose, Moorish-style Scotty's Castle

Central Coast

CALIFORNIA'S SPANISH HERITAGE is highly visible in this pleasant coastal area. Several of the 21 missions, established by Franciscan friars in the 18th and early 19th centuries, are located here. These, as well as the Spanish Colonial capital at Monterey, preserve vestiges of the state's rich Colonial past. Besides historic sights, the rugged shoreline along the Pacific Ocean harbors beach resorts and large areas of natural beauty.

The 1929 Spanish Colonial-style County Courthouse, Santa Barbara

Santa Barbara ⑫

🚶 90,200. ✈ 🚆 209 State St. 🚌 1020 Chapala St. 🚢 34 W Carrillo. 🚢 Stearns Wharf. 🛈 12 E Carrillo St, (805) 965-3023. 📅 I Madonnari Italian Street Painting Festival (May); Fiesta (Aug).

SANTA BARBARA IS a Southern Californian rarity: a city with a single architectural style. Following a devastating earthquake in 1925, the entire center was rebuilt according to strict rules that dictated Mediterranean-style architecture. Santa Barbara is today a quiet administrative center with a sizable student population, which lends the city an informal flavor.

Often called the "Queen of the Missions," **Santa Barbara Mission** is the most visited in the state. The tenth mission built by the Spanish, it was founded in 1786 on the feast day of St. Barbara – four years after the colonists established a garrison here. The present structure took shape after the third adobe church on the site was destroyed by an earthquake in 1812. Its twin towers and the blend of Roman, Moorish, and Spanish

styles, were the inspiration for what came to be known as Mission Style. This is the only California mission that has been in continuous use since it was founded.

The beautifully landscaped Sacred Gardens were once a working area for Native Americans. The surrounding living quarters now display a rich collection of mission artifacts. The church's Classical façade was designed by Padre Antonio Ripoll, who was influenced by the Roman architect Vitruvius Pollio (around 27 BC). Its Neo-Classical interior has imitation marble columns, while the reredos has a painted canvas backdrop and carved wooden statues. The **County Courthouse** on Figueroa Street is still in use. In the Assembly Room are murals depicting California history. The **Museum of Art**, close by, has an outstanding collection that includes Asian and American

art, antiquities, and photographs. To its south is the **Lobero Theater**. This graceful 1924 structure stands on the site of the city's original theater. Farther east is the **Presidio**. Built in 1782, this was the last in a chain of four Spanish forts erected along the coast. Other sights include the **Paseo Nuevo**, a colorful outdoor shopping center, and the Historical Museum, housed in two adobe buildings. Among the many artifacts on display here is a statue of the 4th-century martyr St. Barbara.

🔒 **Santa Barbara Mission**
2201 Laguna St. 📞 (805) 682-4713. 🚌 22. ⏰ 9am–5pm daily. **Donation.** ♿ 🎁
🏛 **Museum of Art**
📞 (805) 963-4364. ⏰ Tue–Sun. 📷

Channel Islands National Park ⑬

🚉 Ventura. 🚌 ⛴ Island Packers, 1867 Spinnaker Dr, (805) 642-1393. **Visitor Center** (805) 658-5730. ⏰ daily.

THE UNPOPULATED volcanic islands of Santa Barbara, Anacapa, San Miguel, Santa Cruz, and Santa Rosa, together comprise the Channel Islands National Park. Access is strictly monitored by park rangers, who issue landing permits from the visitor center. Camping is allowed on all the islands, but visitors must book two weeks in advance. They must also bring their own food and water supplies, since none is available on any of the five islands.

Day trips to Anacapa Island, nearest the mainland, offer an insight into this unique coastal ecosystem. All the islands' rock pools are rich in marine life, and the surrounding kelp forests provide shelter for more than 1,000 plant and animal species. The islands' many sea caves make sea kayaking an exciting experi-

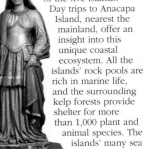

Statue of the 4th-century martyr St. Barbara

ence. The snorkeling and scuba diving here are considered to be among the best on the entire Pacific Coast.

Wildlife on these islands is plentiful and includes sea lions, elephant seals, cormorants, and gulls. Depending on the time of year, visitors can spot gray whales, dolphins, and California brown pelicans on the passage across the Santa Barbara Channel.

La Purísima Concepción Mission in Lompoc Valley

Lompoc Valley ⑭

☒ ▭ *Lompoc.* ℹ *111 S I St, Lompoc, (805 736-4567).*

ONE OF THE world's major producers of flower seed, Lompoc Valley is surrounded by hills and flower fields, and is a blaze of color between late spring and mid-summer each year. Marigolds, sweet peas, asters, lobelia, larkspur, nasturtiums, and cornflowers are just some of the varieties grown here. A map of the area's flower fields is distributed by Lompoc town's Chamber of Commerce. The Civic Center Plaza, between Ocean Avenue and C Street, has a display garden where all the varieties of flowers are labeled and identified.

California's 11th mission, **La Purísima Concepción**, located 3 miles (5 km) northeast of Lompoc, was declared a State Historic Park during the 1930s. The early 19th-century buildings have now been perfectly reconstructed, and the entire complex provides a real insight into the missionary way of life.

Visitors can view the priests' living quarters, furnished with authentic pieces in the elegant residence building. The simple, narrow church is decorated with colorful stencilwork. The adjacent workshops at one time produced cloth, candles, leather goods, and furniture for the mission.

The mission's gardens also have been faithfully restored. The numerous varieties of fruit, vegetables, and herbs that are now grown here were all common in the 19th century. Visitors can also view the system that provided the mission with water.

🏛 La Purísima Concepción Mission

2295 Purisima Rd, Lompoc. ☎ *(805) 733-3713.* ☐ *9am–5pm daily.* ● *Jan 1, Thanksgiving, Dec 25.* ⬛

San Luis Obispo ⑮

🏠 *43,000.* ☒ 🚃 ▭ ℹ *1037 Mill St, (805 541-8000).*

THIS SMALL CITY, situated in a valley in the Santa Lucia Mountains, developed around the **San Luis Obispo**

Mission de Tolosa, founded on September 1, 1772, by Father Junípero Serra *(see p692).* Fifth in the chain of 21 missions, and also one of the wealthiest, it is still in use as a parish church. Beside the church, the mission's museum displays Chumash Indian artifacts such as baskets, vessels, and jewelry, the padre's bed, and the mission's original altar.

In front of the church is Mission Plaza, a landscaped public square bisected by the tree-lined San Luis Creek. During the 1860s, bullfights and bear-baiting took place here; today it hosts many of the city's less bloody events.

Just west of the Plaza, is the Ah Louis Store. Founded in 1874 by a Chinese cook, and railroad laborer, it became the center of a then thriving Chinatown and served as a post office, bank, and store. The property is still owned by the Louis family, but it is now a gift shop.

🏛 San Luis Obispo Mission de Tolosa

751 Palm St. ☎ *(805) 781-8220.* ☐ *9am–5pm Mon–Fri.* ● *Jan 1, Easter, Thanksgiving, Dec 25.*

MISSION ARCHITECTURE

Santa Barbara Mission

The 21 missions established along El Camino Real were adaptations of Mexican Baroque architecture. Designed by friars, these provincial versions were built of adobe bricks and wood by unskilled Native Americans. Over the years they decayed or were shaken by earthquakes, but many have been carefully restored. Distinctive features include massive walls covered with white lime cement, small window openings, rounded gables, and tiered bell towers. The early 20th-century Mission Revival style is a more elegant version of the original. Today, most missions offer public tours.

Hearst Castle™ ⓰

Tile detail

Perched on a hill above the village of San Simeon, Hearst Castle™ was the private playground and museum of media tycoon William Randolph Hearst. One of California's top tourist attractions, its three guest houses are superb buildings in their own right, but the highlight of the tour is the twin-towered Casa Grande (the "Big House"). Designed by the Paris-trained architect Julia Morgan and built in stages from 1922 to 1947, its 115 rooms hold numerous artworks and epitomize the glamor of the 1930s and 40s.

Casa Grande
Casa Grande's "poured concrete" façade is in the Mediterranean Revival style. It is embellished with ancient architectural fragments.

The Theater, the walls of which are lined with damask, has 50 seats. The lamps inside are held by gilded caryatids.

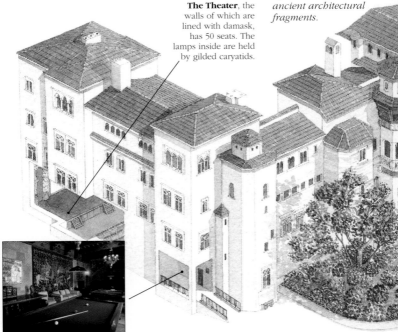

★ **Billiard Room**
This room features an early 16th-century millefleurs tapestry of a stag hunt.

STAR FEATURES

* ★ The Assembly Room
* ★ Billiard Room
* ★ Gothic Study
* ★ Refectory

WILLIAM RANDOLPH HEARST

The son of a multimillionaire, W.R. Hearst (1863–1951) was an ebullient personality who made his own fortune in magazine and newspaper publishing. He married Millicent Willson, an entertainer from New York, in 1903. On his mother's death in 1919, Hearst inherited the San Simeon property. He began to build the castle and grounds as a tribute to his mother, and then lived there with his mistress, the actress Marion Davies. The couple entertained royally at San Simeon over the next 20 years. When Hearst suffered problems with his heart in 1947, he moved to a house in Beverly Hills, where he died in 1951.

Portrait of Hearst, age 31

★ **Gothic Study**
Hearst ran his media empire from the Gothic Study. His most prized books and manuscripts were kept behind grilles.

Main entrance

★ **The Assembly Room**
features a 16th-century French fireplace. Italian choir stalls line the walls, which are hung with Flemish tapestries.

★ **Refectory**
Tapestries and choir stalls cover the walls of the massive dining hall. Its long, medieval table has cathedral seats and is decorated with silver candlesticks.

VISITORS' CHECKLIST

750 Hearst Castle Rd. 📞 (805) 927-2020, (800) 444-4445. 🚌
🕐 8am–4pm daily. 🚫 Jan 1, Thanksgiving, Dec 25. 📷 ♿ call ahead. 🎫 🚶 obligatory.
🌐 www.hearstcastle.org

Exploring Hearst Castle
Visitors must take one of the four guided tours, of which Tour One is best for first-timers. In spring and autumn, evening tours feature actors or "guests" in 1930s costume.

La Casa Grande was built from reinforced concrete to withstand California's earthquakes. This gilded playhouse for Hearst's many famous guests has scores of bedrooms, an Assembly Room, a Billiard Room, two pools, and a theater, where up to 50 guests could watch film premieres. Hearst himself lived in the sumptuous, third-floor Gothic Suite. The exquisite heated indoor **Roman Pool** was entirely covered with mosaics of hammered gold and Venetian glass.

The magnate transformed the California hillside into a veritable Garden of Eden, laying 127 acres (51 ha) of gardens. Fan palms, Italian cypresses, and huge 200-year-old oaks were hauled up at great expense. Five greenhouses and 4,000 fruit trees supplied plants and fruit. Ancient and modern statues were collected to adorn the terraces. Among the finest are four statues of Sekhmet, the Egyptian goddess of war, dating from 1350 to 1200 BC. The 104-ft (32-m) white marble **Neptune Pool** is flanked by colonnades and the façade of a reproduction Greek temple.

A great lover of the outdoors, Hearst had a covered bridlepath built, so that he could ride in all weather. There was also a private zoo on Camp Hill that once had lions, bears, elephants, leopards, and pumas. Zebras, giraffes, ostriches, and even a baby elephant were free to wander the grounds. The three guesthouses – Casa del Mar, Casa del Sol, and Casa del Monte – are luxurious mansions in their own right.

Big Sur ⓱

CALIFORNIA'S WILDEST LENGTH of coastline was named El Pais Grande del Sur, the "Big Country to the South," by Spanish colonists at Carmel *(see p692)* in the late 18th century, and since then, Big Sur has been attracting hyperbole. The novelist Robert Louis Stevenson called it "the greatest meeting of land and sea in the world," and the 100 miles (160 km) of breathtaking mountains, cliffs, and rocky coves still leave visitors groping for adjectives.

The scenic Highway 1 was constructed across this rugged landscape during the 1930s, but otherwise Big Sur has been preserved in its natural state. There are no large towns and very few signs of civilization in the area. Most of the shore is protected in a series of state parks that offer dense forests, broad rivers, and crashing surf, all easily accessible within a short distance of the road.

Crashing surf and rocky cliffs, typical of the Big Sur coastline

Point Lobos State Reserve
This is the habitat of the Monterey cypress, the only tree to survive the region's mixture of fog and salt spray. Its branches are shaped by the strong sea winds.

Point Sur Lighthouse sits atop a volcanic cone. It was manned until 1974 but is now automated.

Bixby Creek Bridge
This picturesque arched bridge was built in 1932. For many years it was the world's largest single-arch span, standing 260 ft (79 m) tall and 700 ft (213 m) long. Hwy 1 was named the state's first scenic highway here in 1966.

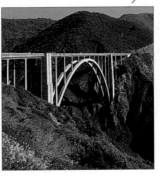

Nepenthe is a lovely resort hidden from the road by oak trees. It has long been frequented by Hollywood movie stars.

KEY

▬▬	Minor road
▬	Scenic route
- -	Hiking trail
▬	National park boundary
🌿	River or lake
Ⓐ	Camping
🔆	Viewpoint

Andrew Molera State Park
Opened in 1972, this park includes 10 miles (16 km) of hiking trails and 2.5 miles (4 km) of quiet, sandy beach.

Julia Pfeiffer Burns State Park
A tunnel under Hwy 1, accessible only on foot, leads to a 100-ft (30-m) high bluff, from which the McWay Creek waterfall spills into the Pacific Ocean.

VISITORS' CHECKLIST

1,500. Nepenthe Park.
(831) 667-2100.

Ventana Wilderness
Many of the steep ridges of this beautiful wilderness, a part of the Los Padres National Forest, are accessible only to experienced hikers. Campsites cover the lower reaches.

The Esalen Institute was set up in the 1960s to hold New Age seminars. Its hot springs were first frequented by Native Americans and still attract visitors.

VENTANA WILDERNESS

Tassajara Creek

ge Rd

Big Creek

LOS PADRES NATIONAL FOREST

Lucia

Nacimiento Fergusson Rd

Plaskett

Los Burros Rd

Plaskett Creek

Antonio River

Lake San Antonio

Nacimiento River

Lake Nacimiento

Alder Creek

San Simeon Point is a natural harbor that was used by William Randolph Hearst to ship in materials for his estate, Hearst Castle™, located on the inland hilltop (see pp688–9).

Jade Cove
This beautiful cove can be reached only by way of a steep path down the cliff face. The removal of jade above the high tide level is prohibited.

0 km 10
0 miles 10

San Simeon

The beautiful Gothic arch of the main altar, Carmel Mission

Carmel ⑱

🏃 24,000. 🚌 Monterey-Salinas Transit (MST), (831) 899-2555. 🛈 137 Crossroads Blvd, (831) 626-1424. 🎭 Carmel Bach Festival, Monterey (Sep–Mar). ⓦ www.carmelmission.org

THIS WEALTHY RESORT, with its art galleries and shops, has one of the area's most spectacular beaches. Among the town's many cultural events is a Bach Festival.

A short drive from town is the **Carmel Mission**, founded in 1770 by the father of California's mission chain, Junípero Serra. The most important of the 21 missions, it served as the administrative center for the state's northern missions. Father Serra, who lived here until his death in 1784, is buried at the foot of the altar. The sarcophagus, one of the finest in the US, depicts Father Serra recumbent in death, surrounded by three mourning priests.

Carmel Mission was abandoned in 1834, and restoration work began in 1924, following the original plans. It now functions as a Catholic church. Its beautiful altar, with a Gothic arch and ornate decoration, is the only one of its kind among the 21 missions in California. The reconstructed living quarters evoke 18th-century mission life; the kitchen still has its original oven from Mexico.

🔒 **Carmel Mission**
3080 Rio Rd, Carmel. 🄲 (831) 624-3600. 🄾 daily upto 4:30pm. ● Thanksgiving, Dec 25. 🖼 🕭 🅿

Monterey ⑲

🏃 35,000. ✈ 🚌 Tyler, Pearl & Munras Sts, (831) 899-2555. 🛈 401 Camino el Estero, (831) 648-5350. 🎭 Monterey Blues Festival (Jul); Monterey Jazz Festival (Sep); Laguna Seca Races (May–Oct).

THE NAVIGATOR Sebastián Vizcaíno landed here in 1602 and named the bay after his patron, the Count of Monterrey. But it was not until the Spanish captain Gaspar de Portolá and Father Serra arrived in 1770, establishing a church and presidio, that Monterey grew into a pueblo. It served as the Spanish Colonial capital of California until the Gold Rush of 1848, when it lost its status to San Francisco.

Monterey still retains its unique character as a fishing port and market town. Today, visitors come to tour its carefully restored historic sites and attend the famous annual jazz festival in September.

In the center of town, a cluster of old buildings form the Monterey State Historic Park. The stately **Colton Hall** was where the California State Constitution was first signed in 1849. It now houses a museum commemorating the event. A short distance to the north, **Larkin House** was built in 1837 by an East Coast merchant, Thomas Larkin. Its architectural style, with two stories of adobe brick, wooden porticoes, and symmetry of plan and elevation, has become representative of the Monterey style. Farther east, **Stevenson House** is where Robert Louis Stevenson lived in 1879. It is now a museum. The Royal Presidio Chapel on Church Street was built in 1794 and is the town's oldest building. To the north are the Old Whaling Station, where mementos of the whaling industry are displayed, and the Custom House, preserved as it was in the 1830s and 40s.

Street sign in Cannery Row

Close by, **Fisherman's Wharf**, once the center of the fishing and whaling industries, is now well known for its seafood restaurants.

Cannery Row, a six-block harbor-front street celebrated by John Steinbeck in his ribald novels *Cannery Row* and *Sweet Thursday*, was once the site of more than 20 fish-packing plants that processed fresh sardines. The canneries thrived in the early 20th century. In 1945 the sardines disappeared, and the canneries were abandoned. The buildings that remain house a collection of eletic restaurants and shops. One notable building, at No. 800, is the old laboratory of "Doc" Ricketts, noted marine biologist, beer drinker, and Steinbeck's best friend. It is now a private club.

The **Monterey Bay Aquarium**, at the end of

THE 17-MILE DRIVE

The Monterey Peninsula has a spectacular coastline, best explored via a toll road, the 17-Mile Drive. The road offers superb views of crashing surf, coastal flora, and the Del Monte Forest. The drive begins at Spanish Bay, a popular picnicking area at the edge of Pacific Grove. Sights include the Carmel Mission; the striking Tor House, built in rock by the poet Robinson Jeffers; Lone Cypress, perhaps the most photographed tree in the world; and Spyglass Hill, a golf course named after a site in Robert Louis Stevenson's novel, *Treasure Island*. Among the other attractions are the exclusive country clubs and championship golf courses.

Spanish Bay, a picnicking area

Cannery Row, is the largest in the US, More than 570 species and 350,000 specimens portray Monterey Bay's rich marine environment. Among the exhibits are an enclosed kelp forest, a rock pool, and a display of live jellyfish. The Outer Bay Wing has a one million-gallon (4.5 million-liter) tank, which re-creates the conditions of the ocean. It contains yellowfin tuna, ocean sunfish, and barracuda. The Research Institute offers visitors a chance to watch marine scientists at work, while the Splash Zone is a hands-on aquarium for kids.

The wealthy resort of **Pacific Grove**, at the end of the peninsula, was originally founded in 1889 as a religious retreat. Today, it is best known for its quaint wooden houses, many now converted into inns, coastal parks, and the beautiful migratory monarch butterflies that arrive between October and April.

➤ **Monterey Bay Aquarium**
886 Cannery Row. 🛈 *(831) 648-4888.* ⭕ *daily.* 🌑 *Dec 25.* 🈂️
🇼 *www.montereybayaquarium.org*

Santa Cruz ⑳

🏠 *252,000.* 🚉 🚌 *920 Pacific Ave.* 🛈 *701 Front St, (831) 425-1234.* 🎏 *Santa Cruz Fungus Fair (Jan); Clam Chowder Cook-Off (Feb).*

Perched at the northern tip of Monterey Bay, Santa Cruz is a lively beach town, backed by densely forested mountains. Surrounded by farmland, it evokes an agri-cultural rather than suburban feel. The town's cosmopolitan character is due to the pres-ence of the large University of California campus, with its students and professors from all over the world.

Much of the downtown area was badly damaged by the Loma Prieta earthquake in 1989. It has recovered since then, and many good book-stores, art galleries, and cafés now line the streets.

The town's highlight is the waterfront, particularly the **Santa Cruz Beach Board-walk**, the last surviving old-

Eroded archway at the Natural Bridges State Park, Santa Cruz

style amusement park on the West Coast. Its main attraction is the Giant Dipper roller coaster, built by Arthur Looff in 1924 and now a National Historic Landmark. The car travels along the 1-mile (1.6-km) wooden track at 55 mph (88 km/h). The carousel near-by has horses and chariots hand-carved by Looff's father, craftsman Charles Looff, in 1911. The ride is accompan-ied by a 100-year-old pipe organ. The park also has 27 other modern rides and an Art Deco dance hall.

The **Museum of Art and History at the McPherson Center**, on Front Street, is a 20,000 sq ft (1,858 sq m) cul-tural center, which opened in 1993. The Art Gallery shows works primarily by local north central artists, while the History Gallery displays vari-ous aspects of Santa Cruz County's past.

Standing on a hill to the northeast of town is a replica of the **Mission Santa Cruz**, founded in 1791. All traces of the original were destroyed by frequent earthquakes, and the present structure was built in 1931. It now houses a small museum.

The scenic Cliff Drive along the coast takes in the **Natural Bridges State Beach**, named for the archways that were carved into the cliffs by ocean waves. One of the original arches still remains, through which waves roll into a small sandy cove. The park also preserves a eucalyptus grove and a nature trail, which shows the stages in the life cycle of the monarch butter-fly. Also along the coast is the Surfing Museum, housed in a lighthouse. The museum has artifacts from every era of Santa Cruz surfing history. Surfboards range from 1930s redwood planks to today's high-tech laminates.

East of downtown, Mystery Spot is a redwood grove, which has been drawing visitors for decades due to various strange events here. Balls roll uphill, parallel lines converge, and the laws of physics seem to be suspend-ed. Part tourist trap, part genuine oddity, this attraction has to be seen to be believed.

🎟️ **Santa Cruz Beach Boardwalk**
400 Beach St. 🛈 *(831) 423-5590.* ⭕ *call ahead for opening times.*

SURFING IN CALIFORNIA

Surfing was originally practiced by the Hawaiian nobility as a religious ceremony; it was introduced to California by Hawaiian George Freeth in 1907. The sport evolved into a truly California pursuit with the Beach Boys' hit song "Surfin" in 1961. Films such as *Ride the Wild Surf* (1964), and *Beach Blanket Bingo* (1965) helped to establish its cultural allure, and beach parties in the style of these films were highly popular in the 1960s. Today, surf culture determines fashion as well as speech.

Surfers on fiberglass boards

San Francisco ㉑

SAN FRANCISCO IS, after New York, the second most densely populated city in the US, with 750,000 people crowded into 47 sq miles (122 sq km). It is located at the tip of a peninsula, with the Pacific Ocean to the west and San Francisco Bay to the east. To the north, Golden Gate Bridge links it to the Marin Headlands. The Greater San Francisco area includes the cities of Oakland and Berkeley. San Francisco is a compact city, and most of the area can be explored on foot. The estimated 43 hills give many of the streets near impossible gradients but offer superb views.

A panoramic view of San Francisco from a penthouse bar on Nob Hill

KEY

▦	Sight/Place of interest
✈	Airport
🚋	Cable car terminal
🚉	Streetcar station
🚇	BART station
⛴	Ferry terminal
ℹ	Tourist information
P	Parking
✝	Church
✡	Synagogue
═	Freeway

GETTING AROUND

The Municipal Railway (Muni) runs San Francisco's public transportation system. Visitors can use one pass – the Muni Passport – to travel on buses, Metro streetcars (electric trams), and the three cable car lines. Buses and streetcars serve all areas, while the high-speed BART (Bay Area Rapid Transit) rail system links the suburbs and outlying regions. Taxis are advised for traveling at night. Ferries run regularly east and north across the bay.

0 meters 750
0 yards 750

SIGHTS AT A GLANCE

Financial District ①
Wells Fargo History Museum ②
Yerba Buena Center
  for the Arts ③
San Francisco Museum of
  Modern Art ④
Union Square ⑤
Chinatown ⑥
Nob Hill p701 ⑦
Fisherman's Wharf ⑧
North Beach ⑨
Alcatraz Island p703 ⑩
Pacific Heights ⑪

Asian Art Museum ⑫
Mission Dolores p705 ⑬
Haight Ashbury ⑭
California Academy of
  Sciences ⑮
MH de Young Memorial
  Museum ⑯
California Palace of the Legion
  of Honor ⑰
The Presidio ⑱
Golden Gate Bridge ⑲

Greater San Francisco
(see inset map)

San Jose ⑳
Palo Alto ㉑
Oakland ㉒
Berkeley ㉓
Sausalito ㉔
Muir Woods ㉕

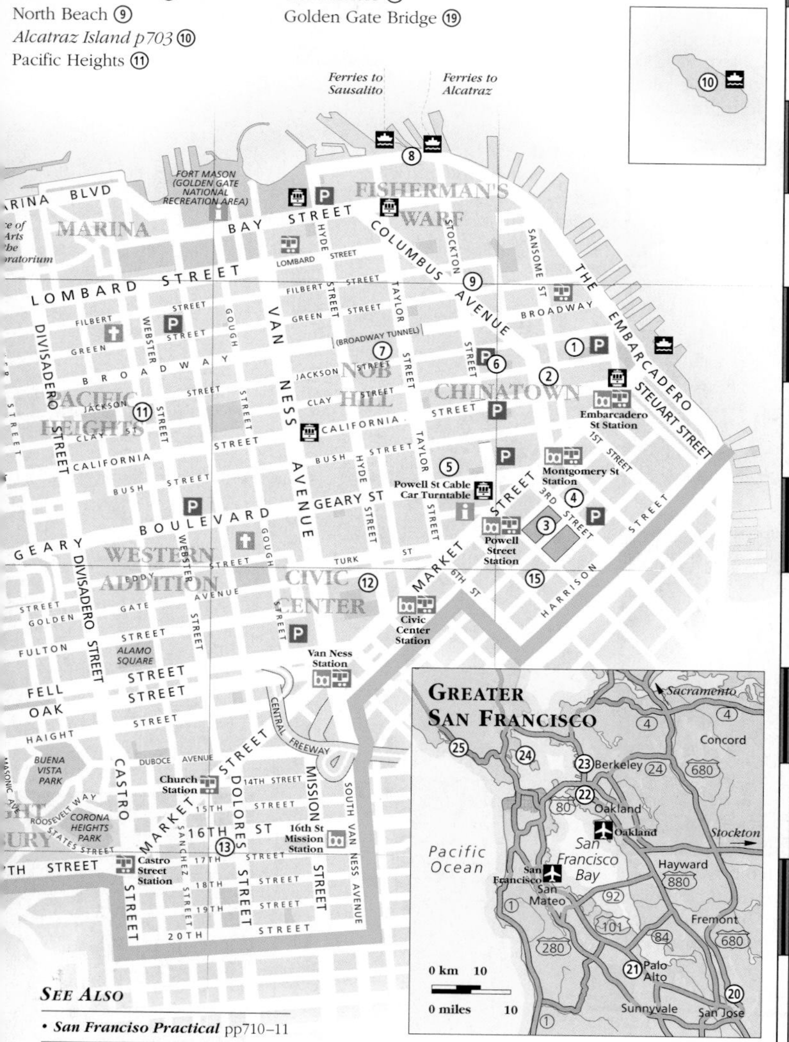

Ferries to
Sausalito

Ferries to
Alcatraz

FORT MASON
(GOLDEN GATE
NATIONAL
RECREATION AREA)

MARINA BLVD

MARINA

ARINA BLVD

e of
Arts
e
oratorium

BAY STREET

FISHERMAN'S
WHARF

LOMBARD STREET

FILBERT STREET

LOMBARD STREET

DIVISADERO STREET

WEBSTER STREET

GREEN

FILBERT STREET

GOUGH STREET

VAN NESS AVENUE

HYDE STREET

GREEN STREET

TAYLOR STREET

STOCKTON STREET

COLUMBUS AVENUE

BROADWAY

SANSOME ST

BROADWAY

THE EMBARCADERO

PACIFIC HEIGHTS ⑪

BROADWAY

JACKSON STREET

CLAY STREET

[BROADWAY TUNNEL]

NOB
HILL ⑦

CHINATOWN

STEUART STREET

CLAY STREET

CALIFORNIA STREET

CALIFORNIA

Embarcadero
St Station

CALIFORNIA STREET

BUSH STREET

TAYLOR STREET

HYDE ST

STREET

Montgomery St
Station

GEARY STREET

GEARY ST

Powell St Cable
Car Turntable

MARKET STREET

1ST STREET

2ND STREET

3RD STREET

Powell
Street Station

Montgomery St
Station ④

WESTERN
ADDITION

BOULEVARD

GEARY

DIVISADERO STREET

GOUGH STREET

TURK ST

ST

CIVIC
CENTER ⑫

HARRISON

GOLDEN GATE AVENUE

FULTON STREET

ALAMO
SQUARE

STREET

Civic
Center
Station

FELL STREET

OAK STREET

Van Ness
Station

HAIGHT STREET

CENTRAL FREEWAY

DUBOCE AVENUE

BUENA
VISTA
PARK

Church
Station

14TH STREET

MISSION STREET

DOLORES STREET

SOUTH VAN NESS AVENUE

VAN NESS AVENUE

ROOSEVELT WAY

STATES STREET

CORONA
HEIGHTS
PARK

16TH ST

15TH

16TH STREET ⑬

16th St
Mission
Station

MASONIC AVE

CASTRO STREET

SANCHEZ STREET

DOLORES STREET

Castro
Street
Station

17TH

18TH STREET

19TH STREET

20TH STREET

URY

STREET

SEE ALSO

• *San Francisco Practical* pp710–11

• *Where to Stay* p724

• *Where to Eat* pp728–9

GREATER
SAN FRANCISCO

Sacramento

4

Concord

4

680

Berkeley ㉓

24

25

㉔

80

Oakland ㉒

Oakland

Stockton

Pacific
Ocean

San
Francisco
Bay

San
Francisco

San
Mateo

92

Hayward

880

101

Fremont

680

280

㉑ Palo
Alto

Sunnyvale

San Jose ⑳

1

0 km   10

0 miles   10

KEY

Area of main map

D   E   F

1
2
3
4
5

The 49-Mile Scenic Drive

Official sign

LINKING THE CITY'S most intriguing neighborhoods, fascinating sights, and spectacular views, the 49-Mile Scenic Drive (79 km) provides a splendid overview of San Francisco. Keeping to the well-marked route is easy: just follow the blue-and-white seagull signs. Some of these are hidden by overhanging vegetation, so you need to be alert. Set aside a whole day for this trip; there are plenty of places to stop to take photographs or admire the views.

The Palace of Fine Arts & the Exploratorium (24)
The grand Neo-Classical building and its modern science museum stand near the entrance to the Presidio.

Stow Lake (5)
There is a waterfall and a Chinese pavilion on the island in this picturesque lake, where you can also rent boats.

Sutro Tower (8)
This distinctive orange-and-white tower is visible from all over the city.

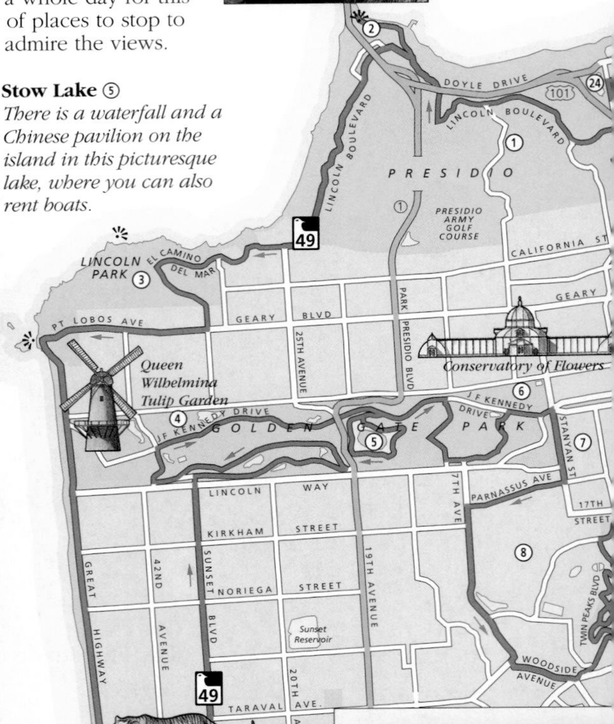

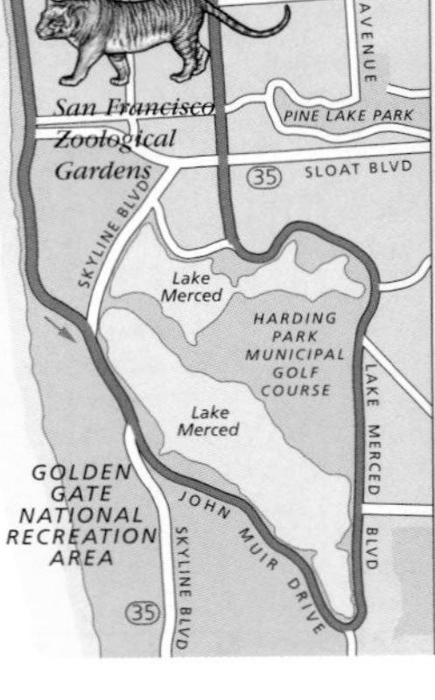

0 km 2

0 miles 1

KEY

— 49-Mile Scenic Drive

✳ Viewpoint

Five-tiered pagoda in Japantown

Coit Tower ⑳
Overlooking North Beach, Telegraph Hill is topped by this tower, which has fine murals and an observation deck.

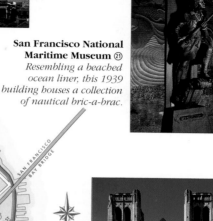

San Francisco National Maritime Museum ㉑
Resembling a beached ocean liner, this 1939 building houses a collection of nautical bric-a-brac.

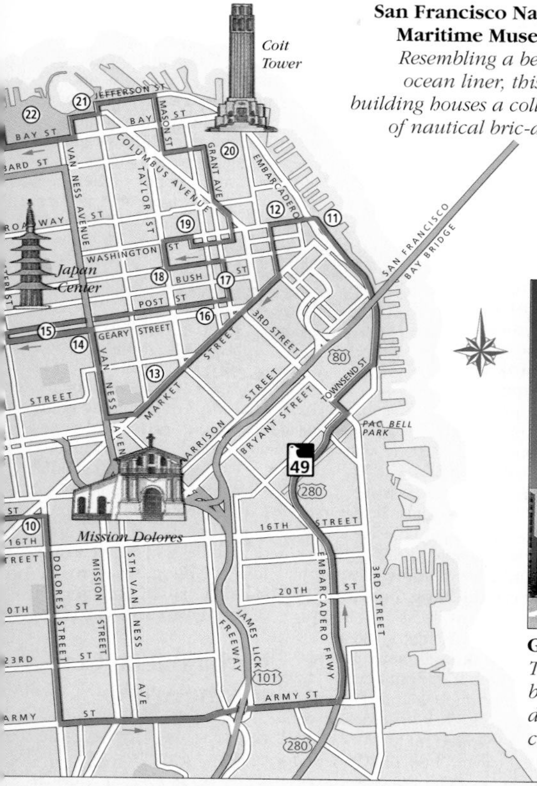

Grace Cathedral ⑱
This impressive cathedral, based on Notre Dame in Paris, dominates the summit of the city's steepest hill, Nob Hill.

Tips for Drivers

Starting point: *Anywhere. The circuit is designed to be followed in a counterclockwise direction starting and ending at any point.*
When to go: *Avoid driving during rush hours: 7–9am, 4–7pm. Most of the views are as spectacular by night as by day.*
Parking: *Use the parking lots that are located around the Financial District, the Civic Center, Japantown, Nob Hill, Chinatown, North Beach, and Fisherman's Wharf. Elsewhere, street parking is usually easily available.*

Finding the Sights

① Presidio *p707*
② Fort Point *p707*
③ California Palace of the Legion of Honor *p706*
④ Queen Wilhelmina Tulip Garden
⑤ Stow Lake
⑥ Conservatory of Flowers
⑦ Haight Street
⑧ Sutro Tower
⑨ Twin Peaks
⑩ Mission Dolores *p705*
⑪ Ferry Building *p698*
⑫ Embarcadero Center *p698*
⑬ Civic Center
⑭ St. Mary's Cathedral
⑮ Japan Center
⑯ Union Square *p699*
⑰ Chinatown Gateway *p700*
⑱ Grace Cathedral *p701*
⑲ Cable Car Barn *p701*
⑳ Coit Tower *p702*
㉑ San Francisco National Maritime Museum *p702*
㉒ Fort Mason
㉓ Marina Green
㉔ Palace of Fine Arts and the Exploratorium *p704*

Transamerica Pyramid, the tallest building on the city's skyline

Financial District ①

Map F3. *Between Washington & Market Sts.* 🚌 *1, 12, 15, 32, 42, 83.* 🚊 *F, J, K, L, M, N.* 🚋 *California St.* **Embarcadero Center** 🚌 *1, 32, 42.* 🚊 *J, K, L, M, N.* 🚋 *California St.*

S̲AN FRANCISCO'S economic engine is fueled by the Financial District, lying at the heart of downtown. The district stretches from the imposing skyscrapers and plazas of the **Embarcadero Center** to staid Montgomery Street, called the "Wall Street of the West." All the main banks, brokers, and law offices are located here.

Completed in 1981 after a decade of construction, the vast Embarcadero Center stretches from Justin Herman Plaza to Battery Street and houses a large number of commercial outlets and offices. A shopping arcade occupies the first three tiers of its four high-rise towers. The splendid foyer of the Hyatt Regency Hotel, located here, has a 17-story atrium.

North of Washington Street, the **Jackson Square Historical District** was once the heart of the business community. Renovated in the early 1950s, this area contains brick, cast-iron, and granite façades dating from Gold Rush days. From 1850 to 1910 it was known as the Barbary Coast, notorious for its brothels and squalor. Today, the buildings are used as showrooms, law offices, and

antique shops; some of the best ones can be seen in Jackson and Montgomery Streets.

Standing adjacent is a soaring San Francisco landmark, the **Transamerica Pyramid**. Capped with a spire on top of its 48 stories, it reaches 853 ft (260 m) and is the tallest building in the city. Its 3,678 windows take cleaners an entire month to wash. Designed by William Pereira, the building stands on what was earlier the site of the historic Montgomery Block, which contained many important offices. Numerous artists and writers took up residence in the block, including the writer Mark Twain, who often visited the Exchange Saloon, located in the building's basement. Farther south, the granite **Bank of America** was originally the Bank of Italy, founded by A.P. Giannini in San Jose. Its 52 floors make it one of the city's tallest skyscrapers, with incredible views from the top. At the district's northeastern corner lies the **Ferry Building**, built in 1903. In the early 1930s, over 50 million passengers a year passed through here, to and from the transcontinental railroad in Oakland or homes across the bay. Its clock tower was inspired by the Moorish bell tower of Seville Cathedral in Spain. With the opening of the Bay Bridge in 1936, it began to deteriorate. A few ferries still cross to Tiburon, Sausalito, and Oakland. On the building's east side stands the Gandhi Monument (1988). Designed by K.B. Patel and sculpted by Z. Pounov and S. Lowe, it bears an inscription of Gandhi's words.

🏛 **Transamerica Pyramid**
600 Montgomery St. ◯ *8:30am–4:30pm Mon–Fri.* ● *public hols.* ♿
🏛 **Bank of America**
555 California St. 🔵 *(415) 433-7500 (Camelian Room).*
🆆 *www.camelianroom.com*

Wells Fargo History Museum ②

Map F3. *420 Montgomery St.* 🔵 *(415) 396-2619.* 🚌 *1, 12, 15, 42.* 🚊 *Montgomery St.* ◯ *9am–5pm Mon–Fri.* ● *public hols.* ♿ 🅿
🆆 *www.wellsfargohistory.com*

F̲OUNDED IN 1852, Wells Fargo & Co. became the greatest banking and transportation company in the West. The company moved people, goods, gold, and mail. The Pony Express was one of their mail ventures. The museum displays splendid stagecoaches – famous for the legendary stories of their heroic drivers and the bandits who robbed them. The best known bandit was Black Bart, who left poems at the scene of his crimes. He was later identified as the mining engineer Charles Boles. Exhibits include a simulated stagecoach ride, Pony Express mail, photographs, gold nuggets, and the imperial currency of the eccentric Joshua Norton, who proclaimed himself Emperor of the United States in 1854.

A splendid old stagecoach at the Wells Fargo Museum

Yerba Buena Center for the Arts ③

Map F3. *Mission, 3rd, Folsom & 4th Sts.* 🔵 *(415) 978-2787.* 🚌 *9, 14, 15, 30, 45, 76.* 🚊 *J, K, L, M, N.* **Center for the Arts Galleries & Forum** ◯ *11am–5pm Tue–Sun (until 8pm first Thu of month).* ● *public hols.* 📷 *(free first Thu of month).* 🚫 ♿ 🅿 🏛 **Zeum** 🛈 *(415) 777-2800.* ◯ *11am–5pm Sat & Sun.* ● *Dec 25.* 📷 ♿ 🅿 *open 11am–5:30pm daily.*
🆆 *www.yerbabuenaarts.org*

T̲HE CONSTRUCTION of the underground Moscone Center, San Francisco's largest venue for conventions, heralded the beginning of ambitious plans for Yerba Buena Gardens, now the Yerba Buena Center for the Arts. New housing, hotels,

Esplanade Gardens in the Yerba Buena Center for the Arts

museums, and shops have sprung up. The center is situated at the heart of SoMa (South of Market), an area that has become the city's "artists' quarter," with its warehouses-turned-studios, bars, and avant-garde theaters. The **Esplanade Gardens** give visitors a chance to wander along paths or relax on benches. Close by, the Martin Luther King Jr. Memorial has words of peace in several languages. The adjacent **Center for the Arts Galleries and Forum** have visual arts galleries and a screening room featuring contemporary art and films. The **Center for the Arts Theater** presents performing arts that reflect the cultural diversity of the city in a 755-seat indoor theater. **Zeum**, located at the Yerba Buena Rooftop, has an ongoing program of events and provides opportunities for youngsters and artists to collaborate in the design and creation of anything from robots to sculptures.

San Francisco Museum of Modern Art [4]

Map F3. 151 Third St. ☎ *(415) 357-4000.* 🚌 *5, 9, 12, 14, 15, 30, 38, 45.* 🚇 *J, K, L, M, N.* 🕐 *11am–9pm Thu, 11am–6pm Fri–Tue. Times may change, please call to confirm.* ● *Wed, Jan 1, Thanksgiving, Dec 25.* 💲 *(free first Tue of month; half-price admission Thu 6–9pm).* ♿ 🛍 [W] www.sfmoma.org

THIS DRAMATIC museum forms the nucleus of San Francisco's reputation as a leading center of modern art. Created in 1935 with the aim of displaying works by 20th-century artists, it moved into its new quarters in 1995. The focus of Swiss architect Mario Botta's Modernist building is the 125-ft (38-m) cylindrical skylight, which channels light down to the first floor atrium court. More than 17,000 works of art are housed in its 50,000 sq ft (4,600 sq m) of gallery space, and it offers a dynamic schedule of changing exhibits from around the world.

The galleries display paintings, sculptures, architecture, design, photography, and media art. Among the highlights are works by Dali, Matisse, and Picasso; Diego Rivera's mural *The Flower Carrier*, a powerful irony on the human cost of luxury, painted in oil and tempera on Masonite in 1935; and Richard Shaw's sculpted figure *Melodius Double Stop* in the California Art section.

Union Square [5]

Map E3. 🚌 *2, 3, 4, 30, 38, 45.* 🚇 *J, K, L, M, N.* 🚡 *Powell–Mason, Powell–Hyde.*

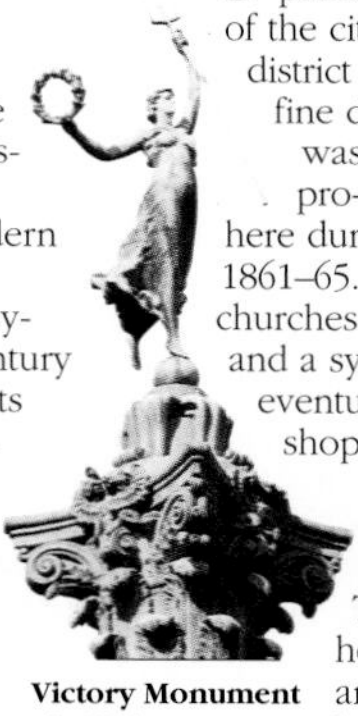

Victory Monument in Union Square

UNION SQUARE, lined with palm trees, is at the heart of the city's main shopping district and has a wealth of fine department stores. It was named after the pro-Union rallies held here during the Civil War of 1861–65. The original churches, gentlemen's clubs, and a synagogue were eventually overtaken by shops and offices. Some of the main stores include Macy's, Saks, and Gump's. The area also houses many antiquarian bookshops and smaller boutiques. Union Square marks the edge of the **Theater District** and is bordered on the west side by the luxurious Westin St. Francis Hotel. At the center of the square there is a bronze statue of the Goddess of Victory, sculpted by Robert Aitken in 1903 to commemorate Admiral Dewey's victory during the Spanish–American War (1898). The **Circle Gallery Building** at 140 Maiden Lane is an art gallery designed by Frank Lloyd Wright. It was the precursor to his Guggenheim Museum in New York *(see p82)*.

CALIFORNIA'S EARTHQUAKES

The San Andreas Fault extends some 600 miles (965 km) along California's coastline and is one of the few sites on Earth where an active plate boundary occurs on land. Each year, the Pacific Plate moves 1–1.6 inches (2.5–4 cm). The terrible fire of 1906 that destroyed San Francisco was caused by an earthquake estimated at 7.8 on the Richter Scale. More recently, the earthquake of October 1989, south of San Francisco, killed 62 people and caused at least $6 billion worth of damage. In 1994, the Northridge quake, magnitude 6.7, rocked Los Angeles. Scientists predict that the next major earthquake, the "Big One," will hit Southern California.

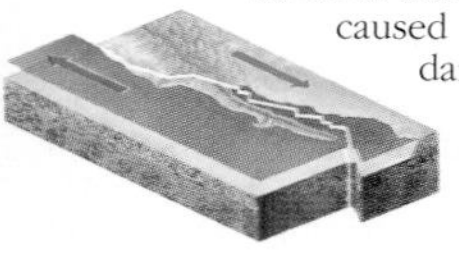

The San Andreas Fault

Colorful oriental architecture along Grant Avenue, Chinatown

Chinatown ⑥

Map F3. 🚋 *1, 2, 3, 4, 15, 30, 45.*
🚃 *all three lines go to Chinatown.*

An estimated 25,000 Chinese migrants settled in the plaza on Stockton Street during the Gold Rush era of the 1850s *(see p654)*. Today, the district evokes the atmosphere of a bustling southern Chinese town, although the architecture and customs are distinctly American hybrids on a Cantonese theme. This densely populated neighborhood has been called the "Gilded Ghetto," because its colorful façades screen a harsher world of sweatshops and cramped living quarters. Cable cars run down two sides of the district.

The ornate Chinatown Gateway, marking the southern entrance to Chinatown, was designed by Clayton Lee as an arch over the start of the main tourist street, **Grant Avenue**. The three-arched structure was inspired by the ceremonial entrances of traditional Chinese villages. It is capped with green roof tiles and a host of propitiatory animals in glazed ceramic.

Dragon lampposts, upturned roofs, and stores selling everything from kites and cooking utensils to antiques, embroidered silks, and gems line Grant Avenue. Most of the buildings were erected after the 1906 earth-

quake in an Oriental Renaissance style. In the 1830s and 40s it was the main thoroughfare of Yerba Buena, the village that preceded San Francisco. A plaque at No. 823 marks the site of the first dwelling, a canvas tent that was built in 1835.

To the east of Grant Avenue is the city's original town square, **Portsmouth Plaza**, which was laid out in 1839. In 1846 marines raised the American flag above the plaza, officially seizing the port as part of the United States. Two years later, it was here that Sam Brannan announced the discovery of gold in the Sierra Nevada Mountains *(see pp718–19)*. It soon became the hub of the new booming city in the 1850s. Today, Portsmouth Plaza is the social hub of Chinatown. In the morning people practice t'ai chi, and from noon to evening gather to play cards.

Running parallel to Grant Avenue, **Stockton Street** is where locals shop. Boxes of the freshest vegetables, fish, and other produce spill over onto crowded sidewalks. The Kong Chow Temple, located here, features fine Cantonese wood carvings.

Chinatown's busy alleys, located between Grant Avenue and Stockton Street, echo with authentic sights and sounds of the Orient. The largest of the four narrow lanes is Waverly Place, also

Dragon's Head at the Chinese Historical Society

known as the "Street of Painted Balconies." Watch for the Tin How Temple, which is brightly decorated with hundreds of gold and red lanterns. Nearby, Ross Alley has the tiny Fortune Cookie Factory, where visitors can see how the famous San Francisco creation is made. The alleys have many old buildings as well as laundries and old-fashioned herbalist shops, displaying elk antlers, sea horses, snake wine, and other exotic wares. Numerous small restaurants, above and below street level, serve cheap and delicious food.

The newly renovated **Chinese Historical Society** has a range of fascinating exhibits including a ceremonial dragon costume and a "tiger fork," a triton that was wielded in one of the battles during the reign of terror known as the Tong Wars. The Tongs were rival Chinese clans who fought over the control of gambling and prostitution in the city in the late 19th century. Other artifacts, documents, and photographs illuminate the daily life of Chinese immigrants in San Francisco. Among these is a yearbook written in Chinese.

🏛 **Chinese Historical Society**
965 Clay St. 📞 *(415) 391-1188.*
🚋 *1, 30, 45.* 🚃 *Powell St.*
🕐 *11am–4pm Tue–Fri & Sun.*
⬤ *public hols.* ⬛ ⬛

Cable Cars

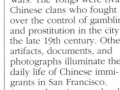

The cable car system was launched in 1873, with its inventor Andrew Hallidie riding in the first car. He was inspired to tackle the problem of transporting people up the city's steep slopes after seeing an accident, where a horse-drawn tram slipped down a

One of the city's cable cars

hill. His system was a success, and by 1889 cable cars were running on eight lines. Before the 1906 earthquake, over 600 cars were in use. With the advent of the internal combustion engine, however, they became obsolete, and in 1947 attempts were made to replace them with buses. After a huge public outcry, the present three lines were retained.

Nob Hill ⑦

Map E3. 🚋 *1, 12, 30, 45, 83.*
🚋 *California St, Powell–Mason,
Powell–Hyde.*

NOB HILL IS the highest
summit of the city itself,
rising 338 ft (103 m) above
the bay. It is San Francisco's
most celebrated hilltop,
famous for its cable cars,
plush hotels, and views. The
steep slopes kept prominent
citizens away until the opening of the California Street
cable car line in 1878. The
rich then flocked to build
homes here, including the
"Big Four" railroad barons,
who were among its richest
tenants. The name "Nob Hill"
is thought to come from the
Indian word *nabob*, meaning
chieftain. Sadly, all the grand
mansions were leveled in the
great earthquake and fire of
1906. The only building that
survived was the home of
James C. Flood, which is now
the Pacific Union Club.
    Nob Hill still attracts the
affluent to its hotels, which
recall the opulence of the
Victorian era and offer fine
views of the city.

Grace Cathedral is the main
Episcopal church in San
Francisco. Designed by Lewis
P. Hobart, this building was
inspired by Notre Dame in
Paris. Preparatory work began
in 1928, but the cathedral was
not completed until 1964. Its
entrance doors are cast from
molds of Ghiberti's "Doors of
Paradise," made for the
Baptistry in Florence.
    A short distance north of
Nob Hill is the **Cable Car
Barn**, erected in 1909, which
garages cable cars at night. It
is a repair shop, museum, and
powerhouse of the cable car
system. Anchored to the
ground floor are the engines
and wheels that wind the

cables through the system of
channels and pulleys beneath
the city's streets. Visitors can
observe them from the mezzanine, then walk down to
look under the street. The
museum also houses an early
cable car and the mechanisms
that control individual cars.

🔒 **Grace Cathedral**
1100 California St. 🎫 *(415) 749-
6300.* 🕐 *Choral evensong 5:15pm
Thu, 3pm Sun; Choral Eucharist 6am,
7:30am, 8:15am, 11am Sun.*
🏛 **Cable Car Barn**
1201 Mason St. 🎫 *(415) 474-1887.*
🕐 *summer: 10am–6pm daily; winter:
10am–5pm daily.* ⚫ *Jan 1, Thanksgiving, Dec 25.* ♿ *mezzanine only.*
Video show. 📷
🌐 www.cablecarmuseum.com

GRACE CATHEDRAL

The interior of this Gothic-style cathedral is replete with
marble and beautiful stained glass. The leaded windows
were designed by Charles Connick, using the blue glass
of Chartres as his inspiration. The rose window has thick
faceted glass, which is illuminated from the inside at
night. Other windows are by Henry Willet and Gabriel
Loire, and include depictions of Albert Einstein and
astronaut John Glenn. The cathedral also features a
13th-century Catalonian crucifix and a 16th-century
Brussels tapestry, and is popular for its choral
evensong, held every Thursday and Sunday.

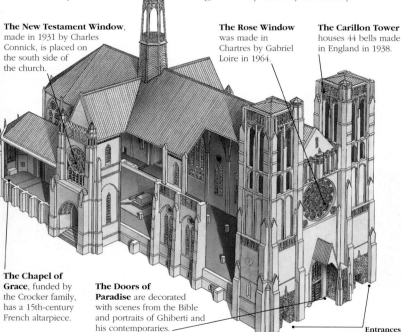

The New Testament Window,
made in 1931 by Charles
Connick, is placed on
the south side of
the church.

The Rose Window
was made in
Chartres by Gabriel
Loire in 1964.

The Carillon Tower
houses 44 bells made
in England in 1938.

**The Chapel of
Grace**, funded by
the Crocker family,
has a 15th-century
French altarpiece.

**The Doors of
Paradise** are decorated
with scenes from the Bible
and portraits of Ghiberti and
his contemporaries.

Entrances

Shops and amusements at Pier 39, Fisherman's Wharf

Fisherman's Wharf ⑧

Map E2. Between the coastline & Beach St. 🚌 *15, 19, 25, 30, 32, 39, 42, 45, 47.* 🚋 *Powell–Mason, Powell–Hyde.*

ITALIAN SEAFOOD restaurants have replaced fishing as the primary focus of Fisherman's Wharf. Fishermen from Genoa and Sicily first arrived here in the late 19th century and founded San Francisco's fishing industry. Since the 1950s, the area has given way to tourism, although brightly colored boats still set out to sea early each morning. The specialty here is the delicious Dungeness crab.

Pier 39 is the Wharf's hub, with restaurants, shops, and specialty stores, set against a backdrop of stunning bay views. Refurbished in 1978 to resemble a quaint wooden fishing village, the pier is also home to groups of sea lions that bask on the docks.

Docked at Pier 45 is the World War II submarine **USS *Pampanito***, which fought several battles in the Pacific, sinking six enemy ships. Visitors can tour the torpedo room, galley, and officer's quarters. To its south on Jefferson Street is **Ripley's Believe It Or Not! Museum**, which displays the cartoonist's collection of curiosities – one of which is a cable car built of 275,000 matchsticks. Farther along Jefferson Street, **The Cannery**, earlier a fruit processing factory, now houses a mall with restaurants, museums, and shops. The **San Francisco National Maritime Museum** on Beach Street, displays ship models, nautical instruments, and photographs illustrating nautical history. A large collection of old ships are moored at the nearby **Hyde Street Pier**. Among the finest is the *C.A. Thayer*, a three-masted schooner built in 1895.

North Beach ⑨

Map E2. 🚌 *15, 30, 39, 45.* 🚋 *Powell–Mason, Powell–Hyde.*

SOUTH OF Fisherman's Wharf is North Beach, also known as "Little Italy." Settlers from Chile, China, and Italy brought their enthusiasm for nightlife to the area, earning North Beach its vibrant reputation and attracting bohemians and writers, including the leading chronicler of the "Beat generation," Jack Kerouac. At the junction of Broadway and Columbus Avenue, the **City Lights Bookstore**, once owned by the Beat poet Lawrence Ferlinghetti, was the first bookshop in the US to sell only paperbacks. **Vesuvio**, south of City Lights, was one of the most popular Beat bars. Welsh poet Dylan Thomas was a patron here, and it is still a favorite with poets and artists. The former **Condor Club** is located on a stretch of Broadway known as The Strip, noted for its "adult entertainment." This landmark establishment was where the area's first topless show was staged in June 1964. **Caffè Trieste**, on the corner of Vallejo Street, is the oldest coffee house in San Francisco and a genuine Beat rendezvous since 1956. Very much a part of Italian-American culture, it offers live opera on Saturday afternoons.

Lombard Street, a little to the north, is renowned as "the crookedest street in the world." Banked at a natural incline of 27 degrees, this hill proved too steep for vehicles to climb. In the 1920s the section close to the summit of Russian Hill was revamped, and eight tight curves were added. There are spectacular views of San Francisco from the summit, especially at night. Close by, the **San Francisco Art Institute** is famous for its Diego Rivera Gallery, which contains an outstanding mural by the famous Mexican muralist created in 1931.

The 210-ft **Coit Tower** lies at the top of Telegraph Hill. The lobby has many Depression-era murals.

SAN FRANCISCO'S MURALS

Coit Tower's mural of Fisherman's Wharf in the 1930s

San Francisco's cosmopolitan heritage comes alive in the bright murals that decorate walls and public places in several parts of the city. Life in the metropolis is one of the major themes. The Mission District has over 200 murals showing every aspect of daily life on the walls of restaurants, banks, and schools. Many of these were painted in the 1970s, when the government paid rebellious young people to create public works of art. One of the best is the *Carnaval Mural* on 24th Street. The city also has three murals by Diego Rivera, the Mexican artist who revived fresco painting in the 1930s and 40s.

Cars negotiating Lombard St, "the crookedest street in the world"

Alcatraz Island ⑩

A LCATRAZ MEANS "pelican" in Spanish and refers to the first inhabitants of this rocky, steep-sided island. In 1859, the US Army established a fort here that guarded San Francisco Bay until 1907, when it became a military prison. From 1934 to 1963 it served as a maximum-security federal penitentiary. Dubbed "The Rock" by prisoners, it housed an average of 264 of the country's most infamous criminals, who were transferred here for disobedience while serving time in prisons elsewhere in the US. Today, Alcatraz is part of the Golden Gate National Recreation Area.

The Cell Block
Prisoners spent between 16 and 23 hours every day alone in stark cells, equipped with only a toilet and bunk. Many cells measured 5 ft by 9 ft (1.5 m by 2.7 m).

Water tower

Prison workshops

Military morgue

Military parade ground

The Post Exchange

Electric maintenance shop

The Military Dorm

The Pier

The Visitor Center is in the barracks building behind the jetty. It houses an information center, bookstore, exhibits, and a multimedia show providing a historical overview of Alcatraz.

Alcatraz from the Ferry
Looming ominously out of the ocean, "The Rock" promised its inmates strict discipline and constant vigilance.

Exercise Yard
Meals and a walk around the exercise yard were the highlights of a prisoner's day. This walled yard appeared in films that were shot here.

FAMOUS INMATES OF ALCATRAZ ISLAND

Al Capone
Al Capone was convicted in 1934 for income tax evasion and spent much of his five-year sentence at Alcatraz in an isolation cell. He left the prison mentally unstable.

Robert Stroud
Stroud spent most of his 17 years here in solitary confinement. Despite assertions to the contrary in the film *The Birdman of Alcatraz* (1962), he was forbidden from keeping birds in his cell.

Anglin Brothers
John and Clarence Anglin and Frank Morris chipped through the walls of their cells, hiding the holes with cardboard grates. They made a raft to escape and were never caught. Their story was dramatized in the film *Escape from Alcatraz* (1979).

George Kelly
George "Machine Gun" Kelly was the prison's most dangerous inmate and has the singular distinction of serving 17 years for kidnapping and extortion.

Haas-Lilienthal House in Pacific Heights, an 1886-Queen Anne mansion

Pacific Heights ⑪

Map D3. 🚌 *1, 3, 12, 19, 22, 24, 27, 28, 29, 30, 42, 43, 45, 47, 49, 83.* 🚋 *California St.*

THE STEEP BLOCKS between **Alta Plaza** and **Lafayette Park** are set in the heart of the exclusive Pacific Heights district. After cable cars linked it with the downtown area in the 1880s, it quickly became a desirable place to live, and many palatial Victorian houses line its quiet streets. Some date from the late 19th century, while others were built after the devastating earthquake and fire of 1906.

The **Haas-Lilienthal House**, an elaborate Queen Anne-style mansion, was built in 1886 for the merchant William Haas. Furnished in Victorian style, it is the only intact private home of the period and houses the headquarters of the Architectural Heritage Foundation. The impressive **Spreckels Mansion** on Washington Street, constructed on the lines of a French Baroque palace, is now home to bestselling novelist Danielle Steele. Close by, Lafayette Park is one of San Francisco's loveliest hilltop gardens, lined with pine and eucalyptus trees. It offers excellent views of the numerous Victorian houses in the surrounding streets. Located across the street from the park, **2151 Sacramento Street** is an ornate French-style mansion, which has a plaque commemorating a visit by the famous author Sir Arthur Conan Doyle in 1923.

At the center of Pacific Heights is Alta Plaza, a landscaped urban park, where the San Franciscan elite come to relax. Set up in the 1850s, this hilltop green has tennis courts and a playground. The stone steps rising from Clay Street on the south side offer overall views of Haight Ashbury.

North of Pacific Heights, the streets drop steeply down to the Marina District, which was created from reclaimed land for the 1915 Panama-Pacific Exposition. The Expo's only surviving monument is the grand **Palace of Fine Arts**. This Neo-Classical building has a large rotunda with allegorical paintings on its dome. It houses the entertaining Exploratorium Science Museum and hosts events such as the May Film Festival.

🏛 **Haas-Lilienthal House**
2007 Franklin St. 🄲 *(415) 441-3004.* ⃝ *noon–3pm Wed & Sat, 11am–4pm Sun.* 🚫 🅿

Asian Art Museum ⑫

Map E4. Larkin at Grove St. 🄲 *(415) 379-8800.* 🚌 *5, 8, 19, 21, 26, 42, 47, 49.* 🚇 *F, J, K, L, M, N.* ⃝ *9am–5pm Tue–Sun (until 9pm Thu).* 🚫 🅵 🔲 🔳 ⅏ www.asianart.org

THE NEW Asian Art Museum is located on Civic Center Plaza in a building that was the crown jewel of the Beaux Arts movement. The former Main Library, built in 1917, has undergone seismic strengthening and adaptive reuse of space to create the largest museum outside Asia devoted exclusively to Asian art. The new museum's exhibits include 12,000 art objects spanning 6,000 years of history and representing over 40 Asian nations. There are also performance venues and a hands-on discovery center. The terrace café overlooks the Civic Center and Fulton Street Mall.

The grand staircase at the Asian Art Museum

THE SOUNDS OF 1960s SAN FRANCISCO

During the late 1960s, and most notably during the 1967 "Summer of Love," young people from all over the country flocked to the Haight Ashbury district. They came not just to "turn on, tune in, and drop out," but also to listen to rock bands such as Janis Joplin's Big Brother and the Holding Company, Jefferson Airplane, and the Grateful Dead, all of whom emerged out of the thriving music scene. Impresario Bill Graham put unlikely pairs such as Miles Davis and the Grateful Dead on the same bill at Fillmore Auditorium. He also brought in big-name performers such as Jimi Hendrix and The Who, making "the Haight" the focus of the rock world.

A 1960s street scene in Haight Ashbury

Mission Dolores ⑬

Map E4. 16th St & Dolores St.
🚋 22. 🚇 J. 📞 (415) 621-8203.
⏰ check for times. ⬤ Thanksgiving,
Dec 25. 🎫 ♿ 📷

PRESERVED INTACT since it
was built in 1791, Mission
Dolores, after which the
surrounding Mission District
is named, is the oldest building in the city and an embod-
iment of San Francisco's
Spanish Colonial roots.
Founded by Father Junípero
Serra as the sixth California
mission, it is formally
known as the Mission of
San Francisco de Asis.
The name Dolores
reflects its
proximity to
Laguna de los
Dolores (Lake
of Our Lady of
Sorrows), an
ancient swamp.
The building is
modest by
mission stan-
dards, but its 4-
ft (1.2-m) thick
walls have
survived.

**Figure of saint
in the mission**

Paintings by Native Americans
adorn the restored ceiling.
There is a fine Baroque altar
and reredos, and a display of
historical documents in the
small museum. Most services
are held in the basilica, built
adjacent to the mission in
1918. The cemetery contains
graves of San Franciscan
pioneers, as well as a mass
grave of 5,000 Native Americans, who died in the measles
epidemics of 1804 and 1826.

**The altarpiece of Mission Dolores,
imported from Mexico in 1780**

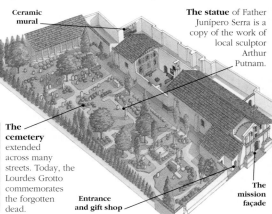

**Ceramic
mural**

The statue of Father
Junípero Serra is a
copy of the work of
local sculptor
Arthur
Putnam.

**The
cemetery**
extended
across many
streets. Today, the
Lourdes Grotto
commemorates
the forgotten
dead.

**Entrance
and gift shop**

**The
mission
façade**

Haight Ashbury ⑭

Map D4. 🚌 6, 7, 33, 37, 43, 66, 71.
🚋 N. **Lower Haight** 🚌 6, 7, 22, 66,
71. 🚋 K, L, M.

STRETCHING FROM Buena Vista
Park to Golden Gate Park,
Haight Ashbury was the
center of the hippie world in
the 1960s. Originally a quiet,
middle class suburb – hence
the dozens of elaborate
Queen Anne-style houses – it
changed dramatically into the
mecca of a free-wheeling,
bohemian community that
defied social norms and
conventions. In 1967, the
"Summer of Love," fueled by
the media, brought some
75,000 young people in
search of free love, music,
and drugs, and it became the
focus of a worldwide youth
culture. Thousands lived here,
and there was even a free
clinic to treat hippies without
medical insurance.

Today, "the Haight" retains
its radical atmosphere and has

settled into being one of the
liveliest and most unconven-
tional places in San Francisco,
with an eclectic mix of
people, second-hand clothing
shops, excellent music and
book stores, and a variety of
excellent cafés.

Buena Vista Park on its
eastern fringe has a mass of
knotted trees and offers magnificent views of the city. The
grand (Richard) Spreckels
Mansion on Buena Vista
Avenue (not to be confused
with the one on Washington

**The Red Victorian Hotel in Haight
Ashbury, a relic of the hippie era**

Street), is a typical late-
Victorian home. It was once
a guest house, and its visitors
included writer Jack London
and journalist Ambrose Bierce.
The **Red Victorian Hotel**,
affectionately dubbed the
"Jeffrey Haight" in 1967, was
a favorite among hippies. It
now caters to a New Age
clientele and offers rooms
with transcendental themes.

Halfway between City Hall
and Haight Ashbury, the
Lower Haight marks the
border of the predominantly
African-American Fillmore
District, which is one of the
liveliest parts of the city.
Unusual art galleries, boutiques, inexpensive cafés, and
bars serve a largely bohemian
clientele. It also has dozens of
houses known as "Victorians,"
built from the 1850s to the
1900s, including cottages
such as the Nightingale
House at 201 Buchanan
Street. Although safe during
the day, the Lower Haight
can be unnerving after dark.

California Academy of Sciences ⑮

Map F3. 875 Howard St near 5th St. **C** (415) 750-7145. **⊟** 5, 9. **⊞** J, K, L. **○** call for times. **W** www.calacademy.org

THE ACADEMY is temporarily located on Howard Street while the building at the southern end of Golden Gate Park undergoes extensive refurbishment; the renovated building is slated to reopen in 2008. Founded in 1853, this is San Francisco's oldest and most popular science museum. It has an outstanding natural history collection, an anthropology section, an aquarium, and a planetarium. The **African Hall**, with its displays of realistic models of animals from Africa's jungles in lifelike dioramas, provides an opportunity to examine big game at close range. The diorama of a watering hole in the African savanna features the changing light and sounds of an African day, compressed into a 20-minute cycle. One of the museum's star exhibits, in its Earth and Space section, is

Tyrannosaurus rex skeleton

The Earth Quake!, where visitors experience earth tremors and learn about their destructive power. The **Morrison Planetarium** has one of the world's most precise star projectors, which transforms the ceiling into the night sky. Popular planetarium shows include "The Sky Tonight" and "Worlds Unseen."

A small percentage of the museum's sizable collection relating to American Indian, Polynesian, Asian, Melanesian, and other cultures is on display at any one time. Navajo and Pueblo artworks are well represented in the superb **Elkus Collection of Native American Art**. Evolutionary history is the subject of the **Life Through Time** section, which has life-sized models of Velociraptors and of a Quetzalcoatlus, the largest flying creature that ever lived. A popular draw is the skeleton of a *Tyrannosaurus rex*.

The enchanting **Steinhart Aquarium**, the oldest and one of the most diverse aquariums in the US, houses more than 8,000 specimens of tide-pool animals, sea mammals, and other aquatic creatures. Prime attractions here include the Giant Pacific octopus and the Sharks of Tropics tank. The **Gem and Mineral Hall** contains more than 1,000 specimens of gemstones and minerals, including a 1,350-lb (612-kg) quartz crystal from Arkansas. A special exhibition shows how gemstones are set to make jewelry. In **Wild California**, naturalistic dioramas portray the landscapes and animals of California, with recorded commentaries helping to explain the scenes.

Lifelike dioramas in the African Hall of the California Academy of Sciences

MH de Young Memorial Museum ⑯

THE DE YOUNG museum is closed for renovation until 2006. Many of its exhibits are on now display at the **California Palace of the Legion of Honor**.

California Palace of the Legion of Honor ⑰

Map C4. 34th Ave & Clement, Lincoln Park. **C** (415) 750-3600. **⊟** 18. **🚻** (415) 863-3330. **○** 9:30am–5pm Tue–Sun. **●** Mon. **🎫** (free on Tue). *Appointment required to see the Achenbach Collection.* **Ø 🔊 🖵 🚹 📷 W** www.thinker.org

INSPIRED BY THE Palais de la Légion d'Honneur in Paris, Alma de Bretteville Spreckels built this museum in the 1920s to promote French art in California. Designed by the architect George Applegarth, it displays European art from the last eight centuries, with paintings by Rembrandt, Monet, and Rubens, and more than 70 sculptures by Rodin. The Achenbach Foundation, a well-known collection of graphic works, occupies a part of the gallery.

The museum's collection of European art is displayed in 19 galleries on the first floor. The portrait *The Impresario* (1877) by Edgar Degas emphasizes the subject's size by making him appear too large for the frame. Claude Monet's beautiful *Waterlilies* (1914–17) is one of a series depicting the lily pond in his gardens in Giverny, near Paris. The original bronze casting of Rodin's *Le Penseur* (1904), which is better known as *The Thinker*, is located at the center of the colonnaded Court of Honor. It is one of the five castings of the statue in collections around the world. The oil-on-canvas *The Tribute Money* (1612) shows the Flemish artist Peter Paul Rubens' typical use of primary colors.

The Presidio ⑱

Map C3. **Visitor Center** 102 Montgomery St. 【 (415) 561-4323.
○ 9am–5pm daily. ● public hols. ⓖ

To THE NORTH of Golden
Gate Park, overlooking
San Francisco Bay, the
Presidio was established as an
outpost of Spain's New World
empire in 1776, and for many
years was a military base. In
1994 it became a national
park, and visitors can now
stroll through its acres of
woodland full of wildlife.

The site has been occupied
longer than any other part of
the city, and remnants of its
military past, including the
barracks, artillery emplace-
ments, and museum, can be
seen. There are also many
hiking trails, bike paths, and
beaches. The coastal path is
one of the city's most popular
walks and picnic areas.

The Presidio Museum,
once housed in a wood-
en building dating from
the 1860s that served
as the hospital, is now
part of the new **Mott
Visitor Center** in the
Main Post area. It
houses artifacts relating
to the Presidio's long
history. Close by, the
Officers' Club was built over
the adobe remains of the
original 18th-century Spanish
fort, still preserved inside the
building. The club sometimes
holds exhibitions; visitors can
phone to check the schedule.
A 19th-century cannon from
the Spanish–American War lies
across the adjoining parade
ground. To the north, close
to the bay, is the large, grassy
Crissy Field, that was
reclaimed from marshland
for the 1915 Panama-Pacific
Exposition. It was used as an
airfield from 1919 to 1936 and
has recently been restored.
The **Military Cemetery**, east
of the visitor center, holds the
remains of 15,000 American
soldiers killed during various
wars. At the park's southeast
corner, the decorative
Arguello Gate has military
symbols on its surface and
marks the entrance to the
former army base, now open
to the public.

**Detail of the 19th-century cannon
located on the Presidio grounds**

At the northwestern tip of the
Presidio, **Fort Point** is an
impressive brick fortress that
once guarded the Golden
Gate during the Civil War
and also survived the 1906
earthquake. The fort was
built in 1861 to protect San
Francisco Bay from attack,
and to defend ships
carrying gold from the
California mines. It is
a good place from
which to view Golden
Gate Bridge. There is
also a museum dis-
playing military
uniforms and arms.
Park rangers dressed in Civil
War costume conduct guided
tours. South of Fort
Point, **Baker Beach** is
one of the city's best
beaches. Farther inland
is the spring-fed
Mountain Lake, now a
delightful picnic spot.

**Detail,
Arguello Gate**

Golden Gate Bridge ⑲

Map B2. Hwy 101, Presidio.
【 (415) 923-2000. ▭ 2, 4,
8, 10, 18, 20, 28, 29, 50, 72,
76, 80. Pedestrians & cyclists
allowed 5am–9pm daily, east
walkway only. ⓖ observation
area only. ▯

NAMED AFTER the part
of San Francisco
Bay called "Golden
Gate" by John Frémont
in 1844, the Golden
Gate Bridge opened in
1937, connecting the
city with Marin County.

It took just over four years to
build, at a cost of $35 million.
This world-famous landmark
offers breathtaking views;
the bridge has six lanes for
vehicles plus a free pedestrian
walkway. Each year, more
than 40 million vehicles cross
it, averaging a daily count
of about 118,000. It is the
world's third largest single-
span bridge, stretching 1.7
miles (2.7 km). When it was
built, it was the world's
longest and tallest suspension
structure, rising 746 ft (227 m)
above the water.

Designed by Chicago-based
engineers Joseph Strauss and
Leon Moisseiff, the bridge is
a remarkable feat of engineering. The mammoth structure
was built to withstand 100
mph (160 km/h) winds. Its
south pier was sunk 100 ft
(30 m) into the seabed, while
each pier supports a 44,000-
ton steel tower. The original
coat of paint lasted for 27
years, but since 1965 it has
needed continuous painting.
The two 7,650-ft (2,332-m)
cables are more than 3 ft
(1 m) thick and contain
80,000 miles (128,744 km)
of steel wire, enough to circle
the earth at the equator three
times. The best views are
available from the Marin
County side.

**The Golden Gate Bridge, with a single
span of 4,200 ft (1,280 m)**

Greater San Francisco

MANY OF THE SETTLEMENTS encircling San Francisco Bay were once summer retreats for the city's residents, but today they are sprawling suburbs or cities in their own right. Two popular destinations in the East Bay are Oakland's museum and Berkeley's famous university. The landmark San Francisco–Oakland Bay Bridge stretches 4.5 miles (7.2 km) and is crossed by 250,000 vehicles a day – even more than the Golden Gate. Farther south, San Jose combines the technology of Silicon Valley with fine museums and Spanish Colonial architecture. To the north is the rocky coastline of the Marin Headlands, with its abundant wildlife.

The Thinker by Auguste Rodin at the Stanford Museum of Art

San Jose ⑳

🏛 846,000. ✈ 🚉 65 Cahill St. 🚌 70 Almeden St. 🚶 180 S Market St, (888) 726-5673. 📷 *Festival of the Arts (Sep).*

THE ONLY OTHER original Spanish Colonial town in California apart from Los Angeles, San Jose was founded in 1777 by Felipe de Neve and has become the state's third largest city. It is now the commercial and cultural center of South Bay and the civic heart of Silicon Valley.

The **Mission Santa Clara de Asis**, on the campus of the Jesuit University of Santa Clara, is a modern replica of the adobe original, first built in 1777. Relics include bells given to the missionaries by the Spanish monarchy. The large **Rosicrucian Egyptian Museum and Planetarium** has an extensive collection of ancient Egyptian artifacts. Displays include mummies, burial tombs, and toys, some of which date to 1500 BC. There are replicas of the sarcophagus in which Tutankhamen was discovered in 1922, and the Rosetta Stone.

At the heart of San Jose, the fascinating **Tech Museum of Innovation** is crowded with hands-on exhibits, encouraging visitors to discover how technological inventions work. Here, the focus is on understanding the workings of computer hardware and software.

The **Winchester Mystery House**, on the outskirts of town, has a remarkable history. Sarah Winchester, widow and heiress of the Winchester Rifle fortune, was told by a medium that the expansion of her farmhouse would exorcise the spirits of those killed by the rifle. She kept builders working 24 hours a day, 7 days a week, for 38 years, until her death in 1922. The result is a bizarre complex of 160 rooms, including stairs that lead nowhere and windows set into floors. The total cost amounted to $5.5 million.

The center of the computer industry, **Silicon Valley** covers about 100 sq miles (260 sq km) from Palo Alto to San Jose. The name refers to myriad businesses rather than a specific location. The seeds of the hardware and software industries were sown in the 1980s at Stanford University, at the Xerox Palo Alto Research Center, and in the garages of pioneers William Hewlett, David Packard, and later Steve Jobs and Stephen Wozniak, who invented the Apple personal computer. Many world-class firms are based here.

Organ, Winchester Mystery House

🚪 **Winchester Mystery House**
525 S Winchester Blvd. 📞 (408) 247-2000. ⏱ *check for times.* ⬤ *Dec 25.* 📷 ♿ *gardens only.* 🔒 📷 💻

Palo Alto ㉑

Stanford University 📞 (650) 723-2053. **Visitor Center** ⏱ *11am–3:15pm except during winter break.* ⬤ *university hols; call ahead.*

AMONG THE most pleasant of the Bay Area suburbs, Palo Alto grew up to serve Stanford University, one of the most reputed centers of education in the US. It was founded in 1891 by the railroad tycoon Leland Stanford in honor of his son who died at the age of 16. The campus covers 8,200 acres (3,320 ha), and is larger than the downtown district of San Francisco. Designed in a mixture of Romanesque and Mission styles, its sandstone buildings are capped by red-tiled roofs. The Memorial Church is decorated with gold-leaf and tile mosaic. The **Stanford Museum of Art** holds one of the largest collections of sculptures by Auguste Rodin, including the impressive *Gates of Hell*.

Oakland ㉒

🏛 387,000. ✈ 🚉 1245 Broadway St. 🚶 (510 874-4800). 📷 *Festival at the Lake (Jun).*

AT ONE TIME a small, working-class suburb of San Francisco, Oakland grew into a flourishing city when it became the West Coast terminus of the transcontinental railroad. Many of the African Americans who worked on the railroad settled here, later followed by the Hispanics, giving Oakland a multicultural atmosphere that continues to this day. Its literary associations, including Jack London and Gertrude Stein, have also enhanced the area as a cultural center.

Jack London Square on the waterfront was named after author Jack London who grew up in Oakland in the 1880s and frequently visited the area. Today, it is a bright promenade of shops, restaurants, and pleasure boats. The Jack London Museum contains books, photographs, and memorabilia. To the east, the **Oakland Museum of California** is dedicated to documenting California's art, history, and ecology. The Cowell Hall of California History has a large collection of Californian artifacts, while the Gallery of California Art is famous for early oil paintings of San Francisco.

To the north, the two blocks of **Old Oakland** (also known as Victorian Row) attract crowds of shoppers. Northern California's only **Mormon Temple**, situated on a hilltop on the eastern edge of the city, offers great views of the Bay Area. Its central ziggurat is surrounded by four towers, all clad with white granite and capped by golden pyramids.

🏛 **Oakland Museum of California**
Oak & 10th Sts. ℹ (510) 238-2200. ◷ 10am–5pm Wed–Sat, noon–5pm Sun. ● Jan 1, Thanksgiving, Dec 25, Mon & Tue. 🎟 (free 2nd Sun). ♿ 🏪 📷 💻 www.museumca.org

Berkeley ㉓

🏠 104,900. ✈ 🚊 🚌 2160 Shattuck Ave. ℹ 1834 University Ave, (800) 847-4823 🎭 Fourth of July Fireworks; Telegraph Ave Book Fair (Jul).

B ERKELEY BEGAN to boom after the earthquake of 1906, when many San Franciscans fled their city and settled on the East Bay. It was the seat of the student uprisings against the Vietnam War in the 1960s, earning itself the nickname "Beserkeley." Many

Model of DNA at the Lawrence Hall of Science, UC Berkeley

stores still hark to the hippie era with psychedelic merchandise, but in recent years Berkeley has begun to change its profile. Stylish restaurants have emerged, as well as a reputation for fine food; it was here that the popular California cuisine was born.

Berkeley is essentially a university town. The **University of California at Berkeley's** reputation for countercultural movements sometimes eclipses its academic reputation, yet with its student body of 30,000, it is one of the country's most prestigious institutions. Founded in 1868, it has at least ten Nobel laureates among its professors. There are many museums, cultural amenities, and noteworthy buildings to visit. The **University Art Museum** includes works by Piccasso and Cézanne among its exhibits. The main campus landmark, the 307-ft (94-m) **Sather Tower** and the splendid **Lawrence Hall of Science** are all outstanding.

To the south, the **Telegraph Avenue** was the center of student protest in the 1960s. Today, this fascinating street swarms with students, musicians, street vendors, and eccentrics. There is also a plethora of bookstores, coffee houses, and cheap eateries. North of the University, **Shattuck Avenue**, nicknamed "Gourmet Ghetto," is known for its restaurants.

🏫 **University of California at Berkeley**
ℹ (510) 642-6000. **University Art Museum** ℹ (510) 642-0808. ◷ Wed–Sun. ● public hols. 🎟 ♿

Sausalito ㉔

🏠 7,300. 🚉 🚌 🚌 ℹ 777 Bridgeway Ave, 4th floor, (415) 332-0505.

I N THIS SMALL town, Victorian bungalows cling to hills rising from San Francisco Bay. Bridgeway Avenue along the waterfront serves as a promenade for the crowds that come to patronize the restaurants and shops and enjoy the views. **Village Fair** is an assembly of trendy shops located in an old warehouse.

🏪 **Village Fair**
777 Bridgeway Ave. ℹ (415) 332-1902. ◷ daily. ● public hols.

Muir Woods ㉕

🚌 Mill Valley. **Visitor Center** Hwy 1, Mill Valley, (415) 388-2595. ◷ 8am–5pm daily

N ESTLING AT the foot of Mount Tamalpais is Muir Woods National Monument, one of the few remaining stands of old-growth coastal redwoods. Before the 19th-century lumber industry boom, these tall trees (the oldest is 1,000 years old) covered the Californian coastline. The woods were named in honor of John Muir, the naturalist responsible for turning Yosemite into a national park (see p718). Muir Beach nearby is a wide expanse of sand, usually crowded during the summer weekends.

Muir Woods, the last remaining redwood forest in the Bay Area

San Francisco Practical Information

S AN FRANCISCO OCCUPIES a compact area, making it a sightseer's dream. Its efficient transportation system has cable cars, buses, Muni Metro, and BART lines. The city prides itself on its variety of cultural and entertainment opportunities, which make it one of the most enjoyable vacation spots in the world. The Civic Center is the main venue for classical music, opera, and ballet, while pop music – in particular jazz and blues – is where the city really excels. There are also diverse theater companies and specialty movie houses.

TOURIST INFORMATION

V ISITORS PLANNING a trip will find the *San Francisco Book*, published twice yearly by the **San Francisco Convention and Visitors' Bureau**, very helpful. It is available free at the **Visitor Information Center** at Hallidie Plaza. Complete listings of what's on are given in the *San Francisco Chronicle* and *Examiner* newspapers; the *Chronicle's* Sunday edition is very useful. Other sources are the weekly newspapers, such as the *San Francisco Weekly* or the *San Francisco Bay Guardian*. These give both listings and reviews, especially of live music, films, and nightclubs. For details on events, call the visitors' bureau's Events Line.

GETTING AROUND

T HE BEST WAY TO explore San Francisco is on foot, although the hills can be strenuous. The city's main sights all lie within 15 to 20 minutes of each other. City taxis are licensed and operate 24 hours a day. **City Cab** and Yellow Cab are good bets.

The San Francisco Municipal Railway or **Muni**, runs the city's transportation system. The Muni Passport, valid for 1, 3, or 7 days can be used for unlimited travel on Muni buses, Muni Metro streetcars, as well as San Francisco's three cable car lines. These are available at the Visitor Information Center.

Buses and streetcars serve all areas. Buses stop only at designated places, every few blocks, and route numbers are printed on the buses. Muni Metro streetcars and

BART trains both use the same underground terminals on Market Street. The high-speed BART trains stop at five downtown stations: Van Ness, Civic Center, Powell, Montgomery, and Embarcadero.

San Francisco's famous cable cars operate from 6:30am to 12:30am daily, at 15-minute intervals. Cars run on three routes: the popular Powell–Hyde line, the Powell–Mason line, and the California line.

Boats and passenger ferries are also a fun way to get around the city's shoreline. The Ferry Building is the terminal for the **Golden Gate Ferries**. Bay sightseeing cruises from Fisherman's Wharf are operated by the **Blue & Gold Fleet**. **Hornblower Dining Yachts** offer lunch on Friday, brunch on weekends, and dinner daily on their cruises.

Other modes of travel include bicycles, which can be rented for around $25 a day or $125 a week. Details of scenic routes are available from the **Start to Finish** rental. Pedicabs and horse-drawn cabs are found on the Embarcadero. Sightseeing bus tours are also available.

SPORTS & OUTDOOR ACTIVITIES

T HE CITY HAS plenty of options for sports fans. The home ground of the San Francisco 49ers is 3-Com Park. Other football teams are supported by local colleges, UC Berkeley, and Stanford University. Two professional baseball teams play in the Bay Area, the National League San Francisco Giants (in Pacific Bell Park) and the American

League Oakland Athletics (in Network Associates Coliseum).

Golfers have a range of courses to choose from, including the municipal links in **Lincoln Park**. Most of the public swimming pools are located in the suburbs; for details contact the **City of San Francisco Recreation and Parks Department**. To swim in the chilly ocean, head out to China Beach. There are tennis courts in almost all the public parks, with the largest ones in Golden Gate Park. **Claremont Resort Spa and Tennis Club** in Berkeley offers fine courts with unlimited playing time even to non-guests.

ENTERTAINMENT

S AN FRANCISCO offers visitors an unending variety of high-quality entertainment. It has an avid film-going community, and one of the best movie houses is the **AMC Kabuki**, an eight-screen complex in the Japan Center, which also hosts the San Francisco **International Film Festival** each May. The main venue for first-run foreign films is the **Opera Plaza**. For theater goers, major shows are staged at Theater District venues, the two largest being the **Curran Theater** for Broadway shows; and the Geary Theater, now home to the **American Conservatory Theater (ACT)**, which performs October through May.

The **San Francisco Opera Association** season runs from September to December; tickets can cost more than $100, but there is a summer season with less expensive tickets. The **Civic Center** complex on Van Ness Avenue offers opera, classical music, and dance. The **San Francisco Ballet** season runs from February to April, while the Yerba Buena Center for the Arts is home to the **LINES Contemporary Ballet**.

Two of the best rock clubs, **Slim's** and **Paradise Lounge**, are opposite one another in the SoMa district. Another popular place is the **Fillmore Auditorium**, the legendary birthplace of psychedelic rock during the 1960s. There are a number of places to hear live jazz, such as **Jazz at Pearl's**, and live blues is played in bars such as **The Saloon**. The annual **San Francisco Blues Festival** attracts blues bands from all over the country.

San Francisco's largest disco is **Polly Esther's**, with its multiple dance floors and mainstream clientele. Some of the most popular clubs are primarily, though rarely exclusively, gay. These include **Rawhide II**, which has square dancing every night.

Piano bars all have nightly live music. One of the best is the Art Deco-style **Top of the Mark** at the top of the Mark Hopkins InterContinental Hotel. **Cobb's Comedy Club** stages a great comedy show.

San Francisco also has a number of free concerts that are regularly staged all over the city. Watch for the San Francisco Symphony Orchestra in late summer at Stern Grove. The San Francisco Opera performs in Golden Gate Park in the "Opera in the Park" event. The summer Shakespeare Festival is also held here.

SHOPPING

SHOPPING IN SAN FRANCISCO is a complete experience that allows a glimpse into the city's culture. The diversity of San Francisco makes buying anything here an adventure. An enormous range of goods is available, from the practical to the more eccentric, but you can take your time in choosing, since browsers are made to feel welcome, particularly in the many small specialty shops and boutiques. Guided shopping tours are available for those who want to be directed to the best shops.

For visitors who want convenience, the numerous shopping centers, such as the Embarcadero Center and Japan Center, are excellent.

Similarly, huge retail department stores such as **Macy's** and **Neiman Marcus** offer an outstanding selection of goods and services.

The city's innovative entrepreneurial spirit is evident in its specialty shops, featuring humorous art at **Smile–A Gallery with Tongue in Chic** and fantasy toys at **FAO Schwartz**.

A mecca for designer wear, the city is home to the famous **Levis Strauss & Co**, which has been making jeans since 1853 and offers factory tours on Tuesdays and Wednesdays to visitors. For discount designer wear, head to the trendy SoMa district.

Book lovers should head for **A Clean Well-Lighted Place for Books**, or the famous Beat hideout **City Lights Bookstore**, which stays open late and is a famous San Francisco institution.

Art lovers will find something to their liking in the city's hundreds of galleries, featuring works by emerging and more established artists as well as expressions of Native American folk artists.

The city is also home to many dedicated "foodies," gastronomes whose liking for fine wine and gourmet meals have resulted in unusual and delicious grocery stores. Regular farmers' markets, held in the center of the city, abound in locally grown fruit and vegetables, while seafood and wines from **Napa Valley Winery Exchange** figure among the city's best buys.

The Wine Country

BORN IN THE SONOMA VALLEY in 1823, when Franciscan priests planted grapes to make sacramental wines, California's wine industry was taken to new heights by the flamboyant Hungarian Count Agoston Haraszthy in 1857. Known as the "Father of California Wine," he planted European grapes in the state's first big vineyard at the revered Buena Vista Winery. Today, in addition to its superb wines and vineyards, the Wine Country is known for its mild climate, rocky landscapes, secluded beaches, redwood groves, and impressive architecture.

View of vineyards in the Sonoma Valley, famous for wineries

Sonoma Valley ㉒

🏠 8,600. ✈ 🚌 90 Broadway & W Napa Sts, Sonoma Plaza. 🛈 453 1st St E, (707) 996-1090. 📷 Valley of the Moon Vintage Festival (late Sep).

NESTLING picturesquely in the crescent-shaped Sonoma Valley are 6,000 acres (2,400 ha) of beautiful vineyards. At the foot of the valley lies the tiny town of Sonoma. This town has had a colorful past, as it was here on June 14, 1846, that about 30 armed American farmers captured Mexican General Mariano Vallejo and his men, to protest the fact that land ownership was reserved for Mexican citizens. They seized control of Sonoma, declared California an independent republic, and flew their own flag, with a crude drawing of a grizzly bear. Although the republic was annulled 25 days later when the United States annexed California, the Bear Flag design was adopted as the official state flag in 1911.

Sonoma's main attractions are its world-famous wineries and meticulously preserved historical sites lining the Spanish-style plaza. Many of the adobe buildings house wine shops, boutiques, and restaurants serving excellent local cuisine. East of the plaza is the restored **Mission San Francisco Solano de Sonoma**, the last of California's 21 historic Franciscan missions (founded by Father José Altimira of Spain in 1823). Today, all that survives of the original building is the corridor of his quarters. The adobe chapel was built by General Vallejo in 1840.

A short drive northward leads to the **Jack London State Historic Park**. In the early 1900s, London, the famous author of *The Call of the Wild* and *The Sea Wolf*, abandoned his hectic lifestyle to live in this tranquil 800-acre (325-ha) expanse of oaks, madrones, and redwoods. The park retains eerie ruins of London's dream home, the Wolf House, mysteriously destroyed by fire just before completion. After London's death, his widow, Charmian Kittredge, built a magnificent home on the ranch, called the House of Happy Walls. Today, the house has been made into a museum, worth a visit for its display of London memorabilia.

🏛 **Mission San Francisco Solano de Sonoma**
E Spain St. 📞 (707) 938-9560. ◯ daily. ● Jan 1, Thanksg., Dec 25. 🎫

🌳 **Jack London Historic State Park**
London Ranch Rd, Glen Ellen. 📞 (707) 938-5216. **Park & Museum** ◯ daily. ● Jan 1, Thanksgiving, Dec 25. 🎫 ♿ museum only. 🎫

Napa Valley ㉓

🏠 115,000. ✕ 🛈 1310 Town Center Mall, Napa, (707) 226-7459. 📷 Napa Valley Mustard Festival (Feb–Apr).

LYING AT the heart of California's wine industry, the 35-mile (56-km) sliver of land known as Napa Valley encompasses the towns of Yountville, Oakville, St. Helena, Rutherford, and Calistoga. More than 250 wineries are scattered across its hillsides and valleys, some dating from the early 19th century. Prominent among these is the **Mumm Napa Valley** winery, partly owned by French champagne producer G.H. Mumm, where wines are made in the classic tradition. To its north, the **Rutherford Hill Winery** features caves dug into the hillsides, for aging wines. Farther north, the modern **Clos Pegase** winery is famed for its distinctive art collection and superior wines.

For a bird's-eye view of the valley, visitors can take hot-air balloon trips over the Wine Country from Yountville or a three-hour luxury tour in the Napa Valley Wine Train, enjoying gourmet cuisine. But the best way to explore the valley is along a scenic 40-mile (64-km) drive, stopping along the way at the B&B inns in the towns of St. Helena and Calistoga. The latter is popular for its spa treatments and good Wine Country

Statue at Clos Pegase

cuisine, prepared with the freshest ingredients. A few miles north of Calistoga, the Old Faithful Geyser spouts jets of boiling mineral water 60 ft (18 m) into the sky, once every 40 minutes. To the west lies the **Petrified Forest**, home of the largest petrified trees in the world – huge redwoods which were turned to stone by a volcanic eruption that took place more than three million years ago.

🪵 Petrified Forest
4100 Petrified Forest Rd. 📞 *(707) 942-6667.* ⏰ *daily.* ● *Thanksgiving, Dec 25.* 🏷 ♿ *limited.*

The Clos Pegase winery designed by Michael Graves, Napa Valley

Russian River Valley ㉔

🚂 *from Healdsburg.* ℹ *16209 1st St, Guerneville, (707) 869-9000.* 🖥 *www.russianriverchamber.com*

Bisected by the Russian River and its tributaries, this valley contains many smaller valleys, dotted with vineyards, apple orchards, redwood groves, family farms, and sandy river beaches. At its hub is the town of **Healdsburg**, with a splendid Spanish-style town square lined with shops, restaurants, and cafés.

Southwest of Healdsburg lies **Guerneville**, a summer haven for San Francisco's gay population. Every September, the town hosts the famous Russian River Jazz Festival at Johnson's Beach, where visitors can take a canoe or raft down the gentle Russian River. Otters and blue herons can be often be seen here.

Hikers and equestrians also flock to Guerneville to visit the 805-acre (330-ha) **Armstrong Redwoods State Reserve**, one of the few remaining old-growth redwood forests in

California. Among its redwoods is a 308-ft (94-m) giant – a 1,400-year-old tree named Colonel Armstrong.

♣ Armstrong Redwoods State Preserve
17000 Armstrong Woods Rd, Guerneville. 📞 *(707) 869-2015, 865-2391.* ⏰ *daily.*

Fort Ross State Historic Park ㉕

📞 *(707) 847-3286.* 🚌 *from Point Arena.* ⏰ *sunrise–sunset daily.* ● *Thanksgiving, Dec 25.* 🏷 ♿ 🖥 *www.mcn.org/one/rrparks/fortress*

On a windswept headland north of Jenner stands this well-restored Russian trading outpost, founded in 1812 (the name "Ross" is a derivative of the Russian word "Rossyia," meaning Russia). The Russians were the first Europeans to visit the region, serving as representatives of a Russian-American Company, established in 1799. They never tried to expand their territory in California and abandoned the fort after 30 years of peaceful trading.

Built in 1836, the house of the fort's last manager, Alexander Rotchev, is still intact. Within the wooden palisade are several other reconstructed buildings. The most impressive is the 1824 Russian Orthodox chapel. Every July, a living history day is held, in which costumed actors recreate life at the outpost.

Town of Mendocino perched on the rocky Mendocino headlands

Mendocino ㉖

🏠 *1,200.* 🚌 ℹ *332 N Main St, Fort Bragg, (707) 961-6300.* 🖥 *www.mendocinocoast.com*

The founders of this fishing village came to California from New England in 1852, building their new homes to resemble those they had left behind. The Mendocino coastline is thus often referred to as "California's New England Coast." Perched on a rocky promontory above the Pacific Ocean, Mendocino retains the picturesque charm of its days as a fishing center. Its heather-covered bluffs, migrating gray whales, and stunning ocean vistas make it a popular tourist center, yet the town seems untarnished by commercialism. It is a thriving arts center with a large number of resident artists and writers. Visitors can stroll around the many exclusive boutiques, art galleries, bookshops, and cafés.

CALIFORNIA WINES

With over 327,000 acres (132,000 ha) of land under viticulture, California produces 90 percent of the nation's wine. Its latitude, proximity to the ocean, and sheltered valleys create a mild climate, ideal for growing grapes. Half the grapes grown here are harvested from the fertile stretch of land bordered by the Sacramento Valley to the north and San Joaquin Valley to the south. The north coast, home to most of the state's 800 wineries, accounts for less than a quarter of California's wine-growing acreage, but produces many of the country's best Sauvignon Blanc, Cabernet Sauvignon, Merlot, and Chardonnay grapes. Chardonnay and Pinot Noir grapes are the mainstays of the central coast region, which extends from the San Francisco Bay Area to Santa Barbara.

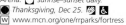

Sparkling Cuvée Napa by Mumm

Northern California

RUGGED AND SPARSELY populated, Northern California has a diverse landscape of dense forests, volcanic mountains, and arid plains. It also has the world's largest concentration of giant redwood trees, now protected by national parks. Scenic routes in the parks offer visitors a chance to view their awesome beauty. To experience the full immensity of the trees, however, it is best to walk around in these majestic groves.

Avenue of the Giants in the Humboldt Redwoods State Park

Humboldt Redwoods State Park ㉗

US Hwy 101. 🚂 Garberville. **Visitor Center** Weott 🛈 (707) 946-2263. ◯ Apr–Oct: 9am–5pm; Nov–Mar: 10am–4pm. ● Thanksg., Dec 25.

THIS PARK HAS the world's tallest redwood trees and the most extensive primeval redwood groves. The tallest individual specimen, the 364-ft (110-m) Dyersville Giant, was blown over by a storm in 1991. Now seen lying on its side, its size appears even more astounding.

The serpentine 33-mile (53-km) **Avenue of the Giants** runs through the 52,000-acre (21,053-ha) park. The visitor center is halfway along the road.

To the north is the town of **Scotia**, built in 1887 to house the workers of the Pacific Lumber Company's massive redwood mill. Scotia is the only complete lumber community still in existence in California. Its small museum traces the history of the town, and of the lumber industry, as well as offers self-guided tours of the lumber mill.

Eureka ㉘

🏨 27,600. ✈ 🚌 🛈 2112 Broadway, (707) 442-3738.

FOUNDED BY gold miners in 1850, Eureka was named after the state's ancient Greek motto, meaning "I have found it." Today, it is the northern coast's largest industrial center, with extensive logging and fishing operations surrounding the state-protected natural harbor. Its Old Town's many restored 19th-century buildings have been converted into fashionable cafés, bars, and restaurants.

Eureka also houses the 1885 Carson Mansion, home of the millionaire lumber baron William Carson, and now a private club. Its Gothic design is enhanced by its redwood construction, painted to resemble stone.

Redwood National Park ㉙

Arcata to Crescent City is 78 miles (125km). US Hwy 101 is the quickest route.
🅦 www.nationalpark.com/redwood

SOME OF THE largest original redwood forests in the world are preserved in this national park. Stretching along the coastline, the 58,000-acre (23,500-ha) park includes many smaller state parks and can be explored along a day-long drive. A two-day trip, however, allows time to walk away from the roads and experience the tranquility of the stately groves, or spot one of the world's last remaining herds of Roosevelt elk.

The park's headquarters are in **Crescent City**, a few miles north of which lies the 9,200-acre (3,720-ha) Jedediah Smith Redwoods State Park, with the most awe-inspiring coastal redwoods. Named after the fur trapper Jedediah Smith, the first white man who walked across the US, it has excellent campground facilities. South from Crescent City, the **Trees of Mystery** grove features unusual looking fiberglass statues of

REDWOODS & THE LUMBER INDUSTRY

The tallest tree on earth, the coniferous coastal redwood (*Sequoia sempervirens*) is unique to the northwest coast. It can live for 2,000 years and reach 350 ft (105 m), with roots that grow up to 200 ft (60 m) horizontally but only 4–6 ft (1–2 m) deep. Its fast growth and resistance to disease makes it ideal for commercial use. By the 1920s, however, logging had destroyed 90 percent of the groves. The Save the Redwoods League was formed, buying land now under state park protection. Lumber firms still own some groves, and their future remains a major environmental issue, both locally and nationally.

Redwood lumber

the mythical lumberjack Paul Bunyan and his faithful ox, Babe *(see p419)*. The park's main attraction is the world's tallest tree, a 368-ft (112-m) giant, standing in the **Tall Trees Grove**. Farther south is Big Lagoon, a freshwater lake stretching for 3 miles (5 km) and two other estuaries. Together, they form the **Humboldt Lagoons State Park**. The headlands at Patrick's Point State Park, at the southern end, are a good place to watch for migrating gray whales in winter.

Weaverville ③⓪

🏠 *3,500.* ✖ 🛈 *317 Main St, (530) 623-6101.*

THIS SMALL RURAL town has changed little since it was founded by gold prospectors 150 years ago. The **Jake Jackson Museum**, in the heart of the small commercial district, traces the history of the town and its surrounding gold mining and lumber region. Next door, the **Joss House State Historic Site** is the country's oldest and best-preserved Chinese temple. Built in 1874, it is a reminder of the many Chinese immigrants who came to the US to mine gold, and stayed on as cheap labor to build the California railroads.

North of Weaverville, the Trinity Alps rise up at the center of beautiful mountain wilderness. The mountains are popular with hikers and backpackers in summer and with cross-country skiers during the winter months.

Mount Shasta ③①

🚉 *Dunsmuir.* 🚌 *Siskiyou.* 🚌 *Shasta.* **Visitor Center** 🛈 *(530) 926-4865.* ◯ *daily.* 🌐 *www.mtshastachamber.com*

AT A HEIGHT of 14,162 ft (4,316 m) Mount Shasta is the second highest of the Cascade Mountains, after Mount Rainier in Washington *(see pp626–7)*. Visible more than 100 miles (160 km) away and usually covered with

Mount Shasta, towering over the town of Shasta below

snow, the summit is a popular destination for adventure sports enthusiasts such as mountaineers. At its foothills lies the picturesque town of **Shasta**, which was once one of the state's largest gold mining camps. Today, Shasta makes a welcome base with plenty of good places to stay.

Lava Beds National Monument ③②

🛈 *(530) 667-2282.* 🚌 *Klamath Falls.* 🛈 ◯ *daily.*

SPREADING OVER 46,500 acres (18,800 ha) of the Modoc Plateau, this eerie landscape of lava flows has over 200 caves and lava tubes – those cylindrical tunnels created by exposed lava turning to stone. Most of the volcanic caves lie near the visitor center, where visitors can take ranger-led or self-guided tours down into the caves. To visit any of the caves, wear sturdy shoes, carry a flashlight, and check first with the visitor center.

The park is also notable as the site of the 1872–73 Modoc War, one of the many conflicts between the US and the Native Americans. For six months a group of Modoc Indians, under the command of "Captain Jack," evaded the US Cavalry from a natural fortress of passageways along the park's northern border. The captain was eventually hanged, and the rest were forced into a reservation in what is now Oklahoma.

Lassen Volcanic National Park ③③

🚌 *Chester, Red Bluff.* **Visitor Center** 🛈 *(530) 595-4444.* ◯ *daily.*

BEFORE THE eruption of Mount St. Helens in Washington in 1980 *(see p629)*, the 10,457-ft (3,187-m) high Lassen Peak was the last volcano to erupt on mainland US. In nearly 300 eruptions between 1914 and 1917, it laid 100,000 acres (40,500 ha) of the surrounding land to waste.

Lassen Peak is considered to be still active. Numerous areas on its flanks show clear signs of the geological processes. The boardwalk trail of Bumpass Hell (named for an early guide, who lost his leg in a boiling mudpot in 1865) leads past a series of steaming sulfurous pools of boiling water, heated by molten rock deep underground. In summer, visitors can take the winding road through the park, climbing more than 8,500 ft (2,590 m) high to Summit Lake. The road continues winding its way through the so-called Devastated Area, a bleak gray landscape of rough volcanic mudflows, which terminates at the Manzanita Lake, and the **Loomis Museum**.

🏛 Loomis Museum
Lassen Park Rd, N Entrance.
🛈 *(530) 595-4444.* ◯ *late Jun– mid-Sep: daily.*

Sulfur springs in Lassen Volcanic National Park

The Gold Country

LOCATED AT THE HEART of California, the Gold Country was once a real life El Dorado, where a thick vein of gold sat waiting to be discovered. Once home of the Miwok and Maidu peoples, the Gold Rush turned this quiet region into a lawless jamboree of gold miners from all over the world. But the boom went bust by 1860. A few years later, the area saw another short-lived boom, when the transcontinental railroad was constructed through the Sierra Nevada Mountains by low-paid laborers, many of whom were Chinese.

Firehouse #1 Museum, a Nevada City landmark

Nevada City 34

👥 *2,855.* 🚆 🚌 ℹ *132 Main St, (530) 265-2692.*

LOCATED AT THE northern end of the Mother Lode gold fields, this picturesque city deserves its reputation as the "Queen of the Northern Mines." But the once thriving city faded into oblivion after the Gold Rush subsided. It was resurrected as a tourist destination a century later with galleries, restaurants, and inns re-creating Gold Rush themes. The town boasts one of the region's most photographed façades in the **Firehouse #1 Museum**, with its dainty balconies and white cupola. It is now a local history museum. Antique mining devices are displayed across the street. Other historic buildings include the Nevada Theater, a performance venue since 1865, and the National Hotel. One of California's oldest hotels, it first opened in the mid-1850s.

Grass Valley 35

👥 *9,000.* 🚆 ℹ *248 Mill St, (530) 273-4667.*

ONE OF THE largest and busiest gold mining towns, Grass Valley employed workers from the tin mines of Cornwall in England. It was their expertise that enabled local mines to stay in business long after the others had fallen quiet. At the entrance to the town's **North Star Mining Museum** are the giant Pelton wheel that increased production in underground mines. Also on view are a stamp mill (for crushing ore) and a Cornish pump which was used to filter out water.

A nugget of gold set inside quartz crystal

Grass Valley also served the nearby **Empire Mine**, the state's richest and longest surviving gold mine. Now a state park, the mine had recovered almost six million ounces of gold when it closed in 1956. Mining equipment and artifacts can be seen in the park and in the museum, but it is Empire Cottage, the mine's owner home that embodies the mine's riches.

🏛 **North Star Mining Museum**
Mill St at Allison Ranch Rd. ☎ *(530) 273-4255.* ○ *May–Oct: daily.*

🏛 **Empire Mine State Park**
☎ *(530) 273-8522.* ○ *daily.* ● *Jan 1, Thanksgiving, Dec 25.* 💲 ♿ ✋

Marshall Gold Discovery State Park 36

☎ *(530) 622-3470.* 🚌 *from Placerville.* ○ *8am–5pm daily.* ● *Jan 1, Thanksg, Dec 25.* 💲 ♿ ✋

THIS PEACEFUL park protects the site where gold was first discovered in 1848. James Marshall spotted shiny flakes in the water channel of a sawmill he and other workers were building for the Swiss entrepreneur John Sutter. Gold miners soon took over Sutter's land leaving him penniless. Within a year, Coloma had turned into a thriving city but then declined, with news of richer deposits elsewhere.

A replica of **Sutter's Mill** stands on the original site, and a statue of Marshall marks his grave. The park's Gold Country Museum features Native American artifacts, films, and other exhibits on the discovery of gold.

Reconstructed Sutter's Mill, Marshall Gold Discovery State Park

Sacramento ③

🚶 🚉 🚌 *30, 31, 32.* ℹ️ *(916) 442-7644.* 🌐 *www.oldsacramento.com*

FOUNDED BY John Sutter in 1839, California's capital city preserves many historic buildings along the waterfront in Old Sacramento. Most of the structures date from the 1860s, when it became the supply point for miners. Both the transcontinental railroad and Pony Express had their western terminus here,

with riverboats providing passage to San Francisco. The **California State Railroad Museum**, at the northern edge of the old town, houses some immaculately restored locomotives. A little away from the old city, the State Capitol stands in a land-scaped park. To its east, Sutter's Fort is a re-creation of the town's original settlement.

🏛 California State Railroad Museum

111 I St. 📞 *(916) 445-6645.* ⏰ *10am–5pm daily.* ● *Jan 1, Thanksgiving, Dec 25.*

CALIFORNIA STATE CAPITOL

Designed in 1860 in grand Renaissance Revival style, this building was completed in 1874. Housing the office of the governor and the state senate chambers, the Capitol also serves as a museum of the state's political and cultural history.

The Capitol Rotunda was restored to its original 19th-century splendor in 1975.

Original 1860 statuary

Entrance

The Historic Offices on the first floor contain a few government offices restored to their turn-of-the-century appearance.

Highway 49 ③

🚌 ℹ️ *542 Main St, Placerville, (530) 621-5885.*

THE GOLD COUNTRY offers one of California's best scenic drives, through rocky ridges and flowing rivers, along Highway 49. Many of the towns it passes through, such as **Sutter Creek**, have survived unchanged since the Gold Rush. Named after John Sutter, this scenic town grew up to service the Old Eureka Mine, owned by Hetty Green, the "Richest Woman in the World." Leland Stanford, the railroad baron, made his fortune here, by investing in the town's Lincoln Mine. He used the money to become a railroad magnate and then the governor of California.

A short drive southeast leads to **Jackson**, a bustling gold mining community that has continued to thrive as a

lumber mill town since 1850. The Amador County Museum, located on a hill above the town, features a range of old mining equipment.

Northward, Highway 49 passes through **Placerville**. Once a busy supply center for the area's mining camps, the town is still a major transportation center. Of interest here are the Placerville History Museum and the El Dorado County Historical Museum, which displays a replica of a 19th-century general store, artifacts from the Chinese settlement, and other local historical exhibits.

Parrots Ferry Bridge along Highway 49

Columbia State Historic Park ③

Hwy 49. ℹ️ *22708 Broadway, (209) 532-0150.*

AT THE HEIGHT of the Gold Rush, Columbia was one of the most important towns in the Gold Country. Most of the state's mining camps disintegrated once the gold ran out in the late 1850s. But Columbia was kept intact by its residents until 1945, when it was turned into a state historic park. Many of the town's buildings are preserved in their original state, like its transportation office, the **Wells Fargo Express Office**, and the restored **Columbia Schoolhouse**. Visitors can buy pans of sand to try panning gold.

🏛 Wells Fargo Express Office & Columbia Schoolhouse

⏰ *10am–4pm daily, Jun–Aug: until 6pm.* ● *Thanksgiving, Dec 25.*

The High Sierras

FORMING A TOWERING WALL AT THE eastern side of central California, the densely forested, 14,000-ft (4,270-m) high Sierra Nevada Mountains were formed 3 million years ago. Known as the High Sierras, these rugged mountains make up one of the state's most popular recreation areas, preserved by a series of national parks.

Skiing at Lake Tahoe's Alpine Meadows Resort

Lake Tahoe ⑩

🚹 South Lake Tahoe, (800) 288-2463

THE DEEP, EMERALD waters of this beautiful lake are set within an alpine valley at the highest point of the High Sierras. For over a century, Lake Tahoe has been a year-round recreational haven, offering water sports, hiking, and camping. South Lake Tahoe, the largest town here, caters to visitors headed for Nevada's casinos. To its west, the inlet of Emerald Bay State Park is the most photo-graphed part of the lake. To the north is the D.L. Bliss State Park with its 1903 Ehrman Mansion. The surrounding peaks are also famous for their ski resorts. The world-class Alpine Meadows and Squaw Valley are well-known because the Winter Olympics were held here in 1960.

Yosemite National Park ⑪

🚋 from Merced. 🚌 Yosemite Valley. 🚐 from Merced. 🛈 PO Box 577, Yosemite, (209) 372-0200. 🔲 daily. 🈳 🅿 🚻 🕚 🅆 www.nps.gov/yose

A WILDERNESS of evergreen forests, high meadows, and sheer granite walls, the 1,170 sq mile (3,030 sq km) Yosemite National Park (established in 1890) protects some of the world's most beau-tiful mountain terrain. Soaring cliffs, rugged canyons, valleys, gigantic trees, and waterfalls all combine to lend Yosemite its incom-parable beauty. Each season offers a dif-ferent experience, from the swelling waterfalls of spring to the russet colors of fall. Numerous roads, bus tours, bike paths, and hiking trails lead visitors from one awe-inspiring panoramic view to another.

Yosemite Valley is a good base from which to explore the park. **Yosemite Museum**, in the village, displays the history of the Native Miwok and Paiute people, along with works by local artists. Nearby is the **Ahwanee Hotel** (see p725). Built in 1927, this is one of the country's best-known hotels. Just to the south of the Valley Visitor Center, the tiny wooden **Yosemite Chapel** (1879) is the sole reminder of the park's Old Village, dating from the 19th century.

Standing nearly 1 mile (1.6 km) above the valley floor, the silhouette of the **Half Dome** cliff has become the symbol of Yosemite. Geologists believe that it is now three-quarters of its original size, rather than a true half. It is thought that 15,000 years ago glacial ice floes moved across the valley, scything off rock, depositing it downstream. A formidable trail leads to the 8,840-ft (2,695-m) summit, offering panoramic views of the valley. The other major cliff, **El Capitan**, standing guard at the valley's western entrance, attracts rock-climbers, who spend days on its sheer face

El Capitan, the world's largest piece of exposed granite, Yosemite NP

to reach the top. But the great Yosemite panorama is best experienced from the 3,215-ft (980-m) high **Glacier Point**. It can be reached only in summer, because snow blocks the road during winter.

Among the park's most recognizable features are the cascading Yosemite waterfalls, the highest in North America. Tumbling from a height of 2,425 ft (740 m) in two great leaps, **Upper** and **Lower Yosemite Falls** are at their peak in May and June, when the snow melts. By September, however, the falls often dry up.

In summer, when the wild-flowers are in full bloom, the park's striking landscape is best explored in the sub-alpine **Tuolumne Meadows** along the Tuolumne River at the Yosemite's eastern edge.

A few miles past Yosemite's southern entrance, **Mariposa Grove** features over 500 giant sequoia trees *(Sequoia-dendron gigantea)*, some more than 3,000 years old.

Tufa spires rising out of Mono Lake, Eastern Sierras

1870s but declined when the gold ran out in 1882. Now protected as a state historic park, Bodie's 170 buildings have been maintained in a state of "arrested decay." The result is an experience of empty streets lined by deserted wooden buildings. The Miner's Union Hall has been converted into a visitor center and a museum.

Nearby **Mono Lake**, covering 60-sq miles (155-sq km), lies at the eastern foot of the Sierra Nevada Mountains and presents an eerie sight of limestone towers rising from the water. Set between two volcanic islands, the lake has no natural outlet, but evaporation and water diversion to Los Angeles, through aqueducts, have caused it to shrink to one-fifth of its size. The lake's water has turned brackish and alkaline, putting the local wild-life and ecosystem in grave danger. In recent years, Mono Lake has been the subject of much environmental debate.

The 1879 Yosemite Chapel, Yosemite National Park

Eastern Sierras ⓯

Bodie State Historic Park 🗺 *from Bridgeport.* 🚏 *End of Hwy 270, (760) 647-6445.* ⵔ *daily.* **Mono Lake** ☎ *(760) 647-3044.* 🚉 *Merced.*

HIGH UP IN the foothills of the eastern Sierras lies **Bodie State Historic Park**, the largest ghost town in California. It was named after the prospector Waterman S. Bodey, who discovered surface gold here in 1859. The town thrived in the mid-

Sequoia & Kings Canyon National Parks ⓰

Ash Mountain, Three Rivers. ☎ *(559) 565-3341.* ⵔ *daily.* 🏛 & *call ahead.* 🅿 🚻 *summer only.* 🅿 🖥 *www.nps.gov/seki*

THESE TWIN national parks preserve lush green forests, magnificent glacier-carved canyons, and granite peaks. America's deepest canyon, the south fork of the Kings River, cuts a depth of 8,200 ft (2,500 m) through Kings Canyon. Roads serve

the western side of the parks; the rest is accessible only to hikers or rented pack-trains of horses or mules.

The parks embrace 34 separate groves of the sequoia tree, the earth's largest living species. **Giant Forest**, at the southern end of Sequoia National Park, is one of the world's largest groves of living sequoias. A 3-mile (5-km) trail from here leads to Moro Rock, a granite monolith affording a 360-degree view of the High Sierras and the Central Valley. To its east lies the marshy Crescent Meadow, bordered by sequoias. Another short trail leads to **Tharp's Log**, a hollowed-out sequoia, home to Hale Tharp, a 19th-century farmer who was introduced to the area by Native Americans.

North of Giant Forest is the world's largest living thing, the 275-ft (84-m) **General Sherman's Tree**. It still grows 0.4 inches (1 cm) every ten years and is rivaled by the third largest sequoia, **General Grant Tree** in Kings Canyon Park. This park also features the Big Stump Trail, lined with tall stumps, left by loggers in the 1880s.

Along the eastern boundary of Sequoia is the 14,496-ft (4,420-m) **Mount Whitney**, one of the highest peaks on the US mainland. A steep trail leads from Whitney Portal Road to the summit, offering a panorama over the High Sierras. The mountain, named in honor of geologist Josiah Whitney, was first climbed in 1873. The lovely green alpine meadows around it are ideal for backpacking in the summer months.

Practical Information

CALIFORNIA IS A VIBRANT and diverse vacation destination. The spirit of the state can be felt in the busy cities of San Francisco, Los Angeles, and San Diego as much as in the quiet wilderness of the Sierra Nevada Mountains. At the center of the film industry, Los Angeles prides itself as the entertainment capital of the world. All over the state visitors needs' are well tended. The state's major tourist spots see a rush of visitors from mid-April to September. But the winter months are equally popular, either for the warm climate of the south or the ski slopes of Lake Tahoe.

TOURIST INFORMATION

ADVANCE INFORMATION can be obtained from the **California Division of Tourism** or the nearest US Consulate. Local Visitors' and Convention Bureaus supply maps, guides, event listings, and discount passes for public transportation and tourist destinations.

PERSONAL SECURITY

SAN FRANCISCO IS one of the safest large cities in the US. Problems are more visible in Los Angeles, although the notorious gangs of the city generally do not bother visitors. Still, as in every big city, visitors can be victims of petty thefts or car crime. Although police patrol regularly in the tourist areas, it is good to be cautious. Safety rules for pedestrians are strictly observed – jay-walking, or crossing the road anywhere except at an intersection, can result in a fine.

NATURAL HAZARDS

IN THE EVENT OF an earthquake, it is most important not to panic. Most injuries occur from falling material. Stand in a doorway, or crouch under a table. In a car, slow down and pull over.

When hiking in the wilderness, be wary of occasionally dangerous wildlife. Also be careful of rapid climatic changes in deserts, where temperatures can drop to below freezing points at high elevations. The Pacific Ocean can often be rough, with a strong undertow.

GETTING AROUND

ALTHOUGH OFTEN more time-consuming, traveling by train, bus, and ferry is an inexpensive way of getting around the state. Within the major cities of San Francisco, Los Angeles, and San Diego, the public transportation network serves parts of the city very well, with shuttle buses, trams, Metro trains, ferries, taxis, and cable cars.

The network of Amtrak railroad lines and connecting bus services serves the state's populous areas. Guided bus tours are a convenient way of sightseeing. Express boat services provide a fast link from Los Angeles to Santa Catalina Island, while others sail more leisurely across San Francisco Bay. Most ferries carry foot passengers and bicycles.

DRIVING IN CALIFORNIA

DRIVING IS the best way to travel around the state. It is best to arrange a fly-drive package before leaving for California. Find out exactly what is included and whether any extra payments may arise when the car is returned. These additions – which may include collision damage waiver, drop-off charges, and rental tax – can double the original fee. Litigation is common in California, so it is best to be fully insured.

In the US, cars are driven on the right side of the road. Seat belts are compulsory. The maximum speed limit is generally 65 mph (104 km/h) In cities, the speed limits are restricted as marked and may vary within a few miles. These controls are rigorously enforced by the Highway Patrol. Drunk driving is a serious offense and carries very heavy penalties. You can turn right on red at traffic lights if there is nothing coming the other way. The first vehicle to reach a stop-sign junction has the right of way.

Parking in California cities is strictly controlled and can be somewhat expensive. In remote areas, drivers should be wary of wildlife that may stray onto the roads.

OUTDOOR ACTIVITIES

CALIFORNIA is practically synonymous with the great outdoors. The deserts, redwood forests, alpine meadows, mountains, lakes, and white beaches all welcome visitors. The state

---

THE CLIMATE OF CALIFORNIA

Apart from the extremes of the north and the deserts, the state's climate is neither oppressive in summer, nor too cold in winter. The Northern Coastal Range is temperate, although wet in winter. To the east, rain turns to snow on the Sierra Nevada Mountains. Central California and the Central Valley have a Mediterranean climate, characterized by seasonal changes in rainfall – a dry summer and a rainy winter – but only moderate changes in temperature. The weather becomes drier and warmer toward the south with soaring temperatures in the desert in summer.

LOS ANGELES

°F/C	Apr	Jul	Oct	Jan
high	70/21	81/27	76/24	65/18
low	50/16	60/16	54/12	46/8
sun	21 days	25 days	23 days	21 days
rain	1 in	0.01 in	0.3 in	2.9 in

32°F / 0°C

has a culture rich with physical activity, and wilderness is never far from any city.

With more than 250 places classified as state parks, wilderness areas, or historic sites, California is a hikers' and campers' paradise. For camping, reserve a site with **State Park Reservations** or **Yosemite Reservations**. There are more than 1 million miles (1.6 million km) of trails in California, the longest being the Pacific Crest Trail, stretching from Canada to Mexico. The **Sierra Club** organizes guided outings and provides detailed maps. Many state parks also allow cyclists on their hiking trails. Outfitters such as **Backroads** lead groups of cyclists on tours of rolling countrysides.

Equestrians find a wide variety of riding trails here. California's 900-mile (1,450-km) coastline offers various beaches. Some have rough waves and rocky shores; others, with white sand, arching waves, and warm water, are ideal for surfing. The best beaches include the **Leo Carrillo State Beach** in Orange County, **Windansea Beach** in La Jolla, and **Corona del Mar** in Newport.

The lakes, rivers, and beaches of California offer a variety of watersports, from slow cruises on houseboats to parasailing and whitewater rafting. Most outfitters that offer river rafting also provide kayak and canoe trips. For more information, contact **American River Touring Association**. The rivers and coastline are feeding grounds for migrating birds. In autumn, ducks, geese, and other shorebirds can be spotted here. The state is also an angler's haven. The rivers and streams of the Sierra Nevada Mountains have plenty of trout. Bass fishing in California's lakes and reservoirs is plentiful throughout the year.

From December through April, gray whales travel 7,000 miles (11,260 kms) from the California coast to Mexico. Ocean cruises offer views of the impressive mammals.

California's great outdoors list also includes island hopping. Five volcanic islands off the coast of Southern California form the Channel Islands National Park, ideal for hiking, exploring rock pools, and spotting whales and dolphins. **Island Packers** is only one of the many outfits that offer island tours.

California is famed for its special interest vacations, the most popular being the tours of the state's missions along El Camino Real. Resident writers often give readings at local writers' workshops such as the **Santa Barbara Writers' Conference**. Institutes such as **Tante Marie's Cooking School** provide lodging, cooking classes, shopping tours, and visits to the Wine Country during week-long intensive courses in summer.

SHOPPING

A MAJOR PLAYER in the global economy, California is known for its casual clothing as well as the best in cutting-edge fashion. It is the largest producer of children's clothing in the US, with Sara's Prints and **Levi Strauss** being among the best. It is equally famous for its sportswear and swimwear, designed by names such as **California Wave**.

Fresh fruit, nuts, and vegetables from the San Joaquin Valley feeds the entire nation. The fine wines of Napa and Sonoma Valleys are available in wineries across the state. Some, such as **Viansa Winery** and **Sebastiani Vineyards**, also sell a wide range of wine related products.

Aside from the shopping districts of L.A. and San Francisco, the state's smaller towns offer a wide range of merchandise and local produce in roadside food stands, wineries, antique shops, and flea markets, where prices tend to be cheaper than in cities.

Where to Stay

Framed by rugged coastal mountains, forested hills, sophisticated urban centers, and a long coastline, California is one of the premier vacation destinations in the world. From budget inns to five-star resorts, there is a wealth of options for travelers to the state. Hotels here have been selected across a wide price range for their excellent facilities and locations.

	Number of Rooms	Restaurant	Children's Facilities	Garden or Terrace	Swimming Pool
LOS ANGELES					
ANAHEIM: *Disneyland Hotel* $$$$ 1150 W Cerritos, CA 92802. **(** (714) 778-6600. **FAX** (714) 956-6597. **W** www.disneyland.com This large hotel with guest rooms or cottages is linked to Disneyland by monorail. The emphasis is on entertainment.	2,290	●	▦	●	▦
BEVERLY HILLS: *Peninsula Beverly Hills* $$$$$ 9882 S Santa Monica Blvd, CA 90212. **(** (310) 551-2888, (800) 462-7899. **FAX** (310) 788-2319. **W** www.peninsula.com Celebrities come to this luxurious five-star hotel.	196	●	▦	●	▦
DOWNTOWN: *Miyako Inn and Spa* $$ 328 E 1st St, CA 90012. **(** (213) 617-2000, (800) 228-6596. **FAX** (213) 617-2700. **W** www.miyakoinn.com This hotel in Little Tokyo has a karaoke lounge and separate spa facilities for men and women. Children under 12 stay free.	174	●			
HOLLYWOOD: *Ramada Inn* $$ 1160 N Vermont, CA 90029. **(** (323) 660-1788, (800) 272-6232. **FAX** (323) 660-8069. **W** www.ramadahollywood.com This chain hotel near Universal Studios has suites and rooms with Internet, free breakfast, and a jacuzzi.	140	●	▦		
LONG BEACH: *Hotel Queen Mary* $$$ 1126 Queen's Hwy, CA 90802. **(** (562) 435-3511, (800) 437-2934. **FAX** (562) 437-4531. **W** www.queenmary.com The famous ocean liner's first-class staterooms have been updated and restored. Breakfast is included.	365	●	▦	●	
MALIBU: *Casa Malibu Inn on the Beach* $$ 22752 Pacific Coast Hwy, CA 90265. **(** (310) 456-2219, (800) 831-0858. **FAX** (310) 456-5418. This hotel is built on its own private beach.	21			●	
PASADENA: *Ritz Carlton Huntingdon Hotel* $$$$ 1401 S Oak Knoll Ave, CA 91106. **(** (626) 568-3900, (800) 241-3333. **FAX** (626) 568-3700. **W** www.ritzcarlton.com This luxury hotel has elegant rooms and a wooden bridge between the two wings overlooking Japanese gardens.	391	●	▦	●	▦
SANTA MONICA: *Four Points Hotel* $$$ 530 W Pico Blvd, CA 90405. **(** (310) 399-9344, (800) 465-4329. **FAX** (310) 399-2504. **W** www.fourpoints.com Offers jacuzzis, a free airport shuttle, and tours.	314	●	▦		▦
VENICE BEACH: *The Cadillac* $ 8 Dudley Ave, CA 90291. **(** (310) 399-8876. **FAX** (310) 399-4536. **W** www.cadillachotel.com This gorgeous Art Deco hotel attracts a young, chic crowd. It is right on the beach, with a sauna, pool tables, and sun terrace.	41			●	
WEST HOLLYWOOD: *Argyle Hotel* $$$$$ 8358 Sunset Blvd, CA 90069. **(** (323) 654-7100, (800) 225-2637. **FAX** (323) 654-1004. **W** www.argylehotel.com Originally built as apartments for film stars, the rooms here are Italian Art Deco in style.	64	●	▦	●	▦
SAN DIEGO COUNTY					
CORONADO: *Hotel del Coronado* $$$$$ 1500 Orange Ave, CA 92118. **(** (619) 435-6611, (800) 468-3533. **FAX** (619) 522-8238. This grand Victorian hotel on the beach has been updated with modern annexes and a spa.	700	●	▦	●	▦
LA JOLLA: *Embassy Suites Hotel* $$$ 4550 La Jolla Village Dr, CA 92122. **(** (858) 453-0400, (800) 362-2779. **FAX** (858) 453-4226. **W** www.embassysuites.com This modern hotel with two-room suites is perfect for families. It offers breakfast and a game room.	335	●	▦		▦

Price categories for a standard double room per night, inclusive of breakfast, service charges, and any additional taxes:

$ under $100
$$ $100–$150
$$$ $150–$200
$$$$ $200–$250
$$$$$ over $250

RESTAURANT
Hotel restaurant or dining room usually open to nonresidents unless otherwise stated.

CHILDREN'S FACILITIES
Indicates cribs and/or a baby-sitting service available. A few hotels also provide children's portions and high chairs in the restaurant.

GARDEN OR TERRACE
Hotels with a garden, courtyard, or terrace, often with tables for eating outside.

SWIMMING POOL
Hotel with indoor or outdoor swimming pool.

	Number of Rooms	Restaurant	Children's Facilities	Garden or Terrace	Swimming Pool
SAN DIEGO: *Marriott Hotel* — $$$$ 333 W Harbor Dr, CA 92101. (619) 234-1500, (800) 228-9290. FAX (619) 234-8678. www.marriott.com A 25-story luxury hotel next to San Diego Bay with exceptional outdoor landscaping and facilities.	1,357	●	■		■
TIJUANA: *Grand Hotel Tijuana* — $$ 4500 Blvd Agua Caliente, CP 22420. (011-52-66) 81-70-00. FAX (011-52-66) 81-70-16. This is a large hotel complex with twin towers. Facilities include tennis courts and Jacuzzis.	423	●	■	●	■
THE DESERTS					
DEATH VALLEY: *Furnace Creek Inn* — $$$$ 1 Main St, CA 92328. (760) 786-2345. FAX (760) 786-2514. www.furnacecreekresort.com This marvelous, historic resort is one of the most stylish places in the desert, with spring-fed pools, tennis, and golf.	68	●	■	●	■
PALM SPRINGS: *The Palm Springs Hilton Resort* — $$$$ 400 E Tahquitz Canyon Way, CA 92262. (760) 320-6868, (800) 522-6900. FAX (760) 320-2126. www.hilton.com Near downtown, this hotel's sports facilities include tennis courts and access to local golf courses.	260	●	■		■
PALM SPRINGS: *Givenchy Hotel and Spa* — $$$$$ 4200 E Palm Canyon Dr, CA 92264. (760) 770-5000, (800) 276-5000. FAX (760) 324-7280. This elegant hotel has a golf course, tennis courts, and a spa.	98	●		●	■
TWENTYNINE PALMS: *Best Western Gardens Inn & Suites* — $ 71487 Twenty Nine Palms Hwy, CA 92277. (760) 367-9141. FAX (760) 367-2584. www.bestwestern.com This lushly landscaped hotel is conveniently located near the main entrance to the Joshua Tree National Park.	84		■		■
CENTRAL CALIFORNIA					
BIG SUR: *Post Ranch Inn* — $$$$$ PO Box 219, Hwy 1, CA 93920. (831) 667-2200, (800) 527-2200. FAX (831) 667-2824. www.postranchinn.com Buildings at this extraordinary resort with fine facilities include tree houses and earth shelters built into the hillside.	30	●		●	■
CARMEL: *Highlands Inn and Restaurant* — $$$$$ Pacific Coast Hwy 1, CA 93923. (831) 624-3801, (800) 682-4811. FAX (831) 626-1574. This rustic hotel is set in woodland on a bluff overlooking the coast. The inn offers excellent ocean views.	142	●	■	●	■
MONTEREY: *Monterey Plaza Hotel and Spa* — $$$ 400 Cannery Row, CA 93940. (831) 646-1700, (800) 334-3999. FAX (831) 646-5937. www.montereyplaza.com Some rooms have balconies with views of Monterey Bay. The hotel is near all the city sights.	285	●	■		
SANTA BARBARA: *Four Seasons Biltmore* — $$$$$ 1260 Channel Dr, CA 93108. (805) 969-2261, (800) 332-3442. FAX (805) 565-8323. www.fourseasons.com/santabarbara A luxury resort since the 1920s, the rooms, suites, and cottages are set in coastal gardens.	213	●	■	●	■
SANTA CRUZ: *Sunset Inn* — $$ 2424 Mission St, CA 95060. (831) 423-7500. FAX (831) 423-7595. This hotel has microwaves and refrigerators in all rooms. Close to excellent restaurants and all corporate businesses.	32		■		
SAN LUIS OBISPO: *The Madonna Inn* — $$$ 100 Madonna Rd, CA 93405. (805) 543-3000, (800) 543-9666. FAX (805) 543-1800. www.madonnainn.com All the rooms have themes – for example, the Caveman Room is made entirely out of rock. Book in advance.	109	●	■	●	

For key to symbols see back flap

		Price categories info		NUMBER OF ROOMS	RESTAURANT	CHILDREN'S FACILITIES	GARDEN OR TERRACE	SWIMMING POOL

Price categories for a standard double room per night, inclusive of breakfast, service charges, and any additional taxes:

- $ under $100
- $$ $100–$150
- $$$ $150–$200
- $$$$ $200–$250
- $$$$$ over $250

RESTAURANT
Hotel restaurant or dining room usually open to nonresidents unless otherwise stated.

CHILDREN'S FACILITIES
Indicates cribs and/or a baby-sitting service available. A few hotels also provide children's portions and high chairs in the restaurant.

GARDEN OR TERRACE
Hotels with a garden, courtyard, or terrace, often with tables for eating outside.

SWIMMING POOL
Hotel with indoor or outdoor swimming pool.

SAN FRANCISCO

Hotel	Rooms	Restaurant	Children's Facilities	Garden or Terrace	Swimming Pool
BERKELEY: *Claremont Resort, Spa, & Tennis Club* $$$$ — 41 Tunnel Road, Oakland, CA 94623. (510) 843-3000, (800) 843-7924. FAX (510) 549-8582. www.claremontresort.com At the foot of the Berkeley Hills, this is the area's grandest hotel.	239	●	■	●	
CHINATOWN & NOB HILL: *Hotel Triton* $$$$$ — 342 Grant Ave, CA 94108. (415) 394-0500, (800) 433-6611. FAX (415) 394-0555. www.hoteltriton.com Small but stylish, this is the newest hip place to stay. You might even run into a rock star or two.	140	●			
DOWNTOWN: *Clift Hotel* $$$$$ — 495 Geary St, CA 94102. (415) 775-4700, (800) 652-5438. FAX (415) 441-4621. www.ianschragerhotels.com Well-appointed rooms, an old-fashioned ambience, and gracious service characterize this fine hotel.	363	●			
FISHERMAN'S WHARF: *Sheraton at Fisherman's Wharf* $$$ — 2500 Mason St, CA 94133. (415) 362-5500, (800) 325-3535. FAX (415) 956-5275. www.sheratonatthewharf.com This family-oriented tourist hotel is also popular with business people and has easy access to many attractions.	525	●	■		■
HAIGHT ASHBURY: *Red Victorian Bed & Breakfast* $$ — 1665 Haight St, CA 94117. (415) 864-1978. FAX (415) 863-3293. www.redvic.com This unique hotel offers New Age accommodation in themed rooms such as the Flower Child Suite; no radios, TVs, or smoking.	18				
MUIR BEACH: *The Pelican Inn* $$$ — 10 Pacifica Way, CA 94965. (415) 383-6000. FAX (415) 383-3424. www.pelicaninn.com Roaring fireplaces, British beers, and gorgeous rooms, some with four-poster beds, are all within walking distance of Muir Woods.	7	●	■	●	
OAKLAND: *Waterfront Plaza Hotel* $$$$ — 10 Washington St, CA 94607. (510) 836-3800. FAX (510) 832-5695. www.waterfrontplazahotel.com Many rooms have fireplaces and views across the bay at this well-appointed hotel at the edge of Jack London Square.	144	●	■	●	
PACIFIC HEIGHTS: *Edward II Inn & Suites* $$$ — 3155 Scott St at Lombard, CA 94123. (415) 922-3000, (800) 473-2846. FAX (415) 931-5784. www.edwardii.com This 1949 house offers free breakfasts and afternoon sherry.	39				
SAN JOSE: *San Jose Hilton & Towers Hotel* $$$ — 300 Almaden Blvd, CA 95110. (408) 287-2100, (800) 445-8667. FAX (408) 947-4489. www.hilton.com This chain hotel is well equipped for the business traveler. Each floor has its own concierge.	355	●	■	●	■

WINE COUNTRY

Hotel	Rooms	Restaurant	Children's Facilities	Garden or Terrace	Swimming Pool
MENDOCINO: *MacCallum House* $$$ — 45020 Albion St (PO Box 206), CA 95460. (707) 937-0289, (800) 609-0492. www.maccallumhouse.com Not all rooms have private baths at this 19th-century inn. Ask for one of the annexes, many of which also have fireplaces.	19	●	■	●	
NAPA: *Silverado Country Club Resort* $$$$ — 1600 Atlas Peak Rd, CA 94558. (707) 257-0200, (800) 532-0500. FAX (707) 257-5400. www.silveradoresort.com Luxurious guest bungalows surround an old mansion set in 1,200 acres (485 ha). Fabulous recreational facilities are also available for guests staying here.	260	●	■	●	■
SONOMA: *Victorian Garden Inn* $$$ — 316 E Napa St, CA 95476. (707) 996-5339. FAX (707) 996-1689. www.victoriangardeninn.com This peaceful Greek Revival farmhouse offers the perfect antidote to a hectic tour of the region's wineries.	5			●	■

THE NORTH

EUREKA: *Quality Inn* — $ — 60
1209 4th St, CA 95501. **C** *(707) 443-1601.* **FAX** *(707) 444-8365.*
W www.qualityinneureka.com Along with a prime location at the heart of Eureka's
Old Town, this hotel offers spacious rooms and suites, plus a sauna.

MOUNT LASSEN: *Mineral Lodge* — $ — 20
PO Box 160 Mineral, CA 96063. **C** *(530) 595-4422.* **W** www.minerallodge.com
This rustic lodge offers motel-style rooms, and a tavern.
It is on the southern fringes of Lassen Volcanic National Park.

MOUNT SHASTA: *Mountain Air Lodge* — $ — 50
1121 S Mount Shasta Blvd, CA 96067. **C** *(530) 926-3411, (800) 727-3704.*
This simple lodge-style hotel is in a wonderful mountain setting.
Ski slopes and water-sports facilities are just a short drive away.

SCOTIA: *Scotia Inn* — $$ — 20
100 Main St, CA 95565. **C** *(707) 764-5684.* **FAX** *(707) 764-1707.* **W** www.scotiainn.com
Built at Scotia's lumber mill, this inn is a showcase of redwood craftsmanship,
with period furnishings such as claw-foot bathtubs.

WEAVERVILLE: *Motel Trinity* — $ — 25
1112 Main St, CA 96093. **C** *(530) 623-2129.* **FAX** *(530) 623-6007.*
Accommodations in this small motel range from single rooms to two-
bedroom suites with kitchenettes. Some rooms have jacuzzis.

GOLD COUNTRY & THE CENTRAL VALLEY

GRASS VALLEY: *Holbrooke Hotel & Restaurant* — $$$ — 27
212 West Main St, CA 95945. **C** *(530) 273-1353, (800) 933-7077.* **FAX** *(530) 273-0434.*
W www.holbrooke.com Rooms in this downtown hotel – a California Historic
Landmark – are named after famous guests.

NEVADA CITY: *National Hotel* — $ — 42
211 Broad St, CA 95959. **C** *(530) 265-4551.* **FAX** *(530) 265-2445.*
W www.thenationalhotel.com This historic building surrounded by pine trees has
been a hotel since 1855. All the rooms have Victorian furnishings.

SACRAMENTO: *Marriott Hotel* — $$$$ — 262
1211 Point E Dr, Rancho Cordova, CA 95742. **C** *(916) 638-1100, (800) 228-9290.*
FAX *(916) 635-8356.* **W** www.marriott.com
This hotel is perfect for the business traveler and the tourist.

SONORA: *Sonora Days Inn & Café* — $$ — 64
160 S Washington St, CA 95370. **C** *(209) 532-2400, (800) 580-4667.*
FAX *(209) 536-1303.* **W** www.sonoradaysinn.com
Housed in an 1890s Spanish-style building in old downtown Sonora; there is
a motel annex at the back.

SUTTER CREEK: *Sutter Creek Inn* — $$ — 17
75 Main St, CA 95685. **C** *(209) 267-5606.* **FAX** *(209) 267-9287.* **W** www.suttercreekinn.com
This English-style country inn has swinging beds that hang by chains from
the ceiling. Some rooms have fireplaces and private patios.

THE HIGH SIERRAS

KINGS CANYON NATIONAL PARK: *Montecito Lodge* **W** www.montecitolodge.com — $$ — 52
PO Box 858, Grant Grove, CA 93633. **C** *(559) 565-3388.* **FAX** *(559) 565-3223.*
Set amid groves of giant sequoias, this is a family-oriented lodge.

LEE VINING: *Best Western Lake View Lodge* — $ — 46
PO Box 345, CA 93541. **C** *(760) 647-6543, (800) 528-1234.* **FAX** *(760) 647-6325.*
W www.bestwestern.com Set on the western shore of Mono Lake, this motel makes
an excellent base for exploring the area. Some rooms have kitchens.

TRUCKEE: *Donner Lake Village Resort* — $$ — 64
Suite 101, 15695 Donner Pass Rd, CA 96161. **C** *(530) 587-6081, (800) 621-6664.*
FAX *(530) 587-8782.* **W** www.donnerlakevillage.com
With its own beach and marina, this resort has two-bedroom suites.

YOSEMITE NATIONAL PARK: *Ahwahnee Hotel* — $$$$ — 123
Yosemite Valley, CA 95389. **C** *(209) 372-1407.* **FAX** *(209) 372-1403.*
W www.yosemitepark.com This is the most stylish of Yosemite's hotels. Rental
bikes and horseback riding are available.

For key to symbols see back flap

Where to Eat

Of all the states in the country, California has perhaps the widest variety of places to eat. "California cuisine" – light food prepared in a range of international styles using locally grown ingredients – is now internationally recognized. The many ethnic cuisines reflect the state's many cultures. In the listings below, "L" indicates lunch and "D" stands for dinner.

Column headings: **Outdoor Eating** | **Vegetarian Specialties** | **Bar Area/Cocktail Bar** | **Fixed-Price Menu** | **Children's Facilities**

LOS ANGELES

BEVERLY HILLS: *Nate 'n' Al's Deli* $
414 N Beverly Dr, CA 90210. ((310) 274-0101. Everyone comes here for fabulous sandwiches, deli items, and dinners. Breakfast is served all day.

BEVERLY HILLS: *Mr. Chow* $$$$$
#44 N Camden Dr, CA 90210. ((310) 278-9911.
Celebritites come to this stylish restaurant for delicious Peking-style cuisine. Favorites include drunken fish and gamblers' duck. Sat & Sun L.

DOWNTOWN: *Cicada* $$$$
617 S Olive St, CA 90014. ((213) 488-9488.
The contemporary Italian cuisine packs in the customers at this beautiful Art Deco restaurant in the Oviatt Hotel. Sun, Mon–Wed L, Sat L.

HOLLYWOOD: *Canter's Deli* $
419 N Fairfax Ave, CA 90036. ((323) 651-2030.
This 24-hour deli has superb sandwiches and diner-style meals.

HOLLYWOOD: *The Gumbo Pot* $
Farmers Market, 6333 W 3rd St, CA 90036. ((323) 933-0358.
Try gumbo stew and enormous po' boys (foot-long sandwiches) at this Cajun fast-food bar, with occasional live Cajun bands. D.

HOLLYWOOD: *Mandalay* $$$$
611 N La Brea Ave, CA 90036. ((323) 933-0717.
This French-Vietnamese restaurant's eclectic menu includes sushi, dumplings, and traditional Vietnamese dishes such as spicy beef salad. L.

LONG BEACH: *M Bar & Grill* $$
213A Pine Ave at Broadway St, CA 90802. ((562) 435-2525.
A fusion of Mediterranean and Latin flavors highlights the cuisine at this trendy café with rotating art exhibits and good live bands. Sat & Sun L.

MALIBU: *Gladstone's 4 Fish* $$$
17300 Pacific Coast Hwy, CA 90272. ((310) 454-3474.
This oceanside seafood restaurant is great fun for families. Portions are huge, but you can take home the leftovers in an aluminum foil sculpture.

PASADENA: *Yujean Kang's* $$$
67 N Raymond Ave, CA 91103. ((626) 585-0855.
Presentation is everything at this very elegant Chinese restaurant.
Try the "lobster with strange flavors." Lunch is a bargain. Tue.

SANTA MONICA: *Schatzi on Main* $$
3110 Main St, CA 90405. ((310) 399-4800.
Hollywood star Arnold Schwarzenegger owns this pleasant restaurant serving Austrian specialties and healthy California cuisine.

VENICE: *Café 50s Diner* $
838 Lincoln Blvd, CA 90291. ((310) 399 1955.
This tiny 1950s café serves sandwiches, salads, hamburgers, milkshakes, and "blue plate special" dinners, such as pot roast, in the evenings.

WEST HOLLYWOOD: *The Rainbow Bar and Grill* $
9015 Sunset Blvd, CA 90069. ((310) 278-4232.
This high-energy hangout for the entertainment industry serves Continental food with Italian flair. It is also a nightclub in the evenings. Sat & Sun.

WESTWOOD/WEST L.A.: *Bombay Café* $$
12021 W Pico Blvd, CA 90025. ((310) 473-3388.
One of the best Indian restaurants in the city, this place serves homecooked dishes from the owner's native city. Busy but worth it. Mon.

	OUTDOOR EATING	VEGETARIAN SPECIALTIES	BAR AREA/COCKTAIL BAR	FIXED-PRICE MENU	CHILDREN'S FACILITIES

Price categories include a three-course meal for one, a glass of house wine, and all unavoidable extra charges such as sales tax and service.
$ under $20
$$ $20–30
$$$ $30–45
$$$$ $45–60
$$$$$ over $60

OUTDOOR EATING
Some tables on a patio or terrace.
VEGETARIAN SPECIALTIES
One menu always includes a selection of vegetarian dishes.
BAR AREA/COCKTAIL BAR
There is a bar area or cocktail bar within the restaurant.
FIXED-PRICE MENU
A fixed-price menu offered at lunch, dinner or both, usually with three courses.
CHILDREN'S FACILITIES
Small portions and/or high chairs available on request.

SAN DIEGO COUNTY

CORONADO: *Poehe's* $$$
1201 1st St, Old Ferry Landing Plaza. (619) 437-4474.
There are lovely views of downtown San Diego from this restaurant, which serves creative Polynesian cuisine. The setting is very Hawaiian, with waterfalls and tropical plants every place you look.

| | ● | ● | | | ● |

LA JOLLA: *Top O' The Cove* $$$$$
1216 Prospect St, CA 92037. (858) 454-7779.
Fabulous coastal views, celebrity customers, and delicious food guarantee the success of this famous restaurant. The cuisine is contemporary French with a Pacific Rim influence. Dress up.

| | ● | ● | | ● | ● |

SAN DIEGO: *Big Kitchen* $
3003 Grape St, CA 92102. (619) 234-5789.
The best breakfast intown and rumored to be where Whoopi Goldberg washed dishes. The staff is good humored, the place is kid friendly, and it's very, very popular. ● *D.*

| | | ● | | | ● |

SAN DIEGO: *Humphrey's* $$$$$
2241 Shelter Island Dr, CA 92106. (619) 224-3577.
Named after Humphrey Bogart and decorated in the style of *Casablanca*, this seafood restaurant serves lobster fresh from the tank.

| | | | ● | | ● |

THE DESERTS

BARSTOW: *Cactus Kitchen* $
1505 E Main St, CA 92311. (760) 256-8806.
American food is offered at this café set in a large Holiday Inn. After a hearty meal, the popular Calico Ghost Town is just minutes away.

| | | | ● | ● | ● |

DEATH VALLEY: *Wrangler Steakhouse* $$
Furnace Creek Ranch, CA 92328. (760) 786-2345 (ext. 250).
This classic steak house offers steaks, chops, chicken, and seafood in a Southwestern setting. There is also a well-stocked salad bar.

| | | ● | ● | | ● |

DEATH VALLEY: *Inn Dining Room* $$$
Furnace Creek Inn, CA 92328. (760) 786-2345 (ext. 253).
There are wonderful mountain views from this popular Continental restaurant set in the Furnace Creek Inn. ● *Mon.*

| | | ● | ● | | ● |

PALM SPRINGS: *Flower Drum* $$
424 S Indian Canyon Dr, CA 92262. (760) 323-3020.
Five chefs serve five regional styles of Chinese cooking. There is a stream filled with fish running through the center of the restaurant. ● *L.*

| | | ● | ● | ● | ● |

CENTRAL CALIFORNIA

BIG SUR: *Nepenthe* $$
Hwy 1, CA 93920. (831) 667-2345.
Originally a honeymoon retreat for Orson Welles and Rita Hayworth, this restaurant offers panoramic views of the coastline. The emphasis is on basic American cuisine.

| | ● | ● | ● | ● | ● |

CARMEL: *The French Poodle* $$$
Junipero & 5th Ave, CA 93921. (831) 624-8643.
This intimate restaurant was selected as one of the best French restaurants in the US by the International Restaurant Rating Bureau. ● *Sun, Mon–Sat L.*

| | | ● | | | |

MONTEREY: *Fresh Cream* $$$$
99 Pacific St, Suite 100C, Heritage Harbor, CA 93940. (831) 375-9798.
This award-winning restaurant, with its harbor views, offers some of the best French food in Northern California. ● *L.*

| | | ● | ● | | |

For key to symbols see back flap

Price categories include a three-course meal for one, half a bottle of house wine, and all unavoidable extra charges such as sales tax and service.
$ under $20
$$ $20–30
$$$ $30–45
$$$$ $45–60
$$$$$ over $60

OUTDOOR EATING
Some tables on a patio or terrace.
VEGETARIAN SPECIALTIES
One menu always includes a selection of vegetarian dishes.
BAR AREA/COCKTAIL BAR
There is a bar area or cocktail bar within the restaurant.
FIXED-PRICE MENU
A fixed-price menu offered at lunch, dinner or both, usually with three courses.
CHILDREN'S FACILITIES
Small portions and/or high chairs available on request.

	OUTDOOR EATING	VEGETARIAN SPECIALTIES	BAR AREA/COCKTAIL BAR	FIXED-PRICE MENU	CHILDREN'S FACILITIES
SANTA BARBARA: *Something's Fishy* $$ 502 State St, CA 93101. ☎ *(805) 966-6607.* The crowd is mixed at this lively Japanese restaurant. Sit at the all-you-can-eat sushi bar or have a Benihana-style dinner cooked and served at your table. ♿ 💳					■
SANTA BARBARA: *The Wine Cask* $$$ 813 Anacapa St, CA 93101. ☎ *(805) 966-9463.* Mediterranean cuisine is offered here and one of the best wine lists in the US. Eat inside under the decoratively painted ceiling or outside in the courtyard. ● *L.* ♿ 🍷 💳	■	●	■		■
SANTA CRUZ: *Crows Nest* $$ 2218 E Cliff Dr, CA 95062. ☎ *(831) 476-4560.* Perched on Santa Cruz harbor jetty, this restaurant serves fresh seafood, steaks, and pastas. The house specialty is Alderwood smoked salmon. ♿ 🍷 ♫ 💳	■	●	■		■
SAN LUIS OBISPO: *Tio Alberto's* $ 1131 Broad St, CA 93401. ☎ *(805) 546-9646.* The specialty is *carne asada* (grilled beef) at this popular, old-style Mexican restaurant. No alcohol is served or allowed. ♿ 💳					
SAN FRANCISCO					
BERKELEY: *Chez Panisse Restaurant* $$$$$ 1517 Shattuck Ave, CA 94709. ☎ *(510) 548-5525.* One of the country's top restaurants, founder Chef Alice Waters is credited with having invented California cuisine here. ● *Sun.* ♿ 🍷 💳		●	■	●	
CHINATOWN & NOB HILL: *Fornou's Oven* $$$ 905 California St, Stanford Court Hotel, CA 94108. ☎ *(415) 989-1910.* The name comes from the large Portuguese tile oven in the center of this Mediterranean-style restaurant. The rack of lamb is wonderful. ♿ 🍷 💳			■		■
DOWNTOWN: *House of Nan King* $ 919 Kearny St, CA 94133. ☎ *(415) 421-1429.* Many consider this the best budget Chinese restaurant in the country. There is an extensive Shanghai menu of braised meats and vegetable dishes. ● *Sun L.*		●			
DOWNTOWN: *Cypress Club* $$$$$ 500 Jackson St, CA 94133. ☎ *(415) 296-8555.* There is no more attractive combination of good food, great style, and indefinably San Franciscan "buzz" than in this popular haunt. ● *L.* ♿ 💳		●	■		
FISHERMAN'S WHARF: *Alioto's* $$$$ Pier 45, CA 94133. ☎ *(415) 673-0183.* Fresh seafood has been served here by the Alioto family since 1930. Fine views of the Golden Gate Bridge. ♿ ♫ 💳		●	■		■
GOLDEN GATE PARK & THE PRESIDIO: *New Eritrea Restaurant* $$ 907 Irving St, CA 94122. ☎ *(415) 681-1288.* This family-owned Eritrean and Ethiopian restaurant has the best all-you-can-eat weekday buffet lunch in the city. The full bar offers African beers. 💳		●	■		
HAIGHT ASHBURY: *Cha Cha Cha* $ 1801 Haight St, CA 94133. ☎ *(415) 386-5758.* You will have to wait for a table at this very popular tapas bar. The menu changes daily and mixes Caribbean, Cajun, and Mexican influences. ♿			■		
NORTH BEACH: *Little Joe's & Baby Joe's* $ 2550 Van Ness, CA 94133. ☎ *(415) 433-4343.* One of the best cheap Italian eating places in the city, Little Joe's is very lively, and the food is good. The garlic squid is particularly popular. ♿ *limited.* 💳		●			■

PACIFIC HEIGHTS: *Café Marimba* $$
2317 Chestnut St, CA 94123. (415) 776-1506.
The brightly painted café in the Marina district makes a perfect backdrop for the innovative southern Mexican specialties served here. ● *Mon.* &

SAN JOSE: *Tied House Café and Brewery* $$
65 N San Pedro St, CA 95112. (408) 295-2739.
Best known for its beers, which are made on the premises, this lively, airy restaurant features especially good seafood dishes. ● *Sun L.*

THE MISSION DISTRICT: *El Nuevo Frutilandia* $
3077 24th St, CA 94110. (415) 648-2958.
The authentic Cuban and Puerto Rican specialties are complemented by a casual Caribbean atmosphere. Serves tropical fruitshakes. ● *Mon.*

WINE COUNTRY

NAPA: *Napa Valley Wine Train* $$$$
1275 McKinstry St, CA 94559. (800) 427-4124. W www.winetrain.com
Gourmet California cuisine is served on this luxury diesel train as you enjoy the views of the beautiful Wine Country. ● *Mon & Tue D.* &

SONOMA: *Ristorante Piatti* $$
405 1st St West, CA 94576. (707) 996-2351.
This bustling Italian bistro is part of a small California chain. The risotto of the day is always delicious, as are the signature pizzas, pasta dishes, and chicken. &

THE NORTH

EUREKA: *Samoa Cookhouse* $
59 Cookhouse Lane, CA 95501. (707) 442-1659.
For a taste of the North Coast woods as they used to be, nothing beats this century-old dining hall, which still serves mountains of good food. &

MOUNT SHASTA: *Michael's* $$
313 N Mount Shasta Blvd, CA 96067. (530) 926-5288.
Delicious sandwiches, light lunches, and Italian dinners have made this restaurant in the Mount Shasta area a favorite for many years. ● *Sun.*

WEAVERVILLE: *La Grange Café* $$
226 N Main St, CA 96093. (530) 623-5325.
Adventurous Californian health food is offered here at moderate prices, including oganic salads and a wide range of vegetarian dishes. ● *Sun.*

GOLD COUNTRY & THE CENTRAL VALLEY

NEVADA CITY: *Country Rose Café* $$
1112 2nd St, CA 95814. (916) 442-4772.
This busy bistro-style café, housed in an 1860s brick building, specializes in French country cuisine, such as sautéed chicken. A classical guitarist often plays on weekends. Reservations are recommended. ♫

SACRAMENTO: *The Firehouse* $$
1112 2nd St, CA 95814. (916) 442-4772.
The original fire pole still stands in this converted fire station, built in the 1850s. The fare is superb with dishes such as glazed duck and filet mignon.
● *Sun, Mon D, Sat L.* &

SONORA: *Banny's Café* $$
83 S Stewart St, Suite 100, CA 95370. (209) 533-4709.
An eclectic mixture of California, Italian, Mediterranean, and Thai cuisine is served from the seasonal menu at this pleasant café. ● *Sun.* &

THE HIGH SIERRAS

SOUTH LAKE TAHOE: *Chevys* $
3678 Lake Tahoe Blvd, CA 95731. (530) 542-1741.
Huge portions of traditional Mexican food and inexpensive cocktails are the main attractions of this popular, casual restaurant.

YOSEMITE NATIONAL PARK: *Abwahnee Dining Room* $$$$
Yosemite Valley, CA 95389. (559) 252-4848.
The soaring ceiling of this beautiful hotel dining room makes up for rather bland food. Steaks and other simple dishes are a safe bet. &

For key to symbols see back flap

ALASKA

FOR MOST VISITORS, *familiar images of Alaska include pristine waterways, towering snowcapped peaks, glaciers calving to form icebergs, and massive grizzly bears feasting on salmon. All this and much more can still be found here on North America's "Last Frontier," where less than one percent of the state's 375 million acres (150 million ha) shows any sign of human habitation.*

Situated at the top of the North American continent and separated from the rest of the country by Canada, Alaska is more than twice the size of Texas, the next largest state. Alaska can be divided into three regions, both geographically and for the purpose of travel. Southeast Alaska, commonly called the Inside Passage, is a long, narrow stretch of islands and channels sandwiched between the Pacific Ocean and Canada's Coast Mountains. Picture-postcard coastal towns, including the state capital Juneau, are linked conveniently by an efficient state-run ferry system.

The bulk of Alaska's land mass, however, lies in the continent's extreme northwest corner, closer to Russia than the "Lower 48" states. The modern city of Anchorage is a good base for exploring the Kenai Peninsula and Denali National Park, or as a jumping-off point for more adventurous destinations such as Kodiak Island and the Alaska Peninsula. To the west of the

Russian doll on sale in Juneau

mainland, the windswept volcanic archipelago of the Aleutian Islands stretches 1,200 miles (1,932 km) west into the Bering Sea.

HISTORY

Alaska's southeast corner is 500 miles (805 km) from the rest of the US, but its farthest reaches a mere 50 miles (80 km) from Russia. As a result, the state's history reflects its role as a bridge and buffer between these two powerful nations. Human history here goes back much farther, since Alaska was the point of entry for some of the first people to set foot in North America, who crossed a land bridge over the Bering Strait 13,000 to 30,000 years ago. While some groups continued their migrations southward, a few remained for millenia, hunting and fishing until the arrival of Western Europeans. The original Alaskans' descendants today include the island-dwelling Aleut, the coastal Tlingit, the Athabascans of the interior, and the Eskimos of artic and western Alaska.

A panoramic view of North America's highest peak, Mount McKinley in Denali National Park

◁ Hawai'i's Makapu'u Beach on southeast O'ahu, backed by the peaks of the Ko'olau Range

A brown bear fishing for salmon at Brooks Camp, Katmai National Park, Alaska Peninsula

The first non-Native settlements were outposts built by Russian fur traders in the late 18th century. Although their far-flung colony stretched as far south as California, it declined as trappers decimated once-huge populations of seals and sea otters. Seen as a liability, Alaska was sold by Russia in 1867 to the US Secretary of State William Seward. The purchase was popularly considered a waste of money and dubbed "Seward's Folly"; however, doubts vanished when the first of many deposits of gold was found near Juneau. More mineral discoveries, including gold in 1898 at distant Nome, as well as vast quantities of copper, and oil at Prudhoe Bay, have all proved the wisdom of Seward's purchase.

ALASKA TODAY

Alaska is home to 635,000 people. Of the population, 16 percent are of Native descent, while the remainder come from diverse backgrounds (only 34 percent of the total are born in the state). It has a population density of just one person per square mile (compared to over 1,000 in New Jersey).

Visitors at Aialik Glacier, one of the main attractions at Kenai Fjords National Park

Alaska's economy depends upon oil from the North Slope, but government jobs, seafood processing, and tourism are also important. Anchorage is a major international hub for air cargo shipments. Over time, there has been a growing awareness to preserve and protect Alaska's unique wilderness from the commercial pressures arising from the state's natural wealth. The vast majority of Alaska is owned by the government, and much of this is protected in national parks and other undeveloped areas stretching from Glacier Bay to the Gates of the Arctic.

KEY DATES IN HISTORY

13,000–30,000 years ago Migratory peoples cross from present-day Siberia into Alaska

1741 Working for the Czar of Russia, Danish explorer Vitus Bering and his crew are the first Europeans to visit Alaska

1867 To ease an economic recession, the Czar of Russia sells Alaska to the US for $7.2 million

1880 Gold is discovered near Juneau

1897 The Klondike Gold Rush hits Skagway

1912 Alaska becomes a US Territory

1942 US Army builds the 1,442-mile (2,322-km) Alaska Highway as an overland link

1959 Alaska becomes the 49th state

1964 Good Friday earthquake destroys much of Anchorage

1968 Oil discovered at Prudhoe Bay

1977 Trans-Alaska pipeline completed

1989 *Exxon Valdez* runs aground on Bligh Reef, spilling 11 million gallons (50 million liters) of oil into Prince William Sound

2001 onwards Alaska is a resource-dependent state, and the potential extraction of oil from the Arctic National Wildlife Refuge continues to stir a national debate

Exploring Alaska

A VAST WILDERNESS OF VIRGIN rivers, towering mountain peaks, abundant wildlife, and calving glaciers, Alaska is by far the largest state in the United States. Its sheer size means that travel takes up a fair proportion of a visitor's time. However, the state has an excellent transportation and tourism infrastructure, which caters to a million visitors each year, most of whom arrive during the brief summer season from late May to early September. Good roads connect Anchorage, Fairbanks, and other cities, but much of Southeast Alaska – including the capital city of Juneau – are inaccessible by road. Ferries, planes, and cruise ships connect coastal towns, while remote bush villages are accessed only by air.

King Salmon Antler's Inn, outside Katmai NP, Alaska Peninsula

SIGHTS AT A GLANCE

Ketchikan ❶
Sitka ❷
Juneau ❸
Glacier Bay National Park ❹
Skagway ❺
Anchorage ❻
Valdez ❼
Seward ❽
Homer ❾
Kodiak Island ❿
Alaska Peninsula ⓫
Aleutian Islands ⓬
Nome ⓭
Fairbanks ⓮
Denali National Park pp742–3 ⓯

SEE ALSO

0 km   250

0 miles   250

Point Lay

B r o o

Wevok
Point Hope   *Noatak*

Noatak   A

RUSSIAN   Kotzebue   Kiana   Amb
FEDERATION   Selav
                 Shishmaref   Lake

                 Wales   Deering

                 Teller

                 Nome   Council
                  ⓭

Gambell   Shaktoolik
        Savoonga
Saint   Unalakleet
Lawrence Island   Camp Kulowiye
                             Kotlik

                 Sheldons   Holy Cross
B E R I N G   Point
                             Yukon
S E A   Hooper Bay
                        Kálskag
                 Aropuk
Saint Matthew Island   Lake   Kash
                 Newtok   Nyac

        Mekoryuk   Dall
                    Lake   Eek
Nunivak Island Kwigillingok
                       Quinhagak
                         Aleknagik
                Platinum   Dillingha
                              N
                          Bechar
Saint Paul Island   Pilot Poi
Pribilof Islands   Port
Saint George Island   Heiden

                 Port Moller
                            Perry
                              Sand Poi
        False Pass
A   l   Akutan   Pauloff
Kiska   e   u   Harbor
Island   t i a n   Dutch Harbor   N
    Kanaga
    Island
Amchitka Island Tanaga Adak Atka ⓬ Nikolski
    P   Island Island Atka   O C   E   A   N
      A   C   I   F   I   C

KEY

- ✈ Airport
- — Major road
- ·—·— International border

MILEAGE CHART

10 = Distance in miles
10 = Distance in kilometers

SKAGWAY						
833 1340	ANCHORAGE					
757 1218	**307** 494	VALDEZ				
960 1544	**127** 205	**429** 690	SEWARD			
1055 1697	**236** 379	**531** 854	**180** 289	HOMER		
712 1145	**360** 579	**362** 582	**484** 779	**582** 936	FAIRBANKS	
833 1340	**237** 382	**504** 811	**364** 585	**473** 761	**121** 195	DENALI NP

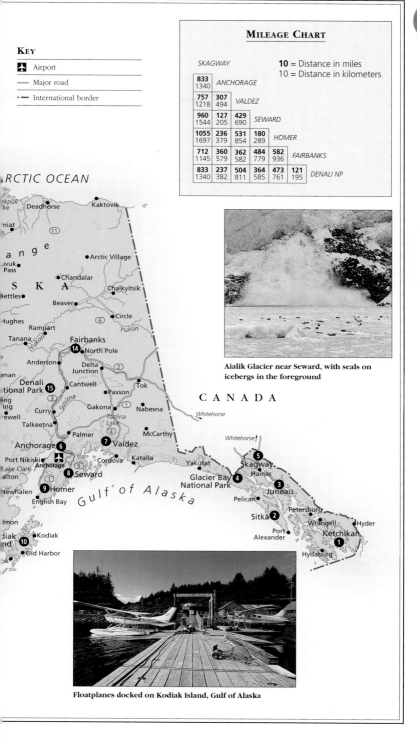

Aialik Glacier near Seward, with seals on icebergs in the foreground

ARCTIC OCEAN

Deadhorse
Kaktovik
ⁿiat
ekpûk
ke

(11)

Arctic Village

n g e

Chandalar
uvuk Pass

S K A

Chalkyitsik

ettles

Beaver

Hughes
Rampart
Circle (6)

Tanana
Yukon
Yukon

Fairbanks
(14) North Pole
Anderson
Delta Junction (2)
Cantwell
Tok

Denali tional Park (15)
Susitna
Paxson
Nabesna

Curry
Gakona (1)
Whitehorse

Talkeetna
Tazlina Lake (4)
McCarthy

Palmer (6)
Valdez (7)
Whitehorse

Anchorage
Anchorage ✈
Cordova
Katalla
Yakutat

Port Nikiski
Seward (8)
Glacier Bay National Park
Skagway (5)
Haines (4)

Lake Clark
Homer (9)
Juneau (3)

Newhalen
English Bay
Gulf of Alaska
Pelican

Sitka (2)
Petersburg

Kodiak
Old Harbor
Wrangell
Hyder
Ketchikan (1)

(10)

Port Alexander

Hydaburg

C A N A D A

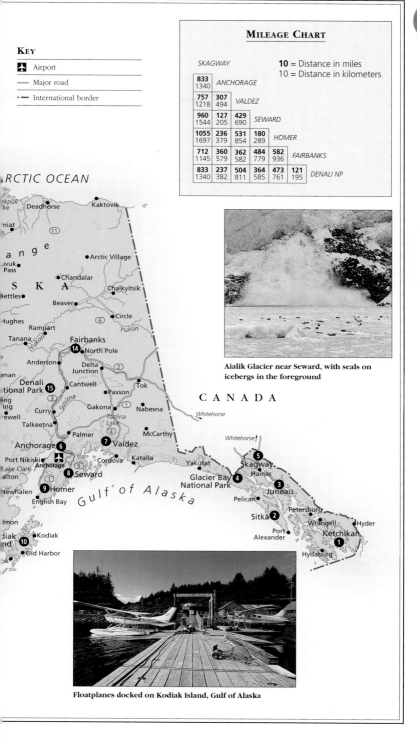

Floatplanes docked on Kodiak Island, Gulf of Alaska

Ketchikan ❶

🏠 9,000. ✈ 🚢 2 miles (3 km) S of downtown. 🛈 131 Front Street, (907) 225-6166.

STRUNG OUT ALONG the waters of the Tongass Narrows and backed by forested hills, Ketchikan is the first stop along the Inside Passage for Alaska-bound cruise ships and ferries. All kinds of watercraft, floatplanes, and kayakers jostle for space along the crowded waterfront. Cruise ships dock outside downtown, providing passengers with easy access to local attractions such as the **Creek Street** precinct. Formerly the heart of a red-light district, the street is lined with colorfully restored wooden houses built on pilings over the water and linked by a boardwalk. The creek below fills up with spawning salmon in late summer.

Even for those who are not planning a trip into the wilderness, the **Southeast Alaska Discovery Center** is definitely worth a visit. Exhibits here relate the human and natural history of the southeast region of Alaska, and also include a fabulous re-creation of a rainforest. Ketchikan's **Totem Heritage Center** displays an incredible collection of more than 30 original totems poles, many more than a century old.

Lying to the north of the city, Tongass Avenue runs along the waterfront all the way to the **Totem Bight**

Totem pole, Sitka

State Historical Park. From here, a trail leads past huge totem poles to a reconstruction of a Native clan house.

🏛 Southeast Alaska Discovery Center
50 Main Street. 📞 (907) 228-6220. 🕐 8am–5pm daily. ● Oct–Apr: Sun & Mon. 🎫 ♿

Sitka ❷

🏠 8,500. ✈ 🚢 7 miles (11 km) N of downtown. 🛈 303 Lincoln St, (907) 747-5940. 🎉 Alaska Day (Oct 18).

FOUNDED BY Russian entrepreneur Alexander Baranof in 1799, Sitka was the capital of Russian America until Alaska was sold to the United States in 1867. Even now, a strong Russian influence survives here. The center of town is dominated by **St. Michael's Cathedral**, a Russian Orthodox cathedral that was rebuilt after the original 1848 structure burned down in 1966. It preserves many Russian artifacts, including the Sitka Madonna, supposedly blessed with healing powers. Beyond St. Michael's is **Sitka National Historic Park**, the site of a fierce week-long battle between the Russians and local Tlingit tribe in 1804. The area is sprinkled with totem poles, and its shores are gently lapped by the waters of Sitka Sound. Native workers display their craft skills at a cultural center throughout the warm summer. The park is

The Russian-style St. Michael's Cathedral, Sitka

also a good place to view the town's natural setting. Islands dot the Sound, and the snow-capped volcano Mount Edgecumbe – often compared to Japan's Mount Fuji – sits majestically on the horizon.

The **Alaska Raptor Center**, across Indian River from the park, rehabilitates bald eagles, owls, and falcons. Visitors are free to walk or join a guided tour. Sitka also has a network of hiking and biking trails for the more adventurous.

🏛 Alaska Raptor Center
1101 Sawmill Creek Rd. 📞 (907) 747-8662. 🕐 Jun–Sep: 8am–4pm Mon–Fri. ● Oct–May. 🎫 ♿

Juneau ❸

🏠 30,000. ✈ 🚢 Auke Bay, 14 miles (22 km) NW of downtown, (907) 465-3940. 🛈 Centennial Hall Visitor Center, 101 Egan Dr, (907) 586-2201.

JUNEAU IS POSSIBLY the most spectacularly located capital city in the US. It is also the most remote, with no road access to the outside world or even to the rest of Alaska. With its large resident population, as well as the 700,000 visitors who arrive during the short summer (late May–early Sep), Juneau is the busy hub of the Inside Passage. Sandwiched between steep-sided forested peaks and the Gastineau Channel, the heart of the city is an intriguing mix of modern high-rise buildings and historic gems such as the **Red Dog Saloon**, and the **Alaskan Hotel**.

Ketchikan's Creek Street, with restored buildings linked by a boardwalk

The best way to appreciate the town's wonderful location is by taking the tramway up **Mount Roberts**, from where the panorama extends across Gastineau Channel. The downtown **Alaska State Museum** contains a fine collection of Russian artifacts as well as Native crafts such as Eskimo masks. Its natural history section exhibits a re-creation of a bald eagle's nest.

Located at the northern end of the city, 13 miles (21 km) from downtown, **Mendenhall Glacier** is an impressive attraction. A part of the massive Juneau Icefield, this slowly retreating 1.5-mile (2.4-km) wide glacier is calving icebergs into Mendenhall Lake. A lakeside visitor center offers interpretive panels describing the forces behind glacial movement. This is the starting point for hiking trails that provide close-up views of the glacier. Rafting is also offered here for adventure seekers.

The scenic White Pass & Yukon Route Railroad near Skagway

🏛 **Alaska State Museum**
395 Whittier St. ☎ (907) 465-2901. ⏰ 8:30am–6:30pm daily. Oct–May: Sun & Mon. ♿ 🅿

🌲 **Mendenhall Glacier**
Off Mendenhall Loop Rd. ☎ (907) 789-0097. ⏰ 8am–6:30pm daily. ● Oct–Apr: Mon–Wed. ♿ 🅿

Glacier Bay National Park ❹

❌ 🚢 from Juneau. ℹ (907) 697-2230. **Glacier Bay Cruiseline**
Departures: Jun–mid-Sep: 8am daily, (800) 451-5952.

GLACIER BAY HAS changed greatly since the British explorer Captain George Vancouver (see p612) found his way through Icy Strait in 1794. During the ensuing 200 years, the glaciers have retreated almost 100 miles (160 km), creating a magnificent waterway indented by long bays and protected by the 5,156-sqmile (13,354-sq-km) national park. Six glaciers reach the sea and break up into massive chunks of ice, which float into a bay inhabited by humpback whales, porpoises, and seals.

Most visitors to Glacier Bay arrive aboard cruise ships. Travelers can also come by way of the hamlet of Gustavus from Juneau, making the short overland trip to Bartlett Cove and Glacier Bay Lodge (see p758) by taxi. From Bartlett Cove, it is 40 miles (64 km) to the nearest glacier in a high-speed catamaran. An onboard park naturalist describes the bay's natural history. The tide-water glaciers are the main highlight of the trip to Glacier Bay National Park.

Skagway ❺

🏔 800. ❌ 🚌 🚢 SW end of Broadway. ℹ Broadway at 2nd Ave, (907) 983-2855.

THE FINAL NORTHBOUND STOP for travelers on the Inside Passage is this little tourist town surrounded by towering peaks. In 1897, thousands of fortune seekers heading for the Klondike goldfields arrived here only to be faced with an almost insurmountable obstacle – the 33-mile (53 km) **Chilkoot Trail**. This trail traversed a harrowing 45-degree slope nicknamed the "Golden Staircase" over the White Pass to the headwaters of the Yukon River. In the following years, Skagway became a lawless outpost, unofficially ruled by the notorious businessman "Soapy" Smith, who died in a famous shootout with a local surveyor outside the City Hall.

Today, Skagway's fortunes rely largely on promoting its colorful history. The whole of the downtown district is protected as the **Klondike Gold Rush National Historic Park**, encompassing false-fronted buildings, old-time saloons, as well as the distinctive Arctic Brotherhood Hall, whose interesting façade is decorated with about 20,000 pieces of driftwood. The **White Pass & Yukon Route Railroad**, which was originally built over the White Pass as an alternative to the Chilkoot Trail, now operates purely for tourists on a scenic three-hour long round-trip to the pass and back.

ALASKA MARINE HIGHWAY

The state-operated ferry service links towns that are inaccessible by road throughout southeast and south central Alaska, extending service as far south as Prince Rupert (British Columbia) and Bellingham (Washington). En route, visitors pass magnificent fjords, towering glaciers, and virgin forests. The comfortable and well-equipped vessels carry vehicles, and feature cabins, dining areas, and onboard naturalists. It is possible to even pitch tents on the outer deck. Bookings should be made well in advance (see p756).

We Drove Alaska's Marine Highway
www.alaska.gov/ferry
1.800.642.0066

Logo, Alaska Marine Highway

Clan house in the Alaska Native Heritage Center, Anchorage

Anchorage ❻

🏛 270,000. ✈ 🚉 🚍 🛈 6th Ave
at F St, (907) 274-3531. 🎪 Alaska
State Fair (late Aug).

L YING BETWEEN Cook Inlet
and the Chugach
Mountains, Anchorage is
Alaska's largest city. Although
this coastal urban sprawl is
often described as being un-
Alaskan, it is still worth
spending a little time in this
northern metropolis, soaking
up the wealth of sights and
taking advantage of its many
services. It also serves as
Alaska's financial and transportation hub. Most of downtown was destroyed by the
1964 Good Friday earthquake
(see p733), when the north
side of 4th Avenue sank 10 ft
(3 m). Interpretive displays at
Earthquake Park, west of
downtown toward the airport,
tell the story of the Big One.
The park offers superb views
over the downtown skyline to
the Chugach Mountains.
    One of Alaska's finest
museums, the **Anchorage
Museum of History and Art**
displays an impressive collection of Alaska-themed
paintings, and an Alaska
Gallery with creative dioramas that chronicle prehistoric
times through the present
day. At the **Alaska Native
Heritage Center**, costumed
actors provide visitors with a
glimpse of Native culture
through dance. An entire
section has been dedicated to
a re-created Native village set
beside a pond. Located 50
miles (80 km) southeast of
the city, **Portage Glacier** is

steadily retreating and is now
out of sight from the visitor
center. A tour boat
plies the lake close
to the glacier.

🏛 Anchorage
Museum of History
& Art
7th Ave at A St. 📞 (907)
343-6173. ⬤ Jun–Aug:
9am–6pm daily; Sep–May:
10am–6pm Tue–Sun. 🎫 ♿

🏛 Alaska Native
Heritage Center
Muldoon Rd. 📞 (907) 330-
8000. ⬤ mid-May–Sep:
9am–6pm daily. ● Oct–
mid-May. 🎫 ♿

Valdez ❼

🏛 4,000. ✈ 🚍 downtown. 🛈 200
Chenega St, (907) 835-2984. **Prince
William Sound Cruises & Tours**
Departures: late Jun–early Sep: daily,
(907) 835-4731. ♿ *limited.*

T HE PICTURESQUE town of
Valdez nestles below
snowcapped peaks along an
arm of Prince William Sound,

a vast bay encompassing
islands, glaciers, and icy waters
teeming with wildlife. This is
North America's northernmost
ice-free port. The **Trans-
Alaska Pipeline**, which runs
above ground for 800 miles
(1,288 km) across the state
from Prudhoe Bay on the
Arctic Ocean, ends here, from
where it is transferred to oil
tankers. The *Exxon Valdez*,
the best known tanker, infa-
mously ran aground in 1989,
spilling millions of gallons
of oil into the Sound. A huge
cleanup effort has attempted
to restore the Sound, and
although there are no obvious
signs of the spill today, its
adverse effect on birds, fish,
and marine mammals
persists. A cruise of the
Sound passes the **Col-
umbia Glacier**, which
is more than 3 miles
(4.8 km) wide at its
250-ft (75-m) high
face, and continously
calves icebergs into
the sea. Check with
the vistor center
for summer tours.

Bronze sculpture,
Valdez Museum

The town's **Valdez
Museum** explores
the Native culture,
the importance of oil for the
local economy, the *Exxon
Valdez* oil spill, and the devastating 1964 Good Friday
earthquake, whose epicenter
lay less than 60 miles (97 km)
from Valdez. The town also
offers great hiking, sea kayaking, and rafting opportunities.

🏛 Valdez Museum
217 Egan Dr. 📞 (907) 835-2764.
⬤ May–Sep: 9am–6pm daily;
Oct–Apr: 1pm–5pm Mon–Sat,
noon–4pm Sat. 🎫 ♿

Re-creation of a traditional miner's cabin, Valdez Museum

The magnificent Exit Glacier in the Kenai Fjords National Park, north of Seward

Seward ⓫

🏔 *3,000.* ✈ 🚉 🚌 🛳 *downtown.*
ℹ *3rd St, (907) 224-80514.*

ONE OF THE only large towns on the Kenai Peninsula, Seward is a charming fishing port at the head of Resurrection Bay, surrounded by the snow-capped Kenai Mountains. One of its main attractions is the **Alaska SeaLife Center**, which exhibits the marine life of the surrounding ocean. The centerpiece is a string of three huge aquariums holding colorful puffins, seals, and sea lions. Smaller tanks provide a home for crabs and octopuses, while a "touch tank" encourages a hands-on approach to exploring sessile life along the tidal zone.

Seward is encircled by the **Kenai Fjords National Park**, a 906-sq-mile (2,347-sq-km) glaciated coastal wilderness. From the gigantic Hardy Icefield, glaciers radiate in all directions, eight of which are "tidewater glaciers," which extend to sea level. Seward's downtown dock is the departure point for boat trips along the park's coastline. These day cruises also provide excellent opportunities for viewing whales, seals, sea lions, porpoises, and large concentrations of photogenic puffins perched on rocky outcrops. The park's most accessible glacier is Exit Glacier, located off the highway, 4 miles (6.4 km) north of Seward. From the end of the access road, a short trail

leads through a forest of stunted trees, suddenly emerging at the improbable sight of a deep-blue river of ice running through the trees.

⚓ Alaska SeaLife Center
Railway Ave. 📞 *(907) 224-6300.*
◯ *May–Sep: 8am–8pm daily;*
Oct–Apr: 10am–5pm daily.
● *Thanksgiving, Dec 25.* 🎫 ♿
⚓ Kenai Fjords National Park
Park 🎫 ♿ Visitor Center 📞 *(907)*
224-3175. ◯ *Mem. Day–Labor Day:*
daily; Labor Day–Mem. Day: Mon–Fri.

Homer ❾

🏔 *4,000.* ✈ 🛳 *Homer Spit.* ℹ *201*
Sterling Hwy, (907) 235-7740. **Central**
Charter Booking Agency *Departures:*
Jun–Sep, (907) 235-7847. ♿ *limited.*

AT THE END OF the Sterling Highway lies Homer, a delightful little hamlet by the water. It was discovered by Homer Pennock, a gold-prospector who arrived here in 1896. Today, this town has become a popular destination

for visitors. Its main focus is **Homer Spit**, a 4-mile (6.4-km) finger of land that juts into Kachemak Bay, with the rugged Kenai Mountains glistening across the water. A busy road traverses the entire Spit, passing beaches strewn with driftwood, a colorful collection of dry-docked boats, fishing-supply stores, and lively restaurants. Known as the "Halibut Capital of the World," fishing is its main attraction. Charter operators and their boats line the Spit; day trips include tackle and bait as well as instruction. Those who manage to hook a 200-lb (90-kg) halibut can arrange to have it frozen and shipped home. The **Fishing Hole** on the Spit is a man-made waterhole stocked with salmon for an easy catch.

The magnificent wilderness of the **Kachemak Bay State Park**, on the bay's opposite shore, can be explored through a number of hiking trails. The best-known of these leads the visitor to the Grewingk Glacier.

Fishermen with a halibut "weigh-in" on Homer Spit

The northern end of Kodiak Island, covered with thick spruce forests

Kodiak Island ⑩

🚹 14,000. ✈ 🚌 downtown.
ℹ Marine Way, (907) 486-4070.

THE SECOND-LARGEST island in
the United States, Kodiak
extends for 100 miles (160
km) across the Gulf of Alaska.
Most of the island is an inaccessible stretch of wilderness
protected by the 2,969-sq-mile
(7,690-sq-km) **Kodiak
National Wildlife Refuge**.
Kodiak Island is famous as
the habitat of about 2,500
Kodiak bears – the world's
largest brown bear – some
of which stand 10 ft (3
m) tall and weigh up to
1,500 lb (675 kg). The
visitor center provides
details on charter flights to
the best viewing spots.

Most of the island's
residents live in the
town of Kodiak, home
of the country's largest
Coast Guard station and its
third-largest fishing fleet. North
America's oldest Russian
building, a storehouse dating
to 1808, is now the excellent
Baranof Museum. A repository of Kodiak's history, the
museum's highlights include a
superb samovar (urn) collection, Aleut kayaks, and photographs of the town after it
was hit by a *tsunami* (massive
tidal wave), triggered by the
1964 Good Friday earthquake
(see p733). To explore the
local fishing industry, follow
Shelikof Street past the harbor
to the canneries, one of
which was converted from a
1945 troop ship.

**Samovar,
Baranof Museum**

🏛 Baranof Museum
Marine Way. 📞 (907) 486-5920.
◯ Jun–Aug: 10am–4pm Mon–Sat;
noon–4pm Sun; reduced hours for
the rest of the year. ◯ Feb. 📷

Alaska Peninsula ⑪

✈ ℹ King Salmon Airport, (907)
246-4250.

DOMINATED BY the Alaska
Range, this remote part
of the state attracts visitors for
its intriguing wilderness
and wildlife viewing
opportunities. In 1912,
the second-largest blast
in recorded history
occurred when the
peninsula's Mount
Novarupta erupted,
covering a 400-sq-mile
(1,036-sq-km) area
with ash and pumice
up to a height of 700 ft
(210 m). The blast was
heard as far away as Seattle,
and the ash that erupted

stayed in the atmosphere for
an entire year, changing
weather patterns worldwide.

The 6,250-sq-mile (16,187-
sq-km) **Katmai National
Park** encompasses the area
where the volcano was most
active. A remnant is the Valley
of 10,000 Smokes, where hot
gases and ash continue to
spew across a lunar-like landscape. Bears and other wildlife abound in the park, most
famously at Brooks Falls.

Adjacent to Katmai, photographers from around the world
gather at the **McNeil River
State Game Sanctuary** to
photograph brown bears
catching salmon as they
struggle up to McNeil River
Falls. Access to the falls is by
air taxi from King Salmon or
Homer *(see p739)*.

🦌 McNeil River State Game
Sanctuary
◯ Best viewing: Jul–mid-Aug. 📷
Permit required from Department
of Fish & Game, (907) 267-2182.

A brown bear at Katmai National Park, Alaska Peninsula

Aleutian Islands

🏔 *14,000.* ✈ 🚢 *Unalaska.* ℹ
*Unalaska Visitors' Bureau, Broadway,
Unalaska, (907) 581-2612.*

B EYOND THE Alaska
Peninsula, the summits of
the Aleutian Range have
created a string of islands that
extend 1,200 miles (1,932 km)
into the Pacific Ocean.
Originally settled by hardy
Aleut seal hunters, the islands
were occupied for more than
a year by the Japanese during
World War II. Today, over half
the archipelago's population
live in the town of **Unalaska**,
set around a picturesque
Dutch Harbor. This town is
North America's number one
seafood producer. The catch
includes crab, halibut, cod,
and pollock. Its harbor is
lined with fishing boats, container cranes, and processing
plants, all catering to this
industry. The **Russian Orthodox Church of the Holy
Ascension**, built in 1827,
dominates the foreshore.

Nome ❸

🏔 *3,600.* ✈ ℹ *Front St, (907)
443-5535.*

F EW WOULD ARGUE with the
local catchphrase that
"there's no place like Nome."
Perched on the edge of the
Bering Sea, closer to Russia
than to Anchorage, the town
was named after an early
cartographer marked this
location as "Name?" on a
map. Later another mapmaker
misread the annotation as
"Nome." Gold was discovered
in nearby **Anvil Creek**
around the same time that
prospectors were moving on

from the played-out Klondike
(see p733) goldfields, and by
the year 1900 approximately
20,000 miners had descended
on this remote outpost.

Although Nome is now a
shadow of its former self, it is
still a fascinating and popular
destination. Friendly staff at
the tourist information office
obligingly indicate historic
relics such as the **Last Train
to Nowhere**, and the rusting
hulks of dredges that have
long since been abandoned.
There are many hiking trails
stretching across the treeless
tundra. Panning for gold
along the beach is another
unique activity.

Fairbanks ❹

🏔 *32,000.* ✈ 🚌 ℹ *1st Ave at
Cushman St, (907) 456-5774.*

S URROUNDED BY sub-arctic
wilderness, Fairbanks is
Alaska's second-largest city
and has one of the largest
populations at this latitude
anywhere in the world.
Located just 150 miles
(241 km) south of the
Arctic Circle, the sun
barely dips below the
horizon at the time of
the summer solstice
(Jun 21). The long
hours of darkness
through winter make
it a good place to
view the aurora
borealis, or
northern lights, a
phenomenon of
dazzling sheets of
light produced in the sky by
electron and proton particles
of the solar wind. Fairbanks is
also known for its extremes in
temperature, which often soar
well above 90° F (32° C) in

**View of the aurora borealis,
or northern lights, Alaska**

summer, but dip below -60° F
(-15° C) in winter.

The city's many unique
attractions include the **Ice
Museum**, where a huge
walk-in freezer holds impressive ice sculptures. Another
museum on the University of
Alaska grounds provides a
home for a 36,000-year-old
mummified bison. At **Pioneer
Park**, historic buildings
collected from around the
state help to re-create
a Gold Rush-era town
on the banks of the
Chena River. One of its
main highlights is a
restored stern-
wheeler, the
Nenana, claimed
to be the world's
second largest
wooden hulled
vessel. Each
summer evening,
Pioneer Park plays
host to a musical
revue, with dancers who are
dressed in period costume.

**Caribou at the Ice
Museum, Fairbanks**

🎪 **Pioneer Park**
Airport Way. 📞 *(907) 459-1087.* ⏰
Jun–Sep: 11am–9pm. ⬤ *Oct–May.* ♿

The Iditarod Trail Sled Dog Race

THE IDITAROD

In March each year, depending on the snowfall, dog
mushers from around the world gather in Anchorage for
the Iditarod Trail Sled Dog Race, one of the world's most
grueling races. After an outbreak of diphtheria in Nome
in 1925, a relay of mushers and their dogs took just six
days to cover 670 frozen miles (1,078 km), delivering a
vaccine that saved hundreds of lives. Today, the race is a
professional production, with top competitors; the racers
become household names, and images of the sled dogs
fighting the elements are beamed worldwide.

Denali National Park ⑮

ALASKA'S TOP ATTRACTION, Denali National Park encompasses 9,375 sq miles (24,281 sq km). The 20,320-ft (6,194-m) high Mount McKinley, North America's highest peak, dominates the landscape, rising 10,000 ft (3,048 m) above the surrounding peaks. The park is home to abundant wildlife, including grizzly bears, moose, and caribou, and wildflowers explode with color across the tundra in July. Only one road penetrates Denali, traversing varied landscapes that include lowlands and high mountain passes. Several hiking trails can be enjoyed in the vicinity of the visitor center. Other activities include sled dog demonstrations, rafting on the Nenana River, and flight-seeing around Mount McKinley.

The Alaska Railroad
Many travelers opt for rail travel when it comes to visiting Denali.

★ Wonder Lake
On a clear day, Mount McKinley is visible from various locations within Denali National Park.

Kantishn

Wonder Lak

Mount McKinley

Alaska Range

Dall Glacier · Yentna Glacier · Lacuna Glacier · Kahiltna Glacier · Kahiltna Glacier

0 km   20

0 miles   20

★ Mount McKinley
View of the snow clad Mount McKinley from Park Road, en route to Wonder Lake. Originally called Denali, "the Great One," by Athabascan Natives, many Alaskans still continue to refer to Mount McKinley by its old name.

★ Whitewater Rafting
Thrills and spills abound on the Nenana River, which flows along the eastern boundary of the national park.

Sanctuary River
Savage River
Teklanika River
Riley Creek
Igloo Creek
Toklat
Eielson Visitor Center
Alaska Range
Cantwell
Nenana River
Alaska Railroad
Eldridge Glacier

Tourists on a park shuttle bus trip

KEY

- - Park boundary
Ⓐ Camping
— Alaska railroad
═ Major road
═ Unpaved road

WILDLIFE VIEWING

One of the major attractions in Alaska is wildlife viewing, and Denali National Park provides great opportunities to see a wide variety of the state's largest and most impressive animals. Grizzly bears,

Mountain goat

moose, Dall sheep, and caribou are routinely sighted by visitors from the park shuttle buses, with drivers stopping to allow viewing and photography. The park is also home to wolves, and while they are not as commonly sighted as many other mammals, spotting these magnificent creatures in the wild is a memorable experience for visitors.

Grizzly bear feeding on berries

Moose wading in water

Caribou are a common sight

STAR SIGHTS

★ Mount McKinley

★ Whitewater Rafting

★ Wonder Lake

HAWAI'I

A TROPICAL ISLAND PARADISE *of golden sand beaches, waterfalls, and lush forests, the Aloha State attracts more than 6 million visitors a year. An isolated archipelago in the middle of the Pacific Ocean, the islands' exotic landscape and luxurious hospitality offer a wealth of experiences from volcanic eruptions and world-class surfing to glimpses of the fascinating cultural heritage of Polynesia.*

Located in the middle of the Pacific Ocean, 2,500 miles (4,000 km) southwest of Los Angeles, the Hawaiian Islands are volcanic in origin. In fact, the islands are still evolving, as is evident from the lava flows on the slopes of 13,796-ft (4,205-m) Mount Kīlauea on the island of Hawai'i or the "Big Island."

Polynesian dancer, a popular attraction

The next largest island, Maui, was formed by the dormant volcano Haleakalā. This, the fastest-growing of the islands, still retains some significant history, especially in the former whaling port of Lahaina. The next island along in the chain, Moloka'i, is well off the tourist trail. Formerly a pineapple ranching center, Moloka'i is famous for the towering cliffs that line its northern coast. Lāna'i, another small island, is also offshore from Maui.

The most popular and developed island is O'ahu, where three-quarters of the population lives and most of the visitors congregate. The center of O'ahu is Honolulu, the state capital

and only big city. Across the ocean from O'ahu sits magical Kaua'i, known as the "Garden Isle" for its verdant rain-forests, kept moist by more than 400 inches (10 m) of annual rainfall.

HISTORY

Hawai'i's historical connections to the US mainland are both distant and contentious. Originally colonized by Polynesians, Hawai'i was a group of independent kingdoms when it was discovered by English sailor Captain James Cook in 1778. Initially welcomed by the natives, Cook was killed by them a year later. Other explorers followed, bringing new, often fatal diseases. By the end of the 18th century, however, the islands had been united into a respected monarchy under the revered monarch, King Kamehameha the Great (ruled 1795–1819).

During the early 19th century, European traders introduced fundamental changes. Christianity was introduced by Puritan missionaries from Boston in 1820, while economically, forestry and whaling gained importance. These proved destabilizing to Native culture, and by the 1880s, white American entrepreneurs, mainly sugar cane and pineapple farmers, acquired control, and the monarchy was overthrown in 1893. After a series of highly complicated political maneuvers, Hawai'i became part of the US in 1898. Much later, in 1993, the US issued a formal apology to the people of Hawai'i for its leading role in the "illegal overthrow of the Kingdom of Hawai'i."

The summit of Maui's Mount Haleakalā

Canoeing and swimming, some of the most popular water activities in Hawai'i

Powerful American plantation owners dominated the first half of the 1900s, and all attempts to unionize the low-paid, mostly Japanese labor force were firmly squelched. Ironically, it took the threat of invasion to make the feudal institutions democratic. On December 7, 1941, Japan attacked Pearl Harbor, instigating America's entry into World War II, and changing Hawai'i forever.

HAWAI'I TODAY

Located midway between mainland US and the Far East, Hawai'i has a diverse population. Of its 1.1 million residents, roughly one-third are non-Asian, one-third are of Japanese descent, and the rest a wide-ranging mix of Filipinos, Chinese, Koreans, and Samoans. Only a few thousand full-blooded indigenous Hawaiians survive today, but the native spirit of "Aloha," a Hawaiian word that simultaneously means hello, goodbye, welcome, and love, is still alive.

The introduction of air travel in 1959 brought Hawai'i within easy reach of the West Coast. As tourism became the chief industry, resort developments proliferated, signaling a new era for island economy. At the same time, a resurgence in Native culture, language, and crafts has softened the harsher edges of the commercial development, so that no matter where you go in the islands, Polynesian roots grow very close to the surface.

Cyclist on a scenic bike ride, away from the crowded beach Waikīkī

KEY DATES IN HISTORY

AD 400 Polynesians migrate to the Hawaiian Islands from the Marquesas Islands

1778 James Cook is the first European to the islands, which he names the Sandwich Islands after his benefactor, the Earl of Sandwich

1795 Reign of Kamehameha begins

1893 With the support of the US Navy, American businessmen overthrow the Kingdom of Hawai'i, declaring an independent republic

1898 Hawai'i is annexed as a US Territory

1941 Japanese bombers attack Pearl Harbor on December 7

1959 Hawai'i becomes the 50th state

1983 Mount Kīlauea begins its present eruption

1993 US government issues a formal apology on the 100th anniversary of the overthrow of the Kingdom of Hawai'i

1996 Citizens vote to convene on the issue of sovereignty

Exploring Hawai'i

THE WORLD'S MOST isolated archipelago, Hawai'i lies 2,500 miles (4,000 km) from the West Coast. The five main islands – O'ahu, Moloka'i, Maui, Hawai'i, and Kaua'i – stretch across over 500 miles (805 km) of the Pacific Ocean. Although most of its six million annual visitors arrive by air in Honolulu, the state capital, travel from one island to another is mainly by inter-island flights. A handful of ferry services and some luxury cruises also link the islands. The most reliable way to explore individual islands is by car, as public transportation is minimal, except on O'ahu.

A secluded swimming spot on the rocky coast of the Ke'anae Peninsula

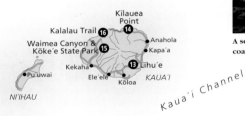

SIGHTS AT A GLANCE

Windsurfers in action at Ho'okipa Beach County Park, near the beach town of Pā'ia on Maui's north shore

Dramatic Honomanū Bay with its clear blue waters, surrounded by lushly forested cliffs

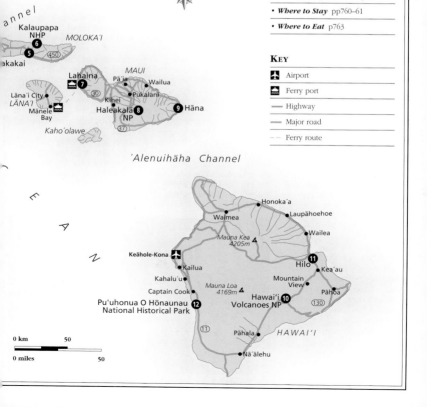

SEE ALSO

- *Practical Information* p757
- *Where to Stay* pp760–61
- *Where to Eat* p763

KEY

✈	Airport
⛴	Ferry port
—	Highway
—	Major road
--	Ferry route

Channel

Kalaupapa
NHP
6
5
MOLOKA'I
akakai
(450)

Lahaina
7
MAUI
Pā'ia
Wailua

Lāna'i City
LĀNA'I
(30)
Kihei
Pukalani

Mānele
Bay
Haleakalā
NP
8
(37)
9 Hāna

Kaho'olawe

'Alenuihāha Channel

Honoka'a
Waimea
Laupāhoehoe

Wailea

Mauna Kea
4205m

Keāhole-Kona ✈

Kailua
11
Hilo
Kea'au

Kahalu'u
Mauna Loa
4169m
Mountain
View

Captain Cook
Pāhoa

Pu'uhonua O Hōnaunau
National Historical Park
12
Hawai'i **10**
Volcanoes NP
(130)

(11)
Pāhala
HAWAI'I

Nā'ālehu

0 km   50
0 miles   50

O'ahu

T HE THIRD LARGEST ISLAND in the archipelago, with an area of 600 sq miles (1,550 sq km), O'ahu is Hawai'i's most visited and most populous island. Three-quarters of the state's million residents live here, most of them in the Greater Honolulu area. Outside the urban areas, with their cultural attractions, O'ahu offers spectacular scenery, with lush plantations, tropical beaches, and a surfers' paradise on the North Shore.

Statue of King Kamehameha, his hand extended in welcome

Honolulu ❶

🏛 371,657. ℹ *HVCB-Honolulu, (808) 923-1811; O'ahu VB, 733 Bishop St, Honolulu, (808) 524-0722.* 🌐 *www.gohawaii.com*

H AWAI'I'S CAPITAL city has two focal points – the historic and business district of downtown Honolulu, and the world famous resort of Waikiki, 3 miles (5 km) to its east. The downtown area, which first gained prominence as a trading port in the early 19th century, today manages to squeeze together towering skyscrapers, a royal palace, Japanese shrines, New England-style missionary houses, a bustling Chinatown, strip joints, and fish markets in a relatively small and compact area.

Dominating downtown's Capitol District is the magnificent Victorian-style **'Iolani Palace**, completed in 1882. The only royal palace in the US, it was designed and first lived in by King David Kalākaua, followed by his sister Queen Lili'uokalani, who reigned for only two years before the monarchy was overthrown in 1893 (*see p744*). Recently used as a movie set, the palace has luxurious interiors and a *koa*-wood staircase.

To its south is the New England-style **Kawaiaha'o Church**, constructed of coral blocks. It was built in 1842, by which time American missionaries had gained many influential local converts to Christianity. The upper gallery has portraits of Hawaiian monarchs, most of whom were baptized, married, and crowned here. Adjacent to the church is the **Mission**

'Iolani Palace crest

Houses Museum, which contains the oldest timber frame house in Hawai'i, built in 1821 by the New England missionary Reverend Hiram Bingham. Housed in three buildings, the museum has a printing house and lovingly preserved interiors.

Nearby is the bronze **Statue of King Kamehameha**, Hawai'i's most revered monarch, who ruled from 1795 to 1819 (*see p744*). The statue, with its feathered cloak and an arm extended in a welcome, is one of Hawai'i's most famous sights.

North of the Capitol District is **Chinatown**, with two marble lions guarding its entrance. The area is an exotic neighborhood of open-air markets, *lei* (flower garland) stands, eateries, and herbal medicine shops. Hawai'i's first Chinese arrived on merchant ships in 1789, followed in 1852 by larger numbers who came to work on O'ahu's sugar plantations. Chinatown's buildings include the Art Deco **Hawai'i Theatre** and the state's oldest Japanese Shinto shrine, the **Izumo Taisha Shrine**, built in 1923.

At Honolulu Harbor, the fascinating **Hawai'i Maritime Center** displays antique canoes and exhibits tracing the exploits of Polynesian navigators. Moored next to it are the *Hōkūle'a*, a modern replica of an ancient Polynesian canoe with sails, and the restored 1878 *Falls of Clyde*, the world's last surviving full-rigged four-masted sailing ship.

Waikiki, originally a place of taro patches and fish ponds, now has one of the world's famous beaches – a sliver of people-packed sand against the backdrop of **Diamond Head** crater. Waikiki bustles with some 65,000 tourists a day who flock here to sunbathe on the golden sand, swim in the sheltered water, and surf the gentle waves. The sandy beach stretches for 2.5 miles (4 km), from the Hilton Hawaiian Village to Diamond Head. The streets and shopping malls are packed with beachwear vendors, honeymooners, Japanese matrons, and boys carrying surfboards. Conspicuous amid the glass and concrete skyscrapers are two stately

The Waikīkī Beach front, lined with high-rise hotels

old hotels – the coral pink **Royal Hawaiian Hotel** and the Colonial-style **Moana Hotel**, Waikiki's oldest.

Several interesting sights are also located in Greater Honolulu. Considered the world's finest museum of Polynesian culture, **Bishop Museum** was created by American businessman Charles Bishop to preserve royal heirlooms left by his wife, a Hawaiian princess. Its priceless exhibits include fabulous ceremonial feather standards, rare *tamate* costumes made of shredded fiber, sacred images, and a *hale* (traditional house) thatched with *pili* grass.

The **National Memorial Cemetery of the Pacific**, located in Punchbowl, the crater of an extinct volcano, has over 33,000 graves. Among those buried here are victims of Pearl Harbor and those killed in the Korean and Vietnam wars.

Pearl Harbor, a place of pilgrimage for many visitors, houses warships, military museums, and memorials. Most significant among these is the **USS *Arizona* Memorial**, which stands perched above the ship of the same name that was sunk during the Japanese bombing on December 7, 1941. Some of the volunteer guides that you will meet here happen to be survivors of that fateful attack, which killed more than 2,000 US officers and men, and destroyed 18 battleships, bringing the United States into World War II (*see p745*).

🚇 **Hawai'i Maritime Center**
Pier 7, Honolulu Harbor.
📞 *(808) 536-6373.* 🚌 *19, 20.*
🕐 *8:30am–8pm daily.* ⬤ *Dec 25.*

🏛 **Bishop Museum**
1525 Bernice St. 📞 *(808) 847-3511.*
🚌 *2.* 🕐 *9am–5pm daily.* ⬤ *Dec 25.*
♿ 🅿 📷 💻 📹 *Craft demonstrations, music & dance recitals: daily.*
🌐 *www.bishopmuseum.org*

🏛 **Pearl Harbor**
7 miles (11 km) NW of downtown
Honolulu. 🚌 *20, 47.* **USS *Arizona* Memorial** 1 Arizona Memorial Drive.
📞 *(808) 422-0561.* 🕐 *7:30am–5pm daily.* ⬤ *Jan 1, Thanksgiving, Dec 25.*
♿ 📷 🌐 *www.nps.gov/usar*

Byodo-In Temple ❷

47-200 Kahekili Hwy (Hwy 83),
Kāne'ohe. 📞 *(808) 239-8811.* 🚗 *on Kahekili Hwy (Hwy 83), then 10-min walk.* 🕐 *8:30am–4:30pm daily.*
⬤ *Dec 25.* 💷 ♿

THIS REPLICA of a 900-year-old Japanese temple in a tranquil and secluded spot is O'ahu's hidden treasure, its bright red walls framed against the backdrop of fluted green cliffs. A curved vermilion footbridge and a three-ton bell lead to the Byodo-In Temple, which houses a beautiful 9-ft (3-m) Buddha. Sunset here is a magical experience, with the cliffs giving off pink and mauve hues.

Hawai'i's Plantation Village ❸

94-695 Waipahu St, Waipahu.
📞 *(808) 677-0110.* 🚗 *Waipahu.*
🕐 *9am–3pm Mon–Fri, 10am–3pm Sat.* ⬤ *public hols.* 💷 ♿

THIS THREE-MILLION dollar restored village portrays a hundred years of sugar plantation culture, from 1840 to 1943. It also contains various re-created buildings from the major ethnic groups that worked in the plantations – Korean, Puerto Rican, and Japanese homes – as well as a Shinto shrine. Personal objects placed in the houses give the impression that the occupants have just left, soon to return. The small on-site museum runs informative walking tours for visitors.

North Shore ❹

🏊 *2,500.* 🚗 ℹ *HVCB, Waikīkī, (808) 924-0266.* 🎎 *O-Bon Buddhist Festival (Jul or Aug).*

THE HUB FOR the North Shore surfing community is **Hale'iwa**. The town's picturesque harbor is flanked by well-appointed public beaches. **Ali'i Beach** is famous for big waves and surfing contests. The adjacent **Hale'iwa Beach Park** is one of the few North Shore spots where it is usually quite safe to swim in winter. At the enchanting annual O-Bon Festival, thousands of floating lanterns are released into the ocean here.

Another popular North Shore spot is the **Waimea Valley Adventure Park**. The valley is a botanical paradise, with 36 gardens, thousands of rare tropical plants, and 30 species of birds. It also has superb cliff-diving shows, when high divers execute their feats from above a 45-ft (14-m) waterfall. Tours of the gardens and of a *hale kahiko* (ancient house) are offered, as is a show on the evolution of the *hula* dance form. The attached Adventure Park features more active forms of entertainment and includes activities such as horseback riding, mountain biking, and kayaking.

🦌 **Waimea Valley Adventure Park**
59-864 Kamehameha Hwy (Hwy 83),
Waimea. 📞 *(808) 638-8511.*
🚗 🕐 *10am–5:30pm daily.* 💷 ♿

Sign for Hale'iwa, O'ahu's surf town

The enchanting Byodo-In Temple, a Buddhist shrine

Moloka'i & Maui

T HE SMALL ISLAND OF Moloka'i, between O'ahu and Maui, is much less developed for tourism than its neighbors. The gentle pace of life, and the spectacular scenery of its flower-decked south coast and of the Kalaupapa National Historical Park, backed by the world's highest sea cliffs, enchant most visitors. Maui, Hawai'i's second largest island, offers lively resorts with a range of water sports, as well as lush plantations and the awesome grandeur of the Haleakalā Volcano.

Moloka'i's isolated Kalaupapa Peninsula, backed by towering cliffs

Kaunakakai ❺

🏃 3,500. 🅸 Ala Malama St & Kamehameha V Hwy (Hwy 450), (808) 553-3876. 🎏 Ka Moloka'i Makahiki (cultural festival, late Jan).

M OLOKA'I'S MAIN TOWN, Kaunakakai, was built in the 19th century as a port for the local sugar and pineapple plantations. Today, commercial agriculture has all but disappeared from the island, and Kaunakakai looks its age. The main street, with its wooden boardwalk, is lined with false-fronted stores. A short distance from the town center, local fishermen throng **Kaunakakai Harbor**, its long stone jetty jutting out into the ocean. About 2 miles (3 km) west of town is the **Kapuāiwa Coconut Grove**, whose 1,000 soaring trees are a majestic sight, silhouetted against the setting sun.

ENVIRONS: East of Kaunakakai begins the **Kamehameha V Highway**, which is among the most beautiful coastal drives in Hawai'i. The 27-mile (44-km) highway takes in ancient sites, picturesque churches, pristine beaches, and sleepy villages tucked away amid tropical flowers and luxuriant rainforests. The road finally twists to a halt at the stunningly beautiful **Halawa Valley** which, with its soaring walls, lush vegetation, idyllic beaches, and shimmering waterfalls, is Moloka'i's most scenic spot.

Kalaupapa National Historical Park ❻

Reached by foot or mule on Kalaupapa Trail: trailhead on Hwy 470, 3 miles (5 km) N of Kualapu'u, between the mule stables & Kalaupapa Overlook. ✈ 🖼 🗺 compulsory. Father Damien Tours, (808) 567-6171. Book well in advance. Visitors must be 16 years of age or older. For Moloka'i Mule Ride, (808) 567-6088, book in advance.

T HE ISOLATED Kalaupapa Peninsula, sealed off from the rest of Moloka'i by a mighty wall of cliffs, is home to the **Kalaupapa National Historical Park**. In 1865, when the imported disease of leprosy seemed to threaten the survival of the Hawaiian people, the peninsula was designated a leper colony, and those afflicted were exiled here. The park now serves as a memorial. The main settlement was at the village of Kalaupapa, on the sheltered western side of the peninsula. The last patients arrived in 1969, when the policy of enforced isolation ended. Kalaupapa's small population today includes a few aging patients who chose to live out their lives here.

South of the village is the precipitous **Kalaupapa Trail**, a favorite with hikers and mule riders who enjoy stupendous views during the 2-mile (3-km) trip. At the center of the peninsula is the **Kauhakō Crater**, with an 800-ft (245-m) deep lake.

On the peninsula's eastern shore is **St. Philomena Church**, in the original leprosy settlement of Kalawao. Shipped out from Honolulu in 1872, the church was later modified by the Belgian priest Father Damien (1840–89), who dedicated his life to caring for the leprosy patients. Father Damien succumbed to leprosy in 1889 and has been beatified by the Pope. His right hand is interred in the church. From the peninsula's eastern side, small islands poke out of the waters of the ocean, next to staggering 2000-ft (600-m) cliffs – the tallest sea cliffs in the world.

St. Philomena Church, where Father Damien's hand is buried

Locals demonstrating their courage at Keka'a Point, Kā'anapali

Lahaina ❼

🏠 9,500. ⚓ Lahaina Harbor. ℹ 648 Wharf St, (808) 667-9193. 🎉 A Taste of Lahaina (food festival, mid-Sep); Halloween Mardi Gras of the Pacific (Oct 31). 🌐 www.visitlahaina.com

ONE OF MAUI'S most popular attractions, this small harbor town was the capital of the Kingdom of Hawai'i until 1845 and a major center of the whaling trade. The area around Front Street has a wealth of well-restored historic sites, evocative of Lahaina's past. Among them is the **Baldwin Home**, Maui's oldest Western-style dwelling, dating from the 1830s, with original furnishings and artifacts. Nearby is the **Chinese Wo Hing Temple**, built in 1912. A favorite landmark is Lahaina's first hotel, the charming 1901 **Pioneer Inn**, still a tourist mecca and hotel.

Docked in the harbor, beside the lighthouse, is the *Carthaginian II*, a 1920s German schooner transformed to look like the kind of small freighter that brought cargo and people to the islands in the 1800s. It has a fascinating museum in the hold, devoted to whales and the whale trade.

Just 6 miles (10 km) north of Lahaina is Maui's biggest resort, **Kā'anapali**, its long white beach lined with hotels. **Pu'u Keka'a**, better known as Black Rock, towers above the beach and overlooks one of Maui's best snorkeling spots. Vintage steam locomotives make the short and scenic trip here from Lahaina. A 20-minute drive north of Kā'anapali is Maui's other major resort, **Kapalua**, with its exquisite crescent bays, blue waters, luxury hotels, golf courses, and beautiful pineapple plantations.

Haleakalā National Park ❽

Haleakalā Crater Road (Hwy 378). 🕐 24 hrs daily. 🎫 🚗 **Park Headquarters** 📞 (808) 572-4400. 🕐 7:30am–4pm daily. 🦯 **Visitor Center** 🕐 sunrise–3pm daily. 🦯 **Cabins** To enter lottery for reservations, write to: Cabins, Haleakalā National Park, Box 369, Makawao, HI 96768.

THE LAND MASS of East Maui is really the top of an enormous volcano that begins more than 3 miles (5 km) below sea level. Haleakalā last spewed molten lava some 200 years ago and is still considered to be active, although not currently erupting. Its summit depression is 7.5 miles (12 km) long and 2.5 miles (4 km) wide. This natural wonder is preserved as part of the national park. The 2-hour drive to the 10,023-ft (3,055-m) **Pu'u 'Ula'ula Summit**, the highest point in Maui, offers a breathtaking view of the entire volcano, with its cinder cones and brightly colored ashes.

The best way to appreciate Haleakalā's scale and varied terrain is to descend 3,000 ft (900 m) into the volcano. The 10-mile (16-km) **Sliding Sands Trail** takes you from the visitor center through scenery that ranges from barren cinder desert to alpine shrubland. Also worth exploring is the **Silversword Loop** where one of the world's rarest plants, the Haleakalā Silversword, thrives. It takes up to 50 years to flower, when it raises a spectacular spike of purplish flowers.

Hāna ❾

🏠 700. ✈ ℹ MVB, Wailuku, (808) 244-3530. 🎉 East Maui Taro Festival (Mar/Apr).

OFTEN CALLED Hawai'i's most Hawaiian town, Hāna continues to lag lazily behind modernity. Its perfect round bay and dreamy climate have made it a prized settlement since ancient times. **Ka'uiki Head**, the large cinder cone on the right flank of the bay, served as a natural fortification.

The **Hāna Cultural Center** presents a *kauhale* (residential compound) in the pre-contact style once unique to this area and exhibits artifacts that give a sense of local history. **Wānanalua Church**, constructed from blocks of coral in 1838, was built by missionaries on top of an existing *heiau* (temple), thus symbolizing the triumph of Christianity over paganism.

The scenic **Hāna Belt Road** twists along the coast to Pā'ia, with views of waterfalls, gulches choked with vegetation, taro fields, botanical gardens, rocky cliffs, and the dramatic Honomanū Bay with its black sand beach.

Pu'u 'Ula'ula Summit in Haleakalā National Park, Maui's highest point

Hawai'i Island

SPREADING OVER 4,035 SQ MILES (10,450 sq km), Hawai'i Island, also known as the Big Island, is more than twice the size of all the other islands combined. Its natural wonders include the earth's most massive mountain, Mauna Loa, which rises over 30,000 ft (9,150 m) from the ocean floor, and Kilauea, the most active volcano on earth, both of which form part of the Hawai'i Volcanoes National Park. Equally fascinating are the island's well-preserved cultural sites within the Pu'uhonua O Hōnaunau National Historical Park.

Hawai'i Volcanoes National Park ❿

Hawai'i Belt Road (Hwy 11).
⬤ 24 hours daily. ♿ ⛺ **Kīlauea Visitor Center** ☎ (808) 985-6000.
⬤ 7:45am–5pm daily. ♿ **Jaggar Museum** ☎ (808) 985-6049. ⬤ 8:30am–5pm daily. ♿ **Volcano Art Center** ☎ (808) 967-7565. ⬤ 9am–5pm daily. ⬤ Dec 25. ♿ ⛩ **Volcano House Hotel** ☎ (808) 967-7321. ♿ 🍴 W www.nps.gov/havo

ENCOMPASSING about a quarter of a million acres, this national park includes the 13,677-ft (4,169-m) summit of

Mauna Loa, 150 miles (240 km) of hiking trails, and vast tracts of wilderness that preserve some of the world's rarest species of flora and fauna. But it is Kilauea Caldera and the lava flows of its furious East Rift Zone that draw most visitors. Two roads – **Crater Rim Drive**, which loops around the caldera, and **Chain of Craters Road**, which descends through the recent outpourings – form a gigantic drive-through museum. The present eruption started in 1983 and produces slow-moving lava, which poses no threat to

visitors. However, you should stay out of closed areas; no one knows how long the flow will continue or where it will next erupt.

East of the park, the **Kīlauea Iki Overlook** gives a view of the crater, which in 1959 filled with bubbling lava,

Lava fountains spewing from Kīlauea during the 1983 eruption

KEY

▬▬ Major road
▬▬ Minor road
■ ■ Hiking trail
❇ Vista

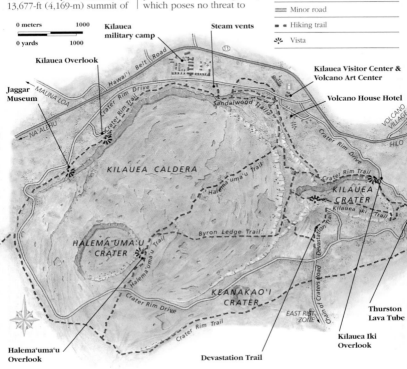

0 meters 1000
0 yards 1000

Kīlauea military camp
Steam vents
Kīlauea Overlook
Jaggar Museum
MAUNA LOA
Hawai'i Belt Road
Crater Rim Drive
Crater Rim Trail
NA'ALEHU
Sandalwood Trail
Kīlauea Visitor Center & Volcano Art Center
Volcano House Hotel
VOLCANO VILLAGE
HILO
Crater Rim Drive
KILAUEA CALDERA
Halema'uma'u Trail
Crater Rim Trail
KILAUEA CRATER
Kīlauea Iki Trail
Byron Ledge Trail
Devastation Trail
HALEMA'UMA'U CRATER
Halema'uma'u Trail
Crater Rim Drive
KEANAKAO'I CRATER
Chain of Craters Road
EAST RIFT ZONE
Thurston Lava Tube
Kīlauea Iki Overlook
Crater Rim Trail
Halema'uma'u Overlook
Devastation Trail

Thurston Lava Tube, formed by the hardening of a lava stream

shooting fire fountains 1,900 ft (580 m) into the air. Across the road from the crater, at the eastern edge of the park, lies the Thurston Lava Tube. This huge tunnel was left behind when a subterranean river of lava drained away. An easy trail runs through the tube and a grove of giant ferns. Nearby, the short Devastation Trail features ghostly remains of a rainforest, wiped out by ash falling from Kīlauea Iki's 1959 eruption. Farther west, the Halemaʻumaʻu Overlook affords views of the once boiling lake of lava. The crater below still steams with sulfurous fumes. This is the home of Pele, the fiery-tempered volcano goddess, who migrated from Kahiki (Tahiti) seeking a dry place for her eternal fires.

Hilo ⑪

🏨 38,000. ✈ 🚌 *Kamehameha Ave, near Mamo St, (808) 961-8744.* ℹ *BIVB, 250 Keawe St, (808) 961-5797.* 🎉 *Merrie Monarch Festival (Mar or Apr).*

ALTHOUGH IT IS the state's second city, "rainy old Hilo" is a contrast to sunny, urban Honolulu. The city's progress has been checked by nature – rain falls 278 days of the year, and two destructive *tsunamis* pounded Hilo in 1946 and 1960. The city has since retreated from the sea, turning the waterfront area into enormous parks, while the rain has made it a natural garden, full of orchids and anthuriums. Hilo's population is largely Japanese and Filipino in ancestry.

The downtown business district, with its restored buildings, is worth exploring on foot. The **Lyman Museum and Mission House** vividly evokes a bygone era – it is preserved as it was in the 1830s, with Victorian furnishings and artifacts.

On the Waiākea Peninsula, jutting into Hilo Bay, the 30-acre (12-ha) **Liliʻuokalani Gardens**, landscaped in Japanese style, while east of downtown are the 80-ft (24-m) high **Rainbow Falls**. The morning sun, filtering through the mist of the waterfall, often creates beautiful rainbows.

The east side of Hilo Bay offers fine snorkeling and swimming at the **James Kealoha Beach Park**; and at the **Richardson Ocean Park**.

Puʻuhonua O Honaunau National Historical Park ⑫

Hwy 160, off Hawaiʻi Belt Rd (Hwy 11). 📞 *(808) 328-2326.* 🕐 *6am–8pm Mon–Thu, 6am–11pm Fri–Sun.* 🏛 👢
Visitor Center 🕐 *8am–4:30pm. Daily orientation talks.*

FROM THE 11th century on, social interactions were regulated by the *kapu* (taboo) system, and even minor infractions, such as stepping on a chief's shadow, were punished by violent death. Lawbreakers could, however, escape punishment by reaching a *puʻuhonua* (place of refuge). The greatest of these was at **Hōnaunau**, a 6-acre (2-ha) temple compound dating from the 16th century, which offered absolution to all those who could swim or run past the chief's warriors. The sanctuary was stripped of power in 1819, after the fall of the *kapu* system. Now partly restored, it provides a glimpse into precontact Hawaiʻi.

Located on a peninsula of black lava, whose jagged shoreline made it difficult for *kapu*-breakers to approach from the sea, the *puʻuhonua's* focal point is the 1650 **Hale O Keawe Heiau**, the temple that once held the bones and therefore the *mana* (sacred power) of great chiefs. Outside it stand Kiʻi – wooden images of gods. As impressive is the great drystone wall, 10 ft (3 m) high and 17 ft (5 m) wide. Built around 1550, it separated the *puʻuhonua* from the palace area inland.

PROFESSOR JAGGAR (1871–1953)

Thomas A. Jaggar was a pioneer in the young science of volcanology. A professor of geology at Massachusetts Institute of Technology, he founded the Hawaiian Volcano Observatory at Kilauea Caldera in 1912. Four years later, he and Honolulu publisher Lorrin Thurston persuaded Congress to preserve the area as a national park. Professor Jaggar developed techniques for collecting volcanic gases and measuring ground tilt, seismic activity, and lava temperatures. The work he initiated has made Kilauea one of the world's best understood volcanoes.

Professor Jaggar on a boat trip

The Hale O Keawe Heiau, a place of spiritual power

Kauaʻi

WIND AND WATER HAVE HAD six million years to transform Kauaʻi, the oldest of the major Hawaiian islands, into a stunning array of pleated cliffs and yawning chasms, cloaked with a mantle of emerald green vegetation. Also known as the "Garden Island," Kauaʻi is Hawaiʻi's most beautiful and irresistible destination. Its highlights include Kīlauea Point's glorious beaches, the dramatic Waimea Canyon, and the soaring cliffs of the Kalalau Trail on the Nā Pali Coast. You can drive anywhere in Kauaʻi in three hours or less.

The shady *koa*-wood veranda at Grove Farm Homestead

Līhuʻe ⓭

🏨 5,500. ✈ 🚌 *Rice St, (808) 241-6410.* 🚩 *KVB, 4334 Rice St, Suite 101, (808) 245-3971.* 🎭 *Kauaʻi-Tahiti Fete (mid-Aug).*

ALTHOUGH LĪHUʻE happens to be the administrative and business center of Kauaʻi, it is actually little more than a plantation village. It was built in the 19th century to serve the Līhuʻe Sugar Mill, whose rusting machinery still dominates the downtown area. Līhuʻe's oceanfront district, with the beautiful Kalapakī Beach, is especially appealing, and the outskirts of town offer such delights as grand plantation mansions and a stunning waterfall.

Within the town, **Kauaʻi Museum** displays a splendid collection of traditional artifacts, including huge *koa*-wood bowls, royal feather standards, and old weapons. It also has exhibits on the island's history and geology. The imposing **Grove Farm Homestead** on Nāwiliwili Road is an early 20th-century mansion, paneled in dark, heavy *koa* wood. A guided tour, which must be reserved in advance, covers the rather formal house, the cramped servants' quarters, and the beautifully scented orchard.

Kalapakī Beach, with gently sloping beautiful white sands and sheltered inshore waters, is the safest beach in the area and especially suitable for families with small children. On its far side, the scenic palm-fringed **Nāwiliwili Beach County Park** is ideal for picnics.

The grand 1930s house known as **Kilohana Plantation**, 1.5 miles (2.5 km) west of Līhuʻe, resembles an English country estate. Visitors can tour the house, which has a restaurant and some shops, and explore the cane fields in old-fashioned horse-drawn carriages. The mansion commands superb views of the Kilohana mountain inland.

ENVIRONS: Just 5 miles (8 km) north of Līhuʻe, a winding road through cane fields leads to the twin cascades of the 80-ft (24-m) **Wailua Falls**. They are best viewed from the roadside parking lot, as the path down the hillside can be slippery. **Menehune Fish Pond** 1.5 miles (2.5 km) south of Līhuʻe, is located in idyllic pastoral landscape. With its ancient stonemasonry, the pond was used to fatten mullet for the royal table.

Kīlauea Point ⓮

Kīlauea Road, off Kūhiō Hwy (Hwy 56), 10 miles (16 km) NW of Anahola. 🚌 *Kīlauea.* 🚩 *KVB, Līhuʻe, (808) 245-3971.*

THE NORTHERNMOST spot on the Hawaiian archipelago, Kīlauea Point is a rocky promontory pounded by mighty waves. The windswept clifftop has been set aside as the **Kīlauea Point National Wildlife Refuge**, where bird-watcher's can spot frigatebirds, Laysan albatrosses, and many other species. A short walk beyond the visitor center leads to the red and white **Kīlauea Lighthouse**, erected in 1913. Approaching the tip of the headland, there are splendid views westward to the fabled **Nā Pali** cliffs. Half a mile (800 m) west of the Kīlauea turn-off on Kalihiwai Road, a red dirt

The twin cascades of Wailua Falls near Līhuʻe

The Pu'u O Kila Lookout, with views of the Kalalau Valley

track leads to the vast but little-visited shelf of glorious yellow sand known as **Secret Beach**. The ocean can be rough for swimming here, but it is a beautiful place to walk, with its dramatic views of the lighthouse and a glorious waterfall at the far end.

🐾 Kīlauea Point National Wildlife Refuge

Kilauea Point. 🅒 *(808) 828-1413.* ◯ *daily.* ◯ *Jan 1, Thanksgiving, Dec 25.* 🈺 ♿

Waimea Canyon & Koke'e State Park ⑮

Kōke'e Road (Hwy 550). 🅒 *Kaua'i Division of State Parks, (808) 274-3444.* **Kōke'e State Park** ◯ *daily.* **Kōke'e Museum** 🅒 *(808) 335-9975. Donation.* ◯ *10am–4pm daily.* 🅿 **Kōke'e Lodge** 🅒 *(808) 335-6061.* 🛏 *Cabins available for rent.*

N̲O VISITOR should leave Kaua'i without taking in the rugged grandeur of Waimea Canyon and the breathtaking views from Kōke'e State Park. Waimea Canyon, known as the "Grand Canyon of the Pacific," was created by an earthquake that almost split Kaua'i in two. The gorge, now 3,000 ft (915 m) deep, is still eroding as landslides and the Waimea River continue to carry away tons of soil. Of the several lookouts dotted along the rim, the **Waimea Canyon Lookout**, despite being the lowest of the lookouts, offers the best canyon views. The more adventurous can take hiking trails to explore in greater depth. The **Kukui Trail** heads sharply down into the canyon as far as the Waimea River – a relatively easy and rewarding trip. At the North End of Waimea Canyon is **Kōke'e State Park**, laced through with more hiking trails. From the park's **Pu'u O Kila Lookout**, the majestic amphitheater of the Kalalau Valley opens out; another view is from the nearby **Kalalau Lookout**. A highlight of the park is the **Alaka'i Swamp**, a bowl-like depression drenched by nearly 42 ft (13 m) of rain every year. Part rainforest, part bog, the area boasts some of Hawai'i's rarest birds, such as the *'i'iwi* or honeycreeper, and the tiny yellow *'anianiau*. A hiking trail leads to the more accessible part of the swamp. Information, hiking advice, and maps are all available at the Kōke'e State Park headquarters.

Kalalau Trail ⑯

Visitors must obtain permission in advance from the State Parks office. **State Parks office** *3060 'Eiwa St, Lihu'e, HI 96766, (808) 274-3444.*

T̲HE PRECIPITOUS cliffs of the Nā Pali Coast make it impossible for the road to continue west of Kē'ē Beach on Kauai's north shore. But hardy hikers can follow the narrow Kalalau Trail for another 11 miles (18 km) to isolated Kalalau Valley. One of the most dramatic hikes in the world, it covers a landscape of almost primeval vastness and splendor. While this is not an expedition to undertake lightly, a half-day round trip to Hanakāpi'ai Valley is within most capabilities and provides an unforgettable wilderness experience.

The trail begins at the end of **Kūhiō Highway**, climbing steeply to **Makana Peak** and affording spectacular views of the rugged coastline. It continues on to **Ke Ahu A Laka**, which was once Hawai'i's most celebrated school for *hula* dancing. The next stop is **Hanakāpi'ai Valley** where in summer a pristine sandy beach replaces the pebbles found at the valley mouth in winter. Wading and swimming here are unsafe, due to dangerous rip currents.

The more challenging part of the trail continues through an abandoned coffee plantation to the **Hanakāpi'ai Falls**, and then to **Pā Ma Wa'a**, an 800-ft (240-m) cliff, which is the highest point on the trail. The trail then dips into several hanging valleys where the streams have still to cut their way down to sea level, before reaching the beautiful campsite at **Hanakoa Valley**, set amid the ruins of ancient taro terraces. For the last 5 miles (8 km), the trail clings perilously to a sandstone cliff. The magical view of **Kalalau Valley** is the trail's reward. Note that there is no food or safe drinking water *en route*.

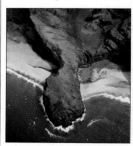

The soaring, pleated cliffs of the Nā Pali Coast, Kalalau Trail

Alaska Practical Information

TRAVELING AROUND THE LARGEST state in the US requires a great deal of advance planning. From endless snowfields, towering mountains, majestic rainforests, sweeping tundra, active volcanoes, and the spectacular "northern lights" to some of the world's most abundant wildlife preserves, Alaska has much to offer its visitors. Although traveling in Alaska is more expensive than in other parts of the country, visitors on a small budget can also have a memorable trip.

TOURIST INFORMATION

THE BEST SOURCE of travel information is the very comprehensive Alaska Vacation Planner, published by the **Alaska Travel Industry Association** (ATIA). The ATIA is run jointly by the state and various travel businesses. Many regional tourism councils also publish brochures on travel in their areas.

GETTING AROUND

VISITORS HAVE A number of transportation options. **Alaska Airlines** flights link larger cities and towns, while smaller "bush" planes take visitors to more remote areas. The state-run **Alaska Railroad** connects Fairbanks, Anchorage, Seward, and Denali National Park. The main intercity bus service, **Alaska Direct BusLine**, has year-round service.

A government-operated ferry service, the **Alaska Marine Highway System** links towns throughout southeast and south central Alaska, with service extending as far south as Prince Rupert in British Columbia and Bellingham, Washington. The large, comfortable, and well-equipped ships carry hundreds of vehicles and feature cabins, multiple dining areas, and onboard naturalists. The pace is relaxed and the atmosphere is very casual; some travelers even sleep under the stars on the outer deck. Book well in advance for this popular ferry service. However, driving within Alaska involves long distances; be especially careful of collisions with Alaska's wildlife.

NATURAL HAZARDS

MOST TRAVELERS visit Alaska in the milder summer season between late May and early-September. Even so, bring a jacket and warm clothes for chilly nights. Summer also brings the worst of Alaska's insects, mainly mosquitoes and blackflies. Backcountry travelers also need to take precautions in bear country. **Park Service** or **Forest Service** rangers can provide safety tips.

FESTIVALS

THERE ARE A number of special events taking place in Alaska at different times of the year. Starting in spring, the famous **Iditarod Trail Sled Dog Race** runs between Anchorage and Nome. April sees the **Alaska Folk Festival** held in Juneau. The **Alaska State Fair** (August) in Palmer is famous for its pumpkins and cabbages, which grow to world-record sizes under the state's 24-hour sunshine. On October 18th, the **Alaska Day Celebration**, the day Alaska was bought from Russia by the US, livens up the Colonial town of Sitka.

OUTDOOR ACTIVITIES

THE VAST MAJORITY of Alaska is set aside as public land, making the state a paradise for hikers, fishermen, and other outdoor enthusiasts. Trekking, mountain climbing, skiing, rafting, kayaking, and whale-watching are some of the activities that visitors can enjoy here. Most tourist offices provide information and details of outdoor pursuits that Alaska has to offer.

THE CLIMATE OF ALASKA

Although situated near the Arctic Circle, weather patterns vary a great deal in Alaska. Winters are cold and dark, but summer with its warm weather and long days is the prime season for visitors. In the state's northern tier, the sun does not set for two months of the year, and there is daylight for as many as 22 hours each day in June at Fairbanks. July is the rainiest month. Most coastal cruises take place in the summer.

ANCHORAGE

°F/C	Apr	Jul	Oct	Jan
		65/18		
32°F	44/7	49/9	43/6	
0°C				19/−7
	27/−3		29/−2	5/−15
☀	15 days	13 days	11 days	10 days
☂	0.7 in	1.8 in	2 in	0.8 in
month	Apr	Jul	Oct	Jan

Hawai'i Practical Information

Tourism is Hawai'i's most important industry. From the bright lights of Waikīkī and Honolulu to the remote waterfalls of Maui's Hāna district, the islands offer something to suit all budgets. The cost of living in Hawai'i is about 40 percent higher than that in the rest of the US; even so, Hawai'i is a year-round destination. However, visitors will enjoy better prices in the off-season, between April and December.

TOURIST INFORMATION

Visitor information desks at all airports provide maps and guides, and all major hotels have a guest services desk. All islands have a branch of the **Hawai'i Visitors' and Convention Bureau** (HVCB), or some other visitors' bureau.

GETTING AROUND

Driving is the best way to get around, since public transportation is limited. Seat belts are mandatory, and children under three must sit in approved car seats. Distances between gas stations can be long, so keep the tank at least half full. Always check the weather – many roads wash out during or after heavy rains.

Allow plenty of time for any trip. The locals move at a leisurely pace, seldom using horns. On narrow roads, pull over to let cars pass.

NATURAL HAZARDS

Visitors should be aware of certain potential dangers that the sun and the ocean pose to health. Thus,

wear a hat and sunglasses, use sunblock cream, and drink plenty of fluids as a protection against the harsh sun.

Ask the lifeguard about ocean conditions, as some beaches can be safe in summer but very dangerous in winter. Swim facing away from the beach, as sudden rogue waves can sweep you out to sea. If you get carried out by a rip current, try to swim with it until it dissipates. Always check for rocks and corals below the surface, and wear protective foot gear. If you cut yourself on coral, clean the cut thoroughly with antiseptic. If you step on a sea urchin, or are stung by a jellyfish, apply a paste of vinegar and meat tenderizer. Although shark encounters are rare, it's best that you check with the lifeguard before swimming.

OUTDOOR ACTIVITIES

Hawai'i offers a plethora of outdoor activities, many focused on the ocean, such as surfing, swimming, fishing, scuba diving, and snorkeling. In addition, sports enthusiasts

DIRECTORY

TOURIST INFORMATION

Hawai'i Visitors' & Convention Bureau
((808) 923-1811.

SNORKELING

Snorkel Bob's
700 Kapahulu Ave,
Honolulu, O'ahu.
((808) 735-7944.

SCUBA DIVING

Bubbles Below
PO Box 157, Eleele, Kaua'i.
((808) 332-7333.

have a variety of opportunities such as horseback riding, hiking, and playing golf on some of the world's best courses.

ENTERTAINMENT

Music and dance are as important to Hawaiians as the air they breathe. Most islands offer extravagant Polynesian shows, with *lū'au*-style meals, and music and dance from other Pacific islands such as Tahiti and Fiji. You can dance the night away in nightclubs in Honolulu and Maui, but also be prepared for earlier nights in other parts of the state.

FESTIVALS

A diverse range of festivals and events take place all through the year. The onset of summer sees **Lei Day** with everyone donning flowered garlands. The **King Kamehameha Day** honors the chief who united the islands. All summer long, there are cultural, music, and food festivals, as well as sports events, from rodeos to canoe races and the grueling **Ironman Triathlon**. Summer draws to a close with the grand **Aloha Week Festivals**.

Winters offer sports and cultural events such as the **Triple Crown of Surfing**, and the **Merrie Monarch Festival** which culminates with the "Olympics" of *hula*.

THE CLIMATE OF HAWAI'I

Hawai'i has two distinct seasons, summer and winter. May to October is hot and dry, while November through April is cooler and wetter. Happily for visitors, there are very few days when Hawai'i's beaches do not beckon. Sudden rains or storms mean the onset of winter, as do the big waves that surfers eagerly await. However, Hawai'i is not all sunshine, and residents in the cooler upcountry areas spend Christmas Eve gathered around the fireplace.

HONOLULU

°F/C

	Apr	Jul	Oct	Jan
	78/25	82/28	82/28	76/24
	68/20	73/22	73/22	68/20
☀	21 days	24 days	22 days	20 days
☂	1.5 in	0.6 in	2.3 in	3.5 in
month	Apr	Jul	Oct	Jan

32°F
0°C

Where to Stay

THESE HOTELS HAVE BEEN selected across a wide price range for their excellent facilities and locations. While Hawai'i is a year-round destination, Alaska's accommodations fill fast during the short and busy summer. This chart lists hotels by region and within this by price category. In the Hawai'i section, figures in parentheses indicate the number of suites available.

	Credit Cards	Number of Rooms	Restaurant	Breakfast Included	Summer Only
ALASKA					
ALASKA PENINSULA: *Brooks Lodge* $$$$$ Katmai National Park. (907) 243-5448, (800) 554-0551. FAX (907) 243-0649. W www.bear-viewing.com A famous hunting lodge located within walking distance of bear-viewing platforms. Has a package that includes the flight from Anchorage and three meals per day. ● *Oct–May.*	■	16	■	●	■
ANCHORAGE: *Hostelling International Anchorage* $ 700 H St. (907) 276-3635. FAX (907) 276-7772. Visitors can walk to downtown and the long-distance bus terminal from this centrally located hostel. There are private rooms in addition to male and female dormitories. The check-in time is 8–11am and after 5pm.		95 beds			
ANCHORAGE: *Hotel Captain Cook* $$$$ 4th Avenue at K St. (907) 276-6000, (800) 843-1950. FAX (907) 343-2298. W www.captaincook.com Located in the heart of downtown, this is Alaska's largest hotel with rooms in three towers. An understated elegance pervades the building.	■	547	■		
DENALI NATIONAL PARK: *Westmark Denali Sourdough Cabins* $$ Parks Hwy. (907) 683-2773, (800) 354-6020. W www.westmarkhotels.com The park visitor center is only a 10-minute walk from this scattering of functional cabins spread throughout the forest. ● *mid-Sep–mid-May.*	■	51	■		■
DENALI NATIONAL PARK: *Kantishna Roadhouse* $$$$$ Park Rd Kantishna. (907) 459-2120, (800) 942-7420. FAX (907) 459-2160. W www.kantishnaroadhouse.com This hotel has an upscale, rustic ambience that extends from the inviting guest rooms to the comfortable communal area of the main lodge. Access is by private bus from the park entrance. ● *mid-Sep–May.*	■	32		●	■
FAIRBANKS: *Springhill Suites* $$$ 575 1st Ave. (907) 451-6552, (888) 287-9400. FAX: (907) 451-6553. W www.springhillsuites.com The standard suite at this Marriott-affiliated property is unequaled in Fairbanks. Its rooms are spacious and tastefully appointed.	■	140	■	●	
FAIRBANKS: *Sophie Station Hotel* $$$$ 1717 University Ave. (907) 479-3650, (800) 528-4916. FAX: (907) 451-6376. W www.fountainheadhotels.com This all-suites hotel features comfortable rooms with kitchenettes, and is close to the airport.	■	148	■		
GLACIER BAY NATIONAL PARK: *Glacier Bay Lodge* $$$ Bartlett Cove. (206) 623-2417, (800) 451-5952. FAX (206) 623-7809. W www.glacierbaycruiseline.com This lodge is set in a forest at the departure point for cruises into Glacier Bay. Most visitors stay as part of a package tour. ● *Oct–May.*	■	56	■	●	■
HOMER: *Land's End Resort* $$$ 4786 Homer Spit Rd. (907) 235-0400, (800) 478-0400. FAX (907) 235-0420. W www.lands-end-resort.com Named for its location at the tip of Homer Spit, this hotel offers splendid views over the ocean from its comfortable rooms.	■	80	■		
JUNEAU: *Alaskan Hotel* $ 167 S Franklin St. (907) 586-1000, (800) 327-9347. FAX (907) 463-3775. W www.ptialaska.net/~akhotel This inexpensive downtown hotel has been popular since it opened in 1913. The old-fashioned rooms here are clean and comfortable.	■	40	■		

		Price category /	CREDIT CARDS	NUMBER OF ROOMS	RESTAURANT	BREAKFAST INCLUDED	SUMMER ONLY

Price categories for a standard double room per night in peak season, and inclusive of all taxes:

$ under $75
$$ $75–$125
$$$ $125–$185
$$$$ $185–$250
$$$$$ over $250

CREDIT CARDS
Major credit cards accepted.
NUMBER OF ROOMS
Number of rooms in the hotel. Hostels offer dormitory-style accommodations; number of beds are indicated in the column.
RESTAURANT
Hotel restaurant or dining room, also open to non residents.
BREAKFAST INCLUDED
Cooked or Continental breakfast included in rates.
SUMMER ONLY
Opens in May or June and is closed by early October.

	CREDIT CARDS	NUMBER OF ROOMS	RESTAURANT	BREAKFAST INCLUDED	SUMMER ONLY
JUNEAU: *Juneau International Hostel* $ 614 Harris St. (907) 586-9559. W www.juneauhostel.org Visitors can check in after 5pm at this friendly and homey hotel which has separate dormitories for men and women, and no TV. There is a midnight curfew.		46 beds			
JUNEAU: *Westmark Baranof* $$$ 127 N Franklin St. (907) 586-2660, (800) 544-0970. FAX (907) 586-8315. W www.westmarkhotels.com This is the grand dame of Juneau hotels. This nine-story downtown gem has beautiful pressed tin ceilings and polished wood furnishings in the lobby. However, the rooms of the Westmark Baranof are modern and well-equipped.	■	196	■		
KETCHIKAN: *Blueberry Hill B&B* $$ 500 Front St. (907) 247-2583, (877) 449-2583. FAX (907) 247-2584. W www.blueberryhillbb.com A budget B&B, within walking distance of downtown. Rooms are brightly decorated and two feature water views.	■	4			
KETCHIKAN: *Cedars Lodge* $$$$ 1471 Tongass Ave. (907) 225-1900, (800) 813-4363. FAX (907) 225-8604. W www.cedarslodge.com With its waterfront setting, this hostelry is preferred by anglers, who head out on guided trips from the lodge's private marina. Some of the units of Cedars Lodge have attached kitchens. ● Oct–Apr.	■	13	■	●	■
KODIAK ISLAND: *Kodiak Inn* $$$ 236 Rezanof Dr, Kodiak. (907) 486-5712. FAX (907) 486-3430. W www.kodiakinn.com Affiliated with the Best Western chain, this is the largest and most modern hotel on Kodiak Island.	■	80	■		
NOME: *Chateau de Cape Nome* $ E 4th Avenue at East N St. (907) 443-2083. Visitors could try skipping Nome's regular hotels to stay in the home of a local family. The atmosphere here is exceptionally warm and friendly.		3	■	●	■
SEWARD: *Seward Windsong Lodge* $$$ Exit Glacier Rd. (907) 224-7116, (888) 959-9590. FAX (907) 224-7118. W www.sewardwindsong.com Overlooking Resurrection River north of Seward, this lodge takes advantage of its delightful surroundings. ● Oct–Apr.	■	108	■		■
SITKA: *Sitka Hotel* $ 118 Lincoln St. (907) 747-3288. FAX (907) 747-8499. W www.sitkahotel.com This attractive yet economical hotel with comfortable rooms has been restored to its 1930s grandeur. The bar is popular with locals.	■	60	■		
SKAGWAY: *Skagway Inn* $$$ 655 Broadway. (907) 983-2289, (888) 752-4929. FAX (907) 983-2713. W www.skagwayinn.com Built in 1897, this charming B&B was originally a bordello for gold miners. Guests enjoy the Victorian ambience and a cozy downstairs bistro.	■	12	■		
VALDEZ: *Aspen Hotel Valdez* $$$ 100 Meals Ave. (907) 835-4445. FAX (907) 835-2437. W www.aspenhotelsak.com A well-maintained hotel in the center of town. Each room is equipped with a microwave, small refrigerators, and voice-mail.	■	78	■	●	

For key to symbols see back flap

Price categories for a standard double room for one night in tourist season (Dec–Apr), including taxes:

ⓢ under $85
ⓢⓢ $85–$150
ⓢⓢⓢ $150–$250
ⓢⓢⓢⓢ $250–$400
ⓢⓢⓢⓢⓢ over $400

CREDIT CARDS
Major credit cards accepted.

NUMBER OF ROOMS
Number of rooms in the hotel (suites shown in parentheses).

RECOMMENDED RESTAURANT
Good restaurant within the hotel.

CHILDREN'S FACILITIES
Hotel has various facilities for young children.

OCEAN VIEW
Ocean-front guestrooms or rooms with spectacular ocean views are available.

	CREDIT CARDS	NUMBER OF ROOMS (SUITES)	RECOMMENDED RESTAURANT	CHILDREN'S FACILITIES	OCEAN VIEW

HAWAI'I

HONOLULU (O'AHU): *Doubletree Alana Waikiki Hotel*   ⓢⓢⓢ
1956 Ala Moana Boulevard, HI 96815. 📞 *(808) 941-7275.* 📠 *(808) 941-7423.*
Ⓦ www.alana-doubletree.com
A favorite with islanders, this is one of the best small hotels and is located near the shoppers' mecca known as the Ala Moana Center. It offers attractively appointed, functional rooms. 🅿 ⛵

| | ■ | 268 (45) | ■ | | ■ |

WAIKĪKĪ (O'AHU): *Royal Garden at Waikīkī*   ⓢⓢ
440 'Olohana St, HI 96815. 📞 *(808) 943-0202, (800) 367-5666.* 📠 *(808) 945-7407.*
Ⓦ www.royalgardens.com
This boutique hotel is truly a breath of fresh air. Half a block from the Ala Wai Canal, it is fairly quiet with beautifully appointed rooms and baths, and an excellent restaurant, the Cascada.

| | ■ | 201 (19) | ■ | ● | |

WAIKĪKĪ (O'AHU): *Radisson Waikīkī Prince Kūhiō*   ⓢⓢⓢ
2500 Kūhiō Ave, HI 96815. 📞 *(808) 922-0811, (800) 333-3333.* 📠 *(808) 921-5507.*
Ⓦ www.radisson.com/waikikihi
Located a block away from the beach and two blocks from Kapi'olani Park, this hotel still seems a long way from the Waikīkī crowds. It offers lovely rooms with marble baths.

| | ■ | 620 (6) | ■ | | ■ |

WAIKĪKĪ (O'AHU): *Halekūlani*   ⓢⓢⓢⓢ
2199 Kālia Rd, HI 96815. 📞 *(808) 923-2311, (800) 367-2343.* 📠 *(808) 926-8004.*
Ⓦ www.halekulani.com
The Halekūlani is the epitome of elegance. Everything is perfect, from the manicured tropical grounds and the tasteful decor to the superb cuisine at La Mer and the beautiful, orchid-design pool.

| | ■ | 412 (44) | ■ | | ■ |

WAIKĪKĪ (O'AHU): *The Royal Hawaiian*   ⓢⓢⓢⓢ
2259 Kalākaua Ave, HI 96815. 📞 *(808) 923-7311, (800) 325-3589.* 📠 *(808) 924-7098.*
Ⓦ www.starwood.com/luxury.com
This elegant Waikīkī landmark, built in 1927, is affectionately known as the Pink Palace of the Pacific.

| | ■ | 526 (54) | ■ | ● | ■ |

WAIKĪKĪ (O'AHU): *Sheraton Moana Surfrider*   ⓢⓢⓢⓢ
2365 Kalākaua Ave, HI 96815. 📞 *(808) 922-3111, (800) 325-3535.* 📠 *(808) 923-0308.*
Ⓦ www. sheraton.com
The splendid "First Lady of Waikīkī" combines modern comforts with high elegance and grandeur. Don't on any account miss the tea on the popular Banyan Veranda.

| | ■ | 791 (46) | ■ | ● | ■ |

KAUNAKAKAI (MOLOKA'I): *Hotel Moloka'i*   ⓢⓢ
Mile Marker 2, Kamehameha V Hwy, PO Box 1020, HI 96748. 📞 *(808) 553-5347.*
📠 *(808) 553-5047.* Ⓦ www.castleresorts.com
This oceanfront, Polynesian-style hotel is a favorite with islanders, offering simple, comfortable lodgings and warm service. Enjoy seaside dining at the Holo Holo Kai restaurant.

| | ■ | 45 | ■ | | ■ |

KAUNAKAKAI (MOLOKA'I): *Moloka'i Shores Suites*   ⓢⓢⓢ
Mile Marker 1, Kamehameha V Hwy, PO Box1037, HI 96748. 📞 *(808) 553-5954,*
(800) 535-0085. 📠 *(808) 553-5954.* Ⓦ www.marcresorts.com
These one-and-two-bedroom condos lie just minutes from the main town. This hotel also offers whale-watching opportunities during winter.

| | ■ | (102) | | | ■ |

HĀNA (MAUI): *Josie's Hāna Hideaway*   ⓢⓢⓢ
PO Box 265, HI 96713. 📞 *(808) 248-7727.* 📠 *(808) 248-8418.*
Each of the houses in this complex has its own special charm and is close to the peaceful village of Hāna. Some have beautiful ocean views, others are surrounded by coconut, banana, and papaya groves.

| | ■ | 12 | | | ■ |

Kā'anapali (Maui): *Kā'anapali Beach Hotel* $$$ 416 (14)
2525 Kā'anapali Parkway, HI 96761. (808) 661-0011, (800) 262-8450.
FAX (808) 667-5978. W www.kbhmaui.com
Great hospitality has earned this low-rise property a reputation as Maui's most Hawaiian hotel. Authentic foods, craft classes, and free children's programs are also available.

Kā'anapali (Maui): *Sheraton Maui* $$$$ 510 (45)
2605 Kā'anapali Parkway, HI 96761. (808) 661-0031, (800) 782-9488.
FAX (808) 661-0458. W www.sheraton-maui.com
Perched on top of Black Rock high above the beach, this hotel has the distinction of having furnishings made from *koa* wood, and a variety of native plants.

Lahaina (Maui): *Lahaina Inn* $$ 9 (3)
127 Lahainaluna Rd, HI 96761. (808) 661-0577, (800) 669-3444.
FAX (808) 667-9480.
Lovingly restored to Victorian elegance, this small inn has individually decorated rooms with private *lānai* on which breakfast is served every morning. David Paul's "Lahaina Grill" is downstairs.

Lahaina (Maui): *Lahaina Shores Beach Resort* $$$ 184 (15)
475 Front St, HI 96761. (808) 661-4835, (800) 642-6284. FAX (808) 661-4696.
W www.lahainashores.com
This seven-story plantation-style resort with fully equipped kitchens is the only beachfront hotel in town. It is also close to the local shops.

Hilo (Hawai'i Island): *Hawai'i Naniloa Hotel* $$ 318 (7)
93 Banyan Dr, HI 96720. (808) 969-3333, (800) 367-5360. FAX (808) 969-6622.
W www.naniloa.com
Located on the lovely Banyan Drive, the Naniloa is as luxurious as it gets in Hilo. There are two pools, a health spa, and a restaurant on the property, and a nine-hole golf course across the street.

Hilo (Hawai'i Island): *Uncle Billy's Hilo Bay Hotel* $$ 143
87 Banyan Dr, HI 96720. (808) 935-0861, (800) 367-5102. FAX (808) 935-7903.
W www.unclebillys.com
A low-rise, family-style Polynesian resort with a nightly *hula* show, where visitors are welcome to experience Hilo as local residents do.

Volcano Village (Hawai'i Island): *Kīlauea Lodge* $$ 11
Old Volcano Rd, PO Box 116, HI 96785. (808) 967-7366. FAX (808) 967-7367.
W www.kilauealodge.com
Built as a YMCA camp in 1938, the refurbished lodge is a mile (1.5 km) from Volcanoes National Park. It also has a fine restaurant. *Cottages: 2*

Līhu'e (Kaua'i): *Aston Kaha Lani Resort* $$$ 74 units
4331 Kaua'i Beach Dr, HI 96766. (808) 822-9331, (800) 922-7866.
FAX (808) 822-2828. W www.radissonkauai.com
A few minutes north of town, this low-rise complex offers a range of condos in a quiet setting beside the beach. The attractive units have fully-equipped kitchens. Free tennis and outdoor barbeques.

Līhu'e (Kaua'i): *Kaua'i Beach Marriott Resort & Beach Club* $$$$ 345 (11)
3610 Rice St, HI 96766. (808) 245-5050, (800) 228-9290.
FAX (808) 245-5049.
Facing the ocean, this luxury resort enjoys a quarter-mile of white-sand beach and the largest pool in the state. Restaurants include the casual Duke's Canoe Club.

Waimea (Kaua'i): *Kē Iki Beach Bungalows* $$$ 10
59-579 Kē Iki Rd, Hale'iwa, HI 96712. (808) 638-8829.
FAX 800) 637-6100. W www.keikibeachbungalows.com
Comfortable beach cottages run by a local resident. Serene, old fashioned, and family-style accomodation for those visitors who prefer quieter comforts.

Waimea (Kaua'i): *Waimea Plantation Cottages* $$$ 50
9400 Kaumuali'i Hwy, PO Box 367, HI 96796. (808) 338-1635. FAX (808) 338-2338.
W www.aston-hotels.com
Step back into old Hawai'i at these wonderfully restored plantation cottages set in coconut groves at the gateway to the Waimea Canyon. Ceiling fans and period furniture.

For key to symbols see back flap

Where to Eat

B OTH ALASKA AND HAWAI‘I OFFER an enormous choice of places
to eat. Restaurants have been selected across a wide range
of price categories for their good value, excellent food,
atmosphere, and location. Restaurants are listed by area and
within these by price. Opening times are indicated by a "B"
for breakfast, "L" for lunch, and "D" for dinner.

	CREDIT CARDS	OUTDOOR TABLES	VEGETARIAN	GOOD WINE LIST	LATE OPENING

ALASKA

ANCHORAGE: *Club Paris*　　　　　　　　　　　　　　$$$
417 W 5th Ave. ☎ *(907) 277-6332.*
The filet mignon with blue cheese stuffing is legendary. Save room for
a slice of just-as-delicious cheesecake. *L, D.* 🅿 🍸 ♿

ANCHORAGE: *Marx Bros Cafe*　　　　　　　　　　　$$$$
627 W 3rd Ave. ☎ *(907) 278-2133.*
An intimate restaurant with an Alaska-sized reputation for presentations
of Alaskan seafood and game. Reservations required. *D.* ● *Mon.* 🅿 ♿

DENALI: *Perch Restaurant*　　　　　　　　　　　　$$$
13 miles S of Visitor Center. ☎ *(907) 683-2523.*
An informal place offering tender cuts of beef and seafood. It has great
views of the Alaska Range. *B, L, D.* ● *Oct–Apr: Mon–Fri.* 🅿 🍸 🚹 ♿

FAIRBANKS: *Pike's Landing*　　　　　　　　　　　　$$$
Airport Way W. ☎ *(907) 479-6500.*
Reserve a table by the window or dine outdoors, overlooking the Chena
River. The wide-ranging menu and casual atmosphere mirror its clientele.
L, D. 🅿 🍸 ♿

HOMER: *Boardwalk Fish & Chips*　　　　　　　　　　$
Homer Spit Rd. ☎ *(907) 235-7749.*
The best halibut and chips in the "Halibut Capital of the World." Also try a
bowl of creamy clam chowder with a side of scallops. *L, D.* ● *Oct–Apr.* 🅿

JUNEAU: *Gold Creek Salmon Bake*　　　　　　　　　$$$
Basin Rd. ☎ *(907) 789-0052, (800) 323-5757.*
Salmon, ribs, and chicken grilled outdoors in traditional style. The set price
includes entertainment and hotel transfers. *L, D.* ● *Oct–Apr.* 🅿 🎵 🚹 ♿

JUNEAU: *Fiddlehead Restaurant & Di Sopra*　　　　$$$$
429 W Willoughby Ave. ☎ *(907) 586-3150.*
Offers earthy dishes like fisherman's stew. Upstairs, Di Sopra presents
local seafood with an Italian twist. *L, D.* 🅿 🍸 ♿

KETCHIKAN: *Annabelle's Keg & Chowder House*　　$$$
326 Front St. ☎ *(907) 225-6009.*
Authentic Alaskan food served in the elegant surroundings. Sourdough
pancakes are a breakfast specialty. ● *Oct–May: B.* 🅿 🍸 ♿

KODIAK ISLAND: *Second Floor Restaurant*　　　　　$$
116 W Rezanof Dr. ☎ *(907) 486-8555.*
Good Japanese cuisine is available at this eatery, which uses local
seafood in the tempura and "Kodiak Rolls." *L, D.* ● *Sat–Sun L.* 🅿

SEWARD: *Ray's Waterfront*　　　　　　　　　　　　$$
Small Boat Harbor, 4th Ave. ☎ *(907) 224-5606.*
Views to snowcapped peaks and walls adorned with trophy fish for a
classic Alaskan ambience. Cedar plank salmon and Thai-style scallops are
favorites here. ● *Oct–Mar.* 🅿 ♿

SITKA: *Van Winkle & Sons*　　　　　　　　　　　　$$
205 Harbor Dr. ☎ *(907) 747-7652.*
A popular place, it is best known for the fresh halibut and chips, but also
has a full seafood menu. *L, D.* 🅿 ♿

SKAGWAY: *Stowaway Café*　　　　　　　　　　　　$$$
2nd Ave. ☎ *(907) 983-3463.*
Well-spaced tables, perfectly grilled fish, and water views make this a
romantic place to enjoy dinner. It is just a few steps from the cruise ship
dock. ● *Oct–Apr.* 🅿 ♿

	CREDIT CARDS	OUTDOOR TABLES	VEGETARIAN	GOOD WINE LIST	LATE OPENING

Price categories include a three-course meal for one, a glass of house wine, and all unavoidable extra charges such as sales tax and service:
$ under $20
$$ $20–30
$$$ $30–45
$$$$ $45–60
$$$$$ over $60

CREDIT CARDS Major credit cards accepted.
OUTDOOR TABLES Garden, courtyard, or terrace with outside tables.
VEGETARIAN A good selection of vegetarian dishes available.
GOOD WINE LIST Extensive list of good wines, both domestic and imported.
LATE OPENING Full menu or light meals served after 11pm.

HAWAI‘I

Restaurant	CC	OT	VEG	WINE	LATE
HALE‘IWA (O‘AHU): *Kua ‘Aina Sandwich* — $ 66-214 Kamehameha Hwy (Hwy 83). (808) 637-6067. If you love burgers and fries, try this humble surfer hangout on O‘ahu's North Shore. A local landmark, it has the best food in town. **P**		●			
HONOLULU (O‘AHU): *Ono Hawaiian Foods* — $ 726 Kapahulu Ave. (808) 737-2275. Second only to a *tūtū's* (grandmother's) kitchen, this small eatery is great for Hawaiian dishes such as *poi, laulau,* and *lomi-lomi* salmon. ● Sun.					
HONOLULU (O‘AHU): *Kincaid's Fish, Chop & Steakhouse* — $$$ 1050 Ala Moana Boulevard (at Ward Warehouse). (808) 591-2005. Kincaid's offers excellent food and first rate service. It is a terrific place to take a break from shopping, but it tends to get extremely busy around noon. **P**	■			●	■
WAIKĪKĪ (O‘AHU): *Duke's Canoe Club* — $$$ 2335 Kalākaua Ave (in the Outrigger Waikīkī). (808) 922-2268. Just steps from Duke Kahanamoku's favorite surfing spot, this is part restaurant, part bar, part museum, and one of the most popular hangouts in town. A varied menu of steak, fish, and salads. **P**	■	●		●	
KAUNAKAKAI (MOLOKA‘I): *Kanemitsu Bakery* — $ 79 Ala Malama St. (808) 553-5855. Meals until 11:30am; bakery open until 6:30pm. Locals say if you haven't been to this bakery, you haven't been to this region at all. Sweet breads are baked daily. Local-style breakfast and lunch. **P**					
HĀNA (MAUI): *Hāna Ranch Restaurant* — $$ Hāna Ranch Center, off Hāna Hwy (Hwy 360). (808) 248-8255. Whether in the light-wood dining room or outside amid the serenity of Hāna, the food is superb, prepared simply with local ingredients. **P**	■	●			
LAHAINA (MAUI): *Longhi's* — $$$ 888 Front St. (808) 667-2288. Created by "a man who loves to eat" (Bob Longhi), this is a Maui institution. The orange juice and coffee alone are worth the trip for breakfast. Specials include *‘ahi* (tuna) torino and shrimp amaretto. **P**	■			●	
LAHAINA (MAUI): *David Paul's Lahaina Grill* — $$$$$ 127 Lahainaluna Rd. (808) 667-5117. Voted "Best Maui Restaurant" eight times by *Honolulu* magazine readers, try Lahaina Grill's superb *kālua* duck, Tequila shrimp, or triple berry pie. **P**	■			●	
HILO (HAWAI‘I ISLAND): *Nihon Restaurant & Cultural Center* — $$ 123 Lihiwai St. (808) 969-1133. Japanese in design, Nihon gives you culture with your sushi. The upstairs dining room offers a beautiful view of Hilo Bay and Lili‘uokalani Gardens. The food here is authentic and delicious. ● Sun. **P**	■	●			
LĪHU‘E (KAUA‘I): *Hamura Saimin Stand* — $ 2956 Kress St. (808) 245-3271. Many feel this restaurant makes Hawai‘i's best noodles. Customers sit at a counter, and even on the hottest day, the *saimin* is absolutely delicious.					
LĪHU‘E (KAUA‘I): *Gaylord's at Kilohana* — $$$ 3-2087 Kaumuali‘i Hwy (Hwy 50). (808) 245-9593. Located at Kaua‘i's legendary plantation estate, Gaylord's offers visitors open-air dining with a varied menu that ranges from pasta to prime rib. **P**	■	●		●	

For key to symbols see back flap

General Index

Acknowledgements

PROOF READER & INDEXER
Glenda Fernandes.

DK LONDON
EDITORIAL & DESIGN ASSISTANCE
Brigitte Arora, Sherry Collins, Jo Cowen,
Caroline Evans, Madeline Farbman, Jacky
Jackson, Pamela Marmito, Ros Walford.

FACTCHECKERS
D. Clancy, Jerry Dean, Paul Franklin, Jill
Metzler, Don Pitcher, Mike Rogers.

SENIOR DTP DESIGNER
Jason Little.

SENIOR CARTOGRAPHIC EDITOR
Casper Morris.

DK PICTURE LIBRARY
Mark Dennis.

PRODUCTION CONTROLLERS
Sarah Dodd, Melanie Dowland.

MANAGING ART EDITOR
Jane Ewart.

PUBLISHING MANAGER
Helen Townsend.

PUBLISHER
Douglas Amrine.

DORLING KINDERSLEY would like to thank the
following people whose contributions and
assistance have made the preparation of this
book possible.

ADDITIONAL CONTRIBUTORS
Ruth & Eric Bailey, Eleanor Berman, Jeremy
Black, Lester Brooks, Patricia Brooks, Tom
Bross, Susan Burke, Richard Cawthorne, Brett
Cook, Donna Dailey, Michelle de Larrabeiti,
David Dick, Susan Farewell, Rebecca Poole
Forée, Paul Franklin, Donald S. Frazier, Bonnie
Friedman, Rita Goldman, Patricia Harris, Ross
Hassig, Carolyn Heller, Pierre Home-Douglas,
Lorraine Johnson, Penney Kome, Philip Lee,
Helga Loverseed, David Lyon, Clemence
McLaren, Guy Mansell, Fred Mawer, Melissa
Miller, Kendrick Oliver, Barry Parr, Ellen Payne,
J. Kingston Pierce, Alice L. Powers, Jennifer
Quasha, George Raudzens, Juliette Rogers, John
Ryan, Alex Salkever, Kem Sawyer, Emma
Stanford, Phyllis Steinberg, Nigel Tisdall, Brian
Ward, Greg Ward, John Wilcock, Ian Williams,
Marilyn Wood, Paul Wood, Stanley Young.

ADDITIONAL ILLUSTRATORS
Ricardo Almazan, Ricardo Almazan Jr, Arcana
Studios, Robert Ashby, William Band, Gilles
Beauchemin, Richard Bonson, Joanne Cameron,
Stephen Conlin, Gary Cross, Richard Draper,
Dean Entwhistle, Eugene Fleurey, Chris Forsey,
Martin Gagnon, Vincent Gagnon, Stephen
Gyapay, Stéphane Jorisch, Patrick Jougla, Nick
Lipscombe, Claire Littlejohn, Luc Normandin,
Lee Peters, Mel Pickering, Robbie Polley,
Kevin Robinson, Hamish Simpson, Mike
Taylor, Pat Thorne, Chris Orr & Associates,
Jean-François Vachon, John Woodcock.

ADDITIONAL PHOTOGRAPHERS
Max Alexander, Peter Anderson, Jaime
Baldovinos, Alan Briere, Demetrio Carrasco,
Philippe Dewet, Philip Dowell, Neil Fletcher,
Bruce Forster, John Heseltine, Ed Homonylo,
Philip C. Jackson, Eliot Kaufman, Alan Keohane,
Dave King, Andrew Leyerle, Neil Lukas, David
Lyons, Norman McGrath, Andrew McKinney,
Tim Mann, Gunter Marx, Neil Mersh, Howard
Millard, Michael Moran, Sue Oldfield, Scot
Pitts, Rob Reichenfeld, Julio Rochon, Kim
Sayer, Neil Setchfield, Mike Severns, Chris
Stevens, Clive Streeter, Giles Stokoe, Scott
Suchman, Matthew Ward, Stephen White-
horne, Linda Whitwam, Francesca Yorke.

PHOTOGRAPHIC &
ARTWORK REFERENCE
Madeline Farbman; Emily Hovland;
Independence National Historic Park: Phil
Sheridan; National Park Service: Tom Patterson;
Philadelphia Convention & Visitors Bureau:
Danielle Cohn, Ellen Kornfield, Marissa Philip,

San Antonio Convention & Visitors Bureau: Angela McClendon; M&A Design: Ajay Sethi, Mugdha Sethi; AirPhoto USA: Brian Garcia, Shannon Kelley.

Photography Permissions

DORLING KINDERSLEY would like to thank the following for their assistance and kind permission to photograph at their establishments (the establishments are listed in chapter order):

Old Merchant's House, East Village, NY; American Museum of Natural History, NY; Museum of American Folk Art, NY; Studio Museum in Harlem, NY; The Cloisters, NY; Columbia University, NY; Rockefeller Group, NY; Massachusetts State House, Boston; Nichols House Museum, Boston; Trinity Church, Boston; Museum of Fine Arts, Boston; Sackler Museum, Boston; New England Aquarium, Boston; Salem Witch Museum, MS; Plimoth Plantation, MS; Mark Twain House, CT; Florence Griswold Museum, CT; Currier Gallery of Art, Manchester; National Air and Space Museum, Washington, DC; National Museum of Natural History, Washington, DC; National Museum of African Art, Washington, DC; National Museum of American History, Washington, DC; Kenmore House, VA; Library of Congress, Washington, DC; South Carolina State Museum, SC; Stone Mountain Park, GA; Shaker Village of Pleasant Hill, Harrodsburg, KY; Graceland, TN; Historic New Orleans Voodoo Museum, New Orleans, LA; Nottoway Plantation, LA; National Voting Rights Museum and Institute, Selma, AL; Elvis Presley Park, Tupelo CVB; Spertus Museum of Jewish Studies, Chicago; Field Museum, Chicago; Oriental Institute Museum, Chicago; Museum of Broadcast Communications, Chicago; University of Notre Dame, IN; Eiteljorg Museum, IN; Franklin Park Conservatory and Botanical Gardens, OH; Detroit Metro CVB, MI; The Detroit Institute of Arts, MI; Circus World Museum, Baraboo, WI; Walker Art Center, MN; The Mammoth Site of Hot Springs, South Dakota Inc., SD; The Nelson Atkins Museum of Art, MO; City Manager, Vince Capell, St. Joseph, MO; Woolaroc Ranch Museum, OK; Oral Roberts University, OK; Cowboy Artists of America Museum, Kerville, TX; Museum of Indian Arts and Culture, Santa Fe; Millicent Rogers Museum, Taos, NM; Las Vegas Natural History Museum; Cedar City Museum, UT; Museum of Northern Arizona, Flagstaff, AZ; Phoenix Museum of History, Phoenix, AZ; Hopi Learning Center, AZ; New Mexico Museum of Natural History and Science, Albuquerque, NM; Albuquerque Museum of Art and History, Albuquerque; Maxwell Museum of Anthropology, Albuquerque, NM; Hubbell Trading Post, NM; Odyssey Maritime Discovery Center, WA; Seattle Art Museum, WA; National Park Service, OR; Museum of Tolerance, Los Angeles, CA; Balboa Park, San Diego; Hearst Castle, San Simeon; Huntington Library, San Marino; Knotts Berry Farm, Buena Park; Museum of Contemporary Art, LA; *Queen Mary,* Long Beach; Sacramento State Capitol; San Diego Aerospace Museum; San Diego Automotive Museum; San Diego Museum of Art; San Diego Zoological Society; Santa Barbara Mission, CA; Wells Fargo History Museum, San Francisco, CA; San Francisco History Center, San Francisco Public Library, CA; University of California, Berkeley; University of California, LA; Winchester Mystery House, San Jose; Valdez Museum, Valdez, AK; Baranof Museum, Kodiak Island, AK; Ice Museum, Fairbanks, AK; as well as all the other churches, museums, hotels, restaurants, shops, galleries and sights too numerous to thank individually.

Picture Credits

t = top; tl = top left; tlc = top left centre; tc = top centre; tr = top right; cla = centre left above; ca = centre above; cra = centre right above; cl = centre left; c = centre; cr = centre right; clb = centre left below; cb = centre below; crb = centre right below; bl = bottom left; b = bottom; bc = bottom centre; bcl = bottom centre left; br = bottom right.

Works of art have been reproduced with the permission of the following copyright holders:

© ALBUQUERQUE MUSEUM OF ART AND HISTORY: Museum Purchase, 1993 General Obligation Bond Estella Loretto *Earth Mother, Offerings for a Good Life (No Wa Mu Stio)*, 1994, 548tl; BELL ATLANTIC BUILDING: *Telephone Men & Women at Work* by Dean Cornwell, 140tl; COLUMBIA UNIVERSITY: 84cla; Courtesy COMMONWEALTH OF MASSACHUSETTS ART COMMISSION: *Civil War Army Nurses Memorial* Bela Pratt, 1911, 138tr; Stained glass window, Main Stair Hall, 1900/details: *Magna Carta seal 43, Seal of the Commonwealth* (pre-1898) 138cl; *Return of the Colours to the Custody of the Commonwealth,* December 22, 1986, mural by Edward Simmons 1902: 139cbl. © Denman Fink: Detail from *Law Guides Florida's Progress*, 1940, 287tl; HISTORIC NEW ORLEANS VOODOO MUSEUM: *Marie Laveau* by Charles M. Gandolfo, 348br; Courtesy FLORENCE GRISWOLD MUSEUM: *The Harpist, A Portrait of Miss Florence Griswold,* by Alphonse Jongers, 1903, 159br; © Georg John Lober: *Hans Christian Anderson*, 1956, 78br. MILLICENT ROGERS MUSEUM: 507tl; HENRY MOORE FOUNDATION: *Reclining Figure: Hand* (1979), the work illustrated on page 76bl has been reproduced by permission of the Henry Moore Foundation; SACKLER MUSEUM, Cambridge, Boston: 149tc; Courtesy KENNETH TREISTER HOLOCAUST MEMORIAL: © Kenneth Treister, *A Sculpture of Love and Anguish,* 1990, 293cl. Courtesy THE SEATTLE ARTS COMMISSION © Jonathan Borofsky: *Hammering Man*, 1988, 617tr. © Victor Arnautoff, *City Life*, Coit Tower, 1934, 702bl. COLLECTION OF SPERTUS MUSEUM: *Flame of Hope* by Leonardo Nierman, 1995, 392crb.

The publisher would like to thank the following individuals, companies and picture libraries for permission to reproduce their photographs:

ALAMY: Joseph Sohm 652; THE AFRICAN AMERICAN MUSEUM IN PHILADELPHIA: 100cla; ATLANTA–FULTON PUBLIC LIBRARY FOUNDATION, INC. COURTESY THE ATLANTA HISTORY CENTER: 260cr;

THE BROOKLYN MUSEUM OF ART: 87bc; BRUCE COLEMAN INC., NEW YORK: Jeff Foott 122-123; BRUCE COLEMAN, LONDON: Raimund Cramm GDT 303br; COLORADO HISTORICAL SOCIETY: William Henry Jackson Collection: *Westward HO!* 1904, 612bl; CONVENTION AND VISITORS ASSOCIATION OF LANE COUNTY, OR: 634tl; CORBIS: 32br, 34br, 38tr, 38cl, 39br, 47b, 49t, 53cra, 95tl, 95b, 127b, 166br, 189tl, 335 (inset), 376-377, 394bl, 433 (inset), 565 (inset), 688br, 730 (inset), 741tr; 752cra, 753bl; AFP 53br; James L. Amos 57tl; Craig Aurness 204bl, 688tr (Hearst Castle, CA Park Service), 692tl; Dave Bartruff 101br, 450tc; Tom Bean 35tl, 41br, 527br; Nathan Benn 56cl; Corbis-Bettman 28br, 43b, 44br, 45t, 46tl, 50tl, 50br, 53tl, 53tc, 53tr, 60cl, 90bl, 94bl, 187 (inset), 193bl, 225cl, 225bc, 226cla, 349br, 393crb, 421cla, 450cla, 511bl, 655ca, 661br; Richard Bickel 108cr; Kristi J. Black 689tl; © Carnegie Museum of Art, Pittsburgh, photo by W. Cody 108bc; Steve Chenn 102bl; L. Clarke 54-55; Jerry Cooke 92cr, 243b; Richard A. Cooke 109b, 188bl, 221b; Lake County Museum 9 (inset), 519br; Richard Cummins 30bc, 103tc, 107tr, 338, 339b, 485tc; Jeff Curtes 595bl; Corcoran Gallery of Art, Washington, D.C.; 2003: *Washington Before Yorktown*, 1824-25, by Rembrandt Peale, 42; *George Washington*, 1796, by Gilbert Stuart, 52clb; Dennis Degnan 105tl; Hulton–Deutsch Collection 140 cr; Jay Dickman 219br; Henry Dittz 665br; Duomo 29br; Peter Finger 90tr, 91tr; Kevin Fleming 189cr, 192t, 225cr, 226br, 227br, 238-239, 407br; Owen Franken 29cl; Michael Freeman 198cl; Raymond Gehman 527tc; Mark E. Gibson 194br; Tod A. Gipstein 189br; Farell Grehan 97br, 165bl; Bob Gomes 29tr; The Solomon R. Guggenheim Foundation, NY: (*Man with Arms Crossed*, 1895-1900, by Cézanne, photo by Francis G. Mayer) 82tr; Liz Haymans 593br; Robert Holmes 104bc, 334-335; Dave G. Houser 712cla; George H. H. Huey 503ca; Swim Ink 48ca; Woolfgang Kaehler 34cl; Catherine Karnow 101tc, 512crb; Steve

Kaufman 579tr; Layne Kennedy 109tr, 380, 421tr; Dave King 552clb; Bob Krist 61bl, 98tr, 103cl, 352bl, 688clb, 689bl; Owaki-Kulla 242, 353bl; Robert Landau 93tl; Larry Lee 32tr; Danny Lehman 35tr; George D. Lepp 39tr; Craig Lovell 32cl; Georgia Lowell 706bl; James Marshall 517bc, 741bl; Francis G. Mayer 44tl, 60tr, 81tl, 94crb; Buddy Mays 91cr, 475br; Joe McDonald 65b; Louis K. Meisel Gallery 8-9; Kelly-Mooney Photography 31tr, 96br, 97tl, 199cr; David Muench 33tl, 56bl, 64, 92bc, 106cla, 126, 188tr, 218br, 219cla, 220cla, 224tr, 436, 527cbr, 755tl; Marc Muench 594tr, 595tl, 595crb; Walley McNamee 53crb; © National Portrait Gallery, Smithsonian Institution, Washington, DC, acquired as a gift to the nation through the generosity of the Donald W. Reynolds Foundation, 2003; 203br (*Lansdowne portrait of George Washington*, 1796, by Gilbert Stuart, photo by Archivo Iconografico, S. A.); Richard T. Nowitz 104tl, 191b, 220br, 221tl; Pat O'Hara 610; Douglas Peebles 33bl, 594cl; The Phillips Collection, Washington, D.C.: (*The Luncheon of the Boating Party*, 1881, by Pierre Auguste Renoir (1841-1919), photo by Francis G. Mayer) 210tl; Charles Philip 35bl; Philadelphia Museum of Arts: 105crb; Neil Preston 269bl; Greg Probst 564-565; Carl & Ann Purcell 94tc; Roger Ressmeyer 286br, 608-609, 629tr; Jim Richardson 33cr; Bill Ross 38bl, 63br; Ron Sanford 437b; Paul A. Souders 224b; Kevin Schafer 56tr; Alan Schein 57br, 92tl, 108tl; Phil Schermeister 378cb, 516bc; Flip Schulke 51tr; Michael T. Sedam 34tr, 611b, 750cla; Leif Skoogfors 102cla, 107clb; Lee Snider 61ca, 91bl, 96clb, 100tr, 101cr, 101cb, 106br, 198tr, 218tl, 227tl; Joseph Sohm; ChromoSohm Inc. 39tl, 41tl, 57cra, 217cra; 486b; Ted Spiegel 57crb; Mark L Stephenson 31crb, 755br; David Stoecklein 500-501; Bequest of Mrs. Benjamin Ogle Tayloe, Collection of the Corcoran Art Gallery: 52ctl; Underwood & Underwood 93bl, 264cla, 381b; Patrick Ward 107br; Ron Watts 32bl, 33tr, 62tr, 93br; David H. Wells 105b; Nick Wheeler 669bcl; Oscar White 53cb; Michael S. Yamashita 96cla, 421b; Bo Zaunders 472-473, 481tl;

THE FRICK COLLECTION: *Lady Meux* by James Abbot McNeill Whistler, 1881, 80bl;

GETTY IMAGES: Jack Dykinga 26-27; Robert Glusic 648-649; Chris Noble 568; © J PAUL GETTY TRUST: *Adoration of the Magi*, 1495-1505, by Andrea Mantegna, 660tl; GRANGER COLLECTION, NEW YORK: 52tc, 52clb, 52bl, 52bc, 52br, 53bl, 501 (inset);

HELLS CANYON ADVENTURES: 641crb, 641bl; HISTORIC NEW ORLEANS COLLECTION: 351cb; HISTORIC NEW ORLEANS VOODOO MUSEUM: *Portrait of Marie Laveau* 348br;

MARY EVANS PICTURE LIBRARY: 27 (inset), 55 (inset), 123 (inset), 239 (inset), 283 (inset), 377 (inset), 473 (inset), 481bl; 609 (inset); 649 (inset); MASTERFILE: Garry Black 432-433; Bill Brooks 40tr; Gail Mooney 35crb; Randy Lincks 41cr; MUSEUM OF FINE ARTS, BOSTON: HU–MFA Expedition *Shawabtis of Taharka* 147tl; Egypt Exploration Fund *Inner Coffin of Nes-mut-aat-neru* 147cl; Ruth & Carl J. Shapiro Colonnade and Vault *John Singer Sargent Murals* 147br; MUSEUM OF INTERNATIONAL FOLK ART, A UNIT OF THE MUSEUM OF NEW MEXICO: Girard Foundation Collection, Photo Michel Monteaux *Toy Horse* Bangladesh, Indian. C. 1960. 547cb;

© 2003 Board of Trustees, National Gallery of Art, Washington, DC: *The Alba Madonna*, 1510, by Raphael (Raffaello Sanzio of Urbino, 1483–1520), Andrew W. Melon Collection: 201tl; NHPA: David Middleton 553 br; NATIONAL MUSEUM OF AMERICAN JEWISH HISTORY: Collection of Congregation Mikveh Israel: 100clb; NATIONAL MUSEUM OF NATURAL HISTORY, WASHINGTON/© SMITHSONIAN INSTITUTION: Dane Penland 202cr; NATIONAL PARK SERVICE, OR: 637tr; NELSON-ATKINS MUSEUM OF ART, KANSAS CITY, MISSOURI: *Shuttlecocks* by Claes Oldenburg and Coosje van Bruggen, 1994: 457tl; NEW ORLEANS METROPOLITAN CONVENTION & VISITORS BUREAU: Ann Purcell 344bl; Carl Purcell 346tl;

ODYSSEY MARITIME DISCOVERY CENTER, WA: 617cl;

PEDRO E. GUERRERO © 2002, Talesin Preservation Inc.: 415tl; © COURTESY OF THE PENNSYLVANIA ACADEMY OF FINE ARTS; PHILADELPHIA: Joseph E. Temple Fund, 2003: *The Fox Hunt,* 1893, by Winslow Homer 103br;

REDFERNS MUSIC PICTURE LIBRARY: 49bc; THE RONALD GRANT ARCHIVE: 666bl; MAE SCANLAN: 202tl; SUPERSTOCK: 174tl;

TERRA GALLERIA PHOTOGRAPHY: 624tl;

© 2002 UNIVERSAL STUDIOS, INC.: 308br, 309tl, 309br;

VIEWFINDERS: Bruce Forster 623cra, 637ca, 637bl, 639bc; Trevor Graves 613tl; Rich Iwasaki 620tc; Pefley 622tr; Bob Poole 632br; Greg Vaughn 620b, 623tl, 628br, 632cra, 633t, 633crb, 635br, 636cla, 636 br, 638b, 640bl, 641tl;

WALLA WALLA CHAMBER OF COMMERCE: 625bl; WALKER ART CENTER, MINNEAPOLIS: *Spoonbridge and Cherry* by Claes Oldenburg and Coosje van Bruggen, 1987-1988, Gift of Frederick R. Weisman in honor of his parents, William and Mary Weisman, 1988: 416tr; © WHITE HOUSE HISTORICAL ASSOCIATION (WHITE HOUSE COLLECTION) 206cla, 206bc, 207tc, 207cr, 207bl (653, 579, 656, 140, 663) Bruce White 195tr (3074); WORDS AND PICTURES: 334bl, 346tl; WORLD PICTURES: 653b, 730-731.

Back Endpaper: CORBIS: Tom Bean, Jan Butchofsky-Houser, Charles Krebs, Owaki-Kulla, Robert Landau, Lester Lefkowitz.

JACKET
Front - DK PICTURE LIBRARY: Matthew Ward bc; GETTY IMAGES: Joseph Pobereskin cl; Ken Reid cr; ROBERT HARDING PICTURE LIBRARY: main image. Back - CORBIS: Dallas and John Heaton tl; David Muench br. Spine - ROBERT HARDING PICTURE LIBRARY

All other images © Dorling Kindersley. For further information see **www.dkimages.com**

urther Reading

TION

nesburg, Ohio Anderson, herwood, Random House, 995.

now Why the Caged Bird ings Angelou, Maya, Random House, 1983.

dnight in the Garden of Good and Evil Berendt, ohn, Random House, 1994.

andelion Wine Bradbury, Ray, Random House, 1985.

Walk in the Woods Bryson, Bill, Random House, 1999.

eakfast at Tiffany's Capote, Truman, Penguin, 1988.

e Awakening Chopin, Kate, Random House, 1985.

e Last of the Mohicans Cooper, James Fenimore, Penguin, 1984.

e Red Badge of Courage Crane, Stephen, Penguin, 1994.

me and Again Finney. Jack, Simon & Schuster, 1995.

e Great Gatsby Fitzgerald, F. Scott, Penguin, 1994.

e Little Shepherd of Kingdom Come Fox, Jr, John, University Press of Kentucky, 1987.

e Scarlet Letter Hawthorne, Nathaniel, Penguin, 1994.

arewell to Arms Hemingway, Ernest, Simon & Schuster, 1995.

he Legend of Sleepy Hollow Irving, Washington, Penguin, 1999.

n the Road Kerouac, Jack, Penguin, 1998.

o Kill a Mockingbird Lee, Harper, Warner Books, 1988.

all of the Wild and Other Stories London, Jack, Penguin, 1995.

River Runs Through It and Other Stories Maclean, Norman, University of Chicago Press, 2001.

onesome Dove McMurtry, Larry, Simon & Schuster, 1986.

Gone With the Wind Mitchell, Margaret, Warner Books, 1993.

Beloved Morrison, Toni, Penguin, 1998.

The Octopus Norris, Frank, Penguin, 1994.

Catcher in the Rye Salinger, JD, Penguin, 1994.

The Jungle Sinclair, Upton, Penguin, 1985.

Uncle Tom's Cabin Stowe, Harriet Beecher, Penguin, 1981.

The Grapes of Wrath Steinbeck, John, Penguin, 2001.

The Adventures of Tom Sawyer, Twain, Mark, Penguin, 1986.

The Color Purple Walker, Alice, Pocket Books, 1990.

Our Town and Other Plays Wilder, Thornton, Penguin, 2000.

A Streetcar Named Desire Williams, Tennessee, Signet, 1989.

Look Homeward Angel Wolfe, Thomas, Simon & Schuster, 1995.

HISTORY & POLITICS

One Nation: America Remembers September 11, 2001 Life Magazine/ Giuliani, Rudolph W, Little Brown & Company, 2001.

The Penguin History of the USA Brogan, Hugh, Penguin, 2001.

An Hour Before Daylight Carter, Jimmy, Simon & Schuster, 2001.

The Civil War: A Narrative Foote, Shelby, Vintage, 1986.

1939: The Lost World of the Fair Gelertner, David, Free Press, 1999.

Dispatches Herr, Michael, Vintage, 1991.

Benjamin Franklin: An American Life Isaacson, Walter, Simon & Schuster, 2003.

Writings Jefferson, Thomas, Library of America, 1984.

Profiles in Courage Kennedy, John F, Perennial Press, 2000.

Profiles in Courage for Our Time Kennedy, Caroline, Hyperion, 2003.

The Columbia Historical Portrait of New York Kouwenhoven, John, Icon, 1972.

John Adams McCollough, David, Simon & Schuster, 2002.

Collected Writings Paine, Thomas, Library of America, 1995.

American Colonies Taylor, Alan, Penguin, 2002.

Civil Disobedience Thoreau, Henry David, Dover, 1993.

Democracy in America Tocqueville, Alexis de, Alfred A. Knopf, 1994.

Writings from The New Yorker White, E.B., Perennial Press, 1991.

All the President's Men Woodward, Bob, and Bernstein, Carl, Simon & Schuster, 1994.

NATURAL HISTORY & TRAVEL

National Audubon Society Field Guide to North American Mammals Whitaker Jr, John O, Alfred A. Knopf, 1996.

North American Wildlife: Wildflowers Reader's Digest Association, 1998.

North American Wildlife: Trees & Non-Flowering Plants Reader's Digest Association, 1998.

America's National Parks Tehabi Books/ Dorling Kindersley, 2001.

National Geographic on Assignment USA National Geographic, 1997.

The Mississippi and the Making of a Nation National Geographic, 2002.

Route 66 Main Street USA Freeth, Nick, Taylor, Paul, Motorbooks Intl, 2001.

Bayou Farewell Tidwell, Mike, Pantheon, 2003.

ART

Twentieth Century American Art Lee Doss, Erika, Oxford University Press, 2002.

Framing America: A Social History of American Art Pohl, Frances K., Thames & Hudson, 2002.

DK Eyewitness Travel Guides

Boston
0-7894-9559-7 $20.00 (US) $30.00 (Canada)
0-7513-6864-4 £10.99 (UK) $32.00 (Australia)

California
0-7894-1451-1 $29.95 (US) $40.00 (Canada)
0-7513-4841-4 £16.99 (UK) $45.00 (Australia)

Chicago
0-7894-9562-7 $20.00 (US) $30.00 (Canada)
0-7513-4825-2 £10.99 (UK) $32.00 (Australia)

Florida
0-7894-9564-3 $25.00 (US) $34.95 (Canada)
0-7513-4831-7 £14.99 (UK) $39.95 (Australia)

Hawaii
0-7894-9732-8 $29.95 (US) $20.00 (Canada)
0-7513-4823-6 £12.99 (UK) $32.00 (Australia)

New England
0-7894-9570-8 $25.00 (US) $34.95 (Canada)
0-7513-6866-0 £14.99 (UK) $39.95 (Australia)

New Orleans
0-7894-9737-9 $20.00 (US) $29.95 (Canada)
0-7513-1317-3 £12.99 (UK) $32.00 (Australia)

New York
0-7894-9382-9 $25.00 (US) $35.00 (Canada)
0-7513-6860-1 £14.99 (UK) $39.95 (Australia)

Pacific Northwest
0-7894-9680-1 $25.00 (US) $35.00 (Canada)
0-7513-6997-7 £15.99 (UK) $42.00 (Australia)

San Francisco
0-7894-9420-5 $20.00 (US) $30.00 (Canada)
0-7513-4842-2 £12.99 (UK) $35.00 (Australia)

Southwest USA & Las Vegas
0-7894-9565-1 $20.00 (US) $30.00 (Canada)
0-7513-6871-7 £14.99 (UK) $39.95 (Australia)

Washington, DC
0-7894-9576-7 $20.00 (US) $29.95 (Canada)
0-7513-2739-5 £9.99 (UK) $32.00 (Australia)

DK Top 10 Guides

Boston
0-7894-9193-1 $10.00 (US) $15.00 (Canada)
0-7513-4851-1 £6.99 (UK) $19.95 (Australia)

Maui, Moloka‘i & Lana‘i
0-7566-0032-4 $10.00 (US) $15.00 (Canada)
1-4053-0274-7 £6.99 (UK) $19.95 (Australia)

Miami & the Keys
0-7894-9185-0 $10.00 (US) $15.00 (Canada)
0-7513-4848-1 £6.99 (UK) $19.95 (Australia)

Orlando
0-7894-8435-8 $10.00 (US) $15.00 (Canada)
0-7513-3762-5 £6.99 (UK) $19.95 (Australia)

New York
0-7894-8351-3 $10.00 (US) $15.00 (Canada)
0-7513-3571-1 £6.99 (UK) $19.95 (Australia)

San Francisco
0-7894-9190-7 $10.00 (US) $15.00 (Canada)
0-7513-4853-8 £6.99 (UK) $19.95 (Australia)

Washington, DC
0-7894-9186-9 $10.00 (US) $15.00 (Canada)
0-7513-4850-3 £6.99 (UK) $19.95 (Australia)

Chicago
0-7566-0031-6 $10.00 (US) $15.00 (Canada)
1-4053-0272-0 £6.99 (UK) $19.95 (Australia)

Las Vegas
0-7894-8354-8 $10.00 (US) $15.00 (Canada)
0-7513-3825-7 £6.99 (UK) $19.95 (Australia)

Upcoming Titles

Top 10 Honolulu & O‘ahu

Top 10 Los Angeles

Top 10 Virgin Islands

Eyewitness Orlando & the Space Coast

Eyewitness Arizona & the Grand Canyon

Highlights of the USA

Mount Rainier National Park, Washington's prime outdoor destination

0 km   250

0 miles   250

Olympic NP

Seattle
WA
Mt. Rainier NP

Portland

Glacier NP

MT

OR

Yellowstone NP

ID
Grand
Teton NP

WY

CA

Reno

NV

Rocky Mt.

Napa Valley
San
Francisco

Sacramento

Yosemite NP

UT

Zion NP

Aspen

Carmel

Death
Valley NP

Las
Vegas

Mesa
Verde N

Sequoia NP

Grand
Canyon NP

Santa

Channel
Islands NP

Los Angeles

Anaheim

Sedona

Albuquerqu

San Diego

Joshua
Tree NP

AZ

Phoenix

NM

Tucson

Carlsbad
Caverns NP

C   A

M E X I C

Las Vegas neon lightening up the Strip

The luxurious Beverly Hills Hotel, a landmark in Los Angeles

Sandstone formations, Zion National Park, Utah

KEY

- Great Cities
- Charming Cities
- Fun Places to Visit
- National Parks